Pocahontas' Descendants

A Revision, Enlargement and Extension
of the List as Set Out by
Wyndham Robertson in His Book
Pocahontas and Her Descendants (1887)

*By Stuart E. Brown, Jr., Lorraine F. Myers,
and Eileen M. Chappel*

*Combined with two volumes of
corrections and additions*

D1431519

Originally published by the Pocahontas Foundation, 1985, 1992
Copyright © 1985, 1992, 1994
by the Pocahontas Foundation
All Rights Reserved
Reprinted as a consolidated edition by
Genealogical Publishing Co., Inc.
Baltimore, 1994
Library of Congress Catalogue Card Number 93-80412
International Standard Book Number 0-8063-1407-9
Made in the United States of America

POCAHONTAS' DESCENDANTS

by

Stuart E. Brown, Jr., Lorraine F. Myers
and Eileen M. Chappel

A revision, enlargement and extension of the list as
set out by Wyndham Robertson in his book

POCAHONTAS AND HER DESCENDANTS
(1887)

THE POCAHONTAS FOUNDATION
1985

ACKNOWLEDGEMENTS

Much of the data included in this volume was obtained from or through the assistance of the following persons and organizations: The Association for the Preservation of Virginia Antiquities; Alderman Library, University of Virginia; George W. Archer, President, The Archer Association, Ltd.; James A. Bear, Jr., Resident Director, Thomas Jefferson Memorial Foundation; Charles L. Bland; Mrs. Charlotte L. Bryant; Nathaniel C. Brydon, Governor, Jamestowne Society; Mrs. Paul C. Bennett, Jr.; Mrs. J. F. Bunnett; Mrs. Carolyn Burke, Editor, Pocahontas Trails Newsletter; Charles T. Burton; Lyle O. Caldwell; Bernard M. Caperton; Mrs. M. E. D. Carson; Hastings E. A. Carson, M.D.; Mrs. Dorothy Carter; J. Gilliam Conrad, Esq.; Margaret Cook, Curator of Manuscripts and Rare Books, Earl Gregg Swem Library, The College of William and Mary in Virginia; Dr. Robert T. Coolidge, Historian, The Monticello Association; Mrs. Roy A. Edwards; Littleton B. Ensey; William Craghead Evans; Bolling Byrd Flood; Bobby Ellis Gilliam; Gordon H. Hawks, M.D.; Mr. and Mrs. Francis W. Hayes, Jr.; Mrs. D. R. Heiss; T. Gibson Hobbs, Jr.; W. Bolling Izard; John Melville Jennings, Director Emeritus, Virginia Historical Society; Mrs. Kathryn Keen; Jane Rives Ledford; Charles S. McCandlish; Robert J. McCandlish, Jr., Esq.; Mrs. Shirley M. McCarty; Mary Sue Mathys; Mrs. Merrill Keith Molsberry; Sir Iain Moncreiffe of that Ilk; North Carolina Division of Archives and History; James S. Patton; Joe A. Randolph; Charles Recker; Kenneth R. Reffeitt, Great Keeper of Wampum, Great Council of the United States, Improved Order of Red Men; Rolfe Robertson; Mrs. Sigourney Romaine; John D. Schaperkotter, Esq.; Dr. George Green Shackelford; Mrs. Linda Wright Smith; Mrs. Courtenay T. Stanley; The Reverend Canon Stephen F. Sidebotham, Rector, St. George's Gravesend; W. Leigh Taylor; Mrs. Inez N. Tomlinson; Virginia State Library; Nettie Watson, The Filson Club, Inc.; Benjamin B. Weisiger III, M.D.; Waverly K. Winfree, Librarian, Department of Manuscript Cataloging, Virginia Historical Society; and Mrs. Robert K. Woltz. Also, Eldridge Hoyle Turner.

CONTENTS

ILLUSTRATIONS

PHOTO CREDITS

Page iv Association for the Preservation of Virginia Antiquities
Page 79-B National Portrait Gallery, Smithsonian Institution,
           Washington, D.C.

INTRODUCTION

This volume is a slight revision and enlargement, and a considerable extension of the list of the descendants of Pocahontas as set out in Wyndham Robertson's splendid work, POCAHONTAS AND HER DESCENDANTS (1887).

Ideally, a list of descendants should include the full name of each descendant, together with that descendant's genealogical dates - - - month, day and year of birth, of death, of marriage(s), and of divorce(s) - - - together with the dates of the birth and death of that descendant's spouse(s), and the names of the parents of the spouse(s), the later being for the purpose of spousal identification. But in this volume, as in most similar volumes, there are many "blanks".

Also this volume probably contains at least a few errors. And any and all suggested additions and/or corrections are both cordially invited and earnestly requested---a supplemental volume (not a replacement volume) will be published in due course.

Please write to The Pocahontas Foundation, P. O. Box 431, Berryville, Virginia 22611.

NUMBERING SYSTEM

The numbering system used in this volume is the same as that employed in RANDOLPH, but with a bit of modification.

Bolling Descendants

According to ROBERTSON:

Pocahontas and John Rolfe had only one child: Thomas Rolfe.

Thomas Rolfe had only one child: Jane Rolfe.

Jane Rolfe, who married Col. Robert Bolling, had only one child: Maj. John Bolling, who had six children.

Normally, under the numbering system employed in RANDOLPH, the digital numbering system, Pocahontas would be 1, Thomas Rolfe would be 11, Jane Rolfe would be 111, and Maj. John Bolling would be 1111.

But since these four persons are common ancestors of all of the Bolling descendants of Pocahontas, the 1111 that would precede the number of each of Maj. John Bolling's descendants is omitted, and the first digits are assigned to Maj. John Bolling's children, with the six children being numbered 1 through 6.

Elwyn (Elwin) Descendants

According to the proponents of the Elwyn (Elwin) descent (see below), Thomas Rolfe had a daughter Anne who married Peter Elwyn. And under the numbering system employed in RANDOLPH, Pocahontas would be 1, Thomas Rolfe would be 11, and Anne Rolfe rather than Jane Rolfe would be 111 since she was older than Jane Rolfe - - - Jane Rolfe would be 112.

But in this volume, since there may be some doubt about the Elwyn descent, Jane Rolfe is given "first billing" (and the number 111), and Anne Rolfe receives a qualified "billing" (and the letter "E" rather than the number 111).

Accordingly, Anne Rolfe's (and Peter Elwyn's) children are numbered E1, E2, etc.

And E1, E2, etc., denote an Elwyn great grandchild of Pocahontas, whereas the numbers 1, 2, etc., denote a Bolling great-great-grandchild of Pocahontas.

An E plus two digits (E11, etc.) denote an Elwyn great-great-grandchild of Pocahontas; and E plus three digits (E111, etc.) denote an Elwyn great-great-great-grandchild of Pocahontas; etc.

Two digits without an E (11, etc.) denote a Bolling great-great-great-grandchild of Pocahontas; three digits without an E (111, etc.) denote a great-great-great-great-grandchild of Pocahontas; etc.

To avoid using rather clumsy phrases such as great-great-etc., one may use $great^2$ for great-great, $great^3$ for great-great-great, etc. For example, a nine digit with no E person would be a $great^{10}$ grandson (or a $great^{10}$ granddaughter) of Pocahontas, and Pocahontas would be that person's $great^{10}$ grandmother. And for those who go in for fractions, a nine digit with no E person, for example, is 1/2048th Pocahontas blood.

And for those persons who descend from Pocahontas through more than one ancestor, the fraction would be increased.

For example, a person might be a $great^7$ granddaughter of Pocahontas, and also a $great^8$ granddaughter of Pocahontas.

As the $great^7$ granddaughter of Pocahontas, the person is 1/512th Pocahontas blood, and as the $great^8$ granddaughter of Pocahontas, the person is 1/1024th Pocahontas blood. And, adding the fractions, the person is 3/1024ths Pocahontas blood.

In the digital numbering system, in order to avoid confusion, the tenth child of a descendant is lettered "x"; the eleventh child is lettered "a"; the twelfth child is lettered "b"; etc., with the letters "x", "a", "b", etc., being used in lieu of digits.

Multi-Descent

A number of persons descend from Pocahontas through more than one ancestor.

In this volume, an attempt is made to see to it that such descendants are not listed and numbered twice. Rather, they are listed and numbered under their father or mother, but not under both, and an attempt is made to see to it that they are appropriately cross-referenced.

Ideally, in a volume such as this, children are numbered chronologically (in order of their births), but in this volume, many birth dates are either unknown or uncertain, and chronological numbering is not attempted.

POCAHONTAS,

ALIAS MATOAKA,

AND HER DESCENDANTS

THROUGH HER MARRIAGE AT

Jamestown, Virginia, in April, 1614,

WITH

JOHN ROLFE, GENTLEMAN;

INCLUDING THE NAMES OF

ALFRIEND, ARCHER, BENTLEY, BERNARD, BLAND, BOLLING, BRANCH,
CABELL, CATLETT, CARY, DANDRIDGE, DIXON, DOUGLAS, DUVAL,
ELDRIDGE, ELLETT, FERGUSON, FIELD, FLEMING, GAY, GORDON,
GRIFFIN, GRAYSON, HARRISON, HUBARD, LEWIS, LOGAN, MARK-
HAM, MEADE, McRAE, MURRAY, PAGE, POYTHRESS, RAN-
DOLPH, ROBERTSON, SKIPWITH, STANARD, TAZEWELL,
WALKE, WEST, WHITTLE, AND OTHERS.

WITH

Biographical Sketches

BY

WYNDHAM ROBERTSON,

AND

ILLUSTRATIVE HISTORICAL NOTES

BY

R. A. BROCK.

J. W. RANDOLPH & ENGLISH,

PUBLISHERS AND BOOKSELLERS,

1302 MAIN ST., RICHMOND, VA.

1887.

POCAHONTAS

The date of Pocahontas's birth is not known - - - estimates
are that it occurred in about 1595 - - - and her mother is identified
only as being one in the series of over 100 wives of Wahunsonacock
(called Powhatan by the English), chief Werowance of the Powhatan
Confederary of Algonquian tribes that occupied much of the tide-
water section of Virginia.

The name Pocahontas was a nickname. Her proper name was
Matoaka. Or according to Strachey, "she was rightly called Amonute",
a name that is sometimes spelled Amonate (and there are several
narrow variations in the spelling of Pocahontas, and some rather
wide variations in the spelling of Matoaka).

On April 5, 1614, in Jamestown, Pocahontas (freshly
baptised Rebecca by the English) was married to John Rolfe, an
innovative, tobacco-growing colonist, who may or may not have been
the John Rolfe who was the son of John and Dorothea Mason Rolfe of
Heacham, and who was christened on May 6, 1585.

John Rolfe

At the time of his marriage to Pocahontas, Rolfe was a
childless widower.

On June 2, 1609, he and his late wife (who probably was
his first wife, and whose name is not known) were among the some
500 persons who left England in Sir George Somers' fleet of nine
ships which were ladened with a "third supply" of provisions and
settlers for the struggling Colony of Virginia.

The fleet, following the Canaries route, entered the
tropics where a number of those aboard succumbed to yellow fever,
and on July 25th, near the Bahamas, the fleet was struck by a
terrific forty-four hour storm, a storm that is believed to have
been the basis for Shakespeare's "The Tempest". The nine ships were
scattered; one, "The Catch", was destroyed; and the "Sea Venture"
(or "Sea Adventure") was so badly damaged that when it finally
reached the islands of Bermuda, it was driven aground and wrecked
(on August 7th).

Fortunately, all of the "Sea Venture's" personnel survived
- - - the lucky ones included the Admiral (Somers); the captain (and
Virginia's Vice-Admiral), Sir Christopher Newport; the Colony's
Lieutenant-Governor, Sir Thomas Gates; and last (and possibly among
the least) John Rolfe and his wife - - - and soon the shipwrecked
party, making use of materials salvaged from the "Sea Venture",
commenced the tedious task of constructing two small ships which
they hoped would carry them on to Jamestown.

Some weeks before the two ships were completed, Rolfe's
wife gave birth to a daughter who, on February 21, 1610, was

christened Bermuda Rolfe, and who probably died before the two ships bearing the surviving members of the shipwrecked party finally quit the islands. And Rolfe's wife died, probably soon after the two ships reached Jamestown on June 2, 1610.

QUERY: Was Pocahontas childless at the time of her marriage to Rolfe?

This question is prompted by claims of descent from Pocahontas through a child or children (name or names not stated) born to Pocahontas prior to her marriage to Rolfe, and there may well be some bases for such claims.

William Strachey wrote, ca. 1612, that Pocahontas is "now marryed to a pryvate Captayne called Kocoum some 2. yeares synce". See MOSSIKER 147-150, and BARBOUR 99 and 264. And by the spring of 1613, when Pocahontas's captivity by the English commenced, she may well have given birth to one or more children. But because of the scarcity of contemporary or near-contemporary written records, the proving or disproving of such a birth, or a line of descent from such a child would be quite difficult.

Thomas Rolfe (b. ca. 1615)

In due course, John Rolfe and Pocahontas had a son, Thomas, the date of whose birth is not known, but who probably was named for Sir Thomas Dale, the Colony's acting Governor. Or Thomas Rolfe may possibly have been named for the London-based Virginia Company's Treasurer, Sir Thomas Smith.

In the Spring of 1616, Dale returned to England aboard the "Treasurer", taking with him a heterogenous group that included a Spanish spy, an Irish traitor, and the John Rolfes plus Pocahontas' sister, her sister's husband, one of her father's tribal councilors-priests, and "several young Indians of both sexes".

On May 31, 1616, the "Treasurer" arrived in Plymouth. And during the months that followed, Pocahontas was made or became the object of a considerable amount of publicity.

But Pocahontas soon sickened as did her baby son Thomas and, most probably, the other Indians.

Possibly because of these illnesses, or possibly pursuant to schedule, the Colony's sponsors, the Virginia Company, made arrangements for the John Rolfes to return to Virginia aboard Capt. Samuel Argall's "George", the flagship of a fleet of three Virginia-bound vessels. But as Pocahontas "was returning homeward" ("towards Virginia"), she died in Gravesend, a Thames River port located some twenty-odd miles downstream from London.

A Briton writing on March 29, 1617, reported the death "last week in Gravesend" of "The Virginian woman", and a cleric, entering in the Gravesend Parish Register a record of Pocahontas' March 21, 1617 burial, referred to her as "a Virginia lady borne".

Because of Thomas' sickness, John Rolfe was "ymportuned" to leave him in Gravesend, but John Rolfe "hadde no * * * intent" of so doing. However, he apparently felt that he could not delay his own previously planned departure, and so both he and Thomas together with Thomas' "attendants" boarded the "George" as it was preparing to set sail for Plymouth, the last English port of call for many Virginia-bound vessals.

En route, on the one hundred and seventy-odd mile trip from Gravesend westward to Plymouth, the "George" encountered "smooth water", but despite this, John Rolfe "found such feare and hazard of (Thomas') health (being not fully recovered of his sickness) and lack of attendance (for they who looked to him hadd need of nurses themselves, and indeed in all or passage pvd no better) that by the advise of Captaine Argal, and Divers who also forsaw the danger and knew the inconvenyence hereof pswade" Rolfe to leave Thomas in Plymouth.

According to Argall, Sir Lewis Stukely, Vice-Admiral of Devon, the shire in which Plymouth was located, "desired the keeping of" baby Thomas Rolfe. John Rolfe, writing in a similar vein, reported that Stukely was "so Nobly mynded toward me, that he most earnestly entreated to have the keping of (Thomas) until my Brother tooke further order". And Thomas, "the lyving ashes of his deceased mother", was left in England until he was "of better strength to endure so hard a passage".

And the probabilities seem to be that not long after John Rolfe departed in the "George", Thomas was in London under the care of his uncle, John Rolfe's merchant brother Henry.

John Rolfe remarried, probably soon after returning to Virginia, his new wife being Joanne or Jane Pierce (also spelled Pyers, Peirce, Perse, Pearsey, etc.), daughter of Capt. William and Joann Pierce, and by his new wife, Rolfe had a daughter Elizabeth.

John Rolfe died sometime between March 10, 1622 (the date of his will) and October 7, 1622, the date upon or prior to which the news of his death reached his brother Henry in England. (MOSSIKER) And John Rolfe may have been killed in the massacre of Good Friday, March 22, 1622, or he may have died of natural causes - - - in his will, he recites that he is "sicke in body, but of perfecte mind and memory".

His will, which was probated in London's prerogative Court of Canterbury on May 31, 1630, by John Rolfe's father-in-law, "William Pyers", i.e., Capt. William Pierce, is set out in full in 58 V 61.

Some time after John Rolfe's death, his widow Jane re-married - - - in the Muster of January 1625, she and her daughter Elizabeth (then four years old) are listed as living with her husband (her daughter's step-father), Capt. Roger Smith.

In September of 1632, at St. James Church, Clerkenwell, London, one Thomas Rolfe married Elizabeth Washington who, it is said, died soon after the birth of their daughter, Anne Rolfe, who, it is said, married (in 1659) Peter Elwyn, and by him had three sons and four daughters.

QUERY: Was this Thomas Rolfe the son of Pocahontas?

This question is discussed hereinafter in the section on the Elwyns.

Ca. 1635, Thomas Rolfe, the son of Pocahontas, returned to Virginia - - - on 6/22/1635, Capt. William Pierce, the father of Thomas Rolfe's step-mother, received a headright grant of land in return for having underwritten the transportation to Virginia of forty persons including Thomas Rolfe.

Years later, on October 10, 1655, Thomas Rolfe fathered a daughter Jane who, according to one source, was named for his step-mother. 6 W(1) 28.

Rolfe's wife (and baby Jane's mother) has not been definitely identified. CHART shows her name as "unknown". OMSS shows her as "Jane Poyers". And Judge Robertson (in ROBERTSON p. 30) writes: "I adopt 'Jane Poythress' (not Poyers)" (and cites reasons that are not altogether convincing).

Judge Robertson's full sentence reads: "I adopt 'Jane Poythress' (not Poyers) whom he is stated in the 'Bolling Memoirs' to have married in England".

The "he" to whom Judge Robertson refers is Thomas Rolfe, and the "Bolling Memoirs" to which Judge Robertson refers were written, in French, in 1764, by Robert Bolling (1738-1775), "who courted the muses and wrote equally well in Latin, French and Italian". Ca. 1803, William Robertson (1750-1829) gave the "Bolling Memoirs" to his son, John Robertson (1787-1873), "as an exercise in translation", and John Robertson's translation made in 1803 eventually "fell into the hands of John Randolph, of Roanoke", who "showed his interest in it by inserting explanatory notes, by interlineation". And in 1868, "a small number of copies" of the translation plus notes were "printed for private distribution" by Thomas H. Wynne under the title "A Memoir of A Portion of The Bolling Family in England and Virginia" (cited herein as MEMOIR).

An examination of MEMOIR does not disclose any "married in England" statement, or anything else pertaining to Thomas Rolfe's wife (and baby Jane's mother), and this leads to the conclusion that the "married in England" statement may have been found in the "Bolling Memoirs" and/or in the 1803 translation.

The phrase "Jane Poyers, of England" appears in OMSS - - - it may have appeared also in the 1803 translation - - - and Judge Robertson may have concluded, rightly or wrongly, that "of England" meant that Jane and Thomas Rolfe were married in England.

Judge Robertson notes, also on p. 30, that "Poyers" is "one of the forms of spelling the modern Pierce or Peirce", and this gives rise to the possibility that the wife of Thomas Rolfe (and the mother of his daughter Jane) may have been related to John Rolfe's third wife (and Thomas Rolfe's step-mohter), or that one or more of the early writers may have confused the wives of the two Rolfes.

In 1675, Thomas Rolfe's daughter Jane married Col. Robert Bolling.

QUERY: Did Thomas Rolfe have a child or children other than Jane Rolfe Bolling, and other than Anne Rolfe who married Peter Elwyn?

This question is prompted by claims of descent from Pocahontas through a child or children of Thomas Rolfe other than Jane Rolfe Bolling and Anne Rolfe Elwyn.

CHART shows "an only daughter" (who married Col. Robert Bolling). OMSS includes the following: "Thomas Rolfe, who married Jane Poyers, of England, and left one child only, a daughter" (who married Col. Robert Bolling). ROBERTSON, p. 29, states that Thomas Rolfe and Jane Poythress "left issue one child only, a daughter" (who married Col. Robert Bolling). And a Deed dated October 1, 1698, recites that "Jane late wife of Robert Bolling * * * was the only daughter of Thomas Rolfe dec'd". 1 V 447.

CHART, OMSS, ROBERTSON, and the October 1, 1698 Deed all are post-Thomas Rolfe creations of one or more of the descendants of Jane Rolfe Bolling, and the financial interests of these descendants would be furthered or at least protected if it could be established that Jane was the only child of Thomas Rolfe (who died intestate).

As noted below in the section on the Elwyns, Mrs. Carson's allegation that Anne Rolfe Elwyn was Thomas Rolfe's daughter merits acceptance. And there is a possibility that Thomas Rolfe had a child or children other than Jane Rolfe Bolling and Anne Rolfe Elwyn. In this connection, see the notes in the Appendix: "The Rolfes of North Carolina" and "Barnett".

Thomas Rolfe died some time between September 16, 1658, when he received a headright grant for 50 acres of land located on the Chickahominy, and October 1, 1698, the date of the Deed noted above.

A marker erected in 1946 by the Virginia Conservation Commission at the site of "Kippax" or "Farmingdale" (located in Prince George County on the south side of the Appomattox River not far from what is now the City of Petersburg) gives Thomas Rolfe's dates as 1615-1680. ROBERTSON-PATTON, p. 18. But the 1680 death date has not been established.

Jane Rolfe Bolling is memorialized by a similar marker at the same site, and James S. Patton, perhaps the best living authority on matters pertaining to the Rolfes and the Bollings, is of the opinion that both Thomas Rolfe and Jane Rolfe Bolling were, and still are buried at "Kippax".

Jane Rolfe (1650-1676)

In 1675, Jane Rolfe married Col. Robert Bolling (12/26/1646-7/17/1709) of "Kippax", son of John and Mary Bolling of London, and in due course, they had "one son, John Bolling, born ye 27th day of Jan'y, 1676". MEMOIR, p. 3.

In 1681, Col. Robert Bolling married, as his second wife, Anne Stith, daughter of Maj. John and Jane Parsons Stith of Brunswick County.

Col. Robert and Ann Stith Bolling's descendants (seven children, etc., etc.) are sometimes referred to as "white" Bollings to distinguish them from the descendants of Colonel Robert and Jane Rolfe Bolling who, in the same context, and because of their descendancy from Pocahontas, are sometimes referred to as "red" Bollings.

John Bolling (1/26/1675*6-4/20/1729)

Maj. John Bolling of "Cobbs" (1/26/1675*6-4/20/1729) m. 12/29/1697 (date of marriage bond), Mary Kennon (6/29/1679-   ), daughter of Dr. Richard and Elizabeth Worsham Kennon of "Conjuror's Neck".

Children of Maj. John and Mary Kennon Bolling:

1 Col. John Bolling
2 Jane Bolling, m. Col. Richard Randolph
3 Mary Bolling, m. Col. John Fleming
4 Elizabeth Bolling, m. Dr. William Gay
5 Martha Bolling, m. Thomas Eldridge
6 Anne Bolling, m. James Murray

COL. JOHN BOLLING

1   Col. John Bolling (1/20/1700*1-9/6/1757) of "Cobbs", m. (1st)
    Elizabeth Lewis, dau. of John and Elizabeth Warner Lewis of
    "Warner Hall". She d. soon after the marriage. No issue. He
    m. (2nd) 8/1/1728, Elizabeth Bland Blair (4/4/1712-4/22/1775),
    dau. of Dr. Archibald Blair of Williamsburg and his third wife
    Mary Wilson of "Ceelys" (Doctor Blair was Mary's third husband,
    her first husband having been William Roscow, and her second
    husband having been Miles Cary). Another source says that
    Elizabeth was the daughter of Dr. Archibald Blair's second
    wife, Sarah (Archer?), widow of Bartholomew Fowler. Elizabeth
    m. (2nd), Richard Bland, Jr. (1710-1766), as his third wife,
    his first wife having been Anne Poythress (1712-1758), and
    his second wife having been Martha Macon Massie. In MEMOIR,
    p. 6, it is reported that Col. John Bolling "died at Cobbs,
    6 Sept'r, 1757, and was buried near his father and mother".
    NOTE: There is a difference of opinion as regards the
    identity of those children of Col. John and Elizabeth Bland
    Blair Bolling who are not named in ROBERTSON or in CHART,
    the difference of opinion being detailed in the Appendix
    note "Children of Col. John and Elizabeth Bland Blair
    Bolling".

11   Thomas Bolling (7/7/1735-8/7/1804) of "Cobbs", m. 11/24/1757,
    Elizabeth ("Betty") Gay (9/ /1738-11/27/1813)(his first
    cousin), dau. of Dr. William and Elizabeth Bolling Gay.
    Thomas, "was born at Varina on the 18 July, 1735", MEMOIR,
    p. 7, the fifth child (see below 19, et seq.)

111   Elizabeth Bolling (10/14/1758-8/12/1830), m. 5/7/1775, William
    Robertson (2/5/1750-11/18/1829), son of Archibald and
    Elizabeth Fitzgerald Robertson

1111   Archibald Robertson (4/16/1776-1861), m. 6/11/1801, Elizabeth
    Meade Bolling (17 -1823)(his mother's first cousin),
    dau. of Archibald Bolling, and his second wife, Jane Randolph

11111 Elizabeth Jane Robertson (1802-1822). Unm.

11112 Rebecca Murray Robertson (1803-1823). Unm.

11113 Pocahontas Anne Robertson (1805-1838), m. 1832, William
    Smith Bolling. No issue. Home: Columbus, Mississippi

11114 Virginia Bolling Robertson (1807-1836), m. 1832, Col. Ralph
    Graves (-1848), C.S.A. He d. in Mississippi

111141 Archibald Bolling Graves (1833-1867), Captain C.S.A. Unm.
    Died in Texas

111142 Virginia Graves (1835-1837)

1112   Thomas Bolling Robertson (2/27/1778-10/5/1828), m. 4/12/1821,
    Lelia Skipwith (4/13/1804-4/28/1844), dau. of Fulwar Skipwith
    and a Flemish Countess. Skipwith was governor of the West
    Florida republic. No issue. Robertson was governor of
    Louisiana. Lelia m. (2nd) Humberstone Skipwith (-9/
    /1863). She was his second wife, and they had issue.
    BP 228

1113   William Robertson, Jr. (6/8/1785-8/20/1855), m. 1809,
    Christina Williams (1/1/1790-9/18/1850), dau. of Frederick
    (1749-5/9/1829) and Ann Williams

11131 Lelia Skipwith Robertson (4/23/1823-8/ /1827)

11132　Ann Robertson (11/22/1810-1847), m. 4/28/1831, Nathaniel G.
　　　　Friend, M.D. (　　-1853), son of Nathaniel and Elizabeth
　　　　Gilliam Friend of "White Hall", Prince George County
111321　William Robert Friend (1832-1889), m. Ella Dunlop Lightfoot
　　　　(1840-1867), dau. of Dr. Philip Lewis and Mary Virginia
　　　　Smith Lightfoot
1113211　Dau., d. inf.
111322　Elizabeth Friend, m. 1860, Francis J. Lynch (1815-1897)
1113221　Virginia Friend Lynch (1861-1934), m. ca. 1880, James
　　　　Alexander Wimbish (1858-1886)
11132211　Lila Taylor Wimbish (1881-1948), m. 1901, Oscar Gustav
　　　　Eckhardt (18　-1960)
111322111　Oscar ("Ox") Gustav Eckhardt, Jr. (1901-1951), m. Edith
　　　　Harrison
1113221111　Lila Taylor Wimbish Eckhardt (1949-　　)
111322112　James Wimbish Eckhardt, M.D. (1905-　　), m. 1931,
　　　　Louise Adams
111322113　Lila Virginia Eckhardt (1907-　　), m. 1930, George
　　　　E. Robinson
1113221131　Patricia Robinson, m. John Tate
1113221132　George E. Robinson, Jr.
1113221133　James Oscar Robinson
1113221134　James Eckhardt Robinson
11132212　James Henderson Wimbish (1884-　　), m. 1936, Ruth
　　　　Cook
111323　Christina Friend, m. Dr. James Archie Wimbish
1113231　Archie Glenn Wimbish (1859-1937), m. Dora
11132311　Tom Wimbish
11132312　Dora Wimbish
11132313　Tina Wimbish
11132314　Glenn Wimbish
11132315　Fannie Wimbish
11132316　Mary Wimbish
111324　Virginia Friend, m. Capt. William McCormack
1113241　Jose McCormack (　　-1931), m. Percy Caldwell
11132411　Virginia McCormack
11132412　William McCormack
11132413　Lillian McCormack
111325　Nathaniel G. Friend, Jr., m. Araminta A. Harrison
1113251　Kate Harrison Friend (1874-1949). Unm.
111326　John Wesley Friend (1842-1915), m. 1875, Hibernia McIlwaine
　　　　(1856-1945)
1113261　Robert McIlwaine Friend (8/26/1876-1968), m. (1st) 4/18/
　　　　1911, Bessie Meade Patterson (2181121)(3/31/1892-1916).
　　　　M. (2nd) 1941, Florence Winfield (1896-　　)
11132611　Bessie Meade Friend (8/6/1912-　　), m. 7/8/1939,
　　　　Francis Elmer Drake (10/13/1908-197　), son of Clarence
　　　　Elmer and Annie Vann Lewis Drake
111326111　Francis Elmer Drake, Jr. (6/10/1941-　　)
111326112　Elizabeth Randolph Meade Drake (3/11/1943-　　), m.
　　　　Leslie Cunliffe
1113261121
1113261122

1113261123
1113261124
11132612 Margaret Patterson Friend (10/29/1913-   ), m. 10/
    29/1942, Rev. William David Stewart (10/5/1913-   ),
    son of William Weldon Thompson and Ada Parks Clotfelter
    Stewart
111326121 Margaret Beverly Stewart (1945-   ), m. James
    Warner Armstrong
1113261211
1113261212
1113261213
1113261214
111326122 Mary Friend Stewart (1947-   ), m. Darrell R.
    Shephard
1113261221
111326123 William D. Stewart, Jr. (1949-   ), m. Margaret
1113261231
1113261232
1113261233
1113262 Hibernia McIlwaine Friend (1879-1957). Unm.
1113263 John Wesley Friend, Jr. (1881-1943), m. 1904, Grace Irving
    Lunsford (1882-   )
11132631 John Wesley Friend III (1905-1916)
11132632 Grace Lunsford Friend (1909-   ), m. 1931, Dr. Clabe
    Webster Lynn (1900-   )
111326321 Clabe Webster Lynn, Jr. (1932-   )
111326322 John Worth Lynn (1936-   ), m. Etta Donman Mann
1113263221 Anne Catherine Lynn (1958-   )
111326323 Jean E. Lynn (1943-   )
111326324 Robert Page Lynn (1944-   )
11132633 Charles Lunsford Friend (191 -   ), m. (1st)   .
    M. (2nd) Rosemary   (1914-   ). No issue
    Children by first wife:
111326331 Emily Rule Friend (1945-   )
111326332 John Wesley Friend (1948-   )
111326333 Jean Rose Friend (1952-   )
111326334 Charles Lunsford Friend, Jr. (1959-   )
11132634 Robert McIlwaine Friend (1915-   ), m. 1943, Ruth
    Johnson
111326341 Carole Ann Friend (1944-   ), m. Frank Douglas
    Pinckney
111326342 Grace Lunsford Friend (1947-   ), m. Everett Theo-
    dore Mullins, Jr.
111326343 Robert McIlwaine Friend, Jr. (1950-   )
11132635 Rose Berry Friend (1916-   ), m. (1st) Dr. Thomas
    Ethelburg Loving (19 -1959). No issue. M. (2nd) Fred
    Whipp
11132636 Hibernia McIlwaine Friend (1917-   ), m. James
    Arthur Richardson, Jr. (1916-   )
111326361 James Arthur Richardson III (1943-   ), m. Brenda
    Bailey
111326362 John Friend Richardson (1947-   ), m. Margie
    Lordman
1113263621 Cricket Richardson

111326363 George Randolph Richardson (1949-   ), m. Debbie
    Maltrotti
111326364 Grace Irving Richardson (1954-   ), m. Beto Samilpas
1113263641 Jenny Rose Richardson
111326365 Cecile Richardson (1956-   )
111326366 Martha Helen Richardson (1958-   )
1113264 Lucy Pryor Friend (1884-1959). Unm.
1113265 Archibald Graham McIlwaine Friend (dau.)(1887-1979), m.
    1914, Rev. James Woodrow Hassell (1886-1979)
11132651 James Woodrow Hassell, Jr. (1915-   ), m. 1947,
    Virginia Senn
111326511 James Woodrow Hassell III (1948-   )
111326512 Hugh Senn Hassell (1951-   )(twin), m.
111326513 Andrew Morrison Hassell (1951-   )(twin), m.
111326514 Dorothy Virginia Hassell (1954-   ), m. Karekin
    Goekjian
111326515 William David Hassell (1956-   )
11132652 Hibernia McIlwaine Hassell (1917-   ), m. 1941,
    Col. Charles Henry Cuthbert IV (1917-   )
111326521 Margaret Collier Cuthbert (1943-   ), m. D. Tilgh-
    man Broaddus
1113265211
1113265212
1113265213
1113265214
111326522 Charles Henry Cuthbert, Jr. (1947-   ), m.
1113265221
111326523 Hibernia McIlwaine ("Mac") Cuthbert (1950-   ), m.
    1976, William J. Langley
111326524 Nathaniel West Cuthbert (1956-   )
11132653 Lucy Friend Hassell (1921-   ), m. 1943, Dr. John
    Woodrow Davis (1918-   )
111326531 John Woodrow Davis, Jr. (1944-   ), m.
111326532 Archibald Graham Davis (1947-   ), m.
111326533 Roger Pryor Davis (1950-   ), m.
111326534 Nancy Winslow Davis (1952-   ), m. Cecil Bilbro
111326535 James Hassell Davis (1954-   )
111326536 Katherine Barwell Davis (1957-   )
11132654 Andrew Morrison Massell (1923-   ), m. 1946, Mary
    Lois Johns (1925-   )
111326541 Elizabeth Graham Hassell (1953-   )
111326542 Jane Mathis Hassell (1955-   ), m. Keith Wishon
11133 William Robertson III (2/18/1813-4/11/1865), m. (1st) ca.
    1835, Mary Anne Caruthers (-9/27/1842). M.
    (2nd) 4/6/1846, Caroline A. Land of Sussex County
    Child by first wife:
111331 Dau., d. inf.
    Child by second wife:
111332 Caroline Gay Robertson (7/8/1849-1937), m. Charles P. Jones
    (1838-1931)
1113321 Caroline Jones (1868-1955), m. Leroy Nutt Blackwell (1864-
    1948)

11133211   LeRoy Nutt Blackwell, Jr., m. Lucie DuBois
111332111 Gay Robertson Blackwell, m. Dean Richard Lally
1113321111 Thomas Arthur Lally, m. Melanie Wood
1113321112 Dean Richard Lally, Jr., m. Janet Olsen
1113321113 Bryan Robertson Lally
1113321114 Charles Alen Lally (1969-1982)
111332112 Ann Gordon Blackwell, m. (1st) David Sanford Tilloston.
           M. (2nd) James McNeill
           Children by first husband:
1113321121 David Sanford Tilloston, Jr.
1113321122 John Blackwell Tilloston
1113321123 James Lee Tilloston
111332113 LeRoy Nutt Blackwell III (1934-1934)
111332114 Rose Yvonne Blackwell, m. Victor Poggie
1113321141 Yvonne Marie Poggie
1113321142 Caroline Gay Poggie
111332115 Lucie Keith Blackwell, m. (1st) Edward Demsey Schmidt.
           M. (2nd) George Park Killian
           Child by first husband:
1113321151 Tracey Ann Schmidt (Killian)
11133212   Charles Claiborne Blackwell, m. Julia Mae Boothe
111332121 Charles Claiborne Blackwell, Jr., m. Helen Poff
1113321211 Charles Claiborne Blackwell III
1113321212 Carol Ann Blackwell
111332122 Robert Boothe Blackwell, m. Sandra Gail Dicus
1113321221 Elizabeth Dicus Blackwell
1113321222 Robert Boothe Blackwell, Jr.
111332123 Richard Cabot Blackwell, m. Judith Turner
1113321231 Sarah Turner Blackwell
1113321232 William Claiborne Blackwell
1113321233 Douglas F. Blackwell
1113321234 Patricia Wilsey Blackwell
11133213   Gordon Blackwell
11133214   Churchill Gordon Blackwell, m.
111332141 Churchill Gordon Blackwell III, m. Susan Casion Park
1113321411 Julia Elizabeth Blackwell, m. Matthew Edward Mays
1113321412 Janet Ellen Blackwell, m. Thomas Russell Turner
1113321413 Lisa Ann Blackwell
111332142 Ann Kent Blackwell, m. Thomas Best
1113321421 Nancy Kent Best
1113321422 Cynthia Anne Best
1113321423 Thomas Andrew Best
1113322   William Bolling Jones (1874-1903). Unm.
1113323   Martha Fairfax Jones, m. William Bartle
11133231   William Bartle, Jr.
1113324   Bessie Jones (1880-1963), m. (1st) 1898, Henry Fairfax
           Lynn, Jr. (1875-1906). M. (2nd) 1908, Winter Owens
           (1875-1966)
           Child by first husband:
11133241   Henry Fairfax Lynn III (1899-19), m. 1922, Mary Eliza
           Dorsey (1902-   )
111332411 Elizabeth Moore Lynn (1923-   ), m. 1947, Kenneth
           Donald Richards (1922-   )

```
1113324111  Donald James Richards (1948-        )
1113324112  Walter Scott Richards (1954-        )
111332412   Henry Fairfax Lynn, Jr. (1925-        ), m. (1st) 1949,
            Natalie Nell Clawson (1928-        ). Div. 1966. M. (2nd)
            1967, Norma Gilmer Schultz (1926-        )
         Children by first wife:
1113324121  Henry Fairfax Lynn III (1950-        ), m. 1973, Barbara
            Gilsdorf (1950-        )
1113324122  James Clawson Lynn (1954-        ), m. 1974, Gretchen
            Sue Hoff (1955-        )
11133241221
1113324123  Charles Andrew Lynn (1958-        )
111332413   Mary Frances Lynn (1926-        ), m. 1948, Joseph A.
            Cheatham, Jr. (1925-        )
1113324131  Joseph A. Cheatham III (1950-        ), m. 1972, Frances
            Mary White (1951-        )
1113324132  Debra Lynn Cheatham (1953-        ),m. 1974, Raymond C.
            Hooker III
11133241321
1113324133  Elizabeth Jean Cheatham (1965-        )
111332414   Caroline Jones Lynn (1928-        ), m. 1949, Thomas M.
            Doyle (1925-        )
1113324141  Thomas M. Doyle, Jr. (1951-        ), m. 1973, Donna M.
            Campbell. Div. 1975
1113324142  Mary Katherine Doyle (1955-        ),m. 1975, Christopher
            N. Rhodes
1113324143  Frances Ann Doyle (1956-        )
111332415   Jean Dorsey Lynn (1929-        ), m. 1949, Briscoe Baldwin
            Brown, Jr. (1927-        )
1113324151  Briscoe Baldwin Brown III (1951-        )
1113324152  Mary Crist Brown (1955-        )
1113324153  William Pendleton Brown (1956-        )
1113324154  Caroline Lynn Brown (1963-        )
1113324155  Edward Dorsey Brown (1971-1972)
         Children by second husband:
11133242    Elizabeth ("Bessie") Winter Owens (1911-        ), m. 1930,
            Bernard Carter Smith (1895-1957)
11133243    Kent Owens (1909-        ), d. young
1113325     Gay Robertson Jones (1882-        ), m. (1st) 1908, Edward
            Kinlock Turner (1867-1922); m. (2nd) M. H. Secrest
         Children by first husband:
11133251    Gay Robertson Turner (1909-        ), m. 1930, Hugh
            Craggs (1904-        )
111332511   Gay Frances Craggs (1937-        ), m. Guy Oliver Wasler
1113325111  Gay Kinlock Wasler
1113325112  Guy Oliver Wasler III
1113325113  Rebecca Lynn Wasler
1113325114  Hugh Craggs Wasler
1113325115  Michael John Wasler
111332512   John Rogers Craggs (1940-        ), m. Elizabeth Emily
            Thomas
1113325121  Scott Turner Craggs
```

1113325122 Kenneth Hugh Craggs
111332513 Barbara Jean Craggs, m. Wilford A. Hammond
1113325131 Walter Allen Hammond
11133252 Edward Beverley Turner (1912-   ), m. 1935,
    Kathleen Marie Goodenough
11134 Thomas Bolling Robertson (10/28/1814-3/31/1887), m. (1st)
    1836, Eliza J. C. Winfree of Chesterfield County; m. (2nd)
    1849, Martha Lindsay Fairfax (5/19/1826-11/24/1909), dau.
    of Henry and Elizabeth Lindsay Fairfax of Prince William
    County
    Child by first wife:
111341 Samuel Winfree Robertson (4/27/1843-1844)
    Child by second wife:
111342 Mary Bernard Robertson (10/27/1850-1925). Unm.
111343 Thomas Lindsay Robertson, M.D. (1852-1927), m. 1887,
    Clarinda Bowyer (1865-   )
1113431 Henry Bolling Robertson (1888-1894)
1113432 Mercer Leyburn Robertson (1895-196), m. Frances Thompson.
    No issue
111344 Thomas Bolling Robertson, Jr. (1854-1907), m. 1891, Lillian
    Hunter Lynn (1870-1947)
1113441 Walter Holmes Robertson (1892-1941), m. 1917, Frances
    Dorsey (1893-   ). Frances Dorsey m. (2nd) 1949,
    Ernest J. Ristedt
11134411 Frances Robertson (1918-   ), m. 1937, John M. Piercy,
    Jr. (1915-1978). M. (2nd) 1983
111344111 John M. Piercy III (1938-   ), m. 1960, Gloria Ann
    Hutcherson (1939-   )
1113441111 Melanie Ann Piercy (1961-   )
1113441112 John M. Piercy IV
1113441113 Michael Vaden Piercy
1113441114 Timothy Davis Piercy
111344112 Gay Lynn Piercy (1944-   ), m. Louis F. Gagnor
1113441121 Louis F. Gagnor, Jr.
1113441122 Jennifer Lynn Gagnor
1113441123 Walter Holmes Robertson Gagnor
11134412 Mary Ann Robertson (1919-   ), m. 1940, Robert
    Billington (1920-   )
111344121 Robin Ann Billington (1941-   ), m. (1st) 1960,
    William E. Toth (1938-   ). M. (2nd) Austin E.
    Starbird
    Children by first husband:
1113441211 Anthony Powell Toth (1961-   )
1113441212 Edward Billington Toth (1963-   )
1113441213 Anne Dorsey Toth
111344122 Robert Billington, Jr. (1944-   ), m.
111344123 Randall Holmes Billington (1948-   ), m. (1st), Lynn
    Fairfax Carr (111344331). M. (2nd) Louann
    Child by first wife:
1113441231 Melissa Billington
111344124 Thomas James Billington (1952-   )
111344125 John Edward Billington (1955-   )

111344126 Jeffrey Robertson Billington (1957-   )
11134413 Rita Holmes Robertson (1926-   ), m. (1st) 1949,
          Dr. Elliott Clarke Haley (1922-1957); m. (2nd) 1959,
          Robert K. Woltz (1919-   )
          Children by first husband:
111344131 Elliott Clarke Haley, Jr. (1949-   ), m. Jane
          Carroll Eggleton
111344132 Timothy Fairfax Haley (1951-   ), m. Anne Mary
          McDonnell
          Children by second husband:
111344133 Lynn Philippe Woltz (1960-   ), m. 1982, John J.
          Bernard
111344134 Rita Robertson Woltz (1961-   )
111344135 Sarah K. Woltz (1964-   )
1113442 Bolling Lynn Robertson (1894-1963), m. (1st) 1918, Marian
          Stoeger (1899-1961). Div. M. (2nd) 1937, Elizabeth
          Averitt Pennick (Meredith)(1895-   )
          Children by first wife:
11134421 Bolling Lynn Robertson, Jr. (1921-   ), m. (1st)
          1947, Edith Clisby. M. (2nd) 1953, Mavis Scott (1921-
          1981)
111344211 Bolling Lynn Robertson III (1948-   )
11134422 Caroline Fairfax Robertson (1923-1982), m. 1947, Thomas
          Gordon Lewis (-1961)
111344221 Marianne Fairfax Lewis (1948-   ), m. (1st)
          Larson. M. (2nd) William Isinger
          Child by first husband:
1113442211 Desiree Lee Larson
          Child by second husband:
1113442212 Robert Davis Isinger II
111344222 Linda Leslie Lewis (1952-   )
1113443 Rolfe Robertson (1896-1939), m. (1st) 1916, Charlotte
          Cochran (1897-   ). M. (2nd) 1922, Anne Peyton
          (1896-1942)
          Child by first wife:
11134431 Charlotte Robertson (1917-   ), m. (1st) 1947,
          Walter Munster (1916-   ). Div. M. (2nd) Amos
          Teasley
          Children by first husband:
111344311 Charlotte Nelson Munster (1949-   ), m. Steve
          Landvoight
1113443111 Maple Landvoight
1113443112 Noel Landvoight
111344312 Catherine Dabney Munster (1952-   ), m. Christopher
          Stilling
111344313 Walter Nelson Munster (1955-   )
          Child by second wife:
11134432 Rolfe Robertson, Jr. (1922-   ), m. 1950, Nancy
          Arthington Gilpin (1928-   )
111344321 Caroline Coxe Robertson (1952-   ), m. 1976, John
          Stewart Cross (1935-   )
1113443211 John Stewart Cross, Jr. (1978-   )

```
1113443212  Jennifer Thorsen Cross (1980-          )
111344322   Anne Peyton Robertson (1953-        ), m. 1976, Joseph
            John Procaccinni (1951-       )
1113443221  Anthony Nicholas Procaccinni (1979-          )
1113443222  Mary Peyton Procaccinni (1982-        )
1113443223  Joseph John Procaccinni III (1984-        )
111344323   Rolfe Robertson III (1955-        ), m. 1980, Debora
            Jeremiah (1955-       )
1113443231  Allison Brooke Robertson (1981-        )
1113443232  Kathryn Scot Robertson (1983-        )
111344324   Nancy Purchas Robertson (1956-        ), m. 1983, Martin
            Michael McNerney (1955-       )
1113443241  Martin Michael McNerney, Jr. (1984-        )
111344325   Charlotte Gilpin Robertson (1959-        ), m. 1982,
            Robert Charles Kettler (1952-       )
1113443251  Milton Taylor Kettler (1983-        )
111344326   James Wyndham Robertson (1963-        )
11134433    Phyllis Hunter Robertson (1924-1980), m. (1st) 1944,
            James Edward Carr.  M. (2nd) Overton Lea Murdock
        Children by first husband:
111344331   Lynn Fairfax Carr (1945-        ), m. (1st) Randall
            Holmes Billington (111344123).  Div. M. (2nd)
            Borton
111344332   James Edward Carr, Jr. (1948-        )
        Children by second husband:
111344333 Luke Lea Murdock (1964-        )
111344334   Elizabeth Murdock (1967-        )(Rolfe Robertson advises
            that Elizabeth was adopted as a young child by foster
            parents)
11134434    Thomas Bolling Robertson III (1925-        ), m. 1949,
            Ann Mary Cleveland (1925-       )
111344341   Thomas Bolling Robertson IV (1950-        ), m. 1982,
            Antoinette Scala
1113443411  Thomas Gailor Robertson (1983-        )
1113443412
111344342   Elizabeth Averett Robertson (1952-        ), m. 1974,
            Laurence Ray Arnold. Div.
111344343   Ruth Cleveland Robertson (1955-        ), m. 1982,
            Steven Abarbanel
11134435    John William Peyton Robertson (1927-        ), m. 1952,
            Edith Brooke (1928-       )
111344351   Elizabeth Bolling Robertson (1954-        ), m. 1981,
            Trace Tinsman
111344352   James Vass Brooke Robertson (1957-        )
111344353   John William Peyton Robertson, Jr. (1960-        )
11134436    Daniel Bruce Robertson (1929-        ), m. 1952, Diane
            Dixon (1930-       )
111344361   Randolph Christian Robertson (1953-        ), m. 1975,
            Diane Thomas
1113443611  Daniel Christian Robertson (1982-        )
1113443612  Lindsay Jane Robertson (1984-        )
111344362   Bruce Dixon Robertson (1957-        )
111344363   Ellen Peyton Robertson (1959-        )
111344364   Jonathan Rood Robertson (1963-        )
```

11134437 Anne Wyndham Robertson (1933-   ), m. 1954, Charles
        Donald Butter (1930-   )
111344371 Nancy Ann Butter (1955-   ), m. Keith Weiser
1113443711 Jessica Weiser (1982-   )
1113443712
111344372 Mary Josephine Butter (1958-   ), m. David Pierson
111344373 Charles Donald Butter, Jr. (1959-   )
111344374 Gretchen Butter (1965-   )
111344375 Daniel Butter (1968-   )
1113444 Rita Fairfax Robertson (1898-1974), m. 1918, John Arthur
        Brashears (1892-1967)
11134441 Lillian Lynn Brashears (1920-   ), m. 1945, John
        Gruet (19   -1954)
111344411 Eileen Lynn Gruet (1946-   )
11134442 Martha Knighton Brashears (1921-   ), m. 1944,
        Samuel James Gibson (1922-   )
111344421 James Randolph Gibson (1944-   )
111344422 Elizabeth Knighton Gibson (1950-   )m. Joseph A. Kohan
111344423 Gail Brashears Gibson (1955-   ), m. Harvey L.
        Zimmerman
11134443 Margaret Fairfax Brashears (1923-   ), m. 1944,
        George Reif (1921-   )
111344431 Gay Frances Reif (1946-   )
111344432 Karen Neely Reif (1950-   )
11134444 Rita Bolling Brashears (1930-   ), m. 1950, Fred
        E. Kuver (1927-   )
111344441 Fred Harwood Kuver (1952-   )
111344442 Nancy Lynn Kuver (1955-   )
111344443 Bethann Kuver (1959-   )
111345 John Walter Robertson (1856-1927), m. 1886, Caroline Mary
        Wyvill. Caroline Mary Wyvill m. (2nd) Frank Vanvleck
1113451 Louise Fairfax Robertson (1889-1968), m. 1914, George
        Twyman Wood, Jr.
11134511 George T. Wood IV (1922-   ), m. 1948, Mimi
        Etheridge
111345111 Lee Robertson Wood (1951-   )
111345112 George T. Wood V (1952-   )
111345113 Renee Wood, m. (1st) John McD. Cavin. M. (2nd) Robert
        Schlatter
        Children by first husband:
1113451131 Stephanie (Renee) Cavin
1113451132 John (James) Cavin
11134512 Walter Wyvill Wood (1928-   ), m. 1956, Caroline Shel-
        burne Crone
111345121 Victoria Armistead Wood (1960-   )
111345122 Walter Wyvill Wood, Jr. (1964-   )
111346 Mercer Leyburn Robertson (1858-1931), m. 1889, Edna Giels
        Simpson (1870-1956)
1113461 Edna Giels Robertson (1890-1967), m. 1915, Herbert H.
        Harrison (1884-   )
11134611 Edna Elizabeth Harrison (1916-   ), m. 1936,
        Worley Cottingham Campbell (brother of husband of
        11134612)

111346111 Harriet Ray Campbell (1937-   ), m.1955, Jerre
           Aiken Fillmore
1113461111 Margaret Fillmore (1956-   ), m. Chas. Owen
           Gaines
1113461112 William Campbell Fillmore (1957-   ), m. Brenda
           Hale
1113461113 Elizabeth Fillmore
111346112 Robert Harrison Campbell (1943-   ), m. Judy Preston
1113461121 Bryan Edward Campbell
1113461122 Bruce William Campbell
11134612 Harriet Harrison (1921-   ), m. (1st) 1943, William
         Bruce Campbell (1920-1968)(brother of husband of
         11134611). M. (2nd) James Henry Clarke
         Children by first husband:
111346121 Martha Ann Campbell (1946-   )
111346122 Sarah Elizabeth Campbell (1949-   )
111346123 William Bruce Campbell (1953-1976)(twin)
111346124 Ellen Campbell (1953-   )(twin)
1113462 Harriet Simpson Robertson (1891-   ), m. 1915, Thomas
        Elmer Chancellor (-1959)
11134621 Thomas Elmer Chancellor, Jr. (1917-   ), m. 1942,
          Precilla Angstman (1917-   )
111346211 Shelley Chancellor (1951-   )
111346212 Robin Chancellor (1952-   ), m. Greg Hagerman
1113462121 Zachery Chancellor Hagerman
1113463 Martha Fairfax Robertson (1893-1967). Unm.
111347 William Robertson (1859-1860)
111348 Henry Fairfax Robertson (1861-1928), m. 1892, Frances El-
        well Robertson (1870-1950)(111363)(his first cousin)
1113481 Nellie Reynolds Robertson (7/14/1894-10/1/1971)(twin), m.
         1917, Samuel Alexander Moore (1881-1925)
11134811 Samuel Alexander Moore, Jr. (11/18/1918-   ), m. (1st)
          1/27/1942, Nathalie Forbes Gardiner (3/1/1917-9/2/1962).
          M. (2nd) 9/1/1966, Lynn Ellen Lucas (1918-   )
          Children by first wife:
111348111 Judith Gardiner Moore (11/20/1944-   )
111348112 Sarah ("Sally") Adelaide Moore (11/29/1952-   )
11134812 Reynolds Robertson Moore (2/18/1925-   ), m. (1st)
          1/31/1946, Agnes Marie Cuevas (9/10/1924-   ). Div.
          M. (2nd) 7/10/1970, Esther Mae Hill (1/10/1927-   ).
          Div.
          Child by first wife:
111348121 Richard Reynolds Moore (9/12/1947-   ), m. 1/30/1968,
           Laurel L. Hoffman (3/17/1947-   )
1113481211 Brian Richard Moore (5/29/1969-   )
1113481212 Melanie Lee Moore (8/13/1974-   )
1113482 Mary Fairfax Robertson (7/14/1894-   )(twin), m.
        6/26/1926, Richard Edgar Waterhouse, Jr. (11/24/1901-2/
        26/1956)
11134821 Frances Waterhouse (3/22/1931-   ), m. 3/25/1954,
          Frederick Robert Richmond, Jr. (1930-   ). Div. 1959
111348211 Charlotte Fairfax Richmond (10/25/1957-   )

111348212 Adelaide Waterhouse Richmond (7/13/1959-   ), m.
    V. Darrell Waldron
11134822 Richard Edgar Waterhouse III (9/11/1934-   ), m.
    1/20/1968, Sidney Helen LaFlavour. Div. 8/ /1979
1113483 Frances Elwell Robertson (2/6/1897-7/12/1920), m. 9/20/
    1919, Frederick Scott Campbell (4/24/1884-3/20/1941)
11134831 William Robertson Campbell (7/11/1920-1959), m. 8/31/
    1941, Elizabeth Ann Moore (12/18/1919-   ). She
    m. (2nd) Ronald Johnson
111348311 Frederick Scott Campbell (9/23/1943-   ), m. 8/4/
    1965, Diane Di Nunzio (11/6/1945-   )
1113483111 Ann Marie Campbell (10/17/1967-   )
1113483112 Lisa Helm Campbell (10/27/1976-   )
111348312 William Moore Campbell (3/11/1955-   ), m. 2/10/
    1973, Peggy Ann Stone (12/30/1956-   )
1113483121 William Robertson Campbell (4/2/1973-   )
1113483122 Jessica Ann Campbell (4/3/1977-   )
111349 Frances Christina Robertson (3/ /1863-8/ /1863)
11134x Powhatan Wyndham Robertson (1865-1934), m. 1888, Margaret
    Lee Stone Chapman (1864-1935). No issue
11134a Murray Robertson (1868-1884)
11134b William Robertson (second of this name)(1/ /1869-6/ /
    1869)
11135 Frances Williams Robertson (11/23/1816-   ), m. (1st)
    4/ /1839, Achilles Swepson Jeffries (1806-1841) of
    Mecklenburg County. M. (2nd) Dr. Robert Gale of Texas
   Children by first husband:
111351 William Wyndham Jeffries (ca. 1840-1852)
111352 Child (ca. 1841 or 2-   )
   Children by second husband:
111353 Lelia R. Gale
111354 Fannie Gale (ca. 1854-   )
111355 Mary Gale (ca. 1857-   )
11136 Frederick Williams Robertson (2/4/1819-8/25/1870, m. (1st)
    2/15/1854, Fanny O. Spain (ca. 1835-1/30/1855), dau. of
    Richard and Mary Harmon Spain of Dinwiddie County. M. (2nd)
    10/29/1867, Charlotte Jane Reynolds (11/15/1826-1/7/1902),
    dau. of Rev. John Reynolds, Jr., and Ann Kettlewell Reynolds.
    Charlotte's first husband (m. 1/4/1855) was William Knox
    Hackett (8/18/1828-1/7/1862), who was mortally wounded at
    Battle of Seven Pines, and by whom she had three children.
   Child by first wife:
111361 Thomas Bolling Robertson (11/26/1854-1878). Unm.
   Children by second wife:
111362 William Frederick Robertson (8/2/1868-12/15/1940), m. 4/
    25/1894, Julia Clay Cox (11/12/1871-11/21/1958), dau. of
    Henry Clay and Julia Bradford Dundrieth Cox
1113621 Frederick Clay Robertson (2/22/1895-11/11/1969), m. 1923,
    Elizabeth Gibson Brown (7/10/1902-   ), dau. of
    Hampton Samuel and Mary Elizabeth Glass Brown
11136211 Mary Elizabeth Robertson (10/23/1925-   ), m. 8/22/
    1947, Edgar Marion Buttenheim (12/23/1922-   )

111362111 Margaret Collier Buttenheim (6/20/1949-   ), m.
           8/29/1976, Kenneth Robert Silk, MD. (5/27/1944-   )
1113621111 David Robertson Silk (7/25/1980-   )
111362112 Anne Robertson Buttenheim (4/25/1951-   )
111362113 Elizabeth Gay Buttenheim (3/12/1955-   )
111362114 Martha Bradford Buttenheim (4/4/1959-   ), m. 7/11/
           1981, Vytas Alfonsas Kisielius (3/8/1956-   )
11136212   Frederick Clay Robertson, Jr. (9/30/1927-   ), m.
           3/17/1951, Virginia Whipple Davidson (8/28/1932-   ),
           dau. of James Marquis and Virginia Norris Whipple
           Davidson
111362121 Bradford Ann Robertson (3/10/1953-   ), m. 8/8/1981,
           Charles Wade Hulcher (10/20/1950-   )
111362122 Susan Rutledge Robertson (1/31/1955-   )
111362123 Frederick Clay Robertson III (5/23/1958-   )
11136213   Bradford Brown Robertson (9/29/1938-3/27/1957)
1113622   Julian Hart Robertson (11/3/1899-   ), m. 4/25/1931,
           Blanche Williamson Spencer (1906-   ), dau. of
           James Harrison and Mary Blanche Williamson Spencer
11136221   Julian Hart Robertson, Jr. (6/25/1932-   ), m.
           8/22/1972, Josephine Vance Tucker (5/16/1943-   ),
           dau. of Robert Edwin and Josephine Vance Spencer Tucker
111362211 Julian Spencer Robertson (9/18/1974-   )
111362212 Julian Hart Robertson III (8/16/1977-   )
111362213 Alexander Tucker Robertson (7/24/1979-   )
11136222   Blanche Spencer Robertson (10/2/1935-   ), m. (1st)
           Benjamin Robert Williamson (9/3/1932-   ), son of
           Carl Levering and Betty Robertson Williamson. Div. 5/ /
           1979. M. (2nd) 1980, Zack Hampton Bacon, Jr. (7/5/1928-
)
           Children by first husband:
111362221 Benjamin Robert Williamson, Jr. (9/18/1956-   )
111362222 Blanche Spencer Williamson (3/19/1958-   )
111362223 Julian Robertson Williamson (1/11/1962-   )
11136223   Wyndham Gay Robertson (9/25/1937-   )
1113623   William Frederick Robertson, Jr. (1/19/1905-1983)(baptized
           William Cox Robertson - name changed in 1911), m. 10/24/
           1931, Elizabeth Orr (1907-   ), dau. of Henry
           Hammett and Emily ("Dolly") Wannamaker Orr
11136231   Julia Robertson (12/4/1932-   ), m. (1st) 7/9/1955,
           Spart James McKinney, Jr. (7/22/1930-   ), son of
           Spart James and Mary Howell McKinney. Div. 1978. M.
           (2nd) Thomas Kennedy Gentles
           Children by first husband:
111362311 Patricia Elizabeth McKinney (3/8/1957-   ), m. 11/
           30/1979, Thomas Jerry Crimminger (10/13/1951-   )
111362312 Katherine Clay McKinney (2/16/1959-   )
111362313 Julia Bradford McKinney (3/18/1956-   )
111362314 Emily Howell McKinney (1/2/1969-   )
11136232   William Frederick Robertson III (5/15/1936-   ), m.
           3/26/1960, Meredith Ann Gibson (11/13/1938-   ),
           dau. of Charles Arnold and Mary Alice Burns Gibson

```
111362321  Elizabeth Burns Robertson (6/18/1961-      )
111362322  William Marsh Robertson (8/20/1963-        )
111362323  Dolly Orr Robertson (5/26/1966-      )
111362324  Mary Anne Robertson (4/4/1969-      )
11136233   Henry Orr Robertson (8/30/1940-         ), m. 2/19/1966,
           Linda Lou Shirley (8/9/1944-         ), dau. of Vernon
           O. and Jane Jones Shirley
111362331  Henry Orr Robertson, Jr. (12/20/1968-      )
111362332  Frederick Olin Robertson (3/1/1972-        )
111362333  Meredith Shirley Robertson (10/16/1975-      )
11136234   Elizabeth Noble Robertson (9/3/1945-        ), m. 1973,
           Jack Davis Mobley (9/7/1938-        ), son of Harold
           Henry and Alma Davis Mobley
111363   Frances Elwell Robertson (5/4/1870-11/21/1950), m. 1/20/
         1892, Henry Fairfax Robertson (4/29/1861-1/12/1928)(her
         first cousin), son of Thomas Bolling and Martha Lindsay
         Fairfax Robertson. For their children, see 111348
11137    Christina Robertson (4/ /1821-post 1871), m. 1844, Dandridge
         C. Williams of Nottoway County (ca. 1812-        ). Lived
         in Alabama
111371   David G. Williams (ca. 1847-        )
111372   Sarah D. Williams (ca. 1848-        )
11138    Wyndham Robertson (3/2/1825-9/6/1866), m. (1st), 9/22/1847,
         Judith M. Pope of Memphis. No issue.  M. (2nd) 7/1/1856,
         Caterina Conte di Carlo (1836-3/10/1931) of Trieste.
         Caterina remarried.  Wyndham is bur. in Trieste in the
         di Carlo tomb.
111381   Wyndham Robertson, Jr. (1857-1942), m. (1st) 1902, Ross
         Girard Black (1886-1966).  M. (2nd) 1914, Emmy Schwenke
         (1894-        ).  Wyndham settled first in Louisiana, and
         later in Texas
         Child by first wife:
1113811  Margaret Nina Robertson (1903-1953), m. Cameron Ellsworth
         Wylie
11138111  Cameron Ellsworth Wylie, Jr. (1934-        ), m.
111381111
111381112
111381113
111381114
1113812  Wyn A. Robertson (1905-        ), m. (1st) 1924, Constance
         Keyworth.  Div.  M. (2nd) 1942, Laura Wilson Adams. No
         issue. Home: California
         Children by first wife:
11138121  Helen Patricia (Trish) Robertson (1925-        ), m. (1st)
          1946, Richard Anderson.  Div. 1952.  M. (2nd) 1954, John
          Williard Griffin.  M. (3rd) 1981, Arthur S. Kuhns
          Children by first husband:
111381211  Cynthia Lynn Anderson (1947-        ), m. 1964, Richard
           Roger Harris. Div.
1113812111  Rooty Darin Harris
111381212  Bradley Kent Anderson (1949-        ), m. (1st) 1966,
           Sandra Lynn Huffman. Div. M. (2nd) 1979, Kathy Jean
           Ruth
```

NOTE. 111381211 and 111381212 were adopted by John
     Williard Griffin, and names were changed to Griffin
     Child by second husband:
111381213 Christopher Sean Griffin (1956-   ), m. 1981,
     Kathleen Louise Philbrick
1113812131 Jay Robert Griffin (1982-   )
11138122 Wyndham Robertson (1927-   ), m. (1st)1949, Gloria
     Atwell. Div. M. (2nd) 1961, Linda Alexander. Home:
     California. M. (3rd) 1973, Linda Bickford
     Children by first wife:
111381221 Jeffry Wyndham Robertson (1950-   ), m. Linda Strawser
111381222 Stephan Eugene Robertson (1953-   )
     Children by second wife:
111381223 Wyndham Robertson III (1962-   )
111381224 Richard A. Robertson (1967-   )
     Child by second wife of 111381:
1113813 Wyndham-Gay Robertson (1915-   ), m. 1948, Harry
     Montague Bedell, Jr. (1925-   ). Div.
11138131 Christina Wyndham Bedell (1950-   ), m. 1974, Charles
     Edward Brehm III
111381311 Alexander Wyndham Brehm (1980-   )
111382 Christina Robertson
111383 Alida Robertson (-1864)
111384 Minnie Gay Robertson
11139 Lelia Skipwith Robertson (1823-1827)
1114 John Robertson (4/13/1787-7/5/1873), m. 4/28/1819, Ann Frances
    Trent (12/10/1799-7/29/1887), dau.of Col. John Archer and
    Elizabeth Montgomery Lewis Trent of "Vue Mont", Cumberland
    County
11141 Powhatan Robertson (9/24/1820-1882), m. (1st) 1853, Lelia
    Bolling Bernard (1827-1873)(11178), dau. of John H. Bernard;
    m. (2nd) 11/25/1879, Kate Harrison Tabb (2415312)(7/18/
    1847-12/12/1915), dau. of George Edward and Mary Harrison
    Randolph Tabb of "Toddsbury", Gloucester County
    Children by first wife:
111411 John Robertson (1855-1872)
111412 John Bernard Robertson (1857-1934). Unm.
111413 Anne Trent Robertson (1860-1891). Unm.
111414 Powhatan Robertson, Jr. (1862-1945). Unm.
111415 Lelia Skipwith Robertson (1864-1865)
111416 Gay Bernard Robertson (1866-1936), m. 1891, Alfred Walton
    Fleming
1114161 Robert Walton Fleming (1894-1945), Captain, U.S.N., m.
    1924, Emma Scott Stitt (1905-   ). She m. (2nd) 1946,
    Warren L. Stephenson (-1971); m. (3rd) 1982,
    Malcolm W. Fraser
11141611 Robert Walton Fleming, Jr. (1925-   ), m. (1st)
    1951, Jane Marie Sullivan. No issue. Div. 1969. M.
    (2nd) 1969, Dorothy Sweat Cox (dau. of Wilson Thomas
    Sweat). No issue. Div. M. (3rd) Virginia
11141612 Edward Stitt Fleming (1930-   ), M.D., m. (1st)
    1952, Anna McCay Page. Div. 1972. M. (2nd) 1972,
    Mariana Moran Parsons. No issue

Children by first wife:
111416121 Edward Stitt Fleming, Jr. (1955-   )
111416122 Edith Page Fleming (1958-   )
111416123 Richard Bland Lee Fleming II (196 -   )
1114162 Richard Bland Lee Fleming (1900-1964), m. 1946, Elizabeth
         Wilson Eastland (1916-   )
111417 Thomas Bolling Robertson (1870-1871)
         Child by second wife of 11141:
111418 Ellen Harrison Robertson (9/15/1880-1969), m. 10/2/1912,
        Rev. Lewis Carter Harrison (12/31/1878-1974), son of
        Pracht Gessner and Julia Wood Riddick Harrison of Richmond
1114181 Kate Tabb Harrison (4/28/1914-   ), m. 8/3/1940, Rev.
        Walter Willett Davis (4/24/1912 or 1913-   ), son of
        William Virginius and Winifred Bonney Davis of Savannah
11141811 Ellen Harrison Davis (1/10/1943-   ), m. 1965, Keith
        Ray Shelton
111418111 James White Shelton (1968-   )
111418112 Julia Bonney Shelton (1969-   )
11141812 Margaret Bonney Davis (1946-   ), m. 1970, Robert
        Andrews
111418121 Katherine Nora Andrews (1979-   )
1114182 Elizabeth Lewis Carter Harrison (12/23/1918 or 1919-   ),
        m. 1946, William B. White (1919-   )
11141821 Katherine Anne Robertson White (1962-   )
11142 Elizabeth Lewis Robertson (1824-1858), m. 1847, Robert Jones
        Barksdale (1821-1878) of "Clay Hill", Amelia County. He
        m. (2nd) Emma Mason
111421 Ann Montgomery ("Nannie") Barksdale (1850-1939), m. 1882,
        Richard Morris Bolling (1841-1921)(21935)
1114211 Rolfe Bolling, d. young
1114212 Mary Frances Monro Bolling (1885-1968), m. 191 , Chris-
        topher Mayer Randolph (1868-1937)
11142121 Richard Bolling Randolph (1918-   ). Unm.
11142122 William Barksdale Randolph (1919-   ), m. 1954,
        Elizabeth Pagr Craven (1922-   )
111421221 Christopher Randolph (1956-   ), m. 1982, Linda
        Bubernak
111421222 Richard Nichols Randolph (1958-   )
111421223 John Bolling Randolph (1963-   )
11142123 Anne Robertson Randolph (1921-   ), m. 1949,
        William Hampton Crom, Jr.
111421231 Nancy Bolling Randolph Crom (1951-   ,)
111421232 Emily Martha Hampton Crom (1953-   )
111421233 Lucy Barksdale Crom (1957-   )
11142124 John Lewis Randolph (1925-   ), m. 1974, Elizabeth
        May Welsh Marney
111422 William Jones Barksdale (1852-ca. 1902). Unm.
111423 John Robertson Barksdale (1854-ca. 1867)
111424 Robert Jones Barksdale, Jr. (1856-1947), m. 1889, Alice
        Carlotta Stith (1868-1953)
1114241 Alice Stith Barksdale (1891-   ). Unm.
1114242 Anne Robertson Barksdale (1893-1984), m. 1926, Bernard
        H. Baylor

11142421 William Barksdale Baylor (1927-   ), m. 1955,
          Margaret Mary Burchenal
111424211 William Barksdale Baylor, Jr. (1956-   )
111424212 Charles Burchenal Baylor (1958-   )
111424213 Anne Courtenay Baylor (1960-   )
111424214 Margaret Burchenal Baylor (1962-   )
1114243   Frances Evans Barksdale (1896-   ), m. 1924, Arthur
          E. Ooghe
11142431 Robert Barksdale Ooghe (1927-   ), M.D., m. (1st)
          1956, Joan Virginia Barritt. Div. M. (2nd)
          No issue
       Children by first wife:
111424311 Virginia Barritt Ooghe (1966-   )
111424312 Robin Barksdale Ooghe (1968-   )
11142432 Arthur Edward Ooghe, Jr. (1932-   ), m. 1953,
          Elizabeth Daniel
111424321 Carol Elizabeth Ooghe (1955-   ), m.
111424322 Marie Diane Ooghe (1958-   )
111424323 Arthur Edward Ooghe III (1962-   )
111424324 Frances Angela Ooghe (1965-   )
1114244   Winifred Elizabeth Lewis Barksdale (1899-   ). Unm.
1114245   Gay Robertson Barksdale (1901-   ), m. 1926, Edward
          Franklin Woodall, Jr.
11142451 Nancy Barksdale Woodall (1928-   ), m. 1948, William
          Barnes Propert
111424511 Christopher Barnes Propert (1952-   ), m.
111424512 Franklin Boyd Propert (1953-   )
111424513 William Barksdale Propert (1955-   )
11142452 Edward Franklin Woodall III (1931-   ), m. 1955,
          Alice Ancarrow
111424521 Mark Robertson Woodall (1957-   )
111424522 Eric Barksdale Woodall (1960-   )
111424523 John Franklin Woodall (1961-   )
1114246   John Robertson Barksdale (1904-1979). Unm.
11143   Thomas Bolling Robertson (1827-1855). Unm.
11144   Anne Frances Robertson (1832-1857). Unm.
11145   Gay Bernard Robertson (1834-1855). Unm.
1115   Rebecca Robertson (10/5/1789-6/8/1791)
1116   Anne Robertson (11/5/1792-ca. 1821), m. 11/23/1813, Dr. Henry
          Skipwith (6/11/1790-11/27/1852), son of Col. Henry and Anne
          ("Nancy") Wayles Skipwith of "Hors du Monde", Powhatan
          County (she was half sister to Mrs. Thomas Jefferson, the
          former Martha Wayles). Dr. Henry Skipwith m. (2nd), in
          Louisiana, Margaret Winter, and by her had six children.
11161   Eliza Bolling Skipwith (1815-1900), m. 4/29/1840, Basil
          Brown Gordon (-10/9/1845) of Falmouth (Stafford
          County) and Baltimore, son of Basil and Ann Campbell Knox
          Gordon of "Windsor Lodge", Culpeper County
111611   Basil Fitzhugh Gordon (1841-1866)
111612   Anne Campbell Gordon (1843-1844)
111613   Henry Skipwith Gordon (10/25/1844-1888), m. 1/9/1866, Mary
          T. Wheeler (1845-1892)

1116131 Basil Brown Gordon (1866-1888)
1116132 Henry Skipwith Gordon, Jr. (1868-1945), m. 1897, Margaret
    Wallach Stewart (1873-1923)
11161321 Henry Skipwith Gordon III (1898-   )
11161322 Henry Skipwith Gordon IV (1900-1967), m.
111613221 Henry Skipwith Gordon V, m. (1st)   . M. (2nd)
         . M. (3rd)
       Child by first wife:
1116132211 Henry Skipwith Gordon VI
11161323 Stewart E. Gordon (1905-   ), m. 1926, Mary Gardiner
    Blake (1906-   )
111613231 Margaret Stewart Gordon (1927-   ), m. 1949, Philip
    Merrill Hildebrandt
1116132311 Philip Merrill Hildebrandt, Jr. (1951-   )
1116132312 Margaret A. Hildebrandt (1952-   ), m. 1975, Bruce
    C. Sampson (1951-   )
1116132313 Grace Brooks Hildebrandt (1956-   )
1116132314 John Stewart Hildrbrandt (1957-   )
111613232 Stewart E. Gordon, Jr. (1929-   ), m. 1953, Helen
    Gifford Graham
1116132321 Katherine S. Gordon (1955-   )
1116132322 Elizabeth G. Gordon (1957-   )
1116132323 Louisa Lee ("Cricket") Gordon (1965-   )
1116132324 Stewart E. ("Chip") Gordon III (1968-   )
11162 Henry Skipwith, Jr. (1816-1894), m. Martha E. Killian (1829-
    1903)
111621 Henry Skipwith III, m. 1868, Jane Dick DuBose
1116211 Anne Robertson Skipwith, m. Thomas Moore Boissat, Jr.
11162111 Thomas Moore Boissat III
1116212 Beatrice DuBose Skipwith, m. L. O. Clark, M.D.
1116213 Edna Earl Skipwith, m. 1905, Rev. Robert H. Harper
11162131 Henry Harper, d. inf.
11162132 Robert E. Harper (1909-197), m. Alma Vaughan
111621321 Robin Harper, d. young
111621322 Robert Skipwith Harper (1943-   ), m.
1116214 Mattie Bell Skipwith, m. 1899, Claude C. Herndon
1116215 Addie G. Skipwith
1116216 John McKowen Skipwith
111622 John Killian Skipwith (1847-1933), m. 1871, Sara Victoria
    Gayle (1848-1923)
1116221 William Henry Skipwith (1875-1882)
1116222 Eliza Bolling Skipwith (1881-1957), m. Vallerie Gaiennic
    Hyams (1871-1952)
11162221 Vallerine Mathilda Hyams, d. young
11162222 John Skipwith Hyams, m. Myrtle Temple. Div.
111622221 (Baby) Hyams
111622222 Ouita Hyams, m. Benjamin Bingham
11162223 Henry M. Hyams, m. Clovis Martin
111622231 Michael Hyams, m. Diana Dalme
1116222311 Michael Hyams, Jr.
1116222312 Scott Hyams
111622232 Dennis Hyams, m. Linda Hampton

```
1116222321  Dennis Hyams, Jr.
1116222322  Denise Hyams
1116222323  David Hyams
1116222  4  Vallerie Gaiennic Hyams, Jr., m. Dorothy L'Herrison
111622241  Gaiennic Hyams, Jr., d.
111622242  John Skipwith ("Buddy") Hyams, m. (1st) Barbara
              M. (2nd) Pennie
111622243  William Henry Hyams, m. Marilyn Orr
1116222431  David Hyams
1116222432  Toni Hyams
111622244  Elizabeth Gayle Hyams, m. James Howell
1116222441  Jay Howell
1116222442  Jeffrey Howell
1116222443  Jonathan Howell
111622245  Robert Genoe Hyams
111622246  Mary Mathilda Hyams, m. Manuel Flores
111622247  Donald Paul Hyams
111622248  James Lester Hyams
111622249  Amy Katherine Hyams
11162225  Sarah Gayle Hyams, m. Rev. Randall ("Randy") Hartwell
              Pyfron
111622251  Sarah Gayle Pyfron
111622252  Valerie Anita Pyfron
111622253  Mary Victoria Pyfron, m.
111622254  Randall Hartwell Pyfron, Jr., m.
1116223  John Killian Skipwith, Jr.
1116224  Sarah Victoria ("Sally") Skipwith, m. James B. Coleman
1116225  Ella D. Skipwith (1874-1965), m. Graham Morris
11162251  Martha Lillian Morris (deceased), m. Earl Hargis (deceased)
111622511  Pattie Jean Hargis, m. Dwayne Manning
1116225111  Sherryl Manning
1116225112  Cindy Manning
11162252  Rev. Lamkin L. Morris, m. Camilla
11162253  Charles Morris, d.s.p.
11162254  Gayle Skipwith Morris, m. Josephine Myrtle Wall
111622541  Thomas Graham Morris
111622542  Michael Wall Morris, m. Nelwyn Taylor
1116225421  Lisa Amanda Morris
111622543  Carol Jane Morris, m. Philip Taylor Morris
111622544  Jonathan Lamkin Morris, m. Theresa Ann Brantley
1116225441  Emily Ann Morris
111622545  David Walter Morris, m. Laurie Diane Madison
111622546  Ellen Amanda Morris
11162255  Jane Bolling Morris, m. George Stanley Wannamer
111622551  Gayle Morris Wannamer, m. Gene LeBlanc
1116225511  Sandra LeBlanc
1116225512  Ella LeBlanc
111622552  George Murray Wannamer
111622553  Jane Elizabeth Wannamer, m. David Tortorich
1116226  Lillian R. Skipwith (1885-1908), m. Dudley C. Sharkey
1116227  Martha Elizabeth Skipwith (1887-1968), m. 1911, Louis
              Henry Cosper (1884-1963)
```

11162271   Louis Henry Cosper III, d. 1 day old
11162272   Martha Elizabeth Cosper (1913-   ), m. 1936, Eldredge
            Linus Carroll, M.D.
111622721 Eldredge Linus Carroll, Jr., M.D. (1939-   ), m.
            Gale Dean Simmons (1940-   )
1116227211 James Linus Carroll (1963-   )
1116227212 John Sherman Carroll (1965-   )
1116227213 Charlotte Marie Carroll (1970-   )
111622722 Sherman Louis Carroll (1945-   ), m. 1969, Dorothy
            Veronica Connell (1946-   )
1116227221 Thomas Eldredge Carroll (1979-   )
1116228 Oliver Gayle Skipwith (1899-1929)
1116229 Inf. d. y.
111622x Inf. d. y.
111622a Inf. d. y.
111622b Inf. d. y.
111622c Inf. d. y.
111623   Wyndham Robertson Skipwith
11163   William Robertson Skipwith, MD. (1819-1847), d.s.p.
11164   Powhatan (Thomas?) Skipwith (1820-ca. 1822)
1117 Jane Gay Robertson (4/1/1795-7/19/1852), m. 5/18/1816, John
       Hipkins Bernard (1/10/1792-4/4/1858) of "Gaymont", son of
       William and Fanny Hipkins Bernard of Caroline County
11171 Gay Robertson Bernard (2/25/1817-1868), m. 1836, Charles
       Tiernan of Baltimore (1797-1886). He m. (1st) Helen
       Magruder. M. (3rd) Mary Spear Nicholas
111711 Anna Dolores Tiernan (1838-1910), m. 1872, John R. Tait
        (1834-1909)
1117111 Arthur M. Tait, d. inf. 1879
1117112 Dorothy Gordon Tait (1883-1933), m. 1911, W. Hill
         Urquhart. No issue. W. Hill Urquhart m. (2nd) Margaret
         (-1961). No issue
111712 Charles Bernard Tiernan (1840-1912). Unm.
111713 Gay Bernard Tiernan (1842-1938), m. 1877, Henry A.
        Fenwick (1831-1885)
1117131 Henry A. Fenwick, Jr. (1878-1906). Unm.
1117132 Charles G. Fenwick (1880-1973), m. 1942, Maria Jose Lynch
         (1908-   )
11171321 Charles Henry Fenwick (1944-   )
11171322 Francis Edmund Fenwick (1945-   ), m.
111713221
1117133 Guy Bernard Fenwick (1881-1953), m. 1913, Margaret Mary
         Griffiss (-1974)
11171331 Guy Bernard Fenwick, Jr. (1914-1970), m. 194 , Eleanor
          Atkinson Brady (1921-   )
111713311 Guy Bernard Fenwick III (1943-   )
111713312 John Abell Brady Fenwick (1944-   ), m. (1st) 1969,
           Ann Young. M. (2nd) Mary G. Addison
111713313 Francis Lightfoot Fenwick (1949-1982)
111713314 George Hunter Fenwick (1951-   )
11171332 John Griffiss Fenwick (1915-1938). Unm.
11171333 Frances Abell Fenwick (1919-   ), m. John Walbach
          Edelen

```
111713331  John Walbach Edelen, Jr.., m. Cecil Locke
111713332  Peter Edelen
111713333  David deB. Edelen
111713334  Gay Bernard Edelen
111713335  William Boggs Edelen
111713336  Stephen F. Edelen
11171334   Henry Robertson Fenwick (1922-1976), m. (1st) Mary Gillian
             Crimmens. Div. 19    . M. (2nd)
111713341  G. Chance Fenwick (1948-      )
111713342  Elizabeth Fenwick
111713343  Carol C. Fenwick
111713344  Martin S. Fenwick
11171335   Charles Cuthbert Fenwick (1924-      ), m. (1st)
             Rosalie Bruce. Div. M. (2nd) Elizabeth White
           Children by first wife:
111713351  Charles Cuthbert Fenwick, Jr. (1948-      ), m.
             Stewart
111713352  H. Bruce Fenwick (1950-      )
111713353  Edwin A. Fenwick (1952-      )
111713354  John G. Fenwick (1954-      )
           Child by second wife:
111713355  Peter Fenwick (1967-      )
1117134    Frank Fenwick (1884-191    )
111714     Laura Cecilia Tiernan (1844-1885), m. 1865, J. Pierce
             Klingle (1835-1892).  He m. (2nd) Georgianna May Morrison
1117141    Susan Juliet Gay Beatrice ("Lily") Klingle (1867-1895),
             m. (1st) 1885, Edward Irving Darling.  M. (2nd) 1895,
             Francis X. Spranger, Jr., M.D.  Francis X. Spranger m.
             (2nd) Augusta Weber
11171411   Nancy Adams Pierce Klingle Darling (1887-1937), m. 1911,
             John Bernard Robb (1881-1965)(1117a6). No issue
11171412   Charles Tiernan Darling (1889-1926), m. (1st) 1907,
             Virginia Gertrude Dickinson (1883-1913), dau. of John
             Saunders and Attaway Lewis Dickinson.  M. (2nd) 1915,
             Columbia Smith (1893-1976), dau. of Allan and Cornelia
             Stuart Smith.  No issue.  Columbia Smith Darling m.
             (2nd) 1934, L. Marshall Walker
111714121  Virginia Klingle Darling (1910-      ), m. 1930,
             Webster Grymes (1892-      )
1117141211 Helen Virginia Grymes (1931-1949)
11172      Anna Skipwith Bernard (2/9/1819-1821)
11173      John Hipkins Bernard, Jr. (1/12/1821-1822)
11174      Sally Savine Bernard (2/5/1823-1831)(twin)
11175      William R. Bernard (2/5/1823-1823)(twin)
11176      Mary Eliza Barnard (7/1/1824-1895), m. 1861, George Guest
             (1806-1879).  George Guest m. (1st) Sallie Hoffman.  M.
             (2nd) Nora Bankhead
111761     Nora Guest (1862-1863)
111762     Bernard Robertson Guest (1864-1948), m. 1896, Eliza
             ("Liela") Laurens Chisolm
1117621    Mary Bernard Guest (1898-1974), m. 1922, C. W. Beattie
             Gwyn. Div.
```

1117622 John Laurens Guest (1899-1953), m. 1929, Ruth Warwick
    (1905-1955)
111763 Frank Barksdale Guest (1867-1926), m. 1907, Caroline
    Randolph Wellford (1880-1972)
1117631 Elisabeth Carter Guest (1908-   ), m. 1938, Herman
    Hollerith
1117632 John Wellford Guest (1919-   )
11177 William Robertson Bernard (12/17/1825-1881). Unm. C.S.A.
    D. and bur. at "Gay Mont"
11178 Lelia Bolling Bernard (7/18/1827-1873), m. 1853, Powhatan
    Robertson (her cousin). For their children, see 11141
11179 Caroline Pocahontas Bernard (2/17/1831-1895), m. 1854,
    Martin Pickett Scott, M.D. (1823-1904), of Fauquier County,
    later of Baltimore
111791 Gay Bernard Scott (1855-1917). Unm.
111792 Elizabeth Blackford Scott (10/10/1864-1/15/1920), m. 8/28/
    1888, William Ballard Preston (9/30/1858-12/6/1901), son
    of James Francis and Sarah Ann Caperton Preston
1117921 Caroline Pocahontas Bernard Preston (1895-1972). Unm.
111793 Lelia Bernard Scott (1859-1948), m. 1894, Richard H. Alvey
    (1859-   )
1117931 Lelia Scott Alvey (1895-1982), m. Henry A. Tilden (-
    1955)
11179311 Caroline Tilden (-1979), m. 1952, John Bemiss
    Simmons
111793111 Virginia Simmons
111793112 Amy Simmons
111793113 Bradford Simmons
111793114 Douglas Simmons
1117932 Richard H. Alvey, Jr. (1897-1983), m.
1117933 Martin Scott Alvey (1898-   ), m. Elma Glass
1117934 Mary Alvey (1900-1984), m. John D. Zadra
1117935 Margaret Scott Alvey (1902-   ), m. (1st) Edwin M.
    Chapman. M. (2nd) Tileston Mudge
11179351 Edwin M. Chapman, Jr., m.
111794 John Bernard Scott (1861-1945), m. 1906, Eleanor Washington
    (1886-1974)
1117941 John Bernard Scott, Jr. (1908-   ), m. 1938, Mary
    F. Lanier
11179411 Gay Lanier Scott (1941-   ), m. (1st) Elliott P.
    Robbins. M. (2nd) 1980, Donald V. Boecker
    Children by first husband:
111794111 Virginia Robbins
111794112 Scott Robbins
11179412 Ann Mason Scott (1945-   ), m. (1st) Leslie D.
    Alderman, Jr. M. (2nd) John Kopelouses
    Children by first husband:
111794121 Leslie D. Alderman III
111794122 Mary Margaret Alderman
1117942 Eleanor Washington Scott (1910-   ), m. 1936, Berry
    Iglehart (-1982)
11179421 Edward Scott Iglehart (1941-   ), m. 1969, Charlotte
    Marguerite Thomas

111794211 Thomas Dylan Scott Iglehart (1971-   )
111794212 Anabel Iglehart
11179422   Robert Eden Iglehart (1944-   ), m. (1st) 1968,
           Deborah Ellen Patterson. Div. M. (2nd) 1984,
111795 Caroline Louisa Scott (1864-1892). Unm.
1117x   Powhatan Bolling Bernard (9/22/1833-1835)
1117a   Helen Struan Bernard (1/11/1836-1901), m. 3/16/1864, Philip
           Lightfoot Robb (1840-1894), son of Capt. (C.S.N.) Robert
           Gilchrist and Fannie Bernard Robb
1117a1 Fannie Bernard Robb (3/18/1867-1950). Unm.
1117a2 Helen Struan Robb (9/21/1869-1955). Unm.
1117a3 Gay Sevigne (Robertson?) Robb (8/13/1873-1936), m. 1910,
           Edwin Carleton Upton (1872-1945)
1117a31 Frances Bernard Robb Upton (1911-1981), m. (1st) 1940,
           Bayard Gordon Poyntz (1911-1949). M. (2nd) 1951, James
           Samuel Patton (1919-   )
1117a32 Robert Carleton Upton (1914-1945), m. 1941, Alberta A.
           Pritchett (1920-   ). She m. (2nd) Barry Buschell
           (-1980)
1117a4 Robert Gilchrist Robb (10/22/1875-1951), m. 1927, Frances
           Randolph Howard (1893-19   )
1117a41 Frances Lightfoot Robb (1928-   )
1117a42 Robert Gilchrist Robb, Jr. (1931-   )
1117a5 Philip Lightfoot Robb, Jr. (5/22/1878-1965), m. 1921,
           Eugenia May Price (1893-1965)
1117a51 Eugenia VanDyke Robb (1923-   )
1117a6 John Bernard Robb (11/2/1881-1965), m. 1911, Nancy Adams
           Peirce Klingle Darling (11171411). No issue
1118 Powhatan Robertson (4/1/1798-10/18/1820). Unm.
1119 Arthur Robertson (4/12/1800-1801 or 1802)
111x Wyndham Robertson (6/26/1803-2/11/1888)(Governor of Virginia),
           m. 8/16/1831, Mary Frances Trigg Smith (8/7/1812-1/12/1890),
           only child of Capt. Francis and Mary Trigg King Smith of
           Abingdon
111x1 William Robertson (6/26/1832-1835)
111x2 Mary Trigg Robertson (4/24/1834-1866), m. 1856, Capt.
           William W. Blackford, C.S.A. (1831-1905)
111x21 Lizzie Robertson Blackford (1856-1932), m. Rev. Arthur S.
           Lloyd (1857-1936)
111x211 Mary Lloyd, m. Edmund Pendleton Dandridge
111x2111 Edmund Pendleton Dandridge, Jr., m. Anne Davis
111x21111 Anne Davis Dandridge
111x21112 Sally Dandridge
111x21113 Edmund Pendleton Dandridge III
111x2112 Elizabeth Lloyd Dandridge, m. Angus McDonald
111x21121 Angus McDonald
111x21122 Dandridge McDonald
111x21123 Mary Lloyd McDonald
111x21124 Edward McDonald
111x212 Rebecca Selden Lloyd (1892-1965), m. Gavin Hadden
111x2121 Gaven Hadden, Jr. (1915-   ), m. 1947, Caryl
           Wolgemuth

```
111x21211  Gavin Hadden III (1947-      )
111x21212  Linda Hadden (1949-      )
111x21213  Susan Gay Hadden (1955-      )
111x21214  Peter Hadden (1962-      )
111x2122   Arthur Lloyd Hadden (1917-      ), m. Katherine Loring
111x21221  Arthur Lloyd Hadden, Jr. (1942-      )
111x21222  Nicholas Loring Hadden (1947-      )
111x21223  Christopher Burchardt Hadden (1949-      )
111x2123   David Hadden (1921-      ), m. 1946, Doris Jeffries
111x21231  David Hadden, Jr. (1947-      ), m. Loris
111x21232  Jeffrey Hadden (1949-      )
111x21233  Ann Hadden (1951-      )
111x2124   John Lloyd Hadden (1923-      ), m.
111x21241  John Lloyd Hadden, Jr.
111x21242  Barbara Hadden
111x21243  Alexander Hadden (1958-      )
111x21244  James Michael Hadden (1962-      )
111x2125   Gay Hadden (1928-      ), m. Richard Armistead Watson
111x21251  Richard Armistead Watson, Jr. (1959-      )
111x21252  Gavin Hadden Watson (1960-      )
111x213    Gay Robertson Lloyd (1888-1962), m. Churchill Jones
             Gibson (1885-1970), D.D.
111x2131   Elizabeth Lloyd Gibson (1914-      ), m. John Weed
             Franklin
111x21311  John Weed Franklin, Jr. (1941-      ), m. Barbara
             Larkin
111x213111
111x213112
111x213113
111x21312  Gay Lloyd Franklin (1943-      ), m. Brian Best
111x213121
111x213122
111x213123
111x21313  Churchill Gibson Franklin (1948-      ), m. Janet
             Halstead
111x213131
111x213132
111x2132   Susan Stuart Gibson (1916-      ), m. Rev. Stephen
             Rintoul Davenport
111x21321  Stephen Rintoul Davenport, Jr. (1942-      ), m. Susan

111x213211 Charles M. Davenport                              '
111x213212
111x21322  Churchill Gibson Davenport (1944-      ), m. Nancy
             Terrel
111x21323  Susan Stuart Davenport (1948-      ), m. Spencer
             Simrill
111x213231
111x213232
111x21324  John Lloyd Davenport (1949-      ).
111x21325  Robert Atkinson Davenport (1951-      ), m. Penelope
             Albritton
```

```
111x2133   Gay Lloyd Gibson (1920-        ), m. Rev. Joseph W.
             Pinder
111x21331  Gay Lloyd Pinder (1946-        )
111x21332  Anne Winston Pinder (1948-        ), m. Thomas Batchelder
111x213321
111x213322
111x213323
111x21333  Joseph W. Pinder, Jr. (1950-        )
111x21334  Churchill Gibson Pinder (1953-        )
111x21335  Elizabeth Lloyd Pinder (1956-        )
111x2134   Churchill Jones Gibson, Jr. (1931-        ), m. Dorothy
             Simons
111x21341  Churchill Jones Gibson III (1961-        )
111x21342  Dorothy Gibson (1964-        )
111x21343  Webster Gibson (1967-        )
111x21344  Gay Gibson (1970-        )
111x214    Elizabeth Blackford Lloyd (1886-1958), m. Charles J.
             Symington
111x2141   Arthur Lloyd Symington, m. Nancy Glover
111x21411  Arthur Lloyd Symington, Jr. (1943-        )
111x21412  Donald Symington (1946-        )
111x21413  Marian Symington (1947-        )
111x21414  Nicholas Symington (1952-        )
111x2142   Charles J. Symington, Jr. (1914-        ), m. Mary Jo
             Finucane
111x21421  Elizabeth Gay Symington (1948-        ), m. Yehuda
             Gelb
111x21422  Katherine Symington (1950-        )
111x21423  Charles Symington (1959-        )
111x2143   Betty Gay Symington (1916-        ), m. Sanford B.
             Kauffman
111x21431  Pamela Byrd Kauffman (1941-        ), m. John Graham
111x214311 Liza Graham
111x214312 Kezia Graham
111x21432  Lelia Symington Kauffman (1943-        ), m.        Norris
111x214321 Levin Norris
111x214322 Timo Norris
111x21433  Robert Sanford Kauffman (1947-        )
111x21434  Margaret Moore Kauffman (1950-        )
111x21435  Virginia Lloyd Kauffman (1952-        )
111x2144   Pamela Symington (1921-        ), m. David Mayer
111x21441  Elizabeth Lloyd Mayer (1948-        )
111x21442  Michael Mayer (1950-        )
111x21443  Anneke Mayer (1953-        )
111x21444  Rebecca Mayer (1956-        )
111x2145   Anne Byrd Symington (1927-        ), m. Thomas Platt
111x21451  Ann Byrd Platt (1952-        ), m. Stewart Pinkerton
111x21452  Charles Platt (1954-        )
111x21453  Timothy Platt (1956-        )
111x21454  Heather Platt (1958-        )
111x215    Arthur S. Lloyd (1882-1883)
111x216    John Lloyd (1890-1922). Unm.
```

111x22 Lucy Landon Blackford (1857-1857)
111x23 Wyndham Robertson Blackford (1858-192), m. Loulie
111x24 Landon Carter Blackford (1859-1862)
111x25 Gay Robertson Blackford (1861-1959). Unm.
111x26 Pelham Blackford (1863-   ), m. Evelyn Baylor (-
          1954)
111x261 Pelham Blackford, Jr. (1905-   ), m. 1936, Franklin
          Carter Neale
111x2611 Franklin Carter Blackford (1946-   ),m. Ray Iseman
111x26111 Catherine Carter Iseman (1972-   )
111x26112 Ann Kenneth Iseman (1975-   )
111x2612 Evelyn Baylor Blackford (1939-   ), m. Paul O'Brien
111x26121 Kimberly Ann O'Brien (1965-   )
111x26122 Evelyn Carter O'Brien (1972-   )
111x262 James Baylor Blackford (1907-1972), m. (1st) Lillian St.
          Clair. M. (2nd) 1957, Susan Gatewood Powers
        Children by first wife:
111x2621 Gay St. Clair Blackford
111x2622 Anne Courteney Blackford
        Children by second wife:
111x2623 Susan Constant Blackford
111x2624 James Baylor Blackford, Jr.
111x263 Frank Robertson Blackford (1912-   ), m. Polly
          Baldwin
111x2631 Frank Robertson Blackford, Jr.
111x2632 John Baldwin Blackford
111x27 Mary Robertson Blackford (1866-1867)
111x3 Elizabeth Bolling Robertson (10/4/1836-1853)
111x4 Francis Smith Robertson, Captain C.S.A. (1/3/1841-1926), m.
          1868, Stella Wheeler (1849-1926)
111x41 Mary Wheeler Robertson (1868-1919), m. Willoughby Reade
111x411 Frank Reade (-1957), m. Jean Cunningham. No issue
111x412 Evelyn Reade, m. (1st) Lee Trenholm. M. (2nd) Paul
          Johnson
111x4121 Reade Johnson, m. Stephen N. Berry
111x41211 Robin Rebecca Berry
111x413 Stella Garland Reade (1900-1929). Unm.
111x414 Mary Willoughby Reade (1905-   ), m. 1924, William
          Copenhaver (-1969)
111x4141 Mary Robertson Copenhaver (1928-   ), m. Nelson Maclin
111x41411 Reade Maclin
111x41412 Caroline Maclin
111x4142 Elizabeth Whitman Copenhaver (1931-   ), m. Roger B.
          Triplett, Jr.
111x41421 Roger B. Triplett III, m.
111x41422 Whit Triplett
111x41423 Clarke Triplett
111x41424 Beth Triplett
111x42 Stella Forester Robertson (1870-   ). Unm.
111x43 Katy Robertson (1877-1950), m. 1926, William Trigg Booker
111x44 Nellie Robertson (1890-1937), m. 1914, James Coleman
          Motley, M.D. He m. (3rd) Elizabeth Buchanan

111x441 Katy Robertson Motley (1917-   ), m. 1936, Homer M.
           Grandstaff (1901-1973)
111x4411 Coleman Motley Grandstaff (1938-   ), m. 1964,
           Joanne Mason
111x44111 James Coleman Grandstaff (1965-   )
111x44112 Elizabeth Ruffin Grandstaff (1967-   )
111x4412 Kenny Armistead Grandstaff (1941-   ), m. (1st) 1960,
           Doris Apperson. M. (2nd) 1974, Lucy Person
        Child by first wife:
111x44121 Kimberly Grandstaff (1963-   )
        Children by second wife:
111x44122 Armistead Wyndham Grandstaff (1978-   )
111x44123 Emily Kellam Grandstaff (1979-   )
111x442 James Coleman Motley, Jr. (1920-1944). Unm.
111x443 Frank Robertson Motley (1926-   ), m. (1st) 1949,
           Caroline Camp. M. (2nd) 1963, Nancy Marshall (1926-   )
        Children by first wife:
111x4431 Mary Robertson Motley (1951-   ), m. 1973, David
           Kalirgis
111x4432 Hugh Camp Motley (1954-   )
111x4433 James Coleman Motley III (1960-   )
        Child by second wife:
111x4434 Frank Robertson Motley, Jr. (1964-   )
111x5 Jane Gay Robertson (8/9/1842-1842)
111x6 Catherine Markham Robertson (2/20/1845-1922), m. James
           Lowery White (1842-1914)
111x61 Wyndham Robertson White (1869-1944),m. Mary Clifton White
111x611 Wyndham R. White, Jr., m. Judith Fernald
111x6111 Wyndham Robertson White III, m. Lois Owen White
111x61111 Allison White
111x61112 Stuart White
111x61113 Wyndham R. White IV
111x6112 Sydney White
111x612 Mary Preston White. Unm.
111x613 Ann Campbell White (-1941)
111x62 Annie Campbell White (1871-1948). Unm.
111x63 Madge Greenway White (1873-1945). Unm.
111x64 William Young Conn White (1876-1950), m. Harriet Harris
           (-1962)
111x641 Kathleen Robertson White (1902-198)
111x642 James Lowery White (1903-1983), m. Clare Stone
111x6421 Martha Stone White, m. James L. Hart
111x64211 Sheila Hart
111x64212 James A. Hart
111x6422 Clare Stone White
111x643 Mary Faulkerson White (1905-1959), m. Fred C. Alexander
111x6431 Fred C. Alexander, Jr., m. 1957, Betsey Jones
111x64311 Frederick Mitchell Alexander
111x64312 Mary White Alexander
111x64313 Margerie Alexander
111x64314 Margaret Alexander
111x6432 William White Alexander, m. Joyce Rinker

111x64321 James White Alexander
111x64322 Laurie Alexander
111x6433 M. R. Alexander
111x644 Madge Greenway White (1907-1981), m. George Emery Baya
111x6441 Madge Greenway Baya (1938-   )
111x6442 Harry P. Baya (1940-   )
111x64421 Matthew Baya (1969-   )
111x64422 Paul Baya (1973-   )
111x645 Harriet Harris White (1910-1979), m. 1944, John Hastings
          Gwathmey (1886-1956)
111x6451 Harriet White Gwathmey (1945-   ), m. John Minor
          Chinn
111x646 William Young Conn White, Jr. (1914-   ), m. Kathleen
          Brown
111x6461 Kathleen Saunders White, m. Benj. F. Sheftall
111x64611 Katherine R. Sheftall
111x6462 William Young Conn White III, m. Kathy
111x6463 James Lowery White
111x65 Pocahontas White (1877-1950), m. William Henry Sargeant
111x66 Frank Robertson White (1879-1963), m. Anita Clark
111x67 Kathleen White (1880-   ), m. 1906, Clarence B. Penn
          1880-1957)
111x671 Kathleen Robertson Penn (1906-   ), m. 1932, Charles
          Joseph Post (1903-   )
111x6711 Penn Robertson Post (1933-   ), m. Janet Bowman
          (1936-   )
111x67111 David Penn Post (1960-   )
111x67112 Kathleen Robertson Post (1962-   )
111x67113 Elizabeth Gay Post (1964-   )
111x6712 Charles Joseph Post III (1938-   ),m. 1960, Vicki
          Crosby (1939-   )
111x67121 Nancy Elizabeth Post (1969-   )
111x67122 Christopher Crosby Post (1974-   )
111x672 Estelle Gilmore Penn (1914-   ), m. 1937, Elvin
          F. Henry (1911-   )
111x6721 William White Henry (1940-   ), m. Virginia Prosise
111x67211 Anne Stuart Henry
111x67212 Markham Robertson Henry
111x6722 Ellen Wilson Henry (1952-   )
111x68 Gay White (1882-   ), m. Thomas Preston Trigg
111x7 Anne Pocahontas Robertson (2/17/1847-1923), m. 1874,
          Connally F. Trigg (1841-1907)
111x8 Wyndham Bolling Robertson (1/16/1851-1923) of Saltville,
          m. 1871, Florence Henderson (1849-1930)
111x81 Eliza Holcombe Robertson (1872-   ), m. 1895,
          Lorenzo Norvell Lee (1868-1937)
111x811 Florence Lee (1896-1896)
111x812 Wyndham Bolling Robertson Lee, m.
111x8121 Carol Holcomb Lee, m. T. E. Farrar
111x81211 Wyndham Bolling Farrar
111x8122 Norvell Harrison Lee, m. Preston Mayo
111x81221 Gay Robertson Mayo, m. Chirstopher Lent

111x82   Wyndham Bolling Robertson, MD. (1875-   ), m. Saida
         Grandy Claiborne
111x821 Wyndham Bolling Robertson III (1900-19   ). Unm.
111x822 Archibald Douglas Robertson (19 -19). Unm.
111x83   Walter Henderson Robertson (1879-1950), m. 1905, Bessie
         White (1878-1954)
111x831 Margie Robertson. Unm.
111x832 Florie Robertson (1907-   ), m. 1930, Gordon
         Milbourne (1902-1977)
111x8321 Walter Robertson Milbourne, m.
111x83211   111x83212   111x83213
111x84   William Robertson (1881-1882)
111x85   Charles Edward Robertson (1884-1884)
111x86   John Rofle Robertson (1885-1888)
111x87   Pocahontas T. Robertson (1891-1927)
111x88   Mary ("Mazie") Smith Robertson, m. George Worden
111x881 Wyndham Robertson Worden (1902-   )
111x882 George Edward Worden (1904-1972)
111x883 Florence Henderson Worden (1906-1921)
111x884 Stuart Barrett Worden (1907-1978), m. Blair Lewis
111x8841 Blair Lewis Worden
111x8842 Florence Worden, m.   Johnson
111x885 Mary Smith Worden (1909-1909)
111x886 Walter Bolling Worden (1910-1948)
111x887 Betsey Holcombe Worden,m. Turner A. Slaughter
111x888 John Bolling Worden, m. Ellen Lewis
111x8881 Lynn Worden, m. Franklin Wayne Wilson
111x88811 Sarah Lewis Wilson
111x88812 Franklin Wayne Wilson III
111x8882 Mary Stuart Worden, m. Bryant Brooks
111x88821 Jennifer Lynn Brooks
111x88822 Kristina Noel Brooks
111a Elizabeth ("Betsey") Robertson (3/10/1780-6/9/1801), m. 1801,
      Henry Lawson Biscoe (-7/19/1810). She d. about six
      weeks after her wedding.
111b Mary ("Polly") Buchanan Robertson (4/24/1783-3/6/1829). Unm.
111c Dead by 5/10/1796
112   Rebecca Bolling (8/19/1763-9/ /1826), m. 11/ /1779, Capt.
      William Murray (her first cousin once removed). For their
      children, see 61
113   Col. William Bolling (5/26/1777-7/17/1845), m. 2/24/1798,
      Mary Randolph (his second cousin) of "Curles". For their
      children, see 219
114   Mary ("Polly") Bolling (1/27/1765-4/10/1826), born deaf. Unm.
115   Thomas Bolling, Jr. (7/1/1766-1/11/1836), born deaf. Unm.
116   John Bolling (1/31/1761-10/11/1783 or 8/29/1783), born deaf.
      Unm.
117   Susanna Bolling (8/18/1771-10/1/1773)
118   Sarah Bolling (12/11/1772-9/1/1773)(twin)
119   Ann Bolling (12/11/1772-9/14/1773)(twin)
11x   William Gay Bolling (10/2/1769-9/2/1771)
11a   Archibald Blair Bolling. Dead by 5/10/1796. No issue

12 John Bolling III of "Chestnut Grove" (6/24/1737-4/ /1800), m.
6/29/1760, Mary Jefferson (10/1/1741-), sister of
President Thomas Jefferson
NOTE: Latrobe, in CHART, states that John Bolling (1737-
1800) was called "The old Indian", and in MEMOIR, pp. 27 and
28, John's brother Robert explains that John "was addicted
to strong drink, and in consequence of that propensity was
familiarly called 'The old Indian'".
121 Martha Bolling, bapt. 11/24/1769, m. 2/20/1794, Peter Field
Archer, son of Field and Elizabeth Archer. The Peter Field
Archers lived in Chesterfield County.
1211 Powhatan Archer, m.   Walthall
1212 Martha Archer, m. (1st) John Bolling, m. (2nd)   Berry
1213 Ellen Archer, m.   Berry
1214 Mary Archer, m. Edward Covington
1215 Lucy Archer, m.   Archer
1216 (son)   1217 (son)   1218 (son)   1219 (son) 121x(dau)
122 John Bolling (3/24/1762-   ) of "North Garden", Albemarle
County, m. Mary Kennon
1221 Evelina Bolling (1790-1863), m. 1808, Alexander Garrett
(1775-1860). She was his second wife. His first wife
was Elizabeth Minor who d. 1806. He was the son of Henry
and Mary Johnson Garrett of Nelson County. Both Alexander
and Evalina are bur. at "Monticello".
12211 Dr. John Bolling Garrett (1809-1855) of "Clover Plains",
Albemarle County, m. (1st), Elizabeth Ann Walker (1811-
1845). M. (2nd), Ann ("Nannie") Hartwell Harrison (1819-
1892)(2424c). Dr. Garrett had children by both wives.
Dr. John Bolling Garrett and his first wife are bur. at
"Monticello".
122111 Evelina Bolling Garrett (11/22/1850-4/18/1917), m. 10/19/
1886, William Byrd Harrison II (9/8/1853-4/12/1927), son
of Capt. Benjamin Harrison Harrison, C.S.A., of "The Rowe",
Charles City County, and his wife, the former Mary ("Molly")
Randolph Page. Home: "Dungeness", Albemarle County
1221111 Mary Randolph Harrison (12/2/1890-12/3/1890)
1221112 William Byrd Harrison III (1/11/1893-   ), m. 7/10/
1919, Eva Moran Detamore (12/14/1893-   ), dau.
of John William and Frances Virginia Moran Detamore of
Albemarle County. The Harrisons lived in Richmond.
12211121 Evelyn Byrd Harrison (5/6/1920-   ) of Charlottesville
12211122 Elizabeth Ashton Harrison (6/18/1921-   ), m.
2/14/1942, Walter Mason Ormes. Div.
122111221 Anne Harrison Ormes (6/22/1943-   )
122111222 Ashton Harrison Ormes (12/8/1948-   )
12211123 William Byrd Harrison IV (9/29/1926-   ), m. 7/17/
1948, Nancy Pope (3/3/1926-   ), dau. of Joseph
Meredith and Grace Robbins Pope of Richmond
122111231 Margaret Jane Harrison (8/2/1949-   )
1221113 Lucius Ashton Harrison of "Dungeness" (7/10/1896-   ),
m. 10/12/1920, Irene B. Waring, dau. of Henry and Irene
Nelson Waring of Charles City County
12211131 Lucius Ashton Harrison, Jr. (3/28/1927-   )
12212 Susan Garrett, m. Dr. Thomas Johnson of the University of
Virginia. No issue

12213 Evalina Kennon Garrott (1813-1843), m. 1835, Alexander
Brown Duke (   ), son of Burnley and Huldah Brown
Duke. Alexander Brown Duke graduated in medicine at the
University of Virginia, and for some years was connected
with Rev. Pike Powers in the conduct of a high school at
Midway in Albemarle County. Dr. Duke died in Savannah,
where he had gone to fight the yellow fever plague, which
cost him his life. Evalina is bur. at "Monticello", and
in DUKE, it is stated that Dr. Duke was bur. at "Monticello"
beside her, but the "Monticello" cemetery records do not
have him listed.
122131 S. J. Duke (d. 1843), bur. at "Monticello"
122132 Sue Duke (   ), m. (before 1875) Maj. Horace Walker
Jones of Charlottesville, son of Dr. Basil and Lucy
Magruder Jones
1221321 Kennon Jones m. Miss Godfrey of Baltimore
12213211 Godfrey Jones
1221322 Horace Walker Jones, Jr., m. 6/10/1896, Hope Grant
Curtis of Rock Island, Ill. He graduated at the Naval
Academy in 1884, and was a Commander in the United
States Navy
12213221 Hope Jones (4/17/1897-   ), m. 12/23/1920, at
Thompson Ridge, N.Y., Edward Phillips Heath. Lived
in Charlottesville
122132211 Edward Phillips Heath, Jr. (10/28/1921-   )(twin)
b. in Houston
122132212 Horace Walker Heath (10/28/1921-   )(twin) b. in
Houston. He was killed while serving in the Naval Air
Corps in World War II
12213222 Horace Walker Jones III (10/5/1900-   ), m. 9/ /1932,
at Groton, Conn., Mildred Phelps. Lived in West Hart-
ford, Conn.
122132221 Curtis Phelps Jones (5/ /1933-   )
122132222 Peter Walker Jones (1936-   )(twin)
122132223 Timothy Jones (1936-   )(twin)
122132224 Horace Walker Jones IV (1945-   )
12213223 Hugh Everett Jones (11/12/1903-   ). Home: New
York City
1221323 Evelyn Bolling Jones, m. Abel Norwood of New Orleans
12213231 Evelyn Norwood
12213232 Mary Randolph Norwood
12213233 Sue Norwood (twin)
12213234 Virginia Norwood (twin)
12213235 Catherine Norwood
1221324 Mary Randolph Jones, m. Dr. John Cochrane. Home: East
Dorset, Vermont
12213241 David Duke Cochrane
12213242 Sara Roberts Cochrane
1221325 Basil Jones. Lived in Chicago
12213251 Basil Jones, Jr.
1221326 Wilhelmina Marshall Jones. Home: East Dorset, Vt.
1221327 James Duke Jones. Home: East Dorset, Vt.
1221328 Sue Johnson Jones, m. Roy Palmer

12214   Clarissa Garrett, m. Dr. Thomas J. Pretlow (ca. 1774-1860)
of Southampton County. They had children
12215   Elizabeth Garrett (-1845), m. Samuel Purcell
1222   Susan Bolling, m. John Scott
12221   Elizabeth Scott, m.   Scott (her first cousin)
12222   Pocahontas Scott, m.   Scott (brother to husband of
12221)
12223   Mary Scott, m.   Scott (widower---husband of 12221)
1223   Kennon Bolling
1224   Mary Bolling, m.   Snelson, and moved to the West
1225   (son)
1226   (dau)
1227   (dau)
        NOTE: CHART (5/10/1796) shows that three of the children
        of 122 were then dead.
123   Edward Bolling (9/17/1772-1835), m. 1794, Dorothea Dandridge
        ("Dolly") Payne (7/10/1777-   ), dau. of Archer and
        Martha Dandridge Payne of "New Market", Goochland County
1231   Powhatan R. Bolling (d. ante 1840), m. 1823, Arminda R. Payne,
        dau. of Archibald Payne
12311   Pocahontas J. Bolling, b. 1830
12312   Elvira G. Bolling, b. 1837
1232   (son)
1233   (son)
1234   (son)
124   Archibald Bolling, m. 1801, Catherine Payne, dau. of Archer
        and Martha Dandridge Payne of "New Market", Goochland County.
        The Archibald Bollings lived in Campbell County
1241   Dr. Archibald Bolling (-1860), m. 5/15/1835, Anne
        E. Wigginton, dau. of Benjamin and Harriett B. Scott
        Wigginton, of Campbell County
12411   John Bolling, d. inf.
12412   William Holcomb(e) Bolling (5/29/1837-7/6/1899), m. 9/18/
        1860, Sallie Spiers White (1/5/1843-11/21/1925), dau. of
        Col. William Allen and Lucy McDaniel Reese White of Bedford
        County
124121 Rolfe Emerson Bolling (8/22/1861-2/3/1936), m. 6/18/1890,
        Annie Stuart Litchfield (2/19/1869-4/12/1944), dau. of
        George Victor and Elizabeth Pannill Peirce Litchfield
1241211 Elizabeth Bolling (12/2/1891-   ), m. 8/18/1915,
        Jorge Eduardo Boyd (3/14/1886-   ), son of Frederico
        and Teodolindo Briceno Boyd of Panama. The Boyds lived
        in Mexico City.
12412111 Lola Elizabeth Boyd (11/24/1916-   )
12412112 Mildred Stuart Boyd (8/23/1921-   )(triplet)
12412113 Edith Bolling (Nelson?) Boyd (8/23/1921-   )(triplet)
12412114 Elena Rolfe Boyd (8/23/1921-   )(triplet)
124122 Gertrude Bolling (5/16/1863-   ), m. 10/14/1885,
        Alexander Hunter Galt (12/5/1860-   ), son of Thomas
        Jefferson and Mary Ann Hunter Galt

JOHN BOLLING

(Son of Jane Rolfe)

1241221 Alexander Bolling Galt (7/21/1890-   )
124123   Annie Lee Bolling (6/15/1865-2/26/1917), m. 6/14/1893,
         Matthew H. Maury of Anniston, Alabama (6/9/1860-   ),
         son of Joseph Frye and Elizabeth Graves Maury
1241231 Anne Bolling Maury (9/2/1900-   ), m. John A.
         Goodloe
12412311 John A. Goodloe, Jr.
12412312 Anne Goodloe
12412313 Matthew Maury Goodloe
12412314 Elizabeth Goodloe
1241232 Lucy Logwood Maury (4/19/1903-   ), m. 2/23/1929),
         John Edward Moeling of Louisiana
124124   William Archibald Bolling (10/11/1867-   ), m.
         10/21/1891, Mary Johnson Keller (3/31/1870-   ),
         dau. of John Esten Cooke and Frances Weir Berry Keller
1241241 John Esten Bolling (12/9/1893-   ), m. 4/1/1918,
         Edith Marion Bourne of New York City
1241242 William Holcombe Bolling (7/31/1896-   ), m.
         12/22/1922, Virginia Gaither of North Carolina
124125   Bertha Bolling (10/11/1869-   ). Unm.
124126   Charles Rodefer Bolling (6/11/1871-6/11/1871)
124127   Edith Bolling (10/15/1872-   ), m. (1st) 4/30/1896,
         Norman Galt of Washington (4/30/1866-1/28/1908), son of
         Matthew W. and Mary Jane Galt. M. (2nd) 12/18/1915,
         President Woodrow Wilson (12/28/1856-2/3/1924, son of
         Joseph Ruggles and Janet Woodrow Wilson. Edith was the
         President's second wife. No issue.
124128   John Randolph Bolling (4/11/1876-   ). Unm.
124129   Richard Wilmer Bolling (10/6/1879-   ), m. 5/9/
         1908, Eleanor Hunter Lutz (7/8/1885-   ), dau . of
         Francis Asbury and Eleanor Sweeting Galt Lutz
1241291 Clara L. Bolling
1241292 Richard Wilmer Bolling, Jr.
1241293 Sterling Ruffin Bolling
1241294 Barbara Bolling
12412x   Julian Brandon Bolling (5/7/1882-   ), m. 6/19/1906,
         Viola Roosevelt Belden (9/10/1882-   ), dau. of
         William Harrison and Elizabeth Roosevelt Jennings Belden.
         No issue.
12412a   Geraldine Bolling (8/12/1885-7/6/1887)
12413   Harriett W. Bolling, m. 9/18/1861, Robert H. Waddell, of
         Attala County, Mississippi
12414   Mary Jefferson Bolling, m. 3/31/1864, Rudolph Tuesler of
         Petersburg. Had issue.
1242   Edward Bolling (-1855), m. Anne Cralle
12421   (son)   12422 (dau)
1243   Alexander Bolling (-1878), m. Susan Gray
12431   (dau)   12432 (dau)   12433 (dau)
1244   Jefferson Bolling, d.s.p.
1245   Catherine Bolling, d.s.p.
1246   Pocahontas R. Bolling, m. (1st) William G. White. M (2nd)
         10/10/1867, Peter J. Hill of Nelson County

1247   (son)
1248   (son)
125   Mary Jefferson Bolling, m. 5/27/1797, Col. Edward P. Archer of
      Powhatan County, son of Field and Elizabeth Archer. Colonel
      Archer, m. (2nd) 1799, Anne Walthall, and had issue.
1251   Peter Jefferson Archer, m. (1st) Martha W. Michaux, dau. of
      Jacob and Mary Ann Eliza Woodson Michaux. M. (2nd) Lucy
      Gilliam
      Children by first wife:
12511 William Segar Archer, m. Mary McIlwaine
125111 Mary Finley Archer, m. 10/25/1905, Beverley Heth Randolph
       (6/25/1868-   )(242383)
1251111 Beverley Heth Randolph (6/23/1908-   )
1251112 Mary Archer Randolph (2/15/1912-   )
12512 Edward Cunningham Archer, M.D., m. Caroline Wooldridge (33242)
12513 John Archer
12514 Michaux Archer, m. Mrs. Smith
12515 Sally Archer, m. Robert Archer
12516 Mary Archer
12517 Katie Archer, m. Robert Dunn
12518 Martha Archer
126   Robert Bolling, m. 1800, Jane S. Payne (-1806), dau. of
      Archer and Martha Dandridge Payne of "New Market", Goochland
      County. No issue. She m. (2nd) James B. Ferguson (541)
127   Thomas Bolling (2/11/1764-   )
128   Jane Bolling (9/17/1765-   )
129   Ann Bolling (7/20/1767-   ), m. 1784, Capt. Howell Lewis
      NOTE: There were a number of persons named Howell Lewis.
12x   (son)
12a   (dau)
13   Col. Robert Bolling, of "Chellowe", Buckingham County (8/17/
      1738-1775), m. (1st) 6/5/1763, Mary Burton (ca. 1749-5/2/1764),
      dau. of William Burton of the "Old Plantation", Northampton
      County; m. (2nd) 5/31/1765 (marriage bond this date) Susannah
      Watson of "The Brooke", Henrico County. Mary Burton died at
      Jordan's. When she married Col. Bolling, she was 15. MEMOIR
      pp. 10 and 40.
131   Mary Burton Bolling (4/301764-8/3/1787), m. 11/4/1781, Robert
      Bolling of "Centre Hill, Petersburg (3/3/1759-   )(of
      the Stith Bollings), son of Robert Bolling of "Bollingbrook",
      and his second wife, Mary Marshall Tabb Bolling (-
      10/14/1814), dau. of Col. Thomas Tabb of "Clay Hill", Amelia
      County. Robert Bolling of "Centre Hill" m. (2nd) 11/4/1790,
      Catherine Stith (-8/9/1795); m. (3rd) 9/1/1796, Sally
      Washington (-10/2/1796); and m. (4th) 11/23/1797,
      Ann Dade Stith (-4/ /1846)

1311   Mary Burton Augusta Bolling (6/18/1789-4/ /1853), m. 10/15/
      1807, John Monro Banister, son of Col. John and Anne Blair
      Banister of "Battersea" (near Petersburg)
13111 William C. Banister (-6/9/1864), m. Caroline Lewis.
      He was killed in the Civil War.
131111 John M. Banister of Petersburg
131112 (dau), m. H. Noltenius of Petersburg
131113 (dau), m. Campbell Pryor of Petersburg
131114 T. Lewis Banister, D.D., of Constableville, N.Y.
13112 Mary Burton Banister, m. German B. Gill of Sussex County
13113 Ann Banister (-8/29/1843), m. Wm. T. McCandlish
13114 Robert B. Banister, Surgeon U.S.N.
13115 John Monro Banister, D.D. (of Huntsville, Ala.), m. Mary
      Louisa Broadnax, dau. of Gen. Wm. H. Broadnax
      NOTE: 13115 had a niece Mary, who married Professor
      Richards of Rollo, Mo.
131151 John M. Banister, Surgeon U.S.A. (in 1889, stationed at
      Fort Sherman, Idado)
131152 William B. Banister, Surgeon U.S.A. (in 1889, stationed
      at Fort Grant, Arizona)
13116 Emily C. Banister (1820-1869), m. Henry Harrison Cocke
      (1794-1873), Captain C.S.N., Commodore U.S.N., of Prince
      George County, son of Walter and Anne Carter Harrison
      Cocke. She was his second wife. His first wife was
      Elizabeth Ruffin.
131161 Ann Harrison Cocke (1860-   ), m. George Mason (1853-
      1923) an attorney of Petersburg
131162 Mary M. Cocke, m. Walter B. Richards
13117 Euretta B. Banister, m. Charles L. Stickney of Greensboro,
      Alabama
13118 Augusta Banister
13119 Helen T. Banister, m. Dr. Robert L. Madison of Lexington
131191 Robert Madison of Sylva, N.C.
131192 Bolling Madison of Knoxville
1312 Dead by 5/10/1796
1313 Dead by 5/10/1796
132 Pocahontas Rebecca Bolling (OMSS shows Pocahontas Watson
      Bolling)(-1803), m. 1783, Col. Joseph Cabell, Jr.
      (-8/31/1831), son of Col. Joseph and Mary Hopkins
      Cabell. He m. (2nd) 10/31/1804, Anne Everard'Bolling Duval
      (-1/26/1834)(162)
1321 Sophonisba E. Cabell (3/4/1784-11/26/1857), m. 9/3/1809,
      Robert Harrison Grayson (3/12/1788-   ), son of Senator
      William Grayson of Virginia and his wife, the former Eleanor
      Smallwood. Moved to Kentucky.
13211 William Powhatan Bolling Grayson (9/9/1810-   ), m. 6/15/
      1837, Susan Dixon, dau. of Capt. Henry Dixon of Henderson
      County, Ky.
132111 Robert Harrison Grayson, d. inf.
132112 Mary Eleanor Grayson (9/24/1839-   ), m. Henry Dixon

```
1321121  Sarah Dixon, m. Edward Irvine
1321l3   Joseph Cabell Grayson (1842-1845)
132114   Susan Baillie Grayson (12/25/1843-          ), m. William
         Norman
1321141  Phelps Norman
132115   Sophonisba Grayson (11/9/1845-          ), m. Young Watson
1321151  Jennie Watson, m. Howell Watson
1321152  Mary Watson, m. Milton Grymes
1321153  Bertha Watson, m. J. Stanley Dennis
132116   Hebe Carter Grayson (5/27/1848-          )
132117   Elizabeth Frances Grayson, d. inf.
132118   Elizabeth Cabell Grayson, d. inf.
132119   William Powhatan Grayson, d. inf.
13211x   Henry Dixon Grayson, d. inf.
13211a   Roger Dixon Grayson (1/28/1858-          ), m. Mamie Grymes
13212    Joseph Cabell Grayson (1812-1824)
13213    Hebe Carter Grayson (1/8/1814-1872), m. (1st) 1/8/1833,
         William Preston Smith of Henderson, Ky. (      -2/12/1850),
         son of John and Chenoe Hart Smith (Chenoe is Indian name
         for Kentucky)
         NOTE: William Preston Smith had his name changed from
         Smith to Preston.  Hebe m. (2nd) 10/31/1852, (her cousin)
         William Peartree Smith of Henderson County, Ky., a des-
         cendant of Obadiah and Mary Burks Smith. No issue.
132131   Sophonisba Grayson Preston (10/27/1833-9/ /1876, m. 4/12/
         1855, (her cousin) Carter Henry Harrison (2/15/1825-10/28/
         1893), son of Carter Henry Harrison (9/30/1796-10/9/1825)
         and his wife, the former Caroline Evaline Russell (1/16/
         1797-8/14/1875).  He was Mayor of Chicago during the
         World's Fair, and was assassinated. Caroline m. (2nd)
         1848, Rev. Thomas P. Dudley.
         Children by first husband:
1321311  Willie Harrison (1856-       ), d. inf.
1321312  Caroline Dudley Harrison (3/28/1857-       ), m. 7/ /
         1887, Heaton Owsley (1856-       ), son of John G.
         Owsley of Chicago
13213121 Lina Harrison Owsley, m. (1st) Paul Bartlett; m. (2nd)
         Philip Thornton Hutchins
13213122 Sophie Preston Owsley (1890-       ), m. 1910, Sterling
         Morton
132131221 Susette Morton (1911-       ), m. Ernest Alfred
         Hammill, Jr.
132131222 Caroline Morton (1915-1921)
132131223 Millicent Morton (1925-1929)
1321313  Carter Henry Harrison, Jr. (4/23/1860-       ), m. 12/14/
         1887, Edith Ogden, dau. of Robert N. Ogden of New Orleans
13213131       (1888-       )
13213132 Carter Henry Harrison III (6/28/1890-       ), m. 1914,
         Lucy Brady Cook
132131321 Lucy Brady Harrison (1915-       )
132131322 Edith Ogden Harrison (1917-       )
```

```
132131323  Caryl Harrison (1920-          )
132131324  Jean Harrison (1923-          )
13213133   Edith Ogden Harrison (1896-        ), m. 1916, Cyrus Edson
             Manierre
132131331  Cyrus Edson Manierre, Jr. (1919-        )
132131332  William Reid Manierre (1923-        )
1321314    Hebe Grayson Harrison (1862-d. inf.)
1321315    Dudley Harrison (1864-d. inf.)
1321316    Randolph Harrison (1866-d. inf.)
1321317    Harry Grayson Harrison (1868-d. inf.)
1321318    William Preston Harrison (4/12/1869-        ), m. 1915, Ada
             Marie Sandburg
13213181   Preston Carter Harrison (1921-        )
1321319    Gracie Harrison (1871-d. inf.)
132131x    Sophonisba Preston Harrison (12/17/1873-        ), m. (1st)
             Barrett Eastman. M. (2nd) Roland Thompson
13214      Robert Bolling Grayson (1815-1816)
13215      Mary Ann Elizabeth Grayson (twin), d. inf.
13216      Robert H. Grayson (twin), d. inf.
13217      Benjamin Blair Grayson, d. inf.
13218      Pocahontas Rebecca Bolling Grayson, d. inf.
13219      Sarah Bolling Grayson, d. inf.
1321x      Eleanor Smallwood Grayson (3/1/1827-        ), m. 11/28/1844,
             Joseph Adams.  Merchant of Hendersontown, Ky.
1321x1     Eleanor Adams (1845-1850)
1321x2     Joseph Grayson Adams (9/21/1849-        )
1321x3     William Smallwood Adams (7/17/1851-        )
1321x4     Ellie Adams, d. inf.
1321x5     John Cabell Adams (8/12/1854-        )
1321x6     Robert Grayson Adams (2/22/1856-        ), m. Martha Elam
1321x61    Baxter Harrison Adams
1321x62    Robert William Adams
1322   Sarah Bolling Cabell (5/29/1786-        ), m. 11/14/1805, Elisha
         Meredith (10/13/1783-        ), son of John and Ann Taylor
         Meredith.  Moved to Kentucky, then to Alabama.
13221      Pocahontas Rebecca Bolling Meredith (9/18/1806-5/6/1838),
             m. 12/18/1827, William O'Neal Perkins (2/28/1791-        )
132211     William Harding Perkins (1829-1870), m. ca. 1848, Louisa
             Hewit of Alabama.  Moved to Mississippi.
1322111    Louisa Perkins
1322112    Wm. O'Neal Perkins
1322113    Elizabeth Perkins
1322114    Thomas H. Perkins
1322115    Sarah Cabell Perkins
132212     Elizabeth Perkins (1831-8/  /1872), m. 10/  /1850, Col.
             James Jackson, C.S.A. (        -1840), son of James and
             Sarah Moore Jackson (widow of Samuel McCulloch). Alabama.
1322121    William Jackson (1851-        ) of Bessemer, Ala., m.
             Sarah J. Weakly, d.s.p.
1322122    Jane Jackson, d. inf.
1322123    Mary Steele Jackson (1854-1861)
```

1322124   Sarah Jackson (1856-1861)
1322125   Eleanor Kirkman Jackson (1858-   ), m. William H.
          Phillips of Alabama
1322126   James Kirkman Jackson (1861-   ). Montgomery, Ala.
1322127   Charles Pollard Jackson (1864-   )
1322128   Robert Andrews Jackson of Evansville, Ind.
1322129   Elizabeth Jackson, d. inf.
132213   Sarah Cabell Perkins (5/23/1834-3/ /1868), m. 1853, George
          Moore Jackson, C.S.A., brother to Col. James Jackson who
          m. Elizabeth Perkins
1322131   Alexander Jackson (7/4/1854-   ) of Colbert County,
          Ala.
1322132   Elizabeth Jackson (1856-1861)
1322133   Jane Jackson (4/10/1858-   ), m. George W. Polk. San
          Antonio.
13221331 Kate Polk, d. inf.
13221332 George W. Polk, Jr.
13221333 Jane Polk
1322134   Martha Jackson (1860-1862)
1322135   Kate Breckinridge Jackson (11/24/1863-   )
1322136   Rufus Polk Jackson (8/24/1861-   ). Texas.
1322137   Richard Harrison Jackson (5/10/1866-   ). U.S.N.
13222   Edward Mosely Meredith, d. inf.
13223   John Taylor Meredith (5/8/1811-1893), m. Elizabeth H. Payne,
          dau. of Daniel and Elizabeth Hooe Winter Payne of Fauquier
          County. Lived at "Greenville", Prince William County.
132231   Richard Winter Meredith (8/18/1839-   )("Black Horse
          Cavalry", C.S.A.), m. Mary Williams of Mississippi.
          Physician, Prince William County.
1322311   Samuel W. Meredith
132232   Elizabeth Daniel Meredith, m. R. H. Hooe
1322321   John M. Hooe
1322322   Robert Hooe
1322323   Daniel Hooe
132233   Elisha E. Meredith (12/26/1848-   ) M.C., m. Sylvia
          Contee of Maryland, dau. of Capt. John Contee, U.S.N.
1322331   Edward Contee Meredith
1322332   William Payne Meredith
132234   Alice P. Meredith
132235   Thomas S. Meredith
132236   J. Cabell Meredith, M.D., Washington, D.C.
13224   Joseph Cabell Meredith (8/29/1813-8/14/1851), Alabama.
13225   Francis Dandridge Meredith (12/15/1815-   ), m. Frances
          Broadnax, dau. of Col. Thomas Broadnax of Williamson County,
          Tenn., formerly of Virginia. Merediths lived in Mississippi.
132251   Sarah Jane Meredith (3/16/1841-   )
132252   Mary Ann Meredith (7/22/1845-   )
132253   Elisha Meredith (2/2/1848-   )
132254   Frances B. Meredith (2/4/1855-   )
132255   George Dandridge Meredith (12/8/1858-   )
13226   Benjamin Cabell Meredith (2/8/1819-1873), Physician, m. (1st)

Margaret J. Broadnax (-9/23/1843)(sister to Frances Broadnax). M. (2nd) Mrs. Cheek. M. (3rd) ca. 1869. Doctor Meredith lived in Washington County, Texas.
Children by first wife:
132261 Margaret J. Meredith (1/14/1843-   )
Children by third wife:
132262 Ben Meredith
13227 Mary Ann Meredith (10/27/1821-2/26/1868), m. 6/13/1839, Shelby W. Chadwick (4/26/1815-4/5/1854). Merchant of Greensboro, Ala.
132271 William Henry Chadwick (10/10/1840-1867), C.S.A.
132272 Shelby Wayne Chadwick (4/26/1842-   ), C.S.A., m. 12/20/1865, Jane Comack of Hale County, Ala. Chadwicks lived in Greensboro.
1322721 Mary E. Chadwick (10/20/1866-   ), m. 11/7/1888, Rev. J. D. Ellis of Marengo, Ala.
13227211 Clara V. Ellis
13227212 Hattie Ellis
13227213 Martha M. Ellis
13227214 George Stowers Ellis
1322722 Mattie Erwin Chadwick (3/6/1868-   ), m. 4/11/1888, J. W. Rodney of Roanoke, Randolph County, Ala.
1322723 John Shelby Chadwick (5/15/1871-   )
1322724 Clara Chadwick (3/9/1874-   )
1322725 David Chadwick (1877-1877)
1322726 Robert Edward Chadwick (5/7/1879-   )
1322727 Francis Peterson Chadwick (8/13/1884-   )
132273 Robert Alvin Chadwick (1844-   ), m. 1868, Nannie Wright. Lived in St. Louis.
1322731 Cabell Wright Chadwick
1322732 Mary Chadwick
132274 Edward Shelby Chadwick (1846-   ). Unm.
13228 Dr. Thomas Jefferson Meredith (2/25/1824-1889), Physician, m. (1st) 12/22/1853, Mary E. Brown. M. (2nd) Bettie   . Lived in Texas.
Children by first wife: (one of the daughters married a Mr. Ware)
132281 Sara Annie Meredith (12/6/1854-   )
132282 Mary Ida Meredith (9/24/1856-   )
132283 Edward Cabell Meredith (1/3/1859-   )
132284 (dau)
Children by second wife:
132285 Stuart Meredith
132286 Minnie Meredith
132287 (dau). Married.
13229 Virginia Meredith (4/25/1826-1877), m. Dr. Daniel Eddins (1/4/1853-1867). Lived in Texas.
132291 Elisha M. Eddins. Marlin, Texas.
132292 Daniel S. Eddins. Marlin, Texas.
132293 Mary Eddins Brown, m.   Brown. Grimes County, Texas
132294 Ella Eddins Scales, m.   Scales

```
1322941   Clayton Scales
1322942   Effie Scales
1322943   Mollie Scales
1322944   Eddins Scales
132295    Elizabeth Eddins, m. 1875, Rev. Reddin Andrews of Texas
132296    Sallie Eddins, m.              Morse.  Waco.
1323    Robert Bolling Cabell, M.D. (1787-10/7/1808), m. 1808,
          Elizabeth Walthall of Chesterfield County, d.s.p.
1324    Joseph Magginson Cabell (changed name to Charles Joseph
          Cabell)(1788-11/23/1810).  Unm.  New Orleans.  Fought three
          duels.
1325    Archibald Cabell, d. inf.
1326    Edward Blair Cabell (5/29/1791-8/29/1850), m. 4/10/1812,
          Harriet Forbes Monroe (4/10/1794-3/22/1857), dau. of Col.
          Joseph Jones Monroe and his wife, who was a Miss Carr.
          Lived in Missouri.
13261   Charles Joseph Cabell (4/26/1813-10/10/1882), m. 9/15/1837,
          Susan Allin, dau. of Col. William Allin
132611  Mary Allin Cabell (5/3/1839-          ), m. 1858, John S.
          Kikendall of Kentucky.  No issue. Lived in Missouri.
132612  Pocahontas Cabell (6/2/1842-          ), m. 9/6/1860,
          Charles Hammond. Missouri.
1326121   Talbott Hammond
1326122   Charles Cabell Hammond
1326123   Mary Cabell Hammond
1326124   Pocahontas Hammond
1326125   Robert Boyd Hammond
132613  Harriet M. Cabell (1845-1847)
132614  Robert Boyd Cabell (2/22/1847-          ), Physician, m.
          (1st) Sarah Spencer. No issue.  M. (2nd) Emma Thomas.
          Lived in Carroll County, Mo.
          Children by his second wife:
1326141   Sarah Spencer Cabell
1326142   Pocahontas Cabell
1326143   Mary Allin Cabell
1326144   Susan Burton Cabell
1326145   William Allin Cabell
132615  Edward Blair Cabell (1852-1869)
132616  William Allin Cabell (6/14/1855-          ), m. 9/25/1883,
          Mrs. Claire McDaniel. No issue. Glasgow, Mo.
132617  James Monroe Cabell (7/3/1858-          ), m. 12/7/1883,
          Mrs. Clara Dengler.  Leadville, Colo.
1326171   Susan Burton Cabell
13262   Emily Monroe Cabell (4/12/1818-          ), m. 5/19/1835,
          Peter T. Abell (7/26/1813) of Bardstown, Ky.  They lived
          in Atchison, Kansas
132621  Susan Emily Abell (11/1/1836-          ), m. 9/28/1853,
          Charles Elijah Woolfork (5/19/1828-          ), a Kentucky
          merchant.
1326211   (son), d. inf.
1326212   (son, d. inf.
```

132622   Harriet M. Abell, d. inf.
132623   Elizabeth J. Abell, d. inf.
132624   Edward Cabell Abell (12/4/1841-   ), m. Fannie Flood.
         Lived in Linn County, Mo.
1326241 John Abell
1326242 Addison S. Abell
132625   Addison Slye Abell (4/21/1844-d. in C.S.A.)
132626   Pocahontas R. Abell (8/4/1846-   ), m. (1st) Dr.
         James White. M. (2nd) 12/19/1879, Rev. Joseph King of
         Missouri.
         Children by first husband:
1326261 Emily White
         Children by second husband:
1326262 Ella King
1326263 May Cabell King
1326264 Addison Abell King
1326265 Ruth Scarritt King
132627   Harriet J. Abell (2/10/1848-   ), m. George M.
         Wyatt. La Salle, Ill.
1326271 Harriet Emily Wyatt
132628   Pamela Davis Abell (7/2/1851-   ), m. Edward Couch.
         Lived near Galveston.
1326281 Hallie Abell Couch, m. Mr. Ingram of Texas.
1326282 (son)
132629   Adela T. Abell, d. inf.
13262x   Ellen Abell (-8/5/1856), m. George Bloom
13262x1 George Bloom
13262x2 Imogen Bloom
13262a   Peter Thompson Abell (1858-   ), m. Maggie Stephenson
13262a1 Cecil Thompson Abell
13263   Jane Browder Cabell (7/14/1823-1/21/1849), m. 11/29/1845,
         Thomas Parke Wilkinson (b. in Prince Edward or Buckingham
         County). They lived in Keysville, Mo.
132631   John Cabell Wilkinson (12/13/1846-   ), m. 1877,
         Margaret Ewing, dau. of Judge Ephraim B. and Elizabeth
         Allen Ewing. The Wilkinsons lived in St. Louis.
1326311 Margaret Ewing Wilkinson
1326312 William Tudor Wilkinson
1326313 Jane Alice Wilkinson
1326314 John Cabell Wilkinson
1326315 Elizabeth Allen Wilkinson
1326316 Florence Ewing Wilkinson
1326317 Dorothy Brevard Wilkinson
13264   John Linneus Cabell (11/7/1825-1/29/1846)
13265   Pocahontas Rebecca Cabell (11/29/1830-11/ /1881), m. 3/15/
         1848, Adamantine Johnson of Brunswick, Chariton County, Mo.
132651   Edward Cabell Johnson (5/29/1849-   ), m. Nannie
         Henry
1326511 Hattie Johnson
1326512 Marie Johnson
1326513 Henry Johnson

1326514 Pocahontas Johnson
132652   Adamantine Johnson, Jr. (1/21/1850-   ), m. (1st)
         Nannie Scott. M. (2nd) Miss Bernard
         Children by first wife:
1326521 Maud Johnson
1326522 Cabell Johnson
         Children by second wife:
1326523 Bernard Johnson
132653   Robert Fisher Johnson (12/25/1852-   ), m. Louisa
         Clinkscales
1326531
1326532
132654   Emma Maud Johnson (10/19/1854-   ), m. Dr. James
         Morrison
1326541 Emily Maud Morrison
1326542 Sarah Johnson Morrison
132655   Maj. Matthias Johnson (1857-d. young)
132656   Nova Zembla Johnson
132657   Pocahontas Cabell Johnson, m. Charles Delaney
132658   Susan Cabell Johnson
13266   Robert Harvey Cabell (12/13/1832-   ), Physician, m.
         (1st) 12/6/1853, Ellen C. Ballentine of Missouri, d.s.p.
         M. (2nd) 8/12/1857, Alice Oliver of Pennsylvania. M. (3rd)
         Sarah Wright. Doctor Cabell practiced in Grundy County,
         Mo.
         Children by second wife:
132661   Hattie F. Cabell
132662   Janie Oliver Cabell
132663   Pocahontas Cabell
132664   Robert Harvey Cabell
132665   Charles J. Cabell
         Children by thrid wife:
132666   Ila Wright Cabell
132667   Marie Wright Cabell
132668   Edward Blair Cabell
132669   Emily Monroe Cabell
13266x   Harriet F. Cabell
1327   Benjamin William S. Cabell (5/10/1793-4/19/1862)(Major Gen-
         eral of Militia), m. 12/16/1816, Sarah("Sallie") Epes
         Doswell (4/27/1802-8/5/1874), dau. of Maj. John and Mary
         Doswell of Nottoway County. The Cabells lived in Pittsyl-
         vania County. He was in War of 1812.
13271   Pocahontas Rebecca Cabell (6/29/1819-2/3/1858), m. 8/25/
         1836, Col. John Tyler Hairston (-1/13/1857),
         son of Col. George and Louisa Hardiman (Hardyman?)
         Hairston. The John Tyler Hairstons lived at "Red Plains"
         in Henry County.
132711   Virginia Hairston (7/4/1837-   ). Unm.
132712   Louisa Hardiman (Hardyman?) Hairston (7/7/1839-   ),
         m. 7/3/1860, Virginius Randolph Williams of Lunenburg
         County.

1327121   Ellen Gertrude Williams (5/16/1861-   ), m. Wythe
          M. Peyton
1327122   Belle Williams (9/ /1866-   )
132713   Elizabeth Lewis Hairston (3/20/1841-   ), m. 11/9/
          1859, Livingston Claiborne of Pittsylvania County
1327131   Leonard Claiborne (10/26/1860-   )
1327132   Elizabeth Cabell Claiborne (2/ /1867-   )
1327133   Pocahontas Bolling Claiborne (3/ /1869-   ), m. E. W.
          Griggs
1327134   Tyler Hairston Claiborne (2/ /1872-   )
1327135   George C. Cabell Claiborne
1327136   Letitia Claiborne
1327137   Livingston Claiborne, Jr. (ca. 1883-5/25/1899)
132714   George Hairston (1843-d. inf.)
132715   Sarah ("Sallie") Epes Doswell Hairston (5/21/1845-   ),
          m. 12/18/1866, James (John?) S. Redd of Henry County,
          C.S.A. (18th Virginia).
1327151   Sarah Hill Redd (8/ /1868-   )
1327152   James S. Redd, Jr. (7/ /1871-   )
1327153   Cabell Redd
132716   Benjamin (George?) Cabell Hairston (2/10/1847-   ),
          m. 11/14/1872, Powell Huse (Ann Powell?) Lash of Stokes
          County, N.C.
1327161   Annie Hairston
1327162   George Cabell Hairston
1327163   Lettie Hairston
132717   Hardiman (Hardyman?) Hairston. Unm.
132718   John Tyler Hairston (1851-   ), m. Elizabeth ("Bettie")
          Brown Dillard
1327181
1327182
132719   Powhatan Bolling Hairston (1853-d. young)
13272   John Roy Cabell (3/24/1823-   ), M.D., m. (1st) 6/19/
          1847, Martha C. Wilson (11/22/1823-6/15/1859), dau. of Col.
          Nathaniel and Winifred Tunstall Wilson. M. (2nd) Mrs. Kate
          Clements. No issue.
          Children by first wife:
132721   Ann Eliza Cabell (3/27/1848-   ), m. John A. Coleman
1327211   Martha W. Coleman
1327212   John Roy Coleman
1327213   Daniel Coleman
1327214   Benjamin Coleman
1327215   Joseph Coleman
132722   William C. Cabell (5/11/1851-   ), M.D., m. Mary
          Watson. They lived in Baltimore.
1327221   Katie Cabell
1327222   Mary Cabell
1327223   John R. Cabell
132723   Mary W. Cabell (8/15/1853-   ), m. O. C. Smith
1327231   Cabell Smith
1327232   Carrington Smith

```
1327233  Roy Smith
132724   Nathaniel W. Cabell (9/3/1855-          ), m. Essie Frederick
1327241  John Roy Cabell
1327242  Benjamin Cabell
1327243  Frederick Cabell
1327244  George C. Cabell
132725   John R. Cabell, Jr. (6/8/1859-          ). Unm.
13273    Virginia J. Cabell (1825-1832)
13274    Gen. William Lewis Cabell (1/1/1827-          ), C.S.A., m.
         7/22/1856, Harriet A. Rector (      -4/16/1887), dau. of
         Maj. Elias and Catharine Duval Rector.  General Cabell was
         Major of Dallas.
132741   Benjamin E. Cabell (11/18/1858-           )
132742   Katie Doswell Cabell, m. 4/24/1889, John R. Currie
132743   John J. Cabell (11/28/1870-      )
132744   Lawrence Du Val Cabell (8/22/1874-        )
132745   Lewis Rector Cabell (1/3/1879)
132746   D. inf.
132747   D. inf.
13275    Dr. Powhatan Bolling Cabell (10/17/1828-12/14/1859), m. 9/
         3/1857, Jane B. Lanier. No issue.
13276    D. inf.
13277    Algernon Sidney Cabell (11/25/1832-          ) Major, C.S.A.,
         m. 12/22/1859, Mary Angela Carroll, dau. of Col. DeRosa
         Carroll, C.S.A., of Arkansas
132771   DeRosa Carroll Cabell (8/ /1861-      )
132772   Sallie Doswell Cabell
132773   Benjamin Cabell
132774   Powhatan Cabell
13278    George Craighead Cabell (1/25/1836-          ), m. (1st) 10/25/
         1859, Mary Harrison Baird (      -9/30/1890), a descen-
         dant of Nathaniel Harrison (1742-1782). M. (2nd) 11/ /
         1892, Ellen Virginia Ashton of Portsmouth.  No issue.
         Children by first wife:
132781   Sarah D. Cabell, m. L. H. Lewis.  Dallas.
1327811  George C. Lewis
1327812  Benjamin H. Lewis
1327813  Archibald L. Lewis
132782   Annie D. Cabell, m. Garland S. Wooding, Danville.
1327821  Jennie Garland Wooding
1327822  Mary Baird Wooding
132783   Dr. Benjamin W. S. Cabell, m. 1/1/1895, Nannie Bradley,
         dau. of Capt. Thomas D. Bradley. Ringold, Va.
132784   George C. Cabell, Jr., m. Katie Graveley. Marlin, Falls
         County, Texas.
1327841  Mary B. Cabell
132785   Powhatan Algernon Cabell
13279    Sarah Epes Cabell (11/25/1838-11/9/1876), m. 2/7/1860,
         Richard Junius Epes (      -12/14/1861) of Lunenburg
         County. M. (2nd) 1/20/1864, Ashley L. Davis of Lunenburg
         County.
```

132791 Junius Epes (3/31/1861-   )
        Children by second husband:
132792 Joseph Cabell Davis (7/30/1867-   )
132793 Mary Pocahontas Davis (8/8/1869-   ), m. 10/ /
          1890, George A. Muncaster of Henderson, Ky.
132794 Sallie Ashley Davis (1875-1878)
1327x   Joseph Robert Cabell (5/28/1840-5/10/1864), m. 12/16/1863,
          Mary Elizabeth Irby. No issue. Commanded 38th Virginia,
          C.S.A. Killed near Drury's Bluff.
1327a   Benjamin Edward Cabell (12/8/1842-3/17/1862). Lieutenant,
          38th Virginia. Died Chimborazo Hospital, Richmond.
1328   Archibald B. Cabell (5/ /1795-1822). Unm. Lost sight in
          early youth. Musical genius.
1329   Nicholas Cabell, d. inf.
132x   Mary Pocahontas Rebecca Cabell (1798-2/4/1821), m. 3/27/1818,
          Peyton Doswell (-12/ /1820) of Nottoway County.
          Moved to Henderson, Ky., where within a year, Mr. and Mrs.
          Doswell and their two children died of the "slow" fever.
132x1   D. inf.
132x2   D. inf.
133   Elizabeth Blair Bolling, m. Maj. Thomas West (1751-1829), son
          of Col. John and Elizabeth Seaton West
1331   Martha West (1796-1828), m. James Saunders Jones (1786-1846),
          son of William Jones (1745-1781) and his wife Elizabeth
          Walker
13311   Elizabeth Bolling Jones (1812-1885), m. 12/18/1828, Dr.
          Glover Davenport Gilliam (5/25/1800-9/22/1852)(b. in
          Buckingham County) of "Landover" (near Naruna), son of
          Richard Holland and Elizabeth Glover Gilliam. Dr. and
          Mrs. Gilliam lived and died in Campbell County.
133111 Martha Virginia Gilliam (1/7/1830-   ), m. Joseph
          Epperson
1331111 Glover Egbert Epperson, C.S.A.
133112 Eloise Glover Gilliam (3/22/1832-2/24/1870), m. Rev.
          Richard Edward Booker, a Baptist minister
1331121 Sallie Love Booker, m. H. T. Booker
1331122 Richard Glover Booker
1331123 Walter T. Booker, m. Fannie Foster
1331124 Norman Courtney Booker, m. Lillian Bell
1331125 Loulie Emma Booker, m. Jesse T. Adams
1331126 George Richard Booker, d. young
133113 James Richard Gilliam (10/3/1833-1855), m. Anne Slaughter
          Davenport (1834-1921), dau. of Richard Glover Davenport
          (1806-1841) and his wife Mary E. Hubbard (1815-1900)
1331131 James Richard Gilliam, Jr. (1854-1917), of Lynchburg, m.
          Jessie Belfield Johnson (1863-1941), dau. of Fontaine
          Dickerson Johnson (1834-1917) and his wife Lucy Ellen
          Burrows (1836-1932)
13311311 James Richard Gilliam III
13311312 Annie Gilliam (1888-1959), m. Charles Edward Conrad
          (1879-1944)

133113121 James Gilliam Conrad (1915-   ), m. (1st) Celeste
     B. Goolsby (1917-1980), m. (2nd) Caroline W. Poindexter
     (1915-   )
     Children by first wife:
1331131211 James Gilliam Conrad, Jr. (1944-   ), m. Kathryn
     B. Ford (1947-   )
1331131212 Robert Bullington Conrad (1946-1967)
133114 Elizabeth ("Queenie") Bolling Gilliam (5/20/1835-1/19/1894),
     m. Dr. Richard M. Price (6/3/1827-6/10/1903), born in
     Virginia, lived in Graham, Texas
1331141 (dau), d. inf., en route to Tennessee, bur. Hollins, in
     the Enon Baptist Church Cemetery
1331142 Nannie Lee Price (9/29/1866-10/24/1896), m. 10/16/1884,
     Jefferson D. Short (8/6/1860-9/28/1941), lived in Graham,
     Texas. He died in Goble, Oregon
13311421 Willie Short (7/4/1885-   )
13311422 Motie Short (4/3/1887-   )
13311423 Maggie Short (7/3/1889-   )
13311424 Lyda Elizabeth Short (1/9 or 19?/1891-11/28/1961), m.
     2/9/1908, Daniel William Carter (5/7/1888-7/4/1963).
     Married at St. Helens, Oregon. Died in Rainier, Oregon.
133114241 Henry Davis Carter (10/25/1909-   )
133114242 Harold Carter (1911-1929)
133114243 Howard William Carter (12/10/1919-   ), m. 1/1/
     1945, Dorothy L. Scates (11/9/1923-   ) of Douglas,
     Kansas. They live in Oregon.
1331142431 Jon-Henry Carter (10/7/1945-   )
1331142432 Claudia E. Carter (9/2/1947-   )
1331142433 Mary Lou Carter (5/26/1949-   )
1331142434 Kathleen J. Carter (10/17/1953-   )
133114244 Helen L. Carter (3/21/1923-   )(twin)
133114245 Herbert Carter (3/21/1923-2/6/1975)(twin)
133114246 Anna Mae Carter (2/7/1927-   )(triplet)
133114247 Robert Carter (2/7/1927-   )(triplet)
133114248 Daniel Carter (2/7/1927-   )(triplet)
13311425 Walter Short (9/10/1892-1900)
13311426 Mary Etta Short (5/24/1894-   )
1331143 Elizabeth Bolling Price, m. Mr. Melton
1331144 Daisy Price, m. Mr. Broyler
1331145 Motie Price, m. Morton Price
1331146 William Jones Price
1331147 Thomas West Price
1331148 Walter Price
1331149 Nathaniel G. Price
133115 Amanda Jones Gilliam (11/27/1836-2/22/1920), m. 7/ /1887,
     Richard E. Adams. No issue.
133116 Mary Victoria Gilliam (6/4/1838-5/10/1840)
133117 Edward Glover Gilliam (3/9/1840-12/9/1891), m. (1st) 1869,
     Emma Plunkett Gilbert ; m. (2nd) 1882, Colie Tynes
     Children by first wife:
1331171 Ella Coleman Gilliam (11/26/1870-5/ /1945), m. C. Edward
     Evans

```
1331172   John Richard Gilliam (5/  /1871-1876)
1331173   Annie Eliza Gilliam (3/24/1872-        ), m. Augustus H.
          Evans
1331174   James Cornelius Gilliam (6/15/1874-        ), m. 3/21/
          1899, Minnie Callaham
1331175   Walter Edward Gilliam (10/14/1878-6/  /1941)
1331176   Fannie Jane Gilliam (3/14/1880-        ), m. 9/  /1909,
          William C. Cook
1331177   Emma Hubbard Gilliam (7/31/1881-        ), m. 12/1/1900,
          Daniel P. Minix
133118    Mary Marshall Gilliam (7/26/1842-1854)
133119    Olivia Ford Gilliam (4/11/1844-2/4/1907), m. Thomas H.
          Wooding
1331191   Martha Susan Wooding, m. Leigh Budwell
1331192   Eliza Gilliam Wooding, m. Silas Carter
1331193   Loulie M. Berger Wooding
1331194   Ella Wilcox Wooding, m. Thos. Carter
1331195   Robert H. Wooding, m. (1st) Virginia Eamons; m. (2nd)
          Elizabeth Carter
1331196   Alice Wooding, m. Silas Carter
1331197   Emma Wooding, m. John Shapard
1331198   Willie Hill Wooding
1331199   Thomas W. Wooding, m. Ethel Booker
133119x   Samuel Josiah Wooding
133119a   Lillian Wooding, m. (1st)           Winston; m. (2nd) J. W.
          Kent
133119b   James Richard Wooding, m. Jane Smith
133119c   West Gilliam Wooding, m. Bessie Moses
133119d   Nathaniel Wooding, m. Ola Reynolds
13311x    Walter Flood (Floyd?) Gilliam (1/27/1846-2/3/1926), m.
          1/30/1866, Jane Lewis Hamlet
13311x1   Armistead Hamlet Gilliam, m. Mrs. Anna Steele Ramsey
13311x2   Eliza Bolling Gilliam, m. Martin Whitlow
13311x3   Sallie Virginia Gilliam
13311x4   Olivia West Gilliam, m. William Jones Abbitt
13311x5   Robert Edward Gilliam, m. Mrs. Annie Holmes Henry
13311x6   Walter Fuqua Gilliam
13311x7   Glover Davenport Gilliam, m. Russie Turner
13311x8   James Chomas Gilliam, m. Sallie Bowman
13311x9   Rosa Maria Gilliam.  Was Principal of Naruna High School
13311xx   Ruth Jane Gilliam
13311a    Emma Josephine Gilliam (4/30/1848-1886), m. (1st) 11/  /
          1865, George Gilbert; m. (2nd) Charles Gooch
          Children by first husband:
13311a1   Rosa Lee Gilbert, m. Dr. J. B. Woodson
13311a2   George W. Gilbert, m. Blanche Robertson
13311a3   Cornelius Gilbert, m. Eva Sanderson
13311a4   Annie Gilbert, m. W. A. Ford
          Children by second husband:
13311a5   John Gooch
13311a6   Emma Josephine Gooch, m. Floyd Knight
13311b    Thomas West Gilliam (11/21/1849-2/2/1924), m. Fannie Diuguid
```

13311b1 Elsie West Gilliam. Served as a missionary.
13311b2 Grace Schenk Gilliam, m. Edward F. Younger
13311b3 Fannie Diuguid Gilliam
13312 Maj. Thomas West Jones, m. Elizabeth Johns
133121 Martha Jane Jones, m. (1st) John Franklin Wood, m. (2nd)
         Patterson Jennings
         Children by first husband:
1331211 William Franklin Wood, m. Rachel McFarland Hunter
13312111 Ann Virginia Wood, m. William Franklin
13312112 John B. Wood, killed in Civil War
13312113 William E. Wood, d. inf.
13312114 Martha Elizabeth Wood, m. Joseph Houston Torrence
133121141 Lenora Zephna Torrence, m. Thomas Lafayette Franklin
1331211411 Carl Burton Franklin. Unm.
1331211412 Eunice May Franklin (5/11/1897-8/30/1983), m. 11/24/
             1920, Samuel Arthur Caldwell (5/20/1893-9/22/1976),
             son of Washington Hunter and Bridget Allie Booth
             Caldwell
13312114121 Samuel Franklin Caldwell (9/30/1921-   ), m.
             12/21/1945, Carol Evelyn Tweedy (1/16/1926-   )
133121141211 Dana Elizabeth Caldwell (10/20/1946-   ), m.
             10/29/1965, William Clarence Mosebrook (2/19/1945-
)
1331211412111 Jeffrey Wade Mosebrook (1/25/1968-   )
1331211412112 Christy Elizabeth Mosebrook (12/2/1970-   )
133121141212 Robert Allen Caldwell (2/20/1949-   ), m. 9/
             11/1971, Barbara Ann Hammock (9/20/1952-   )
1331211412121 Robert Sherwood Caldwell (2/20/1974-   )
1331211412122 Jacob Daniel Caldwell (5/21/1978-   )
133121141213 Arthur Ray Caldwell (3/10/1952-   ), m. 8/21/
             1971, Sandra Kay Bates (7/10/1952-   )
1331211412131 Tobie Kay Caldwell (9/11/1972-   )
1331211412132 Stacey Rae Caldwell (8/18/1976-   )
1331211412133 Arthur Ray Caldwell, Jr. (9/5/1980-   )
13312114214 Barry Evans Caldwell (4/8/1963-   )
13312114122 Elva Lenora Caldwell (6/12/1922-5/2/1979)(triplet), m.
             2/19/1951, Wyatt Matthew Witt (7/26/1929-   )
133121141221 Wyatt Matthew Witt, Jr. (10/6/1952-   ), m.
             7/26/1975, Darlene Farley (3/19/1954-   )
1331211412211 Jason Edward Witt (3/10/1976-   )
1331211412212 Heather Lenora Witt (6/15/1980-   )
133121141222 Melvin Douglas Witt (11/1/1957-   ), m. 7/14/
             1978, Elizabeth Terrell (12/24/1960-   )
1331211412221 Angel Marie Witt (4/30/1979-   )
13312114123 Edna Caldwell (6/12/1922-6/12/1922)(triplet), d. at
             birth
13312114124 Emma Caldwell (6/12/1922-6/12/1922)(triplet). d. at
             birth
13312114125 Lyle Ould Caldwell (9/21/1923-   ), m. 4/1/1960,
             Mildred Christine Eubank (9/10/1932-   )
13312114126 Christine May Caldwell (5/16/1926-   ), m. 7/26/
             1952, Harry Lloyd Layne (7/6/1930-   )

133121141261 Judy May Layne (9/2/1955-   ), m. 5/24/1975,
                Richard Lee Foltz (3/11/1951-   )
1331211412611 Rodney Arthur Foltz (12/27/1977-   )
1331211412612 Sarah Virginia Foltz (12/28/1979-   )
133121141262 Lois Marie Layne (10/19/1962-10/19/1962)
13312114127 Margaret Virginia Caldwell (5/7/1928-   ), m.
                8/2/1975, Walter Lee Mitchell, Jr. (12/31/1926-   )
13312114128 (dau), d. inf.
13312114129 Mary Ellen Caldwell (3/8/1941-   ), m. 10/6/1962,
                Merwyn Albert Ewers (5/5/1940-   )
1331211413 Daniel Thomas Franklin. Unm.
1331211414 Jesse William Franklin, m. Josephine Carwile
13312114141 Lenora Franklin, m. Robert Clark
133121141411 Donna Clark
133121141412 Mark Clark
133121141413 Dianne Clark
13312114142 Elizabeth Ann Franklin, m. Paul Bryant
133121141421 Paulus Elson Bryant
133121141422 Jesse Landon Bryant
13312115 Washington Hunter Wood, killed in Civil War
13312116 Edward Hunter Wood, m. Betty Hunter
13312117 Sarah Emeline Wood, m. Thomas Henry Alfred Cheatham
13312118 Jesse Jones Wood (6/13/1850-3/5/1928), m. Mary Bridget
                Robertson (8/2/1860-12/1/1923). They are bur. New
                Concord Presbyterian Church, Concord, Va. Their infant
                son is bur. Old Concord Presbyterian Church, Spout
                Spring, Va. Mary was a sister to Mittie Jackson
                Robertson.
133121181 (son) d. inf.
13312119 Nancy ("Nannie") Mae (May?) Wood, m. Thomas Davis Gilmer
                Evans (1842-1911)
133121191 Anna McFarland Evans, m. Daniel Hugh Booth (6/4/1875-
                          ), son of Thomas Anderson and Eliza Evans
                Booth
1331211911 Alice May Booth, m. Rasworth Thomas Wright, son of
                Naomi Rasworth and Willie Ann Campbell Wright
13312119111 Hugh Rasworth Wright
13312119112 Linda Gale Wright, m. Calvin Samuel Smith, son of
                Robert Walker and Marian Lee Jordan Smith
133121191121 Calvin Samuel Smith II
133121191122 Thomas Ray Smith
13312119113 Charlotte Ann Wright
133121192 Thomas William Evans (1880-1959), m. Laura Adalyn Evans
                (-1944)
1331211921 Edith Evans, m. Stuart Trice
1331211922 William David Evans (1899-1963), m. Florence Esther
                Godsey (1902-   )
133121192211 Lena Ray Evans (1948-   ), m. (1st) 1969,
                James Ailor; m. (2nd) Garry Hunt Drunson
13312119222 James Ray Evans (1921-1946)
13312119223 David Fulton Evans (1924-1983), m. 1941, Pauline
                Craghead
133121192231 James David Evans (1944-   ), m. Judy Ann Drew

```
1331211922311  Jonathan Evans
1331211922312  Patrick Evans
133121192232   Susan Elizabeth Evans (1947-          ), m. (1st)
                 Richard Jackson; m. (2nd), William Wilburn
               Children by first husband:
1331211922321  Pauline Elizabeth Jackson
1331211922322  Charlie Richard Jackson
133121192233   Frances May Esther Evans, m. Larry A. Grubbs
1331211922331  Jessie Davis Grubbs
1331211922332  Cynthia Gayle Grubbs
133121192234   William Gradhead Evans, m. Lisa Gayle Franklin
1331211922341  William Matthew Evans
1331211922342  Laura Aleigh Evans
13312119224    Robert Saunders Evans, m. (1st) 1967, Madeline Ann
                 Kane; m. (2nd) Caroline Reese Lueby
1331211x   Adaline McFarland Wood, m. John Randolph Caldwell
1331211a   William Franklin Wood, Jr. (10/10/1836-2/11/1941), m.
               Mittie J. Robertson (9/4/1865-6/18/1940)(sister to Mary
               Bridget Robertson)
1331211a1  Robert Franklin Wood (3/26/1891-2/18/1922). Unm.
1331211a2  David Pharr Wood (3/19/1894-10/29/1917).  Unm.
1331211a3  William Hocker Wood (6/16/1896-8/14/1972), m. Mary Lee
               McNair (4/25/1903-12/12/1970)
1331211a31  Barbara Wood
1331211a32  Mary Lee Wood
1331211a33  Laura Wood
1331211a34  Ann Wood
1331211a35  Jane Wood
1331211a36  Rachel Wood
1331211a37  William Wood
1331212  Nancy Franklin Wood, m. (1st) Horatio DePriest; m. (2nd)
             Joel W. Franklin
         Children by first husband:
13312121 (son)          13312122 (son)          13312123 (son)
         Children by second husband:
13312124  Owen Walker Franklin (moved to Missouri). Unm.
13312125  Mary Ann Franklin, m.          Jones. D. young
13312126  Ida Franklin.  Unm.
13312127  Hattie Elizabeth Franklin (2/7/1858-1/31/1939). Unm.
            Blind. Teacher.
13312128  Paxton Saunders Franklin (8/3/1860-5/20/1926), m. in
            Fauquier County, Elizabeth Robertson Puckett (5/4/1868-
            4/29/1944).  Both b. in Campbell County. (She had one
            brother, William T. Puckett).
133121281  Ruth Calesta Franklin (11/12/1893-Spring 1927), m. Edward
             Owen. No children.
133121282  Arthur William Franklin (4/6/1890-7/10/1943), m. Hattie
             Evans. No children.
133121283  Arrah Neal Franklin (4/1/1897-9/13/1958), m. Ernest
             Jones
1331212831          1331212832          1331212833
```

133121284 Ethel Frost Franklin (9/11/1894-6/8/1982), m. 11/24/1913,
          John Boyce Litchford (4/10/1889-12/12/1960)
1331212841 Arlene Elizabeth Litchford (9/5/1914-   ), m.
          Onyx Stuart Metz (8/4/1915-   )
13312128411 Onyx Richard Metz (1/13/1940-   ) of Foster City,
          Calif., m. Gloria Christine Sullivan
133121284111 John Richard Metz (1/25/1963-   ), m. 12/29/1983,
          Susan Gail Curling (11/3/1958-   )
133121284112 Karen Christine Metz (10/3/1966-   )
133121284113 Bryan Stuart Metz (5/22/1970-   )
13312128412 Franklin Hunter Metz (6/7/1947-   ), m. Barbara
          Ann Davidson
133121284121 Julie Ann Metz (1/1/1969-   )
133121284122 Frosty Elizabeth Metz (12/7/1971-   )
133121284123 Franklin Hunter Metz, Jr. (4/30/1973-   )
1331212842 Franklin Boyce Litchford (10/20/1922-   ), m.
          12/18/1948, Marion Rosalie Williams (10/10/1929-   )
13312128421 Charlotte Ann Litchford (1/31/1950-   ), m. 10/
          3/1969, Lewis Albert Bryant, Jr. (12/27/1948-   )
133121284211 Lewis Albert Bryant III (4/17/1971-   )
13312128422 Franklin Boyce Litchford, Jr. (1/29/1956-   )
13312128423 William Edwin Litchford (10/4/1958-   )
1331212843 James Paxton Litchford (7/13/1932-   ), m. Margery
          Pauline Bean
13312128431 John Albert Litchford (5/28/1956-   ), m. Jane
          Durice Fariss
133121284311 John Thomas Litchford (12/12/1979-   )
13312128432 Phyllis Arlene Litchford (12/18/1958-   )
13312128433 Margaret Anne Litchford (4/7/1964-   ), m.
          Anthony Kendall Lerner
133121285 Ernest Paxton Franklin (2/22/1899-6/14/1954), m. Ella
          Franklin
1331212851 (son)
133121286 Owen Walker Franklin (1/26/1900-   ), m. 2/ /
          1926, Iona ("Ona") Harper
1331212861 Evelyn Christine Franklin, m. Clarence Hunter Caldwell
13312128611 JoAnn Caldwell, m. Gerald Williamson
133121286111 Jerry Williamson
133121286112 Karen Williamson
13312128612 Allen Wayne Caldwell, m. Teresa Snyder
133121286121 Ryan Scott Caldwell
1331212862 Harold Owen Franklin, m. Juanita Hughes
13312128621 Scarlet Franklin, m. David Bohan
133121286211 Christopher Bohan
13312128622 Robin Franklin, m. David Keese. No issue

1331212863 Wilmoth Cornelia Franklin, m. Jesse Lyle Moore. Div.
13312128631 Ronald Lyle Moore, m. Debra Kay Burnett. No issue
1331212864 Audrey Delores Franklin, m. James Thomas Steele, Jr.
13312128641 Cheryl Ann Steele
13312128642 Wanda Kay Steele
13312128643 James Thomas Steele III

13312128644 Michael Wayne Steele
13312128645 Gregory Scott Steele
1331212865 Mary Kathaleen Franklin, m. (1st) Curtis Jamerson. Div.
            M. (2nd) Wallace Gunter
            Child by first husband:
13312128651 Jeffery Michael Jamerson
1331212866 Alvan Holmes Franklin, m. (1st) Jacqueline Horton. Div.
            M. (2nd) Sandra Galliger. No issue
133121287 Nannie Mae Franklin (10/17/1904-   ), m. Harry W.
            Davidson
1331212871 (son)
133121288 Ida Morgan Franklin (12/14/1905-12/ /1973), m. (1st)
            Clyde Trent. M. (2nd) Roy Binkley. No children from
            second husband.
            Child by first husband:
1331212881 (son)
133121289 Elizabeth Leftwich Franklin (6/4/1909-   ), m.
            3/30/1929, Powhatan Moorman Cox (4/18/1904-   )
1331212891 Owen Talmadge Cox (1/21/1936-   ), m. Janet
            Noel
13312128911 Elizabeth Ann Cox (5/12/1960-   )
13312128912 Donna Gay Cox (8/3/1962-   ), m. Leland Vaughan
            Dobyns
133121289121 Michael Vaughan Dobyns (1/29/1984-   )
13312128913 Lisa Gayle Cox (11/11/1964-   )
13312128914 Lee Talmadge Cox (5/25/1966-   )
1331212892 Loretta Anne Cox (10/23/1939-   ), m. Preston
            Eugene Davis
13312128921 Nathalie Anne Davis (5/31/1966-   )
13312128922 Pamela Lynn Davis (5/22/1968-   )
1331212893 Carole Lee Cox (3/23/1944-   ), m. Carroll Page
            Amiss. No issue
1331212894 Patricia Moorman Cox (11/7/1947-   ), m. Danny
            Lee Burchett
13312128941 Chad Lee Burchett (11/20/1978-   )
13312128x John Henry Franklin (4/21/1911-8/ /1974), m. Grace
            Franklin
13312128x1 John Preston Franklin, m. Evelyn Childress Bailey
13312128x11 John Lewis Franklin
13313 Mary Ann Jones, m. Thomas Rollins Marshall

1332   Elizabeth Bolling West, m. 4/26/1815, Dr. Joel Walker Flood
     (7/11/1789-4/ /1858) of Buckingham County, son of Major
     Henry and Polly Flood
13321   Henry de la Warr Flood (8/14/1816-4/21/1892), m. 2/14/1838,
     Mary Elizabeth Trent
133211   Maj. Joel Walker Flood, C.S.A., (1/9/1839-1916), m. (1st)
     ca. 1862, Ella Faulkner, dau. of Charles James Faulkner
     (7/6/1806-11/1/1884) of "Boydville" near Martinsburg
     (now W.Va.) M. (2nd) Jennie Pleasants. No issue. M.
     (3rd) Sallie Whiteman Delk (6/18/1852-10/15/1927) of
     Norfolk. Major Flood and family lived at "Selmo" near
     Appomattox.
     Children by first wife:
1332111   Henry ("Hal" or "Harry", never Henry) Delaware Flood
     (9/2/1865-12/8/1941), M.C., m. Anna Portner (5/23/1888-
     8/1/1966), dau. of Robert Portner (-1906)
13321111   Bolling Byrd Flood (5/22/1915-   ), m. Marie
133211111   Robert Flood (8/31/1955-   ), m. 7/31/1982, Amy
     House
13321112   Eleanor Flood (8/13/1917-8/14/1975), m. Walter Horton
     Schoellkopf
133211121   Walter Horton Schoellkopf, Jr.
133211122   Anna Portner Schoellkopf
133211123   Henry Flood Schoellkopf
13321113   (son) d. inf.
13321114   (dau) d. inf.
1332112   Holmes Boyd Flood (d. about 6 years of age)
1332113   Eleanor Bolling Flood, m. 9/15/1886, Richard Evelyn Byrd
     (1860-1925), son of William and Jennie Rivers Byrd of
     Austin, Texas
13321131   Harry Flood Byrd (6/8/1887-1966), Governor of Virginia
     and U. S. Senator, m. 10/7/1913, Anne Douglas Beverley
     (1887-   ), dau. of James Bradshaw and Anne
     Douglas Gray Beverley
133211311   Harry Flood Byrd, Jr. (12/20/1914-   ), U. S.
     Senator, m. 8/9/1941, Gretchen Bigelow Thomson (12/
     27/1917-   ), dau. of Paul Jones and Gretchen
     Bigelow Thomson of Winchester
1332113111   Harry Flood Byrd III (7/16/1942-   )
1332113112   Thomas Thomson Byrd (1946-   )
1332113113   Beverley Bryd (1949-   ), m. George Partridge
     Greenhalgh III (1946-   ), son of George
     Partridge Greenhalgh, Jr., and his wife, the former
     Sybilla Burwell ("Billy") Jacobs. Div. Issue.
133211312   Westwood Beverley Byrd (6/24/1916-3/20/1952). Unm.
133211313   Bradshaw Beverley Byrd (10/30/1920-   ), m. (1st)
     Martha Robinson of Winchester. Div. M. (2nd) 1963,
     Shirley Deane of England. Div.
     Children by first wife:
1332113131   Anne Robinson Byrd
1332113132   Westwood Beverley Byrd, m. 1981, John Fairbanks McDermid
     of Washington, D. C.

```
                Child by second wife:
1332113133  Bradshaw Beverley Byrd, Jr.
133211314   Richard Evelyn Byrd II (4/26/1923-        ), m. Helen
                Bradshaw of Massachusetts
1332113141  Richard Evelyn Byrd III
1332113142  Lucy Byrd, m. George H. Carter, son of Allen M. and
                Dixie Carter
1332113143  William Benton Byrd
13321132    Richard Evelyn Byrd, Jr., Admiral, U.S.N., (10/25/1888-
                1957), m. 1915, Marie Donaldson Ames of Boston
133211321   Richard Evelyn Byrd III (1920-         )
133211322   Bolling Byrd (1922-        ), m. William A. Clarke of
                Swathmore, Pa.
133211323   Catherine Byrd (1924-        ), m. Richard A. Breyer of
                Los Angeles
1332113231  Robert Byrd Breyer (1948-         )
1332113232  Katherine Ames Breyer (1950-        )
133211324   Helen Byrd (1926-        ), m. Lawrence J. Stabler of
                Radnor, Pa.
1332113241  David Stabler (1951-         )
1332113242  Ann Blanchard Stabler (1954-        )
13321133    Thomas Bolling Byrd (1889-2/  /1968), m. (1st) 10/27/1917,
                Margaret Lewis (1889-1920), dau. of Henry Llewellyn
                Dangerfield and Carter Penn Freeland Lewis of "Audley".
                M. (2nd) Elizabeth Miller, widow of Gen. William Mitchell
                (by whom she had one son and one daughter).
                Child by first wife:
133211331   Margaret Lewis ("Maggie") Byrd (4/13/1920), m. Harry
                Farnum Stimpson, Jr., of Dedham, Mass.
1332113311  Harry Farnum Stimpson III, m.            Blackwell
                Child by third wife:
1332114     Joel West Flood (8/2/1894-1964), M.C.
1332113211  Richard Evelyn Byrd IV (1950-           )
1332113212  Leverett S. Byrd (1952-          )
1332113213  Ames Byrd (1953-         )
1332113214  Harry Flood Byrd II (1955-         )
1332113221  Evelyn Byrd Clarke (1948-         )
1332113222  Marie Ames Clarke (1950-         )
1332113223  Eleanor Clarke (1953-         )
1332113224  Richard Byrd Clarke (1958-         )
134    Linnaeus Bolling (1773-7/7/1849)(son of Susan Watson Bolling),
           m. 12/16/1793, Mary Markham, dau. of Col. Bernard and Mary
           Harris Markham of Chesterfield County (at the time of the
           marriage, Mary was "not of age")
1341   Mary Bolling, m. Dr. James Madison Cobbs of Bedford
13411    (son)
1342   Susannah Pocahontas Bolling (        -1849), m. 1842, Robert
           Thruston Hubard of "Saratoga", Buckingham County, son of
           Dr. James T. Hubard and his wife, the former Susan Wilcox,
           dau. of Susan Watson (widow and second wife of Robert Boll-
           ing of "Chellowe") and Dr. Edmund Wilcox, Susan's second
           husband
```

13421 William T. Hubard (-1844), m. 1/10/1865, Eliza Cabell
      Calloway (1/23/1844-   ), dau. of Dr. Paul Carrington
      and A. E. D. Manson Calloway
134211 Paul Carrington Hubard
134212 Eliza Calloway Hubard
134213 Susan Markham Hubard, m. 11/3/1890, Rev. George S. Somerville
1342131   Churchill Knox Somerville
134214 Addis Hubard
134215 Louisa Hubard
134216 Anna Hubard
134217
13422 Edward Wilcox Hubard, Rector of Broomfield Parish
13423
13424
13425
13426
13427
13428
1343   Philip A. Bolling, m. (1st) Mary Eppes (-1867), dau.
      of John Wayles Eppes and his second wife, the dau. of Hon.
      Wilie Jones of Halifax, N.C. His first wife was Maria, dau.
      of Thomas Jefferson; m. (2nd) 1868, the widow Griswold (nee
      Tappan, of Boston). See 15 GCHSM 77
      Child by first wife:
13431 John Eppes Bolling (8/ /1840-12/ /1840)
1344   Robert Bolling, m. (1st) 9/ /1821, Sarah Hobson of Cumber-
      land County; m. (2nd) Mary Watkins (1811-1840) of Powhatan
      County; m. (3rd) Martha Brackett of Cumberland County
      Child by first wife:
13441 Pocahontas Bolling, m. Rev. William Clarkson Meredith (1823-
      11/1/1875), son of Dr. Reuben and Lucretia Clarkson Mere-
      dith of Hanover County. Pocahontas was the Reverend's
      first wife. He m. (2nd) Elizabeth Hanson Cushing, (3rd)
      Elizabeth Wartzwelder, and (4th) Fannie Randolph Page
      Child by first wife:
134411 Pocahontas Meredith (9/14/1854-6/7/1896), m. 8/23/1883,
      Robert Fauntleroy Turner (1858-6/9/1889), son of Edward
      Carter and Sarah Jane Beverley Turner. Pocahontas was
      Turner's second wife
1344111 Mary Bolling Turner (9/3/1884-7/29/1939), m. Archibald
      Magill Smith (2/10/1877-   ), son of Charles
      Magill and Katherine Sterling Smith. Archibald remarried
      after Mary's death.
13441111 Pocahontas Meredith Smith (8/19/1906-   )
13441112 Charles Magill Smith (10/5/1908-   ), m. 4/13/1935,
      Cynthia Sanborn, dau. of Cummings Avery and Mary Moore
      Sanborn
134411121 Cynthia Sanborn Smith (8/25/1936-   )
134411122 Pocahontas Meredith Sterling Smith (10/6/1937-   )
134411123 Tamara Magill Smith (1/29/1943-   )
13441113 Katharine Sterling Smith (9/2/1912-   ), m. 9/1/
      1939, Hortaio Nash Ogden (6/22/1909-   ), son of

James Davison Hill and Martha Beard Ogden
134411131 Mary Turner Ogden (9/14/1942-   )
13441114 Archibald Magill Smith, Jr. (2/27/1920-   )
      Children by third wife:
13442 Susan Bolling (1848-   )
13443 Robert Bolling (1850-   )
1345 Linnaeus Bolling, Jr., M.D., m.   Harris, dau. of
      James Harris of Buckingham County
13451
13452
13453
135 Powhatan Bolling (1767-1802)(son of Susan Watson Bolling),
      d.s.p.
136 (son)
14 Mary Bolling (7/16/1744-1775), m. 10/8/1761, Richard Bland III
      (2/20/1730*1-1766), son of Richard and Anne Poythress Bland of
      "Jordan's Point", Prince George County
141 Richard Bland (7/23/1762-3/26/1806), m. ca. 1787, Susannah
      Poythress, dau. of Peter and Elizabeth Bland Roythress
1411 Richard Bland, m. (1st)   , m. (2nd)   Ledbetter
14111 (son)
14112 (son)
14113 (dau)
14114 (dau)
1412 John Bolling Bland (1798-1863), m. (1st) Mary Eppes; m. (2nd)
      1840, Rachel Reed (1816-1841); m. (3rd) Elizabeth Cargill
      Children by first wife:
14121 Magdalen Bland
14122 Robert Bland
14123 John Theodorick Bland, m. 3/26/1857, in Petersburg, Va.,
      Priscilla Read Watkins
141231 John Bolling Bland (3/21/1858-   ), m. 10/9/1882,
      Harriotte Henderson Osborne of Louisville, Ky., dau. of
      John Dunlop and Harriotte Henderson Graves Osborne
1412311 John Osborne Bland (7/2/1883-   ), m. 10/20/1915,
      Ethel Swann Bacon
14123111 Mary Bacon Bland (2/28/1917-   )
14123112 John Osborne Bland, Jr. (1/16/1921-   )
1412312 Emily Graves Bland (1/28/1890-   ), m. 10/9/1918,
      John Henry Aaron of Wilmington, Delaware
14123121 John Bland Aaron (8/20/1919-   )
14123122 Henry Osborne Aaron (12/18/1923-   )
141232 Charles Watkins Bland (1/8/1860-   ), m. 6/ /1915,
      Janie Patrick. No issue.
141233 Robert Bland, d. inf.
141234 Henry Bland, d. inf.
14124 William Bland
      Child by second wife:
14125 Rachel Bland (1841-1864), m. James D. Proctor (1832-1900)
1413 Sarah Bland, m. Thomas Bott
14131 (son)
14132 (son)

14133 (dau)
1414   Theodorick Bland, m. Mary Harrison
14141 Theodorick Bland, Jr.
14142 Susannah Poythress Bland, m. Edward Temple
14143 Sally Bland
14144 Anne Bland
14145 Mary Bland
1415   Mary Bland, m. Elgin Russell
142   Ann Bland (1765-   ), m. (1st) John Morrison. No issue. M.
       (2nd) Peter Woodlief
1421   Hannah Woodlief, m. Dr. Hardaway
14211 (son)
1422   Anna Woodlief, m.   Jeffrey
14221 (son)
14222 (son)
1423   Elizabeth Woodlief, m. Dr. Shadrach Alfriend
14231 (son)
14232 (son)
14233 (son)
14234 (dau)
143   Elizabeth Bland, m. William Poythress
1431
1432
144   (dau)
15   Sarah Bolling (6/16/1748-   ), m. Judge John Tazewell of
       Williamsburg, youngest son of Capt. William and Sophia Harman-
       son Tazewell (brother of Henry Tazewell, the father of Little-
       ton Waller Tazewell, U. S. Senator and Gov. of Va.)
151   Elizabeth Tazewell, m. Samuel Griffin, M.D., Member of Congress
       1789-95
1511   (son)
152   Littleton Tazewell, m. Catherine Boush Nivison, widow of
       William Nivison, and dau. of Samuel Boush of Norfolk
1521   Sarah Bolling Tazewell, m.   Goode of Mecklenburg.
       GOODE 465 says not Hon. W. O. Goode.
153   William Tazewell, MD. (of Richmond)(-1840), m. Mary
       Page Tanner (1784-1877). OMSS shows that William Tazewell
       m. Mary Bolling
1531   Willianna Blair Tazewell
1532   Catherine Nivison Tazewell, m. (1st) E. Ambler; m. (2nd)
       Edward Scott Gay (416) of Atlanta. For their children,
       see 416.
1533   Henrietta Watkins Tazewell, m. C. I. Fox
15331 (son)
15332 (son)
15333 (son)
1534   Mary Louisa Tazewell, m. Dr. J. B. Southall. He m. (2nd)
       Mary's sister (1536)
15341 (dau)
1535   Sally Bolling Tazewell, m. Dr. George Fitzgerald
15351 (son)
15352 (son)
15353 (dau)

15354 (dau)
1536 Martha Jefferson Tazewell, m., after the death of her sister (1534), Dr. J. B. Southall
1537 Jane Rebecca Tazewell
1538 Anne ("Nancy") Rosalie Tazewell, m. Andrew Lewis Ellett, son of James B. and Sallie Drewry Ellett. Home: Richmond
15381 Tazewell Ellett (1/6/1856-5/19/1914). MC.
153811 Tazewell Ellett, Jr. (1886-   ), m. 1916, Susie C. McGuire (1889-1947), dau. of Francis Howe McGuire, Jr. and Helen Pauling Nolting McGuire
1538111 Helen McGuire Ellett (1918-   ), m. 1941, Dr. Felix Claudius Feamster
15381111 Robert Tazewell Feamster (1948-   )
15381112 Catherine Cantrell Feamster (1950-   )
1538112 Tazewell Ellett III (1922-   ), m. 1948, Marguerite Rucker (1926-   ), dau. of Edmund H. and Elizabeth Harrison Rucker. Lives in Richmond.
15381121 Susan Elizabeth Ellett (1950-   ), m., div. and lives in Richmond
15381122 Edmund Tazewell Ellett (1952-   ), m. 1977, Alice Lee Withers. Lives in Alexandria
153811221 Elizabeth Pender Ellett (1980-   )
15381123 Robert Scott Ellett (1954-   ), m. 1979, Mary G. Campbell. Lives in Pittsboro, N.C.
1538113 Josephine Scott Ellett (1926-   )
15382 Andrew Lewis Ellett, Jr.
15383 Ida Ellett, m.   Stegar
15384 Nannie Ellett, m.   Fleming
1539 Isabella Tazewell
153x (son)
153a (son)
153b (son)
154 (son)
155 (dau)
156 (dau)
16 Archibald Bolling of "Red Oak", "Retreat" (on the line between Buckingham and Campbell Counties), and "Mount Athos" (3/20/1749*50-7/ /1827)(this birth date is doubtful---see CABELL p. 250-1), m. (1st) 1770, his first cousin once removed, Sarah Cary (2/23/1753-10/ /1773)(246), dau. of Col. Archibald and Mary Randolph Cary of "Ampthill". M. (2nd) 2/17/1774, his first cousin once removed, Jane Randolph (216), dau. ·of Richard Randolph (21) of "Curles", and his wife, the former Anne ("Nancy") Meade. M. (3rd) 1797, Maria Taylor, widow of John Carter Byrd. M. (4th) 1802, Sarah Ellyson Woodson (8/4/1749-   ), widow of James Clark, and dau. of Charles Woodson and his second wife, Agnes Parsons Richardson (she was the widow Richardson). Sarah Ellyson Woodson, a member of the Curles Meeting of Friends, was disowned in 1771 for marrying Clark (out of unity)---her parents did not consent to the marriage.

Children by first wife:
  NOTE: These children are listed below (and out of order) as
  166 and 167.
Children by second wife:
161 Sarah Bolling, m. 1792, Joseph Cabell Megginson of "Clover
     Plains", Buckingham County (1/28/1771-4/11/1811), son of
     Capt. William and Elizabeth Cabell Megginson
1611 William Cabell Megginson (4/17/1794-11/2/1847), m. 11/15/
      1821, Amanda M. Bocock, dau. of John T. Bocock of Bucking-
      ham (later Appomattox) County
16111 Joseph Megginson (1822-1840)
16112 John Megginson (9/9/1824-11/18/1867), m. 1867, Sarah ("Sally")
       Smith of Tennessee
161121 William Megginson
161122 Thomas Megginson
161123 Henry Megginson
16113 Mary Megginson (6/20/1826-12/8/1830), m. 1850, Capt. Jeter
       Davidson of Buckingham
161131 Caroline Davidson (9/28/1852-   )
161132 Charles Davidson
161133 Maria Davidson
161134 Francis Davidson (1858-   )
161135 Antonia Davidson (1856-   )
16114 Judith T. Megginson (11/19/1828-   ). Unm.
16115 Sarah B. Megginson (2/4/1831-1863), m. 12/23/1857, Jesse
       Carter of Appomattox
161151 William Carter (1858-   )
161152 Charles Carter (1860-   )
161153 Albion Carter (10/ /1861-   )
16116 Martha Megginson (1/18/1834-   )(twin), m. 5/1/1866,
       Matthew Farrar (-10/25/1868) of Fluvanna County
161161 William Farrar (8/1/1867-   )
16117 Jane Megginson (1834-   )(twin), m. 12/24/1867, Peleg
       Bosworth of Amherst County
161171 Amanda E. Bosworth
16118 Maria L. Megginson (7/24/1837-   ), m. 11/28/1867,
       Thomas Farrar (-1868) of Fluvanna County
161181 Thomas Farrar
16119 William Megginson (10/28/1839 or 1840-   ), m. 12/24/
       1871, Martha McCraw of Buckingham County
1611x Pocahontas Megginson (8/29/1842-   ), m. (1st) 11/
       14/1865, George Christian (-7/22/1866), of
       Appomattox. M. (2nd) 10/16/1872, Benjamin Farrar of
       Nashville
1611a Frances D. Megginson (12/6/1844-   ), m. 11/14/1865,
       Dr. William N. Horsley of Nelson
1611a1 William Horsley (8/7/1866-   )
1611a2 Rolfe Horsley (2/12/1867-   )
1611a3 Amy Horsley (10/10/1871-6/4/1874)
1612 Elizabeth C. Megginson (1796-   ), m. 11/ /1820, William
      Berkeley of Buckingham County

16121   Joseph Berkeley, m. Almira Virginia Megginson (16142), dau.
         of (his uncle) Joseph Cabell Megginson
1613 Archibald Bolling Megginson (3/9/1798-2/6/1851), m. (1st)
         10/21/1824, Ann R. White (8/1/1807-10/8/1829), dau. of
         Joseph White of Amherst (Nelson?) County. M. (2nd) 5/22/
         1833, Elizabeth H. (N.?) Roberts (2/4/1807-   ), dau.
         of John Roberts of Bent Creek, Appomattox County
         Children by first wife:
16131   Jane Courtney Megginson (11/30/1825-   ), m. 5/6/1851,
         James Douglas Campbell (3/8/1825-10/ /1865, son of Robert
         Smith Campbell
161311   Mary Campbell, m. 3/31/1871, H. Garland Brown of Roanoke.
         They had eleven children.
161312   Archibald Campbell (1853-   ), m.
1613121   Campbell (1888-   )
161313   Clara Campbell
161314   Alice Campbell, m. 10/5/1883, (her cousin) Walton B.
         Megginson (1/15/1855-   )(16187)
16132   Mary A. Megginson (5/28/1827-   )
16133   Robert H. Megginson (8/8/1829-9/2/1829)
         Children by second wife:
16134   John G. Megginson (4/17/1834-   )
16135   Fanny E. Megginson (2/26/1836-12/30/1868)
16136   Sarah H. Megginson (10/10/1838-   )
16137   Benjamin Megginson (7/14/1840-9/4/1849)
16138   Olivia A. Megginson (12/17/1841-   )
16139   Lewis A. Megginson (12/22/1843-   ), m. 12/24/1871,
         Ann D. Wright
1613x   Joseph C. Megginson (6/16/1846-   )
1613a   Archibald B. Megginson (4/21/1849-   )
1614 Joseph Cabell Megginson (2/11/1800-3/28/1858), m. 11/15/1826,
         Almira Montgomery (9/14/1804-4/13/1831), dau. of Capt. Joseph
         Montgomery of "Rockfish", Nelson County. Mr. and Mrs.
         Megginson moved to Texas.
16141   Sarah J. E. Megginson (10/9/1827-8/ /1871), m. 9/13/1845,
         Hamilton L. Blaine
161411   Catherine V. Blaine (5/11/1849-   ), d.s.p.
161412   Mary F. L. Blaine (6/11/1853-   )
161413   Jessie B. Blaine, m. William Arrington
161414   Berkeley Blain
161415   Henry Blaine
161416   Charles Blaine
161417   Roberta Blaine
16142   Almira Virginia Megginson (6/15/1829-   ), m. (her
         cousin) Joseph Berkeley (16121)
1615 Samuel B. Megginson (1/14/1802-prior to 1872), m. 6/10/1828,
         Mary A. Johnston (Johnson?)(3/19/1809-   ), dau. of
         Christopher (Christian?) Johnston of Appomattox
16151   Joseph Cabell Megginson (8/14/1829-   ), m. (1st) 7/1/
         1855, Eliza S. Alvis (10/12/1823-   ). M. (2nd) Sally
         Spencer

```
        Children by first marriage:
161511  William S. Megginson
161513
161514
        Children by second marriage:
161515
161516
161517
161518
16152   Sarah J. Megginson (11/10/1845-          ), m. Thomas David-
          son
161521
161522
16153   Samuel F. Megginson (12/11/1850-        )
1616    Jane Randolph Megginson (1804-prior to 1835), m. Dr. Nathaniel
          R. Powell of Nelson County
16161   Sally Powell, d. young. Unm.
16162   (dau), d. young. Unm.
1617    John Randolph Megginson (5/1/1806-7/  /1875), m. 1/8/1835,
          Mary R. Dunn, dau. of William J. Dunn of Appomattox County
16171   Sarah E. Megginson (2/9/1836-          ), m. 1/3/1856, James
          R. Phelps
161711  Ada B. Phelps (1857-           )
161712  Lee Phelps
161713  Alice Phelps
161714  Elizabeth Phelps
16172   (son) Archibald B. Megginson (2/21/1838), m. (1st) Helen
          Brady of Scottsville
16173   (dau)
1618    Benjamin Cabell Megginson (7/31/1809-4/20/1887) of Nelson
          County, m. (1st) 5/25/1837, Fanny Blain (1819-3/11/1879),
          dau. of Capt. Alexander Blain of Albemarle County. M. (2nd)
          8/18/1880, Maria C. Hening, of Powhatan
        Children by first wife:
16181   Pocahontas B. Megginson (9/7/1842-9/12/1864), m. 7/10/1861
          or 1862, Dr. William H. (or J.) Hening of Powhatan County
161811  Benjamin C. Hening (9/15/1863-         ), m. 6/1/1892,
          Peachy Fleet Bagby
16182   Joseph A. Megginson (1844-1863)
16183   Sarah L. Megginson (12/19/1845-8/7/1870), m. 4/5/1867, Ben-
          jamin J. (or F.) Farrar of Nashville, formerly of Fluvanna
          County
161831  Laura Farrar (6/14/1869-          ), m. 11/9/1892, Rev.
          Mayo Cabell Martin, son of Rev. Thomas Ferdinand and
          Cornelia Mayo Cabell Martin
16184   Ella O'C. Megginson (12/6/1847-1/7/1863)
16185   Benjamin H. Megginson (1/1/1850-5/10/1852)
16186   Robert Craig Megginson (2/7/1852-          ), m. 9/29/1879,
          Annie L. Moon
161861  Carrie L. Megginson (8/1/1880-        )
161862  Pocahontas M. Megginson (10/5/1882-        )
```

161863   Mamie Lyle Megginson (9/14/1884-   )
161864   James Craig Megginson (1086-1890)
161865   Laura Barita Megginson (11/10/1890-   )
16187   Walton (Walter?) B. Megginson (1/15/1855-   ), m.
         10/5/1883, (his cousin) Alice Campbell (161314)
161871   Mattie Blain Megginson (5/29/1889-   )
161872   Clara Virginia Megginson (3/31/1893-   )
16188   Mary Frances Megginson (5/23/1859-4/7/1888), m. 5/10/1880,
         William D. Moon
161881   Fannie Edna Moon (6/9/1881-   )
161882   Carrie Lottie Moon (4/5/1884-   )
161883   William Richard Moon (5/ /1887-   )
16189   Elizabeth J. Megginson (3/19/1870-11/23/1877)
1618x   Alexander Megginson (6/14/1844-1/4/1863)
         Children by second wife:
1618a   Eliza Park Megginson (6/12/1881-   )
1618b   Benjamin Cabell Megginson (9/25/1882-   )

162   Anne Everard Bolling (-1834), m. (1st), Samuel Shepherd
       Duval, son of Samuel and Lucy Claiborne Duval of "Mt. Com-
       fort", Henrico County, served as an officer in the Revolution,
       and apparently moved to Kentucky. Anne m. (2nd) 10/31/1804,
       Col. Joseph Cabell, Jr. (-8/31/1831), son of Col.
       Joseph and Mary Hopkins Cabell. The first wife of Col.
       Joseph Cabell, Jr., was Pocahontas Rebecca Bolling (132).
       Colonel Cabell emigrated from Virginia to Kentucky in the
       early 1800's
       Children by first husband:
1621   Samuel Shepherd Duval, Jr., living in Barren County, Ky.,
       in 1855
16211   Jennie Duval, m. John Posey Cabell (16243). GRABOWSKII
       217 shows Jennie as the dau. of 162, but it seems more
       likely that she was the dau. of 1621
1622   Archibald Bolling Duval, living in Barren County, Ky., in
       1855
       Children by second husband:
1623   Jane Randolph Cabell (8/29/1805-6/23/1833), m. 5/6/1824,
       Philip T. Allin (5/5/1803-11/23/1849) of Harrodsburg, Ky.
16231   Joseph Cabell Allin (3/14/1825-   ), m. (1st) Susan
       A. Smith, dau. of Obadiah Smith of Henderson, Ky. No
       issue. M. (2nd) Mrs.   Brown, of Louisville. No issue
16232   Mary Ann Allin (8/2/1827-   ), m. 9/23/1849, Rev.
       Stephen A. Collier, of "The Crab Orchard", Ky.
162321   Elizabeth Cabell Collier
162322   William A. Collier
162323   Susan Harrison Collier
162324   Stephen B. Collier
162325   John Collier
162326   Cabell Collier
162327   "Pattie" Collier
162328   Mary Collier
16233   Thomas Grant Allin (8/2/1829-3/17/1832)

16234 Elizabeth Randolph Allin (12/13/1831-   ), m. 7/12/
  1852, Dr. Edwin G. Hall (Colonel, C.S.A.) of West Point, Ky.

162341 Joseph Cabell Hall (6/3/1854-9/30/1855)

1624 John Breckinridge Cabell (1/5/1808-7/18/1862), m. (1st) 1/26/
  1830, Mary Coalter Wardlow (-6/19/1835). M. (2nd)
  4/25/1839, Martha Posey, dau. of Capt. John Posey of Henderson, Ky.

```
        Children by first wife:
16241   d. inf.
16242   d. inf.
        Children by second wife:
16243   John Posey Cabell (8/19/1841-        ), m. (1st) 2/28/1871,
        Sarah Elizabeth Trumbo.  M. (2nd) 12/12/1876, Jennie Duval,
        dau. of Samuel Shepherd Duval.  Mr. & Mrs. Cabell lived in
        Corsicana, Texas.
        Child by first wife:
162431  Elizabeth Cabell (mother and child both died in two years)
        Children by second wife:
162432  Samuel Shepherd Cabell (8/19/1878-        )
162433  Archibald Bolling Cabell (4/17/1881-         )
162434  John Posey Cabell (1/13/1884-          )
162435  Calvin S. Cabell (11/5/1886-          )
16244   Mary Frances Cabell (11/13/1845-        ), m. 12/18/1862,
        Calvin W. Woodbridge.  Several children d. inf.
162441  Louisa Woodbridge (10/16/1867-        )
162442  Kate Woodbridge (4/18/1871-          )
162443  Mary Woodbridge (11/12/1875-          )
16245   Sears Cabell, M.D. (5/10/1848-        ), m. 11/15/1870,
        (his cousin) Althaea Spalding Cabell (16267)
162451  William Nicholas Cabell (1/11/1875-          )
162452  Robert Bolling Cabell (1877-1884)
162453  Sears Cabell (7/29/1878-          )
162454  John Breckinridge Cabell (1880-1881)
162455  Frank Murray Cabell (2/1/1882-          )
162456  Allie Spalding Cabell (6/13/1884-          )
162457  George Wilson Cabell (7/28/1886-          )
162458  Ellen Cabell (9/13/1888-          )
162459  Susan Cabell (4/10/1892-          )
1625    Elizabeth Robertson Cabell (5/13/1809-9/23/1852), m. (1st)
        4/4/1826, James B. Pollitt (        -10/28/1832).  M. (2nd)
        3/13/1834, Archibald Dixon (4/2/1802-4/23/1876), (U. S.
        Senator from Kentucky), son of Warren Dixon
        Children by first husband:
16251   Ann Ballard Pollitt (1/4/1828-        ), m. 3/23/1852,
        Lafayette Jones, M.D. (        -1866), of Henderson County,
        Ky.
162511  Elizabeth Pollitt Jones (7/8/1854-          )
162512  Mary Ballard Jones (3/24/1856-          )
16252   Virginia James Pollitt (12/18/1829-3/13/1893), m. 2/27/1849,
        William McClain
162521  William Pollitt McClain (12/17/1849-        ), m. Mary
        Garland, dau. of Dr. Richard Garland of Virginia
162522  James Ballard McClain (9/15/1851-        ), a journalist
        of London, England
162523  Virginia McClain (7/22/1856-        ), m. Lee Sehon of
        Louisville
162524  Kate Atkinson McClain (8/  /1858-        ), m. Charles
        H. Le Sueur, of Louisville
```

162525 Rebecca Dixon McClain (2/ /1860-   ), m. Dr. Rufus
         Bowman of Florida
162526 Elizabeth McClain (1861-   ), m. R. Lee Suter of
         Louisville
162527 Henry Jackson McClain (12/ /1864-   )
162528 Annie McClain (10/ /1867-   )
162529 Archibald McClain (9/ /1886-   )
16252x d. young
16252a d. young
16252b d. young
16252c d. young
16253 Susan Pollitt (9/14/1831-5/12/1835)
     Children by second husband:
16254 Wynn Dixon (2/6/1835-d. young)
16255 Rebecca Hart Dixon (5/28/1839-   ), m. 9/ /1860,
         John Young Brown of Hardin County, Kentucky (M.C., and
         Governor of Kentucky)(6/28/1835-1/11/1904) son of Thomas
         Dudley and Elizabeth Young Brown. His first wife was Lucie
         Barbee, dau. of Col. Thomas Barbee (1839-1858)
162551 Elizabeth Cabell Brown (6/6/1861-11/23/1866)
162552 Archibald Dixon Brown (4/ /1863-4/30/1895), m. 1889, Virginia
         Marshall of Henderson, Ky. Div. 4/ /1895. He was shot
         and killed 4/30/1895.
162553 John Young Brown, Jr. (7/21/1865-   ), m. Cora Smith
         of Louisville
162554 Virginia Singleton Brown (5/11/1867-   ), m. Edward
         F. Humphries of Louisville
162555 Susan Dixon Brown (4/26/1869-10/20/1894)
162556 Vance Brown (twin)(11/21/1870-d. inf.)
162557 Dudley Brown (twin)(11/21/1870-d. inf.)
162558 Evelyn Cabell Brown (4/4/1872-   ), m. John Rodman of
         Memphis
16256 Susan Belle Dixon (12/20/1840-2/28/1884), m. (1st) Cuthbert
         Powell, son of Dr. Llewellyn Powell of Louisville. M. (2nd)
         Maj. John J. Reeve, C.S.A., of Richmond
     Children by first husband:
162561 Elizabeth Powell (d. age 16)
162562 Susan Ballard Powell (6/16/1860-   ), m. J. Hawkins
         Hart of Henderson County, Ky.
     Children by second husband:
162563 Margaret Caskie Reeve (6/3/1871-   )
162564 Mary Gilmore Reeve (11/13/1872-   )
162565 John D. Burr Reeve (12/18/1875-   )
162566 Kate Reeve (2/27/1882-   )
16257 Archibald Dixon (3/4/1844-   ), m. Margaret Herndon of
         Frankfort, Ky.
162571 Margaret Herndon Dixon (10/11/1865-   ), m. Edward A.
         Jonas of London, England
1625711 Archibald Edward Jonas
162572 Wynn Dixon (12/27/1866-   ), m. 7/10/1894, Margaret
         McCreery, of Owensboro, Ky.

162573 Archibald Dixon, Jr. (8/ /1868-   )
162574 Julia Ballard Dixon (8/ /1871-   )
16258   Henry Cabell Dixon (9/19/1845-   )
16259   Joseph Cabell Dixon (12/26/1848-   ), m. Lucy
        Alves of Henderson, Ky.
162591 James Alves Dixon (1/25/1881-   )
162592 Susan Reeve Dixon (8/ /1883-   )
162593 Maria Davis Dixon (8/7/1886-   )
162594 Margaret Herndon Dixon (9/19/1892-   )
1625x   Wynn Dixon (4/5/1851-12/ /1860)
1626   Robert Bolling Cabell II (2/22/1812-12/27/1876), m. (1st)
        1/31/1833, Anne E. Herndon (-2/ /1834). M. (2nd)
        4/16/1835, Eleanor Hart, dau. of Capt. William Hart of
        Henderson, Ky.
        Child by first wife:
16261   Anne E. Cabell (1/16/1834-d. young)
        Children by second wife:
16262   Mary Elizabeth Cabell (1/14/1836-11/2/1837)
16263   Jane Randolph Cabell (3/27/1838-9/4/1839)
16264   Pocahontas Rebecca Cabell (6/16/1840-9/18/1872), m. 1869,
        David B. Barbee of Henderson, Ky.
162641 David Hart Barbee (2/2/1872-   )
16265   Mary Philip Cabell (4/6/1843-10/31/1873), m. 1868, Col.
        Livingston G. Taylor, C.S.A. (-6/12/1877)
162651 Mary Cabell Taylor (10/31/1873-   )
16266   Susan Cowan Cabell (11/6/1845-   ), m. 2/22/1866,
        John P. Beverley of Henderson, Ky.
162661 Robert Cabell Beverley (12/4/1868-   )
162662 Elizabeth Edwin Beverley (10/25/1870-   ), m. John
        P. Crossly of California
1626621
1626622
162663 Eleanor Hodge Beverley (5/12/1874-   )
162664 Susan Beverley (10/5/1879-   )
162665 Harry S. Beverley (8/2/1885-   )
16267   Althaea Spalding Cabell, m. 11/15/1870, (her cousin) Sears
        Cabell, M.D. (5/10/1848-   )(16245)
16268   Laura Bradford Cabell (2/24/1851-   )
16269   Caroline Allin Cabell (1/8/1854-d. inf.)
1626x   Robert Bolling Cabell (8/9/1859-d. inf.)
1626a   Inah Gabriella Cabell (6/27/1858-   )
1626b   Joseph Benjamin Cabell (5/3/1862-   )
1627   George Washington Cabell (10/16/1814-12/15/1864), m. 1/8/
        1837, Mary R. Williams, of Henderson County, Ky.
16271   Elizabeth Randolph Cabell (8/13/1838-9/21/1838)
16272   Sarah Jane Cabell (10/13/1839-9/2/1841)
16273   Joseph J. Cabell (2/12/1842-   ), m. 4/23/1863, Rhoda
        Williams (-6/24/1868)
162731 George B. Cabell (7/26/1865-   )
162732 Louisa Cabell (10/31/1867-   ), m. 8/14/1885, W. S.
        Cheatham
16274   John Edward Cabell (10/12/1843-   )

```
16275   Martha J. Cabell (5/24/1846-9/24/1847)
16276   Robert Harrison Cabell (6/12/1847-      ), d.s.p.
16277   George Washington Cabell (9/3/1849-         ), m. Laura
        B. Wilson of College Corner, Ohio
162771  Sears Cabell
16278   Mary F. Cabell (10/12/1851-      ), d.s.p.
16279   Nancy Bolling Cabell (3/11/1853-       ), d.s.p.
1627x   Richard Randolph Cabell (10/31/1855-         ), m. Sallie
        McKendricks of Henderson County, Ky.
1627a   Virginia Margaretta Cabell (10/5/1857-        ), m. 5/8/
        1878, George W. McKendrick, of Henderson County, Ky.
1627a1  Mary C. McKendrick (2/24/1880-          )
1627a2  Calvin C. McKendrick (12/26/1884-          )
1627b   William Henry Cabell (1/31/1860-        )
1628    Joseph H. Cabell (11/23/1815-5/15/1816)
1629    William Nicholas Cabell (11/1/1817-9/10/1820)
162x    Richard R. Cabell (3/9/1822-10/9/1843).  Unm.
162a    Mary Ann Hopkins Cabell (3/28/1824-         ), m. 9/2/1845,
        Dr. E. L. Willard, "a gentleman of Northern birth".  Dr.
        and Mrs. Willard lived in San Francisco.
162a1   Joseph Cabell Willard (6/  /1846-d. inf.)
162a2   Mary Josephine Willard (5/5/1848-d. young)
162a3   Emory Cabell Willard, d.s.p.
162a4   Lory Willard
162a5   Evanda Willard, d.s.p.
162b    George C. Cabell (4/16/182  -d. inf.)
        Several other children of Col. Joseph Cabell died in
        infancy.  It is said that by his two wives, he had a
        total of thirty-nine children.
163     Elizabeth Meade Bolling (        -1823), m. 1801, Archibald
        Robertson (1111)
164     John R. (B.?) Bolling (1784-1851).  Bur "Centre Hill", Pow-
        hatan County.
165     Blair Bolling (1792-1839), m. (1st) 1824, M. A. (J?) Webster.
        M. (2nd)  1827, Penelope Storrs, dau. of Gervas Storrs of
        "Hunslet Hall", Henrico County, and of his second wife, Martha
        Trueheart.  OMSS shows J. Webster
1651    Archibald Bolling, m. 2/  /1852, Eliza Trueheart Armistead
16511   (son)
16512   (son)
16513   (son)
16514   (son)
16515   (dau)
1652    John Bolling, m. (1st) 10/  /1855, Maria Page Armistead.  M.
        (2nd) Julia B. Tinsley
16521   (son)
16522   (son)
16523   (son)
16524   (son)
16525   (dau)
16526   (dau)
16527   (dau)
```

1653 Mary Susan Bolling, m. (1st) 8/ /1851, Gervas Storrs Burton
     (1823-1855), son of Edwin Burton and Susannah Pleasants
     Storrs Burton. M. (2nd) Dr. J. C. Macon
     NOTE: In PLEASANTS, p. 236, it is stated that "Susannah
     Storrs, married Samuel Coleman æ his first wife". Perhaps
     this Susannah Storrs and Susannah Pleasants Storrs who
     married Gervas Storrs Burton were one and the same. In
     PLEASANTS, the name Gervas (Storrs) is spelled Gervais.
16531 Mary Agnes Burton (9/5/1852-7/5/1911), m. John Daniel
     Shepperson (2/2/1851-12/1/1921), son of John Shepperson
     and Martha B. Daniel Shepperson. Their plantation in
     Charlotte County was called "College Hill".
165311 Martha Daniel Shepperson (11/7/1878-   ), m. 9/14/
     1904, James Henry Grant
1653111 James H. Grant (9/27/1906-   ), m. Elsie Ingram
     Michaux
16531111 James H. Grant, d. young
16531112 James Henry Grant (5/9/1938-   )
16531113 William Michaux Grant (4/27/1943-   )
1653112 Mary Agnes Grant (8/17/1908-   )
1653113 John Shepperson Grant (3/3/1911-   )
165312 Mary G. Shepperson (1880-   ). Unm.
165313 Rebecca S. Shepperson (1882-   ), d. young
165314 Lucy Shepperson (1884-   ). Unm.
165315 Gay Bolling Shepperson (1887-   )
165316 Edmonia Blair Shepperson (12/5/1888-   ), m. 10/15/
     1923, Robert Alexander Charmside
1653161 Martha Brooke Charmside (12/6/1925-   )
1653162 Robert Alexander Charmside, Jr. (2/2/1927-   )
165317 Dr. Archibald Bolling Shepperson (3/20/1897-7/24/1962), m.
     12/12/1923, Phillippa Alexander Bruce, dau. of Philip A.
     and Bettie T. Taylor Bruce. Dr. Shepperson was head of
     the English Department at University of Virginia.
1653171 Phillipa A. Bruce Shepperson (10/1/1934-   )
16532 Dr. Gervas Storrs Burton, Jr. (4/16/1854-5/25/1892), m. (1st)
     1/16/1878, Lucy Emily Frantz, of Botetourt County, dau. of
     Thornton P. and Sarah J. Pettit Frantz. M. (2nd) 12/14/
     1886, Edmonia Anne Brugh, of Botetourt County (1863-1898),
     dau. of Benjamin Franklin and Estaline Reid McClure Brugh
     Children by first wife:
165321 Loula Hortense Burton (12/18/1878-10/15/1959), m. (1st),
     Dr. Charles H. Davis. M. (2nd) Charles Grant. No children
     by either husband.
165322 Otis Munford Burton (11/9/1881-   ), m. Mrs. Polly
     McAlexander, who died in 1955. No children.
     Children by second wife:
165323 Gervas Storrs Burton (10/25/1887-   ) in Wellington,
     Kansas and died unmarried in Charlotte County
165324 Blair Bolling Burton (5/30/1889-12/7/1963), born in
     Buchanan, Botetourt County, Va., died in Prince Edward
     County, m. 6/8/1913 in Prince Edward County, Virginia
     Juanita Rice, dau. of Charles M. and Sarah E. Allen Rice

1653241   Edmonia Blair Burton (9/22/1914-   ), m. 10/12/1935,
          Lonnie Edward McKay (12/2/1910-   )
16532411 Peggy Joyce McKay (3/2/1938-   ), m. 5/11/1957,
          Dorsey L. Glass, Jr. (4/25/1928-   )
165324111 Edward Lee Glass (3/12/1959-   )
165324112 Susan Blair Glass (3/10/1961-   )
165324113 Sandra Joyce Glass (3/10/1961-   )
165324114 Lisa Gayle Glass (7/6/1962-   )
1653242   Charles Gervas Burton (10/8/1917-   ), m. 12/24/
          1938, Laura Gladys Jones
16532421 Juanita Lee Burton (6/20/1942-   )
16532422 Nancy Ann Burton (8/9/1944-   )
1653243   Virginia Juanita Burton (5/19/1919-   ), m. 5/12/
          1950, Harvey A. Bowen II (-10/29/1954)
1653244   Roy Smith Burton (11/20/1920-   ), m. 3/17/1962,
          Mrs. Ruth
165325   Gilmer Brugh Burton (8/18/1890-9/16/1969), m. 12/28/1911,
          Eula Gage Thomas (4/30/1889-7/24/1974), dau. of Cephalas
          B. and Maggie Caroline Smith Thomas
1653251   Charles Thomas Burton (10/6/1912-   ), m. (1st)
          2/17/1935, Flora E. Horne (1911-1/7/1937), dau. of
          Burdette H. and Lillie E. Pollard Horne
          NOTE: Charles Thomas Burton (1653251) advises that
          Dr. J. C. Macon, a Roman Catholic, placed his wife's
          two surviving children (16531 and 16532) in a Catholic
          Orphanage in Richmond where they remained until they
          could take care of themselves; that Gervas Storrs
          Burton, Jr., completed the classical course at Hampden-
          Sidney College in 1872, and was graduated from Baltimore
          Dental College in 1875; and interned in the office of
          Dr. C. B. F. Jankins in Fincastle; thatboth of his
          marriages are recorded in Betetourt County; and that
          for both, he gave his birthplace as Richmond, and the
          names of his parents as G. S. and M. S. Burton.
16532511 Donald Eugene Burton (12/25/1936-   ), m. 6/28/
          1958, Carol Ann Brickey (1/8/1939-   ), dau. of
          James H. and Sudie Huffman Brickey
165325111 Stephen Roger Burton (8/4/1959-5/24/1972)
165325112 Lonna Kay Burton (10/9/1961-   )
1653251   Charles Thomas Burton, m. (2nd) 6/6/1942, Frances Dobyns
          Barksdale (11/15/1917-   ), dau. of Peter and Annie
          Childredd Barksdale
16532512 William Thomas Burton (8/28/1948-   )
1653252   Margaret Antonia Burton (9/15/1914-   ), m. 8/11/
          1934, Ernest Living St.Clair (7/24/1911-   ), son of
          Lauriston E. and Jessie J. Loving St.Clair
16532521 Mary Louise St.Clair (3/27/1935-   ), m. 1957, Donald
          G. Bryant (12/18/1934-   ), son of Dave Bryant
165325211 Dawn Denise St.Clair (6/24/1960-   ), m. 3/10/1982,
          Robert Lee Hartless (6/15/1956-   ), son of
          William R. and Anne Elizabeth Gunter Hartless
165325212 Kevin David St.Clair (6/18/1965-   )

16532522 Michael Loving St.Clair (10/28/1942-   ), m. 2/22/
          1964, Judith Gaynelle Miller (9/22/1942-   ), dau.
          of James R. Miller
165325221 David Michael St.Clair (9/9/1969-   )
165325222 Angela C. St.Clair (6/28/1969-   )
16532523 Margaret Ernestine St.Clair (11/26/1947-   ), m.
          5/10/1969, James B. Trent (3/31/1948-   ), son of
          James H. Trent
165325231 Ashleigh Ross Trent (9/8/1976-   )
165325232 Matthew Barry Trent (8/7/1982-   )
1653253   Virginia Catherine Burton (12/11/1916-   ), m. 9/
          18/1934, Frank A. Woolwine (11/27/1910-11/24/1982), son
          of John W. and Lillian Wainwright Woolwine. No children.
1653254   George Russell Burton (1918-10/1/1922)
1653255   Carrie Elizabeth Burton (7/19/1920-6/1/1981), m. (1st)
          Frank Rocker. No children. Div. M. (2nd) 9/12/1945,
          Vincent J. Shedwell (2/10/1919-3/10/1978), son of
          Charles and Margaret   Shedwell
16532551 Rebecca Shedwell (5/10/1946-   ), m. Peter Lafe
          Scales (1/8/1946-   )
165325511 Timothy Shaun Scales (1/27/66-   )
165325512 Brian Anthony Scales (2/18/1969-   )
16532552 Sandra Shedwell (5/7/1950-   )
16532553 Catherine Marie Shedwell (9/17/1951-   ), m. 5/4/
          1968, Tunis Hampton Wells, Jr. (1/9/1949-   ),
          son of T. H. Wells, Sr.
165325531 Rebecca Wells (3/17/1969-   )
1653256   Ralph Munford Burton (6/8/1922-   ), m. (1st) 1947,
          Reba Louise Johnson (1917-   ). Div. He m. (2nd)
          11/6/1965, Martha Jane Breech, dau. of Maria Breech.
          No children by either wife.
1653257   Thelma Gage Burton (6/15/1924-   ), m. (1st) Michael
          David
16532571 Mildred Ruth David (5/8/1951-   ), m. 7/3/1970,
          Darrell H. Arnold (3/21/1947-   ). Mildred was
          adopted by Thelma's second husband.
165325711 Melinda Diane Arnold (3/22/1973-   )
165325712 Chris Arnold (7/21/1977-   )
1653257   Thelma Gage Burton, m. (2nd) 1959, Ralph Wellington
          Evans (4/29/1926-   ), son of Harlan W. and Leola
          Shanholtzer Evans
1653258   Helen Ruth Burton (11/14/1926-   ), m. 12/26/1944,
          Frank Mathias Camper (12/12/1926-8/3/1979), son of
          William E. and Bessie Booze Camper
16532581 Patricia Faye Camper (8/4/1947-   ), m. (1st)
          5/4/1968, William Edward Smith (1/26/1947-   ),
          son of Maynard H. Smith. She m. (2nd), Sterling
          Johnson (9/9/1947-   )
16532582 Nancy Ann Camper (2/23/1949-   ), m. 10/3/1970,
          Richard Leon McClure (11/15/1946-   ), son of
          Oscar F. and Elizabeth Dooley McClure

```
165325821  Allen McClure (2/8/1972-              )
165325822  Michael McClure (4/18/1973-           )
165325823  Leanna McClure (8/12/1976-            )
16532583   Billie Eugene Camper (7/8/1950-              ), m. 8/29/1970,
           Kathie Ann Hall (11/29/1950-          ), dau. of Raymond
           Hall
165325831  Mary Beth Camper (9/20/1972-             )
165325832  James Matthew Camper (7/31/1976-         )
165325833  Heather Nicole Camper (7/21/1980-        )
16532584   Victoria Louise Camper (6/3/1952-            ), m. 9/15/
           1973, David A. Duffy
165325841  Brennan Duffy (4/4/1978-              )
165325842  Darin Duffy (5/11/1983-               )
16532585   Diana Marie Campe4 (1/5/1958-               ), m. 8/22/1981,
           C. Layne Wilson (6/20/1956-            )
165325851  Cary Wilson (6/3/1983-                )
1653259    Dorathy Agnes Burton (7/20/1929-            ), m. 1/1/1948,
           James Raymond Bishop (7/16/1924-          ), son of James
           E. and D. Epperly Bishop
16532591   David Raymond Bishop (2/21/1924-         )
165325911  Heather Brook Bishop (8/25/1978-          )
16532592   James Robert Bishop (3/12/1952-             ), m. Katherine
165325921  Patrick Eli Bishop (8/29/1978-           )
16532593   Linda Lee Bishop (6/28/1960-            ), m. 6/2/1978,
           Donald R. Marshall, Jr. (11/8/1956-         ), son of
           Donald R. Marshall
165325931  Jessica Marshall (12/21/1979-             )
16532594   Terri Jo Bishop (5/9/1968-            )
165325x    Gilmer Brugh Bruton, Jr. (5/14/1932-           ), m. (1st)
           4/1/1952, Evelyn Dooley (1933-1959), dau. of Roy Dooley.
           He m. (2nd) 8/ /1960, Alyce L. Singer (2/14/1920-     ).
           He m. (3rd) 1967, Mrs. Jean Avona (Pope)(11/20/1924-   ).
           No children by any of his wives.
165326     Mary Estelle ("Mamie") Burton (3/11/1892-9/2/1940), m. (1st)
           5/15/1912, Melvin Ross Vandergrift (1891-1949), son of
           Samuel and Lottie Old Vandergrift
1653261    Courtney Burton Vandergrift (4/11/1913-8/27/1983), m.
           1935, E. Beatrice McDaniel. No children, but adopted a
           son.
1653262    Curtis Edison Vandergrift, m. Mildred
16532621   Clark Edison Vandergrift, m. 7/17/1965, Zarilda Jean Cox
16532622   Joan Elfreda Vandergrift, m. Arthur C. Price
16533      (dau)
1654    Paulina Bolling
1655       (son)
1656       (son)
1657       (son)
1658       (dau)
1659       (dau)
165x       (dau)
166     Archibald Bolling, dead by 5/10/1796
```

167 Sarah Bolling, dead by 5/10/1796
168 (son)
169 (son)
16x (son)
16a (son)
16b (dau)
16c (dau)
     NOTE: 166 and 167 are children of the first wife (Sarah
     Cary) of Archibald Bolling (16)
17   Anne Bolling (2/7/1752-   ), m. William Alexander
     Dandridge II (4/6/1750-   ), son of Capt. Nathaniel
     West (of the Royal Navy) and Dorothea Spotswood Dandridge
     (dau. of Alexander Spotswood)
171 John Dandridge, m.   Underwood
1711 Bolling Dandridge, m.
17111 (son)
172 William Alexander ("Dover") Dandridge (1772-1842), m. Nancy
     Pulliam (1782-   ), born Goochland County
1721 William Alexander ("Little Dover") Dandridge (1812-1865),
     born Hanover County, settled in Henry County near Martins-
     ville, m. (1st) Sarah Nickols (sister of Greenberry Nickols).
     M. (2nd) 1847, Mary Jane Hamner (-1879), dau. of
     Nancy House Hamner, born Brunswick County, died Tate County,
     Miss. After second marriage, William Alexander Dandridge
     moved to "Locust Grove" plantation, near Spencer, Virginia.
     Children by first wife:
17211 Thomas West Dandridge
17211 Dr. Thomas West Dandridge (ca. 1836-ca. 1880), died Madison,
     North Carolina. In the Civil War, he served with the
     "Texas Rangers"
17212 Dr. Robert Bolling Dandridge (8/6/1838-   ), m. 12/
     /1866, Susan Rangeley, dau. of John and Mary Webster
     Rangeley of Rangeley, Virginia. Dr. Dandridge's home was
     near Horsepasture, Va.
172121 William R. Dandridge
172122 John Thomas Dandridge
172123 Harry C. Dandridge
172124 Una Dandridge, m. Kelsey Puckett
172125 Annie Dandridge. Worked in Washington, D.C.
17213 Clay Dandridge (ca. 1840-18   ), m. Mattie Dodd, dau. of
     Nathaniel and Maria Woodson Dodd of Rockingham County, N.C.
     During the Civil War, Clay Dandridge served in the 42nd
     Virginia Cavalry. After the death of his wife shortly
     after the birth of their only child, Nathaniel, he moved
     to Missouri, where he married again.
172131 Nathaniel ("Nat") Dandridge, m.   Watson of S.C.
1721311 Nell Dandridge
17214 John ("Dude") Dandridge. 42nd Virginia Infantry, C.S.A.
     Died of typhoid fever during the War, at Corbin's Planta-
     tion, near Fredericksburg
17215 Sarah Virginia Dandridge (8/20/1845-12/7/1908), m. 1874,

Samuel Wall of Stokes, N.C. (6/28/1847-11/14/1900). First
lived on an old plantation near Sandy Ridge, N.C., and
later moved to Winston, N.C.

172151 Thomas Dandridge
172152 Elizabeth Roseboro Dandridge
172153 Samuel S. Dandridge
172154 Nannie Spottswood Dandridge
172155 Robert Edward Dandridge
       Children by second wife:
17216 Nannie Anderson Dandridge (4/15/1848-6/4/1922), m. 5/18/
     1869, Peter Washington Dalton of Patrick County, son of
     James Hunter and Nancy Critz Dalton
172161 Edgar Elliot Dalton
172162 Harry Lee Dalton
172163 Charles Dalton
172164 Ada Dalton
172165 Nannie Anderson Dalton
172166 Hunter Dalton
172167 Irene Dalton
17217 Mary Pocahontas Dandridge (7/24/1849-10/29/1915), m. 12/23/
     1873, James W. Wilborn. They settled in Senatobia, Miss.
172171 Willie Wilborn
172172 Durward Wilborn
172173 Marcus Wilborn
172174 Bessie Wilborn
17218 Emma Louise Dandridge. Unm. Moved to Mississippi.
17219 Martha Washington Dandridge, m. 8/1/1888, J. W. Thornton of
     Littleton, N.C.
172191 Dandridge Thornton
172192 Martha Thornton
172193 Mary Thornton
1721x Bessie Lee Dandridge (9/ /1865-   ), m. 5/26/1881,
     Walter G. Compton of Paris, Arkansas (5/15/1865-   )
1721x1 Dandridge Compton
1721x2 Mary Compton
1721x3 Anna Lou Compton
1721x4 Walter George Compton
1721a James Spottswood Dandridge (1/27/1851-19   ), m. 1/4/1881,
     Mary Cathey. Home: Tate County, Miss.
1721a1 Cathey Spottswood Dandridge
1721a2 Jimmie Ophelia Dandridge
1721a3
1721a4
1721a5
1721a6
1721b Samuel Hamner Dandridge (1/1/1885-   ), m. 12/4/1890,
     Nannie Cathey. Home: Thyatira, Miss.
1721b1 Mildred Hamner Dandridge
1721b2 William Cathey Dandridge
1721b3 Lightie Louise Dandridge
1721b4 George Samuel Dandridge
1721b5 James Spottswood Dandridge (-1903)

1721c George Gilmer Dandridge (1/29/1853-   ), m. 12/23/
      1879, Mattie Norfleet. Home: Paris, Arkansas
1721c1 Merle Dandridge
1721c2 Jessie Dandridge
1721c3 Beatrice Dandridge
1721c4 Edward Dandridge
1721c5 George Gilmer Dandridge
1721c6 Samuel Clark Dandridge
1721c7 Pattie Dandridge
1721c8 Martha Washington Dandridge
1721c9 Zelia Lightfoot Dandridge
1721cx James Spottswood Dandridge
1721d Walter Alexander Dandridge. Unm. Moved to Mississippi.
173 Nathaniel West Dandridge (1/14/1771-7/26/1847), m. 7/13/1797,
    Martha H. Fontaine (Fountaine) (7/4/1781-9/12/1845)(niece
    of Patrick Henry)
1731 Charles Fontaine Dandridge, m.   McGhee
1732 William Fontaine Dandridge, m.   Stith
17321
1733 Eliza Anne Dandridge, m. W. Hereford
1734 Martha Lightfoot Dandridge (6/3/1850-   ), m. R. Bolton
1735 Nathaniel West Dandridge, Jr., m. H. Wylie
1736 Rosalie Spotswood Dandridge, m. W. D. Bradford
1737 Harry Bolling Dandridge
174 Dorothy Ann (Dorothea Anne?) Dandridge, m. 5/29/1800, Fre-
    derick William James. Surety: William S. Dandridge.
    Witness: Archibald B. Dandridge. Goochland County Marriage
    Register 75. James d. in Madison County, Alabama, 2/ /
    1825.
        NOTE: The following data is from the "Jones-Ganrud
    Volume of Alabama Records":
            The August 1, 1840, Huntsville (Alabama)
    Democrat reports the death, "in the 26th year of her
    age, at this place on Wednesday the 15th instant after
    a painful illness of 16 days Mrs. Elizabeth G. wife of
    Samuel Martin, merchant. The deceased was a native of
    Botetourt County, Virginia, and daughter of Frederick
    W. and Dorothy Ann James late of that place, whence
    she early emigrated to Madison County, Ala. and thence
    in 1836 to this place where he has since resided."
    The Democrat copied its notice from the Macon
    Mississippi Intelligencer.
            In the Madison County (Alabama) Deed Book
    I & J, page 493, there is an agreement dated August
    16, 1824, between Frederic W. James and William B.
    Johnson "in consequence of a marriage then shortly
    meant to be solemnized between the said William B.
    Johnson and Martha Ann, daughter of said Frederic
    W. James"---"he having seven other children, and on
    the 4th day of September following the marriage was
    solemnized".
            In the Madison County (Alabama) Orphans
    Court Minute Book No. 4, page 81, on December 1,
    1826, "George S. Smith resigns and John R. B.

Eldridge is appointed guardian of Catharine James, Mary L. James and Richard James, infant children of Frederic W. James, dec'd."

In Madison County (Alabama) Orphans County Minute Book 6, page 268, there appears the final settlement of John B. Eldridge as administrator of Frederick W. James in which are named the following children of James: Alfred T. James; Martha, wife of William B. Johnson; Mary, wife of Morgan Utz; Archibald B. James; Marion James; Elizabeth G. James; Jane C., wife of Larkin Bradford; and Richard B. James. See, also, Book No. 7, page 203.

Probate File No. 2, Madison County (Alabama) contains a letter addressed to Col. Jesse W. Garth, at Huntsville, from Nathaniel W. Dandridge, Thomas Bolling Dandridge and William J. Dandridge stating that in 1824 Alfred James was in Virginia on his father's business and lost his horse; they bought another for him from Richard G. Lamkin of Henry Co., Va. Sworn to March 15, 1830. One bill for "Capt. F. W. James". There is also the "Receipt of W. T. Bolling, June 6, 1831, for boarding a negro man".

1741   Alfred Turpin James (11/19/1802-   )
1742   William Dandridge James (6/20/1803-8/28/1804)
1743   Martha Ann James (2/9/1805-   ), m. 9/14/1824, William B. Johnson
17431   Frederick Valentine Johnson (11/28/1826-   ), m. Cornelia Ann Harris
174311   Isabella May Johnson (5/10/1850-   ), m. 7/6/1875, W. N. Cowan
174312   Ann Letitia Johnson (4/6/1852-10/20/1917), m. 12/8/1878, Charles Askin
174313   Eliza Jane Johnson (7/26/1854-3/28/1875)
174314   Sue Emma Johnson (12/15/1857-2/18/1932), m. 9/29/1889, James M. Irvin

MATOAKA ALS REBECCA FILIA POTENTISS : PRINC : POWHATANI IMP : VIRGINIÆ .

Ætatis suæ 21 A.
1616.

Matoaks als Rebecka daughter to the mighty Prince
Powhatan Emperour of Attanougskomouck als virginia
converted and baptized in the Christian fauth, and
S: Pass: sculp: wife to the worff Mr Joh: Rolff. Compton Holland excud:

174315   George Robinson Johnson (1/17/1860-   ), m. 3/ /
         1912, Corrine Lewis
174316   Frederick Harris Johnson (10/23/1862-   )
174317   Mary Cornelia Johnson (10/11/1866-9/25/1885)
174318   Jessie Lee Johnson (12/15/1869-   )
17432   Elizabeth Ann Johnson (11/5/1828-5/22/1861)
17433   Isabella Marion Johnson (8/25/1830-9/25/1849)
17434   Henrietta Snow Johnson (6/2/1832-8/23/1854)
17435   Helen St. Mawr Johnson (1/22/1835-8/29/1835)
17436   William Bennett Johnson (2/14/1838-   )
17437   Martin Van Buren Johnson (10/18/1840-1/25/1858)
17438   James Osgood Andrew Johnson (12/15/1844-1/17/1852)
1744   Richard Henry James (9/15/1806-9/15/1806)
1745   Mary Lavinia James (1/1/1808-6/28/1856), m. in Cumberland
         County, Morgan Utz. Her guardian was John R. B. Eldridge
1746   Isabella Marion James (10/16/1811-2/23/1830), m. 7/23/1828,
         Lawrence Banks
1747   Archibald Bolling James (9/7/1813-   ), m. Ann Eliza
         Harris
1748   Elizabeth Goode James (1/7/1815-6/15/1840), m. 9/28/1835,
         Samuel Martin. Elizabeth was born in Botetourt County;
         moved to Madison County, Alabama; and in 1836, moved to
         Macon, Mississippi
1749   Lucy Ambler James (b. and d. 1816)
174x   Jane Catherine James (8/11/1817-6/6/1840), m. 1/22/   ,
         Larkin Bradford
174a   Richard Bland James (5/29/1820-12/11/1885), m. (1st) 1839,
         Sarah Bransford; m. (2nd) 10/5/1851, Sarah Ann Howard
         (-7/1/1861)
     Children by first wife:
174a1   Mary Catherine James (12/27/1840-6/28/1910)
174a2   Marion Isabella James (8/30/1842-5/5/1903), m. (1st) 1859,
         N. W. Hawkins; m. (2nd) 1875, Henry J. Ford
174a3   John Henry James (7/31/1844-6/30/1885), m. (1st) Alice Cook
         Connally; m. (2nd)
     Child by first wife:
174a31   Thomas Brewster James (4/5/1872-12/12/1926), m. 4/4/1900,
         Laura Octavia Branum (11/29/1880-8/13/1971), dau. of
         William Peter and Mary Ellen Moon Branum
174a311 Ruth Lawler James (1/1/1903-   ), m. Earl Clarence
         Worley
174a3111 Ruth Geraldine Worley (12/15/1921-   ), m. (1st)
         William Penn; m. (2nd) Karl Elam, son of Benjamin and
         Nettie Louise Stevenson Elam; m. (3rd) Edwin Vessel
     Child by first husband:
174a31111 Earl William Penn (11/25/1940-   ), m. (1st) Linda
         Stone; m. (2nd) Marsha Barr
     Children by first wife:
174a311111 Donna Penn (5/19/1959-   ), m. Larry Henson
174a311112 Kathy K. Penn (10/14/1960-   )
174a311113 William Harvey Penn (6/29/1962-   )

```
            Children by second husband:
174a31112  Patricia Ann Elam (7/6/1946-           ), m. Dale Bernius
174a311121  Debbie Bernius (2/15/1964-        )
174a311122  Mary Ruth Bernius (10/6/1966-        )
174a311123  Dale Bernius, Jr. (12/31/1970-         )
174a311124  Robin Henry Bernius (6/22/1979 -       )
174a31113  Jacqueline L. Elam (9/9/1948-          ), m. Daniel
            Rosier, Jr.
174a311131  Michael Rosier (7/11/1966-         )
174a311132  Charles Rosier (10/4/1967-         )
174a311133  Kelley Rosier (3/4/1969-          )
174a311134  Daniel Rosier (3/9/1970-         )
174a31114  Rhonda G. Elam (11/11/1951-          ), m. Gary Bennett
174a311141  Bridgett Lorene Bennett (5/13/1973-        )
174a311142  Gary Reid Bennett (1/3/1976-         )
174a311143  Kristi Lynn Lawson Bennett (1/3/1980-          )
174a31115  Jon H. Elam (5/9/1955-          )
174a31116  Wayne K. Elam (10/12/1956-          )
174a3112  Laura Jacqueline Worley (4/29/1924-          ), m. Elwyn
            Glenn ("Bill") Blevins
174a31121  Daniel Glenn Blevins (1/19/1950-          ), m. (1st)
            Betty Holbert; m. (2nd) Elizabeth De Fee
        Child by first wife:
174a311211  Birdgett Dyan Blevins (9/7/1970-          )
        Child by second wife:
174a311212  Shelley Marie Blevins (1/5/1979-          )
174a3113  Earl Clarence Worley, Jr. (1/31/1927-          ), m. Ruth
            Helen Sims
174a31131  Earl Clarence Worley, III (10/2/1954-          ), m. Ann
            McKeroy
174a311311  Jeffrey Brent Worley (9/10/1978-          )
174a31132  Bruce M. Worley (3/10/1957-         ), m. Elizabeth
            Stevenson
174a311321  Brandy Michele Worley (1/3/1977-          )
174a3114  James Bruce Worley (5/3/1933-         ), m. (1st) Mae
            Nelson; m. (2nd) Mary Long; m. (3rd) Mary Clyde Reeves
        Children by first wife:
174a31141  Vicki Jo Worley (7/27/1955-          )
174a31142  Sharon Kay Worley (6/26/1956-         ), m. Otis Ray
174a311421  Carrie Nicole Ray (5/12/1973-         )
174a31143  James Bruce Worley, Jr. (7/24/58-         ), m. Tina Kay
            Williams
174a311431  Heather Lynne Worley (9/28/1980-          )
174a312  Bertha Mildred James (7/29/1905-          ), m. 7/3/1921,
            Albert Cotton Jordan (12/27/1900-1/24/1976), son of John
            Thomas and Rebecca Sanders Jordan
174a3121  Mary Joyce Jordan (3/19/1927-          ), m. (1st) Edward
            Francis Burke, Jr. (1/2/1924-          ), son of Edward
            Francis and Nettie Louise Stevenson Burke
174a31211  Sherry Marie Burke (2/3/1947-          ), m. (1st) Howard
            Newton
```

174a312111 Alicia Ann Newton (-1965)
174a31212   Susan Fay Burke (4/27/1953-   ), m. (2nd) George
            Douglas Butler
174a312121 Brandice Marie Butler (10/1/1976-   )
174a312122 Jared George Butler (12/6/1982-   )
174a31213   Karen Frances Burke (6/27/1957-   ), m. Ronald
            Espinoza
174a312131 Desiree Octavia Espinoza
174a312132 Branum Edward Espinoza (11/29/1983-   )
174a3122 Carolyn Fay Jordan (11/13/1932-   ), m. 8/20/1950,
            David Grayson Burke (10/24/1925-   ), son of
            Edward Francis and Nettie Louise Stevenson Burke
174a31221   Deborah Joyce Burke (3/31/1951-   ), m. (1st) Byron
            Craig Giese (7/12/1952-   ), son of Byron Lee
            and Edythe Love Giese; m. (2nd) Wesley Wheeler (4/14/
            1948-   ), son of Robert and Mary Wheeler
          Children by first husband:
174a312211 Laura Michele Giese (3/28/1972-   )
174a312212 Byron Craig Giese II (2/19/1976-   )
174a31222   Donna Mildred Burke (4/13/1952-   ), m. John
            Clyde Hall (8/7/1950-   ), son of William and
            Rhonda Hall
174a31223   David Grayson Burke, Jr. (5/22/1953-   ), m. (1st)
            Diana McGlothlin, dau. of Harvey and Dorothy McGlothlin;
            m. (2nd) Lorna Diane Cochrane (3/18/1958-   ),
            dau. of William and Carol Cochrane
          Child by first wife:
174a312231 David Grayson Burke III (4/9/1973-   )
174a313   Alice Edna James (10/9/1910-   ), m. Thomas
            Pickens
174a3131   Edna Doris Pickens (12/3/1931-   ), m. Fred Frank
            Horn
174a31311 Fred Frank Horn, Jr. (10/5/1954-   ), m. Donna
            Frank
174a313111 Wesley Frank Horn (5/12/1977-   )
174a31312   James Tracey Horn (5/8/1959-   )
174a31313   John Horn (10/15/1960-   )
174a31314   Michael Horn (9/23/1966-   )
174a3132   Virginia Lorene Pickens (12/8/1933-   ), m. (1st)
            Arvin Leigh Compton; m. (2nd) Hollis Morrow
          Children by first husband:
174a31321   Arvin Leigh Compton, Jr. (1/23/1955-   )
174a31322   Thomas Jeffrey Compton (8/16/1957-   ), m. Lisa
            Henderson
174a31323   Edna Jane Compton (10/10/1958-   ), m. Ray
            Wilkerson
174a313231 Holly Edna Wilkerson (1/7/1978-   )
174a3133   Sandra Gale Pickens (1/23/1941-   ), m. Carl
            Collins
174a314   Virgil Connally James (2/27/1913-1931)
174a315   Thomas Brester James, Jr. (2/5/1920-   )

```
            Child by second wife:
174a32   (son)
            Children by second wife:
174a4    Alfred Bolling James (9/21/1852-4/2/1906), m. 1/14/1874,
            Mary Jackson Curry
174a41   Blanche B. James (8/30/1875-          )
174a42   Walter Bland James (8/15/1880-   /  /19  )
174a5    Arabella Elizabeth ("Betty") James (7/1/1854-5/11/1898)
174a6    Frances Ann James (3/15/1859-8/15/1915), m. (1st) 12/14/
            1880, Rolant Alexander Gooch (         -3/16/1883); m.
            (2nd) 1887, James Monroe Kerr
            Children by first husband:
174a61   Howard Bland Gooch (11/1/1881-  /  /19  ), m. 9/27/1906,
            Augusta Ernestine Albies.  No issue.
174a62   Roland Alexander ("Ellie") Gooch (9/9/1883-1966), m. (1st)
            Augustus H. Longmoor (        -4/29/1908).  She m. (2nd)
            3/11/1914, John W. O'Neill
            Children by second husband:
174a621  James Leo O'Neill (3/8/1915-11/20/1983), m. 5/15/1942,
            Eloise Skipper (4/14/1916-          )
174a6211 Margaret ("Peggy") Skipper O'Neill (5/26/1943-        ),
            m. (1st) Richard Alan Garner.  Div., m. (2nd) James
            Alexander O'Reilly and lives in Kensington, Md.
            Children by first husband:
174a62111 Charles Everett Garner (9/18/1962-          )
174a62112 Neil Patrick Garner (7/12/1965-          )
174a6212 Eleanor Patricia ("Patsy") O'Neill (10/3/1947-        ),
            m. Thomas Richard Brock (11/25/1947-          )
174a62121 Elizabeth Skipper Brock (12/26/1974-          )
174a62122 Patricia Claire Brock (12/20/1977-          )
174a6213 John Alexander O'Neill (3/14/1950-          ), m. (1st)
                       ; m. (2nd)                    , and
            lives in Medea, Pa.
            Child by first wife:
174a62131 John Alexander O'Neill, Jr.
174a622  John William O'Neill (4/10/1917-1950), m. Cola Allen (now
            deceased)
174a6221 Sarah Ann O'Neill (10/10/1940?-        ), m. Gene Ray-
            mond Wilson.  Lives in California
174a62211 Elizabeth Paige Wilson
174a62212 William Wilson
174a62213 Deborah Ann Wilson
174a62214 Keith Marion (or Marion Keith) Wilson
            Children by second husband:
174a63   Alfred Thomas Kerr (1/10/1889-1950), m. 1/31/1918, Kate
            French Stewart (1/29/1888-7/10/1954)
174a631  Jane Snow Kerr (11/10/1918-11/1/1929), d. of polio
174a632  Alfred Thomas Kerr, Jr. (12/3/1920-1/23/1983), m. 5/12/
            1943, Lillian Bernice Hester (7/27/1923-          )
174a6321 Robert William Kerr (2/10/1945-          ), m. (1st) 6/6/
            1967, Olivia Louise Shwab (4/9/1946-          ).  Div.  M.
            (2nd) 7/9/1977, Paula Fason Triff (12/19/19  -      )
```

```
          Child by first wife:
174a63211  Robert Davidson Shwab Kerr (4/12/1971-              )
          Child by second wife:
174a63212  Lindsay Marie Kerr (6/9/1978-              )
174a6322   Howard James Kerr (9/11/1947-              ), m. 12/28/1968,
          Elizabeth Cox Waitzman (7/28/1949-              )
174a63221  Lacy Elizabeth Kerr (5/19/1970-              )
174a63222  Shelby Jennifer Kerr (11/9/1972-              )
174a63223  Richard Thomas Kerr (4/9/1978-              )
174a6323   Jane Hester Kerr (12/6/1951-              ), m. 10/15/1971,
          Thomas Allan Wingo (10/16/1948-              )
174a63231  Christin Kerr Wingo (3/12/1974-              )
174a63232  Caroline Elizabeth Wingo (3/7/1977-              )
174a63233  Kerry Virginia Wingo (7/6/1979-              )
174a633    Kathryn Ann Kerr (7/23/1923-              ), m. 1/24/1953,
          Howard Morgan Keen (11/22/1925-              )
174a6331   James Howard Keen (3/24/1954-              )
174a6332   Stewart Hamilton Keen (7/26/1957-              )
174a6333   Rebecca Jane Keen (7/3/1959-              ), m. 10/8/1983,
          Jay Mark Faulkner (3/30/1956-              )
174a634    Howard James Kerr (11/28/1925-3/4/1945). Drowned
174a64     Julian Hawke Kerr, d. when 3 weeks old
174a65     William ("Willie") Appleman Kerr (8/30/1897-3/20/1908)
          (twin).  Drowned
174a66     Twin to Willie, lived one hour
175   Jane Butler Dandridge, m. Rev. Joseph Davies Logan, son of
      James and Hannah Brown Logan.  Their two children below were
      adopted by Jane's aunt, Mary Dandridge, and her husband,
      George Woodson Payne  of "Dungeness"
1751  James William Logan, m. Sarah Anne Woodville Strother
17511  Joseph Davies Logan, of Salem, m. Georgine Willis (1861-
              ), dau. of Col. George and Sally Innes Smith Willis
175111  James Fielding Lewis Logan, m. Jean Markley
1751111  Jean Dandridge Logan
175112  Maud Matthews Logan (1890-              ), m. Garland J.
          Hopkins
175113  Sally Logan (1887-              )
175114  Anna Clayton Logan (1888-              )
175115  John Lee Logan (1892-              )
1752  Mary Woodville Logan
176
177
178
179
17x
18   Edward Bolling (9/9/1746-8/10/1770) of Goochland County.  Unm.
19   John Bolling (5/1/1729-5/24/1736)
1x   Archibald Bolling (1/26/1730*1-6/20/1749)
1a   Robert Bolling (11/10/1732-5/26/1736)(first of name)
1b   Elizabeth Bolling (7/10/1734-7/31/1735)(first of name)
1c   Sarah Bolling (8/22/1740-4/27/1747)(first of name)
1d   Ann Bolling (8/19/1742-4/2/174?)
```

le Elizabeth Bolling (6/24/1753-7/29/1754)(second of name)
lf Jane Bolling (7/6/1754-7/31/1754)
lg Rebecca Bolling (7/6/1754-d. young)
lh Elizabeth Bolling (3/21/1756-8/7/1756)(third of name)
li

JANE BOLLING

(2)

Wife of Richard Randolph of "Curles"

2 Jane Bolling (1698-1767), m. 1713*4, Col. Richard Randolph (5/
/1689-12/17/1748) of "Curles", son of William and Mary Isham
Randolph of "Turkey Island". Colonel Richard died while on a
trip to England

21 Richard Randolph of "Curles" (1725*6-6/5/1786), m. 12/27/1750,
Ann ("Nancy") Meade (-12/9/1814), dau. of David and
Susan Everard Meade of Nansemond County

The following is found in an old prayer book (copy in
VHS): "Richard Randolph of Curles departed this life June
5, 1786 - In the Sixty-First year of his Age", and "Ann
Randolph, wife of the above Richard, died at S. East, on
Dec. 9, 1814 in the 82nd year of her age".

211 Richard Randolph III (3/31/1757-3/16/1799), Officer of
Cavalry, Revolutionary War, m. 12/15/1785, Maria Beverley
(12/15/1764-10/2/1824), dau. of Robert and Maria Carter
Beverley. She m. (2nd) 8/12/1800, Maj. Gawin Lane Corbin
who adopted Maria's last child by Richard, and named the
child Gawin Lane Corbin, Jr.

2111 Richard Randolph IV (9/2/1786-7/13/1787)

2112 Richard Randolph IV (10/7/1788-   )

2113 Robert Beverley Randolph (11/10/1790-4/ /1869), Lieut. U.S.N.,
m. 3/23/1834, (his first cousin) Eglantine (Maria?) Beverley,
dau. of Peter Randolph and Lovely St. Martin Beverley

21131 Lovely St. Martin Randolph, m. A. Parrish

211311 Guy Parrish   211312 Clara Parrish   211313 Adele Parrish

21132 Euphrasie Randolph   21133 Carrie Randolph

21134 Maggie Randolph   21135 Robert Randolph

2114 William Byrd Randolph (3/29/1792-1814). On board ship
"Chesapeake" when taken; lost on "Wasp". Unm.

2115 Maria Beverley Randolph (4/4/1794-1845), m. Philip DuVal, Jr.
(9/28/1789-1847), son of Benjamin and Elizabeth Warrock
DuVal. Home: Richmond (he was a pharmacist)

21151 Rev. Benjamin DuVal II (ca. 1815-ca. 1878), m. Agnes Slade
of North Carolina. Methodist Missionary to Honduras

211511 Ida DuVal, m.   . No issue

211512 Mary Mebane DuVal, m. Julian Peace

211513 Lelia DuVal, m. Norton Anderson

211514 Willie DuVal, d. young

211515 Elizabeth DuVal, m.   (in Honduras). GRABOWSKII 166

21152 Robert Randolph DuVal (1817-5/25/1875), m. 6/6/1849, Sallie
Dandridge Cooke (3/18/1828-12/14/1887), dau. of John Rogers
and Maria Pendleton Cooke. DuVal was a druggist in Richmond

211521 Maria Pendleton DuVal (10/4/1852-12/29/1943). Unm. Principal of Stuart Hall, Staunton, and Owner-Principal of
St. Hilda's School for Young Ladies, Charles Town, W.Va.

211522 Florence Beverley DuVal (3/4/1855-   ). Unm.

211523 Willie (dau) Randolph DuVal (8/ /1857-5/ /1864)

211524 Katherine Cooke DuVal (9/15/1859-3/9/1937), m. 1893, Carter
Henry Harrison, Jr. (2424611). No issue. Lived at "Oakhurst", University (Charlottesville)

211525 Robert Randolph DuVal, Jr. (2/11/1862-1864)
211526 Sarah Esten DuVal (7/28/1866-   ). Unm. "Oakhurst"
211527 Philip St. John DuVal (9/9/1868-   ), m. 1897, Louise
        Payne. No issue. Home: "Orapax", King William County
211528 Edmund Pendleton Randolph DuVal (12/4/1871-   ), m.
        7/14/1905, Katherine Cole (4/21/1880-4/11/1944), dau. of
        James Reid and Mary Parrish King Cole of Dallas. No issue.
        Adopted two sisters, naming them Elizabeth ("Betty") Ran-
        dolph DuVal and Virginia Pendleton DuVal
21153   Maria Midgely DuVal (-1874). Unm.
21154   James McPherson (Powhatan?) DuVal (-1884). Apothecary
21155   Rev. William Randolph DuVal (5/ /1822-6/25/1850). Unm.
        Episcopal

2116   Mary Midgeley Randolph (4/29/1796-   )
2117   Peter Beverley Randolph (1/22/1798-   )
2118   Gawin Lane Corbin, Jr., M.D. (9/17/1799-1874), m. 1837,
        Elizabeth Hines, dau. of Robert and Anne Elliott Hines of
        Smithfield. Corbin was born c. Randolph (see note under
        211).
21181   Dr. Philip Sin Physic Corbin (1838-1874), m. 2/16/1860,
        Martha Eliza Brown Brinkley (9/7/1839-5/31/1877), dau. of
        Jackson and Martha Amanda Parker Brinkley of Nansemond
        County
211811 Dr. Luther Carroll Corbin (1/22/1861-9/14/1924). Unm.
211812 Gawinae Corbin (3/27/1864-7/14/1941), m. 11/31/1883, John
        William Sowers (7/26/1859-1/26/1932), son of William
        Joseph and Mahala Elizabeth Clark Sowers
2118121 William Corbin Sowers (11/1/1884-   ), m. 12/10/
        1913, Estelle Park Morgan (9/15/1889-   ), dau. of
        Benjamin Walker and Nannie Woodson Morgan
21181211 William Corbin Sowers, Jr. (6/5/1915-   ). Unm.
21181212 Mary Jane Sowers (1/14/1918-   ), m. 7/15/1942,
        Addison Peter Marsh, Jr. (7/23/1917-   ), son of
        Addison Peter and Constance Fischer Marsh
211812121 Mary Addison Marsh (9/9/1943-   )
21181213 Walker Morgan Sowers (7/30/1921-   ), m. 1/15/1943,
        Margaret Virginia Spencer (3/2/1923-   ), dau. of
        Leonard Ray and Cecil Elsie Carter Spencer. No issue.
2118122 Alvin Marion Sowers (11/15/1887-   ), m. 11/11/
        1914, Myrtle Blanche Sheets (12/22/1884-   ), dau.
        of Silas H. and Bertha Marrow Sheets
21181221 Alvin Marion Sowers, Jr. (6/9/1917-   ), m. 4/9/
        1939, Helen Corinne Swindler (4/13/1915-   ),
        dau. of Madison Calvin and Maude Grace Pugh Swindler
211812211 John Morrow Sowers (10/25/1940-   )
211812212 Paul Madison Sowers (8/10/1942-   )
21181222 William Carroll Sowers (10/8/1919-   )
21181223 Robert Eugene Sowers (9/21/1923-   )
2118123 Raymond St. Physic Sowers (12/4/1892-   ), m.
        Virginia Southworth. Home: Charleston, W.Va.
2118124 Princess Gawinae Sowers (1/22/1895-   ), m. 5/22/
        1922, Reuben Orville Thomas (5/22/1898-   ), son
        of William O. and Belle Fox Thomas. Div.

21181241 William Corbin Thomas (1/16/1926-   )
21181242 Reuben Orville Thomas, Jr. (3/25/1928-   )
21181243 Stafford Hundley Thomas (9/9/1930-   )
2118125   Miriam Ethel Sowers (9/10/1897-   ), m. 2/17/1916,
          William Thomas Howard (9/17/1893-   ), son of
          Ernest Oscar and Ella Virginia Goodwin Howard
21181251 Katherine Howard (11/24/1920-   ), m. 6/20/1942,
          Robert Munford Biggs, Jr. (7/21/1920-   )
21181252 William Thomas Howard, Jr. (5/20/1926-   )
2118126   Reginald Carroll Sowers (3/8/1903-8/11/1918). Unm.
2118127   Shirley May Sowers (5/18/1907-   ), m. 3/2/1926,
          Curtis Parke Harrell (12/17/1904-   ), son of
          Theodore Curtis and Ruth Rodgers Brinkley Harrell
21181271 Sally Brinkley Harrell (1/22/1927-   )
21181272 Malcolm Cloeman Harrell (4/5/1928-   )
21181273 Philys Corbin Harrell (10/8/1934-   )
211813   Dr. Marion Xerxes Corbin (11/8/1866-9/29/1935), m. 11/12/
          1896, May Thirza Williams (10/21/1869-   ), dau. of
          David Edward and Alice Rebecca Guy Williams
2118131   Gawin Lane Corbin III (2/19/1898-   ), m. 6/30/
          1931, Kathleen Culbertson (3/9/1902-   ), dau. of
          Richard Watt and Anna Maria Johnstone Culbertson
21181311 Richard Johnstone Corbin (10/6/1932-   )
21181312 Alice Guy Corbin (4/2/1939-   )
2118132   Marian Thirza Corbin (7/13/1899-   ), m. 12/8/1925,
          Carl Ingman Aslakson (4/23/1896-   ), son of Frank
          Theodore and Minnesota Ella Inmundson Aslakson
21181321 Richard Corbin Aslakson (8/7/1928-   )
2118133   Elizabeth Tayloe Corbin (6/11/1902-   ), m. 2/19/
          1925, Albert Sidney Lawton (6/17/1900-   ), son
          of William Henry and Mary Elma Wiggins Lawton
21181331 Elizabeth Tayloe Lawton (12/30/1925-   )
21181332 Marian Corbin Lawton (4/3/1929-   )
21181333 Susan Catherine Lawton (12/22/1931-   )
2118134   Cary Randolph Corbin (4/2/1908-6/11/1910)
2119   Richard Randolph Corbin (4/11/1801-10/4/1853), m. (1st) 6/4/
          1821, Catherine Moore Fauntleroy (8/7/1802-1825), dau. of
          Thomas and Isabella Lorimer Fauntleroy of "Waltham", Middle-
          sex County. M. (2nd) 6/28/1827, Mary King Mallory (-
          10/5/1853) of Norfolk
       Children by first wife:
21191 Gawin Lane Corbin (ca. 1822-6/17/1888). Unm.
21192 Edmonia Fauntleroy Corbin (1825-2/5/1917), m. 9/30/1845,
          Robert Otway Carter, M.D. (1/3/1810-3/7/1874), son of
          Robert Charles and Harwar Beale Carter
211921 Robert Corbin Carter (8/11/1846-   ). C.S.A. Unm.
211922 Edmonia Beverley Carter (10/3/1847-4/17/1879), m. 1/14/
          1869, Judge Charles Bowen Howry (5/14/1844-7/20/1928),
          C.S.A., son of Judge James Moorman and Narcissa Bowen
          Howry
2119221 Lucien Beverley Howry (10/27/1867-   ). Unm.
2119222 Willard Carter Howry (6/18/1874-12/24/1919). Unm.
2119223 Maude Howry (6/22/1878-8/1/1878)
211923 Otway Lane Carter (1/24/1849-12/14/1917), m. 6/19/1873,
          Fanny Lovie McKie (-3/7/1926) of Mississippi

2119231 Capt. Charles Otway Carter (3/21/1874-11/7/1931), m. (1st)
3/13/1899, Virginia Pearl Burford (8/9/1875-10/3/1908)
No issue. M. (2nd) 9/14/1910, Florence Annie Price (5/
2/1890-4/18/1925). No issue.
2119232 Capt. Bracton Cleve Carter (10/2/1877-11/ /1915), m. 3/
19/1910, Bertha Ann McCleskey. No issue.
2119233 Fannie Lovie Carter (9/25/1887-   ). Unm.
2119234 Beverley (dau.) Carter (2/12/1891-   ). Unm.
211924   Anna Fauntleroy Carter (10/7/1850-4/18/1872). Unm.
211925   St. Leger Landon Carter (5/2/1854-   ). Unm.
211926   Mary Harwar Carter (3/25/1857-   ), m. 9/1/1880,
James Melmoth Sloan (12/4/1850-9/16/1916), son of Rev.
Alexander and Sarah Ann Moffatt Sloan
2119261 Isla Sloan (12/10/1882-   ), m. 12/4/1912, Mark
McCausland Anderson (2/2/1873-6/18/1928), son of Dr.
Richard and Laura McCausland Anderson. No issue.
2119262 Lucia Landon Sloan (7/4/1885-   ), m. 12/4/1913,
Henry Harold Hopkins (9/20/1883-3/29/1933), son of
Lorenzo Dow and Effie Elliott Fry Hopkins
21192621 Henry Melmoth Hopkins (1/14/1915-   ). Unm.
2119263 Melmoth Sloan (7/31/1887-5/3/1889)
2119264 Berkeley Carter Sloan (4/9/1890-   ). Unm.
2119265 Eugene Williams Sloan (9/14/1893-   ), m. 2/11/1937,
Grace Edminston Switzer (6/11/1906-   ), dau. of
Roland Woodhill and Stella Cook Switzer. No issue.
2119266 Mildred Sloan (11/21/1896-   ), m. 6/17/1922, George
Dock, Jr. (1/20/1895-   ), son of Dr. George
and Laura McLemore Dock
21192661 Donald Stone Dock (8/8/1927-   )
2119267 William Carter Sloan (7/13/1899-   ), m. 1/2/1933,
Ann Emily Post (8/8/1912-   ), dau. of William
Rolla and Edith Thompson Post of Grosse Point, Mich.
21192671 Berkeley Carter Sloan (12/15/1933-   )
21192672 Ann Sloan (11/7/1935-   )
2119268 Mary Carter Sloan (11/16/1902-   ), m. 3/4/1929,
Isaac Caldwell Orr, Jr., son of Charles Jordan and Mary
Ann Caldwell Orr. No issue.
211927   Charles Cleve Carter (5/21/1861-10/13/1861)
211928   Beverley (son) Carter (ca. 1867-1889)
21193   Charles Corbin, m.   . Died in Texas.
211921   Roberta Edmonia Corbin
21194   Frances Corbin (1830-4/10/1865), m. Perkins
211941   Clara Perkins, m. Frederick B. Philbrook
211942   Florence Isabel Perkins, m. John B. Core of Boston
21195   Fillmore Mallory Corbin (3/4/1832 or 1833-3/3/1931), m. (1st)
1878-79, Lula Hebe Carradine, dau. of James and Mary Hewitt
Carradine of Yazoo City, Miss. M. (2nd) 5/5/1891, Effie
Ewing (4/5/1870-   ), dau. of John McKinley and
Margaret Irvin Ewing of Bloomington
    Children by first wife:
211951   Alice Richardson Corbin (4/16/1881-   ), m. 10/14/
1905, William Penhallow Henderson (6/4/1877-   ), son
of William Oliver and Sallie Augusta Legallie Henderson

2119511   Alice Oliver Henderson (1/27/1907-   ), m. (1st)
          12/20/1922, later divorced, John Ganson Evans (1/4/1902-
                        ), son of Karl Kellogg and Mabel Ganson
          Evans of Buffalo. M. (2nd) 6/3/1938, Edgar Lewis Rossin
          (3/9/1901-3/18/1948), son of Alfred Samuel and Clara
          Lewisohn Rossin of New York City. No issue (had had a
          son by his first wife).
          Children by first husband:
21195111 Natalie Sarah Evans (1/8/1924-   ), m. 6/27/1947,
          William Henry Mauldin (10/29/1921-   )(cartoonist),
          son of Sidney Albert and Edith Watrina Bemis Mauldin
          of New Mexico and Arizona
211951111 Andrew Edgar Mauldin (9/3/1948-   )
21195112 Nancy Ganson Evans (1/8/1924 or 2/23/1925-   ), m.
          6/10/1947, Robert William Janes (9/24/1916-   ),
          son of Robert Bullis and Marie Klotz Janes of Oak Park,
          Ill. No issue.
21195113 Letitia Ellicott Evans (11/6/1926-   )
211952   Mallory Corbin, d. inf.
211953   Richard Beverley Corbin, d. inf.
          Children by second wife:
211954   Margaret Corbin (4/13/1893-   ), m. 6/14/1922,
          Eugene Little Young (9/19/1887-   ), son of William
          Little and Margaret Wheeler Young of Kansas City. No issue.
211955   Richard Ewing Corbin (6/14/1895-9/17/1930). Unm.
211x   Lucy Beverley Corbin (9/1/1804-8/19/1836), m. 3/18/1823, Rev.
          John Goodall (1789-5/23/1840) of James City County (whose
          first wife was Martha Burwell Diggs of York County
211x1   Junius Goodall (4/22/1824-10/11/1828)
211x2   Louisa Anna Hester Goodall (1/8/1827-10/29/1832)
211x3   Anna Byrd Corbin Goodall (11/23/1829-1/6/1919). Unm.
211x4   Lucy Corbin Goodall (9/24/1832-10/3/1833)
211x5   Hester Morris Goodall (10/1/1833-1/30/1908), m. 5/13/1861,
          Capt. Edward Payson Reeve (7/17/1832-6/10/1898), C.S.A.,
          son of John Flavel and Elizabeth Purvall Grubbs Reeve
211x51   Anna Byrd Reeve (4/9/1862-8/5/1911), m. 4/5/1888, Robert
          Edgar Bruce (4/29/1865-7/20/1936), son of Charles Lucien
          and Susan Elizabeth Hines Bruce
211x511   Robert Edgar Bruce, Jr. (3/2/1889-   ), m. 10/21/1914,
          Amelia Scott Buck (11/9/1889-   ), dau. of Walker
          Davidson and Hettie Hunter Buck
211x5111 Robert Edgar Bruce III (3/6/1923-   )
211x5112 Anna Byrd Bruce (5/27/1928-1/2/1932)
211x512   Payson Reeve Bruce (9/13/1891-   ). Unm.
211x513   George Ashton Bruce (8/7/1894-3/18/1915). Unm.
211x514   John Goodall Bruce (5/25/1898-   ), m. 10/23/1926,
          Anne Benjamin Gunn (11/25/1900-   ), dau. of Acors
          Rathburn and Mary Eliza Quarles Gunn
211x5141 John Goodall Bruce, Jr. (10/19/1927-   )
211x5142 Benjamin Byrd Bruce (5/28/1930-6/30/1930)
211x5143 George Rathbun Bruce (2/25/1932-   )
211x5144 Arthur Chilton Bruce (2/28/1933-   )

211x515 Hester Beverley Bruce (3/18/1900-   ). Unm.
211x516 Charles Corbin Byrd Bruce (8/3/1904-   ), m. (1st)
          Ruby Wanda Fennelle. M. (2nd) 1/31/1938, Roberta Niobe
          Hanes (3/9/1911-   ), dau. of James Benjamin and
          Mary Lee Killian Hanes. No issue.
          Child by first wife:
211x5161 Wanda Beverley Bruce (9/29/1928-   )
211x52   Lucy Corbin Reeve (7/12/1865-8/31/1940). Unm.
211x53   Bessie Reeve (10/4/1868-3/3/1886). Unm.
211x54   John Goodall Reeve (9/7/1871-8/11/1872)
211x55   Maude Stuart Reeve (10/14/1972-   ). Unm.
211x6   Catherine Carter Goodall (2/23/1836-7/9/1836)
211a   John Tayloe Corbin II (8/21/1806-3/1/1809)
211b   Anna Byrd Corbin (11/26/1808-2/3/1847), m. 11/29/1831, Rev.
          William Henry Shield (4/16/1807-10/10/1883), son of Samuel
          and Maria Drummond Shield of York County. Nine children.
          Rev. Shield m. (2nd) Susan Ann Howard, and had nine children
          by her also. He was murdered in Russia.
211b1   Lelia Anna Shield (11/18/1832-4/24/1878), m. (1st) 11/15/
          1854, Robert Edmund Wynne. No issue. M. (2nd) 12/16/1857,
          Lt. William Randolph Fleming (1/7/1832-11/9/1992), C.S.A.,
          son of Tarlton and Rebecca Elizabeth Coles Fleming of
          Goochland County
211b11   William Randolph Fleming, Jr. (3/4/1859-5/8/1898). Unm.
211b12   Henry Corbin Fleming (11/11/1860-5/6/1931), m. Lottie
          Webster of Richmond, Ind.
211b13   Orlando Fairfax Fleming (12/9/1861-3/1/1934), m. 7/30/
          1885, Belle Henley Harbold (6/25/1867-   ), dau. of
          Jacob William and Belle Henley Harbold
211b131 Lelia Byrd Fleming (5/16/1886-   ), m.11/24/1906,
          Melville Franklin Wayland (3/17/1886-   ), son
          of Burrus Franklin and Marie Thoressa Booten Wayland
211b1311 Beverley Fairfax Wayland (11/28/1907-   ), m. 2/3/
          1933, Helen Veronica Murphy (10/11/1910-   ),
          dau. of Arthur Nicholas and Irene Elizabeth Miller
          Murphy of Washington, D. C.
211b13111 William Randolph Wayland (10/2/1934-   )
211b13112 Beverley Ann Wayland (11/25/1941-   )
211b1312 Reith Hartwell Wayland (3/14/1909-8/17/1909)
211b1313 Catherine Randolph Wayland (7/17/1910-   ), m.
          5/13/1933, George Earl Grace Moffatt (11/26/1909-   ),
          son of Albert Grace and Margaret Virginia Rea Moffatt
211b13131 George Earl Grace Moffatt, Jr. (7/7/1936-   )
211b1314 Elizabeth Fleming Wayland (10/30/1912-   ), m. 9/
          25/1937, Edward Roosevelt Clarkson (2/11/1903-   ),
          son of Albert Edward and Charlotte Green Clarkson of
          Waltham, Mass. No issue.
211b132 Bessie Taliaferro Fleming (3/6/1892-   ), m. 4/14/
          1917, John Bascom Dey (5/3/1892-   ), son of Rev.
          Bascom and Hettie Lee Morris Dey
211b1321 John Bascom Dey, Jr. (5/31/1931-7/15/1931)
211b133 Sims Shield Fleming (7/8/1893-   ), m. 9/2/1907,
          Ernest Ashby Shafer (1/24/1885-   )

211b1331 Dorothy Elizabeth Shafer (8/31/1909-   ), m. 8/
          25/1940, Richard Powell Harris (11/11/1905-   ),
          son of Ritchie Breckenridge and Josephine Marian Spicer
          Harris
211b1332 Virginia Ashby Shafer (4/10/1911-   ). Unm.
211b1333 Louise Fleming Shafer (12/9/1912-   ), m. 2/29/
          1940, Ashby French Johnston
211b13331 Ashby French Johnston, Jr. (6/ /1943-   )
211b1334 Mary Taliaferro Shafer (8/8/1914-   ), m. 6/2/
          1931, James Thrift Dawson (4/20/1911-   ), son
          of Haywood Monticello and Laura Eunice Wilhoit Dawson.
          No issue.
211b1335 Ernest Orlando Shafer (10/10/1915-   ). Unm.
211b1336 Mildred Sims Shafer (4/26/1918-   ), m. 4/1/
          1939, Leroy Albert Yocum
211b1337 Margaret Henley Shafer (11/1/1919-   )
211b1338 Catherine Shafer (7/29/1923-   )
211b1339 Charles William Shafer (1/18/1925-   )
211b14   Thomas Mann Fleming (9/2/1862-9/10/1863)
211b15   Tarlton Beverley Fleming (10/3/1866-5/10/1898). Unm.
211b16   Charles Spotswood Fleming (9/19/1871-   ), m. 9/5/
          1907, Rosa Lee Carpenter (8/21/1883-   ), dau. of
          William A. and Rebecca Anne Lohr Carpenter
211b161   William Earle Fleming (7/31/1909-   ), m. 2/20/
          1936, Ann Stafford
211b1611 Virginia Fleming (1937-   )
211b162   Virginia Rose Fleming (1/30/1912-   )
211b163   Lelia Rebecca Fleming (3/30/1919-   )
211b17   Samuel Shield Fleming (10/6/1873-10/27/1943). Unm.
211b2   Dr. William Henry Shield, Jr. (7/15/1834-10/12/1894), C.S.A.
          Unm.
211b3   Orlando Fairfax Shield (12/5/1835-5/3/1862), C.S.A. Unm.
          Killed at Seven Pines.
211b4   Lucy Beverley Corbin Shield, d. inf.
211b5   Maria Randolph Shield, d. inf.
211b6   Caroline Sims Shield (11/20/1839-5/25/1907), m. 8/ /1876,
          Woodford Broaddus Henley (12/20/1834-2/14/1909), son of
          Richardson and Mary Ann Taliaferro Henley
211b61   Lelia Anna Henley (2/ /1878-   ). Unm.
211b62   Woodford Beverley Henley (6/19/1880-   ), m. Mary
          Waddell. No issue.
211b63   Richardson Corbin Henley (2/ /1887-   )
211b7   Robert Saunders Shield (2/15/1842-1842)
211b8   Samuel Corbin Shield (3/17/1844-1/4/1920), m. Sally B.
          Yarborough of Richmond
211b81   Son, d. inf.
211b82   Dau, d. inf.
211b83   Dau, d. inf.
211b84   Samuel Corbin Shield, Jr. (-1942)
211b9   Edmonia Midge Shield (5/4/1845-   )
212   David Meade Randolph (3/14/1759-9/23/1830), m. Mary ("Molly")
          Randolph of "Tuckahoe" (2411). He was Officer of Cavalry,
          Revolutionary War. U.S. Marshall for Virginia.

2121 Richard Randolph (10/30/1782-1859), m. Elizabeth McGibbon
      Gibbon
2122 William Beverley Randolph (6/11/99-5/15/68), m. 5/21/16,
      Sarah Lingan, dau. of Gen. James M. Lingan
21221 James Lingan Randolph (6/11/17-9/17/88, m. 11/23/48, Emily
      Strother, dau. of Col. John Strother
212211 John Strother Randolph (11/1/49-11/7/50)
212212 Beverley Strother Randolph (7/17/51-   ), m. 9/20/82,
      Mary Jewett
212213 Edmund Strother Randolph (4/30/55-8/25/66)
212214 Lingan Strother Randolph (5/13/59-3/7/22), m. 10/15/90,
      Fanny Robbins (2/18/67-   ), dau. of Orlando
      Douglas and Fanny Magruder Robbins
2122141 James Robbins Randolph (8/4/91-   )
2122142 Orlando Robbins Randolph (7/11/94-   ), m. 10/24/
      23, Jean Graham McAllister (12/6/97-   ), dau. of
      Joseph Thompson and Virginia Richards Anderson McAllister
21221421 Beverley Randolph (dau)(12/5/24-   )
21221422 Jean Graham Randolph (10/7/29-   )
2122143 Emily Randolph (1/13/97-   ), m. 10/12/18, Stapleton
      Conway Deitrick, son of S. C. and Elsie Taylor Deitrick
21221431 Stapleton Conway Deitrick, Jr. (8/6/19-   )
21221432 Frances Randolph Deitrick (7/13/22-   )
21221433 Lingan Randolph Deitrick (4/26/25-   )
21221434 Elsie Payne Deitrick (4/26/25-   )
21221435 Emily Lynn Deitrick (11/18/26-   )
2122144 Lingan Strother Randolph, Jr. (2/12/03-   ), m.
      5/9/31, Anne Elizabeth Wallace (4/13/10-   ), dau.
      of John Overton and Anne Elizabeth Walker Wallace
21221441 Joan Overton Randolph (4/25/33-   )
21221442 Lingan Strother Wallace Randolph (1/8/36-   )
21222 Martha Jane Randolph (11/16/18-   ), m. 6/23/40,
      Charles Ferdinand Codwise
212221 Mary Byvanck Codwise (7/18/42-3/1/90), m. Maj. Malbone F.
      Watson
212222 Beverley Randolph Codwise (6/5/44-   ), m. Mary
      Evelyn Russell
212223 Jane Randolph Codwise
21223 William Moray Randolph (1/24/21-11/14/90), m. 6/5/51, Sarah
      Seymour, dau. of Felix Seymour
212231 William Seymour Randolph (9/28/57-   ), m. 10/19/81,
      Lucy Cunningham
212232 Felix Seymour Randolph (3/29/59-   ), m. 9/22/91,
      Lelia Little
212233 Richard Beverley Randolph (5/28/61-   ). Unm.
212234 Emma Stark Randolph (3/1/63-   ), m. 6/5/90, Ben-
      jamin Daily
212235 Mary Meade Randolph (6/28/70-   ), m. 4/20/92, Albert
      Livingston Johnson
21224 Emma Beverley Randolph (5/5/23-10/9/64), m. 6/1/55, Henry
      Stark
21225 Cornelia Patterson Randolph (2/10/25-   ). Unm.

21226   Richard Randolph (1/29/27- 2/9/93). Unm.

21227   Mary Meade Randolph (9/23/28-   ), m. 9/13/55, W. W.
       Turner

21228   Harriet Isabel Randolph (7/19/30-7/5/97), m. 6/14/60, John
       A. Pickett

212281   George Randolph Pickett (3/31/61-10/31/85). Unm.

21229   Elizabeth Gibbon Randolph (4/1/33-   ), m. 10/28/63,
       Washington Custis Calvert

2122x   David Meade Randolph (7/30/36-8/3/37)

2123   David Meade Randolph (-1825)

2124   Burwell Starke Randolph (1800-10/22/54), d.s.p.

2125   (son)

2126   (son)

2127   (dau)

2128   (dau)

213 Brett Randolph (7/20/1766-1/23/1828), m. 11/21/1789, Lucy
     Beverley (2/24/1771-1854), dau. of Robert and Maria Carter
     Beverley of "Blandfield". Brett d. at "Goshen", Lowndes
     County, Miss., and bur. at "Oakleigh", near Greensboro, Ala.

2131   (son)(11/24/1790-12/13/1790)

2132   Capt. Edward Brett Randolph (1/9/1792-8/4/1848), m. 6/7/
     1825, (his first cousin), Elizabeth Bland Beverley (12/14/
     1804-7/29/1880), dau. of Carter and Jane Wormeley Beverley
     of "The Cedars", Columbus, Miss. Captain and Mrs. Randolph
     lived at "Goshen", near Columbus

21321   Virginia Beverley Randolph (7/19/1827-2/12/1865), m. 1850,
      George Wisner Sherman (1817-8/18/1865), son of Sherman and
           Sutherland Sherman of "Burnt Hills", Saratoga
      County, N.Y.

213211   Edward Randolph Sherman (1851-1927). Unm.

213212   Hugh Sutherland Sherman (7/11/1852-5/10/1905). Unm.

213213   George Wormeley Sherman (10/9/1859-5/31/1929), m. 6/3/1888,
      Hallie Antionette Bowen (4/12/1860-6/20/1945), dau. of
      Matthew Irvin Keith and Maria Tabitha Conant Bowen of
      Aberdeen, Miss.

213231   Beverley Randolph Sherman (4/1/1890-6/ /1908). Unm.

2132132 Mary Ita Sherman (9/19/1891-   ), m. 4/22/1914,
      Thomas Bailey Hardy (3/7/1884-   ), son of Thomas
      William and Sarah Elizabeth Bailey Hardy of Lunenburg
      County. No issue.

2132133 Hugh Sutherland Sherman II (4/12/1894-   ), m. 1924,
      Elizabeth Nelson Anderson (6/27/190), dau. of Frank-
      lin Yates and Frances Rosamond Shelton Anderson of Mem-
      phis and St. Louis

21321331 Elizabeth Randolph Sherman (11/26/1926-   )

2132134 George Wormeley Sherman, Jr. (5/5/1899-4/23/1942). Unm.

213214   Beverley Sherman (2/4/1863-8/22/1866)

213215   Virginia Randolph Sherman (2/9/1865-1/2/1888), m. 10/14/
      1883, Joseph Johnston White (11/2/1862-6/14/1937), son of
      George M. and Nancy McDavid Morgan White of Granville
      County, N.C.

2132151 Sherman White (9/23/1886-5/7/1888)

2132152   Edward Randolph White (12/26/1887-   ), m. 11/10/
          1909, Mary Adelaide Graves (7/31/1888-   ), dau.
          of Capt. John Edmond and Frances Beverley Lamb Graves
          of Charles City County
21321521 Edward Randolph White, Jr. (12/25/1912-   ), m.
          4/16/1935, Mary Ellen Barnes (1/25/1916-   ), dau.
          of Augustus and Marguerite Williams Barnes
213215211 Edward Randolph White III (9/5/1939-   )
213215212 Marguerite Barnes White (9/13/1941-   )
213215213 Augustus Barnes White (1/6/1943-   )
21321522 Frances Beverley White (2/14/1920-   ), m. 3/28/
          1940, William Ransom Johnson Dunn, Jr., (4/18/1917-
              ), son of William Ransom Johnson and Mary Wescott
          Cobbs Dunn of Birmingham
213215221 Mary Beverley Dunn (4/18/1941-   )
213215222 William Ransom Johnson Dunn III (6/17/1943-   )
2133 Dr. Robert Carter Randolph (7/22/1793-4/6/1854), Asst.Surgeon,
      U.S.N., m. 6/12/1826, (his first cousin), Anne Tayloe
      Beverley (3/31/1808-9/15/1889), dau. of Carter and Jane
      Wormeley Beverley, (her first husband was Capt. Benjamin
      Farrar, by whom she had one child, Benjamin Farrar, Jr.).
      Dr. and Mrs. Randolph moved to Greensboro, Ala.
21331 Jane Wormeley Randolph (10/26/1828-d. young)
21332 Richard Randolph (6/17/1830-9/11/1866), m. 3/5/1857, Florence
      Estelle Goffe (1843-6/30/1906), dau. of George and Louisa
      C. Gardner Goffe of Alabama
213321 Robert Carter Randolph (6/11/1858-4/8/1859)
213322 Rittenhouse S. Randolph (1/27/1860-12/27/1862)
213323 Smith Randolph (6/27/1862-d. inf.)
213324 Richard Rutherford Randolph (6/6/1865-   ), m. (1st)
       4/25/1889, Mary Etta King (9/16/1871-8/12/1910), dau. of
       Peyton Griffin and Mary Alabama Tarrant King of Birming-
       ham. M. (2nd) 7/31/1912, Sue Sanderson Blodgett (2/16/
       1888-   ), dau. of Austin and Susan Clark Sanderson
       of Texas
       Children by first wife:
2133241 Helen Rosa Randolph (6/4/1890-   ), m. 4/25/1913,
        Judge Thomas Alexander Murphree (12/1/1883-9/5/1945),
        son of Lindsey Sylvester and Martha Hendricks Murphree
        of Blunt County
21332411 Florence Murphree (5/23/1929-   )
2133242 Richard Rutherford Randolph, Jr. (1/11/1900-   ),
        m. 8/23/1934, Lillian Beverley Fant (2/21/1909-   ),
        dau. of Neuitt and Mary Gaston Smith Fant of Walhalla,
        S.C.
21332421 Richard Rutherford Randolph III (9/7/1939-   )
21332422 John Neuitt Randolph (7/2/1944-   )
2133243 Mary Etta Randolph (11/3/1903-   ), m. 2/5/1923,
        Stephen Beasley Coleman (9/23/1903-   ), son of
        Thomas Wilkes and Carolyn Arnold Beasley Coleman of
        Anniston
21332431 Helen Rose Coleman (11/9/1923-   ), m. 8/31/1945,

James Jackson Monaghan (7/20/1921-   ), son of
Bernard Andrew and Mary Frances Jackson Monaghan of
Birmingham
21332432 Stephen Beasley Coleman, Jr. (8/7/1941-   )
Children by second wife:
2133244 Beverley Randolph (6/21/1915-   ), m. 11/19/1942,
Mary Virginia Bruce (11/14/1921-   ), dau. of Lamar
Earl and Frances Boing Bruce of Dunham
21332441 Shirley Bruce Randolph (9/8/1943-   )
21332442 Lynn Carole Randolph (10/28/1946-   )
2133245 Robert Carter Randolph (9/3/1918-   ), m. Lee
Weaver (2/14/1918-   ), dau. of John B. and
Elizabeth Ray Weaver of Birmingham
21332451 Jean Susan Randolph (6/ /1947-   )
2133246 Nancy Randolph (11/19/1921-   )
21333 Lucy Beverley Randolph (2/ /1834-   ), m. John William
Taylor, son of James Langhorne and Mary Taylor
213331 Anne Randolph Taylor (4/28/1855-   ), m. 11/ /1872,
Dr. Albert Thomas Henley, son of Robert and Eveline Hartwell Henley of Demopolis, Ala.
2133311 Taylor William Henley (1873-1881)
2133312 John Woodson Henley (9/16/1876-   ). Unm.
21334 Robert Carter Randolph, Jr. (5/24/1839-10/3/1898), m. 7/14/
1863, Sarah Julia Pickett (7/13/1843-1/31/1920), dau. of
Col. Albert James and Sarah Smith Harris Pickett of Montgomery, Ala.
213341 Jane Beverley Randolph (6/12/1866-12/19/1938), m. 11/20/
1889, Herbert Paschal Candler (4/6/1858-9/3/1926), son
of Judge Albert T. and Susan Paschal Candler
2133411 Albert Randolph Candler (1/30/1890-5/7/1921), m. 11/12/
1913, Roberta Hails (12/21/1893-   ), dau. of Robert
and Susan Anna Felder Hails of Montgomery
21334111 Albert Randolph Candler, Jr. (9/23/1914-   ), m.
8/7/1946, Louise Blackburn (4/10/1924-   ), dau.
of Clarence Flinn and Lula Waller Blackburn of Ramer,
Ala.
213341111 Susan Blackburn Candler (10/10/1948-   )
21334112 Robert Hails Candler (10/20/1916-   ), m. 10/11/
1939, Nancy Cornelia Sorrell (4/6/1920-   ), dau.
of Franklin Ivan and Julia Carr Sorrell of Monterey,
Mexico
213341121 Robert Hails Candler, Jr. (7/13/1943-   )
213341122 Nancy Randolph Candler (2/27/1947-   )
21334113 Beverley Randolph Candler (1/17/1921-   ), m. 3/14/
1942, Gustave Joseph Rauschenbach, Jr. (2/19/1914-   ),
son of G. J. and Josephine Rauschenbach of Paterson,
N. J.
213341131 Beverley Randolph Rauschenbach (6/30/1947-   )
213341132 Roberta Hails Rauschenbach (10/22/1949-   )
213342 George Coston Randolph (1/20/1869-10/ /1948), m. 11/21/
1911, Katherine Elizabeth Hatch, dau. of Col. Lemuel
Durant and Willie F. (McRae) Hatch of "Ramblers Rest",
Perdido Beach, Ala. No issue.

213343   Sarah Pickett Randolph (10/10/1872-10/14/1915). Unm.
213344   Robert Carter Randolph III (5/21/1883-   ). Unm.
21335   Anne Tayloe Randolph (7/28/1843-   ), m. 2/6/1866,
         Maj. Richard Inge Hill (4/24/1832-1/23/1899), son of
         Gabriel Long and Elizabeth Inge Murphy Hill of Greene
         County, Ala.
213351   Mary Elizabeth Hill (1/10/1867-11/18/1930), m. 10/24/1900,
         William Read Rogan (2/7/1837-4/9/1911), son of Francis
         and Martha Lytle Read Rogan of Rogana, Tenn.
2133511 Clarissa Randolph Rogan (11/22/1901-   ), m. George
         Montroy Ross (8/13/1902-   ), son of George Hubbard
         and Elizabeth Lee Hearn Ross of Colbert County, Ala.
         No issue.
213352   Jennings Murphy Hill (12/10/1868-5/4/1946)
213353   Rittenhouse Moore Hill (11/16/1872-11/23/1890). Unm.
213354   Richard Randolph Hill (1/1/1871-1/10/1944). Unm.
213355   Annie Randolph Hill (10/17/1877-   ). Unm.
213356   Harriet Beverley Hill (11/30/1880-   ). Unm.
21336   Harriet Beverley Randolph, m. Rittenhouse Moore of Mobile
213361   Helen Moore (d. ca. 1944), m. (1st) Captain Thomas. M.
         (2nd) Adm. Mark Bristol, U.S.N., Retired. No issue
213362   Amanda ("Nannie") Moore, m. Dr. Henry Coldwaithe of Panama
         and Mobile. No issue.
213363   Rittenhouse Moore, Jr. (d. after 1945)
21337   (son)(12/25/1840-lived only a few hours)
2134   Richard Randolph (5/20/1795-1/31/1885)
2135   Victor Moreau Randolph (7/24/1797-1/28/1876), Commodore C.S.N.,
         m. 6/20/1825, Augusta Ellen Granbery (5/2/1802-10/4/1839),
         dau. of John and Susanna Butterfield Stowe Granbery of
         Norfolk. Augusta d. in Lowndes County, Mississippi, at
         home of her mother-in-law. Victor and his wife lived in
         Greene County, Alabama
21351   John Granbery Randolph (4/18/1826-8/ /1852). Unm.
21352   Brett Randolph (2/19/1829-1/21/1899), m. 5/11/1858, Emma
         Herndon (1/1/1840-5/4/1913), dau. of Thomas Horde and Emma
         Toulmin Herndon
213521   Augusta Granbery Randolph (7/25/1859-1/28/1941), m. 10/2/
         1878, at Blount Springs, John Bradley Reid (10/ /1848-
         9/27/1918), son of Rufus and Anne Perry Reid of Marion,
         Ala.
2135211 Emma Toulmin Reid (8/21/1881-   ), m. 12/19/1905,
         Henry Scudder Ryall (11/23/1875-   ), son of Henry
         Clay and Frances Bomar Ryall of Shelbyville, Tenn.
21352111 Henry Scudder Ryall, Jr. (7/4/1907-   ), m. 9/1/
         1929, Hazel Sawyer (12/19/1907-   ), dau. of
         Clayton Charles and Adelaide Forest Sawyer of Waycross,
         Ga.
213521111 Adelaide Ryall (1/29/1931-   )
213521112 Ann Reid Ryall (12/18/1933-   )
21352112 James Bomar Ryall (8/20/1910-   ), m. 7/12/1941,
         Imogene Walker Hinton (4/16/1916-   ), dau.
         Leonard Walker and Lula Emaline Byrd Hinton of Arkansas
213521121 James Bomar Ryall, Jr. (12/19/1942-   )
213521122 Emma Scudder Ryall (11/25/1945-   )

21352113 John Reid Ryall (12/2/1912-   ), m. 12/10/1938,
          Mary Hardy (7/21/1910-   ), dau. of Hugh Miles
          and Claudia Rives Hardy of Pleasant Hill, Ala.
213521131 Mary Reid Ryall (5/10/1940-   )
2135212   Anne Perry Reid (9/27/1883-6/12/1912), m. 6/5/1907, Dr.
          John Wade Watts (1880-8/9/1946), son of Thomas H. Watts
          and Jomice Eddin Watts of Montgomery, Ala.
21352121 Jane Watts (6/12/1912-6/12/1912)
2135213   Augusta Randolph Reid (11/11/1885-   ), m. 9/7/1909,
          William Lee Roueche (4/27/1881-   ), son of William
          Henry and Caroline Strong Lee Roueche of Marietta
21352131 William Lee Roueche, Jr. (11/11/1910-   )
21352132 Augusta Randolph Roueche (12/18/1912-   ), m. 6/8/
          1935, Arthua C. Parker III (9/22/1909-   ), son
          of Arthur C. II and Susie Bell Parker of Memphis. No
          issue
21352133 Caroline Strong Roueche (9/13/1915-   ), m. 6/12/
          1937, Robert Leroy Hume (7/2/1909-   ), son of
          Frederick LeRoy and Blanche Goodnow Hume of Birmingham
213521331 Caroline Lee Hume (11/4/1941-   )
21352134 John Reid Roueche (8/16/1917-   ). Unm.
21352135 Brett Emmett Roueche(5/26/1924-   )
2135214   Brett Randolph Reid (7/1/1888-10/21/1969), m. 10/24/1910,
          Rufus Absolom Russell (10/29/1878-1/8/1944), son of Rufus
          Alanson and Nancy Tyson Russell of Florida
21352141 Anne Reid Russell (6/17/1912-   ), m. 4/19/1938,
          Edwin Joseph Greenhalgh (2/28/1911-   ), son of
          Edwin and Evelyn Benners Greenhalgh of Birmingham
213521411 Thomas Edwin Greenhalgh (1/22/1942-   )
213521412 Russell Joseph Greenhalgh (1/13/1947-   )
21352142 Rufus Augustus Russell (5/9/1915-   ), m. 12/ /
          1942, Bernice Garvey (7/ /1905-   ), dau. of
                     and Nadine Carter Garvey of Louisiana; m.
          (2nd) 1/24/1959, Dorothy Greenleaf
213521421 Nadine Carter Russell (10/5/1943-   )
21352143 Herndon Brett Russell (8/3/1919-   ), m. Margaret
          Eppely
213521431 Brenda Anne Russell (4/13/1950-   )
213521432 Don Randolph Russell (5/31/1951-   )
213521433 Scott Reid Russell (5/22/1953-   )
2135215   John Bryan Reid (9/27/1895-   ), m. (1st) Ione
          Harrison, dau. of George Edward and Kate Odom Harrison
          of Birmingham. M. (2nd) 6/13/1941, Madelon Calais (3/
          23/1903-   ). No issue
          Children by first wife:
21352151 John Bryan Reid, Jr. (12/28/1918-   ), m. 5/2/
          1942, Virginia Ann Richardson (5/1/1919-   ),
          dau. of Charles Ritter and Mabel Frances Clarke Richard,
          son of Pittsburgh. No issue
21352152 George Harrison Reid (5/23/1926-   ). Unm.
2135216   Oliver Fowlkes Reid (9/24/1898-   ), m. 7/12/1924,
          Byrd Taliaferro Conway (12/23/1903-   ), dau. of
          Alfred Taliaferro and Elizabeth LeRoy Hart Conway of
          Athens and Atlanta, Ga.
21352161 Robin LeRoy Reid (4/23/1923-   )

21352162 Anne Randolph Reid (4/23/1931-   )
213522 John Randolph (9/6/1861-6/8/1935), m. 11/10/1891, Margaret
        Lillian ("Maggie")Bell (12/30/1868-3/3/1895), dau. of
        William and Phedora Harris Bell. Home: Montgomery, Ala.
2135221 Phedora Randolph (8/23/1892-   ), m. 10/1/1913,
        Peter M. Nicrosi (3/16/1888-5/8/1944), son of John
        Baptiste and Jennie Kelly Nicrosi
21352211 Margaret Randolph Nicrosi (12/23/1914-   ). Unm.
21352212 John Baptiste Nicrosi II (12/22/1916-   ), m.
        11/27/1943, Frances Manning Sledge (9/14/1918-   ),
        dau. of Walter Kells and Evelyn Lock Parker Sledge of
        Montgomery
2135222 Jule Thweatt Randolph (12/11/1893-   )
2135223 John Brett Randolph (1/6/1895-   )
213523 Brett Randolph, Jr. (10/5/1863-12/14/1864)
213524 Emma Randolph (3/7/1866-   ), m. 1/21/1890, in Bir-
        mingham, William Clarence Agee (7/5/1858-12/17/1924), son
        of Noah Alfred and Caroline Forney Hunley Agee
2135241 Lucy Randolph Agee (7/3/1893-   ), m. 11/18/1914,
        James Graham Melvin (9/13/1889-   ), son of Stewart
        Bishop and Mary Martha Tillman Melvin of Selma
21352411 Comdr. Clarence Agee Melvin, U.S.N. (1/30/1916-   ),
        m. 6/5/1940, Emily Louise Tilley (4/26/1921-   ),
        dau. of Comdr. Benjamin Franklin, U.S.N., and Harriet
        Buchanan Tilley
213524111 Emily Agee Melvin (5/3/1941-   )
213524112 John Tillman Melvin III (1/12/1946-   )
21352412 Claude Mallory (dau.) Melvin (1/20/1918-   ), m.
        7/24/1942, David Reynolds Pruet (2/6/1918-   ), son
        of David C. and Gertrude Reynolds Pruet of Sylacauga, Ala.
21352413 John Tillman Melvin II (5/15/1924-9/7/1944). Killed in
        W.W.2 (B24 in which he was gunner collided with another
        B24 in Massachusetts).
2135242 Ann Hunley (Hundly?) Agee (12/18/1894-   ), m. 10/25/
        1916, Eugene Perrin Elebash (7/18/1893-2/5/1946), son of
        LeGrand Charles and Margaret Stilt Elebash of Selma
21352421 Emma Randolph Elebash (8/31/1917-   ), m. 7/31/1942,
        Edward Hunter Hurst (12/18/1916-   ), son of Samuel
        Thomas Hurst and Jule Brown Hunter Hurst of Fort Valley,Ga.
213524211 Ann Randolph Hurst (3/21/1943-   )
213525212 Jean Perrin Hurst (6/13/1946-   )
21352422 Eugene Perrin Elebash, Jr. (5/13/1920-   ), m. 10/24/
        1942, Jane Cornelia Nobles (4/8/1921-   ), dau. of
        Dr. William Daniel and Claude Coles Crockett Nobles of
        Pensacola
213524221 Eugene Perrin Elebash III (2/4/1945-   )
21352423 Hunley (Hundly?) Agee Elebash (7/27/1923-   )
21352424 Clarence Couch Elebash (10/23/1925-   )
2135243 Emma Herndon Agee (9/9/1900-   ), m. 4/4/1923, William
        Watkins Vaughan (12/11/1899-   ), son of Watkins
        Mabry and Erin Lockhart Osborn Vaughan of Selma
21352431 Herndon Vaughan (10/23/1925-   )
21352432 Erin Lockhart Vaughan (4/29/1933-   )

2135244 William Clarence Agee, Jr. (7/22/1902-4/22/1943), m.
         5/8/1923, Faye Orlena Seale (7/17/1901-   ), dau. of
         Steven Farmer and Molly Farish Seale of Selma
21352441 Faye Seale Agee (12/4/1923-   ). Unm.
213525 Lucy Virginia Randolph (2/23/1869-7/17/1894). Unm.
213526 Herndon Randolph (3/20/1871-7/2/1871)
213527 Fannie Toulmin Randolph (9/18/1874-   ), m. 7/5/1899,
         John Phillips Evans (10/12/1875-1/26/1918), son of George
         Alexander and Emily Phillips Evans of Columbus and
         Birmingham
2135271 Randolph Evans (4/17/1901-   ), m. 11/1/1924, Mintor
         ("Noona") Peyton Bibb (11/23/1902-   ), dau. of
         Walter and Florence Spiers Bibb of Millbrook, Ala.
21352711 Florence Bibb Evans (4/1/1934-   )
21352712 Ann Randolph Evans (2/11/1938-   )
21352713 Peyton Bibb Evans (8/27/1939-   )
21352714 Randolph Evans, Jr. (9/4/1945-   )
2135272 Richard Stanton Evans (5/17/1905-   ), m. 3/4/1935,
         Nancy Heidelburg Foote (4/14/1909-   ), dau. of
         Thomas M. and Clara Buskin Foote of Mississippi. No issue
2135273 Frances Randolph Evans (4/2/1914-   ), m. 2/2/1936,
         Alexander VanHoose Davies (9/18/1909-   ), son of
         William Allen George and Anna VanHoose Davies of Birmingham
21352731 Frances Beverley Davies (4/26/1940-   )
213528 Tremlet Herndon Randolph (5/4/1876-3/ /1901), m. 9/21/
         1897, Chester Francis Mattison (5/6/1876-2/6/1911), son of
         John Lafayetteand Elizabeth Sproull Mattison of Jacksonville
2135281 Emma Agee Mattison (8/30/1898-   ), m. 6/28/1922,
         Robert Lee Lott, Jr. (5/15/1901-   ), son of Robert
         Lee Lott of Birmingham
21352811 Robert Lee Lott III (5/29/1927-   )
21352812 Nancy Bowling Lott (11/7/1931-   )
213529 Virginia Meade Randolph (5/14/1881-8/11/1914), m. 6/17/
         1903, Hugh Culverhouse McIlwain (8/3/1877-   ), son
         of Samuel Pinckney and Mary Ann Culverhouse McIlwain of
         Alabama
2135291 Hugh Herndon McIlwain (8/3/1904-   )
2135292 Virginia Randolph McIlwain (4/11/1905-   ), son of
         John Stanley and Mary Ella Chapman Frazer of Alabama.
         No issue
21353   Col. Edward Ryland Randolph (10/28/1835-5/6/1903), C.S.A.,
         m. 2/2/1870, Kate Withers (-1901)
213531 Ryland Randolph (1872-10/3/1906), m.
2135311 Ormond Randolph (supposed lost at sea)
213532 Victor Moreau Randolph II (9/17/1877-   ), m. Grace
         Mattie Burwell
2135321 Victor Moreau Randolph III (7/28/1910-   ), m. 5/
         29/1936, Olive Henkel (1/9/1911-   ), dau. of
         James Oliver and Helen Isla Huggins Henkel of Crawford,
         Miss.
21353211 Victor Moreau Randolph IV (7/25/1942-   )
21353212 James Ryland Randolph (5/31/1944-   )
2136   John Thomson Randolph (1/27/1800-8/23/1819)
2137   Benjamin Franklin Randolph (7/27/1801-9/8/1802)

2138 Benjamin Franklin Randolph (2/2/1803-7/15/1890), m. 2/10/
      1829, (his first cousin), Anna Page Corbin (6/13/1803-7/
      28/1885), dau. of Francis and Anna Munford Beverley Corbin
      of "The Reeds"
21381 Anna Munford Randolph (1/19/1835-11/18/1842)
21382 Lucy Randolph, d. age 3 or 4 yrs.
21383 Maria Randolph, d. inf.
21384 Capt. Edward Brett Randolph (3/5/1837-7/1/1904), C.S.A.,
      m. (1st) 12/14/1858, Corinne Albert Pickett (2/15/1839-
      1867), dau. of Albert James and Sarah Smith Harris Pickett
      of Montgomery. M. (2nd) Mary Sayre (11/16/1847-4/23/1913)
      Children by first wife:
213841 Edward Brett Randolph, Jr., d. inf.
213842 Corinne Pickett Randolph (1867-3/25/1890), m. 11/5/1889,
      Loderick ("Larry") W. Dimick (Dimmock?) of Sheffield,
      Ala. Div. No issue
      Children by second wife:
213843 Carolyn Sayre Randolph (10/12/1874-   ). Unm.
213844 Lucy Beverley Randolph (8/15/1876-   ). Unm.
21385 Maj. Francis Corbin Randolph (12/6/1839-5/24/1905), C.S.A.,
      m. 12/6/1866, Sarah Tayloe Nicolson (2/19/1846-7/ /1926),
      dau. of Robert Wormeley and Mary Ann Shearer Nicolson of
      Uniontown, Ala.
213851 Mary Nicolson Randolph (11/27/1867-3/24/1926), m. (1st)
      Dr. James Reed Jordan (-3/ /1897). No issue.
      M. (2nd) 8/3/1915, Christopher Claude Cobbs (8/23/1863-
      3/8/1937), son of John Lewis Cobbs and Dorothy (Piques
      or Pegeas) Cobbs. No issue
213852 Anne Page Randolph (12/5/1869-   ), m. 6/4/1895,
      Cecil Howard Willcox (12/31/1865-4/24/1917), son of
      Cyprian Porter and Mary Frances Smythe Willcox of
      Athens, Ga.
2138521 Eleanor Randolph Willcox (9/3/1896-   ), m. 1/12/
      1918, Capt. Walter Fossine Coachman, Jr.
21385211 Anne Page Coachman (3/8/1920-   )
213853 Eleanor Wormeley Randolph (4/10/1871-8/25/1892), m. 12/1/
      1891, Francis Avery Cobbs (1867-8/11/1938), son of Richard
      Hooker and Frances Avery Cobbs of Greensboro. No issue
213854 Sallie Cary Randolph (12/29/1873-12/1/1874)
213855 Elizabeth Bland Randolph (2/16/1876-5/4/1890)
213856 Evelyn Byrd Randolph (7/9/1878-6/2/1940), m. 12/10/1902,
      Harris Russell Willcox (12/10/1862-   ), son of
      Cyprian Porter and Mary Frances Smythe Willcox
2138561 Harris Russell Willcox, Jr. (8/5/1904-6/23/1913)
213857 Emily Nicolson Randolph (9/13/1880-   ), m. 12/3/1903,
      William Livingston Stewart (5/20/1877-3/12/1938), son of
      Arthur Sidney and Mary Jane Clark Stewart of Montgomery.
      No issue
213858 Francis Corbin Randolph, Jr. (9/3/1882-   ), m. 12/7/
      1915, (he was her second husband), Laura Elmore Fitz-
      patrick (1879-   ), dau. of Maj. John and Emma Fitz-
      patrick of Elmore, Ala. No issue

2139 Ryland Randolph (7/29/1805-6/9/1833), died of cholera at
    Lexington, Ky. Unm.
213x Theodorick Beverley Randolph (7/1/1807-   ), m. 7/ /1852,
    in Greensboro, Ala., Sarah Brand (1/6/1830-1/29/1877)
213x1 Lucy Meade Randolph (9/27/1853-12/22/1855)
213x2 Dr. John Randolph (druggist) (7/10/1855-3/12/1891), m.
    10/16/1879, Catherine Erwin Jones (8/16/1856-4/23/1897),
    dau. of Allen Cadwallader and Catherine Erwin Jones of
    Greensboro
213x21 Sarah Randolph (10/28/1880-   ), m. 11/30/1910, James
    Washington Otts (10/16/1878-9/17/1937), son of Dr. J.N.D.
    and Lelia McCrary Otts. No issue
213x22 Catherine Erwin Randolph (5/16/1882-   ), m. 4/3/
    1907, Thomas Hamilton Jones (12/19/1877-2/28/1934), son
    of Madison and Alice McLean Jones of Greensboro. No issue
213x23 Julia Jones Randolph (12/16/1884-   ). Unm.
213x3 Meade Randolph (8/5/1857-8/28/1858)
213x4 Lee Randolph. Unm.
213x5 Theodorick (dau.) Bland Randolph, m.   No issue
213x6 Edward Brett Randolph (12/24/1865-12/4/1901), m. 12/12/
    1889, Mary Louise Stickney (10/18/1866-   ), dau.
    of Charles Lefebore Stickney and Eurretta Blair Bannister
    of Greensbori, Ala. No issue. She m. (2nd) Leo T. Randolph
213x7 William Randolph. Unm.
213x8 Maria Withers Randolph (5/31/1872-   ), m. 2/20/1894,
    Thomas Volney Boardman (1/10/1872-4/10/1922), son of Henry
    and Carrie Osborn Boardman
213x81 Carolyn Osborn Boardman (8/28/1896-   ), m. C.C.
    McDonnell
213x811 Sarah Randolph McDonnell, m. Capt. Robert Kratz of Norris-
    town, Pa.
213x82 Bland Randolph Boardman (3/10/1900-   ), m. 6/17/
    1924, Dudley Chipley Thornton (9/26/1886-   ), son
    of Harry Hyer and Isabella Knowles Thornton of Pensacola
213x821 Margaret Knowles Thornton (9/21/1927-   )
213x83 Margaret Earle Boardman (5/24/1902-   ), m. Joseph
    Utley MacKethan, son of Alfred Augustus MacKethan of
    Fayetteville, NC
213x84 Thomas Volney Boardman (12/2/1904-   ), m. 9/29/
    1927, Dorothy Moore Cochran (3/13/1901-   ), dau. of
    Negley Dakin and Nettie Belle Moore Cochran of Toledo
213x841 Thomas Volney Boardman, Jr. (12/20/1930-   )
213x842 John Randolph Boardman (8/20/1933-   )
213x843 Sally Cochran Boardman (2/22/1938-   )
213a Ann Maria Randolph (3/2/1811-7/20/1845). Unm.
214 Ryland Randolph (3/5/1770-1815), m. 7/7/1795, in Halifax,
    N.C., Elizabeth Frazier (Fraser?)
2141 Ryland Randolph
21411
2142 (dau)
21421
215 Susan Randolph (4/10/1753-11 or 12/3/1781), m. 4/6/1776,

Benjamin Harrison, Jr. (VI), of "Berkeley" (-1799),
son of Benjamin (V) (ca. 1740-1791)(the Signer) and Elizabeth
Bassett Harrison. No issue. Susan was the second wife,
the first wife (m. 1785), Anna Mercer (9/6/1760-8/28/1787),
died eight days after the birth of her son, Benjamin Harrison
(VII), the only child of Benjamin Harrison, Jr. (VI).

216 Jane Randolph (11/19/1755-3/ /1796), m. 10/1/1774, Archibald
Bolling of Buckingham County (3/20/1749-   ), son of
John and Elizabeth Blair Bolling. For children see (16).
Jane was Archibald's second wife

217 Ann Randolph (2/21/1764-1/ /1820), m. 5/12/1782, Brett
Randolph, Jr. (222)

218 Elizabeth ("Betty") Randolph (3/8/1768-   ), m. 2/28/
1789, David Meade of "Woodland", son of David and Susanna
Everard Meade

2181 John Everard Meade (7/16/1792-12/27/1854), m. Rebecca Wormeley Beverley (9/4/1803-1/5/1867), dau. of Carter and Jane
Wormeley Beverley of "Cedar Level", Prince George County

21811 Elizabeth Randolph ("Bessie") Meade (9/4/1831-11/11/1912),
m. 11/8/1855, David Callendar (5/5/1831-7/28/1910), of
Petersburg, formerly of Glasgow, Scotland, son of Thomas
and Margaret Ormiston Callendar

218111 Thomas Meade Callendar (10/13/1856-6/25/1922), m. 10/8/
1884, Bessie Haskins Wills (10/15/1861-10/29/1943), dau.
of Henry Wirt and Ella Rose Garland Wills

2181111 David Callendar (3/27/1886-2/3/1914). Unm.

2181112 Ella Garland Callendar (2/8/1888-   ), m. 2/6/1920,
William Judson Moore (3/17/1881-   ), son of Henry
Lewis and Alice Rose Wynn Moore

21811121 William Judson Moore, Jr. (7/30/1926-2/4/1934)

21811122 Thomas Callendar Moore (1/10/1929-   )

2181113 Henry Wills Callendar (9/10/1890-10/27/1911). Unm.

2181114 Bessie Wills Callendar (9/15/1894-   ). Unm.

218112 Margaret Beverley (Meade?) Callendar (4/20/1859-   ),
m. 6/25/1889, Dr. John Kinnier Patterson (3/16/1839-2/20/
1905)

2181121 Bessie Meade Patterson (3/31/1892-1916), m. 4/18/1911,
Robert McIlwaine Friend (1113261)(8/26/1876-1968), son
of John Wesley and Hibernia McIlwaine Friend. For their
children, etc., see 1113261

21811211 Bessie Meade Friend (8/6/1912-   ), m. 7/8/1939,
Francis Elmer Drake (10/13/1908-   ), son of
Clarence Elmer and Annie Vann Lewis Drake

218112111 Francis Elmer Drake, Jr. (6/10/1941-   )

218112112 Elizabeth Randolph Meade Drake (3/11/1943-   )

21811212 Margaret Patterson Friend (10/29/1913-   ), m. 10/
29/1942, Rev. William David Stewart (10/5/1913-   ),
son of William Weldon Thompson and Ada Parks Clotfelter
Stewart. No issue

218113 Lottie Ruffin Callendar (2/14/1861-3/18/1861)

218114 Charlotte Ruffin (Meade?) Callendar (12/25/1862-   ),
m. 8/26/1884, Charles Hodges Constable (2/16/1856-2/18/
1906), son of William Stephenson and Hansen Hodges Constable

2181141   Eleanor Beverley Constable (10/8/1886-   ), m. 6/16/
        1908, William Preston Hoy (2/12/1876-3/23/1927), son of
        Patrick Crawford and Nannie Elizabeth Jackson Hoy
21811411 William Preston Hoy, Jr. (3/18/1909-9/30/1932). Unm.
21811412 Charlotte Beverley Hoy (10/9/1913-   ), m. 5/25/
        1938, Rev. Boyd Roberts Howarth (5/3/1910-   ),
        son of Boyd Jefferson and Grace Roberts Dixon Howarth
218114121 Beverley Roberts (son) Howarth (2/3/1944-   )
2181142 William Reginald Constable (10/3/1900-10/9/1900)
2181143 Frances Hansen Constable (11/22/1901-12/27/1915)
2181144 Charles Hodges Constable (5/10/1904-6/12/1904)
218115   John Meade Callendar (8/20/1865-   ). Unm.
218116   David Meade Callendar (6/6/1870-1/17/1941), m. 7/29/1908,
        Loulie Anderson (12/17/18 -   ), dau. of Clifford
        Combrelling and Mary Corinne Cannon Anderson. No issue
21812 Charlotte Stockdale Meade (5/23/1833-3/24/1918), m. 5/26/
        1852, Sgt. Julian Calx Ruffin, CSA (7/14/1821-5/16/1864),
        son of Edmund and Susan Travis Ruffin of Prince George
        County. He was killed in action at Drury's Bluff. Home:
        "Ruthven", Prince George County
218121   Julian Meade Ruffin (5/7/1853-11/11/1938), m. 7/19/1887,
        Mary Ruffin (1/21/1869-11/16/1938), dau. of Charles
        Lorraine and Henrietta Harrison Ruffin. The Julian
        Meade Ruffins lived at "Marlbourne", Hanover County
2181211 Hester ("Hettie") Ruffin (6/9/1888-4/8/1907). Died of
        typhoid fever. Unm.
2181212 Charlotte ("Lottie") Meade Ruffin (12/26/1890-   ),
        m. 6/25/1912, Dr. Luther Hepburn Apperson (5/31/1890-
        ), son of James Robert and Mary Virginia
        Lipscomb Apperson
21812121 Julian Ruffin Apperson (5/17/1914-   ), m. 1940,
        Rachel Bracken
218121211 Julian Ruffin Apperson, Jr. (1/1/1941-   )
218121212 Adrianna Meade Apperson (5/19/1944-   )
218121213 James Ward Apperson (1947-1948)
21812122 Mary Meade Apperson (4/10/1917-   ), m. Robert
        Linwood Powell
218121221 Beverley Meade Powell (2/19/1944-   )
218121222 Robert Linwood Powell, Jr. (1945-   )
2181213 Julian Meade Ruffin, Jr. (7/13/1892-   ), m. 6/6/
        1931, Lois Miller Gayle (9/4/1899-   ), dau. of
        Seth and Attie Broaddus Gayle
21812131 Lois Gayle Ruffin (7/28/1932-   )
21812132 Marion Bruce Ruffin (11/18/1934-   )
21812133 Jane Beverley Ruffin (12/4/1937-   )
2181214 Mary Beverley Ruffin (12/27/1893-   ). Unm.
2181215 Jane Skipwith Ruffin (4/25/1895-10/5/1895)
2181216 Elizabeth Randolph Ruffin (5/29/1896-10/30/1906). Died
        of typhoid fever
2181217 Jane Skipwith Ruffin (1/20/1898-   ). Unm.
2181218 Charles Lorraine (dau) Ruffin (3/22/1899-   ), m.
        10/20/1925, George Wright, Jr. (11/30/1894-1946), son of
        George and Loulie Brooke Evans Wright

```
21812181   George Wright III (2/8/1928-          )
21812182   Julian Meade Wright (5/3/1930-        )
21812183   Charlotte Lorraine Wright (8/2/1935-        )
2181219    Virginia Powell Ruffin (8/3/1901-          ), m. 8/27/
           1932, John Elmo Cowles, son of Charles Miles and Elizabeth
           Waterman Cowles
21812191   Mary Ruffin Cowles (9/27/1933-        )
21812192   Virginia Powell Cowles (3/24/1935-        )
218121x    Edmund Sumter Ruffin (12/13/1902-7/13/1903), d.s.p.
218121a    John James Ruffin (1/12/1909-          ), m. 10/15/1932,
           May Langhorne Puller (9/15/1909-          ), dau. of Tribble
           Meredith and Mary Austin Timberlake Puller
218121a1   John James Ruffin, Jr. (12/3/1934-        )
218121a2   Elizabeth Randolph Ruffin (4/14/1939-        )
218121a3   Julian Meade Ruffin (1946-        )
218122     Jane Ruffin (10/29/1856-4/16/1944). Unm.
218123     Bessie Callendar Ruffin (5/19/1859-2/7/1941), m. 4/24/1889,
           Roland Faulconer Broaddus (2/5/1856-12/4/1914), son of
           Alexander Woodford and Fanny Ellen Croxton Broaddus
2181231    Roland Ruffin Broaddus (2/28/1890-3/18/1906)
2181232    Louise Everard Broaddus (5/15/1894-          ), m. 3/6/1918,
           Harry Edgar Miller (7/7/1893-          ), son of Joseph
           Medford and            Edwards Miller
21812321   Roland Broaddus Miller (12/8/1918-        )
21812322   Elizabeth Whiteman Miller (12/18/1920-        )
21812323   Harry Edgar Miller (11/24/1922-        )
21812324   Bessie Ruffin Miller (5/8/1935-        )
2181233    Alexander Woodford Broaddus (3/10/1897-          ), m. 10/
           24/1936, Jane Elizabeth Campbell (1/24/1909-        ), dau.
           of Dr. Walker Aylett and Rose Campbell Tilghman Campbell
21812331   Woodford Meade Broaddus (8/3/1937-        )
21812332   David Tilghman Broaddus (3/12/1943-        )
218124     Edmund Sumter Ruffin (4/19/1861-          ), m. 4/30/1895,
           Cordelia Willing Waller (9/8/1868-          ), dau. of
           Richard Willing and Jane Brodnax deJarnette Byrd of
           Norfolk, and widow of Dr. William Cary Judson Waller
2181241    Edmund Sumter Ruffin, Jr. (5/29/1896-          ), m. 4/17/
           1926, Jennie Morrison Brooke (7/17/1900-          ), dau.
           of William Throckmorton and Mary Goode Brooke
21812411   Jean Morrison Ruffin (1/18/1927-        )
21812412   Cordelia Byrd Ruffin (5/28/1929-        )
21812413   Edmund Sumter Ruffin III (3/6/1934-        )
2181242    Jane Byrd Ruffin (7/22/1897-          ), m. 4/30/1918,
           Reginald Buchanan Henry, M.D., U.S.N. (5/23/1881-        ),
           son of James Buchanan and Louisa Anderson Henry
21812421   Evelyn Byrd Henry (2/21/1919-          ), m. 9/14/1946,
           George Harris Sargeant, Jr. (7/1/1912-          ), son of
           George Harris and Evelyn Byrd Trigg Sargeant of Norfolk
218124211  Evelyn Byrd Sargeant (8/1/1948-        )
218124212  Jane Byrd Sargeant (9/17/1949-        )
21812422   Reginald Buchanan Henry, Jr. (7/18/1926-        )
2181243    Richard Willing Bryd Ruffin (10/27/1898-          ), m.
```

4/18/1931, Eleanor Randolph Garnett (2/2/1909-   ),
dau. of Theodore Stanford and Eleanor Randolph Garnett
21812431 Eleanor Randolph Ruffin (5/13/1933-   )
21812432 Cordelia Byrd Ruffin (5/11/1937-   )
21812433 Lelia Garnett Ruffin (3/1/1942-   )
2181244 Julian Meade Ruffin (8/26/1900-   ), M.D., m. 6/22/
1929, Lucy Landon Noland (10/4/1903-   ), dau. of
Fenton and Lucy Landon Cooke Noland
21812441 Lucy Landon Ruffin (11/24/1930-   )
21812442 Jane Byrd Ruffin (5/11/1932-   )
21812443 Judith Meade Ruffin (9/10/1935-   )
2181245 Cordelia Byrd Ruffin (2/25/1904-   ), m. 2/18/1928,
Thomas Johnson Michie, Jr., son of Thomas Johnson and
Emily Hewson Michie
21812451 Cordelia Ruffin Michie (6/21/1929-   )
21812452 Thomas Johnson Michie III (6/12/1931-   )
21812453 Emily Hewson Michie (1/13/1938-   )
2181246 Robert deJarnette Ruffin (6/2/1908-   ),m. 9/1/1937,
Mary Elizabeth Nixon (8/20/1908-   ), dau. of
Robert and Winifred Smith Nixon
21812461 Mary Nixon Ruffin (5/1/1939-   )
21812462 Robert deJarnette Ruffin, Jr. (1/2/1941-   )
21812463 Richard Willing Byrd Ruffin (8/3/1942-   )
218125 Rebecca Beverley Ruffin (11/19/1863-   ), m. 6/14/1905,
Henry Harrison Christian (6/18/1851-4/22/1929), son of
Dr. William Albert and Anna Martha Harrison Christian
2181251 Charlotte Meade Christian (4/24/1906-   ), m. 11/8/
1941, Beverley Kennon Patton (9/20/1904-   ), son
of James Boyd and May Beverley Williams Patton
21812511 Rebecca Beverley Patton (1947-   )
21813 Eleanor Beverley ("Nellie") Meade (12/18/1834-1/18/1867), m.
6/23/1857, Rev. William Henry Platt, D.D., of Petersburg.
She was his second wife. His first wife, by whom he had
three children, was Cornelia Cuthbert of Mobile. He m.
(3rd) Indiana Meade, by whom he had one child.
218131 Cornelia Gholsen Platt (01/5/1944), m. Andrew
Wesley Kent
218132 John Meade Platt (12/2/1862-   ), m. 1923, Lama Holt
(1873-   ), dau. of George Taylor and Josephine Fox
Holt. No issue
21814 Carter Randolph Meade (11/9/1836-6/24/1837)
21815 Jane Wormeley Meade (4/15/1838-6/24/1839)
21816 John Everard Meade, Jr. (3/16/1841-12/31/1862). Died of
pneumonia during the Civil War. Unm.
2182 Mary Thornton Meade
2183 Anne Charlotte Meade, m. 2/12/1818, Dr. John Y. Stockdell
(1797-ca. 9/ /1840), d. in his 49th year
21831 Mary Thornton Stockdell (1821-   ), m. William Allen
Harrison
218311 Anna Harrison, m. Edward Cunningham Harrison (2424135)
218312 Charlotte Harrison
218313 William Harrison, m. Lelia Sweeney

```
2183131  William A. Harrison
2183132  Clara H. Harrison
218314   Virginia Harrison
218315   John Harrison
218316   Carter Harrison, m. Clara Sweeney
218317   Robert Harrison
21832    John Meade Stockdell (1819-        )
21833    William Everard Stockdell (1824-      )
21834    Ryland Randolph Stockdell (1826-      )
21835    (son)
21836    (son)
21837    Elizabeth Rebecca Stockdell (1820-        )
21838    Charlotte Stockdell (1823-      )
21839    (dau)
2183x    (dau)
2183a    (dau)
2184   Rebecca Meade, m. James Lea
21841    (son) Killed 6/6/1840 at age of 10.  Run over by train
21842    (son)
21843    (son)
21844    (dau)
21845    (dau)
21846    (dau)
2185   (son)
2186   (son)
2187   (son)
2188   (son)
2189   (son)
218x   (son)
```

219 Mary Randolph (7/5/1774-8/8/1863), m. 2/24/1798 (her second
cousin), Col. William Bolling (113)(5/26/1777-7/16/1845),
son of Thomas and Elizabeth Gay Bolling. He owned farms
known as "Pocahontas" and "Ware's". First lived at "Cobbs"
(where he was born), then at "Bolling Hall", Goochland
County. "Pocahontas" was part of the "Bolling Hall" tract,
and in 1836, was given to daughter Ann, and the house (no
longer standing) was built for her. "Ware's" became the
"Bolling Island" house, and was lived in by William after
his marriage (his family gave him "Bolling Island").

2191 Anne Meade Bolling (1804-4/29/1845), m. 8/4/1824, in Goochland County, Joseph Kendall Weisiger (ca. 1801-1/19/1878)
(b. Chesterfield County, d. Manchester, Va.), son of Daniel
and Sarah Branch Weisiger. The Joseph Kendall Weisigers
lived early in their married life at "Bolling Island", and
later at "Pocahontas", both in Goochland County. Still
later, he lived in Richmond, and he m. (2nd) 12/24/1846,
in Northampton County, Mrs. Catherine Jones, widow of John
W. Jones

21911 Mary Randolph Weisiger (6/20/1825-1/15/1898), m. 10/6/1845,
in Goochland County, Charles D. McIndoe (11/17/1821-12/8/
1891). Lived at "Moldavia" (at 5th & Main Streets) in
Richmond. Both bur. Hollywood Cemetery, Richmond

219111   (son), m. Ann Bolling
219112   Charles D. McIndoe, Jr., m. Mary Randolph
219113   Joseph McIndoe
219114   Jane Rolfe McIndoe, m. Maurice Norvell Langhorne
2191141   Charles Maurice Langhorne of Richmond, m. 8/12/1905, Mary
          Louise Alexander (-8/3/1906)
21911411 Charles Maurice Langhorne, Jr. (8/3/1906-8/4/1906) twin
21911412 Louise Langhorne (8/3/1906-   ) twin
219115   Junius Randolph McIndoe, d. 9/9/1858, when about 2 years old
219116   Alice Royall McIndoe
219117   Ann Meade McIndoe (-5/5/1882), m. Rufus Sarvay
21912   Junius Kendall Weisiger (1827-4/22/1869), served in Ellett's
          and Crenshaw's Regiments, C.S.A.
21913   William Bolling Weisiger (9/18/1829-9/20/1911)(b. "Bolling
          Hall", Goochland County, d. in Memphis), m. 2/13/1851,
          Sarah ("Sally") Nelson Anderson (2/14/1831-4/18/1913), dau.
          of Benjamin Boynton and Mary Burdette Nelson Anderson of
          "Fairfield", Goochland County
219131   William Bolling Weisiger, Jr. (-12/25/1917), m.
          10/22/1874, in Memphis, Ann Brown
219132   Cary Nelson Weisiger (11/2/1856-1947)(b. Goochland County),
          m. 5/5/1881, Elizabeth Hughes Humphreys (1854-1937), of
          Clarksville, Tenn., dau. of Robert West and Mary Walton
          Meriwether Humphreys
2191321   Cary Nelson Weisiger, Jr. (1/22/1882-6/3/1965)(b. Memphis,
          d. Charlottesville, Va.), m. 5/ /1906, Mary Louise Little
          (11/1/1884-   )(b. New York), dau. of William Cyrus
          and Mary R. Senior Little
21913211 Margaret Page Weisiger (11/26/1907-   )(b. St. Louis),
          m. 1935, Rev. Harry Evans Proctor (11/29/1905-4/ /1979)
          (b. Wilmington, Delaware, d. Arlington, Va.)
219132111 Ernest William Proctor II (12/26/1936-   )(b. New
          Haven, Conn.), m. 4/ /1961, Judith C. Ross
2191321111
2191321112
2191321113
2191321114
2191321115
219132112 Sarah Nelson Proctor (6/13/1939-   )(b. Washington,
          D.C.), m. 7/ /1959, George Henry Brannan, Jr.
2191321121
2191321122
2191321123
2191321124
219132113 Margaret Page Proctor (6/29/1943-   )(b. Washington,
          D.C.), m. 3/ /1968, Timothy P. Hagan
2191321131
2191321132
2191321133
219132114 Mary Stewart Proctor (3/12/1946-   )(b. Washington,
          D.C.), m. 4/ /1976, Bernard E. Fedewa

2191321141
2191321142
21913212   Rev. Cary Nelson Weisiger III (1/11/1910-   )(b. St.
           Louis), m. 8/28/1937, at Madison, Conn., Elizabeth
           Whitney Forbes (9/5/1912-   )(b. Ridgewood, N.J.)
219132121 Cary Nelson Weisiger IV (9/8/1938-   ), m. (1st)
           1960, Kathleen Knoch; m. (2nd) 10/29/1976, Mrs.
           Elaine Green. By a previous marriage, Elaine Green
           Weisiger had two children who were adopted by Cary
           Nelson Weisiger VI: Kasi Green Weisiger (12/10/1969-
                ), and Tana Green Weisiger (12/18/1972-   )
           Children by first wife:
2191321211 James N. Weisiger (5/4/1961-   )
2191321212 Andrew P. Weisiger (12/7/1962-   )
2191321213 Joseph W. Weisiger (7/20/1964-   )
219132122 Mary Whitney Weisiger (6/14/1941-   ), m. 10/ /1965,
           Gerry B. Andeen
2191321221 Ashley Ruth Andeen (3/11/1968-   )
2191321222 Laura Elizabeth Andeen (1/23/1970-   )
2191321223 David Gerry Andeen (2/25/1973-   )
219132123 John Bolling Weisiger (11/28/1943-   ), m. 1966, Susan
           Towle
2191321231 Cynthia Weisiger (8/23/1967-   )
219132124 Ruth Whitney Weisiger (6/26/1951-   ), m. 4/ /1979,
           Farhad Farivar
21913213   Carter Byrd Weisiger (12/26/1917-   )(b. St. Louis),
           m. (1st) 5/21/1943, at Miami, Audrey Vivian (5/27/1922-
           8/28/1974)(b. Pushthrough, Newfoundland, d. Norfolk, Va.),
           dau. of Norah G. and Bessie Rowsell Vivian; m. (2nd) 9/
           27/1975, in Norfolk, Va., Ruth Loving Weed (12/4/1919-
)(b. Blackstone, Va.)
           Children by first wife:
219132131 Jane Randolph Weisiger (2/20/1945-   ), m. 4/8/
           1970, Handord N. Lockwood IV
2191321311 Carter Lockwood (5/22/1982-5/22/1982)
219132132 Louise Alden Weisiger (3/7/1947-   ), m. (1st) 12/27/
           1969, John Harris, div. 1977; m. (2nd) 2/16/1980, Daniel
           E. Perry
           Child by first husband:
2191321321 Rebecca Harris (4/4/1974-   )
           Child by second husband:
2191321322 Daniel Carter Perry (10/9/1982-   )
219132133 Ann Vivian Weisiger (3/6/1950-   ), m. 6/10/1972,
           John H. Bell
2191321331 Audrey Vivian Bell (11/24/1974-   )
2191321332 David Nelson Bell (1/15/1980-   )
21913214   Mary Randolph Weisiger (6/11/1920-   )(b. St. Louis)
2191322   Mary Humphreys Weisiger (10/4/1886-12/17/1977)(b. Memphis),
           m. 6/2/1910, in St. Louis, Thomas William White III (8/2/
           1883-3/19/1946)(d. St. Louis), a well known attorney of
           St. Louis

21913221 Thomas William White IV (6/13/1918-   )(b. St. Louis), m. 9/26/1953, in St. Louis, Joan Wallace Woods (2/9/1931-   ), dau. of Leonard R. Woods

219132211 Cary Randolph White (10/27/1954-   ), m. 10/4/ 1980, John David Schaperkotter (1951-   )

219132212 Thomas William White V (3/4/1958-   ), m. 4/9/ 1983, Elizabeth E. Keyes

219132213 Mary Wallace White (11/26/1960-   )

219132214 Joan Woods White (11/5/1962-   )

2191323 Elizabeth West Weisiger (1892-   ), m. 1915, Hamilton Day Whitelaw

2191324 Lucy Page Weisiger (1894-   ), m. 1924, Joseph Hays McNaughter

219133 Lewis Weisiger

219134 Mary Randolph Weisiger, m. Alfred Ball Carter, Jr. (1853-   ), son of Alfred Ball and Betty Randolph Carter

219135 Anne Meade Weisiger, m. 9/10/1885, in Memphis, Everett Frederick Adams

219136 Lucy Page Weisiger, m. 6/25/1885, Lee Coulter

219137 Baynham Weisiger

219138 Edmund Withers Weisiger (-7/25/1916), m. in Memphis, Pearl Mansfield (-10/8/1938)

219139 Benjamin Cary Weisiger, d. 4/13/1854, inf., at "Bolling Hall"

21913x Joseph Kendall Weisiger, d. inf.

21914 Powhatan Weisiger (ca. 1834-   ),m. 11/3/1857, in Petersburg, Va., Josephine White (ca. 1838-   ). Powhatan Weisiger served in Richmond City Ambulance Corp. Troop E of the 4th Regiment, Crenshaw's Regiment and Ellett's Regiment, C.S.A.

219141 Pauline White ("Lina") Weisiger (8/4/1858-   )

219142 Powhatan Weisiger, Jr. (1862-12/29/1862)

21915 Ryland Randolph Weisiger (6/7/1837-5/24/1920)(b. Goochland County, d. Powhatan County), m. 6/7/1859, at Georgetown, D.C., Mary Abbott(?) Moulder (6/3/1836-3/5/1907). Ryland Randolph Weisiger was Captain in the 86th Virginia Militia, C.S.A. Both bur. Grace Church, Genito

219151 George Abbott Weisiger (2/22/1861-8/3/1924)(b. Georgetown, D.C.), m. 9/21/1893, in Amelia County, Va., Elizabeth ("Betty") Coleman (-9/23/1923). He bur. Grace Church, Genito

2191511 George Abbott Weisiger, Jr. (12/1/1904-9/27/1913)(d. Powhatan County). Bur. Grace Church, Genito

2191512 Elizabeth Coleman Weisiger (6/12/1898-9/25/1913)(d. Powhatan County). Bur. Grace Church, Genito

219152 Mary Randolph Weisiger (9/7/1862-3/25/1868)(b. New River Springs, Va.)

219153 Richard Wilmer Weisiger (4/23/1864-12/29/1945)(b. at "Bolling Hall", Goochland County, d. Powhatan County), m. Louise Brown Sult (1879-4/25/1945). Both bur. Grace Church, Genito

219154 John Richardson Weisiger (2/10/1866-12/23/1947)(d. Centralia, Va.)

219155 Bessie Abbott Weisiger (7/10/1867-7/7/1945)(b. Georgetown,
        d. Centralia, Va.), m. 8/17/1893, William Old
2191551 Sinclair B. Old (10/3/1894-   )
2191552 Nannie Leigh Old (12/1/1895-   )
2191553 Bessie Old (8/16/1897-   )
2191554 William Old (8/16/1897-   )
219156 Joseph Kendall Weisiger (4/3/1868-10/ /1962)(b. Radford,
        Va., d. Chester, N.J.), m. 12/22/1898, in Powhatan County,
        Carrie Graves (11/6/1867-3/ /1941)(d. Wyckoff, N.H.),
        dau. of Robert and Mary Jane Watkins Graves
2191561 Kendall F. Weisiger (12/10/1903-   )(b. Powhatan
        County), m. 4/14/1928, in Brooklyn, Dorothy Gest
21915611 Richard K. Weisiger (12/23/1929-   )(b. Brooklyn),
        m. 12/27/1958, at Ramsey, N.J., Janet Baird
219156111 Glen R. Weisiger (6/7/1962-   )
219156112 Beth J. Weisiger (2/7/1964-   )
219156113 Carin D. Weisiger (9/15/1965-   )
219156114 Diana F. Weisiger (8/24/1964-   )
21915612 Doris C. Weisiger (2/18/1932-   )(b. in Brooklyn),
        m. 11/16/1952, at Wyckoff, N.J., Edmund H. Moore
219156121 Edmund H. Moore IV (6/9/1959-   )
219156122 Carol L. Moore (7/31/1960-   )
219156123 Scott K. Moore (6/20/1962-   )
21915613 Lora A. Weisiger (9/3/1936-   )(b. in Brooklyn), m.
        3/1/1955, at Wyckoff, N.J., Douglas Feick
219156131 Linda S. Feick (8/31/1955-   ), m. 9/23/1978,
        Scott Murphy
219156132 Tamara L. Feick (7/1/1960-   )
219156133 Doulgas K. Feick (5/24/1962-   )
21915614 Ryland H. Weisiger (8/7/1938-   )(b. Brooklyn), m.
        7/6/1968, in Ridgewood, N.J., Cathleen Wieland
219156141 Kristin S. Weisiger (10/6/1972-   )
219156142 Gretchen K. Weisiger (9/11/1974-   )
219156143 Wendy E. Weisiger (12/16/1976-   )
219157 Clarence Duncan Weisiger (5/25/1870-12/7/1953)(b. Pulaski
        County, d. Blackstone, Va.), m. 12/26/1906, Fleeta Chappell
        Jones (8/2/1887-9/12/1958)
2191571 Clarence Duncan Weisiger, Jr. (10/28/1907-5/7/1969)(b. and
        d. Amelia County), m. 9/8/1930, at Chatham, Va., Katherine
        Watson (12/5/1905-   )(b. Chatham, Va.)
21915711 Anne Bolling Weisiger (6/4/1931-   )(b. Charlottesville),
        m. 7/12/1952, Robert Allen Quicke (5/1/1930-   )(b.
        Petersburg, Va.)
219157111 Sarah Randolph Quicke (1/31/1953-   ), m. 8/11/1973,
        Richard Waddell Cobbs
2191571111 Richard Waddell Cobbs, Jr. (1/11/1975-   )
2191571112 Katherine Randolph Cobbs (3/31/1977-   )
2191571113 Virginia Courtney Cobbs (4/27/1981-   )
219157112 Elizabeth Bolling Quicke (3/23/1954-   )
219157113 Robert Allen Quicke, Jr. (9/27/1957-   ), m. 7/25/
        1981, Elizabeth Chandler Connelly

219157114 Courtney Duncan Quicke (4/17/1959-   )
21915712 Katherine Graves Weisiger (6/2/1933-   ), m. 10/2/
          1954, Thomas Stark III (1/19/1932-   )
219157121 Martha Cary Stark (8/27/1958-   ), m. 7/26/1980,
          Steven Jon Cronemeyer
219157122 Thomas Stark IV (7/2/1964-   )
219157123 Elizabeth Anne Stark (12/20/1967-   )
21915713 Martha Watson Weisiger (11/22/1936-   ), m. 8/9/
          1958, Edward Shelton Fraher, Jr. (11/22/1932-   )
219157131 Edward Shelton Fraher III (10/30/1962-   )
219157132 Katherine Watson Fraher (12/9/1963-   )
219157133 Clarence Duncan Fraher (7/19/1969-   )
21915714 Sarah Duncan Weisiger (8/1/1938-   ), m. 12/28/
          1957, Robert Cannon Irby, Jr. (8/10/1935-   )
219157141 Robert Cannon Irby III (9/15/1958-   ), m. 6/7/
          1980, Joan Marie Broomell
219157142 Stuart Duncan Irby (9/26/1959-   )
219157143 Bruce Watson Irby (11/14/1960-   )
2191572 Frances Chappell Weisiger (2/28/1910-   )(b. Amelia
          County), m. Alvin Dawson Blount
21915721 Jean Dawson Blount (5/26/1949-   ), m. 7/24/1971,
          Robert Bruce Hudson (11/23/1949-   )
219157211 Katherine Abbott Hudson (9/1/1977-   )
219157212 John Kendall Hudson (4/28/1981-   )
2191573 Mary Abbott Weisiger (5/17/1912-   )(b. Amelia
          County), m. Oswald Epes Shell
21915731 Charles Franklin Shell (7/27/1939-   ), m. 12/19/
          1964, Jane Bruce Hillsman (6/26/1942-   )
219157311 Elizabeth Abbott Shell (6/16/1968-   )
219157312 Catherine Hillsman Shell (10/26/1970-   )
21915732 Randolph Weisiger Shell (10/18/1940-11/6/1967), m. Joanne
          Henkel
219157321 Randolph Weisiger Shell, Jr. (1958-   )
2191574 Ryland Randolph Weisiger (8/24/1915-   )(b. Amelia
          County), m. 3/25/1944, Marian Rose Verona (6/6/1918-   )
21915741 Marian Victoria Weisiger (10/3/1952-   )
21915742 Elizabeth Abbott Weisiger (11/22/1953-   )
219158 William Percy Weisiger (1/10/1872-12/24/1942)(b. Pulaski
          County, d. Powhatan County), m. 6/7/1906, in Wythe
          County, Ida Sult (3/28/1882-4/11/1972). Both bur. Grace
          Church, Genito
2191581 Anna Abbott Weisiger (5/11/1908-   )
2191582 James Coley Weisiger (5/24/1916-   )(b. Powhatan
          County), m. 2/14/1946, Addie Holladay (5/5/1919-   )
          (b. Manning, S.C.)
21915821 William Bolling Weisiger (11/30/1946-   ), m. Donna
          Green
219158211 Christine Michele Weisiger (10/11/1972-   )
219158212 Kimberly Ann Weisiger (1/1/1974-   )
21915822 James Kendall Weisiger (9/15/1952-   ), m. 8/16/1974,
          in Yoakum, Texas, Laurel Lee Koether
219158221 Sean Kendall Weisiger (8.15/1977-   )

21915823 Wanda Louise Weisiger (3/15/1957-   ), m. Robert
          Edward Shue
21915824 Barry Meade Weisiger (11/9/1959-   ), m. Debby
          Coley Buchanan
21915825 Janet Mavis Weisiger (6/19/1961-   ), m. 2/19/
          1983, John Ignatius Simpson III
219159 Louis Eggleston Weisiger (6/11/1873-10/6/1933)(b. Pulaski
        County, d. Powhatan County), m. 12/7/1905, in Richmond,
        Mary Montague Hancock (12/16/1875-6/2/1927)(b. and d.
        Powhatan County)
2191591 Nancy Peyton Weisiger (11/27/1906-10/24/1974)(b. Powhatan
         County, d. Acton, Mass.), m. 4/2/1945, Henley Granville
         Rouillard
2191592 Louis Wilson Weisiger (7/22/1910-   )(b. Powhatan
         County), m. (1st) 9/27/1941, Violet Mary Graham; m. (2nd)
         8/2/1952, Virginia Wittenbraker. Div. M. (3rd) 5/21/1960,
         Margaret Kuyk (2/19/1911-   )
         Child by first wife:
21915921 Mary Helms Weisiger (6/16/1942-   ), m. Jonathan
          Elber
219159211 Nathaniel Graham Elber (9/16/1967-   )
2191593 Ellie Hancock Weisiger (3/11/1914-   )(b. Powhatan
         County), m. 6/4/1938, Edward J. Lefeber, M.D. (6/1/1911-
)(b. Wawatosa, Wis.)
21915931 Edward James Lefeber, Jr., M.D. (1/12/1941-   ), m.
          11/18/1967, Faith Gabrielson (9/2/1942-   )
219159311 Karin Elizabeth Lefeber (10/12/1976-   )
21915932 Robert Randolph Lefeber (8/13/1943-   )
21915933 John Courtney Lefeber (8/21/1945-   )
21915934 Ann Elizabeth Lefeber (9/9/1947-   ),m. 11/25/1967,
          Philip Wayne Botik (12/16/1941-   )
21915935 Donald Louis Lefeber (3/20/1953-   ), m. 3/12/1977,
          Rose York-Quijano (10/7/1953-   )
21915936 Nancy Ellen Lefeber (12/21/1954-   ), m. 5/29/1976,
          Michael Burke Hughes (10/24/1953-   )
2191594 Levin Powell Weisiger (10/10/1915-2/27/1973)(b. and d.
         Powhatan County), m. (1st) 6/1/1950, Grace Louise Ger-
         melman. Div. M. (2nd) 6/18/1964, Mary P. Ludlam (11/16/
         1918-10/2/1976)
2191595 Randolph Abbott Weisiger (6/24/1918-7/7/1919)(d. Powhatan
         County)
21915x Lilly Wilson Weisiger (3/1/1877-2/9/1947)(d. Onancock, Va.),
        m. 10/28/1896, Rev. Frank Rideout
21915x1 Mary Abbott Rideout (1898-   )
21915x2 Frank A. Rideout (10/7/1901-   )
21915x3 Lily Wilson Rideout (3/15/1908-   )
21915a Mattie Duncan Weisiger (12/26/1879-   ), m. 6/23/
        1904, J. E. Jackson
21915a1 Margaret Bolling Jackson
21915a2 Edward Randolph Jackson
21915a3 Lily Wilson Jackson
21916 George Harris Weisiger (1840-2/25/1900), m. (1st) 4/10/1861,

Caroline Booth; m. (2nd) Virginia Wilmer(?). He was a lieutenant in F Co., 24th Regiment, C.S.A. He d. in Richmond. Which wife was the mother of his two children is not known.

219161 Virginia C. Weisiger (1867-   ), m. 6/3/1890, in Richmond, William L. Murray

219162

21917 Richard Wilmer Weisiger (11/ /1841-12/11/1862), m. 11/19/1862, in Chesterfield County, Bettie Gregory. A member of the Richmond Light Infantry Blues, he was killed in the Civil War.

21918 Joseph Albert Weisiger, d. inf.

2192 William Albert Bolling (2/21/1799-10/30/1884), born deaf, m. (1st) 1/23/1833 (at "White Hall", Buckingham County), Eliza Hunt Christian of Appomattox (ca. 1812-8/18/1853); m. (2nd) Elvira Arminda Bolling

21921 William Bolling, b. ca. 1835, m. Virginia Louise ("Jennie") Baker (-1/25/1882) at "Silver Springs", Louisa County

219211 Ernest Lee Bolling (-6/25/1934), m. Mary Celeste Winston (-10/21/1946)

2192111 Thomas Winston Bolling (-6/28/1968), m. 1931, Loreta Elizabeth Blaker of Greenbrier County, W.Va.

21921111 Winston Blaker Bolling, m. 1930, Barbara Hastings

21921112 John Ernest Bolling, m. Elizabeth Johnson

219211121 Kristine Bolling

219211122 John Ernest Bolling, Jr.

21922 Mary Elizabeth ("Lizzie") Bolling (12/29/1836-12/12/1909), m. (1st) 2/7/1856 (MB) Powhatan F. Jones of Louisa County; m. (2nd) 3/2/1871, Robert Skipwith (9/30/1810-4/27/1904) (6121). "Lizzie" was murdered, and their home was burned in 1909.

Child by first husband:

219221 George Fleming Jones (ca. 1859-9/25/1862?) General, C.S.A.

21923 Anne Meade Bolling (b. ca. 1848), m. 1867, Sterling B. Claiborne

219231 Nena Claiborne, m.   Hager

219232 Laurie Claiborne, d. young

219233 (son). Studied for Episcopal ministry at Seminary in Alexandria.

21924 Susan Christian Bolling, b. ca. 1849, m. 9/21/1870, George Henry King, Jr.

219241 Mary Meredith King (3/15/1872-   ), m.   Johnston

2192411 (dau)(ca. 1898-   )

219242 Richard Bolling King (12/1/1874-   )

219243 Annie Randolph King (4/10/1877-   )

219244 Susan Christian King (12/26/1881-   )

219245 George Henry King, Jr. (9/2/1883-   )

219246 Robert Skipwith King (3/26/1887-   )

21925 Thomas Albert Bolling (1852-1934), m. Jennie Mitchell (-ca. 1895)

219251 Thomas Albert ("Press") Bolling, Jr. (1881-1957), m. Mamie A. Hodges (-1978 or 1979)

NOTE: The information on 21925, et seq., was supplied by
Mamie A. Hodges Bolling.
2192511 Pearl Ann Bolling (1929-   ), m. (1st)   Rickman.
Div. M. (2nd) John R. Schell. No issue by second husband
Children by first husband:
21925111
21925112
21925113
2192512 Preston James Bolling (1934-   ), married four times,
(div. from fourth wife)
21925121
21925122
21925123
2192513 Thomas Albert Bolling III (1937-   ), m. (1st) Frances
. Div.
21925131 Troy Bolling
219252 Arthur Bolling (1883-   ), m. Lillie
219253 John C. Bolling (1885-   ), m.   Cannon of
Caroline County. Living in Hopewell in 1931.
2192531 Irene Bolling of Arlington
2192532 Johnny Bolling of Portsmouth
219254 Walter Bolling (1887-prior to 1974), m. Bessie Lane (-
1974). No issue. (Bessie Lane was an aunt of Mamie A.
Hodges above)
219255 Nathan(iel ?) Bolling (1890-   ), m.
2192551 (dau)
2192552 (dau)
219256 Jenny Bolling (ca. 1892-d. age 22), m.   Stock
2192561 Willie Stock
2192562 Linette Stock, m.   Gentry
21926 D. inf.
2193 Thomas Bolling (2/5 or 7/1807-3/18/1889) of "Bolling Hall"
(he settled on "Bolling Island"), Goochland County, m.
2/7/1832 (at Campbell County, home of her maternal grandmother), Mary Louisa Morris (8/11/1810-5/4/1852), eldest
dau. of Richard Morris of "Taylor's Creek", Hanover County,
and his wife, the former Mary Watts of Campbell County.
Mary Louisa was b. at Flat Creek, Campbell County.
21931 Virginia Randolph Bolling (11/17 or 18/1838-7/11/1899), m.
4/17/1861, Alexander Quarles Holladay, C.S.A. (1839-1909),
son of Alexander Richmond and Patsy Quarles Poindexter
Holladay of "Prospect Hill", Spotsylvania County
219311 Mary Stuart Holladay (1862-   ),m. 1883, Rev. Peyton
Harrison Hoge (2424452)
219312 William Waller Holladay
219313 Julia Cabell Holladay, m.   Pickell
219314 A. Randolph Holladay (1869-1949)
219315 Charles Bolling Holladay (1873-   ). Home (1928):
Wilmington, Delaware
21932 Julia Calvert ("Pink") Bolling (8/3 or 4/1834-6/21/1923),
m. 2/27/1861 (at "Bolling Island"), Rev. Philip Barraud
Cabell of Nelson County (6/16/1836-3/16/1904), son of

Nathaniel Francis and Anne Blaws Cocke Cabell of "Liberty
Hall". Both Julia and Philip are bur. at "Liberty Hall"
219321 Elizabeth Nicholas Cabell (1862-1862)
219322 Joseph Hartwell Cabell (12/24/1863-12/ /1955), m. (1st)
      Swing. Div. M. (2nd) 2/17/1896, Meta Logan, dau.
    of General Logan, C.S.A.; m. (3rd) Louise Groesbeck, dau.
    of Judge Croesbeck of Cincinnati
    Children by second wife:
2193221 Francis Cabell (-2/ /1927), m.   .
    Lt. (Air Force), killed in flying accident
21932211 (son)
2193222 Honoria Muldropp Cabell, m.   . Has children
    Child of third wife:
2193223 Mary Groesbeck Cabell, m. George Selden Somerville (-
    1974). No issue
219323 Francis Barraud Cabell (7/14/1866-11/22/1893). Killed
    himself in Cincinnati. Bur. at "Liberty Hall"
219324 Philip Mason Cabell (1/4/1869-ca. 1940), m. 10/15/1894,
    Nannine Dove Sioussat of Washington, D. C.
2193241 Calvert Cabell, m. (1st) James Osbourne; m. (2nd) Igor
    Moravsky (-1976)
21933   Mary Elizabeth Bolling (5/1/1833-6/19/1833). Bur. "Bolling
    Hall"
21934   William Randolph Bolling (10/17/1836-9/23/1839). Bur.
    "Bolling Hall"
21935   Richard Morris Bolling (3/7/1841-1921), m. 10/24/1882, Ann
    ("Nannie") Montgomery Barksdale (4/6/1850-6/1/1939). Both
    bur. "Bolling Hall". For their children, etc., see 111421
21936   Thomas Bolling, Jr. (9/7/1844-4/15/1912), m. 1877, Sally
    B. Aylett (4/25/1855-   ), dau. of Patrick and
    Rutherford Aylett. His gravestone in Hollywood
    gives his birthdate as 9/7/1846. B. "Bolling Island"
219361 Randolph Bolling (12/23/1877-   ), m. (1st) Sally
    B. Stokes; m. (2nd) 11/ /1905, Suzie Ann Estelle
    Peppett of Canada
    Children by second wife:
2193611 Estelle Randolph Bolling (11/30/1906-197?), m. (1st)
    Dr. Willard E. Austen; m. (2nd) Henry DeRham. No issue
2193612 Thomas B. Bolling (5/7/1908-   )
2193613 Josephine Peppett Bolling (11/9/1909-   )
21937   William Bolling (5/1/1846-5/2/1847). B. "Bolling Island",
    bur. "Bolling Hall"
21938   Helen Wilmer Bolling (5/1/1848-12/27/1848). D. in Richmond,
    b. "Bolling Island", bur. "Bolling Hall"
21929   Louisa Morris Bolling (1/3/1850-7/3/1879). Bur. Hollywood.
2193x   Charles Edward Bolling (5/3/1852-6/22/1929). B. "Bolling
    Island" (his mother d. at his birth), bur. Hollywood. M.
    (1st) Imogene Burrows Warwick, dau. of Corbin and Margaret
    Bradfute Warwick; m. (2nd) Parke Bagby
2194   Jane Rolfe Bolling (5/1/1817-2/28/1867), m. 7/7/1847, her
    first cousin once removed, Robert Skipwith (1810-1904)(6121).
    She was his first wife. No issue

2195   Mary R. Bolling (4/3/1809-1/18/1870), born deaf
2196
2197
2198
2199
219x
21x   Sarah Randolph (4/30/1772-d. 8/ /1829 at "South East", Pow-
       hatan County), m. 1/20/1814 (MB), William Mewburn of England
       (-6/ /1829)
21x1   William Mewburn, Jr. (ca. 1818-ca. 1833) d.s.p.
21a   Susan Randolph (10/14/1751-6/11/1752)
21b   Mary Randolph (10/9/1760-12/18/1772)
21c   Ann Randolph (8/19/1762-7/ /1763)
22   Brett Randolph (9/4/1732-9/4/1759), m. 7/14/1753, in London,
       Mary Scott of Gloucester Shire. They lived in Gloucester-
       shire, England. He died at Dursley, England
221   Henry Randolph (10/7/1758-   ), of "Warwick", Chester-
       field County, m. ca. 1780, Lucy Ward, dau. of Seth and Mary
       Goode Ward
2211   Henry Randolph (ca. 1784-10/26/1840 or 1837), of "Warwick",
       m. (1st) Caroline Matilda Smith (-9/25/1808), dau.
       of Major Smith of Manchester. No issue. M. (2nd) Eliza
       Griffin Norman (1785-10/7/1825) of a Henrico County family
       from Pennsylvania, and of the Society of Friends. M. (3rd)
       Mrs.   Perry, a descendant of Thomas Tinsley, a planter
       who emigrated to Virginia from Yorkshire near the close of
       the 17th Century
     Children by second wife:
22111 Henry Seth Ward Randolph (7/15/1810-7/26/1874) of Mount
       Prospect, Henrico County, m. 1835, Deborah Perry, dau. of
       Benjamin and Anna Perry of Schaghticoke (now Hart's Falls),
       Rensselear County, N.Y.
221111 Anna Louise Randolph (7/15/1836 or 1837-   ), m. 1865,
       Rev. William T. Price of Marlins Bottom, Pocahontas County,
       son of James and Margaret Poague Price
2211111 William Randolph Price (1866-   ), d. young
2211112 James Ward Price (1868-   )
2211113 Andrew Gatewood Price (1871-   )
2211114 Susan Alexander Price (1873-   )
2211115 Norman Randolph Price (1875-   )
2211116 Calvin Wells Price
2211117 Anna Virginia Price (1882-   )
221112 Virginia Randolph (1842-   ), m. 6/20/1859, James B.
       Mallory (-12/4/1874) of Brunswick County, son
       of William and Martha Mallory
2211121 William Young Mallory (9/30/1860-   )
2211122 Virginia Perry Mallory (2/16/1863-   )
2211123 James Baugh Mallory (8/2/1865-   )
2211124 Edwin Morrison Mallory (11/16/1867-   )
2211125 Louise Randolph Mallory (3/2/1870-   )
221113 Lucy Ward Randolph (5/12/1847-   ), m. 6/24/1875, Rev.
       Robert Hanson Fleming (10/12/1846-   ), son of William
       Wier and Margaret Lewis Fleming

2211131 Mary Randolph Fleming (1877-   )
221114   Joseph Randolph (1850-   ), d. young
221115   Henry Randolph (1854-   ), m. 1877, Anna Slater of
          Richmond
2211151 Henry Ward Randolph (1878-   )
2211152 Ruth Slater Randolph
22112   Benjamin Randolph, d. young
22113   Joseph Williamson Randolph (8/19/1815-   )(born at "War-
          wick" on the James River), a Richmond bookseller and pub-
          lisher, m. 11/26/1842, Honoria Mary Tucker (22313)
221131   Capt. Joseph Tucker (Tucker St. Joseph?) Randolph (9/19/
          1844-5/30/1864), C.S.A. Killed near Bethesda Church
          (Cold Harbor)
221132   Norman Vincent Randolph (11/2/1846-   ), m. (1st)
          4/16/1873, Louisa Whelan Reed (-3/17/1877), dau.
          of William B. and Louisa Whelan Reed. M. (2nd) Janet
          Henderson (4/29/1848-   ), dau. of Richard A. and
          Janet Cleiland Homer Weaver
          Children by first wife:
2211321 Cornelia Whelan Randolph (3/24/1874-   )
2211322 Nora Mary Randolph (5/20/1875-7/7/1876)
2211323 Norman Vincent Randolph, Jr. (9/15/1876-   )
          Children by second wife:
2211324 Joseph Williamson Randolph (12/14/1881-2/14/1883)
2211325 Janet Cleiland Randolph (11/15/1884-   )
2211326 Meta Lee Randolph (9/10/1886-   )
22114   William Randolph, d. young
22115   Elizabeth Anna Randolph (2/21/1819-11/2/1885), m. Richard
          Channing Hall of Richmond, son of Jacob and Catherine
          Eliza Moore Hall
221151   Catherine Eliza Hall (1848-   ), m. 1869, George
          Brown
2211511 Elizabeth Brown (1868-   ), d. young
2211512 Kate Randolph Brown (1879-   )
221152   Mary Norman Hall (1850-   ), m. 12/17/1872, Andrew
          Rufus Yarbrough of Richmond, son of William James and
          Ophelia Yarbrough
2211521 Lilian Moore Hall Yarbrough (9/26/1873-   )
2211522 Rufus Norman Yarbrough (6/25/1882-   )
221153   Lucy Hall, d. young
221154   Channing Hall, d. young
221155   Virginia Dean Hall, m. 1883, James McCall Fox
2211551 Richard Fox (1886-   )
221156   Fannie MacMurdo Hall, m. 1886, Walter Wren
22116   Lucy Ward Randolph (2/14 or 16/1821-10/27/1853)(d. in
          Henderson, Ky.), m. Robert Goode Saunders (10/22/1808-ca.
          1859) of Norfolk, son of Tarlton and Sally Bland Goode Lyle
          Saunders
221161   James Randolph Saunders, d. young
22117   Mary Goode Randolph (11/13 or 15/1823-   ), m. William
          Henry Hammond of Petersburg, son of Joel Hammond of North
          Carolina

221171 Henry Randolph Hammond (1851-   )
221172 Lula Douglass Hammond, d. young
        Children by third wife (of 2211):
22118   Anna Grantland Randolph, d. young
22119   Capt. William Tinsley Randolph (ca. 1825-ca. 1855), U.S.A.,
        d.s.p., killed in Mexico
2212   Mary Randolph (5/25/1785-10/15/1865), m. (1st) 9/21/1805,
        George Washington Thornton (b. ca. 1760-75-d. ca. 1815) of
        "Rumford", Stafford County, son of Maj. George and Mary
        Alexander Thornton. M. (2nd) 11/12/1817, James Francis
        Maury (11/13/1786-10/24/1841), son of Abraham and Mildred
        Washington Thornton Maury
22121   Henry Randolph Thornton (2/23/1807-11/21/1862), m. (1st)
        6/28/1829, Maria Agnes Bradford. M. (2nd) 9/7/1848, Ellen
        Thom, dau. of George Slaughter and Margaret Hansbrough
        Thom of Culpeper County. Ca. 1833, Thornton sold "Rumford",
        and moved to Livingston, Ala.
        Children by first wife:
221211 George Thornton (1840-1880), m. 1860, Fannie Rew
2212111 Bradford Thornton
2212112 Maria Agnes Thornton
2212113 Kate Garrison Thornton
2212114 Henry Williams Thornton
2212115 Lillie Thornton
2212116 Fannie Thornton
221212 Alexander Cunningham Thornton
221213 Samuel Bradford Thornton, d. young
        Children by second wife:
221214 Reuben Thom Thornton
221215 Hortense Randolph Thornton
221216 Henry Ward Thornton
221217 Margaret Virginia Thornton, m. John S. Johnston
2212171 Reuben Thornton Johnston
2212172 Emmie Holmes Johnston
2212173 Ellen Thom Johnston
221218 Lucie Cobbs Thornton
221219 Seth Brett Thornton, d. young
22122   Lucy Ward Thornton (3/21/1811-9/22/1840), m. Richard Adams
        (2/7/1800-6/11/1851) of Richmond, son of Samuel Griffin
        and Catharine Innes Adams. Adams' first wife was Mary
        Selden, dau. of Col. Miles Selden, Jr.
221221 Mary E. Adams, m. (1st)   Pope; m. (2nd) Brig. Gen.
        George Wythe Randolph (3/10/1818-4/3/1867), C.S.A.(2414b),
        son of Gov. Thomas Mann Randolph
221222 Catherine Adams
221223 Samuel Goode Adams of Mobile, m. Mary Campbell of Mobile
2212231 Lucy Thornton Adams
2212232 Mary Toulmin Adams, m. Joseph Rich of Mobile
22123   Mary Goode Thornton (1813-   ), m. (1st) Lieut. Alex-
        ander Cunningham Maury (ca. 1806-10/ /), son of Philip
        P. and E. Cunningham Maury. M. (2nd) Rev. John Jackson
        Scott, son of Joseph Adams and Mary McNish Scott. No issue

22124   Capt. Seth Brett Thornton, U.S.A. (5/28/1815-8/18/1847),
        killed in the War with Mexico
     Children by second husband:
22125   Capt. Thomas Francis Maury (2/ /1819-5/2/1862), C.S.A.,
        of Kemper County, Miss., m. 5/ /1847, Ann R. Jenkins,
        dau. of Richard Jenkins of Virginia
221251 Seth Thornton Maury (2/19/1848-   ) of Temple Junction,
        Bell County, Texas, m. 12/2/1879, Kate Stevenson
2212511 Lillian Maury (9/6/1883-6/1/1884)
2212512 Zaidee Eliza Maury (12/10/1886-   )
221252 Richard Randolph Maury (2/ /1850-   ) of China Springs,
        McLennan County, Texas, m. 1/1/1880, Ida Clements
2212521 Annie Lena Maury (8/16/1881-   )
2212522 Lottie Stewart Maury (5/29/1883-   )
2212523 Thomas Joseph Maury (12/10/1884-   )
221253 Thomas Fontaine Maury (twin)(5/ /1851-   ), m. Florence
        Heddin
2212531 Cora G. Maury (7/29/1884-   )
2212532 Maggie Fontaine Maury (7/27/1886-   )
221254 Edward (Edmund?) Kimbrough Maury (twin)(5/ /1851-   ),
        m. Nannie Foster
2212541 Caroline Elizabeth Maury (11/7/1882-   )
2212542 Annie Richard Maury (4/19/1885-   )
221255 Jeanette Williams Maury (2/22/1853-   ), d. young
221256 John A. Maury (12/ /1854-   )
221257 Mary Lucy Maury (2/23/1856-   ), m. James B. Stevens
        of Oenaville, Bell County, Texas
2212571 William Henry Stevens (1/13/1885-1886)
2212572 Annie Goode Stevens (7/11/1886-   )
221258 James Woodville Maury (5/6/1858-   ) of China Springs,
        Texas. Unm.
221259 Bettie Greene Maury (10/9/1860-   ), d. young
22125x Francis Alexander Maury (5/5/1862-   ), d. young
22126   James Woodville Maury (1/4/1821-   ) of Shuqulak,
        Noxube County, Miss.
22127   James Woodville Maury (3/18/1823-   ), m. 2/22/1848,
        Rachel Kittrell Harris, dau. of Richard and Elizabeth
        Harris of South Carolina
221271 Richard Harris Maury (12/6/1848-12/24/1875)
221272 James Francis Maury (3/22/1850-   ), m. 8/1/1881,
        Willie Irene Allen
2212721 Aline Maury (2/1/1883-   )
2212722 Harris Maury (3/3/1885-   )
221273 Edward Fontaine Maury (5/27/1852-   ), m. Mary L.
        Shelton
2212731 James Berkley Maury (3/11/1878-   )
2212732 Francis Lewis Maury (11/28/1880-   )
2212733 Richard Henry Maury (12/23/1882-   )
221274 Matthew Henry Maury (4/16/1854-   ), m. 12/21/1875,
        Mary J. Galbraight
2212741 Richard Harris Maury (1/10/1877-   )
2212742 Kate Galbraight Maury (9/3/1879-   )

2212743 Clara Kittrell Maury (5/11/1881-   )
2212744 Henry Francis Maury (9/23/1883-   )
2212745 Annie Maury (4/23/1884-   )
2212746 Nellie Maury (9/23/1885-   ), d. young
22128 Catherine Mildred Maury (8/11/1825-   ), d. young
22129 Agnes Gray Maury (11/26/1828-   ), d. young
2212x Gilbert Lafayette Maury (2/7/1831-   ) of Pushmataha,
       Ala., m. Eliza Sears Scott (1/8/1841-   ), dau. of
       James Scott
2212x1 Oscar Fontaine Maury (7/8/1864-   )
2212x2 James Woodville Maury (12/3/1868-   )
2212x3 Julia R. Maury (8/31/1870-   )
2212x4 Charles D. Maury (7/4/1872-   )
2212x5 Dabney Herndon Maury (7/5/1874-   )
2212x6 Ernest Caleb Maury (1/22/1880-   )
2212x7   Maury (9/9/1883-   )
2213 Brett Randolph, d. young
2214 Robert Goode Randolph, d. young
2215 Catherine Cochrane Randolph (1797-12/12/1852), m. Josiah
      Bartlett Abbott (1/1/1793-9/23/1849) of "High Meadow",
      Henrico County
22151 Capt. Walter Raleigh Abbott (4/19/1838-6/13/1862), C.S.A.,
       of Lynchburg, m. Elizabeth Duval of Richmond. He was
       killed at Malvern Hill.
221511 Walter Raleigh Abbott, d. young
22152 Virginia Abbott (3/30/1855-   ), m. Claiborne Watkins
       of Richmond, son of Henry W. and Judith F. Watkins
221521 Walter Abbott Watkins (4/3/1857-   )
221522 Charles Hunter Watkins (9/26/1858-   )
221523 Randolph Watkins (8/30/1860-   )
221524 Claiborne Watkins (5/3/1863-   )
221525 Kate Watkins (6/16/1866-   )
221526 Henry Watkins (4/22/1869-   )
221527 Virginia Watkins (6/6/1870-   )
221528 Elizabeth Watkins (12/28/1872-   )
221529 Adelaide Watkins (4/22/1875-   )
2216 Lucy Randolph, d. young
2217 Lucy Goode Randolph, d. young
2218 Georgiana (Georgina?) Washington Randolph, d. unm.
2219 Lucy Ward Randolph, d. young
221x Susan Frances Randolph, m. Alexander Lithgow Botts (7/20/
      1799-1860) of New York, son of Benjamin Gaines and Jane
      Tyler Botts. Both Benjamin Gaines and Jane Tyler Botts
      perished in the Richmond Theatre fire of December 26, 1811.
221x1 Mary Page Botts, d. young
221x2 Lucy Botts
221x3 Jane Botts, m. Henry Chadwick of Brooklyn, son of James
       Chadwick of Manchester, Eng.
221x31 Richard Westlake Chadwick, d. young
221x32 Susan Mary Chadwick (8/5/1851-   ), m. Thomas Slaight
        Eldridge
221x33 Rose Virginia Chadwick, d. young

221x4 William Henry Botts (11/19/1822-9/ /1867), m. Evelina
      Oddie, dau. of John Ward Oddie of New York
221x41 Rosalie Botts (1845-   ), m. George W. Bates
221x411 Minnie Bates
221x412 William Bates
221x413 Frederick Bates
221x414 Thomas Bates
221x415 Alison Bates
221x42 John A. Botts (10/ /1847-   ), m. Julia Thompson
221x421 Asbury H. Botts
221x422 Adelaide Botts
221x423 Stella Botts
221x424 Julia May Botts, d. young
221x425 Frank Botts
221x426 Edna Botts
221x427 Henry Botts
221x428 Arthur Botts
221x43 Edwin Thorne Botts
221x44 Beverly Randolph Botts
221x45 Elizabeth Botts
221x5 Thomas Lawson Botts (4/14/1828-6/5/1854) of New York, m.
      Catharine Martha Hamilton of New York
221x51 Ella Frances Botts (10/29/1852-   ), m. Henry Sickles
221x511 William Sickles
221x52 Thomas Botts (7/19/1854-   ) of New York
221x6 Alexander Botts
221x7 Julian Botts of New York, m. Harriet Bishop
221x71 Lydia Frances Botts (1/2/1859-   )
221x72 Cora Botts (1865-   )
221x8 Randolph Botts, m. Cornelia Osborne of Brooklyn
221x81 John Botts
221x82 Emma Botts
221x83 D, young
221x84 D, young
221x9 Steven King Botts of Brooklyn, m. Mary Gaffney of Ireland
221x91 Virginia Brooks Botts
221x92 Henry Chadwick Botts
221x93 John Minor Botts
221x94 Kate Botts
221xx Virginia Ann Botts, m. Beverly Blair Botts of Harrisonburg,
      son of John Minor Botts. Beverly Blair Botts, m. (2nd)
      Charlotte Lewis, dau. of Gen. Samuel H. Lewis
      Children by first wife:
221xx1 Beverly Botts, d. young
221xx2 Susan Botts, d. young
221a Lucy Randolph, d. young
221b Percy Brett Randolph, d. young
222 Brett Randolph, Jr. (b. prior to 1759-1/22/1828), d. in
      Mississippi, m. (his first cousin), Ann Randolph of "Curles"
      (217). They lived in Powhatan County
2221 Richard Kidder Randolph, Jr. (4/26/1794-9/26/1846), m. 1/28/
      1818 or 1819, Elizabeth Jane ("Betsey") Montague (1800-

1/30/1853) of Powhatan County, dau. of Mickelborough and
Anne Carter Vaughan Montague. In 1835, they moved to Greene
County, Ala.

22211   Brett Noel Randolph, d. 10/18/1836, age 14 years, 4 months
22212   George W. Randolph (1823-1851), m. 1849, Cornelia Fleming
       of Alabama
22213   Montague Mickelborough Randolph, MD. (8/4/1825?-1/14/1909),
       m. late 1853 or early 1854, Cornelia K. Wright (12/17/
       1836?011/2/1911). They lived in Panola County, Miss.
       He graduated from the Medical College of Missouri at St.
       Louis
222131   Ann E. Randolph (1856-   )
222132   Nancy W. ("Nannie") Randolph (1859-   )
222133   John M. Randolph (1862-   )
222134   Alice Randolph (1864-   )
222135   Virginia Randolph (1866-   )
222136   R. M. Randolph (1868-   )
222137   Addie Randolph (1871-   )
222138   George Washington Randolph (1874-5/21/1955), m. Isabella
       ("Belle") Aldridge (12/8/1876-8/14/1941), dau. of Mattson
       Lafayette and Joanah Wooten Aldridge
2221381   Chastine Morris Randolph (11/1/1901-   ), m. 12/8/
       1921, Clair Belle Eubanks (9/3/1904-   ), dau. of
       Buddy and Annie Paul Berry Eubanks
22213811   Dorothy Pearl Randolph (1/2/1926-   ),m. 8/17/1947,
       John Pitts, Jr. (1/25/1925-   ), son of John L.
       and Ruth McCoy Pitts
222138111   John Randolph Pitts (11/4/1953-   )
222138112   Joe McCoy Pitts (8/1/1956-   ), m. Maribeth Thomas
       (1/20/1959-   ), dau. of Lent Thomas, Jr. and Mary
       Ruth Mobley Thomas
2221381121   Joe McCoy Pitts, Jr. (12/5/1974-   )
2221381122   Jennifer Ruth Pitts (9/14/1977-   )
22213812   Clemmie Cornelia Randolph (5/9/1923-   ), m. 5/
       26/1944, Robert M. McCulley (6/4/1918-   ), son of
       John W. and Bessie Lazenby McCulley
222138121   Ronald M. McCulley (2/28/1945-   ), m. 6/26/1965,
       June Woodruff (6/17/1947-   ), dau. of Bryant
       and Verna McKee Woodruff
2221381211   Ronald Bart McCulley (4/12/1967-   )
2221381212   Bard Woodruff McCulley (10/19/1969-   )
2221381213   Allyson Randolph McCulley (1/11/1971-   )
2221382   Richard Montague Randolph (1/28/1904-   ), m. 4/15/
       1924, Mary Gibson (4/11/1903-   ), dau. of MacKintosh
       and Elizabeth Wilkerson Gibson
22213821   George G. Randolph (2/15/1926-   ), m. 8/19/1951,
       Miriam Nell Clement (4/10/1929-   ), dau. of
       Benjamin F. and Alma Carpenter Clement
222138211   Debbie Ann Randolph (12/17/1954-   ), m. 2/24/1978,
       Gregory Holland (7/2/1955-   ), son of Raymond
       and Virginia Purdy Holland
222138212   Richard C. Randolph (10/8/1957-   ), m. 5/21/1983,

           Rae Ann Harper (11/5/1954-   ), dau. of Jack
           and Cynthia Wheelock Harper
222138213 Miriam Susan Randolph (3/27/1964-   )
22213822   Malcolm M. Randolph (5/26/1928-   ), m. 1/14/1956,
           Betty Jo Burns (7/9/1930-   ), dau. of Alonzo and
           Myrtle Pitcock Burns
222138221 Mary Macy Randolph (5/16/1957-   ), m. 11/23/
           1976, Raymond Belk (1/26/1947-   ), son of
           Gordye and Jessie Breazeale Belk
222138222 Lori Lynn Randolph (9/14/1960-   ), m. 9/17/1983,
           Benjamin B. Watts (6/24/1958-   ), son of Thomas
           H. Watts, Jr., and Mary Francis Barnes Watts
2221383   Armead Randolph (1905-   ), d. inf.
2221384   Joe Aldridge Randolph (9/6/1907-   ), m. 12/22/
           1961, Violet Webb
2221385   Max Morris Randolph (1910-1918)
2221386   Cornelia Randolph (1913-1914)
22214   Richard Ryland Randolph (1827-   ), d. inf.
22215   Thomas E. Randolph, M.D. (1829-   ), m. 3/17/1857,
           Nancy Jordan Taylor. He served through the entire war
           in Virginia under General Lee's command, and d. in Vicks-
           burg, Miss.
22216   Ann E. Randolph (1831-   ), d. inf.
22217   Emily Vaughan Randolph (1835-   ), d. inf.
22218   Lucy A. Randolph (1839-1869), m. 1863, Rev. J. B. Barry.
           She d. Eureka, Miss.
222181   Hattie Barry
222182   Lucy Barry
222183   Kidder Barry
22219   Maria S. Randolph (1842-   ), m. (1st) 1859, Greene
           Middleton, who was killed in battle during the Civil War.
           She m. (2nd) S. W. Mills, and moved to Hillsboro, Texas
           Child by first husband:
222191   Frank M. Middleton
           Children by second husband:
222192   Sidney Mills
222193   Clara Mills
2222   Howard Randolph, m.   Meade (Kentucky)
2223   Patrick Randolph, m.   Meade
2224   Brett Randolph (twin of Patrick)
2225   Ann Meade Randolph (4/21/1787-6/28/1836), m. 2/7/1822, in
           Powhatan County, Joseph Michaux (4/3/1771-9/ /1837), son
           of Joseph and Judith Woodson Michaux. Ann was Joseph's
           second wife. He was b. in Cumberland County, and d. in
           Prince Edward County
22251   Richard Randolph Michaux, m. (1st) Anna Davis; and (2nd)
           her sister, Sallie Davis. The Davises were from Granville
           County, N.C. Michaux was a Methodist minister
22252   John LaFayette Michaux (9/3/1824-7/6/1898), D.D., m. 1/23/
           1855, Sarah McLemore Macon (10/26/1831-1/17/1894), dau. of
           George Washington and Eleanor (Ellen) M. Green Macon. Rev.
           Michaux was b. at "St. Domingo", Cumberland County, and d.
           in Greensboro, N.C.

222521 Leonidas Macon Michaux (1856-1926), m. Loulie Miller, dau.
     of Dr. John and Sarah Borden Miller of Goldsboro, N.C.
2225211 Mary Michaux of Goldsboro, N.C.
2225212 (dau)
2225213 Leonidas Macon Michaux
22252131 Leonidas Macon Michaux
222521311 Leonidas Macon Michaux, Jr.
222522 Edward Randolph Michaux (1859-1931), M.D. No issue
222523 John Summerfield Michaux (12/28/1861-8/18/1953)(b. near
     Brinkleyville, Halifax County, N.C., d. Greensboro), m.
     10/21/1903, Lola Carraway (7/26/1874-4/8/1971), dau. of
     Rev. Paul J. and Mattie Foster Carraway
2225231 Mildred Randolph Michaux (5/18/1907-2/21/1982), m. 10/19/
     1929, William Caswell Drake (4/22/1908-4/16/1963). He
     was b. in Halifax County, N.C., and d. in Raleigh
22252311 Marcia Randolph Drake (6/7/1932-   ), m. 9/17/1954,
     Paul C. Bennett, Jr., M.D.
222523111 Anna Michaux Bennett
222523112 Paul C. Bennett III
2225232 John Summerfield Michaux, Jr., d.s.p.
2225233 Paul C. Michaux, d.s.p.
2225234 Lola Michaux (11/30/1908-   ), m. 5/10/1930, Louis
     LeGrand Glascock (12/13/1907-   ). Both of them
     were born and died in Greensboro
22252341 Gail Glascock, m. Edward Kemm
22252342 Louis L. Glascock, m. Mary Louise Norwood
222524 Lucy Evelyn Michaux (1864-1936), m. (1st) Will F. Moss;
     and (2nd) Thomas McConnell, D.D. No issue
222525 Annie Glenn Michaux (1875-1961), m. 1906, Thomas Crocker
2225251 Macon Crocker
22252511 Mary Ann Crocker, m. Ashley S. James, Jr.
2225252 Michaux H. Crocker
22252521 Michaux H. Crocker, Jr.
222525211 Michaux H. Crocker III
2225253 Lucy Crocker
22253 Daniel Meade ("Meade") Michaux
2226 Mary Susan Randolph, m. Frank Watkins
223 Susannah Randolph, m. 1/23/1783, Dr. Charles Douglas (10/11/
     1752-   ) of Essex, England (Scotland?)
2231 Susannah Mary Ann Douglas (5/ /1785-   ) m. (1st)
         Wallace. M. (2nd) 6/2/1808, Capt. John Tucker of
     Bermuda
22311 Susan Jane Tucker (6/20/1810-   ), m. (1st) Andrew
     McDonald Jackson, Purser, U.S.N. M. (2nd) Henry Chandler
     Holt, Surgeon, U.S.N.
22312 John Randolph Tucker (1/31/1812-   ), Admiral, C.S.N.
22313 Honoria Mary Tucker, m. 11/26/1842, Joseph Williamson
     Randolph (22113)
22314 (son)
2232 Archibald Heatly Douglas (12/25/1786-   )
2233 Charles Brett Douglas (12/31/1789-   )(twin)
2234 Abbadore Douglas (12/31/1789-   )(twin)

2235 Eliza Randolph Douglas (1791-   )
224 Richard Randolph (8/17/1754-9/8/1775)
225 (dau)
23 John Randolph of "Matoax", Chesterfield County (6/29/1742-10/
    28/1775), m. 3/9/1769, Frances Bland (9/24/1752-1788), dau.
    of Col. Theodorick (1719-1784) and Frances Bolling Bland
    (1724-1774) of "Cawson's", Prince George County (Theodorick
    was the son of Richard and Elizabeth Randolph Bland of "Jordan's";
    and Frances Bolling was the dau. of Drury Bolling of "Kippax",
    who was, in turn, the son of Robert and Anne Stith Bolling.
    Following the death of Frances Bolling, Theodorick married
    Elizabeth Randolph Yates. No issue.) Following the death
    of John Randolph, Frances Bland Randolph m. 9/22/1777, St.
    George Tucker, and had five children
231 Richard Randolph of "Bizarre" (3/9/1770-6/14/1796), m. 12/31/
    1789, his cousin, Judith Randolph (2417), dau. of Thomas Mann
    and Ann Cary Randolph of "Tuckahoe"
2311 John (or Henry) St. George Randolph, d.s.p. A deaf, "a hope-
    less lunatic" (ECKENRODE 187)
2312 Theodorock (or Thomas) Tudor Randolph (1796-1815), d.s.p.
    Perhaps died of dissipation (ECKENRODE 171, 187). Always
    called Tudor.
2313 (son)
2314 (dau)
232 Theodorick Bland Randolph (1/22/1771-2/14/1792), d.s.p.
233 John Randolph of Roanoke (6/3/1773-5/24/1833), d.s.p.
234 Jane Randolph
24 Mary Randolph (11/21/1727-11/25/1781), m. 5/31/1744, Archibald
    Cary of "Ampthill", Chesterfield County (1/24/1720*1-9/ /
    1787), son of Henry and Anne Edwards Cary
241 Anne Cary (2/ /1745-1786), m. 11/18/1761, Thomas Mann Ran-
    dolph of "Tuckahoe", Goochland County (1740*1-11/20/1793),
    son of William and Maria Judith Page Randolph. Thomas m.
    (2nd) Gabriella Harvie by whom he had a child, Thomas Mann
    Randolph III
    NOTE: Thomas Mann Randolph named one son of each of his
    two marriages Thomas Mann Randolph. Thomas Mann Randolph
    (1792-1851), the son of his second marriage to Gabriella
    Harvie (and who was not a descendant of Pocahontas), in-
    herited "Tuckahoe", and m. (1st) Harriet Wilson, and (2nd)
    Lucinda ("Lucy") Ann Patterson. Gabriella (ca. 1771-post
    1800) was the dau. of Col. John Harvie. After Randolph's
    death, she m. Dr. John Brockenbrough.
    Children by first wife:
2411 Mary ("Molly") Randolph (8/9/62, m. David Meade Randolph
    (212)
2412 Henry Cary Randolph (1769-   ), d.s.p.
2413 Elizabeth Randolph (1765-   ), m. 10/15/1784, Robert
    Pleasants (-ca. 1796), of "Four Mile Creek",
    son of Robert and Mary Webster Pleasants of "Curles"
24131 Robert Pleasants
24132 Elizabeth Randolph Pleasants (3/25/1787-   ), m. 5/1/
    1810, Maurice Langhorne Miller

241321   George B. Miller
241322   Daniel Eppes Miller
24133   Ann Pleasants (5/1/1790-   )
24134   Mary Webster Pleasants (4/25/1792-1844), m. 2/14/1810, John
     Garland Mosby (5/17/1785-12/26/1857), of "Woodland", Pow-
     hatan County, son of Col. Wade and Susanna Trueheart Mosby
241341   Juliet Mosby (-1813)
241342   Elizabeth Mosby (-1816)
241343   Susan Mosby (-1826)
241344   Louisa Mosby (-1863), m. Rev. William McLain (8/8/
     1806-1873), son of Joseph and Betsy Runyon McLain
2413441   William Mosby McLain
2413442   Elizabeth McLain
2413443   Mary Webster McLain
2413444   Lewis Randolph McLain, m. Harriett Rutledge Ravenel
2413445   John Speed McLain
241345   Mary Randolph Mosby (ca. 1852-   ), m. Patrick Theodore
     Moore (ca. 1822, Ireland-10/1/1875)
2413451   Mary Webster Moore (ca. 1852-   ), m. Dr. Robert
     Cowden
2143452   Kathleen (Katherine?) Moore (1856-1928), m. George Alfred
     Lathrop (1850-1908)
24134521   George Alfred Lathrop, Jr. (1876-1924), m. Blanche Nesbitt
24134522   Patrick Theodore Moore Lathrop (1881-1919), m. Constance
     Davies
241345221   Kathleen R. Lathrop
24134523   Mary Randolph Lathrop (1885-   )
24134524   Carrol Currie Lathrop (5/27/1895-   ), m. 11/20/1920,
     Ruth M. Shackley (5/18/1903-   ), dau. of Charles
     Shackley of Sheffield, England
24134525   Whitmel Forbes Lathrop (9/4/1897-   ), m. 12/21/
     1925, Margaret Pomainville (12/29/1903-   ), dau.
     of Dr. F. X. Pomainville of Wisconsin Rapdis, Wisc.
     Home: Chicago
241345251   Nancy Randolph Lathrop (9/14/1926-   )
241345252   Patrick Moore Lathrop (5/29/1928-   )
2413453   Margaret ("Maggie") Moore (1857-   ), m. Walter Palmer
24134531   Eliza M. Palmer
2413454   William R. Moore (ca. 1860-   ), m. Edith Emmert
2413455   John Moore
2413456   Patrick Theodore Moore, Jr.
241346   Virginia Cary Mosby (ca. 1827-   ), m. 5/6/1852,
     John Adair Pleasants (5/17/1826-11/19/1893). He was
     born in Woodford County, Kentucky. They lived in Rich-
     mond, Va.
2413461   Mary Webster Moore Pleasants (2/21/1853-3/13/1854)
2413462   Louise McLain Pleasants (10/24/1855-2/19/1931)
2413463   Catherine ("Kate") Noble Pleasants (4/8/1857-12/30/1925),
     m. 4/18/1877, Edmund Christian Minor
24134631   Louise McLain Minor (3/3/1878-5/27/1880)
24134632   Catherine ("Kate") Pleasants Minor (11/5/1879-9/30/1887)
24134633   Virginia Adair Minor (7/19/1882-   ), m. 9/8/1907,
     Edward Gilchrist

241346331 Catherine Caroline Gilchrist (1909-   )
24134634 Edmund Christian Minor, Jr. (1/10/1885-10/22/1890)
24134635 Caroline Minor (1887-   ), m. 1914, Richard S. Ely
241346351 Richard Edmund Minor Ely (1915-   )
241346352 Adair Anderson Ely (1921-   )
241346353 Anna Morris Ely (1923-   )
24134636 Annie Hyde Minor (12/3/1890-1922)
2413464 Lydia Mosby Pleasants (5/18/1860-1923), m. 1893, Benjamin
          Ladd Purcell
24134641 Martha Webb Purcell (1894-   ), m. 1920, Philip S.
          Barba
241346411 William Philip Barba (1922-   )
24134642 John Adair Purcell (1900-   )
24134643 Lydia Mosby Purcell (1902-   )
24134644 Benjamin Ladd Purcell, Jr. (1903-1905)
241365 Rosalie Harrison Pleasants (9/6/1864-   ), m. 1893,
          William Wharton Archer
24134651 Adair Pleasants Archer (8/31/1894-10/6/1918), d. at
          Camp Grant, Ill. of influenza while serving in the
          Army during World War I
24134652 Sheppard Archer (1898-   ), d. inf.
24134653 William Wharton Archer, Jr. (6/13/1902-   ), m.
          Mary Ann Lindsay
24134654 Edmund Minor Archer
241347 Lydia Octavia Mosby (ca. 1828-   ), m. 10/6/1852,
          Matthew Franklin Pleasants (9/17/1829-11/2/1906). Lived
          in Richmond.
2413471 Isabella Adair Pleasants (10/21/1853-   ), m. 10/16/
          1888, Reginald Gilham. No issue
2413472 Virginia Mosby Pleasants (1/10/1856-   )
2413473 McLain Pleasants (6/21/1860-6/29/1903), m. 4/12/1893,
          in Albemarle County, Hester Roberta Kyle
24134731 Matthew Franklin Pleasants (5/4/1894-   ), m.
          Helene Frances Schreck
24134732 Roberta Kyle Pleasants (11/30/1896-   ), m. 1917,
          Cassius Moncure Chichester
241347321 Roberta Kyle Pleasants Chichester
24134733 Catherine Sellars Pleasants (9/25/1898-   ), m. 1922,
          Charles Melcher Butterworth, Jr.
241347331 Roberta Kyle Butterworth (1923-   )
241347332 Charles Melcher Butterworth III
2413474 Matthew Pleasants (7/22/1865-d. age 2)
2413475 John Adair Pleasants (5/14/1870-1/7/1904)
241348 John Speed Mosby (-1833)
241349 Juliet Mosby (-1813)
24134x Elizabeth Mosby (-1816)
24134a Susan Mosby (-1826)
24135 Margaret Pleasants (8/15/1793-   )
2414 Thomas Mann Randolph (5/17/1768-6/20/1828), of "Edge Hill",
          Governor of Virginia (1819-1822), m. 2/23/1790, Martha
          ("Patsy") Jefferson (9/27/1772-10/10/1836), dau. of Presi-
          dent Thomas and Martha Wayles (Skelton) Jefferson (widow

of Bathurst Skelton). Randolph inherited "Varina", and for several years, resided at it during the winter months. MEMOIR 29-30.

24141 Anne Cary Randolph (1/23/1791-2/11/1826), m. 9/19/1808, Charles Lewis Bankhead (1788-1835)

241411 John Warner Bankhead (12/1/1810-11/21/1897), m. 11/3/1832, Elizabeth Poindexter Christian (1814-1895)

2414111 Archer Christian Bankhead (9/15/1833-4/2/1906), m. 6/10/1857, Mary Graves Chambers

24141111 John Warren Bankhead (2/25/1859-10/19/1916), m. 11/4/1886, Selma Presca Purgahn

241411111 Charles Archie Bankhead (4/28/1887-1/1/1976), m. (1st) 1/5/1909, Vera Reese; m. (2nd) 3/14/1928, Nora Belle Ogden

2414111111 Lowell Carey Bankhead (10/14/1909-5/11/1979), m. 1/30/1937, Erma Lee Green

24141111111 Warren Lee Bankhead (2/23/1943-2/23/1943)

24141111112 Lowell Carey Bankhead, Jr. (10/14/1947-   ), m. 9/15/1968, Charla Marie Rockett

241411111121 Lowell Carey Bankhead III (9/15/1972-   )

241411111122 Chandra Rose Lee Bankhead (4/30/1976-   )

2414111112 Audrey Louise Bankhead (5/16/1913-   ), m. 4/21/1935, Joseph Eugene Howard

24141111121 Sharon Jo Ann Howard (10/31/1939-   ), m. 7/14/1962, Steven George Stockwell

241411111211 Tod Howard Stockwell (1/1/1966-   )

241411111212 Charlton Howard Stockwell (5/29/1967-   )

24141111122 Kristen Audell Howard (7/4/1947-   ), m. 4/4/1971, David Samuelson Druker

241411111221 Michael David Druker (10/8/1977-   )

241411111222 Mara Bankhead Druker (5/22/1981-   )

2414111113 Iris Jean Bankhead (5/5/1916-   ), m. 3/14/1936, Wilford Cameron Caldwell

24141111131 Stanley Terrill Caldwell (4/1/1942-5/20/1958)

24141111132 Randolph Cary Caldwell (8/23/1945-   ), m. 3/10/1972, Roxanne Kay Garlick

241411111321 Terrill Cameron Caldwell (9/27/1973-   )

241411111322 Cary Randolph Caldwell (2/14/1977-   )

2414111114 Selma Elizabeth Bankhead (5/10/1918-   ), m. 11/26/1938, Richard Philip West

24141111141 Stephen Matthew West (10/30/1939-   ), m. (1st) 1963, Lois Ione Kleiber. M. (2nd) 1968, Linda Gregory

Child by first wife:

241411111411 Jeffrey Stephen (West) Grouda (5/ /1964-   )

Children by second wife:

241411111412 Richard Austin West (5/22/1971-   )

241411111413 Ruth Ann West (6/23/1972-   )

24141111142 Penny Jeanne West (3/11/1946-   ), m. (1st) 1966, Duane Raymond Lamoureaux. M. (2nd) 1968, Erich Kurt Hutzler

Child by second wife:
241411111421 Megan Wayles Hutzler (11/20/1969-   )
241411112 John Warren Bankhead, Jr. (12/23/1888-12/28/1918), m.
        5/29/1909, Minnie Kirk
2414111121 Robert Eugene Bankhead (4/22/1913-4/28/1968), m. 7/2/
        1938, Eva Lena James
241411121 Deanna Marlene Bankhead (11/29/1942-   ), m. 11/
        11/1961, Kenneth Wayne Taylor
241411112111 Matthew Brent Taylor (6/20/1964-   )
241411112112 James Kirk Taylor (9/6/1968-   )
2414111122 Pauline Bankhead (4/29/1918-   ), m. 10/23/1937,
        Paul Edward Bramblett
241411112221 Sherrilee Bramblett (10/10/1940-   ), m. 8/31/
        1968, Delbert M. Berry
241411112211 Paul Edward Berry (7/20/1971-   )
241411112212 Robert Lee Berry (8/6/1973-   )
241411113 Selma Pauline Bankhead (8/29/1893-12/24/1916), m. 10/
        8/1909, Ansel Sanderson
2414111131 Genevie Sanderson (1/5/1913-   ), m. 8/9/1934,
        Lewis Olie Erickson
241411111311 Charles Ansel Erickson (1/8/1939-   ), m. (1st)
        7/20/1960, Barbara Jean O'Connor. M. (2nd) 12/26/
        1964, Kathryn Mae Hoon
        Children by second wife:
241411113111 Kristina Marie Erickson (8/2/1965-   )
241411113112 Karin Maria Erickson (11/10/1966-   )
2414111312 John Lewis Erickson (11/8/1942-   ), m. 6/6/1970,
        Sarah Kathleen Turner
241411113121 Thomas Jeffrey Erickson (9/20/1973-   )
241411113122 Michael John Erickson (10/17/1976-   )
2414111132 Marjorie Sanderson (1/18/1916-   ), m. 10/27/
        1945, Clifford A. Orcutt
241411111321 Pamela Sue Orcutt (6/8/1952-   ), m. 12/28/1973,
        Edward Lee Trehearn
241411114 Jay Houchins Bankhead (10/28/1899-12/17/1926)
241411115 Mary Clara Bankhead (10/31/1901-9/19/1945), m. (1st),
        Samuel Owens. M. (2nd) Edwin Conrad
24141112 Thomas Randolph Bankhead (1863-1936), m. 1891, Elizabeth
        ("Betty") Haynie
241411121 William Chambers Bankhead (1894-   ), m. 1914,
        Agnes Temple
2414111211 Marie Elizabeth Bankhead (1923-   ), m. 1946, Lloyd
        Miller
241411112111 Warren Randolph Miller (1947-   )
241411112112 Michael Reginald Miller (6/29/1956-   ), m. 8/9/
        1980, Calda Ray Shaw
241411122 Thomas Jefferson Bankhead (1897-1975), m. 1920, Blanche
        Kerr
2414111221 Robert Wayne Bankhead (1925-1942)
241411123 Katherine Bankhead Bankhead (1901-   ), m. 1920,
        Karl Emil Zuber
2414111231 Frieda Bell Zuber (1925-   ), m. 1950, Obed Hall, Jr.

24141112311 Jeannine Bankhead Hall (1953-   ), m. 8/12/1978,
              David Martin Osborn
24141112312 Karl Obed Hall (7/4/1955-   )
24141113 Elizabeth Chambers Bankhead (1865-6/12/1958), m. 1886,
          William Everett Bell
241411131 Mary Elizabeth Bell (12/3/1886-11/29/1969), m. Horace
           Leonard Hutchison
2414111311 Lucy Elizabeth Hutchison (1912-   ), m. 1941,
            Frank Humbewtel
2414111312 Horace Leonard Hutchison, Jr. (2/9/1915-   ), m.
            11/2/1946, Alice Elizabeth Dimmick
24141113121 Janet Elizabeth Hutchison (1/1/1949-   ), m.
             6/12/1971, Robert Carson Glenn, Jr.
241411131211 Roger Christopher Glenn (2/14/1974-   )
24141113122 Hal Thomas Hutchison (5/10/1950-   )
24141113123 Mary Lynn Hutchison (3/12/1954-   )
24141113124 Susan Frances Hutchison (10/19/1957-   )
2414111313 Everett Bell Hutchison (1918-12/5/1982), m. 1950,
            Virginia Casey
24141113131 Thomas Casey Hutchison (8/13/1952-   ), m. 10/
             24/1972, Mary Elizabeth Brooks
241411131311 Keri Lee Hutchison (8/11/1974-   )
241411131312 Thomas Casey Hutchison, Jr. (1/26/1977-   )
24141113132 Holly Elizabeth Hutchison (1/4/1956-   )
24141113133 Patricia Anne Hutchison (8/24/1957-   ), m. 8/11/
             1973, Neal C. Ramhorst
24141113134 Kenneth Todd Hutchison (2/25/1963-   )
241411132 William Bell, Jr. (1887-   ), m. Alma Arnoldy
2414111321 William Everett Bell III (1927-   )
241411133 Emily Carr Bell (1/25/1891-6/2/1972), m. 11/23/1910,
           Frank F. Marr
2414111331 William Lee Marr (9/3/1911-   ), m. 9/25/1931,
            Thelma Morrison
24141113311 Nancy Lee Marr (12/4/1932-   ), m. 4/16/1952,
             Richard Louis Urbina
241411133111 Laura Lee Urbina (4/26/1953-   )
241411133112 William Nicholas Urbina (1/11/1955-   )
24141113312 John Randolph Marr 5/18/1938-   )
2414111332 Helen Elizabeth Marr (2/24/1914-   ), m. 11/
            21/1943, Arthur A. Townsend
24141113321 John David Townsend (5/6/1955-   ), m. (1st) 5/
             21/1977, Raelynn Carol Pratt. M. (2nd) 11/21/1981,
             Jane Cole Abbott
241411134 Helen Catherine Bell (4/2/1893-   ), m. 5/14/1912,
           Ulysus Earl Mitchell
2414111341 John William Mitchell (6/1/1914-   ), m. 12/3/
            1943, Margaret Ames
24141113411 John William Mitchell, Jr. (5/30/1944-   ), m.
             3/22/1968, Aletha Sue Bishop
241411134111 John William Mitchell III (6/27/1972-   )
241411134112 Amy Aletha Mitchell (2/2/1977-   )
24141113412 Robert Ames Mitchell (12/16/1948-   ), m. 9/30/
             1972, Frances Lincoln

2414111342 Leonard Bell Mitchell (9/30/1916-   ), m. Louise
            Quissenberry
24141113421 Leonard Bell Mitchell, Jr. (9/5/1945-   )
24141113422 Earl Spencer Mitchell (10/15/1946-   )
2414111343 Betty Jane Mitchell (2/10/1928-9/25/1981), m. 11/23/
            1949, George Solberg
24141113431 Robert M. Solbert (4/26/1951-   ), m. 12/22/1972,
            Marion Patrice Walker
241411134311 Jennifer Leigh Solbert (8/19/1976-   )
241411134312 Michael Paul Solbert (11/7/1978-   )
241411134313 Nathaniel James Solbert (2/2/1982-   )
24141113432 Janet Solbert (3/3/1954-   )
241411135 Robert Griffith Bell (3/8/1902-   ), m. (1st) 1931,
            Hortense Lucks. M. (2nd) 5/21/1952, Kathleen Wheeler
            Bair
        Children by first wife:
2414111351 Robert Griffith, Jr. (5/26/1936-   ), m. (1st)
            5/7/1960, Donna Dorothy DeWitt. M. (2nd) Peggy Conway
        Children by first wife:
24141113511 William Bell (1961-   )
24141113512 Robert Bell (1964-   )
        Children by second wife:
24141113513 Michael Bell (1970-   )
24141113514 Matthew Bell (1972-   )
2414111352 Randolph Bankhead Bell (4/26/1945-   )
241411136 Kenneth Cary Bell (1904-   ), m. Martha Jane Brown
2414111361 Kenneth Cary Bell, Jr. (1942-   ), m. (1st) 6/6/
            1969, Bette Jon Fitzpatrick. M. (2nd) 11/27/1976,
            Sue Anne Wiens
        Children by second wife:
24141113611 Cary Jane Anne Bell (2/11/1978-   )
24141113612 Kenneth Cary Bell III (1/15/1981-   )
24141114 Benjamin Chambers Bankhead (1867-1928), m. Kate Smith
24141115 Archie Cary Bankhead (1874-1921), m. 1901, Grace Major
241411151 Mary Clio Bankhead (1901-   )
241411152 Benjamin Nelson Bankhead (1907-   ), m. Betty
            Varweek
2414111521 Judith Ann Bankhead (1937-1942)
2414111522 Mary Elizabeth Bankhead (1940-   )
2414111523 Thomas Randolph Bankhead (1942-   )
2414111524 Jeanne Bankhead (1945-   )
2414112 Dr. Cary Randolph Bankhead (3/5/1835-3/12/1907), m. 1860,
            Amanda Ellen Errett
24141121 Elizabeth Bankhead (12/27/1860-6/5/1863)
24141122 Martha Bankhead (11/20/1862-10/28/1930)
24141123 Dr. Joseph Errett Bankhead (9/21/1864-12/ /1941), m.
            (1st) Laura Hughes. M. (2nd) Elizabeth Cake
        Child by second wife:
241411231 Ellen Cary Bankhead (2/12/1905 (second wife)-1/25/1977),
            m. (1st) Robert Benton Mackey. M. (2nd) William B.
            Weakley
        Children by first wife:

2414112311 Joseph Benton Mackey (1928-   ), m. 1949, Jean Smith
24141123111 Joellen Mackey (6/20/1952-   )
2414112312 Betsy Cake Mackey (1934-   )
24141124 Mary Archer Bankhead (2/12/1867-7/27/1944), m. 1887,
          Mark Miller Gillum
241411241 Cary Randolph Gillum (1889-1953), m. Ruth Stark
2414112411 Mildred Gillum (1913-   ), m. Ross Elgin
2414112412 Rachel Errett Gillum (1917-   ), d. inf.
241411242 Rachel Errett Gillum (1891-1917), m. Clinton Talbert
          Yates
2414112421 Mark Milton Yates (1913-   )
24141125 Charles Lewis Bankhead (11/15/1869-11/29/1949), m. 1915,
          Margaret Cheatwood
241411251 Charles Lewis Bankhead III (1/21/1925-   ), m.
          1946, Margaret Clark Omohundro
2414112511 Michael Errett Bankhead (7/31/1947-   ), m. 9/16/
          1972, Janet Elaine Lovell
24141125111 Shelley Marie Bankhead (7/28/1974-   )
24141125112 Reid Hamilton Bankhead (6/22/1978-   )
2414112512 Margaret Elaine Bankhead (7/6/1949-   ), m. 5/28/
          1972, Benjamin Franklin Jeans
24141125121 Matthew Seth Jeans (4/29/1974-   )
24141125122 Carey Elizabeth Jeans (10/11/1975-   )
2414112513 Mary Bankhead (1953-   ), d. inf.
2414112514 Mary Leigh Bankhead (8/2/1954-   ), m. 5/18/1974,
          Douglas Mackey Burns
24141126 Ellen Cary Bankhead (9/26/1871-4/29/1962), m. 1892,
          Clemence Griffith Smith, M.D.
241411261 Kathryn Smith (9/7/1893-5/21/1957),m. 1916, Willard
          Moyer
2414112611 William Bankhead Moyer (1919-   ), m. 1944 Atha
          Bell Peacock
2414112612 Anne Cary Moyer (1926-   ), m. (1st) 1944, Billie
          Waers. M. (2nd) Bob Davis
          Children by first wife:
24141126121 Anne Randolph Waers (10/27/1946-   )
24141126122 David Moyer Waers (5/12/1951-   )
24141126123 Jeff Waers
2414112613 Jane Randolph Moyer (4/30/1931-   ), m. 1/14/1952,
          William Emmet Banks IV
24141126131 Katherine Banks
24141126132 Scott Banks
241411262 Ellen Clemence Smith (1895-4/6/1946), m. Dr. Paul Edgar
          Hamilton
2414112621 Richard Edgar Hamilton (4/10/1923-   ), m. Ima Jean
          Tiffin
24141126211 Gary Paul Hamilton (4/15/1952-   )
24141126212 Mark Roger Hamilton (11/10/1957-   )
24141126213 Scott Lester Hamilton (2/19/1960-   )
2414112622 Ann Hamilton (12/16/1929-   ), m. 1947, Thomas
          Mett Beauchamp
24141126221 Lynne Beauchamp (3/23/1949-   ), m. 6/25/1967,
          William Eugene Woods

241411262211 Troy Paul Woods (3/4/1975-   )
241411262212 Todd Michael Woods (8/13/1980-   )
24141126222   Thomas Lawrence Beauchamp (3/27/1951-   ), m.
              6/5/1971, Susan Elisabeth Smoker
241411262221 Thomas Lawrence Beauchamp, Jr. (6/25/1974-   )
241411262222 Ted Michael Beauchamp (6/4/1982-   )
241411262223 Lori Hamilton Beauchamp (5/7/1959-   ), m. 2/14/
              1981, Douglas Jay Tarwater
241411262231 Andrew Ross Tarwater (7/31/1981-   )
241411263   Mary Emily Smith (1901-7/1/1975), m. 1925, Frank Wirt
              Minor
241411264   (child) Smith, d. inf.
24141127   Henry Russell Bankhead (9/9/1873-1/19/1946), m. 1901,
              Edythe Kemble
241411271   Martha Lu Bankhead (1/13/1906-   ), m. (1st) 1/11/
              1926, Charles Lester Stouffer. M. (2nd) 10/7/1968,
              Ernest Benjurman Crosley
           Child by first husband:
2414112711   Martha Jane Stouffer (12/4/1926-   ), m. (1st)
              6/30/1946, Edward Henry Smith. M. (2nd) 7/1/1972,
              Winston Peter Jaskowiak
           Children by first husband:
24141127111 Edythe Lu Smith (9/25/1947-   ), m. (1st) 7/4/
              1969, Charles Carter Gaffney. M. (2nd) 4/26/1974,
              Thomas Howard Anderfore Turner III
           Child by first husband:
241411271111 Michael Charles Gaffney (1/12/1970-   )
           Child by second husband:
241411271112 Thomas Howard Anderfore Turner IV (9/25/1976-   )
24141127112 Katherine Jayne Smith (3/26/1950-   ), m. 4/12/
              1970, Fred Willis Neff
24141127112 Kenneth Edward Neff (12/7/1971-   )
241411271122 Andrea Katherine Neff (8/22/1978-   )
24141127113 Edward Henry Smith, Jr. (10/30/1953-   )
24141127114 Mary Elizabeth Smith (3/12/1957-   ), m. 2/22/
              1976, Ralph Michael Destrini
24141127115 Carl Kemble Smith (5/12/1960-   )
241411272   Charles Kemble Bankhead (1908-   ), m. 1936, Billie
              Bradshaw
24141128   Fannie Warren Bankhead (8/16/1875-11/10/1879)
24141129   Cary Randolph Bankhead, Jr. (1/2/1878-11/21/1935), m.
              1905, Mary Lucilla Miller
241411291   Henry Miller Bankhead (9/21/1906-8/ /1956), m. 1942,
              Annette Gasser
2414112911   Barbara Bankhead (9/21/1932-   ), m. 2/2/1957,
              Frank Edwin Booker
24141129111 Thomas Randolph Booker (2/21/1958-   )
24141129112 Elizabeth Lenore Booker (1/25/1960-   )
24141129113 Leigh Ann Booker (3/8/1961-   )
24141129114 Susanne Melinda Booker (5/22/1962-   )
24141129115 Robert Frank Booker (3/3/1969-   )
24141129116 Rachel Eleanor Booker (8/31/1971-   )

2414112912   Malvern Miller Bankhead (8/15/1933-   ), m. 12/
             26/1955, Sheila Jo-Ann Walsh
             Jennifer Ann Bankhead (1/24/1963-   )(adopted)
24141129121 Henry Miller Bankhead (10/13/1964-   )
24141129122 Joseph Randolph Bankhead (2/5/1969-   )
24141129123 Benjamin Lewis Bankhead (7/24/1971-   )
2414112913   William Marion Bankhead (6/14/1936-   ), m. 7/15/
             1957, Verna Ruth Page
24141129131 Jodie Marie Bankhead (6/13/1959-   ), m. David
             Paul Tomczak
241411291311 Krista Marie Tomczak (8/22/1979-   )
241411291312 David Paul Tomczak, Jr. (7/18/1980-   )
24141129132 Ruth Anette Bankhead (4/11/1961-   )
24141129133 William Page Bankhead (10/16/1963-   )
2414112914   Bettie Bankhead (9/30/1939-   ), m. 5/7/1958, James
             Hoyle Branson
24141129141 Deborah Marie Branson (2/7/1959-   )
24141129142 Denise Lynn Branson (6/17/1960-   )
24141129143 Kevin Matthew Branson (6/17/1960-   )
241411292   Cary Randolph Bankhead III (10/20/1910-   ), m. 10/
             25/1941, Katherine Bernice Lubke
2414112921   Robert Randolph Bankhead (10/29/1942-   ), m.
             7/22/1972, Martha C. Harrold
24141129211 William Randolph Bankhead (4/9/1977-   )
24141129212 Mary McFarland Bankhead (6/1/1980-   )
2414112922   Thomas Alfred Bankhead (6/2/1945-   ), m. 3/20/
             1976, Judith K. Lemon
24141129221 Laura Kay Bankhead (10/2/1977-   )
24141129222 Sarah Anne Cary Bankhead (10/26/1979-   )
241411293   Marion Swain Bankhead (12/12/1912-11/14/1915)
241411294   Joseph Russell Bankhead (11/2/1917-   ), m. 7/11/
             1941, Kathryn G. Jones
2414112941   Terry Jo Bankhead (1/24/1943-   ), m. 8/6/1961,
             Keith Mitchell
24141129411 Brian Keith Mitchell (11/9/1962-   )
24141129412 Joseph Blake Mitchell (3/17/1964-   )
24141129413 Kerri Renee Mitchell (3/20/1967-   )
2414112942   James Lewis Bankhead (4/4/1945-   ), m. 12/12/1967,
             Kay Collier
24141129421 Noel Keith Bankhead (7/5/1968-   )
24141129422 Nicholas Andrew Bankhead (10/16/1973-   )
2414112x   Katie Clyde Bankhead (2/11/1880-7/28/1960)
2414112a   Bessie Guy Bankhead (10/23/1883-12/12/1962)
2414113   Martha Jefferson Bankhead (1837-1891), m. 1858, Kinzea
             Howard Norris
24141131   Elizabeth Bankhead Norris (1858-1898), m. Peter Norton
241411311   Natalie Norton, m. (1st) Eugene Schmierle. M. (2nd)
             William Dallet
24141132   Mollie Norris (1860-   ), m. (1st) Eugene Wells. M.
             (2nd) James Augustus Sublette
             Children by first husband:
241411321   Howard Custis Wells (1881-1950), m. Meta Fragstein

241411322 Dixie Annette Wells, m. Alfred Lund
24141133   Ellen B. Norris (1862-   ), m. Emmanuel Daniels
24141134   Charles A. Norris (1866-1921), m. (1st) Harriet Amos.
           M. (2nd) Anne C. P. Carter Clark (24141331)
24141135   John Bankhead Norris (1868-1901)
2414114   Thomas Jefferson Bankhead (1839-1863) (Civil War)
241412   Thomas Mann Randolph Bankhead (1811-7/1/1851), m. Elizabeth
           Pryor (-1880)
241413   Ellen Monroe Bankhead (9/3/1812-1/6/1838), m. 7/7/1832,
           John Coles Carter (1800-1876), of "Redlands", Albemarle
           County. He m. (2nd) Margaret Rachel Higginbotham Coleman,
           and had issue.
2414131   Anne Cary Carter (4/19/1833-1/12/1915), m. 9/8/1852,
           Henry Preston (11/20/1828-7/17/1899) of "Walnut Grove",
           Washington County, son of John and Margaret Brown
           (Preston) Preston
24141311   Mary Coles Preston (2/9/1854-3/27/1914). Unm.
24141312   Margaret Brown Preston (9/9/1855-5/9/1926). Unm.
24141313   Ellen Bankhead Preston (3/3/1857-3/3/1923), m. 4/24/1889,
           Otway Giles Bailey (5/25/1854-1930)
241413131 Preston H. Bailey (5/25/1891-10/11/1918), m. 6/19/1917,
           Elizabeth Marie Leftwich
2414131311 Margaret Preston Bailey (1918-   ), m. 1941,
           Robert Jacobson
24141313111 Betty Rea Jacobson (1942-   )
241413132 Otway Giles Bailey, Jr. (1895-   ), m. 1923, Ellen
           Verena De Ford
2414131321 Otway Giles Bailey III (1924-   ), m. 1948,
           Elsie Watson
24141313211 Anne Lynne Bailey (1950-   )
24141313212 Barbara Leigh Bailey (1955-   )
2414131322 Ellen Olivia Bailey (1926-   ), m. 1950,
           Curtis Geannini
24141313221 David Curtis Geannini
24141313222 Stephen Philip Geannini
24141313223 Giles Anderson Geannini
2414131323 Jeanne Bailey (1928-   ), m. 1952, Robert Pierce
           Whitman
24141313231 Robert Pierce Whitman, Jr. (1953-   )
24141314   Elizabeth Madison Preston (10/5/1858-1/4/1906), m. 7/18/
           1900, her cousin, Dr. James White Cummings (9/19/1855-
           7/9/1924), son of David C. and Elizabeth Wilson White
           Cummings. No issue. He was a physician in Abingdon.
           He remarried: Fannie S.   , and had children.
24141315   Henry Preston, Jr. (7/29/1861-12/14/1921), m. Mary Helen
           ("Nellie") Carson (11/13/1863-   )
241413151 Sidney Preston (1891-1938). Twin
241413152 Henley Preston (1891-   ). Twin
241413153 Anne Carter Preston (1893-   )
241413154 Henry Preston III (1895-   ), m. 1930, Leta P.
           Wilson
2414131541 Henry Donald Preston (1933-   ), m. 1952, Nancy
           Neal

241413155 Robert Carson Preston (1902-1941)
24141316 Anne Cary Preston (2/18/1863-1931), m. 6/7/1899, Albert
          Pendleton Killinger (12/1/1854-   ) of Smyth County.
          No issue
24141317 Isaette Randolph Preston (11/5/1865-6/18/1916), d.s.p.
24141318 Percy Thomas Preston (10/11/1875-4/2/1941), m. 9/7/1905,
          Corinne Roane Wills (4/1/1875-   )
241413181 Virginia Wills Preston (1906-1928), m. Albert Basil
          Wilson, Jr.
2414131811 Elizabeth Ann Wilson (6/23/1931-   ), m. 8/27/
          1951, Dwight Eugene Bogle
24141318111 Keith Eugene Bogle (8/9/1952-   )
24141318112 Barbara Ann Bogle (10/10/1953-   )
24141318113 Jerry Wayne Bogle (12/11/1954-   )
2414131812 Albert Percy Wilson (7/5/1933-   ), m. 7/8/1956,
          Betty Lou Umbarger
2414131813 Charlotte Louise Wilson (12/13/1937-   )
241413182 Percy Thomas Preston, Jr. (1909-   ), m. 1933,
          Mary Marguerite Carter
241413183 Elizabeth Madison Preston (1913-   ), m. 1940,
          Kyle Roosevelt Ferris
24141319 Jane Craighead Preston (8/1/1863-d.s.p. 1/23/1907)
2414131x Eugenia Fannie Preston (1/31/1868-1/4/1913), m. 10/2/
          1889, Charles Cummings Gibson (12/14/1863-10/26/1920.
          No issue. He remarried: Bessie P.
2414132 Robert Hill Carter (1835-1854)
2414133 John Coles Carter, Jr. (1837-1902), m. (1st) Mary Ann
          Pollard. M. (2nd) Sarah Elizabeth Calvert
24141331 Anne C. P. Carter (1865-1952), m. (1st) Edward J. Clark.
          M. (2nd) Charles A. Norris (24141134)
          Child by first husband:
241413311 Carter Bankhead Clark (1903-1963), m. Merlie King
2414133111 Bankhead Clark
24141332 Mary Bankhead Carter (1863-1939)
241414 William Stuart Bankhead (1/30/1826-11/ /1898), m. (1st)
          1850, Martha Jane Watkins (d. 1851). M. (2nd) 1854,
          Barbara Elizabeth Garth (d. 1867). M. (3rd) Catharine
          Gilchrist Garth
          Child by first wife:
2414141   Bankhead, d. inf.
          Children by second wife:
2414142 Anne Cary ("Nannie") Randolph Bankhead (1856-1900), m.
          1873, J. Harvey Gilchrist
24141421 Katie Frank Gilchrist (10/19/1876-2/10/1968), m. 9/29/
          1896, Lawson Sykes
241414211 (dau) Sykes, d. inf.
241414212 Lelia Scaife Sykes (10/7/1905-   ), m. 2/16/1934,
          David Lawson Martin
2414142121 Lawson Sykes Martin (7/18/1936-   ), m. 11/24/
          1962, Donie De Bardeleben Neal
24141421211 Virginia Larkin Martin (9/2/1963-   )
24141421212 Anne Randolph Martin (1/19/1965-   )(twin)

24141421213 Ellen Pratt Martin (1/19/1965-   )(twin)
24141421214 Donie Neal Martin (1/4/1970-   )
2414143 William Stuart Bankhead, Jr., d. inf.
2414144 (dau) Bankhead, d. inf.
2414145 Elizabeth Garth Bankhead (8/28/1865-4/9/1942), m. 1886,
          William Edgar Hotchkiss (1855-1962)
24141451 Cary Randolph Hotchkiss (5/18/1887-3/3/1978)
24141452 Anna Frances Hotchkiss (11/18/1889-11/26/1943), m. 9/5/
          1911, Campbell Houston Gillespie
241414521 Campbell Houston Gillespie, Jr. (8/7/1913-   ), m.
          1937, Mary Ruffin McMurdo (241424334)
2414145211 Campbell Houston Gillespie III (8/21/1938-   ), m.
          9/1/1962, Mary Bert Patillo
24141452111 Maryanna Keeval Gillespie (5/1/1968-   )
24141452112 Cary Ruffin Gillespie ((4/14/1970-   )
2414145212 Robert McMurdo Gillespie (7/29/1945-   ), m. 11/
          7/1981, Susan (Estes) Robinson
241414522 Stuart Edgar Gillespie (9/13/1919-   ), m. (1st)
          1942, Layle Church. M. (2nd) 8/7/1958, Dorothy
          (Hastings) Wellman
          Children by first wife:
2414145221 Clark Patton Gillespie (4/13/1944-   ), m. 8/2/
          1972, Anne Marie Varn
          Teresa Marie Gillespie (2/6/1961-   )(adopted)
24141452211 Kelly Elizabeth Gillespie (8/23/1973-   )
24141452212 Patricia DeAnne Gillespie (2/24/1975-   )
24141452213 Adam Stuart Gillespie (9/18/1980-   )
2414145222 Layle Christine Gillespie (2/7/1946-   )
          Julia Elizabeth (Wellman) Gillespie (1/18/1947-   ),
          (adopted), m. 6/30/1973, James Henderson Collins
          1 James Henderson Collins, Jr. (1/6/1977-   )
          2 Kimberleigh Pamela Collins (10/21/1979-   )
          Anna Kate (Wellman) Gillespie (3/25/1950-   ), m.
          Ayers
2414145223 William Stuart Gillespie (9/6/1950-   )
24141453 Elizabeth Bankhead Hotchkiss (7/29/1891-2/27/1944), m.
          1924, Virgin James
24141454 Rev. David Stuart Hotchkiss (6/28/1894-8/23/1935), m.
          12/22/1919, Martha Maddox Smith
241414541 David Stuart Hotchkiss, Jr. (10/5/1920-   ), m.
          Beryl
241414542 Martha Jane Hotchkiss (5/28/1924-4/15/1973), m. 12/19/
          1942, Robert Tweedy McWhorter
2414145421 Robert Tweedy McWhorter, Jr. (9/28/1943-   ), m.
          10/27/1967, Kathleen Marie Morrison
24141454211 Cary Bankhead McWhorter (4/3/1973-   )
2414145422 Roger Barton McWhorter II (9/9/1945-   ), m. 7/6/
          1969, Barbara Hudson
24141454221 Elizabeth Randolph McWhorter (12/14/1971-   )
24141454222 Roger Barton McWhorter III (9/28/1973-   )
2414145423 Martha Stuart McWhorter (6/25/1947-   ), m. 3/7/
          1970, John Thomas Terry

24141454231 Katherine Stuart Terry (8/17/1976-   )
24141454232 Virginia Garth Terry (8/30/1980-   )(twin)
24141454233 Ellen Wayles Terry (8/30/1980-   )(twin)
241414543 William Edgar Hotchkiss III (8/24/1926-   ), m.
           9/8/1951, Jean Downes Hinson
2414145431 Jean Randolph Hotchkiss (9/6/1952-   ), m. 6/23/
           1973, Gene Ray Harris
24141454311 William Randolph Harris (4/28/1975-   )
2414145432 David William Hotchkiss (12/9/1953-   ), m. 6/23/
           1978, Elizabeth Ann Stophel
2414145433 Thomas Odus Hinson Hotchkiss (11/12/1955-   ), m.
           5/12/1979, Edna Kathleen Schell
24141454331 Shelley Louise Hotchkiss (6/29/1981-   )
2414145434 William Edgar Hotchkiss IV (11/20/1958-   )
2414145435 Stuart Andrew Hotchkiss (2/13/1961-   )
2414145436 Mae Stone Hotchkiss (5/1/1963-   )
24141455 William Edgar Hotchkiss, Jr. (1/26/1899-7/4/1959), m.
           5/18/1922, Mary (Beard) Walker
241414551 William Bankhead Hotchkiss (12/19/1923-   ), m. 8/
           31, 1947, Jo Vaughan Paulus
2414145511 Nancy Vaughan Hotchkiss (10/25/1949-   ), m. 3/20/
           1970, Jimmy Burch Aston, Jr.
24141455111 Jennifer Elizabeth Aston (1/21/1972-   )
24141455112 Amy Gail Aston (9/30/1974-   )
2414145512 Charles William Hotchkiss (7/31/1951-   )
241414552 Cary Randolph Hotchkiss II (8/23/1931-   ), m. 2/
           26/1953, Charlotte Taylor Shackelford
2414145521 Ellen Garth Hotchkiss (9/29/1954-   ), m. (1st)
           9/10/1976, John Claude Morris III. M. (2nd) 7/18/
           1981, Theodore Straub
           Child by first husband:
24141455211 John Claude Morris IV (6/20/1977-   ), name changed
           to John Bankhead Morris Straub
2414145522 Michael Cary Hotchkiss (7/22/1957-   )
2414145523 Elizabeth Bankhead Hotchkiss (2/27/1963-   ), m.
           2/23/1982, John Daniel Wyker III
24141456 Charles Wilcox Hotchkiss (7/22/1903-12/14/1952), m. 7/
           3/1929, Gene Marie Fennel
241414561 Gene Bankhead Hotchkiss (10/7/1930-   ), m. 5/19/
           1953, Wilburn Craft
2414145611 Rebecca Lecky Craft (7/30/1954-   ), m. 11/15/
           1981, William Neal Mitchell
241414562 John Fennel Hotchkiss (3/20/1938-   )
           Child by third wife:
2414146 Stuart Gibbons Bankhead (1869-   )(approx.), d. inf.
24142 Col. Thomas Jefferson Randolph (9/12/1792-10/8/1875), m.
           3/10/1815, Jane Hollis Nicholas (1798-1871), dau. of
           Wilson Cary Nicholas
241421 Margaret Smith Randolph (3/7/1816-12/20/1842), m. 9/2/
           1839, William Mann Randolph (-1850)(241x1)
           NOTE: Descendants of Margaret Smith Randolph are listed
           as descendants of their father, William Mann Randolph.

241422   Martha ("Patsy") Jefferson Randolph (7/20/1817-7/16/1857),
         m. 12/22/1834, John Charles Randolph Taylor (5/30/1802-
         1/6/1875), son of Bennett and Susan Beverly Randolph
         Taylor
2414221   Col. Bennett Taylor (8/15/1836-4/9/1898), m. 6/19/1866,
         Lucy Colston (3/9/1842-   ), dau. of Edward and
         Sarah Jane Brockenbrough Colston
24142211   Patsy Jefferson Taylor (3/24/1867-11/20/1903)
24142212   Raleigh Colston Taylor (6/22/1869-4/11/1952), m. 1907,
         Mary Tayloe
241422121   Raleigh Colston Taylor, Jr. (2/13/1909-4/19/1959), m.
         1940, Margaret Lamb
2414221211   Jane Colston Taylor (7/8/1941-   ), m. 2/12/
         1966, William Hanks Gaede
24142213   Lewis Randolph Taylor (9/22/1871-4/12/1945), m. 9/10/
         1901, Natalie Dorsey Sefton
241422131   Bennett Taylor III (5/14/1904-   ), m. 6/8/1935,
         Anne Spottswood Harrison
241422132   Lewis Randolph Taylor, Jr. (3/11/1909-5/3/1976), m.
         6/7/1941, Carolyn Douthat
2414221321   Susan Randolph Taylor (8/3/1949-   ), m. 11/15/
         1975, James Addison Martin, Jr.
24142213211   Steven Randolph Martin (5/16/1979-   )
241422133   Walter Dorsey Taylor (12/5/1916-   ), m. Emily
         Rawlings
2414221331   Emily Hume Taylor (7/6/1942-   ), m. 4/16/1966,
         Bradford Willis Gile
24142213311   Bradford Willis Gile, Jr. (1/20/1969-   )
24142213312   Emily Hume Gile (3/23/1973-   )
2414221332   Walter Dorsey Taylor, Jr. (12/23/1945-   ), m. 6/8/
         1968, Linda Sue Bohon
24142213321   Linda Bohon Taylor (8/2/1971-   )
24142213322   Martha Randolph Taylor (10/16/1975-   )
24142213323   Lucy Colston Taylor (1/21/1981-   )
24142214   John Charles Randolph Taylor, Jr. (8/21/1874-   ), m.
         6/18/1907, Mary Grammer Leigh (-1/27/1962)
241422141   Martha Jefferson Taylor (12/10/1910-   ), m. 9/8/
         1964, Edgar Stedman
241422142   John Charles Randolph Taylor III (9/22/1914-   ),
         m. 12/9/1944, Mary Farrant Ferebee
2414221421   John Charles Randolph Taylor IV (3/26/1946-   )
2414221422   Randolph Emery Taylor (10/1/1947-   )
241422143   William Leigh Taylor (5/7/1919-   ), m. 1/24/1942,
         Norma Pamplin
2414221431   Mary Leigh Taylor (12/9/1942-   ), m. 7/10/1965,
         Philip Wilson Shepard
24142214311   Jennifer Leigh Shepard (4/29/1969-   )
24142214312   Douglas Carey Shepard (5/16/1972-   )
2414221432   William Leigh Taylor, Jr. (2/26/1947-   )
2414221433   Charles MacLellan Taylor (9/2/1949-   ), m. 9/11/
         1977, Alice Whitcomb Clark

24142214331 Alice Theresa Taylor (10/24/1977-   )
24142214332 Joanna Leigh Taylor (2/8/1983-   )
2414221434   Martha Jefferson Taylor (1/9/1954-   ),m. 9/17/
             1977, Mark Irvin Raper
24142214341 Carter Jefferson Raper (10/27/1983-   )
241422144 Mary Leigh Taylor (8/1/1922-   ), m. 1/13/1951,
             Martin Nisbet Shaw, Jr.
2414221441   Christopher Gordon Shaw (2/28/1953-   )
2414221442   Margaret Hope Shaw (1/19/1956-   )
24142215   Edward Colston Taylor (2/22/1877-6/23/1940), m. Jessie
             Alwine
241422151   Edward Colston Taylor, Jr. (3/21/1911-   ), m.
             9/9/1972, Alys (Shanks) Cremer
24142216   Jane Brockenbrough Taylor (1/29/1881-11/11/1955)
2414222   Jane Randolph Taylor (4/2/1838-1/12/1917)
2414223   Susan Beverley Taylor (2/8/1840-9/22/1900), m. John
             Sinclair Blackburn
24142231   Richard Scott Blackburn (4/29/1875-4/4/1946), m. Ruth
             Darwin
241422311   John Sinclair Blackburn (3/31/1916-5/27/1935)
241422312   Gertrude Blackburn (6/10/1918-1977), m. George F. Fowler
241422313   Ruth Blackburn (5/17/1920-   ), m. Walter Thomas
             Nobles
2414223131   Charlotte Ruth Nobles (11/3/1949-   )
24142232   Charlotte Moncure Blackburn (1881-7/27/1917), m. 12/23/
             1909, Thomas Shepherd
241422321   John Blackburn Shepherd
2414223211   James Shepherd
241422322   Arnold Page Shepherd
2414223221   Richard Shepherd
241422323   Edward Lippert Shepherd (7/22/1917-   )(twin). (On
             death of mother, Charlotte Moncure Blackburn Shepherd
             was adopted by Mr. & Mrs. Eustace Williams. Name
             changed to Blackburn Edward Williams.)
241422324 Moncure Shepherd (7/22/1917-9/9/1917)(twin of preceding)
24142233   John Sinclair Blackburn, Jr. (1881-1900)
2414224 Jefferson Randolph Taylor (12/27/1842-4/15/1919), m. Mary
             Hubard Bruce (1857-1909), dau. of Edward C. and Eliza
             Thompson Hubard Bruce
24142241   Martha Randolph Taylor (5/31/1892-1/11/1968), m. 4/6/
             1935, George Hyndman Esser, Sr.
24142242   Mary Cary Taylor (8/10/1894-1/2/1923), m. 9/4/1920,
             George Hyndman Esser, Sr.
241422421   George Hyndman Esser, Jr. (8/6/1921-   ), m. 6/20/
             1953, Mary Parker
2414224211   Mary Cary Esser (9/16/1955-   )
2414224212   John Parker Esser (11/1/1957-   )
2414224213   George Randolph Esser (9/8/1960-   )
241422422   Jefferson Randolph Cary Esser (12/28/1922-   ), m.
             7/18/1953, Kathryn Swanson
2414224221   Jefferson Randolph Esser (4/26/1954-   ), m. 10/
             4/1980, Carolyn Patricia Smith

2414224222 Karyn Ann Esser (4/16/1957-   )
2414224223 Douglas Swanson Esser (4/1/1963-   )
2414225 Margaret Randolph Taylor (11/14/1843-2/12/1898), m. 11/9/
        1887, William Lewis Randolph. She was his second wife.
        See 241x12
2414226 Stevens Mason Taylor (7/6/1847-1/10/1917), m. 2/7/1882,
        Mary Mann Page
24142261 Page Taylor (1/25/1885-5/1/1983), m. 6/26/1913, Edwin
        Kirk
241422611 Mary Mann Page Kirk (9/9/1915-   ), m. 6/6/1942,
        James Charles Moyer
2414226111 Margaret Randolph Moyer (9/16/1944-   )
2414226112 Stevens Mason Moyer (6/6/1947-   )
2414226113 Elizabeth Duncan Moyer (10/23/1952-   ), m. 4/30/
        1982, Michael Christopher Powanda
241422612 Edwin Roger Kirk (6/27/1917-   ), m. 9/21/1946,
        Charlotte Louise Homrighaus
2414226121 Charlotte Louise Kirk (7/26/1949-   )
2414226122 Elizabeth Page Kirk (7/24/1953-   )
24142262 Mary Randolph Taylor (1886-1887), d. inf.
24142263 Margaret Randolph Taylor (6/9/1888-   )
24142264 Olivia Alexander Taylor (10/31/1890-   )
2414227 Cornelia Jefferson Taylor (3/29/1849-3/3/1937)
2414228 Moncure Robinson Taylor (2/23/1851-12/7/1915), m. 1901,
        Lucie Madison Willis
24142281 John Bird Taylor (3/4/1903-   ), m. 10/4/1930, Mildred
        Powell Bronaugh
241422811 Moncure Robinson Taylor II (11/8/1932-   ), m. 3/22/
        1957, Patsie Harline Williams
2414228111 Moncure Robinson Taylor III (11/6/1957-   )
2414228112 John Harper Taylor (11/7/1959-   )
2414228113 Minor Bronaugh Taylor (6/4/1961-   )
2414228114 Lawrence Colston Taylor (5/27/1969-   )
241422812 Mildred Lee Drewry Taylor (7/17/1936-   ), m. 9/7/
        1963, Claude Crisp Farmer, Jr.
2414228121 Claude Crisp Farmer III (3/28/1965-4/1/1965)
2414228122 Taylor Bronaugh Farmer (1/3/1968-   )
2414228123 Paul Crisp Farmer (6/3/1971-   )
241422813 Lucie Bronaugh Taylor (12/14/1938-   ), m. 9/21/
        1958, Louis John Carnesale
2414228131 Louis Vincent Carnesale (1/16/1963)(twin)
2414228132 John Lawrence Carnesale (1/16/1963)(twin)
2414228133 Carrie Lee Carnesale (4/28/1969-   )
2414228134 Virginia Powell Carnesale (6/1/1975-   )
2414229 Edmund Randolph Taylor, Sr. (7/12/1853-6/16/1919), m. 7/
        7/1892, Julia Paca Kennedy
24142291 Juliana Paca Taylor (1/31/1894-   )
24142292 Elizabeth Gray Taylor (6/10/1895-1/19/1978)
24142293 Edmund Randolph Taylor, Jr. (10/5/1898-   ), m.
        12/26/1924, Alice Hunt
241422931 Edmund Randolph Taylor III (10/21/1925-   ), m.
        5/29/1954, Patricia Ann Kilmartin

2414229311 Patricia Taylor (8/1/1959-   )
24142294 Margaret Beverley Taylor (9/1/1904-   )
241422x Sidney Wayles Taylor (11/27/1854-8/4/1856)
241422a John Charles Randolph Taylor (5/8/1857-d.s.p. 6/8/1863)
241422b Charlotte Taylor (12/17/1845-5/17/1846)
241423 Mary Buchanan Randolph (11/23/1818-10/24/1821)
241424 Caryanne Nicholas Randolph (4/22/1820-7/24/1857), m. 12/
        28/1840, Col. Francis Gildart Ruffin, son of William and
        Frances Gildart Ruffin (1816-1892). Colonel Ruffin m.
        (2nd) 3/27/1860, Ellen S. Harvie, and had issue
2414241 Spencer Roane Ruffin (1841-   ), d. inf.
2414242 Jefferson Randolph Ruffin (11/16/1842-12/9/1907)
2414243 William Roane Ruffin (7/3/1845-5/27/1899), m. 4/7/1870,
        Sally Walthall McIlwaine (8/30/1831-   ), dau. of
        James and Fannie Susan Dunn McIlwaine
24142431 James McIlwaine Ruffin (2/22/1871-11/21/1936), m. 10/31/
        1901, Anne Lillian Nichols (1/ /1878-   ), dau. of
        William and Nora Pratt Nichols
241424311 James McIlwaine Ruffin, Jr. (8/3/1902-8/8/1961), m. 7/
        27/1929, Jean Fairfax Dickey
2414243111 Page Dickey Ruffin (7/27/1930-   ), m. (1st) 10/
        14/1950, Richard Anthony Myers. M. (2nd) 7/16/1964,
        Dean Hale Case. M. (3rd) 1/15/1977, William Haig
        Rowe. M. (4th) 9/11/1982, Ronald L. McFall
        Children by second husband:
24142431111 Michael Dean Case (8/2/1966-   )
24142431112 Toni Page Case (5/16/1968-   )
2414243112 Jean Fairfax Ruffin (1/26/1946-   ), m. 3/6/1971,
        Louis Ruben Wegner
2414243121 Wendi Charlotte Wegner (9/28/1975-   )
2414243113 Jane McIlwaine Ruffin (1/26/1946-   ), m. (1st)
        4/16/1966, James R. Knapp. M. (2nd) 6/14/1973,
        Clayton Hartzell
        Child by second husband:
2414243131 David McKinley Hartzell (11/21/1975-   )
241424312 William Nichols Ruffin (10/9/1905-10/26/1979), m. Naomi
        Fulford
2414243121 William Nichols Ruffin, Jr. (3/9/1938-   ), m.
        9/10/1960, Dorothy Leonard Gill
24142431211 Anna Sutherland Ruffin (9/22/1962-   )
24142431212 Robert Nichols Ruffin (5/21/1964-   )
2414243122 Thomas Randolph Ruffin (7/22/1947-   ), m. 8/10/
        1969, Bonnie Susan Bowman
24142431221 Susan Randolph Ruffin (4/5/1970-   )
24142431222 Robin Gayle Ruffin (6/25/1974-   )
24142432 Francis Gildart Ruffin (8/21/1874-2/12/1898)
24142433 Caryanne Randolph Ruffin (5/31/1876-11/5/1945, m. 12/3/
        1901, Robert Montagu McMurdo, son of Capt. and Madelein
        Baxter McMurdo
241424331 Sally Roane McMurdo (12/5/1904-   ), m. 6/8/1929,
        William Wardlaw Williston
2414243311 Anne Cary Williston (4/24/1934-   ), m. 6/16/1956,
        Charles Henry Nowlin

24142433111 Elizabeth Anne Nowlin (5/15/1963-6/16/1963)
24142433112 William Charles Nowlin (10/1/1964-   )
24142433113 Margaret Anne Nowlin (11/4/1966-   )
2414243312   Margaret Randolph Williston (9/10/1937-   ), m.
             9/14/1957, Ernest John Laidlaw, Jr.
24142433121 Gillian Randolph Laidlaw (4/10/1979-   )
241424332   Madeline Montagu McMurdo (9/8/1906-   ), m. 9/3/
             1932, Herbert Bruce Whitmore
2414243321   Caryanne Randolph Whitmore (5/24/1937-   ), m. 9/
             17/1977, William Lars Ericson
2414243322   Bruce Gray Whitmore (5/7/1944-   ), m. 11/18/1972,
             Carol Elizabeth Rugg
24142433221 Robert Gray Whitmore (7/7/1978-   )
24142433222 Daniel Bruce Whitmore (1/8/1981-   )
241424333   Robert Montagu McMurdo, Jr. (10/31/1911-   ), m.
             (1st) 6/6/1942, Bettie W. Seabury. M. (2nd) 11/20/
             1982, Frances Elizabeth Driver Jennings
        Children by first wife:
2414243331   Jane Vaughan McMurdo (10/31/1944-   ), m. 7/22/
             1967, William Demord Bagwell
24142433311 Keith Montagu Bagwell (5/19/1972-   )
24142433312 Kirk Seabury Bagwell (4/24/1975-   )
2414243332   Martha Seabury McMurdo (2/4/1948-   )
2414243333   Sally Ruffin McMurdo (9/4/1951-   ), m. 7/11/1981,
             Peter J. Minnich
24142433331 Joseph Robert McMurdo Minnich (2/25/1983-   )
241424334   Mary Ruffin McMurdo (10/14/1913-   ), m. 1937,
             Campbell Houston Gillespie, Jr. (241414521)
             NOTE: See 2414145211 and 2414145212 for children of
             Mary Ruffin McMurdo Gillespie
24142434   William Roane Ruffin, Jr. (3/8/1878-6/26/1943), m. 1919,
             Martha Cocke Taylor
24142435   John Francis Walthall Ruffin (5/17/1880-5/22/1952), m.
             10/19/1910, Sarah McElroy Osborne, dau. of Dr. Osborne
             and Virginia McElroy
241424351   John Francis Walthall Ruffin, Jr. (9/2/1911-   ), m.
             6/5/1937, Jane Barnes
2414243511   Sara Jane Ruffin (6/5/1939-   ), m .2/1/1964,
             Michael Kennerley
24142435111 Elizabeth Anne Kennerley (11/28/1970-   )
24142435112 Michael Andrew Ruffin Kennerley (4/26/1972-   )
2414243512   Elizabeth Anne Ruffin (6/12/1941-   ), m. 6/30/
             1962, Ivor Lee Balyeat
24142435121 Jonathan Lee Balyeat (4/13/1970-   )
24142435122 Nicholas Barnes Balyeat (12/20/1974-   )
24142435123 Peter Randolph Balyear (2/20/1979-   )
241424352   William Roane Ruffin III (11/13/1912-   ),m. 6/30/
             1945, Jane Evans
2414243521   William Roane Ruffin IV (2/6/1948-   ), m. 8/10/
             1974, Mary Lou Neurohr
24142435211 Jane Best Ruffin (8/7/1980-   )
24142435212 Elizabeth Kathleen Ruffin (10/12/1981-   )

24142435221 Elizabeth Evans Ruffin (4/15/1953-   ), m. 8/27/
       1977, Howard Lynn Douglas
24142435221 William Howard Douglas (11/28/1980-   )
241424353 Sidney Matthews Ruffin (6/5/1915-   ), m. 6/26/
       1943, Harriet Martin
2414243531 Nicholas Cary Ruffin (8/20/1944-   )
2414243532 Martha Martin Ruffin (3/11/1947-   ), m. 4/8/1972,
       Bruce Lawrence Ackerman
2414243533 Caryanne Randolph Ruffin (8/9/1951-   )
2414243534 Harriet Fox Ruffin (7/12/1954-   )
241424354 Virginius Osborne Ruffin (3/12/1918-   ), m. 6/16/
       1951, Nancy Diefenbeck
24142436 Mary McIlwaine Ruffin (12/17/1883-5/5/1951)
24142437 Sally Walthall Ruffin (2/17/1886-1/21/1966)
24142438 Wilson Cary Nicholas Ruffin (7/5/1888-12/17/1892)
2414244 Wilson Cary Nicholas Ruffin (3/19/1848-2/22/1919), m.
       4/20/1875, Mary Winston Harvie, dau. of John and Mary
       Blair Harvie
24142441 John Harvie Ruffin (1/15/1876-5/3/1961), m. 4/7/1907,
       Laura Virginia Walters
241424411 Nelson Randolph Ruffin (4/3/1910-   )
24142442 Ellen Harvie Ruffin (9/24/1877-11/3/1977), m. 6/27/1906,
       James M. Featherston
241424421 Ellen Ruffin Featherston (5/26/1907-7/10/1941), m. 7/7/
       1932, William Franklin Taylor
2414244211 Ellen Ruffin Taylor (12/24/1933-   ), m. 11/23/
       1954, John Rodney Stevens
24142442111 Laura Lynn Stevens (8/3/1957-   )
24142442112 Ellen Elizabeth Stevens (5/5/1959-   )
24142442113 John Rodney Stevens, Jr. (12/16/1961-   )
2414244212 Ada Lee Taylor (4/30/1940-   ), m. 11/18/1972,
       Richard J. Thomas
24142443 Wilson Nicholas Ruffin, Jr. (9/15/1879-6/2/1951), m. 8/
       18/1910, Martha Pearl Woods
24142444 Francis Gildard Ruffin (1881-1883)
24142445 Lewis Rutherford Ruffin (10/29/1884-8/18/1907)
24142446 Cary Randolph Ruffin (12/22/1886-8/19/1914)
24142447 William Pickett Ruffin (4/19/1889-4/24/1915)
24142448 Mary Blair Harvie Ruffin (6/13/1892-   )
2414245 George Randolph Ruffin (1849-1915), m. 1883, Amarilla
       (Bell) Gholson
24142451 William Ragsdale Ruffin (1884-   ), d. inf.
24142452 Mary Hellen Ruffin (4/9/1886-9/22/1972), m. 3/5/1913,
       Fred Marshall
241424521 Mary Bell Marshall (3/26/1914-   ), m. 9/ /1942,
       Robert D. Sard
2414245211 David Paul Sard (11/10/1943-   ), m. Sarah Dooley
24142452111 Kristen Anna Sard (4/2/1966-   )
2414245212 Frederick Marshall Sard (2/27/1946-   )
2414245213 Hannah Belloch Sard (5/31/1951-   )
241424522 George Randolph Ruffin Marshall (7/7/1915-3/20/1964), m.
       8/21/1954, Olga di Nicola

2414245221 Mary Helen Ruffin Marshall ((12/25/1955-   ), m. 10/
            23, 1977, Joseph Fragola
2414245222 George Randolph Ruffin Marshall (3/25/1957-   )
2414245223 Clara Ann Marshall (1/13/1959-   )
241424523   Caroline Margaret Marshall (4/24/1927-   ), m. 7/
            14/1950, Armand William Kitto, Jr.
2414245231 Katherine Babette Kitto (7/31/1951-   ), m. 9/28/
            1973, Joseph Kott III
24142452311 Paul Thomas Kott (7/18/1975-   )
2414245232 Laurence Bridger Kitto (9/7/1953-   ), m. 5/21/
            1977, Elizabeth Elliot
2414245233 Robert Marshall Kitto (1/31/1955-   )
2414245234 Jonathan Bell Kitto (8/23/1958-   )
2414246   Francis Gildart Ruffin, Jr. (1/6/1852-1/12/1902), m. 1887,
            Margaret Ellen Henry (8/26/1861-   ), dau. of
            Thomas and Mary Nugent Henry
24142461 Frances Ruffin (2/27/1889-6/23/1972), m. 1/8/1914, Joseph
            Francis Durham
241424611 Mary Frances Durham (11/4/1914-1978), m. (1st) 9/3/1938,
            Paul deVendal Chaudron. M. (2nd) Samuel P. Militano
            Child by first husband:
2414246111 Lucia Marie Chaudron (6/24/1939-   ), m. 3/21/1963,
            Heino Kristall
            Child by second husband:
2414246112 Michael Francis Militano (9/29/1944-   ), m. 9/
            29/1965, Nancy Helen Hiler
24142461121 Angela Marie Militano (12/16/1966-   )
24142462 Mary Henry Ruffin (5/5/1890-1981), "Sister Miriam", Sister
            of Charity
24142463 Ellen Randolph Ruffin (7/10/1892-   ), "Sister Rita",
            Sister of Charity
24142464 Thomas Henry Ruffin (10/31/1894-8/18/1964)(twin), m.
            1924, Anna Cecilia Kelly
241424641 Joseph Henry Ruffin (4/10/1926-   ), m. 9/4/1948,
            Waurine Bradley
2414246411 Joan Charlene Ruffin (6/7/1949-4/23/1977), Michael
            Woodrow Sharp
24142464111 Jennifer Elizabeth Sharp (1/24/1979-   )
2414246412 Margaret Cecilia Ruffin (7/4/1950-   ), m. 6/3/
            1972, Kerry Bruce Miller
24142464121 Justin Thomas Miller (12/11/1972-   )
24142464122 Graham Ryan Miller (1/22/1975-   )
241424642 Child
24142465 Thomas Jefferson Ruffin (10/31/1894-9/12/1975)(twin)
24142466 Caroline Randolph Ruffin (4/27/1897-10/ /1919)
24142467 Elizabeth de l'Esprit Ruffin (6/ /1901-3/ /1903)
2414247 Benjamin Randolph Ruffin, d. inf.
2414248 Eliza McDonald Ruffin (7/26/1853-4/20/1904)
2414249 Cary Randolph Ruffin (7/24/1857-8/27/1910), m. Ethel
            Patterson
            NOTE: Name changed to Cary Ruffin Randolph just before
            his marriage to Ethel Patterson.

241425 Mary Buchanan Randolph (12/17/1821-6/23/1884)
241426 Eleonora (Ellen) Wayles Randolph (12/1/1823-8/15/1896),
      m. 5/1/1859, second wife of William Byrd Harrison (1800-
      1870), son of Benjamin and Betsy Page Harrison. See
      24247.
2414261 Evelyn Byrd Harrison (3/14/1860-3/16/1860)
2414262 Jane Nicholas Randolph Harrison (6/26/1862-8/16/1926, m.
      12/31/1892, Alexander Burton Randall
24142621 Burton Harrison Randolph Randall (10/13/1893-9/29/1971),
      m. (1st) 8/25/1919, Louise Florentine Monganaste. M.
      (2nd) 8/31/1935, Anne Holloway
      Child by first husband:
241426211 Edith Richards Randall (8/3/1920-   ), m. 3/3/1946,
      John J. Kotz
2414262111 Randall Michael Kotz (11/15/1952-   )
2414262112 Nancy Margaret Kotz (12/10/1958-   ), m. 5/9/
      1978, Kenneth Harris Shore
24142621121 Janice Lynn Shore (7/9/1981-   )
2414263 Jefferson Randolph Harrison (12/9/1863-5/11/1931)
241427 Maria Jefferson Carr Randolph (2/2/1826-7/12/1902), m.
      1848, Charles Mason
2414271 Jefferson Randolph Mason (7/12/1850-7/29/1888)
2414272 Lucy Wiley Mason (3/4/1852-7/18/1922), m. 4/26/1881,
      Edward Jacquelin Smith
24142721 Charles Mason Smith (7/29/1882-1/2/1933), m. 11/10/1914,
      Emma Copeland Lawless
241427211 Jacquelin Randolph Smith (10/21/1915-   ), m. 11/
      10/1939, Angus Slater Lamond
2414272111 Cary Randolph Lamond (8/1/1940-   ), m. (1st) 11/
      10/1962, Francis Patrick Dillon. M. (2nd) 3/31/1977,
      Joseph Antony Michael Lynch
      Children by first husband:
24142721111 Cary Randolph Dillon (4/23/1963-   )
24142721112 Francis Patrick Dillon, Jr. (5/10/1966-   )
2414272112 Jacquelin Ambler Lamond (9/22/1942-   ), m. 4/18/
      1970, Peter Mueller Schluter
24142721121 Jane Randolph Schluter (3/25/1972-   )
24142721122 Charlotte Mueller Schluter (6/19/1973-   )
24142721123 Anne Ambler Schluter (8/12/1976-   )
2414272113 Angus Slater Lamond, Jr. (4/17/1946-   ), m. (1st)
      11/6/1970, Sandra Delayne Taylor. M. (2nd) 6/1/1974,
      June Hollis Altman
      Children by second wife:
24142721131 Ann Randolph Lamond (8/23/1978-   )
24142721132 Angus Slater Lamond III (2/19/1981-   )
2414272114 Lucy Mason Lamond (7/28/1947-   ), m. 12/7/1978,
      Donald Bruce Falkenberg
241427212 Cary Ambler Smith (7/28/1917-   ), m. 8/15/1935,
      Addison Gordon Billingsley, Jr.
      Cary Copeland Billingsley (9/27/1948-   )(adopted),
      m. 10/ /1974, Richard Charles Shomo
24142722 William Taylor Smith (8/24/1885-ca. 1940), m. 9/10/1914,
      Ellen Dickinson Wallace

241427221 Lucy Randolph Smith (11/6/1915-   ), m. (1st) 1934,
           Stiles Morrow Decker, Jr. M. (2nd) Douglas Hammond
        Children by first husband:
2414272211 Randolph Morrow Decker (2/28/1935-   )
2414272212 Joel Porter Decker (4/5/1936-   )
2414272213 Diane Lewis Decker (3/17/1943-   )
2414272214 Christine Cary Decker (3/17/1951-   )
2414273 John Enoch Mason (7/11/1854-12/10/1910), m. 11/24/1885,
         Kate Kearney Henry
24142731 Flora Randolph Mason (4/16/1887-4/29/1972), m. (1st)
          4/2/1917, George B. Nicholson. M. (2nd) 10/24/1931,
          Joseph Parkes Crockett
24142732 Charles T. Mason (2/7/1893-11/6/1896)
24142733 Thomas Jefferson Mason (4/14/1896-10/21/1918)
2414274 Wilson Cary Nicholas Mason (1856-1866)
241428 Caroline Ramsay Randolph (1/15/1828-d.s.p. 6/28/1902)
241429 Col. Thomas Jefferson Randolph II (8/29/1829-8/8/1872), m.
        (1st) 7/20/1853, Mary Walker Meriwether (4/29/1833-10/4/
        1863), dau. of Francis Thornton Meriwether and his wife,
        the former Margaret ("Peggy") Douglas Meriwether. M.
        (2nd) 1865, Charlotte Nelson Meriwether, dau. of Thomas
        Warner and Anne Carter Nelson Meriwether
        Children by first wife:
2414291 Francis (Frank) Meriwether Randolph (10/22/1854-9/8/1922),
         m. 1/17/1883, Charlotte Nelson Macon (-5/24/1935),
         dau. of George W. and Mildred Nelson Meriwether Macon
24142911 Margaret Douglas Randolph (3/17/1884-2/15/1955). Unm.
24142912 Mildred Nelson Randolph (10/27/1885-1/16/1886), d.s.p.
24142913 Carolina Ramsay Randolph (10/28/1886-8/16/1971), m. 8/
          1/1906, Edward H. Joslin. No issue
24142914 Charlotte Nelson Randolph (5/5/1888-   ), m. 1/25/
          1919, Gilbert Thomas Rafferty, Jr. of Pittsburg. She
          lives (lived) at "Clover Fields"
241429141 Caroline Randolph Rafferty (7/23/1919-   ), m.
           Richard White Hall of Keswick, Va.
241429142 Anne Rafferty (9/16/1920 or 1921?-   ), m. 6/9/
           1947, Silas A. Barnes of Crozet, Va.
2414291421 Charlotte Randolph Barnes (11/13/1949-   ), m. 9/
            2/1972, Ralph Kellogg Dammann
2414291422 Sarah Lee Barnes (8/4/1952-   ), m. 9/13/1975,
            John Reeves Frizzell III
241429143 Frances Douglas Rafferty (4/13/1922-1/7/1982)
241429144 Doris Rafferty (6/9/1925 or 1927?-   ), m. 3/27/
           1951, Robert Coles, Jr. of Jenkintown, Pa.
2414291441 Robert Coles III (5/7/1952-   )
2414291442 John Coles (11/26/1953-   )
2414291443 Margaret Douglas Coles (4/19/1955-   ), m. 6/21/
            1980, William Anderson
2414291444 Edward Joslin Coles (5/3/1956-   )
2414291445 Caroline Coles (6/15/1959-   )
2414292 Thomas Jefferson Randolph III (10/23/1855-9/30/1884),
         d.s.p.

2414293 Margaret Douglas Randolph (8/6/1857-12/17/1880), d.s.p.
2414294 Francis Nelson Randolph (10/4/1858-12/15/1880), d.s.p.
2414295 Jane Hollins Randolph (8/1/1861-11/30/1862),d.s.p.
2414296 George Geiger Randolph (8/15/1863-12/23/1893), d.s.p.
         Children by second wife:
2414297 Mary Walker Randolph (6/14/1866-12/9/1957), m. 10/20/
            1894, Dr. William Mann Randolph (241x123)
            NOTE: The descendants of Mary Walker Randolph are
            listed 241x1231 through 241x1238 as descendants of
            their father, William Mann Randolph, 241x123.
2414298 Charlotte Nelson Randolph (12/28/1868-11/1/1870)
24142x   Jane Nicholas Randolph (10/11/1831-8/26/1868), m. 4/24/
            1854, Robert Garlick Hill Kean (1828-1898)
24142x1 Lancelot Minor Kean (1/11/1856-1/8/1931), m. (1st) 5/25/
            1880, Elizabeth Tucker Prescott. M. (2nd) 10/3/1911,
            Martha Foster Murphy
         Children by first wife:
24142x11 Jane Randolph Kean (5/19/1881-10/18/1948), m. 12/21/1903,
            John Samuel Butler, Jr.
24142x111 John Samuel Butler III (1/26/1905-3/9/1973), m. 6/9/
            1934, Miriam Elizabeth Leguene
24142x1111 Miriam Elizabeth Butler (5/21/1938-   ), m. 3/19/
            1960, Richard Joseph Moore
24142x11111 Richard Joseph Moore, Jr. (8/21/1961-   )
24142x11112 Sean Butler Moore (9/9/1962-   )
24142x11113 Patrick Edward Moore (8/16/1964-   )
24142x11114 Jefferson Randolph Kean Moore (8/16/1964-   )
24142x11115 Miriam Elizabeth Moore (9/9/1977-   )
24142x11116 Sarah Archer Leigh Moore (12/18/1979-   )
24142x112 Lancelot Kean Butler (7/16/1906-5/23/1957), m. 12/25/
            1939, Eddy Louise Hood
24142x113 Jane Randolph Butler (10/26/1908-1/28/1963), m. 3/15/
            1941, Wesley C. Lancaster
24142x1131 Wesley Cary Lancaster (3/19/1943-3/20/1943)
24142x1132 Susan Jane Lancaster (6/15/1944-   )
24142x1133 William Joseph Lancaster (10/29/1945-   )
24142x114 Joseph Edmund Butler (1/29/1912-   ), m. 4/25/1937,
            Boyd Evelyn Phillips
24142x12 Lancelot Minor Kean, Jr. (9/9/1884-6/23/1885)
24142x13 Lancelot Minor Kean (3/ /1886-4/ /1886)
24142x14 (son) Kean (1886-1891), d. inf.
24142x15 Mary Evalina Sanfrosa Prescott Kean (7/30/1891-   ),
            m. 1/15/1927, Constant Southworth
24142x16 Elizabeth Caroline Hill Kean (1/12/1896-4/25/1969), m.
            6/3/1920, Raymond H. Campbell
24142x161 Elizabeth Eva Campbell (1/6/1921-   )
24142x162 Althee Marion Campbell (9/21/1922-   ), m. 3/25/1942,
            Francis Thomas Moore
24142x1621 Francis Thomas Moore, Jr. (3/15/1947-   )
24142x1622 Roy Victor Moore (5/26/1948-   )
24142x1623 Terry Carol Moore (11/7/1952-   ), m. 1/24/1973,
            Christopher Joseph Bode

24142x16231 Christopher Joseph Bode, Jr. (10/3/1973-   )
24142x16232 Sean Patrick Bode (3/25/1975-   )
24142x16233 Kyle Michael Bode (3/31/1980-   )
24142x1624   Patricia Ellen Moore (11/-2/1955-   )
24142x1625   Renee Ersel Moore (8/23/1961-   )
24142x163   Raymond Henry Campbell, Jr. (5/27/1924-   ), m. 6/
             18/1948, Betty Cantelli
24142x1631   Kristen Marie Campbell (7/13/1949-   )
24142x1632   Michael Raymond Campbell (1/14/1955-   )
24142x164   Ruth Virginia Campbell (7/7/1925-   ), m. 6/30/
             1960, Claude Benoit Walker
24142x1641   Jacques Doak Walker (3/18/1962-   )
24142x1642   Dantin Kean Walker (11/11/1963-   )
24142x165   Martin Bradburn Campbell (10/26/1928-   )
             Child by second wife:
24142x17   James Louis Randolph Kean (5/17/1913-   ), m. 11/16/
             1940, Mary Louise McCarter
24142x171   James Louis Randolph Kean, Jr. (6/18/1942-   )
24142x172   Susan Foster Kean (10/1/1949-   )
24142x173   John Michael Kean (1/28/1952-   )
24142x174   Thomas Jefferson Kean (1/8/1954-   )
24142x2   Martha (Pattie) Cary Kean (4/11/1858-3/5/1939), m. 4/27/
             1882, John Speed Morris (1855-1929)
24142x21   Robert Kean Morris (4/12/1883-12/14/1961), m. (1st) 8/30/
             1906, Meta Elaine Thomas. M. (2nd) 4/18/1925, Louise
             Newcom (Richards) Baughman
             Children by first wife:
24142x211   Dorothy Elaine Morris (7/14/1907-4/8/1971), m. (1st)
             11/3/1930, Janvier L. Lamar. M. (2nd) Daniel W. Smith.
             M. (3rd) Raymond Price
             Child by first husband:
24142x2111   Dorothy Elaine Lamar (8/20/1932-   ), m. Fred
             Rogers Saunders
24142x21111 Daniel Price Saunders (2/15/1963-   )
24142x21112 Patricia Morris Saunders (10/29/1966-   )
             Children by second husband:
24142x2112   Bonnycastle Smith (1940-   ), m.   McCabe
24142x21121 (child) McCabe, name unknown
24142x21122 (child) McCabe, name unknown
24142x21123 (child) McCabe, name unknown
24142x2113   Daniel W. Smith, Jr. (2/15/1942-   ), m. (1st) 8/
             20/1964, Joyce Ann Reynolds. M. (2nd) 11/30/1974,
             Nancy Jean Smith
             Child by first wife:
24142x21131 Leslie Jeanne Smith (4/30/1968-   )
24142x212   Robert Kean Morris, Jr. (12/24/1917-   ), m. 2/14/
             1946, Muriel Ellen Walker
24142x2121   Robert Kean Morris III (12/12/1946-   )
24142x2122   Cynthia Anne Morris (6/13/1949-   )
24142x22   Mary Randolph Morris (2/5/1885-8/2/1955), m. 5/12/1909,
             Allen Melancthon Sumner
24142x221   Margaret Page Sumner (2/21/1910-   ), m. 9/24/1932,
             Burton Francis Miller

24142x2211　Margaret Page Miller (9/13/1933-　　　), 11/12/1955,
　　　　　　Robert Sanders Hinton, Jr.
24142x22111　Robert Sanders Hinton III (1/6/1959-　　)
24142x22112　Jeffrey Brady Hinton (4/7/1963-　　)
24142x22113　Richard Francis Hinton (1/26/1966-　　)
24142x2212　Adelaide Randolph Miller (2/4/1935-　　　　), m. (1st)
　　　　　　3/31/1956, Gordon Conrad Coiner. M. (2nd) 11/15/
　　　　　　1980, Kitchel Ludy
　　　　　Children by first husband:
24142x22121　Patricia Jane Coiner (1/10/1958-　　)
24142x22122　Gordon Conrad Coiner, Jr. (6/13/1963-　　　)
24142x22123　Elizabeth Randolph Coiner (12/22/1969-　　　)
24142x22124　Burton Grayson Coiner (12/22/1969-　　)
24142x22125　Margaret Page Coiner (12/22/1969-　　　)
24142x23　Page Waller Morris (7/1/1886-9/19/1956), m. 6/20/1910,
　　　　　　Frederick Campbell Stuart Hunter II
24142x231　Frederick Campbell Stuart Hunter III (3/14/1911-　　),
　　　　　　m. 1/1/1939, Dorothy Dulany
24142x2311　Grace Page Hunter (1/15/1941-　　　)
24142x232　John Morris Hunter (1/17/1916-　　　　), m. 1/23/1943,
　　　　　　Juliet King Lehman
24142x24　William Sylvanus Morris (5/5/1888—9/6/1947, m. 8/2/
　　　　　　1923, Pearl Lenore Oberg
24142x241　Mary Elizabeth Morris (3/28/1924-4/14/1962)
24142x25　Pattie Nicholas Morris (4/9/1893-10/18/1980), m. 4/28/
　　　　　　1920, Horace King Hutchens
24142x251　Katherine King Hutchens (2/25/1921-　　　), m. (1st)
　　　　　　6/6/1942, George William Wiley. M. (2nd) 10/12/1973,
　　　　　　William Joseph Ermisch
　　　　　Child by first husband:
24142x2511　John Hutchens Wiley (11/30/1948-　　)
24142x26　Adelaide Prescott Morris (4/28/1896-11/23/1958), m. 4/
　　　　　　21/1919, Thomas Ross Cooley
24142x261　Adelaide Morris Cooley (3/6/1920-2/9/1974), m. (1st)
　　　　　　5/8/1943, Hal Waugh Smith. M. (2nd) 3/31/1955, Burnett
　　　　　　Laurence Gadeberg
　　　　　Children by first husband:
24142x2611　Ross Emerson (Smith) Gadeberg (5/10/1949-　　)(name
　　　　　　changed), m. (1st) 1/5/1974, Deborah Lynn McBride.
　　　　　　M. (2nd) 2/12/1978, Margaret Rose Andresen
　　　　　Child by second wife:
24142x26111　Michael Emerson Gadeberg (6/27/1980-　　)
24142x2612　Margaret Waugh (Smith) Gadeberg (6/3/1950-　　　)
　　　　　　(name changed), m. Michael Antony Morrow
24142x26121　Adelaide Lee Morrow (5/24/1969-　　)
24142x2613　Adelaide Leigh (Smith) Gadeberg (2/15/1952 (name
　　　　　　changed), m. 6/30/1972, William James Cleese
24142x262　Mary Lawrence Cooley (5/21/1930-　　　　), m. 1/8/1951,
　　　　　　Hugh Sommerville Aitken
24142x2621　Mary Lawrence Aitken (10/28/1951-　　　　), m. 4/14/
　　　　　　1974, Michael A. Yaniello
24142x26211　Christina Marie Yaniello (9/19/1974-　　　)

24142x2622 Elizabeth Sommerville Aitken (11/11/1952-   ), m.
            4/28 /1971, Frank Peter Cruikshank
24142x26221 Elizabeth Marie Cruikshank (7/26/1972-   )
24142x26222 William Francis Cruikshank (4/5/1974-   )
24142x2623 Hugh Wylie Aitken (6/26/1955-   )
24142x2624 William Ormond Aitken (4/25/1961-   )
24142x2625 Thomas Ross Cooley Aitken (10/28/1964-   )
24142x2626 Margaret Randolph Aitken (1/18/1966 -   )
24142x263 Margaret Ross Cooley (12/14/1931-8/24/1940)
24142x3 Jefferson Randolph Kean, M.D. (6/27/1860-9/4/1950), m.
            (1st) 10/10/1894, Louise Hurlbut Young. M. (2nd) 3/24/
            1919, Cornelia Butler Knox
         Children by first wife:
24142x31 Martha Jefferson Kean (8/7/1895-11/1/1978), m. 12/5/1917,
            William Chason
24142x311 William Randolph Chason (4/8/1919-   )
24142x312 Louise Young Chason (9/11/1921-   )
24142x313 Robert Leonard Chason (10/30/1923-   ), m. 3/7/
            1945, Shirley Lucille Flynn
24142x3131 Patricia Lucille Chason (8/11/1955-   ), m. 6/8/
            1974, Timothy L. Bladon
24142x31311 Sara Elizabeth Bladon (9/16/1976-   )
24142x3132 Carol Randolph Chason (1/18/1962 -   )
24142x314 Helen Borodell Chason (7/16/1928-   ), m. 11/21/
            1945, John Wesley Crump
24142x3141 Sheila Kean Crump (9/13/1946-   ), m. 6/22/1968,
            Carson Lee Fifer, Jr.
24142x32 Robert Hill Kean (7/5/1900-   ), m. 12/26/1927,
            Sara Rice Elliott
24142x321 Jefferson Randolph Kean (2/18/1930-   ), m. (1st)
            7/13/1957, Barbara Miller. M. (2nd) 4/24/1971, Leah
            Jones Stevens
         Child by first wife:
            Robert Hill Kean II (7/5/1961-   )(adopted)
24142x3211 Evelina Southworth Kean (11/5/1964-   )
24142x322 Margaret Young Kean (9/24/1938-   ), m. 6/17/1961,
            Edward Alexander Rubel
24142x3221 Daniel Martin Rubel (3/16/1965-   )
24142x3222 Stephen Elliott Rubel (12/12/1966-   )
24142x3223 Sarah Rice Rubel (9/13/1968-   )
24142x4 Robert Garlick Hill Kean (12/26/1862-1883), m. (1st) Jane
            Randolph. M. (2nd) Adelaide Navarro Demarest
         Children by second wife:
24142x41 Evalina Moore Kean
24142x42 Caroline Hill Kean
24142x43 Marshall Prescott Kean
24142x44 Otho Vaughan Kean
24142x5 Lewis Randolph Kean (8/17/1864-8/17/1864)
24142x6 George Randolph Kean (4/6/1866-d.s.p. 8/27/1869)
24142a   Wilson Cary Nicholas Randolph, M.D. (10/26/1834-4/26/1907),
            m. (1st) 11/11/1858, Anne Elizabeth ("Nannie") Holladay
            (1839-1888), dau. of John Zachary and Julia Ann Minor
            Holladay. M. (2nd) 6/10/1891, Mary McIntire (1855-1937)

Children by first wife:

24142a1 Virginia Minor Randolph (11/28/1859-1/28/1937), m. 7/1/
1884, George Scott Shackelford
24142a11 Virginius Randolph Shackelford (4/15/1885-1/19/1949), m.
11/10/1910, Peachy Gascoigne Lyne
24142a111 Virginius Randolph Shackelford (8/24/1911-7/25/1912)
24142a112 Lyne Moncure Shackelford (5/22/1914-   ), m. 10/
2/1948, Elizabeth Burrow Dixon
24142a1121 Lyne Moncure Shackelford, Jr. (11/17/1952-   ),
m. 11/13/1974, Marguerite Lynn Simpson
24142a11211 Mary Elizabeth Shackelford (6/1/1979-   )
24142a113 Virginius Randolph Shackelford, Jr. (1/15/1916-   ),
m. 8/7/1943, Carroll Kem
24142a1131 Virginius Randolph Shackelford III (7/27/1946-   ),
m. 9/27/1975, Jane Lee Schwartzschild
24142a11311 Virginius Randolph Shackelford IV (1/17/1979-   )
24142a1132 Carroll Preston Shackelford (1/30/1948-   ), m. 10/
24/1980, James Richard Geisler
24142a1133 Mary Gascoigne Lyne Shackelford (5/19/1953-   ),
m. 4/22/1978, James Stuart Chaffee Burke
24142a1134 Kem Moncure Shackelford (10/22/1954-   )
24142a114 George Green Shackelford (12/17/1920-   ), m. 6/9/
1962, Grace Howard McConnell
24142a12 Nannie Holladay Shackelford (2/23/1887-2/15/1945), m.
10/1/1913, Rev. Karl Morgan Block
24142a121 Virginia Randolph Block (5/5/1915-   ), m. 1/3/1941,
Wayne Horton Snowden
24142a1211 Wayne Scott Snowden (4/6/1946-   ), m. 10/17/
1969, Nancy Helen Jones
24142a12111 Diana Styles Snowden (3/3/1978-   )
24142a12112 Susanne Maria Snowden (3/22/1980-   )
24142a1212 Randolph Fort Snowden (9/12/1949-   ), m. 9/19/
1970, Janet Fake
24142a12121 Christian Randolph Snowden (3/18/1979-   )
24142a12122 Carey Holladay Snowden (12/3/1981-   )
24142a122 Karl Morgan Block, Jr. (1/16/1921-8/29/1979), m. 6/2/
1945, Marion Lambert Niedringhaus
24142a1221 Karl Morgan Block III (4/6/1946-   ), m. 1976,
Priscilla Beliveau
24142a12211 Sally Sutherland Block (4/28/1977-   )
24142a12212 Brian Block (7/20/1979-   )
24142a1222 Lambert Stafford Block (1/26/1948-   ), m. 1971,
Lucille Lanning
24142a12221 Gerard Lambert Block (10/5/1981-   )
24142a1223 Nancy Holladay Block (10/17/1949-   ), m. 11/27/
1979, Miodrag Zeibert Cvitkovic
24142a12231 Anna Linden Cvitkovic (10/3/1980-   )
24142a1224 Florence Parker Block (4/25/1951-   ), m. 7/ /1972,
John Henry Lloyd
24142a12241 Jessica May Lloyd (11/12/1973-   )
24142a12242 Joseph Marion Lloyd (11/4/1975-   )
24142a12243 Philip Marion Lloyd (10/20/1981-   )

24142a1225 Warne Niedringhaus Block (6/8/1955-   ), m. 4/24/
            1982, Lisa Koch
24142a1226 Anne Randolph Block (2/11/1959-   ), m. 7/ /1981,
            Earl Gerfen
24142a1227 Marion Lambert Block (2/11/1959-   )
24142a1228 Amy Carter Block (4/25/1963-   )
24142a1229 Andrew Minor Block (7/29/1965-   )
24142a13 George Scott Shackelford, Jr. (1/27/1897-7/31/1965), m.
            2/26/1927, Mary Evelyn Fishburn
24142a131 Mary Parker Shackelford (1/19/1929-   ), m. 1951,
            John Crosland, Jr.
24142a1311 Mary Parker Crosland (1/4/1954-   ), m. 7/21/1979,
            William Oliver Tankard
24142a1312 John Crosland III (1/30/1957-   )
24142a132 George Scott Shackelford III (9/20/1933-   ), m.
            9/10/1960, Virginia Ria Thomas
24142a1321 William Scott Shackelford (5/12/1962-   )
24142a1322 George Randolph Shackelford (11/7/1964-   )
24142a1323 Virginia Travis Shackelford (3/17/1967-   )
24142a14 Margaret Wilson Shackelford (10/28/1898-7/13/1963), m.
            12/5/1923, Frank Stringfellow Walker
24142a141 Anne Carter Walker (4/4/1925-   ), m. 10/14/1948,
            Atwell Wilson Somerville
24142a1411 Atwell Wilson Somerville, Jr. (11/24/1949-   )
24142a1412 Frank Walker Somerville (2/21/1952-   )
24142a1413 Anne Carter Somerville (1/3/1954-   )
24142a142 Virginia Randolph Walker (4/23/1927-   ), m. 9/19/
            1949, Andrew Henry Christian
24142a1421 Andrew Henry Christian, Jr. (9/19/1950-   ), m. 9/
            10/1977, Jennifer Jenkins
24142a1422 Scott Shackelford Christian (9/3/1953-   )
24142a1423 Virginia Randolph Christian (5/19/1957-   )
24142a143 Margot Shackelford Walker (8/8/1931-   ), m. 12/18/
            1954, Cary Hill Humphries
24142a1431 Raleigh Green Humphries (2/6/1956-   ), m. 9/6/
            1981, Betty Scott Whitlow
24142a1432 Cary Hill Humphries, Jr. (2/6/1958-   ),m. 6/21/
            1980, Susan Lynn Murphy
24142a1433 Robert Walker Humphries (7/30/1960-   )
24142a144 Frank Stringfellow Walker, Jr. (10/11/1935-   ), m.
            12/3/1960, Bernice Spathey
24142a1441 Susan Stringfellow Walker (1/22/1964-   )
24142a1442 Margaret Austin Walker (2/27/1967-   )
24142a2 Wilson Cary Nicholas Randolph, Jr. (8/1/1861-3/1/1923), m.
            1/2/1890, Margaret Henderson Hager
24142a21 John Hager Randolph (7/16/1893-6/12/1981), m. 8/15/1917,
            Grace Lee
24142a211 Margaret Lee Randolph (9/15/1919-11/24/1976), m. 1/2/
            1946, William Moreau Platt, Jr.
24142a2111 William Moreau Platt III (1/4/1955-   ), m. 7/7/
            1979, Rebecca Ann Hylton
24142a212 John Hager Randolph, Jr. (7/27/1921-   ), m. 9/7/
            1946, Rebecca Holmes Meem

24142a2121 Beverley Langhorne Randolph (4/25/1948-   )
24142a2122 Rebecca Hutter Randolph (7/22/1949-   )
24142a213 Cary Ann Randolph (4/12/1925-   ), m. 4/23/1949,
          Carroll Marcus Cooper
24142a2131 Carroll Marcus Cooper, Jr. (7/17/1950-   )
24142a2132 Margaret Lee Cooper (2/24/1953-   )
24142a3 Mary Buchanan Randolph (1865-1900), d.s.p.
24142a4 Julia Minor Randolph (2/19/1866-7/10/1946), m. 9/26/1891,
          William Porterfield
24142a41 Mary Elizabeth Porterfield (7/17/1893-5/8/1965)
24142a42 Virginia Randolph Porterfield (8/23/1897-7/22/1898)
24142a43 John Porterfield (3/7/1900-7/5/1916)
24142a44 Wilson Randolph Porterfield (2/17/1903-4/ /1977), m. 7/
          30/1931, Mary Hamilton Cook
          Children by second wife:
24142a5 Elizabeth McIntire Randolph (1/9/1893-2/28/1966), m. 8/19/
          1917, Thomas Jeffries Betts
24142a51 Mary McIntire Betts (5/29/1920-   ), m. 9/30/1944,
          Walter Stratton Anderson, Jr.
24142a511 Virginia Randolph Anderson (12/20/1947-   ), 2/19/
          1983, Mats Ake Sigvard Sanuelsson
24142a512 Thomas Stratton Anderson (7/27/1951-   ), m. 9/5/
          1981, Mina Roustayi
24142a52 Elizabeth Hill Betts (3/29/1923-   )
24142b Meriwether Lewis Randolph (7/17/1837-2/1/1871), m. 1869,
          Anna T. Daniel (1851-1873)(244122)
24142b1 Meriwether Lewis Randolph, Jr. (1870-3/ /1877), d.s.p.
24142c Sarah Nicholas Randolph (10/10/1839-4/25/1892), d.s.p.
24143 Ellen Wayles Randolph (8/30/1794-7/26/1795)
          NOTE: The third child of Martha Jefferson Randolph was
          Ellen Wayles Randolph. (She died an infant and the next
          child (4th) born after the death of her infant sister
          was given the same name.)
24144 Ellen Wayles Randolph (10/13/1796-4/21/1876), m. 5/27/1825,
          Joseph Coolidge, Jr. (1798-1879), son of Joseph Coolidge
          and Elizabeth Bullfinch
241441 Ellen Randolph Coolidge (3/30/1826-5/9/1894), d.s.p., m.
          1/24/1855, Edmund Dwight (1824-1900)
241442 Elizabeth Bullfinch Coolidge (1827-6/9/1832)
241443 Joseph Randolph Coolidge (1/29/1828-2/9/1925), m. 12/18/
          1860, Julia Gardner (1841-1921). He purchased "Tuckahoe".
2414431 Joseph Randolph Coolidge, Jr. (5/17/1862-8/8/1928), m. 10/
          28/1886, Mary Hamilton Hill
24144311 Joseph Randolph Coolidge III (12/13/1887-9/22/1936), m.
          7/30/1913, Anna Lyman Cabot
241443111 Julia Coolidge (3/8/1914-   )
241443112 Joseph Randolph Coolidge IV (2/17/1916-   ), m.
          11/8/1952, Peggy Stuart
24144312 Julia Gardner Coolidge (9/6/1889-6/22/1961), m. 6/10/
          1910, Henry Howe Richards
241443121 Henry Howe Richards, Jr. (3/15/1911-   ), m. 6/21/
          1952, Mary Pauline Choate

241443122   Hamilton Richards (9/15/1913-   ), m. 10/8/1937,
            Edith Lewis
2414431221 Hamilton Richards, Jr. (2/14/1939-   ), m. 7/4/
            1968, Joanne Feldman
24144312211 Benjamin Lewis Richards (3/13/1976-   )
2414431222 James Lincoln Richards (10/22/1942-   ), m. 6/12/
            1965, Deborah Ann Davis
24144312221 Christine Richards (12/22/1969-   )
2414431223 Anne Hallowell Richards (11/7/1946-   ), m. 6/6/
            1981, John Hamilton Coolidge (2414431541)
241443123   Tudor Richards (2/15/1915-   ), m. 8/10/1949,
            Barbara G. Day
2414431231 Francis Tudor Richards (2/15/1952-   )m. 5/31/1980,
            Amy Goble
2414431232 Victoria Day Richards (11/18/1956-   ), m. 6/10/
            1979, Peter Hingston
24144312321 Honor Christine Hingston (10/27/1981-   )
2414431233 Robert Gardner Richards (11/7/1960-   )
241443124   Anne Hallowell Richards (9/13/1917-   ), m. 4/3/
            1966, John Robert Knowlton Preedy
241443125   John Richards II (3/15/1932-   ), m. 6/14/1955,
            Carol Meredith Cameron
2414431251 Laura Elizabeth Richards (11/2/1956-   ), m. (1st)
            6/19/1976, Harvey Milton Millier. M. (2nd) 6/21/1980,
            John Joseph McWilliams III
2414431252 Pamela Moore Richards (6/3/1958-   )
2414431253 Christopher Cameron Richards (5/4/1963-   )(twin)
2414431254 John Timothy Richards (5/4/1963-   )(twin)
2414431255 Catherine Coolidge Richards (6/11/1964-   )
24144313   Mary Eliza Coolidge (12/10/1890-8/21/1935)
24144314   Hamilton Coolidge (9/1/1895-10/27/1918)
24144315   John Gardner Coolidge (12/12/1897-3/5/1984), m. 6/12/
            1918, Mary Louise Hill
241443151   Natalie McLean Coolidge (4/30/1919-3/24/1965), m. 11/
            23/1941, John Wilbur Keller
2414431511 Jeremy Keller (8/23/1942-   ), m. (1st) 1969,
            Justin Hartman. M. (2nd) 8/23/1978, Giuliana Reed
2414431512 Natalie Russell Keller (5/30/1945-   ), m. 5/30/
            1981, Milford H. Sprecher
24144315121 Eliza McLean Sprecher (8/9/1978-   )
2414431513 Peter Gardner Keller (7/17/1949-   )
2414431514 Mary Hill Keller (8/30/1955-   ), m. George Ebanks
24144315141 Marissa Keller Ebanks (6/5/1980-   )
241443152   Mary Hamilton Coolidge (7/8/1921-   ), m. (1st)
            6/4/1942, Albert Lamb Lincoln, Jr. Div. M. (2nd)
            2/18/1968, George Nichols. M. (3rd) 8/30/1975, Donald
            S. Pitkin
            Children by first husband:
2414431521 Albert Lamb Lincoln III (3/16/1945-   ), m. 3/23/
            1968, Joan Millar
24144315211 Joshua Lincoln (4/29/1970-   )
24144315212 Daniel Lincoln (1/10/1972-   )

24144315213 Jessica Lincoln (4/14/1976-   )
2414431522   Christine Lincoln (9/16/1947-   ), m. 9/4/1971, James
             Danneskiold
2414431523   Matthew Dehon Lincoln (11/30/1948-   )
241443153   Olivia Hill Coolidge (4/8/1923-   ), 6/17/1950,
             Harry William Dworkin
2414431531   Michael Hill Dworkin (5/28/1953-   )
2414431532   Victoria Gail Dworkin (4/29/1955-   )
2414431533   Thomas Adam Dworkin (6/11/1959-   )
241443154   Hamilton Coolidge II (11/11/1924-   ), m. 10/16/
             1948, Barbara Fiske Bowles
2414431541   John Jamilton Coolidge (2/21/1950-   ),m. 6/6/
             1981, Anne Hallowell Richard (2414431223)
2414431542   Linda Bowles Coolidge (3/7/1952-   ), 7/17/1982,
             Lawrence W. Berndt
2414431543   Hope McLean Coolidge (8/20/1953-   )
2414431544   Malcolm Hill Coolidge (4/20/1956-   )
24144316   Eleanora Randolph Coolidge (1/31/1899-   ), m. 6/20/
             1921, Charles Enoch Works
241443161   Charles Chandler Works (3/25/1923-   )
241443162   John Hamilton Works (3/29/1925-   ), m. (1st)8/
             27/1950, Ellen Linnea Johnson.   M. (2nd)
             Children by first wife:
2414431621   Linnea Coolidge Works (8/17/1952-   ), m. 6/30/
             1976, Theron Gilbert Bowles
24144316211 Valerie Linnea Bowles (5/17/1978-   )
24144316212 Andrea Lillian Bowles (10/15/1980-   )
2414431622   John Hamilton Works, Jr. (7/13/1954-   ), m. 10/
             15/1983, Angela Marie DeMeo
2414431623   David Aaron Works (9/3/1956-   )
241443163   Josephine Randolph Works (4/28/1929-   ), m. 12/
             20/ 1949, Willis Lloyd Turner
             Michael Turner (9/25/1958-   )(adopted)
             Erika Edith Turner (8/10/1960-   )(adopted)
24144317   Oliver Hill Coolidge (8/5/1900-   ), m. 8/31/1925,
             Elizabeth Ten Eyck Brooks
241443171   Oliver Hill Coolidge, Jr. (3/13/1927-   ),m. 12/
             29, 1956, Lee (Leonarda) McGrath
2414431711   Peter Brian Coolidge (10/3/1957-   )
2414431712   Liza Hill Coolidge (5/27/1959-   ), m. 6/24/1978,
             Donald Green Neafsey
24144317121 Daniel Glenn Neafsey (11/6/1978-   )
241443172   Peter Jefferson Coolidge (8/24/1928-2/14/1934)
241443173   Henry Ten Eyck Coolidge (5/14/1935-   ), m. 1/9/
             1959, Camilla Starnes Tedford
2414431731   Henry Ten Eyck Coolidge, Jr. (10/4/1959-   )
2414431732   John Vincent Coolidge (2/20/1962-   )
24144318   Roger Sherman Coolidge (9/30/1904-   ), m. 7/1/1950,
             Barbara Litchfield Milne
241443181   Bayard Randolph Coolidge (8/16/1951-   ), m. 7/5/
             1980, Kathleen Maureen Parker
2414431811   Elizabeth Anne Coolidge (12/11/1981-   )

2414431812 Charles Randolph Coolidge (3/27/1983-   )
2414432 John Gardner Coolidge (7/4/1863-2/28/1936), m. 4/29/1909,
         Helen Granger Stevens
2414433 Archibald Cary Coolidge (3/6/1866-1/14/1928)
2414434 Charles Apthorp Coolidge (1/10/1868-1/11/1868)
2414435 Harold Jefferson Coolidge (1/22/1870-7/31/1934), m. 2/19/
         1903, Edith Lawrence
24144351 Harold Jefferson Coolidge, Jr. (1/15/1904-   ), m.
         (1st) 1/25/1931, Helen Carpenter Isaacs. M. (2nd) 5/
         26/1972, Martha Thayer Henderson
         Children by first wife:
241443511 Nicholas Jefferson Coolidge (2/12/1932-   ), m. (1st)
         7/11/1959, Sarah Flanagan Gordon. M. (2nd) 6/26/1977,
         Eliska Hasek
         Children by first wife:
2414435111 Nicole Rousmaniere Collidge (5/29/1961-   )
2414435112 Peter Jefferson Coolidge (4/17/1963-   )
         Child by second wife:
241443512 Thomas Richards Coolidge (1/29/1934-   ), m. 5/8/
         1965, Susan Lane Freiberg
2414435121 Laura Jefferson Coolidge (6/27/1967-   )
2414435122 Anne Richards Coolidge (2/10/1969-   )
2414435123 Thomas Lawrence Coolidge (7/6/1973-   )
241443513 Isabella Gardner Coolidge (6/1/1939-   )
24144352 Lawrence Coolidge (1/17/1905-1/3/1950), m. 1/16/1932,
         Victoria Stuart Tytus
241443521 Robert Tytus Coolidge (3/30/1933-   ), m. 9/10/
         1960, Ellen Leonard Osborne
2414435211 Christopher Randolph Coolidge (4/4/1962-   )
2414435212 Miles Cary Coolidge (12/22/1963-   )
2414435213 Matthew Perkins Coolidge (12/31/1966-   )
241443522 Lawrence Coolidge, Jr. (3/2/1936-   ), m. 6/22/
         1963, Nancy Winslow Rich
2414435221 David Steward Coolidge (8/7/1964-   )
2414435222 Edward Winslow Coolidge (6/30/1967-   )
2414435223 Elizabeth Appleton Coolidge (10/12/1969-   )
241443523 Nathaniel Silsbee Coolidge (1/24/1939-   ), m. 6/14/
         1961, Camilla Cutler
2414435231 Richard Lawrence Coolidge (4/6/1965-   )
2414435232 Hilary Coolidge (9/9/1966-   )
2414435233 Joanna Coolidge (4/19/1970-   )
24144353 Emily Fairfax Coolidge (10/13/1907-   ), m. (1st)
         10/3/1927, Harry Adsit Woodruff. M. (2nd) 11/17/1962,
         Thomas Archibald Stone
         Children by first wife:
241443531 Edith Lawrence Woodruff (4/25/1932-   ), m. 7/2/
         1952, Kenneth Bradish Kunhardt
2414435311 Kenneth Bradish Kunhardt, Jr. (3/1/1954-   ), m.
         5/8/1982, Denise Daria Williams
2414435312 Linda Lawrence Kunhardt (12/27/1955-   )
2414435313 Christopher Calve Kunhardt (7/1/1959-   )

2414435314 Timothy Woodruff Kunhardt (10/2/1964-   )
24144352 John Woodruff (11/9/1935-6/22/1947)
2414436 Julian Lowell Coolidge (9/28/1873-3/5/1954),m. 1/17/1901,
        Theresa Reynolds
24144361 Jane Revere Coolidge (7/17/1902-   ), m. 6/5/1930,
        Walter Muir Whitehill, Jr.
241443611 Jane Coolidge Whitehill (12/2/1931-12/20/1952), m. 12/
        20/1952, William Rotch
2414436111 Jane Revere Rotch (10/31/1959-   )
2414436112 William Rotch, Jr. (5/2/1962-   )
2414436113 Sarah Aldis Rotch (12/20/1965-   )
241443612 Diana Whitehill (8/1/1934-   ), m. 10/30/1954,
        Charles Christopher Laing
2414436121 Diana Randolph Laing (8/3/1957-   )
2414436122 Julia Gardner Laing (10/4/1958-   ), m. 6/25/1979,
        Jonathan Peevers
24144361221 Charlotte Emma Peevers (12/11/1979-   )
24144361222 Camilla Peevers (1/7/1982-   )
2414436123 Christopher Stephens Laing (3/8/1961-   )
24144362 Julian Gardner Coolidge (9/30/1903-2/18/1907)
24144363 Archibald Cary Coolidge II (12/10/1905-   ), m. (1st)
        6/27/1927, Susan Thistle Jennings. M. (2nd) 6/14/1946,
        Margaret Olivia Ensor
241443631 Archibald Cary Coolidge III (6/9/1928-   ), m. 6/21/
        1951, Lillian Dobbell Merrill
2414436311 Lillian Merrill Coolidge (5/21/1953-   ), m. 10/26/
        1974, Kimberly Bryan Boyer
24144363111 Eliza Boyer, d. inf.
2414436312 Emily White Coolidge (8/5/1955-   ), m. 12/23/1976,
        Stephen Conway
2414436313 Sarah Revere Coolidge (4/16/1957-   ), m. 9/2/1978,
        David Coleman
2414436314 Archibald Cary Coolidge IV (11/4/1959-   )
2414436315 Anne Edwards Coolidge (3/14/1963-   )
2414436316 John Jennings Coolidge (6/24/1967-   )
2414436317 Alexander Reynolds Coolidge (8/3/1969-   )
241443632 Joel Coolidge (11/21/1929-11/21/1929)
241443633 Susan Thistle Coolidge (4/3/1931-   ), m. 5/8/1954,
        Henry Hammond Barnes
2414436331 Henry Hammond Barnes, Jr. (3/11/1955-   )
2414436332 Nancy Susan Barnes (8/27/1957-   )
2414436333 Deborah Coolidge Barnes (6/12/1961-   )
241443634 Julian Lowell Coolidge (9/1/1933-   ), m. 9/13/
        1958, Gail Becker
2414436341 Margaret Olivia Coolidge (5/9/1959-   )
2414436342 David Andrew Coolidge (8/3/1961-   )
241443635 Elizabeth Crane Coolidge (11/29/1939-   ), m. 6/17/
        1960, Lewis Holmes Miller, Jr.
2414436351 Susan Thistle Miller (7/12/1962-   )
2414436352 Lewis Holmes Miller III (11/10/1964-   )
24144364 Margaret Wendell Coolidge (10/17/1907-   ), m. 12/10/
        1938, Charles Stacy French

241443641 Helena Stacy Franch (11/16/1941-   ), m. 9/23/1962,
           Bertrand Israel Helperin
2414436411 Jeffrey Arnold Halperin (5/5/1963-   )
2414436412 Julia Stacy Halperin (3/17/1967-   )
           Charles Ephraim French (10/30/1943-   )(adopted)
24144365   Elizabeth Peabody Coolidge (8/30/1909-   ), m. 2/27/
           1933, Charles Joseph Moizeau
241443651 Charles Julian Moizeau (2/7/1934-   ),m. 8/27/1960,
           Gail Stark Fisher
2414436511 Catherine Elizabeth Moizeau (11/22/1961-   )
2414436512 Margaret Theresa Moizeau (1966-   )
241443652 Elizabeth Peabody Moizeau (9/14/1937-   ), m. (1st)
           6/9/1957, Sylvain Merenlender. M. (2nd) 10/22/1972,
           Frederick Shima
           Child by first husband:
2414436521 Havazalet Merenlender (12/ /1957-   )
24144366   Rachel Revere Coolidge (2/21/1911-   ), m. 10/3/
           1936, Frederick Milton Kimball
241443661 Rachel Revere Kimball (10/20/1938-   ), m. 9/16/
           1980, John E. Allen
2414436611 Sarah Revere Allen (1980-   )
241443662 Carolyn Coolidge Kimball (9/7/1940-   ), m. 9/15/
           1962, Bryant Franklin Tolles, Jr.
2414436621 Thayer Coolidge Tolles (8/7/1965-   )
2414436622 Bryant Franklin Tolles III (7/11/1968-   )
241443663 Margaret Revelle Kimball (9/2/1945-   )
241443664 Cynthia Fifield Kimball (9/2/1945-   ), m. 8/26/
           1972, Richard Lloyd Merriam
2414436641 Priscilla Anne Fifield Merriam (12/2/1975-   )
2414436642 Scott Roger Kimball Merriam (6/17/1978-   )
2414436643 Lillian Cynthia Coolidge Merriam (10/4/1981-   )
24144367   John Philips Coolidge (12/16/1913-   ), m. 5/25/1935,
           Mary Elizabeth Welch
241443671 Mary Elizabeth Coolidge (3/19/1936 —   ), m. 8/6/
           1955, William Bradford Warren
2414436711 John Coolidge Warren (5/16/1956-   )
2414436712 Sarah Robbins Warren (1/4/1958-   )
24144368   Theresa Reynolds Coolidge (5/21/1915-   ), m. 12/
           2/1967, William Tracy Ceruti
241444   Dr. Algernon Coolidge (8/22/1830-1/4/1912), m. 7/15/1856,
           Mary Lowell (1833-1915)
2414441   Dr. Algernon Coolidge II (1/24/1860-8/16/1939), m. 12/15/
           1896, Amy Peabody Lothrop
24144411   Anne Coolidge (11/4/1897-   ), m. 1946, Edward
           W. Moore
24144412   Algernon Lothrop Coolidge (5/24/1900-11/16/1927)
24144413   Thornton Kirkland Coolidge (10/11/1906-   )
2414442   Francis Lowell Coolidge (11/20/1861-9/2/1942), m. 11/19/
           1901, Alice Brackett White
2414443   Sydney Coolidge (3/8/1864-6/6/1939), m. 8/18/1890, Mary
           Laura Colt
24144431   Mary Lowell Coolidge (12/9/1891-10/8/1958)

24144432 Sydney Coolidge, Jr. (11/9/1894-2/17/1958), m. 8/19/
          1917, Lucy Kent Richardson
241444321 Sydney Coolidge III (5/20/1919-   ), m. 5/22/1954,
          Adele Chevillat
241444322 Mary Elizabeth Coolidge (4/16/1923-   ), m. 1948,
          Raymond L. Barnett
2414443221 Patricia Elizabeth Barnett (8/15/1949-   )
2414443222 Sydney Louis Barnett (8/19/1952-   )
24144433 Edmund Jefferson Coolidge (4/13/1899-8/11/1974), m. 1940,
          Elizabeth Francesca Bender
241444331 Edmund Dwight Coolidge (1/22/1943-   )
241444332 Katherine TenBrinck Coolidge (9/7/1946-   ), m. (1st)
          Elwood Lenny. M. (2nd)
241444333 Marta Elizabeth Coolidge (10/29/1948-   )
24144434 Thomas Buckingham Coolidge (7/2/1901-   ), m. (1st)
          6/24/1924, Ellen Whitney Watson. Div. M. (2nd) 2/15/
          1944, Helen Knight
          Children by first wife:
241444341 Thomas Coolidge (2/20/1926-   )
241444342 John Lowell Coolidge (7/24/1927-   )
241444343 Richard Warren Coolidge (8/11/1930-   )
          Children by second wife:
241444344 Algernon Knight Coolidge (9/30/1945-   )
241444345 Robert Buckingham Coolidge (4/6/1947-   )
24144435 John Lowell Coolidge (12/19/1902-12/11/1918)
24144436 Helen Coolidge (5/24/1904-9/ /1976), m. Arthur Maxwell
          Stevens
241444361 Amy Stevens, m. Steven Wexler
2414443611   Wexler
          Timothy Stevens (adopted)
24144437 Francis Lowell Coolidge (12/4/1906-1/15/1972), m. 5/17/
          1940, Helen Read Curtis
241444371 Mary Coolidge (5/21/1942-   ), m. (1st) 6/26/1965,
          Thomas Benham Helliar. M. (2nd) 12/28/1975, Salvatore
          Pace
          Child by first husband:
2414443711 Trevor Lowell Helliar (10/21/1970-   )
          Child by second husband:
2414443712 Salvatore Pace, Jr. (12/ /1976-   )
214444372 Georgina Lowell Coolidge (10/5/1943-   ), m. 7/ /
          1970, Philip Bogetto
2414443721 Christina Randolph Bogetto (1971-   )
2414443722 Curtis Lowell Bogetto (3/17/1973-   )
241444373 Francis Lowell Coolidge (8/4/1945-   )
241444374 Ellen Randolph Coolidge (8/4/1945-   ), m. 6/13/
          1970, Stephen Bradner Burbank
2414443741 Peter Jefferson Burbank (4/19/1981-   )
24144438 Philip Coolidge (8/25/1908-5/23/1967)
2414444   Ellen Wayles Coolidge (1/24/1866-4/29/1953)
2414445   Mary Lowell Coolidge (8/24/1868-5/3/1957), m. 6/14/1898,
          Frederick Otis Barton
24144451 Frederick Otis Barton, Jr. (1/5/1899-   )

24144452   Ellen Randolph Barton (8/21/1900-2/5/1922)
24144453   Mary Lowell Barton (12/5/1901-   ), m. 7/7/1927,
           Edward Delos Churchill
241444531 Mary Lowell Churchill (10/15/1930-   ), m. (1st)
           6/25/1955, John Herd Hart. M. (2nd) 3/11/1960, Robert
           Lynn Fischelis
           Children by second husband:
2414445311 Peter Conway Fischelis (4/20/1962-   )
2414445312 William Churchill Fischelis (4/21/1964-   )
2414445313 Mary Lowell Fischelis (5/29/1968-   )
241444532 Frederick Barton Churchill (12/14/1932-   ), m. 5/
           23/1981, Sandra Riddle
241444533 Edward Delos Churchill (5/5/1934-   ), m. 6/18/
           1971, Ellen Buntzie Ellis
2414445331 Eric Coolidge Churchill (12/20/1974-   )
2414445332 Eva Lowell Churchill (2/7/1977-   )
241444534 Algernon Coolidge Churchill (8/15/1937-   ), m.
           10/31/1959, Ann Marshall Chapman
2414445341 Susan Lowell Churchill (5/22/1960-   )
2414445342 David Lawrence Churchill (11/14/1962-   )
24144454   Francis Lowell Barton (6/4/1903-   ), m. (1st) 2/24/
           1930, Elizabeth Harris. M. (2nd) Phyllis M. (Saunders)
           Simpson
           Children by first wife:
241444541 James Harris Barton (4/10/1934-   ), m. 6/12/1957,
           Alberta Vaughan Castellanos
2414445411 Matthew Vaughan Barton (5/16/1961-   )
2414445412 Patrick Lowell Barton (2/19/1964-   )
241444542 Elizabeth Lowell Barton (5/13/1937-   ), m. 9/1/
           1962, Garrett Gregory Gillespie
2414445421 Melanie L. Gillespie (1/18/1968 (adopted) -   )
2414445422 Garrett Gregory Gillespie, Jr. (6/29/1971-   )
241445   Philip Sydney Coolidge (8/22/1830-9/19/1863), (Major, U.S.
           Army, killed in War between the States)
241446   Thomas Jefferson Coolidge (8/26/1831-11/17/1920), m. 11/4/
           1852, Mehitable Sullivan Appleton
2414461   Marian Appleton Coolidge (9/7/1853-2/15/1924), m. 11/16/
           1876, Lucius Manilius Sargent
24144611   Hetty Appleton Sargent (10/28/1877-6/27/1921), m. 6/7/
           1905, Francis Lee Higginson, Jr.
241446111 Francis Lee Higginson III (6/5/1906-   ), m. (1st)
           10/10/1927, Dorothy Jucas. Div. M. (2nd) 1935, Harriet
           Beecher Scoville. Div. M. (3rd) 1/30/1959, Katherine
           Dues Hobson
           Child by second wife:
2414461111 Francis Lee Higginson IV (8/12/1937-   ), m. 7/22/
           1961, Cornelia Parker Wilson
           Children by third wife:
24144611111 Francis Lee Higginson V (5/3/1962-   )
24144611112 James Samuel Higginson (9/26/1965-   )
2414461112 John Higginson (5/2/1939-   ), m. 7/8/1967, Linda
           Windover Reismeyer

241446111121 Hadley Scoville Higginson (3/16/1969-   )
241446112 Joan Higginson (3/7/1908-   ), m. (1st) 6/16/1928,
 Alexander Mackay-Smith. M. (2nd) 9/19/1971, Sigourney
 Bond Romaine
  Children by first husband:
2414461121 Alexander Mackay-Smith, Jr. (3/31/1929-   ), m.
 2/6/1949, Virginia Leigh Ribble
24144611211 Mark Sargent Mackay-Smith (12/5/1949-   ). Name
 changed to Alexander Mackay-Smith III
24144611212 Francis Higginson Mackay-Smith (10/7/1951-   ), m.
 1/23/1971, Janet Leslie Hills
241446112121 Gillian Frances Mackay-Smith (9/15/1982-   )
24144611213 Catherine Cook Mackay-Smith (7/15/1954-   )
24144611214 Virginia Leigh Mackay-Smith (4/14/1956-   )
24144611215 Anne Carter Mackay-Smith (11/19/1957-   )
24144611216 Mary Alexandra Mackay-Smith (9/10/1960-   )
24144611217 Helen Susanne Mackay-Smith (11/17/1962-   )
24144611218 Barbara Joan Mackay-Smith (10/9/1964-   )
2414461122 Mehitable ("Hetty") Mackay-Smith (8/22/1931-   ), m.
 9/29/1961, Charles Calvert Abeles
24144611221 Nathaniel Calvert Abeles (6/26/1962-   )
24144611222 Damaris Sargent Abeles (3/28/1964-   )
24144611223 Jessica Appleton Key Abeles (5/17/1969-   )
2414461123 Matthew Page Mackay-Smith (9/15/1932-   ), m. 6/16/
 1958, Wingate Eddy
24144611231 Wingate Joan Mackay-Smith (3/10/1960-   )
24144611232 Juliet Higginson Mackay-Smith (3/15/1962-   )
24144611233 Emily Austin Mackay-Smith (2/19/1968-   )
2414461124 Frances Lee Mackay-Smith (9/23/1934-4/15/1935)
2414461125 Amanda Joan Mackay-Smith (1/25/1940-   ), m. (1st)
 8/19/1961, Jacobus Egbert DeVries. M. (2nd) 11/27/
 1972, James David Barber
 Luke David Barber (11/13/1976-   )(adopted)
2414461126 Justin Mackay-Smith (9/24/1945-   ), m. 11/23/
 1964, Meredith Mason Stone
24144611261 Joshua Dabney Mackay-Smith (2/6/1969-   )
24144611262 Seth Wentworth Mackay-Smith (8/15/1972-   )
241446113 Griselda Higginson (1/6/1915-   ), m. (1st) 1/16/
 1935, Abram Stevens Hewitt. Div. M. (2nd) 12/ /1954,
 Robert N. Cunningham. M. (3rd) 8/27/1977, James
 Lawrence Basil Williams
  Child by first husband:
2414461131 Camilla C. Hewitt (3/26/1936-   )
2414462 Eleanora Randolph Coolidge (9/21/1856-12/19/1912), m.
 6/18/1879, Frederick Richard Sears, Jr.
24144621 Frederick Richard Sears III (3/30/1881-1/ /1948), m.
 1925, Norma Fontaine
24144622 Eleanora Randolph Sears (9/28/1882-3/26/1968)
2414463 Sarah Lawrence Coolidge (1/2/1858-12/27/1922), m. 6/2/1880,
 Thomas Newbold
24144631 Mary Edith Newbold (2/19/1883-10/28/1969), m. 6/3/1916,
 Gerald Morgan

241446311 Gerald Morgan, Jr. (6/2/1923-   ), m. 9/19/1953,
            Mary Emily Dalton
2414463111 David Gerald Morgan (10/7/1956-   )
2414463112 John Dalton Morgan (3/11/1959-   )
2414463113 Nancy Morgan (8/15/1961-   )
241446312 Thomas Newbold Morgan (5/6/1928-   )
24144632   Thomas Jefferson Newbold (3/26/1886-1/21/1939), m. 1/21/
            1914, Katherine Hubbard
241446321 Thomas Jefferson Newbold, Jr. (11/2/1914-3/3/1960), m.
            8/29/1942, Mary Dell Mathis
2414463211 Thomas Jefferson Newbold III (10/7/1943-   ), m.
            6/22/1974, Donna Clare Marshall
24144632111 Amanda Lucille Newbold (5/2/1976-   )
2414463212 Peter Mathis Newbold (4/29/1948-7/4/1953)
241446322 Thomas Newbold (1/4/1916-   ), m. 10/14/1945, Mary
            Noreen Maxwell
2414463221 Thomas Newbold, Jr. (6/7/1947-   )
2414463222 John Cunningham Newbold (6/1/1950-   )
2414463223 Peter Jefferson Newbold (6/1/1950-   )
2414463224 Alexander Maxwell Newbold (8/1/1954-   )
2414463225 Richard Coolidge Newbold (8/1/1954-   )
2414463226 Robert Hubbard Newbold (8/24/1960-   )
241446323 Katherine Newbold (3/6/1918-   ), m. 3/12/1955,
            George Hale Lowe III
2414463231 Jonathan Newbold Lowe (1/4/1960-   )
241446324 Sarah Hubbard Newbold (3/23/1922-10/6/1962), m. 4/27/
            1957, Charles Alan Krahmer
2414463241 Frances Penelope Krahmer (2/19/1960-   )
241446325 Herman LeRoy Newbold (7/8/1924-   ), m. (1st)
            6/12/1948, Mary Cheney Crocker. M. (2nd) 5/17/1980,
            Cynthia B. Newbold
            Children by first wife:
2414463251 Beth Wyman Newbold (1/16/1955-   )
2414463252 David LeRoy Newbold (8/22/1956-   )
2414463253 Stephen Randolph Newbold (2/15/1959-   ), m. 7/3/
            1982, Christine Marie Nigro
2414463254 Susan Crocker Newbold (4/8/1961-   )(twin)
2414463255 Wendy Jefferson Newbold (4/8/1961-   )(twin)
24144633   Julia Appleton Newbold (11/1/1891-5/10/1972), m. 4/19/
            1913, William Redmond Cross
241446331 Emily Redmond Cross (2/10/1914-   ), m. 3/13/1940,
            Sir John Kenyon Vaughan-Morgan
2414463311 Julia Redmond Vaughan-Morgan (1/14/1943-   ), m.
            4/3/1962, Henry Walter Wiggin
24144633111 Lucy Redmond Wiggin (8/25/1965-   )
24144633112 Caroline Julia Wiggin (11/25/1970-   )
2414463312 Deborah Mary Vaughan-Morgan (9/1/1944-   ), m. 5/
            3/1966, Michael Whitfield
24144633121 Nicholas John Whitfield (1/31/1968-   )
24144633122 Mark David Whitfield (8/27/1971-   )
24144633123 Melanie Katherine Whitfield (2/24/1976-   )
241446332 Richard James Cross (3/31/1915-   ), m. 6/28/1939,
            Margaret Whittemore Lee

2414463321 Richard James Cross, Jr. (6/28/1940-   ), m. 10/
            29/1969, Anne Marie Dyman
24144633211 Donna Louise Cross (12/16/1971-   )
24144633212 John Dyman Cross (12/24/1974-   )
2414463322 Margaret Lee Cross (3/8/1942-   ), m. 1/2/1976,
            William Martin Brodsky
24144633221 Sarah Newbold Cross (10/27/1977 (given mother's name)
24144633222 Rachel L. Brodsky (4/20/1979-   )
2414463323 Alan Whittemore Cross (7/11/1944-   ), m. 8/31/
            1968, Marion Morgan Johnson
24144633231 Julia Marion Cross (4/4/1972-   )
24144633232 Katherine Lee Cross (10/23/1974-   )
24144633233 Caroline W. Cross (2/22/1979-   )
24144633234 Susannah H. Cross (2/22/1979-   )
2414463324 Anne Redmond Cross (3/10/1948-   )
2414463325 Jane Randolph Cross (2/18/1953-   )
241446333   William Redmond Cross, Jr. (4/26/1917-   ), m. 6/
            14/1958, Sally Curtis Smith
2414463331 William Redmond Cross III (7/21/1959-   )
2414463332 Pauline Curtis Cross (10/19/1960-   )
2414463333 Frederick Newbold Cross (12/4/1962-   )
241446334   Thomas Newbold Cross (2/19/1920-   ), m. 3/22/
            1946, Patricia Geer Townsend
            John Townsend Cross (5/28/1951-   )(adopted)
            Katherine Newbold Cross (9/28/1954-   )(adopted)
2414463341 Peter Redmond Cross (8/19/1955-   )
241446335   Mary Newbold Cross (8/5/1925-   ), m. 6/2/1951,
            Donald Pond Spence
2414463351 Alan Keith Spence (6/6/1952-   ), m. 8/26/1978,
            Pamela W. Hughes
2414463352 Sarah Coolidge Spence (8/14/1954-   )
2414463353 Laura Newbold Spence (10/5/1959-   ), m. 10/16/
            1982, Adam Miller Ash
2414463354 Katherine Beckett Spence (8/22/1961-   )
2414464   Thomas Jefferson Coolidge, Jr. (3/6/1863-4/4/1912), m.
            9/30/1891, Clara Amory
24144641   Thomas Jefferson Coolidge III (9/17/1893-8/6/1959), m.
            8/20/1927, Katherine Hill Kuhn
241446411   (son) Coolidge (9/1/1928-9/4/1928)
241446412   Catherine Coolidge (9/16/1930-   ), m. (1st) 5/
            29/1965, John Winthrop Sears. M. (2nd) 10/4/1978,
            John Lastavica
241446413   Thomas Jefferson Coolidge IV (10/6/1932-   ), m.
            6/30/1978, Gloria A. (Geary) Dyett
241446414   John Linzee Coolidge (12/10/1937-   ), m. 1/5/
            1973, Elizabeth Graham O'Donahoe
24144642   Amory Coolidge (3/23/1895-4/2/1952)
24144643   William Appleton Coolidge (10/22/1901-   )
24144644   John Linzee Coolidge (3/21/1905-5/22/1917)
24145   Cornelia Jefferson Randolph (7/26/1799-2/24/1871), d.s.p.
24146   Virginia Jefferson Randolph (8/22/1801-4/26/1882), m. 9/11/
            1824, Nicholas Philip Trist (1800-1874)

241461   Martha Jefferson Trist (5/8/1826-8/8/1915), m. 10/12/1858,
        John Woolfolk Burke (1/21/1825-1907), son of John Muse
        Burke and Sophia F. Woolfolk
2414611   Nicholas Philip Trist Burke (7/16/1859-2/12/1907), m. 1/
        18/1901, Jane Revere Reynolds, dau. of John Philip and
        Jane Minot Revere Reynolds
24146111 Jane Revere Burke (11/14/1904-4/15/1920)
24146112 John Randolph Burke (4/19/1906-   ), m. (1st) 3/22/
        1941, Phyllis Brewster. M. (2nd) 10/6/1965, Agnes
        (Hayes) Honeycutt
        Child by first wife:
241461121 Nicholas Randolph Burke (10/6/1942-   ), m. 11/8/
        1975, Claire Juliette (Geszty)Gardiner
2414612   Frances Maury Burke (3/25/1861-1/18/1933)
2414613   John Woolfolk Burke, Jr. (2/9/1863-8/1/1865)
2414614   Harry Randolph Burke (10/14/1864-11/21/1947), m. 4/19/
        1898, Rosella Gordon Trist, dau. of Nicholas Browse and
        Augustine Gordon Trist
24146141 Nicholas Browse Trist Burke (2/28/1899-1/28/1930), m.
        9/1/1928, Mary Weeden Smith
24146142 Ellen Coolidge Burke (5/10/1901-12/29/1975)
24146143 Rosella Trist Burke (11/30/1903-   ), m. 11/3/1924,
        Robert Edwin Graham, son of Robert Montrose and Alice
        Henderson Graham
241461431 Robert Montrose Graham II (2/6/1926-   ), m. (1st)
        11/27/1950, Hazel Delmer. M. (2nd) 10/26/1969,
        Patricia Shemonek
        Child by first wife:
2414614311 Martina Trist Graham (5/9/1958-   )
241461432 Rosella Trist Graham (1/13/1930-   ), m. (1st) 2/3/
        1951, Richard Charles Lamb. M. (2nd) 8/1/1963, Walter
        Gerald Schendel, Jr.
        Children by first husband:
2414614321 John Graham Lamb (11/23/1951-   )
2414614322 Elizabeth Randolph Lamb (12/7/1953-   ), m. 10/
        25/1980, Martin Francis Casey
        Child by second husband:
2414614323 Walter Gerald Schendel III (5/24/1964-   )
24146144 Gordon Trist Burke (1/6/1907-11/7/1964), m. 4/19/1926,
        Cornelia Lee Baum (12/21/1904-   ), dau. of Daniel
        and Harriet H. Hackett Baum
241461441 Nicholas Gordon Trist Burke (10/20/1930-   ), m.
        (1st) 4/19/1954, Betty Ann Clayton. M. (2nd) 1/17/
        1975, Joan Ruth Arnold
        Harriet Holland Hackett Burke (3/26/1940-   )(adopted)
2414615   Virginia Randolph Burke (10/20/1866-12/29/1953)
2414616   Ellen Coolidge Burke (10/11/1868-9/30/1941), m. 6/7/1902,
        Charles Brown Eddy (11/29/1872-   ), son of James
        Henry and Maria Nancy Brown Eddy
24146161 Martha Jefferson Eddy (6/28/1903-   ), d. inf.
24146162 James Henry Eddy (1/28/1907-3/29/1971), m. 10/28/1939,
        Phyllis Audrey Merian

    Phyllis Merian Eddy (12/13/1944-   )(adopted), m.
    6/24/1967, Nicholas Radcliffe Orem
    James Henry Eddy, Jr. (9/14/1946-   )(adopted), m.
    3/15/1969, Terry West James
    James Henry Eddy III (6/18/1971-   )(adopted)
24146163 Charles Brown Eddy, Jr. (10/19/1908-   ), m. 11/23/
    1946, Mary Elizabeth Hillard
241461631 Ellen Hillard Eddy (9/8/1947-   ), m. 7/13/1974,
    Alan Thorndike
2414616311 Nicholas Peter Thorndike (6/1/1978-   )
2414616312 Edward Hillard Thorndike (12/12/1981-   )
241461632 Charles Brown Eddy III (6/1/1950-   )
24146164 John Burke Eddy (11/15/1910-8/20/1974), m. 1/6/1945,
    Elizabeth Westcott
241461641 Stephen Burke Eddy (10/28/1945-   ), m. 8/29/1970,
    Susan Lorraine Osborn
241461642 Susan Westcott Eddy (8/30/1948-   ), m. (1st)
    8/27/1971, Thomas Richard Fuller. M. (2nd) 7/21/1979,
    Raymond Parker
    Child by second husband:
2414616421 John Robert Parker (2/4/1981-   )
2414617 Edmund Jefferson Burke (12/10/1870-11/14/1942), m. 4/13/
    1903, Gertrude Lucy Storey (241b422)
24146171 John Woolfolk Burke III (5/20/1904-3/29/1905)
24146172 Martha Jefferson Burke (3/18/1907-10/14/1957)
241462 Thomas Jefferson Trist (1828-   ), m. (1st) Ellen
    Dorothea (Strong) Lyman. M. (2nd), Sophia Knabe, d.s.p.
241463 Hore Browse Trist (2/20/1832-1896), m. 1861, Anna Mary
    Waring
2414631 Nicholas Browse Trist (4/1/1862-1928), m. (1st), Delia
    Porter. M. (2nd) Alice Cooke. M. (3rd) 6/19/1920,
    Kathleen B. Watts
    Child by second wife:
24146311 Mary Cooke Trist (2/24/1888-1969), m. (1st) 9/23/1908,
    Albert R. Kenny. M. (2nd) 10/ /1949, Edward Joseph
    Rudel
    Children by first husband:
241463111 Katherine Mary Kenny (6/2/1909-10/2/1966), m. 8/23/
    1934, John William Fulton
2414631111 John William Fulton, Jr. (5/15/1936-   ), m. Lotus
    Pua Keonaona
24146311111 Lilianaikiwai Fulton (4/11/1975-   )
24146311112 Maile Katherine Fulton (11/8/1977-   )
241463112 Virginia Jefferson Kenny (2/11/1911-5/30/1960), 6/8/
    1935, Seward Davis, Jr.
2414631121 Virginia Jefferson Davis (5/17/1936-   ), m. 4/
    29/1966, Richard Duckworth Irwin
24146311211 Christopher Jefferson Irwin (4/5/1968-   )
24146311212 Katherine Seward Irwin (5/24/1970-   )
2414631122 Katherine Roy Davis (7/3/1939-   ), m. 10/13/
    1962, James William Flynn, Jr.
24146311221 Virginia Kenny Flynn (10/16/1964-   )

```
             James William Flynn III (6/28/1970-        )(adopted)
2414632   George Waring Trist (11/16/1863-1884). Unm.
2414633   Hore Browse Trist,Jr. (9/12/1865-        ), d. inf.
2414634   Mary Helen Trist (9/12/1872-3/6/1959)
24147    Mary Jefferson Randolph (11/2/1803-d.s.p. 3/29/1876)
24148    James Madison Randolph (1/17/1806-d.s.p. 1/23/1834)(born
             in the White House)
24149    Benjamin Franklin Randolph (7/14/1808-2/18/1871), m. 11/13/
             1834, Sarah Champe Carter (1810-1896), dau. of Robert Hill
             and           Coles Carter
241491   Isaetta Carter Randolph (3/24/1836-12/9/1888), m. 11/13/
             1860, James Lenaeus Hubard (1835-1913)
2414911  Benjamin (Franklin) Randolph Hubard (2/2/1862-3/7/1942),
             m. Mary Neil Grub
24149111 Thomas James Hubard (11/15/1892-6/3/1968), m. 9/8/1924,
             Lora Stella Letsinger
241491111 Wiley Nelson Hubard (6/29/1925-        ), m. (1st) 7/3/
             1947, Grace Jeanette Cupp. M. (2nd) 6/19/1964, Anie
             Renie Kemp
         Children by first wife:
2414911111 Sherry Lorraine Hubard (12/10/1948-        ), m. 8/5/
             1964, Jack Miles
24149111111 Samuel Christopher Miles (5/2/1965-        )
24149111112 Timi Lanay Miles (7/27/1967-        )
24149111113 Amber Marie Miles (11/13/1970-        )
2414911112 Wiley Dan Hubard (7/17/1952-        )
2414911113 Deborah Gail Hubard (8/25/1955-        ), m. 8/28/1971,
             Steve Carnes
24149111131 Nicole Rochelle Carnes (4/3/1978-        )
241491112 Mary Crissie Hubard (7/21/1927-        ), m. (1st) 8/18/
             1945, Elmo E. Williams. M. (2nd) 6/24/1972, Raymond
             Earl Tillery
         Children by first husband:
2414911121 Jean Kay Williams (11/21/1946-        ), m. 6/11/1966,
             Turner Louis Jones III
24149111211 Amanda Kay Jones (1/15/1969-        )
24149111212 Anita Melanie Jones (8/1/1971-        )
2414911122 Larry Dean Williams (12/29/1948-1/23/1961)
241491113 Lora Stella Hubard (2/10/1933-        ), m. (1st) 11/1/
             1950, James French. M. (2nd), Don Hair
         Children by first husband:
2414911131 Thomas James French (12/12/1951-        )
2414911132 Gary Steven French (5/22/1953-        ), m. 9/23/1972,
             Christine Tillery
24149111321 Jonathan Steven French (6/7/1979-        )
         Child by second husband:
2414911133 Cindy Janice Hair (10/14/1957-        ), m. Theodore
             Clinton Morse II
24149111331 Theodore Clinton Morse III (7/ /1975-        )
24149111332 Kenny Allen Eugene Morse (8/ /1977-        )
24149111333 Christopher Lee Morse (9/ /1978-        )
24149112 Robert Thruston Hubard (10/2/1902-11/4/1952), m. (1st)
             Emily Bolen. M. (2nd), Alice Hensley
```

241491121 Benjamin Randolph Hubard II (8/2/1923-8/4/1952), m.
2/7/1946, Margaret Hellard
2414911211 John Robert Hubard (11/19/1946-   ), m. 1/25/
1967, Carolyn Caldwell
24149112111 John Robert Hubard, Jr. (6/3/1968-   )
24149112112 Angela Kay Hubard (5/13/1970-   )
24149112113 Jason Robert Hubard (4/10/1976-   )
2414911212 Benjamin Randolph Hubard III (10/4/1947-   ), m.
6/17/1966, Norma Lee Beall
24149112121 Benjamin Randolph Hubard IV (9/20/1967-   )
241491122 Robert King Hubard (1/18/1925-   ), m. (1st) 3/3/
1958, Irene Stumpf. M. (2nd) 3/17/1978, Frances Ruth
Riehenberger
    Children by first wife:
2414911221 Robert Kule Hubard (9/18/1958-   )
2414911222 Terry Keith Hubard (3/2/1964-   )
241491123 Ramona Jean Hubard (7/3/1927-   ), m. (1st) 3/10/
1946, Alonzo Stokes. M. (2nd) 8/14/1969, Robert
Sharp
    Children by first husband:
2414911231 Wesley Ann Stokes (1/28/1947-   ), m. 10/10/1967,
Rodney Schilz
24149112311 Karen Elizabeth Schilz (6/24/1968-   )
24149112312 Matthew Schilz (3/12/1971-   )
2414911232 Barbara Jean Stokes (9/14/1950-   ), m. Bobby McCoy
24149112321 Carrie Ann McCoy (9/3/1973-   )
24149112322 Erin Keiley McCoy (4/3/1975-   )
2414911233 Robert Alonzo Stokes, Jr., m. 8/14/1976, Mary Vasquez
24149112331 Desideria Cloe Stokes (1/7/1978-   )
    Child by second wife:
241491124 Thomas Carr Jefferson Hubard (11/6/1945 (2nd wife)-12/
7/1967)
2414912 Susan Bolling Hubard (10/5/1863-2/20/1894), m. 1888, John
Slaughter
24149121 Charles Hubard Slaughter (4/16/1889-5/4/1977), m. 9/18/
1914, Evelyn Morman Meech
24149122 Isaetta Randolph Slaughter (10/12/1892-11/4/1979), m.
4/15/1912, Harry Benjamin Munday
241491221 Harry Benjamin Munday, Jr. (2/1/1913-12/9/1979), m.
Pauline Vaughan
241491222 Mary Frances Munday (1/23/1930-   ), m. 10/25/
1952, Robert Lawrence Warwick
2414912221 Stephen Lawrence Warwick (9/8/1965-   )
2414913 James Thruston Hubard (4/17/1865-6/18/1882)
2414914 Robert Thruston Hubard (10/31/1866-1/3/1923), m. (1st)
1897, Leila C. Moss. M. (2nd), Mary Brennan Swift
(-1/3/1923)
    Children by first husband:
24149141 Robert Thruston Hubard, Jr. (1898-1899)
24149142 Martha Randolph Hubard (4/29/1900-   ), m. 1/26/1920,
Louis Elsinger
241491421 James Hubard Elsinger (5/1/1924-   ), m. 8/6/1949,
Jo Ann Fossett

2414914211 Patricia Ann Elsinger (7/2/1953-   )
           Child by second husband:
24149143   Stephen Swift Hubard (4/14/1914-3/6/1956)(2nd wife)
2414915   Sarah Champe Hubard (8/18/1868-1/1/1903)
2414916   Mary Randolph Hubard (5/7/1870-8/25/1930), m. 10/28/1896,
           Edward Miles Mathewes
24149161   Eliza Peronneau Mathewes (9/15/1897-4/15/1898)
24149162   Edward Miles Mathewes, Jr. (12/19/1898-3/4/1906)
24149163   Mary Randolph Hubard Mathewes (8/16/1902-3/12/1943)
24149164   Clelia Peronneau Mathews (8/2/1906-7/3/1967), m. 9/23/
           1933, Thomas Richard Waring
241491641 Mary Randolph Waring (6/20/1939-   ), m. (1st) 3/15/
           1958, Kenneth J. Elder . M. (2nd) 9/22/1962, Robert
           Eugene Berretta
2414916411 Thomas Waring Elder (added name Berretta)(12/9/1960-)
2414916412 Mary Randolph Berretta (12/7/1964-   )
241491642 Thomas Waring (3/5/1944-   ), m. 11/29/1975, Janice
           Virginia Duffie
2414916421 Joseph Ioor Waring (10/20/1979-   )
2414916422 Katherine Peronneau Waring (5/5/1981-   )
2414916423 Thomas Richard Waring II (7/12/1983-   )
24149165   James Hubard Mathewes (6/16/1908-2/16/1975), m. 11/25/
           1939, Elizabeth Gaillard Lowndes
2414917   Isaetta Carter Hubard (4/18/1872-3/3/1952), m. 1/28/1916,
           Beverley Landon Ambler
2414918   Bernard Markham Hubard
2414919   Ellen Wayles Hubard, m. Robinson
241491x   Jefferson Randolph Hubard (3/14/1877-1925), m. 11/18/
           1908, Louise Moore
241491x1   Agnes Moore Hubard (8/2/1909-10/10/1910)
241491a   Archibald Blair Hubard (7/21/1879-5/26/1952), m. 10/28/
           1905, Carlotta D. Barney
241491a1   Randolph Bolling Hubard (1/15/1906-   ), m. 5/2/
           1936, Ina Walker Cochran
241491a11 John Bolling Hubard (4/20/1937-   ), m. 5/29/1970,
           Margaret Bate Cobb
241491a111 Randolph Bolling Hubard II (10/3/1971-7/24/1980)
241491a112 Robin Mitchell Hubard (7/28/1974-   )
241491a113 John Randolph Hubard (5/7/1981-   )
241491a12 Cynthia Ann Hubard (3/17/1942-   ), m. (1st) 3/14/
           1964, Samuel Bartow Strang III. M. (2nd) 6/15/1972,
           James Craig Ziegler
241491a121 Samuel Bartow Strang IV (9/22/1964-   )
241492   Lewis Carter Randolph (6/13/1838-5/29/1887), m. 1/29/1867,
           Louisa Hubard, only dau. of Robert Thruston Hubard
2414921   Robert Carter Randolph (12/11/1867-7/9/1939), m. 10/31/
           1906, Letitia Lawrence
2414922   Louise Hubard Randolph (5/22/1869-8/23/1951)
2414923   Sarah Champe Randolph (7/1/1871-1/1/1959), m. 6/24/1908,
           Randolph Warren Hammerslough
2414924   Susan Bolling Randolph (8/28/1874-4/19/1929)
2414925   Benjamin Franklin Randolph (9/9/1876-3/31/1951)

2414926 Lewis Carter Randolph (7/28/1877-8/29/1934), m. 9/6/1906,
     Dorothy Atkins
24149261 John Randolph (4/23/1915-   )
2414927 Eugene Jefferson Randolph (3/19/1880-10/6/1950), m. 2/28/
     1902, Anne Elizabeth Carrier
24149271 Hubard Carrier Randolph (12/21/1902-10/28/1929)
24149272 Catharine Carrier Randolph (7/22/1904-   ), m. 10/3/
     1931, Edgar Reid Russell
241492721 Catharine Randolph Russell (6/25/1933-   ), m. 6/27/
     1957, James Leake Little. Div. 11/17/1962
2414927211 Catharine Randolph Little (5/17/1958-   )
24149273 Elizabeth Carrier Randolph (11/10/1905-   ), m. (1st)
     10/8/1927, William Lord Rivers. M. (2nd) 3/9/1946,
     Monroe Stanley Bobst
        Child by first wife:
241492731 William Lord Rivers, Jr. (8/10/1933-   ), m. (1st)
     7/11/1959, Gayle Musick. M. (2nd) 10/10/1973, Silvia
     (Willis) Griffin
        Child by first wife:
2414927311 Laura Blake Rivers (2/15/1961-   )
2414928 Janet Thruston Randolph (1/27/1884-4/19/1951)
2414x Meriwether Lewis Randolph (1/31/1810-9/24/1837), m. 4/9/
     1835, Elizabeth Martin
2414x1 Lewis Jackson Randolph (3/ /1836-1840)
2414a Septimia Anne Randolph (1/3/1814-9/14/1887), m. 8/13/1838,
     Dr. David Scott Meikleham (/16/1904-11/20/1949)
2414a1 William Morland Meikleham (12/11/1839-7/27/1889), m. (1st)
     4/25/1865, Fannie Cassidy (1845-1885). M. (2nd) 6/8/1887,
     Isabella Parlby Cuthbert
     Children by first wife:
2414a11 William Arabin Meikleham (3/1/1866-11/12/1942), m. 1/28/
     1903, Margaret Breckenridge
2414a12 Thomas Mann Randolph Meikleham (2/14/1869-4/10/1954), m.
     10/7/1896, Agnes Dash
2414a121 Frances Louise Meikleham (8/4/1902-7/20/1977)
2414a122 Martha Randolph Meikleham (5/8/1905-9/15/1919)
2414a13 Frank Sydney Meikleham (5/28/1872-9/14/1872)(twin)
2414a14 Henry Parish Meikleham (5/28/1872-7/23/1937)(twin), m.
     (1st) 6/9/1897, Virginia Grafton. Div. 1912. M. (2nd)
     1/16/1926, Juliet (Howell) Graves
2414a2 Thomas Mann Randolph Meikelham (12/30/1840-4/7/1922). Unm.
2414a3 Esther Alice Meikelham (11/12/1842-9/4/1843)
2414a4 Esther Alice Meikelham (12/28/1843-2/6/1927). Unm.
2414a5 Ellen Wayles Meikelham (8/29/1846-2/22/1913). Unm.
2414b George Wythe Randolph (3/10/1818-4/3/1867), m. 4/10/1852,
     Mary Elizabeth (Adams) Pope (1830-1871)(221221)
2415 William Randolph (1/16/1770-5/5/1848), m. 9/11/1792, Lucy
     Bolling Randolph (11/7/1775-3/6/1841), dau. of Gov. Beverley
     and Martha ("Patty") Cocke Randolph of "Green Creek", Cum-
     berland County
24151 Col. Thomas Beverley Randolph (4/31/1793-12/12/1867), U.S.A.,
     m. 5/31/1814, Maria Barbara Mayer, dau. of Christopher Bar-
     tholomew and Maria Barbara Mayer of Lancaster, Pa.

241511 William Mayer Randolph (1815-1875), m. 1842, Mary Eleanor
      Pitts
2415111 Mary St. Mayer Randolph (1844-1870), m. William Wallace
      Harney (1831-1912), son of John Hopkins and Martha
      Wallace Harney
24151111 William Randolph Harney (1/24/1869-   ), m. 10/10/
      1900, Jane Bratton Montague (11/20/1879-   ), dau.
      of James Robert and Fanny Bernard Preston Montague. No
      issue
241512 Susan Burkhart Randolph (1817-1867)
241513 Martha Elizabeth Randolph (4/6/1818-6/5/1890), m. 9/3/
      1839, Col. John High("Hoch") Keim (1/26/1817-10/29/1858),
      son of DeBenville and Mary High Keim of Reading
2415131 DeBenville Randolph Keim (1/1/1841-   ), m. 6/15/1872,
      Jane A. Sumner Owen (2/18/1844-11/22/1912), dau. of
      Galusha and Betsey P. Denison Owen of Hartford
24151311 Elizabeth Randolph Keim (8/1/1873-   ), m. 6/25/
      1895, Charles Willauer Kurtz
241513111 Emily Randolph Kurtz (10/17/1897-   )
241513112 Maria Elizabeth Kurtz (1900-   )
241513113 Charles Randolph Kurtz (
24151312 Harriet Virginia Keim (7/9/1875-   )
24151313 DeBenville Keim (7/ /1880-1883)
24151314 John Owen Keim, d. inf.
2415132 Mary High Keim (12/4/1842-8/2/1891), m. (1st) 1866,
      William Wirt Mills (-6/20/1867). M. (2nd) 12/
      15/1870, Abner K. Stauffer
    Children by first husband:
24151321 William Wirt Mills, Jr. (7/17/1867-   ), m. 11/15/
      1898, Nellie Coleman (2/ /1879-   ). She was born
      in Aldershot, Eng.
    Children by second husband:
24151322 John Keim Stauffer (7/22/1874-   )
24151323 Anna Keim Stauffer (4/7/1877-   )
24151324 Mary Virginia Stauffer (11/21/1878-   ), m. Rev.
      Wallace Martin
24151325 Frederick Randolph Stauffer (8/28/1881-   )
2415133 Edward Tudor Keim (8/8/1844-   ), m. (1st) 7/9/1867,
      Emma L. Bloomfield of New Jersey. M. (2nd)   .
      M. (3rd) 3/5/1913, Mrs. John Alexander
    Children by first wife:
24151331 Randolph Keim (7/29/1869-9/12/1891)
24151332 Edward Peyton Keim (8/1/1871-   )
24151333 Martha E. R. Keim (12/12/1875-   )
24151334 Carl DeBenville Keim. d. inf.
24151335 Griffith Keim
24151336 DeBenville Keim (7/ /1880-   )
2415134 Virginia Randolph Keim (5/4/1846-2/ /1896), m. 2/4/1869,
      James Allaire Millholland (12/8/1842-12/8/1911), son of
      James and Fanny Curtis Millholland of Mount Savage, Md.
24151341 Fanny Randolph Millholland (1/2/1870-11/21/1917), m.
      6/6/1894, William Milner Roberts, Jr. (1/21/1865-4/2/
      1946), son of William Milner and Elizabeth ("Betty")
      Humbird Roberts

241513411 Virginia Millholland Roberts (12/25/1895-   ), m.
           9/12/1920, William Hunter Oswald (7/21/1895-   ),
           son of Richard Willing and Elizabeth Woodin Hanly
           Oswald
2415134111 William Hunter Oswald, Jr. (4/23/1921-   ), m. 10/
            24/1942, Jean Ann Nutt (9/2/1922-   ), dau. of
            Arthur and Ann Josephine Dewey Nutt
24151341111 William Hunter Oswald III (8/17/1943-   )
2415134112 Milner Robert Oswald (1/13/1925-   )
2415134113 Virginia Randolph Oswald (1/21/1927-   )
2415134114 Thomas Woodin Oswald (8/29/1931-   )
241513412 Elizabeth Humbird Roberts (11/21/1898-   ), m. 2/
           12/1923, Robert Edward Lee Barnard, son of James G.
           and Mary Easter Barnard
2415134121 Robert Edward Lee Barnard, Jr.
2415134122 Frederick Roberts Barnard
241513413 Fanny Curtis Roberts (2/10/1900-   ), m. 6/16/
           1920, Frank Minnium Wilson, M.D., son of Dr. Jacob
           Jones and Josephine McConnick Wilson
2415134131 Frank Minnium Wilson, Jr.
2415134132 Fanny Roberts Wilson
2415134133 William McConnick Wilson
241513414 Eleanor MacDonald Roberts (10/5/1903-   ), m. 1/22/
           1927, Samuel Bradford (-3/16/1934), son of
           Samuel W. and Cornelia (Norris) Bradford
2415134141 Eleanor MacDonald Bradford (2/8/1928-   ), m. 7/18/
            1946, Wilton Holmes Sykes (11/24/1925-   ), son
            of S. Lua and Beatrice Minerva Holmes Syckes of
            Cumberland, Md.
24151341411 Cornelia Bradford Syckes (5/9/1947-   )
241513415 Martha Wharton Roberts (8/23/1905-   ), m. 10/28/
           1933, Arthur Ford Jones (8/9/1903-   ), M.D., son
           of Dr. Emmett Lee and Annie Rebecca Ford Jones of
           Cumberland, Md.
2415134151 Arthur Ford Jones, Jr. (10/13/1934-   )
2415134152 Nancy Philippa Jones (1/22/1938-   )
241513416 Helen Dickey Roberts (11/8/1906-   ), m. 6/20/
           1931, John Myers Berry (10/30/1907-   ), son of
           Peter Edmund and Mabel Myers Berry
2415134161 Peter Edmund Berry (3/27/1934-   )
2415134162 David Humbird Berry (1/11/1938-   )
241513417 William Milner Roberts III (11/10/1907-7/1/1934)
241513418 Frederick Humbird Roberts (10/5/1907-   ), m. 9/23/
           1938, Mary Catherine Askey (6/14/1911-   ), dau.
           of William Harrison and Christiana Adela Hast Askey
           of Cumberland, Md.
2415134181 Adela Jane Roberts (7/25/1942-   )
2415134182 William Milner Roberts IV (10/19/1945-   )
24151342 James Allaire Millholland, Jr. (11/10/1871-12/23/1875)
24151343 Anne Keim Millholland (8/8/1873-   ), m. 11/2/1898,
          VanLear Perry Shriver (12/11/1872-   ), son of
          Henry and Sarah VanLear Perry Shriver

241513431 VanLear Perry Shriver, Jr. (9/20/1899-   ), m.
          1/12/1929, Marie Boggs McBride (6/21/1909-   ),
          dau. of William and Emma Boggs McBride. Div.
2415134311 Sally VanLear Shriver (4/12/1930-   )
2415134312 VanLear Perry Shriver III (11/24/1934-   )
241513432 Beverley Randolph Shriver (11/23/1903-   ), m.
          2/5/1930, Mary Elizabeth Armstrong (12/7/1903-   ),
          dau. of Frederick Serles and Susan Brainard Armstrong
2415134321 Beverley Randolph Shriver, Jr. (11/10/1931-   )
24151344 Lewis Curtis Millholland (3/23/1875-6/4/1945), m. 4/16/
          1902, Minnie Martin West (6/21/1879-   ), dau. of
          Thomas Hilleary and Fannie Hennon West
241513441 Lewis Curtis Millholland, Jr. (11/14/1905-   ), m.
2415134411 Lewis Curtis Millholland III (8/11/1930-   )
2415134412 Phyllis Ann Millholland (9/28/1931-   )
2415134413 William Keffer Millholland (12/29/1939-   )
241513442 Fannie West Millholland (1/14/1906-   )
24151345 John Keim Millholland (12/30/1876-   ), m. 7/18/
          1898, Estelle Kilham Devries (3/21/1876-   ), dau.
          of William and Anna Mary Humbird Devries
241513451 Virginia Keim Millholland (6/22/1899-   ), m. 6/9/
          1920, Clarence Hobard Osborne (7/13/1896-   ), son
          of George and Loretta Gilly Osborne
2415134511 John Hobart Osborne (8/4/1921-7/25/1941)
2415134512 William Devries Osborne (5/1/1923-   )
2415134513 George Richard Osborne (7/7/1928-   )
2415134514 Estelle Millholland Osborne (4/13/1931-   )
241513452 John Keim Millholland, Jr. (8/8/1902-   ), m. 3/3/
          1930, Mildred Marie Douglas (7/25/1912-   ), dau.
          of George Albert and Frances Raetelle Douglas
2415134521 Marie Joan Millholland (2/20/1931-   )
2415134522 John Keim Millholland III (9/23/1932-   )
241513453 William Devries Millholland (8/14/1904-   ), m. 10/
          18/1926, Josephine Betty Dunn (4/11/1906-9/17/1937),
          dau. of William James and Adehlia Honeywood Dunn
2415134531 Gay Ann Millholland (3/24/1931-   )
2415134532 Josephine Keim Millholland (7/24/1933-   )
241513454 Anna Mary Millholland (10/16/1910-5/7/1929), m. 4/16/
          1926, Alton Wallin (8/8/1902-   ), son of Richard
          W. and Corrine Williams Wallin
2415134541 Anna Mary Wallin (3/20/1929-   )
24151346 Allen Campbell Millholland (7/14/1878-   )
24151347 Randolph Millholland (2/6/1880-   ), m. 6/8/1904,
          Jean Humbird Roberts (7/24/1881-   ), dau. of
          William Milner and Elizabeth Humbird Roberts
241513471 Randolph Millholland, Jr. (9/21/1906-   ). Unm.
241513472 Betty Millholland (12/28/1910-   ), m. 10/2/1937,
          Elihu Holland Joyner (11/15/1902-   ), son of
          Elihu and Sarah Catherine Holland Joyner
2415134721 Jean Holland Joyner (7/30/1938-   )
2415134722 Elihu Holland Joyner, Jr. (6/26/1942-   )
24151348 Virginia Randolph Millholland (10/11/1881-9/25/1882)

2415134'J Nona Millholland (6/21/1883-   ), m. (1st) 3/4/1905,
       Dr. Thomas Benton McDonald (2/22/1871-1924), son of John
       and Mary Jane Benton McDonald. M. (2nd) Johnson R.
       Morgan (-11/22/1935), son of Thomas P. and
       Edith Johnson Morgan. No issue
241513491 Col. Thomas Benton McDonald, Jr. (6/19/1907-   ),
       m. 5/31/1934, Marion Farrar Warren (8/30/1912-   ),
       dau. of John Trenholm and Grace Hortense Tomer Warren
2415134911 Thomas Benton McDonald III (12/20/1935-   )
2415134912 Warren Randolph McDonald (9/27/1938-   )
241513492 Nancy Day McDonald (-11/23/1911)
241513493 Anna Randolph McDonald (8/22/1918-   ), m. 6/14/
       1941, Lt. Col. Ogden Nelson Pratt (5/15/1912-   ),
       son of Willis Hadley and Agnes Fossum Pratt
2415134931 Douglas McDonald Pratt (6/11/1942-   )
2415134x William McIlvaine Millholland (5/24/1885-   ), m.
       11/28/1906, Estelle Llewelyn, dau. of John Wesley and
       Delphia Hansel Llewelyn
2415134x1 Alma Llewelyn Millholland (2/1/1908-   ), m. 11/
       20/1927, Charles Lawrence Cullen (11/13/1906-   ),
       son of Harold Dempster and Bessie Mae French Cullen of
       Birmingham
2415134x11 Lewis Keim Cullen (2/2/1932-   )
2415134x12 Norma Jean Cullen (8/13/1935-   )
2415134x2 Harrietta Ann Millholland (3/15/1914-   ), m. 7/10/
       1936, William Cosa Jordan (7/23/1912-   ), son of
       Rupert Clyde and Willa Olivia Bailey Jordan
2415134x21 William Michael Jordan (4/1/1941-   )
2415134a Beverley Millholland (9/21/1886-   )
2415134b Martha Randolph Millholland (1/7/1889-   )
2415135 Anne Heister Keim (3/9/1849-1851)
2415136 Peyton Randolph Keim (3/23/1850-1/ /1904), m. (1st) 8/
       19/1876, Lillie Seymour (-5/23/1891) of Milan,
       Ill. M. (2nd) 10/1/1892, Nellie Beauregard Williams
       (1/3/1861-12/30/1893), dau. of Mortimer Lyles and Sarah
       Williams Phelps Williams of Georgetown, D.C. M. (3rd)
       4/17/1895, Annie Adelaide Hurkamp (1862-1939), dau. of
       John G. and Catherine Elizabeth Hardent Hurkamp of Fre-
       dericksburg. No issue
24151361 Lillie M. Keim (-5/25/1889)
24151362 Seymour DeBenville Keim (10/14/1878-   ), m. 1908,
       Rosalind Laughna of Bridgeport, Conn.
24151363 Elsie Loraine Keim (2/19/1889-   ). Unm.
24151364 Anna Randolph Keim (12/26/1893-   ), m. 8/31/1929,
       John James Barsam (11/23/1886-   ), son of John and
       Margaret Dingshian Barsam of Troy, N.Y. No issue
2415137 Thomas Beverley Keim (1/11/1852-   ), m , 5/31/1876,
       Elizabeth Morris Cox (1/1/1851-   ), dau. of William
       Penny and Mary Elizabeth Morris Cox
24151371 William Penny Cox Keim (12/25/1880-   )
24151372 Mary Morris Keim (6/2/1882-2/1/1885)
24151373 Thomas Beverley Keim, Jr. (2/26/1884-   )

24151374 Henry May Keim (11/9/1888-4/22/1889)
2415138   John Randolph Keim (11/15/1853-1854)
2415139   John Otto Keim (3/28/1855-   ), m. Ella Boreaf
24151391 Shuster Boreaf Keim (1887-   )
24151392 Ella Boreaf Keim (8/ /1891-11/ /1891)
24151393 Charles Carver Keim
241513x   Frederick Sherwood Jessup Keim (1/7/1857-1858)
241513a   Anna Sherwood Keim (4/18/1859-1/23/1873)
241514   Lucy Jane Randolph (9/28/1819-1872), m. 1836, Gen. William
          High Keim (6/13/1813-5/18/1862), son of DeBenville and
          Mary High Keim. No issue recorded
241515   George Lewis Randolph (1821-   )
241516   Susan Beverley Randolph (9/2/1823-3/9/1882), m. 4/11/1852,
          Samuel Richardson Millar (5/3/1817-10/ /1861, son of
          Isaac and Ann Hall Richardson Millar
2415161   George Randolph Millar (7/3/1854-10/21/1857)
2415162   Samuel Rolfe Millar (5/31/1857-2/13/1930), m. 10/3/1882,
          Bertha Marie Riedel (12/25/1857-9/20/1927), dau. of
          Jacob and Susanna Gramm Riedel
24151621 Susan Beverley Millar (5/1/1884-   ), m. (1st)
          1904, Rudolph Maxmillian Ruthardt. M. (2nd) 11/23/1917,
          Alfred Pochon. Susan's three children by Ruthardt
          were adopted by Pochon, and given his name .
241516211 Virginia Elizabeth Pochon (12/5/1905-   ), m. 10/4/
          1933, Harry ("Hal") Ustance Oxenham (3/29/1906-   )
          of Dovercourt, Eng.
2415162111 Peter Rolfe Oxenham (6/5/1934-   )
241516212 Erica Millar Pochon (1/21/1907-   ), m. 10/6/1928,
          Capt. George Francis Mentz, U.S.N.
2415162121 Susan Beverley Mentz (12/1/1929-   )
2415162122 George Francis Mentz, Jr. (9/5/1931-   )
241516213 Rolfe Millar Pochon (8/21/1908-   )
241516214 Alfred Pochon, Jr. (2/1/1919-8/ /1919)
241516215 Beverley Randolph Pochon (2/1/1922-   )
241516216 Susan Beverley Pochon (3/ /1924-3/ /1924)
241516217 Catherine Dubois Pochon (9/20/1926-   )
24151622 Elizabeth Anne Millar (10/13/1885-   )
24151623 Florence Virginia Millar (7/9/1887-   ), m. 10/3/
          1907, Gen. Samuel Gardner Waller (3/26/1881-   ),
          son of Nelson Samuel and Rebecca Beanson Allen Gardner
          Waller. No issue
24151624 Col. Samuel Rolfe Millar, Jr. (2/12/1889-   ), m.
          1/19/1934, Mrs. Dorothy Treece Angus (10/16/1896-   ),
          dau. of William Ferris and Cara May Perry Treece. No
          issue. Dorothy has a daughter by her first marriage.
24151625 Bertha Randolph Millar (2/24/1892-   ), m. 11/16/
          1921, Charles Edward Loizeaux (1/22/1889-   ), son
          of Joshua Duse and Catherine Lorraine Thomson Loizeaux
241516251 Charles Edward Loizeaux, Jr. (3/19/1923-   )
241516252 Elaine Millar Loizeaux (7/25/1925-   )
241517   Peyton Randolph (-1847). Killed in Mexico.
241518   Christopher Mayer Randolph (1830-1868), m. 2/19/1856, Emily
          Susan Keim (-1/27/1860), dau. of DeBenville and Mary
          High Keim

2415181 William Keim Randolph (2/19/1857-   )
241519   Thomas Mann Randolph (-1877)
24151x   Anne Cary Randolph
24151a   Margaret Wetherell Randolph, d. inf.
24151b   Charles Wetherell Randolph
24152   Anne Cary Randolph (10/30/1794-1/20/1877), m. 10/31/1825,
         William Strother Jones, Jr. (10/7/1783-7/13/1845), son of
         Capt. William Strother and Frances Thornton Jones of
         "Vaucluse", Frederick County. The first wife of William
         Strother Jones, Jr. was Anna Maria Marshall (8/8/1788-11/
         25/1823) by whom he had issue.
241521   William Randolph Jones (10/1/1826-1839)
241522   Francis Buckner Jones (6/4/1828-   ), m. 8/31/1853,
         Susan Peyton Clark
2415221 Louisa Peyton Jones (2/16/1855-3/4/1939), m. 11/9/1882,
         C. Gratton Crawford (10/4/1858-   ), son of Rev.
         William Anderson and Elizabeth Eleanor Leche Crawford
24152211 Dr. Francis Randolph Crawford (8/21/1884-   ), m.
         5/17/1917, Martha Paxton Moffett (1/15/1891-   ),
         dau. of Rev. Alexander Stuart and Carrie Lena Crawford
         Moffett
24152212 Elizabeth Eleanor Crawford (4/18/1887-   ), m. 6/18/
         1913, Bishop John Long Jackson (3/28/1884-   ),
         son of Edward Thornton and Helen Steele Long Jackson
241522121 Eleanor Pendleton Jackson (3/18/1918-   ), m. 9/29/
         1942, John Ely Burleson (9/21/1911-   ), son of
         Rt. Rev. Hugh L. and Helen Steele Ely Burleson
24152213 Louisa Morrow Crawford (1/21/1894-   ). Unm.
2415222 William Randolph Jones (4/13/1857-   ). Unm.
2415223 Anne Cary Randolph Jones (12/22/1860-   ). Unm.
2415224 Frances Buckner Jones (10/19/1862-   ), m. Joseph
         Marx Barton. No issue
241523   Thomas Beverley Jones (3/24/1830-   ), d. inf.
241524   Beverley Randolph Jones (12/12/1832-11/3/1912), m. 6/1/
         1854, Rebecca J. Tidball, dau. of Alexander S. and
         Millicent S. McGuire Tidball of Winchester
2415241 Lucy Bolling Randolph Jones (4/8/1855-9/7/1940). Unm.
2415242 Alexander Tidball Jones (4/4/1857-12/17/1928), m. 10/12/
         1898, Emily Carr Whittle (11/5/1851-5/6/1940), dau. of
         Bishop Fortesque McNeece Whittle of Richmond
24152421 Frances McNeece Whittle Jones (5/15/1900-   ). Unm.
2415243 Anne Cary Randolph Jones (7/3/1859-6/30/1908), m. 2/25/
         1879, Robert Hume Lewis (11/12/1843-12/12/1921), son of
         Capt. (U.S.N.) James Battaile and Anne Catherine Hume
         Lewis
24152431 Rebecca Hune Lewis (1/5/1881-   ), m. 10/3/1900,
         Rev. Charles Noyes Tyndell (5/2/1876-   ), son of
         Charles Henry and Martha Wilson Noyes Tyndell
241524311 Cary Noyes Tyndell (7/23/1901-   ), m. 12/18/
         1924, Peyton Jacquelin Marshall III (2/3/1896-   )
2415243111 Peyton Jacquelin Marshall IV (11/7/1927-   )
2415243112 Cary Randolph Marshall (1/7/1932-   )

241524312 Rebecca Jean Wyndell (7/29/1903-   ). Unm.
24152432 Anne Hume Lewis (3/24/1883-   ), m. 11/5/1910,
      Robert Lemmon Burwell (3/3/1878-   ), son of
      Elliott Hall and August Somervell Sollers Burwell
241524321 Robert Lemmon Burwell, Jr. (5/6/1912-   ), m. 12/
      22/1939, Elise Frank, dau. of Comdr. (U.S.N.) Arthur
      William and Mabel Elise Droste Frank
2415243211 Mary Elise Burwell (10/10/1942-   )
241524322 Cary Randolph Burwell (1/3/1915-   ), m. 6/27/1938,
      Francis Edward Carter, Jr., son of Francis Edward and
      Lucile Alvey Carter of Episcopal High School,
      Alexandria
2415244 Edward McGuire Jones (6/7/1861-1926), m. 10/7/1910, Mary
      E. Halderman. No issue
2415245 Susan Millicent Jones (5/17/1866-12/1/1927), m. 10/11/
      1899, Harry Lee Doll (3/22/1853-11/13/1910), son of
      Christian Wolff and Margaret Ann Harlan Doll
24152451 Rebecca Doll (9/22/1901-   ). Unm.
24152452 Rev. Harry Lee Doll, Jr. (7/31/1903-   ), m. 10/11/
      1933, Delia Frances Gould (12/8/1908-   ), dau. of
      William Proctor and Mary Eliza Perry Gould
241524521 Millicent Scott Doll (5/1/1936-   )
241524522 Mary Chotard Doll (5/1/1939-   )
241524523 Rebecca Tidball Doll (3/13/1946-   )
2415246 Elizabeth Holmes Jones (4/26/1870-5/9/1947). Unm.
2415247 (son)(unnamed) Jones (8/28/1871-8/28/1871)
2415248 Mary Strother Jones (10/12/1873-   ). Unm.
2415249 Beverley Randolph Jones, Jr. (10/26/1876-11/13/1913). Unm.
24153 William Fitzhugh Randolph (3/29/1796-7/16/1859), m. 9/11/
      1817, Jane Cary Harrison (2/9/1797-11/28/1883)(24242),
      dau. of Randolph and Mary Randolph Harrison of "Clifton"
241531 Mary Harrison Randolph (2/1/1819-4/3/1907), m. 4/2/1840,
      George Edward Tabb (1/3/1810-6/15/1867), son of Thomas
      Todd and Lucy Armistead Smith Tabb of "Toddsbury"
2415311 Ellen Randolph Tabb (10/6/1845-11/26/1926), m. 4/23/1870,
      Dr. Thomas Barkwell Lane (5/23/1840-10/19/1910), son of
      Walker Cardiner and Mary Anna Henry Barkwell Lane of
      Mathews County
24153111 Mary Randolph Lane (2/19/1871-   ). Unm.
24153112 George Edward Todd Lane (5/29/1872-4/23/1936). Unm.
24153113 Thomas Barkwell Lane, Jr. (11/16/1879-10/9/1943), m. (1st)
      4/14/1909, Emily Gay Baker (3/19/1868-10/25/1934), dau.
      of Richard Henry and Nannie May Baker of Norfolk. No
      issue. M. (2nd) 5/29/1937, Gertrude Leonard Bush (4/2/
      1878-   ), dau. of Rev. Franklin Leonard and Mary
      Walker Bush of Southboro, Mass. No issue
24153114 Rev. Henry Gardiner Lane (3/18/1881-   ), m. 10/9/
      1907, Annie Taylor Gordon (3/12/1883-   ), dau. of
      John Addison and Fannie Fife Gordon Gordon of Fre-
      dericksburg. No issue
2415312 Kate Harrison Tabb (7/18/1847-12/12/1915), m. 11/25/1879,
      Powhatan Robertson (-10/12/1882)(11141), son of
      Judge John and Anne Trent Robertson of Richmond

2415313 Nannie Tabb (8/17/1849-9/7/1854)
2415314 Frederick Tabb (9/4/1854-10/20/1854)
2415315 Georgia Tabb (11/21/1855-10/9/1862)
2415316 George Randolph Tabb (11/18/1860-12/8/1896), m. 12/21/
         1885, Juliet Jeffries Tabb (12/8/1860-3/13/1946), dau.
         of Capt. (C.S.A.) Robert Mayo and Charlotte Elizabeth
         Jeffries Tabb of Richmond
24153161 George Edward Tabb (10/21/1886-4/25/1898)
24153162 James Jeffries Tabb (3/6/1889-   ), m. (1st) 8/23/
         1919, Elizabeth Gibbons Smart (7/10/1898-   ), dau.
         of Edmund Dickerson and Allison Smart Smart of Richmond.
         M. (2nd) 10/16/1936, Dorothy Peple (12/16/1903-   ),
         dau. of Charles Anthony and Louise Hardy Peple of
         Richmond
         Children by first wife:
241531621 James Jeffries Tabb, Jr. (7/18/1920-   ). Unm.
         Children by second wife:
241531622 Charles Anthony Peple Tabb (2/25/1939-   )
24153163 George Randolph Tabb, Jr. (4/21/1892-   ), m. 11/4/
         1929, Jane Ellen Bell (2/4/1892-   ), dau. of
         William Franklin and Jane Henderson Breckenridge Bell
         of Baltimore (Govanstown)
241531631 Jane Randolph Tabb (11/6/1934-   )
24153164 Charles Brock Tabb (1/6/1894-   ), m. 8/30/1924, Gay
         Buford Lewis (8/12/1897-6/5/1930), dau. of Warren Field-
         ing and Annie Deane Burch Lewis. No issue
241532   William Eston Randolph (5/7/1820-7/30/1898) of "Benlomen",
         Cumberland County, m. (1st) 5/1/1850, Lavinia Epes of
         Lunenburg County. M. (2nd) 5/1/1860, Susan Wellford
         Randolph (7/8/1835-12/18/1897)(242173), dau. of Dr. Robert
         Carter and Lucy Nelson Wellford Randolph of "New Market",
         Clarke County
         Children by first wife:
2415321 Sarah Lavinia Randolph (4/2/1854-9/15/1869)
2415322 Epes Randolph (8/16/1856-8/22/1921), m. 1/14/1886,
         Eleanor Gridley Taylor. No issue
         Children by second wife:
2415323 Phillipa Randolph (4/20/1861-11/17/1929), m. 11/8/1899,
         Henry Clay Somerville, M.D. (6/8/1834-7/30/1918), son
         of James and Elizabeth Mauzy Somerville of Bloomery
24153231 Susan Randolph Somerville (1/24/1901-   ), m. 10/8/
         1927, Gwynne Harrison Jones (8/10/1902-   ), son
         of George Lorraine and Florence Cox Jones of Berryville
241532311 Gwynne Harrison Jones, Jr. (10/15/1928-   )
241532312 Henry Somerville Jones (3/5/1931-3/30/1931)
241532313 George Lorraine Jones II (12/23/1932-   )
241532314 Susan Randolph Jones (9/10/1935-   )
241532315 Mary Somerville Jones (9/7/1945-   )
24153232 Mary Beverley Somerville (2/11/1903-   ), m. 8/15/
         1931, Thomas Wallace Whitaker (8/13/1904-   ), son
         of Walter Raymond and Mary Dunne Whitaker of California
241532321 Thomas Wallace Whitaker, Jr. (6/18/1933-   )

241532322 Mary Beverley Whitaker (3/31/1935-   )
2415324 Robert Carter Randolph, Jr. (1863- d. inf.)
2415325 Henry Isham Randolph (4/21/1866-4/24/1935), m. 10/10/1894,
      Marion Ada Phelps (6/4/1874-   ), dau.of John Bennett
      and Mary Augusta Crocker Phelps of Evanston, Ill.
24153251 Eston Harrison Randolph (6/7/1896-2/16/1899)
24153252 Marion Ada Randolph (5/26/1897-3/19/1898)
24153253 Epes Randolph (1/1/1906-   ), m. 9/10/1940, Virginia
      West (9/5/1911-   ), dau. of Ezra Elwood and Ella
      Homeyer West of Huntington, Ind. The Randolphs lived
      in California.
241532531 Robert Earl Randolph (2/3/1942-   )
24153254 Mary Randolph (4/16/1907-   ), m. 8/20/1938, James
      Struthers Edgar (2/5/1909-   ), son of Charles and
      Margaret Porter Munro Edgar of Richmond
241532541 James Struthers Edgar, Jr. (6/24/1941-   )
241532542 Randolph Munro Edgar (10/1/1943-   )
241532543 Susan Wellford Edgar (12/7/1945-   )
2415326 Isabella Randolph (11/2/1867-7/5/1934). Unm.
2415327 Jane Cary Randolph, d. inf.
2415328 Benjamin Burn Randolph, d. inf.
2415329 Lucy Wellford Randolph (1873- d. inf.)
241533 Maj. Beverley Randolph (6/26/1823-11/19/1903) of "The
      Moorings", Clarke County, m. 8/1/1847, Mary Conway
      Randolph (8/19/1825-9/7/1905)(242141), dau. of Dr.
      Philip Grymes and Mary B. O'Neale Randolph of Clarke
      County
2415331 Beverley Randolph, Jr. (5/28/1848-3/2/1865). Killed in
      action
2415332 Nathaniel Burwell Randolph (10/28/1850-1/3/1874)
2415333 Philip Grymes Randolph (5/31/1852-2/16/1902), m. 12/9/
      1880, Ruth Caroline O'Fallon (4/15/1859-10/27/1891),
      dau. of Benjamin and Sally Champe Carter O'Fallon of
      St. Louis
24153331 Nathaniel Burwell Randolph (8/30/1881-   ), m.
      10/12/1910, Irene Alta Niedringhaus (7/2/1884-8/27/
      1946), dau. of William Frederick and Mary Bittner
      Niedringhaus of St. Louis
241533311 William Frederick Niedringhaus Randolph (10/11/1911-
      ), m. 9/20/1947, Lucy Ann Tate (1/14/1922-
      ), dau. of Lemuel Hall and Lida Chester
      Hammontree Tate of Memphis
2415333111 Ann Tate Randolph (5/27/1948-   )
241533312 Ruth Caroline Randolph (8/27/1914-   ), m. 6/18/
      1938, John Lamb Gillis (5/23/1911-   ), son of
      John Daniel and Mary Lamb Gillis of St. Louis
2415333121 John Lamb Gillis, Jr. (6/13/1939-   )
2415333122 Carol Randolph Gillis (12/10/1941-   )
2415333123 Ann Carter Gillis (5/25/1942-   )
241533313 Irene Randolph (8/15/1921-   )
2415334 Mary Harrison Randolph (3/5/1854-   ), m. (1st) 6/
      26/1877, Percy William Charrington (6/9/1844-7/18/1894),

son of Edward and Georgiana Mary Trice Baumgartner
Charrington of Surrey, Eng. M. (2nd) 3/ /1902, Ernest
Astley Cooper (8/22/1857-1/1/1942). No issue
    Children by first husband:
24153341 Percy Randolph Charrington (6/5/1878-2/15/1891)
24153342 Mary Virginia Charrington (7/26/1880-   ), m. (1st)
    7/24/1902, Col. Gerald Keith Matchett (3/1/1866-3/16/
    1932), son of Henry Horace and Emily Rose Palmer
    Matchett of England. No issue. M. (2nd) 9/19/1934,
    Arthur John Coleridge Mackarness (4/30/1865-   ),
    son of (Bishop of Oxford) John Fielder and Alethea
    Buchanan Mackarness. No issue
25143343 Georgiana Randolph Charrington (11/9/1881-   ), m.
    5/23/1907, William Conway Whittle III (6/27/1881-8/2/
    1927)(652135)
24153344 Edward Beverley Charrington (11/17/1882-7/10/1909)
24153345 Arthur Mowbray Randolph Charrington (11/8/1887-   ),
    m. 4/29/1915, Mary Elizabeth Wilbur (11/2/1889-   ),
    dau. of William Nelson and Elizabeth Mason Fitch Wilbur
    of Devon, Pa.
241533451 Arthur Mowbray Randolph Charrington, Jr. (3/11/1916-
          ), m. 9/9/1939, Frances Irving Glover (5/16/
    1916-   ), dau. of Warren Irving and Annabelle
    Englis Glover of Edgewood, N.J.
2415334511 Peter Randolph Charrington (9/9/1942-   )
2415334512 Arthur Mowbray Randolph Charrington III (1947-   )
241533452 Elizabeth Mason Fitch Charrington (5/31/1917-5/ /1948),
    m. 4/29/1943, Carlyle Forrest Nicol, Jr. (4/23/1919-
          ), son of Carlyle Forest and Amelia Catherine
    Ames Nicol of Boston
2415334521 Virginia Randolph Nicol (5/27/1945-   )
2415334522 Arthur Charrington Ames Nicol (7/11/1946-   )
2415335 William Fitzhugh Randolph (1/19/1856-4/3/1915), m. 4/21/
    1881, Rebecca Rosalie O'Fallon (11/1/1861-4/3/1935),
    dau. of Benjamin and Sally Champe Carter O'Fallon of
    St. Louis
24153351 Mary Carter Randolph (12/27/1881-   ), m. 2/18/
    1914, Cyrus Wiley Grandy III (12/5/1878-   ), son
    of Cyrus Wiley and Mary Selden Grandy, Jr. of Norfolk
241533511 Mary Carter Grandy (7/11/1915-   ), m. 11/26/1936,
    Hartwell Henry Gary, Jr. (6/15/1911-   ), son of
    Hartwell Henry and Cary Baldwin Preston Gary of
    Birmingham
2415335111 Hartwell Henry Gary III (11/16/1937-   )
2415335112 Wiley Grandy Gary (10/16/1940-   )
2415335113 Ballard Preston Gary (6/19/1942-   )
2415335114 William Fitzhugh Randolph Gary (10/27/1944-   )
241533512 Caroline Selden Grandy (2/13/1919-   ), m. 12/11/
    1941, Stockton Heth Tyler, Jr., son of Maj. Stockton
    Heth and Nell Louise Serpell Tyler of Norfolk
2415335121 Caroline Grandy Tyler (10/30/1942-   )
2415335122 Sallie Carter Tyler (7/4/1945-   )

241533513   Cyrus Wiley Grandy IV (3/22/1920-   ), m. 11/13/
            1943, Ann Sterrett (3/10/1916-   ), dau. of Rev.
            Henry Hatch Dent and Helen Margaret Black Sterrett
2415335131 Carter (dau) Randolph Grandy (10/27/1944-   )
2415335132 Cyrus Wiley Grandy V (6/12/1946-   )
2415335133
24153352   Beverley Randolph (12/9/1883-10/7/1918), m. 11/ /1916,
            Harriet Shields (7/6/1886-10/14/1918), dau. of Dr.
            Charles and Margaret New Shields of Richmond. Mr. and
            Mrs. Randolph died in the flu epidemic.
241533521   D. inf.
24153353   Benjamin O'Fallon Randolph (5/18/1885-   ), m. 6/
            7/1911, Matilda Fontaine Jones (3/13/1885-   ), dau.
            of Lorraine Fauquhar and Matilda Fontaine Berkeley Jones
241533531   Mary Carter Randolph (2/16/1914-   ), m. 10/12/
            1936, Beverley Tucker Nelson, Jr. (3/31/1925-   ),
            son of Beverley and Gwen A. Moore Nelson
2415335311 Mary Carter Randolph Nelson (5/13/1938-   )
2415335312 Thomas Nelson (5/13/1938-   )
2415335313 Page (dau) Nelson (10/9/1939-   )
241533532   Edward Fairfax Randolph (7/31/1915-   ), m. 10/16/
            1937, Margaret Matheson (10/24/1916), dau. of Malcolm
            and Julia Robertson Culbertson Matheson of Alexandria
2415335321 Edward Fairfax Randolph, Jr. (12/11/1928-   )
2415335322 Malcolm Matheson Randolph (6/25/1942-   )
241533533   Jane Cary Randolph (5/21/1917-   ), m. 5/ /1948,
            Benjamin Harrison III (12/3/1909-5/7/1984), son of Dr.
            Gwynn Page and Phoebe Virginia Westwater Harrison of
            "Longwood", Clarke County
2415335331 Jane Cary Harrison, m. Philip A. Embury, son of Edward
            Coe and Marguerite Haynes Embury
2415335332 Nancy Randolph Harrison, m. D'Arcy Scott Thorpe of
            Canada
24153353321 Virginia Jane Scott Thorpe (6/27/1980-   )
24153353322 D'Arcy Randolph Scott Thorpe (5/21/1983-   )
2415335333 Benjamin Harrison, m. Sharon Estep, dau. of George S.
            and Marilyn Joyce Heyward Estep
24153353331 Mary Christine Harrison (3/12/1983-   )
241533534   Benjamin O'Fallon Randolph, Jr. (8/6/1922-12/24/1944).
            Killed in Belgium (Infantryman)
24153354   William Fitzhugh Randolph, Jr. (10/8/1886-   ), m.
            10/19/1916, Katherine Essex Gratz (11/18/1887-   ),
            nee Hensley (adopted by her mother's aunt and uncle,
            Anderson Gratz)
241533541   Katherine Gratz Randolph (9/22/1917-   ), m. 8/9/
            1941, Ford William Thompson, Jr. (8/15/1917-   ),
            son of Ford William and Gladys Maria Gertrude Gale
            Thompson of St. Louis
2415335411 Katherine Randolph Thompson (9/22/1942-   )
2415335412 Gladys Gale Thompson (5/30/1944-   )
241533542   Rosalie Fitzhugh Randolph (12/14/1919-   )
241533543   William Fitzhugh Randolph III (7/25/1923-1/1/1925)

24153355 Eston Randolph (3/4/1888-   ), m. 5/21/1922, Blanche
          Rose Turner (7/3/1896-   ), dau. of Valentine Coval
          and Beatrice Clark Turner of St. Louis
241533551 Eston Randolph, Jr. (11/25/1925-   )
24153356 Percy Charrington Randolph (7/16/1898-   ), m.
          12/15/1921, Jean McNeil Carson, dau. of Joseph Loung-
          heed and Jean McNeil Carson of Riverton, Warren County
241533561 Beverley Randolph (1/20/1922-   )
241533562 Jean McNeil Randolph (5/26/1926-   )
2415336   William Eston Randolph (12/7/1857-4/28/1910). Unm.
2415337   Robert Carter Randolph (8/4/1859-8/14/1859)
2415338   Jane Cary Randolph (1861-3/15/1983)
2415339   Lucius Wilton Randolph, d. inf.
241533x   Julian Harrison Randolph (8/4/1864-5/8/1891). Unm.
241533a   Virginius Cary Randolph (-11/11/1867)
241534   Lucius Burwell Randolph, m. Isadora Preston
2415341   Emma K. Randolph
2415342   Jackson Randolph
2415343   Virginius Randolph
2415344   Eliza P. Randolph
241535   Virginius Randolph, m. (1st) Isabella Pitts. M. (2nd)
          Eliza Madison Preston
       Children by second wife:
2415351   Preston Randolph
2415352   William F. Randolph
24153521 William F. Randolph, Jr.
24153522 Jane Cary Harrison Randolph
2416   Archibald Cary Randolph, d.s.p.
2417   Judith Randolph, m. Richard Randolph (231) of "Bizarre"
2418   Ann Cary ("Nancy") Randolph (1774-1837), m. Gouverneur Morris
       (1752-1816) of New York. Lived at "Bizarre"
24181   Gouverneur Morris, Jr., m. Martha ("Patsy") Jefferson Cary
        (241c7)
2419   Jane Cary Randolph of "Tuckahoe", m. Thomas Eston Randolph,
       son of William and Elizabeth Little Randolph of "Dungeness"
24191   William Eston Randolph, d.s.p.
24192   Thomas Mann Randolph, m. Susan Brown
241921   Thomas Eston Randolph (1823-   ), d.s.p.
241922   William Brown Randolph
241923   Marian Randolph, m. Joseph Yates Porter
2419231   Joseph Yates Porter, Jr., m. Louise Curry
24192311   Marian Porter
24192312   William Randolph Porter
24192313   Joseph Yates Porter
241924   Jane Cary Randolph
24193   Mary Elizabeth Cleland Randolph (1/16/1801-4/15/1835), m.
        11/28/1822, Francis Wayles Eppes (1801-5/30/1881). He m.
        (2nd) Susan Margaret Ware (widow Couch), dau. of Nicholas
        Ware, by whom he had issue
241931   Jane Cary Eppes (1823-1890). Unm.
241932   Dr. John Wayles Eppes (1825-1908), m. 1854, Josephine
         Bellamy

2419321   Frances E. Eppes, d. inf.
2419322   Eliza Wayles Eppes (1857-1898), m. 1878, Alexander Kennedy
24193221 Margaret Kennedy (1880-   ), m. William Blanc
24193222 Josephine Bellamy Kennedy (1882-   ), m. 1908, Marion
            Howard Bradley
241932221 Annie Ward Bradley (1911-d. inf.)
241932222 Marion Howard Bradley (1915-   )
24193223 Alexander Kennedy
24193224 Agnes Kennedy, m. 1917, James Washington Herburt
241932241 Eliza Eppes Herburt
241932242 Julia Frances Herburt
241932243 Agnes Kennedy Herburt
24193225 Florence Kennedy
24193226 John Wayles Kennedy, m. 1921, Laura Cooms Hebb
241932261 John Wayles Kennedy, Jr. (1922-   )
241932262 Margaret Coombs Kennedy (1924-   )
241932263 Alexander Kennedy (1926-   )
241933   Thomas Jefferson Eppes (1827-1869), m. 1861, Theodosia
            Burr Bellamy
2419331   Thomas Jefferson Eppes, Jr. (1861-   ), m. (1st) Kate
            Edna Shaler. M. (2nd) Mrs. Mamie J. Gones
24193311 Thomas Jefferson Eppes, m. Katherine Davis
24193312 Edna Eppes, m. Dr. Ralston Lattimore
241933121 Edna Eppes Lattimore (9/9/1816-   )
241933122 William Lattimore (6/8/1818-   )
241933123 Harry Hays Lattimore (3/18/1824-   )
2419332   Victoria Eppes (1862-   ), m. (1st) Carlton M.
            Marshall. M. (2nd) Arthur B. Harrison
2419333   Mary Eppes (1864-   ), m. George Morrison
24193331 Theodosia Bellamy Morrison, m. 12/29/1909, D. Shephard
            Shine, Jr. (12/19/1885-   ), son of D. Shephard
            and Caroline Matilda Eppes Shine
241933311 D. Shephard Shine III (7/17/1914-   )
241933312 Theodosia Morrison Shine (6/5/1916-   )
2419334   Francis Eppes (1865-   ), m. 1892, Alberta R. Wharton
24193341 Francis Eppes (1894-   ), m.
241933411 Alberta Eppes (1923-   )
241933412 Francis Eppes (1925-   )
24193342 Mary Eppes (1896-   )
2419335   Paul Eppes (1866-d. young)
2419336   Randolph Eppes (1868-   ), m. 1898, Sadie Mays
24193361 Edith Eppes (1896-   ), m. 1920, Haskell Harris Bass
241933611 Edith Bass (1921-   )
241933612 Elinor Bass (1923-   )
24193362 Patty Eppes (1903-   ), m. 1922, Edward Baldwin Young
241933621 Meta Baldwin Young (1924-   )
241934   Rev. William Eston Eppes (1830-1896), m. 1854, Emily Ban-
            croft. M. (2nd) Augusta Kollock
       Children by first wife:
2419341   Matilda Bancroft Eppes (1855-   )
2419342   Elizabeth Cleland Eppes (1867-1881)
2419343   Francis Eppes (1859-1921), m. 1881, Mary Margaret Bancroft

```
24193431   Frederick Eppes (1882-    )
24193432   William Eston Eppes (1885-1918). Unm.
24193433   James Bancroft Eppes (1888-    ), m. 1908, Elizabeth
             Williford
241934331  Elizabeth Eppes, d. inf.
241934332  Caroline Frances Eppes (1910-    )
241934333  James Bancroft Eppes, Jr. (1912-    )
241934334  Emily Eppes (1914-    )
241934335  Mary Eppes (1921-    )
241934336  Williford Eppes (1923-    )
24193434   Lillie Jeanerette Eppes (1890-    )
24193435   John Wayles Eppes (1892-    ), m. 1915, Mary Lou
             Lemon
241934351  John Francis Eppes (1921-    )
2419344    James Bancroft Eppes (1860-1861)
2419345    Lucy Randolph Eppes (1861-    ), m. 1881, Edward
             Bancroft
24193451   Lucy Eppes Bancroft (1882-1883)
24193452   Irene Scott Bancroft (1883-    )
24193453   Dr. Edward Bancroft (1886-    )
24193454   Emily Cleland Bancroft (1888-    )
24193455   Matilda Eppes Bancroft (1893-    ), m. 1928, Thomas
             Richards
241934551  Thomas Edward Richards (1932-    )
2419346    Jane Cary Eppes (1863-d. inf.)
2419347    William Eston Eppes (1864-    ), m. 1889, Irene Ada
             Bancroft
24193471   Adele Evelyn Eppes (1890-    ), m. 1913, James W.
             Lockett
241934711  Martha Ann Lockett (1914-    )
241934712  Evelyn Eppes Lockett (1916-d. inf.)
241934713  Frances Lockett (1917-    )
241934714  James William Lockett (1920-    )
241934715  Randolph Eppes Lockett (1922-    )
241934716  Frederick Buckner Lockett (1930-    )
24193472   William Randolph Eppes (1892-    ), m. 1919, Marion
             McCorkle
24193473   Arthur Beverley Eppes (1893-    ), m. 1921, Nora
             Nedra Reddick
24193474   Irene Ada Eppes (1895-    )
24193475   Catherine Eppes (1897-    ), m. 1925, Joseph Forrester
             Buckner
241934751  Emily Bancroft Buckner (1926-    )
241934752  Joseph Forrester Buckner (1928-    )
24193476   Thomas Jefferson Eppes (1899-    ), m. 1919, Camille
             Hamilton
241934761  Gloria Camille Eppes (11/13/1926-    )
24193477   William Eston Eppes (1901-1919)
24193478   Marion Theresa Eppes (1904-    ), m. 1928, William
             Byrd Moss
241934781  William Lee Moss (1929-    )
241934782  Mary Catharine Moss (1931-    )
```

24193479 Benjamin Scott Eppes (1906-   ), m. 1932, Frances
          Crane
241934791 Frances Eppes (1934-   )
2419348 John Wayles Eppes (1866-1874)
2419349 Emily Bancroft Eppes (1868-1873)
241934x Edward Bancroft Eppes (1868-1918), m. 1908, Jennie Kendall
241934x1 John Kendall Eppes (1916-   )
241934a Maria Jefferson Eppes (1871-1916)
241935 Mary Elizabeth Eppes (1832-1903)
241936 Francis Eppes (1835-d. inf.)
24194 Harriet Tucker Randolph (1802-11/28/1832), m. 2nd wife,
        Dr. Lewis Byrd Willis. See 241b3
24195 Lucy Beverley Randolph, m. 2nd wife, John Parkhill
241951 Harriet Parkhill, d.s.p.
24196 James Henry Randolph, m. (1st), Margaret Howard. M. (2nd)
        Elizabeth Beard
      Children by first wife:
241961 Arthur Lee Randolph (1848-7/31/1884), m. Genevieve Vallee
2419611 Vallee Randolph, m. (1st), Clara Eggleston. M. (2nd)
        Anna
2419612 Mary Page Randolph, m. Lawrence Grant
2419613 Arthur Lee Randolph, m. Eleanor Oviatt
24196131 Eleanor Randolph
24196132 Genevieve Vallee Randolph (5/8/1920-1/6/1923)
2419614 Agalaie C. Randolph, d. inf.
241962 Thomas Hayward Randolph (6/ /1845-11/16/1916), m. Julia
        Church Croom
2419621 Margaret Hayward Randolph, m. 2nd wife, Judge James B.
        Whitfield
24196211 Mary Croom Whitfield
24196212 James B. Whitfield
24196213 Julia Whitfield
24196214 Margaret Whitfield
24196215 Randolph Whitfield, m. Shirley McPhaul
2419622 George Beverley Randolph (9/3/1875-12/19/1877)
2419623 Annie Porter Randolph (-3/ /1931), m. Thomas M.
        Dozier
2419624 Dr. James Henry Randolph, m. (1st), Evelyn Winthrop. M.
        (2nd) Elizabeth Hamilton
      Children by first wife (of 2419624):
24196241 James Henry Randolph, Jr.
24196242 John Winthrop Randolph
24196243 Barbara Hope Randolph
      Children by second wife (of 2419624):
24196244 Patricia Louise Randolph
2419625 Hayward Randolph, m. Luella Clark
24196251 Elizabeth Clark Randolph, m. Dr. George Calloway
241962511 Nancy Randolph Calloway
24196252 John Randolph
241963 Jane Cary Randolph (12/4/1841-4/30/1881), m. Capt. William
        H. Whitner
241964 Mary Lucia Randolph (6/11/1843-2/7/1853)

241965 James Henry Randolph, Jr. (5/25/1849-1/17/1879), d.s.p.
    Children by second wife (of 24196):
241966 Maria Beard Randolph, m. John Chipman
241967 Elizabeth Beard Randolph, m. John M. Cook
241968 Lucy Beverley Randolph (7/21/1863-1/ /1905), m. 7/17/
    1888, Rev. Theodore Du Bose Bratton. He m. (2nd), Ivy
    Perrin Gass
2419681 William Du Bose Bratton (5/18/1889-   ), m. Ivy
    Gass, his step-sister
24196811 Theodore Du Bose Bratton (7/ /1916-   )
24196812 Lucy Randolph Bratton (9/ /1918-   )
24196813 William Du Bose Bratton (8/ /1920-   )
24196814 John Gass Bratton (1/ /1927-   )
2419682 Elizabeth Bratton (3/25/1891-1892)
2419683 John Randolph Bratton (9/3/1892-   ), m. Ann Lewis
24196831 Anne Bratton
24196832 John Bratton
24196833 Lewis Palmer Bratton
2419684 Randolph B. Bratton (11/18/1895-   ), m. Eula Boulware
24196841 Randolph Bratton
24196842 Lucy Beverley Bratton
24196843 Isabel Bratton
2419685 Harriet Bratton, d. inf.
2419686 Lucy Bratton, d. inf.
2419687 Marion Bratton (4/13/1899-   ), m. Harris Brister
24196871 Harris Brister (7/ /1921-   )
24196872 Ivy Bratton Brister (6/ /1924-   )
24196873 Theodore Bratton Brister (5/ /1930-   )
2419688 Mary Means Bratton (3/4/1901-   ), m. Robert Connor
24196881 Robert Connor (1923-   )
24196882 Elizabeth Randolph Connor (1926-   )
24196883 Theodore Bratton Connor (1930-   )
2419689 Isabelle Bratton (4/5/1903-   ), m. Parham Bridges
24196891 Parham Bridges (9/ /1928)
241969 Mary Lucia Randolph (7/29/1858-4/14/1864)
24196x Constance Randolph 3/19/1859-4/8/1864)
24196a John Beard Randolph (8/28/1861-5/9/1864)
24197 Mary Page Randolph (9/11/1811-1/10/1889)
24198 Dr. Arthur Moray Randolph, m. Laura Harrison Duval, dau. of
    Gov. (of Florida) William Pope and Nancy Hynes Duval
241981 James Henry Randolph (8/12/1847-6/12/1860)
241982 Elizabeth Randolph (-1/27/1933), m. B. F. Whitner
2419821 B. F. Whitner
2419822 Daughter Whitner, m. Sydney Chase
241x Dr. John Randolph, m. Judith Lewis of Amelia County
241x1 William Mann Randolph, m. 9/2/1839, Margaret Smith Randolph
    (3/7/1816-12/20/1842)(241421)
241x11 Jane Margaret Randolph (5/1/1840-6/27/1914), m. 11/8/1860,
    Edward Clifford Anderson (1/17/1839-9/27/1876)
241x111 Jefferson Randolph Anderson (9/4/1861-7/17/1950), m. 11/
    27/1895, Ann Page Wilder
241x1111 Page Randolph Anderson (9/27/1899-   ), m. 4/2/1921,
    Henry Norris Platt

241x11111 Henry Norris Platt, Jr. (3/23/1922-   ), m. 6/26/
           1953, Lenore Guest MacLeish
241x111111 Henry Norris Platt III (6/12/1954-   )
241x111112 Lenore McCall Platt (5/17/1956-   )
241x111113 Martha Hillard Platt (4/29/1959-   )
241x111114 Caroline Anderson Platt (11/23/1961-   )
241x11112 Ann Page Platt (11/22/1924-   ), m. 7/1/1950, Thomas
           Elliott Allen
241x111121 Page Randolph Allen (9/6/1951-   ), m. (1st) 6/19/
           1970, William Scott Morris. M. (2nd) Nathaniel
           Owings
241x111122 James Elliott Allen (7/26/1953-   )
241x111123 Samuel Wilder Allen (11/9/1956-   )
241x111124 Abigail Brewster Allen (2/14/1960-   )
241x111125 Mary Davis Allen (4/11/1963-   )
241x11113 Jefferson Davis Platt (5/13/1929-   ), m. 8/22/1971,
           Veronica Chisholm
241x1112   Jefferson Randolph Anderson, Jr.(9/3/1900-11/30/1903)
241x1113   Joseph Randolph Anderson (3/22/1905-   ), m. 11/15/
           1930, Edith O'Driscoll Hunter
241x11131 Page O'Driscoll Anderson (11/7/1932-   ), m. 4/26/
           1953, James Eggleston Hungerpillar
241x111311 Susan Page Hungerpillar (2/23/1954-   ), m. 5/12/
           1979, George J. Oelschig, Jr.
241x1113111 Edith Page Oelschig (11/29/1982-   )
241x111312 James Randolph Hungerpillar (11/25/1956-   )
241x111313 John Colin Hungerpillar (3/18/1959-   )
241x112   Col. George Wayne Anderson (7/10/1863-12/30/1922), m. 12/
           21/1889, Estelle Marguerite Burthe
241x1121   Edward Clifford Anderson (11/26/1893-   ), m. 1/12/
           1922, Isabel Scott
241x11211 George Wayne Anderson III (5/1/1927-   ), m. 10/
           4/1952, Virginia Lee Richardson
241x112111 Cary Randolph Anderson (6/30/1953-   ), m. 1/22/
           1983, Thomas Edward Trainor
241x112112 Edward Clifford Anderson II (12/2/1958-   )
241x11212 Elizabeth Strother Anderson (4/11/1929-   ), m. 12/
           6/1952, Jonathan Bryan III
241x112121 Robert Carter Bryan (1/31/1954-   )
241x112122 Isabel Scott Bryan (4/5/1955-   )
241x112123 John Randolph Bryan (3/8/1959-   )
241x11213 Isabel Scott Anderson (9/27/1932-   ), m. (1st) 12/
           29/1962, James Turner Sloan, Jr. M. (2nd) 5/24/1968,
           Harvey Wilkinson Fitzgerald
           Children by first husband:
241x112131 Louise Williams Sloan (6/24/1963-   )
241x112132 Edward Anderson Sloan (7/16/1965-   )
           Children by second husband:
241x112133 Isabel Scott Fitzgerald (6/28/1969-   )
241x112134 Caroline Harris Fitzgerald (1970-   )
241x1122   George Wayne Anderson, Jr. (6/30/1896-11/1/1918). Killed
           in Argonne. World War I

241x1123 Cary Nicholas Anderson (2/4/1903-   ), m. 4/10/1926,
          Manfred Keller
241x11231 Estelle Wayne Keller (6/7/1927-   )
241x11232 Ursula Sophie Keller (9/26/1928-   ), m. 9/8/1951,
          Irenee DuPont May
241x112321 Sophie Christine May (8/2/1953-   ), m. 6/16/1973,
          Peter Charles Rupert Gerard
241x112322 Irenee DuPont May (8/6/1954-   )
241x112313 Wilson Cary Nicholas May (4/21/1965-   )
241x113 Eliza Clifford Anderson (10/24/1864-9/11/1876)
241x114 Margaret Randolph Anderson (8/21/1866-5/3/1941), m. (1st)
          11/24/1893, Abbott Lawrence Rotch. M. (2nd) 11/1/1919,
          Henry Parkman, Jr.
          Children by first husband:
241x11141 Elizabeth Rotch (1895-6/29/1895)
241x11142 Margaret Randolph Rotch (6/14/1896-3/19/1945), m. 6/31/
          1916, James Jackson Storrow
241x11421 James Jackson Storrow II (5/17/1917-   ), m. (1st)
          6/26/1940, Patricia Blake. M. (2nd) 12/15/1962, Linda
          Eder
          Children by first wife:
241x114211 Gerald Blake Storrow (7/15/1944-   )
241x114212 Peter Storrow (9/26/1946-   ), m. Nancy
241x114213 Arthur Rotch Storrow (6/7/1948-   ), name changed to
          James Jackson Storrow III
241x114214 Margaret Randolph Storrow (1/4/1955-   )
241x11143 Arthur Rotch (2/1/1899-2/6/1973), m. 4/30/1935, Alice
          Gedney Storrow
241x11431 Ann Storrow Rotch (1/28/1937-   ), m. 7/16/1960,
          Henry G. Magendantz
          Eric Ashley Magendantz (4/1/1967-   )(adopted)
          Christopher Lawrence Megendantz (12/12/1968-   )(adopted)
241x114311 Nicholas Alexander Magendantz (11/28/1973-   )
241x114312 Elisa Margaret Magendantz (10/11/1976-   )
241x11432 Abbott Lawrence Rotch (3/8/1939-   ), m. 8/31/1963,
          Emily Beaumelle Roe
241x114321 Elizabeth Ann Rotch (10/23/1964-   )
241x114322 Arthur Randolph Rotch (8/11/1966-   )
241x114323 Andrew Lawrence Rotch (2/6/1970-   )
241x11433 Edward Cabot Rotch (7/9/1941-   )
241x1144 Katherine Lawrence Rotch (5/26/1906-3/30/1966), m. 6/17/
          1925, Malcolm Whelen Greenough
241x11441 Malcolm Whelen Greenough, Jr. (6/11/1926-   ), m.
          (1st) 2/7/1948, Sarah Eden Browne. M. (2nd) 11/29/
          1969, Catherine Royce McKenna
          Children by first wife:
241x114411 Katherine Lawrence Greenough (11/16/1949-   )
241x114412 Sarah Eden Greenough (5/25/1951-   ), m. 6/17/1978,
          Nicolai Cikovsky
241x114413 Margaret Randolph Greenough (7/19/1954-   )
241x114414 Malcolm Whelan Greenough III (9/16/1957-   )
          Children by second wife:

241x114415 Charles William Greenough (3/12/1971-   )
241x114416 Andrew Scollay Greenough (6/26/1973-   )
241x114417 George Pelham Greenough (5/6/1976-   )
241x11442 Lawrence Rotch Greenough (12/16/1930-4/17/1964), m.
        4/14/1956, Pamela Antoinette Marguerite Seddon
241x114421 Elizabeth Tiffany Greenough (5/31/1957-   )
241x114422 Lawrence Rotch Greenough, Jr. (6/2/1959-   )
241x115 Sarah Randolph Anderson (5/21/1872-1/17/1960)
241x12 William Lewis Randolph (12/20/1841-6/7/1892), m. 1866,
        Agnes Dillon. M. (2nd) 1887, Margaret Randolph Taylor
        (2414225)
        Children by first wife:
241x121 Margaret Gibson Randolph (11/19/1866-9/13/1872)
241x122 Thomas Jefferson Randolph IV (7/21/1868-2/18/1926), m.
        (1st) 11/14/1895, Laura Lester. M. (2nd) Nancy Clifton
        de Marclay
        Children by first wife:
241x1221 Laura Lester Randolph (2/9/1899-3/19/1969), m. 12/18/
        1920, Alfred Wright Thompson
241x12211 Randolph Hines Thompson (7/13/1924-   ), m. 6/30/
        1951, Sarah Beauvois L'Engle
241x122111 Michael L'Engle Thompson (6/26/1955-   )
241x1222 Martha Jefferson Randolph (9/23/1900-8/23/1969), m.
        6/9/1920, John Porter Stevens
241x12221 Martha Randolph Stevens (7/23/1921-7/29/1935)
241x12222 Laura Randolph Stevens (11/23/1931-   ), m. (1st)
        10/14/1950, Frank Kohler Peeples. Div. M. (2nd) 8/3/
        1961, Donald Allan Devendorf
241x122221 Martha Stevens Peeples (12/10/1951-   ), name changed
        to Devendorf in 1961
241x122222 Daryn Stewart Peeples (4/15/1954-   ), name changed
        to Devendorf in 1961
        Child by second husband:
241x122223 Meredith Randolph Devendorf (10/11/1970-   )
241x123 Dr. William Mann Randolph (1/14/1870-1/25/1944), m. 10/
        20/1894, Mary Walker Randolph (2414297)
241x1231 Carolina Ramsay Randolph (9/23/1895-3/1/1958)
241x1232 Sarah Nicholas Randolph (12/8/1896-8/17/1974), m. 3/29/
        1919, Lucian King Truscott, Jr.
241x12321 Mary Randolph Truscott (5/3/1920-   ), m. (1st) 4/
        28/1942, Robert Wilbourn. Div. M. (2nd) 12/14/1957,
        Graeme Grant Bruce
241x12322 Lucian King Truscott III (9/17/1921-   ), m. 4/16/
        1946, Anne Harloe
241x123221 Lucian King Truscott IV (4/12/1947-   ), m. 3/17/
        1979, Carol Troy
241x123222 Francis Meriwether Truscott (1/28/1949-   ), m. 1/3/
        1970, Deborah Newell Jackson
241x1232221 Christopher Harloe Truscott (8/8/1978-   )
241x1232222 Lucas Randolph Truscott (10/28/1981-   )
241x123223 Susan Harloe Truscott (1/19/1953-   ), m. 6/5/1971,
        Allan Moscowitz

241x1232231 Rachel Moscowitz (1971-   )
241x1232232 Sara Moscowitz (6/25/1972-   )
241x123224 Mary Randolph Truscott (8/7/1959-   ), m. 4/11/
         1981, Robert Frank Spicknall
241x1232241 Ian Harloe Spicknall (8/7/1981-   )
241x123225 Virginia Anne Truscott (5/12/1961-   ), m. 8/16/
         1980, Kevin Edward Roland Butcher
241x12323 James Joseph Truscott (12/26/1930-   ), m. 8/31/
         1957, Helen Kelly Haydock
241x123231 James Joseph Truscott, Jr. (8/1/1958-   )
241x123232 Thomas Haydock Truscott (11/30/1959-   )
241x123233 Patrick Moore Truscott (7/16/1962-   )
241x123234 Sarah Randolph Truscott (1/6/1968-   )
241x1233 Agnes Dillon Randolph (4/13/1898-   ), m. (1st) 5/25/
         1925, George Marvin. M. (2nd) 12/28/1934, Edward Buff-
         man Hill
241x1234 William Lewis Randolph II (7/10/1899-1/7/1906)
241x1235 Lt. Thomas Jefferson Randolph V (10/7/1900-   ), m.
         4/24/1930, Augusta Lyell Blue
241x12351 Virginia Hyland Randolph (5/10/1931-   ), m. 12/28/
         1957, Landry Thomas Slade
241x123511 Lyell Landry Slade (9/19/1959-   )
241x123512 Lawrence Randolph Slade (8/9/1964-   )
241x123513 William Learned Slade (2/10/1967-   )
241x12352 William Mann Randolph III 94/20/1933-   ), m. 1/28/
         1956, Maria Teresa Osma
241x123521 Helen Augusta Randolph (3/14/1958-   )
241x123522 Elizabeth Virginia Randolph (9/15/1959-   )
241x123523 Peter Jefferson Randolph (3/6/1961-3/9/1961)
241x123524 Susan Carolina Randolph (2/5/1964-   )
241x123525 Thomas Joseph Randolph (7/30/1965-   )
241x1236 Mary Walker Randolph (4/30/1903-   )
241x1237 Hollins Nicholas Randolph II (6/14/1904-11/21/1976), m.
         8/22/1933, Mary Virginia Hoge
241x12371 Hollins Nicholas Randolph, Jr. (6/2/1934-   ), m.
         7/18/1957, Nancy Lee Wilson
241x123711 Bonnie Sue Randolph (1/8/1858-   ), m. 10/26/1979,
         Henry Harrison Smith III
241x123712 Martha Christine Randolph (12/31/1959-   )
241x123713 Hollins Nicholas Randolph III (9/28/1961-   )
241x123714 Angel Marie Randolph (3/16/1971-   )
241x12372 Thomas Jefferson Randolph VI (10/8/1936-   ), m.
         12/20/1958, Marie Spitler
241x123721 Thomas Jefferson Randolph VII (2/11/1960-   )
241x123722 William Franklin Randolph (7/8/1963-   )
241x123723 John Michael Randolph (4/23/1972-   )
241x1238 Francis Meriwether Randolph (4/22/1906-10/19/1978), m.
         12/21/1935, Leonne Gouaux
241x12381 Thomas Mann Randolph (9/24/1936-   ), m. 11/24/
         1960, Evelyn Adele Morash
241x123811 Margaret Elizabeth Randolph (8/26/1961-   )
241x123812 Hugh Jefferson Randolph (10/16/1962-   )

241x123813 Aileen Ann Randolph (3/17/1964-   )
241x123814 Timothy Lawrence Randolph (9/23/1966-   )
241x123815 Matthew Thomas Randolph (2/8/1969-   )
241x12382 William Lewis Randolph (9/28/1940-   ), m. (1st)
         12/ /1961, Brenda Theresa Cherami. M. (2nd) 7/3/
         1976, Dana Grafton Kroyer
241x123821 Katherine Randolph (12/ /1962-   )
241x123822 Joseph Adam Randolph (11/28/1963-   )
241x123823 Frances Margaret Randolph (9/8/1966-   )
241x12383 Michael Joseph Randolph (12/19/1942-   )
241x124 Hollins Nicholas Randolph (2/25/1872-4/29/1938), m. 10/
         17/1899, Caroline Tyson Walter
241x125 Arthur Dillon Randolph (2/9/1874-11/6/1874)
241x126 Agnes Dillon Randolph (7/12/1875-12/3/1930)
241x2 James Randolph
241x3 Dr. Stith L. Randolph
241x4 Julia Randolph
241x5 Virginia C. Randolph, m.   Omahundro
241a George Washington Randolph, d.s.p.
241b Harriet Randolph, m. Richard S. Hackley, Consul at Cadiz
241b1 Harriet Randolph Hackley, m. Capt. Andrew Talcott
241b11 Nannie Talcott, m. Count Bolas Laskig
241b12 Mary Talcott, Sister in Episcopal Church
241b13 Fannie Talcott, Sister in Episcopal Church
241b14 Richard Talcott
241b15 Col. Thomas Mann Randolph Talcott, C.S.A. (3/7/1838-   ),
         m. 1/7/1864, Nannie Carrington McPhail (10/5/1837-   );
         dau. of John Blair and Anne Cabell Carrington McPhail
241b151 Mary Talcott
241b152 Harriet Talcott
241b153 Eva Talcott
241b154 Augusta Talcott, m. Dr. Truman Alfred Parker of California
241b1541 Augusta Parker
241b1542 Truman Alfred Parker, Jr.
241b1543 Randolph Talcott Parker
241b1544 Nancy Carrington Parker
241b155 Jennie McPhail Talcott
241b2 William Beverley Randolph Hackley, m. Matilda R. Folker
241b21 Charlotte Hackley, m. Angelo Paul Spencer
241b211 Marion Spencer
241b212 Lilly Charlotte Spencer, m. Fred A. Sweet
241b213 Lucia Beverley Spencer, m. Lt. Comdr. F. H. Young
241b214 Randolph R. Spencer
241b3 Lucia Beverley Hackley, m. Dr. Lewis Byrd Willis. See 24194
241b31 Lewis Byrd Willis, Jr., m. Elizabeth Maclay
241b32 William R. Willis, d.s.p.
241b4 Martha Jefferson Hackley, m. Richard D. Cutts
241b41 Richard Malcolm Cutts (10/18/1846-2/3/1886),m. 10/ /1876,
         Emily Turner
241b411 Alice Gertrude Cutts (12/15/1877-   ), m. John Twiggs
         Myers, U.S.M.C.
241b412 Richard Malcolm Cutts, Jr. m. Margaret

241b4121 Richard Malcolm Cutts III
241b4122 Alice Cutts, m. 6/ /1930, John Tillotson Wainwright
241b41221 John Tillotson Wainwright III (7/ /1931-   )
241b42 Anna Gertrude Cutts (10/14/1848-11/27/1912), m. 1/6/1870,
          Moorefield Storey, son of Charles William and Elizabeth
          Moorefield Storey
241b421 Elizabeth Moorefield Storey (2/16/1871-   ), m. 10/8/
          1895, Dr. Robert W. Lovett
241b4211 Gertrude Lovett (9/17/1896-   ),m. 6/19/1916, Henry
          Sprague Sturgis
241b42111 Elizabeth Moorefield Sutrgis (10/20/1917-   )
241b42112 Henry Sprague Sturgis, Jr. (5/31/1920-   )
241b42113 Robert Lovett Sturgis (1/26/1923-   )
241b422 Gertrude Lucy Storey (10/21/1872-   ), m. 4/13/1903,
          Edmund Jefferson Burke (2414617)
241b423 Richard Cutts Storey (4/30/1875-6/10/1931), m. 7/7/1898,
          Anna W. Ladd
241b4231 Katherine Ladd Storey (7/3/1899-   ), m. 6/1/1922,
          Theodore L. Storer
241b42311 Anna Ladd Storer (11/22/1923-   )
241b4232 Richard Cutts Storey, Jr. (10/27/1902-   ), m. 1/19/
          1929, Mabel Bayard Thayer
241b42321 Ruth Bayard Storey (11/15/1929-   )
241b42322 Richard Cutts Storey (10/16/1930-   )
241b42323 Bayard Thayer Storey (7/ /1932-   )
241b4233 Moorefield Storey II (1/27/1905-   )
241b4234 William Ladd Storey (9/25/1907-   )
241b4235 John Cutts Storey (3/6/1930-   )
241b424 Katherine Storey (12/30/1879-10/14/1920), m. 1/4/1904,
          Malcolm Donald
241b4241 Alexander Donald (7/24/1905-   ), m. 9/17/1932,
          Barbara Pond
241b4242 Barbara Donald (3/4/1909-   )
241b425 Charles Moorefield Storey (3/4/1889-   ), m. 6/24/1913,
          Susan Jameson Sweetser
241b4251 Charles Moorefield Storey, Jr. (6/11/1914-   )
241b4252 Anderson Storey (8/1/1917-   )
241b4253 Susan Jameson Storey (5/17/1919-   )
241b4254 Gertrude Storey (7/2/1923-   )
241b4255 James Moorefield Storey (4/12/1931-   )
241b43 Lucia Beverley Cutts (3/15/1851-   ). Unm.
241b44 Harriet Randolph Cutts (-1856)
241b45 Harry Madison Cutts (9/4/1858-2/22/1919), m. 11/ /1891,
          Marion Belcher
241b451 Dorothy Madison Cutts (12/27/1892-   ), m. 1920, John
          B. Wills
241b452 George Belcher Cutts (5/ /1895-   ), m. 12/ /1928,
          Priscilla Whipple
241b4521 Robert Whipple Cutts (12/26/1931-   )
241c Virginia Randolph (1/31/1786-   ), m. 1805, Wilson
        Jefferson Cary (1784-1823)
241c1 Wilson Miles Cary (1806-1877), m. 1831, Jane Margaret Carr
        (34533)

241c11   Sarah Nicholas Cary (1832-1893), m. 1855, James Howard
      McHenry
241c111   Juliana H. McHenry (-1901)
241c112   Wilson Cary McHenry, m. Edith Dove
241c1121   Howard McHenry, m. Frances Garrison
241c1122   Edith Dove McHenry
241c113   John McHenry, m. Priscilla Pinkney Stewart
241c1131   John McHenry
241c1132   James McHenry, m. Marjorie Hambelton Ober Keyser. She
      m. (1st) 241c1143
241c1133   Julia Howard McHenry, m. 1925, Robert Lee Randolph, Jr.
      (1895-   ), son of Robert Lee and Phoebe Waite
      Elliott Randolph
241c11331   Robert Lee Randolph
241c11332   Priscilla Stewart Randolph
241c1134   Priscilla Pinkney McHenry, m. Duncan Forbes Thayer
241c11341   Priscilla Stewart Thayer
241c11342   Cornelia Van Rensselaer Thayer
241c114   Ellen McHenry, m. R. Brent Keyser
241c1141   Ellen Keyser, M. James Bruce
241c11411   Ellen Bruce
241c11412   Louise Este Bruce
241c1142   Juliana Brent Keyser, m. Gaylord Lee Clark
241c11421   Juliana Gaylord Clark
241c11422   Letitia Lee Clark
241c11423   Mathilde Keyser Clark
241c11424   Gaylord Lee Clark
241c11425   Sally Cary Clark
241c1143   W. McHenry Keyser, m. Marjorie Hambleton Ober. She
      m. (2nd) 241c1132
241c11431   Robert Brent Keyser
241c11432   W. McHenry Keyser
241c115   Sophia McHenry, m. Charles Morton Stewart
241c1151   Sophia McHenry Stewart, m. George Martin Gillet
241c11511   George Martin Gillet
241c11512   James McHenry Gillet
241c1152   Charles Morton Stewart, m. Lillie Emerson Van Leuven
241c11521   Charles Morton Stewart (1933-   )
241c1153   Margaret Stewart
241c12   Virginia Cary (1833-d. inf.)
241c13   Hetty Cary (1836-1892), m. (1st) 1865, John Pegram, Brig.
      Gen. C.S.A. M. (2nd) 1879, Henry Newell Martin (1848-
      1897)
241c14   Virginia Randolph Cary (1837-d. inf.)
241c15   Wilson Miles Cary, Maj. C.S.A.
241c16   John Brune Cary (1840-1917), m. 1867, Frances Eugenia
      Daniel
241c161   Hetty Cary, m. Fairfax Harrison (241c521)
241c17   Jane Margaret Cary (1843-   )
241c18   Sydney Carr Cary (1845-1896), m. 1885, Pauline Playford
241c181   Gwendolen Cary
241c2   Jane Blair Cary (1808-1888), m. 1831, Rev. Edward Dunlap
      Smith

241c21 Archibald Cary Smith (1873-1911)
241c3 Mary Randolph Cary (1811-1887), m. 5/21/1829, Orlando
    Fairfax (1806-1882)
241c31 Virginia Fairfax (-1832)
241c32 Edith Fairfax (-1839)
241c33 Orlando Cary Fairfax (-1836)
241c34 Monimia Fairfax (12/27/1837-   ), m. 5/19/1866, George
    Davis (3/1/1820-2/23/1896) of New Hanover County, N.C.,
    son of Thomas Frederick and Sarah Isabel Eagles Davis,
    Atty. Gen. C.S.A.
241c341 Mary Fairfax Davis, m. Minor Fairfax Heiskel Gouverneur
241c3411 Fairfax Heiskel Gouverneur, m. Caroline Jeffress
241c34111 Minor Fairfax Heiskel Gouverneur
241c34112 Sallie Thornton Gouverneur
241c34113 Caroline Gouverneur
241c34114 Jane Fairfax Gouverneur
241c3412 Esther Gouverneur
241c342 Monimia Cary Davis (11/10/1876-   ), m. Donad S.
    MacRae (5/3/1861-   ), son of Donald and Julia Norton
    MacRae
241c3421 Monimia Fairfax MacRae (-1980). Unm.
241c3422 Donald MacRae, d.
241c34221 Donald MacRae, d. at age of 17
241c3423 Colin MacRae, M. D. (6/12/1907-12/11/1975), m. 10/10/
    1942, Elizabeth Clarke Brown-Serman (2/20/1919-   ),
    dau. of Stanley and Marion Montagu Clarke Brown-Serman.
    Dr. MacRae practiced in Alexandria, Va. She m. (2nd)
    Francis W. Hayes, Jr.
241c34231 Elizabeth Fairfax MacRae (8/3/1943-   ), m. 9/3/
    1966, Frederick Caskey Gouldin (7/4/1943-   ),
    son of James D. C. and Jane Caskey Gouldin. Frederick
    is Prof. of Engineering at Cornell
241c342311 Ann Caskey Gouldin (2/7/1972-   )
241c342312 Cary Fairfax Gouldin (8/20/1973-   )
241c34232 Marion Montague MacRae (4/21/1945-   ). Attorney in
    Washington, D.C., living in Alexandria
241c34233 Cary Davis MacRae (11/17/1947-   ), m. 3/23/1974,
    John Douglas McDaniel (6/11/1947-   ), son of
    Thomas McDaniel and Helen Jordan McDaniel
241c342331 Douglas Fairfax McDaniel (9/11/1976-   )
241c342332 Katherine Randolph McDaniel (9/19/1978-   )
241c3424 George Davis MacRae (   ), m. Serena Chesnut
    Randolph. They live in Banner Elk, N.C.
241c34241 Davis MacRae (4/10/1949-   )
241c34242 Kate MacRae (9/3/1950-   )
241c34243 Colin MacRae (10/6/1951-   )
241c34244 Douglas MacRae (8/30/1952 or 1953-   )
241c35 Jane Cary Fairfax
241c36 Randolph Fairfax (1842-1862)
241c37 Ethelbert Fairfax (1845-1865)
241c38 Mary Edith Fairfax, m. 1877, John Jaquelin Ambler Moncure,
    M.D.

241c381 Rosamond Cary Moncure (1882-   )
241c382 Orlando Moncure (1883-   )
241c383 Randolph Moncure (-1886)
241c4 Anne Mantia Cary (1813-1822)
241c5 Archibald Cary (1815-1854), m. 1838, Monimia Fairfax, dau.
       of Thomas Fairfax
241c51 Falkland Fairfax Cary, d.s.p.
241c52 Constance Fairfax Cary, m. 11/26/1867, Burton Norvell
       Harrison (7/14/1838-3/29/1904), son of Jesse Burton and
       Frances Brand Harrison
241c521 Fairfax Harrison (3/13/1869-   ), m. Hetty Cary
       (241c161)
241c5211 Constance Harrison
241c5212 Ursula Harrison
241c5213 Richard Harrison
241c522 Francis Burton Harrison (12/18/1873-   ), m. (1st)
       Mary Crocker, dau. of Charles Crocker. M. (2nd) Mabel
       Judson, dau. of Henry Judson
241c5221 Virginia Randolph Harrison
241c5222 Barbara Burton Harrison
241c5223 Burton Harrison
241c5224 Frances Fairfax Harrison
241c523 Archibald Cary Harrison (10/21/1876-   ), m. Helen
       Bates Walley, dau. of George Phillipps Walley
241c5231 Mary Harrison
241c53 Clarence Cary, m. Elizabeth Potter
241c6 Ellen Randolph Cary (1817-1901)
241c7 Martha ("Patsy") Jefferson Cary (1820-1873), m. 1842,
       Gouverneur Morris (24181)
241c8 Sally Newsum Cary (1822-d. inf.)
241c9 Louisa Hartwell Cary (1823-d. inf.)
242 Jane Cary, m. Thomas Isham Randolph (ca. 1728-   ) of
       "Dungeness"
2421 Archibald Cary Randolph (1769-11/14/1813), m. 4/6/1797, Lucy
       Burwell (11/20/1777-3/22/1810) of "Ben Lomond" (d. at "Carter
       Hall")
24211 Thomas Isham Randolph II (1797-1805). Killed by lightning
       at "Ben Lomond"
24212 Nathaniel Randolph, d. inf.
24213 Nathaniel Randolph, d. age 6 years
24214 Dr. Philip Grymes Randolph (11/1/1801-3/12/1836), m. ca.
       1824, Mary B. O'Neale, dau. of William and Rhoda O'Neale
       of Washington, D.C.
242141 Mary Conway Randolph (8/19/1825-9/7/1905)(d. at "The
       Moorings", Clarke Co. Va.), m. 8/1/1847, Beverley
       Randolph (241533)
242142 Henrietta Eaton Randolph (5/9/1827-5/19/1894), m. 5/8/1850,
       Rev. William Henry Pendleton (9/30/1817-3/8/1873), son of
       William and Susan Snodgrass Pendleton of Berkeley Co. Va.
2421421 Lucy Randolph Pendleton (6/26/1851-7/10/1926)(b. "Leeds
       Manor", Fauquier Co., d. "The Grove", Fauquier Co.) Unm.
2421422 Susan Randolph Pendleton (4/9/1853-1/26/1936)(b. "Leeds
       Manor"). Unm.

2421423 Mary Randolph Pendleton (10/5/1854-11/29/1856)
2421424 Philip Randolph Pendleton (1/4/1858-4/15/1875)
2421425 Henrietta Grymes Randolph Pendleton (3/10/1860-9/17/1925).
         Unm.
2421426 Ellen Shepherd Pendleton (3/21/1862-1899), m. 1893, Lionel
         B. Perry Ayscough
24214261 Henrietta Randolph Ayscough, m. William E. Virts
242142611 Stuart Virts
2421427 Garnett Peyton Pendleton (10/8/1864-5/15/1939), m. 10/2/
         1895, William Dabney Wirt (7/24/1857-3/16/1930), son of
         William and Betty Selina Payne Wirt of Oak Grove
24214271 Henrietta Mary Randolph Peyton Wirt (2/15/1901-   ).
         Unm.
24214272 Elizabeth Garnett Pendleton Wirt (2/27/1903-   ), m.
         9/27/1941, Porter Lane Mattox (10/10/1888-   ), son
         of Henry Brennel and Abbie Porter Mattox
2421428 Rev. William Henry Kinckle Pendleton (1/17/1867-   ),
         m. 7/28/1897, Elizabeth Forrer Chapman (6/12/1869-   ),
         dau. of Col. William Henry and Josephine MacCrae Jeffries
         Chapman
24214281 Elizabeth Randolph Pendleton (12/8/1898-   )
24214282 William Henry Chapman Pendleton (7/27/1900-12/6/1909)
24214283 Robert Randolph Pendleton (6/5/1902-3/12/1931)
24214284 Cary Verdier Pendleton (1/27/1904-5/19/1943)
24214285 Joseph Pendleton (3/11/1909-d. at birth)
24214286 Josephine Chapman Pendleton (11/10/1911-   ), m. 12/21/
         1940, Guy Marvin Fenstermacher (9/20/1906-   ), son
         of Frank Hiram and Jennie Bell Brodt Fenstermacher
242142861 William Pendleton Fenstermacher (3/24/1944-   )
2421429 Robert Carter Pendleton (2/2/1870-2/15/1891).   Unm.
242142x "Little Sister" Pendleton, b. and d. 7/20/1856
24215   Susan Grymes Randolph of "Saratoga" Clarke Co. (1803-7/3/
         1858), m. 10/1/1829 (his second wife), Dr. Robert Powel
         Page (1/11/1794-3/ /1849) of "The Briars", son of John
         and Maria Horsemanden Byrd Page
242151   Elizabeth Burwell Page (1839-1863).   Unm.
242152   Mary Frances Page (5/24/1840-1/15/1878)(b. and d. at "The
         Briars"), m. 9/18/1867, John Esten Cooke (11/3/1830-9/
         27/1886), son of John Rogers and Maria Pendleton Cooke
2421521 Susan Randolph Cooke (7/11/1868-   )(b. at "Saratoga"),
         m. 9/23/1893, Rev. Charles Henry Lee (12/20/1866-2/5/
         1938), son of Col. Richard H. and Evelyn Byrd Page Lee
         of Clarke Co., Va.
24215211 Lucy Carter Lee (10/3/1895-   )
24215212 Elsie Frances Lee (7/5/1897-   ), m. 6/1/1821, Ralph
         Frederick Skylstead (7/5/1897-   ), son of Olaf George
         and Anne Gaelmacdeh Trope Skylstead
242152121 Suzannehea Skylstead (1/10/1924-   )(b. Honolulu)
242152122 Elsie Page Lee Skylstead (3/2/1926-   )
24215213 Alice Dandridge Lee (6/24/1904-   ), m. 7/18/1934,
         Rear Adm. Dwight Harvey Day, U.S.N., Ret. (1/31/1901-
         ), son of Carlyle Harwood and Marguerita Dwight
         Day
242152131 Susan Randolph Day (2/5/1937-   )
242152132 Dwight Harvey Day, Jr. (7/10/1940-   )

242152133 Lucy Page Lee Day (11/13/1943-   )
2421522 Edmund Pendleton Cooke (5/23/1870-1905)(b. "The Briars").
Unm.
2421523 Dr. Robert Powell Page Cooke (10/12/1874-   )(b. "The
Briars"), m. 11/2/1912, Nell Page Jones (11/1/1888-   ),
dau. of Sturgeon and Page Helm Jones
24215231 Sallie Page Cooke (4/16/1914-10/20/1920)(b. and d. Front
Royal, Va.)
24215232 Mary Estes Cooke (2/6/1919-   ), m. 2/27/1943,
Chester Bernard Goolrick, Jr. (3/30/1917-   ), son
of C. B. and Virginia Ward Maitland Goolrick of Fredericksburg
242152321 Chester Bernard Gookrick III (5/4/1946-   )
242152322 Robert Cooke Goolrick (8/4/1948-   )
24215233 Anne Pendleton Cooke (12/29/1923-   )
242153 Lucy Randolph Page (3/1/1842-8/3/1893)(b. "The Briars", d.
"The Glen"), m. 2/28/1867, Capt. William Page Carter (9/
6/1836-11/20/1913), son of Thomas Nelson and Anne Willing
Page Carter
242154 Robert Powell Page III (8/22/1846-8/31/1930)(b."The Briars",
d. "Saratoga"), m. 9/28/1873, Agnes Atkinson Burwell (9/
28/1850-1/22/1921)(b. "Carter Hall", d. "Saratoga"), dau.
of George Harrison and Agnes Atkinson Burwell
2421541 Agnes Rogers Page (6/17/1875-   )(b. "Saratoga")
2421542 Mary Frances Page (10/21/1876-   )(b. "Saratoga")
2421643 Robert Powell Page IV (1/30/1879-6/6/1949)(b. "Saratoga"),
m. 6/17/1980, Helen White Hamilton (1/22/1884-   ),
dau. of James M. and Ida Lee Hamilton
24215431 Robert Powell Page V (10/10/1909-   )
24215432 Maj. James Hamilton Page (12/12/1910-   ), m. 7/22/
1947, Muriel Charlotte VanDusen (4/6/1914-   ), dau.
of Lewis H. and Muriel Lund VanDusen of Philadelphia
242154321 Helen Hamilton Page (1/15/1948-   )
24215433 Peter Mayo Page (3/31/1919-2/14/1943), Air Service, U.S.
M.C. Killed in action, in southwest Pacific while
piloting a torpedo plane
2421544 George Burwell Page (5/18/1880-11/24/1908)(b. "Saratoga")
2421545 Nathaniel Burwell Page (11/17/1882-1/4/1928), m. 3/17/
1908, Henrietta Mary King Welton (7/7/1882-   ), dau.
of Louis Morris and Ella Morse King Welton of San Antonio,
Texas
24215451 Henrietta King Page (9/19/1910-   )(b. "Sararoga"),
m. 5/26/1930, John Henderson Farrar (12/1/1905-   ),
son of Dr. William and Harriet Purcell Henderson Farrar
242154511 John Henderson Farrar, Jr. (9/9/1931-   )
24215452 Nathaniel Burwell Page, Jr. (2/17/1913-   ), m. 7/8/
1942, Mary Virginia Gordon (5/4/1922-   ), dau. of
John W. and Catherine Ann Mitchell Gordon
242154521 Mary Catherine Page (4/1/1943-   )
242154522 Frances Byrne Page (10/24/1944-   )
242154523 Henrietta King Page (4/23/1947-   )
2421546 Susan Randolph Page (11/28/1886-   ), m. 1/4/1910,
Roland Green Mitchell (4/4/1873-2/3/1933)(b. The Glen"),
son of Henry Post and Rebecca Simons Price Mitchell

24215461 Henry Post Mitchell (3/17/1911-   ), m. 9/26/1936,
          Mary Cary Harrison. See 24216432
24215462 Agnes Page Mitchell (8/5/1914-   )(b. "The Glen"). Unm.
24215463 Roland Green Mitchell, Jr. (10/4/1916-   )(b. "The
          Glen"), m. 5/1/1948, Virginia Stuart Watkins (1920-   )
          (b. "Annfield"), dau. of William Bell and Gladys Alden
          Mackay-Smith Watkins of "Annfield"
242154631 Virginia Page Mitchell
24216   Mary Cary ("Polly") Randolph (4/12/1806-1/22/1855)(d. "Long-
          wood"), m. 3/ /1824, Dr. Mathew Page (ca. 1800-1/17/1837),
          son of Gwynne and Hereford Page
242161   Archibald Cary Page (1/15/1828-1/1/1903). Unm. C.S.A.
          Soldier
242162   Gwynne Page (1833-5/28/1850). Killed by a horse
242163   Dr. William Meade Page (6/22/1831-5/9/1906), m. Emily
          Carrington
2421631   Emily Page, m. Hamilton Sheppard
2421632   Louise Page, d.s.p.
242164   Mattilla ("Mattie") Cary Page (8/26/1835-8/31/1898)(b. and
          d. "Longwood"), m. 2/4/1858, Dr. Benjamin Harrison (2/18/
          1824-5/11/1898), son of Benjamin and Mary Willing Page
          Harrison
2421641   Dr. Benjamin Harrison, Jr. (5/28/1859-9/10/1900)(b. "Hazel-
          wood"). Unm.
2421642   Mary Cary Harrison (2/5/1861-12/6/1907)(b. "Longwood", d.
          "Hazelwood"), m. Dr. Archibald B. Bevan (1859-3/1/1931).
          No issue. Dr. Bevan m. 2nd, Mary Meade and had 1 dau.
          who d. inf.
2421643   Dr. Gwynne Page Harrison (4/13/1878-8/12/1914), m. 2/20/
          1909, Phoebe Virginia Westwater (2/21/1890-   ), dau.
          of James and Virginia Gulick Westwater. She m. (2nd),
          Hugh Nelson (4424d22); m. (3rd) 1935, Walter Roesler
24216431 Benjamin Harrison III (12/3/1909-5/7/1984), m. 5/ /
          1948, Jane Cary Randolph (241533533)
24216432 Mary Cary Harrison (2/29/1911-   ), m. 9/26/1936,
          Henry Post Mitchell. See 24215461
24216433 Virginia Gwynne Harrison (11/29/1913-   )
242165   Roberta Page (1830-9/25/1835). D. from burns when dress
          caught fire
242166   Phillippa B. Page (-2/3/1832)
24217   Dr. Robert Carter Randolph (12/1/1807-1/14/1887)(b. "Carter
          Hall", d. "Waverley"), m. 4/28/1830, Lucy Nelson Wellford
          (4/28/1810-2/1/1882), dau. of William and Susan Robinson
          Nelson Wellford
242171   Bettie Burwell Randolph (3/13/1831-4/24/1899), m. 2/18/
          1862, Warren Collier Smith (8/10/1824-1/6/1888), son of
          Dr. Philip and Louisa Collier Christian Smith
2421711   Robert Randolph Smith (12/1/1864-5/25/1909), m. 10/14/
          1896, Elizabeth ("Bettie") Mackey Smith (3/4/1873-   ),
          dau. of William Dickerson and Agnes Pickett Williams
          Smith of "Smithfield", Clarke Co.
24217111 Robert Randolph Smith, Jr. (11/4/1902-   )(b. "Silver
          Spring"), m. 11/25/1939, Mary Rogers (12/24/1909-   ),
          dau. of William Herbert and Rachel Harless Rogers

242171111 Mary Randolph Smith (3/5/1941-   )
242171112 Robert Randolph Smith III (8/17/1942-   )
242171113 Ruth Rogers Smith (11/23/1944-   )
24217112 Elizabeth Mackey Smith (7/26/1897-   ). Unm.
24217113 Agnes Williams Smith (8/22/1899-9/25/1918). Unm.
24217114 Susan Wellford Smith (2/1/1901-   ). Unm.
24217115 Louisa Collier Smith (12/29/1904-   ). Unm.
24217116 Ann Williams Smith (8/11/1907-   ). Unm.
2421712 Warren Collier Smith (6/28/1866-3/25/1895)(b. "Summerfield")
2421713 Lucy Wellford Smith (7/2/1870-8/20/1908)
2421714 Susan Burwell Smith (1/26/1869-11/30/1937). Unm.
2421715 Betty Randolph Smith (9/4/1871-1/7/1896)
242172 Dr. Archibald Cary Randolph II (4/13/1833-3/30/1887), m.
        9/29/1881, Susan Randolph Burwell (8/15/1849-   ),
        dau. of Nathaniel and Dorothy Willing Page Burwell,
        widow of Col. Mathis Winston Henry
2421721 Dr. Archibald Cary Randolph III (9/14/1885-   ), m.
        (1st), 4/26/1910, Eva ("Terry") Randolph Dulany (10/3/
        1887-2/4/1933), dau. of Richard Hunter and Eva Virginia
        Randolph Dulany. M. (2nd), 1934, Rebecca Anne Dulany
        8/6/1884-   ), sister of first wife. No issue.
        M. (3rd), 9/3/1941, Theodora Ayer (9/27/1905-   ),
        dau. of Charles Fanning and Sara Theodora Isley Ayer.
        No issue
     Children by first wife:
24217211 Dorothy Willing Randolph (2/22/1911-   ), m. 12/26/
        1935, William Beverley Mason, Jr., Lt. USNR (7/13/
        1908-   ), son of Dr. William Beverley and Agnes
        Gray Kennedy Mason
242172111 William Beverley Mason III (12/12/1936-   )
242172112 Randolph Dulany Mason (8/1/1942-   )
24217212 Lt. Richard Hunter Dulany Randolph, USNR (4/10/1912-   )
24217213 Capt. Archibald Cary Randolph IV, U.S. Air Transport
        Command (1/25/1915-   ), m. 5/1/1940, Elizabeth
        Anne Leith (11/11/1916-   ), dau. of Louis Cayle
        and Eva Virginia Rawlings Leith of Middleburg
242172131 Rebecca Anne Dulany Randolph (6/14/1941-   )
242173 Susan Wellford Randolph (7/8/1835-12/18/1897), m. 5/1/
        1860, second wife of William Eston Randolph (241532)
242174 Col. William Wellford Randolph (2/20/1837-5/6/1864), m.
        9/9/1863, Ada Stuart (10/27/1841-3/28/1914), dau. of
        Dr. Richard Henry and Julia Calvert Stuart of King
        George County
2421741 William Wellford Randolph, Jr. (7/16/1864-1/24/1924), m.
        10/31/1893, Julia Edmond Taylor (5/20/1869-6/14/1947),
        dau. of George Edmund and Elizabeth Frazer Taylor
24217411 Calvert Stuart Randolph (5/29/1895-   ), m. (1st)
        3/12/1918, Mildred Patterson Betts, dau. of Clement
        Herbert and Lily Patterson Betts. No issue. M. (2nd)
        Helen Bell
     Child by second wife:
242174111 Calvert Stuart Randolph, Jr.

24217412 William Wellford Randolph III (7/8/1902-   ), m. 6/4/
          1927, Kathryn Fowler Williams (1/25/1899-   ), dau.
          of George Wesley and Garetta Hughlett Williams
242174121 Susan Charlotte Randolph (5/16/1938-   )
24217413 Katharine Randolph (11/26/1903-   ), m. (1st), 10/25/
          1924, Stuart Allan Prevost (6/27/1896 or 97-   ), son
          of Joseph and Amy Simpson Prevost of Canada. Div. 1935.
          M. (2nd) 8/10/1935, John Parmelee Coffin (7/10/1904-
               ), son of Charles Wellington Dutcher and Eliza-
          beth Pratt Parmelee Coffin. No issue. Lived Short Hills,N.J.
          Child by first husband:
242174131 Patricia Randolph Prevost (9/16/1927-   ), m. 7/31/
          1948, William Howard Taylor, son of Harry Augustus
          Taylor. Lived in Orange, N.J.
2421741311 William Randolph Taylor (7/9/1949-   )
242175   Philip Burwell Randolph (9/3/1838-11/21/1857)(b. "New
          Market", d. while a student at University of Virginia)
242176   Capt. Robert Carter Randolph, Jr., C.S.A. (7/14/1840-10/
          19/1864)(b. "New Market"). Killed in battle "Cedar Creek"
242177   Thomas Hugh Burwell Randolph (4/5/1843-4/23/1900)(b. "New
          Market", d."Powhatan"), m. 2/4/1868, Eliza Page Burwell
          (8/30/1845-4/29/1928)(b. "Carter Hall", d. "Powhatan"),
          dau. of George Harrison and Agnes Atkinson Burwell of
          "Carter Hall"
2421771   Robert Carter Randolph III (11/16/1869-2/20/1928)(b. and
          d. "Powhatan"), m. 11/14/1906, Isabel Wurts Harrison (11/
          30/1880-10/2/1939)(b. "Huntington", d. "Powhatan"), dau.
          of Henry Huntingdon and Margaret Byrd Page Harrison of
          Philadelphia
24217711 Margaret Harrison Randolph (11/11/1908-4/9/1926)(b.
          "Powhatan")
24217712 Robert Carter Randolph IV (3/2/1912-   ), m. Susan
          Gordon Dabney Bolling, dau. of Albert Stuart and
          Susan Gordon Dabney Bolling (Mrs. Bolling m. 2nd, Henry
          Stuart Lewis). Mrs. Randolph m. (2nd)   Meredith
242177121
242177122
242177123
242177124
242177125
242178   Isham Randolph (3/25/1848-8/2/1920)(b. "New Market"), m.
          6/15/1882, Mary Henry Taylor (11/18/1859-12/8/1935), dau.
          of George Edmund and Elizabeth Frazer Taylor
2421781   Col. Robert Isham Randolph (4/14/1883-   ), m. 10/
          17/1912, Martha Amelia Ackerman Maclean (4/23/1884-   ),
          widow of George Alexander Maclean, dau. of Alfred and
          Jane Charlotte Adams Ackerman. The Randolphs lived in
          Santa Barbara, Calif. He wrote THE RANDOLPHS OF VIRGINIA
2421782   Rev. Oscar deWolf Randolph (9/28/1885-   ), m. 6/19/
          1911, Alice Laurie Crawford (8/26/1886-   ), dau. of
          Rev. Angus and Susie Brown Crawford. The Randolphs
          lived in Ardmore, Pa.
24217821 Oscar deWolf Randolph, Jr. (1/7/1913-1/7/1913)

24217822   Angus Crawford Randolph, M.D. (8/23/1914-   ), m.
        12/20/1941, Marjorie Armstrong McLernon (4/1/1914-   ),
        dau. of George Justus and Marjorie Pleasants Armstrong
        McLernon of Tampico, Mexico. They lived in Winston-
        Salem

242178221 Marjorie Armstrong Randolph (10/10/1942-   ). Lived
        in Baltimore, Md.

242178222 Angus MacDonald Crawford Randolph (9/16/1946-   ).
        Lived in Baltimore, Md.

24217823 Mary Isham Randolph (7/10/1917-   ), m. 6/8/1940,
        James Edward Poindexter (2/15/1915-   ), son of
        Gordon Wallace and Mary Morse Byrd Poindexter of Warren-
        ton, N.C. Lived in Columbus, Miss.

242178231 Mary Boyd Poindexter (10/20/1942-   )

242178232 James Randolph Gordon Poindexter (1/16/1945-   )

2421783   Spotswood Wellford Randolph (8/5/1892-   ), m. (1st),
        5/17/1916, Deborah Beatrice White (6/24/1882-   ),
        dau. of William Francis and Catharine Stringfellow White
        of Chicago. Div. 4/21/1936. M. (2nd) 6/10/1937, Carmen
        Hevia Santos (6/23/1894-   ), dau. of Timolio Ale-
        jandro and Mary Onderdonk Long Santos of Ecuador.
        (Spotswood Wellford Randolph was second husband of Carmen
        Hevia Santos). Lived in Baltimore, Md.
        Children by first wife:

24217831 Jean Wellford Randolph (2/2/1918-   ), m. 6/14/1939,
        Lawrence Reid Houston (1/14/1913-   ), son of David
        Franklin and Helen Beall Houston of Washington, D.C.
        Lived in Washington, D.C.

242178311 David Lawrence Houston (6/15/1947-   )

24217832 Spotswood Wellford Randolph, Jr. (10/20/1919-   ),
        m. 7/15/1944, Elsie Mary Smith (7/29/1923-   ), dau.
        of Ernest Everett and Caroline Phillips Smith of Cam-
        bridge. Lived in Lutherville, Md.

242178321 Spotswood Wellford Randolph III (2/21/1945-   )

24217833 Deborah Phyllis Cary Randolph (11/27/1922-   ), m.
        4/1/1944, William Russell Peabody (8/12/1916-   ),
        son of Charles Cockman and Margaret Davidson Peabody
        of Cambridge. Lived in Providence, R.I.

2421784   George Taylor Wellford Randolph (1/2/1895-5/4/1897)

242179   Lucy Wellford Randolph (3/13/1850-2/5/1854)

24217x   Polly Cary Randolph (7/19/1851-1/31/1935). Unm.

24217a   Catharine Isham Randolph (1854-d. inf.)(b. in Millwood)

24218   Lucy Burwell Randolph (12/31/1809-7/27/1877), m. 12/31/
        1929, Rev. Eleazer Carter Hutchinson (12/25/1804-   ),
        son of Eleazer and Sarah Talcott Hutchinson

242181   William Talcott Hutchinson, d. inf.

242182   D. inf.

242183   D. inf.

242184   D. inf.

242185   D. inf.

242186   Lewis Burwell Hutchinson (9/26/1832-9/17/1910), m. (1st),
        10/4/1860, Elizabeth Gearhart. M. (2nd) 2/6/1867, Adeline
        Kincaid Hughes

Children by first wife:
2421861 A. Carter Hutchinson (8/14/1861-   ), m. 1/24/1906,
       Mary E. Flaugher
24218611 Randolph Hutchinson (11/15/1906-   ), m. Lorna
       Christie
24218612 Edmond Hutchinson (10/22/1910-   ), m. Winona Brazeal
24218613 Catherine Hutchinson (10/22/1911-   )
       Children by second wife (of 242186):
2421862 William Talcott Hutchinson (1870-   ), m. 1/5/1894,
       Donnie Brown
24218621 Lucille Hutchinson (8/27/1898-   ), m. 9/17/1918,
       Herman Farris Middlecoff
242186211 Cary Middlecoff (1/8/1921-   )
242186212 Penelope Lucille Middlecoff (6/16/1933-   )
24218622 Cary Hutchinson (6/27/1901-   ), m. 3/25/1926,
       Penelope Snyder (3/26/1905-   )
242186221 Cary Brown Hutchinson (5/10/1930-   )
2421863 Lewis Randolph Hutchinson (9/12/1874-   ), m. 1/7/
       1898, Mary Clyde Smith (1/16/1874-   )
24218631 Maude Estella Hutchinson (3/13/1899-3/29/1914)
24218632 Lucy May Hutchinson (1/21/1901-   ), m. 12/31/1919,
       Richard Doyle Mills
242186321 Earl Ronald Mills (9/28/1920-   )
242186322 Alice Mills (1/21/1922-   )
242186323 Charles Henry Mills (8/15/1923-   )
242186324 Mary Jane Mills (9/17/1925-   )
242186325 Jimmie Ray Mills (11/7/1927-   )
24218633 Randolph Clifton Hutchinson (6/11/1903-   ), m. 6/
       19/1927, J. Ehrman Hayes
24218634 Althea Clyde Hutchinson (5/6/1906-   ), m. 5/9/1928,
       Thomas Grosen
242186341 Thomas Grosen, Jr. (4/21/1930-   )
24218635 Charles Raymond Hutchinson (11/4/1911-   )
242187 Robert Randolph Hutchinson (8/27/1837-11/21/1910), m. 6/7/
       1865, Mary S. Mitchell
2421871 Cary Talcott Hutchinson (3/4/1866-   ), m. 4/22/1922,
       Hebe Heth Harrison, dau. of Julien and Lavinia Heth
       Beverley Harrison. No issue. He was her third husband.
       See 2424538
2421872 Randolph Burwell Hutchinson (10/17/1867-   )
2421873 David Mitchell Hutchinson (10/13/1869-   ), m. Mary
       B. Luney
24218731 Marjorie Hutchinson (9/12/1907-   )
24218732 Lucy Carter Hutchinson (1/7/1912-   )
2421874 William Christy Hutchinson (2/22/1871-   )
2421875 Mary Randolph Hutchinson (12/20/1872-   ),m. 5/12/1897,
       Lindell Gordon, son of Robert C. and Anne Elizabeth
       Lindell Gordon
24218751 Mary Randolph Gordon (3/11/1898-   ), m. 3/31/1921,
       John Gates Williams
242187511 Ann Cary Williams (12/30/1921-   )
24218752 Lindell Gordon, Jr. (3/18/1899-   ), m. 4/22/1927,
       Maud Miller Street

242187521 Maud Wells Gordon (5/22/1928-   )
242187522 Mary Christie Gordon (2/13/1932-   )
2421876 Lucy Carter Hutchinson (2/15/1875-   )
2421877 Archibald Grymes Hutchinson (3/13/1876-3/2/1936)
2421878 Martha Hutchinson (9/26/1880-   ), m. 4/21/1919,
        Eugene Andrews
24218781 Robert Randolph Andrews (6/15/1920-   )
24218782 Mary Mitchell Andrews (5/9/1922-   )
242188 Mary Talcott Hutchinson, m. Robert Anderson of Scotland
2421881 Daisy Anderson, d.s.p.
2421882 Randolph Anderson, d.s.p.
2421883 Donald Anderson, d.s.p.
2421884 Mary Talcott Anderson, m.

THOMAS BOLLING of "Cobbs"

(11)

2422 Thomas Randolph of Amelia County and "Dungeness" (4/20/1760-
  11/5/1811)(twin), killed in Battle of Tippecanoe, m. (1st)
  Mary Skipwith, dau. of Col. Henry and Anne Wayles Skipwith.
  M. (2nd) Catherine Lawrence
  Child by first wife:
24221 Elizabeth Randolph, m. (1st)   Watkins. M. (2nd) E. S.
  Symington of Indianapolis
  Child by second wife:
24222 Mary S. Randolph, m. William Sheets
2423 Isham Randolph of "Dungeness"(and "Clay Bank")(4/20/1760)
  (twin), m. 1795, Ann Randolph Coupland (1777-1853), dau. of
  Co. David O'Shields and Anne Harrison Coupland
24231 Jane Randolph
24232 Mary Carter Randolph (1797-1857), m. 12/16/1816, Gen. William
  Harvie Richardson (1795-1876) of "Westham", Henrico County,
  son of Maj. George Parke and Frances Bacon Whitlock
  Richardson
242321 Col. William H. Richardson, Jr. (-1/24/1870)
24233 Lucy Anne Randolph (1799-1857), m. Thomas I. West of
  "Bellefield", Henrico County
24234 Elizabeth Meade Randolph (1803-1882), m. Alexander William
  (V.?) Trent of Cumberland
24235 Juliana Randolph (1805-1858), m. 2/1/1827, Thomas Nelson
  Page of "Shelly" (10/5/1792-1835), son of Mann and Elizabeth Nelson Page
242351 Mann Page (4/21/1835-   )
24236 Fanny Peyton Randolph (1811-1867), m. 1827, William Nelson
  Page of "Ca Ira", Cumberland County (2/28/1803-   ),
  son of Maj. Carter and Lucy Nelson Page
24237 Judith Ellen Randolph (1813-1877), m. George Taylor Swann
24238 David Coupland Page Randolph (1804-1888), m. 1857, Harriet
  Randolph Page of "Union Hill", Cumberland County (2441x)
242381 Mary A. Page Randolph (6/5/1860-   )
242382 David Coupland Page Randolph, Jr. (2/14/1865-   ), m.
  Nancy Cartwell
242383 Beverley Heth Page Randolph (6/25/1868-   ), m. 10/25/
  1905, Mary Finley Archer (125111), dau. of William Segar
  and Mary McIlwaine Archer
2423831 Beverley Heth Randolph, Jr. (6/23/1908-   )
2423832 Mary Archer Randolph (2/16/1912-   ), m. Henry Armistead Boyd
24238321 William N. Boyd
24238322 Randolph Boyd
24238323 Henry A. Boyd
2424 Mary Randolph (2/1/1773-1853), m. 3/20/1790, Randolph
  Harrison (2/11/1768*9-9/23/1839), of "Clifton", Cumberland
  County, son of Carter Henry and Susannah Randolph (of
  "Dungeness") Harrison
24241 Thomas Randolph Harrison (2/27/1791-11/12/1833), m. 12/2/
  1812, at Cartersville, Va., Elizabeth Maria Cunningham
  (-1869), dau. of John Cunningham and Mary Burleigh.
  They lived at "Dover", Goochland County
242411 John Cunningham Harrison (1812-   )

242412   Mary Burleigh Harrison (1815-1885). Unm.
242413   William Mortimer Harrison (8/14/1817-1865), m. 1840,
         Caroline Rivers Lambert (1817-1909), dau. of Gen. William
         and Mary Ann Pickett Lambert
2424131 Thomas Randolph Harrison (1/10/1842-8/13/1920), m. 6/20/
         1888, Gertrude Strachan (5/10/1865-   ), dau. of
         Rev. John Alexander Strachan and Emily Ann Adkins
24241311 Emily Randolph Harrison (4/7/1889-   ), m. 4/24/
         1918, Charles Hill Carter (5/1/1868-   ), son of
         Charles and Frances ("Fanny") Page Nelson Carter
242413111 Charles Hill Carter, Jr. (8/16/1919-   ), m. Helle
         Margarethe Klingemann (1933-   ), of Copenhagen
2424131111 Charles Hill Carter III (1962-   )
2424131112 Robert Randolph Carter (1964-   )
2424131113 Harriet Emily Carter (1965-   )
242413112 Gertrude Randolph Carter (9/25/1921-   ), m.
         Madison Macon. They lived in Richmond
242413113 Shirley Harrison Carter (3/29/1929-   ), m. Nancy
         Jane Jones. They live in Charles City County
24241312 William Mortimer Harrison (1/2/1892-   ), m. 7/10/
         1920, Isabel Parker, dau. of Surry Parker and Ida Jane
         Whatley
242413121 William Mortimer Harrison (12/20/1921-   )
242413122 Surry Parker Harrison (3/31/1923-   )
242413123 Isabel Parker Harrison (12/10/1926-   )
2424132 Mary Harrison (2/21/1844-d.s.p.6/28/1918), m. Maj.
         Augustus Harrison Drewry
2424133 William Lambert Harrison (1/8/1846-2/16/1919). Unm.
2424134 John Strobler Harrison (9/8/1850-10/12/1920)
2424135 Edward Cunningham Harrison (6/30/1847-1/31/1908), m.(1st)
         Anna Harrison (218311), dau. of William Allen and Mary
         Thornton Stockdell Harrison. M. (2nd) Sue Ruffin Wilcox,
         dau. of Edmund Ruffin and Mary Cooke Smith
     Children by first wife:
24241351 Edward Mortimer Harrison (1884-   ), m. 1912, Lavinia
         Carter (1881-   ), dau. of Beverley R. and Maria
         Anderson Carter
242413511 Lavinia Carter Harrison (1915-   )
242413512 Edward Mortimer Harrison, Jr. (1920-   )
242413513 Archie Harrison (1922-   )
24241352 Hugh Thornton Harrison (1886-   ), m. 12/1/1908, Grace
         Dorothea Dutro (3/31/1884-   ), dau. of Thomas Corwin
         Dutro
242413521 Dorothea Dutro Harrison (12/29/1909-   ), m. 6/15/
         1933, Lt. Robert E. Van Meter (1905-   ), son of
         Maurice Van Meter
2424135211 Robert Harrison Van Meter (4/14/1934-   )
242413522 Hugh Randolph Harrison (5/27/1915-   )
2424136 Archibald Harrison (1850-3/6/1929)
2424137 Elizabeth ("Lizzie") Cunningham Harrison of "Westover"
         (1852-   ), m. Robert Carter Wellford, son of A. N.
         and Elizabeth Carter Wellford

24241371 Armistead Wellford, m. Katy Davis, dau. of Dabney Davis
24241372 Caroline Wellford
24241373 Robert Carter Wellford II , d.s.p.
24241374 William Harrison Wellford, m. Ida Dulany Beverley, dau.
          of Hill and Rebecca Dulany Beverley. The Wellfords lived
          at "Sabine Hall"
24241375 Elsie Wellford
24241376 John Wellford
2424138   Jane Cary Harrison (6/20/1854-4/18/1909), m. 5/22/1888,
          John Augustine Ruffin of "Evelynton" (2/25/1853-   ),
          son of Edmund and Mary Cooke Smith Ruffin
24241381 Susan Harrison Ruffin (5/5/1889-   ), m. 9/12/1923,
          Lyon Gardiner Tyler of "Sherwood Forest" (8/24/1853-
          2/13/1935), son of John and Julia Gardiner Tyler. His
          first wife, by whom he had issue, was Annie Baker
          Tucker (4/8/1857-11-2/1921), dau. of Henry St. George
          and Elizabeth Gilmer Tucker of Charlottesville
242413811 Lyon Gardiner Tyler, Jr. (1/3/1925-   ), m. Lucy
          Pope
2424138111 Susan Selina Tyler
242413812 Harrison Ruffin Tyler (11/9/1928-   ), m. Frances
          Payne ("Paynie") Bouknight of South Carolina ("Mulberry
          Hill" plantation). The Harrison Ruffin Tylers live at
          "Sherwood Forest"
2424138121 Julia Gardiner Tyler (ca. 1962-   )
2424138122 Harrison Ruffin Tyler, Jr. (ca. 1963-   )
2424138123 William Bouknight Tyler (ca. 1964-   )
242413813 Henry Tyler (1/27/1931-   )
24241382 Caroline Kirkland Ruffin (5/7/1891-   ), m. 11/9/1921,
          Richard Brown Saunders (12/12/1888-   ), son of
          Edmund Archer and Martha Ann Brown Saunders
242413821 Carol Harrison Saunders (11/18/1922-   ), m. George
          Robinette of Ronmount, Pa.
242413822 Martha Brown Saunders (3/15/1924-   ), m.   Roney
          of Silvermine, Conn.
242413823 Richard Ruffin Saunders (3/14/1926-   )
242413824 Edmund Harrison Saunders (11/24/1929-   )
24241383 Mary Harrison Ruffin (8/13/1893-   ), m. 12/21/1924,
          Albert George Copland
242413831 Albert Ruffin Copland (9/19/1925-   )
242413832 John Augustine Ruffin Copland (2/4/1927-   )
242413833 Jane Harrison Copland (7/23/1929-   )
242413834 George Forbes Copland (5/13/1931-   )
242413835 Mary Blackwell Copland
24241384 John Augustine Ruffin, Jr. (8/17/1895-   ), m. 11/6/
          1924, Mary Ball Saunders (5/28/1891-   ), dau. of
          Edmund Archer and Martha Ann Brown Saunders
242413841 Mary Ball Ruffin (3/25/1926-   )
242413842 John Augustine Ruffin III (2/10/1928-   )
242413843 Edmund Saunders Ruffin (1/16/1930-   )
242413844 Martha Saunders Ruffin (4/14/1931-   )
242413845 Archer Harrison Ruffin (1/28/1934-   )

2424139   Caroline Rivers Harrison (1856-   ), m. (1st), Jaquelin
        M. Douthat, son of Robert and Mary Ambler Marshall Douthat.
        M. (2nd), James Pinckney Harrison, son of William Henry
        Harrison and Lucy Anne Powers
24241391 Caroline Rivers Harrison
24241392 William Mortimer Harrison (1893-   ), m. Martha Baker
        Bass
24241393 Wayles Randolph Harrison, m. Sue Lewis Brown
242413931 Caroline Brown Harrison
242413932 Wayles Randolph Harrison, Jr.
242413933 Sue Lewis Harrison
24241394 James Pinckney Harrison, Jr. (1896-   ), m. Nellie
        Atkins Meade (1900-   )
242413941 Ellen Roxane Harrison (1930-   )
242413942 James Pinckney Harrison III (1932-   )
242414 Elizabeth Cunningham Harrison (1819-   ), m. Col.
        Archibald Cary Page. See 24418
242415 Jane Cary Harrison (1821-d.s.p.), m. Rev. Hugh Roy
        Scott, d.s.p.
242416 Edward Cunningham Harrison (3/10/1823-1/1/1854), m. 6/10/
        1848, Sara Roane (-4/28/1874), dau. of Sen.
        William H. Roane and Sara Anne Lyons
2424161 Mary Lyons Harrison (4/16/1849-   ), m. 1/23/187 ,
        Freeman Cady, d.s.p.
2424162 Edward Cunningham Harrison (9/25/1851-1/24/1925), m.
        10/16/1875, Marie Louise Harrison (8/30/1855-   )
        (2424662)
24241621 Edward Cunningham Harrison, Jr. (7/2/1876-   )
24241622 Carter Henry Harrison (12/1/1877-   ), m. 11/23/192 3,
        Alice Ogilvie McLaurin (24246635)
242416221 Carter McLaurin Harrison (2/21/1925-   )
24241623 Sara Roane Harrison (6/14/1879-   ), m. 4/25/1912,
        George Champion Ruffin, Jr. (9/20/1885-   ), son of
        George Champion and Alice Teller Cocke Ruffin
242416231 George Champion Ruffin III (3/11/1913-   ), m.
        6/16/1936, Edith V. Williams
242416232 Edward Harrison Ruffin (9/27/1914-   )
242416233 Marie Louise Ruffin (3/31/1917-   )
242416234 Julien Beckwith Ruffin (6/23/1919-   )
24241624 Channing Williams Harrison (10/14/1882-   ), m. 9/
        17/1917, Rebecca Leigh
24241625 John Williams Harrison (10/5/1889-3/25/1911)
242417 Thomas Randolph Harrison (9/30/1824-10/29/1905), m. 1844,
        Julia Wickham Leigh (3/6/1828-2/23/1916), dau. of Ben-
        jamin Watkins and Julia Wickham Leigh
2424171 Benjamin Watkins Leigh Harrison (9/30/1850-d.s.p.1/15/
        1877)
2424172 Edward Cunningham Harrison (1/25/1852-8/ /1855)
2424173 Chapman Leigh Harrison (1/17/1856-3/13/1925), m. 11/ /
        1880, Mary Ida Nance, dau. of Eaton and Anne Eliza Vaiden
        Nance
24241731 Elizabeth Leigh Harrison (6/18/1883-   )

24241732 Watkins Leigh Harrison (11/22/1884-10/1/1916), m. 12/
          28/1910, Josephine T. Hollahan (7/11/1890-   ),
          dau. of Patrick J. and Julia T. Whelen Hollahan
242417321 Thomas Leigh Harrison (8/21/1915-   )
24241733 Eaton Nance Harrison (10/10/1886-8/30/1892)
24241734 Eliza Cunningham Harrison (1/25/1888-   ), m. 8/3/
          1915, Calvin Hooker Goddard
242417341 Eliza Cunningham Goddard (3/26/1917-   )
242417342 Mary Woodbridge Goddard (12/2/1921-   )
24241735 Thomas Randolph Harrison (1/4/1891-   ), m. 6/27/
          1916, Susie Ruffin Coleman (3/16/1893-   ), dau. of
          Richard Logan and Sarah Powell Coleman
242417351 Thomas Randolph Harrison, Jr. (4/19/1921-   )
242417352 Sarah Powell Harrison (12/7/1925-   )
242417353 Richard Logan Harrison (1/24/1927-   )
24241736 Julia Wickham Harrison (10/1/1893-   ), m. 3/10/
          1915, James Grover McCann (1/28/1886-   ), son of
          Gideon Monroe and Mary Willis Walker McCann
242417361 James Grover McCann, Jr. (1/31/1916-   )
242417362 Wickham Nance McCann (8/27/1917-   )
24241737 Edward Eaton Harrison (1/8/1895- 1961), m. 10/18/1919,
          Kendall Wisegar Lipscomb (8/13/1897- 1942), dau. of
          Willard and Frances Minor Terry Lipscomb
242417371 Edward Eaton Harrison, Jr. (9/6/1920-   )
242417372 Chapman Leigh Harrison (10/2/1925-   )
24241738 Archibald Chapman Harrison (4/5/1898-   ), m. 6/16/
          1925, Mildred Carrington Williams (11/13/1898-   ),
          dau. of Wm. Reid and Caroline Henderson Powell Williams
242417381 Archibald Chapman Harrison, Jr. (5/22/1926-   )
242417382 Caroline Reid Harrison (7/16/1931-   )
24241739 William Nance Harrison (11/27/1900-   ), m. 4/12/
          1924, Lula Banks Richards (12/8/1902-   ), dau. of
          Franklin Thomas and Mary Alice Willis Richards
242417391 Leigh Randolph Harrison (6/12/1929-   )
242417392 Benjamin Willis Harrison (7/16/1933-   )
2424173x Anne Harrison (3/ /1906-   ), m. 10/17/1925, William
          Francis La Porte (4/6/1902-   ), son of Frank Morton
          and Florence M. Daugherty La Porte
2424173x1 Anne Harrison La Porte (7/19/1926-   )
2424173x2 Frances Leigh La Porte (1/23/1932-   )
2424174   Julia Wickham Harrison (1/9/1862-   ), m. 1/18/1887,
          Robert Emmet Richardson (8/15/1854-   ), son of
          Andrew Peyton and Lucy Newsteb Richardson
24241741 Catherine Cary Richardson (12/31/1887-4/7/1892)
24241742 Lucia Peyton Richardson (6/9/1890-5/3/1892)
24241743 Elizabeth Meriwether Richardson (2/11/1893-   ), m.
          7/ /1924, James M. Bowcock
24241744 Thomas Randolph Richardson (3/18/1895-3/6/1933), m.
          12/17/1924, Laura Ann Martindale
242417441 Julia Wickham Richardson (9/19/1928-   )
242417442 Elizabeth Randolph Richardson (5/18/1933-   )
24241745 Julian Leigh Richardson (11/20/1898-   ), m. (1st)
                    . M. (2nd), Clara Day

24241746 Daughter Richardson, twin of above, d. young
24241747 Richard Cunningham Richardson (9/16/1902-   ), m.
          4/ /1930, Meade B. Laird
2424175   Dr. Archibald Cunningham Richardson (1/6/1864-1/17/1926),
          m. 6/15/1892, Anne Elizabeth Warfield (10/31/1865-   )
24241751 Mary Randolph Harrison (3/1/1893-   ), m. 6/15/1920,
          Thomas Donaldson (1891-   ), son of Frederick and
          Sophie Davis Donaldson
242417511 Thomas Donaldson, Jr. (8/4/1921-   )
242417512 Anne Warfield Donaldson (10/3/1924-   )
242417513 Lucy Donaldson (3/30/1926-   )
24241752 Julia Leigh Harrison (5/25/1894-   )
24241753 Alice Cunningham Harrison (12/24/1897-   ), m. 4/25/
          1925, John William Scott, Jr. (1899-   ), son of
          Dr. John William and Caroline Preston Thornton Scott
242417531 Julia Leigh Harrison Scott (3/18/1928-   )
242417532 Caroline Preston Thornton Scott (4/13/1929-   )
242417533 John William Scott III (8/12/1935-   )
242418   Dr. Burleigh Cunningham Harrison (1827-d.s.p. 1886)
242419   Randolph W. Harrison, d. inf.
24241x   Archibald Taylor Harrison (1829-5/5/1889), m. 1/13/1864,
          Mary Montgomery Orgain, dau. of Richard Griffin and
          Martha Edloe Orgain
24241x1   William Allen Harrison (10/16/1864-8/25/1907)
24241x2   Archibald Cary Harrison (8/6/1866-   ), m. 10/20/1897,
          Martha Cary Dew
24241x21 Archibald Cary Harrison, m. Lucy Butler
24241x211 William Allen Harrison
24241x212 Archibald Cary Harrison
24241x22 Page Harrison
24241x23 Elizabeth Dew Harrison
24241x24 Mattie Corbin Harrison, m. G. Hudgins
24241x3   Burleigh Carter Harrison (12/5/1870-   ), m. 12/22/
          1898, Emma W. Shelton
24241x31
24241x32
24241x33
24241x34
24241x35
24241x36
24241x37 ,
24241x38
24241a   Randolph Harrison (1831-1896), m. Eliza Thompson
24241a1   William Mortimer Harrison
24241a2   Lillias Harrison (1863-1934), m. John J. Knapp (1857-1915)
24241a21 John Harrison Knapp (1885-   ), m. 1914, Maitland
          Marshall (2364752)
24241a211 John Marshall Knapp (2/14/1915-4/7/1920)
24241a212 Elizabeth Maitland Knapp (8/19/1917-   )
24241a213 William Marshall Knapp
24241a214 Jaquelin Randolph Knapp
24241a3   Sara (Tazie) Harrison (5/6/1865-8/26/1934), m. Edward
          Walter Eberle, Rear Admiral, U.S.N., (8/17/1864-7/16/1929)

24241a31 Edward Randolph Eberle (1890-1935), m. Mildred North
24241a311 Edward Randolph Eberle, Jr. (7/25/1917-   )
24241a312 Mildred Randolph Eberle (7/25/1920-   )
24241a4 Thomas Randolph Harrison
24241a5 Randolph Harrison
24241a6 McPherson Harrison
24242 Jane Cary Harrison (2/9/1797-11/28/1883), m. 1820, William
       Fitzhugh Randolph (24153)
24243 Archibald Morgan Harrison (9/6/1794-3/17/1842), m. (1st)
       2/27/1817, Catharine ("Kitty") Heth, dau. of Capt. Henry
       ("Harry") and Nancy Hare Heth. M. (2nd) 11/22/1837,
       Euphania Claiborne ("Fanny") Taylor (7/27/1819-7/10/
       1897), dau. of Thomas and Lucy Harrison Singleton Taylor
    Children by first wife:
242431 Henry Heth Harrison (2/15/1820-   ), m. Sarah Frazer,
       dau. of James Frazer and Elizabeth Frazer
2424311 Catharine Heth Harrison. Unm.
2424312 Margaret Carter Harrison. Unm.
242432 Lavinia Beverley Harrison (7/11/1827-9/14/1902), m. 12/7/
       1848, Dr. Richard Kidder Taylor (1/20/1826-1/6/1905),
       son of Thomas Taylor and Luch Harrison Singleton
2424321 Kate Heth Taylor (7/20/1852-2/28/1928), m. 12/11/1878,
       Dabney B. Stephens
24243211 Gertrude H. Stephens (9/30/1882-8/16/1926), m. 10/10/
       1907, Roy G. Miller
242432111 Katharine E. Miller (10/21/1908-   ), m. 9/3/1931,
       Alvin W. Oehler
242432112 Roy G. Miller, Jr. (3/24/1913-   ), m. 10/25/1934,
       Helen Kean
24243212 John S. Stephens (5/27/1885-   ), m. 5/24/1914, Nadine
       May
2424322 Fannie Ellis Taylor (3/15/1854-d. young)
2424323 Lizzie Robertson Taylor, d. inf.
2424324 Lavinia Beverley Taylor, d. inf.
2424325 Mollie Orgain Taylor, d. inf.
2424326 Lucy Harrison Taylor (10/8/1863-   ), m. 1/17/1888,
       John S. Kennedy
2424327 Virginia Randolph Taylor (12/10/1865-10/6/1925). Unm.
2424328 Warner Gibson Taylor (1/29/1868-   ), m. 5/26/1904,
       Eva Grant
24243281 Warner Gibson Taylor, Jr. (11/3/1905-   ), m. 12/
       28/1929, Emma Osmun
2424329 Harry Heth Taylor (12/19/1872-d.s.p.7/30/1934)
242433 Catharine ("Kitty") Heth Harrison (1889-   ), m. 1854,
       Prof. Robert Morrison
2424331 Ellis Morrison, m. Margaret Guy
24243311 Kate Morrison
24243312 Berta Morrison
2424332 Berta Morrison, m. James R. Micou
242434 Randolph Harrison (5/30/1825-5/30/1825)
24244 Rev. Peyton Randolph Harrison (11/19/1800-1887), m. (1st)
       1825, Jane Cary Carr (1809-1858), dau. of Dabney and
       Elizabeth Carr. M. (2nd) 1863, Ellen M. Smith

242441   Elizabeth Carr Harrison (1826-1847), m. Rev. J. M. P. Atkinson
242442   Randolph Harrison, M.D. (1829-1863), m. Rosalie Freeland
2424421   Child (-1863)
242443   Rev. Dabney Carr Harrison (1830-1862), m. 1855, Sally Pendleton Buchanan
2424431   Jane Carr Harrison (1856-1864)
2424432   Dabney Carr Harrison (1858-   ), m. 1899, Ellen Robinson Riley
24244321   William Riley Harrison (1900-1924)
24244322   Dabney Carr Harrison (1906-   )
2424433   Nannie Spotswood D. Harrison (1860-1898)
242444   Peyton Randolph Harrison (1832-1861), Lt. C.S.A., killed Battle Manassas, m. 1854, Sarah Forrest Hunter (1933-1926)
2424441   Jane Cary Harrison (1856-1928), m. 1881, Rev. Edward Davis Washburn
24244411   Edward Davis Washburn
24244412   Peyton Washburn
24244413   Emory Washburn
2424442   Edmund Pendleton Harrison, m. Caroline Henderson
24244421   Sarah Hunter Webster Harrison (1893-   )
24244422   Carolyn Webster Harrison (1897-   )
24244423   Edmund Pendleton Harrison, M. D. (1900-   )
2424443   Peyton Randolph Harrison, m. (1st), Lillian Gorham. M. (2nd), Nannie Spotswood Byrd
       Children by first wife:
24244431   Lillian Gorham Harrison, m. 1912, Forrest Augustus Brown
242444311   Sarah Harrison Brown
242444312   Forrest Washington Brown
242444313   Peyton Randolph Brown
242444314   David Hunter Brown
242444315   Lillian Gorham Brown
       Children by second wife:
24244432   Holmes Boyd Harrison (1899-1911)
24244433   Peyton Randolph Harrison (1905-   )
24244434   Ann Spotswood Harrison (1909-   )
242445   Virginia Randolph Harrison (1833-1895), m. 1855, Rev. William James Hoge (1825-1864)
2424451   Mary Swift Hoge (1855-   ), m. 1880, Rev. DeLacey Wardlaw, son of T. DeLacey Wardlaw and Sarah Louise Fisher
24244511   Virginia Randolph Wardlaw (8/1/1881-   ), 5/5/1908, James Williams Adamson
242445111   Mary Virginia Adamson (7/6/1910-   ), m. 6/20/1933, Charles Edouard Howriet
242445112   Jessie Bruxton Adamson (7/14/1912-   )
242445113   George DeLacey Adamson (5/16/1914-9/9/1915)
242445114   Elizabeth Randolph Adamson (1/12/1917-   )
24244512   Blanche Lewis Wardlaw (8/6/1883-   ), m. 12/28/1909, Frank Reeves Webb
24244513   Mary Louise Wardlaw (6/4/1886-   ), m. 8/22/1912, William McKeon Thomson

```
242445131   Donald Wardlaw Thomson (7/8/1913-      )
242445132   DeLacey Alexander Thomson (8/5/1914-      )
242445133   William McKeon Thomson (6/27/1916-     )
242445134   Addison Hoge Thomson (3/1/1918-     )
242445135   Randolph Murray Thomson (10/6/1921-     )
242445136   David McKeon Thomson (9/5/1928-     )
24244514   Caroline Cunningham Wardlaw (7/19/1891-        ), m. 9/15/
            1920, John Jay Naugle
242445141   John Jay Naugle, Jr.. (11/9/1922-      )
242445143   Frederick Barent Naugle (3/6/1924-     )
242445144   Thomas DeLacey Wardlaw Naugle (9/10/1929-     )
2424452   Rev. Peyton Harrison Hoge (1/6/1858-       ), m. 8/22/
          1883, Mary Stuart Holladay (219311)
24244521   Virginia Randolph Bolling Hoge (1/8/1884-        ), m.
           8/9/1906, Emidio San Germano
242445211   Mary Randolph San Germano (6/7/1907-      ), m. 10/23/
            1926, Warwick M. Anderson
2424452111  Mary Stuart Anderson (9/14/1927-      )
24244522   William Lacey Hoge (11/25/1885-       ), m.  6/9/1914,
           Emily Tryon Mengel
242445221   Emily Tryon Hoge (2/6/1916-      )
242445222   Mary Holladay Hoge (11/21/1917-      )
242445223   William Lacey Hoge, Jr. (12/13/1922-       )
24244523   Mary Stuart Hoge (2/21/1887-       ), m. 4/29/1909,
           George Harrison Houston
242445231   Peyton Hoge Houston (12/20/1910-      )
242445232   George Harrison Houston (9/29/1914-      )
242445233   Mary Stuart Houston (10/29/1918-     )
24244524   Peyton Harrison Hoge (1/28/1889-      ), m. 4/17/1913,
           Blanche Weissinger Smith
242445241   Peyton Harrison Hoge (4/17/1914-      )
242445242   Nell Hunt Hoge (1/20/1920-     )
24244525   Elizabeth Addison Hoge (8/13/1897-        ), m. 10/22/
           1913, Edmund Taylor Meriwether
242445251   Elizabeth Meriwether (3/7/1915-       )
242445252   Mary Hoge Meriwether (10/4/1921-     )
24244526   Evelyn Cary Hoge (8/13/1897-      ), m. 5/18/1921,
           George Jackson Mead
242445261   George Nathaniel Jackson Mead (11/30/1922-      )
242445262   Mary Randolph Mead (1/2/1925-     )
242445263   Peyton Hoge Mead (9/7/1927-     )
242446   William Wirt Harrison (1837-      ), m. 1859, Emily
         Taylor
2424461   Emily Harrison (1860-     )
2424462   Wythe Harrison (1861-     )
2424463   Peyton Harrison
2424464   Randolph Harrison
2424465   Lucy Harrison
2424466   Taylor Harrison
2424467   William Harrison
242447   Mary Clifton Harrison (1839-1862), m. Robert W. Hunter
242448   Nancy Addison Harrison (1841-1862)
242449   Henry St. George Tucker Harrison (1844-1914), m. 1877,
         Marion Maxwell Jenifer (1855-      )
```

2424491 Peyton Randolph Harrison (1878-   ), m. 1915, Elsie
         Adkins Corbin
24244911 Ann Randolph Harrison (1918-   )
2424492 Daniel Jenifer Harrison (1880-   ), m. 1913, Virginia
         Meade
24244921 Daniel Jenifer Harrison (1915-   )
2424493 Bessie Jenifer Harrison (1882-   ), 1910, John R.
         Caulk
24244931 John R. Caulk (1913-   )
24244932 Marion Elizabeth Caulk (1914-   )
2424494 Dabney Carr Harrison (1884-   ), m. 1921, Mary Marbury
24244941 Dabney Carr Harrison (1922-   )
24244942 Courtenay Jenifer Harrison (1925-   )
2424495 Emily Clifton Harrison (1888-   )
2424496 Charlotte Lisle Harrison (1890-   )
2424497 Henry Tucker Harrison (1892-   ), m. 1924, Leola
         McCullers
24244971 Trilby Jenifer Harrison (1925-   )
24244972 Henry Tucker Harrison (1928-   )
2424498 Campbell Jenifer Harrison (1893-   )
2424499 Lillie Tripp Harrison (1894-   )
242449x Ruth Ellen Harrison (1898-   )
24244x Williana Irving Harrison (1847-   ), m. J. Lisle Turn-
         bull
24244x1 Janet Graeme Turnbull
24244x2 Graeme Turnbull
24244x3 Rosalie Randolph Turnbull (1879-   ), m. 1902, Alexander
         Winchester Carroll
24244x31 Anne Harrison Carroll (1903-   )
         Children by second wife:
24244a Samuel Graeme Harrison, m. Alice Marquand
24244a1 Samuel Graeme Harrison, Jr.
24244a2 Randolph Harrison
24244a3 Ellen Harrison
24245 Randolph Harrison, Jr. of "Glentivar", Cumberland County
         (2/27/1796 or 9-1844), m. 9/6/1821, Henningham Carrington
         Wills (1801-1864), married at "Wilton", Logan County,
         Kentucky. Both bur. at "Clifton", Cumberland County
242451 Elizabeth Harrison (3/1/1823-4/ /1861), m. 11/ /1847,
         Alexander B. Gordon of Baltimore, son of Samuel and
         Susannah Fitzhugh Knox Gordon
2424511 Randolph Harrison Gordon (10/2/1848-12/10/1915)
2424512 Henningham Gordon, son (2/3/1852-12/8/1920)
2424513 Margaret Gordon (11/18/1850-d.s.p. 12/10/1925)
2424514 Emily Gordon (7/20/1855-8/19/1901), m. 12/31/1877,
         Admiral Thomas McLean (10/25/1849-   ), son of
         Charles and Anne Tilden Waters McLean
24245141 Elizabeth Harrison McLean (4/14/1879-   )
24245142 Charles McLean (7/20/1881-10/3/1903)
24245143 Emily Gordon McLean (8/ /1887-   )
24245144 Anne Waters McLean (2/24/1893-   ), m. 6/3/1917),
         Nathaniel Edward Griffin

242451441 Nathaniel Edward Griffin (4/2/1921-   )
242451442 Thomas McLean Griffin (9/10/1924-   )
2424515 Nicholas Gordon
242452 Anne Louisa Harrison (1829-1905), m. Alexander Burton Hagner
         (1826-1915) of Annapolis
242453 Julien Harrison (2/6/1827-3/31/1865) of "Millview", Gooch-
         land County, m. 6/7/1849, Lavinia Beverley Heth (3/31/
         1827-   ), dau. of John and Margaret L. Pickett
         Heth. M. (2nd) 1866, Elizabeth ("Lilly") Johnston
         (7/9/1845-   ), dau. of Stephen and Elizabeth
         Anderson Johnston
      Children by first wife:
2424531 Heth Harrison (1850-d.s.p.)
2424532 Frances Cadwallader Harrison (1/12/1850*52-6/20/1916),
         m. 1/12/1875, William Maury Hill (3/30/1848-1/3/1918),
         son of Lewis and Mary Elizabeth Maury Hill
24245321 Mary M. Hill
24245322 Julien H. Hill
24245323 Lilly H. Hill
24245324 William M. Hill
24245325 Mildred Hill
2424533 Louisa Hagner Harrison (4/19/1854-d. young), d.s.p.
2424534 Julien Harrison (2/11/1856-   ), d.s.p.
2424535 Virginia C. Harrison (1/26/1861-6/20/1932), m. 10/ /1891,
         W. E. Addison
24245351 Julien H. Addison, m. Isabelle Sanderson
242453511 Virginia Harrison Addison
2424536 Walter Harrison (3/1/1863-   ), d.s.p.
      Children by second wife:
2424537 Beverley Randolph Harrison (2/9/1865-   ), m. Mary
         Berry
24245371 Taylor Harrison
24245372 Fannie B. Harrison, m.   Webster
24245373 Rosalie Harrison, m.   Mahone
24245374 Julien Harrison
24245375 Lilly Harrison
      Children by second wife:
2424538 Hebe Harrison (7/7/1867-   ), m. (1st) 1888, Upton
         Muir (1863-   ). M. (2nd), Louis E. McComas. M.
         (3rd) 4/22/1922, Cary Talcott Hutchinson (1866-   )
         (2421871)
      Children by first husband:
24245381 Elizabeth Harrison Muir, m. (1st), William Waters. M.
         (2nd) Charles Lee of Coral Gables
242453811 Hebe Harrison Waters (7/17/1917-   )
242453812 Elizabeth Darragh Waters (5/1/1919-   )
24245382 Peter Upton Muir (1/3/1898-   )
2424539 Elizabeth Harrison (6/29/1869-5/30/1921), m. 3/ /1898,
         John Watts Kearny (1845-1933), and was his second wife
24245391 Elizabeth Anderson Kearny (1899-   ), m. Ford Hibbard
24245392 Peter B. Kearny
242453x Peyton Randolph Harrison (3/3/1873-4/15/1926), m. 1903,
         Louise Thomas Wheat (1880-   ) of New Jersey

242453x1   Julien Harrison (1905-   ) of Cleveland
242453x2   Ann Harrison (1905-   ), m. 4/26/1930, Edward Moody
           Seay (1900-   )
242453a   Alexander Hagner Harrison (1873-   ), d. inf.
242453b   Bernard Johnston Harrison (1/31/1875-   ), m. 6/19/1901,
           Jane Dashiell Randolph (3/13/1876-   ), dau. of John
           Field and Virginia Dashiell Bayard Randolph
242453b1   John Randolph Harrison (3/15/1905-   ), m. (1st)
           11/30/1929, Emily B. McFadden. M. (2nd) Elizabeth
           Buckner Cary
242453b11 Josephine C. Harrison (9/30/1930-   ), m.   Evarts
242453b111
242453b112
242453b113
242453b114
242453b115
242453b12 Randolph Harrison (5/28/1932-   ), m.
242453b121 Randolph Harrison, Jr.
242453b122 Alexander Harrison
242453b123 Elsie Harrison
242453b13 Carter Henry Harrison (6/ /1935-   )
242453b2   Bernard Johnston Harrison, Jr. (12/16/1907-   ), m.
           9/13/1930, Martha B. Kountz
242453b21 Carter H. Harrison
242453b22 Peyton R. Harrison
242453b23 Virginia Harrison
242454   Randolph Harrison III (1831-1894) of "Elk Hill", Goochland
         County, m. 1853, at Christ Church Norfolk, Elizabeth Gate-
         wood Williamson (1835-1918) of Norfolk
2424541 Randolph Harrison IV (1854-1907) of "Elk Hill", m. 1880,
         Mary Ann Troup (1861-1897) of Portland, Oregon. He is
         bur. in Cedar Grove Cemetery, Williamsburg, and she is
         bur. in the family plot of the Masonic Cemetery at
         Vancouver, Wash.
24245411 Elizabeth Cary Harrison (1884-d. at age 14 in Portland,
          Ore.)
24245412 Mary Louise Harrison (1887-1950) of Dallas, Tex., m.
          1921, Thomas Hugh Mercer. Bot are bur. in Cedar Grove
          Cemetery
242454121 Elizabeth Harrison Mercer (1924-   ) of Houston,
           Tex., m. John Hart Chess and lived in Williamsburg
2424541211 John Hart Chess, Jr., m. Marcia
24245412111 Theresa Chess (1975-   )
24245412112 Son
242454122 Jean Bright Mercer (1927-   ) of Dallas, Tex., m.
           in Dallas, Charles Clayton Sorrells
2424541221 Becky Ann Sorrells, m. 1975, Charles Francis Payne,
            Jr., and lived in Dallas, Tex.
2424541222 Mary Lucille Sorrells, m. 1973, Dr. Joe Glickman, Jr.
            and lived in Dallas, Tex. and had two children
24245412221
24245412222

24245413 Virginia Troup Harrison of Portland, Ore. (1890-1973),
          m. 1913, Charles Sea Floyd (1889-1927) of Severance,
          Kansas. He d. in Berkeley, Calif., and is bur. in
          Ashland Cemetery, St. Joseph, Mo. She is bur. at
          Sunset View Cemetery, El Cerrito, Calif.
242454131 Charles Harrison Floyd (1914-   ) of Washington, D.C.
242454132 Mary Randolph Floyd (1918-1937) of West Point, N.Y. is
          bur. in Berkeley, Calif. She m. 1940, Benjamin Frank-
          lyn Kegg (1919-   ) of Carson City, Nev.
2424541321 Marilyn Randolph Kegg (1941-   ), m. 1962, at
          Oakland, Calif., John Fincher Hart (1937-   ) of
          Amarillo, Tex. Div. 1973. She m. (2nd) Steiner
          Pedersen
          Children by first husband:
24245413211 Christopher Harrison Hart (1964-   ) Oakland,
          Calif.
24245413212 Karen Anne Hart (1965-   ) Walnut Creek, Calif.
          Wendy Lynne Hart (1967-   ) Thu Duc, S. Vietnam
          (adopted)
2424541322 Robert Franklyn Kegg (1946-1959) of Berkeley and San
          Francisco, Calif.
2424541323 Terry Harrison Kegg (1956-   ) of Berkeley, Calif,
          m. 1978, Rhonda Lee Davidson (1957-   ) of Oakland,
          Calif.
2424541324 Christy Ann Kegg (1961-   )of Berkeley, Calif.
2424542   Mary Galt Harrison (1855-1913), m. (1st) Gordon Webb of
          N.Y. M. (2nd) 1885, William Hartwell Macon of Hanover
          Co. (1852-   ). She is bur. in Cedar Grove
          Cemetery, Williamsburg
          Children by first husband:
24245421 Louisa Alexander Webb (1877-1880)
24245422 Susan Gordon Webb (1879-1952) of "Hampstead" New Kent
          Co., m. (1st) Dr. John Blair Spencer (1906-   ).
          M. (2nd) Admiral Leigh Noyes
          Children by first husband:
242454221 Margaret Gordon Spencer, m. Seymour St. John, former
          Head Master of Choate School, and lives in Florida and
          Rhode Island
242454222 Mary Webb Spencer (-1973), m. Edward Dissette,
          U.S.N.
2424542221 Blair Spencer Dissette, M.D., m. George Jamarik and
          lives at Round Hill
24245422211 James Leigh Dissette Jamarik, m. Deborah
242454222111 Tobias Spencer Dissetts Jamarik (1977-   )
          Children by second husband:
24245423 William Hartwell Macon (1886-   ) of "Clover Lea"
          Hanover County, d. inf.
24245424 Randolph Harrison Macon (1887-1971) born at "Clover Lea"
          and d. in St. Louis, Mo.
242454241 Jane Macon, m. J. M. Schnarr and lived in Richmond
          Heights, Mo.
242454242 William Hartwell Macon III of St. Louis, Mo.

24245425   Nora Criena Macon (1889-   ) of Farmington
24245426   Helen Stanley Gordon Macon (1892-1893)
24245427   Elizabeth Randolph Macon (1895-1939) of Williamsburg
2424543   Thomas Gatewood Harrison (1857-1857)
2424544   Gabriel Williamson Harrison (1858-1899) of "Elk Hill",
           m. 1889, Sarah ("Sallie") Webb Burrus of New Kent Co.
           (1857-1948)
24245441   Randolph Williamson Harrison (1889-1946), m. 1915,
           Carrie Esther Clements (1895-1936)
242454411 Esther Gordon Harrison (1917-   ), m. Elliot Logan
           Hovel (1912-   ) of San Antonio, Tex.
2424544111 Richard Elliot Hovel (1946-   ), m. 1968, Karma
           Kidd
24245441111 William Richard Hovel
24245441112 Lacy Elyse Hovel
2424544112 Dorothy Auverne Hovel (1949-   ), m. 1973, William
           J. Watkins
24245441121 David Preston Watkins
24245441122 Lisa Brandon Watkins
24245442   Carter Beverley Harrison (1890-   )
24245443   Sarah (Sadie) Webb Harrison (1892-1979), m. Judge William
           J. Parker of Norfolk, Va.
242454431 Gabrielle Harrison Parker, m. J. William Hubbard, Jr.,
           and lives in Charleston, W. Va.
2424545   Carolin (Cary) Heth Harrison (1859-1906) of "Elk Hill",
           Goochland Co., m. in Portland, Ore., Sallie Belle Stroud
           (1862-1948)
24245451   Clifford Cary Harrison (1890-1965) of Portland, Ore., m.
           (1st) Harriet Hulett. M. (2nd) Alta
24245452   Annie Jordan Harrison (1892-1972) of Portland, Ore., m.
           1918, Willis Glaze Telfer (1884-1957) of Wisconsin
242454521 Sara Anne Telfer (1919-   ), m. 1942, Joseph F.
           Bunnett (1921-   )
2424545211 Alfred Boulan Bunnett (1946-   ) Portland, Ore.,
           m. 1970, Nancy Hubbell of Downers Grove, Ill.
24245452111 Samuel Harrison Bunnett (1982-   ) Minneapolis,
           MN
24245452121 William Alexander Bunnett (1981-   ) Pt. Reyes
           Station, Calif.
2424545212 David Telfer Bunnett (1948-   ) Portland, Ore., m.
           1978, Wendy Friefeld of Point Reyes Station, Calif.
2424545213 Peter Silvester Bunnett (1951-1972) Portland, Ore.
242454522 Lelia Randolph Telfer (1921-   ) Oakland, Calif.,
           m. (1st) Ray Heath. Div. M. (2nd) Cameron Pearson of
           Portland, Ore.
           Children by first husband:
2424545221 Charles Heath (1953-   ) Portland, Ore.
2424545222 Cary Ellen Heath (1955-   ) Portland, Ore.
242454523 William Harrison Telfer (1924-   ) of Seattle,
           Wash., m. 1950, Mary Andrus (1923-   ) of Orange,
           N.J.
2424545231 Sally Telfer (1954-   ) of Philadelphia, Pa.,
           m. 1977, Yutaka Matsuura Ishizaka

2424545232 Abby Telfer (1958-   ) of Bryn Mawr, Pa.
2424546 Lelia Beverley Harrison (1860-1931), m. 1887, Edmund
         Ruffin of "Weyanoke", Hanover Co.
24245461 Anne Harrison Ruffin (1889-   ) of Richmond, Va.
24245462 Randolph Ruffin (-1976?)
24245463 Roulac Ruffin (1901-1961) in Norfolk
24245464 Lelia Beverley Ruffin (1903-   )
2424547 Carter Beverley Harrison (1861-ca. 1915), m. 1892, Carrie
         Sumter Stowe of Lenoir, N.C.
24245471 Elizabeth Gatewood Harrison (1895-1922), m. Joseph C.
          Blaisdell, Jr. and lived in Des Lacs, N. Dak.
242454711 Elizabeth Harrison Blaisdell
24245472 Sarah Stowe Harrison (1897-1970), m. Yancey D. Moore
242454721 Harriet Sumter Moore, m. Gordon Lee Lipscomb
2424547211 Sarah Harrison Lipscomb
2424547212 Hester Johnstone Lipscomb
2424547213 Gordon Lipscomb
242454722 Beverley Lipscomb, m. Grady Pearson
2424547221 Jan Pearson
242454723 Ann Randolph Lipscomb, m. James Helms
2424547231 Allison Randolph Helms
2424547232 Elizabeth Helms
24245473 Mary Hartley Harrison, m. Roger Wilson
242454731 Dau.
24245474 Louisa Harrison (-1970), m. John Davis
          Cary Venable Davis (adopted)
24245475 Cary Garnett Harrison (1898-   ). Unm.
24245476 Charlotte Randolph Harrison, m. Weaver Myers and lives
          near Washington, D. C.
2424548 Elizabeth Randolph Harrison (1864-1865)
2424549 Elizabeth Williamson Harrison (1866-1866)
242454x Robert Tunstall Harrison (1867-c. 1921). Unm.
242454a Henningham Harrison (1869-   ), m. (1st) Elizabeth
         Charles. M. (2nd)   Binns. In 1894, he was living
         in Caperton, W. Va. He was bur. in Cedar Grove Cemetery,
         Williamsburg, Va.
242454a1 Gabriella Galt Harrison (ca. 1915-   )
242455 William Morton (Mortimer?) Harrison (1825-1826)
242456 Mary Randolph ("Polly") Harrison (1826-1834)
242457 Henningham Harrison (1828-1829)
24246 Carter Henry Harrison (8/28/1792-10/ /1843), m. 1/16/1819,
       Janetta Fisher, dau. of George and Ann Ambler Fisher.
       Harrison was b. at "Glenlivar", Cumberland County. The
       Harrison's four eldest children were b. in Richmond
242461 Henry Harrison (1823-   ), m. 1844, Jane St. Clair
        Cochrane (1821-1870)
2424611 Carter Henry Harrison, Jr. (1831-1917), m. 1896, Katherine
         Cooke Duval (211524). No issue. He was b. at "Eastwood"
2424612 Judge George M. Harrison (-1910), m. 1874, Betty
         Kent
24246121 Fannie Harrison, m. James Quarles
242461211 Caroline Quarles
242461212 Francis Quarles

24246122 J. Kent Harrison, m. Cornelia Summerville
242461221 Joseph Kent Harrison, Jr.
242461222 Billy Kent Harrison
24246123 Rose H. Harrison, m. Clarke Worthington
2424613 Dr. Jaquelin Ambler Harrison (-1874), m. Ella Gold
2424614 Henry Harrison (-1899). Unm.
2424615 William Boyd Harrison, m. Janet Withers
24246151 Clara Harrison, m. Lt. W. N. Edwards, U.S.N.
2424616 Maria Boyd Harrison (1853-1870)
2424617 Janetta Harrison, m. Thomas D. Ranson
24246171 Thomas D. Ranson
24246172 Margaret Randolph Ranson
24246173 Henry Harrison Ranson
2424618 Rose St. Clair Harrison, m. (1st), Dr. B. R. Ranson. M.
          (2nd), Carter Page Johnson
2424619 Randolph Harrison (1/25/1858-2/16/1928), m. 11/17/1897,
          Julia Halsey Meem (9/4/1876-   ), dau. of John G.
          and Aurelia Halsey Meem
24246191 Randolph Harrison, Jr. (11/24/1897-   )
24246192 Jaquelin Ambler Harrison (7/1/1900-5/5/1902)
24246193 Aurelia Halsey Harrison (3/5/1905-   )
24246194 Julia Meem Harrison (6/28/1906-   ), m. 10/24/1931,
          Dr. James Winston Watts
242461x Edward C. Harrison, m. Mrs. Grace Leonard
242461a Margaret Harrison (-1892). Unm.
242461b Beverley Randolph Harrison, m. Laura Tafft
242461b1 Beverley Randolph Harrison, Jr.
242461b2 Carter H. Harrison
242461b3 Edward C. Harrison
242462 Elizabeth ("Betsy") Ambler Harrison, m. William H. Fitzhugh.
          See 242463. Betsy was b. at "Eastwood"
2424621 Betty Fitzhugh, m. John W. Daniel
242463 Mary Ann (Marianna?) Harrison (4/26/1839-   ), m.
          William H. Fitzhugh. See 242462. Mary Ann was b. at
          "Clifton"
2424631 William Fitzhugh
2424632 Carter Fitzhugh, m. Isabella Scribner
2424633 Thomas Fitzhugh
2424634 Nannie Fitzhugh
2424635 Alice Fitzhugh
2424636 Mary Fitzhugh
2424637 Nannie Fitzhugh
2424638 Edmonia Fitzhugh
2424639 Alexander Fitzhugh
242464 Edward Jaquelin Harrison (1824-1897), m. (1st), Betty
          Conrad. M. (2nd), Sally Powell. M. (3rd) Susan Mathews
          Ficklin
      Children by second wife:
2424641 Julia Randolph Harrison, m. Ambrose Ford
24246411 George Ford
24246412 Sally Ford
24246413 Gertrude Ford
2424642 Edward Jaquelin Harrison, m. (1st), Irene Anderson. M.
          (2nd), Jane Thompson

```
24246421   Jaquelin Ambler Harrison, m. Amandus H. Sharbaugh
242464211  Amandus Sharbaugh, Jr.
24246422   Courtland Harrison, m. Leola Snodgrass
242464221  Kathleen Virginia Harrison
242464222  Theodore Courtland Harrison
24246423   Virginia Harrison, d. inf.
24246424   Adele Harrison, d. inf.
           Children by second wife:
24246425   Harry St. George Tucker Harrison,m. Carroll Winifred
           Duval
24246426   Carter Henry Harrison
24246427   Edward Jaquelin Harrison
24246428   Janie Judith Harrison
24246429   Hildreth Vernon Harrison
2424642x   Elizabeth Powell Harrison
2424642a   Edmund Randolph Harrison
2424643    Raleigh Colston Harrison
2424644    Powell Brooke Harrison, m. Angeline Bacon Gomillion
24246441   Mary Spann Harrison, m. James Morgan Cullum
242464411  James Morgan Cullum, d. inf.
242464412  Angeline Harrison Cullum
24246442   Caroline Virginia Harrison
24246443   Powell Brooke Harrison, m. Nell Bickham
242464431  Powell Brooke Harrison
242464432  Mary Elizabeth Harrison
24246444   Annie Randolph Holmes Harrison, m. Oliver Perry Lightsey
2424645    Annie Holmes Harrison, m. Joseph S. Payne
24246451   Julia Mosby Payne, m. William Nance
242464511  Louise Wyatt Nance
242464512  Julia Payne Nance
24246452   Marie Powell Payne, m. Thomas D. Neal, Jr.
242464521  Thomas D. Neal, Jr.
242464522  Randolph Harrison Neal
24246453   Joseph S. Payne, m. Rachel Irwin
242464531  Joseph Samuel Payne
242464532  Ruth Irwin Payne
24246454   Jaquelin Harrison Payne, m. Katherine De Mott
242464541  Katherine De Mott Payne, d. inf.
242464542  Jaquelin Harrison Payne
24246455   William Overton Payne, m. Rachel Shepherd
24246456   Annie Holmes Payne, m. Gordon Barbour Ambler
242464561  Gordon Barbour Ambler, Jr.
           Children by third wife of 242464:
2424646    James Burwell Harrison, m. Isabella Wright Clarke
24246461   Isabella Harrison
24246462   William Wright Harrison
2424647    Henry Jaquelin Harrison
2424648    Bessie Ambler Harrison, m. James Overton Winston
24246481   William Alexander Winston
24246482   James Overton Winston
24246483   Jaquelin Ambler Harrison Winston
24246484   Randolph Harrison Winston
2424649    Katharine Davenport Harrison, m. James Thomas Rodgers
```

24246491 Benjamin Harrison Rodgers
242465 Capt. George Fisher Harrison, C.S.A. (1821-   ), m. (1st)
     Sally   . M. (2nd) Rebecca Conrad. M. (3rd) Mrs.
     Susan Mathews. M. (4th) Eula Holmes
       Children by first wife:
2424651 Janetta Harrison, m. W. H. P. Morris
2424652 George Harrison, m. Clara Skelton
2424653 John Harrison, m. Mary Wingfield
       Children by second wife:
2424654 Bessie Harrison, m. C. V. Cavitt
2424655 Holmes Harrison
2424656 Sallie Harrison
2424657 Nannie Harrison, m. B. T. Turner
2424658 Rebecca Harrison
2424659 Mary Harrison
242465x Henrietta Harrison
242465a Birdie Harrison
242465b Susie Harrison
       Child by fourth wife:
242465c Louisa P. Harrison
242466 Carter Henry Harrison, Jr. (1831-   ), m. Alice Burwell
     Williams
2424661 Carter Harrison, m. Byrd Swift
24246611 Fred Harrison
24246612 Alice Harrison
24246613 Eloise Harrison
24246614 Mary Harrison
2424662 Marie Louise Harrison, m. Edward Cunningham Harrison
     (2424162)
2424663 Elizabeth Ambler Harrison, m. Marcellus Foute McLaurin
24246631 John McLaurin
24246632 Harrison McLaurin
24246633 King McLaurin
24246634 Carter McLaurin
24246635 Alice Ogilvie McLaurin, m. Carter Henry Harrison (24241622)
2424664 John W. Harrison, m. May K. Willson
24246641 Eliza Harrison
24246642 Randolph Harrison
24246643 Alpheus E. W. Harrison
242467 Randolph Harrison (1820-   )
24247 Mary Randolph ("Polly") Harrison (1804-1857), m. 1st wife
     of William Byrd Harrison of "Upper Brandon", son of Ben-
     jamin Harrison and Betsy Page. See 241426
242471 Randolph Harrison of "Ampthill", Cumberland County, m.
     Harriet Heilman
242472 Benjamin Harrison Harrison, m. Mary ("Polly") Randolph
     Page (242491)(1830-   ), dau. of Nelson and Lucie
     Cary Harrison Page. The Harrisons lived at "The Rowe",
     Charles City County
2424721 William Byrd Harrison II (9/8/1853-4/12/1927), m. 10/19/
     1886, Evelina Bolling Garrett (11/22/1850-4/18/1917),
     dau. of John Bolling and Nannie Harrison Garrett. For
     their children, see 122111

2424722 Lucia Cary Harrison (1856-1898), m. Edmund Randolph Cocke, son of William Armistead and Elizabeth Randolph Preston Cocke. Lucia was Edmund's second wife.

2424723 Benjamin Harrison Harrison, Jr. (1858-1911) of "Upper Brandon", m. 1902, Mattie Cary Nelson (1882-   ), dau. of Thomas Carter and Mary Walker Nelson of Charles City County

24247231 Benjamin Harrison Harrison III (1903-   ) of "The Rowe", m. 1936, Margaret Elizabeth Redwood of Richmond, d.s.p.

24247232 Randolph Page Harrison (1905-   )

24247233 Mann Page Harrison (1911-   ), m. 1944, Kathleen Kennon (1914-   ) of County Down, Ireland

242472331 Brian David Harrison (1945-   ) of Exeter, Devon, England

2424724 Nelson Page Harrison (1855-1855)

242473 Charles Shirley Harrison, d.s.p.

242474 Dr. George Byrd Harrison, m. 1876, Jane Wenthall Stone, dau. of Dr. Robert Stone

2424741 William Evelyn Harrison (1877-1909)

2424742 Margaret Ritchie Harrison, m. 1/22/1920, Edmund Randolph Cocke (8/4/1884-   ), son of Edmund Randolph and Lucia Cary Harrison Cocke

24248 Susanna Isham Harrison (9/13/1806-1/14/1891), m. 12/15/1937, Rev. Samuel Wilson Blain (2/9/1807-   ), son of Rev. Daniel and Mary Hanna Blain

242481 Daniel Harrison Blain (11/20/1838-10/14/1906), m. 1/30/ 1867, Mary Louisa Mercer (1839-1916), dau. of John C. and Mary Waller Mercer

2424811 Rev. John Mercer Blain (4/30/1869-1932), m. 1898, Claudia Lacy Grier (1869-1963), dau. of Dr. John Grier

24248111 Daniel Blain III (12/17/1898-   ), m. 1936, Sara Logan Stair

242481111 Daniel Blain IV (1938-   ), m. Dale Van Sciver

2424811111 Stacy Wister Blain

2424811112 Travis Van Sciver Blain

24248112 Mary Grier Blain (10/27/1900-1906)

24248113 Margaret Cary Blain (10/14/1903 or 1908-   ), m. 1929, Raymond Fitch Kepler

242481131 Mercer Raymond Kepler (1931-   ), m. Grace Thompson

2424811311 David Mercer Kepler

2424811312 Steven Kepler

2424811313 Daniel Kepler

242481132 Thomas Fitch Kepler (1933-   ), m.

2424811321 Thomas Fitch Kepler, Jr.

2424811322 James Blain Kepler

2424811323 John Harold Kepler

242481133 John Erdman Kepler (1937-   ), m. Toyoko

2424811331 Kenneth Raymond Kepler

2424811332 Bobby Kepler

2424811333 Michael Kepler

2424811334 Paul Kepler

242481134 William Grier Kepler (1941-   ), m. Lucilla

```
2424811341  Chris Kepler
2424811342  Kenny Kepler
2424811343  Kelly Kepler
24248114   Elizabeth Grier Blain (3/10/1909-          ), m. 1935, James
             Baker Woods, Jr.
242481141  Daniel Blain Woods (1936-1956)
242481142  Agnes Lacy Aoods (1937-         ), m. 1961, Anthony White
             Dick, Jr.
2424811421  Anthony White Dick III (1963-          )
2424811422  Elizabeth Grier Dick (1966-       )
2424811423  Daniel Woods Dick (1970-        )
242481143  James Baker Woods III (1940-1966), m. 1962, Sheena Lane
             Warren
2424811431  James Blain Woods (1964-          )
242481144  John Mercer Woods (1949-         ), m. 1972, Diana Rice
2424811441  Kristin Mercer Woods (1976-       )
2424811442  James Baker Woods (1978-        )
2424812    Randolph Harrison Blain (1/12/1871-1923)(born in Christian-
             burg and died in Lexington), m. 8/23/1899, Jean Throck-
             morton Forman (1877-1947)(born in Maysville, Ky., d. in
             Flushing, N.Y.).  Both are bur. in the Blain family plot
             of the Stonewall Jackson Cemetery in Lexington
24248121   Mary Louisa Blain (8/14/1900-1977), m. 10/ /1921,
             Harold Bradford Christie of N.Y.C.
242481211  Mary Louise Christie (4/ /1929-        )
24248122   Stanton Forman Blain (7/22/1902-1972), m. Dorothy Gwinn
             of Goshen, dau. of James Floyd Gwinn
242481221  James Stanton Forman Blain (5/8/1925-          )
242481222  Marion Jean Blain (2/14/1927-       )
24248123   Susanna Randolph Blain (6/15/1908-          ), m. 7/ /
             1928, William Lamar G. Sargent
242481231  William Sargent (6/ /1929-          )
242481232  Randolph Harrison Sargent (11/ /1930-          )
24248124   Jean Thorckmorton Blain (11/22/1910-          ), m. (1st)
             1934, George H. Scheele, Jr. of N.Y.C. (1911-1973).  M.
             (2nd), Louis S. Bock of Poughkeepsie, N.Y.
         Children by first husband:
242481241  Robert Blain Scheele (1940-          ), m. 1963, Marianne
             Male of Pittsburgh, Pa. (1941-          ), lives in
             Madison, Wisc.
2424812411  Lynn Ellen Scheele (1967-          )
2424812412  Michael Eric Scheele (1970-          )
242481242  Richard Stanton Scheele (1943-          ) of N.Y.C.  Unm.
24248125   Randolph Harrison Blain III (2/16/1914-        )
24248126   Cary Mercer Blain (8/3/1915-1971), m. (1st) Gerald Rice,
             widowed.  M. (2nd), Robert Newell
2424813    Samuel Stuart Blain (10/18/1872-1957), m. 6/18/1908, in
             Roanoke, Jean Maurice Vaughan (1882-1951)
24248131   Mary Mercer Blain (9/2/1909-          ), d.s.p.
24248132   Ann Morton Blain (6/12/1911-          ), m. 1937, Jack
             Gerald Weldon (1911-        ) of N.Y.C.  Live in St.
             Petersburg, Fla.
```

242481321 Ann Stuart Weldon (1942-   ),m. 1972, in New
           Orleans, La., Kenneth Wilbur Michael
2424813211 Kenneth Wilbur Michael, Jr. (1973-   )
24248133   Samuel Wilson Blain (12/29/1913-   ), m. 1948, in
           Roanoke, Early Wells (1924-   ), lives in Roanoke
242481331 Wilson Edward Blain (1951-   )
242481332 Virginia Barbour Blain (1954-   )
242481333 Stuart Wells Blain (1956-   )
24248134   Mary Fraser Blain (12/11/1915-   )
24248135   Jean Vaughan Blain (11/14/1920-   ), m. 1945, in
           Roanoke, Charles Hyatt Shields, Jr. (1917-   ),
           of Richmond
242481351 Charles Hyatt Shields III (1956-   ), m. 1980, in
           Richmond, Karen Leigh Perry (1957-   )
2424814   Hugh Mercer Blain (12/26/1874-   ), m. 8/ /1901,
           Mary Moore Winston
24248141   Elizabeth Winston Blain (11/28/1902-   )
24248142   Hugh Mercer Blain (8/ /1905-   )
24248143   Martha Randolph Blain (9/7/1908-   )
2424815   Daniel Blain (11/23/1877-1879)
2424816   Robert Waller Blain (1879-   ),m. 12/19/1916, Mary
           Logan Bagby
24248161   Mercer Shipman Blain (10/26/1917-   )
2424817   Rev. Cary Randolph Blain (1882-   ), m. 8/10/1923,
           Margaret Minnick
242482   Mary Randolph Blain (9/12/1840-   )
242483   Randolph Harrison Blain (8/16/1842-6/9/1929)
242484   Charlotte Elizabeth Blain (7/4/1844-   ), m. 6/30/1869,
           Col. Charles Richardson
2424841   William Dorrington Richardson, d.s.p.
2424842   Samuel Blain Richardson, m. Nannie Erickson
2424843   Lavinia Dandridge Richardson
242485   Lucia Cary Harrison Blain (1/17/1848-9/21/1931)
24249   Lucia ("Lucy") Cary Harrison (1809-1842), m. 1829, Nelson
           Page (11/8/1801-1850), of "The Fork" Cumberland Co. She
           was his first wife. He m. (2nd) Marie Hamilton. No issue
242491   Mary ("Polly") Randolph Page (1830-   ), m. Col. Ben-
           jamin Harrison (242472)
242492   Lucius Carter Page (1842-   ), d. inf.
2424x   Catharine Lilbourne Harrison (1811-1898), m. 1831, John S.
           McKim of Baltimore
2424x1   Emily McKim
2424x2   Mary Randolph McKim (-1911)
2424x3   Margie Telfair McKim, d.s.p.
2424x4   Telfair McKim, d.s.p.
2424x5   Carter Henry McKim, m. Miss Phillips of Staunton
2424x6   Rev. Randolph Harrison McKim of Washington, D. C., m. (1st),
           Agnes Phillips. M. (2nd) Mrs. Annie Brooke
           Child by first wife:
2424x61   Kate McKim, m. Henry G. Rathbone of England
2424x62   Duncan McKim, d.s.p.
2424x63   Telfair McKim
2424x64   Eleanor McKim

2424a Willianna Mortimer Harrison (1813-1847), m. 1836, Henry Page
       Irving and moved to California
2424a1 James H. Irving, d. young
2424a2 Joseph Kinkaid Irving (-1864)
2424a3 Henry Page Irving, Jr., d. inf.
2424b Virginia Randolph Harrison (1815-1830)
2424c Ann ("Nannie") Hartwell Harrison (1819-1892), m. 1847 at
       "Upper Brandon", Dr. John Bolling Garrett of "Clover
       Plains", Albemarle County. For their children, see 12211
2424d William Mortimer Harrison (9/23/1802-5/19/1811), d.s.p. He
       was drowned
243 Elizabeth Cary, m. Robert Kincaid, "an Irishman"
2431 Mary J. Kincaid, m. Charles Irving
24311 (son)
24312 (son)
24313 (son)
24314 (son)
24315 (son)
24316 (dau)
24317 (dau)
24318 (dau)
2432 (son)
2433 (son)
2434 (dau)
2435 (dau)
2436 (dau)
244 Mary Cary (12/4/1766-1/26/1797), m. 4/12/1773, first wife of
      Carter Page of "The Fork", Cumberland County, Major of
      Cavalry, Revolutionary War, son of Gov. John and Jane Byrd
      Page. His second wife was Lucy Nelson
2441 John Cary Page of "South Grove", later "Union Hill", both
      Cumberland County (5/9/1784-   ), m. 10/12/1808, Mary
      Anna Trent, dau. of Dr. Alexander C. Trent of "Barley Hill",
      Cumberland County
24411 Lavinia Anderson Page, m. 1832, Dr. Edward Fisher
244111 George Fisher, m. 1864,   Woodfin
244112 John Page Fisher, d.s.p. 1863
244113 Nannie Ambler Fisher, m. 1858, William H. Kennon
244114 Eliza Page Fisher, d.s.p. 1867
244115 Charles Fisher
244116 Edward Fisher
24412 Mary Anna Page (5/26/1811-   ), m. 1845, John Daniel
244121 Lucy Daniel, m. 1869, Francis Kinckel (244171) of "Broom-
       field", Cumberland County
244122 Anna T. Daniel, m. 1870, Meriwether Lewis Randolph (24142b)
24413 Virginia Randolph Page 8/17/1813-   ), m. 1833, Thomas
      Hobson
244131 Mary Anna Hobson (1834-   ), m. Mann Page, Jr. (24468)
244132 Caroline Hobson, d.s.p.
244133 Joseph Hobson, d.s.p.
244134 Virginia Page Hobson, m. Richard Archer
244135 Thomas Hobson, Jr., d.s.p.
244136 Ellen Hobson, m.   Nash

```
244137   Clara Hobson
244138   Alexander Hobson
244139   Cary Hobson
24414    Eliza Trent Page (10/19/1815-9/16/1838).  Unm.
24415    Ellen Cary Page (6/19/1817-5/19/1837).  Unm.
24416    Alexander Trent Page (11/21/1819-4/4/1845), m. 1840, Martha
           Henderson
244161   Martha Henderson Page, m. 1867,          Stewart
24417    Maria Willis Page (1/18/1822-1862), m. 1843, Rev. Wm. H.
           Kinckel
244171   Francis Kinckel, m. 1869, Lucy Daniel (244121)
244172   Anna Kinckel, m. 1870, J. P. Williams
244173   William Kinckel
244174   Maria Kinckel
244175   John P. Kinckel
244176   J. Carrington Kinckel
244177   Alexander Gilmer Kinckel
244178   Frederick Kinckel
24418    Col. Archibald Cary Page (4/22/1824-        ), m. (1st)
           Lucy Trent.  M. (2nd) Lizzie Trent.  M. (3rd) Elizabeth
           Cunningham Harrison (242414)
         Children by first wife:
244181   William H. Page
244182   John C. Page
         Child by second wife:
244183   Archibald Cary Page, Jr.
24419    Carter Page (3/25/1826-5/31/1826)
2441x    Harriet Randolph Page (4/15/1827-        ), m. 1857, David
           Coupland Randolph (24238).  For their children, see 24238
2441a    John Cary Page, Jr. (2/22/1830-        ), m. (1st), Nellie
           Eppes.  M. (2nd), Julia Trent
2441a1   Willie J. Page
2441a2   Mary A. Page
2441a3   Martha Burke Page
2441b    Edward Trent Page (5/20/1833-        ), m. 1854, Bettie
           Nicholas, dau. of J. S. Nicholas
2441b1   Nannie Nicholas Page
2441b2   Mary Byrd Page
2441b3   John Nicholas Page
2441b4   Edward Trent Page
2441b5   Bessie Coupland Page
2442     Henry Page (9/29/1785-        ), m. 12/23/1813, Jane B. Deane
24421    Mary Cary Page (10/27/1814-        ), m. 12/30/1840, Rev.
           George McPhail
244211   Jane McPhail, d.s.p.
244212   Mary McPhail, m. Rev.      Davis
244213   Henry McPhail
244214   Lillian McPhail, m. Rev.        Irving
24422    Thomas Deane Page (7/27/1816-        ), m. 1846, Isabella
           Catlett
244221   Fannie Catlett Page, m. 10/28/1874, William McCown
244222   Henry Page (12/27/1849-        ), m. 1/9/1878, Maude G.
           Crews
```

244223 Jane Deane Page (1851-6/8/1855)
244224 Thomas Deane Page (10/20/1853-   )
244225 Calmere Catlett Page (4/24/1856-   )
244226 Carter Page (-8/30/1876)
244227 Isabella Page (4/22/1859-   )
244228 John Cary Page (2/12/1861-   )
24423 Carter Page (5/4/1818-   ), m. (1st), Betty Byers. M.
        (2nd) Sarah Bell Miller
     Children by first wife:
244231 Henry Cary Page, d. inf.
244232 Elizabeth Deane Page (9/10/1854-   )
     Children by second wife:
244233 Henry Page (10/1/1856-   )
244234 Isaac Newton Page (2/ /1858-   )
244235 Eglantine Page (1860-   )
244236 James Page (1863-   )
244237 Virginia Lee Page (1865-d. inf.)
244238 Catharine Page, d. inf.
24424 Eliza Wallace Page (7/2/1820-   ), m. 1851, Jonathan
        Clark Temple
24425 Rev. James Jellis Page (7/7/1822-   ),m. 12/16/1851,
        Virginia Newton
244251 Wood Newton Page (11/13/1852-7/22/1894), m. Ellie Mason
2442511 Ellie Wood Page, m. A. A. Morson Keith
24425111 A. A. Morson Keith, m. Ellie Wood Page
244251111 Ellie Wood Page Keith (9/10/1921-   )
244251112 James Keith (4/25/1923-   )
244251113 Thomas Randolph Keith (12/22/1930-   )
244252 Henry Deane Page (11/2/1854-   )
244253 Sarah Bell Page (7/28/1856-   )
244254 Thomas Carter Page (12/8/1858-   )
244255 Mary Wallace Page (11/17/1860-   )
244256 Lilla Leigh Page (5/7/1868-   )
24426 Anne Catharine Page (1/13/1825-   ), m. 1850, Dr. Charles
        A. Williams
244261 Jane Clark Williams (8/14/1852-   ), m. 1/1/1874, Henry
        M. Hatton
2442611 Son Hatton, d. inf.
2442612 Herbert McPhail Hatton (9/18/1877-   )
244262 Lucy Washington Williams (12/22/1855-   )
244263 Henry Page Williams, d.s.p.
244264 Charles Williams, (2/3/1866-   )
24427 Martha Belle Page (2/17/1827-   ), d.s.p.
24428 (son)
2443 Carter Page, Jr. (12/9/1786-11/7/1789)
2444 Lavinia Randolph Page, d. inf.
2445 Carter Page, Jr. (10/10/1790-8/30/1791)
2446 Dr. Mann Page (10/26/1791-1850), m. 12/12/1815, Jane F.
        Walker, dau. of Francis Walker and Jane F. Nelson. Dr.
        Page and wife lived at Keswick in Albemarle County
24461 Maria Page (12/ /1816-6/15/1837). Unm.
24462 Ella Page (9/18/1818-11/14/1882). Unm.

24463   Francis Walker Page (11/17/1820-7/12/1846), m. 9/4/1844,
       Anna E. Cheesman, dau. of Benjamin F. and Maria S. Whitte-
       more Cheeseman
244631 Francis Walker Page, Jr.
24464   Carter Henry Page (11/21/1822-   ), m. 1857, Leila
       Graham, dau. of William Graham
244641 Leila Graham Page (1858-   )
244642 William Graham Page (7/ /1860-   )
244643 Carter Henry Page, Jr. (1864-   )
244644 Mary Bowdoin Page (1866-   )
24465   John Cary Page (1824-1828)
24466   Frederick Winslow Page (11/2/1826-   ), m. 12/24/
       1850, Anne Kinloch Meriwether, dau. of Thomas Walker and
       Anne Carter Nelson Meriwether
244661 Jane Walker Page (9/22/1851-   ), m. 1/ /1875, Thomas
       Walker Lewis
2446611 Frederick Page Lewis (11/ /1875-d.s.p. 7/22/1893)
2446612 Dr. Archibald Cary Lewis (7/12/1877-   ), m. 1914,
       Ruth Dillon Hatton (Hastin?)
2446613 Alice Page (Douglas?) Lewis (7/19/1879-   ), m. 10/ /
       1903, Ashton Blair Jones
24466131 Alice Page Jones (2/19/1905-   )
24466132 Ashton Blair Jones, Jr. (12/27/1906-   )
24466133 Walker Lewis Jones (9/14/1912*11?-   )
24466134 Archibald Lewis (Cary?) Jones (6/ /1914?-   )
2446614 Thomas Walker Lewis, Jr. (8/ /1881?-   ), m. 1912,
       Agnes Thomas of Memphis
24466141 Thomas Walker Lewis III (9/30/1914-   )
24466142 Frank Nelson Lewis (4/1/1923-   )
2446615 Isabel Money Lewis (9/22/1883-   ), m. 10/14/1911,
       Archibald Dexter Davis of Tennessee
24466151 Mildred Page Davis (9/2/1912-   )
24466152 Archibald Dexter Davis, Jr. (3/14/1918-   )
2446616 Jane Page Lewis (1885-1886)
2446617 Anne Kinloch Lewis (9/22/1888 or 8/ /1887?-   ), m.
       1921, Roger Scott Warren of Virginia
24466171 Annette Page Warren (1/13/1924-   )
24466172 Hugh Nelson Warren (12/14/1927-   )
2446618 Frank Nelson Lewis, Capt. U.S.A. (6/5/1890-1/24/1919).
       Died in France of injuries suffered in the Argonne
2446619 Mildred Nelson Page Lewis (11/7/1893-   ), m. 9/22/1916,
       Orton (Osten?) Everett Duling of West Virginia
24466191 Anne Lewis (Nelson?) Duling (5/18/1918-   )
24466192 Jane Page Duling (10/21/1920-   )
24466193 Orton (Osten?) Everett Duling, Jr. (5/30/1922-   )
244661x Dr. Philip Meriwether Lewis (9/10/1898-   ), m. 12/ /
       1925, Ruth Kitchins
244661x1 Jean Lewis (9/8/1926-   )
244661x2 Meriwether Lewis (dau)(5/10/1929-   )
244662 Eliza M. Page (8/1/1853-1871)
244663 Annie Nelson Page (9/15/1855-   ), m. 1/13/1875,
       Nathaniel Ragsdale Coleman (64173)
244664 Frederick Kinloch Page (7/24/1857-1926), m. Flora Temple
       Lewis, dau. of William Stanford and Frances M. Campbell
       Lewis

```
2446641   William Douglas Page (8/30/1879-          ), m. 8/11/1924,
            Margaret Caldwell Brady
2446642   Evelyn Mabrey Page (12/17/1881-          ), m. Grigsby Cave
            Shackelford
24466421  Evelyn Byrd Shackelford, m. Thomas Murfee
244664211  Thomas Murfee, Jr. (1930-          )
244664212  Evelyn Byrd Murfee (1934-          )
24466422  Flora Kinloch Shackelford, d.s.p. 1934
24466423  Jane Byrd Shackelford, m. 1934, Judge Plunkett Beirne
2446643   Frederick Byrd Page (9/22/1883-          ), m. 11/1/1915,
            Anne Randolph Radford
2446644   Frances Campbell Page (9/20/1886-          ), m. (1st), Hugh
            Stockdell Morrison.  M. (2nd) Henry W. Mann
          Children by first husband:
24466441  Frances Page Morrison
24466442  Elizabeth Madison Morrison
24466443  Flora Lewis Morrison, m. 1932, Caperton Beirne
          Child by second husband:
24466444  Eleanor Mann
2446645   Robert Shackelford Page (9/14/1888-          ), m. 1913,
            Pattie Aline Moring
24466451  Aline Moring Page
24466452  Robert Shackelford Page, Jr.
244665    William Douglas Page (6/11/1859-d.s.p. 1878)
244666    Evelyn Byrd Page (9/21/1862-11/11/1937), m.(1st) 7/19/1882,
            John Mabrey Coleman (64178).  M. (2nd), John Clifford
            Howlett
244667    Mildred Nelson Page (6/27/1865-          )
24467     Jane Walker Page (10/18/1828-d.s.p. 1/29/1845)
24468     Mann Page, Jr. (5/1/1831-10/  /1864), m. 5/  /1854, Mary
            Anna Hobson (244131)
244681    Charlotte Nelson Page (1862-          )
24469     Charlotte Nelson Page (3/25/1833-d.s.p. 1849)
2446x     William Wilmer Page (1836-11/6/1857)
2446a     Thomas Walker Page (4/  /1837-          ), m. 1861, Nannie
            Watson Morris, dau. of James and Caroline Pleasants Morris
2446a1    Ella Rives Page (1862-          )
2446a2    James Morris Page (1864-          )
2446a3    Thomas Walker Page, Jr. (1866-          )
2446a4    Constance Morris Page (1868-          )
2446a5    Mann Page (1872-          )
2446a6    Rose Morris Page (1876-          )
2446b     Richard Channing Moore Page, Author of the "Page Family in
            Virginia" (1/2/1841-          ), m. 4/30/1874, Mary Elizabeth
            Fitch
2447      William Page (8/21/1793-12/26/1793)
2448      Mary Isham Page (12/30/1794-12/26/1811). Lost life in burn-
            ing of Richmond theatre
245       Henry Cary
246       Sarah Cary (          -10/  /1773), m. 1770, Archibald Bolling
            (16).  She was his first wife
25     Jane Randolph, m. Col. Anthony Walke, Jr., of "Fairfield",
          Princess Anne County (1/3/1726-          ), son of Anthony and
```

Annlee Armistead Walke. Colonel Anthony Walke, Jr., m. (2nd)
Mary Mosely, and had issue
251 Rev. Anthony Walke III, the "Fox-hunting Parson", M. Va. Con-
vention 1788, m. (1st), Anna McColley McClennahan (McClanahan?).
M. (2nd) Mrs. Anne Fisher (nee Newton). M. (3rd)
Children by first wife:
2511 Edwin (Edward?) Walke, m. Sarah Massenburg
25111 (son)
25112 (son)
25113 (dau)
25114 (dau)
25115 (dau)
2512 David Meade Walke, m. Elizabeth Boush
2513 John Nelson Walke, m. (1st) Miss Land. M. (2nd), Anna M.
Baylor
25131 Dr. Frank Anthony Walke, m. (1st), Miss Anne Baylor. M.
(2nd), Miss Isabelle Tunstall
25132 (dau)
Children by second wife (of 251):
2514 Anthony Walke IV, m. (1st), Jane Ritson. M. (2nd), Ann
Livingston
25141 (son)
25142 (son)
25143 (son)
25144 (dau)
25145 (dau)
2515 Jane E. Walke, m. Richard Watson
2516 Susan M. Walke, m. 11/20/1819, Charles Hansford Sheild. He
m. (2nd), Mary Dole Woten, and (3rd), Cornelia Armistead
25161 Robert Anthony Sheild, d. inf.
25162 Rev. Charles Henry Sheild (11/16/1824-1/16/1894), m. (1st)
Jane Cary Randolph Barton (3/23/1832-3/25/1869), dau. of
David Barton, Esq., of Winchester. M. (2nd), Martha Walker
Barton (1834-5/5/1890), his sister-in-law
Child by first wife:
251621 Charles Hansford Sheild, Jr. (1796-1868). Lawyer of Louisville
Child by second wife:
251622 George Norton Sheild
25163 Anne Walke Sheild (1/6/1822-   ), m. 5/14/1846, Robert
John McCandlish, son of Thomas Coleman and Mary Peters
McCandlish
251631 Charles Sheild McCandlish, m. Elizabeth Putnam, dau. of
Douglas Putnam of Marietta, Ohio
2516311 Randolph Walke McCandlish (1893-1970), m. Frances Archer
25163111 Randolph Walke McCandlish, Jr. (1920-1980), m. Rachel
Hanson
251631111 Anthony Walke McCandlish
251631112 Carolyn Hanson McCandlish
25163112 Charles Sheild McCandlish, Jr. (1922-   ), m.
Winifred Thompson
251631121 Charles Sheild McCandlish III, m. Anne Leake
2516311211 Charles Sheild McCandlish IV
251631122 Susan Randolph McCandlish, m. Gordon Murdock

2516311221 (dau)
2516311222 (son)
251631123   Thomas Wickham McCandlish, m. Nancy Friedberg
2516311231 (dau)
2516311232 (dau)
251631124   Ellen Archer McCandlish, m. John Melville
25163113   Frances Archer McCandlish (1924-   ), m. Frank L.
            Strond (Mt. Lakes, N.J.)
251631131   Robert Strond
251631132   Frances Strond
251631133   Elizabeth Strond
251631134   Susan Strond
251631135   Katherine Strond
2516312   Elizabeth McCandlish (-1965). Unm.
2516313   Mary Putnam McCandlish (1890-1981), m. Henry Archer
25163131   Mary Archer (1920-   )(Thibodeax, La.)
25163132   Ellen Archer (1922-   )(Saudi Arabia)
25163133   Charles Henry Archer (1925-   )(New Orleans)
2516314   Douglas Putnam McCandlish (died very young)
251632   Upton Beall McCandlish (7/6/1848-5/31/1915), m. 9/3/1875,
            Margaret Lindsay Landstreet (1855-12/ /1918 or 1919)
2516321   Lindsay McCandlish (1877-1912), m. Elizabeth Rick
25163211   Jane Randolph McCandlish (-2/28/1979), m. Harold
            Boyer. No issue
25163212   Elizabeth Lee McCandlish, d. unm.
2516322   Robert J. McCandlish, m. Jane Charlton Graves
25163221   Sarah McCandlish, m. Richard H. Crane
251632211 Jane Crane, m. Thomas McSwain
2516322111 Kimberley McSwain
2516322112 Kristin McSwain
251632212 Richard H. Crane, Jr., m. Donna Campbell. They adopted
            Erin Crane
25163222   Robert J. McCandlish, Jr., m. Josephine Sutton
251632221 Rebekah McCandlish, m. Lawrence Loring Burckmyer
2516322211 Sarah Lindsay Burckmyer
2516322212 Charles Loring Burckmyer
251632222 Charles McCandlish,m. Mary Williams Smith
2516322221 Robert J. McCandlish II
2516322222 Caroline Nash McCandlish
2516323   Edward Gerstell McCandlish (3/10/1887-12/6/1946), m.6/
            21/1919, Maybelle Bowen (8/8/1889-11/3/1973)
25163231   Margaret Belle McCandlish (3/30/1920-   ), m. 1/21/
            1943, Roy Anson Edwards (5/11/1911-   ). Adopted
            Lorenna Jean Edwards (12/3/1947-   ), m. Charles J.
            Rothert, and they had Ryan Charles Rothert (10/29/1972)
251632311 Douglas Roy Edwards (12/24/1952-10/22/1977), m. Gail
            Lynne Pardo (1/12/1957-   )
251632312 Carol Evelyn Edwards (10/16/1954-   ), m. (1st)
            Charles A. Pearce (no issue). M. (2nd) 8/14/1981,
            Daniel Alan Lindsay (5/26/1955-   )
2516323121 Philip Alan Lindsay (4/15/1983-   )
251632313 Keith Anson Edwards (8/12/1955-   ), m. Catherine
            S. Heid
2516323131 Anson Daniel Heid-Edwards (2/13/1979-   )
25163232   Edward Lindsay McCandlish (10/21/1921-   ). Unm.

25163233 Phoebe Grey McCandlish (3/3/1923-   ), m. (1st)
          Floyd M. Young (no issue). M. (2nd) William Corcoran.
          M. (3rd) 3/17/1952, Edward Wetzler (deceased). M. (4th)
          5/28/1966, Gilbert Klaes. No issue
251632331 Mary Jane Corcoran (3/28/1950-   )(name changed to
          Mary Jane Wetzler), m. Michael Christopher Neal
2516323311 Jeffrey Todd Neal (8/1/1967-   )
2516323312 Jody Michael Neal (7/30/1969-   )
2516323313 Julie Marie Neal (1/21/1973-   )
251632332 Nancy Hope Wetzler, m. Kerry Mormann
251632333 Raymond Edwin Wetzler (8/7/1956-   ), m. Dondi Lee
          Medlin
2516323331 Brittany Nicole Wetzler (10/18/1983-   )
25163234 David Bowen McCandlish (10/21/1924-   ), m. 7/23/
          1960, Dorothy Jean Welderly (3/31/1924-   )
251632341 Stephen Claude McCandlish (6/22/1962-   )
251632342 Peter David McCandlish (6/16/1964-   )
251632343 Karen Louise McCandlish (3/5/1966-   )
25163235 Doris King McCandlish (6/14/1926-   ), m. 3/22/1952,
          Charles A. Kurzius (d. 2/ /1983)
251632351 Mathew Charles Kurzius (3/25/1952-   ), m. Teresa
          Kotz
2516323511 William Mathew Kurzius (1/22/1983-   )
251632352 Hope Marie Kurzius (11/5/1957-   ), m. Edward P.
          Helbig. Div.
2516323521 Jennifer Willow Helbig (1/16/1976-   )(known as
          Jennifer Kurzius)
251632353 Brian Glen Kurzius (10/9/1959-   )
25163236 Anne Walke McCandlish (2/15/1928-   ), m. 4/3/1947,
          (1st), Ronald Marshall. M. (2nd) 1955, Donald Sheely
          (4/16/1929-   )
251632361 Ronald Edward Marshall (11/5/1952-   )(name changed
          to Ronald Edward Sheely), m. Joyce Jones
2516323611 Karen Rejoyce Sheely (9/18/1979-   )
2516323612 Kristen Praise Sheely (7/30/1981-   )
251632362 Annette Ray Sheely (8/9/1956-   ), m. 3/17/1984,
          Kipling Williams
251632363 Janet April Sheely, m. Vaatuia Tavui (legally changed
          from Vaatuia Melepai), a native of Samoa (4/27/1953-)
2516323631 Malani Donald Tavui (8/6/1984-   )
25163237 Ralph McCandlish (7/9/1931-d. at birth)
25163238 Evelyn Hope McCandlish (7/30/1932-   ), m. 7/1/1955,
          Frank Milton Rider
251632381 John Frederick Rider III (3/22/1956-   )
251632382 Karl Thomas Rider (9/10/1958-   )
251632383 Mark David Rider (1/15/1965-   )
25163239 Jean Landstreet McCandlish (2/5/1936-   ), m. 4/13/
          1957, William Robert Hoffman (11/18/1932-   )
251632391 Janice Elaine Hoffman (12/16/1963-   ), m. 4/18/1984,
          William Marshall Tate (5/19/1959-   )
251632392 Debra Jean Hoffman (10/1/1963-   ), m. 2/18/1982,
          Jeffrey Miller (8/13/1962-   )
2516324 Katherine McCandlish, m. Frederick D. Richardson
25163241 Evelyn Randolph Richardson, m. George Macatee, Jr.

251632411 George Frederick Macatee,m. Mary Locke
2516324111 Mary Locke Macatee
251632412 John Randolph Macatee. Unm.
251632413 Phyllis Lee Macatee. Unm.
25163242 Phyllis Walke Richardson, m. Henry Lyle Millan
251632421 John Alden Millan. Unm.
2516325 Evelyn McCandlish, m. Ralph K. Tallant. No issue
2516326 Ruth McCandlish, m. (1st) Robert D. Graham (deceased).
     M. (2nd) Ralph K. Tallant (deceased)
     Child by first husband:
25163261 Roberta Graham, m. Frank M. Carter
251632611 Anne Lindsay Carter, m. James Lillard. No issue
251632162 Frank Graham Carter. Unm.
251633 Ann ("Nannie") Walke McCandlish, d. unm.
251634 Sarah Sheild McCandlish (1855-5/6/1910), m. Thomas Hardaway
     Hawks (1855-3/4/1914), son of Joseph and Rebecca Hawks
2516341 Anne Sheild Hawks (3/28/1887-1932). Unm.
2516342 Thomas Holmes Hawks (2/7/1889-6/25/1969), m. 8/1/1914,
     Fanny Ada Holmes (10/4/1887-12/2/1973), dau. of James
     and Cora Holmes
25163421 Thomas Hardaway Hawks (6/2/1915-9/21/1977), m. (1st),
     Olive Lorraine Lewis (3/26/1916-   ). M. (2nd)
     Marion Mutch. M. (3rd) Ethel
    Child by first wife:
251634211 Shiela Holmes Hawks (7/30/1939-   ). Unm.
    Child by second wife:
251634212 Charlotte Hawks (10/22/1948-   ). Unm.
    Child by third wife:
251634213 Sheryl Hawks (7/11/1961-   ). Unm.
25163422 Gordon Holmes Hawks, M. D. (3/31/1917-   ), m. 6/
     4/1949, Winifred Beatrice Medland (6/19/1923-   ),
     dau. of Charles and Winnifred Medland. Dr. Hawks, a
     resident of Toronto, winters in Vero Beach, Florida
251634221 Thomas Holmes Hawks (2/25/1954-   ), m. 5/19/1981,
     Catherine Thomson (4/21/1956-   ), dau. of
     Donald and Barbara Thomson
251634222 Sally Elizabeth Hawks (7/26/1958-   ). Unm.
25163423 Helen Anne Hawks (1/2/1926-   ), m. 10/2/1948, David
     Lane Roby (2/3/1927-   ), son of Frank and Rhea
     Roby
251634231 Helen Anne Roby (12/7/1949-   ), m. 7/1/1976,
     Douglas Bryce, son of Douglas and Elizabeth Bryce
2516342311 Douglas Bryce (5/7/1979-   )
2516342312 Andrew Bryce (5/26/1982-   )
251634232 David Lane Roby (1/26/1953-   ). Unm.
251635 Robert Coleman McCandlish, m. (1st)   . M.
     (2nd)   No issue
    Children by first wife:
2516351 Henry McCandlish
2516352 Anne McCandlish
251636 Mary Peters McCandlish, d. inf.
25164 Sarah Eliza Sheild (6/4/1827-1853)

25165   William Francis Sheild (3/24/1830-   ), m. 12/9/1868,
         Mrs. Lizzie Armistead Booker
251651   William Walke Sheild of Norfolk
251652   Howard Sheild
2517   (son)
2518   (son)
2519   Anne Walke. Unm.
251x
251a
251b

252   (son)
253   (dau)
26   Elizabeth Randolph, m. ca. 1765, Col. Richard Kidder Meade
     (7/14/1746-2/9/1805), son of David Meade and Susannah Everard
     Meade. He was Aide to General Washington. Elizabeth's
     children died before her death, leaving no descendants. The
     Colonel m. (2nd) 12/10/1780, Mary Grymes (11/9/1753-6/16/1813),
     widow of William Randolph of "Chattsworth".
261   (son), d. inf.
262   (dau), d. inf.
263   (dau), d. inf.
27   Ryland Randolph. Unm. Died "an old bachelor" at "Turkey
     Island"
28   (son)
29   (dau)

John Randolph.
OF ROANOKE.

MARY BOLLING

3 Mary Bolling (1711-8/10/1744), m. 1/20/1727, Col. John Fleming
(11/ /1697-11/6/1756, of "Mount Pleasant", Goochland (now
Powhatan) County, eldest son of Col. Charles and Susannah
Tarleton Fleming of New Kent County. Colonel John's sister
Judith Fleming, m. (1st) 10/16/1712, Thomas Randolph of
"Tuckahoe", m. (2nd) 1733, Nicholas Davies of Goochland County

31 Col. Thomas Fleming (-1777). Unm. Served in French and
Indian War, and in Revolution (as Colonel, 9th Virginia Regiment). Will probated 7/21/1777, Goochland County

32 Col. John Fleming (-4/21/1767), m. Susannah Skelton

321 Capt. John Fleming. Killed Battle of Princeton 1/3/1777. Unm.

322 Mary Fleming, m. (1st) Warner Lewis, Jr. (1747-1791), son of
Col. Warner and Eleanor Bowles Lewis of "Warner Hall",
Gloucester County (Mary was his second wife, his first wife
was Mary Chiswell by whom he had four children). M. (2nd)
Ellis, a Methodist preacher. No issue.

3221 Julia Lewis, m. Thomas Throckmorton of Williamsburg. No
issue.

3222 John Lewis, m. Eleanor Lewis (his cousin). No issue.

3223 Philip Warner Lewis. Unm.

3224 Caroline Lewis (6/28/1783-4/6/1811), m. Charles Barrett. No
issue.

323 Susanna ("Sukey") Fleming, m. 1779, Capt. Addison Lewis of
Gloucester County (2/5/1756-1820)

3231 Susan Lewis (3/17/1782-11/12/1865), m. 1798, William Powell
Byrd (1777-), of "Whitehall", on the Ware River,
in Gloucester County, son of Col. William (of "Westover")
and Mary Willing Byrd

32311 Addison Lewis Byrd (1799-1842), m. 1821, Susan Coke (4/5/
1805-4/10/1882), dau. of Dr. John and Rebecca Minor Coke
of Williamsburg

323111 William Powell Byrd (1823-1852), m. 1846, Martha McKensie
of Richmond

3231111 Jane Byrd (8/1/1848-4/24/1935), m. William Miller of
Mathews County

323112 Rebecca Minor Byrd (8/11/1830-11/15/1861), m. 1859,
Robinson Nottingham (-4/ /1917) of Eastville,
Virginia. No issue. She was his first wife.

323113 Mary Willing Byrd (7/31/1833-7/5/1905), m. (1st) 3/ /1852,
John Thomas Fitchett (1831-11/15/1854), son of George and
Mary Seth Fitchett. M. (2nd) George W. Miester (-
1868). No issue.
Child by first husband:

3231131 Mary Seth Fitchett (2/16/1854-8/28/1935), m. 11/3/1875,
Edwin Leroy Adair (1/7/1852-1/10/1881), son of John
William and Margaret Littleton Savage Adair of Accomac

32311311 Mabel Littleton Adair (9/24/1876-   ), m. 9/24/
          1904, Victor Clayton Jefferis (11/19/1876-   ), son
          of Edwin Clayton and Maria Armstrong Jefferis of Wilming-
          ton, Del.
323113111 Mary Adair Jefferis (12/1/1910-   ), m. 11/23/
          1935, W. Latimer Snowdon (5/20/19-7-   ), son
          of Richard Ward and Mary Latimer Snowdon
32311312 Edwina Leroy Adair (10/12/1877-3/4/1929), m. (1st) 7/31/
          1900, Warner H. Smith, son of Allen Smith. M. (2nd)
          1914, David Allen Nease of St. Louis. No issue.
32311313 John William Adair (11/31/1878-   ), m. 1899,
          Margaret L. Calahan of Wilmington. No issue.
323114   Addison Lewis Byrd, Jr. (12/ /1836-   ). Unm.
32312 Mary Willing Byrd, m. Richard C. Coke of Williamsburg
323121 Rebecca Francis Coke, m. (her cousin) Fielding Lewis
          Marshall (1819-1902). She was his first wife.
3231211 Col. Richard Coke Marshall, C.S.A. (7/5/1844-4/5/1914),
          m. 1866, Mary Catherine Wilson (9/12/1843-7/1/1891)
32312111 Myra Marshall, d. young
32312112 Samuel Wilson Marshall of Dallas (his cousin), m. Agnes
          Harwood Nelson
323121121 Eleanor Warner Marshall, m. N. Beverly Tucker
323121122 Samuel Wilson Marshall, Jr.
32312113 Rebecca Coke Marshall, m. (her cousin) Marion Lewis
          Marshall (9/9/1867-12/ /1925) of Fauquier County.
          She was his first wife.
323121131 Maj. Richard Jaquelin Marshall (6/16/1895-   )
323121132 Catherine Wilson Marshall
323121133 Capt. St. Julien Ravenel Marshall, U.S.M.C., m. Marion
          Russell, dau. of Capt. Robert Russell, U.S.N.
3231211331 (dau)
3231211332 (dau)
32312114 Susan Lewis Marshall (4/26/1870-   ), m. (her
          cousin) Robert Stribling Marshall (12/27/1871-   )
323121141 Richard Coke Marshall (11/22/1900-   ), m. 3/
          /1924, Sara Reid Embry White, dau. of Hugh and Jean
          McIlwaine White
3231211411 Richard Coke Marshall, Jr. (8/1/1925-   )
3231211412 Jean McIlwaine Marshall (6/25/1929-   )
323121142 Mary Douthat Marshall (8/26/1902-   ), m. 1926,
          Joseph Reid Anderson Hobson, Jr., son of Joseph Reid
          Anderson and Anne Camm Hobson
3231211421 Susan Lewis Hobson (2/11/1931-   )
3231211422 Anne Colston Hobson (3/19/1933-   )
323121143 Addison Lewis Marshall (1903-1903)
323121144 Robert Stribling Marshall, Jr. (9/25/1905-   ),
          m. 6/16/1934, Betsy Ross Nicholson, dau. of Mrs.
          Elizabeth Ball Nicholson
323121145 Myra St. Julien Marshall (1/12/1909-   ), m.
          12/27/1933, Edward Vernon Brush, Jr., of Portsmouth
323121146 Susan Lewis Marshall (2/17/1911-   ), m. 4/28/
          1934, Wayt B. Timberlake, Jr., of Staunton

32312115   Fielding Lewis Marshall of Augusta, Ga., m. Freda Darby
           Jackson
323121151 Fielding Lewis Marshall, Jr.
323121152 Freda Darby Marshall
323121153 Richard Coke Marshall
323121154 George Jackson Marshall
32312116   Gen. Richard Coke Marshall, Jr., U.S.A., m. Louise Booker
323121161 Laura Winder Marshall, m. Edgar Derry Fisher of Baltimore
323121162 Richard Coke Marshall III, m. 2/16/1934, Florence Stuart
           Beale, dau. of Dr. Robert Somerville and Sophie Clark-
           son Stuart Beale of Washington, D.C.
323121163 Mary Mallory Marshall, d. inf.
32312117   St. Julien Ravenel Marshall (11/23/1881-   ), m.
           11/24/1908, Marie Stuart Lewis of "Buena Vista", Clarke
           County
323121171 St. Julian Ravenel Marshall, Jr. (7/24/1910-   ).
           Unm.
323121172 John Lewis Marshall (6/23/1912-5/25/1927)
32312118   Rev. Myron Barrand Marshall, m. Elizabeth Barrand Niemyer
323121181 Louise Chandler Marshall
323121182 Elizabeth Barrand Marshall
323121183 Catherine Wilson Marshall
323121184 Myron Barrand Marshall, Jr.
323121185 Hermon Calvert Marshall
323121186 Richard Coke Marshall
323121187 Helen St. Julien Marshall
323121188 John Marshall
323121189 Arthur Niemyer Marshall
3231212   Margaret Lewis Marshall, m. Cornelius B. Hite. No issue.
3231213   Mary Willing Byrd Marshall, m. (1st) J. R. Yates (-
           1876). M. (2nd) 1887, Count Eugene de Mitkiewicz. No
           issue.
           Child by first husband:
32312131   Margaret Yates, d. age 19. Unm.
3231214   Susan Lewis Marshall, m. Bowles E. Armistead. No issue.
           She was his first wife.
3231215   Thomas Marshall (11/ /1850-9/13/1893), m. Maud Wolcott
           Griswold Barhydt, dau. of David Parish and Sophia Gris-
           wold Hackley Barhydt. He was her first husband.
32312151   Sophy Griswold Marshall (6/9/1881-   ), m. 5/9/
           1903, Julien Jaquelin Mason (1869-1914) of New York City
323121511 Maud Marshall Mason (2/6/1907-   ), m. Capt.
           Robert W. Raynsford, U.S.A. (8/1/1898-   )
3231215111 Robert Wayne Raynsford, Jr. (7/13/1935-   )
323121512 Julien Jaquelin Mason, Jr. (9/6/1908-   ). Unm.
32312152   David Parish Bardydt Marshall (1882-   ), m. Agnes
           Lilley Dunlap
323121521 Thomas Marshall (3/2/1916-   )
323121522 David Parish Bardydt Marshall, Jr. (6/22/1919-   )
3231216   Evelyn Byrd Marshall. Unm.
3231217   Fielding Lewis Marshall (-1/24/1933), m. Caroline
           B. Gwatkin

32312171 Mary Blackford Marshall, m. Richard F. Amphlett of
          England (-1917). He was killed in action in
          France.
323121711 Mary Marshall Amphlett
323121712 Richard John Marshall Amphlett
323121713 Caroline Amphlett
3231218 Rebecca Francis Marshall, m. Charles Reid Nash of Ports-
          mouth (-4/11/1918)
32312181 Rebecca Coke Nash, m. Comdr. J. Paulding Murdock, U.S.N.
323121811 Rebecca Marshall Murdock, m. Kenneth L. Carter of Quebec
323121812 Mary Paulding Murdock
32312182 Nancy Collins Nash, m. Comdr. Logan Cresap, U.S.N.
323121821 Logan Cresap, Jr.
323121822 Charles Nash Cresap
32312183 Florence Nash, m. Fenwick Hall Murray of West River,
          Maryland
323121831 Nancy Cheston Murray
323121832 Fenwick Hall Murray, Jr.
323121833 Mary Byrd Marshall Murray
32312184 Mary Byrd Marshall Nash (-1905). Unm.
3231219 Agnes Marshall, m. William Pickett Helm
32312191 William Pickett Helm, Jr.
32312192 Virginia Helm
32312193 Margaret Helm
32312194 (son)
32312195 Rebecca Helm, d. in childhood
323121x Eleanor Warner Marshall, d. in childhood
32313 Jane Otway Bryd, m. George Wythe McCandlish of Williamsburg
323131 Susan Lewis McCandlish, m. Dr. Philip Alexander Taliaferro
          of Gloucester County, son of Warner Throckmorton and Leah
          Seddon Alexander Taliaferro. No issue.
323132 Jane Otway Byrd McCandlish, m. John B. Dougherty of Wil-
          mington, Del.
3231321 George Byrd Dougherty
3231322 Charles Dougherty
3231323 Otway Dougherty
3231324 Byrd Dougherty
3231325 Addison Lewis Dougherty
3231326 Evelyn Bryd Dougherty
3231327 Fielding Lewis Dougherty
323133 Evelyn Byrd McCandlish
323134 Mary Willing McCandlish (-1876). Unm.
32314 Dr. Samuel Powell Byrd (1807-12/25/1863) of "Whitehall",
          Gloucester County, m. (1st) Catherine Carter Corbin (widow
          of Dr. L. E. W. Fauntleroy), dau. of Richard and Rebecca
          Farley Corbin. M. (2nd) Mary Lewis Brooke, dau. of Dr.
          Matthew Whiting and Elizabeth Lewis Brooke. No issue.
          Children by first wife:
323141 Susan Lewis Byrd (1/18/1835-5/3/1898), m. 10/2/1858,
          Tazewell Thompson (9/26/1834-5/10/1914), son of William
          Henry and Mary Sawyer Thompson of Camden County, N.C.
          The Tazewell Thompsons lived at "Erin" in Gloucester County

3231411   Powell Byrd Thompson (5/3/1859-   ), m. 10/7/1907,
          Helen Parsons, dau. of James Thomas and Maria Reeder
          Parsons of St. Mary's County, Maryland
32314111 Anne Byrd Thompson (10/4/1911-   ), m. 10/19/1935,
          Louis Stoll Nixdorff, son of Frank Singleton and Bertha
          Nixdorff
32314112 Tazewell Thompson (8/29/1912-   )
3231412   Mary Sawyer Thompson (5/17/1860-   ). Unm.
3231413   Tazewell Thompson, Jr. (4/9/1869-11/30/1886)
3231414   William Henry Thompson (10/14/1872-   ), m. 10/8/1900,
          Janet Wortley Tatem, dau. of William Henry and Mary Etta
          Chamberlain Tatem of Camden County, N.C.
32314141 Susan Lewis Byrd Thompson (1/19/1904-   ), m. 10/
          29/1927, Osborne LeRoux Goforth, son of Melmith LeRoux
          and Mary Jane LeVan Goforth
32314142 Tazewell Franklin Thompson (12/7/1907-   ), m. 10/
          6/1934, Martha Lankford, dau. of Dr. Livins and Lucy
          Jones Lankford
32314143 William Henry Thompson, Jr. (5/10/1913-   )
323142   Capt. Richard Corbin Byrd, C.S.A. (9/9/1837-1925), m. 1860,
          (his cousin) Ann Gordon Marshall of "Oak Hill", Fauquier
          County
3231421   Samuel Powell Byrd (6/23/1861-1891), m. 1890, Fannie
          Johnson
32314211 Ann Powell Byrd (1891-   ), m. Dr. Alan Churchill
          Woods of Baltimore
3231422   Richard Corbin Byrd, Jr. (7/29/1863-6/11/1909), m. Annie
          Tazewell Walke (10/27/1872-   ), dau. of Richard
          (Jr.) and Annie Nivison Bradford Walke
32314221 Richard Walke Byrd (8/19/1899-   ). Unm.
3231423   Lewis Marshall Byrd (3/11/1866-   ), m. 11/18/
          1903, (his cousin) Sallie Innes Williams of Orange County
32314231 John Williams Byrd (1/15/1905-   ). Unm.
32314232 Lewis Innes Byrd (3/8/1907-   ). Unm.
3231424   Mary Brooke Byrd (1/22/1868-   ). Unm. Home:
          "Zanoni", Gloucester County
3231425   Fanny Marshall Byrd (10/15/1869-   ), m. 9/18/1894,
          Corbin Griffin Waller (1860-3/5/1923)
32314251 Sally Tazewell Waller (6/26/1895-   ), m. 6/11/
          1919, Addison Leech Luce (12/1/1894-   ), son of
          Wilson Ayres and Ann Isabel Leech Luce of Erie, Pa.
323142511 Isabel Byrd Luce (5/18/1920-   )
323142512 Sally Tazewell Luce (3/7/1925-   )
323142513 Caroline Ayres Luce (10/7/1928-   )
323142514 Addison Leech Luce, Jr. (11/23/1931-   )
32314252 Ann Marshall Byrd Waller (9/28/1896-   ), m.
          Thomas M. Whittemore of Charleston, S.C.
323142521 Thomas Marshall Whittemore (3/ /1924-   )
322142522 Hart Waller Whittemore (10/   /1926-   )
32314253 Katharine Corbin Waller (1/11/1899-   ). Unm.
32314254 Fanny Byrd Waller (11/22/1901-   ). Unm.

32314255 Corbin Griffin Waller, Jr. (1/7/1907-   ). Unm.
3231426 Ann Gordon Byrd (4/4/1876-   ), m. 9/5/1900, Roland
    Hanmer Clark (1874-   ), son of Henry Walker and
    Fanny Elizabeth Hunt Clark of New Rochelle, N.Y.
32314261 Elizabeth Hunt Clark (9/17/1901-   ), m. 9/5/
    1923, John Samuel Wallis, son of Mrs. Thomas P. Moore
    of Carlisle, Pa.
323142611 Mather Clark Wallis
32314262 William Evelyn Byrd Clark (5/30/1903-   ). Unm.
32314263 Ann Gordon Clark (1/9/1912-   ). Unm.
33 Judge William Fleming (7/6/1736-2/15/1824 or 1828), m. 10/5/
    1766, Elizabeth ("Bettie") Champe, dau. of Col. John Champe
    of King George County
331 Lucy Champe Fleming, m. 1/1/1794, John Markham of Goochland
    County (1/20/1770-   ), son of Col. Bernard and Mary
    Harris Markham of "Ware",Chesterfield County. The Flemings
    went to Kentucky.
3311 Bernard Markham
3312 William Fleming Markham
33121 Rev. Thomas R. Markham (1829-1894), a Presbyterian minister
    of New Orleans
33122 William F. Markham of Huntersville, Texas
331221 Thomas Osborne Markham, MD.
3313 George Markham
3314 Linnaeus Markham
3315 Hugh Markham
3316 John Markham
3317 Mary Markham
3318 Judith Markham, m.   Burke of Tennessee
3319 Virginia Markham, m. Jesse Claiborne
331a Osborne Markham
331b Martha Markham
331c Norborne Markham
331d Champe Markham
332 Mary Bolling Fleming (1779-1/22/1812), m. 2/8/1799, Capt.
    Beverley Chew Stanard, C.S.A. (1779-7/11/1823) of Chesterfield
    County. He m. (2nd) Elizabeth Smith Watts. No issue.
3321 John Champe Stanard (8/6/1805-6/24/1884) of "Roxbury", Caroline
    County, m. 9/15/1829, Sarah Taliaferro Thornton (8/6/1804-
    10/4/1890), dau. of Philip and Sarah Taliaferro Conway
    Thornton
33211 Jane Stith Stanard (5/12/1831-ca. 1917). Unm.
33212 Capt. Robert Conway Stanard (2/18/1833-10/27/1861), C.S.A.,
    m. 1857, Martha Virginia Cowan (11/2/1838-10/ /1920), dau.
    of William and Mary Elizabeth Johns Cowan of Memphis.
    Martha m. (2nd) Col. William B. Wooldridge (33241)
332121 William Glover Stanard (10/2/1858-5/6/1933), m. 4/17/1900,
    Mary Mann Page Newton (-6/5/1929), dau. of
    Bishop John Brockenborough and Roberta Page Williamson
    Newton of Richmond. No issue.
332122 Robert Conway Stanard, Jr. (10/23/1861-10/23/1924), m. 12/
    /1892, Mrs. Wistar Langhorne, nee Louise Belle Morris

(2/10/1856-1/ /1898), dau. of Dr. Sylvanus and Laura
Page Waller Morris
3321221 Virginia Morris Stanard (1/8/1894-   ), m. 4/14/1918,
George Lester Forbes (7/4/1892-   ), son of Walter
Tillon and Lillian Cannon Forbes of Atlanta
33212211 Virginia Stanard Forbes (4/1/1921-   ), m. 7/8/
1944, William Lawton Maner, Jr. (11/16/1918-   ),
son of William Lawton and Katherine Norborne Bell
Maner of Allendale, S.C.
332122111 William Lawton Maner III (1/24/1949-   )
33212212 Dr. George Lester Forbes, Jr. (8/19/1923-   ), m.
9/11/1948, Ruth Alice Wright (5/25/1922-   ),
dau. of Earl Franklin and Anna Allene Dick Wright of
Akron. No issue.
33212213 Robert Stanard Forbes (6/8/1926-   )
3321222 Mary Louise Stanard (7/16/1897-   ), m. 2/12/1927,
William Franklin Oliver (8/16/1893-   ), son of
Dr. George Hansford and Katherine Cunningham Oliver of
Irvington
33212221 Katherine Langhorne Oliver (5/15/1937-   )
33213 Maj. Philip Beverley Stanard (2/2/1835-5/6/1878), C.S.A.,
m. Rose Christian, dau. of John Christian of Lexington
332131 Robert Conway Stanard, m. Louise Stark, d.s.p.
332132 Lucy Jordan Stanard, m. George Wright (-1923).
She was his first wife.
3321321 Lawrence Beverley Wright (11/1/1880-   ), m. 7/31/
1906, Gertrude Madeline Peterson. Div.
33213211 Robert Stanard Wright (12/18/1909-   )
33213212 Evelyn May Wright (7/29/1911-   )
3321322 Robert Orlando Wright (9/24/1882-d. young). Unm.
332133 Sally Champe Stanard (d. age 18 years). Unm.
332134 Philip Beverley Stanard, Jr. (2/25/1868-7/21/1895), m.
1/27/1892, Annie James Reilly (11/2/1869-   ). She
m. (2nd) W. S. McClanahan
3321341 Hugh Conway Stanard (12/4/1892-   ), m. 9/9/1922,
Wanda Fern Engle (2/1/1892-   ), dau. of George
Adam and Anna Jane Dunn Engle of Newton, Iowa. No issue.
332135 George Stanard, d. young. Unm.
332136 James Christian Stanard, d. young. Unm.
332137 Lewis Thornton Stanard, m. Mary Carrington, dau. of Dr.
George Carrington of Richmond. No issue.
332138 Rosa Hazeltine Stanard, m. Charles Towson of White Plains,
N.Y.
332139 John Champe Stanard, d. age 17 years
33214 John Champe Stanard. Went West.
33215 Mary Bolling Stanard (3/20/1837-1910), m. Sidney H. Owens
332151 Stanard Owens, m. Mary Pratt, dau. of Rev. Pratt
3321511 Pratt Owens
33216 Sarah Julia Stanard (3/11/1838-1910), m. Henry French East-
ham, C.S.A., of Rappahannock County. No issue.
33217 Eliza Lavinia Stanard (12/15/1841-10/1/1843)

33218 Eliza Lavinia Stanard (7/3/1844-ca. 1922)
3322   Robert Beverley Stanard. Unm.
3323   William Fleming Stanard. Unm.
3324   Julia Ann Stanard (1809-4/7/1839), m. Dr. Archibald Logwood
      Wooldridge, son of William and   Logwood Wooldridge
      of Chesterfield County. Julia was Archibald's second wife
      ---he m. first Elizabeth Perrott Stanard, Julia's aunt, of
      Chesterfield County.
33241 Col. William Beverley Wooldridge, C.S.A., m. Martha Virginia
      Cowan (11/2/1838-10/29/1920), dau. of William and Mary
      Johns Cowan of Memphis. Martha m. (1st) Capt.Robert Conway
      Stanard (33212)
332411 Julia Stanard Wooldridge (-3/7/1938). Unm.
332412 Archer Wooldridge, d. 18 years of age
332413 Ellen Beverley Wooldridge. Unm.
332414 Mary Johns Wooldridge. Unm.
33242 Caroline Wooldridge, m. Dr. Edward Cunningham Archer of
      Powhatan County (12512)
332421 Elizabeth Temple Archer, d. unm.
332422 Emily Fowler Archer
332423 Robert Temple Archer
332424 Edward Cunningham Archer, Jr., d. young and unm.
332425 Mary Bolling Archer, m. William Phlegar Manuel of South
      Carolina
3324251 Virginia Jennie Manuel, d. unm.
3324252 Fannie Manuel, m.   Graham
3324253 William Phlegar Manuel, Jr.
3324254 John Manuel
332426 John Walthall Archer, m. 2/20/1884, Virginia Hening Floyd,
      dau. of   and Elizabeth Abbott Floyd of
      Powhatan County
3324261 Caroline Wooldridge Archer (4/16/1888-   ), m. 10/
      9/1915, Frank Deane Hill, Jr. (4/27/1878-   ), son
      of F. D. and Lelia Palmer Hill of Richmond
33242611 Virginia Archer Hill (4/20/1920-   )
33242612 Frank Deane Hill III (7/9/1926-   )
3324262 Elsie Selden Archer (10/5/1890-   ), m. 6/22/1910,
      Walter Wingate Allen (4/22/1887-   ), son of Thomas
      Moore Allen and Mattie F. Thatcher Allen of Semora, N.C.
33242621 Helen Floyd Allen (12/2/1911-   ), m. 5/16/1942,
      Albert Eugene Plant (12/22/1905-   ), son of
      Albert Frederick and Sarah Anne Schools Plant of Ports-
      mouth. No issue.
33242622 Elsie Archer Allen (9/11/1914-   ), m. 7/14/1933,
      Samuel Green (1/26/1896-   ), son of Norman and
      Edith Weinger Green of Baltimore
332426221 Samuel Archer Green (7/4/1935-   )
332426222 Floyd Allen Green (12/15/1938-   )
332426223 Lisa Green (8/18/1945-   )
33242623 Ann Vernon Allen (2/10/1919-   ), m. 9/6/1941,
      Charles Nelson Euroughty (7/31/1916-   ), son
      of Cameron and Annie Louise Doeppe Euroughty of Richmond

332426231 Charan Lynn Euroughty (10/31/1945-   )
3324263 John Stanard Archer (11/18/1884-   ), m. Jeannette
    Baird Jacobs
33242631 Floyd Archer
33242632 Dr. John Stanard Archer, Jr. of Richmond
3324264 Abbott Floyd Archer (5/22/1886-   ), m. 6/5/1912,
    Edith Gray Spratley (8/1/188-   ), dau. of William
    Walter and Virginia Lee Cowardin Spratley of Richmond
33242641 Edith Stanard Archer (3/15/1915-   ), m. 6/23/
    1945, Parvin Everett Cantrell (2/28/1906-   ),
    son of Parvin Leonard and Stella Alice Mills Cantrell
    of Richmond
332426411 Trudy Lee Cantrell (10/27/1946-   )
33242642 Abbott F. Archer, Jr. (8/14/1918-   )
33242643 Walter Gray Archer (44/1924-   )
3324265 Virginia Randolph Archer (1/28/1898-   ), m. 9/
    22/1923, James Ashley Gills (9/23/1885-   ), son
    of Jeptha Winston and Nancy Laventhia Gills of Amelia
33242651 Carolyn Floyd Gills (1/19/1908-   ). Unm.
332427 William Wooldridge Archer
332428 Jane Stanard Archer
33243 Julia Ann Wooldridge, m. Robert Temple Taylor, C.S.A., of
    Richmond
332431 Emily F. Taylor
3325 Elizabeth Fleming Stanard (- before 8/ /1874),
    m. Samuel Overton Eggleston (4/24/1797-8/8/1874). He m.
    (1st) 2/23/1825, Mrs. Caroline Wooldridge Elam of Virginia
    (-9/10/1836) who bore him a son, Marcellus Archer
    Eggleston (8/25/1836-   ). Two children of Samuel's,
    Jacqueline and Anne, d. inf., but whether they were children
    of Elizabeth or of Caroline is not known.
33251 Robert Stanard Eggleston
33252 William Fleming Eggleston (1841-12/ /1913), m. 2/21/1861,
    Mary Chambers Bibb, dau. of David Porter and Mary Betts
    Bibb of Alabama
332521 Robert Stanard Eggleston II, d. inf.
332522 Eliza Lockhart Eggleston (1869-   ), m. 12/1/1910,
    Benjamin Bartow Smith
332523 Mary Julia Bibb Eggleston, d. young
332524 Martha Cousins Eggleston, m. W. K. Browne
332525 Richard Henry Eggleston, m. Daisy A. Carpenter
3325251 Richard Fleming Eggleston
3325252 Louise Jerome Eggleston
333 (son)
334 Caroline Fleming
335 Jenny Fleming
336 Mary Fleming, m.   Strange
34 Richard Fleming. No issue.
35 Charles Fleming (-ca. 1793), Captain, 17th Virginia
    Regiment, and Lieutenant-Colonel in the State Line. Unm.
36 Mary Fleming, m. 3/20/1748, William Bernard, son of Robert and
    Elizabeth Bernard of Goochland County

361   Daniel Bernard, m.   Branch
3611 Cyrus Bernard (-5/15/1821), Midshipman, U.S.N.
      Prisoner of war at Algiers, killed in a duel at Havana.
3612 Christopher Bernard, Sergeant of Richmond Volunteers (War
      of 1812)
36121 (dau), m.   Branch
361211 Cyrus A. Branch of James City County
362   John Bernard, m. (1st) Miss Clopton, m. (2nd) Miss Norvell
     Children by first wife:
3621
3622

     Children by second wife:
3623
3624
363   Mary Bernard, m. Archibald Branch
3631 Christopher Branch
3632 Mary Branch
3633 Cyrus Branch
364   Elizabeth Bernard (dead by 5/10/1796), m.   Goode
      NOTE: This information, from Latrobe's CHART, does not
      seem to tally with GOODE. See GOODE, 50F, and pp. 468
      and 470
3641 Lucy Goode
365   Robert Bernard, dead by 5/10/1796
366   Thomas Bernard (1756-6/12/1834), m. Mary Hicks (1772-5/7/1847),
      dau. of Meshack Hicks. Marriage bond 12/28/1792. Thomas was
      b. in Cumberland County. He and Mary died in Leesburg, High-
      land County, Ohio, and are bur. in Pleasant Hill Cemetery,
      Fairfield Township.
367   Richard Bernard. Unm.
368   Jane Bernard. Unm.
369   William Bernard, dead by 5/10/1796
36x (dau)
37   Caroline Fleming, m. (1st) James Deane ("an old bachelor") of
      Chesterfield County, m. (2nd) 1764, James Fyrie of "Blandford",
      Prince George County. Deane was sometimes spelled Deans.
     Child by first husband:
371   Mary Deane, m. Edmund Randolph Yates. He m. (2nd) Elizabeth
      Murray (621)
3711 (dau) dead by 5/10/1796
38   (son) (predeceased his father)

4 Elizabeth Bolling (1709-ca. 1766), m. Dr. or Maj. William Gay
     of Henrico and Chesterfield Counties
41 Capt. William Gay of "Fairfield", Cumberland and Powhatan
     Counties, m. (1st) 9/20/1769, Frances Trent, dau. of Alexander
     Trent. M. (2nd) widow Ward (nee Eggleston). M. (3rd) 1/14/
     1783, in Amelia County, Judith Scott (-10/3/1827), dau.
     of John Scott ward of George Carrington
     Children by first wife:
411 William Alexander Gay (1778-1831) of Powhatan and Buchanan
      Counties, m. ca. 1802, Lucy Harrison Coupland (10/24/1784-
      1863), dau. of Ann Harrison and Col. David O'Shields Coup-
      land of Nansemond County
4111 Peter Field Gay, M.D. (1806-1866) of "Longwood", Charles City
       County, m. 1844, Ann Manning Christian
41111 (dau)
41112 (dau)
41113 (dau)
41114 (dau)
4112 B. Franklin Gay, m.   Baptist
41121 (son)
41122 (son)
41123 (son)
41124 (son)
41125 (son)
41126 (dau)
41127 (dau)
4113 William A. Gay (1803-1857). Unm.
4114 David Coupland Gay (1805-   ), m. Mrs. Sarah Nicholson
      of Vicksburg, Miss., d.s.p. See 39V175
4115 Benjamin Carter Gay (1818-1867), m. Elizabeth Cary
      NOTE: 4112 and 4115 may be the same person.
4116 Willis Walter Gay (1813-   ). Unm.
4117
4118
4119
411x
412 Elizabeth Gay (1772-   ), m. 1795, Peter Efford Bentley
     (-1857)
4121 Eliza Gay Bentley, m. Daniel Harris
4122 Wm. Field Benltey, m. Sarah Dupree
41221 (son)
41222 (son)
4123 Fanny Trent Bentley, m. Wm. Houston
4124 Efford Bolling Bentley (9/21/1801-   ), m. Lucy Williamson-
      son Chamberlayne, dau. of William Boyd and Ann Williamson
      Mosby Chamberlayne
41241 Efford Bolling Bentley, Jr. (4/26/1846-12/8/1848)
41242 Anne Chamberlayne Bentley (6/13/1848-4/30/1930)
41243 Lucy Parke Bentley (1/11/1854-8/22/1859)
41244 Henry Alexander Bentley (12/13/1855-9/1/1859)
4125 John Gay Bentley, m. Judith Bolling Thompson (5131)
4126 Maria Buchanan Bentley, m. 9/13/1826, Daniel Bates Friend
      (7/2/1802-6/28/1875), son of John and Judith Cary Bates
      Friend

```
41261   John Osborne Friend (10/2/1827-        ), m. Ellen C.
412611   Ellen Maria Pruet (Brent?) Friend (12/21/1854-        )
41262   Efford Bentley Friend (11/26/1828-7/8/1880)
41263   David Henry Friend (8/20/1830-7/24/1832)
41264   Elizabeth Gay Friend (7/15/1833-        )(twin)
41265   William Field Friend (7/15/1833-3/22/1845)(twin)
41266   Pocahontas Cary Friend (12/8/1835-7/11/1836)
41267   Maria Frances Friend (1/17/1838-5/28/1839)
41268   Daniel Bates Friend (10/30/1841-        )
41269   Ann Maria Friend (9/19/1843-6/10/1910), m. 1/15/1878, Joseph
          Greer McEwen (1/15/1842-11/6/1909).  She was his second
          wife.  His first wife was Isabella Goff Lane
412691   Robert Campbell McEwen (3/8/1879-        )
412692   Daniel Friend McEwen (2/17/1884-7/28/1885)
4126x   Sarah Lavinia Friend (4/10/1847-        )
```

ELIZABETH ("BETTY") GAY

(42)

Wife of Thomas Bolling of "Cobbs"

```
4127  Alex'r Willis Bentley, M.D., m.              Peters
4128  Lavinia Bentley, m. William Roper
4129  (dau)
```
        NOTE: For child of second wife (placed out of order), see
        41d
      Children of third wife:
```
413   Thomas Bolling Gay (ca. 1786-before 1850), m. 10/23/1811,
```
        Eliza Royall Archer, dau. of Maj. Peter Field Archer (1756-
        1814) of Powhatan County, and his first wife, Frances Tanner
        (d. 1797)
```
4131  Ellen Gay, m. Jacob Skein
41311 (son)
41312 (dau)
4132  Delia Gay (ca. 1821-              )
4133  William Gay, m.              Jackson
41331 (dau)
41332 (dau)
41333 (dau)
41334 (dau)
41335 (dau)
4134  Eliza S. Gay (ca. 1831-           )
4135  Powhatan A. Gay (ca. 1834-          )
4136  Virginia F. Gay (ca. 1840-          )
4137  Thomas Bolling Gay, C.S.A. (ca. 1823-4/  /1865), d. at Camp
```
        Douglass
```
4138  Charles S. Gay
414   Neale Buchanan Gay, m. Martha Talley
4141  William Gay, m. Sarah Bruce
4142  Neale B. Gay, Jr., m. Mary Bunn
41421 (son)
41422 (son)
41423 (son)
41424 (son)
41425 (dau)
41426 (dau)
4143  Martha Gay, m.              Perkins
41431 (son)
4144  Pocahontas V. Gay
4145  Ann Caroline Gay
415   Mary Buchanan ("Polly") Gay (1794-1879), m. Col. Gideon A.
```
        Strange of Fluvanna (d. 1838). For a later Gideon A. Strange,
        see GOODE 250. OMSS shows Colonel Strange's initial as B.
```
4151  William Gay Strange
416   Edward Scott Gay (1794-1874), m. 1840, Catherine Nivison
```
        Tazewell (1532), widow of E. Ambler. Gay was her second
        husband.
```
4161  Matoaca Gay, a distinguished society writer, under the nom
```
        de plume of "Bric-a-Brac". Unm.
```
4162  Louisa Tazewell Gay, m. Robert C. White
4163  Edward Scott Gay, Jr., m. Sarah ("Sallie") Mahulda Ewell,
```
        dau. of Dr. Ewell of Texas. Home: Atlanta

41631   Edward Scott Gay III, m. Helen Hendricks Hobbs (1/13/1892-
          5/8/1965), dau. of Arthur Greenwood Hobbs, M.D., and his
          wife, the former Lillie Hendricks
416311   Edward Scott Gay IV, m. Carroll Payne Smith
4163111 Edward Gay
4163112 Arthur Gay
4163113 Carroll Gay
41632   Louise Cary Gay (3/11/1884-   ), m. (1st) Sidney G.
          Stubbs; m. (2nd) 11/11/1909, John Wilson Somerville, M.D.
          (7/12/1881-   )(born in Culpeper, practices in Atlanta)
41633   Ewell Gay
416331   Frank L. Gay
4164   Caroline Scott Gay, m. Charles P. Winston (-1/1/1887)
4165   Minnie Wellford Gay. Unm.
4166   Kate Rolfe Gay, d. 1861
4167   Sally Bolling Gay, m. George Fitzgerald
41671
41672
41673
41674
417   Ann H. Gay, m. Charles H. Scott
4171   (son)
418   Charles Scott Gay (1802-1872), m. Margaret Lewis Erskine,
          dau. of Henry and Agatha Estill Erskine. Home: "Gaymont",
          near Staunton.
4181   Charles Wyndham Gay, C.S.A., killed in battle. Unm.
4182   Henry Erskine Gay. Unm.
4183   Frances ("Fannie") Bolling Gay, m. 1875, Richard Henry Catlett,
          son of Robert and Ann Tutt Catlett. Frances was Richard's
          second wife. His first wife was (?) Jennie Friend Daniel
          (see GOODE, p. 485).
41831   Margaret Erskine Catlett (2/27/1878-4/6/1958), m. 12/6/1906,
          Lawrence Washington Howe Peyton (1/27/1872-6/11/1949) of
          Staunton, son of Col. John Lewis and Henrietta Clark
          Washington Peyton
418311   Betty Washington Peyton (9/3/1914-   ), m. 4/23/1938,
          William Grosvenor Davis (10/30/1913-   ), son of
          Dudley and Alice Mason Grosvenor Davis
4183111 Alice Grosvenor Davis (6/4/1941-   ), m. 9/22/1960,
          Franco Codognato
4183112 Margaret Peyton Davis (3/24/1948-   ), m. 8/30/
          1969, Peter P. Brower
418312   Richard Catlett Peyton (-1969), m. Carolyn
418313   John Peyton
418314   Lawrence Peyton
41832   Fannie Gay Catlett, m. Livingston Waddell Smith of Lexington
          (Prof. W. & L Univ.)
418321   Amey Pendleton Smith
418322   Elizabeth Smith
4184   Lizzie E. Gay. Unm.
4185   William Patton Gay. Unm.
4186   Agatha Estill Gay. Unm.

4187   Caroline Scott Gay, m. W. M. Allen
4188   John R. Gay. Unm.
4189   Margaret Gay. Unm.
419   Sally Gay, m. 1808, Maj. James Boswell Ferguson (541). She
       was his second wife.
4191   Judith Gay Ferguson (1801-1839), m. John A. Carr, U.S.N.,
       grandson of Martha Jefferson and Dabney Carr
41911 (son)
4192   Rebecca Pocahontas Ferguson, m. 10/22/1833, John Meriwether
       Vaughan, M.D. (1805-1/3/1855), son of Nicholas Meriwether
       and Ann Randolph Pleasants Vaughan
41921 John Meriwether Vaughan, Jr. (9/21/1851-7/10/1913, m. 1880,
       Nannie Woodson Fuqua
419211 Elizabeth Langhorne Vaughan (9/4/1882-9/11/1950), m. 3/2/
       1905, Judge William Morgan Smith (1872-1946)
4192111 Nancy Vaughan Smith (12/31/1905-   ), m. Charles
       Campbell Hundley
41921111 Charles Campbell Hundley, Jr. of Farmville
4192112 Elizabeth Langhorne Smith (1/4/1907-   ), m. Stanley
       Vance Munsey
41921121 Elizabeth Vaughan Munsey
41921122 Anne Stafford Munsey of Richmond
4192113 Virginia Meriwether Smith (8/6/1908-   ), m. Richard
       Dunn Marks of Charlottesville
41921131 Dr. Richard Dunn Marks, Jr.
4192114 Rebecca Pocahontas Smith (11/23/1911-   ), m. Joshua
       Benjamin Davis. They live in War, W.Va.
41921141 Nancy Vaughan Davis
41921142 Dr. Robert Nicholas Davis
41921143 William Morgan Davis
41921144 Anne Meriwether Davis
41921145 Lee Langhorne Davis
4192115 Robbie Gay Smith (5/17/1915-   ), m. George James
       Whitlock. Home: "Morven", Cartersville, Va.
41921151 Frances Langhorne Whitlock
41921152 Margaret Elizabeth Whitlock
4192116 Frances Ferguson Smith (4/11/1919-   ), m. Otha
       Goodloe May of Vienna, Va.
41921161 Nancy Goodloe May
41921162 Judith Morgan May
4192117 Meriwether Vaughan Smith (12/2/1921-   ), m. 9/25/
       1944, Barbara Hope Almond of Norfolk County. Home:
       "Pocahontas Farm", Cumberland County
41921171 William Morgan Smith II
41921172 Meriwether Vaughan Smith
4192118
4192119
419211x
419211a
419211b
419211c

419212   Rebecca Pocahontas Vaughan (1883-   ), m. Andrew D.
         Graham of Goshen, Va.
4192121 Anne Meriwether Graham, m. Rev. Roy Coker
4192122 Andrew D. Graham, Jr.
4192123 Joseph B. Graham
4192124 Rebecca Pocahontas Graham, m. Dr. Francis I. Catlin of
         Baltimore
419213   William Fuqua Vaughan (1886-1960), m. (1st) Florence Pope
         (-1918). M. (2nd) Eugenia Pope (a sister of
         his first wife)
         Children by first wife:
4192131 William Meriwether Vaughan
4192132 Nancy Belle Vaughan
         Children by second wife:
4192133 Fred Pope Vaughan
4192134 Robert Vaughan
4192135 Flora Jean Vaughan
4192136 James Ferguson Vaughan
419214   Annie Randolph Briscoe Vaughan (9/28/1894-   ), m.
         Samuel Waverly Putney of Farmville
4192141 Anne Randolph Briscoe Putney (1915-   ), m. William
         E. Flory. Home: "Belair", Woodbridge, Va.
41921411 William E. Flory, Jr. (1947-   )
41921412 Anne Randolph Flory (1949-   )
4192142 Samuel Waverly Putney, Jr. (1917-   ), m. Grace
         Waring. Home: Farmville
41921421 Grace Lee Putney (1942-   )
41921422 Samuel Waverly Putney III (1946-   )
41921423 Lucy Meriwether Putney (1947-   )
41921424 William Waring Putney (1952-   )
4192143 Nellie Floyd Putney (1918-   ), m. John Vernon
         Casteen, Jr., of Chesapeake, Va.
41921431 Carolyn Lee Casteen (1942-   )
41921432 Anne Putney Casteen (1945-   )
4192144 Dr. William Witt Putney, D.V.M. (1920-   ), m. Elaine
         Mappa (Mapps?) Home: Van Nuys, Calif.
41921441 William Witt Putney III (1946-   )
41921442 James Lee Putney (1949-   )
4192145 Meriwether Vaughan Putney (1922-   ), m. Dorothy
         Martin. Home: Saluda, Va.
41921451 Dorothy Meriwether Putney (1952-   )
41921452 Meriwether Vaughan Putney, Jr. (1958-   )
4192146 Dr. Blake Fuqua Putney (1923-   ), m. Marie Flinker
41921461 Blake Fuqua Putney, Jr. (1953-   )
41921462 Thomas Ferguson Putney (1955-   )
41921463 Barbara Marie Putney (1957-   )
4192147 Myrtle Alice Putney (1926-1938)
4192148 Julian Taylor Putney (1928-   ), m. (1st) Gladys
         Dowdy. M. (2nd) 1962, Joyce London
         Children by first wife:
41921481 Julian Taylor Putney, Jr. (1952-   )

41921482 Lloyd Madison Putney (1956-   )
41921483 Debra Putney (1957-   )
41921484 Denise Putney (1958-   )
         Child by second wife:
41921485 James Terrell Putney (1963-   )
41922 Robert Ferguson Vaughan (2/ /1842-   ), m. 1874, Eliza-
         beth Lily Morton (7/ /1848-   ). Goochland County.
419221 Allen M. Vaughan (9/ /1875-   )
419222 Elsie Vaughan (6/ /1874-   ), m.   Carter
         NOTE: One source gives the name Elspeth instead of
         Elsie, and another source gives the name Gay instead
         of Elsie.
419223 Robert Ferguson Vaughan, Jr. (3/ /1882-   )
419224 Anne Randolph Vaughan (2/ /1990-   )
419225 Harry K. Vaughan (8/ /1883-   )
419226 Elizabeth M. Vaughan (4/ /1887-   )
41923 Sally Vaughan (1845-   ), m. 1873, Edward Briscoe
419231 Marie Briscoe (4/24/1875-1961), m. ca. 1895, Edward
         Crocker. She was poet Laureate of Maryland
4192311 Edward Crocker, Jr. (1896-1918)
4192312 Dorothy G. Crocker (6/27/1898-   ), m. Charles
         Lewis Lea (-8/20/1962)
41923121 Charles Lewis Lea, Jr. (12/2/1927-   )(twin)
41923122 Sally Vaughan Lea (12/2/1927-   )(twin)
41923123 Dorothy Cooke Lea (10/10/1930-   )
4192313 Douglas Vaughan Crocker (9/19/1900-   ), m. Margaret
         Herbert Mather
41923131 Margaret Mather Crocker
41923132 Edward Briscoe Crocker
41923133 Douglas Vaughan Crocker
41923134 Robinson Poe Crocker
4192314 John Hanson Crocker (1/30/1902-   ), m. Carolyn
         Ellicott MacCoun
41923141 Carolyn Crocker
41923142 Joan Crocker
41923143 Virginia Vaughan Crocker
41923144 John Hanson Crocker, Jr.
4192315 Nannette Frances Crocker (4/23/1903-1960), m. Randolph
         Fenton
41923151 Nanette Fenton
41923152 Maria Fenton
41923153 Randolph Fenton, Jr.
419232 Frances Briscoe (1877-   )
41924 Susan Gay Vaughan (1840-   ). Unm.
41925 Annie Randolph Vaughan (1847-   ), m. Calvin Wilson
         (ca. 1846-   ). Cumberland County
419251 Annie Randolph Wilson (1872-1951). A Presbyterian miss-
         ionary in China
419252 Pocahontas G. Wilson (3/ /1874-1948), m. Richard Cunning-
         ham Wight (1873-   ) of Halifax County, son of William
         Washington and Arianna Peyton Cunningham

```
4192521   Arianna Cunningham Wight (1899-          )
4192522   Pocahontas Wilson Wight (1904-          ), m. Richard Coles
          Edmunds, son of Henry Hurt and Louise Gilmer Riely
          Edmunds
41925221  Richard Coles Edmunds, Jr. (1931-        ), m. Nancy Page
          Hall
419252211 Marietta Page Edmunds (1958-            )
419252212 Elizabeth ("Betty") Randolph Edmunds (1961-          )
41925222  Anne Randolph Edmunds (1935-            )
41925223  Elizabeth Wight Edmunds (1937-          ), m. St. George
          Tucker Grinnan III
419252231 Louise Dabney Grinnan (1961-            )
4192523   Elizabeth Trent Wight (1907-            ), m. William F.
          Brown of Winston-Salem
4192524   Richard Cunningham Wight (1910-          ), m. Estella
          Churchill Cooke
41925241  Richard Cunningham Wight III (1947-          )
41925242  William Churchill Wight (1954-          )
4192525   Virginia Wight (1913-        ), m. Anderson Wade Lamb
41925251  Pocahontas Gay Lamb (1946-        )
41925252  Virginia Archer Lamb (1948-          )
419253    John Park Wilson (1875-1955)
419254    Elvira Peachy Wilson (5/  /1878-1931)
419255    Meriwether Wilson (1880-d. young)
419256    William Calvin Wilson (9/  /1883-        ), m. Olive Gwynne
4192561   William Calvin Wilson, Jr., m.
41925611
41925612
41925613
41925614
41925615
41925616
41925617
4192562   Emily Wilson, m. Jack Terry
41925621
4192563   John Park Wilson, m.
419257    Julian Mosely Wilson (11/  /1885-1950), m. Alys Clemmitt
419258    Elizabeth Trent Wilson, m. Wilfred Campbell McLauchlin.
          They were missionaries to Japan and China.
4192581   Elizabeth Trent McLauchlin (1918-1960), m. A. Taylor Seay
41925811  Marguerite Seay
41925812  Wilfred Seay
41925813  Elizabeth Wilson Seay
4192582   Annie Randolph McLauchlin (1920-          ), m. Rev. John
          Davidson of Marion, S.C.
41925821  John McLauchlin
41925822  Anne McLauchlin
4192583   Catherine Campbell McLauchlin, m. Rev. Lyle Peterson.  They
          were missionaries to Kochi, Japan
41925831  Anne Peterson, m. W. C. Morris of Kingsport, Tenn.
41925832  Mary Ellen Peterson
41925833  Richard Peterson
```

41925834 Daniel Peterson
419259 Gay Wilson, m. Ed S. Currie. They were missionaries to
     China and Formosa. Retired to Montreat, N.C.
4192591 Gay Currie (1920-   ), m. Joe Fox, Director of
     Peace Corps in British Borneo
4192592 Ed S. Currie, Jr., M.D. (1922-   ), m. Elinor
4192593 Lucy Calvin Currie (1923-1925)
4192594 John R. Currie (1925-1928)
4192595 David Currie (1931-   )
4192596 Anne Randolph Currie (1935-   ), m. Jack Leggoe of
     Philadelphia
41925961 Currie Randolph Leggoe (1962-   )
4193 Maj. James Boswell Ferguson, C.S.A., m. 12/22/1858, Emma
     Cabell Henry (2/14/1838-   ), dau. of Col. John
     Henry, and grand-dau. of Patrick Henry
41931 Elvira H. Ferguson (12/13/1859-   )
41932 James Boswell Ferguson, Jr., m. Dora Horner
4194 Mary Frances ("Fanny") Ferguson, b. ca. 1818. Unm.
4195 William Gay Ferguson, M. Margaret Bryce, nee Pickett
41951 (son)
41952 (dau)
4196 Robert Ferguson
41x (son)
41a (son)
41b Frances Gay (1788-1861). Unm.
41c Caroline H. Gay. Unm.
41d John Gay, d. 1797. He was the son of Capt. William Gay's
     second wife, the widow Ward (nee Eggleston)
42 Elizabeth ("Betty") Gay (9/ /1738-11/27/1813), m. Thomas
     Bolling of "Cobbs" (11)
43 Mary Gay, m. 1770, Neale ("Ugly Neale") Buchanan of "Ettrick
     Banks", Chesterfield County
44 John Gay, d. in the East Indies. No issue.
45 (dau). No issue.

5 Martha Bolling (1713-10/23/1749), m. 1737, (her first cousin), Thomas Eldridge, Jr. (1710-12/4/1754), of Henrico and Sussex Counties, son of Thomas and Judith Kennon Eldridge of "Rochdale", located twelve miles from Richmond. Thomas Eldridge, Jr., practiced law in Amelia County, and later moved to Prince George County, and died in Sussex County. He m. (2nd) Elizabeth Jones, dau. of James III and Sarah Edmunds Jones of Surry County. Thomas Eldridge, Jr., and Elizabeth Jones Eldridge had children including Aristotle, Howell and Sarah who m. Col. Thomas Edmunds of Brunswick (MB 11/25/1771-28 V 167). After the death of Thomas Eldridge, Jr., Elizabeth Jones Eldridge m. Col. Drury Stith of Brunswick County (she was his second wife).

For material on the Eldridges, see 46 V 172 and 267.

THE READ CONNECTION

MEADE, Vol. II, 28, states that Rev. Clement Read (son of Col. Isaac Read) married " a descendant of Pocahontas,--- a Miss Edmunds, of Brunswick---by whom he had thirteen children". And GOODE 195 states: "Miss Edmunds was a descendant of Pocahontas. Thomas Eldridge, according to Mr. Brock, m. Martha Bolling (b. 1713, d. Oct. 23, 1749). Their eldest son, Thomas, m. H. E. Read, and their (italicized) eldest dau., Sarah, m. Col. Thos. Edmunds".

"Miss Edmunds" was Clarissa, daughter of Sarah Eldridge and her husband, Col. Thomas Edmunds, and MEADE and GOODE were apparently laboring under the impression that Sarah Eldridge was the daughter (granddaughter?) of Pocahontas-descendant Martha Bolling (1713-10/23/1749), the first wife of Thomas Eldridge, Jr.

However, ROUSE 336, shows quite conclusively that Sarah Eldridge "who married 1771 Capt. Thomas Edmunds", and who was born in 1754 (several years after the death of Martha Bolling Eldridge), was the daughter of Thomas Eldridge, Jr.'s second wife, Elizabeth Jones, who was not a descendant of Pocahontas.

51 Thomas Eldridge III (1730's-   ) who probably moved to Goochland County, m. Winifred Jones Miller, dau. of William Miller, Sheriff of Goochland County in 1741, and his wife, Mary Heath Miller, dau. of Thomas Heath and Winifred Jones Heath, dau. of Robert Jones, Jr., and his wife Sarah Garlington (dau. of Christopher Garlington, Jr., and his wife Margaret). Thomas Heath's mother was Mary Lee, dau. of Capt. William Lee and grand-dau. of Col. Richard Lee
NOTE: There is some confusion concerning the wife or wives of Thomas Eldridge III. One source states that he married, first, Winifred Jones of Goochland County, and that he married, second, in 1776, Winifred Anne Miller Povall, dau. of William Miller and widow of Robert Povall. And GOODE says that he married H. E. Read (see above).

511   Thomas Eldridge IV (Will prob. Madison County, Ala., in 1822)
5111   John Bolling Eldridge
5112   Mary Miller Eldridge
5113   Martha Bolling Eldridge
5114   Winifred Jones Eldridge
5115   Sally Eppes Eldridge
5116   William Miller Eldridge
5117   Elizabeth Susan Eldridge
512   Judith Eldridge (1774-1852), m. 4/3/1794, Henry Cox (1774-
      1821) of Nottoway County, son of Henry and Ann Harris Cox
      (Cumberland County MB). Ann Harris Cox was the dau. of
      Benjamin and Ann Eppes Harris. Henry and Judith Eldridge
      Cox moved to Madison County, Ala. (Huntsville)
5121   Winifred Miller Cox (1798-1802)
5122   Ann Harris Cox (1800-   ), m. 1816, William Stratton
      Jones (1796-1870), son of Thomas Speck and Prudence Jones
      Jones of Amelia County (Thomas Speck Jones, a son of Peter
      Jones of Dinwiddie County, was a Colonel in the Revolution).
      William Stratton Jones moved to Madison County, Ala., in
      1813, and he and his wife moved to Franklin County, Ala.,
      in 1819
51221 Martha Bolling Cox Jones (1813-   ), m. Rev. Richard
      Henderson Rivers
51222 Henry Cox Jones(1821-1913), m. Martha Louisa Keyes
512221 William Stratton Jones
512222 George Presley Jones, m. Mary Bliss
5122221 George Bliss Jones
512223 Henry Cox Jones, Jr.
512224 John R. Jones
512225 Robert Jones, m. Annie Pollard
5122251 Franklin Pollard Jones
5122252 Judith Eldridge Jones
512226 Wade Keyes Jones
512227 Bertha Jones, m. Lindsay Melbourne Allen
5122271 Nellie May Allen
512228 Nellie R. Jones
512229 Jennie Keyes Jones, m. William Jones Kernachan
5122291 Henry Jones Kernachan
51222x John Simmons Jones, m. Virginia Lusk
51222a Bertha Jones, m. Charles Dunn Cushing
51222b Martha Bolling Jones, m. Thomas Sadler Jordan
51222b1 Henrietta Jordan, m. Louis Nebel
51223 William Stratton Jones, Jr. (1823-   ), m. Harriet
      Hutchens Harris
51224 Amelia Ann Harris Jones (1825-   ), m. Hon. Richard
      Sharp Watkins
51225 Thomas Speck Jones (1827-   ), m. Eliza P. Perry
51226 John Peyton Jones (1832-d. inf.)
51227 Evalina Eldridge Wyatt Jones, m. Dr. John King Clark
51228 Richard Eppes Jones (1839-d. inf.)
51229 Edward Sturdivant Jones (1844-   ), m. Ann Stratton
      Reynolds

5123 Martha Bolling Cox (1803-1818)
5124 Henry Cox, Jr. (1805-1839), m. (1st) Matilda Moore. No issue.
    M. (2nd) Sarah A. Steward
51241 Judith Ann Cox
51242 Martha Jane Cox
5125 Thomas Eldridge Cox (1807-1818)
5126 Judith.Eldridge Cox (1810-1852), m. John Harris
5127 Vincent P. Cox (1815-1832)
5128 Sarah Eldridge Cox (1815-1819)
513 Winifred Jones Eldridge (1776-   ), m. Rev. David Thompson
5131 Judith Bolling Thompson, m. John Gay Bentley (4125)
5132 John Eldridge Thompson, m. Blanche B.
514 John Rolfe Bolling Eldridge (1783-1868), d. Madison County,
    Ala. (Huntsville), m. Susan Miller (1788-1844)
5141 William Eldridge. Moved to Ohio
5142 John M. Eldridge, m. Frances Powell, dau. of Peyton Powell
    (Revolutionary soldier) and his wife Elizabeth Biscoe
51421 Sarah Eldridge, m. Albert Jones of Huntsville
51422 Mary Miller Eldridge, m. Norman Jones
51423 Pocahontas Eldridge
51424 Frances Lawson Eldridge
515 Sarah ("Sally") Eppes Eldridge, m. (1st) Thomas Hill. M. (2nd)
    George Moseley (Will recorded Madison County, Ala.)
   Child by first husband:
5151 Winifred Jones Thompson Hill, m. (her cousin), John Rolfe
    Bolling Johnson
   Children by second husband:
5152 George Moseley, Jr.
5153 Joseph Eldridge Moseley
5154 George Miller Moseley

258

516 Jane Eldridge, m. John Johnson
52   **Jenny Eldridge (1740-in the 1800's).** Unm.
53   John Bolling Eldridge (4/22/1741-   ). Unm.
54   Judith Eldridge (3/11/1742*3-   )(twin), m. James Ferguson
     of "Fairfield", Goochland County (he made his will in 1769 in
     Amelia County)
541 Maj. James Boswell Ferguson, m. (1st) Jane S. Payne Bolling
     (-1806)(widow of Robert Bolling)(126). M. (2nd)
     Sally Gay (419). For Maj. James Boswell Ferguson's children
     by Sally Gay, see 419.
5411 Jane Elvira Ferguson (4/6/1806-9/8/1898), m. 1827, Peachy R.
     Grattan (11/7/1801-9/8/1881), son of Maj. Robert Grattan of
     Rockingham County and his wife, the former Martha Divers
     Minor Grattan (or Elizabeth Gilmer Thornton. See LM, p.174).
54111 Elizabeth Gilmer Grattan (4/11/1837-   )("The Saint").
     Unm.
54112 Sally Gay Grattan (8/10/1838-   )(twin)("The Wit"),
     m. Otho H. Kean. Had issue
54113 Lucy Gilmer Grattan (8/10/1838-10/14/1890)(twin)("The
     Beauty"), m. W. F. Alexander. Had issue
54114 James Ferguson Grattan (77/11/1840-1879), m. Miss Morris.
     No issue
54115 George Gilmer Grattan (10/12/1844-   ). Killed at
     the Battle of Seven Pines
54116 (dau)
54117 (dau)
54118 (dau)
54119 (dau)
5411x (dau)
5412 Robert Bolling Ferguson. Settled in St. Louis ca. 1840, and
     died there.
5413 (son)
5414 (son)
5415 (son)
5416 (dau)
5417 (dau)
5418 (dau)
542 (son)
55   Mary Eldridge (3/11/1742*3-living in November 1792)(twin),
     m. 1760, Thomas Branch (ca. 1730-7/4/1815) of "Hannah Spring",
     Chesterfield County, son of Matthew Branch (-ca. 1766)
     and Elizabeth Goode Branch of Henrico County
551 Maj. Bolling Branch (-11/4/1829) of Buckingham County,
     m. (1st) 2/20/1800*1 in Chesterfield County, Rebecca Graves
     (-8/7/1815), dau. of Arthur Graves. The Major m.
     (2nd) 6/3/1817, Mary H. Bell (9/22/1781-8/15/1822), dau. of
     Henry and Rebecca Harrison Bell. See (552)
     Children by first wife:
5511 Mary Susan Branch (11/9/1801-1890), m. John F. Wiley (d.
     before 1903, in Gerrardstown, W.Va.)
55111 George Wiley (was living in 1896 in Paineville, Amelia
     County), m.

551111 Arthur Skelton Wiley of New York
55112 William F. Wiley, m. Mary Evans
55113 Harvey Wiley
55114 Dr. John B. Wiley, m. Nannie S. Murry. For children, see 6133
55115 (son)
55116 (son)
55117 Rebecca Wiley, m. Dr. M. F. T. Evans
55118 (dau)
55119 (dau)
5512 William Arthur Branch (9/30/1805-1893). He d. in Albemarle
     County
5513 Sarah Graves ("Sally") Branch (2/19/1808-   ), m. Capt.
     Edward Gregg
5514 Robert Bolling Branch (11/30/1803-2/12/1827). Died in Rich-
     mond
5515 Thomas Branch (2/15/1811-4/26/1817)
     Child by second wife:
5516 Wiley Harrison Branch (7/28/1821-d. age 15 mos., 2 days)
     NOTE: Family Bible notes death of Bolling Henry Bell Branch
     on 8/20/1822.
552 Matthew Branch (ca. 1776-ca. 1828), lived, d., and was bur. at
     "Tower Hill", Buckingham County, m. (1st) Martha Cox; m. (2nd)
     Rebecca Bell (1/18/1777-12/31/1858), dau. of Henry and Rebecca
     Harrison Bell of "Cold Comfort". Rebecca Harrison Bell was
     the dau. of Benjamin Harrison of "Horn's Quarter". "Tower
     Hill" adjoins "Cold Comfort" (both are near the village of
     Dillwyn), and "Cold Comfort" adjoins "Belmont" which is on
     Hatcher's Creek, fifteen miles below Buckingham Court House.
     "Belmont" was built by Colonel Bell who married a daughter of
     Archibald Cary, and who, from 1761 to 1770, was Clerk of the
     Buckingham County Court. "Horn's Quarter" (part in Bucking-
     ham County, and part in Cumberland County) lies on both sides
     of Willis' River, six and one-half miles northwest from
     Cumberland Court House.
     All of the children of Matthew Branch were born at "Tower
     Hill".
    Child by first wife:
5521 Mary ("Polly") Branch,m. Thomas May. Lived and died at
     Buckingham Court House.
55211 Sarah May, m. Robert Page
55212 Martha May
55213 Mary May
55214 (son)
55215 (son)
55216 (son)
    Children by second wife:
5522 Henry Bell Branch (5/13/1793 or 1798-7/17/1842), m. his first
     cousin, 9/18/1823, Susan Cary Bell (5/15/1805-5/16/1864,
     dau. of Henry Cary and Susan P. Mosley Bell of Buckingham
     County. Henry Bell Branch failed as a merchant in Caira,
     Cumberland County, and moved to Missouri where he soon died.

Susan Cary Bell m. (2nd) Judge Nathaniel Harris Price (and they had three daughters)

55221 Col. Harrison Bell Branch (8/22/1824-8/28/1893), m. 10/25/ 1853, at Weston, Mo., Lucretia Matilda Perry (3/15/1829- 2/4/1900), dau. of Elias H. and Angelina Waters Perry of St. Joseph, Mo. Col. Branch b. Buckingham County, Va., d. St. Joseph, and is bur. in Mount Maria Cemetery, St. Joseph

552211 Lucretia Bell Branch (1854-d. inf.)

552212 Susan Bell Branch (9/1/1855-3/30/1926), m. at St. Joseph, Alfred B. Sowden (9/20/1848-4/28/1903). Susan Bell Branch b. Weston, Platte County, Mo., d. Hollywood, Calif. Alfred B. Sowden b. London, England, d. St. Joseph

5522121 Alfred Harrison Sowden (3/16/1884-), b. St. Joseph. Unm.

5522122 "Baby" Sowden (3/5/1888-3/21/1888), b. St. Joseph

552213 James Harrison Branch (2/18/1863-10/24/1923), m. 9/4/1901, at Kansas City, Catherine Mulkey Drips (7/24/1880-), b. Kansas City, dau. of Andrew Jackson and Florence Jane Winship Drips. James Harrison Branch b. St. Joseph, d. Los Angeles.

5522131 Catherine Mulkey Branch (10/19/1904-), b. Kansas City, m. (1st) 2/2/1924, Walter MacDonald. No issue. M. (2nd) 7/28/1933, in Riverside, Calif., William Ray Benedict (5/11/1894-), b. Beverley Hills, Calif., son of Pierce Edson and Viola Leone Colkerton Benedict

55221311 Catherine Branch Benedict (6/7/1937-) b. Los Angeles, m. 1/21/1956, in Santa Barbara, Calif. Conrad Wayne Lalicker (5/13/1935-), b. Kansas, son of Clyde Russell and Lelia Frances Elizabeth Wise Lalicker

552213111 William Benedict Lalicker (12/2/1956-), b. Los Angeles

552213112 Loris Catherine Lalicker (7/10/1958-), b. Los Angeles

552213113 Russell Stephan Lalicker (2/10/1961-), b. Los Angelse

55221312 Sharon Rae Benedict (12/27/1941-), b. Los Angeles, m. 4/25/1959, at Santa Barbara, Kenneth Marshall Nelson (11/17/1938-), b. Salt Lake City, son of Merlyn and Maria Marshall Nelson

552213121 Susan Gaye Nelson (3/10/1960-), b. Santa Monica, Calif.

5522133 Lucretia Harrison Branch (5/3/1909-) b. Kansas City, m. 2/27/1943, at Pacific Palisades, Calif., Richard Barker Hershey (3/20/1908-), b. Los Angeles, son of Charles Wesley and Louise Durfee Hershey

55221331 Richard Barker Hershey II (1/12/1944-), b. San Diego

55221332 Harrison Branch Hershey (11/18/1945-), b. San Diego

5522134   James Harrison Branch, Jr. (4/6/1911-   ) b. Kansas
          City, m. 1943, Loris Todtman. No issue
5522135   Mary Jane Branch (7/17/1913-   ), b. Kansas City,
          m. 4/2/1930, at Beverley Hills, Joseph Paul Popkin
          (2/27/1906-   ), son of George and Isabel Platt
          Popkin
55221351 Pamela Branch Popkin (5/24/1941-   ) b. Los Angeles,
          m. 7/7/1962, John Ernest Ford III
55221352 Paula Branch Popkin (7/15/1949-   ), b. Los Angeles
55222   Matthew Graham Branch (4/10/1833-   ), b. Buckingham
          County, d. Salt Lake City, en route to California
55223   Henry Cary Branch (2/15/1827-3/15/1903), m. (1st) 11/4/1851,
          Dorothy Ann Perry (3/10/1829-3/11/1872), of Platte County,
          Mo. (b. Montgomery County, Md.), dau. of Elias and Angeline
          Waters Perry of Platte County. M. (2nd) 11/20/1872, Emily
          Wailes Wilcoxen (8/31/1831-1/19/1924), (b. Frederick, Md.;
          d. St. Louis), dau. of Horatio and Sarah Attilda Wayles
          Wilcoxen. Henry Cary Branch was born, raised and educated
          in Buckingham County. At fifteen years of age he went with
          his parents to Missouri. He resided in Platte Coumty; in
          Leavenworth County, Kansas; and for eleven years, in Saline
          County, Mo. In 1877, he settled five miles from Lexington
          on a 180 acre farm. D. Lexington, and is bur. in Mashpelah
          Cemetery, Lexington
          Children by first wife:
552231   Acquilina Perry Branch (1/24/1855-d. after 1903), m. in
          Platte, Mo., Andrew P. Tucker of Saline County, Mo.
5522311   Charles Tucker, m. Olive Graham of Lincoln, Neb.
55223111 Morrison Graham Tucker (Oklahoma City), m. Gladys
552231111 Susanne Tucker
552231112 John Tucker
5522312   Jesse Norris Tucker, m. Fay Spencer of Ft. Worth. Lived
          in Texas
55223121 J. Norris Tucker, Jr., M.D., m. Leah   . Houston.
552231211 J. Norris Tucker III
552231212 Brooke Tucker
55223122 Dorothy T. Tucker, m. Judge Frank M. Wilson of Waco
552231221 Martha Fay Wilson, m. O. Cleveland Witt
5522312211 Robert Cameron Witt, age 22 mos. 3/1962
552231222 Frank M. Wilson, Jr. Kileen, Texas
5522313   Robert Tucker, m. (1st)   , div., m. (2nd)
                    . Lived in Calif.
          Child by first wife:
55223131 Wesley Tucker. Fort Worth
552231311 Mary Tucker
552231312 Bill Tucker
5522314   Boyd Branch Tucker, m. Virginia Bunting. Fort Worth
55223141 Mary Tucker, m.   Muse. Austin
552231411
552231412
55223142 Boyd Branch Tucker, Jr.

55223143 Lucille Tucker, m.
552231431
552231432
552231433
552232 James Cary Branch (2/7/1857-3/25/1933) of Saline County,
        Mo., m. Hattie Emma Robertson (2/21/1861-10/30/1929),
        dau. of John and Nancy T.Robertson
5522321 Wallace Turpin Branch (12/19/1885-7/27/1954), m. at
        Fort Worth, 6/4/1912, Gertrude Adams (4/1/1890-   ),
        (b. Amarillo, Potter Co., Texas), dau. of Joseph Warren
        and Jeanetts Woods Adams
55223211 Harriet Adams Branch (2/9/1914-   ), m. J. C.
        Jenkins
552232111 Janet Carole Jenkins (1/15/1940-   )
552232112 Sally Jean Jenkins (1/7/1947-   )
55223212 Dorothy Jean Branch (12/10/1920-   ), m. Russell
        A. Nelson
552232121 Henry Allen Nelson (2/16/1957-   )
552232122 Ann Jeanette Nelson (11/14/1943-   )
552232123 Laura Louise Nelson (9/19/1959-   )
5522322 Nancy Dorothy Branch (2/16/1888-7/12/1945), m. 6/24/1914,
        Walker Coward Fletcher (baptized Walter Catron Fletcher)
        (9/11/1879-   ), son of George and F. Z. Meeks
        Fletcher
55223221 Walker Coward Fletcher, Jr. (12/8/1929-   ), m.
        Marjorie Ruth Sherlock (2/19/1933-   ), dau. of
        Mr. and Mrs. Alva Merle Sperlock of Rossville, Ind.
552232211 John Merle Fletcher (12/3/1956-   )
552232212 Steven Walker Fletcher (9/9/1958-   )
552232213 Nancy Ruth Fletcher (1/31/1960-   )
552232214 Lucy Anne Fletcher (8/1/1961-   )
5522323 Charles Henry Branch (9/16/1890-7/23/1958), m. 11/2/1921,
        in Los Angeles, Grace Myra Fowler (10/23/1898-   ),
        (b. Virginia City, Storey County, Nev.), dau. of Henry
        B. and Lillian Hancock Fowler
55223231 Barbara Branch (6/23/1923-   )
5522324 John Robertson Branch (7/2/1894-   ), m. 4/24/
        1917, in Belen, N.M., Elsa Becker
55223241 Margaret ("Peggy") Esther Branch (8/14/1921-   ),
        m.
552232411 (dau)
552232412 (dau)
552232413 (dau)
55223242 John Robertson Branch (4/2/1923-   ), m.
552232421 (son)
5522325 James Cary Branch, Jr. (10/16/1905-6/ /1959), m. (1st)
                    , div. M. (2nd) 6/25/1941, in Denver, Colo.,
        Margaret Rebecca Green (5/30/1914-1955),(b. Mountain Grove,
        Mo.), dau. of Charles Llewellyn and Mary Bessie Dorton
        Green. M. (3rd) two years before his death, a widow with
        four children

Children by first wife:
55223251 Charles James Branch (7/16/1934-   ), b. Elbow Lake,
          Minn.)
55223252 (dau)
          Child by second wife:
55223253 Jerry Dorton Branch (1/24/1947-   ), b. Ogden,
          Utah
552233 Susan Elizabeth Branch (3/4/1859-3/17/1936), m. 4/27/1881,
          Robert Mitchell Howe (1/26/1859-3/19/1942) of Fayette
          County, Mo., son of John Ross and Nancy Jane Mitchell
          Howe. Susan Elizabeth Branch b. Leavenworth County,
          Kansas Territory, and bur. Lexington, Mo. She was her
          parents 13th child
5522331   Jane Hortense Howe (7/24/1882-11/24/1884)
5522332   Henry Branch Howe (9/4/1884-   ), m. 5/27/1920,
          at Wellington, Mo., Grace Lee Mann, eldest dau. of Dr.
          John A. and Sally Dodd Mann
55223321 Sally Sue Howe (12/19/1921-   ), Birmingham,
          Ala., m. 4/15/1950, (as his second wife) George William
          Henry Haines, Jr. (6/14/1916-   ), son of George
          William Henry and Alice Ruth Smith Haines of Jacksonville,
          Fla.
552233211 Henry Branch Haines (3/8/1961-   ), b. Jacksonville
55223322 Henry Branch Howe, Jr. (8/5/1924-   ), b. Atlanta,
          m. 9/1/1951, Margaret Anne Haden (1/15/1928-   ),
          b. Charlottesville, Va.
552233221 Stephen Jeffrey Howe (7/29/1955-   ), b. Char-
          lottesville
552233222 Barbara Lynn Howe (7/2/1958-   ), b. Winston-
          Salem, N.C.
552233223 Allan Howe
5522333 Robert Lee Howe (2/17/1887-11/20/1966), m. 10/3/1915,
          Frances Astoria Munson of Michigan. Robert Lee Howe d.
          Independence, Mo.
55223331 Robert Munson Howe (10/18/1916-   ), m. 12/27/1956,
          Mary Lucas Hall of Virginia
5522334 Charles Howe (2/28/1891-1891)(twin). D. Elma, Wash., at
          age one month
5522335 John Bell Howe (2/28/1891-   )(twin), b. Elma,
          Wash., m. (1st) 7/9/1923, Frances G. C. Simmons of New
          York. M. (2nd) 9/16/1953, Mrs. Mabel Olive Thuilard
          (4/7/1887-   ), b. Berkshire, N.Y. John Bell
          Howe's home: Lakeland, Fla. No children by second wife.
          Child by first wife:
55223351 Patricia Simmons Howe (5/20/1928-   ), b. New York,
          m. (1st) Robert L. Rogers of Jamaica, N.Y. He served
          in Marine Corps during World War II, was captured at
          Corregidor, and was a prisoner of the Japanese for
          forty-one months. M. (2nd) 1953, Willis B. Casey of
          N.Y. Home: Florida
          Children by first husband:

552233511 Betsy Rogers
552233512 Bobby Rogers
           Children by second husband:
552233153 David Casey
552233514 John Burton Howe Casey
5522336   Samuel Teller Howe (12/14/1893-   ), b. at the home
           of his grandparents Howe, six miles southwest of
           Lexington, Mo., m. Lucy Pearl Copas Sampson (he was her
           second husband) (1/14/1894-Autumn 1961) of Hopkinsville,
           Ky.
55223361   Robert Jeral Howe (4/21/1925-   ), b. Tulsa,
           m. (1st) Betty Baxter. Div., m. (2nd) Martha Daniel
           (10/24/1930-   ), b. Swink, Colo.
552233611 Ronald Jerald Howe (9/8/1954-   ), b. Tulsa
552233612 Daniel Wray Howe (9/18/1955-   ), b. Tulsa
55223362   Samuel Teller Howe, Jr. (10/17/1926-   ), b. Tulsa,
           m. Marjorie Lee Wadley (6/26/1928-   ), b. Monett,
           Mo.
552233621 Judith Lee Howe (4/24/1947-   ), b. Tulsa, m. 1966,
           Don Hoddard. Lives in Attica, Kans.
552233622 Linda Ann Howe (12/27/1948-   ), b. Falboris,Tx.
552233623 Martha Jean Howe (12/21/1949-   ), b. Fremont, Tx.
5522337   Clayton Brown Howe (4/1/1898-   ), b. near Lexington,
           Mo., m. 10/5/1925, in Colorado Springs, Colo, Daisie Dean
           Winifred Simmons (5/22/1899-   ) b. Logan County,
           Ark., dau. of James and Lettie Ann Smith Simmons
55223371   Wallace Brady Howe (8/5/1926-   ), m. 8/24/1948,
           Lola Spenny (11/20/1925-   ), dau. of Oval Howard
           and Virgie Lee Norris Spenny
552233711 Sally Howe (7/9/1965-   ), b. Rolla, Mo.
55223372   Rosamond Arlene Howe (2/1/1928-   ), m. 2/2/1948,
           John Nelson Warfield (11/21/1925-   ), son of
           Mrs. Alice Warfield
552233721 Daniel Lawrence Warfield (9/14/1950-   )
552233722 Nancy Rose Warfield (6/3/1955-   )
552233723 Thomas Edward Warfield (8/5/1958-   )
55223373   Beverly Pavlowa Howe (2/28/1929-   ), m. 8/29/1947,
           Lewis Austin West (2/6/1928-   ), b. Worth County,
           Mo., son of Raymond Arthur and Beulah Iona Patrick West
552233731 Ann Clayton West (10/7/1956-   )
552233732 Elizabeth Howe West (3/27/1958-   )
55223374   Maurice Dorien Howe (9/6/1930-   ), m. 10/4/1952,
           Helen Mary Draskovich, dau. of Matthew Frank and Mary
           Stepetic Draskovich (who came to U.S. in 1909 from
           Croatia)
552233741 Cynthia Gail Howe (11/15/1955-   )
552233742 Dana Linn Howe (4/7/1957-   )
552233743 David Brian Howe (8/15/1959-   )
552233744 Susan Mary Howe (7/17/1962-   )
5522338   Melvin Perdue Howe (8/29/1903-   ), m. 7/27/1942,
           Joan Esther Anderson (4/22/1915-   ), dau. of
           Victor C. and Esther Macadam Anderson. No issue. Home:
           Marathon, Fla.

552234   Henry Harding Branch (12/7/1861-6/19/1931)(b. Leavenworth
      County, Kansas, d. Lincoln, Neb.), m. 11/10/1894 Bennita
      Wood of Kansas City, dau. of Ben and Amanda Riddle Wood.
      With his brother, Charles Waters Branch, Henry Harding
      Branch owned a shoe store, ca. 1896, in Lincoln
5522341   Ben Wood Branch (11/24/1897-12/15/1898)
5522342   Henry Harding Branch, Jr. (10/13/1904-1/28/1955)(b.
      Kansas City, Mo., d. Pulaski, Giles County, Tennessee),
      m. (1st) 2/24/1926, Helen Ryons (she m. second, Judge
      Lloyd S. Nix, of Los Angeles); m. (2nd) 4/20/1944, in
      Kansas City, Bennita Branch McKinney McGuire (5522391)
      (3/26/1909-   ), dau. of Dr. James William and
      Anna Branch McKinney of Kansas City. (Henry Harding
      Branch, Jr. was Bennita Branch McKinney McGuire's second
      husband)
      Children by first wife:
55223421   Bennita Branch, b. Lincoln, Neb.
55223422   Henry Harding Branch, III (9/2/1929-9/22/1962, b. Lincoln,
      Neb.
552235   Charles Waters Branch (3/1/1865-1/2/1939)(b. Leavenworth
      County, Kansas, d. Lincoln, Neb.), m. 11/9/1892 (his first
      cousin), May Perry (5/21/1865-1/1/1956) of St. Joseph,
      Mo.(b. Petaluma, Calif., d. Lincoln, Neb.), dau. of Elias
      H. and Annie M. Riddle Perry
5522351   Perry Waters Branch (8/18/1898-   ) b. Lincoln,
      Lancaster County, Neb., m. 9/28/1922, at Lincoln, Neb.,
      Latta Watson (5/28/1902-   ) b. Friend, Neb.,
      dau. of Edward Garland and Mary Olive Latta Watson
55223511   Perry Waters Branch, Jr. (7/23/1924-   )b. Lincoln,
      Neb., m. 12/27/1946, Mary Lou Holtz (6/1/1924-   )
      b. Lincoln, Neb., dau. of Harold F. and Vina E. Kohler
      Holtz
552235111   Suzanne Latta Branch (2/5/1949-   ), b. Lincoln,
      Neb.
552235112   Sarah Kohler Branch (12/22/1950-   ), b. in
      Rochester, N.Y.
55223512   Jeanne Latta Branch (5/30/1927-   ), b. Lincoln,
      Neb., m. 8/25/1948, in Lincoln, John E. Boman (5/17/
      1926-   ), b. Lincoln, son of Eric E. and Mary
      Minerva Strom Boman
552235121   Jeanne Latta Boman (10/23/1949-   ), b. Lincoln,
      Neb.
552235122   Kim Branch Boman (12/12/1952-   ), b. Lincoln,
      Neb.
552235123   Debra Ann Boman (4/13/1954-   ), b. Lincoln,
      Neb.
552235124   Joni Joakim Boman (8/5/1955-   ), b. Lincoln,
      Neb.
55223513   Latta Watson Branch (2/12/1931-4/26/1940), b. Lincoln,
      Neb.
552236   Virginia Bell ("Virgie") Branch (7/15/1868-8/25/1931), b.

Lexington, Saline County, Mo., d. Alliance, Neb., bur. in
Green Wood Cemetery, Alliance, m. 9/16/1902, William
Harrison Rust (10/31/1874-8/25/1922)(b. near Waverly, Neb.,
d. Alliance), son of William Wall and Mary Rosa Rust

5522361 Hall Wood Rust (11/29/1903-   ) b. Waverly, Lancaster County, Neb., m. Clara Irene Tice (3/1/1911-
) b. at Alliance, Neb., dau. of Walter Ellis
and Martha Priscilla Colwick Tice

55223611 Bonnie Jean Rust (12/14/1929-   ), m.
Sulzbach of South Dakota (brother to husband of 55223613)

55223612 William Ellis Rust (9/21/1931-   ), m. Winnie

552236121 Terry Rust (dau)

552236122 Tom Rust

552236123 Julia Rust

55223613 Lois Elaine Rust (7/26/1933-   ), m.
Sulzbach of South Dakota (brother to husband of 55223611)

55223614 Charles Woodrow Rust (11/29/1935-   )

552237 Benjamin Augustus Branch (2/25/1872-4/15/1872), b. Saline
County, Mo.

Children by second wife:

552238 Cary Glover Branch (9/15/1873-1/17/1956), (b. Saline County,
Mo., d. age 82, Giles Co., Tenn.), m. 7/18/1904, Estelle
Adams (12/4/1883-   ), of Odessa, Mo., dau. of Noah
P. and Mary Muir Adams

5522381 Richard Kerens Branch (2/14/1906-   ) b. Lexington,
Mo., m. 4/16/1922, Mildred Warner. Lives in Calif.

5522382 Cary Glover Branch, Jr. (9/24/1908-   ) b. Lexington, Mo., m. (1st) 8/2/1937, Annie Chapman; m. (2nd)
before 1961, Eva Mae Trail. No issue. He is an attorney in Los Angeles

5522383 Mary Lillian Branch (8/23/1913-   ) b. Independence,
Mo. Lives in Calif.

5522384 Anna Estelle Branch (9/14/1915-   ) b. Trenton,
Grundy County, Mo., m. before 1961, Austin C. Neal

55223841 Mary Catherine (Kathy) Neal (b. before 1961-   )

552239 Anna Ewing Branch (10/15/1877-7/31/1913)(b. Lexington, Mo.,
d. Kansas City, Mo.), m. 4/15/1903, at Lexington, Dr.
James William McKinney (6/1/1875-12/7/1952) (b. & d.
Kansas City), son of William Franklin and Sarah Storey
McKinney

5522391 Bennita Branch McKinney (3/26/1909-   ) b. Kansas
City, Kansas, m. (1st) 6/22/1933, at Kansas City, Kansas,
John Sargent McGuire (10/10/1903-   )(b. Thayer,
Mo.); m. (2nd) 4/20/1944, at Kansas City, Mo., Henry
Harding Branch, Jr. (5522342)(10/13/1904-1/28/1955)(b.
Kansas City, Mo., d. Pulaski, Giles County, Tenn.), son
of Henry Harding and Bennita Wood Branch. (She was his
second wife)

Children by first husband:

55223911 Bennita Ann McGuire (3/10/1937-   ) b. Kansas City,
Kan., m. 9/27/1955, in Memphis, Thomas William Harrison
(6/17/1914-   ) b. Lawrence County, Tenn., son of
Walter and Marcella Rogers Harrison

552239111 Brenda Ann Harrison (5/3/1956-   ) b. Pulaski,
    Giles County, Tenn.
552239112 Terry William Harrison (8/21/1957-   ) b. Pulaski,
    Giles County, Tenn.
552239113 Gregory Branch Harrison (3/10/1959-   ) b. Pulaski,
    Giles County, Tenn.
55223912 Patricia Kathleen McGuire (1940-   )
5522392 Anna Branch McKinney (6/18/1913-   ) b. Kansas City,
    Kan., m. 10/21/1933, in Kansas City, Kan. Wilbur Monroe
    Broyles (3/8/1909-   ) b. Kansas City, Kan., son
    of John Edward and Lou Etta Shepard Broyles
55223921 James Patrick Broyles (11/5/1939-   ) b. Kansas
    City, Mo.
55223922 Julia Lou Broyles (7/21/1947-   ) b. Kansas City,
    Mo.
55223x Katherine Wilcoxen Branch (10/2/1879-5/4/1965)(b.Lafayette
    County, Mo ., d. Santa Monica, Calif.). Unm.
55223a Martha Harrison Branch (12/1/1882-   )(b. Elm Forest,
    near Lexington, Mo.), m. 11/20/1906, in Kansas City, Mo.,
    Henry Long Sparks, Jr. (4/24/1882-9/17/1918)(b. Marshall,
    Saline County, Mo., d. St. Louis)
55223a1 Martha Harrison Sparks (9/23/1907-   ) b. St. Louis,
    m. 1/19/193 , in St. Louis, Claude Lourie Hough II (4/
    4/1910-   ) b. Muskogee, Okla., son of Claude
    Lourie and Nancy Lee Hough
55223a11 Claude Lourie Hough III (12/19/1935-   ) b. St.
    Louis, m. 8/22/1959, at Burlington, Vermont, Barbara
    Cox (7/12/1936-   ) b. Middleton, N.Y., dau. of
    Elliott H. and Vera W. Cox. In 1961, Claude was a jet
    pilot in the U.S. Air Force, stationed at Cape Cod, Mass.
55223a111 Marjorie Ellen Hough (8/21/1962-   )(b. Otis Air
    Force Base, Cape Cod)
55223a12 Nancy Lee Hough (9/19/1939-   ) b. St. Louis
55223a13 Susan Bradford Hough (7/16/1944-   ) b. Washington,
    D. C.
55223a2 Emily Branch Sparks (11/2/1912-   ) b. St. Louis,
    m. 10/20/19 , in St. Louis, Charles Benjamin Baucam
    (6/9/1910-   ), b. Kenton, Tenn., son of B. R.
    and Jattye Tilghman Baucam
55223a21 Martha Tilghman Baucam (2/21/1947-   ) b. St.
    Louis.
55223b
55223c
55224 David Bell Branch (11/5/1830-1855)(b. in Buckingham County,
    killed in Nevada), m.   Virts. It is said he was
    operating a relay station, working for the Government and
    furnishing horses for the express, and was killed by Mexicans.
    When captured by a posse, the Mexicans were found to have
    David's horses and paraphernalia, and were hanged on the
    spot.
552241 Henry Virts Branch

55225 Martha Edwards Branch ("Aunt Puss")(12/28/1836-   ), m.
       10/4/1860, Rev. William Bradford (9/30/1826-12/7/1895)(b.
       Scioto County, Ohio, d. Oklahoma City). He was a Methodist
       minister.
552251 Eldest child (7/30/1861-10/8/1867)(b. near Carrolton, Mo.)
552252 Susan Bell Bradford (-8/1/1865)
552253 Will L. Bradford (-7/28/1934)
552254 Lou Bell Bradford (-5/9/1935)
552255 Hattie Bradford (-3/15/1948). Unm.
552256 Alvin C. Bradford
55226 Louisa Rebecca Branch (10/6/1838-1/15/1861)(b. Cumberland
       County, bur. in Carrolton, Mo.), m. 10/4/1860, Dr. William
       B. Glover (-d. 12/7/1895, aged 70 years), of
       Carrolton, Mo. No issue. Dr. Glover married, second,
       Virginia B. Perdue (1/2/1830-5/10/1883)(55243). Louisa
       bur. Carrolton.
55227 George Nicholas Branch (9/15/1841-   )(b. Cumberland
       County), m.   Keys. The story goes that he went
       to San Antonio, and married the daughter of a horse rancher.
       He and his father-in-law, after being missing for about
       thirty days, were found dead, and were believed to have been
       killed by robbers.
552271 (dau), m. George Lee _____.
5523 Eliza Rebecca Bolling Branch (1/20/1797-d. after 1858), m.
       (1st) Dr. James Austin; m. (2nd) Young Pankey (4/16/1788-5/
       25/1833) of Manchester, Va., son of Stephen and Elizabeth
       Kelso Pankey
     Children by second husband:
55231 Virginia Bell Pankey (-7/19/1852), m. Joseph Pen-
       dleton Winston
552311 Virginia Bell Winston (-7/19/1852). She was
       murdered, with her mother, on 7/19/1852, in Richmond, by
       a black servant nurse named Jane Williams. The incident
       created a great sensation
552312 Charles P. Winston (was living at 618 East Broad St.,
       Richmond, in 1900)
55232 Lavinia Cary Pankey (-3/30/1897), m. (his second
       wife) Paul Jones
552321 Lizzie Bell Jones (1/11/1859-   ), m. Jack Walker
       Johnson. They lived in Birmingham, Ala.
5523211 Jack Walker Johnson (5/5/1887-   )
5523212 Cary Fannin Johnson (1/27/1891-   )
5523213 Dorothy Rolfe Johnson (10/8/1893-   )
5523214 Josephine Ballard Johnson (8/14/1895-   )
5523215 Paul Jones Johnson (8/17/1897-   )
55233 David Young Pankey, lived in Kennett, Mo., m. (1st) 1852,
       Sallie Betts Jones, dau. of Paul and Mary Watkins Walton
       Jones; m. (2nd) Tennie Miller. No issue. M. (3rd) Addie
       Gregory; m. (4th) Minnie Smith (a widow)
     Children by first wife:
552331 Sally Belle Pankey, m. Wyley Scruggs

5523311 Cassie Scruggs, m. Lucy Vancleves
55233111 Wyley Scruggs
55233112 Sam Scruggs
552332 Mary Jones Pankey (1856-1933), b. Clarkton, Mo., m. 1872,
      Thomas Edward Baldwin (1849-1904)
5523321 Sally Baldwin, m. Luther Tatum
5523322 Thomas Edward Baldwin
5523323 Earnest Baldwin
5523324 Dr. Paul Jones Baldwin (2/23/1880-   ), m. 6/17/
      1914, Elizabeth Brasfield (10/31/1884-   ), dau. of
      Hugh Robb and Julia Eaton Wilson Brasfield of Unionville,
      Mo.
55233241 Elizabeth Baldwin (5/29/1915-   ), m. 2/5/1940, Fred
      Rigdon
55233242 Thomas Edward Baldwin (5/25/1916-   ), m. 1/7/1942,
      Alice Switzler. All children born in Kennett, Mo.
552332421 Thomas Edward Baldwin, Jr. (6/30/1944-   )
552332422 William Warren Baldwin (3/10/1946-   )
552332423 Virginia Royall Baldwin (8/17/1947-   )
552332424 Mary Josephine Baldwin (9/10/1952-   )
55233243 Julia Catherine Baldwin (9/22/1919-   ), m. 8/12/
      1944 in Washington, D. C., Edward Dickinson Taylor (3/
      15/1899-   ), son of Charles Albert and Ann
      MacRorie Taylor
552332431 Julia Ann Taylor (10/22/1949-   )
552332432 Catherine Elizabeth Taylor (3/8/1954-   )
55233244 Paul Baldwin, Jr. (7/23/1922-   ), m. 4/4/1948,
      Juanita Baughman. All children born in San Diego.
552332441 Elizabeth Ann Baldwin (5/10/1949-   )
552332442 Judith Baldwin (10/21/1950-   )
552332443 David Baldwin (1952-   )
552332444 Suzanne Baldwin (1955-   )
552333 Henry Young Pankey
552334 David Ballard Pankey, m. Josephine Rayburn. He was a cashier
      of the Bank of Kennett, Mo.
5523341 Hugh Pankey
552335 Lillian Pankey
      Child by third wife:
552336 Charles Pankey
      Child by fourth wife:
552337 Lavinia Blanche Pankey
55234 d. inf.
55235 d. inf.
55236 d. inf.
55237 d. inf.
55238 d. inf.
5524 Virginia Branch (4/23/1802-12/12/1893)(d. Springfield, Mo.,
      and is bur. in Hazelwood Cemetery, Springfield), m. Josiah
      Perdue (-1859)(bur. in Ray County, Mo.)
55241 Elizabeth Travis Perdue (1824-   ), m. Robert Rives
      of Virginia. He was killed in Atlanta, during the Civil
      War.

55242   Melvin Perdue (10/23/1826-9/17/1911)(b. Buckingham County,
         d. Overland Park, Kan., bur. at Little Grove Cemetery,
         Saline County, Mo.), m. 10/6/1833, in Saline County, Mo.,
         Harriet Dianna Lewis (2/25/1841-4/6/1899)(b. Marshall,
         Mo., d. Springfield, Mo.) (Melvin was her second husband;
         her first husband was John James Snoddy)

552421   Mary Virginia Perdue (7/27/1884-   )(b. Saline County,
         Mo.), m. 6/11/1906, in Saline County, Mo., Joseph Earl
         Leonard (5/10/1885-2/29/1960). She is bur. in Oakmont
         Cemetery, Lafayette, Calif.

5524211 Mary Virginia Leonard (7/22/1907-   )(b. Springfield,
         Mo.(, m. 7/ 3/1929, George Harvey Cruikshank

5524212 Melvin Perdue Leonard (4/16/1909-   )(b. Spring-
         field, Mo.), m. 1/10/1939, Joada Day

5524213 Lewis Earl Leonard (4/30/1911-   )(b. Springfield,
         Mo.), m. 6/21/1937, Florence Hiatt

5524214 Margaret Lewis Leonard (8/17/1915-   )(b. Cedar
         Rapids, Iowa), m. 10/5/1946, George Reed

5524215 Jas. Wesley Leonard (6/1/1917-   )(b. Cedar Rapids,
         Iowa), m. 1/18/1947, Libby McKay

55243   Virginia B. Perdue (1/2/1830-5/10/1883)(bur. at Malta Beach,
         Saline County Mo.), m. in Mo., Dr. William B. Glover (
              -10/7/1895). She was his second wife; he m. (1st)
         Louisa Rebecca Branch (10/6/1838-1/15/1861)

55244   Mary Clay Perdue, d. in her teens

55245   Lavinia Perdue, d. in her teens

55246   Sarah Perdue, m. in Saline County, Mo., James Bohannon

55247   Katherine Perdue, m. in Carroll County, Mo., William Austin
         of Carrolton, Mo.

55248   Judith Perdue, m. in Saline County, Mo., William Brown of
         Higginsville, Mo.

55249   Martha Perdue, m. in Ornick, Mo., Charles Jones of Saline
         County, Mo.

5524x   Henry Clay Perdue (12/12/1836-after 1881), m. (1st) 6/1/
         1861, Mary E. Ballard (-4/26/1879); m. (2nd) Cora
         Cunningham
      Children by first wife:

5524x1 Henry D. Perdue (3/3/1863-   )

5524x2 Minnie Perdue (2/27/1865-   )

5524x3 Mary E. Perdue (12/12/1868-   )

5524x4 Emmett Perdue (8/3/1873-   )

5524x5 Melvin Perdue (7/28/1877-   )
      Children by second wife:

5524x6 Eno Perdue

5524x7 Wilbur Perdue

5525   Emily Anne Branch (before 1804-after 1858)(d. "Tower Hill"),
         m. (1st) Rev. Henry Ally (-d. after 1923, at "Tower
         Hill"); m. (2nd), after 1827, Dr. Carter H. Bradley.

55251   Carter H. Bradley, Jr., M.D. Lived in Louisiana.

5526   Martha Nelson Branch (11/6/1812-7/9/1844), m. 5/9/1833, as
         his second wife, Dr. John Wesley Langhorne (9/24/1808-5/9/
         1881). She is bur. in Lexington, Mo.

55261   Maurice Moulson Langhorne (7/22/1834-6/22/1898)(b. Cumberland County), m. 10/13/1859, Ann Maria Wallace (9/10/1836-8/25/1920)(b. Independence, Mo.). He was in the gold rush, and published a weekly newspaper at Columbia, Calif.

552611 Mary Langhorne (8/18/1860-5/1/1917), m. 10/5/1887, her third cousin, William Leitch (9/23/1850-5/28/1909)(b. Buckingham County, d. Mt. Ida Plantation)

5526111 Col. William Branch Leitch (12/28/1889-4/2/1953), bur. in Arlington National Cemetery

5526112 Virginia Fuqua Leitch (6/22/1891-   )(b. St. Joseph, Mo.), m. Harold R. Palmer

552612 John Shelby Langhorne (2/15/1867-   ), m. 7/22/1898, Josephine Allen (8/10/1871-4/28/1937)

552613 Samuel Wallace Langhorne (10/13/1869-11/22/1917), m. Josephine Frances McCarthy

5526131 Hazel Frances Langhorne (4/14/1896-   )

552614 Ann Maurice Langhorne (7/11/1876-2/7/1937), m. 12/29/1905, Ralph Cary Noll

55262   Samuel Wesley Langhorne (1/19/1836-1/5/1927), m. 10/27/1872, Alice L. Leonard (3/16/1848-10/5/1927). He was the first circuit judge in the State of Montana.

552621 Alice Lorena Langhorne (7/8/1873-1917), m. 5/12/1897, Robert M. Cory (1870-   )

552622 Maurice Leonard Langhorne (11/19/1875-9/28/1911)

552623 Helen Martin Langhorne (9/28/1877-   ), m. 4/11/1900, in Helena, E. K. Preuitt (9/3/1874-   )

552624 Samuel Langhorne

552625 John Langhorne

552626 Harry Branch Langhorne

55263   Ann Rebecca Langhorne (10/15/1837-   )

55264   Mary Eliza Langhorne (9/7/1839-1/28/1927), m. 10/7/1886, J. P. Martin

5527   David Mann Branch (7/21/1809-12/18/1869)(d. St. Louis, Mo.), m. 5/25/1837, by the Reverend William J. Armstrong of Richmond, Sarah Ellen Harris (10/21/1813-4/21/1875)(d. St. Louis, Mo.), dau. of Benjamin James and Sarah Ellyson Harris. David Mann Branch built, in 1839, the house at No. 1 East Main Street (corner of Rouchee Street) in Richmond, Virginia, that was afterwards occupied by Ellen Glasgow, the novelist. He was a tobacco merchant in Richmond, and in 1857, he removed with his family to St. Louis. Their family Bible contains a full record of the family through 1933. Data for the years 1933 through 1963 have been furnished by living members of the family.

55271   Micajah Young Branch (11/17/1838-9/26/1842). He was bur. first at Richmond, Va., and reinterred in the family plot in Bellfontaine Cemetery, St. Louis

55272   Rebecca Bell ("Aunt Bell") Branch (8/12/1839-6/24/1926)(b. Richmond, d. Washington, D.C., and is bur. in St. John's Cemetery near Ellicott City, Md.). Unm.

55273   Julia Norman Branch (9/30/1840-6/10/1930)(b. Richmond, d. 3151 Mount Pleasant Street, N.W., Washington, D.C., and

is bur. in Friends Cemetery, Lincoln, Loudoun County,
Virginia), m. (1st) 10/18/1865, James Glasgow Archer (9/5/
1842-1/12/1869), son of Thomas and Susan R. Glasgow Archer.
M. (2nd) 11/12/1878, at the residence of, and by her brother,
the Rev. Henry Branch, in Hamilton, Va., James Mahlon Hoge
(2/15/1839-7/17/1924)(b. "Pleasant Valley Farm", near
Hamilton), son of Isaac and Rachel Neil Scofield Hoge
        Child by first husband:
552731 Ellen Glasgow Archer (7/18/1866-10/30/1929)(b. Clearbrook,
        Penna., d. 3151 Mount Pleasant Street, N.W., Washington,
        D.C.), m. 4/11/1889, Rev. James Arringdale Dorritee (5/
        18/1859-1/20/1906)(b. Baltimore, d. Corpus Christi, Texas).
        Both bur. in Charlotte, N.C., from Westminster Presbyterian
        Church, where he was minister.
5527311 James Arringdale Dorritee (2/14/1890-11/6/1933)(b. Balti-
        more, d. Blue Ridge Summit, Md., and is bur. in Friends
        Cemetery at Lincoln, Loudoun County, Va.), m. ca. 1916,
        Frances Towner (living in Washington, D. C. in 1957)
55273111 Frances Dorritee (1916 or 1917-1937)(b. Washington, D.C.
        or Clarendon, Va., d. Blue Ridge Summit, Md.), m. ca.
        1937,   Jacobson, a retired fireman
552731111 James Jacobson (1937-   )
5527312 Jeanette Dorritee (8/18/1891-7/26/1907)(d. Charlotte, N.C.)
5527313 Bell Branch Dorritee (5/9/1894-7/31/1907)(d. Charlotte,
        N.C.)
5527314 Hannah Dorritee (6/7/1898-3/15/1957)(b. Charlotte, N.C.,
        d. Leesburg, Loudoun County, Va.), m. 6/20/1918, by the
        Rev. Henry Branch in Washington, D.C., Rex Walton Lauck
        (1/10/1895-12/29/1945)(b. Keyser, W.Va., d. Washington,
        D.C.), son of William and Eltinge Spangler Lauck
55273141 Rex Walton Lauck (9/25/1919-   )(b. Washington,
        D.C.), m. 11/3/1951, in Washington, D. C., Mary Emily
        MacInnis (5/28/1929-   )(b. Duluth, Minn.), dau.
        of Thomas Chalmers and Naomi Mitchell MacInnis
552731411 Jett MacInnis Lauck (3/10/1953-   )(b. Washing-
        ton, D. C.)
552731412 Dorritee Lauck (11/18/1954-   )(b. Washington, D.C.)
552731413 Margaret Ellen Lauck (5/2/1957-   )(b. Washing-
        ton, D.C.)
55273142 Ellen Eltinge Lauck (5/5/1921-   )(b. Washington,
        D.C.), m. 12/30/1950, in Chevy Chase, Md., Ignacio Gon-
        zalez Monreal (5/20/1920-   )(b. San Luis Potosi,
        Mexico), son of Victor Gonzalez and Anastacia Monreal
552731421 Nancy Lee Gonzalez Monreal (7/27/1952-   )(b.
        Mexico City)
552731422 Ellen Leigh Gonzalez Monreal (1/28/1954-6/5/1954)(b.
        Mexico City, d. Celaya, Guanajuato, Mexico, and is
        bur. in Celaya Cemetery)
552731423 Victor Walton Gonzalez Monreal (10/26/1955-   )
        (b. Mexico City)
552731424 Rebecca Bell Gonzalez Monreal (12/27/1956-   )(b.
        Mexico City)

552731425 Sarah Ellen Gonzalez Monreal (7/28/1958-   )(b.
Mexico City)
Children by second husband:
552732 Julia Branch Hoge (1/4/1880-9/16/1929)(b. "Pleasant Valley
Farm" near Hamilton, Loudoun County, Virginia, d. in Leesburg, Virginia). Unm.
552733 Lewis Clark Hoge (8/27/1884-   ), m. 6/11/1912, in
Charles Town, W.Va., Harriet Holladay Tyler (-
2/9/1961)(b. San Francisco, Calif., d. Richmond, and is
bur. in Spring Hill Cemetery, Lynchburg), dau. of Jesse
and Harriet Ewing Holladay. She m. (1st) John Duval Tyler
of Lynchburg, Va. and had two children: Mrs. Ellis Mills
of Leesburg, Va., and Duval Holladay Tyler of Aldie, Va.
Her father owned the Pacific Steamship Co., the first line
to run from San Francisco to the Orient. Lewis Clark Hoge
and Harriet Holladay Tyler were div. in the early 1930's.
No issue. For years, he operated the "Red Apple Market"
at Overlook Orchards, near Leesburg, and was known on
radio and television as Arthur Godfrey's "Old Man of the
Mountains".
55274 Rev. Henry Branch (1/8/1842-6/2/1933)(twin)(b. Richmond,
Va., d. "Overlea Farm", near Hamilton, Loudoun County,
Va., and is bur. in St. John's Cemetery, near Ellicott
City, Md.), m. 2/16/1971, at Cabell's Dale, Boone County,
Mo., Melissa Maurice Jewell (nee Jarvis)(12/13/1845-4/25/
1918)(b. New Orleans, d. 3302 Clifton Avenue, Walbrook,
Baltimore), dau. of Nathan and Ellen Alvarez Jarvis (later
Mrs. Frederick Rector Conway). She was the widow of Dr.
William B. Jewell (1844-1865) of Columbia, Mo.
552741 Benjamin Harrison Branch (12/10/1871-9/11/1956)(b. New
Haven, Conn., d. Hamilton, Va.), m. at "Overlea Farm",
near Hamilton, Loudoun County, Va., 11/10/1915, Rachel
Neill Hoge (12/5/1874-4/16/1944)(b. "Pleasant Valley Farm",
d. "Overlea Farm"), youngest dau. of Isaac Craven and
Elmina Rogers Holmes Hoge
5527411 Benjamin Harrison Branch, Jr. (8/27/1919-   )(b.
Leesburg, Virginia), m. 9/8/1947, at Limona, Hillsborough
County, Fla., Marjorie Lee Browne (12/25/1920-   ),
eldest dau. of Colbert Blocker and Grace Hughes Browne
55274111 James Hoge Branch (12/6/1954-   )(b. Washington,
D.C.)
55274112 Millicent Anne Branch (7/30/1957-   )(b. Washington,
D.C.)
552742 Charles Branch (3/24/1873-7/20/1896)(b. "Eudora Manse",
Loudoun County, Va., drowned in Bush River, Md.).
552743 Henry Branch (2/26/1874-7/18/1874)(d. "Eudora Manse",
Loudoun County, Va., and is bur. in Catoctin Churchyard,
near Warner's Cross Roads, Loudoun County, Va. See 552748.
552744 Rev. Charles Henry Hardin Branch (8/6/1875-9/11/1935)(b.
"Eudora Manse", Loudoun County, Va., d. Tampa, Fla.), m.
6/1/1904, at Collinsville, Ill., Elizabeth Hertzog Reed

(-2/8/1957)(d. Front Royal, Va.), dau. of
Robert Sigerson and Elizabeth A. Collins Reed

5527441   Dr. Charles Henry Hardin Branch (2/14/1908-   )(b.
Hopkinsville, Ky.), m. 12/11/1937, in Riverside, Calif.,
Irma Smith. He is Professor and Head of the Department
of Psychiatry, College of Medicine, University of Utah,
Salt Lake City

55274411   Robert Hardin Branch (12/12/1939-   )
55274412   Alan Henry Branch (8/28/1942-   )
5527442   Elizabeth Hertzog Branch (2/20/1910-   )(b. Hopkinsville, Ky.), m. 6/1/1935, in Tampa, Fla., Charles Edward
("Ned") Johnson, Jr., of Sperryville, Rappahannock County,
Va.

55274421   Charles Edward Johnson III (6/14/1936-   )
55274422   Elizabeth Hertzog Johnson (9/22/1939-   ), m. at
Sperryville, 8/15/1959, Harold Wayne Jones

552745   Rebecca Bell ("Desiree") Branch (12/30/1878-9/30/1963)(b.
Hamilton, Va., d. Ellicott City, Md.), m. 12/15/1904, at
Ellicott City, Louis Thomas Clark (11/28/1872-12/3/1957
(d. Ellicott City), son of James Thomas and Mary Frances
Dorsey Clark. All of their children were born at "Font
Hill", Howard County, Maryland.
NOTE: "Desiree's" mother, who had been raided in New
Orleans, especially wanted a daughter---she had had four
sons. "Desiree" may have been the daughter's real name.

5527451   Louis Dorsey Clark (9/26/1905-   ), m. 12/24/1931,
at St. Paul's Rectory, Baltimore, by Dr. Arthur B. Kin-
solving, Helen M. Gambrill (10/31/1906-   )(b.
Baltimore), dau. of Prof. J. Montgomery and Maude May-
field Gambrill

55274511   Michael Dorsey Clark (11/5/1937-   )(b. Baltimore)
55264512   Judith Montgomery Clark (4/25/1947-   )(b. Baltimore)

5527452   Henry Branch Clark (10/21/1906-   ), m. 2/11/1933,
at Baltimore, by the Rev. C. H. Hardin Branch, Charlotte
Spence, dau. of John Moore and Nellie Carrison Spence

5527453   James Thaddeus Clark (1/25/1908-   ), m. 6/1/1946,
in Milledgville, Ga., Mary Floyd Pennington (11/21/1909-
          ), dau. of Marvin Emory Pennington

55274531   Bernie Pennington Clark (8/6/1948-   )(b. Washington,
D. C.)

55274532   Molly Branch Clark (11/20/1949-   )(b. Washington,
D. C.)

55274533   Desiree Branch Clark (4/22/1954-   )(b. Washington,
D. C.)

5527454   Millicent Clark (6/7/1909-   ), m. at Johnstown,
Pa., 7/17/1929, John Rogers Hammond (11/1/1905-   )
(b. Howard County, Md.), son of Edward Mackinaw and Mary
Rebecca Rogers Hammond

55274541   John Rogers Hammond (5/23/1930-   ), m. in Borger,
Texas, 12/15/1951, Helen Anne Lambert (7/16/1931-   ),
dau. of John W. and Margaret Lambert

552745411 Mary Melissa Hammond (10/15/1952-   )(b. Radford,
          Va.)
552745412 Deborah Ann Hammond (11/29/1953-   )(b. Radford,
          Va.)
552745413 John Rogers Hammond III (3/25/1955-   )(b. Dover,
          N.J.)
552745414 Janet Lynn Hammond (9/17/1957-   )(b. Borger,
          Texas)
55274542 Sally Millicent Hammond (3/3/1932-   ), m. 5/12/
          1956, at Ramsey, N.Y., William Edward Brown (3/26/1930-
                    ), son of William Henry and Helen Brown
55274543 James David Hammond (9/14/1938-   )
55274544 Edward Dorsey Hammond (7/29/1946-   )
5527455 Mary Dorsey Clark (7/11/1910-   )
5527456 Desiree Branch Clark (11/4/1911-   )
5527457 Charles Branch Clark (6/5/1913-   ), m. near
          Ellicott City, Md., 5/26/1945, Adelaide Snowden Hodges
          Clark, dau. of Edward Tabot and Adelaide Snowden Hodges
          Clark . Charles and Adelaide were div. before 1958.
55274571 Adelaide Snowden Hodges Clark (4/28/1946-   )(b.
          Baltimore)
55274572 Charles Branch Clark (9/25/1947-   )
5527458 Marian Gassoway Clark (11/18/1911-   ), m. 8/28/
          1937, at "Mt. Ida", Ellicott City, Md., by the Rev.
          Andrew Allen, Robert Farnsworth Howard (6/16/1912-   ),
          son of Brig. Gen. Harold Palmer and Helen Ella Lynde
          Taylor Howard
55274581 Helen Melissa Howard (1/22/1943-   ), m. 1961
55274582 John Farnsworth Howard (9/3/1945-   )
55274583 Ann Clark Howard (2/16/1950-   )
5527459 Nathan Jarvis Clark (4/13/1916-   ), m. at Mt.
          Vernon, N.Y., 8/12/1944, Marjory Davis Murphy (2/18/
          1921-   )(b. Dobbs Ferry, N.Y.), dau. of Herbert
          Hayes and Eva Davis Murphy. They adopted 6/19/1951, in
          New York City, Cathy Jarvis Clark (4/27/1951-   )
55274591 Susan Davis Clark (11/9/1955-   )(b. White Plains,
          N.Y.)
552745x Basil Crawford Clark (10/16/1917-   ), m. in New
          York, N.Y., 8/26/1944, Joan Johnston, dau. of Lyle Tesson
          and Sue Rosenburg Johnston
552745x1 Carolyn Johnston Clark (9/10/1947-   )
552745x2 Jan Branch Clark (1/29/1952-   )
552745a Betsy Chinn Clark (10/31/1920-   ), m. 10/27/1945,
          Philip Caldwell
552745a1 Lucy Hamphill Caldwell (6/6/1949-   )
552745a2 Desiree Branch Caldwell (6/15/1956-   )(b. Detroit)
552746   Dr. Joseph Robson Bromwell Branch (2/28/1883-   )(b.
          Ellicott City, Md.), m. in East Orange, N.J., 9/5/1915,
          LeRoy Erwin Pope of Macon, Ga., dau. of William Henry and
          Oliva Marfort Pope. Home: Crescent, Ga.
5527461 Anne Erwin Branch (8/19/1916-   )(b. Kuling, China),
          m. (1st) 6/19/1937, George Vance Maree; m. (2nd) 9/28/
          1939, at Las Vegas, Frederick W. Sutlerle

Child by second husband:

55274611 Mary Ann Sutlerle (12/22/1942-   )(b. Phoenix)
5527462 Henry Branch (1/30/1919-11/30/1945)(b. Macon, Ga., d.
Memphis), m. in Fresno, Calif. 9/2/1943, Ruth Allyne
Gade, dau. of Capt. and Mrs. John A. Gade. No issue.
She m. (2nd)
552747 Eleanor Chinn Branch (7/10/1885-   )(b. Hamilton,
Va.), m. 10/30/1912, Lee Owings Warfield (6/23/1881-4/22/
1959), son of Joshua Dorsey and Elizabeth Polk Warfield
5527471 Millicent Jarvis Warfield (2/6/1914-   )(b. Baltimore), m. 6/18/1938, in Sykesville, Md., by Rev. William
C. Milne, James Deer Sadler, son of George Dewy and
Adeline Sadler
55274711 Charlotte Ann Sadler (9/8/1939-   )(b. Sykesville)
55274712 Robert Dale Sadler (5/16/1943-   )
5527472 Lee Owings Warfield, Jr. (12/5/1916-   )(b. Ellicott
City, Md.), m. 7/23/1942, Beatrice Barrett
55274721 Lee Owings Warfield III (2/9/1949-   )(twin)
55274722 Carter Stone Warfield (2/9/1949-   )(twin)
5527473 Henry Branch Warfield (11/3/1924-   )(b. "Solopha",
near Sykesville, Md.), m. 7/14/1956, in Baltimore, Dickens
Waddell (8/27/1925-   ), dau. of Frederick Dickens
and Beatrice DeWett Waddell
55274731 Charles Alexander Warfield (5/26/1959-   )
55274732 DeWett Waddell Warfield (10/18/1961-   )
5527474 Eleanor Chinn Warfield (7/5/1927-   )(b. "Solopha",
near Sykesville, Md.), m. 5/1/1948, Wilbur Agnew White,
son of Emory and   White
55274741 Eleanor Lee White (3/2/1949-   )
55274742 David Emory White (7/10/1954-   )
55274743 Timothy Owen White (1/3/1959-   )
552748 Millicent Jarvis Branch (7/12/1887-8/14/1887)(d. Hamilton,
Va., and is bur. in Catoctin Graveyard near Warner's
Cross Roads, Loudoun County, Va., in the same grave as
her brother, Henry Branch (552743). The grave is marked
only by arborvitae trees, and is located toward the center
of the graveyard.)
55275 Charles Branch (1/8/1842-1/6/1915)(twin)(b. Richmond, d.
Webster Groves, Mo.), m. 10/20/1870, in St. Louis, Mary
Glasgow, dau. of William and Sarah Low Glasgow
552651 Anna Lane Branch (10/13/1871-1/11/1910)(b. and d. St.
Louis). Unm.
552752 Sarah Glasgow Branch (8/12/1873-10/29/1960)(b. St. Louis),
m. 10/15/1908, Alfred Walker Jones, son of Alfred Walker
and Julia Lawrence Jones (5/18/1875-4/10/1948). No issue.
552753 Henry Branch (2/5/1875-6/9/1904)(b. St. Louis). Unm.
552754 David Mann Branch (6/8/1877-3/15/1930)(b. St. Louis). Unm.
55276 Benjamin Harrison Branch (8/2/1846-8/15/1870)(b. Richmond,
d. in St. Louis)
5528 Judith Sarah Branch (1812-   ), m. after 1827, George W.
Nichols. No issue. He is said to have been very wealthy,
and avidly devoted to fox hunting.

5529 Augusta Young Branch (1817 or 1820-9/10/1855)(bur. in Helena, Ark.), m. 6/14/1836, in Buckingham County, Absolom Harper Kenneday (4/20/1811-10/15/1867)(b. Davidson County, N.C., d. Memphis), son of William and Sarah Kenneday

55291 William Henry Kenneday (11/29/1836-10/19/1913)(b. in the Branch home in Buckingham County, bur. Memphis), m. 11/29/1859, at Napoleon, Ark., Laura Elizabeth Rudd (9/29/1841-2/18/1917)(b. Louisville, bur. in Elmwood Cemetery, Memphis)

552911 Rosaline Bell Kenneday (6/13/1862-7/17/1956)(b. Napolean, Ark., bur. in Memphis), m. 11/29/1881, Edward Bondurant Mosley (10/ /1857-10/22/1920)(b. and d. Memphis)

5529111 William Nelson Mosley (11/7/1882-1/6/1929)(b. and bur. in Memphis)

5529112 Edward Bondurant Mosley, Jr. (6/20/1886-8/25/1959)(b. and bur. in Memphis)

55292 Annis Lavinia Kenneday (7/2/1838-)(b. in her grandparents' home in Buckingham County, bur. in Helena, Ark.), m. (1st) Thomas Caulk; m. (2nd) Dr. William B. Eubank (bur. in Helena, Ark.)

Child by first husband:

552921 Harper Theodore Caulk (8/ /1859-10/ /1860)(bur. in Helena, Ark.)

Child by second husband:

552922 Annis Branch Eubank (9/15/1864-)(b. Helena, Ark.), m. 1885, in Memphis, Frederick Huntington

5529221 Elizabeth Lavinia Huntington (10/ /1886-1926)(b. Memphis, d. Chicago), m. 1921, Lucius Parsons Warrens

55293 David Young Kenneday (2/1/1841-9/17/1867)(b. Davidson City, N.C., bur.in Memphis). Unm.

55294 Absolom Early Kenneday (7/30/1843-1930)(b. Davidson City, N.C., bur. in Memphis), m. Eva Virginia Apperson Wade (a widow, with two daughters, Jessie and Eva, whom he adopted)

552941 Augusta Kenneday (1869-1873)

552942 Edmund Kenneday (1871-1873)(bur. in Memphis)

552943 Susie Kenneday (1873-1873)(bur. in Memphis)

55295 Rosaline Augusta Kenneday (9/19/1853-10/26/1882)(b. Oxford, Miss.), m. 11/19/1871, William Arnold Rudd (9/1/1843-8/6/1878)(b. Lexington, Kentucky, bur. in Memphis)

552951 Emma Young Rudd (12/18/1873-8/ /1875)(b. and bur. in Memphis)

552952 Laura Virginia Rudd (11/13/1875-8/27/1959)(bur. in Memphis). Unm.

552953 Blanche Chilton Rudd (5/4/1878-)(b. Memphis), m. 6/22/1902, in Memphis, Edward Barnes Karr (9/17/1878-6/19/1958)(b. Newport, Rhode Island, d. Ossining, N.Y.)

5529531 Edward Rudd Karr (2/20/1903-2/27/1941)(b. Memphis, d. a casualty at Fort Benning, Ga., and is bur. in Arlington National Cemetery), m. 9/19/1934, Janet Barkley Henney. No issue.

5529532 Frances Graham Karr (2/17/1905-)(b. Memphis), m. 8/19/1941, in Ossining, N.Y., Raymond White Holbrook

5529533 Erwin Hamilton Karr (11/6/1914-11/15/1914)(bur. at Hastings-on-Hudson, New York)

552x Lavinia Cary Branch (1802-   ), m. Robert Graham

553 William Branch

554 Mary Branch, m.   Drew

NOTE: Benjamin B. Weisiger III, M.D., identifies Mary Drew as a child of (55), noting that she (of Buckingham County) received a slave in a three-way deed with her father, Thomas Branch, and Bolling Branch.

555? Sarah Branch, m. 1798, Daniel Weisiger (4/15/1776-6/26/1848) of "The Grove" near Manchester, Chesterfield County, son of Samuel and Mary Kendall Weisiger

NOTE: Sarah Branch's number is followed by a ? for the reason that there is some doubt that she was the daughter of Thomas and Mary Eldridge Branch.

ROBERTSON, stating that Thomas and Mary Eldridge Branch had three sons, identifies two: Bolling (551) and Matthew (552). And it is believed that the third son (553) was named William. See, also, 26 W(1)114.

There were other Branches named Thomas who were contemporaries of the Thomas Branch who married Mary Eldridge. One of these, Thomas Branch who married Miss Hayes, made in 1803, a gift of a slave to each of the following children: Elizabeth Branch, Thomas Branch, Jr., Richard Hayes Branch, Catharine C. Branch, Anne Branch, Rebecca G. Branch, and William Hayes Branch. And Dr. Weisiger states that this Anne Branch apparently was the Nancy Branch who married David Weisiger in 1806.

As regards Miss Hayes, GOODE 84 and 84A states that she was the daughter of Richard Hayes of Amelia County (b. 1710 or 20), and that by Mr. Branch, she had (1) a daughter who married "Capt. Weisiger", (2) a son ("Capt. Branch of Buckingham County"), and (3) a daughter (Mrs. Gunn). GOODE 134 identifies "Capt. Weisiger" as David Weisiger, a Captain in the War of 1812.

Dr. Weisiger writes "it is * * * suspected" that Sarah Branch Weisiger was the daughter of Thomas and Mary Eldridge Branch. And John D. Schaperkotter, Esq., writes that "the only available Thomas Branch to have a daughter marry in 1798 as Sarah Branch did Daniel Weisiger would appear to be Thomas Branch who married Mary Eldridge".

Sarah Branch Weisiger and her husband Daniel had the following children:

(a) Mary B. Weisiger (-4/6/1839), m. 4/3/1821, Joseph Albert Royall of Powhatan County. They had three children.

(b) Joseph Kendall Weisiger, m. Pocahontas-descendant Anne
Bolling (2191). For their children, see 2191.
(c) William Washington Weisiger (ca. 1803-5/4/1868), m.
11/14/1831, Sarah Ann Patteson (1814-1863), dau. of
James Anderson and Martha Patteson. The had nine
children.

Daniel Weisiger, m. (2nd) 2/13/1815, Seignora Tabb Smith,
and had issue.

56 Rolfe Eldridge (12/29/1744 or 5-1806), of "Subpoena", Buckingham County, m. (MB 11/26/1773 Brunswick County), Susannah
Everard Walker (1754-3/27/1821), dau. of Col. George Walker,
originally of Elizabeth City County, and his wife, the former
Mary Meade
561 Rolfe Eldridge, Jr. (1780-1861) of "Rolfeton", Buckingham
County, m. 12/16/1808, Mary Moseley, dau. of Benjamin and
Mary Branch Moseley
5611 Susanna Eldridge, m. Dr. James Austin
5612 Lucy Eldridge, m. Rev. James H. Fitzgerald
5613 Elizabeth Eldridge, m. Bernard Austin
5614 Delia Eldridge, m. Robert Kincaid Irving (-1894).
They lived at "Rolfeton". Had issue. Grandchildren: Mrs.
H. C. Thornton, Delia E. Brock, Robert K. Brock
56141 Joseph Kincaid Irving. See 56361.
5615 William Moseley Eldridge, m. Katherine Nixon
5616 Mildred Kidder Eldridge (d. 1902, age 79), m. 1867, William
Meredith Cabell (12/2/1823-   ), son of Col. Edward
A. and Mary Rice Garland Cabell. No issue. Lived near
Buckingham C.H.
5617 Benjamin Eldridge, m. Elizabeth Perkins
56171 Benjamin Rolfe Eldridge, m. Letitia Terry of Bedford County
561711 Edward F. Eldridge
561712 Eliza Eldridge, m. Robert J. Antrim
5618 John Eldridge, m. 1857, Sarah Perkins Moseley, dau. of Col.
Grandison Moseley (1830-1903). Lived near Buckingham C.H.
56181 Paul Eldridge, m. 1886, Bessie Duncan
56182 Grandison Moseley Eldridge (1886-1899)
56183 William Moseley Eldridge, m. 1891, Emma Morton
56184 Elizabeth Fearn Eldridge, m. 1900, A.D. Barnes
56185 Rolfe Eldridge, m.
56186 John Eldridge, m. 1903, Lillian Moorman, dau. of Joel Thomas
Moorman, a descendant of Charles and Elizabeth Moorman who
came to Virginia ca. 1704
5619 Frances Eldridge, m. Samuel Anthony Glover
56191 Rolfe Eldridge Glover (living in 1928)
561x Mary Eldridge. Unm.
561a Martha Bolling Eldridge. Unm.
562 Susanna Everard Eldridge, m.   Webber

563 Thomas Kidder Eldridge (1804-12/19/1864), m. ca. 1820, Mary
     Hales Ayres (6/8/1803-7/2/1869), dau. of Rev. John and
     Elizabeth Bransford Ayres. Mary Hales Ayres was born in
     Buckingham County
5631 Delia Eldridge. This may not be correct.
5632 Ann Elizabeth Eldridge (1821-1844), m. Thomas Henry Garnett
56321 Thomas Garnett, m.   Wright
56322 Mary Garnett, m. Capt. W. I. Raisin
5633 John Rolfe Eldridge (4/7/1825-12/19/1894), m. Eliza Hanes,
     dau. of Col. Elijah and Mary Jane Brown Hanes

WILLIAM BOLLING of "Bolling Hall"

(113)

56231 Annie Eldridge, m. J. E. Connor
563311 Renna Connor, m. John Chambers Ayres, son of William Leake
       and Martha Holman Chambers Ayres
56332 Mary Eldridge. Unm.
56333 Rolfe Eldridge, d. young
56334 Martha Eldridge, m. Julian Smith
56335 Kidder Eldridge. Unm.
56336 Susan Eldridge, m. E. C. Sawyer
56337 Josephine Eldridge. Unm.
56338 Erie Eldridge, d. at age of 13 mos.
56339 Virginia Eldridge, m. E. L. Holman
5634 David Walker Eldridge (ca. 1827-   ), m. Amanda Hocker
56341 Ernest Eldridge, d. young
56342 Blanche Eldridge, m. E. T. Driscoll
56343 Pocahontas Eldridge, m. Lee Cobb
56344 Thomas Eldridge, m. Maud Fore
56345 George Eldridge, m. Pearl Gill
56346 Robert Eldridge, m. Caroline Vaughan
56347 Margaret Eldridge, d. young
56348 Miriam Eldridge, d. young
5635 Susan Bolling Eldridge (ca. 1830-   ), m. Peter Sipe
56351 Nora Sipe, m. Brown Jones
56352 Mary Sipe. Unm.
56353 Henry Sipe. Unm.
56354 Florence Sipe, m. Rev. A.S.J. Rice
56355 Katherine Sipe, m. Edward Patterson
56356 Charles Sipe, m. Mrs. Gill
5636 Courtney Wythe Eldridge (2/24/1833-2/5/1928)(b. at "Subpoena",
       Buckingham County, d. at "Dunleith", Buckingham County), m.
       12/16/1857, in Buckingham County, Capt. John Clark Turner
       (9/23/1823-10/14/1906), (b. and d. in Buckingham County),
       son of Fleming and   Turner.
56361 Ida Clark Turner (12/5/1858-5/ /1949), m. 10/19/1881,
       Joseph Kincaid Irving (1855-11/ /1931) of Howardsville,
       Va. See 56141.
563611 Joseph Kincaid Irving, Jr. (12/4/1882-8/9/1948), m. 10/19/
       1915, Dorothy Wingfield (12/15/1890-12/12/1981)
5636111 Dorothy Irving (7/23/1916-   ), m. 10/9/1948, Bernard
       Vincent Rosenberger (7/27/1913-   ), son of William
       and   Rosenberger of Lynchburg
56361111 Sarah Alexander Rosenberger (6/3/1953-   ), m. 10/14/
       1976, Corbin George Eissler (1948-   )
563611111 Sarah Adele Eissler (1983-   )
56361112 Mary Boland Rosenberger (1/23/1955-   ), m. 1977,
       Cruger Smith Ragland (5/17/1954-   )
563611121 William Cruger Ragland (3/18/1981-   )
563611122 Charles Alexander Ragland (12/3/1982-   )
56361113 William Rosenberger II (4/16/1956-   )
56361114 Joseph Irving Rosenberger (4/4/1959-   ), m. 11/5/1983,
       Ann Fowler (3/20/1958-   )
563612 Courtney Irving (9/13/1883-6/7/1965). Unm.
563613 John Turner Irving (6/19/1885-3/5/1965). Unm.

563614 Charles Robert Irving, M.D. (2/ /1888-11/11/1976), m.
        1917, Elizabeth Logan Bentley (10/9/1892-   )
56362 Eldridge Turner (11/30/1862-4/3/1945), m. (1st) Ida Renshaw;
        m. (2nd), Vivian Land (11/25/1886-1/24/1978), dau. of Walter
        J. and Mary Cleo Matheny Land of Hot Springs, Ark., and St.
        Louis
        Children by first wife:
563621 Eldridge Turner, Jr. (11/11/1892-10/24/1971), m. 1918,
        Elizabeth ("Bessie") Hoyle (12/1/1899-9/4/1968)
5636211 Eldridge Hoyle Turner (9/22/1919-   ), m. 8/15/1947,
        Dorothy Williams (8/29/1921-   )
56362111 Eldridge Hoyle Turner, Jr. (11/5/1953-   ). Unm.
56362112 Judith Lenora Turner (2/14/1958-   ), m. 9/8/1979,
        Derwin Otis Cooper (5/1/1957-   )
563621121 Craig Andrew Cooper (7/17/1984-   )
5636212 Gladys Kingsley Turner (12/29/1922-   ), m. 10/ /1948,
        Charles Eugene Roberts
        Conrad Allison Roberts (10/ /1954-   )(adopted)
        Courtney Elizabeth Roberts (8/ /1957-   )(adopted)
56362121 Jean Louise Roberts (1/ /1958-   )
563622 Geraldine Renshaw Turner (10/27/1890-1/ /1972)(oldest of
        the three children), m. Frederick Howard Twining (10/23/
        1885-   )
5636221 Frederica Twining. Unm.
5636222 Grace Eldridge Twining (-10/ /1971), m. James
        Eades. No issue
5636223 Courtney Twining, m. Julian Guffin
56362231 J. Fred Guffin
56362232 Warren Howard Guffin
56362233 Gordon Webster Guffin
563623 Grace Turner, m. Percy Fletcher. No issue
        Children by second wife (of 56362):
563624 Mary Vivian Turner (6/29/1923-   ). Unm. Home:
        Howardsville, Va.

563625   Leighton Land Turner (10/18/1924-   ). Unm. Home:
         Howardsville, Va.
56363   John Courtney Turner (1/21/1865-2/8/1932), m. 9/7/1902, Ella
         Henningham Jones (12/15/1872-12/16/1953), of Louisa County,
         dau. of James Edward and Ella Carrington Smith Jones
563631   John Carrington Turner (6/6/1903-ca. 1963), m. Pat Owens
5636311 Patricia Anne Turner, m. James Anderson
5636312 John Carrington Turner, Jr.
563632   James Henningham Turner (5/3/1905-   ), m. Virginia
         Hitchcock
5636321 James Henningham Turner, Jr., m. Wilma
56363211 James Henningham Turner III
56363212 Ann Turner
563633   Courtenay Eldridge Turner (6/17/1908-   ), m. 8/24/
         1936, Virginia Dare McCarthy (1/8/1905-   ), dau. of
         John Joseph and Mary Margaret Jarrett McCarthy of Coving-
         ton, Va. They live in Charlottesville
5636331 Courtenay McCarthy Turner (7/15/1942-   ), m. 4/30/
         1971, Richard Arthur Stanley (9/4/1939-   ), son of
         Rev. Dr. Clifford Leland and Helen Louise Tighe Stanley
5636332 Kathleen Virginia Turner (8/16/1944-   ), m. 11/6/1970,
         Bruce Robert Lowrie Stuart (12/22/1943-   ), son of
         Robert and Joy Crozier Lowrie (and the adopted son of
         Jack Lord Stuart)
56363321 Christopher Courtenay Lowrie Stuart (9/14/1971-   )
56363322 Keena Dare Stuart (3/14/1975-   )
56364   Thomas F. Turner (1867-   ), m. Margaret ("Maggie") S.
         Ayres, dau. of Nathan W. Ayres, and grand-dau. of Col. John
         B. Ayres
563641   Benjamin Turner, d. prior to 12/19/1955
56365   Harry Towles Turner (1869-12/7/1955). Unm.
56366   Mary Jane Turner (2/4/1872-8/15/1958). Unm.
56367   Rolfe Eldridge Turner (7/16/1876-   ), m. L. Churchill
5637   Mary Virginia Eldridge (ca. 1834-   ), m. Robert Hales,
         M.D., son of Dr. Peter and   Jennings Hales
56371   Jemima Hales
56372   Annie Hales, m.   Cheatham
56373   Peter Hales. Unm.
56374   Courtney Hales. Unm.
56375   Susan Hales. Unm.
5638   Patsy (Ann?) Eldridge (ca. 1844-   ) was an invalid.
         Unm.
564   Courtenay Tucker Eldridge, m. John Price Williams
5641 John Rolfe Williams (ca. 1824-   )(b. Buckingham County),
      m. 1848, Susan Campbell
5642 Susanna Williams (b. Buckingham County)
5643 Mary Jane Williams (ca. 1827-   )(b. Buckingham County)
5644 Elizabeth Williams (ca. 1829-   )(b. Buckingham County)
5645 Warner Archer Williams (ca. 1830-ca. 1880)(b. Buckingham
      County, d. Henderson, Ky.), m. 4/6/1857, in Collirene,
      Lowndes County, Ala., Jane Emily Rives. Practiced dentistry

in Mobile, Ala., then moved to Pleasant Hill, Lowndes County, after marriage. Ca. 1865 moved to Corydon, Ky., because of economic chaos in Ala. Eventually moved practice to Henderson, Ky.

56451　Green Rives Williams (1/16/1858-　　　　)(b. Lowndes County, Ala.), m. 1884, Mary Lillian Smith

56452　Warner Eldridge Williams (1/17/1859-12/28/1931)(b. Pleasant Hill, Lowndes County, Ala., d. Henderson, Ky.), m. 6/30/1902, in Henderson, Harriet Emily Burst. Warner Eldridge Williams was sent to live with uncle in Birmingham during Battle of Selma. Family moved to Henderson, Ky. Warner went to live with uncle in Texas. Attended Univ. of Chicago Dental School. Went back to Texas to practice Dentistry. When eyesight failed, he moved to Henderson, Ky., to run a general store.

564521　Charles Warner Williams (4/4/1903-9/　/1982)(twin)(b. Henderson, Ky., d. Indiana)

564522　John Rives Williams (4/4/1903-　　　　)(twin)(b. and d. Henderson, Ky.)

564523　Florence Eldridge Williams (9/20/1914 or 1915-　　　　)(b. Henderson, Ky.), m. 12/25/1941, in Henderson, Robert Stanley Williams

5645231　Jane Rives Williams (11/11/1942-　　　　)(b. Louisville), m. (1st) Charles Maury Eppihimer; m. (2nd) 2/11/1969, in Honolulu, Hobert Lynn Ledford

56452311　Jill Elaine Ledford (7/17/1963-　　　　)(b. Jefferson County, Ky.). Born Eppihimer. Adopted and took name of Ledford.

56452312　Hobert Lynn Ledford, Jr. (10/28/1972-　　　　)(b. Jefferson County, Ky.)

56452313　Daniel Rives Ledford (12/31/1973-　　　　)(b. Jefferson County, Ky.)

5645232　Buford Shelby Williams (6/12/1948-　　　　)(b. Jefferson County, Ky.), m. Rita Needy

56453　John Price Williams (3/4/1862-　　　　)(b. Lowndes County, Ala.)

56454　George Jefferson Williams (4/18/1864-　　　　)b. Lowndes County, Ala.)

56455　Thomas Claudius Williams (1/2/1866-　　　　)(b. Lowndes County, Ala.)

5646　Pocahontas Williams (ca. 1832-　　　　)(b. Buckingham County)

5647　Thomas Eldridge Williams (6/14/1833-9/　/1913)(b. Buckingham County , d. Dallas), m. Elizabeth Martha Rives

5648　George Williams (ca. 1836-　　　　)(b. Dallas)

5649　Daniel Claude Williams (ca. 1838-　　　　)(b. Dallas)

565　David Walker Eldridge. Unm.

566　George Wythe Eldridge. Unm.

567　Mary Meade Eldridge. Unm.

568　Nancy Eldridge. Unm.

569　Jane Pocahontas Eldridge. Unm.

56x　Martha Bolling ("Patsy") Eldridge. Unm.

57   Sarah Eldridge (1740-   ), m. 6/9/1762, Col. George Rives
    (ca. 1737-1795), son of George and Frances Tatum Rives. They
    lived in Surry and Sussex Counties.

571 Judith Rives (10/29/1762-   ), m. (MB 1/6/1790) Thomas
    Blunt of "Blackwater", Sussex County

5711 Sally Blunt, m. Vivante Quinitchet

5712 Eldridge Blunt

5713 Pamela Blunt, m. Nat Colyer (Collier), son of Mrs. Sarah
    Williamson Colyer

5714 Thomas Blunt, m. Evelyn Colyer (Collier), sister of Nat
    Colyer (Collier)

5715 Judith Blunt, m.   Edwards

57151 Susan Edwards

57152 Henrietta Edwards

572 Capt. Thomas Eldridge Rives (12/15/1764-ca. 1832) of Sussex
    County, m. Keziah Tucker, dau. of Rev. Wright Tucker of
    Dinwiddie County

5721 Thomas Wright Rives (11/13/1815-6/11/1895), m. (1st) Martha
    Houston of Marshall County, Mississippi; m. (2nd) 7/22/1856,
    Virginia A. Moore of Macon, Tennessee. Prior to 1848, Rives
    moved to LaGrange, Tennessee.

    Children by first wife:

57211 Anna Rives, m. Rev. John Schwar (Episcopal minister)

572111 Mary Houston Schwar, m. Frank P. Poston of Tennessee

5721111 Frank Poston. Unm.

5721112 Kate Poston. Unm.

57212 Mollie Rives, m. David H. Poston, brother of Frank P. Poston

572121 Anna Rives Poston, m.   Halsey. Waco.

57213 d. inf.

    Children by second wife:

57214 Elizabeth Moore Rives (-10/9/1901), m. 1/23/1879,
    John W. Jones, M.D. (-5/ /1901)

572141 Leroy Rives Jones (-5/ /1904), d.s.p.

572142 Thomas Emmett Jones (11/19/1881-   ) of Brinkley,
    Ark.

572143 Margaret Louise Jones (11/4/1885-   ), m. Hugh Curt-
    wright. New York, N.Y.

572144 Norma Jones (8/25/1892-   ), m. Roy Coppedge. New
    York, N.Y.

57215 William H. Rives, d. young

57216 Thomas Wesley Rives (6/18/1861-5/31/1904), m. Margaret
    Elizabeth Mason, dau. of Major and Mrs. Armistead Thompson
    Mason of Benton County, Mississippi, originally from near
    Petersburg. Mr. and Mrs. Thomas Rives lived in Memphis.

572161 Virginius Mason Rives (11/9/1882-   ), m. 11/3/1908,
    Beulah Griffin

5721611 Virgunius Mason Rives (8/29/1909-   )

5721612 Malcolm Eldridge Rives (8/21/1911-   )

572162 Harry William Rives (3/26/1885-   ), m. 12/24/1909,
    Marie Dietz. Denver.

5721621 (dau)

572163 Daniel Minge Rives (8/23/1887-   ), m. 12/18/1908,
       Elizabeth Hoff. Greenwood, Miss.
5721631 Daniel Minge Rives (1914-1925)
572164 Elizabeth Moore Rives (2/9/1889-   ), m. 4/2/1915,
       Arthur Pickard
572165 Thomas Wright Rives (1/28/1891-   ), m. 6/ /1914,
       Mattie Mae Peeples. No issue. Michigan City, Miss.
572166 Virginia Susan Rives (12/15/1892-   ), m. W. C. Jones
       of Memphis
5721661 Thomas Rives Jones (11/30/1914-   )
572167 John Armistead Rives (7/1/1895-   ), m. 11/24/1924,
       Gertrude Stegbauer. No issue. Michigan City, Miss.
572168 Margaret Evelyn Rives (4/30/1897-   ). Memphis.
572169 Frank Edward Rives (10/24/1899-   ), m. 10/10/1925,
       Dorothy Friedel. Memphis.
57216x Alice Louise Rives (10/19/1901-   ), m. 9/5/1925,
       Edward W. Havens. Memphis.
57217 Harry Warren Rives (-ca. 1915), m. Georgia Ore
      of "near Mt. Pleasant, Texas"
572171
572172
572173
5722 (son) d. inf.
573 Martha Rives (3/22/1767-   ), m. John Wilkinson (3/22/
    1761-2/23/1823), a Revolutionary soldier, son of William
    (of Sussex) and Elizabeth Stith Wilkinson (of Brunswick).
    William Wilkinson's mother was Agnes Bolling.
5731 William Wilkinson (6/1/1780-   )
5732 Wiley Wilkinson (5/9/1783-   )
5733 Anne Wilkinson (8/12/1787-   )
5734 Stith Wilkinson (4/6/1791-   )
5735 Thomas Wilkinson (10/27/1794-   )
5736 Henry Wilkinson (5/10/1797-8/6/1883), m. 1827, Ann Eliza
    Kirkland (5/6/1810-5/20/1871)
57361 Ada Virginia Kirkland Wilkinson (4/6/1844-10/4/1884), m.
    1862, James Jabez Robinson (9/25/1833-   )
573611 Carlotta Robinson, m. James Orlando James
574 Capt. George Rives (1/10/1769-   ) of Sussex County,
    m. (1st) Patsy Goodwin; m. (2nd) Mrs. Sarah Williamson Colyer
    (Collier) of South Carolina
    Children by first wife:
5741 Amy Goodwin Rives, m.   Browder
57411 Liza Browder
57412 Adeline Browder
5742 Thomas Peterson Rive, M.D. (8/7/1797-8/9/1840), m. (1st)
    1827 (MB 4/5/1827), Martha Dillard; m. (2nd) 9/12/1831,
    Martha Ann Nicholson (-4/9/1880) of South-
    ampton County. Dr. Rives and family lived in Sussex County.
    Children by second wife (order of birth not known):
57421 Col. George Stith Rives, C.S.A. (12/13/1832-2/12/1887), m.
    (1st) Mrs. Williamson (born Ellis); m. (2nd) Virginia

Saunders (11/30/1840-12/9/1906), dau. of Robert J. Saunders.
Portsmouth.
Children by first wife:
574211 Ada Anne Rives (7/2/1855-   ), m. J. A. Tinker
574212 Agnes Rebecca Rives (6/2/1858-   ), m. 3/3/1879, Lewis
       E. Benster
5742121 Percy Hope Benster (1887-8/25/1925), m.   Marshall
57421211 Edgar Marshall
5742122 Elsie Benster (7/7/1890-   ), m. 8/14/1915, Cecil Hall
       Banks
57421221 Agnes Banks (9/9/1918-   )
       Children by second wife:
574213 Hattie Birdsong Rives (6/28/1863-6/10/1908), m. 9/ /1884,
       Dr. Jacob Eley Kelly (-1/ /1888). She was his
       second wife.
5742131 Hattie Jake Virginia Kelly (8/29/1885-   ), m. 4/11/
       1923, Roderick McCullough Thomas of Baltimore
574214 Robert Stith Rives (7/19/1867-4/ /1912) of Richmond. Unm.
57422 Joseph P. Rives
57423 Thomas Rives
57424 Anne S. Rives, d. inf.
57425 Emily Rives, d. inf.
5743 John Eldridge Rives, m. Virginia Lewis. They lived in Sussex
       County.
57431 Jane Rives
57432
57433
57434
57435
5744 Sarah Martha Thweatt Rives, m. 1820 (MB 6/9/1820)(her first
       cousin) Eldridge Blunt
       Children by second wife:
5745 Rev. George Rives (9/28/1818-9/30/1895), m. 9/ /1841, Ann
       Pollard, dau. of John and Ann Morris Pollard, of Petersburg
57451 George Edwin Rives (11/11/1842-   ), C.S.A., m. 9/ /
       1865, Mary Virginia Loudoun of Portsmouth, dau. of Herbert
       Farrand and Missouri Jarvis Loudoun
574511 George Hubert Rives (11/30/1866-   ), m. (1st) Mattie
       May Sargent of Brandon, Vermont; m. (2nd) Anne Twyford
       Children by first wife:
5745111 George Andrew Rives (3/26/1902-   ). Rockford, Ill.
574512 Edwin Montgomery Rives (7/24/1868-3/3/1871)
574513 Blanche Loudon Rives (4/24/1870 -   ), m. Charles Pond.
       Beaufort, N.C.
5745131 Hubert Pond
5745132 John Richard Pond
57452 Annie Peyton Rives (8/16/1844-3/29/1925), d.s.p.
57453 Mary Louisa Rives (12/31/1845-6/30/1915), d.s.p.
57454 Alice Montgomery Rives (4/8/1848-   1849)
57455 Hettie Everlina Rives (9/2/1849-   ), m. Robert Epes
       Bland of Prince George County

57456   Arthur Williamson Rives (11/22/1850-10/27/1924), m. Leonora
        Holland of Southampton County, dau. of Thomas Carr and
        and Angeline Norfleet Holland. Norfolk.
574561   Louis Hubert Rives (1/19/1894-   ), m. (1st) 12/4/
        1915, Gladys Rose Lambert (-3/21/1920); m. (2nd)
        6/2/1923, Mildred Denna Lee
5745611 Louis Hubert Rives (4/15/1919-   )
574562   Norfleet Williamson Rives (3/15/1896-   ). Raleigh,
        N.C.
574563   Hettie Rives, m. Virginius Butts. Norfolk.
574564   Nellie Rives, m. Palmer King. Valdosta, Ga.
574565   Annie Rives, m.   Bryant
5745651 Marguerite Bryant
574566   Arthur Rives, m. Jack Mingle
57457   Andrew Pollard (11/18/1852-12/15/1924), m. 11/21/1883,
        Florence Edwards (10/10/1858-12/4/1926), dau. of William
        Henry Edwards (10/8/1805-12/9/1859), M.D., of Surry County,
        and his second wife, Mrs. Albina Amanda Drew Holleman
574571   Sterling Edwards Rives (10/4/1884-   ), m. 12/12/1918,
        Pattie Ruth Bailey
5745711 Sterling Edwards Rives (1920-   )
574572   Mabel Pollard Rives (12/29/1885-   ), m. 11/23/1910,
        Frank Pond
5745721 Edward Rives Pond (10/20/1913-   )
5745722 Florence Rives Pond (4/6/1917-   )
574573   Ruth Albina Rives (1/30/1888-   ), m. 1/20/1926,
        John Daniel Pond. Surry County.
57458   Marion Poindexter Rives (5/17/1854-   ). Unm.
57459   Ruth Rives (1/12/1856-   ), m. 4/8/1890, Joseph Roper
        Johnson of Dinwiddie County. No issue.
5745x   Herbert Arnold Rives (9/22/1857-1/22/1886), d.s.p.
5745a   John Hicks Rives (2/20/1859-1862), m. 2/23/1888, Annie Darden,
        dau. of Capt. James Jackson and Sarah Elizabeth Musgrave
        Darden
5745a1 Frank Herbert Rives
5745a2 James Darden Rives (5/16/1891-   ), M.D., m. 1921,
        Grace Sebrell. Richmond.
5745a21 James Darden Rives, Jr. (10/31/1923-   )
5745a3 John Hicks Rives (12/10/1893-   ), m. 5/4/1918,
        Annie Boyd Chanler. Richmond.
5745a4 Annie Elizabeth Rives, m. 8/8/1924, James Hubert Fentress.
        Richmond.
5745a5 Marion Poindexter Rives. Norfolk.
5745b   Thomas Stanley Rives (8/21/1860-1862)
5745c   Addie Aurelia Rives (1/25/1864-1865)
5746 Edwin Williamson Rives (1819-5/27/1846), m. Indiana Scott,
      dau. of Henry and Caroline Scott of Sussex County
57461   Sarah Evelyn Rives (9/2/1845-6/12/1925), m. William Daniel.
        Farmville.
574611   George Watkins Daniel (11/18/1866-   ), m. 10/13/1915,
        Hettie M. Lankford

574612 William Rives Daniel (3/23/1868-   )
574613 Anna Spencer Daniel (3/16/1870-4/7/1923), d.s.p.
574614 Elizabeth Daniel (7/17/1873-   ). Farmville.
574615 Sallie Lancaster Daniel (3/18/1876-11/15/1901), d.s.p.
574616 Kate Price Daniel (9/24/1878-   ), m. 10/29/1912,
        C. Stuart Woods
574617 Mary Rives Daniel (5/7/1881-   ), m. 1915, S. B. White
574618 Evelyn Keeling Daniel (11/21/1883-   ), m. 3/1/1914,
        C. L. Goodloe
574619 Edwin John Daniel (12/29/1888-   ), d.s.p.
575 Nancy Rives (ca. 1772-   ), m. Stith Parham, Jr.
5751 Nancy Parham, m. Dr. Edward Winfield
576 Frances Rives (8/20/1774-   )
577 Eldridge Rives (5/6/1776-d. young)
578 Pamela Rives (5/31/1778-   ), m. Thomas Lewis (MB Sussex
        County 11/7/1818)
5781 Nancy Lewis
5782 Pamela Lewis
58 Martha Eldridge (10/23/1749-   ), m. John Harris of Gooch-
        land
59 Jane Eldridge, m. John Robinson

ANN MEADE BOLLING

(2191)

6 Anne Bolling (1715 or 1718-1800), m. ca. 1742, (her first cousin once removed), James Murray of "Athol Braes" near Petersburg, in what is now Prince George County (Amelia County?)

61 William Murray, M.D. (5/6/1752-1815), m. 1777, Rebecca Bolling (see 112). Dr. William Murray inherited "Athol Braes", and was called the "Duke of Athol". Lived at "Grove Brook", Amelia County, and later at "Woodstock", Powhatan County

611 Anne ("Nancy") Murray (1780-1837), m. Dr. Thomas Robinson, a refugee from Ireland ca. 1800. Settled in Petersburg.

6111 William Murray Robinson (1807-1878), m. Sarah A. Mills of Petersburg. Div. 1865. He moved to N.Y.City in 1850, and changed his name.

61111 Rev. Thomas Robinson (of Roman Catholic Church)

61112 Andrew Robinson, m.

61113 Nannie Robinson, m. Edward Trent "Ned" Robinson, son of Anthony and Rebecca Webb Couch Robinson. She died a few months after her marriage. He m. (2nd) Constance Warwick McDowell

6112 Robert Emmett Robinson, M.D. (1810-12/10/1865), m. (1st) Adeline Dewees of Philadelphia. M. (2nd) Indiana Henley (-7/9/1841, age 23). M. (3rd) Virginia E. Stainback (b. ca. 1824)

Children by third wife:

61121 Robert Emmett Robinson, Jr. (ca. 1845-ca. 1877). Killed accidentally. Survived by two or three children.

61122 Mary Murray Robinson, b. ca. 1844, m. Smiley. Lived in St. Louis. Had one or two children.

6113 Powhatan Robinson, m. Anne Eason. No children.

6114 Rebecca Murray Robinson, b. 1804. Unm.

6115 (son), d. young

6116 (son), d. young

6117 (dau), d. young

612 Mary ("Polly") Murray (1791-1871), m. 1803, George Nicholas Skipwith (-1820), of "Hickory Hall", Cumberland County, nephew of Col. Henry Skipwith (1751-1815)

6121 Robert Skipwith (1810-1904), m. (1st) 1847, Jane Rolfe Bolling (2194). M. (2nd) 1871, Mary Elizabeth ("Lizzie") Bolling (21922)

6122 William Murray Skipwith, Captain, Powhatan Rifles, C.S.A. Killed July 1861 at Battle of Rich Mountain, d.s.p.

6123 George N. Skipwith, M.D. (ca. 1818-8/ /1874), m. Maria Louisa Brooks

61231 George N. Skipwith, Jr.

6124 Cornelia Lotte Skipwith (-1825), m. James M. Whittle (6523)

61241 Matoaca Skipwith, m. Col. W. E. Sims

6125 Thomas Bolling Skipwith (-1873), m. Emma Darrieux (Doring?)

61251 Thomas Bolling Skipwith

6126 (dau)

6127 (dau)

613 William Murray, Jr. (1795-1866), m. Rebecca Martha Skelton
      (1804-1858)
6131 Rebecca B. Murray
6132 Matoaca Murray, m. Judge C. L. C. Gifford of Newark, N.J.
61321 (son)
61322 (son)
61323 (dau)
6133 Nannie S. Murray, m. Dr. John B. Wiley (55115)
61331 Arthur S. Wiley
61332 M. Murray Wiley
61333 Sally Wiley
61334 John Flemming Wiley
61335 Matoaka Wiley
6134 Louisa S. Murray
6135 Mary Murray
6136 Cornelia S. ("Nina") Murray
6137 Gay Bernard Murray, m. Lewis E. (E.A.?) Rawlins
61371 (son)
61372 (dau)
61373 (dau)
6138 (son)
614 Rebecca Bolling Murray (-4/26/1864). Unm. She and 615
      were inseparable. 615 died several years after 614. Both
      bur. at Genito.
615 Martha Murray. Unm.
616 Thomas Murray, b. ca. 1788 (living 1809). Unm.
617 Bolling Murray (ca. 1796-1821). Unm.
618   d. inf. Dead in 1796.
619   d. inf. Dead in 1796.
61x   d. inf. Dead in 1796.
62 John Murray (9/13/1744-   ), m. Susan Yates. John Murray
      owned large estates in Mecklenburg County near what is now
      Chase City.
621 Elizabeth Murray, m. 1783, Edmund Randolph Yates of Amelia and
      Mecklenburg Counties, son of Rev. William and Elizabeth Ran-
      dolph Yates
6211 Mary Deane Yates, m. William Hamlin
6212 Elizabeth Caroline Yates
6213 John Murray Yates, m. Ann Bailey (a widow - Mrs. Wood). He
      acquired under his father's will the tract of land in Meck-
      lenburg County known as "Mill Grove"
62131 John Murray Yates, Jr., m. a widow Boswell
621311 Littleton Yates
621312 John Murray Yates
62132 Edmund Randolph Yates, m. in Calif. (He emigrated to Calif-
      ornia in 1849).
621321
621322
621323
621324
621325
621326

621327
621328
621329
62133 William Morinp Yates, m.   Cralle of Halifax County
621331 (dau)
621332 (dau)
62134 Joseph A. Yates, d. unm. of Lunenburg County
62135 Benjamin Lewis Yates (1827-   ), m. Sophia M. Ralls of
       Albemarle County
621351 John L. Yates, m. Mary Frances Cooksey, dau. of Charles and
        Evelyn Adeliade Royal Cooksey. He was Clerk of Lunenburg
        County from 1878 to ?
6213511 Elliott Yates, d. young
6213512 Mamie Murray Yates, m. Dr. Edwin L. Kendig (State Senator)
62135121 Edwin Kendig, Jr.
6213513 Helen Yates, m. Dr. Dennis Kendig
62135131 Frances Yates Kendig
62135132 John Dennis Kendig
621352 C. N. Yates
621353 B. L. Yates, Jr.
621354 Anna Yates, m.   Moore
621355 George M. Yates
621356 Joseph M. Yates
621357 Addie M. Yates
621358 William A. Yates
621359 L. E. Yates
62136 Louise Murray Yates, d. unm.
62137 Ann Bailey Yates, m. Henry Tucker
621371 John Murray Tucker, killed in the Confederate service, in
        the Civil War
621372 Maria L. Tucker, m. Dr. John A. Watson of Mecklenburg County
621373 Anne Bailey Tucker. Unm.
62138 Mary E. Yates, m. (1st) John H. Tisdale of Mecklenburg County
621381 Richard E. Tisdale
621382 Addie M. Tisdale
62139 Martha J. Yates, m. (1st) Dr. Leroy Murrell; m. (2nd) William
       Campbell of Petersburg
       Children by first husband:
621391 Louisa Yates Murrell
621392 Ellen Murrell
       Child by second husband:
621392 William Lee Campbell (-ca. 1923)
6213x Susan Dean Yates, m. Daniel W. Tisdale of Lunenburg County
6213x1 J. A. Tisdale
6213x2 Fannie M. Tisdale
6213x3 Henrietta Tisdale
6213x4 Ann Bailey Tisdale
6213x5 Robert Lee Tisdale
6214 Susanna Randolph Yates
622 Anne Bolling Murray, m. 1786, Jesse Brown
6221 Hester Brown
6222 Samuel Alfred Brown

6223 Dead by 5/10/1796
623 Susanna ("Sukey") Murray, m. 1788, Theodoric Bland Ruffin
6231 Jane Bland Ruffin
6232 William Frederick Ruffin
6233 Dead by 5/10/1796
624 James Murray, m. Jane Doan
6241 John Murray
6242
6243
625 Margaret ("Peggy") Murray (unm. 5/10/1796), m.   Elam
626 William Yates Murray (unm. 5/10/1796)
627 John Murray (unm. 5/10/1796)
63 Anne Murray (8/30/1746-1779), m. Neale ("Pretty Neale") Buchanan
631 Ann Buchanan, m.   Cross. Married in Scotland.
6311 (dau) Cross, m. Robert Yuilee. Had issue.
632 (son). Dead by 5/10/1796
633 (dau). Dead by 5/10/1796
634 (dau). Dead by 5/10/1796
64 Margaret ("Peggy") Murray (2/8/1748*9-10/12/1779), m. Thomas
      Gordon, son of Rev. Alexander Gordon. He m. (2nd) Elizabeth
      Baird, and they had issue
641 Ann (or Nancy) Gordon (1778-   ), m. Col. Henry Embra Cole-
      man (ca. 1764-   ) of "Woodlawn", Halifax County, son of
      Col. John and Mary Embra Coleman of Halifax County
6411 Elizabeth Anne Coleman (-8/29/1821), m. 9/29/1813,
      Charles Baskerville (1788-3/22/1834) of "Lombardy Grove",
      Halifax County, son of William and Mary Eaton Baskerville.
      He m. (2nd) 1823, Lucy Goode (-12/11/1868), by whom
      he had five children.
    Children by first wife:
64111 Col. William Baskerville (4/10/1816-1895) of "Buena Vista",
      Mecklenburg County, m. (1st) 1839, Susan Jiggitts. M.
      (2nd) Mrs. Alice Sturdivant (-1909)
    Children by first wife:
641111 Elizabeth Anne Baskerville (1841-1880), m. Capt. John W.
      Lewis of Milton, N.C.
6411111 John Willis Lewis (1860-1887)
6411112 Susanna Lewis, m. Hiram Foard of Leaksville, N.C.
64111121 Elizabeth B. Foard, m. Walter M. Millner
64111122 Warner W. Foard
6411113 W. Meriwether Lewis, m. Mary W. Cosby. No issue.
6411114 William Baskervill Lewis, m. Margaret ("Maggie") Watkins
64111141 William B. Lewis
64111142 Charles L. Lewis
64111143 Claudia L. Lewis
64111144 Warner M. Lewis
6411115 Lucy Alice Lewis, m. F. H. Gregory of New York
6411116 Mary Lewis
6411117 Kate Lewis
641112 David Edward Jiggits Baskerville (1843-1909), m. (1st)
      Mary Hinton. M. (2nd) Lucy Jones

Children by first wife:
6411121   David E. Baskervill, d. age 18
6411122   Elizabeth Baskervill, m. Channing Ross of Abingdon, Va.
6411123   George Sumner Baskervill, m.
6411124   Mary Hinton Baskervill, m. Prof. Otis Johnson of Ohio
6411125   Alice Baskervill
6411126   William Baskervill
6411127   Sadie Baskervill
641113   Charles Baskervill (1845-1894), m. Alice M. Sampson
6411131   Susan R. Baskervill, m. Rev. A. P. Saunders, a missionary
        to Greece
64111311   Charles Baskervill Saunders
64111312   A. Pierce Saunders
64111313   Hugh Saunders
6411132   Caroline Baskervill, m. Rev. Frank Hartman of Staunton
6411133   William Baskervill, m. (1st) Kate Lansing. M. (2nd)
        Catherine Jones
      Children by first wife:
64111331   Caroline Baskervill
64111332   William Baskervill
6411134   Alice M. Baskervill, m. George Robson of Scranton, Pa.
64111341   George Robson
64111342   Charles B. Robson of Davidson, N.C.
6411135   Thornton S. Baskervill (1879-   ), m. Mary Mann
64111351   Thornton Baskervill
64111352   Frances Baskervill
64111353   Alice M. Baskervill
64111354   Mary M. Baskervill
6411136   Lucy Baskervill of Davidson, N.C.
6411137   Ellen Baskervill of Shanghai, China
6411138   Elizabeth Baskervill of Orangeburg, N.C.
6411139   Gordon Coleman Baskervill of Burkeville, Va.
641114   Lucy Alice Baskervill (1848-1872), m. John K. Lockett
6411141   William H. Lockett (1869-   )
6411142   John R. Lockett, m. Mary Baptist
6411143   Lucy Baskervill Lockett (1872-1875)
641115   Rev. Henry Embra Coleman Baskervill, m. (1st) Julia T.
     Blanton. M. (2nd) Emma Reid
      Children by first wife:
6411151   Julia T. Baskervill, m.   Hensel of Minnesota
64111511   Virginia Hensel (1902-   )
6411152   Howard C. Baskervill (ca. 1885-   ), killed in Persia
     in a Revolution (1909)
      Children by second wife:
6411153   Emma R. Baskervill, m.
64111531
64111532
64111533
6411154   Rev. Robert Walter Baskervill, m. Nettie M. Anderson
6411155   Charles Edward Baskervill, m. Mary V. Phelps of Nebraska
6411156   Ernest Baskervill
641116   John Gordon Baskervill, m. Sadie Maglenn of Charlotte

6411161 Anne L. Baskervill (1878-1896)
6411162 William Sumner Baskervill, m. Ellie R. Mullen
64111621 Charles Gordon Baskervill
64111622 Virginia R. Baskervill
64111623 William R. Baskervill
6411163 James M. Baskervill (twin), m. Leone Wagner
6411164 John G. Baskervill (-1893)(twin)
6411165 Edgar McComb Baskervill (1886-   )
6411166 Sadie M. Baskervill (1888-   )
6411167 Grace E. Baskervill (1894-   )
6411168 Lily Hall Baskervill (1898-   )
641117 James Riddick Baskervill (1858-1875). Unm.
641118 Rev. George Sumner Baskervill, D.D., m. Bessie Campbell of
         Malcom, Iowa
6411181 John Campbell Baskervill
         Children by second wife (of 64111):
641119 Lilian Gordon Baskervill (1862-   ), m. Rev. Henry
         Tucker Graham, President of Hampden-Sidney College
6411191 Alice Sturdivant Graham (1895-   ), m. Henry Bedinger,
         a Presbyterian minister, and former President of Flora
         McDonough College in N.C.
64112 Capt. Henry Embra Coleman Baskervill, C.S.A. (10/14/1817-
         1/14/1900), m. (1st) 2/10/1846, Isabella Alston Hamilton
         (6/22/1823-7/3/1854), dau. of Patrick and Mary Eaton
         Baskervill Hamilton of "Burnside", Granville County, N.C.
         M. (2nd) 1866, Eugenia Buffington (-3/20/1871),
         dau. of Col. P. C. Buffington of (near) Huntington, W.Va.
         M. (3rd) 1876, Mrs. Margaret A. Humphries (nee Stribling)
         (-1/21/1884). Captain and Mrs. Baskervill lived
         in Richmond.
         Children by first wife:
641121 Patrick Hamilton Baskervill (1848-   ), m. Elise M.
         Skelton
6411211 Jno. Skelton Baskervill (1876-1879)
6411212 Hamilton Meade Baskervill (1882-   )
641122 Isabella A. H. Baskervill (1850-1863)
641123 Mary Eaton Baskervill (1852-3/3/1855), d. scarlet fever
641124 Henry E. C. Baskervill (1854-3/6/1855), d. scarlet fever
         Child by second wife:
641125 Henry Eugene Baskervill (1867-   ), m. Ethel Marsh
         of Easton, Pa.
6411251 Henry Coleman Baskervill
64113 Mary Anne (Alice?) Elizabeth Baskervill (7/14/1819-7/6/1873),
         m. 5/12/1837, Richard Venable Watkins of "Mount Mayo",
         Halifax (originally Charlotte) County, son of Capt. William
         Morton and Elizabeth Woodson Venable Watkins
641131 Charles Baskervill Watkins, C.S.A., m. (1st) Mary Womack;
         m. (2nd) Ella Womack
         Child by first wife:
6411311 Julia Watkins, m. William Blanks of Clarkesville, Va.
         Children by second wife:
6411312 Baskervill Watkins

6411313 Mary Watkins, m. Rev. Mr. Reeves
6411314 Cabell Watkins, m. Joel Wall of Boydton, Va.
6411315 Emily Watkins, m. and lived in Norfolk, Va.
6411316 Louisa Watkins, m. Charles Russell of Clarkesville, Va.
641132 William M. Watkins, C.S.A., killed in Civil War
641133 Richard Venable Watkins, Jr., C.S.A., killed in Civil War
641134 Thomas Algernon Watkins, m. Maria Carrington (Watkins?)
 Red, dau. of William Watkins and Paulina Edmonia Carrington Read of "Greenfield"
641135 John Sims Watkins, D.D., m. Mary Coleman of Fredericksburg
641136 Elizabeth Ann Watkins, m. Thomas Read Carrington, son of
 William and Jane Watkins Carrington
641137 Lucy Baskervill Watkins, m. Elisha Betts, "a mésalliance",
 says one of the cousins; "they lived at 'Lombardy Grove'
 and had many children"
641138 Mary Baskervill Watkins, m. Henry S. Reynolds of Norfolk
6411381 Richard Reynolds
6411382 A. C. L. Reynolds
6411383 Tom Reynolds
6411384 Mary Reynolds, m. John Reid of Norfolk
6411385 Maria Reynolds, m. Senator Saxon Holt of Va.
6411386 Nannie Reynolds
6411387 Margaret Reynolds, m. Mr. Aylor
641139 Clement Watkins, d. inf.
64113x Margaret Watkins, d. inf.
64113a Henrietta Maria Watkins, d. inf.
64113b Isabella Watkins, d. inf.
64113c Henry Joel Watkins (10/9/1849-1921), m. Rose Overby. He
 M.A. Hampden-Sydney, Supt. Schools in Charlotte and Halifax Counties
64113c1 Henry Joel Watkins, Jr., m. Marguerite Richmond, an English
 girl
64113c2 John Overby Watkins, m. Eva Tuggle of Texas
64113c21 Eva Watkins
64113c22 John Overby Watkins, Jr.
64113c23 Douglas Watkins
64113c3 Richard Venable Watkins, m. Christine Boog of Alaska
64113c4 Imogene Watkins
64113d Sarah Alice Watkins, d. unm.
64113e Virginia Douglas Watkins, m. Judge William Randolph Barksdale of Halifax. No issue
64113f Nellis Watkins, m. Henry Paul Carrington (1848-1900) of
 "Bellevue", son of Gen. George and Sally Tucker Carrington
64113f1 Virginia Carrington, m. Peter Williams
64113f11 Peter Williams, Jr.
64113f12 Nannie Williams
64113f13 Nellie Carrington Williams
64113f2 Nancy Carrington, m. John C. Lawson, son of John J. and
 Eliza Craddock Lawson
64113f21 John C. Lawson, Jr.
64113f3 Nellie Carrington, unm.
64113f4 Henry Paul Carrington, Jr., m. Miss McKenzie. No issue

64113g   Julia Watkins, m. Tazewell Morton Carrington, son of William
        Tucker and Bettie Lewis Morton Carrington
64113g1   Richard Venable Carrington, m. Delia Davenport
64113g11   Richard Venable Carrington, Jr.
64113g12   Delia Davenport Carrington
64113g13   Charles Davenport Carrington
64113g2   Tazewell Morton Carrington, Jr., m. Carter Ingram
64113g21   Tazewell Morton Carrington III
64113g22   Bettie Lewis Carrington
64113g3   William Tucker Carrington II
64114   Maj. Charles Baskervill, C.S.A. (2/14/1821-6/23/1890), m.
        (1st) 11/17/1841, Margaret Haynes Freear, dau. of Betty
        Eaton Freear. M. (2nd) Mrs. Brooks. The Charles Basker-
        vills moved ca. 1852 to Mississippi.
     Children by first wife:
641141   Bettie Eaton Baskervill (-1886), m. George Williams
6411411   Charles Baskervill Williams, m. Norma Blackwood
64114111   Charles Roper Williams
64114112   George B. Williams
6411412   Margaret Baskervill Williams, Thomas Tate of Brooksville,
        Miss.
64114121   Samuel Malcolm Tate (1886-   ), m. Margaret
        Simpson
641141211   William Simpson Tate
64114122   Betty Baskervill Tate, m. John Holman
64114123   Thomas Tate, Jr.
64114124   William Bethea Tate
6411413   Samuel Ballard Williams, m.   Peck
641142   Mary Ann Baskervill, m. Anthony Whitfield. No issue
641143   Charles Baskervill III, m. Augusta Louisa Johnston
6411431   Charles Baskervill IV (6/8/1870-   ) of New York City,
        m. Mary Boylan Snow, dau. of George H. Snow of Raleigh
64114311   Charles Baskervill V
64114312   Elizabeth Baskervill
641144   Sarah Coleman Baskervill, m. John J. Du Puy. No issue
641145   Alice Baskervill (1850-   ), m. 1871, John D. Young
        of Columbus, Miss.
6411451   Bettie Freear Young, m. Robert Pollard
64114511   Robert Pollard, Jr. (1905-   )
64114512   John D. Pollard (1906-   )
64114513   James Pollard (1907-   )
64114514   Alice Baskervill Pollard (1909-   )
64114515   Charles Alexander Pollard (1913-   )
6411452   Alexander Franklin Young
6411453   Sarah Du Puy Young, m. Ernest Bell. No issue
6411454   Laura Whitfield Young, m. Robert Perkins
6411455   Mary Anthony Young, m. Price Perkins McLemore II of LeFlore
        County, Miss.
64114551   Price McLemore III (1906-   )
64114552   Baskervill Young McLemore (1907-   )
6412   Mary Margaret Coleman, m. Richard Logan

64121   (son)
64122   (son)
64123   (son)
64124   (son)
64125   (son)
64126   Elizabeth H. Logan, m. Marcellus French
641261 Sarah Henry French (7/29/1861-   ), m. 8/20/1883,
           Charles Craddock Carrington, son of George Cabell and
           Sarah Winston Henry Carrington
6412611 Margaret Logan Carrington, m. Charles Halifax Stebbins,
           son of Charles and Charlotte Carter Walden Stebbins
64126111   Margaret C. Stebbins
64126112   Sally French Stebbins
64126113   Frederica Cary Stebbins
64126114   Charlotte Carter Stebbins
64126115   Charles Harvey Stebbins
6412612 George Cabell Carrington, m. Louise Cary Stebbins, sister
           of Charles H. Stebbins
64126121   Dr. George Cabell Carrington, Jr., m. Miss Alexander
641261211 Louise Carrington, m. Paul Carrington Hubard
6412613 Sarah Henry Carrington, m. James F. Dorrier
6412614 Marcellus F. Carrington
6412615 Charles Reid Carrington, m. Kizzie McDaniel
6412616 William Lorria Carrington
6412617 Elizabeth F. Carrington
6412618 Alice Cary Carrington, m. William B. Settle
6412619 Winifred W. Carrington
64127   (dau)
64128   (dau)
64129   (dau)
6413 John Coleman, m. (1st) Elizabeth Clark. M. (2nd) Mary Love
64131   (dau), m. Mark Alexander
641311 Bettie Alexander, m. Gen. Herbert of Baltimore, Md.
6414 Thomas Gordon Coleman (3/23/1802-8/4/1862), m. 5/6/1828,
           Ann Sims Clark (1/27/1807-1/ /1899)
64141   John Clark Coleman, M.D. (3/9/1829-6/12/1898), m. 1/22/1861,
           Ann Lightfoot Edmunds (1841-   ), dau. of John Richard
           and Mildred Carrington Coles Edmunds
641411 John Coleman of Winston-Salem
641412 Henry Edmunds Coleman (of Huntington, W.Va.), m. Daisy
           Chalmers, dau. of John W. and Julia Henry Chalmers of
           Halifax
6414121
6414122
6414123
6414124
64142   Henry Embry Coleman (7/4/1830-   ), m. 5/11/1852,
           Ella Mackay Alexander
64143   Priscilla Sims Coleman (11/23/1831-12/9/1851)
64144   Capt. Thomas Gordon Coleman, Jr., C.S.A. (1833-8/30/1862),
           (killed at second Battle of Bull Run), m. 11/25/1856,

Isabella Alexander Rives (1/12/1836-3/4/1899), dau. of
    Judge Alexander and Isabella Bachem Wydown Rives
641441   Priscilla Sims Coleman (10/31/1857-   ), m. 10/27/
    1886, William Henry Seamon (12/4/1859-   ), son of
    Henry and Mary Virginia McNash Seamon
6414411 William Henry Seamon (8/4/1888-   ), m. 7/6/1920,
    Caroline Frances Hopkins of "Sherwood", Talbot County,
    Md.
6414412 Alexander Rives Seamon (1/28/1890-ca. 9/26/1918). Killed
    in the Argonne.
6414413 Isabel Gordon Seamon (8/21/1891-   ), m. 12/6/1915,
    Dr. Henry Coleman Chalmers
64144131 Rives Coleman Chalmers (7/28/1918-   )
64144132 Thomas Gordon Chalmers (7/15/1920-   )
641442 Alexander Rives Coleman (6/1/1860-11/18/1876)
64145 Martha Elizabeth Coleman (11/11/1834-4/10/1880), m. 6/20/
    1835, William Marshall Ambler, son of Col. John and
    Catherine Bush Ambler
6415 Henrietta Maria Coleman, m. Rev. John Clark of Halifax
    County
64151 Betty Clark, m.   Garrett. Residence: Clover, Va.
64152 Rev. William M. Clark, of St. James Church, Richmond, Va.
64153 (son)
6416 Henry Embry Coleman, m. (1st) Miss Eaton, dau. of John R.
    and Susan Somerville Eaton. No issue. M. (2nd) Miss Turner
    Children by second wife:
64161 Mrs. Philip Brine of Richmond
64162 Mrs. Charles Bethel of News Ferry, Va.
64163 (dau)
64164 (son)
6417 Dr. Ethelbert Algernon Coleman (1812-   ), of "Creek-
    side, Halifax County, m. (1st) Elizabeth Sims. M. (2nd)
    Martha Frances ("Fanny") Ragsdale
    Child by first wife:
64171 Bettie Sims Coleman, m. 11/4/1857, John Clark, C.S.A. of
    "Banister Lodge", Scottsburg, Va., son of William Howson
    and Elvira Ann Henry Clark
    Children by second wife:
641711 Elvira Ann Clark (2/10/1859-   ), m. Robert Nelson
6417111 Elizabeth Sims Nelson (3/26/1886-   )
6417112 Virginia Lafayette Nelson (10/26/1887-   )
6417113 Ellie Clark Nelson (9/10/1889-   )
6417114 Robert Williams Nelson (4/13/1894-   )
641712 Maria Wilson Clark (1860-   )
641713 Mary Bailey Clark, d. young
641714 John Clark II (1867-   )
641715 Angelina Johns Clark (1869-   )
641716 Phoebe Howson Clark (1871-   )
641717 Ethelberta Coleman Clark (10/9/1874-   )
64172 Mrs. Thomas Edmonds of Danville, Va.
64173 Nathaniel Ragsdale Coleman of "Riverside", Halifax County
    (7/19/1843-12/29/1917), m. 1/13/1875, Anne Nelson Page
    (9/15/1855-7/ /1936)

641731 Frances Page Coleman (7/25/1876-   ), m. 11/18/
        1901, Roger Henry Williams (7/27/1874-   ), son
        of Prf. Henry Shaler and Harriet Hart Wilcox Williams
6417311 Coleman Shaler Williams (10/18/1903-   ), m. 6/24/
        1930, Dora Jones Hancock (6/13/1904-   ), dau.
        of Prof. Charles and Lucy Anne Jones Hancock
64173111 Nathaniel Coleman Williams (10/8/1933-   )
64173112 Catherine McIntyre Williams (12/25/1938-   )
6417312 Gordon Page Williams (7/19/1908-   )
6417313 Roderick Otis Williams (8/14/1912-   ), m. 6/19/
        1937, Mary Dorothy Culver (7/1/1914-   ), dau.
        of Rudolph Clark and Dorothy Farmem Culver of New York
        City
64173131 Alan Stuart Williams (9/29/1944-   )
6417314 Douglas Williams (5/12/1918-   ), m. 6/21/1941,
        Priscilla Mary deForest (10/23/1919-   ), dau.
        of Johnston and Mary Elizabeth Ogden deForest of Long
        Island
64173141 Priscilla Page Williams (4/3/1944-   )
641732 Nathalie Page Coleman (2/10/1878-   ), m. 9/6/
        1901, Rev. George MacLaren Brydon, D.D. (6/27/1875-   ),
        son of Robert and Ellen Dame Brydon
6417321 Capt. George MacLaren Brydon, Jr., U.S.N. (8/7/1902-   ),
        m. 6/9/1932, Cleland Harris (6/10/1905-   ), dau.
        of Alexander Barret Browning and Mary Taylor Harris of
        "Woodville", Goochland County
64173211 Cleland Page Brydon (3/15/1933-   )
64173212 Carter Randolph Brydon (dau) (11/18/1936-   )
64173213 David MacLaren Brydon (1/19/1939-   )
6417322 Anne Page Brydon (7/29/1904-   )
6417323 Robert Brydon II (10/30/1906-   ), m. 5/20/1933,
        Jean Whittet Wood (6/22/1908-   ), dau. William
        Price and Sudie Rucker Wood
64173231 Robert Carter Brydon (12/31/1936-   )
64173232 Jean Wood Brydon (11/2/1939-   )
6417324 Nathaniel Coleman Brydon (12/12/1910-   ), m.
        6/26/1937, Grace Langhorne Slater (9/29/1908-   ),
        dau. of Horace and Sallie Atkinson Bidgood Slater
64173241 Nathaniel Coleman Brydon, Jr. (10/14/1944-   )
641733 Robert Brydon, Jr. (12/1/1876-   ), m. 5/3/1905,
        Olive Pearl Guerrant (4/2/1880-   ), dau. of
        Joseph Bascom and Lizzie Frances Osborne Guerrant
6417331 Earl Guerrant Brydon (8/24/1906-   ), m. 6/26/
        1932, Willa Mae Williams (6/8/1909-   ), dau. of
        Thomas Henry and Eliza Marie White Williams
64173311 Patricia Page Brydon (3/2/1936-7/15/1937)
64173312 Robert Earl Brydon (12/10/1938-   )
64173313 Elizabeth Ilane Brydon (1/12/1941-   )
6417332 Ellen Page Brydon (1/6/1915-   )
641734 Mary Evelyn Brydon, M.D. (6/2/1878-4/13/1930), m. 9/5/1925,
        George Ladeen Mackay (2/13/1857-   ), son of Daniel
        and Margaret Deacon Mackay of Scotland

641735   Ellen Dane Brydon (12/13/1879-   ), m. 10/4/1910,
         William Edgar Murrie (9/30/1871-   ), son of McAden
         and Laura Martha Flippen Murrie
6417351 Robert Brydon Murrie (8/28/1911-   ). Unm.
6417352 Laura Flippen Murrie (1/30/1913-   ), m. 8/30/
         1936, William Clyde Rodgers (8/16/1913-   ), son
         of William Clyde and Florina Humphreys Rodgers
64173521 Laura Humphreys Rodgers (9/21/1937-   )
64173522 Ellen Dame Rodgers (7/15/1943-   )
6417353 Ellen Dame Murrie (10/6/1915-   )
6417354 William Edgar Murrie (10/6/1917-6/7/1919)
6417355 Hilda MacLaren Murrie (8/19/1920-   )
641736   Carter Page Brydon (5/1/1881-   ), m. 12/10/1919,
         Minnie Nunley (widow of Raymond Levin Holt)(12/7/1885-
                      ), dau. of William P. and Ella Swain Nunley.
         No issue.
641737   Margaret Page Brydon (9/11/1883-5/31/1942). Unm.
641738   Lucy Nelson Brydon (7/6/1886-   ). Unm.
641739   Nona Irving Brydon (5/8/1889-7/5/1889)
64174   R. S. Coleman of Paces P.O., Va.
64175   J. A. Coleman of Winston P.O., Va.
64176   A. M. Coleman of Winston P.O., Va.
64177   H. E. Coleman of News Ferry, Va.
64178   John Mabrey Coleman (10/11/1850-6/1/1915), m. 7/19/1882,
         Evelyn Byrd Page (9/21/1862-11/11/1937), (244666), dau. of
         Frederick Winslow and Anne Kinloch Meriwether Page of
         "Millwood", Albemarle County. She m. (2nd) John Clifford
         Howlett. No issue.
641781   Mary Channing Coleman (7/11/1883-   ). Unm.
641782   Dr. (Dentist) John Mabrey Coleman, Jr. (7/24/1885-   ),
         m. (1st) 9/5/1911, Evelyn Johnson Harrison (5/5/1889-   ),
         dau. of John Prosser and Molly Walsh Harrison of Newport
         News. M. (2nd) 8/10/1923, Mary Isabel Patten (2/19/1888-
                      ), dau. of William Edgar and Millicent
         Jessip Patten of Binghampton, N.Y.
         Children by first wife:
6417821 Evelyn Harrison Coleman (8/28/1912-   ), m. 5/
         24/1939, Hugh Casey Harwood (4/26/1901-   ), son
         of Richard Kirby and Helen Casey Harwood of Newport News.
         No issue.
6417822 John Mabrey Coleman III (5/20/1915-   ), m. 10/6/
         1945, Rebecca Elizabeth Harris (7/25/1917-   ),
         dau. of Grady Garland and Rebecca Elizabeth Valentine
         Harris of Brunswick County
64178221 Rebecca Valentine Coleman (9/13/1946-   )
         Children by second wife:
6417823 Frances Page Coleman (4/5/1926-   )
641783   Frederick Page Coleman (5/1/1888-   ), m. 5/23/1917,
         Rebecca Bolling Bland (5/13/1887-   ), dau. of
         John Blackwood and Martha Perkins Bland of Amelia County
6417831 Martha Page Coleman (9/23/1920-   ), m. 2/16/1946,
         Brigham Abithal Morgan (9/6/1916-   ), son of

Alexander R. and Mary Brigham Morgan of Dover, Tenn.
No issue.
6417832 Mary Channing Coleman (1/17/1923-   )
641784   Nathaniel Ragsdale Coleman (1/11/1892-   )
641785   Evelyn Byrd Coleman (6/2/1899-   ) of Escanaba,
Mich. Unm.
64179   T. G. Coleman of Bedford City, Va.
6418   Sarah Embry Coleman, m. David Chalmers of Halifax County
64181   Joseph W. Chalmers of Houston, Va.
6419   Charles Coleman, m. (1st) Sarah Eaton, dau. of John R. and
Susan Somerville Eaton. M. (2nd) Alice Sydnor
Child by first wife:
64191   Col. Henry Eaton Coleman, m.   Logan
Children by second wife:
64192   Mrs. John Tabb of Gloucester, Va.
64193   Mrs. Charles A. Snowdon of Baltimore
641x   Jane C. Coleman, m. Charles Eaton Hamilton (1816-   ),
son of Patrick and Mary Eaton Baskervill Hamilton. He m.
(2nd) Mrs. Sally A. Watkins
641x1   Patrick Hamilton, m. Sally Payne
641x2   Henrietta M. Hamilton (1943-   ), m. Samuel Tarry
of Woodsworth, Granville County, N.C.
641x21   Charles Hamilton Tarry
641x22   Lucy Davis Tarry
641x23   Euphemia Tarry
641x24   Samuel Tarry
641x3   Euphemia Alston Hamilton (1845-   ), m. Dr. John
Drake of Clarksville, Va.
641x4   Henry E. Coleman Hamilton, d. unm.
641x5   Charles Hamilton, d. young
641x6   Edward Tarry Hamilton, m.   Powell
641x61   (son)
641x62   (son)
641x63   (son)
641x7   Rebecca Hamilton, m. O. C. Farrar
641x71   Lizzie Farrar
641x72   Thomas Farrar
641x73   Edward Farrar
65   Mary Murray (2/22/1754-1823), m. (1st) Alexander Gordon, a
merchant of Petersburg. M. (2nd) Col. William Davies, son
of Rev. Samuel Davies
Child by first husband:
651   Margaret ("Peggy") Gordon, m. (1st) William Knox (-1809),
of Philadelphia. He d. in Petersburg. M. (2nd) Col. Grief
Green of "Park Forest", Mecklenburg County
6511   Mary Ann Knox, m. 1/17/1816, Dr. Thomas Goode (10/31/1787-
4/2/1858), of Hot Springs, Bath County, son of Col. Samuel
and Mary Armistead Burwell Goode of "Whitby"
65111   Col. Thomas Francis Goode, C.S.A. (6/28/1825-1/6/1905), m.
11/27/1860, Rosa Cowles Chambers (2/6/1842-1/20/1921)
651111   Edward Chambers Goode (3/1/1862-6/25/1933), m. 5/20/1885
(1st) Maria Belle Morton, dau. of William Morton of

```
         Clarksville, Va.; m. (2nd) Mrs. Alice M. Finch
      Children by first wife:
6511111  Rose Chambers Goode, m. Charles S. McCullough of Darling-
           ton, S.C.
65111111  Edward Goode McCullough (11/6/1923-8/21/1953)
6511112  Mabel Laird Goode, m. Judge John H. Frantz of Knoxville,
           Tenn. No issue.
6511113  Marguerite Keen Goode (        -7/10/1930)(d. in Greens-
           boro, N.C.), m. Thomas Holt Laird
65111131  Louise Holt Laird
65111132  Mary Chambers Laird, m. Lt. Col. Melvin William Kernkamp
           of Minnesota
651111321  Thomas Laird Kernkamp
651111322  Laura Marguerite Kernkamp
651111323  Mary Carolyn Kernkamp
65111133  Chambers Goode Laird, m. Marie Louise Couterier of Mebane,
           N.C.
651111331  Thomas Holt Laird II
6511114  Benjamin Douglas Goode (        -5/18/1928), m. (1st)
           Maude Butterworth; m. (2nd) Louise McKay
65111141  Louise Elizabeth Goode, m. Robert McChesney Sterrett of
           Virginia
651111411  Robert McChesney Sterrett, Jr.
651111412  David Gordon Sterrett
65111142  Belle Morton Goode, m. Hampton Gray, Jr., of West Virginia
651111421  Lynne McKay Gray
651111422  William Stuart Gray
65111143  Douglas Morton Goode, m. Edward Lowell Dodge of Arlington,
           Mass.
651111431  Randolph Lowell Dodge
651111432  Debra McKay Dodge
651111433  Stephen Goode Dodge
65111144  Rose Chambers Goode, m. Boyd Dennison of Virginia
651111441  Marion Scott Dennison
651111442  Douglas Goode Dennison
651111443  John Emory Dennison
6511115  Virginia Morton Goode, m. Dr. H. Frank Starr of Greensboro
65111151  Elizabeth ("Betty") Starr, m. James Jackson of Rock Hill,
           S.C.
65111152  Dr. H. Frank Starr, Jr., m. Ellen Ross Izlar of Winston-
           Salem
651111521  Virginia Ellen ("Ginny") Starr
651111522  Elizabeth Ross ("Betty") Starr
651111523  Frances Camille Starr
6511116  Gordon Murray Goode (6/28/1893-        ). Served with
           Battery F of the 74th Artillery in World War I. Unm.
651112  Kate Tucker Goode (11/22/1863-11/19/1917). Unm.
651113  Marion Knox Goode (5/24/1865-9/30/1954), m. 11/4/1885,
           Philip J. Briscoe (2/ /1865-        ), of Knoxville, son
           of Philip J. and Martha Briscoe of Mississippi
6511131  Thomas Goode Briscoe (1886-6/28/1887)
```

6511132   Charlotte James Briscoe, m. Charles W. Bateson of New York
65111321 Philip Briscoe Bateson, m. Houston Tissier Trippe of
          Texas
65111322 Charles Edward Bateson (1/14/1916-   ). Reported
          missing while with the U.S. Air Force in the Pacific in
          1941. When his plane was last seen it was headed out
          to sea in pursuit of a Japanese plane. On the cockpit
          of his plane he had lettered: "Lone wandering, but not
          lost".
6511133   Rose Chambers Briscoe, m. Hannon Schoolfield of Danville
65111331 Marion Goode Schoolfield
65111332 Lucille Schoolfield, m. Harley Brown Weatherley of
          Tennessee
651113321 Harley Brown Weatherley, Jr.
6511134   Marion Knox Briscoe, m. William Shaw of Boston
65111341 Sylvia Shaw, m. Jerry Martone
651113411 Geraldine Martone
651114   Thomas Francis Goode, Jr. (5/27/1869-1/ /1941). Unm.
651115   St. John Chambers Goode (7/27/1879-   ), m. Lucille
          Randolph Pleasants
6511151   Virginia Chambers Goode
6511152   William Sterling Goode, m. Susan Wiles Fitzhugh
6511153   Mary Louise Goode, m. Alan Gray Hutcheson
65111531 Alan Gray Hutcheson, Jr.
6511154   Katherine Randolph Goode
6511155   John Chambers ("Jimmy") Goode, m. Aurelia Virginia Wyland
65112   Samuel Goode (1827-   ), m. Mary Gatewood Massie,
          dau. of Col. Samuel and Eugenia S. Massie
651121   Mary Eugenia Goode
651122   Nellie Pleasants Goode
651123   William Alfred Goode
651124   Aurelia Goode
651125   Florine Goode
65113   Martha W. Goode, m. 1842 (her first cousin), Samuel Goode
          Jones (9/20/1815-   ), of Sewanee, Tenn., son of
          Thomas W. and Mary Armisteade Goode Jones. Samuel m.
          (2nd) 1862, Aurie Elmore of Sewanee, Tenn., and had seven
          children by her.
651131   Col. Thomas Goode Jones, C.S.A. (11/26/1844-   ), m.
          12/20/1866, Gena C. Bird
6511311   Marshall Bird Jones (11/3/1869-   )
6511312   Gena Moore Jones (11/26/1871-   )
6511313   Martha Goode Jones (8/10/1874-   )
6511314   Carrie Bird Jones (8/25/1876-   )
6511315   Gordon Houston Jones (6/15/1880-   )
6511316   Thomas Goode Jones (6/9/1885-   )
651132   Mary Virginia Jones (4/6/1847-   ), m. 6/21/1866,
          Dr. William Gesner of Birmingham, son of Abraham Gesner,
          M.D.
651133   Samuel Goode Jones, Jr. (10/2/1849-5/16/1854)
651134   Lucy Spotswood Jones (8/3/1851-2/1/1879), m. 11/24/1869,
          F. H. Armstrong

651135   Edwin Francis Jones (12/21/1853-   ) of Montgomery,
        m. 4/18/1820, Bertha Stubbs
6511351 Samuel Baytop Jones
651136   Carter Jones (9/19/1855-   )
651137   Martha Goode Jones (11/13/1856-2/8/1859)
651138   Charles Pollard Jones (6/13/1858-   )
65114 Lucy Goode, m. ca. 1850, Col. George William Brent, C.S.A.,
       (8/ /1821-1872), of Alexandria, son of George and Eliza-
       beth Parsons Brent
651141   Thomas Goode Brent (2/3/1852-   )
651142   Lucy Brent, m. (1st) William G. Howard. M. (2nd) Robert
       T. Thorp of Boydton, Va.
651143   Samuel Gordon Brent (6/28/1855-   )
651144   Mary E. Brent (9/2/1857-   ), m. Charles A. Read
       of Atlanta
651145   George G. Brent (1/3/1860-   )
651146   Alice V. Brent (11/8/1863-   )
651147   Cornelia W. Brent (11/18/1863-   )
651148   Jessie Innis Brent (1/15/1870-   )
65115 Margaret Knox Goode (-1868), m. 10/ /1860, William
       Phillips Garland of Lynchburg (ca. 1834/40-1863), son of
       James and Sarah J. Burch Garland
651151   Willie Phillips Garland (dau) (3/ /1863-   )
65116 Ellen Goode, m. William G. Friend of Charlotte County. No
       issue.
65117 Sophia Goode. Unm.
65118 Isabella Goode. Unm.
65119 Alice Goode, m. Dr. William Crump (-ca. 1869), of
       Culpeper County and Ivy Depot, Albemarle County
651191   Sallie Crump, m. Rev. Mr. Goodwin
651192   Alice Crump
651193   William Crump of Texas
651194   Ellen Crump
651195   Mary Crump
6512 Sophia Knox, m. John Buford of Mecklenburg County
65121
65122
6513 William Alexander (D.?) Knox
6514 Eliza Whittle Knox, d. unm.
6515 John F. O. (C.?) Knox of Mecklenburg County
6516 Henry Green
6517 (son)
    Child by second husband:
652 Mary Ann Davies, m. 1804, Fortescue Whittle of (near) "Whittle's
    Mill", Mecklenburg County
6521 William Conway Whittle (1/6/1805-1878), Commander U.S.N.,
    Commodore C.S.N., m. 6/17/1833, Elizabeth Beverley Sinclair
    (7/26/1812-8/30/1855), dau. of Commodore Arthur Sinclair,
    Jr., and his wife, the former Sarah ("Sally") Skipwith
    Kennon
65211 Arthur Sinclair Whittle (4/18/1835-9/3/1855). Unm.
65212 Mary Davies Whittle (1/2/1838-7/8/1858). Unm.

65213 Lt. William Conway Whittle, Jr. (1/16/1840-1/5/1920), C.S.N.,
m. 11/13/1872, Elizabeth Calvert Page (12/10/1846-8/13/
1921), dau. of Gen. Richard Lucian and Alexina Taylor Page
652131 Alexina Page Whittle (4/11/1874-   ). Unm.
652132 Richard Page Whittle (6/28/1875-   ). Unm.
652133 Elizabeth Sinclair Whittle (2/15/1877-   )
652134 Mary Beverley Whittle (2/9/1879-   ), m. 3/30/1910,
James Cabell Dabney (10/8/1875-   ), son of Dr.
William Cecil and Jane Bell Minor Dabney
6521341 Elizabeth Calvert Page Dabney (3/5/1911-   )
6521342 Mary Beverley Dabney (9/10/1912-   )
6521343 William Minor Dabney (1/6/1919-   ). Unm.
652135 William Conway Whittle III (6/27/1881-8/2/1927) of Norfolk,
m. 5/23/1907, Georgiana Randolph Charrington (11/9/1881-
)(24153343)
6521351 William Conway Whittle IV (3/23/1908-   ), m. 10/5/
1946, Elizabeth Morrison Meredith (3/5/1914-   ),
dau. of George Minor and Elizabeth Madison Morrison
Meredith of Virginia Beach. No issue.
6521352 Georgiana Charrington Whittle (3/23/1908-   ). Unm.
6521353 Beverley Randolph Whittle (11/4/1914-   ), m. 1/21/
1939, Nell Serpell Tyler (12/3/1915-   ), dau. of
Maj. Stockton Heth and Nell Louise Serpell Tyler of
Norfolk
65213531 Beverley Randolph Whittle, Jr. (12/23/1939-   )
65213532 Mary Harrison Randolph Whittle (2/26/1944-   )
65213533 Nell Tyler Whittle (9/25/1946-   )
652136 Edmonia Lee Whittle (4/17/1885-   )
65214 Sarah Kennon Whittle (12/15/1841-   ), m. 1884, Frederick W. Baker. No issue.
65215 Jane Eliza Whittle (2/22/1844-11/18/1912), m. 9/6/1872, Rev.
David Barr (8/26/1843-6/25/1922), son of George R. and
Sarah Rodefer Barr
652151 Sadie Barr (12/21/1873-12/21/1873)
652152 William Arthur Barr (3/8/1875-12/15/1913), m. 9/10/1902,
Frances Whittle Greene (10/25/1881-   ), dau. of
Augustus Newport and Elena Moore Mitchell Greene. No issue.
652153 Elizabeth Beverley Barr (9/19/1876-   ), m. 9/3/1900,
John Nichols Githens (1860-1/28/1921), son of Samuel B.
and Amanda Sickels Githens
6521531 Katherine Beverley Githens (7/4/1903-   ). Unm.
6521532 Elizabeth Sinclair Githens (8/30/1907-   ), m. 10/
2/1925, Leo Charles Nunley (3/31/1905-   ), son of
Franklin Pierce and Jennie Elizabeth James Nunley
65215321 Patricia Ruth Sinclair Nunley (8/27/1926-   )
65215322 John Randolph Nunley (7/15/1931-9/15/1931)
652154 Beverley Ray Barr (4/16/1878-11/24/1912), m. George Eugene
Clancey of Texas. She died in Philippines in childbirth.
6521541 D. inf.
652155 Jennie Whittle Barr (12/21/1880-11/16/1883)
65216 Beverley Kennon Whittle (7/2/1845-10/28/1877). Unm.

65217   Elizabeth Beverley Whittle (2/20/1847-11/2/1911), m. 4/16/
        1873, John Coles Terry (10/28/1844-2/25/1926), son of
        Joseph Matley and Catherine Thompson Coles Terry
652171 Joseph Dandridge Terry (2/3/1874-2/8/1911). Unm.
652172 Elizabeth Beverley Terry (5/28/1875-2/8/1911). Unm.
652173 Catherine Thompson Coles Terry (1/5/1877-8/3/1877)
652174 John Coles Terry, Jr. (8/4/1879-3/3/1927), m. 6/14/1914,
        Elizabeth Huger (2/6/1882-   ), dau. of Col. Frank
        and Julia Trible Huger
6521741 Aurelia Huger Terry (2/2/1915-   ),m. 9/30/1944,
        Lt. John Robb Reed, Jr. (2/19/1902-   ), son of
        John Robb and Theresa Mitchel Reed of Austin. No issue.
6521742 Frank Huger Terry (7/20/1918-   )
6521743 Elizabeth Beverley Whittle Terry (11/28/1921-   )
652175 Grace Fortescue Terry (8/9/1882-   ), m. 11/17/1915,
        Dr. Philip St. Leger Moncure (1/27/1867-   ), son
        of St. Leger Landon and Lucy George Olivier Moncure. No
        issue.
65218   Judge Stafford Gorman Whittle (12/5/1849-9/11/1931), m.
        11/4/1880, Ruth Staples Drewry (10/27/1861-5/22/1923),
        dau. of Dr. Henry Martyn and Flora Ruth Redd Drewry of
        Henry County
652181 Stafford Gorman Whittle, Jr. (11/2/1881-1/16/1942). Unm.
652182 Henry Drewry Whittle (1/22/1883-   ), m. 4/12/1922,
        Flora Overton Redd (11/10/1891-   ), dau. of John
        Edward and Cora Lee Barksdale Redd
6521821 Henry Drewry Whittle, Jr. (4/20/1924-   )
6521822 John Redd Whittle (11/27/1925-   )
6521823 Ruth Stafford Whittle (10/14/1929-   )
652183 Flora Redd Whittle (12/10/1884-   ). Unm.
652184 Elizabeth Sinclair Whittle (6/27/1886-   ), m. 6/7/
        1913, Col. James David Johnston, Jr. (9/16/1869-1940),
        son of James David and Mary Ann Fowler Johnston
6521841 Elizabeth Whittle Johnston (3/11/1915-   ), m. 3/15/
        1941, Dr. John Macky Baldwin, Jr. (11/18/1914-   ),
        son of John Macky and Florence Cooper McClelland Baldwin
        of Norfolk
65218411 John Macky Baldwin III (7/22/1944-   )
6521842 James David Johnston III (5/21/1918-   )
6521843 Ruth Fowler Johnston (6/1/1923-   )
6521844 Stafford Gorman Whittle Johnston (11/14/1927-   )
652185 Ruth Drewry Whittle (6/23/1888-2/20/1919), m. 4/19/1911,
        Robert Thruston Hubard III (6/2/1876-   ), son of
        Robert Thruston II and Sallie Edmunds Hubard
6521851 Sallie Edmunds Hubard (6/1/1913-   ), m. 6/24/1939,
        Walter Lee Penn, Jr. (12/18/1907-   ), son of Walter
        Lee and Caroline Lightfoot Lee Dillard Penn
65218511 Walter Lee Penn III (6/24/1940-   )
6521852 Robert Thruston Hubard IV (11/25/1914-   )
6521853 Ruth Whittle Hubard (9/25/1918-   )
6521854 Mary Stafford Hubard (9/25/1918-   )
652186 Beverley Kennon Whittle (4/30/1890-   ), d. inf.

652187 Kennon Caithness Whittle (10/12/1891-   ), m. 10/20/
        1920, Mary Holt Spencer (9/25/1898-   ), dau.of
        James Harrison and Blanche Williamson Spencer
6521871 Mary Holt Whittle (1/2/1923-   )
6521872 Stafford Gorman Whittle III (9/29/1924-   )
6521873 Kennon Caithness Whittle, Jr. (3/15/1932-   )
652188 Conway Davies Whittle (1/20/1894-1899)
652189 William Murray Whittle (3/4/1896-   ), m. 4/19/1922,
        Alice Hairston Glenn (ca. 1902-   ), dau. of James
        Dodge and Sarah Hairston Glenn of North Carolina
6521891 Sara Hairston Whittle (1/17/1924-   ), m. 8/4/
        1944, William Clarence Kluttz, Jr. (6/24/1917-   ),
        son of William Clarence and Josephine Branch Craige
        Kluttz
65218x Arthur Sinclair Whittle (11/9/1897-   ), d. inf.
65218a Randolph Gordon Whittle (5/4/1900-   ), m. 10/3/1928,
        Josephine Edmonds Parrott (1/10/1905-   ), dau. of
        John Henry and Josephine Cromwell Parrott
65218a1 Randolph Gordon Whittle, Jr. (5/16/1930-   )
65218a2 John Parrott Whittle (5/22/1935-   )
65218a3 Josephine Edmonds Whittle (3/21/1940-   )
65219 Conway McNiece Whittle (11/11/1851-11/5/1888), m. 12/9/1880,
        Rosalie Beirne Tams (3/21/186), dau. of William Henry and
        Marie Antoinette Smith Tams of Staunton
652191 William Tams Whittle (2/16/1882-8/15/1882)
652192 Rosalie Beirne Whittle (2/4/1885-   ), m. 12/1/1909,
        Alfred Pembroke Thom, Jr. (12/3/1883-   ), son of
        Alfred Pembroke and Virginia Williamson Tunstall Thom
6521921 Lt. Col. (Medical Corps) Alfred Pembroke Thom III (9/25/
        1911-   ), m. 9/19/1936, Constance Margaret
        Haigh (9/15/1914-   )
65219211 Constance Fielding Thom (10/24/1939-   )
6521922 Conway Whittle Thom (6/10/1913-   )
652193 Mary Conway Whittle (4/8/1888-2/14/1890)
6521x Gilberta Sinclair Whittle (11/13/1853-12/25/1939). Unm.
6522 Fortescue Whittle
6523 James M. Whittle, m. (1st) Mary Coles, dau. of Col. Isaac
        Coles of Pittsylvania County. M. (2nd) Cornelia Lotte
        Skipwith (6124)
65231 (dau)
65232 (dau)
6524 Conway D. Whittle, m. Gilberta Sinclair, dau. of Com. W.
        Sinclair, U.S.N.
6525 John S. Whittle, Surgeon, U.S.N., m. (1st) Jane Patterson.
        M. (2nd) Anne Southgate, dau. of Wright Southgate of
        Norfolk. Whittle died at sea (off the coast of South
        America) of yellow fever.
65251 (son)
6526 Lewis Neale Whittle, m. Sarah M. Powers of Macon, Ga.
65261 (son)
65262 (son)

65263 (son)
65264 (son)
65265 (son)
65266 (dau)
65267 (dau)
65268 (dau)
65269 (dau)
6526x (dau)
6526a (dau)
6526b (dau)
6527 Stephen Decatur Whittle, m. Anne ("Nannie") Randolph Taylor,
      dau. of George Taylor of "Horn Quarter", King William County
      (and granddaughter of John Taylor of Caroline)
65271 Kate Whittle
65272 Anne Whittle
65273 Fortescue Whittle
65274 Mary Whittle
6528 Francis McNeece Whittle, Bishop of Virginia, m. Emily Fairfax
6529 Powhatan Bolling Whittle, Colonel, C.S.A. Lost an arm in
      the war. Home: Valdosta, Ga.
652x (dau)
652a (dau)
652b (dau)
653 Elizabeth Julia Davies
66 James Murray, Jr. (7/10/1743-   ), m. Martha Ward. She
      m. (2nd) Jerman Baker, attorney-at-law of Petersburg. James
      Murray, Jr. owned large estates in Mecklenburg County near
      what is now Chase City
661 Mary Murray, m. Edmund Harrison
6611 Dead by 5/10/1796
6612 Dead by 5/10/1796
6613 Dead by 5/10/1796
6614 Dead by 5/10/1796
6615 Edmonia Harrison (15 mos. old ca. 5/10/1796)
67 Thomas Murray (1/13/1757-   ). No issue.

The Elwyns (Elwins)

The following appears on page xxxi of Vol. I of Conway Robinson's ABSTRACT OF THE PROCEEDINGS OF THE VIRGINIA COMPANY OF LONDON (1888) published as Vol. 7 of the COLLECTIONS OF THE VIRGINIA HISTORICAL SOCIETY (New Series):

It is claimed in America that the descendants of Pocahontas are limited to those springing from the marriage of Robert Bolling with Jane, daughter of Thomas Rolfe, but it has been alleged that the latter left a son, Anthony, in England, whose daughter, Hannah, married Sir Thomas Leigh, of County Kent, and that their descendants of that and of the additional highly respectable names of Bennet and Spencer are quite numerous. See Deduction in the RICHMOND STANDARD, January 21, 1882.

Anthony Rolfe, Hannah's father, was born in 1600, and hence, was too old to have been a son of Thomas Rolfe, but he is a central figure in the Pocahontas-descent allegation propounded, after extensive study, by Florence Miriam Elizabeth Dorothea Wright Carson (Mrs. Hilding Carson), a lady of culture and intelligence.

Mrs. Carson concludes that the Thomas Rolfe who married Elizabeth Washington was Pocahontas' son, noting parenthetically that Capt. Samuel Argall's "widowed mother had remarried one Lawrence Washington, who resided near Maidstone, Kent". Argall was the gentleman who engineered and effected the capture of Pocahontas, and as Mrs. Carson notes, he and John Rolfe were "old friends", giving Argall "good reason to keep in touch with" Thomas Rolfe, and "it is possible that Thomas knew" Argall's mother, "and met some of the younger members of the Washington family".

Mrs. Carson writes that in 1633, a daughter was born to Thomas and Elizabeth Washington Rolfe; "it is likely that Thomas's wife Elizabeth died in childbirth"; and "the facts that have been handed down to each succeeding generation of the Elwyn family of Norfolk" are that "Thomas Rolfe took his baby daughter to Tuttington, Norfolk, where his father's cousin, Anthony Rolfe, was living".

As regards "facts * * * handed down", Mrs. Carson notes that the "unusual longevity in the Elwyn family" with "so many of its members having lived well beyond their ninetieth year" which "has meant that sometimes it took only three generations to bridge two centuries or more. But this has enabled parents to pass on to their children by word of mouth as well as in other ways a great deal of family history and tradition from their own members of what they were taught in their childhood and youth".

Mrs. Carson writes: that Anthony Rolfe "and his wife Mary had lost their first child, Mary, and had a second little

daughter Maria, who was born in 1632 and was, therefore, only a
year older than Thomas' baby".

Mrs. Carson writes that Thomas left his baby daughter
at Tuttington, and that Anthony adopted her "and had her christened
Anne in Tuttington Church as a member of his own family"; that
"Maria Rolfe died when she was two years old"; that "subsequently"
Anthony and Mary Rolfe "had two sons, Clement and Anthony, born
in 1635 and 1636 respectively, and finally a daughter, Hannah, born
in 1638. Clement died at the age of two * * * but Anthony lived
to graduate from Caius College".

Mrs. Carson reports that in 1659, Anne Rolfe married
Peter Elwyn V (1623-1695)(eldest son of Peter Elwyn IV of Thuring,
Norfolk), and in 1650, Hannah married Sir Thomas Leigh of Adding-
ton, Surrey.

Mrs. Carson continues: "when Anthony Rolfe died the
bulk of what he had to leave was inherited by the eldest of
Anne and Peter Elwyn's daughters, Ann, who married William Bulwer
of Wood Dalling. From this it would seem that she was Anthony's
favourite grandchild, and no doubt he felt that his own daughter,
Lady Leigh, was already well provided for".

Mrs. Carson writes: "when Anne Rolfe married in 1659
her 'goods and chattels' must have included the beautiful portrait
of her grandmother Princess Pocahontas in her Court dress and also
the 'Pocahontas Vase', and these became heirlooms in the Elwyn
family from then on for more than 250 years. In fact, the Vase
remains in the family * * * but the portrait was sold about 1926
by the then head of the family, Fountain Peter Elwin, he being
the last of the entail and the last male Elwin in the direct line
of the senior branch of Elwins".

It appears that Mrs. Carson is not correct in concluding
that the goods and chattels of Anne Rolfe "must have included" the
portrait (which is now owned by The National Portrait Gallery).
Monroe H. Fabian, Curator, Department of Paintings and Sculpture
at The National Gallery writes: "As far as we can tell from a
physical examination of the painting, it was probably not painted
until sometime in the eighteenth century".

As regards the sale of the portrait, Mrs. Carson reports
"that in 1893, when the World's Columbian Exposition, commemorating
the 400th anniversary of the discovery of America, was held in
Chicago, a deputation was dispatched to England by the Organisers
to visit my Great-Uncle HASTINGS ELWIN. They brought with them
a blank cheque and told my Great-Uncle that he might fill this in
for any amount he wished if in return he would part with the
POCAHONTAS portrait so that it might be put on view at the
Exposition for all Americans to see. This, however, was something
he would never have agreed to do, but in any event it was an im-
possibility since the portrait was entailed, together with other

heirlooms, for a further generation. It was left to his heir to
take a different line of action at a later date when the financial
problems of the day must have made the sale of the portrait too
attractive to be lightly dismissed".

The "heir" who took "a different line of action", and
sold the portrait was Fountain Peter Elwin (1862-1955), and ca.
1926 (at the time of the sale of the portrait), he wrote a lengthy
letter setting forth his knowledge as regards the portrait's pro-
venance, giving a bit of family genealogy, and stating: "The
family of Elwyn have no descent from the marriage of Rolfe & the
Princess Pocahontas".35 V 433.

As regards the truth of this "no descent" statement,
Elwin and Mrs. Carson are in disagreement.

As regards the portrait, Mrs. Carson writes: "Fortunately
for POCAHONTAS's English descendants a good copy of it had been
made (in water-colours) by the artist Joseph Nash who had married
Rebecca Elwin, one of the daughters of Col. Fountain Elwin, round
about 1830. A further copy was allowed to be made before the portrait actually left England in 1926 and is believed to be in the
possession of Lord Fairfax, whose ancestor was connected with the
early days of the Virginia Colony. The copy made by Joseph Nash
has been handed down in his family and is now owned by his great-
granddaughter who lives in Norfolk (Dorothy Fountain Stokes, nee
Nash, of Thompson, near Thetford, Norfolk)."

In further, and general support of her allegation, Mrs.
Carson reports: "Members of the Elwyn family have always been
immensely proud of their descent from Pocahontas and the fact that
her blood ran in their veins".

And she writes: "the Pocahontas descent in the Elwin
family has always been easily discernible in the characteristic
features of the Elwyns since the marriage of her granddaughter
Anne Rolfe to Peter Elwyn in 1659. It has been said that until
then most Elwyns had the fair hair and blue eyes of their Anglo-
Saxon and Norman ancestry, but certainly since then the majority
of those in the direct line have had the very dark brown eyes of
Pocahontas and the high-bridged nose of her people. These features
were particularly noticeable in portraits painted during the
XVIIIth and XIXth Centuries of the many children and grandchildren
of Peter Elwin IX even after more than two hundred years! To
mention one such case, the biographer of my Great-Uncle (Rev.)
Whitwell Elwin (who was born in 1816) stated 'Among his direct
ancestors he counted John Rolfe, who introduced tobacco-planting
into Virginia and married the celebrated Pocahontas'. Whitwell
Elwin's 'pronounced nose' and 'rich brown eyes' are said to have
closely resembled those features of the Indian 'Princess'. This
could also be said of most of his brothers and sisters, of whom

my own Grandmother was one. I myself am a brown-eyed descendant,
but my daughter, Patricia Frances Anne nee Carson m. D'Omer A.
Lemieux of Ottawa, Canada, has the real 'Pocahontas eyes' although
she was born more than 300 years after Pocahontas's death and
eleven generations later! In many instances the facial likeness
handed down in the Elwyn family has been remarkable, so much so
that some of the old portraits of Elwyns could well be paintings
of modern descendants wearing the period clothes of their
ancestors."

The Fountain Peter Elwin denial might be at least a bit
self-serving, and despite this denial, Mrs. Carson's allegation
that Thomas Rolfe was the father of Anne Rolfe Elwyn merits
acceptance.

Mrs. Carson has furnished considerable details regarding
the descendants of Peter and Anne Rolfe Elwyn, and these descendants are included hereinafter, but with a slightly different numbering system---the letter "E" is prefixed to each number, and the
numbers E1, E2, E3, etc., are assigned to the children of Peter and
Anne Rolfe Elwyn.

Thus, if Mrs. Carson's allegation is correct, E1 would
be a great grandchild of Pocahontas, etc.

E1   Peter Elwyn VI (1660-2/5/1720*1), of Tuttington and Aylsham.
      Gonville & Caius College 1678/9. M. 1680, Anne Scambler
      (bapt. 11/30/1660, d. 9/26/1697), only dau. of Thomas and
      Elizabeth Marsham Scambler of Hevingham, and gt. gt. grandau.
      of Bishop Scambler of Norwich and Peterborough. Elwyn bought
      the Booton Estate in 1713 from his son-in-law Christopher
      Layer. High Sheriff 1720. Will Norwich Archdeaconry. Elwyn
      bur. Tuttington Church
E11   Peter Elwyn (4/ /1681-1681)
E12   Peter Elwyn (VII)(1685-9/15/1731), admitted to Gonville &
      Caius College 5/8/1703, and to the Middle Temple 5/15/1706
      or 1707. He m. 1710 Anne Chute (d. 8/ /1756, age 63), 2nd
      dau. of Thomas and Elizabeth Chute of South Pickenham,
      Norfolk; and gt. granddau. of Chaloner Chute, Speaker of
      the House of Commons. Both Peter and Anne bur. Tuttington
      Church. D.s.p.
E13   Anne Elwyn (1685-6/30/1731), m. 9/18/1705, James Tennant (d.
      7/21/1733, age 61), of Rougham, Norfolk. Both bur. St.
      John's Church, Maddermarket, Norwich.
E14   Elizabeth Elwyn (1683?-   ), m. Christopher Layer
      (-1723) of Booton, son of John and Elizabeth
      Marsham Layer. Christopher, a Jacobite, was executed at
      Tyburn 5/17/1723
E141 Anne Layer
E142 Elizabeth Layer
E143 Mary Clementina Layer (her godparents were James the Pre-
      tender and his wife Clementina)
E15   Thomas Elwyn (1688-   )(admitted Gonville & Caius College
      3/31/1705; and to the Middle Temple 11/27/1706 or 8).
      Apparently, Elwyn predeceased his father
E2   Fountain(e) Elwyn (1661-8/29/1720) of Thurning, Norfolk, m.
      2/16/1697, at Norwich, Anne Hastings (1674-10/ /1767), dau.
      of Robert Hastings of Barney, Norfolk (who was a descendant
      of Edward I through Sir Hugh Hastings and his wife Ann
      Despencer). Both bur. Thurning Church. Fountain's will
      proved 1721. Anne's will proved 1767.

E21 Hewett Elwyn (1698-bur. 9/2/1727), m. 1726, Ann Elwyn of
Thurning (his cousin). Her will prob. 1/2/1730

E22 Anne Elwyn (1699-1763), m. Riches Repps Brown of Fulmodeston
(1697-7/22/1767)

E221 (son)
E222 (son)
E223 (son)
E224 (dau)
E225 (dau)
E226 (dau)

E23 Peter Elwin (VIII)(1701-1782) of Thurning. Gonville & Caius
College; and Gray's Inn (1720). M. ca. 1728, Philippa Marsham (1703-1784), 4th dau. of Thomas and Dorothy Gooch Marsham of Stratton Strawless. Peter inherited the Booton
Estate from his uncle Peter Elwyn (VII) in 1731, and he inherited the Thurning Estate from his father in 1720. Peter,
who also lived at Saxthorpe Hall, moved to Booton Hall ca.
1742. His portrait by Dom van der Smiffen is known as
"The Blue Coat" portrait.

E231 Peter Elwin (IX)(1730-1798), Squire of Thurning, Booton and
Saxthorpe, m. (1st) 1751, Margaret Paston (1726-1767), dau.
of Sir Edward Paston of Barningham, Norfolk. She is bur.
at Bade, Norfolk. Peter m. (2nd) 1768, Susannah Bell (1752-
1834), dau. of William Bell of Oulton near Saxthorpe. Her
portrait by Philip Reinagle (1780), was sold at Christies
194. Peter was a Fellow at Gonville & Caius College, and
13th in descent from Edward III through John of Gaunt and
his third wife Katherine (nee Roet), widow of Sir Thomas
Sivynford. Peter's portrait by Philip Reinagle (1780) is
known as "The Red Coat" portrait. Peter possessed the
Booton portrait (35 V 432), and was the last Elwin to live
at Booton Hall.
Children, etc., by first wife:

E2311 Peter Elwin (X)(1751-   ), m. Martha   (-
1808), widow of William Moore. Elwin died before his father,
and never inherited the estates. Martha is bur. at Dalton

E23111 (dau)
E23112 (dau)
E2312 (son), d. young
E2313 (dau)
E2314 (dau)
E2315 (dau)
E2316 (dau)
E2317 (dau)
E2318 (dau)
E2319 (dau)
NOTE: E2311 may have had another daughter by his first wife.
Children, etc., by second wife:

E231x Marsham Elwin (1784-1831), Squire of Booton and Thurning,
and Captain of the Norfolk Militia, m. 1809/10, Emma Louisa
Whitwell (1781-1870), widow of Sir George Berney Brograve,
and dau. of Edward Whitwell of Yorkshire, and of his wife,

Mary, dau. of Sir John Mylne. Whitwell, Colonel of the
1st King's Dragoon Guards, was, at the time of the French
Revolution, envoy to the Court at Versailles. Emma is
said to have sat upon the knees of Marie Antoinette. The
Booton portrait was at Thurning Hall during Marsham's
residency. 35 v 432.

E231x1   Hastings Elwin (1811-1902), Squire of Booton (commencing
in 1831), m. Appolonia Mary ("Minnie") Wodehouse, dau.
of Edmund Wodehouse (M.P. for Norfolk) and sister of Sir
Philip Wodehouse, Governor of Bombay, and later, 1st Earl
of Kimberley. No issue. Hastings gave the Booton portrait to his brother Whitwell, and upon Hastings death,
he was succeeded as Squire by his great nephew, Fountain
Peter Elwin.

E231x2   Marsham Elwin (1812-1860), Pembroke College, Cambridge,
and Lincoln's Inn. M. Emily Wyatt, dau. of T. Wyatt of
Willenhall, Warwickshire. No issue. She remarried after
Marsham's death.

E231x3   Whitwell Elwin (1816-1/1/1900) of Norfolk (Gonville &
Caius College 1834), m. 1838, his cousin, Frances Mary
Rebecca Elwin (-1898) of Bath (E23714), third
dau. of Lt. Col. Fountain Elwin and his wife Charlotte
McGlashan Elwin. No issue. Whitwell Elwin succeeded
his cousin Rev. Caleb Elwin in the family living, and
was Rector of Booton for 50 years (1850-1900). Editor
of The Quarterly for some years. Rebuilt Booton Church
and Rectory at his own expense. The Booton portrait
was kept in the Rectory. 35 V 433.

E231x31   Fountain Jeremy Elwin (1830-1869), m. 1860, Esther Tobin
of Bath. She remarried following his death.

E231x311   Fountain Peter Elwin (1862-1955), m. Amy Singer (-
194), Sculptress. No issue. He was last Squire of
Booton, and last male Elwin in the direct line, Senior
Branch of the Elwin family of Norfolk. The Booton
property was devised by will to Lady Emily Lutyens, a
descendant of the Bulwers of Wood Dalling (early 15th
Century) who had inter-married with the Elwins several
times. Fountain's grandfather Whitwell left him the
Booton portrait, and ca. 1926, Fountain sold the portrait to Francis Burton Harrison. 35 V 432-3.

E231x312   Esther Mary Elwin (1864-1955). For many years, a nursing
Sister at University College Hospital, London. Bur.
Enfield.

E231x313   Charlotte Elwin (1866-   ), m. Richard James of
Enfield

E231x3131 Richard James

E231x314   Emma Elwin (1868-19). Unm.

E231x32   Rev. Hastings Philip Elwin (1845-1874)(M.A. Cambridge).
Unm.

E231x33   Rev. Warwick Elwin (1849-1908)(Pembroke College). Succeeded
his father as Rector of Booton. Died abroad, bur. Las
Palmas, Canary Islands.

E231x34   Rev. Edward Fenton Elwin (1853-1921). (M.A. Cambridge).
          Unm. Member of Community of St. John's, Cowley. Died
          in India.
E231x35   Frances Margaret Elwin (1858-1875). Unm.
E231x4   Charles Elwin (1919-1919)
E231x5   Peter James Elwin (1827-1908), m. his cousin, Sarah Lucy
          Lloyd of Bawdeswell Hall, Norfolk. He was Rector of
          Itteringham, Norfolk   '
E231x6   Emma Louisa Elwin (1814-1904), m. 1834, Arthur Martin a
          Beckett, of Sydney, Australia, son of William à Beckett,
          Chief Justice of Victoria (Australia)
E231x61   William à Beckett
E231x611 Mary à Beckett
E231x612 Jean à Beckett, m.
E231x6121 (dau)
E231x613 Elwin à Beckett (189   -   ), m. Bertram Barton (1883-
          1919)
E231x6131 Bertram M. Barton
E231x61311 Andrew Charles Barton
E231x61312   ?   Virginia Barton
E231x61313 Mary Barton
E231x61314 Marsham Barton
E231x61315 Hugh Barton
E231x61316 Nan Barton
E231x62   Arthur à Beckett, m.
E231x621 Arthur Martin a Beckett (1883-   ), m. Nancy
          Campbell
E231x6211 Martin a Beckett. Unm.
E231x6212 Elwin a Beckett. Unm.
E231x622 John a Beckett, m.
E231x623 Hastings a Beckett (-1969), m. Edith
E231x6231
E231x6232
E231x6233   '
E231x624 Madge a Beckett, m.   Beesley ?
E231x6241 (son)
E231x6242 (son)
E231x6243 (son)
E231x63   (dau), m.   McCarthy
E231x631 Maud McCarthy (1860-1949). Boer War. Florence Nightin-
          gale Medal. World War I. Matron in charge, Royal Army
          Nursing Service. Dame of the Order of the British
          Empire. Unm.
E231x632 Marsham McCarthy, Surgeon, New Zealand. With RAMC in
          World War I
E231x633 Hastings McCarthy
E231x634 Mabel McCarthy, m. Frank Coles
E231x6341 Mabel Coles (18 -   ). Unm.
E231x6342 Eileen Coles (189 -   ), m. Guy Laschles. She d.
          in childbirth in Africa
E231x6343 Charles Elwin Coles (189 -   ), m.
E231x63431

E231x63432
E231x63433
E231x63434
E231x6344 William Coles. Killed.
E231x7 Mary Ellen Elwin (1820-   ), m. 1845, Rev. George Edward
        Symonds, Vicar of Thaxted, Essex, 1859. Rural Dean from
        1863.
E231x71 Edward Symonds (1846-   ). B.A. Oxon 1869. In
        Holy Orders. M.
E231x72 Henry Symonds (1850-   ). In Holy Orders, m.
        White. Succeeded father as Vicar of Thaxted.
E231x721 Henry Symonds (1879-1970). In Holy Orders. C. R. Mir-
        field, Yorks.
E231x722 Hilda Symonds (1889-   ). Unm.
E231x723 Sybil Symonds (1890-   ), m. Herbert Moore (1880-
        ), son of Weaver Moore of Boling
E231x7231 Michael Moore (1915-   ), m. Ella White, widow
        (nee Clark)
E231x72311 Elizabeth Moore (1946-   ), m. 1965, Michael
        Parkinson, M.S.
E231x723111 Andrew Moore (1967-   )
E231x723112 (son)
E231x72132 Peter Elwin Moore (1949-   )
E231x7232 Richard Moore (1920-   ), m. M   Dre
        of   ?
E231x72321 Carolyn Moore (1951-   ). Sheffield Univ. 1969
E231x72322 Oliver Moore (1953-   ). Scholar of Eton College
        1966, Balliol College, Oxford, 1971.
E231x72323 Victoria Josephine Moore (1960-   )
E231x72324 Isabelle Marie Moore (1962-   )
E231x72325 Josephine Marie (1967-   )
E231x7233 (son) M.A. Pembroke
E231x724 (dau)
E231x73 Edmund Symonds (1853-   )
E231x8 Rosellen Elwin (1821-1882), m. 1856, Rev. John H. Backhouse,
        Vicar of Laverton 1877
E231x81 John Backhouse (1857-1873)
E231x82 Arthur Backhouse (1862-19   ), m.   Porter. He was
        a Colonel, Regular Army
E231x821 Rev. Thomas Porter Backhouse, M.A. (1898-1971). Rector
        of Cloister St. Edmund, Norfolk. Hon. Cannon of Norwich
        Cathedral. Unm.
E231x9 Eliza Susannah Elwin (1823-1922), m. 1860, Rev. John Wright
        (1793-1893). (Trinity College, Cambridge). Vicar of Great
        Malvern. Rector of Falmouth, He died three weeks before
        his 100th birthday.
E231x91 Hastings Elwin Wright (1861-1897), m. 1890, Florence Amy
        Henderson (-1939, in her 74th year), dau. of George
        and Emily Henderson of Hove, Sussex. He M.I. Mech. E.-
        Served in India, G.I.P. Railway until 1889
E231x911 Marsham Elwin Wright (3/29/1891-1970, m. (1st) Margaret
        Gleeson (-1938). M. (2nd) Mary Ellen   (no

issue by second wife). He was educated in England as a
Civil Engineer. Emigrated to Canada 1910. Fought in
France and Belgium with Royal Canadian Artillery, World
War I. Returned to U.S.A. on demobilisation in 1919
Children by first wife:

E231x9111 John Marsham Wright (3/ /1922-   ), m. 194 ,
  Victoria   of Vancouver, Canada, then serving
  with U.S. Army Nursing Corps in Alaska. Nursing Degree,
  Seattle University. He b. Minneapolis, served with
  American Army overseas, World War II. Transferred to
  Alaska Communications Corps 1946. Served in Alaska and
  Arizona. Seattle University Degree. Retired 196 from
  U.S. Army. No issue.

E231x9112 Margaret Mary Wright (6/ /1923-   ), m. 1941,
  George Edmund ("Judd") Fisher (-196),
  U.S. Navy (Air) She b. Minneapolis

E231x91121 George Edmund ("Buddy") Fisher II (1943-   ), m.
  11/ /1969, Angela Elaine Irwin, dau. of Mr. & Mrs.
  Jam. Perry Irwin of Decatur, Georgia

E231x911211 Child (1971-   )

E231x91122 Judy Fisher (1944-   ), m. 1962, Patrick M.
  McCaffrey, U. S. Navy

E231x911221 (19   -   )
E231x911222 (19   -   )

E231x91123 Janet Fisher (1949-   ), m. 1/ /1971, Robert
  of Pensacola

E231x911231 John   (10/21/1971-   )

E231x91124 D. inf.
E231x91125 D. inf.

E231x91126 John Fisher (1956-   )

E231x912 Percy Elwin Wright (7/3/1892-   ), m. 193 ,
  Margaret Sester. He in British Expéditionary Force,
  France, 1915-18 (R. C. Artillery). St. John's College,
  Oxford as Russian Scholar. Sec./Interpreter British
  Section International Famine Relief Organization, Russia
  1922/23. A.D.C. to Sir James O'Grady, Governor of
  Tasmania 1924. No issue.

E231x913 Francis Elwin Wright (10/ /1893-2/ /1913). Trained
  as Civil Eng.

E231x914 Florence Miriam Elizabeth Dorothea Wright (6/ /1896-
      ), m. 1/ /1921, Hilding Carson (-
  1924), son of Knut Axel Carson of Oestersund and Stock-
  holm. He fought in France with British Expeditionary
  Force, World War I. B. in Sweden and d. in London

E231x9141 Hastings Elwin Axel Carson (9/ /1923-   ). Twin.
  M. 1955, in Jamaica, Frances Ann Fussell (1924-   ),
  twin dau. of William Fussell of Ampfield, H   ,
  and Mabel Gertrude Fussell. London Univ. and Charing
  Cross Hospital. M.D.B.S. London. D.P.H. London. M.D.
  London. Rockefeller Fellowship, S. M. Harvard. Capt.
  RAMC with British Army of Occupation in Germany.
  Fellow of the Faculty of Cummunity Medicine (London)

1972. Medical Officer British Colonial Medical Service
Jamaica. Medical Officer of Health Local Government
Service London from 1956.

E231x91411 Sara Jane Carson (8/ /1957-   )
E231x91412 Jonathan William Elwin Carson (5/31/1959-   ).
Queen's Scholar Westminster School, May 1972
E231x91413 David Hastings Elwin Carson (5/17/1964-   )
E231x9142 Patricia Frances Anne Carson (9/ /1923-   ).
Twin. M. in Cathedral, Apia, Western Samoa 11/18/1967,
a widower, Omer Adrian Lemieux, M.A. Ph.D., M.B.E., of
Ottawa, Canada. She joined United Nations Hdqtrs.
Staff New York 1945. Served with Mission to the Congo
(Admin. Sec.), and Mission to Western Samoa (Admin.
Sec.) 1963-1968. He United Nations Statistical Expert.
(Previously Director for many years of Federal Bureau
of Census Statistics, Ottawa).
E231x92 Edyth Elwin Wright (1863-19   ), m. Frederick Goodsall,
M.D.
E231x921 Flora Alice Goodsall (-1966 Christmas Day). Unm.
Served in World War I as an Ambulance Driver in the
Balkans. Decorated for services. In World War II,
drove an ambulance in London throughout the War
E231x922 Ellen Irene Goodsall
E231x923 Elwyn Freda Goodsall, m. (1st) Rhys Williams (-
19   ), Senior Master Monmouth School. M. (2nd) 1940,
Ralph Stock (-196   )
E231x9231 Elwyn Stock (1942-   ), m. 1968, Simon Taylor, eldest
son of Julian Taylor, F.R.C.S. She b. in California
E231x92311 Linnet Elwin Margaret Taylor (5/15/1973-   )
E231x93 Flora Mirabel Wright (1866-1956), m. Philip Ribboul of
Australia. No issue.
E231a
E231b
E231c
E231d
E231e
E231f
E231g
E231h
E231i
E231j
E231k
E231l
E231m
E231n
E231o
E231p
E232 Elizabeth Elwin (1730-1740)
E233 Philippa Elwin (1931-1732)
E234 Philippa Elwin (1733-1733)
E235 Thomas Elwin (1734-1796) of Baconsthorpe, m. Frances Jones
E236 Fountain Elwin (1736-1737)

E237   Fountaine Elwin (9/ /1737-1833), m. 1778(?), Anne Marie
        Gibson (-1810), dau. of   Gibson of Bath.
        Fountaine Elwin in British Army, Lt.Col., became Military
        Private Secretary to his cousin's husband, Gen. William
        Tryon, and was with him in America when General Tryon was
        Governor of North Carolina. Elwin left the army and
        settled in 1771 in Bath, thus founding the Bath branch of
        the Elwin family. Entered Grays Inn 1800.
E2371   Fountain Elwin (1779-1846) of Bath, m. 1807, Charlotte
        McGlashan (-1853), dau. of Dr. Ian McGlashan
        of Bath. Fountain Elwin was Lt. Col. 44th Regt. of Foot,
        and Knight of the Crescent. Entered Gray's Inn 1833.
E23711 Eliza Maria Elwin (1807-   ), m. 1830, John Evered,
        Barrister
E237111 Elwin Evered (B.A. St. John's Cambridge 1854).
E237112 Everard Robert Fountain Evered (M.A. Cambridge 1860)
E23712 John Fountain Elwin, M.D. FRCS (1809-   )(twin) of
        Bath, m. 1838, Elizabeth (-1855), youngest dau.
        of Thomas Cherbourg Bligh, M.P., and widow of John Cuming
        of Dublin. She died in Naples.
E237121 John Elwin (1841-   )
E237122 Theodore Elwin (1843-   ), Surveyor, City of Sydney,
        Australia, m. Madeline McCarthy
E2371221 Basil Elwin
E2371222 Cyril Elwin
E2371223 Constance Elwin
E2371224 Frances Elwin
E23713 Charlotte Ann Elwin (1809-   )(twin), m. 1850, John
        Edridge of Bath
E23714 Frances Mary Rebecca Elwin (-1898) of Bath, m.
        1838, (her cousin) Whitwell Elwin of Norfolk (E231x3)
E2372   Henry Elwin, British Army, killed at Badajoz. Unm.
E2373   Thomas Henry Elwin, Rector of E. Barnet 1827. Previously
        in British Army. M. ca. 1820, Elizabeth Garrow, dau. of
        Sir William Garrow, Baron of the Court of the Exchequer
E23731 Thomas Savage Elwin (1822?-1839). Died in Dominica.
E23732 George Harvey Elwin (1824-1870)
E23733, et al.
E2374   Charlotte Anne Elwin, m. Dr. Thomas. Henry Reed, Surgeon of
        Enfield
E23741 William Reed
E23742 Fountain Reed
E23743 Edward Reed
E23744 Martha Reed
E2375   Rebecca Dorothy Elwin, m. Joseph Nash, artist, son of Rev.
        Oakey Nash, Rector of Throwley, Kent
E23751 Joseph Nash II (1835-   ), artist, m. Laura Thomas
        (1851-1918), dau.of G. H. Thomas of "The Graphic"
E237511 Elwin H. T. Nash, M.D., D.P.M. (7/ /1872-11/ /1941)
        (Medical Officer of Health, Wimbledon), m. Monica Olden-
        shaw (9/ /1877-4/ /1951), dau. of Walter and Annie
        Oldenshaw

E2375111 Laura M. Elwin Nash (9/ /1900-   ), m. 1925, Ambrose
          Gilbert Goslin (1888-1970) of Newfoundland, son of W. G.
          and Armine Nutting Gosling of Canada.
E2375112 Thomas Nash (-1963), Deputy Headmaster, Canford
          School, Dorset, m. Gwendolen Osmaston
E23751121 Anthony Nash (-1956?)
E23751122 Stephen Nash, Diplimatic Service
E2375113 Joseph Nash (-19), Brigadier, Indian Army, m.
          Jennifer Rickard. No issue.
E2375114 Edward Nash (-1952). Unm.
E2375115 Philip Nash (1906-   ), m. Rachel Hall. He was
          with Indian Civil Service, Advisor and Private Secretary
          to Sir Hubert Rance, Governor of Burma. Escaped from
          Burma to India on foot in World War II. Later with
          BBC as Director of Overseas Broadcasts.
E23751151 Georgina Nash, with BBC, London
E237512   Whitwell Tryon Nash (1874-1948), m. Hilda Barton (1883-
          1948). He was a Civil Engineer in India. Moved to
          Canada.
E2375121 Everard Tryon Whitwell Nash, M.D. (10/ /1907-   ),
          m. (1st) Gertrude Harvey (1910-1953). M. (2nd) Veronica
          Sivaley (1914-   ). He practiced in Victoria,
          Vancouver Island, until 1974. No issue by second wife.
          Children by first wife:
E23751211 Monica Mary Nash (1936-   ), m. 10/ /1956
          Robert P. Herron of Calgary, Canada
E237512111 Steven Herron (7/10/1957-   )
E237512112 Patricia Herron (9/11/1958-   )
E237512113 Susan Herron (3/19/1960-   )
E237512114 Jennifer Herron (5/24/1961-   )
E237512115 Paul Herron (5/1/1962-   )
E237512116 Kevin Herron (4/2/1964-   )
E237512117 Christopher Herron (6/18/1965-   )
E237512118 Kathleen Herron (2/8/1968-   )
E23751212 John Michael Nash (12/ /1937-   ), m. 6/ /1973,
          Robyn
E237512121 (dau)
E23751213 Beatrice Nash (10/ /1940-   ), m. 10/ /1964,
          Lawrence Foort
E237512131 Karen Foort (10/2/1965-   )
E237512132 Julia Ann Foort (4/28/1967-   )
E237512133 Jennifer Lynn Foort (8/30/1974-   )
E23751214 Susan Nash (10/ /1943-   ), m. 2/ /1967, Robert
          Brasset
E237512141 William Brasset (12/22/1968-   )
E237512142 Paul Brasset (10/23/1972-   )
E237512143 Christopher Brasset (7/28/1974-   )
E237512144 Heather Marie Brasset (3/13/1977-   )
E23751215 Peter Joseph Nash (2/ /1949-   ), m. 10/ /1970,
          Moira Lee (2/ /1951-   )
E237512151 Michael Peter Nash (2/ /1977-   )

E23751216 Dorothy Nash (6/ /1952-   ), m. 9/ /1973,
           Brasset (her sister's brother-in-law)
E237512161 Aimee Jean Brasset (7/21/1974-   )
E237512162 Betsy Lynne Brasset (2/ /1976-   )
E2375122   John Nash (1909-1912)
E2375123   Elwin Peter Whitwell Nash (10/1/1913-   ), Ph.D.
           Jesuit Priest, President and Principal, Campion College.
           University of Regina, Saskatchewan.
E2375124   Charles Warwick Whitwell Nash (1917-   ), Engineer,
           m. 1942, Bernadette Corcoran (1919-   )
E23751241 Rita Nash (7/22/1944-   )
E23751242 Teresa Nash (4/27/1947-   )
E23751243 Paul Charles Nash (2/14/1961-   )
E2375125   Andrew Joseph Whitwell Nash (11/ /1918-   ),Ph.D.
           Professor of Forestry, Columbia University, U.S.A., m.
           1960, Lorna MacFarlane of Canada
E237513   Fountain Nash (1876-1915), Major, Northumberland Fusiliers,
           World War I, m. Ella Handley
E2375131   Neville Nash (6/ /1911-   ), m.
E23751311 Diana Nash (1948-   ), m. Charles Wiseman Clarke
E237513111 Thomas Charles Clarke (1974-   )
E237513112 (child)(1977-   )
E23751312 Catherine Nash (1950-   )
E23751313 Phyllida Nash (1952-   ), Actress
E2375132   Dorothy Fountain Nash (1906-   ), m. 196 , Cosby
           Stokes. Home: Thompson, near Thetford, Norfolk
E237514   Laura Nash, m. Thomas Pandy
E237515   Foster Nash (1917-   ), m. Alice Aldrich
E23752   Mary Nash
E2376   Philippa Mary Elwin (-1883), m. Henry Owen, Indian
           Civil Service
E23761   Charles Henry Owen (1865-   ). Unm.
E23762   Edward Henry Owen (1869-   )(MA, Jesus College,
           Cambridge). Vice Principal Leamington College, m.
E237621   E. C. Everard Owen (1880?-   )
E237622, et al.
E238   Anne Elwin (1738-   ), m. 1759, Rev. Thomas Batchelor
           of Herstead
E239   Dorothy Elwin (1739-1826), m. 1764, Rev. John Longe (ca.
           1731-1806) of Spixworth Hall, Norfolk, Chaplain to George
           III
E2391   (son)
E2392   (son)
E23x   Hastings Elwin (1741-1741)
E23a   Hastings Elwin (1742-1833)(Gray's Inn 1770), m. 1774, Eliza-
           beth Diana Woolhead of Herts. He was second Elwin to settle
           in Bath
E23a1   Hastings Elwin (17 -   ), Barrister, sometime Attorney
           General, West Indies. Married twice.
E23a2   Fountain Elwin (17 -), Vicar of Octagon Chapel, Bath,
           m. 1809
E23a21   Fountain Hastings Elwin (1809-   )(Lincolns Inn 1841)

E23a3 (dau)
E23a4 (dau)
E23b Robert Elwin (1744-1745). Born at Booton.
E23c Elizabeth Elwin (1745-1745)
E23d Robert Elwin
E24 Fountain Elwin (1703-4/ /1735), m. Elizabeth Fleetwood (ca. 1710-12/9/1732), dau. of Smith Flertwood of Wood Dalling, and gr. dau. of Major-General Charles Fleetwood, son-in-law of Oliver Cromwell. She is bur. at Wood Dalling Church. He is bur. at Thurning.
E241 Fleetwood Elwin (1729-1729), bur. Wood Dalling Church
E25 Caleb Elwin (1704-1776) of Thurning, m. (1st) Elizabeth (bur. 8/23/1766), dau. of Sir Philip Astley of Norfolk; m. (2nd) 11/27/1766, Elizabeth (-12/12/1797), dau. of Rev. John Thomison, Rector of Swanton Morley. Caleb did not have any children.
E26 Hastings Elwin, Will prob. 3/29/1738.
E27 Mary Elwin, m. Rev. Jonathan Wrench of Aylsham
E28 Elizabeth Elwin (-6/19/1759), m. William Wake, son of Robert Wake of Thurning. Wake, Governor of Bombay (1741), died in 1750 while returning to England, and is bur. Cape of Good Hope.
E281 Marguerite (Margaret ?) Wake, m. William Tryon (1729-1/27/ 1788), a lieutanant in the first regiment of Footguards, and son of Charles Tryon of Bullwick Park, Northamptonshire, and his wife Lady Mary, dau. of Robert Shirley, 1st Earl Ferrers. Tryon, who became a general, served as Governor of North Carolina, and later, as acting Governor of New York.
E2811 Dau. fell in love with an officer of the Life Guards, and while attempting an elopement from her father's house via a rope ladder from an upstairs window, she fell, and was fatally impaled on the spikes of the palisade below.
E29 Joyce Elwin (-1772), m. Rev. Thomas Sayer (- 1757) of Wickmere, Norfolk. No children.
E3 Ann Elwyn (1662 or 3-), m. ca. 1680, William Bulwer of Wood Dalling. Following Ann's death, Bulwer remarried twice.
E31 Edward Bulwer (1681 or 2-). Unm.
E32 (dau)
E33 (dau)
E4 Mary Elwyn. Unm. Will dated 8/13/1695.
E5 Hannah Elwyn, m. Nicholas (Richard ?) Salter
E6 Esther Elwyn, m. Thomas Chute of South Pickenham
E7 Caleb Elwyn

APPENDIX

The Rolfes of North Carolina

     SEVENTEENTH CENTURY COLONIAL ANCESTORS OF MEMBERS OF THE
NATIONAL SOCIETY COLONIAL DAMES XVII CENTURY 1915-1975 compiled
in 1976 by Mary Louise Marshall Hutton reports, p. 216, that Thomas
Rolfe (b. ca. 1615) who married Jane Poythress lived in both
Virginia and North Carolina.

     This report was, most probably, based upon the will of
Thomas Rolfe "of Yawpim", dated 10/15/1688, and probated 2/2/1690*
1 in North Carolina. Signing by a mark, the decedent makes a
single bequest (of a gun to his cousin John Lovett), and leaves
the remainder of his estate to his wife Elizabeth whom he also
names Executrix. Witnesses are Rebecca Wyate, Lawrence Cruise,
Henderson Walker and Thomas Longe. And Richard Plater was the
Clerk of the Court. See ABSTRACT OF NORTH CAROLINA WILLS COMPILED
FROM ORIGINAL AND RECORDED WILLS IN THE OFFICE OF THE SECRETARY OF
STATE by J. Bryan Grimes (1967), p. 319.

     The names of several other 17th and 18th Century Rolfes
appear in this ABSTRACT on pages 40, 41, 46, 100, 123, 161, 167,
189, 193, 201, 244, 288, 336, and 372.

     A number of persons claim descent from Pocahontas through
one or more of the North Carolina Rolfes, but the evidence presently
at hand does not appear sufficient to either establish or dises-
tablish such a descendancy.

Barnett

Mrs. Frances McMahill Molsberry of 940 San Eduardo Avenue, Henderson, Nevada 89015, writes that there is in the Barnett family a strong tradition of descent from Pocahontas, and Mrs. Molsberry furnishes the following information:

The book AUTOBIOGRAPHY OF MARY A. BARNETT AND HISTORY OF THE BARNETT FAMILY OF JOHNSON COUNTY (1923), p. 49, includes the statement: "some historians claim there were 12 children" born to Thomas Rolfe and Jane Poythress "but we can only trace three: Jane who married Colonel Robert Bolling; Anna, who married a Frenchman, William Barnett, who came to America in 1662; and one son, John Rolfe. All we know of the son's family is we have been told that his grandson, Thomas Rolfe, visited at Edinburg, sixty or seventy years ago, and returned south". Edinburg is in Johnson County, Indiana.

At least one later writer describes Barnett as a Huguenot, and another describes him as English.

It is said that Anna (Ann? Anne?) Rolfe, m. William Barnett in 1664, and that they had twelve children including Jane Barnett (b. 1665), John Barnett (1687-1756), and Henry J.("Harry") Barnett (ca. 1704-ca. 1798). The latter was born in Spottsylvania County, later Orange County, and died in Nicholas County, Kentucky, of blood poisoning---at the time of his death, he was in the process of moving his residence to Kentucky.

NOTE: Some of these dates are a bit difficult to accept.

Henry J. ("Harry") Barnett m. (1st) Jane Morrow, and (2nd) Mary Grundy, and by his second wife, he had a son:

John Perry Barnett (7/23/1764-9/8/1828), m. 2/16/1783, Elizabeth Self. He was born in Orange County, and died in Johnson County, Indiana.

John Perry and Elizabeth Self Barnett had a son:

William Barnett (9/27/1786-9/24/1854), m. 2/29/1808, Nancy Kerlin (5/14/1793-12/1/1831). He was born in Orange County, and drowned in the Ohio River.

On the "main road" south of Indianapolis there is a ca. 1912 monument to Nancy Kerlin Barnett which states that her husband "was the great, great, great grandson of Pocahontas and John Rolfe".

Children of Col. John and Elizabeth Bland Blair Bolling

MEMOIR, the 1868 printed edition of the manuscript written ca. 1764 by Robert, one of the children of Col. John and Elizabeth Bland Blair Bolling, states that there were "many children, some of whom died in their infancy", and names the following (who survived John Bolling, who died on 9/6/1757):

> Thomas Bolling, b. 7/18/1735
> John Bolling, b. 6/ /1737
> Robert Bolling, b. 8/28/1738
> Mary Bolling, b. 7/28/1744
> Edward Bolling, b. 9/9/1746
> Archibald Bolling, b. 3/20/1749 (the year 1749 is O.S.)
> Sarah Bolling, b. 6/16/1748
> Anne Bolling, b. 2/7/1752

MEMOIR also notes that Archibald, Sarah and Anne were second children of the same name, and thus MEMOIR accounts for a total of eleven children.

CHART, written in 1796, names seven of the eight children who are named in MEMOIR (LATROBE does not name Edward Bolling who died in 1770). And CHART states that there were "eleven other children all of whom died at different ages, without issue".

In OMSS, in an "Extract from the Cobbs family bible", the following children are named:

John	Mary
Archibald	Edward
Robert	Sarah 2nd of this name
Elizabeth	Archibald " "
Thomas	Ann " "
John 2nd of this name	Eliza " "
Robert " "	Jane
Sarah	Rebecca
Ann	Eliza 3rd " "

ROBERTSON, written ca. 1886, lists only seven of the above eighteen---ROBERTSON lists only those descendants of Pocahontas who had children---and the seven listed in ROBERTSON are the same as those listed in MEMOIR except for Edward Bolling who is listed in MEMOIR, but who did not have any children, and hence is not listed in ROBERTSON.

VOLTA LIST

The Volta list was recently brought to light by James S. Patton who has made an exhaustive study of the Bollings, and who has incorporated many of his findings into articles, etc.,

that have appeared in the GOOCHLAND COUNTY HISTORICAL SOCIETY
MAGAZINES.

The below comments on the Volta list were written by
Mr. Patton in 1965:

"The following (i.e., the Volta list)(is) from the
Bolling Files at the Volta Bureau for the Deaf, Washington, D.C.
Much of their information was collected by a Mrs. Pratt (of Mass.)
for Dr. Alexander Graham Bell in connection with his interest in
the history of early schooling for the deaf of which Thomas Bolling and his son, William, were pioneers. Mrs. Pratt talked and
corresponded with members of the Bolling family in and around
Richmond and Goochland County in the Spring of 1900. A search
was made for family Bibles and from the following records it
appears one or more were available at the time, but not now
extant. There is no indication of the possessors at the time
she copied the record".

"The search in 1900 by Mrs. Pratt was for Bibles that
had been at Bolling Hall. She was directed all around the family
---first to Richard M. Bolling, the eldest grandson of Col. Wm.
Bolling, who it was thought would have inherited them along with
the portraits. He directed the search to Robert Skipwith in Powhatan County whose first wife had been Jane Rolfe Bolling, in-
heritor of Bolling Hall. His second wife was Mary Elizabeth
Bolling (Jones) daughter of Wm. Albert Bolling. Thomas Albert
Bolling, son of Wm. Albert, living at Goochland C.H. in 1900 was
thought to have had his grandfather's Bible but when questioned
about it, it was denied---he thought his sister, Mrs. Susan King
had the leaves from the old Bible. She did not have them. It
was also suggested that Tom Bolling, Jr., of Richmond had the
Bible or Bibles but he did not. It is my theory that Robert
Skipwith was in possession of them and in the destruction of his
home by fire in 1909, five years after his death, when his wife
Lizzie perished in the fire, it (or they) were destroyed".

NOTE: Three of Thomas Bolling's children, and two of
William Bolling's children were born deaf. Mrs. Pratt was "Annie
C. Pratt of Chelsea, Massachusetts, a professional genealogist".
7 GCHSM 13.

The Volta list names eighteen children:

V 1   John Bolling (5/1/1729-5/24/1736)
V 2   Archibald Bolling (1/26/1730*1731-6/20/1749)
V 3   Robert Bolling (11/10/1732-5/27/1736)
V 4   Elizabeth Bolling (7/10/1734-7/31/1735)
V 5   Thomas Bolling (7/7/1735-8/7/1804), m. Elizabeth Gay
        NOTE: In his diary, Thomas Bolling shows his birth date
        as the 18th, and the 18th is also given in MEMOIR.
V 6   John Bolling (6/24/1737-4/ /1800)(2nd of the name), m. Mary
        Jefferson

V 7 Robert Bolling (8/17/1739-1769)(2nd of the name), m. Mary
     Burton
       NOTE: In MEMOIR, Robert gives his birth year as 1738.
       The proper date of his death is 1775.
V 8 Sarah Bolling (8/22/1740-4/27/1747)
V 9 Ann Bolling (8/19/1742-4/2/174)
V x Mary Bolling (7/16/1744-   ), m. Richard Bland
V a Edward Bolling (9/9/1746-8/10/1770). Unm.
V b Sarah Bolling (6/16/1748-   )(2nd of the name), m. John
     Tazewell
V c Archibald Bolling (3/20/1749*1750-   )
V d Ann Bolling (2/7/1752-   )(2nd of the name), m. Wm.
     Dandridge
V e Elizabeth Bolling (6/24/1753-7/29/1754) (2nd of the name)
V f Jane Bolling (twin)(7/6/1754-7/31/1754)
V g Rebecca Bolling (twin)(7/6/1754-lived 25 days & 8 hours)
V h Elizabeth Bolling (3/21/1756-8/7/1756) (3rd of the name)

        The eighteen children shown in the Volta list appear to
be the same as the eighteen children listed in OMSS, and this
suggests that Mrs. Pratt and the preparer of OMSS examined the
same source, i.e., what OMSS refers to as "the Cobbs family
bible".

Price List

        The PRICE list, written ca. 1961, names twenty-one
children:

        P 1 Meotaka ("Meta") Bolling, b. 7/3/1729 in Goochland
County, m. James Sullivan (Sr.)(who later remarried, and moved to
South Carolina).

        P 2 Archibald Bolling, b. 6/1/1730, in Goochland County,
d. young.

        P 3 William Bolling, b. 4/5/1731, in Goochland County,
d. 1776, while serving as a Colonel in the Revolutionary Army.
M. 1/1/1755, at "Curles", Henrico County, his first cousin once
removed, Amelia Randolph, b. 6/15/1739 at "Curles", Henrico County,
d. 9/5/1780, Henry County (where she is buried).

        P 4 Elizabeth Bolling (twin of William), b. 4/5/1731,
in Goochland County.

        P 5 Jared Bolling, b. 6/3/1732, in Goochland County (in
records name is also spelled Gerald, Gerrard, Jarid, Jarrat,
Jarratt, Jarrett, Jarrot, and Jarrott). Said to have moved to N.C.

        P 6 Martha Bolling, b. 7/15/1733, in Henrico County.

        P 7 Dorothea (Dorothy) Bolling, b. 6/30/1734, in Henrico
County.

P 8 Benjamin Bolling (twin of Dorothy), b. 6/30/1734, in Henrico County, d. 1832 in Russell County.

P 9 Thomas Bolling, b. 7/7/1735, in Henrico County, d. 8/7/1804, m. Elizabeth Gay.

P x John Bolling, b. 6/24/1737, in Henrico County, d. 1797, m. 6/29/1760, Mary, sister to Thomas Jefferson.

P a Robert Bolling, b. 8/17/1738, in Henrico County, d. 1775, m. (1st) Mary Burton, (2nd) Susannah Watson.

P b Jane Bolling, b. 7/13/1740, in Henrico County, m. William Hopkins.

P c Rodney Bolling, b. 9/18/1742, in Henrico County, d. 11/19/1778, in Henry County, m. 8/10/1764, Elizabeth Anderson.

P d Rolfe Bolling, b. 7/16/1744, in Henrico County.

P e Mary Bolling (twin of Rolfe Bolling), b. 7/16/1744, in Henrico County, d. 1775, m. 1761, Richard Bland.

P f Edward Bolling, b. 9/9/1746, in Henrico County, d. 8/10/1770. Unm.

P g Sarah Bolling, b. 6/16/1748, in Henrico County, m. John Tazewell.

P h Archibald Bolling, b. 3/20/1749*50, in Chesterfield (from Henrico) County, d. 1822. M. (4 times).

P i Anne Bolling, b. 2/7/1752, in Chesterfield County (from Henrico), m. William Dandridge.

P j Powhatan Bolling, b. 4/16/1754, in Chesterfield (from Henrico) County.

P k James Bolling, b. 1/9/1756, in Chesterfield (from Henrico) County.

Included in this list of twenty-one are the same seven who are named in ROBERTSON; plus Edward Bolling, plus Archibald (the first of the name) who is mentioned in MEMOIR and in CHART, plus an additional twelve children (P 1, P 3, P 4, P 5, P 6, P 7, P 8, P b, P c, P d, P j and P k).

None of the additional twelve are mentioned in the will of Col. John Bolling, or in MEMOIR or CHART or OMSS or ROBERTSON, and this non-mention suggests that the PRICE list be scrutinized carefully.

The author of PRICE, Judge Zelma Wells Price, who traces
her own lines (four) of descent from Pocahontas through William and
Amelia Randolph Bolling states that her (the Price) list of the
children of Col. John and Elizabeth (Bland)Blair Bolling is based
upon "an old and faded sheet which has been in the hands of John
Tarpley Bolling for more than a hundred years, and said to be in
the handwriting of John Tarpley Bolling, (and which) shows twenty
children as having been born to John Bolling, and gives their names
and birth dates". PRICE, Vol. VI, Part 1, pp 60-1.

John Tarpley Bolling, one of Judge Price's antecedents,
was the son of John and Mary Tarpley Bolling, and the grandson of
William and Amelia Randolph Bolling. For the spouse and other
children of John Tarpley Bolling, see PLEASANTS, pp. 45-6.

Judge Price also sets out in PRICE affidavits made by
Ara Janet Bolling Stegall, another descendant of John and Mary
Tarpley Bolling. (Vol. VI, Part 1, p. 10 and pp. 65-71); and an
affidavit made by Martha Ellender (Ellen) Weatherbee Edmundson,
another descendant of John and Mary Tarpley Bolling. Ibid, pp.
72-3.

Judge Price also cites SOUTH CAROLINIANS IN THE REVO-
LUTION compiled and edited by Sara Sullivan Ervin, a descendant
of Samuel, a son of William Bolling; and she cites some family
records furnished by Sara Sullivan Ervin. Ibid, p. 10. Judge
Price also cites Sara Bolling Powell's FAMILY TRACE OF BOLLINGS
(ca. 1931) which concerns some of the descendants of William
Bolling. Ibid, p. 14. NOTE: FAMILY TRACE OF BOLLINGS appears
to be confused, and of little value.

And finally, Judge Price cites Mary Caroline Bradshaw
Bolin's MY BRADSHAWS AND THEIR ALLIED FAMILIES (1964), which
includes the genealogy of the descendants of Benjamin Bolling---
according to Judge Price and to Mary Caroline Bradshaw Bolin,
Benjamin Bolling was a son of John and Elizabeth (Bland) Blair
Bolling.

A close reading of PRICE and of its pertinent authorities
indicates that all of the statements identifying the additional
twelve as children of Col. John and Elizabeth Bland Blair Bolling
emanated from the same source. And the accuracy of the source is
highly suspect.

Accordingly, the Volta list (and not the Price list)
merits acceptance, and one must note, in passing, that if the Volta
list is correct, it would have been biologically difficult if not
impossible for Elizabeth Bland Blair Bolling to have been the
mother of the Price list's P 1, P 3, P 4, P 5, P 7, P 8, P b,
P c, P j and P k.

She could, however, have been the mother of P 6 and P d,
and if one of these is added to the Volta list, the total number

of children would be nineteen (ROBERTSON states the total as nineteen). But which one should be added? Unless and until this
question is answered, it would not seem proper to add either P 6
or P d.

As regards the remaining eleven of the additional twelve,
the names of P 1, P d and P j (Meotaka, Rolfe and Powhatan) strongly
suggest that these three might be descendants of Pocahontas.

Could the additional twelve or the additional eleven
or at least some of them be children of Col. John Bolling by some
lady other than Elizabeth Bland Blair?

Some Virginia genealogists refer to the additional twelve
as the "mysterious Bollings", and equally mysterious is the Price
list's Amelia Randolph (6/15/1739-9/5/1780).

According to Judge Price, Amelia m. 1/1/1755, at "Curles",
her first cousin once removed, William Bolling (4/5/1731-1776), and
Amelia was a half-sister to Mary Randolph (7/5/1774-8/8/1863) who
m. William Bolling (7/26/1777-7/17/1845) of "Bolling Hall". PRICE,
Vol. VI, Part 1, p. 7.

Mary Randolph (1774-1863) was the daughter of Richard and
Anne Meade Randolph, and if Mary Randolph (1774-1863) and Amelia
Randolph (1739-1780) were sisters (through Richard Randolph), Amelia
would be a descendant of Pocahontas.

However, no mention of Amelia Randolph (1731-1780) or of
William Bolling (1731-1776) has been found in any of the many
pages written about the Randolph family.

OMSS

OMSS shows the following data (the numbers, which do not appear in OMSS, are those employed in this volume):

(11a) Archibald Blair Bolling
(12211) Dr. John Bolling Garrett had children by both wives
(12212) no children
(122131) Susan Duke, m. Jones
(12214) had children
(1223) Kennon Bolling
(1224) Mary Bolling, m. Snelson, and moved to the West
(219115) d. when about two years old
(219139) Benjamin Cary Weisiger, d. inf.
(21913x) Joseph Kendall Weisiger, d. inf.
(21914) to be Pauline White ("Lina") Weisiger
(21934) middle name Randolph
(232) Theodorick Bland Randolph
(234) Jane Randolph
(245) Henry Cary
(336) Mary Fleming, m. Strange
(511) married
(513) m. Thomson
(516) m. John Johnson

SHORT TITLE INDEX AND BIBLIOGRAPHY

Short Title Index

BARBOUR- Barbour, Philip L. POCAHONTAS AND HER WORLD (1979)

BP- Slaughter, Philip. A HISTORY OF BRISTOL PARISH, VA. (2nd ed.)
    (1879)

CABELL- Brown, Alexander. THE CABELLS AND THEIR KIN (1939)

CHART- Chart (Pedigree) included on page 113 of Vol. I of the two
    volume THE VIRGINIA JOURNALS OF BENJAMIN HENRY LATROBE
    1795-1798 (1977)

GCHSM- GOOCHLAND COUNTY HISTORICAL SOCIETY MAGAZINE

GOODE- Goode, G. Brown. VIRGINIA COUSINS (1887)

GRABOWSKII- Grabowskii, Bessie Berry. THE DUVAL FAMILY OF VIRGINIA
    (1931)

LM- Anderson, Sarah Travers Lewis Scott. LEWISES, MERIWETHERS AND
    THEIR KIN (1938)

MEADE- Meade, William. OLD CHURCHES, MINISTERS AND FAMILIES OF
    VIRGINIA (1857)

MEMOIR- Bolling, Robert. A MEMOIR OF A PORTION OF THE BOLLING
    FAMILY IN ENGLAND AND VIRGINIA (1868)

MOSSIKER- Mossiker, Frances. POCAHONTAS: THE LIFE AND THE LEGEND
    (1976)

OMSS- An old manuscript (early 19th Century) now or formerly in
    the possession of Robert T. Coolidge, Historian of The
    Monticello Association, and probably used in the preparation
    of MEMOIR.

PLEASANTS- Miller, Norma Carter; and Miller, George Lane. PLEASANTS
    AND ALLIED FAMILIES (1980)

PRICE- Price, Zelma Wells. OF WHOM I CAME, FROM WHENCE I CAME,
    WELLS-WISE, RISH-WISE AND OTHERWISE; A COMPILATION OF
    THE GENEALOGIES OF THE FAMILIES OF BOLLING, COLQUITT,
    GABLE, NORMAN, RISH, ROBERTSON, WEATHERBEE, WELLS (AND)
    WOFFORD, WITH NUMEROUS RELATED AND CONNECTING FAMILIES
    (ca. 1961)

RANDOLPH- Randolph, Robert Isham. THE RANDOLPHS OF VIRGINIA (ca.
    1936)

ROBERTSON- Robertson, Wyndham. POCAHONTAS, ALIAS MATOAKA, AND HER
    DESCENDANTS (1887)

ROBERTSON-PATTON- Robertson, Julian Hart; and Patton, James S.
    THE FAMILY OF WILLIAM AND ELIZABETH BOLLING
    ROBERTSON OF RICHMOND, VIRGINIA. 1585-1981
    (1981)

ROUSE- Read, Alice (Mrs. Shelly Rouse). THE READS AND THEIR
    RELATIVES (1930)

V- VIRGINIA MAGAZINE OF HISTORY AND BIOGRAPHY

VG- THE VIRGINIA GENEALOGIST

W(1)- WILLIAM & MARY COLLEGE QUARTERLY. FIRST SERIES

WOODWARD- Woodward, Grace Steele. POCAHONTAS (1969)

Bibliography

NOTE: Books, etc., relied upon in whole or in part are noted
either in the text, or in the Short Title Index, or in the
following list. The many other books, etc., examined during
the preparation of this volume are not noted for the reason that
the pertinent data which they contained was considered to be
either repetitious or wholly inaccurate.

Ackerly, Mary Denham, 1885- "OUR KIN";THE GENEALOGIES OF SOME OF
   THE EARLY FAMILIES WHO MADE HISTORY IN THE FOUNDING AND DEVELOP-
   MENT OF BEDFORD COUNTY, VIRGINIA (1930)

Ayres, Nellie Frances. AYRES KIN AND KIN TO KIN (1961)

BEVERLEY FAMILY BIBLE - 16 VG 130

Bland, Charles L. A VISION OF UNITY. THE BLAND FAMILY IN ENGLAND
   AND AMERICA 1555-1900 (1982)

Bolling, Edward Watson. THE BOLLING DESCENDANTS OF JOHN ROLFE AND
   POCAHONTAS (1974)
        A cloth bound book concerning the descendants of Benjamin
        Bolling (d. 1832). Includes many of the author's personal
        reminiscences. Gives the date of the birth of Benjamin
        Bolling as 1736.

Bolling, Hattie L. BOLLINGS (ca. 1975)
        A paper bound book concerning the descendants of Benjamin
        Bolling (d. 1832). Gives his birth date as 1734.

Branch, Benjamin H., Jr. THE BRANCH, HARRIS, JARVIS, AND CHINN BOOK (1963)

Brock, Robert Alonzo. DOCUMENTS, CHIEFLY UNPUBLISHED, RELATING TO THE HUGUENOT EMIGRATION TO VIRGINIA AND TO THE SETTLEMENT AT MANAKIN-TOWN (1886)

Carlton, Florence Tyler. A GENEALOGY OF THE KNOWN DESCENDANTS OF ROBERT CARTER OF COROTOMAN (1982)

COLLECTED PAPERS TO COMMEMORATE FIFTY YEARS OF THE MONTICELLO ASSOCIATION OF THE DESCENDANTS OF THOMAS JEFFERSON (1965)

COLLECTED PAPERS OF THE MONTICELLO ASSOCIATION OF THE DESCENDANTS OF THOMAS JEFFERSON. Vol. II (1984)
    Vol. II includes a list of "Descendants of Thomas Jefferson and His Wife, Martha Wayles" that up-dates a similar list that was included in the 1965 volume. Both volumes include biographical and genealogical material on some of the descendants.

Childs, James Rives. RELIQUES OF THE RIVES (1929)

Coke, Ben H. JOHN MAY, JR., OF VIRGINIA: HIS DESCENDANTS AND THEIR LAND (1975)

Early, R. H. CAMPBELL CHRONICLES AND FAMILY SKETCHES EMBRACING THE EARLY HISTORY OF CAMPBELL COUNTY, VIRGINIA 1782-1926 (1927)

Howe, Daisie Dean Winifred Simmons. SOME MID-WEST DESCENDANTS OF REBECCA MATAOKA POCAHONTAS (1960)
    Descendants of Matthew Branch (1776-1928), and his second wife. Book includes biographical material on some of the descendants.

McCullough, Rose Chambers Goode. YESTERDAY WHEN IT IS PAST (1957)

McGill, John. THE BEVERLEY FAMILY OF VIRGINIA (1956)

Meriwether, Nelson Heath. THE MERIWETHERS AND THEIR CONNECTIONS. (1964)

Patton, James Samuel. THE FAMILY OF WILLIAM & ELIZABETH BOLLING ROBERTSON (1975)

Pedigo, Virginia C. HISTORY OF PATRICK AND HENRY COUNTIES, VIRGINIA (1933)

POCAHONTAS TRAILS NEWSLETTER. A Quarterly Publication of the Pocahontas Trails Genealogical Society, an organization "open to all interested persons". Dues: $10.00 annually. Meetings: semi-annually, usually in Northern California. Address: 3628 Cherokee Lane, Modesto, California 95356.

Randolph, Wassell. GEORGE ARCHER I OF THE UMBERSLADE ARCHERS OF
HENRICO COUNTY, VIRGINIA, AND HIS DESCENDANTS (1965)

Rolfe, John. A TRUE RELATION OF THE STATE OF VIRGINIA (1951)
An excellent "biographical sketch" of John Rolfe by
John Melville Jennings is to be found in this reprint.

Sorley, Merrow Egerton. LEWIS OF WARNER HALL (ca. 1937)

TODAY AND YESTERDAY IN THE HEART OF VIRGINIA (1935)
Reprint of March 29, 1939 edition of the FARMVILLE
HERALD.

Weisiger, Benjamin B. III. THE WEISIGER FAMILY (ca. 1984)

Extensive use was made of E. G. Swem's VIRGINIA HISTORICAL INDEX
(2 vols.)(1934), and of the magazines indexed therein; of the
post-Swem issues of THE VIRGINIA MAGAZINE OF HISTORY AND BIO-
GRAPHY; and of THE VIRGINIA GENEALOGIST.

Glossary

The name of a county appearing alone, i.e., unaccompanied
by the name of its state, designates a Virginia county.

MB means marriage bond.
MC means Member of Congress.
"Hollywood" refers to Richmond's Hollywood Cemetery.

Old Style dates are denoted by an asterisk placed
between the old style year date and the new style year date, viz.,
1/25/1675*6 or 1730*1731.

Spelling Variations

Sometimes, in this volume, a person's name will be
spelled one way in one place, and another way in another place,
viz., Ann/Anne, Bettie/Betty, Courtenay/Courtney, Eliza/Elizabeth,
Elwyn/Elwin, Embra/Embry, Julian/Julien, Lenaeus/Linnaeus, Sallie/
Sally, Susan/Susanna/Susannah, Theodoric/Theodorick, etc. And
sometimes a nick-name such as Nancy, Patsy, Peggy, etc., will be
used in one place and not in another.

Index

NOTE: The name of the spouse of a Pocahontas descendant is indexed even though that spouse is not a descendant of Pocahontas, but the name of a parent of such a spouse is not indexed unless, of course, that parent is a descendant of Pocahontas.

Barba, Philip S. 24134641
Barba, William Philip 241346411
Barbee, David B. 16264
Barbee, David Hart 162641
Barbee, Pocahontas Rebecca Cabell 1626
Barber, Amanda Joan Mackay-Smith Devries 2414461125
Barber, James David 2414461125
Barhydt, Maud Wolcott Griswold 3231215
Barksdale, Alice Carlotta Stith 111424
Barksdale, Alice Stith 1114241
Barksdale, Ann ("Nannie") Montgomery 111421,21935
Barksdale, Anne Robertson 1114242
Barksdale, Elizabeth Lewis Robertson 11142
Barksdale, Frances Dobyns 1653251
Barksdale, Frances Evans 1114243
Barksdale, Gay Robertson 1114245
Barksdale, John Robertson 111423
Barksdale, John Robertson 1114246
Barksdale, Robert Jones 11142
Barksdale, Robert Jones, Jr. 111424
Barksdale, Virginia Douglas Watkins 64113e
Barksdale, William Jones 111422
Barksdale, William Randolph 64113e
Barksdale, Winifred Elizabeth Lewis 1114244
Barnard, Elizabeth Humbird Roberts 241513412
Barnard, Frederick Roberts 2415134122
Barnard, Robert Edward Lee, Jr. 2415134121
Barnard, Robert Edward Lee 241513412

Barnes, A. D. 56184
Barnes, Anne Rafferty 241429142
Barnes, Charlotte Randolph 2414291421
Barnes, Deborah Coolidge 2414436333
Barnes, Elizabeth Fearn Eldridge 56184
Barnes, Henry Hammond 241443633
Barnes, Henry Hammond, Jr. 2414436331
Barnes, Jane 241424351
Barnes, Mary Ellen 21321521
Barnes, Nancy Susan 2414436332
Barnes, Sarah Lee 2414291422
Barnes, Silas A. 241429142
Barnes, Susan Thistle Coolidge 241443633
Barnett, Anna Rolfe p. 326
Barnett, Elizabeth Self p. 326
Barnett, Henry J. ("Harry") p. 326
Barnett, Jane p. 326
Barnett, Jane Morrow p. 326
Barnett, John p. 326
Barnett, John Perry p. 326
Barnett, Mary A. p. 326
Barnett, Mary Elizabeth Coolidge 241444322
Barnett, Mary Grundy p. 326
Barnett, Nancy Kerlin p. 326
Barnett, Patricia Elizabeth 2414443221
Barnett, Raymond L. 241444322
Barnett, Sydney Louis 2414443222
Barnett, William p. 326
Barnett, William (1786-1854) p. 326
Barney, Carlotta D. 241491a
Barr, Beverley Ray 652154
Barr, Rev. David 65215
Barr, Elizabeth Beverley 652153
Barr, Frances Whittle Greene 652152
Barr, Jane Eliza Whittle 65215
Barr, Jennie Whittle 652155
Barr, Marsha 174a31111
Barr, Sadie 652151
Barr, William Arthur 652152
Barrett, Beatrice 5527472
Barrett, Caroline Lewis 3224
Barrett, Charles 3224
Barritt, Joan Virginia 11142431
Barry, Hattie 222181
Barry, Rev. J. B. 22218
Barry, Kidder 222183
Barry, Lucy 222182
Barry, Lucy A. Randolph 22218
Barsam, Anna Randolph Keim 24151364
Barsam, John James 24151364
Bartle, Martha Fairfax Jones 1113323
Bartle, William 1113323
Bartle, Willia, Jr. 11133231
Bartlett, Lina Harrison Owsley 13213121
Bartlett, Paul 13213121
Barton, Alberta Vaughan Castellanos 241444541

Barton, Andrew Charles E231x61311
Barton, Bertram E231x613
Barton, Bertram M. E231x61311
Barton, Elizabeth Harris 24144454
Barton, Elizabeth Lowell 24144454
Barton, Elizabeth Lowell 241444542
Barton, Ellen Randolph 24144452
Barton, Elwin a Beckett E231x613
Barton, Frances Buckner Jones 2415224
Barton, Francis Lowell 24144454
Barton, Frederick Otis 2414445
Barton, Frederick Otis, Jr. 24144451
Barton, Hilda E237512
Barton, Hugh E231x61315
Barton, James Harris 241444541
Barton, Jane Cary Randolph 24162
Barton, Joseph Marx 2415224
Barton, Marsham E231x61314
Barton, Martha Walker 25162
Barton, Mary E231x61313
Barton, Mary Lowell 24144453
Barton, Mary Lowell Coolidge 2414445
Barton, Matthew Vaughan 2414445411
Barton, Nan E231x61316
Barton, Patrick Lowell 2414445412
Barton, Phyllis M. Saunders Simpson 24144454
Barton, Virginia E231x61312
Baskervill, Alice 6411125
Baskervill, Alice M. 6411134
Baskervill, Alice M. 64111353
Baskervill, Alice M. Sampson 641113
Baskervill, Anne L. 6411161
Baskervill, Bessie Campbell 6411118
Baskervill, Bettie Eaton 641141
Baskervill, Mrs.   Brooks 64114
Baskervill, Caroline 6411132
Baskervill, Caroline 64111331
Baskervill, Charles 641113
Baskervill, Maj. Charles 64114
Baskervill, Charles Edward 6411155
Baskervill, Charles Gordon 64111621
Baskervill, David E. 6411121
Baskervill, Edgar McComb 6411165
Baskervill, Elizabeth 6411122
Baskervill, Elizabeth 6411138
Baskervill, Ellen 6411137
Baskervill, Ellie R. Mullen 6411162
Baskervill, Elsie M. Skelton 641121
Baskervill, Emma R. 6411153
Baskervill, Emma Reid 641115
Baskervill, Ernest 6411156
Baskervill, Ethel Marsh 641125
Baskervill, Eugenia Buffington 64112
Baskervill, Frances 64111352
Baskervill, Grace E. 6411167
Baskervill, George Sumner 6411123
Baskervill, Rev. George Sumner 6411118
Baskervill, Gordon Coleman 6411139
Baskervill, Hamilton Meade 6411212
Baskervill, Henry Coleman 6411251
Baskervill, Henry E. C. 641124
Baskervill, Capt. Henry Embra Coleman 64112
Baskervill, Rev. Henry Embra Coleman 641115
Baskervill, Henry Eugene 641125
Baskervill, Howard C. 6411152
Baskervill, Isabella A. H. 641122
Baskervill, Isabella Alston Hamilton 64112
Baskervill, James M. 6411163
Baskervill, James Riddick 6411117
Baskervill, Jno. Skelton 6411211
Baskervill, John Campbell 6411181
Baskervill, John G. 6411164
Baskervill, John Gordon 64116
Baskervill, Julia T. 6411151
Baskervill, Julia T. Blanton 641115
Baskervill, Leone Wagner 6411163
Baskervill, Lilian Gordon 641119
Baskervill, Lily Hall 6411168
Baskervill, Lucy 6411136
Baskervill, Lucy Alice 641114
Baskervill, Margaret A. Stribling Humphries 64112
Baskervill, Margaret Haynes Freear 6411
Baskervill, Mary Anne (Alice?) Elizabeth 64113
Baskervill, Mary Eaton 641123
Baskervill, Mary Hinton 6411124
Baskervill, Mary M. 64111354

Benedict, William Ray 5522131
Bennett, Anna Michaux 222523111
Bennett, Bridgett Lorene 174a311141
Bennett, Gary 174a31114
Bennett, Gary Reid 174a311142
Bennett, Kristi Lynn Lawson 174a311143
Bennett, Marcia Randolph Drake 22252311
Bennett, Paul C., Jr., M.D. 22252311
Bennett, Paul C. III 222523112
Bennett, Rhonda G. Elam 174a31114
Benster, Agnes Rebecca Rives 574212
Benster, Elsie 5742122
Benster, Lewis E. 574212
Benster, Percy Hope 5742121
Bentley, Dr. Alexander Willis 4127
Bentley, Anne Chamberlayne 41242
Bentley, Efford Bolling 4124
Bentley, Efford Bolling, Jr. 41241
Bentley, Eliza Gay 4121
Bentley, Elizabeth Gay 412
Bentley, Elizabeth Logan 563614
Bentley, Fanny Trent 4123
Bentley, Henry Alexander 41244
Bentley, John Gay 4125, 5131
Bentley, Judith Thompson 4125
Bentley, Lavinia 4128
Bentley, Lucy Parke 41243
Bentley, Lucy W. Chamberlayne 4124
Bentley, Maria Buchanan 4126
Bentley, Peter Efford 412
Bentley, Mrs.   Peters 4127
Bentley, Sarah Dupree 4122
Bentley, William Field 4122
Berkeley, Almira Virginia Megginson 16121
Berkeley, Almira Virginia Megginson 16142
Berkeley, Elizabeth C. Megginson 1612
Berkeley, Joseph 16121
Berkeley, Joseph 16142
Berkeley, William 1612
Bernard, Anna Skipwith 11172
Bernard, Mrs.   Branch 361
Bernard, Caroline Pocahontas 11179

Bernard, Christopher 3612
Bernard, Mrs.   Clopton 362
Bernard, Cyrus 3611
Bernard, Daniel 361
Bernard, Elizabeth 364
Bernard, Gay Robertson 11171
Bernard, Helen Struan 1117a
Bernard, Jane 368
Bernard, Jane Gay Robertson 1117
Bernard, John 362
Bernard, John Hipkins 1117
Bernard, John Hipkins, Jr. 11173
Bernard, John J. 111344133
Bernard, Lelia Bolling 11141, 11178
Bernard, Lynn Philippe Woltz 111344133
Bernard, Mary 363
Bernard, Mary Eliza 11176
Bernard, Mary Fleming 36
Bernard, Mary Hicks 366
Bernard, Mrs.   Norvell 362
Bernard, Powhatan Bolling 1117x
Bernard, Richard 367
Bernard, Robert 365
Bernard, Sally Savine 11174
Bernard, Thomas 366
Bernard, William 36
Bernard, William 369
Bernard, William R. 11175
Bernard, William Robertson 11177
Bernius, Dale 174a31112
Bernius, Dale, Jr. 174a311123
Bernius, Debbie 174a311121
Bernius, Mary Ruth 174a311122
Bernius, Patricia Ann Elam 174a31112
Bernius, Robin Henry 174a311124
Bernot, Lawrence W. 241443542
Bernot, Linda Bowles Coolidge 2414431542
Berretta, Mary Randolph 241491641
Berretta, Mary Randolph Waring Elder 241491641
Berretta, Robert Eugene 241491641
Berretta, Thomas Waring Elder 2414916411
Berry, Mr. 1212
Berry, Mr. 1213
Berry, David Humbird 2415134162

Berry, Delbert M. 24141111221
Berry, Helen Dickey Roberts 241513416
Berry, Ellen Archer 1213
Berry, John Myers 241513416
Berry, Martha Archer Bolling 1212
Berry, Mary 2424537
Berry, Paul Edward 241411112211
Berry, Peter Edmund 2415134161
Berry, Reade Johnson 111x4121
Berry, Robert Lee 241411112212
Berry, Robin Rebecca 111x41211
Berry, Sherrilee Bramblett 24141111221
Berry, Stephen N. 111x4121

Best, Ann Kent Blackwell 111332142
Best, Brian 111x21312
Best, Cynthia Anne 1113321422
Best, Gay Lloyd Franklin 111x21312
Best, Nancy Kent 1113321421
Best, Thomas 111332142
Best, Thomas Andrew 1113321423
Bethel, Mrs. Charles 64162
Betts, Elisha 641137
Betts, Elizabeth Hill 24142a52
Betts, Elizabeth McIntire Randolph 24142a5
Betts, Lucy Baskerville Watkins 641137
Betts, Mary McIntire 24142a51
Betts, Mildred Patterson 24217411
Betts, Thomas Jeffries 24142a5
Bevan, Dr. Archibald B. 2421642
Bevan, Mary Cary Harrison 2421642
Beverley, Anne Douglas 13321131
Beverley, Anne Tayloe 2133
Beverley, Eglantine (Maria?) 2113
Beverley, Elizabeth Bland 2132
Beverley, Elizabeth Edwin 162662
Beverley, Ida Dulany 24241374
Beverley, John P. 16266
Beverley, Lucy 213
Beverley, Maria 211
Beverley, Rebecca Wormeley 2181
Beverley, Robert Cabell 162661
Beverley, Susan Cowan Cabell 16266
Beverly, Eleanor Hodge 162663
Beverly, Harry S. 162665
Beverly, Susan 162664
Bibb, Mary Chambers 33252
Bibb, Mintor ("Noona") Peyton 2135271
Bickford, Linda 11138122
Bickham, Nell 24246443
Biggs, Katherine Howard 21181251
Biggs, Robert Munford, Jr. 21181251
Bilbro, Cecil 111326534
Bilbro, Nancy Winslow Davis 111326534
Billingsley, Addison Gordon, Jr. 241427212
Billingsley, Cary Ambler Smith 241427212
Billington, Jeffrey Robertson 111344126
Billington, John Edward 111344125
Billington, Louann 111344123
Billington, Lynn Fairfax Carr 111344123, 111344331
Billington, Mary Ann Robertson 11134412
Billington, Melissa 1113441231
Billington, Randall Holmes 111344123, 111344331
Billington, Robert 11134412
Billington, Robert, Jr. 111344122
Billington, Robin Ann 111344121
Billington, Thomas James 111344124
Bingham, Benjamin 111622222
Bingham, Ouita Hyams 111622222
Binkley, Ida Morgan Franklin Trent 133121288
Binkley, Roy 133121288
Binns, Miss 242454a
Bird, Gena C. 651131
Biscoe, Elizabeth ("Betsey") Robertson 111a
Biscoe, Henry Lawson 111a
Bishop, Aletha Sue 24141113411
Bishop, David Raymond 16532591
Bishop, Donna 16532591
Bishop, Dorathy Agnes Burton 1653259
Bishop, Harriet 221x7
Bishop, Heather Brook 165325911
Bishop, Gabriel James 165325922
Bishop, James Raymond 1653259
Bishop, James Robert 16532592
Bishop, Katherine 16532592
Bishop, Linda Lee 16532593
Bishop, Patrick Eli 165325921

Campbell, Raymond H. 24142x16
Campbell, Raymond Henry, Jr. 24142x163
Campbell, Robert Harrison 111346112
Campbell, Ruth Virginia 24142x164
Campbell, Sarah Elizabeth 111346122
Campbell, Susan 5641
Campbell, William 62139
Campbell, William Bruce 11134612
Campbell, William Bruce 111346123
Campbell, William Lee 621393
Campbell, William Moore 111348312
Campbell, William Robertson 11134831
Campbell, William Robertson 1113483121
Campbell, Worley Cottingham 11134611
Camper, Billie Eugene 16532583
Camper, Diana Marie 16532585
Camper, Frank Mathias 1653258
Camper, Heather Nicole 165325833
Camper, Helen Ruth Burton 1653258
Camper, James Matthew 165325832
Camper, Kathie Ann Hall 16532583
Camper, Mary Beth 165325831
Camper, Nancy Ann 16532582
Camper, Patricia Faye 16532581
Camper, Victoria Louise 16532584
Candler, Albert Randolph 2133411
Candler, Albert Randolph, Jr. 21334111
Candler, Beverley Randolph 21334113
Candler, Herbert Paschal 213341
Candler, Jane Beverley Randolph 213341
Candler, Louise Blackburn 21334111
Candler, Nancy Cornelia Sorrell 21334112
Candler, Nancy Randolph 213341122
Candler, Roberta Hails 2133411
Candler, Robert Hails 21334112
Candler, Robert Hails, Jr. 213341121
Candler, Susan Blackburn 213341111
Cannon, Miss 219253
Cantelli, Betty 24142x163
Cantrell, Edith Stanard Archer 33242641
Cantrell, Parvin Everett 33242641
Cantrell, Trudy Lee 332426411
Cargill, Elizabeth 1412
Carnes, Deborah Gail Hubard 2414911113
Carnes, Nichole Rochelle 24149111131
Carnes, Steve 2414911113
Carnesale, Carrie Lee 2414228133
Carnesale, John Lawrence 2414228132
Carnesale, Louis John 241422813
Carnesale, Louis Vincent 2414228131
Carnesale, Lucie Bronaugh Taylor 241422813
Carnesale, Virginia Powell 2414228134
Carpenter, Daisy A. 332525
Carpenter, Rosa Lee 211b16
Carr, James Edward 11134433
Carr, James Edward, Jr. 111344332
Carr, Jane Cary 24244
Carr, Jane Margaret 241c1
Carr, John A. 4191
Carr, Judith Gay Ferguson 4191
Carr, Lynn Fairfax 111344331, 111344123
Carr, Phyllis Hunter Robertson 11134433
Carradine, Lula Hebe 21195
Carraway, Lola 222523
Carrier, Anne Elizabeth 2414927
Carrington, Mrs.   Alexander 64126121
Carrington, Alice Cary 6412618
Carrington, Bettie Lewis 64113g22
Carrington, Carter Ingram 64113g2
Carrington, Charles Craddock 641261
Carrington, Charles Davenport 64113g13
Carrington, Charles Reid 6412615
Carrington, Delia Davenport 64113g1
Carrington, Delia Davenport 64113g12
Carrington, Elizabeth Ann Watkins 641136
Carrington, Elizabeth F. 6412617
Carrington, Emily 242163
Carrington, George Cabell 6412612
Carrington, Dr. George Cabell, Jr. 64126121
Carrington, Henry Paul 64113f
Carrington, Henry Paul, Jr. 64113f4
Carrington, Julia Watkins 64113g
Carrington, Kizzie McDaniel 6412615
Carrington, Louise 641261211

Carrington, Louise Cary Stebbins 6412612
Carrington, Mrs.   McKenzie 6411314
Carrington, Marcellus F. 6412614
Carrington, Margaret Logan 6412611
Carrington, Mary 332137
Carrington, Nancy 64113f2
Carrington, Nellie 64113f3
Carrington, Nellie Watkins 64113f
Carrington, Richard Venable 64113g1
Carrington, Richard Venable, Jr. 64113g11
Carrington, Sarah Henry 6412613
Carrington, Sarah Henry French 641261
Carrington, Tazewell Morton 64113g
Carrington, Tazewell Morton, Jr. 64113g2
Carrington, Tazewell Morton III 64113g21
Carrington, Thomas Read 641136
Carrington, Virginia 64113f1
Carrington, William Lorria 6412616
Carrington, William Tucker II 64113g3
Carrington, Winifred W. 6412619
Carroll, Alexander Winchester 24244x3
Carroll, Anne Harrison 24244x31
Carroll, Charlotte Marie 1116227213
Carroll, Dorothy Veronica Connell 111622722
Carroll, Eldridge Linus 11162272
Carroll, Eldridge Linus, Jr. 111622721
Carroll, Gale Dean Simmons 111622721
Carroll, James 1116227211
Carroll, John Sherman 1116227212
Carroll, Martha Elizabeth Cosper 11162272
Carroll, Mary Angela 13277
Carroll, Rosalie Randolph Turnbull 24244x3
Carroll, Sherman Louis 111622722
Carroll, Thomas Eldredge 1116227221
Carson, David Hastings Elwin E231x91413
Carson, Florence Miriam Elizabeth Dorothea Wright
     E231x914, p. 5, 310, 311, 312, 314
Carson, Frances Ann Fussell E231x9141
Carson, Hastings Elwin Axel E231x9141
Carson, Hilding E231x914
Carson, Jean McNeil 24153356
Carson, Jonathan William Elwin E231x91412
Carson, Mary Helen ("Nellie") 24141315
Carson, Patricia Frances Anne E231x9142, p. 313
Carson, Sara Jane E231x91411
Carter, Mr. 419222
Carter, Albion 161153
Carter, Alfred Ball, Jr. 219134
Carter, Alice Wooding 1331196
Carter, Anna Fauntleroy 211924
Carter, Anna Mae 133114246
Carter, Anne C. P. 24141331
Carter, Anne Cary 2414131
Carter, Anne Lindsay 251632611
Carter, Bertha Ann McCleskey 2119232
Carter, Beverley 211928
Carter, Beverley 2119234
Carter, Capt. Bracton Cleve 2119232
Carter, Cary Randolph Burwell 241524322
Carter, Charles 161152
Carter, Charles Cleve 211927
Carter, Charles Hill 24241311
Carter, Charles Hill, Jr. 242413111
Carter, Charles Hill III 2424131111
Carter, Capt. Charles Otway 2119231
Carter, Claudia E. 1331142432
Carter, Daniel 133114248
Carter, Daniel William 13311424
Carter, Dorothy L. Scates 133114243
Carter, Edmonia Beverley 211922
Carter, Edmonia Fauntleroy Corbin 21192
Carter, Eliza Gilliam Wooding 1331192
Carter, Elizabeth 1331195
Carter, Ella Wilcox Wooding 1331194
Carter, Ellen Monroe Bankhead 241413
Carter, Elsie Vaughan 419222
Carter, Elspeth Vaughan 419222
Carter, Emily Randolph Harrison 24241311
Carter, Fannie Lovie 2119233
Carter, Fanny Lovie McKie 211923
Carter, Florence Annie Price 2119231
Carter, Francis Edward, Jr. 241524322
Carter, Frank Graham 251632612
Carter, Frank M. 25163261

Chapman, Edwin M. 1117935
Chapman, Edwin M., Jr. 11179351
Chapman, Elizabeth Forrer 2421428
Chapman, Margaret Lee Stone 11134x
Chapman, Margaret Scott Alvey 1117935
Charles, Elizabeth 242454a
Charmside, Edmonia Blair Shepperson 165316
Charmside, Martha Brooke 1653161
Charmside, Robert Alexander 165316
Charmside, Robert Alexander, Jr. 1653162
Charrington, Arthur Mowbray Randolph 24153345
Charrington, Arthur Mowbray Randolph, Jr. 241533451
Charrington, Arthur Mowbray Randolph III 2415334512
Charrington, Edward Beverley 24153344
Charrington, Elizabeth Mason Fitch 241533452
Charrington, Frances Irving Glover 241533451
Charrington, Georgiana Randolph 24153343, 652135
Charrington, Mary Elizabeth Wilbur 24153345
Charrington, Mary Harrison Randolph 2415334
Charrington, Mary Virginia 24153342
Charrington, Percy Randolph 24153341
Charrington, Percy William 2415334
Charrington, Peter Randolph 2415334511
CHART p. 327, 330
Chase, Sydney 2419822
Chase, Mrs.   Whitner 2419822
Chason, Carol Randolph 24142x3132
Chason, Helen Borodell 24142x314
Chason, Louise Young 24142x312
Chason, Martha Jefferson Kean 24142x31
Chason, Patricia Lucille 24142x3131
Chason, Robert Leonard 24142x313
Chason, Shirley Lucille Flynn 24142x313
Chason, William 24142x31
Chason, William Randolph 24142x311

Chaudron, Lucia Marie 2414246111
Chaudron, Mary Frances Durham 241424611
Chaudron, Paul de Vendal 241424611
Cheatham, Mr. 56372
Cheatham, Annie Hales 56372
Cheatham, Debra Lynn 1113324132
Cheatham, Elizabeth Jean 1113324133
Cheatham, Frances Mary White 1113324131
Cheatham, Joseph A., Jr. 111332413
Cheatham, Joseph A. III 1113324131
Cheatham, Louisa Cabell 162732
Cheatham, Mary Frances Lynn 111332413
Cheatham, Sarah Emeline Wood 13312117
Cheatham, Thomas Henry Alfred 13312117
Cheatham, W. S. 162732
Cheatwood, Margaret 24141125
Cheesman, Anna E. 24463
Cherami, Brenda Theresa 241x12382
Chess (son) 24245412112
Chess, Elizabeth Harrison Mercer 242454121
Chess, John Hart 242454121
Chess, John Hart, Jr. 2424541211
Chess, Marcia 2424541211
Chess, Theresa 24245412111
Chevillat, Adele 241444321
Chichester, Cassius Moncure 24134732
Chichester, Roberta Kyle Pleasants 24134732
Chichester, Roberta Kyle Pleasants 241347321
Chinn, Harriet White Gwathmey 111x6451
Chinn, John Minor 111x6451
Chipman, John 241966
Chipman, Maria Beard Randolph 241966
Chisholm, Veronica 241x11113
Chisolm, Eliza ("Liela") Laurens 111762
Choate, Mary Pauline 241443121
Christian, Andrew Henry 24142a142
Christian, Andrew Henry, Jr. 24142a1421
Christian, Ann Manning 4111
Christian, Charlotte Meade 2181251
Christian, Eliza Hunt 2192
Christian, Elizabeth Poindexter 241411
Christian, George 1611x
Christian, Henry Harrison 218125
Christian, Jennifer Jenkins 24142a1421
Christian, Pocahontas Megginson 1611x
Christian, Rose 33213
Christian, Rebecca Beverley Ruffin 218125
Christian, Scott Shackelford 24142a1422
Christian, Virginia Randolph 24142a1423
Christian, Virginia Randolph Walker 24142a142

Christie, Harold Bradford 24248121
Christie, Lorna 24218611
Christie, Mary Louise [24248121]
Christie, Mary Louisa Blain 24248121
Church, Layle 241414522
Churchill, Algernon Coolidge 241444534
Churchill, David Lawrence 2414445342
Churchill, Dr. Edward Delos 24144453
Churchill, Edward Delos 241444533
Churchill, Ellen Buntzie Ellis 241444533
Churchill, Eric Coolidge 2414445331
Churchill, Eva Lowell 2414445332
Churchill, Frederick Barton 241444532
Churchill, Miss L. 56367
Churchill, Mary Lowell 241444531
Churchill, Mary Lowell Barton 24144453
Churchill, Sandra Riddle 241444532
Churchill, Susan Lowell 2414445341
Chute, Anne E12
Chute, Esther Elwyn E6
Chute, Thomas E6
Cikovsky, Nicolai 241x114412
Cikovsky, Sarah Eden Greenough 241x114412
Claiborne, Anne Meade Bolling 21923
Claiborne, Elizabeth Cabell 1327132
Claiborne, Elizabeth Lewis Hairston 132713
Claiborne, George C. Cabell 1327135
Claiborne, Jesse 3319
Claiborne, Leonard 1327131
Claiborne, Letitia 1327136
Claiborne, Livingston 132713
Claiborne, Livingston, Jr. 1327137
Claiborne, Nena 219231
Claiborne, Pocahontas Bolling 1327133
Claiborne, Laurie 219232
Claiborne, Saida Grandy 111x82
Claiborne, Sterling B. 21923
Claiborne, Tyler Hairston 1327134
Claiborne, Virginia Markham 3319
Clancey, Beverley Ray Barr 652154
Clancey, George Eugene 652154
Clark, Adelaide Snowden Hodges 5527457
Clark, Adelaide Snowden Hodges 55274571
Clark, Adelaide Snowden Hodges Clark 5527457
Clark, Alice Whitcomb 2414221433
Clark, Angelina Johns 641715
Clark, Anita 111x66
Clark, Ann Gordon 32314263
Clark, Ann Gordon Byrd 3231426
Clark, Ann Sims 6414
Clark, Anne C. P. Carter 24141134, 24141331
Clark, Bankhead 2414133111
Clark, Basil Crawford 552745x
Clark, Beatrice DuBose Skipwith 1116212
Clark, Bernie Pennington 55274531
Clark, Betsy Sims 552745a
Clark, Bettie Sims Coleman 64171
Clark, Betty 64151
Clark, Carolyn Johnston 552745x1
Clark, Carter Bankhead 2414133311
Clark, Charles Branch 5527457
Clark, Charles Branch 55274572
Clark, Charlotte Spence 5527452
Clark, "Desiree" 552745
Clark, Desiree Branch 55274533
Clark, Desiree Branch 5527456
Clark, Dianne 13312114143
Clark, Donna 13312114411
Clark, Edward J. 24141331
Clark, Elizabeth 6413
Clark, Elizabeth Hunt 32314261
Clark, Elvira Ann 641711
Clark, Ethelberta Coleman 641717
Clark, Evalina Eldridge Wyatt Jones 51227
Clark, Gaylord Lee 241c1142
Clark, Gaylord Lee 241c11424
Clark, Helen M. Gambrill 5527451
Clark, Henrietta Maria Coleman 6415
Clark, Henry Branch 5527452
Clark, James Thaddeus 5527453
Clark, Jan Branch 552745x2
Clark, Joan Johnston 552745x
Clark, Rev. John 6415
Clark, John 64171
Clark, John II 641714

Corbin, Elsie Adkins 2424491
Corbin, Fillmore Mallory 21195
Corbin, Frances 21194
Corbin, Gawin Lane 21191
Corbin, Dr. Gawin Lane, Jr. 2118
Corbin, Gawin Lane III 2118131
Corbin, Gawinae 211812
Corbin, John Tayloe II 211a
Corbin, Kathleen Culbertson 2118131
Corbin, Lucy Beverley 211x
Corbin, Lula Hebe Carradine 21195
Corbin, Dr. Luther Carroll 211811
Corbin, Mallory 211952
Corbin, Margaret 211954
Corbin, Marian Thirza 2118132
Corbin, Dr. Marion Xerxes 211813
Corbin, Martha Eliza Brown Brinkley 21181
Corbin, Mary King Mallory 2119
Corbin, May Thirza Williams 211813
Corbin, Dr. Philip Sin Physic 21181
Corbin, Richard Beverley 211953
Corbin, Richard Ewing 211954
Corbin, Richard Johnstone 21181311
Corbin, Richard Randolph 2119
Corbin, Roberta Edmonia 211931
Corcoran, Bernadette E2375124
Corcoran, Mary Jane 251632331
Corcoran, Phoebe Grey McCandlish Young 25163233
Corcoran, William 25163233
Core, Florence Isabel Perkins 211942
Core, John B. 211942
Cory, Alice Lorena Langhorne 552621
Cory, Robert M. 552621
Cosby, Mary W. 6411113
Cosper, Louis Henry 1116227
Cosper, Louis Henry III 11162271
Cosper, Martha Elizabeth 11162272

Cosper, Martha Elizabeth Skipwith 1116227
Couch, Edward 132628
Couch, Hallie Abell 1326281
Couch, Pamela Davis Abell 132628
Coulter, Lee 219136
Coulter, Lucy Page Weisiger 219136
Coupland, Ann Randolph 2423
Coupland, Lucy Harrison 411
Couterier, Marie Louise 65111133
Covington, Edward 1214
Covington, Mary Archer 1214
Cowan, Isabella May Johnson 174311
Cowan, Martha Virginia 33212, 33241
Cowan, W. N. 174311
Cowden, Mary Webster Moore 2413451
Cowden, Dr. Robert 2413451
Cowles, John Elmo 2181219
Cowles, Mary Ruffin 21812191
Cowles, Virginia Powell 21812192
Cowles, Virginia Powell Ruffin 2181219
Cox, Ann Harris 5122
Cox, Barbara 55223a11
Cox, Carole Lee 1331212893
Cox, Donna Gay 13312128912
Cox, Dorothy Sweat 11141611
Cox, Elizabeth Ann 13312128911
Cox, Elizabeth Leftwich Franklin 133121289
Cox, Elizabeth Morris 2415137
Cox, Henry 512
Cox, Henry, Jr. 5124
Cox, Janet Noel 1331212891
Cox, Judith Ann 51241
Cox, Judith Eldridge 512
Cox, Judith Eldridge 5126
Cox, Julia Clay 111362
Cox, Lee Talmadge 13312128914
Cox, Lisa Gayle 13312128913
Cox, Loretta Anne 1331212892
Cox, Martha 552
Cox, Martha Bolling 5123
Cox, Martha Jane 51242
Cox, Matilda Moore 5124
Cox, Owen Talmadge 1331212891
Cox, Patricia Moorman 1331212894
Cox, Powhatan Moorman 133121289
Cox, Sarah A. Steward 5124
Cox, Sarah Eldridge 5128

Cox, Thomas Eldridge 5125
Cox, Vincent P. 5127
Cox, Winifred Miller 5121
Cox, Zarilda Jean 165325621
Craft, Gene Bankhead Hotchkiss 241414561
Craft, Rebecca Lecky 2414145611
Craft, Wilbur 241414561
Craggs, Barbara Jean 111332513
Craggs, Elizabeth Emily Thomas 111332512
Craggs, Gay Frances 111332511
Craggs, Gay Robertson Turner 11133251
Craggs, Hugh 11133251
Craggs, John Rogers 111332512
Craggs, Kenneth Hugh 1113325122
Craggs, Scott Turner 1113325121
Craghead, Pauline 13312119223
Cralle, Miss 62133
Cralle, Anne 1242
Crane, Donna Campbell 251632212
Crane, Frances 24193479
Crane, Jane 251632211
Crane, Richard H. 25163221
Crane, Richard H. Crane, Jr. 251632212
Crane, Sarah McCandlish 25163221
Craven, Elizabeth Page 11142122
Crawford, Alice Laurie 2421782
Crawford, C. Gratton 2415221
Crawford, Elizabeth Eleanor 24152212
Crawford, Dr. Francis Randolph 24152211
Crawford, Louisa Morrow 24152213
Crawford, Louisa Peyton Jones 2415221
Crawford, Martha Paxton Moffett 24152211
Cremer, Alys Shanks 241422151
Cresap, Charles Nash 323121822
Cresap, Comdr. Logan 32312182
Cresap, Logan, Jr. 323121821
Cresap, Nancy Collins Nash 32312182
Crews, Maude G. 244222
Crimmens, Mary Gillian 11171334
Crimminger, Patricia Elizabeth McKinney 111362311
Crimminger, Thomas Jerry 111362311
Crocker, Annie Glenn Michaux 222525
Crocker, Carolyn 41923141
Crocker, Carolyn Ellicott MacCoun 4192314
Crocker, Dorothy G. 4192312
Crocker, Douglas Vaughan 4192313
Crocker, Douglas Vaughan 41923133
Crocker, Edward 419231
Crocker, Edward, Jr. 4192311
Crocker, Edward Briscoe 41923132
Crocker, Joan 41923142
Crocker, John Hanson 4192314
Crocker, John Hanson, Jr. 41923144
Crocker, Lucy 2225253
Crocker, Macon 2225251
Crocker, Margaret Herbert Mather 4192313
Crocker, Margaret Mather 41923131
Crocker, Marie Briscoe 419231
Crocker, Mary 241c522
Crocker, Mary Ann 22252511
Crocker, Mary Cheney 241446325
Crocker, Michaux H. 2225252
Crocker, Michaux H., Jr. 22252521
Crocker, Michaux H. III 222525211
Crocker, Nannette Frances 4192315
Crocker, Robinson Poe 41923134

Crocker, Thomas 222525
Crocker, Virginia Vaughan 41923143
Crockett, Flora Randolph Mason Nicholson 24142731
Crockett, Joseph Parkes 24142731
Crom, Anne Robertson Randolph 11142123
Crom, Emily Martha Hampton 111421232
Crom, Lucy Barksdale 111421233
Crom, Nancy Bolling Randolph 111421231
Crom, William Hampton, Jr. 11142123
Crone, Caroline Shelburne 11134512
Cronemeyer, Martha Cary Stark 219157121
Cronemeyer, Steven Jon 219157121
Croom, Julia Church 241962
Crosby, Vicki 111x6712
Crosland, John 24142a131
Crosland, John III 24142a1312
Crosland, Mary Parker 24142a1311
Crosland, Mary Parker Shackelford 24142a131

Fleming, Virginia 11141611
Fleming, Virginia 211b1611
Fleming, Virginia Rose 211b162
Fleming, Judge William 33
Fleming, William Earle 211b161
Fleming, Lt. William Randolph 211b1
Fleming, William Randolph, Jr. 211b11
Fletcher, Mr. 563623
Fletcher, Grace Turner 563623
Fletcher, John Merle 552232211
Fletcher, Lucy Anne 552232214
Fletcher, Marjorie Ruth Sherlock 55223221
Fletcher, Nancy Dorothy Branch 5522322
Fletcher, Nancy Ruth 552232213
Fletcher, Steven Walker 552232212
Fletcher, Walker Coward 5522322
Fletcher, Walker Coward, Jr. 55223221
Fletcher, Walter Catron 5522322
Flinker, Marie 4192146
Flood, Amy House 133211111
Flood, Anna Portner 1332111
Flood, Bolling Byrd 13321111
Flood, Eleanor 1332112
Flood, Eleanor Bolling 1332113
Flood, Eliza Bolling West 1332
Flood, Ella Faulkner 133211
Flood, Fannie 132624
Flood, Henry ("Hal" or "Harry") Delaware 1332111
Flood, Henry de la Warr 13321
Flood, Holmes Boyd 1332112
Flood, Jennie Pleasants 133211
Flood, Dr. Joel Walker 1332
Flood, Maj. Joel Walker 133211
Flood, Joel West 1332114
Flood, Mrs. Marie 13321111
Flood, Mary Elizabeth Trent 13321
Flood, Robert 133211111
Flood, Sallie Whiteman Delk 133211
Flores, Manuel 111622246
Flores, Mary Mathilda Hyams 111622246
Flory, Anne Randolph 41921412
Flory, Anne Randolph Briscoe Putney 4192141
Flory, William E. 4192141
Flory, William E., Jr. 41921411
Floyd, Charles Harrison 242454131
Floyd, Charles Sea 24245413
Floyd, Mary Randolph 242454132
Floyd, Virginia Hening 332426
Floyd, Virginia Troup Harrison 24245413
Flynn, James William, Jr. 2414631122
Flynn, Katherine Roy Davis 2414631122
Flynn, Shirley Lucille 24142x313
Flynn, Virginia Kenny 2414631221
Foard, Elizabeth B. 64111121
Foard, Hiram 6411112
Foard, Susanna Lewis 6411112
Foard, Warner W. 64111122
Folker, Matilda R. 241b2
Foltz, Judy May Layne 133121141261
Foltz, Richard Lee 133121141261
Foltz, Rodney Arthur 1331211412611
Foltz, Sarah Virginia 1331211412612
Fontaine, Martha H. 173
Fontaine, Norma 24144621
Foort, Beatrice Nash E237512213
Foort, Jennifer Lynn E237512133
Foort, Julia Ann E237512132
Foort, Karen E237512131
Foort, Lawrence E23751213
Foote, Nancy Heidelburg 2135272
Forbes, Elizabeth Whitney 21913212
Forbes, George Lester 3321221
Forbes, Dr. George Lester, Jr. 33212212
Forbes, Robert Stanard 33212213
Forbes, Ruth Allene Wright 33212212
Forbes, Virginia Morris Stanard 3321221
Forbes, Virginia Stanard 33212211
Ford, Ambrose 24246441
Ford, Annie Gilbert 13311a4
Ford, George 24246411
Ford, Gertrude 24246413
Ford, Henry J. 174a2

Ford, John Ernest III 55221351
Ford, Julia Randolph Harrison 2424641
Ford, Kathryn B. 1331131211
Ford, Marion Isabella James Hawkins 174a2
Ford, Pamela Branch Popkin 55221351
Ford, Sally 24246412
Ford, W. A. 13311a4
Fore, Maud 56344
Forman, Jean Throckmorton 2424812
Fossett, Jo Ann 241491421
Foster, Fannie 1331123
Foster, Nannie 221254
Fowler, Ann 56361114
Fowler, George F. 241422312
Fowler, Gertrude Blackburn 241422312
Fowler, Grace Myra 5522323
Fox, C. I. 1533
Fox, Gay Currie 4192591
Fox, Henrietta Watkins Tazewell 1533
Fox, James McCall 221155
Fox, Joe 4192591
Fox, Richard 2211551
Fox, Virginia Dean Hall 221155
Fragola, Joseph 2414245221
Fragola, Mary Helen Ruffin Marshall 2414245221
Fragstein, Meta 241411321
Fraher, Clarence Duncan 219157133
Fraher, Edward Shelton, Jr. 21915713
Fraher, Edward Shelton III 219157131
Fraher, Katherine Watson 219157132
Fraher, Martha Watson Weisiger 21915713
Frank, Donna 174a31311
Frank, Elise 241524321
Franklin, Alvan Holmes 1331212866
Franklin, Ann Virginia Wood 13312111
Franklin, Arrah Neal 133121283
Franklin, Arthur William 133121282
Franklin, Audrey Delores 1331212864
Franklin, Barbara Larkin 111x21311
Franklin, Carl Burton 133121411
Franklin, Churchill Gibson 111x21313
Franklin, Daniel Thomas 133121413
Franklin, Elizabeth Ann 13312114142
Franklin, Elizabeth Leftwich 133121289
Franklin, Elizabeth Lloyd Gibson 111x2131
Franklin, Elizabeth Robertson Puckett 13312128
Franklin, Ella 133121285
Franklin, Ella Franklin 133121285
Franklin, Ernest Paxton 133121285
Franklin, Ethel Frost 133121284
Franklin, Eunice May 133121412
Franklin, Evelyn Childress Bailey 13312128x1
Franklin, Evelyn Christine 1331212861
Franklin, Gay Lloyd 111x21312
Franklin, Grace 13312128x
Franklin, Grace Franklin 13312128x
Franklin, Harold Owen 1331212862
Franklin, Hattie Elizabeth 13312127
Franklin, Hattie Evans 133121282
Franklin, Ida 133121286
Franklin, Ida Morgan 133121288
Franklin, Iona ("Ona") Harper 133121286
Franklin, Jacqueline Horton 1331212866
Franklin, Janet Halstead 111x21313
Franklin, Jesse William 133121141 4
Franklin, Joel W. 1331212
Franklin, John Henry 13312128x
Franklin, John Lewis 13312128x11
Franklin, John Preston 13312128x1
Franklin, John Weed 111x2131
Franklin, John Weed, Jr. 111x21311
Franklin, Josephine Carwile 133121141 4
Franklin, Juanita Hughes 1331212862
Franklin, Lenora 13312114141
Franklin, Lenora Zephna Torrence 133121141
Franklin, Lisa Gayle 133121192234
Franklin, Mary Ann 13312125
Franklin, Mary Kathaleen 1331212865
Franklin, Nancy Franklin Wood DePriest 1331212
Franklin, Nannie Mae 133121287
Franklin, Owen Walker 13312124

Fletcher, Grace Turner 563623
Fletcher, Percy 563623

Gary, Ballard Preston 2415335113
Gary, Hartwell Henry, Jr. 241533511
Gary, Hartwell Henry III 2415335111
Gary, Mary Carter Grandy 241533511
Gary, Wiley Grandy 2415335112
Gary, William Fitzhugh Randolph 2415335114
Gass, Ivy 2419681
Gasser, Annette 241411291
Gay, Agatha Estill 4186
Gay, Ann Caroline 4145
Gay, Ann H. 417
Gay, Ann Manning Christian 4111
Gay, Arthur 4163112
Gay, Mrs. Baptist 4112
Gay, Benjamin Carter 4115
Gay, Bolling 4137
Gay, Caroline H. 41c
Gay, Caroline Scott 4164
Gay, Caroline Scott 4187
Gay, Carroll 4163113
Gay, Carroll Payne Smith 416311
Gay, Catherine Nivison Tazewell 416
Gay, Catherine Nivison Tazewell Ambler 1532
Gay, Charles S. 4138
Gay, Charles Scott 418
Gay, Charles Wyndham 4181
Gay, David Coupland 4114
Gay, Delia 4132
Gay, Edward 4163111
Gay, Edward S. 4163
Gay, Edward Scott 1532, 416
Gay, Edward Scott, Jr. 4163
Gay, Edward Scott III 41631
Gay, Edward Scott IV 416311
Gay, Mrs. Eggleston Ward 41
Gay, Eliza Royall Archer 413
Gay, Eliza S. 4134
Gay, Elizabeth 412
Gay, Elizabeth ("Betty") 11, 42, p. 328, 330
Gay, Elizabeth Bolling 4, p. 6
Gay, Elizabeth Cary 4115
Gay, Ellen 4131
Gay, Ewell 41633
Gay, Frances 41b
Gay, Frances ("Fannie") Bolling 4183
Gay, Frances Trent 41
Gay, Frank L. 416331
Gay, Franklin 4112
Gay, Helen Hendricks Hobbs 41631
Gay, Henry Erskine 4182
Gay, Mrs. Jackson 4133
Gay, John 41d
Gay, John 44
Gay, John R. 4188
Gay, Judith Scott 41
Gay, Kate Rolfe 4166
Gay, Lizzie E. 4184
Gay, Louisa Tazewell 4162
Gay, Louise Cary 41632
Gay, Lucy Harrison Coupland 411
Gay, Margaret 4189
Gay, Margaret Lewis Erskine 418
Gay, Martha 4143
Gay, Martha Talley 414
Gay, Mary 43
Gay, Mary Buchanan ("Polly") 415
Gay, Mary Bunn 4142
Gay, Matoaca 4161
Gay, Minnie Wellford 4165
Gay, Neale Buchanan 414
Gay, Neale Buchanan, Jr. 4142
Gay, Dr. Peter Field 4111
Gay, Pocahontas V. 4144
Gay, Powhatan A. 4135
Gay, Sally 419, 541
Gay, Sally Bolling 4167
Gay, Sarah Bruce 4141
Gay, Sarah ("Sallie") Mahulda Ewell 4163
Gay, Sarah Nicholson 4114
Gay, Thomas Bolling 413
Gay, Thomas Bolling 4137
Gay, Virginia F. 4136
Gay, Dr. (or Maj.) William 4, p. 6

Gay, Capt. William 41
Gay, William 4133
Gay, William 4141
Gay, William A. 4113
Gay, William Alexander 411
Gay, William Patton 4185
Gay, Willis Walter 4116
Gayle, Lois Miller 2181213
Gayle, Sara Victoria 111622
Geannini, Curtis 2414131322
Geannini, David Curtis 24141313221
Geannini, Ellen Olivia Bailey 2414131322
Geannini, Giles Anderson 24141313223
Geannini, Stephen Philip 24141313222
Gearhart, Elizabeth 242186
Geisler, Carroll Preston Shackelford 24142a1132
Geisler, James Richard 24142a1132
Gelb, Elizabeth Gay Symington 111x21421
Gelb, Yehuda 111x21421
Gentles, Julia Robertson McKinney 11136231
Gentles, Thomas Kennedy 11136231
Gentry, Mr. 2192562
Gentry, Linette Stock 2192562
Gerald, Sophie Christine May 241x112321
Gerard, Charles Rupert 241x112321
Gerfen, Anne Randolph Block 24142a1226
Gerfen, Earl 24142a1226
Germano, Emidio San 24244521
Germano, Mary Randolph San 242445211
Germano, Virginia Randolph Bolling Hoge 24244521
Germelman, Grace Louise 2191594
Gesner, Mary Virginia Jones 651132
Gesner, Dr. William 651132
Gest, Dorothy 2191561
Gholson, Amarilla Bell 2414245
Gibson, Elizabeth 2121
Gibson, Anne Marie E237
Gibson, Charles Cummings 2414131x
Gibson, Dr. Churchill Jones 111x213
Gibson, Churchill Jones, Jr. 111x2134
Gibson, Churchill Jones III 111x21341
Gibson, Dorothy 111x21342
Gibson, Dorothy Simons 111x2134
Gibson, Elizabeth Knighton 111344422
Gibson, Elizabeth Lloyd 111x2131
Gibson, Eugenie F. Preston 2414131x
Gibson, Gail Brashears 111344423
Gibson, Gay 111x21344
Gibson, Gay Lloyd 111x2133
Gibson, Gay Robertson Lloyd 111x213
Gibson, James Randolph 111344421
Gibson, Martha Knighton Brashears 11134442
Gibson, Mary 2221382
Gibson, Meredith Ann 11136232
Gibson, Samuel James 11134442
Gibson, Susan Stuart 111x2132
Gibson, Webster 111x21343
Giese, Byron Craig 174a31221
Giese, Byron Craig II 174a312212
Giese, Deborah Joyce Burke 174a31221
Giese, Laura Michele 174a312211
Gifford, C. L. 6132
Gifford, Matoaca Murray 6132
Gilbert, Annie 13311a4
Gilbert, Blanche Robertson 13311a2
Gilbert, Cornelius 13311a3
Gilbert, Emma Josephine Gilliam 13311a
Gilbert, Emma Plunkett 133117
Gilbert, Eva Sanderson 13311a3
Gilbert, George 13311a
Gilbert, George W. 13311a2
Gilbert, Rosa Lee 13311a1
Gilchrist, Anne ("Nannie") Cary Randolph Bankhead 2414142
Gilchrist, Catherine Caroline 241346331
Gilchrist, Edward 24134633
Gilchrist, J. Harvey 2414142
Gilchrist, Katie Frank 24141421
Gilchrist, Virginia Adair Minor 24134633
Gile, Bradford Willis 2414221331
Gile, Bradford Willis, Jr. 24142213311
Gile, Emily Hume 24142213312
Gile, Emily Hume Taylor 2414221331

Gilham, Isabella Adair Pleasants 2413471
Gilham, Reginald 2413471
Gill, Mrs. 56356
Gill, Dorothy Leonard 2414243121
Gill, German B. 13112
Gill, Mary Burton Banister 13112
Gill, Pearl 56345
Gillespie, Adam Stuart 24141452213
Gillespie, Anna Frances Hotchkiss 24141452
Gillespie, Anne Marie 2414145221
Gillespie, Campbell Houston 24141452
Gillespie, Campbell Houston, Jr. 241414521,
  241424334
Gillespie, Campbell Houston III 2414145211
Gillespie, Cary Ruffin 24141452112
Gillespie, Clark Patton 2414145221
Gillespie, Dorothy Hastings Wellman 241414522
Gillespie, Elizabeth Lowell Barton 241444542
Gillespie, Garrett Gregory 241444542
Gillespie, Garrett Gregory, Jr. 2414445422
Gillespie, Layle Christine 2414145222
Gillespie, Layle Church 241414522
Gillespie, Kelly Elizabeth 24141452211
Gillespie, Mary Bert Patillo 2414145211
Gillespie, Mary Ruffin McMurdo 241414521, 241424334
Gillespie, Maryanna Keeval 24141452111
Gillespie, Patricia De Anne 24141452212
Gillespie, Robert McMurdo 2414145212
Gillespie, Stuart Edgar 241414522
Gillespie, Susan Estes Ribonsin 2414145212
Gillespie, William Stuart 2414145223
Gillet, George Martin 241cl1151
Gillet, George Martin 241cl11511
Gillet, James McHenry 241cl11512
Gillet, Sophia McHenry Stewart 241cl1151
Gilliam, Amanda Jones 133115
Gilliam, Anna Steele Ramsey 13311x1

Gilliam, Anne Slaughter Davenport 133113
Gilliam, Annie 13311312
Gilliam, Annie Eliza 1331173
Gilliam, Annie Holmes Henry 13311x5
Gilliam, Armistead Hamlet 13311x1
Gilliam, Colie Tynes 133117
Gilliam, Edward Glover 133117
Gilliam, Eliza Bolling 13311x2
Gilliam, Elizabeth ("Queenie") Bolling 133114
Gilliam, Elizabeth Bolling Jones 13311
Gilliam, Ella Coleman 1331171
Gilliam, Eloise Glover 133112
Gilliam, Elsie West 13311b1
Gilliam, Emma Hubbard 1331177
Gilliam, Emma Josephine 13311a
Gilliam, Emma Plunkett Gilbert 133117
Gilliam, Fannie Diuguid 13311b
Gilliam, Fannie Diuguid 13311b3
Gilliam, Fannie Jane 1331176
Gilliam, Dr. Glover Davenport 13311
Gilliam, Glover Davenport 13311x7
Gilliam, Grace Schenk 13311b2
Gilliam, James Cornelius 1331174
Gilliam, James Richard 133113
Gilliam, James Richard, Jr. 1331131
Gilliam, James Richard III 13311311
Gilliam, James Thomas 13311x8
Gilliam, Jane Lewis Hamlet 13311x
Gilliam, Jessie Belfield Johnson 1331131
Gilliam, John Richard 1331172
Gilliam, Lucy 1251
Gilliam, Martha Virginia 133111
Gilliam, Mary Marshall 133118
Gilliam, Mary Victoria 133116
Gilliam, Minnie Callaham 1331174
Gilliam, Olivia Ford 133119
Gilliam, Olivia West 13311x4
Gilliam, Robert Edward 13311x5
Gilliam, Rosa Maria 13311x9
Gilliam, Russie Turner 13311x7
Gilliam, Ruth Jane 13311xx
Gilliam, Sallie Bowman 13311x8
Gilliam, Sallie Virginia 13311x3
Gilliam, Thomas West 13311b
Gilliam, Walter Edward 1331175
Gilliam, Walter Flood (Floyd?) 13311x
Gilliam, Walter Fuqua 13311x6

Gillis, Ann Carter 2415333123
Gillis, Carol Randolph 2415333122
Gillis, John Lamb 241533312
Gillis, John Lamb, Jr. 2415333121
Gillis, Ruth Caroline Randolph 241533312
Gills, Carolyn Floyd 33242651
Gills, James Ashley 3324265
Gills, Virginia Randolph Archer 3324265
Gillum, Cary Randolph Bankhead 241411241
Gillum, Mark Miller 24141124
Gillum, Mary Archer Bankhead 24141124
Gillum, Mildred 241411241l
Gillum, Rachel Errett 2414112412
Gillum, Rachel Errett 241411242
Gillum, Ruth Stark 241411241
Gilpin, Nancy Arthington 11134432
Gilsdorf, Barbara 1113324121
Githens, Elizabeth Beverley Barr 652153
Githens, Elizabeth Sinclair 6521532
Githens, John Nichols 652153
Githens, Katherine Beverley 6521531
Glascock, Gail 22252341
Glascock, Lola Michaux 2225234
Glascock, Louis L. 22252342
Glascock, Louis LeGrand 2225234
Glascock, Mary Louise Norwood 22252342
Glasgow, Mary 55275
Glass, Dorsey L., Jr. 16532411
Glass, Edward Lee 165324111
Glass, Elma 1117933
Glass, Lisa Gayle 165324114
Glass, Peggy Joyce McKay 16532411
Glass, Sandra Joyce 165324113
Glass, Susan Blair 165324112
Gleeson, Margaret E231x911
Glenn, Alcie Hairston 652189
Glenn, Janet Elizabeth Hutchison 24141113121
Glenn, Robert Carson, Jr. 24141113121
Glenn, Roger Christopher 241411131211
Glickman, Dr. Joe, Jr. 2424541222
Glickman, Mary Lucille Sorrells 2424541222
Glover, Frances Eldridge 5619
Glover, Frances Irving 241533451
Glover, Louisa Rebecca Branch 55226
Glover, Nancy 111x2141
Glover, Rolfe Eldridge 56191
Glover, Samuel Anthony 5619
Glover, Virginia B. Perdue 55226, 55243
Glover, Dr. William B. 55226, 55243
Goble, Amy 2414431231
Goddard, Calvin Hooker 24241734
Goddard, Eliza Cunningham 242417341
Goddard, Eliza Cunningham Harrison 24241734
Goddard, Mary Woodbridge 242417342
Godfrey, Miss 1221321
Godsey, Florence Esther 1331211922
Goekjian, Dorothy Virginia Hassell 111326514
Goekjian, Karekin 111326514
Goffe, Florence Estelle 21332
Goforth, Osborne LeRoux 32314141
Goforth, Susan Lewis Byrd Thompson 32314141
Gold, Ella 2424613
Goldwaithe, Amanda ("Nannie") Moore 213362
Goldwaithe, Dr. Henry 213362
Gomillion, Angeline Bacon 2424644
Gones, Mrs. Mamie J. 2419331

Gooch, Augusta Ernestine Albies 174a61
Gooch, Charles 13311a
Gooch, Emma Josephine 13311a6
Gooch, Emma Josephine Gilliam Gilbert 13311a
Gooch, Frances Ann James 174a6
Gooch, Howard Bland 174a61
Gooch, John 13311a5
Gooch, Roland Alexander 174a6
Gooch, Roland Alexander ("Ellie") 174a62
Goodall, Anna Byrd Corbin 211x3
Goodall, Catherine Carter 211x6
Goodall, Hester Morris 211x5
Goodall, Rev. John 211x
Goodall, Junius 211x1
Goodall, Louisa Anna Hester 211x2
Goodall, Lucy Beverley Corbin 211x
Goodall, Lucy Corbin 211x4

Harrison, Henningham 242457
Harrison, Henningham Carrington Wills 24245
Harrison, Henrietta 242465x
Harrison, Henry 242461
Harrison, Henry 2424614
Harrison, Henry Heth 242431
Harrison, Henry Jaquelin 2424647
Harrison, Henry St. George Tucker 242449
Harrison, Henry Tucker 2424497
Harrison, Henry Tucker 24244972
Harrison, Herbert H. 1113461
Harrison, Heth 2424531
Harrison, Hetty Cary 241c161
Harrison, Hetty Cary 241c521
Harrison, Hildreth Vernon 24246429
Harrison, Holmes 2424655
Harrison, Holmes Boyd 24244432
Harrison, Hugh Randolph 242413522
Harrison, Hugh Thornton 2421352
Harrison, Ione 2135215
Harrison, Irene Anderson 2424642
Harrison, Irene B. Waring 1221113
Harrison, Isabel Parker 24241312
Harrison, Isabel Parker 242413123
Harrison, Isabel Wurts 2421771
Harrison, Isabella 24246461
Harrison, Isabella Wright Clarke 2424646
Harrison, J. Kent 24246122
Harrison, James Burwell 2424646
Harrison, James Pinckney 2424139
Harrison, James Pinckney, Jr. 24241394
Harrison, James Pinckney III 242413942
Harrison, Jane Carr 2424431
Harrison, Jane Cary 24153
Harrison, Jane Cary 242442
Harrison, Jane Cary 2415335331
Harrison, Jane Cary 2424138
Harrison, Jane Cary 242415
Harrison, Jane Cary 2424441
Harrison, Jane Cary Carr 24244
Harrison, Jane Cary Randolph 241533533
Harrison, Jane Dashiell Randolph 242453b
Harrison, Jane Nicholas 2414262
Harrison, Jane St. Clair Cochrane 242461
Harrison, Jane Thompson 2424642
Harrison, Jane Wenthall Stone 242474
Harrison, Janet Withers 2424615
Harrison, Janetta 2424617
Harrison, Janetta 2424651
Harrison, Janetta Fisher 24246
Harrison, Janie Judith 24246428
Harrison, Dr. Jaquelin Ambler 2424613
Harrison, Jaquelin Ambler 24246192
Harrison, Jaquelin Ambler 24246421
Harrison, Jean 132131324
Harrison, Jefferson Randolph 2414263
Harrison, John 2424653
Harrison, John Cunningham 242411
Harrison, John Randolph 242453b1
Harrison, John Strobier 2424134
Harrison, John W. 2424664
Harrison, John Williams 24241625
Harrison, Josephine C. 242453b11
Harrison, Josephine T. Hollahan 24241732
Harrison, Joseph Kent, Jr. 242461221
Harrison, Julia Halsey Meem 2424619
Harrison, Julia Leigh 24241752
Harrison, Julia Meem 24246194
Harrison, Julia Randolph 2424641
Harrison, Julia Wickham 24241736
Harrison, Julia Wickham 2424174
Harrison, Julia Wickham Leigh 242417
Harrison, Julien 242453
Harrison, Julien 2424534
Harrison, Julien 2424537h
Harrison, Julien 242453x1
Harrison, Kate C. Duval 2424611
Harrison, Kate Tabb 1114181
Harrison, Katharine Davenport 2424649
Harrison, Katherine Cooke DuVal 211524
Harrison, Kathleen Kennon 24247233
Harrison, Kathleen Virginia 242464221
Harrison, Kendall Wisegar Lipscomb 24241737
Harrison, Laura Tafft 242461b
Harrison, Lavinia Beverley 242432
Harrison, Lavinia Beverley Heth 242453

Harrison, Lavinia Carter 24241351
Harrison, Lavinia Carter 242413511
Harrison, Lelia Beverley 2424546
Harrison, Leigh Randolph 242417391
Harrison, Lelia Sweeney 218313
Harrison, Leola McCullers 2424497
Harrison, Leola Snodgrass 24246422
Harrison, Rev. Lewis Carter 111418
Harrison, Lillian Gorham 2424443
Harrison, Lillian Gorham 24244431
Harrison, Lillias 24241a2
Harrison, Lillie Tripp 2424499
Harrison, Lilly 24245375
Harrison, Louisa 24245474
Harrison, Louisa Hagner 2424533
Harrison, Louisa P. 242465c
Harrison, Louise Thomas Wheat 242453x
Harrison, Lucia Cary 2424722
Harrison, Lucius Ashton 1221113
Harrison, Lucius Ashton, Jr. 12211131
Harrison, Lucy 2424465
Harrison, Lucy (Lucia?) 24249
Harrison, Lucy Brady 132131321
Harrison, Lucy Brady Cook 13213132
Harrison, Lucy Butler 24241x21
Harrison, Lula Banks Richards 24241739
Harrison, McPherson 24241a6
Harrison, Mabel Judson 241c522
Harrison, Mann Page 24247233
Harrison, Margaret 242461a
Harrison, Margaret Carter 2424312
Harrison, Margaret Elizabeth Redwood 24247231
Harrison, Margaret Jane 122111231
Harrison, Margaret Ritchie 2424742
Harrison, Maria Boyd 2424616
Harrison, Marie Louise 2424162, 2424662
Harrison, Marie Louise Harrison 2424162, 2424662
Harrison, Marion Maxwell Jenifer 242449
Harrison, Martha B. Kountze 242453b2
Harrison, Martha Baker Bass 24241392
Harrison, Martha Cary Dew 24241x2
Harrison, Mary 1414
Harrison, Mary 2424614
Harrison, Mary 2424132
Harrison, Mary 241c5231
Harrison, Mary 2424659
Harrison, Mary Ann (Marianna?) 242463
Harrison, Mary Ann Troup 2424541
Harrison, Mary Berry 2424537
Harrison, Mary Burleigh 242412
Harrison, Mary Cary 24215461
Harrison, Mary Cary 2421642
Harrison, Mary Cary 24216432
Harrison, Mary Christine 24153353331
Harrison, Mary Clifton 242447
Harrison, Mary Crocker 241c522
Harrison, Mary Elizabeth 242464432
Harrison, Mary Galt 2424542
Harrison, Mary Hartley 24245473
Harrison, Mary Ida Nance 2424173
Harrison, Mary Louise 24245412
Harrison, Mary Lyons 2424161
Harrison, Mary Marbury 2424494
Harrison, Mary Montgomery Orgain 24241x
Harrison, Mary Murray 661
Harrison, Mary ("Polly") Randolph 24247
Harrison, Mary ("Polly") Randolph Harrison 24247
Harrison, Mary ("Polly") Randolph Page 242472, 242491
Harrison, Mary Randolph 2424
Harrison, Mary Randolph 24241751
Harrison, Mary Randolph 1221111
Harrison, Mary Randolph ("Polly") 242456
Harrison, Mary Spann 24246441
Harrison, Mary Thornton Stockdell 21831
Harrison, Mary Wingfield 2424653
Harrison, Mattie Cary Nelson 2424723
Harrison, Mattie Corbin 24241x24
Harrison, Mattilla ("Mattie") Cary Page 242164
Harrison, May K. Willson 2424664
Harrison, Mildred Carrington Williams 24241738
Harrison, Nancy Addison 242448
Harrison, Nancy Pope 12211123
Harrison, Nancy Randolph 2415335332
Harrison, Nannie 2424657
Harrison, Nannie Spotswood Byrd 2424443

Harrison, Nannie Spotswood D. 2424433
Harrison, Nell Bickham 24246443
Harrison, Nellie Atkins Meade 24241394
Harrison, Nelson Page 2424724
Harrison, Page 24241x22
Harrison, Peyton 2424463
Harrison, Peyton R. 242453b22
Harrison, Rev. Peyton Randolph 24244
Harrison, Peyton Randolph 242444
Harrison, Peyton Randolph 2424443
Harrison, Peyton Randolph 24244433
Harrison, Peyton Randolph 242453x
Harrison, Peyton Randolph 2424491
Harrison, Phoebe Virginia Westwater 2421643
Harrison, Powell Brooke 2424644
Harrison, Powell Brooke 24246443
Harrison, Powell Brooke 242464431
Harrison, Preston Carter 13213181
Harrison, Raleigh Colston 2424643
Harrison, Randolph 1321316
Harrison, Randolph 2424
Harrison, Randolph 24241a
Harrison, Randolph 24241a5
Harrison, Randolph 242434
Harrison, Dr. Randolph 242442
Harrison, Randolph 2424464
Harrison, Randolph 2424a2
Harrison, Randolph 242453b12
Harrison, Randolph 2424619
Harrison, Randolph 24246642
Harrison, Randolph 242467
Harrison, Randolph 242471
Harrison, Randolph, Jr. 24245
Harrison, Randolph, Jr. 242453b121
Harrison, Randolph, Jr. 24246191
Harrison, Randolph III 242454
Harrison, Randolph IV 2424541
Harrison, Randolph Page 24247232
Harrison, Randolph W. 242419
Harrison, Randolph Williamson 24245441
Harrison, Rebecca 2424658
Harrison, Rebecca Conrad 242465
Harrison, Rebecca Leigh 24241624
Harrison, Richard 241c5213
Harrison, Richard Logan 242417353
Harrison, Robert 218317
Harrison, Robert Tunstall 242454x
Harrison, Rosalie 24245373
Harrison, Rosalie Freeland 242442
Harrison, Rose H. 24246123
Harrison, Rose St. Clair 2424618
Harrison, Ruth Ellen 242449x
Harrison, Sallie 2424656
Harrison, Sallie Belle Stroud 2424545
Harrison, Sally 242465
Harrison, Sally Pendleton Buchanan 242443
Harrison, Sally Powell 242464
Harrison, Samuel Graeme 24244a
Harrison, Samuel Graeme, Jr. 24244al
Harrison, Sara Roane 242416
Harrison, Sara Roane 24241623
Harrison, Sara (Tazie) 24241a3
Harrison, Sarah Forrest Hunter 242444
Harrison, Sarah Frazer 242431
Harrison, Sarah Hunter Webster 24244421
Harrison, Sarah Powell 242417352
Harrison, Sarah Stowe 24245472
Harrison, Sarah ("Sadie") Webb 24245443
Harrison, Sarah ("Sallie") Webb Burrus 2424544
Harrison, Sharon Estep 2415335333
Harrison, Sophonisba Preston 132131x
Harrison, Sophonisba Grayson Preston 132131
Harrison, Sue Lewis 242413933
Harrison, Sue Lewis Brown 24241393
Harrison, Sue Ruffin Wilcox 2424135
Harrison, Surry Parker 242413122
Harrison, Susan Mathews 242465
Harrison, Susan Mathews Ficklin 242464
Harrison, Susan Randolph 215
Harrison, Susanna Isham 24248
Harrison, Susie 242465b
Harrison, Susie Ruffin Coleman 24241735

Harrison, Taylor 8494466
Harrison, Taylor 24245371
Harrison, Terry William 552239112
Harrison, Theodore Courtland 242464222
Harrison, Thomas Gatewood 2424543
Harrison, Thomas Leigh 242417321
Harrison, Thomas Randolph 242417
Harrison, Thomas Randolph 24241a4
Harrison, Thomas Randolph 24241735
Harrison, Thomas Randolph 2424131
Harrison, Thomas Randolph 24241
Harrison, Thomas Randolph, Jr. 242417351
Harrison, Thomas William 55223911
Harrison, Trilby Jenifer 24244971
Harrison, Ursula 241c5212
Harrison, Victoria Eppes Marshall 2419332
Harrison, Virginia 24246423
Harrison, Virginia 242453b23
Harrison, Virginia C. 2424535
Harrison, Virginia Gwynne 24216433
Harrison, Virginia Meade 242492
Harrison, Virginia Randolph 241c5221
Harrison, Virginia Randolph 242445
Harrison, Virginia Randolph 2424b
Harrison, Virginia Troup 24245413
Harrison, Virginia Westwater 2421643
Harrison, Walter 2424536
Harrison, Watkins Leigh 24241732
Harrison, Wayles Randolph 24241393
Harrison, Wayles Randolph, Jr. 242413932
Harrison, William 218313
Harrison, William 2424467
Harrison, William Allen 24241x211
Harrison, William Allen 21831
Harrison, William Allen 24241x1
Harrison, William Boyd 2424615
Harrison, William Byrd 24247
Harrison, William Byrd 241426
Harrison, William Byrd II 122111, 2424721
Harrison, William Byrd III 1221112
Harrison, William Byrd IV 12211123
Harrison, William Evelyn 2424741
Harrison, William Lambert 2424133
Harrison, William Mortimer 24241392
Harrison, William Mortimer 242413
Harrison, William Mortimer 24241a1
Harrison, William Mortimer 24241312
Harrison, William Mortimer 242413121
Harrison, William Mortimer 2424d
Harrison, William Morton (Mortimer?) 242455
Harrison, William Nance 24241739
Harrison, William Preston 1321318
Harrison, William Riley 24244321
Harrison, William Wirt 242446
Harrison, William Wright 24246462
Harrison, Williana Irving 24244x
Harrison, Williana Mortimer 2424a
Harrison, Willie 1321311
Harrison, Wythe 2424462
Harrold, Martha C. 2414112921
Hart, Christopher Harrison 24245413211
Hart, Eleanor 1626
Hart, J. Hawkins 162562
Hart, James A. 111x64212
Hart, James L. 111x6421
Hart, John Fincher 242454321
Hart, John Herd 241444531
Hart, Karen Anne 24245413212
Hart, Marilyn Randolph Kegg 2424541321
Hart, Martha Norton White 111x6421
Hart, Mary Lowell Churchill 241444531
Hart, Sheila 111x64211
Hart, Susan Ballard Powell 162562
Hartless, Dawn Denise St. Clair 165325211
Hartless, Roger Lee 165325211
Hartman, Caroline Baskervill 6411132
Hartman, Rev. Frank 6411132
Hartman, Justin 2414431511
Hartzell, Clayton 2414243113
Hartzell, David McKinley 24142431131
Hartzell, Jane McIlwaine Ruffin Knapp 2414243113
Harvey, Gertrude E2375121
Harvie, Mary Winston 2414244

Hoyle, Elizabeth ("Bessie") 563521

Hutchinson, Lewis Randolph 2421863
Hutchinson, Lorna Christie 24218611
Hutchinson, Lucille 24218621
Hutchinson, Lucy Burwell Randolph 24218
Hutchinson, Lucy Carter 24218731
Hutchinson, Lucy Carter 2421876
Hutchinson, Lucy May 24218632
Hutchinson, Marjorie 24218732
Hutchinson, Martha 2421878
Hutchinson, Mary B. Luney 2421873
Hutchinson, Mary Clyde Smith 2421863
Hutchinson, Mary E. Flaugher 2421861
Hutchinson, Mary Randolph 2421875
Hutchinson, Mary S. Mitchell 242187
Hutchinson, Mary Talcott 242188
Hutchinson, Maude Estella 24218631
Hutchinson, Penelope Snyder 24218622
Hutchinson, Randolph 24218611
Hutchinson, Randolph Burwell 2421872
Hutchinson, Randolph Clifton 24218633
Hutchinson, Robert Randolph 242187
Hutchinson, William Christy 2421874
Hutchinson, William Talcott 2421811
Hutchinson, William Talcott 2421862
Hutchinson, Winona Brazeal 24218612
Hutchison, Alice Elizabeth Dimnick 2414111312
Hutchison, Everett Bell 2414111313
Hutchison, Hal Thomas 24141113122
Hutchison, Holly Elizabeth 24141113132
Hutchison, Horace Leonard 241411131
Hutchison, Horace Leonard, Jr. 2414111312
Hutchison, Janet Elizabeth 24141113121
Hutchison, Kenneth Todd 24141113134
Hutchison, Keri Lee 241411131311
Hutchison, Lucy Elizabeth 2414111311
Hutchison, Mary Elizabeth Bell 24141113131
Hutchison, Mary Elizabeth Brooks 24141113131
Hutchison, Mary Lynn 2414111323
Hutchison, Patricia Anne 24141113133
Hutchison, Susan Frances 24141113124
Hutchison, Thomas Casey 24141113131
Hutchison, Thomas Casey, Jr. 241411131312
Hutchison, Virginia Casey 2414111313
Hutzler, Erich Kurt 24141111142
Hutzler, Megan Wayles 24141111421
Hutzler, Penny Jeanne West Lamoureaux 24141111142
Hyams (baby) 111622221
Hyams, Amy Katherine 111622249
Hyams, Barbara 111622242
Hyams, Clovis Martin 1116222223
Hyams, David 1116222431
Hyams, Davis 1116222323
Hyams, Denise 1116222322
Hyams, Dennis 111622232
Hyams, Dennis, Jr. 1116222321
Hyams, Diana Dalme 111622231
Hyams, Donald Paul 111622247
Hyams, Dorothy L'Herrison 11162224
Hyams, Eliza Bolling Skipwith 1116222
Hyams, Elizabeth Gayle 111622244
Hyams, Gaiennic, Jr. 111622241
Hyams, Henry M. 11162223
Hyams, James Lester 111622248
Hyams, John Skipwith 11162222
Hyams, John Skipwith ("Buddy") 111622242
Hyams, Linda Hampton 111622232
Hyams, Marilyn Orr 111622243
Hyams, Mary Mathilda 111622246
Hyams, Michael 111622231
Hyams, Michael, Jr. 1116222311
Hyams, Myrtle Temple 11162222
Hyams, Ouita 111622222
Hyams, Robert Genoe 111622245
Hyams, Sarah Gayle 11162225
Hyams, Scott 1116222312
Hyams, Toni 1116222432
Hyams, Vallerie Gaiennic 1116222
Hyams, Vallerie Gaiennic, Jr. 11162224
Hyams, Vallerie Mathilda 11162221
Hyams, William Henry 111622243
Hylton, Rebecca Ann 24142a2111

-I-

Iglehart, Anabel 111794212
Iglehart, Berry 1117942
Iglehart, Charlotte Marguerite Thomas 11179421
Iglehart, Deborah Ellen Patterson 11179422
Iglehart, Edward Scott 11179421
Iglehart, Eleanor Washington Scott 1117942
Iglehart, Robert Eden 11179422
Iglehart, Thomas Dylan Scott 111794211
Ingram, Mr. 1326281
Ingram, Carter 64113g2
Ingram, Hallie Abell Couch 1326281
Irby, Bruce Watson 219157143
Irby, Joan Marie Broomell 219157141
Irby, Mary Elizabeth 1327x
Irby, Robert Cannon, Jr. 21915714
Irby, Robert Cannon III 219157141
Irby, Sarah Duncan Weisiger 21915714
Irby, Stuart Duncan 219157142
Irvin, James M. 174314
Irvin, Sue Emma Johnson 174314
Irvine, Edward 1321121
Irvine, Sarah Dixon 1321121
Irving, Rev. 244214
Irving, Charles 2431
Irving, Dr. Charles Robert 563614
Irving, Courtney 563612
Irving, Delia Eldridge 5614
Irving, Dorothy 5636111
Irving, Dorothy Wingfield 563611
Irving, Elizabeth Logan Bentley 563614
Irving, Henry Page 2424a
Irving, Henry Page, Jr. 2424a3
Irving, Ida Clark Turner 56361
Irving, James H. 2424a1
Irving, John Turner 563613
Irving, Joseph Kincaid 56141, 56361
Irving, Joseph Kincaid, Jr. 563611
Irving, Joseph Kincaid 2424a2
Irving, Lillian McPhail 244214
Irving, Mary J. Kincaid 2431
Irving, Robert Kincaid 5614
Irving, Willianna Harrison 2424b
Irwin, Angela Elaine E231x91121
Irwin, Christopher Jefferson 24146311211
Irwin, Katherine Seward 24146311212
Irwin, Rachel 24246453
Irwin, Richard Duckworth 2414631121
Irwin, Virginia Jefferson Davis 2414631121
Isaacs, Helen Carpenter 24144351
Iseman, Ann Kenneth 111x26112
Iseman, Catherine Carter 111x26111
Iseman, Franklin Carter Blackford 111x2611
Iseman, Ray 111x2611
Ishizaka, Sally Telfer 2424545231
Ishizaka, Yutaka Matsuura 2424545231
Isinger, Marianne Fairfax Lewis Larson 111344221
Isinger, Robert Davis II 1113442212
Isinger, William 111344221
Izlar, Ellen Ross 65111152

-J-

Jackson, Alexander 1322131
Jackson, Andrew McDonald 22311
Jackson, Charles Pollard 1322127
Jackson, Charlie Richard 1333121922322
Jackson, Deborah Newell 241x123222
Jackson, Edward Randolph 21915a2
Jackson, Eleanor Kirkman 1322125
Jackson, Eleanor Pendleton 241522121
Jackson, Elizabeth 1322129
Jackson, Elizabeth 1322132
Jackson, Elizabeth Eleanor Crawford 24152212
Jackson, Elizabeth Perkins 132212
Jackson, Elizabeth ("Betty") Starr 65111151
Jackson, Freda Darby 32312115
Jackson, George Moore 132213
Jackson, J. E. 21915a

Luce, Addison Leech 32314251
Luce, Addison Leech, Jr. 323142514
Luce, Caroline Ayres 323142513
Luce, Isabel Byrd 323142511
Luce, Sally Tazewell 323142512
Luce, Sally Tazewell Waller 32314251
Lucks, Hortense 241411135
Ludlam, Mary P. 2191594
Ludy, Adelaide Randolph Miller Coiner 24142x2212
Ludy, Kitchel 24142x2212
Lueby, Caroline Reese 13312119224
Lund, Alfred 241411322
Lund, Dixie Annette Wells 241411322
Luney, Mary B. 2421873
Lunsford, Grace Irving 11132623
Lusk, Virginia 512229

Lutz, Eleanor Hunter 124129
Lyman, Ellen Dorothea Strong 241462
Lynch, Cary Randolph Lamond Dillon 2414272111
Lynch, Elizabeth Friend 111322
Lynch, Francis J. 111322
Lynch, Joseph Antony Michael 2414272111
Lynch, Marie Jose 1117132
Lynch, Virginia Friend 1113221
Lyne, Peachy Gascoigne 24142a11
Lynn, Anne Catherine 111326322
Lynn, Barbara Gilsdorf 1113324121
Lynn, Bessie Jones 1113324
Lynn, Caroline Jones 111332414
Lynn, Charles Andrew 1113324123
Lynn, Dr. Clabe Webster 11132632
Lynn, Clabe Webster, Jr. 111326321
Lynn, Etta Donman Mann 111326332
Lynn, Elizabeth Moore 111332411
Lynn, Grace Lunsford Friend 11132632
Lynn, Gretchen Sue Hoff 1113324122
Lynn, Henry Fairfax, Jr. 1113324
Lynn, Henry Fairfax, Jr. 111332412
Lynn, Henry Fairfax III 11133241
Lynn, Henry Fairfax III 1113324121
Lynn, James Clawson 1113324122
Lynn, Jean Dorsey 111332415
Lynn, Jean E. 111326323
Lynn, John Worth 111326322
Lynn, Lillian Hunter 111344
Lynn, Mary Eliza Dorsey 11133241
Lynn, Mary Frances 111332413
Lynn, Natalie Nell Clawson 111332412
Lynn, Norma Gilmer Schultz 111332412
Lynn, Robert Page 111326324

-Mc-

McAlexander, Polly 165322
McAllister, Jean Graham 2122142
McBride, Deborah Lynn 24142x2611
McBride, Marie Boggs 241513431
McCabe, Mr. 24142x2112
McCabe, Bonnycastle Smith 24142x2112
McCaffrey, Judy Fisher E231x91122
McCaffrey, Patrick M. E231x91122
McCandlish, Ann Banister 13113
McCandlish, Ann ("Nannie") Walke 251633
McCandlish, Anne 2516352
McCandlish, Anne Leake 251631121
McCandlish, Anne Walke 25163236
McCandlish, Anne Walke Sheild 25163
McCandlish, Anthony Walke 251631111
McCandlish, Caroline Nash 2516322222
McCandlish, Carolyn Hanson 251631112
McCandlish, Charles 251632222
McCandlish, Charles Sheild 251631
McCandlish, Charles Sheild, Jr. 25163112
McCandlish, Charles Sheild III 251631121
McCandlish, Charles Sheild IV 2516311211
McCandlish, David Bowen 2516323u
McCandlish, Doris King 25163235
McCandlish, Dorothy Jean Welderly 25163234
McCandlish, Douglas Putnam 2516314
McCandlish, Edward Gerstell 2516323
McCandlish, Edward Lindsay 25163232

McCandlish, Elizabeth 2516318
McCandlish, Elizabeth Lee 25163212
McCandlish, Elizabeth Putnam 251631
McCandlish, Elizabeth Rick 2516321
McCandlish, Ellen Archer 251631124
McCandlish, Evelyn 2516325
McCandlish, Evelyn Byrd 323133
McCandlish, Evelyn Hope 25163238
McCandlish, Frances Archer 2516311
McCandlish, Frances Archer 25163113
McCandlish, George Wythe 32313
McCandlish, Henry 2516351
McCandlish, Jane Charlton Graves 2516322
McCandlish, Jane Otway Byrd 32313
McCandlish, Jane Otway Byrd 323132
McCandlish, Jane Randolph 25163211
McCandlish, Jean Landstreet 25163239
McCandlish, Josephine Sutton 25163222
McCandlish, Karen Louise 251632343
McCandlish, Katherine 2516324
McCandlish, Lindsay 2516321
McCandlish, Margaret Belle 25163231
McCandlish, Margaret Lindsay Landstreet 251632
McCandlish, Mary Peters 251636
McCandlish, Mary Putnam 2516313
McCandlish, Mary Williams Smith 251632222
McCandlish, Mary Willing 323134
McCandlish, Maybelle Bowen 2516323
McCandlish, Nancy Friedberg 251631123
McCandlish, Peter David 251632342
McCandlish, Phoebe Grey 25163233
McCandlish, Rachel Hanson 25163111
McCandlish, Ralph 25163237
McCandlish, Randolph Walke 2516311
McCandlish, Randolph Walke, Jr. 25163111
McCandlish, Rebekah 2516322221
McCandlish, Robert Coleman 251635
McCandlish, Robert J. 2516322
McCandlish, Robert J., Jr. 25163222
McCandlish, Robert J. II 2516322221
McCandlish, Robert John 25163
McCandlish, Ruth 2516326
McCandlish, Sarah 25163221
McCandlish, Sarah Sheild 251634
McCandlish, Stephen Claude 251632341
McCandlish, Susan Lewis 323131
McCandlish, Susan Randolph 251631122
McCandlish, Thomas Wickham 251631123
McCandlish, Upton Beall 251632
McCandlish, William T. 13113
McCandlish, Winifred Thompson 25163112
McCann, James Grover 24241736
McCann, James Grover, Jr. 242417361
McCann, Julia Wickham Harrison 24241736
McCann, Wickham Nance 242417362
McCarter, Mary Louise 24142x17
McCarthy, Mr. E231x63
McCarthy, Hastings E231x633
McCarthy, Josephine Frances 552613
McCarthy, Mabel E231x634
McCarthy, Madeline E237122
McCarthy, Marsham E231x632
McCarthy, Virginia Dare 563633
McCarty, Maud E231x631
McClain, Annie 162528
McClain, Archibald 162529
McClain, Elizabeth 162526
McClain, Henry Jackson 162527
McClain, James Ballard 162522
McClain, Kate Atkinson 162524
McClain, Mary Garland 162521
McClain, Rebecca Dixon 162525
McClain, Virginia 162523
McClain, Virginia James Pollitt 16252
McClain, William 16252
McClain, William Pollitt 162521
McClennahan (McClanahan?), Anna McColley 251
McCleskey, Bertha Ann 2119232
McClure, Allen 165325821
McClure, Leanna 165325823
McClure, Michael 165325822
McClure, Nancy Ann Camper 16532582
McClure, Richard Leon 16532582

Murrie, Ellen Dane Brydon 641735
Murrie, Hilda MacLaren 6417355
Murrie, Laura Flippen 6417352
Murrie, Robert Brydon 6417351
Murrie, William Edgar 641735
Murrie, William Edgar 6417354
Muse, Mr. 55223141
Muse, Mary Tucker 55223141
Musick, Gayle 241492731
Mutch, Marion 25163421
Myers, Alice Gertrude Cutts 241b411
Myers, Charlotte Randolph Harrison 24245476
Myers, John Twiggs 241b411
Myers, Page Dickey Ruffin 2414243111
Myers, Richard Anthony 2414243111
Myers, Weaver 24245476

-N-

Nance, Julia Mosby Payne 24246451
Nance, Julia Payne 242464512
Nance, Louise Wyatt 242464511
Nance, Mary Ida 2424173
Nance, William 24246451
Nash, Mr. 244136
Nash, Alice Aldrich E237515
Nash, Andrew Joseph Whitwell E2375125
Nash, Anthony E23751121
Nash, Beatrice E23751213
Nash, Bernadette Corcoran E2375124
Nash, Catherine E23751312
Nash, Charles Reid 3231218
Nash, Charles Warwick Whitwell E2375124
Nash, Diana E23751311
Nash, Dorothy E23751216
Nash, Dorothy Fountain E2375132, p. 312
Nash, Edward E2375114
Nash, Ella Handley E237513
Nash, Ellen Hobson 244136
Nash, Dr. Elwin H. T. E237511
Nash, Elwin Peter Whitwell E2375123
Nash, Dr. Everard Tryon Whitwell E2375121
Nash, Florence 32312183
Nash, Foster E237515
Nash, Fountain E237513
Nash, Georgina E23751151
Nash, Gertrude Harvey E2375121
Nash, Gwendolen Osmaston E2375112
Nash, Hilda Barton E237512
Nash, Jennifer Rickard E2375113
Nash, John E2375122
Nash, John Michael E23751212
Nash, Joseph E2375, p. 312
Nash, Joseph E2375113
Nash, Joseph II E23751
Nash, Laura E237514
Nash, Laura M. Elwin E2375111
Nash, Laura Thomas E23751
Nash, Lorna MacFarlane E2375125
Nash, Mary E23752
Nash, Mary Byrd Marshall 32312184
Nash, Michael Peter E237512151
Nash, Moira Lee E23751215
Nash, Monica Mary E23751211
Nash, Monica Oldenshaw E237511
Nash, Nancy Collins 32312182
Nash, Neville E2375131
Nash, Paul Charles E23751243
Nash, Peter Joseph E23751215
Nash, Philip E2375115
Nash, Phyllida E23751313
Nash, Rachel Hall E2375115
Nash, Rebecca Coke 32312181
Nash, Rebecca Dorothy Elwin E2375, p. 312
Nash, Rebecca Francis Marshall 3231218
Nash, Rita E23751241
Nash, Robyn E23751212
Nash, Stephen E23751122
Nash, Susan E23751214
Nash, Teresa E23751242
Nash, Thomas E2375112
Nash, Veronica Sivaley E2375121
Nash, Whitwell Tryon E237512

Naugle, Caroline Cunningham Wardlaw 24244514
Naugle, David Randolph 242445143
Naugle, Frederick Barent 242445142
Naugle, John Jay 24244514
Naugle, John Jay, Jr. 242445141
Naugle, Thomas De Lacey Wardlaw 242445144
Neafsey, Daniel Glenn 24144317121
Neafsey, Donald Green 2414431712
Neafsey, Liza Hill Coolidge 2414431712
Neal, Anna Estelle Branch 5522384
Neal, Austin C. 5522384
Neal, Christopher Michael 251632331
Neal, Donie De Bardeleben 2414142121
Neal, Jeffrey Todd 2516323311
Neal, Jody Michael 2516323312
Neal, Julie Marie 2516323313
Neal, Marie Powell Payne 2424652
Neal, Mary Catherine (Kathy) 55223841
Neal, Mary Jane Corcoran 251632331
Neal, Mary Jane Wetzler 251632331
Neal, Nancy 2414131541
Neal, Randolph Harrison 242464522
Neal, Thomas D., Jr. 24246452
Neal, Thomas D., Jr. 242464521
Neale, Franklin Carter 111x261
Nease, Edwina Leroy Adair Smith 32311312
Nebel, Henrietta Jordan 51222a1
Nebel, Louis 51222a1
Needy, Rita 5645232
Neff, Andrea Katherine 241411271122
Neff, Fred Willis 24141127112
Neff, Katherine Jayne Smith 24141127112
Neff, Kenneth Edward 241411271121
Nelson, Agnes Harwood 32312112
Nelson, Ann Jeanete 552232122
Nelson, Beverley Tucker, Jr. 241533531
Nelson, Dorothy Jean Branch 55223212
Nelson, Elizabeth Sims 6417111
Nelson, Ellie Clark 6417113
Nelson, Elvira Ann Clark 641711
Nelson, Henry Allen 552232121
Nelson, Kenneth Marshall 55221312
Nelson, Laura Louise 552232123
Nelson, Mae 174a3114
Nelson, Mary Carter Randolph 241533531
Nelson, Mary Carter Randolph 2415335311
Nelson, Mattie Cary 2424723
Nelson, Page 2415335313
Nelson, Robert 641711
Nelson, Robert Williams 6417114
Nelson, Russell A. 55223212
Nelson, Sharon Rae Benedict 55221312
Nelson, Susan Gaye 552213121
Nelson, Thomas 2415335312
Nelson, Virginia Lafayette 6417112
Nesbitt, Blanche 24134521
Neurohr, Mary Lou 2414243521
Nevison, Catharine 152
Newbold, Alexander Maxwell 2414463224
Newbold, Amanda Lucille 24144632111
Newbold, Beth Weyman 2414463251
Newbold, Christine Marie Nigro 2414463253
Newbold, Cynthia B. 241446325
Newbold, Cynthia B. Newbold 241446325
Newbold, David Leroy 2414463252
Newbold, Donna Clare Marshall 2414463211
Newbold, Herman LeRoy 241446325
Newbold, John Cunningham 2414463222
Newbold, Julia Appleton 2414463223
Newbold, Katherine 241446323
Newbold, Katherine Hubbard 24144632
Newbold, Mary Cheney Crocker 241446325
Newbold, Mary Dell Mathis 241446321
Newbold, Mary Edith 24144631
Newbold, Mary Noreen Maxwell 241446322
Newbold, Peter Jefferson 2414463223
Newbold, Peter Mathis 2414463212
Newbold, Richard Coolidge 2414463225
Newbold, Robert Hubbard 2414463226
Newbold, Sarah Hubbard 241446324
Newbold, Sarah Lawrence Coolidge 2414463
Newbold, Stephen Randolph 2414463253
Newbold, Susan Crocker 2414463254
Newbold, Thomas 2414463

Pollard, Robert, Jr. 64114511
Pollitt, Ann Ballard 16251
Pollitt, Elizabeth Robertson Cabell 1625
Pollitt, James B. 1625
Pollitt, Susan 16253
Pomainville, Margaret 24134525
Pond, Barbara 241b4241
Pond, Blanche Loudoun Rives 574513
Pond, Charles 574513
Pond, Edward Rives 5745721
Pond, Florence Rives 5745722
Pond, Frank 574572
Pond, Hubert 5745131
Pond, John Daniel 574573
Pond, John Richard 5745132
Pond, Mabel Pollard Rives 574572
Pond, Ruth Albina Rives 574573
Pope, Mr. 221221
Pope, Eugenia 419213
Pope, Florence 419213
Pope, Jean Avona 165325x
Pope, Judith M. 11138
Pope, Le Roy Erwin 552746
Pope, Lucy 242413811
Pope, Mary E. Adams 221221
Pope, Mary Elizabeth Adams 2414b
Pope, Nancy 12211123
Popkin, Joseph Paul 5522135
Popkin, Mary Jane Branch 5522135
Popkin, Pamela Branch 55221351
Popkin, Paula Branch 55221352
Porter, Delia 2414631
Porter, Joseph Yates 241923
Porter, Joseph Yates 24192313
Porter, Joseph Yates, Jr. 2419231
Porter, Louise Curry 2419231
Porter, Marian 24192311
Porter, Marian Randolph 241923
Porter, William Randolph 24192312
Porterfield, John 24142a43
Porterfield, Julia Minor Randolph 24142a44
Porterfield, Mary Elizabeth 24142a41
Porterfield, Mary Hamilton Cooke 24142a44
Porterfield, Virginia Randolph 24142a42
Porterfield, William 24142a4
Porterfield, Wilson Randolph 24142a44
Portner, Anna 1332111
Posey, Martha 1624
Post, Ann Emily 2119267
Post, Charles Joseph 111x671
Post, Charles Joseph III 111x6712
Post, Christopher Crosby 111x67122
Post, David Penn 111x67111
Post, Elizabeth Gay 111x67113
Post, Janet Bowman 111x6711
Post, Kathleen Robertson 111x67112
Post, Kathleen Robertson Penn 111x671
Post, Nancy Elizabeth 111x67122
Post, Penn Robertson 111x6711
Post, Vicki Crosby 111x6712
Poston, Anna Rives 572121
Poston, David H. 57212
Poston, Frank 5721111
Poston, Frank P. 572111
Poston, Kate 572112
Poston, Mary Houston Schwar 572111
Poston, Mollie Rives 57212
Potter, Elizabeth 241c53
Povall, Winifred Anne Miller 51
Powanda, Elizabeth Duncan Moyer 2414226113
Powanda, Michael Christopher 2414226113
Powell, Beverley Meade 218121221
Powell, Cuthbert 16256
Powell, Elizabeth 162561
Powell, Frances 5142
Powell, Jane Randolph Megginson 1616
Powell, Mary Meade Apperson 21812122
Powell, Dr. Nathaniel R. 1616
Powell, Robert Linwood 21812122
Powell, Robert Linwood, Jr. 218121222
Powell, Sally 16161
Powell, Sally 242464

Powell, Sara Bolling p. 331
Powell, Susan Ballard 162562
Powell, Susan Belle Dixon 16256
Powers, Sarah M. 6526
Powers, Susan Gatewood 111x262
Powhatan p. 1
Poyers, Jane p. 4, 5
Poyntz, Bayard Gordon 1117a31
Poyntz, Frances Bernard Robb Upton 1117a31
Poythress, Elizabeth Bland 143
Poythress, Jane p. 4, 5, 325, 326
Poythress, Susannah 141
Poythress, William 143
Pratt, Anna Randolph McDonald 241531493
Pratt, Annie C. p. 328, 329
Pratt, Douglas McDonald 2415134931
Pratt, Mary 332151
Pratt, Lt. Col. Ogden Nelson 241513493
Pratt, Raelynn Carol 24141113321
Preedy, Anne Hallowell Richards 241443124
Preedy, John Robert Knowlton 241443124
Prescott, Elizabeth Tucker 24142x1
Preston, Anne Carter 2414131
Preston, Anne Carter 24141353
Preston, Anne Cary 24141316
Preston, Caroline Pocahontas Bernard 1117921
Preston, Corinne Roane Wills 24141318
Preston, Eliza Madison 241535
Preston, Elizabeth Blackford Scott 111792
Preston, Elizabeth Madison 24141314
Preston, Elizabeth Madison 241413183
Preston, Ellen Bankhead 24141313
Preston, Eugenie F. 2414131x
Preston, Hebe Carter Grayson 13213
Preston, Henley 241413152
Preston, Henry 2414131
Preston, Henry, Jr. 24141315
Preston, Henry III 241413154
Preston, Henry Donald 2414131541
Preston, Isadora 241534
Preston, Isaette Randolph 24141317
Preston, Jane 24141319
Preston, Judy 111346112
Preston, Leta P. Wilson 241413154
Preston, Margaret Brown 24141312
Preston, Mary Coles 24141311
Preston, Mary Helen ("Nellie") Carson 24141315
Preston, Mary Marguerite Carter 241413182
Preston, Nancy Neal 2414131541
Preston, Percy Thomas 24141318
Preston, Percy Thomas, Jr. 241413182
Preston, Robert Carson 241413155
Preston, Sidney 241413151
Preston, Sophonisba Grayson 132131
Preston, Virginia Wills 241413181
Preston, William 13213
Preston, William Ballard 111792
Pretlow, Clarissa Garrett 12214, p. 333
Pretlow, Dr. Thomas J. 12214, p. 333
Preuitt, E. K. 552623
Preuitt, Helen Martin Langhorne 552623
Prevost, Katharine Randolph 24217413
Prevost, Patricia Randolph 242174131
Prevost, Stuart Allan 24217413
Price, Andrew Gatewood 2211113
Price, Anna Louise Randolph 221111
Price, Anna Virginia 2211117
Price, Arthur C. 165325622
Price, Calvin Wells 2211116
Price, Daisy 1331144
Price, Dorothy Elaine Morris Lamar Smith 24142x211
Price, Elizabeth Bolling 1331143
Price, Elizabeth ("Queenie") Bolling Gilliam 133114
Price, Eugenia May 1117a5
Price, Florence Annie 2119231
Price, James Ward 2211112
Price, Joan Elfreda Vandergrift 165325622
Price, Morton 1331145
Price, Motie 1331145
Price, Motie Price 1331145
Price, Nannie Lee 1331142
Price, Nathaniel G. 1331149
Price, Norman Randolph 2211115

Randolph, Anne Cary 24141
Randolph, Anne Cary 24151x
Randolph, Anne Cary 241
Randolph, Anne Cary 24152
Randolph, Anne Elizabeth Carrier 2414927
Randolph, Anne Elizabeth Wallace 2122144
Randolph, Anne Page 213852
Randolph, Anne Randolph 217, 222
Randolph, Anne Robertson 11142123
Randolph, Anne Tayloe 21335
Randolph, Anne Tayloe Beverley 2133
Randolph, Annie Porter 2419623
Randolph, Archibald Cary 2416
Randolph, Archibald Cary 2421
Randolph, Dr. Archibald Cary II 242172
Randolph, Dr. Archibald Cary III 2421721
Randolph, Capt. Archibald Cary IV 24217213
Randolph, Armead 2221383
Randolph, Arthur Dillon 241x125
Randolph, Arthur Lee 2419613
Randolph, Arthur Lee 241961
Randolph, Dr. Arthur Moray 24198
Randolph, Augusta Ellen Granbery 2135
Randolph, Augusta Granbery 213521
Randolph, Augusta Lyell Blue 241x1235
Randolph, Barbara Hope 24196243
Randolph, Benjamin 22112
Randolph, Benjamin Burn 2415328
Randolph, Benjamin Franklin 2138
Randolph, Benjamin Franklin 2137
Randolph, Benjamin Franklin 24149
Randolph, Benjamin Franklin 2414925
Randolph, Benjamin O'Fallon 24153353
Randolph, Benjamin O'Fallon, Jr. 241533534
Randolph, Betsey Montague 2221
Randolph, Bettie Burwell 242171
Randolph, Betty Jo Burns 22213822
Randolph, Maj. Beverley 241533, 242141
Randolph, Beverley 241533561
Randolph, Beverley 21221421
Randolph, Beverley 2133244
Randolph, Beverley 24153352
Randolph, Beverley, Jr. 2415331
Randolph, Beverley Heth 125111, 242383
Randolph, Beverley Heth 1251111
Randolph, Beverley Heth, Jr. 2423831
Randolph, Beverley Langhorne 24142a2121
Randolph, Beverley Strother 212212
Randolph, Blanche Rose Turner 24153355
Randolph, Bonnie Sue 241x123711
Randolph, Brenda Theresa Cherami 241x12382
Randolph, Brett 213
Randolph, Brett 21352
Randolph, Brett 22
Randolph, Brett 2213
Randolph, Brett 2224
Randolph, Brett, Jr. 213523
Randolph, Brett, Jr. 217
Randolph, Brett, Jr. 222
Randolph, Brett Noel 22211
Randolph, Burwell Starke 2124
Randolph, C. 2118
Randolph, C. M. 1114212
Randolph, Calvert Stuart 24217411
Randolph, Calvert Stuart, Jr. 242174111
Randolph, Carmen Hevia Santos 2421783
Randolph, Carolina Ramsay 24142913
Randolph, Carolina Ramsay 241x1231
Randolph, Caroline Matilda Smith 2211
Randolph, Caroline Ramsay 241428
Randolph, Caroline Tyson Walter 241x124
Randolph, Carolyn Sayre 213843
Randolph, Carrie 21133
Randolph, Cary Ann 24142a213
Randolph, Caryanne Nicholas 241424
Randolph, Cary Ruffin 2414249
Randolph, Catharine Carrier 24149272
Randolph, Catharine Isham 24217a
Randolph, Catherine Cochrane 2215
Randolph, Catherine Erwin 213x22
Randolph, Catherine Erwin Jones 213x2
Randolph, Catherine Lawrence 2422
Randolph, Charles Wetherell 24151b
Randolph, Charlotte Nelson 2414298
Randolph, Charlotte Nelson 24142914
Randolph, Charlotte Nelson Macon 2414291

Randolph, Charlotte Nelson Marguethen 241429
Randolph, Chastine Morris 2221381
Randolph, Christopher 111421221
Randolph, Christopher Mayer 1114212
Randolph, Christopher Mayer 241518
Randolph, Clair Belle Eubanks 2221381
Randolph, Clara Eggleston 2419611
Randolph, Clemmie Cornelia 22213812
Randolph, Constance 24196x
Randolph, Corinne Albert Pickett 21384
Randolph, Corinne Pickett 213842
Randolph, Cornelia 2221386
Randolph, Cornelia Fleming 22212
Randolph, Cornelia Jefferson 24145
Randolph, Cornelia K. Wright 22213
Randolph, Cornelia Patterson 21225
Randolph, Cornelia Whelan 2211321
Randolph, Dana Grafton Kroyer 241x12382
Randolph, David Coupland 2441x
Randolph, David Coupland Page 24238
Randolph, David Coupland Page, Jr. 242382
Randolph, David Meade 212
Randolph, David Meade 2123
Randolph, David Meade 2122x
Randolph, David Meade 2411
Randolph, Debbie Ann 222138211
Randolph, Deborah Beatrice White 2421783
Randolph, Deborah Perry 22111
Randolph, Deborah Phyllis Cary 24217833
Randolph, Dorothy Atkins 2414926
Randolph, Dorothy Pearl 22213811
Randolph, Dorothy Willing 24217211
Randolph, Edmund Strother 212213
Randolph, Capt. Edward Brett 2132
Randolph, Capt. Edward Brett 21384
Randolph, Edward Brett 213x6
Randolph, Edward Brett, Jr. 213841
Randolph, Edward Fairfax 241533532
Randolph, Edward Fairfax, Jr. 2415335321
Randolph, Col. Edward Ryland 21353
Randolph, Erlantine (Maria?) Beverley 2113
Randolph, Eleanor 24196131
Randolph, Eleanor Gridley Taylor 2415322
Randolph, Eleanor Oviatt 2419613
Randolph, Eleanor Wormeley 213853
Randolph, Eleonora (Ellen) Wayles 241426
Randolph, Eliza Griffin Norman 2211
Randolph, Eliza Madison Preston 241535
Randolph, Eliza P. 2415344
Randolph, Eliza Pape Burwell 242177
Randolph, Elizabeth 2413
Randolph, Elizabeth 241982
Randolph, Elizabeth 24221
Randolph, Elizabeth 26
Randolph, Elizabeth ("Betty") 218
Randolph, Elizabeth Anna 22115
Randolph, Elizabeth Anne Leith 24217213
Randolph, Elizabeth Beard 24196
Randolph, Elizabeth Beard 241967
Randolph, Elizabeth Bland 213855
Randolph, Elizabeth Bland Beverley 2132
Randolph, Elizabeth Carrier 24149273
Randolph, Elizabeth Clark 24196251
Randolph, Elizabeth Frazier (Fraser?) 214
Randolph, Elizabeth Gibbon 21229
Randolph, Elizabeth Gibbon 2121
Randolph, Elizabeth Hamilton 2419624
Randolph, Elizabeth Jane ("Betsey") Montague 2221
Randolph, Elizabeth McIntire 24142a5
Randolph, Elizabeth Martin 2414x
Randolph, Elizabeth May Welsh Marney 11142124
Randolph, Elizabeth Meade 24234
Randolph, Elizabeth Page Craven 11142122
Randolph, Elizabeth Virginia 241x123522
Randolph, Ellen Wayles 24143
Randolph, Ellen Wayles 24144
Randolph, Elsie Mary Smith 24217832
Randolph, E. Mary Adams Pope 2414b
Randolph, Emily 2122143
Randolph, Emily Nicolson 213857
Randolph, Emily Strother 21221
Randolph, Emily Susan Keim 241518
Randolph, Emily Vaughan 22217
Randolph, Emma 213524
Randolph, Emma Beverley 21224
Randolph, Emma Herndon 21352

Simmons, Daisie Dean Winifred 5522337
Simmons, Douglas 111793114
Simmons, Frances G. C. 5522335
Simmons, Gale Dean 111622721
Simmons, John Bemiss 11179311
Simmons, Virginia 111793111
Simons, Dorothy 111x2134
Simpson, Edna Giels 111346
Simpson, Janet Mavis Weisiger 21915825
Simpson, John Ignatius III 21915825
Simpson, Margaret 64114121
Simpson, Phyllis M. Saunders 24144454
Simrill, Spencer 111x21323
Simrill, Susan Stuart Davenport 111x21323
Sims, Elizabeth 6417
Sims, Matoaca Skipwith 61241
Sims, Ruth Helen 174a3113
Sims, Col. W. E. 61241
Sinclair, Elizabeth Beverley 6521
Sinclair, Gilberta 6524
Singer, Alyce L. 165325x
Singer, Amy E231x311
Sioussat, Nannine Dove 219324
Sipe, Charles 56356
Sipe, Florence 56354
Sipe, Mrs. Gill 56356
Sipe, Henry 56353
Sipe, Katherine 56355
Sipe, Mary 56352
Sipe, Nora 56351
Sipe, Peter 5635
Sipe, Susan Bolling Eldridge 5635
Sivaley, Veronica E2375121
Skein, Ellen Gay 4131
Skein, Jacob 4131
Skelton, Clara 2424652
Skelton, Elsie M. 641121
Shelton, Rebecca Martha 613
Skelton, Susannah 32
Skipper, Eloise 174a621
Skipwith, Addie G. 1116215
Skipwith, Anne Robertson 1116
Skipwith, Anne Robertson 1116211
Skipwith, Beatrice DuBose 1116212
Skipwith, Cornelia Lotte 6124, 6523
Skipwith, Edna Earl 1116213
Skipwith, Eliza Bolling 11161
Skipwith, Eliza Bolling 1116222
Skipwith, Ella D. 1116225
Skipwith, Emma Darrieux (Doring?) 6125
Skipwith, Dr. George N. 6123
Skipwith, George N., Jr. 61231
Skipwith, George Nicholas 612
Skipwith, Dr. Henry 1116
Skipwith, Henry, Jr. 11162
Skipwith, Henry III 111621
Skipwith, Jane Dick DuBose 111621
Skipwith, Jane Rolfe Bolling 2194, 6121, p. 328
Skipwith, John Killian 111622
Skipwith, John Killian, Jr. 1116223
Skipwith, John McKowen 1116216
Skipwith, Lelia 1112
Skipwith, Lillian R. 1116226
Skipwith, Maria Louisa Brooks 6123
Skipwith, Martha E. Killian 11162
Skipwith, Martha Elizabeth 1116227
Skipwith, Mary 2422
Skipwith, Mary Elizabeth ("Lizzie") Bolling Jones 21922, 6121, p. 328
Skipwith, Mary ("Polly") Murray 612
Skipwith, Matoaca 61241
Skipwith, Mattie Bell 1116214
Skipwith, Oliver Gayle 1116228
Skipwith, Pennie 111622242
Skipwith, Powhatan (Thomas?) 11164
Skipwith, Robert 21922, 2194, 6121, p. 328
Skipwith, Sara Victoria Gayle 111622
Skipwith, Sarah ("Sally") Victoria 1116224
Skipwith, Thomas Bolling 6125
Skipwith, Thomas Bolling 61251
Skipwith, William Henry 1116221
Skipwith, William Murray 6122
Skipwith, Dr. William Robertson 11163
Skipwith, Wyndham Robertson 111623
Skylstead, Elsie 242152122
Skylstead, Elsie Francis Lee 24215212

Skylstead, Ralph Frederick 24215212
Skylstead, Suzannehea 242152121
Slade, Agnes 21151
Slade, Landry Thomas 241x12351
Slade, Lawrence Randolph 241x123512
Slade, Lyell Landry 241x123511
Slade, Virginia Hyland Randolph 241x12351
Slade, William Learned 241x123513
Slater, Anna 221115
Slater, Grace Langhorne 6417324
Slaughter, Betsey Holcombe Worden 111x887
Slaughter, Charles Hubard 24149121
Slaughter, Evelyn Morman Meech 24149121
Slaughter, Isaetta Pandolph 24149122
Slaughter, John 2414912
Slaughter, Susan Bolling Hubard 2414911
Slaughter, Turner A. 111x887
Sledge, Frances Manning 21352212
Sloan, Ann 21192672
Sloan, Ann Emily Post 2119267
Sloan, Berkeley Carter 2119264
Sloan, Berkeley Carter 2119267
Sloan, Edward Anderson 241x112132
Sloan, Eugene Williams 2119265
Sloan, Grace Edminston Switzer 2119265
Sloan, Isabel Scott Anderson 241x11213
Sloan, Isla 2119261
Sloan, James Melnoth 211926
Sloan, James Turner, Jr. 241x11213
Sloan, Louise Williams 241x112131
Sloan, Lucia Landon 2119262
Sloan, Mary Carter 2119268
Sloan, Mary Harwar Carter 211926
Sloan, Melmoth 2119263
Sloan, Mildred 2119266
Sloan, William Carter 2119267
Smart, Elizabeth Gibbons 24153162
Smiley, Mr. 61122
Smiley, Mary Murray Robinson 61122
Smith, Adelaide Leigh 24142x2613
Smith, Adelaide Morris Cooley 24142x261
Smith, Agnes Williams 24217113
Smith, Amey Pendleton 418321
Smith, Ann Williams 24217116
Smith, Archibald Cary 241c21
Smith, Archibald Magill 1344111
Smith, Archibald Magill, Jr. 13441114
Smith, Barbara Hope Almond 4192117
Smith, Benjamin Bartow 332522
Smith, Bernard Carter 11133242
Smith, Bettie 2421711
Smith, Bettie Burwell Randolph 242171
Smith, Bettie Smith 2421711
Smith, Betty Randolph 2421715
Smith, Blanche Weissinger 24244524
Smith, Bonnie Sue Randolph 241x123711
Smith, Bonnycastle 24142x2112
Smith, Cabell 1327231
Smith, Calvin Samuel 13312119112
Smith, Calvin Samuel II 133121191121
Smith, Carl Kemble 24141127115
Smith, Caroline Matilda 2211
Smith, Carolyn Patricia 2414224221
Smith, Carrington 1327232
Smith, Carroll Payne 416311
Smith, Cary Ambler 241428212
Smith, Charles Magill 13441112
Smith, Dr. Charles Mason 24142721
Smith, Clemence Griffith 24141126
Smith, Columbia 11171412
Smith, Cora 162553
Smith, Cynthia Sanborn 13441112
Smith, Cynthia Sanborn 134411121
Smith, Daniel W. 24142x211
Smith, Daniel W., Jr. 24142x2113
Smith, Dorothy Elaine Morris Lamar 24142x211
Smith, Rev. Edward Dunlap 241c2
Smith, Edward Henry 2414112711
Smith, Edward Henry, Jr. 24141127113
Smith, Edward Jaquelin 2414272
Smith, Edwina Leroy Adair 32311312
Smith, Edythe Lu 24141127111
Smith, Eliza Lockhart Eggleston 332522
Smith, Elizabeth 418322
Smith, Elizabeth ("Bessie") Winter Owens 11133242
Smith, Elizabeth Langhorne 4192112

-Y-

A

MEMOIR

OF

A PORTION

OF

The Bolling Family

IN

ENGLAND AND VIRGINIA.

PRINTED FOR PRIVATE DISTRIBUTION,

RICHMOND, VA.
W. H. WADE & CO.
1868.

CORRECTIONS
and
ADDITIONS
to

POCAHONTAS'
DESCENDANTS

by
Stuart E. Brown, Jr., Lorraine F. Myers
and Eileen M. Chappel

THE POCAHONTAS FOUNDATION
1992

Acknowledgements

Much of the data included in this volume was obtained from or through the assistance of the following persons and organizations: Richard Jeffery Alfriend III; Theodoric Bolling Alfriend; Sarah Dudley Alfriend Blackford; John A. Blakemore; Rev. Lineous Preston Bland, Jr.; LuLu Lee Morris Boggs; Georgia Bohle; Todd Bolen; Maj. Gen. Alexander R. Bolling, Jr.; Chester T. Bolling; William W. Boykin; Carolyn Fay Jordan Burke; Elizabeth Rives Allen Callaway; Thea M. Carpenter; Melinda Marshall Price Childress; Mary Archer Talcott Dodson; John Frederick Dorman; Pamela Hutchison Garrett; Georgia Department of Archives and History; James Roy Gordon; Mary Agnes Grant; Daniel M. Hawks; Katherine Stirling Cross Haygood; Eleanor Washington Scott Iglehart; Jefferson Randolph Kean; Carroll Shannon Blair Keiger; Keith A. Kelly; William D. Loving; Mary Bell Archer Mapp; Buelah Mae Weber Meredith; William Meredith; Patricia Mitchell; Martha Coleman Morgan; Thomas F. Norris, Jr.; Mollie Glass Pamplin; James S. Patton; William Archer Price; Joe A. Randolph; David R. Ransome; Dr. Helen R. Rountree; Parke Rouse, Jr.; Elizabeth Averett Robertson Arnold Rowe; Frances Robertson Piercy Seeley; Susan Rutledge Robertson Selby; Gus M. Sellars; Lisa Guignon Shinberger; Katherine Maury Stringer; John Hale Stutesman, Jr.; George Russell Talcott; Helen Sue Crabtree West Teague; William Thorndale; Irene M. Throop; Frances R. Trapnell; Jean Adams Trent; David P. Werlich; Elizabeth Wiggams (Library, National Maritime Museum, Greenwich); and Pamela Yancey Sparrow Williamson.

"blue" Bollings

The "additional twelve" children reported by some to have been produced by Col. John Bolling and by his wife Elizabeth Bland Blair Bolling (see POCAHONTAS' DESCENDANTS pages 329-332) have been referred to as the "mysterious" Bollings and some genealogists refer to all persons as "blue" Bollings who are among or are descended from the "mysterious" Bollings and who are neither "red" Bollings nor "white" Bollings (their last name may be spelled Bolling, Bolen, Bolin, etc.).

Introduction

Additions and corrections to POCAHONTAS' DESCENDANTS are included in this volume.

Any other suggestions as regards additions or corrections to POCAHONTAS' DESCENDANTS or to this volume are cordially invited and earnestly requested.

Please write to The Pocahontas Foundation, P. O. Box 431, Berryville, Virginia 22611.

Contents

Some Notes on Some Places

"Bolling Island" - Goochland County.

"Chellowe" - a photograph of a drawing appears in 19 V 21.

"Cobbs" - Chesterfield County on north side of the Appomattox
River, about nine miles below Petersburg.

"Conjuror's Neck" - five miles below Petersburg on north side of
the Appomattox River, and at mouth of Swift Creek.

"Jordan's"/Jordan's Point - Samuel Jordan, at an early date,
erected a dwelling on this tract which in 1657 came
into the hands of the Bland family. In Prince George
County on Virginia Primary Highway 156, running from
the southern end of the Ben Harrison Bridge to Virginia
Primary Highway 10, and then a bit on beyond.

"Kippax" - ca. 1900 dwelling (1001 Bland Avenue, Hopewell)
erected on the site of the Bolling home. Some years
ago, the gravestone of Col. Robert Bolling (1646-1709)
was moved to the family mausoleum in Blandford
Cemetery.

"Rolfe House"/"Smith's Fort Plantation" - Thomas Rolfe owned this
tract. Located on south side of James River in Surry
County, nearly opposite Jamestown. Present house dates
from early 18th Century.

"Varina" - said to be site of the home of Pocahontas and John
Rolfe. North side of James River, about six miles
east of Richmond.

Alexander R. Bolling, Jr.

On page 119 of his book, THE BOLLING FAMILY - EIGHT
CENTURIES OF GROWTH, General Bolling writes that "almost all
persons bearing the name of Bolling or related to that family
enthusiastically claim blood connections to Princess Pocahontas".
And on page 17 of his AN ADDENDUM he writes "that the majority of
Bolling/Bowling/Bolin/Bolen in America, though related to the
former occupants of Bolling Hall in Bradford, England, have no
relationship whatsoever to Pocahontas".

Errata POCAHONTAS' DESCENDANTS

NOTE: These changes are to be made in POCAHONTAS' DESCENDANTS.
       If a number is omitted, all names under that number are
       to be omitted from the Index to POCAHONTAS' DESCENDANTS.

2119, 211x, 211a and 211b are the numbers of four persons who are
    not descendants of Pocahontas and these persons as well as
    their descendants, all shown on pages 88-92 and numbered
    2119-211b9, are to be omitted.

Other Errata

Page iii Short Title. Pocahontas (dePasse engraving) in on
    page 79B.

Page 4 Omit "Judge" in lines 23, 26, 29 and 30.

Page 5 Omit "Judge" in lines 6 and 8.

Page 6 Jane Rolfe's dates: (1655-1676).

1251111 and 1251112 are to be omitted.

1332113113 Byrd (instead of Bryd).

1332113211 through 1332113214 are out of place and an arrow
    should show that they follow 133211321.

1332113221 through 1332113224 are out of place and an arrow
    should show that they should follow 133211322.

165316 through 1653162 Chermside (instead of Charmside).

2118 "a" instead of "c" (third line).

21811211 through 218112112 are to be omitted.

2221 Omit "Jr." This change is to be shown in the Index to
    POCAHONTAS' DESCENDANTS.

2312 Theodorick (instead of Theodorock).

241349 through 24134a are to be omitted.

241413181 Omit (d. 1928). Add m. 1928.

24142x41 through 24142x44 are to be omitted.

241491 Add (13423) at end of paragraph.

241492 Add (13426) at end of paragraph.

2415335321 1937 (instead of 1928).

242152321 Goolrick (instead of Gookrick).

552745 Raised (instead of raided).

58 is to be omitted.

6411121 through 641138 and 64114 through 6411452 probably should
be Baskerville and not Baskervill. This probable change
should be shown in the text as well as in the Index to
POCAHONTAS' DESCENDANTS.

Page 332 Last paragraph. Amelia Randolph born 1739.

Index Errata

Harrison, Archie 242413513

Robertson, John William Peyton, Jr. 111344353

Tinsman, Trace 111344351

Varweek instead of Varteek

The Elwyns (Elwins), The Booten Hall Portrait and Madame Zuchelli

On pages 310, et seq., of POCAHONTAS' DESCENDANTS an
explanation is made of the theory presented by Florence Miriam
Elizabeth Dorothea Wright Carson to the effect that Thomas, the
son of Pocahontas, had a daughter Anne, who was born in England,
and who married Peter Elwin V (1623-1695).

This theory is disputed by William Thorndale in his article
"Two Rolfe Negatives" appearing in the July-September 1990 issue
of THE VIRGINIA GENEALOGIST. And in the article Mr. Thorndale
approves the writing of Fountain Peter Elwyn (1862-1955) that
"The family of Elwyn have no descent from the marriage of Rolfe &
the Princess Pocahontas". 35 V 433.

As regards the Booten Hall portrait, mention is made "in
some undated journal supposed to have belonged to Peter Elwin"
(1729-1798), that Madame Zuchelli presented the portrait to that
Elwin.

Mr. Thorndale's further investigation reveals that Thomas
and Sarah Zuchelli were living at St. Marylebone ca. 1789-93.

But where did Madame Zuchelli (whoever she was) get the
painting and when, for whom and by whom was it done?

ADDITIONAL BIBLIOGRAPHY

NOTE: Books, etc., relied upon in whole or in part are noted either in the text, or in the following list, or in the Additional Short Title Index.

AMERICAN HISTORY ILLUSTRATED October 1978. Article: "An American Princess in London" by Gail Diane Cox

Barnett, Mary A. AUTOBIOGRAPHY OF MARY A. BARNETT AND HISTORY OF THE BARNETT FAMILY OF JOHNSON COUNTY (INDIANA). (1923)

Bibles in possession of William Archer Price: Bible of Thomas Jefferson Archer and Bible of Willie Eileen Archer (Mrs. Robert Watkins Price)

Bingham, Barry. DESCENDANTS OF JAMES BINGHAM OF COUNTY DOWN, NORTHERN IRELAND (1980)

Bolen, Todd; and Strange, Lois Bolen. THE BOLLING, BOWLIN, BOLEN FAMILY, IN AMERICA BEFORE 1800 (1987)

Bolling, Alexander R., Jr. THE BOLLING FAMILY -- EIGHT CENTURIES OF GROWTH (1990). Plus AN ADDENDUM.

Bradshaw, Mary Caroline. MY BRADSHAWS AND THEIR ALLIED FAMILIES (1964)

Brown, Stuart E., Jr. POCAHONTAS (1989)

Burns, Marilyn J. POCAHONTAS BLOOD (1983)
   An Index to ROBERTSON

CALENDER OF VIRGINIA STATE PAPERS. VOL. V, page 90

CHESTERFIELD COUNTY, VIRGINIA, WILL BOOK 4, page 244

DALLAS COUNTY, ALABAMA, MARRIAGE RECORDS. Book P, page 273; Book OO, page 137; and Book 11, page 242

DALLAS COUNTY, ALABAMA, GENEALOGICAL RECORDS. Vol. III, page 22

Ervin, Sara Sullivan. SOUTH CAROLINANS IN THE REVOLUTION

THE FILSON CLUB HISTORY QUARTERLY Vol. 27 (1953). Article: "Descendants of Ann Clark, Wife of Owen Gwathmey" by John Frederick Dorman

Grimes, J. Bryan. ABSTRACT OF NORTH CAROLINA WILLS COMPILED FROM ORIGINAL AND RECORDED WILLS IN THE OFFICE OF THE SECRETARY OF STATE (1967)

Groves, Joseph A. ALSTONS AND ALLSTONS OF NORTH AND SOUTH
    CAROLINA (1901), page 266

Groves, Joseph A. Letter 11/21/1899 to Mrs. J. H. P. Gilham

HEARST'S SUNDAY AMERICAN, Atlanta, April 12, 1931. Article on
    Bentleys, etc.

Hutton, Mary Louise Marshall. SEVENTEENTH CENTURY COLONIAL
    ANCESTORS OF MEMBERS OF THE NATIONAL SOCIETY COLONIAL DAMES
    XVII SEVENTEENTH CENTURY 1915-1975 (1976)

Jones, Kathleen Paul; and Gandrud, Pauline Jones. ALABAMA
    RECORDS Vol. 208. September 1962, page 22

Jones, Mrs. Mary Cunningham. Application for Membership Virginia
    Society Colonial Dames of America (1899)

Knorr, Catherine Lindsay. MARRIAGE BONDS AND MINISTERS' RETURNS
    OF CHESTERFIELD COUNTY, VIRGINIA, 1771-1815, page 5

Latrobe, Benjamin Henry. THE VIRGINIA JOURNALS OF BENJAMIN HENRY
    LATROBE 1795-1798 (1977)

Lawrence, James R. FROM POCAHONTAS TO THE BOLLINGS AND KRIMMS
    (1986)

MAGAZINE OF VIRGINIA GENEALOGY Vol. 23, No. 4, p. 39-41. Portion
    of article: "Genealogy from Classified Ads Abraham, Anderson,
    Cary, Dabney, and Jennings" by John G. Bell

MAGAZINE OF VIRGINIA GENEALOGY Vol. 23, No. 3, p. 3-16. Article:
    "The Descendants of Pocahontas: An Unclosed Case" by Elizabeth
    Vann Moore and Richard Slatten

Montague, George William. HISTORY AND GENEALOGY OF PETER
MONTAGUE, OF NANSEMOND AND LANCASTER COUNTIES, VIRGINIA, AND
    HIS DESCENDANTS 1621-1894 (1894)

POCAHONTAS TRAILS QUARTERLY Vol. 4, No. 2. Article: "My Story"
    by William Aubrey Rolfe

Potter, Maud. THE WILLISES OF VIRGINIA. A GENEALOGICAL ACCOUNT
    OF THE DESCENDANTS OF COLONEL FRANCIS WILLIS OF GLOUCESTER
    COUNTY, COLONEL HENRY WILLIS OF FREDERICKSBURG AND WILLIAM
    WILLIS OF SOUTHSIDE CRANY CREEK (1964)

Powell, Sara Bolin. FAMILY TRACE OF BOLLINGS (ca. 1931)

Randolph, Grady Lee. "THE RANDOLPHS OF VIRGINIA" (AFTER THE
    AMERICAN REVOLUTION)(1990)

Randolph, Wassell. PEDIGREE OF DESCENDANTS OF HENRY RANDOLPH I
    (1623-1673) OF HENRICO COUNTY, VIRGINIA (1957)

Rountree, Helen C. POCAHONTAS'S PEOPLE: THE POWHATAN INDIANS OF VIRGINIA THROUGH FOUR CENTURIES (1990)

Rountree, Helen C. THE POWHATAN INDIANS OF VIRGINIA: THEIR TRADITIONAL CULTURE (1989)

Thompson, Ralph E.; and Thompson, Matthew R. DAVID THOMPSON 1592-1628. THE FIRST YANKEE (1979)
    Apparently fiction as regards Pocahontas

Trube, Mattie Ellen Brown. YOUR FAMILY AND MINE (1967-1973)

22 V 332

34 V 161. "A Beverley-Randolph Family Bible (Record)"

93 V 14. Article: "From Virtue to Fitness: The Accomodation of a Planter Family to Postbellum Virginia" by John Burdick

96 V 193. Article: "Trip to the Virginia Springs. An Extract from the Diary of Blair Bolling, 1838". Edited by E. Lee Shepherd

99 V 81. Article: "Pocahontas and the Mission to the Indians" by David R. Ransome

34 VG 209. Article: "Two Rolfe Negatives" by William Thorndale

VOLTA BUREAU FOR THE DEAF, BOLLING FILES. Washington, D. C.

Walthall, Malcolm Elmore. THE WALTHALL FAMILY (1963), pages 21, 56, 57, 77 and 78

Watson, Walter A. NOTES ON SOUTHSIDE VIRGINIA (1925)

Weisiger, Benjamin B. III. CHESTERFIELD COUNTY, VIRGINIA, WILLS 1774-1795.

Werlich, David P. ADMIRAL OF THE AMAZON. JOHN RANDOLPH TUCKER. HIS CONFEDERATE COLLEAGUES AND PERU (1990)

West, Sue Crabtree. THE MAURY FAMILY TREE. DESCENDANTS OF MARY ANNE FONTAINE (1690-1755), AND MATTHEW MAURY (1686-1752) AND OTHERS (1971)

Winfree, Waverly K. GUIDE TO MANUSCRIPT COLLECTIONS IN THE VIRGINIA HISTORICAL SOCIETY. Papers pertain to:
        165 Blair Bolling (1791-1839)
        2193a Charles Edward Bolling (1852-1929)
        134 Linnaeus Bolling (1773-1849)
        Robert Bolling (b. 1759) who married 131 Mary Burton Bolling (1764-1787)
        113 William Bolling (1777-1849)

Wulfeck, Dorothy Ford. MARRIAGES OF SOME VIRGINIA RESIDENTS
1607-1800. Ser. 1, Vol. 6 (1967).

20 W(1) 207

Additional Short Title Index

MEMORIAL - 1833 manuscript: Memorial of Brett Randolph, Jr.
   (222). Reproduced herein

Corrections and Additions to POCAHONTAS' DESCENDANTS

1 Col. John Bolling. Elizabeth Lewis (1st wife) bapt. 5/7/1706.
  Richard Bland, Jr. (d. 1776).

111326111 Francis Elmer Drake, Jr., m. Christine Whyte
1113261111 David Lawrence Drake
1113261112 Jennifer Ruth Drake

1113261121 Rebecca Beverly Cunliffe
1113261122 Charlotte Meade Cunliffe
1113261123 Nathaniel Isaac Cunliffe
1113261124 William Jacob Cunliffe
1113261125 Robert John Joshua Cunliffe

111326123 William David Stewart, Jr.

111326513 Andrew Morrison Hassell II

111326521 Margaret Collier Cuthbert, m. David Tilghman Broaddus
1113265211 Susanna Everard Broaddus
1113265212 David Tilghman Broaddus
1113265213 Charles Cuthbert Broaddus
1113265214 Sarah Peyton Skipwith Broaddus
111326522 Charles Henry Cuthbert V, m. Elizabeth Morrell Allen
1113265221 Richard McIlwaine Cuthbert
111326523 Hibernia McIlwaine ("Mac") Cuthbert, m. William John
           Langley, M.D.
1113265231 William John Langley III
1113265232 Hibernia McIlwaine Langley
111326524 Nathaniel West Cuthbert, m. 1987, Bridget Maureen
           Burton

111326531 John Woodrow Davis, Jr., m. Joanna Arduino
1113265311 Christopher Charles Davis
1113265312 Kevin Kelly Davis
1113265313 Deborah Denise Davis
111326532 Archibald Graham Davis, m. (1st) Eleanor Braxton Cline
           (Div.). M. (2nd) Donna Tew
   Child by first wife:
113265321 John Lynch Davis
   Child by second wife:
1113265322 Ginger Blair Davis
111326533 Roger Pryor Davis, m. Bonnie Jean Fettes
1113265331 Amy Christina Davis
1113265332 James Woodrow Davis
1113265333 Catherine Jean Davis
111326534 Nancy Winslow Davis (1952-   ), m. William Cecil
           Bilbro
1113265341 William Christopher Bilbro
1113265342 Katherine Davis Bilbro
1113265343 James Hassell Bilbro

111326536 Katherine Burwell Davis, m. John Russell Perkins
1113265361 Elizabeth Winslow Perkins
11132654 Andrew Morrison Hassell

1113265421 Christine Jane Wishon (5/27/1986-   )
1113265422 Steven Wishon (4/   /1988-   )

1113321 Caroline Land Jones, m. Leroy Nutt Blackwell
111332112 Ann Gordon Blackwell, m. (1st) David Sanford
            Tillotson. M. (2nd) James N. McNeill
1113321121 David Sanford Tillotson, Jr., m. 4/23/1988, Barbara
            Ann Ely
1113321122 John Blackwell Tillotson (1956-1983)
1113321123 James Lee Tillotson
1113321221 Elizabeth Dicus Blackwell, m. Alec Breckenridge

1113324112 Walter Scott Richards, m. Diane Fortney
11133241121 Emily Mary Richards
11133241122 Philip Scott Richards
11133241123 Kyle Fortney Richards

11133241211 Julie Anne Lynn Gilsdorf
11133241212 Jacob Lynn Gilsdorf
11133241221 Tiffany Anne Lynn
1113324123 Charles Andrew Lynn, m. 1983, Cathy Hickman Hazlewood
11133241231 Charles Andrew Lynn, Jr.
11133241232 James Daniel Lynn

111332413 Mary Frances Lynn, m. Joseph Augustus Cheatham, Jr.
1113324131 Joseph Augustus Cheatham III, m. Frances Mary White
11133241311 Elizabeth Ann Cheatham
11133241312 Robert Cheatham

11133241321 Pamela Elizabeth Hooker
11133241322 Timothy Anderson Hooker
11133241323 Jonathan Anderson Hooker

1113441 Walter Holmes Robertson (1892-1941), m. 1917, Frances
          Lynn Dorsey (1893-   ). Frances Lynn Dorsey m.
          (2nd) 1949, Ernest J. Ristedt
11134411 Frances Robertson (1918-   ), m. 1937, John Morpott
          Piercy, Jr. (1915-1978). M. (2nd) 1983, Conway
          Loomis Seeley (1905-   )
111344111 John Morpott Piercy III (1937-   ), m. 1960, Gloria
          Ann Hutcherson (1938-   )
111344112 Gay Lynn Piercy (1941-   ), m. Louis Fernand Gagnon
1113441121 Louis Fernand Gagnon, Jr.
1113441122 Jennifer Lynn Gagnon
1113441123 Walter Holmes Robertson Gagnon

1113441311 Patrick Robert Haley
1113441312 Andrew Clarke Haley (2/11/1987-   )

1113441321 Meegan Anne Haley
1113441322 Timothy Sean Haley

111344135 Sarah Lyle Woltz

11134431 Charlotte Robinson, m. (1st) Walter Nelson Munster
          (1916-   ). Div. M. (2nd) Amos Teasley

111344313 Walter Nelson Munster, Jr., m. Coleen Gavin

111344342 Elizabeth Averett Robertson (1952-   ), m. 1974,
           Laurence Ray Arnold. Div. M. (2nd) Charles Daniel
           Rowe

11134811 Samuel Alexander Moore, Jr. (11/18/1918-11/5/1985)

1113621 Frederick Clay Robertson, m. Elizabeth Gibson Brown (d.
         1987)

Pocahontas Memorial Association

     The Pocahontas Memorial Association, formed in Washington,
D. C., on September 7, 1906, wished to erect at Jamestown a
statue of Pocahontas.

     The statue by William Ordway Partridge of New York would
cost $10,000.00.

     A membership fee of $1.00 was charged and the Association
sold badges, pins, buttons, photographs of "The Marriage of
Pocahontas", postcards, plates and official ribbons but the
Association was not able to have the statue ready for the 1907
celebration.

     Five years later, on November 18, 1912, Senator Swanson of
Virginia made a speech aimed at raising an additional $5,000.00
to pay the balance due to Mr. Partridge and finally, in 1922, the
statue was erected.

1113621112 Barbara Bradford Silk

111362112 Anne Robertson Buttenheim, m. 1988, Dat Duthink
111362113 Elizabeth Gay Buttenheim, m. 1988, James Edward
           Maxwell

1113621141 Andrew Kisielius
1113621142 Julia Gay Kisielius
11136212 Frederick Clay Robertson, Jr. (d. at 5/4/1988)

1113621211 Charles Clay Hulcher
1113621212 Carter Robertson Hulcher (d. at 3 months 1986)
111362122 Susan Rutledge Robertson, m. Edwin David Selby

111362221 Benjamin Robert Williamson, Jr., m. 5/14/1988
           Caroline Costner Crook

111362321 Elizabeth Burns Robertson, m. 6/23/1985, Jean Melancon

111381223 Wyndham Robertson III, m. Linda Alexander
1113812231 Richard Alexander Robertson II
1113812232 Wendy Robertson
111381224 Richard Alexander Robertson, m. Laura Joanne Wilder

1114212 Mary Frances Munro Bolling. Add, at end, (2415185).

11142122 Elizabeth Page Craven and Elizabeth Page Craven
          Randolph

1114241 Alice Stith Barksdale (d. 1983). Unm.

11142421 William Barksdale Baylor m. (2nd) Elizabeth Cushing
          Herring

111424215 Margo Hazen Baylor

111424513 William Barksdale Propert, m. 1977 Valerie Jean Hanson
1114245131 Matthew Barksdale Propert (12/20/1982-   )
1114245132 Emily Boyd Propert (5/1/1987-   )

111622241 Valery Gaiennie Hyams III

1117133 Guy Bernard Fenwick, m. Margaret Mary Griffiss (b. 1890)

111713351 Charles Cuthbert Fenwick, Jr., m. 1970 Ann Stewart
1117133511 Margaret Elizabeth Fenwick
1117133512 Charles Cuthbert Fenwick III
1117133513 Emily Stewart Fenwick
111713352 H. Bruce Fenwick, m. Susan Clarke

111793113 Bradford Simmons, m.
1117931131 Brian Simmons
111793114 Douglas Simmons, m. Melania

111x212 Rebecca Selden Lloyd, m. Gavin Hadden (1888-1956)
111x2121 Gavin Hadden, Jr. (d. 1982)
111x21211 Gavin Hadden III, m.
111x212111 Rebecca Hadden (1975-   )

111x212112 Melissa Hadden (1977-   )
111x212113 Gavin Hadden IV (1981-   )
111x21212 Linda Hadden, m. Ty Shen (1946-   )
111x212121 Christopher Shen (1976-   )
111x212122 Victoria Shen (1978-   )
111x212123 Sarah Shen (1981-   )
111x21213 Susan Gay Hadden, m. Theodore Woodcock (1942-   )
111x212131 Rebecca Woodcock
111x212132 Elizabeth Woodcock

111x21222 Nicholas Loring Hadden, m.
111x212221
111x212222

111x21231 David Hadden, Jr., m. Lynn Carter
111x212311 John David Hadden (1981-   )
111x212312 Katherine Carter Hadden (1982-   )
111x212313 Alexander Carter Hadden (1987-   )
111x21232 Jeffrey Allister Hadden
111x21233 Ann Aspinwall Hadden, m. Samuel Richard Munoff (1952-)
111x212331 Alison Munoff (1984-   )
111x212332 Anthony A. Munoff (1987-   )
111x2124 John Lloyd Hadden, m. Katherine Folk (1920-   )
111x21241 John Lloyd Hadden, Jr. (1953-   ), m. Susan Dibble
111x212411 Reilly Alexander Hadden (1984-   )
111x21242 Barbara Hadden (1955-   )

111x2125 Gay Lloyd Hadden, m. Richard Armistead Watson (1928-   )

111x213321 Myra Gibson Batchelder
111x213322 Abigail Winston Batchelder
111x213323 Anne Lloyd Batchelder

111x21334 Churchill Gibson Pinder, m. Sally Reeves Gambill

111x411 Frank Reade, m. Jean Cunningham (-1988)

111x4412 Kenny Armistead Grandstaff II

111x4431 Mary Robertson Motley, m. David Gregory Kalergis
111x44311 James George Kalergis
111x44312 Hugh Camp Kalergis
111x44313 David Gregory Kalergis, Jr.
111x4432 Hugh Douglas Camp Motley, m. Kathleen Buchanan
111x44321 Sheila Motley
111x4433 James Coleman Motley III, m. Sandra Jackson
111x44331 James Coleman Motley IV
111x44332 Caroline Camp Motley

111x6442 Harry P. Baya, m.
111x64421 Matthew J. Baya.
111x64422 Paul E. Baya

111x812 Wyndham Bolling Robertson Lee, m. Margaret Francis
         Downing

111x81212 Beverley Norvell Farrar

111x81221 Gay Robertson Mayo, m. Christopher Lent (Div.)
111x812211 Dale Lent
111x812212 Larry Lent
111x81222 Michael Max Mayo, m.
111x812221 Patricia Mayo

111x813 Francis Lee
111x814 Lucy Norvell Lee

111x8882 Mary Stuart Worden (11/17/1955-   ), m. Bryant Brooks
111x88821 Jennifer Lynn Brooks (3/13/1978-   )
111x88822 Kristina Noel Brooks (12/23/1981-   )
111x88823 Bryant Worden Brooks (12/22/1985-   )

121 Martha Bolling, m. Field Archer (2/15/1773-1820), son of
     Edward Archer (d. 1/3/1790) and his wife Mary Walthall
     (b. 12/17/1742), and grandson of Field Archer (d. 1784) and
     his wife Elizabeth Royall (d. 1785)

         NOTE: Field and Elizabeth Archer had a son Field Archer
         born 7/1/1734 (Bristol Parish Register) but he is not
         mentioned in his father's will (1784), an indication
         that he may have died before 1784. Is this Field Archer
         (b. 7/1/1734) the one who married Martha Bolling? Or
         was she married to Peter Field Archer, a son of Field
         Archer (b. 7/1/1734)?

1211 Powhatan Bolling Archer (1806-12/3/1896), m. 12/18/1831,
      Margaret Jones Walthall. He m. (second) 10/21/1847,
      Elizabeth Featherstone Price (1/10/1810-2/18/1890). Miss
      Walthall and Miss Price were first cousins, being grand-
      daughters of Thomas and Elizabeth Featherstone Walthall.
      Miss Walthall's parents were Henry and Elizabeth Batte
      Walthall. Miss Price's parents were David and Cynthia
      Walthall Price (m. 12/9/1799)
   By first wife:
12111 Edwin Archer
12112 Jacob Archer
12113 William Archer
12114 Littleton Archer
12115 Thomas Jefferson Archer, m. Reeder Manning. No surviving
       issue

By second wife:
12116   Alexander Hamilton Archer (8/11/1850-3/8/1921), m. 6/4/
           1873 India Manning (9/30/1849 or 1850-1/18/1926).
           Mannings were sisters, daughters of Indiana Thompson and
           James Manning, Jr.

           In 1875, Thomas Jefferson Archer and Alexander Hamilton
           Archer purchased "Happy Retreat" in Dayton, Marengo
           County, Alabama. Home burned in 1944.

Blair Bolling List

        The collections of the Virginia Historical Society include a
manuscript, "Memoirs of the Bolling Family by Robert Bolling of
Buckingham Continued by Blair Bolling of Richmond, Va. 1833",
that contains a list, "copied from the Cobbs Family Bible", of
the children of Col. John Bolling and of his wife Elizabeth Bland
Blair.

        This Blair Bolling list ("BB") differs from the Volta list
as reported on pages 328 and 329 of POCAHONTAS' DESCENDANTS in
the following respects, and only in the following respects:

        Archibald Bolling - BB gives birth date 6/26/1730 (instead
of 1/26/1730*1731), and death year 1747 (instead of 1749).
        Elizabeth Bolling - BB gives Eliza (instead of Elizabeth),
and day of birth date 19 (instead of 10).
        Robert Bolling - BB gives birth year 1738 (instead of 1739).
        Ann Bolling - BB gives death year 1747.
        Edward Bolling - BB gives day of death 18 (instead of 10).
        Archibald Bolling - BB gives birth year 1750 (instead of
1749*1750)(2nd of that name).
        Jane Bolling - BB gives birth and death dates 8/6/1754-
7/29/1754 (instead of 7/6/1754-7/31/1754).
        Rebecca Bolling - BB gives birth date 8/6/1754 (instead of
7/6/1754) "survived five days only".

        Despite these differences, BB seems to confirm the validity
of the Volta list.

        These differences are not shown in POCAHONTAS' DESCENDANTS
or in this volume.

121161   Bessie Manning Archer (5/26/1874-7/13/1932), m. 11/28/
         1899, Edward Taylor Eppes
121162   India Reeder Archer (11/30/1879-12/31/1892)
121163   Willie Eilleen Archer (3/8/1882-1/28/1919), m. 4/27/1904,
         Robert Watkins Price (6/29/1878-11/8/1939), son of
         Robert William Price (12/27/1846-3/20/1896) and his
         wife, Martha Josephine Watkins (10/1/1856-11/28/1909)
1211631 Robert Watkins Price, Jr. (8/5/1907-7/3/1909)
1211632 Alexander Archer Price (12/3/1908-6/20/1909)
1211633 William Archer Price (11/30/1910-   ), m. 10/3/1936
         Rosalie Pettus (11/19/1913-   ), dau. of Erle Pettus
         (2/4/1877-7/5/1960) and his wife, Ellelee Chapman (8/
         19/1883-11/12/1972)
121164   Alexander Hamilton Archer, Jr. (1/25/1886-10/11/1937), m.
         5/20/1913, Mary Alabama Horn (12/21/1887-1969) near
         Uniontown, AL., dau. of Davis and Margaret McKnight Horn.
         Archer was a merchant of Dayton, AL
1211641 Alexander Hamilton Archer III (b. 2/19/1914), m. 12/13/
         1935 Frances Tibbs at Linden, AL (b. 2/14/1915 at
         Demopolis, AL), dau. of Albert Alexander and Frances
         Rembert Tibbs
12116411 Alexander Hamilton Archer IV (b. 9/7/1936 at Demopolis,
         AL), m. at Oak Ridge 8/31/1957 Winifred Trent (b.
         Charlottesville 3/20/1940), dau. of Floyd Perry and
         Irene Palmer Trent
121164111 Alexander Hamilton Archer V (b. 1/5/1961 at Opelika,
         AL)
12116412 Taylor Manning Archer (b. 11/17/1941 at Demopolis, AL)
12116413 Frances Anne Archer (b. 3/7/1946 at Oak Ridge)
12116414 Dave Tibbs Archer (b. 11/4/1948 at Oak Ridge)
1211642 Davis Manning Archer (11/12/1916-11/6/1943)(b. near
         Uniontown, AL), killed in action in Italy in World War
         II
1211643 Taylor Clements Archer (b. 11/14/1918 near Uniontown,
         AL), m. (1st) at Dandridge, TN 5/7/1954 Elizabeth
         Carpenter; m. (2nd) at Linden, AL 7/14/1958 Mary Rhodes
         (b. 6/5/1919 at Jefferson, AL), dau. of Dr. Charles
         Eugene and Leila Compton Rhodes
12116431 Terry Alan Archer (b. 12/31/1954 at Oak Ridge)
1211644 Margaret India Archer (b. 12/28/1921 near Uniontown,
         AL), m. at Bessemer, AL 4/28/1940 William Edward
         Auton, son of Wilkie Maughan and Rachel Maria Blake
         Auton
12116441 Davis Maughan Auton (b. 2/17/1945 at Gulfport, MS)
12116442 William Edward Auton, Jr. (b. 7/4/1950 at Birmingham)
12116443 Roy Blake Auton (b. 1/19/1959 at Bessemer)

1216 Field Archer
1217 Edward Archer

         On 10/14/1790, Field and Edward Archer, orphans of
         Edward Archer, chose Archibald Walthall as their
         guardian.

122 John Bolling. His wife, Mary Kennon, was the dau. of Col.
     William Kennon.

1221112 William Byrd Harrison III (d. 4/12/1927)

1222 Susan Barthurst Bolling, m. 1818 Dr. John Scott III, son of
     John (Jr.) and Elizabeth Rose Scott
12221 Elizabeth Rose Scott (-1872), m. Edward Scott III
12222 Pocahontas Bolling Scott (7/22/1825-12/5/1912), m. 10/22/
     1852 Charles Alexander Scott III, son of Charles

     Alexander Scott, (Jr.)(2/21/1810-1865) and Elizabeth
     Lewis Hudson Scott
122221 Daniel Scott
122222 Elizabeth Rose Scott, m. 11/19/1874 Thomas Perkins Gantt
122223 Frances Bathurst Scott (7/7/1859-3/13/1941), m. 10/18/
     1877 (or 11/18/1877) William Meade Lewis (3/26/1851-
     3/11/1932), son of Zachary R. Lewis
1222231 Elizabeth Rose Lewis (d. 1982/3)
1222232 Mary Bolling Lewis, m. John Cabell Doswell, jr.
1222233 Charles Scott Lewis, m. Marie Cranz
12222331 John Bolling Lewis II (d. 1979), m. 1955 Nancy Rose
     Creath
122223311 Nancy Meriwether Lewis (1956-   )
122223312 John Bolling Lewis III (1958-   )
1222234 John Bolling Lewis, m. (1st) _____ , m. (2nd)
     Blanche Strickland
1222235 William Meade Lewis, Jr., m. Patsy Johnson
1222236 Edward Bathurst Lewis, m. _____ Booker
1222237 Howell Lewis, m. Louise Bell
1222238 Nancy Langhorne Lewis, m. Walter Leake
1222239 Zachary Robert Lewis, m. Anita Warfield
122223x Daniel Scott Lewis (2/8/1883-12/15/1970), m. 10/18/1922
     Rachel Hill Spencer (b. 12/11/1898)
122223x1 Eleanor Louise Lewis (5/13/1930-   ), m. 9/9/1950
     James Boyer Ebert (7/1/1924-   )
122223x11 Nancy Lewis Ebert (8/10/1956-   ), m. 6/19/1982 Dr.
     Verne Allen Gray
122223x12 James Boyer Ebert, Jr. (12/11/1962-   )
122223a Robert Spencer Lewis, m. Sara A. _____
122223a1 Robert Spencer Lewis, Jr.
122223a2 Kevin Lewis
122224 Mary B. Scott
122225 Annie Langhorne Scott, m. 9/4/1885 Z. B. Lewis, Jr.
12223 Mary Kennon Scott, m. (as second wife) Edward Scott III

123 Edward Bolling m. Goochland County 2/17/1794.

124 Archibald Bolling (1774-   )

1241 Dr. Archibald Bolling (b. 11/5/1801).

124123   Anne Lee Bolling (b. 6/15/1867)(b. Wytheville, bur.
           Roanoke), m. Matthew Hawes Maury (d. 10/10/1930)(b.
           Owingsville, Ky., bur. Roanoke), son of Dr. Joseph
           Fry Maury and his wife, the former Elizabeth Blades
           Graves.
1241231   Anne Bolling Maury (b. Dayton, Tn.), m. John Allan
           Goodloe (7/16/1894-   )(b. Big Stone Gap), son
           of John Mills Goodloe and his wife, the former
           Elizabeth Byron Ferguson.
12412311   John Allan Goodloe, Jr. (3/8/1924-   )(b. Big
           Stone Gap), m. 9/4/1948 Joyce Hill (2/22/1927-   )
           (b. Danville), dau. of Aubrey Carl Hill and his wife,
           the former Agnes Pearl McNew.
124123111 Martha Bolling Goodloe (10/28/1952-   )(b.
           Richmond).
124123112 John Allan Goodloe III (8/8/1954-   )(b. Richmond).
124123113 Melinda Payne Goodloe (9/25/1958-   )(b. Richmond).
124123114 Mary Stuart Goodloe (11/2/1960-   )(b. Richmond).
12412312   Anne Lee Goodloe (2/12/1925-   )(b. Big Stone Gap),
           m. 8/12/1950 Kim Brooks Williams (8/19/1926-   )
           (b. Gloucester, Va.), son of William Albert Williams
           and his wife, the former Bessie Winston.
124123121 Anne Maury Williams (11/8/1951-   )(b. Richmond).
124123122 Kim Brooks Williams, Jr. (12/7/1954-   )(b.
           Baltimore).
12412313   Matthew Maury Goodloe (1/24/1926-   )(b. Big Stone
           Gap), m. 9/6/1952 Mary Jane Hogan (b. Seneca, Il.,
           5/1/1932), dau. of Martin Joseph Hogan and his wife,
           Zeta Margueritte Murphy.
124123131 Matthew Maury Goodloe, Jr. (9/29/1953-   )(b.
           Chicago).
124123132 Mark Holcombe Goodloe (3/19/1956-   )(b. Chicago).
124123133 Thomas Martin Goodloe (11/1/1959-   )(b. Chicago).
124123134 John Edward Goodloe (1/2/1961-   )(b. Chicago).

12412314   Elizabeth Spottswood Goodloe (9/14/1928-   )(b.
           Chester, Chesterfield County), m. 9/25/1948 Robert
           McCandlish Evans (7/21/1917-   )(b. Saluda), son
           of William Dunbar Evans and his wife, the former
           Virginia McCandlish.
124123141 Robert McCandlish Evans, Jr. (9/20/1951-   )(b.
           Lisbon, Portugal).
124123142 John Goodloe Evans (9/27/1953-   )(b. Richmond).
124123143 Elizabeth Bolling Evans (8/2/1955-   )(b. New York
           City).
124123144 Anne Fontaine Evans (2/24/1960-   )(b. Miami).
1241232   Lucy Logwood Maury (4/9/1903-   )(b. Dayton, Tn.),
           m. 2/23/19____, John Edward Moeling (12/31/1902-   )
           b. Lake Charles, La.), son of Walter Goos Moeling and
           his wife, the former Rose Green.
12412321   Lucy Maury Moeling (7/27/1934-   )(b. Chicago), m.
           Leslie Ralph Bishop (3/8/1928-   )(b. Chicago),
           son of Craig Leighton Bishop and his wife, the former
           Gladys Weisenberg.

124123211 John Leslie Bishop (10/19/1961-   )(b. Chicago).
124123212 Lucy Moeling Bishop (9/28/1963-   )(b. Chicago).
12412322 Sally Green Moeling (8/10/1937-5/28/1965)(b. Chicago),
    bur. Montgomery, Al.), m. Paul Pickard.
124123221 Elizabeth Moeling Pickard (5/29/1959-   ).

124127 Edith Bolling (d. 12/28/1961), and Edith Bolling Galt and
    Edith Bolling Galt Wilson

125 Mary Jefferson Bolling (1775 or 1779 -   ), m. Col. Edward
    P. Archer in Chesterfield County

1251 Peter Jefferson Archer (b. 3/21/1798), m. 12/22/1825 Martha
    Woodson Michaux (10/1/1801-1/22/1847).
12511 William Segar Archer (7/12/1843-6/18/1930), m. 1/17/1867
    Mary Finley McIlwaine of Petersburg, dau. of James R.
    McIlwaine and his wife, the former Frances Susan
    Walthall Dunn.
125111 Mary Finley Archer (5/17/1875-   ), m. 10/25/1905
    Beverley Heth Page Randolph (6/25/1868-1945)(242383).
    For children, etc., of Beverley Heth Page Randolph, see
    under his number.
125112 Liesa Bolling Archer (4/22/1886-1/25/1971), m. George
    Russell Talcott, Jr. (12/9/1882-12/ /1917)(241b161).
    For children, etc., of Liesa Bolling Archer Talcott,
    see under his number.
125113 James McIlwaine Archer (2/1/1868-10/17/1929), m. Memphis
    2/17/1909 Elva Sanford Bell of Memphis (11/27/1878-
    10/3/1933), dau. of Charles Nathaniel Bell (1856-1918).
1251131 Mary Bell Archer (6/28/1914-   ), m. Richmond
    6/9/1937 John Aydelotte Mapp (4/20/1913-   ),
    son of George Walter Mapp and his wife, the former
    Mildred Aydelotte.
12511311 Elva Archer Mapp (8/14/1956-   ).
125114 Peter Jefferson Archer (7/5/1871-2/27/1935), m. 11/11/
    1908 Cornelia Whelan Randolph (3/24/1874-11/9/1950),
    dau. of Norman Vincent Randolph and his wife, the former
    Louisa Whelan Reed.
1251141 Mary McIlwaine Archer (5/5/1915-   ), m. 6/21/1939
    John Grant Armistead, Jr. (11/8/1912-3/21/1978), son of
    John Grant Armistead and his wife, the former Rosalie
    Fontaine Jones.
12511411 John Grant Armistead III (7/25/1941-   ).
12511412 Peter Jefferson Armistead (5/27/1943-   ).
12511413 Robert Fontaine Armistead (6/7/1946-   ).
1251142 Norman Randolph Archer, m. Dorothy Bryant, and has one
    or more children.
125115 Martha Elizabeth Archer (b. 4/3/), m. John Durburrow
    Blair III, son of Adolphus Blair of Richmond and his
    first wife, the former Ellen Gray Beirne. For a note
    on Adolphus Blair, see 1 V 339.

1251151   John Durburrow Blair IV (1/27/1893-5/30/1976), m.
Genevieve Venable Lathrop (8/11/1892-1/27/1978), dau.
of Charles Pickett Lathrop and his wife, the former
Louisa Barksdale.
12511511   John Durburrow Blair V (12/18/1923-   ), m. Mary
Jackson Shepherd (11/11/1925-   ).
125115111 John Durburrow Blair VI (8/1/1950-   ), m. Karen
Margaret _____.
1251151111 Mary Winston Blair (5/7/1982-   ).
125115112 James Shepherd Blair (4/8/1952-   ).
125115113 Christopher Pickett Blair (12/10/1954-   ), m.
Kimberly Goodwin Livick.
125115114 Martha Elizabeth Blair (7/29/1958-   ), m. Ronald
Scott Thomas.
12511512   Charles Lathrop Blair (10/8/1926-   ), m. Patsy
Carroll Shannon (12/10/1928-   ), dau. of Dr.
Howell Franklin Shannon and his wife, the former
Evie Cuba Flannery of Richmond.
125115121 Carroll Shannon Blair (2/19/1954-   ), m. Joseph
Lee Keiger, III (10/9/1954-   ), son of
Joseph Lee Keiger, Jr., and his wife, the former
Martha Elizabeth James of Winston-Salem.
1251151211 Catherine Blair Keiger (6/13/1981-   ).
125115122 Charles Lathrop Blair, Jr. (4/6/1956-   ), m. Leslie
Kay Crickenberger (12/17/1956-   ), dau. of
Samuel Wilson Crickenberger and his wife, the former
Elizabeth Wood Bazemore.
1251151221 John Kemper Blair (9/13/1982-   ).
1251151222 Samuel Reed Blair (8/28/1985-   ).
1251152 William Archer Blair.
125116
125117
125118
125119
12512   Edward Cunningham Archer (b. 8/4/1829). For children,
etc., of Edward Cunningham Archer, see under 33242.
12513   John Walthall Archer (3/11/1827-3/9/1852)(d. Richmond).
12514   Jacob Michaux Archer (b. 12/22/1832), m. Miss_____
of Alabama.
125141   Dau., m. _____ Coleman.
1251411 Mattie Evelyn Coleman, m. Hudson Ford Bell.
12515   Sarah Walthall ("Sally") Archer (b. 4/3/1834), m. Robert
P. Archer of Amelia.
12516   Mary Susan Archer (b. 2/16/1831).
12517   Catharine Jefferson Archer (b. 8/10/1838).
12518   Martha Woodson Michaux Archer (b. 8/31/1840)(twin).
12519   Pocahontas Bolling Archer (b. 8/31/1840)(twin).
126 Jane S. Payne (10/20/1780-6/ /1806).

12x Samuel Bolling (ca. 1785-   )
12a Nancy Bolling, m. John Sizemore

126 Robert Bolling (1776-   ), m. Jane S. Payne (10/20/1780-
6/ /1806)

131   Mary Burton Bolling (4/30/1764-8/3/1787), m. 11/4/1781,
        Robert Bolling of "Centre Hill", Petersburg (3/3/1759-   )
        (of the Stith Bollings), son of Robert Bolling of "Bolling-
        brook", and his second wife, Mary Marshall Tabb Bolling
        (6/25/1737-10/14/1814), dau. of Col. Thomas Tabb of "Clay
        Hill", Amelia County. Robert Bolling of "Centre Hill" m.
        (2nd) 11/4/1790, Catherine Stith (1769-8/9/1795); m. (3rd)
        9/1/1796, Sally Washington (1777-10/2/1796); and m. (4th)
        11/23/1797, Ann Dade Stith (1778-3/18/1846)

1311   Mary Burton Augusta Bolling (d. 4/11/1853), m. John Monro
        Banister (b. 1783-d. 1/26/1832)

131113 Anne Banister m. Campbell Pryor of Petersburg.
1311131 Caroline Banister Pryor m. _____ Baker.
13111311 Caroline Banister Pryor Baker.
13114   Robert B. Banister, Surgeon U.S.N

13115   John Monro Banister, Jr. (3/14/1818-3/29/1907) b. Peters-
        burg, m. 2/1/1848 Mary Louisa Brodnax (3/20/1831-6/2/
        1897), dau. of William Henry and Anne Elizabeth Withers
        Brodnax

131151 John Monro Banister, III, Surgeon U.S.A. (in 1889,
        stationed at Fort Sherman, ID). M. (1st) Alice White,
        m. (2nd) Maude Edmundson.
    Child by first wife:
1311511 Alice Mary Banister, m. Herbert Buell of Raleigh, N.C.
    Children by second wife:
1311512 Maude Edmundson Banister.
1311513 John Monro Banister IV.
1311514 Edwin Banister.
1311515 Percival Banister.

131152 William Brodnax Banister, Surgeon U.S.A. (in 1889,
        stationed at Fort Grant, AZ). M. Mary C. Noltenius

1311521 William C. Banister.

131153 Robert Bolling Banister (5/19/1849-   ), m. Corrilla
        Nations

1311531 Mary Louisa Banister, m. T. H. Aldrich, Jr., of
        Birmingham.

131154 Ann Withers Banister (2/4/1857-   ). Unm.
131155 Mary Louisa Banister (9/10/1859-5/30/1947) b. Birmingham,
        d. Tampa, FL, m. 1/9/1883 Sterling Sidney Lanier of Mont
        Vale Springs, TN (7/24/1860-9/25/1917), son of Sidney
        Cooke Lanier (b. 1818 in SC) and his wife Mary Theodora
        Brown Russell
1311551 Mary Banister Lanier (1/10/1885-3/1/1980) b. Birmingham,
        d. Brownwood, TX, m. 11/7/1914 James Theus Munds (10/
        20/1875-7/13/1935 of Wilmington, NC, son of James
        Cassidey and Eliza Hill Lord Munds

13115511   Mary Lanier Munds (4/6/1917-   )(an only child), m.
           Rev. Aubrey Clement Maxted (4/17/1914-12/26/1989), son
           of Edward George and Sallester Sarah Ramage Maxted
131155111 Mary Melanie Maxted (11/30/1940-   ), m. Jesse
           Dailey Smith (5/27/1936-   )
1311551111 Mary Stephanie Smith (3/29/1961-   ), m. Gary
           Gene Gillette (12/20/1951-   )
1311551112 Laura Katharine Smith (5/28/1963-   ), m. Don
           Kennedy (8/27/1962-   )
13115511121 Melanie Miranda Kennedy
13115511122 Anthony Don Kennedy
1311551113 Ronald Paul Smith (12/1/1967-   )
131155112 Margaret Irene Maxted (2/13/1943-   ) of Houston, m.
           9/5/1974 William Allen Throop
1311551121 Stephen Patrick Throop
1311551122 Rebecca Marie Throop
1311551123 Phillip Nathan Throop
131155113 James Ramage Maxted (3/7/1945-   ), m. 9/1/1979 Mary
           Elizabeth Barringer (3/10/1952-   )
1311551131 Michael Cassidey Maxted
1311551132 Catherine Amelia Maxted
1311552 Monro Banister Lanier (12/9/1886-   ), m. 4/20/1910
           Katherine Beverly Leach
1311553 Sterling Sidney Lanier, Jr. (9/23/1888-   ), m. 6/24/
           1916 Elizabeth Anne Wilkinson
1311554 Russel D'Lyon Lanier (12/30/1889-   ), m. at Fort
           Monroe 7/21/1917 Martha Henrietta Gibson
1311555 Anne Banister Lanier (12/25/1899-   ), m. 6/20/1925
           Dr. William Campbell Blake
13115551 William Campbell Blake, Jr.

13115552 Anne Blake, m. William Harper of Tampa
1311556 Reginald Banister Lanier (4/30/1902-   ). Unm.
131156 Augusta Bolling Banister (1/25/1864-   ), m. Robert
           Slaughter of Lynchburg

1311561 Robert Slaughter, Jr.
1311562 Monro Banister Slaughter.

131157 Blair Banister (7/24/1866-   ), m. Marian Glass of
           Lynchburg (sister to Carter Glass)

1311571 Margaret Glass.

131158 Ellen Gordon Banister (6/4/1869-   ), m. Gustav H.
           Stalling of Lynchburg

1311581 Marie Overbeck Stalling.
1311582 Gustav H. Stalling, Jr.

131159 Reginald Heber Banister (7/5/1871-   ). Unm.

13116 Henry Harrison Cocke (b. Surry County, d. Dinwiddie
           County).

131163   Emily Cocke.
131164   Henry Harrison Cocke, Jr.

1322   Sarah Bolling Cabell (5/29/1786-   ) of "Repton", m. 11/
         14/1805 Elisha Meredith (10/13/1783-5/14/1861)(b. Coffe-
         delilah Community, MS), son of John and Ann Taylor
         Meredith. Moved to KY, to AL, and then to MS.
13221 Pocahontas Rebecca Bolling Meredith (9/18/1806-5/6/1838)
         (b. Hanover County, VA, d. Franklin County, AL), m.
         Franklin County 12/18/1827 William O'Neal Perkins (2/28/
         1791-11/2/1840) of Franklin County.
 See below, 132214.
132211 Thomas Harding Perkins (12/18/1829-8/1/1873), m. 7/5/
         1848 Louisa Hewitt (11/12/1832-5/18/1859), dau. of
         Patrick Henry and Elizabeth Armistead Hewitt of AL.
         Moved to MS.
1322111 Louisa Perkins (5/20/1849-10/13/1878), m. 11/16/1875
           Paul D. Owens.
1322112 William O'Neal Perkins (9/15/1850-9/ /1878).
1322113 Eliza Beth Pocahontas Perkins (2/16/1852-   ), m. 12/
         16/1868 Will J. Nelson.
1322114 Thomas Harding Perkins (9/12/1856-10/16/1878).
1322115 Sarah Cabell Perkins (9/18/1857-   ), m. 12/11/1877
           James Daniel Parmer (7/11/1855-   ).
13221151   Calvin Perkins Parmer (d. 7/26/1880, about 2 years
           old).
13221152   John Hewitt Parmer (d. 9/6/1882, about 2 or 3 years
           old).
13221153   James Daniel Parmer (d. 7/11/1883, a young child).
13221154   Ellen Cabell Parmer, m. 5/17/1922 James C. Farrell.
132211541   James Parmer Farrell (ca. 1923-   ). Home: Memphis.
132212 Elizabeth Ann Perkins (1/26/1832-8/18/1872), m. 10/5/1850
           Col. James Jackson, C.S.A., son of James and Sarah Moore
           Jackson (widow of Samuel McCulloch) of "The Forks",
           Franklin County, AL.

132214 Mary Magdalene O'Neal Perkins (9/9/1828-8/9/1835).
13222   Edward Moseley Meredith (6/24/1808-7/11/1824)(b. VA, d.
         Fayette County, KY).
13223   John Taylor Meredith (5/8/1811-1893)(b. Fayette County,
         KY, d. Prince William County, VA), m. Sumter County, AL,
         1838 Elizabeth Hooe Payne, dau. of Daniel and Elizabeth
         Hooe Winter Payne of Fauquier County. Lived at "Green-
         ville", Prince William County.
132231 Richard Winter Meredith (8/18/1839-   )(b. Sumter
         County, AL, d. West Texas, TX)("Black Horse Cavalry",
         C.S.A.), m. Mary Williams of MS. He was a physician,
         Prince William County.
1322311 Samuel W. Meredith.
132232 Elizabeth Daniel Meredith (8/14/1846-after 1908)(d. near
         Manassas, VA), m. Robert Howson Hooe.
1322321 John Meredith Hooe.

1322322   Robert Virginius Hooe.
13223221 John Robert Hooe (8/14/1899-   ). Home: Manassas, VA.
1322323   Daniel Payne Hooe.
1322324   Howson Hooe (d. age 16).
132233   Elisha Edward Meredith (12/26/1848-1/29/1900)(d.
          Manassas) M.C., m. Sylvia Contee of Maryland, dau. of
          Capt. John Contee, U.S.N.

132234   Alice Payne Meredith. Born VA.
132235   Thomas Semmes Meredith (8/12/1860-7/22/1922).
132236   John Cabell Meredith (1/27/1862-9/22/1920), M.D., Wash-
          ington, DC.
13224   Joseph Cabell Meredith (8/29/1813-8/14/1851)(b. Fayette
          County, KY, d. Greensboro, AL). Unm.
13225   Francis Dandridge Meredith (12/15/1815-10/9/1890)(b.
          Fayette County, KY, d. Chatfield, Navarro County, TX), m.
          Williamson County, TN 2/6/1840 Frances Brodnax (1/24/
          1820-1/26/1897), dau. of John P. and Jane Sharpe Brodnax.
          The Merediths lived in Sumter County, AL, from 1840 to
          1854 when they moved to Neshoba County, MS, and in 1873,
          they journeyed to Texas and to their permanent home in
          Navarro County. Family burials in Dresden Cemetery,
          Oakwood Cemetery (Corsicana), and in the family cemetery
          in Chatfield

132254   Frances Brodnax Meredith (2/4/1855-   )

132255   George Dandridge Meredith (12/8/1858-10/1/1943)(b.
          Neshobo County, d. Chatfield), m. Chatfield 12/24/1894
          Clare Randolph McCants (6/22/1871-10/1/1953)(b. Butler,
          GA, d. Chatfield), dau. of Jeremiah A. and Nellie Clay
          Edwards McCants of GA. Home: Chatfield. Raised and
          trained horses.
1322551   Frances Daniel Meredith (4/10/1896-   )(b. Chatfield),
          m. Chatfield 9/8/1918 Joseph Marchbanks Hodge (2/4/
          1893-   )(b. Chatfield), son of Robert Lewis and
          Mary Page Pannill Hodge. The Hodges came to Chatfield
          in 1850.
13225511 Frances Thelma Hodge (11/3/1922-   ), m. 8/14/1948
          Robert Nelson Jones (1/18/1924-   )(b. Schuykill
          Haven, PA).
1322552   Clara Nelle Meredith (3/5/1907-   ), m. (1st) Chat-
          field 10/19/1927 Cecil Latham Manning (10/19/1903-7/3/
          1965); m. (2nd) 7/19/1966 Charles C. Bradbury (5/11/
          1902-   ) of Fort Worth.

13226   Benjamin Cabell Meredith (2/8/1819-10/2/1873)(b. Fayette
          County, AL, d. Chappel Hill, TX). Physician. M. (1st)
          2/16/1842 Margaret Jane Brodnax (5/28/1822-9/23/1843)(d.
          Sumter County, AL)(sister to Frances Brodnax). M. (2nd)
          3/17/1857 Mrs. Evelyn Cheek. M. (3rd) 1860 Caroline
          _____ (b. 1824 TN). M. (4th) 2/14/18   Laura Lee
          Bell (b. 1847, AL). Doctor Meredith lived in Washington
          County, TX

Children by first wife:
132261 Margaret Jane Meredith (1/14/1843-1867)(d. yellow fever),
        m. 4/21/1867 Charles Morton of Brenham, TX.
   Children by third wife:
132262 Ben Meredith (1858-   ). Later lived in California and
        near Waxahachie, TX.
13227 Mary Ann Meredith (10/27/1821-2/26/1868), m. Sumter
        County, AL, 6/13/1839 Shelby Wayne Chadwick (4/26/1815-
        4/5/1854). Merchant of Greensboro, AL.
132271 William Henry Chadwick (10/10/1840-11/1/1867)(d. yellow
        fever, Washington County, TX).
132272 Shelby Wayne Chadwick, Jr. (4/26/1842-   )(d. Havanna,
        AL), C.S.A., m. 11/20/1865 Jane Comack of Hale County,
        AL. Chadwicks lived in Greensboro.

132273 Robert Alvin Chadwick (1844-1928), m. 1868 Nannie Wright
        (1844-   ). Lived in St. Louis.

132274 Edward Shelby Chadwick (1846-12/ /1927)(d. Mobile). M.
        in Denver.
13228 Thomas Jefferson Meredith (2/25/1824-2/20/1889)(b. Fayette
        County, KY, d. Navarro County, TX), M.D. M. (1st)
        Neshobo County, MS, 12/22/1853 Mary Elizabeth Brown (12/
        21/1832-7/30/1866)(d. yellow fever), dau. of George D.
        and Lucy Ann Greer Brown of Neshobo County, MS. M. (2nd)
        Neshobo County 10/17/1867 Mary Elizabeth Alderman (2/21/
        1836-3/21/1919), dau. of John and Elizabeth McDuffie
        Alderman of "Shady Grove" near Philadelphia, Neshobo
        County, MS. Dr. Meredith received his medical training
        at the University of Louisville. He and his wife lived
        in Neshobo until 1859 when they followed his brother
        Benjamin and his sister and her husband, Dr. Daniel
        Eddins, to Washington County, TX. In 1870, Dr. Meredith
        and his family moved back to Raleigh, Dawson and
        Corsicana, Navarro County, TX. Dr. Meredith and his
        second wife are bur. Oakwood Cemetery, Corsicana.
132281 Sarah Ann Meredith (12/6/1854-   )(b. MS), m. Joseph
        Newsome.
1322811 Joseph Park Newsome.
132282 Mary Ida Meredith (9/24/1856-1921)(b. MS), m. Joseph B.
        Park.
132283 Edward Cabell Meredith (2/3/1859-4/18/1860)(b. MS).
132284 Lucy Bolling Meredith (5/29/1861-1/1/1900), m. ca. 1882
        William Thompson Ware (1851-1893).
1322841 Agnes Ormond Ware (11/30/1885-11/27/1935). Unm.
1322842 Mary Meredith Ware (2/9/1855-1969), m. 11/22/1905 Robert
        Henry King.
13228421 Robert Henry King, Jr. (4/14/1904-   ), m. Irene
        McCarthy.
13228422 Emmy Lou King (9/18/1910-   ), m. 1937 Roy Louis
        Patton.
1322843 William Howell Ware (4/ /1888-6/4/1955).

1322844   Meredith Ware (10/4/1889-12/29/1967), m. 8/ /1913
        Carrie Arnold.
13228441   William Ware (1915-   ).
13228442   Mary Cabell Ware (1916-   ), m. (1st) 1937 G. Wallace
        Savage (-1948); m. (2nd) 1954 Frank Alson Metts
        (-1956).
13228443   Ida Bolling Edith Ware (1919-   ), m. (1st) 1939
              Jeffcoat; m. (2nd) 1944 William Irby Chamness.
1322845   Lilly Belle Cabell Meredith (10/24/1864-1937), m. James
        B. Buchanan.
13228451   Lucia Lee Buchanan (1/2/1886-1936).
132286   Petie Harrison Meredith (8/19/1872-11/19/1848)(b.
        Raleigh, TX, d. Galveston), m. 4/16/1893 Lochridge Lee
        Boyd (10/30/1870-2/17/1928)(b. KY, d. Mayfield, KY).
1322861   Lima Ross Boyd (1/29/1894-   ), m. 4/21/1917 Ernest H.
        Canon.
1322862   Joseph Meredith Boyd (1/7/1896-3/15/1956), m. 1/6/1925
        Bernice Mason.
1322863   Ervin Neblett Boyd (8/15/1898-7/18/1967), m. (1st) 12/
        26/1916 Aline Pryor; m. (2nd) 1931 Caroline Wise.
1322864   Lochridge Lee Boyd (1/22/1900-5/10/1969), m. Ethel

1322865   Cabell Gordon Boyd (10/25/1904-   ), m. (1st) ca.
        1930 Lavona Burris; m. (2nd) 5/ /1945 Juanita Thompson.
1322866   Ophelia Jane Boyd (10/4/1906-   ),m. 12/26/1931 Thomas
        Redington Chase.
1322867   Kitty Elizabeth Boyd (1/10/1910-   ), m. ca. 1944
        Homer B. Kline.
132287   Minnie Ellen Meredith (1/6/1874-2/20/1952)(b. Raleigh,
        d. Galveston, TX), m. 4/25/1909 Albert Dunning Brown
        (8/23/1877-3/21/1925)(b. Sedalia, MO, d. Texas City,
        TX), son of Elder Peter and Mary Elizabeth Shanks Brown.
        Mr. and Mrs. Brown bur. Oakwood Cemetery, Corsicana.
1322871   Albert Harrison Meredith Brown (1910-1910). Bur. Roger
        Mills County, OK.
1322872   Mattie Ellen Brown (10/14/1911-   )(b. Hammond, OK),
        m. Galveston 9/4/1937 (div. 1950) Robert Clement Trube,
        Jr., (11/24/1910-   ), son of Robert Clement and
        Elsie M. Schuster Trube.
13228721   Robert Clement Trube III. Home: Houston.
13228722   Jane Meredith Trube, m. 1963 (div. 1968) William Voris
        Bunker, Jr. Home: Tallahassee.
132287221   John Robert Bunker (12/11/1963-   ).
132287222   Constance Grace Bunker (6/28/1965-   ).
132287223   Meredith Ann Bunker (5/16/1966-   ).
1322873   Byron Addison Brown (4/30/1914-   ), m. 8/ /1946
        Evelyn Schlather Williamson (1/ /1911-   ). Home:
        Galveston.
132288   Thomas Stuart Meredith (3/7/1878-9/ /1960)(b. Corsicana,
        TX), m. 12/6/1897 Lavinia Alice Stewart (12/11/1871-5/
        /1960). Both born in Navarro County, TX. Last half
        of lives spent in and near Long Beach, CA. Bur. Garden
        Grove, CA.
1322881   Thomas Jefferson Meredith (9/13/1898-   ), m. (1st)

1920 Alice Brown; m. (2nd) Bessie Abbott.

1322882 William Henry Meredith (8/13/1900-   ), m. 8/30/1920
         Pluma Ewing.
1322883 Edward Ludwig Meredith (6/6/1902-   ), m. 1/4/1924
         Clara Mathis.
1322884 Martha Lillian Meredith (9/1/1904-   ), m. 3/14/1921
         J. C. Ewing.
1322885 Harold Franklin Meredith (9/14/1911-   ), m. 1/20/
         1940 Mary Jane McKibbens.
132289   Bessie M. Meredith (12/17/1875-1879). Bur. Corsicana, TX.
13228x   John Elisha Meredith (12/23/1879-1880). Bur. Corsicana,
         TX.
13229 Virginia Meredith (4/25/1826-1877)(b. Franklin County, AL;
         d. Independence, TX), m. 1/4/1853 (as his second wife)
         Dr. Daniel Eddins (1808-1867)(b. SC, d. Brenham, TX,
         yellow fever)(his first wife was Elizabeth Shivers of
         Greene County, AL). The first six children were by the
         first marriage:
         Henrietta Eddins (d. 3/4/1852, bur. Old Greensboro
         Cemetery).
         Nancy Eddins (1834-1838, bur. Old Greensboro Cemetery).
         Mary E. Eddins (ca. 1836-   )(b. AL, d. Grimes County,
         TX), m. ca. 1860 George H. Brown of MS (1832-   ).
         Jo Ann Eddins (1836-1838, bur. Greensboro).
         William D. Eddins (1841-1848, bur. Greensboro).
         Ellen Eddins (1848-ante 1890), m. George C. Scales
         (1840-   )(b. GA).
    The next children were by the second marriage:
132297   Daniel Eddins (1854-1854)(bur. Greensboro, AL).
132298   Elizabeth Eddins (1855-   )(d. Waco, TX), m. 8/17/1875
         Dr. Reddin Andrews (1/18/1848-   )(d. Waco), son of
         Reddin and Martha Box Andrews. In 1888, Dr. Andrews be-
         came Presidnet of Baylor University.
1322981 Mae Decima Andrews (1876-   ), m. Webberville, TX,
         1898 William Thomas Wood.
13229811 Sue Agnes Wood (b. Bastrop, TX), m. Ed Bristow. Home:
         San Antonio.
13229812 May Bess Wood, m. Leland Antes.
132298121 Leland Antes, Jr., of Austin.
13229813 Hallie Jack Wood, m. Bill Green.
132298131 Son. Houston.
132298132 Son. Dallas.
1322982 William Andrews (ca. 1880-   ), m. Mary Lou Kennedy
         of Bastrop, TX.
13229821 Travis Andrews (1904-   ).
13229822 William Andrews, Jr. (d. Houston).
13229823 Jack Andrews. Living in Abilene.
1322983 Daniel Andrews (12/23/1882-   )(twin), m. 12/28/1913
         Ruth Ford of Tyler, TX.
13229831 Ruth Dana Andrews (8/20/1916-   ), m. 8/3/1933 Russell
         Alvin Williams (-3/23/1960).
132298311 Ruth Ann Williams (6/8/1934-   ), m. Lloyd Richard
         Reeder.
1322983111 Ruth Ellen Reeder (5/25/1953-   ).

1322983112 Lloyd Richard Reeder, Jr. (12/23/1954-   ).
1322983113 Michael Ray Reeder (10/24/1956-   ).
1322983114 Susan Elizabeth Reeder (9/28/1959-   ).
132298312 Russell Alvin Williams, Jr. (6/16/1937-   ), m. 8/11/
          1968 Bessie Louise Rogers.
1322983121 Russell Alvin Williams III (3/2/1970-   ).
1322983122 Kimberly Suzanne Williams (9/28/1972-   ).
132298313 Daniel Walter Williams (1939-2/14/1941).
132298314 Ida Jane Williams (4/13/1942-   ), m. 1/30/1966
          Robert Dale Harvey.
1322983141 Jennifer Jane Harvey (11/5/1969-   ).
1322983142 Robert Dale Harvey, Jr. (4/ /1971-   ).
132298315 Tommy Jon Williams (11/12/1950-   ).
132298316 Randy Alvin Williams (12/30/1952-   ).
13229832 Daniel Eddins Andrews, Jr. (8/14/1921-   ), m. 4/1/
          1944 Mary Lou Ellen Wade.
132298321 Mary Elizabeth Andrews (3/21/1951-   ), m. 7/4/
          1971   .
132298322 Daniel Eddins Andrews III (2/1/1950-   ).
1322984 Reddin Andrews (12/23/1882-d. young)(twin).
1322985 Robert Andrews (ca. 1885-d. 18 months).
1322986 Virginia Meredith Andrews (ca. 1889-4/3/1964), m. 1/30/
          1910 Joseph T. Christian (d. 7/6/1959).
13229861 Joseph T. Christian, Jr. (12/5/1910-   ), m. 9/11/
          1936 Bernardine Henderson.
132298611 Virginia Evelyn Christian (11/11/1942-   ), m.
          8/3/1962 Irving Hayes, Jr.
1322986111 Richard Christian Hayes (6/7/1968-   ).
132298612 Sybil Faye Christian (1/21/1947-   ) D.V.M., m.
          7/16/1972 Dr. Donald H. Heise.
13229862 Madeline Elizabeth Christian (8/7/1914-9/15/1954), m.
          6/8/1939 Henry Alvin Jacobs.
132298621 Joseph Alvin Jacobs (7/24/1940-   ).
1322987 Josephus Green Andrews (5/14/1891-1950)(b. Lampassas,
          TX, bur. Dallas), m. 12/23/1913 Eula Lee Seay.
13229871 Josephus Green Andrews, Jr. (11/8/1914-   ), m.
          10/3/1936 Florence Crandall.
132298711 Lawrence Ross Andrews (3/16/1939-   ), m. 12/31/
          1960 Glenda Faye Hudson.
1322987111 Michelia Jo Andrews (3/24/1964-   ).
1322987112 Deborah Lynn Andrews (5/20/1966-   ).
1322987113 Lawrence Duane Andrews (4/ /1968-   ).
132298712 Charles Phelps Andrews (1/2/1941-   ), m. 12/8/
          1962 Colleen Frances Chambless.
1322987121 Jason Don Andrews (6/4/1968-   ).
1322987122 Mark Phelps Andrews (12/3/1970-   ).
1322988 Alice Morse Andrews (2/28/1895-   )(twin)(b. Bastrop,
          TX), m. (1st) 9/16/1917 Charles Albert LaReau (-
          d. ante 1929); m. (2nd) 10/16/1929 Oscar Jackson
          McCants (12/27/1875-5/9/1941)(bur. Chatfield, TX).
13229881 Charles Albert LaReau, Jr. (6/8/1919-   ), m.
          Betsy Crume.
132298811 John Albert LaReau (7/12/1944-   ), m. 1967 Pamela
          Karen Nansley. Home: Carrollton, TX.

1322988111 Britt LaReau (1/15/1970-   ).
1322989 Richard Warren Andrews (2/28/1895-   )(twin), m. 8/15/
         1925 Alvaree   . No issue.
132299 Sarah Eddins (1859-ca. 1947), m. George Morse.
1322991 Eddins Morse.
1322992 Katherine Morse.
1322993 Elizabeth Morse.
1322994 George Morse.
1322995 Sally Morse.
13229x Elisha Meredith Eddins (b. ca. 1860, d. Marlin, TX), m.
         Mattie Hinkle.
13229x1 Jesse Eddins.
13229a Daniel Stonewall Eddins (b. ca. 1862)(d. Waco, TX), m.
         Mamie Harrison.
13229a1 Alice Eddins, m. Carl Geyer. Home: Alexandria, LA.
13229a11 Carl Geyer, Jr., m. Katherine
13229a111 Katherine Blake Geyer.
13229a112 Carl Geyer III (ca. 1960-   ).

1327212 John Roy Cabell Coleman (twin), m. Helen Louise Hobart.
13272121 Martha Coleman (4/15/1915-   ), m. (1st) Richmond
         11/5/1938 Charles Amandus Howland; m. (2nd) "Locust
         Hill", Reidsville, NC, 12/26/1954 Carl Hilarius
         Morgan.
132721211 Charles Wilson Howland, m. Nancy Phillips. Home:
         Madison, Wisc.
1327212111 Karin Joylene Howland.
13272122 Lila Coleman (-   ), m. Harry Heard. Home:
         Danville
132721221 Helen Lee Heard (-   ), m. Hubert Etheridge.
         Home: Danville
1327212211 Ann Etheridge (-   ). Home: New York, NY.
1327212212 Janet Etheridge (-   ). Home: San Anselmo, CA.
1327212213 Tom Etheridge (-   ). Home. San Anselmo, CA.
1327212214 Patricia Etheridge, m. Monte Plott. Home: Atlanta
13272123 Hobart Cabell Coleman (-   ), m. Louise Lyles.
1327213 Daniel Coleman (twin).

133117 Emma Plunkett Gilbert Gilliam, dau. of Cornelius Gilbert
         and his wife, the former Eliza C. Stone.

1331173 Anne Eliza Gilliam (3/24/1873-11/10/1959), m. 3/6/1895
         Augustus Hunter Evans, son of John William Evans (Sr.)
         and his wife, the former Martha P. Wilkes.
13311731 Ruth Augusta Evans (3/12/1906-   ), m. 12/31/1924
         Clifford Morgan Trent, son of Powhatan Glover Trent,
         M.D., and his wife, the former Mary Ida Holley.
133117311 James Edward Trent (1/15/1926-   ), m. 3/20/1950
         Jean Adams, dau. of Leonard Boyd Adams and his wife,
         the former Robbie Shackelford.
1331173111 Douglas Morgan Trent (8/9/1956-   ).
1331173112 David Allen Trent (1/27/1958-   ).

134   Linnaeus Bolling (d. 1/7/1836). His wife, the former Mary
       Markham (1776-1825).   His name is sometimes spelled
       Lenaeus.
1342   Susannah (Susan?) Pocahontas Bolling (b. 1815), m. 4/16/
       1834 (by Rev. Cobbs) Robert Thruston Hubard (1808-1871).
13422 Edmund Wilcox Hubard.
13423 James Lenaeus Hubard (1835-1913), C.S.A., m. Isaetta
       Carter Randolph (241491). For their children, etc.,
       see under her number.
13424 William Hubard, C.S.A.
13425 Robert Thruston Hubard, Jr. (or II)(1839-1921), m. Sallie
       Edmunds (1850-1916).
134251 Robert Thruston Hubard III, m. Ruth Drewry Whittle
       (652185). For their children, etc., see under her
       number.
Note: 13425 ("Colonel") also had daughters.
13426 Louise (Louisa?) Hubard, m. Dr. Lewis Carter Randolph
       (241492). For their children, etc., see under his
       number.
13427 Philip Hubard.
13428 Bolling Hubard (d. 1896). Acquired "Chellowe" in 1933.

14   Mary Bolling (b. at "Cobbs", living in April 1801), m.
       Richard Bland III (d. 1776).

141   Richard Bland IV, m. 12/17/1787 Susannah Poythress (10/13/
       1769-   )
1411   Richard Bland V (12/21/1793-   )
14112 Peter Bland (1835-   ).*
14113 John Bland (1844-   ).*
       *Named in 1850 Census for Prince George County. There may
       have been other children born after 1850.
1412   John Bolling Bland (b. July 1798). M. (1st Mary Epes.
14122 Robert Epes Bland (1836-   ), m. Hettie _____.
14123 John Theodorick Bland (b. 1826).
14124 William Epes Bland (1/8/1828-7/16/1877)(from tombstone in
       Bland family cemetery at "Jordan's Point"), m. Sarah
       Russell (1/8/1844-6/7/1905).
141241 William Epes Bland (3/13/1864-7/4/1866).
141242 John Theodorick Bland (11/29/1866-6/29/1868).
141243 Mary Brook Bland (9/13/1868-5/19/1895), m. Richard E.
       Hite (his first wife).
141244 Sarah Russell Bland (10/18/1870-8/ /1904), m. Richard
       E. Hite (his second wife).
141245 Robert Epes Bland (7/29/1872-   ).
141246 Magdalen Picket Bland (6/19/1875-5/3/1958).
141247 William Epes Bland (5/26/1877-8/6/1877).
14125 Rachel (Magdalen?) Bland. Rachel's mother (Rachel Reed
       Bland) died when Rachel was two weeks old. 21 Virginia
       Genealogical Society Quarterly, No. 4, p. 156.
1413   Sarah Tazewell Bland (3/2/1796-   ).

1414   Theodorick Bland (9/24/1804-2/28/1859), M.D., m. Mary
       Brooke Harrison (6/6/1809-8/3/1860), dau. of John Harrison
       of "Woodlawn", Brunswick County. Dr. Bland's tombstone
       is in Bland Cemetery at "Jordan's Point".
14141   Theodorick Bland, Jr. (6/21/1846-5/30/1899). Unm.
14142   Susannah Poythress Bland (10/22/1837-d. young).
14143   Sally Bland (1/8/1844-6/7/1905).
14144   Anne Bland (11/28/1851-4/18/1900).
14145   Mary Cocke Bland (12/7/1839-   ).
14146   John Harrison Bland (10/6/1835-d. young).
14147   Susan Poythress Bland (3/25/1845-   ), m. Edward
       Temple.
14148   Pocahontas Harrison Bland (11/14/1842-   ).
14149   Dau. (5/ /1848-d. age 10 days).
1414x   Mary Susannah Bland (8/30/1849-10/8/1909)(b. "Jordan's",
       Prince George County, d. Petersburg), m. Petersburg 1/17/
       1871 George Ajax Armistead (7/31/1848-9/22/1934)(b.
       Prince George County, d. City Point), son of Fabian
       Armistead and his wife, the former Virginia Harrison.
1414x1 Virginia Harrison Armistead (1871-1875).
1414x2 George Clayton Armistead (5/27/1873-10/2/1958)(b.
       Petersburg, d. Roanoke), m. Mary White Graff (b. 6/14/
       1914 Buckeystown, MD.).
1414x21 George Clayton Armistead, Jr. (1/7/1916-   )(b.
       Roanoke), m. 1/11/1947 Margaret Skinner (12/28/1925-
             ), dau. of William Skinner and his wife, the
       former Margaret Bottomly of Holyoke, MA. Home: Pelham
       Manor, NY.
1414X211 George Clayton Armistead III (1/13/1949-   )(b. New
       York).
1414x212 Margaret Bottomly Armistead (6/1/1956-   ).
1414x213 William Skinner Armistead (12/2/1953-   ).
1414x22 Mary Bland Armistead (12/28/1917-   )(b. Roanoke).
1414x23 Anne Armistead (6/14/1920-   )(b. Roanoke).
1414x24 John Graff Armistead (1/13/1924-   )(b. Roanoke), m.
       11/21/1953 Maria von Mebes Perts (2/22/1928-   )
       (b. Riga, Latvia), dau. of Michael Constantine Akimoff-
       Peretz of St. Petersburg, Russia.
1414x241 Maria von Mebes Armistead (4/16/1960-   )(b.
       Washington, DC), m. Alexandria 8/7/1982 Mark David
       Frenaux, son of Charles Ray Frenaux and his wife,
       the former Evelyn Forman of Denver.
1414x242 Elizabeth Bland Armistead (9/19/1962-   )(b. San
       Diego), m. 9/28/1985 William Ronald Andrews, son of
       James Richard Andrews and his wife, the former
       Carol Grubbs.
1414x25 Theresa Simmons Armistead (8/16/1928-   ), m.
       Roanoke 7/22/1953 John Conrad Bouldin (7/14/1930-   )
       (b. Virginia), son of William Kennon Bouldin.
1414x251 John Conrad Bouldin, Jr. (3/2/1956-   )(b. Lynchburg).
1414x252 Robert Armistead Bouldin (12/1/1959-   )(b. Lynch-
       burg), m. 6/1/1985 Norcross, GA, Lisa Elaine Crum,
       dau. of Raymond Huff Crum and his wife, the former
       Joyce Kuhne.

1414x253 Mary Luciel Bouldin (7/31/1962-   )(b. Alexandria).
1414x3   Theodorick Bland Armistead (1874-1877).
1414x4   Mary Jeffrey Armistead (9/26/1876-2/9/1955)(b. Prince
         George County, d. Petersburg). Unm.
1414x5   John Clayton Armistead (12/17/1878-9/19/1964)(b. Prince
         George County, d. Petersburg), m. Petersburg 4/6/1904
         Estelle Ruffin Marks (d. 12/3/1957)(b. Prince George
         County, d. Petersburg), dau. of Richard Marks of
         Petersburg. No issue.
1414x6   Ann Harrison Armistead (1880-1882).
1414x7   Infant (1882-1882).
1414x8   Infant (1884-1884)(twin).
1414x9. Infant (1884-1884)(twin).
1414xx   Jeanne Banister Armistead (1888-1888).
1414xa   Sallie Bland Armistead (5/14/1890-8/8/1976 or 1967)(b.
         "Jordan's", Prince George County, d. Alexandria), m.
         City Point 6/20/1916 Thomas Fendol Norris (1/12/1877-
         1/7/1954)(b. Fluvanna County, d. Charlottesville), son
         of James Bernard Norris and his wife, the former Eliza
         Ellen Marshall of Charlottesville.
1414xa1 Thomas Fendol Norris, Jr.(5/31/1918-   )(b. Wilming-
         ton, DE), m. Charlottesville 1/9/1943 Margaret Nan
         Fletcher (5/28/1921-   )(b. Chatteroy, WV), dau.
         of Charles Lawrence Fletcher and his wife, the former
         Mary Virginia Bounds of Big Stone Gap.
1414xa11 Margaret Fletcher Norris (10/31/1946-   )(b.
         Charlottesville), m. Johnson City, TN, 8/25/1969 John
         Wayne Dotson (5/15/1946-   )(b. Tennessee), son of
         Woodrow W. Dotson and his wife, the former Evelyn M.
         Giles of Kingsport, TN.
1414xa111 James Richard Dotson (10/28/1972-   )(b. Spartan-
         burg, SC).
1414xa112 Virginia Anne Dotson (8/23/1974-   )(b. Spartan-
         burg, SC).
1414xa12 Mary Anne Norris (9/13/1948-   )(b. Charlottesville),
         m. Johnson City, TN 8/5/1970 Donald Blaine Sturgill
         (10/15/1946-   )(b. Wise County), son of S.
         Blaine Sturgill and his wife, the former Nannie
         Ellison.
1414xa121 Christopher Blaine Sturgill (5/18/1975-   )(b. Big
         Stone Gap).
1414xa122 Thomas Harold Sturgill (9/6/1979-   )(b. Norton,
         VA).
1414xa13 George Bernard Norris (3/6/1953-   )(b. Charlottes-
         ville).
1414xa2 John Armistead Norris (7/13/1922-   )(b. Wilmington,
         DE), m. Waynesville, NC, 7/21/1957 Allen Wilkerson
         Hart, dau. of Humes H. W. Hart and his wife, the former
         Lillian Mae Allen of Waynesville.
1414xa3 George Armistead Norris (10/14/1924-6/20/1944)(b. Wil-
         mington, DE, d. Grove, England).
1414xa4 Theodoric(k) Bland Norris (8/16/1927-   )(b.
         Harrisonburg), m. Erwin, TN 6/29/1955 Kathleen
         ("Kathy") Whitson (6/23/1929-   )(b. Tennessee),

dau. of David W. Whitson and his wife, the former
Belle Peake of Erwin.

1414xa41 Patricia Bland Norris (1/27/1958-   )(b. Washing-
ton, DC), m. Fairfax County 9/9/1978 Michael David
Lewis (2/7/1957-   )(b. Fort Bragg), son of Grover
Houston Lewis, Jr., and his wife, the former Elouise
D. George of Alexandria.

1414xa42 Priscilla Anne Norris (12/6/1959-   )(b. Washington, DC).

1414xa43 Mary Armistead Norris (9/15/1962-   )(b. Washington, DC).

1415 Mary Bolling Bland (10/16/1802-   ).

1416 Mary Burton Bolling Bland (10/22/1788-d. age 4 mos.).

1417 Elizabeth Bland (8/20/1790-10/17/1790).

1418 Ann Poythress Bland (11/27/1791-6/22/1806).

1419 Peter Poythress Bland (12/8/1800-   ).

142   Ann Poythress Bland (5/27/1765-   ). M. (1st) John
Morrison, and possibly had a son by Morrison. M. (2nd)
Peter Woodlief II, son of Peter Woodlief (d. 1777) of
"Deep Bottom".

   Children by second husband:

1421 Hannah Woodlief, m. Dr. Peter Manson Hardaway (living as
late as 1825, d. prior to 1831), son of William E.
Hardaway.

14211 Son.

1422 Ann Woodlief (1793-1860)(bur. Elmwood Cemetery, Norfolk),
m. Dr. Richard Jeffery (-1824), son of Capt.
Aaron Jeffery of Norfolk County, Captain of the brig
Bell.

14221 Dr. Richard Woodlief Jeffery (3/13/1815-   )(bur.
Blandford Cemetery). Surgeon in both U.S. and Confederate Navies. Unm.

14222 Aaron Jeffery (d. ca. 1865), m. Margaret Roberta (1825-
). During the Civil War, Aaron worked in
Richmond at the Tredegar Iron Works. He was survived
by his wife and seven children.

142221 Anna W. Jeffery.

142222 Robert Archer Jeffery.

142223 Fanny W. Jeffery.

142224 Mary Jeffery.

142225 Richard W. Jeffery II.

142226 Roberta A. Jeffery.

142227 Aaron Jeffery.

14223 Sally T. Jeffery.

1423 Elizabeth Bland Woodlief (1798-1874)(bur. Blandford
Cemetery), m. 2/27/1816 Dr. Shadrack Alfriend (-
1826)(University of Maryland Medical School), son of
Maj. John Alfriend and his wife, the former Martha
Manson.

14231 Peter Woodlief Alfriend (d. 8/6/1870). Unm.

14232 John Alfriend (1819-1873) of Petersburg (apothecary and
druggist)(bur. Blandford Cemetery), m. 6/8/1858 Eliza
Prentis Vickery (1834-1879)(bur. Blandford Cemetery),
dau. of Jacob and Anne W. Vickery.

142321   Rev. John Shadrack Alfriend (1859-1941), m. Eliza
          ("Lily") Daingerfield.
1423211   John Shadrack Alfriend, Jr., m. Eliza Harrison.
14232111 Rev. John Daingerfield Alfriend. M. (1st) Kitty Little
          Dupuy. M. (2nd) Nancy Clarke.
14232112 Gertrude Bolling Alfriend, m. Robert A. Kimbrough III.
14232113 Genevieve Harrison Alfriend, m. James C. Bryan.
1423212   Margaret Alfriend. Unm.
142322   Rev. Richard Jeffery Alfriend (10/1/1860-1/6/1923), m.
          10/12/1885 Mary Emily Hume (1869-1952).
1423221   Emily Hume Alfriend (10/23/1886-9/21/1972), m. 6/2/1908
          Hunter Ripley Rawlings (9/25/1883-2/29/1964).
14232211 Hunter Ripley Rawlings, Jr. (1/1/1911-   ), m.
          4/11/1942 Evelina Tucker Trapnell (9/13/1913-   ).
142322111 Hunter Ripley Rawlings III (12/14/1944-   ), m.
          1967 Irene M. Kukawa (6/ /1945-   ).
1423221111 Elizabeth Tucker Rawlings (5/25/1967-   ).
1423221112 Hunter Ripley Rawlings IV (8/1/1971-   ).
142322112 Rebecca Trapnell Rawlings (3/20/1948-   ), m. 1/1/
          1977 Mark Norman Jones (7/22/1952-   ).
1423221121 Marcus Colston Jones (3/16/1979-   ).
1423221122 Gordon Rawlings Jones (5/10/1983-   ).
1423221123 Frederica Tucker Jones (2/28/1985-   ).
142322113 Anne Tucker Rawlings (10/15/1953-   ), m. 5/25/
          1975 Kenneth A. Hindman (2/19/1951-   ).
1423221131 Matthew Rawlings Hindman (12/17/1982-   ).
1423221132 Laura Elizabeth Hindman (9/20/1984-   ).
14232212 Frances Bland Rawlings (11/29/1912-   ), m. 1/28/
          1939 Frederick Holmes Trapnell (4/6/1909-11/15/1979).
142322121 Frances Bland Trapnell (4/1/1942-   ), m. 4/12/
          1969 Robert Edwin Gayle (7/15/1942-   ).
1423221211 Robert Holmes Gayle (9/23/1972-   ).
142322122 Jane Brockenbrough Trapnell (5/29/1947-   ), m.
          8/7/1971 Martin Browne of England (5/27/1945-   ).
1423221221 Clinton Dodgson Browne (6/2/1973-   ).
1423221222 Holmes Trapnell Browne (8/26/1975-   ).
142322123 Emily Marshall Trapnell (7/30/1948-   ).
14232213 Elizabeth Claxton Rawlings (8/22/1915-7/8/1974), m.
          4/30/1938 James Elbert Simmons (5/23/1912-1/26/1984).
142322131 James Elbert Simmons, Jr. (12/14/1941-   ), m.
          5/15/1976 Sarah Parry Williams (12/27/1944-   ).
1423221311 David Harrison Simmons (12/19/1978-   ).
1423221312 Andrew Parry Simmons (6/26/1981-   ).
142322132 Elizabeth Bolling Simmons (7/29/1945-   ), m. 5/11/
          1968 Paul Becknell Keister (3/31/1942-   ).
1423221321 Paul Seeley Keister (9/24/1971-   ).
1423221322 Matthew Bolling Keister (8/31/1973-   ).
1423221323 Tyler Montgomery Keister (9/18/1976-   ).
142322133 William Harrison Simmons (10/22/1949-   ), m. Alcira
          Simmons of Argentina.
14232214 Emily Hume Rawlings (1/28/1919-   ), m. 2/22/1941
          Walter Dorsey Taylor (12/5/1915-   ).
142322141 Emily Hume Taylor (7/6/1943-   ), m. 4/16/1964
          Bradford Willis Gile (11/16/1943-   ).

1423221411 Bradford Willis Gile, Jr. (1/20/1969-   ).
1423221412 Emily Hume Gile (3/23/1973-   ).
142322142   Walter Dorsey Taylor, Jr. (12/23/1946-   ), m. 6/8/
            1968 Linda Sue Bohan (6/10/1948-   ).
1423221421 Linda Bohan Taylor (8/2/1971-   ).
1423221422 Martha Randolph Taylor (10/16/1975-   ).
1423221423 Lucy Colston Taylor (1/21/1981-   ).
14232215 Mary Blair Rawlings (10/18/1928-   ), m. 8/29/1952
            John Livingstone Gibson (8/16/1923-   ).
142322151 Mary Blair Gibson (9/10/1955-   ).
142322152 John Livingstone Gibson III (5/25/1960-   ).
1423222 Infant (b. & d. 3/21/1888).
1423223 Eliza Prentis Alfriend (1889-1904).
1423224 Margaret Bland Alfriend (1891-1968), m. Henry Vance
            Boykin (1882-1960).
14232241 Richard Alfriend Boykin (4/7/1918-   ), m. Margaret
            Rumble (8/23/1925-   ).
142322411 Richard Alfriend Boykin, Jr. (6/23/1946-   ), m.
            (1st)_____, m. (2nd) Anna _____.
    Children by first wife:
1423224111 Richard Alfriend Boykin III.
1423224112 Kathleen Boykin.
142322412 Jeffery Boykin, m. Lynn _____.
1423224121 Shayne Boykin.
142322413 Margaret ("Meg") Boykin, m. (1st) _____ Kello;
            m. (2nd) Donald Kimmell.
    Children by first husband:
1423224131 Wilson Kello.
1423224132 Robin Kello.
142322414 Kate H. Boykin.
142322415 William W. Boykin, m. (1st) Elizabeth B. Rucker (10/2/
            1948-7/14/1982), m. (2nd) Lynn L. _____.
1423224151 William W. Boykin, Jr. m. _____ (div.).
14232241511 Sean Boykin.
14232241512 Mirabai Boykin.
1423224152 Elizabeth Boykin, m. Philip S. Newswanger.
14232241521 Caitlin Elizabeth Newswanger (11/23/1985-   ).
1423225 Richard Jeffery Alfriend, Jr. (1894-1971), m. Miriam F.
            Whitehead (1899-7/4/1962).
14232251 Richard Jeffery Alfriend III (1920-   ). M. (1st)
            Sue Ennis Landon (1928-   ). M. (2nd) Rachel
            Kaebnick (1934-   ). No issue second marriage.
    Child by first wife:
142322511 Sue Landon Alfriend (1956-   ).
14232252 Dr. Robert Whitehead Alfriend (1921-   ), m. Olivia
            Ann Coleman (1932-   ). No issue.
14232253 Katherine Whitehead Alfriend (1924-1981). M. (1st)
            Harold Charles Roati (deceased). M. (2nd) Stanley
            Sorem.
    Children by first husband:
142322531 Harold Charles Roati, Jr. (1953-   ).
142322532 Dr. Sarah ("Sally") Bolling Roati (1957-   ), m.
            David Schoem.
142322533 Richard Jeffery Roati (1958-   ).

1423226   John Samuel Alfriend (1897-1974), m. 6/18/1922 Harriet
        L. Sanderlin.
1423227   Virginia Blair Alfriend (2/14/1900-1983), m. Richard
        Custis Mapp, son of Richard Ames Mapp and his wife,
        the former Margaret Anne Talmage.
14232271 Richard Custis Mapp, Jr. (4/2/1023-   ), m. Martha
        Griffin Cory (10/23/1923-   ), dau. of Herbert
        Hope Cory, and his wife, the former Lelia Norfleet.
142322711 Stephen Richard Mapp (4/19/1950-   ).
142322712 Susan Cory Mapp (12/17/1951-   ),m. Mr.
        Moriarity.
142322713 Martha Catherine Mapp (4/5/1953-   ), m. Mr. Swartz.
142322714 Richard Custis Mapp III (10/10/1955-   ).
142322715 Joseph Anthony Mapp (12/11/1957-   ).
142322716 Michael Benedict Mapp (6/29/1961-   ).
14232272 Anne Talmage Mapp (7/29/1927-   ), m. 7/11/1953
        Samuel Edgar Ketner (9/7/1927-   ), son of Robert
        Monroe Ketner and his wife, the former Ruby Hardy.
142322721 Anne Talmage Ketner (2/11/1955-   ), m. 7/10/1980
        Stephen Mark Allan (7/23/1955-   ), son of George
        Wallace Allan and his wife, the former Frances
        Elizabeth Brown.
1423227211 Elsbeth Anne Allan (12/31/1981-   ).
142322722 Rebecca Hardy Ketner (4/2/1959-   ),m. 12/5/1976
        Daniel Urban Colohan (12/18/1954-   ), son of Eric
        James Colohan and his wife, the former Gertrude
        McAdam.
1423227221 Jason Eric Colohan (6/30/1978-   ).
142322723 Samuel Edgar Ketner, Jr. (7/7/1967-   ).
14232273 John Alfriend Mapp (12/8/1932-   )(twin), m.
        12/22/1956 Betty England Fox (1/19/1934-   ), dau.
        of John Elwood Fox and his wife, the former Elizabeth
        Trent.
142322731 John Alfriend Mapp, Jr. (9/24/1959-   ).
142322732 Thomas Fox Mapp (5/7/1962-   ).
142322733 Virginia Ashby Mapp (2/23/1968-   ).
14232274 Virginia Blair Mapp (12/8/1932-   )(twin), m. Allan
        Charles Barbour Richardson, son of Charles Frederick
        Bardsley Richardson and his wife, the former Mary
        Gertrude Barbour.
142322741 David Barbour Richardson (9/2/1960-   ).
142322742 Andrew Fraser Richardson (12/13/1961-   ).
142322743 Michael Hume Richardson (2/25/1966-   ).
1423228 Theodoric Bolling Alfriend (6/26/1906-   ),m. 1927
        Jessie Hunter de Treville (2/4/1907-   ).
14232281 Theodoric Bolling Alfriend, Jr., m. Mary Ames Bolton.
142322811 Harry Bolling Alfriend.
142322812 Virginia de Treville Alfriend.
14232282 Jesse Hunter Alfriend, m. Barbara Rouse Berean.
142322821 Emily Elizabeth Alfriend.
142322822 Jesse H. Alfriend, Jr.
142322823 John Samuel Alfriend.
142322824 Lisa Hunter Alfriend, m. Mr. Freeman.
142322825 Sarah Rouse Alfriend.

1423229 Mary Blair Alfriend (7/30/1903-   ). Unm.
142323   Jacob Vickery Alfriend (1862-8/6/1864).
142324   James Vickery Alfriend (1866-1951), m. Marie Louise Hume.
1423241 Pocahontas Alfriend, m. Daniel Luther Dole.
1423242 Elizabeth Vickery Alfriend, m. J. Warren McLaughlin.
1423243 James Vickery Alfriend, Jr.
142325   William Wilson Alfriend (4/24/1868-12/24/1942), m. Sarah
         Wilmotte Dudley (7/23/1871-1/8/1955), dau. of William
         Robert Dudley and his wife, the former Sarah Berrymore.
1423251 Rev. William Jeffery Alfriend (10/28/1890-4/24/1969), m.
         Mary Virginia Bethell (11/12/1890-1/15/1972), dau. of
         Henry Bethell and his wife, the former Alice Coleman.
14232511 William Jeffery Alfriend, Jr. (9/23/1918-   ), m.
         Lillian Gish (2/19/1922-   ).
142325111 Mary Price Alfriend (7/30/1944-   ), m. Brooks
         Kennedy, son of Donald Kennedy and his wife, the
         former Carol Brooks.
1423251111 Christopher Kennedy (1969-   ).
1423251112 Catherine Kennedy (1971-   ).
142325112 Sarah Lillian Alfriend (10/28/1948-   ), m.
         James Carego.
1423251121 Sarah Elizabeth Carego (1975-   ).
1423251122 Maria Carego (1981-   ).
142325113 William Jeffery Alfriend III (10/2/1959-   ).
14232512 Jula Bethel Alfriend, m. Theron Jay Owen.
14232513 Jane Alfriend.
14232514 Anne Alfriend.
1423252 Sarah Dudley Alfriend (9/25/1903-   ), m. Rev. Ambler
         Mason Blackford (9/26/1888-   ), son of Launcelot
         M. Blackford and his wife, the former Eliza Chew
         Ambler.
14232521 Elizabeth Randolph Bland Blackford (10/12/1941-   ),
         m. John Scriver Freeman, son of Alvin Z. Freeman and
         his wife, the former Margaret Worcester.
142326   Anne Peters Alfriend (1869-10/17/1871).
142327   Bessie Alfriend (d. inf. 1869).
14233   Ann Rosa Alfriend (1821-1905). Unm.
14234   Richard Jeffery Alfriend (-12/18/1859), m. Susie
         Strachen.
142341   Virginia Alfriend. School Teacher.
142342   Theophilus Alfriend (d. 2/25/1895). Became ill while a
         student at the Episcopal Seminary, and died of con-
         sumption shortly thereafter.
143   Elizabeth Blair Bland (5/29/1770-   ).

145   John Bolling Bland (12/6/1767-7/30/1777)

15 Sarah Bolling (living August 1798).

1531 Willianna Blair Tazewell. Unm.

1538 Anne ("Nancy") Rosalie Tazewell, m. 1851 Andrew Lewis
      Ellett (1822-   ).

16 Archibald Bolling (b. 1750). Sarah Cary (d. 4/7/1773). M.
    (2nd) 10/1/1774. M. (3rd) Maria Taylor Page Byrd 5/13/1797.
    M. (4th) 9/29/1802.
161 Sarah Bolling (11/29/1775-   ).

16113 Mary Megginson and Mary Megginson Davidson (d. 1880)

161181 Thomas Farrar, Jr.

1613a Archibald Bolling Megginson, Jr.
1614 Joseph Cabell Megginson, Jr.

161512

1618b Benjamin Cabell Megginson, Jr.

162 Anne Everard Bolling (b. 3/13/1778).

162453 Sears Cabell, Jr.

16257 Archibald Dixon, Jr.

162573 Archibald Dixon III

1626x Robert Bolling Cabell III

16277 George Washington Cabell, Jr.

1627x Sarah McKendrick and Sarah McKendrick Cabell

164 John Randolph Bolling (8/7/1784-3/24/1851).

165 Blair Bolling (b. 3/3/1791-d. 8/3/1839 "Centre Hill" grave-
     yard), m. Margaret Ann (?) Webster (1805-1825) of Henrico
     County, dau. of Ann S. Pleasants Webster (96 V. 194). M.
     (2nd) 3/7/1827 Penelope A. Storrs (1807-5/29/1849 age 43
     "Centre Hill" graveyard).
     "Centre Hill" near Fine Creek Mills. Cemetery on bank of
     James River about 1/2 mile from the house surrounded by an
     iron fence, which has been knocked down, along with two
     table top tombstones, by a fallen tree. Four marked
     graves. 19th Century Bolling family home. Gervas (Guvas)
     Storrs second wife was Margaret Trueheart (b. 1775).

1651 Archibald Bolling (1827-1897), m. 1852 Eliza P. Trueheart
      Armistead (ca. 1828-1862), dau. of Jesse Scott Armistead
      and his wife, the former Martha Storrs Trueheart.
16511 Stanhope Bolling (1852-1927). Unm.
16512 Blair Bolling (1852-1917). Unm.
16513 Wyndham Bolling (1854-1922).
16514 Maria ("Mattie") Bolling (1856-1936). Unm.
16515 Randolph Bolling (1860-1891).

1652 John R. Bolling (8/7/1784-3/24/1851). First wife, Maria
      Page Armistead (1831-8/28/1859), dau. of Jesse Scott
      Armistead and his wife, the former Martha Storrs Trueheart

    Child by first wife:
16521 Maria Page ("Ditz") Bolling, m. Ed Walker
16522 (son)
16523 (son)
16524 (son)
16525 (son)
16526 (dau)
16527 (dau)

16531 Mary Agnes Burton (9/5/1852-7/13/1911), m. 1/23/1878 John
      Daniel Shepperson (2/2/1851-12/1/1921), son of Captain
      John Shepperson and his wife, the former Martha Bass
      Daniel. Their plantation in Charlotte County was called
      "College Hill".
165311 Martha Daniel Shepperson (11/7/1878-1/14/1968), m. 9/14/
      1904 James Henry Grant III (2/11/1876-3/21/1937).
1653111 James Henry Grant IV (9/27/1906-5/17/1976), m. 7/30/1932
      Elsie Ingram Michaux (12/28/1907-11/12/1983).

16531111 James Henry Grant, d. young

16531112 James Henry Grant V (5/9/1938-   ), m. 6/20/1965
      Charlotte Darden Thorne (6/12/1941-   ).

165311121 Page Bolling Grant (12/29/1966-   ).
165311122 James Henry Grant VI (6/12/1969-   ).
16531113 William Michaux Grant (4/27/1943-   ), m. 6/22/1968
      Patricia Ann Gunnell (8/23/1947-   ).
165311131 William Michaux Grant II (1/14/1969-   ).
165311132 Patricia Shepperson Grant (12/30/1971-   ).
1653112 Mary Agnes Grant (8/17/1908-   ).
1653113 John Shepperson Grant (3/3/1911-9/3/1982).
165312 Mary Grisley Shepperson (2/12/1880-4/10/1970). Unm.
165313 Rebecca Storrs Shepperson (1882-5/9/1883).
165314 Lucy Shepperson (2/1/1884-4/18/1958). Unm.
165315 Gay Bolling Shepperson (8/14/1887-11/17/1977).
165316 Edmonia Blair Shepperson (12/5/1888-11/17/1969), m.
      10/15/1923 Robert Alexander Chermside (8/4/1883-   ).
1653161 Martha Brooke Chermside (12/6/1925-2/24/1981), m. 12/28/
      1958 William Wallace Scott Chapman (7/8/1917-   ).

16531611 William Wallace Scott Chapman, Jr. (9/20/1959-   ).
16531612 Dolly Blair Chapman (8/24/1960-   ).
1653162   Robert Alexander Chermside, Jr. (2/2/1927-   ), m.
          Caroline Pace.
165317   Dr. Archibald Bolling Shepperson (3/20/1897-7/24/1962),
          m. 12/12/1923 Phillippa Alexander Bruce (8/10/1897-
          6/17/1972), dau. of Philip A. Bruce and his wife, the
          former Bettie T. Taylor. Dr. Shepperson was head of the
          English Department at the University of Virginia.
1653171   Phillippa Alexander Bruce Shepperson (10/1/1934-   ),
          m. 9/27/1958, Tiffney Haley Armstrong. The Armstrongs
          adopted two children: Shepperson Haley Armstrong (3/29/
          1969-   ), and Phillippa Armstrong (7/29/1971-).

165322   Otis Munford Burton, m. Mary Alexander
165323   Gervas Storrs Burton III

1653252   Margaret Antonia Burton, m. Ernest Loving St. Clair

165325211 Dawn Denise Bryant
165325212 Kevin David Bryant

16532571 Mildred Ruth David/Evans

16532585 Diana Marie Camper

165325x   Gilmer Brugh Burton, Jr.

16532621 Curtis Edison Vandergrift, Jr., m. Zarieda Jean Cox

1654 Paulina S. Bolling (10/23/1839-3/3/1857). "Centre Hill"
      graveyard

166   Archibald Cary Bolling (7/20/1771-1/9/1795). D.s.p.
167   Sarah Cary Bolling (3/30/1773-7/2/1774).
168   John Bolling (1780-1781).
169   Richard Bolling (1787-1787).
16x   Richard Bolling (second of the name)(1788-1788).
16b   Mary Kennon Bolling (1789-1789).
16c   Mary Jane Bolling (1793-1797).
17 Anne Bolling (living August 1802).
1711 Bolling Dandridge, m. Elizabeth Ann _____.

17511 Joseph Davies Logan, m. Georgine Willis. In THE WILLISES
       OF VIRGINIA by Maud Potter, Logan's middle name is given
       as David and Mrs. Logan's first name is given as
       Georgina. She was the dau. of George Willis of "Wood
       Park", Orange County, and of his second wife, Sally Innes
       Smith.

21   Richard Randolph, Jr.

211   Maria Beverley. B. at "Blandfield", d. Williamsburg.

211c   Richard Randolph IV
211d   John Tayloe Randolph II

2115   Maria Beverley Randolph, m. Philip DuVal, Jr., son of
       Philip and Elizabeth Warrock DuVal

2125   James Randolph
2126   Maury Randolph

   Markers referred to below under 213, under 2133-213323, and
under 21337-2133x in the Randolph Cemetery located two miles east
of Greensboro, Alabama, on land owned in 1984 by William L.
"Fuzzy" York.

213   Brett Randolph. Obituary of 2/26/1828 from the Richmond
      Enquirer states that he died "near Columbus, State of
      Mississippi" on 1/26/1828. Marker indicates that his wife,
      Lucy Beverley Randolph (d. 9/15/1854, Montgomery, AL).

2132   Capt. Edward Brett Randolph (d. 1898).

2133   Robert Carter Randolph, M.D. Marker, which has initials
       "R.C.", indicates: (7/21/1793-4/7/1854)(b. Prince Edward
       County, VA, d. at "Oakleigh", Greene County, AL).
     Another marker indicates the grave of B.C.B. Farrar (d. 1/28/
     1828, age 3).
21331   Jane Wormeley Randolph. Marker, which does not include
        "Wormeley", indicates: (10/26/1828-8/9/1862)(b. at
        "Oakleigh", Greene County, AL).
21332   Richard Randolph. Marker indicates: d. 9/11/1868, age 36
        (b. Adamson, MS, d. near Greensboro).
213322   Rittenhouse S. Randolph. Marker, which does not include
         initial "S", indicates: (d. 12/27/1862, age 2 years, 11
         months).
213323   Smith Randolph. Marker indicates: (d. 9/3/1861, age 4
         years, 2 months, 24 days).

21332421   Richard Rutherford Randolph III, m. 11/20/1963 Natasha
           Margaret Blinov, dau. of Benjamin Demetri and Mary
           Lou McKenzie Methvin Blinov
213324211   Richard Rutherford Randolph IV
213324212   Ryland McKenzie Randolph

   Markers indicate graves of two infant children (not named)
of Robert Carter Randolph and his wife, the former Ann Tayloe
Beverley and of their below-listed twin daughters, Rebecca
Randolph and Ann Bland Randolph. It may be assumed that one of
the unnamed infants is 21337.

21335   Anne Tayloe Randolph, b. Culpeper County, d. Sheffield, AL

     There would then be three new numbers:
21338   Inf. bur. Randolph Cemetery, near Greensboro, AL.
21339   Rebecca Randolph (twin of 2133x). Inf. bur. Randolph
        Cemetery near Greensboro, AL.
2133x   Ann Bland Randolph (twin of 21339). Inf. bur. Randolph
        Cemetery near Greensboro, AL.

21352   Brett Randolph, m. Emma January Herndon

213521111   Hazel Adelaide Lawyer Ryall (b. 1/29/1931), m. 3/21/
            1953 Daniel McIntire Beall (b. 1/14/1929)
2135211111 Daniel McIntire Beall, Jr. (b. 2/24/1954)
2135211112 Cynthia Ann Beall (b. 2/26/1956)
213521112   Ann Reid Ryall (b. 12/20/1933), m. 6/13/1953 James
            Lamar Gibson (b. 3/4/1929), son of John and Annie
            Gillis Gibson
2135211121 James Lamar Gibson, Jr. (b. 9/6/1956)
2135211122 Henry Clayton Gibson (b. 6/6/1959)

213521121   James Bomar Ryall, Jr., m. 12/27/1966 Linda Marie
            Pritchett (b. 4/29/1946), dau. of Eulon Chandler and
            Thelma Lena Phillips Pritchett
2135211211 James Bomar Ryall III (b. 6/29/1968)
2135211212 Kathryn Ashley Ryall (b. 11/22/1969)
213521122   Emma Scudder Ryall, m. 6/30/1967 James George Gammons
            (b. 11/10/1943), son of Willard Thomas and Laura
            Myrtle Ramey Gammons
2135211221 James Bartley Gammons (b. 8/26/1969)

213521123   Sarah Byrd Ryall (b. 5/8/1947)

21352113   John Reid Ryall (d. 7/8/1952)
213521131   Mary Reid Ryall, m. 6/8/1955 Louis Daniel McMillion,
            Jr. (3/27 or 11/30/1939), son of Louis Daniel and
            Lisa Cothran McMillion
2135211311 Mary McMillion (b. 4/17/1956)
2135211312 Louis Daniel McMillion III (b. 3/27/1959)
2135211313 John Reid McMillion (b. 11/21/1969)

2135213   Augusta Randolph Reid (d. 5/28/1955), m. William Lee
          Roueche (b. 7/15/1959)
21352131 William Lee Roueche, Jr., m. 6/16/1934 Ruth Manasco
          (b. 10/22/1912), dau. of Oscar and Beulah Christine
          Manasco
213521311 Sarah Ruth Roueche (b. 11/7/1935), m. 6/6/1954 Edwin
          Ayers Murdock (b. 2/21/1933), son of Albert A. and
          Ethel George Murdock
2135213111 Matthew Ayers Murdock (b. 8/5/1959)
2135213112 Susannah Augusta Murdock (b. 12/24/1964)
213521312 William Lee Roueche III (b. 9/19/1938), m. 7/3/1969

```
                Charis Coffman (b. 5/5/1948), dau. of Charles
                Douglas and Avis Marjorie Metcalf Coffman
2135213121  Catherine Avis Roueche (b. 2/7/1970)
213521313   Mary Christine Roueche (b. 4/9/1944), m. 5/4/1963
                Gerald Joaquin Harris (b. 8/1/1938), son of Leslie
                Ewert and Rachel Fernandez Harris
2135213131  David Joaquin Harris (b. 2/2/1965)
2135213132  Michael Joseph Harris (b. 4/8/1969)
213521314   Marguerite Victoria Roueche (b. 8/15/1947), m. 2/  /
                1964 Charles Armand Waller, son of John and Dorothy
                Waller
2135213141  Denise Lynn Waller (b. 2/17/1965)
2135213142  Jenise Lee Waller (b. 6/2/1967)
2135213143  Charles Armand Waller, Jr. (b. 9/  /1969)

213521331   Caroline Lee Hume, m. 5/  /1964 Arnold Clifford Ristad
                (b. 9/14/1938), son of Harold and Adele Plant Ristad
2135213311  John Mark Ristad (b. 3/11/1965)
2135213312  Robert Eric Ristad (b. 9/26/1968)

21352134    John Reid Roueche, m. 9/9/1950 Virginia Wadsworth
                (b. 7/14/1917), dau. of Herbert Alonzo and Antoinette
                Norman Wadsworth
213521341   Reid Wadsworth Roueche (b. 8/13/1952)
213521342   Lee Norman Roueche (b. 5/16/1955)
213521343   Jane Randolph Roueche (b. 9/25/1957)
21352135    Brett Emmett Roueche, Jr. (b. 11/24/1953)
213521351   Georgia Ann Roueche (b. 1/15/1948), m. 4/27/1963,
                Daniel Rainey
213521352   Augusta Randolph Roueche (b. 8/22/1951)
213521353   Brett Emmett Roueche, Jr. (b. 11/24/1953)
213521354   Arthur Bradford Roueche (b. 12/9/1955)

2135214     Brett Randolph Reed, m. Rufus Absolom Russell, Jr., son
                of Rufus Absolom Russell

21352142    Rufus Absolom Russell III, m. (2nd) Dorothy Greenleaf
                (b. 11/7/1920)

   Children by second wife:
213521422   John Randolph Russell (b. 5/2/1964, d. inf.)
213521423   Elizabeth Greenleaf Russell (b. 1/6/1962)
21352143    Herndon Brett Russell, m. 1/18/1949 Margaret Louise
                Epperle (b. 6/21/1930), dau. of Aloysius and Blanche
                Moore Epperle

2135215     John Bryan Reid, m. (1st) 12/20/1916, Ione Harrison
                (b. 12/16/1895), dau. of George Edgar and Katherine
                Odum Harrison, m. (2nd) Madelon Calais (d. 3/21/1961)
21352151    John Bryan Reid, Jr., m. (2nd) 1/16/1951, Barbara Jean
                Hillyer (b. 7/20/1929), dau. of Roy M. and Jo Ann
                Dowdle Hillyer
213521511   Linda Reid (b. 9/13/1943), m. 8/10/1966, Michael S.
                King
```

213521512   Ellen Clarke Reid (b. 2/28/1945), m. 4/25/1965, George
            Price Davis III (b. 8/17/1942), son of George Price
            Davis, Jr., and his wife Thelma Hanslip
2135215121 Sarah Ellen Davis (b. 2/22/1967)
213521513   Laura Reid (b. 10/22/1947), m. 1/11/1969 Robert Iron-
            sides Johnston, Jr. (b. 7/19/1947)
213521514   John Bryan Reid III (b. 7/21/1952)
213521515   Victor Randolph Reid (b. 6/14/1954)
21352152   (Capt.) George Harrison Reid, m. 11/16/1965 Evelin Svec
            (b. 11/22/1932)
213521521   John Bryan Reid IV (b. 5/13/1962)
213521522   Brett Elizabeth Reid (b. 8/24/1963)
213521523   Camilla Reid (b. 8/2/1966)
2135216   Oliver Fowlkes Reid (d. 10/24/1966)
21352161   Robin Leroy Reid, m. Carolyn Walker
21352162   Anne Randolph Reid, m. (1st) 1/2/1954 W. Jackson Jones
            III (b. 8/15/1967), son of Otis Warner and Rosalie
            Wilson Jones, m. (2nd) 12/12/1969 John B. Coker (b.
            1/20/1915), son of John Bethell and Minna Offenhanden
            Coker
213521621   Thomas Randolph Jones (b. 10/6/1955)
21352163   Marion Ethel Reid (b. 5/27/1948)
21352164   Brett Bradley Reid (b. 1/10/1950)
21352165   John Randolph Reid (b. 12/9/1951)

2135221   Phedora Randolph, m. Peter Marie Nicrosi

213522121   Frances Sledge Nicrosi (b. 2/3/1950)
213522122   Carolyn Randolph Nicrosi (b. 7/ /1957)
2135222   Jule Thweat Randolph, m. 7/ /1930 Guy Roy Brightwell
            (b. 7/18/1873), son of W. T. and Helen Fleming
            Brightwell
2135223   John Brett Randolph, Jr. (d. 8/21/1959)

2136 John Thomson Randolph (d. near Fort Montgomery, AL). About
      eight months prior to his death, he left Virginia with his
      brother. 34 V 72.

213x Theodorick Beverley Randolph. In 1848, living in Greene
      County, AL.

213a Anna Maria Randolph. A marker in Randolph Cemetery near
      Greensboro, AL, indicates the name "Anna", and (d. 3/5/
      1849, age 38).

2141 Robert Ryland Randolph in 1810 lived in Tuscaloosa County,
      AL.

217 Anne Meade Randolph (d. 1/20/1820), m. Brett N. Randolph,
     Jr. Issue under father 222. 34 V 72.

218 Elizabeth Meade Randolph, m. David Meade, Jr.

218113 Charlotte Ruffin Meade Callendar

2181144 Charles Hodges Constable, Jr.

21812 **Charlotte Stockdell Meade.**

218124 Edmund Sumpter Ruffin, m. Cordelia Willing Byrd Waller

2181243 Richard Willing Byrd Ruffin

2191 Joseph Kendall Weisiger, son of Mary Kendall Weisiger

219132124 Ruth Whitney Weisiger, m. Farhad Farwar

2191324 Lucy Page Weisiger, m. Joseph Hayes McNauger

219136 Lucy Page Weisiger, m. Lee A. Coulter

21915612 Doris C. Weisiger, m. Edmund H. Moore III

2191593 Ellie Hancock Weisiger, m. Edward James Lefeber

219245 George Henry King III

219251 Thomas Albert Bolling, Jr., m. Mary A. Hodges

21931 Mary Virginia Randolph Bolling (11/18/1838-7/12/1899), m.
4/7/1861 Alexander Quarles Holladay (11/8/1838-3/13/1909)
(bur. Raleigh, NC). Colonel, 19th Virginia, C.S.A.

219311 Mary Stuart Holladay (2/3/1862-   )(b. Richmond), m.
8/22/1883 Rev. Peyton Harrison Hoge

219312 William Waller Holladay (9/7/1864-   )(b. Richmond).
M. (1st) Maggie Murchison Williams (1865-1889). M.
(2nd) 10/18/1896 Fannie Pritchard (10/12/1878-   )
(b. Raleigh, NC). Home: Wilmington, NC. Had issue.

219313 Julia Cabell Holladay (1869-   ), m. James Marion
Pickel.

219314 A. Randolph Holladay (2/ / or 3/ /1868)(b. at "Bolling
Island"). Unm.

219315 Charles Bolling Holladay (2/12/1873-   )(b. Richmond),
m. 11/14/1901 Emma Louise Swift. Home: Wilmington, DE.
Had issue.

21935 Robert Morris Bolling, m. Ann Montgomery Barksdale, dau.
       of Robert Jones and Elizabeth Lewis Robertson Barksdale

2194   Jane Rolfe Bolling, m. Robert Skipwith (9/30/1810-4/27/
       1904), son of George Nicholas and Mary Murray Skipwith

2195   Mary Randolph Bolling

22 Mary Scott, "a native of Wales", m. "sometime in the year
    1752 being then about 20 years of age". She d. 11/ /1779.
    MEMORIAL.
221 Henry Randolph (d. 2/9/1804)(b. Dursley, d. Chesterfield
    County). M. Chesterfield County 11/30/1782 Lucy Ward
    (1765/66-6/12/1848). She is bur. Shockoe Hill, Richmond.
    She m. (2nd) John Higginbotham.

2211 Henry Randolph, Jr. (1784-10/26/1840)(b. Chesterfield
      County, d. Hanover County), m. (1st) Caroline Matilda
      Delia Smith (bond 1/11/1808). M. (2nd) Henrico County
      4/20/1809 Elizabeth Griffin Norment

    NOTE: The following persons are descendants of Honoria Mary
          Tucker Randolph (22113 and 22313):
          A. Royall Turpin of Richmond - great-grandson
          Janet Randolph Turpin Ayers of Richmond - great-
          granddaughter

2211321 Cornelia Whelan Randolph, m. 11/11/1908 Peter Jefferson
         Archer (7/5/1871-2/27/1935)(125114). Children under
         father.

22113212 Norman Randolph Archer, m. Dorothy Delores Bryant (5/
          30/1922-   ), dau. of Darrell Victor and Celia
          Cantone Bryant

2212 Mary Goode Randolph (b. "Warwick", Chesterfield County, d.
      Pensacola), m. Fredericksburg, VA, James Francis Maury (b.
      Madison County, VA, d. Jefferson County, MO), first son of
      Abraham Maury and his wife, the former Mildred Washington
      Thornton.
22121 Henry Randolph Thornton (d. 11/27/1862), m. 6/18/1828 or
       7/26/1828 Mary Agnes Bradford (d. 7/5/1847).
22122 Lucy Ward Thornton, m. 7/15 or 18/1829, Richard Adams, who
       m. 4/15/1821 (his first wife) Mary W. Selden (d. 9/22/
       1826).
221221 Mary Elizabeth Adams (2/26/1826-   ).
221222 Catherine Innes Adams (6/4/1834-3/23/1851)(d.
        Williamsburg).
221223 Samuel Griffin Adams (9/24/1831-   ).
221224 Maria Critenton Adams (7/14/1840-   ).

22123 Mary Goode Thornton, m. 6/12/1834 Alexander Cunningham
       Maury (d. 6/23/1840, age 36)(d. Sumter, AL). M. (2nd)
       Rev. John Jackson Scott (d. 7/28/1886)

22125   Capt. Thomas Francis Maury (2/9/1819-   )(b. Virginia),
        m. 4/25/1847 Ann Richard Jenkins (b. Virginia)(1850
        Census gives her age as 23).
221251 Seth Thornton Maury (2/20/1848-10/18/1928)(b. Alabama),
        m. Kate Elizabeth Stevenson.
2212511 Lillian Maury (b. Temple, TX).

The Rolfes of North Carolina (Continued)

In a lengthy article, "The Descendants of Pocahontas: An
Unclosed Case", in the August 1985 issue (Vol. 23, No. 3) of the
Magazine of Virginia Genealogy, Elizabeth Vann Moore and Richard
Slatten explore and suggest the possibility that Pocahontas' son,
Thomas Rolfe, was the same person as Thomas Relfe (Roelfe?/
Rolfe?/Roelph?) who, ca. 1665, received a patent to 750 acres in
North Carolina on the south side of the Pasquotank River.

The writers of the article indicate that Thomas Relfe had at
least two sons, Thomas and William, and the writers of the
article suggest the possibility that William was the father of
Thomas Rolfe of "Yawpim".

Third Marriage (?) of Thomas Rolfe

In the April 1986 issue (Vol. 4, No. 2) of Pocahontas Trails
Quarterly, in "My Story" by William Aubrey Rolfe, Mr. Rolfe
reports information sent to him by Dan Rolph "of Lexington", and
"learned (by Dan Rolph) from a lady in Florida" (Miss Ruth
Dunnington).

This information is that Thomas Rolfe married Oi Poi
(Uconoco) a daughter of Powhatan's brother, Upechancanough. That
their son Thomas Rolfe, Jr. (called Powhatan) was born in 1654,
and in 1688, married Sylvania Eleanor Penn. That William Penn
Rolfe, son of Thomas Rolfe, Jr., and of his wife, the former
Sylvania Eleanor Penn, was born in 1700, and in 1738 married an
Indian, Minnie Hawaitha. That William Penn Rolfe and his wife,
the former Minnie Hawaitha, had a daughter Wanetta (Juanita) who
was born in 1740, and who married William Wesley Weyland.

2212512   Zaidee Elizabeth Maury (12/14/1886-   )(b. Temple, TX),
          m. Kelly Sherman DeBusk (d. ca. 1954).
22125121 Maurine Zada DeBusk (11/10/1907-   )(b. Temple, TX),
          m. Mr. Elkins (d. ca. 1967).
221251211 Son
22125122 Helen Bernice DeBusk (8/6/1912-   )(b. Temple, TX).
          M. twice.
221251221 Son (by second marriage).
22125123 Kelly Sherman ("Buster") DeBusk, Jr. (2/23/1915-   )
          (b. Temple, TX).
221252   Richard Randolph ("Dick") Maury (1/12/1850-ca. 1940)(b.
          Alabama), m. 1/2/1880. Home: China Spring, TX.
2212522   Lottie Stewart Maury (5/25/1884-   ), m. Thomas Lee
          Tennison (1/28/1874-   ) of St. Clair County, AL.
22125221 Thomas Maury Tennison (12/2/1913-   ).
22125222 Richard Henry Tennison (7/29/1917-   ).
22125223 Harry Lee Tennison (8/1/1919-   ), m. Gloria
          DePoister Lupton (11/6/1923-   ).
221252231 Kit Marie Tennison (4/26/1952-   ).
221252232 Lee Lupton Tennison (7/23/1954-   ), m. 4/21/1979
          Mary Margaret Penn.
221252233 Jil Maury Tennison (7/30/1955-   ), m. 6/21/1978
          Bradford Shaw Barnes.
2212522331 Benjamin Shaw Barnes (2/16/1980-   ).
2212523   Thomas Joseph ("Joe") Maury, m. Nola _____. No
          issue.
2212524   Mary Maury (d. age 12).
2212525   Ruby Maury (d. young).
2212526   John Macain Maury, d.s.p.
221253   Thomas Fontaine ("Fletcher") Maury (5/6/1851-d. ca. 1929)
          (twin)(bur. Dallas), m. 1/30/1883 Florence Heddin.
          Maury, a farmer and a newspaperman (Tribune Waco Times),
          wrote under the pen name of "Junius".
2212531   Cora G. Maury (b. China Spring, TX), m. Bosqueville,
          Bosque County, TX, William Henry Guinn (1881-1955), son
          of Samuel Guinn and his wife, the former Texanna
          Loggins.
22125311 Florence Melvina Guinn (3/10/1911-   )(b. West
          Texas), m. Otis Thompson of Laurel, MS.
221253111 Charles Bowen Thompson (6/10/1937-   )(b. Houston),
          m. Barbara Harris.
2212531111 Charles David Thompson (1/23/1964-   )(b. Houston).
221253112 James Robert Thompson (8/14/1939-   )(b. Houston).
22125312 Samuel Lafayette Guinn (5/20/1912-5/27/1967)(b. Waco),
          m. Helen Coulter of Parksville, KY.
221253121 Sidney Leon Guinn (7/8/1947-   )(b. Houston).
22125313 William Henry Guinn, Jr. (12/13/1913-   )(b. Waco),
          m. Evelyn Ray of Houston.
          Adopted child: Robert Ray (1/4/ca. 1943-   ).
22125314 Fred Wilson Guinn (11/19/1916-   )(b. Houston).
2212532   Maggie Fontaine Maury (7/26/1885-7/ /1968)(d. Lancaster,
          SC), m. 1904 Summey Ray Ferguson (1883-   )(b.
          China Spring, TX), son of John Ferguson .
22125321 Lucile Marvyne Ferguson (2/25/1911-   )(b. Waco),

         m. 9/12/1931 Dr. Jay Dill Pittman (10/4/1904-   )
         (b. Rising Faun, GA), son of John Green Pittman, M.D.,
         and his wife, the former Emily Louise Youngblood.
2212533 Thomas Fontaine Maury, Jr. (5/3/1888-d. ca. 1895).
2212534 William Edward Maury (ca. 1890-1949), m. Ola Mae Pate.
22125341 Thomas Fletcher Maury (1922-   )(b. Dallas), m.
         1/22/1945 Georgia Lee Wallace (b. Dallas 12/6/1926),
         dau. of James Samuel Wallace and his wife, the former
         Esther Magnolia George.
221253411 Donna Gail Maury (2/6/1948-   )(b. Dallas).
2212535 Preston Maury (b.9/3/1892, d. young).
2212536 James Woodville Maury (2/25/1895-6/ /1962), m. Grace
         Presley. No issue.
221254   Edmund Kimbro ("Ned") Maury (5/6/1851-1939)(twin), C.S.A.
         When the War ended, he and some of his kin walked from
         Mississippi to Texas, a journey that took six months.
         When he got back to Texas, he sent for his mother who
         was in Alabama. He was burned to death when his house
         caught fire. Bur. China Spring, TX, as is his mother.
         M. (1st) 11/24/1882, Nannie Foster (d. in childbirth).
         M. (2nd) Fannie Ida Chambers (the widow Holliman)(d.
         1/31/1943)(b. Alabama).
      Children by first wife:
2212541 Caroline Elizabeth Maury (b. 11/7/1883, d. young).
2212542 Annie Richard Maury (d. 8/8/1965)(b. and bur. China
         Spring, TX), m. 12/5/1904, Archie "Can" Hatfield (7/15/
         1880-12/12/1941)(b. Tennessee, bur. Waco), son of
         Archie Can Hatfield and his wife, the former Polly
         Ann Robinet.
22125421 Clint Allen Hatfield (9/20/1905-5/29/1945)(b. Rock
         Creek, TX, bur. China Spring). D.s.p.
22125422 Edward Kimbro Hatfield (6/2/1907-   ). M. (1st)
         6/10/1930 Lillie May Powers (8/10/1908-   )(b.
         Valley Mills, TX), dau. of Mack Powers and his wife,
         the former Annie Lee Smith. M. (2nd) 9/10/1948 Edith
         McDonnal (b. Waco), dau. of Paul McDonnal and his
         wife, the former Etta Ward.
221254221 Barbara Ellen Hatfield (2/2/1930-   )(b. Valley
         Mills), m. Earl Gary.
22125423 Nannie Ree Hatfield (7/13/1908-   ), m. 2/5/1928
         Robert Cecil Granger (4/17/1905-   )(b. Wortham
         Bend, TX), son of Robert Edward Granger and his wife,
         the former Lela Annie Wortham.
221254231 Cecil Ned Granger (b. China Spring), m. 8/24/1957
         Nancy Barbara White (b. El Paso), dau. of Paul White
         and his wife, the former Louise Smith.
2212542311 Nancy D'Ette Granger (12/2/1959-   )(b. Bryan,
         TX).
2212542312 Tressa Lynn Granger (1/2/1961-   )(b. Austin).
2212542313 Van Ned Granger (1/12/1963)(b. Austin).
221254232 Nancy Rae Granger (5/31/1941-   )(b. China Spring),
         m. 7/23/1960 Charles Earnest Ferguson (b. China
         Spring), son of John Ferguson and his wife, the
         former Lula Lane Eichelberger.

2212542321 Charles Scott Ferguson (5/29/1961-   )(b. Clifton, TX).
2212542322 Patricia Dee Ferguson (4/9/1965-   )(b. Clifton, TX).
22125424 Edna Louise Hatfield (8/29/1910-   )(b. Rock Creek, TX), m. 12/5/1929 Walton Earl Mathews (b. China Spring), son of John Mathews and his wife, the former Mary Joy. No issue.
22125425 Willie Earl Hatfield (10/4/1912-   )(b. Bosqueville, Bosque County, TX), m. Thelma Lee Hammons (b. Waco), dau. of John Hammons and his wife, the former Verna Lee Paig.
221254251 Margaret Ann Hatfield (10/1/1940-   )(b. Waco).
22125426 Gladys Dudley Hatfield (9/5/1915-   )(b. Bosqueville), m. 6/9/1938 Loyd Lee Reed (8/28/1914-   )(b. Valley Mills), son of Robert Reed and his wife, the former Ida Heart.
221254261 Marsha Carol Reed (2/10/1942-   )(b. Waco).
2212543 Lucy Maury (1/1/1888-   ), m. 1918 Waco, James E. Carpenter (d. 11/13/1966). No issue.
      Children by second wife:
2212544 Flora Lee Maury (1900-   ). M. (1st) Joe Samuel McFall (b. Waco), son of Elias Joshua McFall and his wife, the former Louise Paralee Threet. M. (2nd) 2/2/1962 Cleon Warren.
22125441 Joe Samuel McFall, Jr. (10/31/1925-   )(b. Speegleville, TX).
22125442 Doris Elizabeth McFall (5/6/1928-   )(b. Speegleville, TX), m. L. C. "Kirk" Bratton, Jr.
221254421 Robert Kirk Bratton (6/4/1953-   )(b. Tucson).
221254422 Barbara Ann Bratton (6/7/1956-   )(b. Waco).
22125443 Mary Ruth McFall (3/26/1932-   )(b. Speegleville), m. Othel Maclin Neely (6/21/1926-   )(b. Tolar, TX), son of Henry Clark Neely and his wife, the former Mae Deering.
221254431 Phillip Park Neely (3/11/1957-   )(b. Waco).
221254432 Elizabeth Lee Neely (3/10/1960-   )(b. Waco).
221254433 Mary Ruth Neely (10/3/1967-   )(b. Waco).
2212545 Mary Elizabeth Maury (3/1/1904-1/31/1950)(d. Houston, bur. China Spring). Unm.
221255 Jeannette Williams Maury (d. 9/9/1854).
221256 John Addison Maury (12/10/1854-   ). Unm.
221257 Mary Lucy Maury (7/23/1856-12/26/1928)(b. Livingston, AL, bur. Temple, TX), m. 11/17/1883 James Benjamin Stevenson (4/21/1854-4/21/1921)(b. Mississippi), son of William Henry Stevenson and his wife, the former Susan Baras.
2212571 William Henry Stevenson II (1/13/1885-1886).
2212572 Annie Goode Stevenson (b. 7/27/1886, d. young).
2212573 Mary Lucy Stevenson (2/21/1888-10/21/1953)(b. near Temple, TX, bur. Washington, DC), m. 6/22/1913 C. C. Shannon.
22125731 Hilda Maury Shannon.
2212574 Frances Fontaine Stevenson (7/7/1889-   )(b. near Temple, TX), m. 9/20/1913 Robert Edwin Griffith

11/26/1883-3/2/1947)(b. Texas, d. Forth Worth, bur. Burleson, TX), son of Edwin Griffith and his wife, the former Betty Fawks.

22125741 Frances Griffith (6/12/1914-   )(b. Burleson), m. 6/15/1946 Jore D. Evaldo.

221257411 Angela David Evaldo (12/22/1951-   )(b. Longview, TX).

221257412 Herta Fontaine Evaldo (9/9/1954-   )(b. Longview).

22125742 Margaret Griffith (3/9/1916-7/6/1927)(b. Burleson).

22125743 Robert Edwin Griffith, Jr. (12/26/1918-   )(b. Burleson), m. 12/16/1950 Mary Vogel.

221257431 David Maury Griffith (11/17/1951-   )(b. Midland, TX).

221257432 Margaret Anne Griffith (3/8/1953-   )(b. Forth Worth).

221257433 Victoria Randolph Griffith (10/5/1955-   )(b. Cemavillo, TX).

2212575 James Benjamin Stevenson, Jr. (3/13/1892-4/5/1969)(b. Bells Falls, near Temple, TX; bur. Cleburne, TX), m. 10/6/1920 Eva Hoskinson (4/27/1905-   )(b. Alva Woods County, OK), dau. of William Addison Hoskinson, and his wife, the former Evaline Spicer.

22125751 Hermione Stevenson (8/2/1921-6/28/1965)(b. Wichita, killed auto accident, bur. Cherryvale, KS), m. 10/13/1940 Gene Arthur Franklin (1/18/1920-   )(b. Erie, KS), son of Arthur William Franklin and his wife, the former Gladys Beulah Whitworth.

221257511 James Arthur Franklin (11/8/1941-   )(b. Wichita), m. Port Angeles, WA, 11/18/1961 Sonia Karolyn Miller (11/28/1944-   )(b. Omaha).

2212575111 Kristen Joy Franklin (10/17/1964-   )(b. Chula Vista, CA).

2212575112 Michelle Avon Franklin (3/7/1967-   )(b. Mountain View, CA).

221257512 John Patrick Franklin (2/7/1943-   )(b. Wichita). M. (1st) 1960 Nancy Greenville. M (2nd) Mazon, IL 6/23/1962 Darlene Elaine Goode (5/7/1940-   )(b. Morris, IL).

Child by first wife:

2212575121 Theresa Ann Franklin (4/27/1961-   ).

Child by second wife:

2212575122 Johanna Susanne Franklin (11/21/1963-   )(b. Morris, IL).

221257513 Jeanne Eleanor Franklin (7/10/1948-   ), m. Morris, IL, 6/24/1966 Jackie Gene Thompson (10/7/1939-   )(b. Galatia, IL).

2212575131 Diane Franklin (10/23/1966-   )(b. Morris).

221257514 Julie Ann Franklin (8/5/1949-   ), m. Morris, IL, 2/17/1968 Rodney LaVerne Wren (3/17/1949-   )(b. Morris, IL).

221257515 Joyce Rosalie Franklin (10/22/1953-10/23/1953)(b. Independence, KS, bur. Cherryvale, KS).

221257516 Joel Brian Franklin (7/20/1956-   )(b. Coffeyville).

22125752 Jeanne Dee Stevenson (7/21/1923-   )(b. Wichita), m.

6/20/1947 Robert Craven Carter Atteberry, Jr. (2/28/
1928-   )(b. Spokane), son of Robert Craven Carter
Atteberry and his wife, the former Irene Ethel Speck.

221257521 Robert Craven Carter Atteberry III (1/28/1949-   )
(b. Guam).

221257522 Penelope Sears Atteberry (11/5/1950-   )(b.
Bremerton, WA).

221257523 Michael Gordon Atteberry (12/18/1952-   )(b. Oakland, CA).

221257524 Allen Addison Atteberry (2/20/1955-   )(b. Guam).

22125753   James Gordon Stevenson (12/6/1925-   ), m. 11/16/
1956 Shirley Anne Mortimer (5/16/1929-   )(b. Kansas
City), dau. of Mark Allen Mortimer and his wife, the
former Lulu Vaughan Morgridge.
    Adopted: Charyl Anne Stevenson (6/21/1953-   )(b.
Wichita).

221257531 Geoffrey Scott Stevenson (1/1/1957-   )(b. Wichita).

22125754   Marjorie Ann Stevenson (5/18/1930-   )(b. Fort
Worth), m. Robert Franklin Hummer (5/13/1922-   )
(b. Chicago), son of Brenton Frank Hummer and his
wife, the former Marie Million.

221257541 Steven Neal Hummer (2/13/1954-   )(b. China Lake,
CA).

221257542 Alissa Marie Hummer (10/22/1956-   )(b. Ridgecrest,
CA).

221257543 Patricia Laurelle Hummer (10/9/1958-   )(b.Santa
Barbara).

221257544 Carolyn Hummer (4/3/1961-   )(b. Santa Barbara).

2212576   Dee Stevenson (4/10/1893-   )(b. near Temple, TX), m.
1934 Sidney Greenhill. No issue.

2212577   Sue Sherwood Stevenson (3/27/1897-   ). Unm.

2212578   Thomas Maury Stevenson (1/18/1900-6/9/1965). Unm.

221258   James Woodville Maury (d. 12/27/1936)(bur. Waco), m. Lula
Randolph Maury (8/31/1870-11/5/1961)(b.Alabama)(2212x3).

2212581   Gilbert Lafayette Maury, Jr. (8/20/1896-   )(b. China
Spring, TX). Unm.

2212582   Harry Randolph Maury (12/18/1897-   ). Unm.

2212583   John Cason Maury (12/18/1900-   ). Unm.

2212584   Virginia Branch Maury (11/13/1902-   ), m. George
L. Case (6/9/1897-11/18/1948)(b. Mooreville, TX).

22125841   James Russell Case (1/11/1921-   )(b. China Spring).
Unm.

22125842   Joseph Harry Case (8/23/1922-   )(b. China Spring),
m. Mary Wilson.

221258421 Jerry Joe Case (2/8/1959-   )(b. China Spring).

221259   Bettie Greene Maury (d. 2/10/1862).

22125x   Francis Alexander Maury (8/5/1862-9/9/1869).

22126   James Woodville Maury (d. 10/17/ or 19/1822). Named for
Rev. John Woodville.

22127   James Woodville Maury (second of this name)(d. Wahalak,
MS). Educated Fredericksburg, VA, and Alabama. C.S.A.
(Co. I, 5th Mississippi). Cotton planter Kemper County,
MS, at "Chestnut Grove" and "Shadyside". M. Sumpter
County, AL, Rachel Kittrell ("Kitty") Harris (10/22/1825-

)(b. Pendleton District, SC).

221271 Richard Harris Maury (d. Kemper County, MS).

221272 James Francis ("Frank") Maury (d. 8/ /1926)(d. Meridian, MS)(bur. Wahalak), m. Willie Irene Allen (adopted dau. of Maj. Allen of Kemper County, MS)(d. in childbirth).

2212721 Aline Maury (d. 1963)(bur. Phoebe, MS), m. Robert F. Bryan (d. within year of marriage).

22127211 Robert F. Bryan, Jr. (d. 1917, age 13 months).

2212722 Richard Harris Maury (3/3/1885-ca. 1960-61)(d. Wahalak). Unm.

2212723 Irene ("Renie") Kittrell Maury (7/7/1889-9/17/1962)(b. Wahala, bur. Lauderdale, MS), m. Clifton Vandevender (b. Shuqualak, MS, 3/2/1889).

22127231 Child (stillborn 12/27/1911).

22127232 Clifton Vandevender, Jr. (1914-1917).

22127233 Child (stillborn 1917).

22127234 Allene Maury Vandevender (1920-1922).

2212724 Henry Fontaine Maury (d. 12/9/1962)(d. Biloxi in Veterans Hospital). Lost leg in World War I (Argonne). M. Illinois 1933 Caroline Echols Harbour, dau. of Dan Harbour and his wife, the former Annie Ashford. No issue.

2212725 James Randolph Maury.

2212726 Son (lived 1 year).

221273 Edward Fontaine Maury (d. 5/11/1945)(b. Sumpter County, AL, d. Durant, MS, bur. Macon, MS), m. Macon, MS 2/15/ 1877 Mary Louise Shelton (d. 1896)(b. Virginia, d. Macon), dau. of Mr. Shelton and his wife, the former Lucy Berkeley.

2212731 James Berkeley ("Berk") Maury (5/11/1878-10/20/1946)(b. Wahalak, bur. Macon), m. 11/5/1912 Renna Agnes Burks (5/13/1889-5/11/   )(b. Ackerman, MS, bur. Macon), dau. of Samuel Burks and his wife, the former Renna Amanda Wood.

22127311 Mary Agnes Maury (10/21/1913-   )(b. Macon), m. 6/23/ 1936 John W. Cox (8/23/1903-   )(b. Charleston, MS), son of John Cunningham Cox and his wife, the former Lillie Selby.

22127312 James Berkeley Maury, Jr. (7/6/1915-   )(b. Macon), m. 7/1/1945 Augusta Genevieve Rogers (10/31/1921-   ) (b. Macon), dau. of Nicholas Newton Rogers and his wife, the former Nellie Smith.

221273121 Jane Rogers Maury (8/10/1946-   )(b. Macon). M (1st) 1/26/1967 Robert Thomas Olson (b. Worcester, MA), son of Mona Lee Raines and William D. Young. M. (2nd) Charles E. Kenner, Jr.

2212731211 Jennifer Olson (9/11/1967-   ).

221273122 James Berkeley Maury III (2/16/1950-   )(b. College Station, TX).

221273123 Carol Augusta Maury (9/20/1954-   )(b. Houston).

2212732 Francis Lewis Maury (11/25/1880-2/22/1959)(b. Wahalak, MS, bur. Mobile). M. (1st)   . M. (2nd) Alice McGill.

Child by first wife:

22127321 Frank Lewis Maury, Jr.
    Child by second wife:
22127322 Mary Alice Maury (name changed to Mary Fontaine Maury),
          m. 12/20/1952 Walter Meeds Smith, son of Raplh Austin
          Smith.
221273221 Brett Smith.
221273222 Charlotte McGill Smith (4/9/1959-   )(b. Mobile).
22127323 L. Garnett ("Rusty") Maury. Lives in Delaware
          (Hercules Powder). M. Betty _____.
221273231 Dau.
221273232 Dau.
221273233 Dau.
2212733 Richard Harris Maury (12/19/1883-7/14/1900)(bur. Macon).
          Unm.
2212734 Joseph Shelton Maury (2/22/1886-9/10/1919)(b. Kemper
          County, MS, bur. Macon), m. Oklahoma City, Elizabeth
          Wright (2/12/1884-2/7/1969)(b. Poinsett County, AR,
          bur. Macon), dau. of Jasper Wright and his wife, the
          former Laura Stevens.
22127341 Joseph Harry Maury (5/27/1909-   )(b. Macon), m. 12/
          31/1933 Oma Wood.
221273411 Shirley Maury, m Robert E. Lindsey.
2212734111 Kathleen Lindsey.
221273412 Patricia Maury, m. Charles Harvey Stovall.
2212734121 Randall Maury Stovall (3/7/1962-   ).
2212734122 Carl Brian Maury (1966-1966).
22127342 Edward Wright Maury (3/5/1911-)(b. Macon). M. (1st)
          Martha Burns. M. (2nd) 9/13/1941 Rose Marie Sasek
          (6/4/1919-   )(b. Leadville, CO), dau. of John
          Sasek and his wife, the former Annie Clements.
    Children by first wife:
221273421 Janet Maury. Adopted by her mother's second husband.
221273422 Elizabeth ("Betty") Maury. Adopted by her mother's
          second husband. "Betty" m. 6/9/1957 Lowell Newton.
2212734221 Michael Lowell Newton (3/14/1958-   )(twin).
2212734222 Cheryl Marie Newton (3/14/1958-   )(twin).
    Children by second wife:
221273423 Richard Maury (5/13/1942-5/13/1942)(b. and d. Belen,
          NM).
221273424 Robert Charles Maury (10/14/1946-   )(b. Albuquer-
          que).
221273425 Linda Sue Maury (7/17/1953-   )(b. Albuquerque).
221273426 William John Maury (12/24/1959-12/25/1959)(b. Albu-
          querque).
22127343 Frank Lewis Maury (4/27/1916-11/29/1958)(b. Macon,
          bur. Tucson), m. Edna Heady of Benson, AZ.
221273431 Frank Lewis Maury, Jr. (8/28/1943-   ), m. and
          has children.
22127344 Joseph Shelton Maury, Jr. (b. 2/4/1920-posthumous
          child)(b. Macon), m. 12/15/1945 Selma Burns (12/9/
          1917-   )(b. Montgomery County, MS), dau. of
          Selmer Burns and his wife, the former Virginia Watson.
221273441 Joseph Shelton ("Bub") Maury III (11/13/1946-   ).
221273442 Thomas Edward Maury (6/3/1952-   )(b. West Point, MS).

2212735 Lucy Kittrell Maury (3/28/1889-   )(b. Wahalak), m.
        10/8/1914 Thomas Sage Humphries (10/9/1885-11/9/1931)
        (b. Atlanta, bur. Durant, MS), son of John Wiley
        Humphries and his wife, the former Laura Virginia
        McCan.
22127351 Laura Louise Humphries (1/3/1917-11/29/1921)(b. and
        bur. Durant).
22127352 John Wiley Humphries II (9/19/1918-   )(b. Durant),
        m. 6/7/1942 Susan Pauline Holder (3/12/1922-   )
        (b. Ebenezer, MS), dau. of Andrew Bowles Holder and
        his wife, the former Missie Bridgeforth.
221273521 Richard Daniel Humphries (6/14/1946-   )(b. Lexing-
        ton, MS).
221273522 Tom Hooke Humphries (6/22/1948-   )(b. Lexington,
        MS).
221273523 Ralph Holder Humphries (12/2/1954-   )(b. Durant).
22127353 Tom Maury Humphries (4/21/1921-   ), m. Myra Broom-
        field, dau. of Mr. Broomfield and his wife, the former
        Evelyn Brown.
221273531 Lucy Humphries (4/21/1957-   )(b. Memphis).
221273532 Laura Brown Humphries (12/1/1959-   )(b. Memphis).
2212736 Susie Campbell Maury (6/14/1893-   )(b. Macon, MS), m.
        2/22/1915 Thomas Harvey Flurry.
22127361 Ruth Celeste Flurry (4/16/1916-   )(b. Montgomery).
221274 Matthew ("Henry") Maury (4/19/1854-12/16/1888)(killed in
        Kemper County, MS, bur. Wahalak). Owned a gin, grist
        and saw mill in Shuqualak, MS. M. Mary Jennie Gathright
        (b. Virginia, bur. Wahalak).
2212741 Richard Harris Maury (killed ca. 1914 when a cow crossed
        in front of an automobile that he was driving).
2212742 Kate Gathright Maury.
2212746 Nellie Maury (bur. Wahalak).
221275 Robert Randolph Maury (5/14/1851-7/30/1851).
221276 Thomas LaFayette Maury (d. 5/4/1856, age 3 months, 4
        days).
22128   Catherine Mildred Washington Maury (d. 8/11 or 18/1825 or
        1826).
22129   Agnes Gray Maury (d. 8/16 or 26/1828 or 1831).
2212x   Gilbert Lafayette Maury (d. 11/24/1898)(b. Fredericksburg,
        VA, bur. Pushmataha). C.S.A. M. 6/4/1860 Choctaw County,
        AL, Eliza Searsm Scott (d. 12/28/1910)(b. Choctaw County,
        bur. Pushmataha), dau. of Rev. James Emanuel Scott and
        his wife, the former Mary Ann Virginia Galloway.
2212x1 Oscar Fontaine Maury (d. 9/6/1945)(b. Crittenden County,
        AR; d. Reno; bur. Ada, OK), m. 12/13/1899 Choctaw
        County, AL, Sadie Flora Rainer (1/30/1879-2/28/1942)(b.
        Pushmataha, bur. Ada), dau. of Frank Rainer and his
        wife, the former Henrietta Baskin.
2212x11 Norman Randolph Maury (11/13/1900-9/4/1923)(b. Cuba,
        AL, d. of typhoid, bur. Ada).
2212x12 Mary Adalyn Maury (9/13/1902-   ), m. 4/29/1929 Ray
        Cotton (3/8/1896-4/19/1957).
        Adopted: Mary Jo Cotton (7/9/1935-   )(b. Louis-
        ville), m. 10/ /1964 Richard O'Connor (9/29/1929-   )

(b. Kansas City), son of R. J. O'Connor and his wife, the former Bertha Brooks.

2212x13 Sadie Pearl Maury (8/9/1904-   )(b. Cuba, AL), m. 6/23/1927 Ed S. Halverson.

2212x131 Edward Ray Halverson (1/13/1932-   )(b. Oklahoma City), m. Billie Jean Wilson (3/21/1930-   )(b. Pontotoc County, OK), dau. of Jesse C. Wilson and his wife, the former Zora P. .

2212x1311 Edward Ray ("Rusty") Halverson, Jr. (5/6/1956-   ) (b. Ada).

2212x1312 Maury Keith Halverson (11/16/1961-   )(b. Ada).

2212x1313 Michael Shawn Halverson (4/7/1967-   )(b. Ada).

2212x14 Oscar LaFayette Maury (1/22/1907-10/3/1963)(b. Stratford, OK, bur. Las Vegas). M. (1st) _____. M. (2nd) Merle Green.

2212x141 Marjorie Maury (1933-   ), m. Dale Garritson (5/16/1930-   ).

2212x1411 Laurie Jean Garritson (4/26/1952-   ).

2212x1412 Allison Garritson (12/28/1958-   ).

2212x1413 Guy Maury Garritson (4/18/1961-   ).

2212x142 Wesley ("Buddy") Maury (1934-   ), m. 8/3/1972 Mary Lucy DiPeso, dau. of Ernest and Lucy DiPeso.

2212x15 Lulu Pauline Maury (2/14/1909-   )(b. Texas), m. L. Jack Birdwell.

2212x151 Donald J. Birdwell (8/17/1936-   )(b. Oklahoma City), m. 11/18/1955 Constance Mercedes Roberson (10/18/1937-   )(b. El Reno, OK), dau. of Cloyd Guy Roberson and his wife, the former Mercedes A. Noah.

2212x1511 David Jay Birdwell (10/21/1956-   )(b. Oklahoma City).

2212x1512 Terri Dawn Birdwell (7/14/1958-   )(b. Oklahoma City).

2212x16 Jessie Shi Maury (7/12/1911-   )(b. Stratford, OK), m. 12/26/1931 Charles C. Benson (1/26/1910-   )(b. Okemah, OK), son of Benjamin Berry Benson and his wife, the former Olive Shumard.

2212x161 Ruth Clarice Benson (5/24/1933-   )(b. Ada), m. 6/20/1953 David W. Beckemeier (9/7/1933-   ), son of Edward Beckemeier and his wife, the former Edna Wakin.

2212x1611 David Charles Beckemeier (2/14/1954-   ).

2212x1612 Timothy Carl Beckemeier (11/28/1957-   ).

2212x1613 Heidi Marie Beckemeier (12/30/1959-   ).

2212x1614 Gretchen Ruth Beckemeier (6/9/1962-   ).

2212x162 Charles Saxon Benson (12/5/1934-   )(b. Okemah), m. 8/19/1957 Irma Jean Smith (11/6/1936-   ), dau. of Jack K. Smith.
    Adopted: Jamie Lynn Benson (1/17/1963·   ), and Julie Ann Benson (7/1/1968-   ).

2212x163 Benny Maury Benson (11/28/1936-   )(b. Okemah), m. 2/14/1960 Wanda Jo Stankewitz (7/15/1938-   )(b. Shawnee, OK), dau. of John Ulys Stankewitz and his wife, the former Edna Ramsey.

2212x1631 Bryan Maury Benson (12/3/1961-   ).

2212x1632 Jo Lynne Benson (1/29/1963-   ).

2212x1633 Laura Beth Benson (8/21/1965-   ).
2212x17 Nora Elizabeth Maury (10/5/1916-   )(b. Stratford),
        m. 10/30/1938 George Ronald Black.
2212x171 Philip Black (11/18/1939-   )(b. Oklahoma City), m.
        1/21/1963 Diana Stevens (b. San Diego), dau. of John
        D. and Ernestine Stevens.
2212x1711 Kari Renee Black (4/19/1964-   )(b. Little Rock).
2212x1712 Jeffrey Philip Black (11/9/1966-   )(Bronxville, NY).
2212x172 Donna Kay Black (1/16/1945-   )(b. Ada), m. 7/ /1964
        John Robert Havgen (b. Amarillo), son of Dr. I. J. and
        Edna Havgen.
2212x1721 Jennifer Paige Havgen (3/11/1968-   )(b. Jackson-
        ville).
2212x2 James Woodville Maury (b. Alabama, d. Tacoma, WA). Unm.
2212x3 Lula Randolph Maury (8/31/1870-11/5/1961)(b.Alabama, bur.
        Waco), m. James Woodville Maury (5/6/1858-12/27/1936)
        (221258). For their children, etc., see under his
        number.
2212x4 Charles Desseso Maury (d. 1939)(b. Pushmataha, d. Butte,
        MT), m. 5/1/1897 Minnie Virginia Wallace (8/19/1871-
        7/3/1966)(b. Toomsuba, MS, bur. Birmingham)(widow of
        James Wilson Coker), dau. of Lawson Wallace and his
        wife, the former Mary Catherine Pigford.
2212x41 Ruby Randolph Maury (4/16/1889-   )(b. Meridian, MS).
        M. (1st) 10/4/1913, Brent, AL, Horace Lee Crabtree (1/
        30/1890-10/6/1930)(b. Franklin County, TN; bur. New
        Brocton, AL), son of Ovia Virgil Crabtree and his wife,
        the former Hallie West. M. (2nd) 2/2/1934 Elvin Curtis
        Jones (d. 1941). No issue by second marriage.
2212x411 Nell Virginia Crabtree (11/9/1914-   )(b. Brent). M.
        (1st) Montgomery 4/11/1933 Howard Milford Brock (12/
        19/1911-11/8/1957)(b. and bur. New Brocton). Killed
        in automobile accident on duty with Alabama State
        Highway Patrol. M. (2nd) 9/23/1975 Clarence Carl
        Bookert (7/16/1914-   ).
2212x4111 Horace Milford Brock (8/24/1934-   ), m. 3/11/1955
        Mary Ruth Bible (4/26/1935-   )(b. Austin), dau.
        of William Lester Bible and his wife, the former
        Hazel Shaffer.
2212x41111 Sandra Ellen Brock (7/16/1956-   )(b. Bangor, ME),
        m. Dallas 6/3/1972 Dale Wayne Cheney (3/5/1953-   )
        (b. Detroit), son of Kenneth Lee Cheney and his
        wife, the former Sylvia Turner.
2212x411111 Christopher Wayne Cheney (11/12/1975-   )(b.
        Birmingham).
2212x41112 Estella Denise Brock (12/7/1959-   )(b. Macon, GA),
        m. 3/19/1976 Richard Carlton Register (1/30/1958-   )
        (b. Lake City, FL), son of Gifford Franklin Register
        and his wife, the former Lois Marie Pepper.
2212x411121 Wendy Denise Register (2/23/1977-   )(b. Valdosta).
2212x411122 Travis Register.
2212x4112 Roslyn Lannell Brock (1/24/1937-   ), m. Birmingham
        7/23/1961 Henry Julius Stern (9/4/1931-   )(b.
        Germany), son of Arnold Stern and his wife, the

former Hedwig Israelson.

2212x41121   Virginia ("Ginger") Howard Stern (4/17/1962-   ) (b. Opelika).

2212x41122   Henry Julius ("Jay") Stern, Jr. (11/19/1963-   )(b. Opelika).

2212x412   Horace Jackson Crabtree (12/7/1918-   )(b. Savannah), m. 12/13/1936 Mildred Byrd (1/1/1917-   )(b. Geneva, AL), dau. of James Robert Ira Byrd and his wife, the former Annie Elizabeth Lammons.

2212x4121   Jacquelyn Crabtree (11/7/1941-   )(b. New Brocton), m. 1/24/1963 Jerry Collins Evans, son of Vachis Nix Evans and his wife, the former Grace Plant.

2212x41211   Jerry Collins ("Cal") Evans, Jr. (12/14/1963-   )(b. Mobile).

2212x41212   Shanda Janeane Evans (7/29/1968-   )(b. Tampa).

2212x4122   Judy Dianne Crabtree (8/12/1947-   ). M. (1st) Tampa 2/2/1967 Richard Andrew Namey (1/21/1947-   ), son of Joseph Andrew Namey and his wife, the former Frances Amy Dills. Div. M. (2nd) Tampa 6/9/1973 Thomas L. Flannery, Jr.

2212x41221   Richard Ashley Namey (9/20/1967-   )(b. Tampa), adopted by Thomas L. Flannery, Jr.

2212x4123   Debra Crabtree (12/22/1951-   )(b. Tuscaloosa)(twin), m. Orlando 10/12/1968 Richard Robert Fain (11/29/1950-   )(b. Pasadena), son of Eugene H. Fain and his wife, the former Barbara L. Noll.

2212x41231   Richard Robert Fain, Jr. (5/28/1969-   )(b. Orlando).

2212x41232   Christine Renee Fain (6/7/1971-   )(b. Miami).

2212x41233   Matthew Jack Fain (7/10/1979-   )(b. Jacksonville).

2212x41234   Creighton Daniel Fain (9/30/1982-   )(b. Jacksonville).

2212x4124   Barbara Crabtree (12/22/1951-   )(b. Tuscaloosa) (twin), m. Orlando 9/12/1970 John Charles ("Rusty") Aubrey (2/11/1948-   )(b. Los Angeles), son of Ralph Aubrey and his wife, the former Eve Young.

2212x41241   John Travis Aubrey (3/5/1976-   )(b. Miami).

2212x41242   Keith Edward Aubrey (8/16/1977-   )(b. Miami).

2212x413   Dorothea Lee Crabtree (5/7/1921-   )(b. Elba, AL), m. 12/25/1940 Charles Roy Burns (9/5/1913-5/ /1979)(b. Cullman, AL, bur. Trussville, AL), son of Lafayette Burns and his wife, the former Jennie Eugene Marlowe. Adopted: Charles Randolph Burns.

2212x414   Ruby Frances Crabtree (5/12/1922-5/9/1929)(bur. New Brocton).

2212x415   Helen Sue Crabtree (1/12/1924-   )(b. New Brocton). M. (1st) Frank Edward Ostman (3/1/1915-11/17/1955)(b. Oakland, bur. Golden Gate National Cemetery), son of John Edward Ostman and his wife, the former Carmen Juarez. M. (2nd) 4/10/1951 Albert Stevenson West (1/20/1922-6/29/1960)(b. Townley, AL, killed in automobile accident), son of Leslie Stephen West and his wife, the former Mattie Ferguson. M. (3rd) Herbert William Teague, Jr. (6/12/1919-   )(b. Anniston), son of Carl C. Teague and Minnie Lee Osborn.

2212x4151 Robert James Ostman (name changed September 1952 to Robert Ostman West (10/30/1945-   )(b. San Francisco). M. (1st) Detroit 12/9/1967 Marjorie Ann Cox (5/15/1947-   )(b. Highland Park, MI), dau. of Willie Cortez Cox and his wife, the former Myrtle Marguerite Lex. M. (2nd) Houston 3/21/1979 Denise Joye Perry Boette (11/8/1948-   )(b. Detroit), dau. of Daniel Bruce Perry and his wife, the former Anita Lillian Blais.

   Children by first wife:

2212x41511 Eric Maury West (2/7/1969-   )(b. San Antonio).

2212x41512 Kathryn Fontaine West (4/20/1971-)(b. Birmingham).

   Children by second wife:

2212x41513 Brian Maxwell West (7/9/1981-   )(b. Houston).

2212x41514 Suzanne Marie West (9/19/1984-   )(b. Houston).

2212x416 Jean Frederica Crabtree (2/18/1925-   )(b. New Brocton). M. (1st) 6/ /1940 James Carl Sharrock, Jr. (10/14/1920-12/14/1954)(b. and bur. Birmingham), son of James Carl Sharrock and his wife, the former Mary Vincent. M. (2nd) 8/16/1965 David ("Smiley") Emerson Messier (10/4/1938-   )(b. Youngstown, PA), son of Ernest Joseph Messier and his wife, the former Mildred Raffensperger.

2212x4161 James Frederick Sharrock (10/6/1941-   )(b. Birmingham), m. 5/5/1961 Barbara Neal Hume (8/19/1939-   ) (b. Rosedale, OK). She had a child by a previous marriage: Jolisa Tyann Hume (4/22/1960-   )(b. Denison, TX).

2212x41611 Kenneth Arlan Sharrock (12/1/1962-   )(b. Denison).

2212x41612 Kelle Renee Sharrock (9/25/1969-   )(b. Denison).

2212x417 Betty Joan Crabtree (8/23/1926-   )(b. New Brocton), m. 11/27/1945 James Forrest West (8/13/1923-   )(b. Townley, AL).

2212X4171 Stephen Forrest West (8/31/1947-   )(b. Birmingham), m. Garden Grove, CA, 10/15/1966 Linda Susan Hansen (11/15/1947-   )(b. Santa Ana), dau. of Gerald Vincent Hansen and his wife, the former Mary Patricia Fitzpatrick.

2212x41711 Erik Stephen West (11/15/1947-   )(b. Santa Ana).

2212x4172 Michael Leslie West (7/15/1950-   )(b. Birmingham), m. San Diego 7/23/1977 Jeannie Austin.

2212x41721 Audrey West (1980-   ).

2212x41722 Michael Austin West (5/8/1982-   )(b. San Diego).

2212x4173 Teresa Joan West (9/4/1957-   )(b. Jacksonville), m. Kennesaw, GA, 3/8/1975 Wesley LaMott King (9/28/1954-   )(b. Philadelphia), son of Wesley Ellington King and his wife, the former Geneva Royal.

2212x41731 Joshua James King (5/26/1978-   )(b. Valdosta).

2212x4174 Lani Dianne West (5/27/1960-   )(b. Honolulu). M. (1st) Marietta, GA, 11/22/1978 H. Douglas Payne. M. (2nd) 12/10/1982 Michael Anthony Nolan.

2212x41741 Lisa Michelle Payne (11/9/1979-   )(b. Marietta).

2212x41742 Stephen Michael Nolan (3/9/1984-   )(b. Marietta).

2212x41743 Jennifer Nichole Nolan (3/6/1985-   )(b. Marietta).
2212x42 Lucie Gaines Maury (11/8/1900-   )(b. Meridian, MS),
    m. 9/9/1923 Samuel Rivers Brice (9/6/1898-3/10/1954)(b.
    Sylacauga, AL, bur. Birmingham), son of Patrick Brice
    and his wife, the former Annie Foley.
2212x421 Byron Barnes Brice (6/16/1925-   )(b. Alabama), m.
    3/11/1945 Rita Elizabeth Brock (1/30/1923-   )(b.
    Fairfield, AL), dau. of Ernest Cole Brock and his
    wife, the former Julia Donho.
2212x4211 Beverly Brock Brice (1/25/1946-   )(b. Birmingham),
    m. Birmingham 12/26/1969 James Carl Cooper (1/4/1945-
)(b. Walker County, AL), son of Col. Carl
    Cooper and his wife, the former James Anna Rutledge.
2212x4212 Linda Dianne Brice (b. 3/11/1947), m. Meridian, MS,
    12/29/1946 Michael Christopher Berndt (12/29/1946-)
    (b. Meridian), son of Earl Michael Berndt and his
    wife, the former Mary Elizabeth Christopher.
2212x42121 Lucie Elizabeth Berndt (8/16/1966-8/17/1966).
2212x42122 Michael Christopher Berndt, Jr. (10/11/1967-   )(b.
    Birmingham).
2212x43 Gilbert Wallace Maury (10/18/1902-8/29/1960)(b. Wapa-
    nucka, OK Territory, bur. Trussville, AL), m. 2/21/1926
    Clarice Adella Parks (10/13/1906-   )(b. Talladega,
    AL), dau. of Lee Otis Parks and his wife, the former
    Kate Morse Freeze.
2212x431 Katherine Virginia Maury (12/22/1926-)(b. Talladega),
    m. 4/17/1943 James Gibson Stringer (4/29/1920-   )
    (b. Tuscaloosa), son of Ernest Gibson Stringer and his
    wife, the former Willie Claudine Sanders.
2212x4311 James Gibson Stringer, Jr. (2/27/1944-   )(b. Talla-
    dega), m. Tuscaloosa 9/3/1966 Mary Helen Roberts (9/
    16/1945-   ), dau. of Milton Boyd Roberts and his
    wife, the former Helen Reid.
2212x43111 Katharine Leigh Stringer (8/20/1971-   )(b. Silver
    Spring, MD).
2212x43112 Michael Boyd Stringer (7/17/1974-   )(b. Manassas).
2212x43113 Laura McLane Stringer (6/16/1976-   ).
2212x4312 Robert Sanders Stringer (1/2/1949-   ), m. 7/26/1975
    Carol Trice (12/15/1950-   ).
2212x43121 Sarah Layne Stringer (5/3/1978-   ).
2212x43122 Stephanie Trice Stringer (7/23/1981-   ).
2212x4313 Virginia Clarice Stringer (3/2/1957-)(b. Talladega),
    m. 8/29/1970 Terry Michael Cromer (1/27/1950   )
    (b. Gadsden, AL), son of Donald Odell Cromer and his
    wife, the former Willodean Yarbrough. Div.
2212x4314 David Lee Stringer (10/25/1953-   ), m. 2/15/1975
    Sharon Gray.
2212x43141 Kelli Renae Stringer (5/23/1981-   ).
2212x43142 Jennifer Lee Stringer (10/19/1983-   ).
2212x4315 Elizabeth Anne Stringer (10/1/1961-   ), m. 7/19/
    1980 Hubert Richard Pair, Jr. (6/15/1957-   ).
2212x43151 Richard Brandon Pair (7/18/1982-   ).
2212x44 Charles Julian ("Bill") Maury (12/15/1906-5/7/1965)(b.
    Stratford, OK Territory, bur. San Pedro, CA), m. Nona

Idella Bonner (10/16/1907-   )(b. Anniston).
2212x441 Charles Julian Maury, Jr. (11/1/1931-   )(b. Anniston),
          m. 3/21/1953 Mae Elizabeth Scarratt (6/6/1933-   )
          (b. Atlanta).
2212x4411 Richard C. Maury (4/12/1954-   )(b. Atlanta).
2212x4412 Elizabeth Ann Maury (12/30/1957-   )(b. Atlanta).
2212x4413 Michael S. Maury (5/14/1959-   )(b. Atlanta).
2212x4414 Nona Christine Maury (11/1/1961-   )(b. Atlanta).
2212x5 Dabney Herndon ("Shing") Maury (d. 6/10/1954)(d. Great
        Falls, MT, bur. Waco).
2212x6 Ernest Linwood Maury (d. 10/22/1960)(b. Pushmataha, bur.
        Birmingham), m. Rosa Mae ("Rosie") Burnette (5/25/1882-
        11/30/1943)(b. Uniontown, AL).
2212x61 Minnie Lee Maury (8/18/1906-   )(b. Pushmataha), m.
         3/2/1935 Isaac Dorriety (7/15/1906-   )(b. Brundidge,
         AL).
2212x611 Maury Odell Dorriety (7/3/1936-   )(b. Birmingham),
          m. 6/25/1966 Roxie Watson of Rossville, GA.
2212x612 William Linwood Dorriety (3/6/1939-   ).
2212x62 Mattie Eliza Maury (1/8/1908-6/30/1951)(b. Pushmataha,
         bur. Sao Paulo, Brazil, where she and her husband were
         missionaries), m. F. Paul Peterson.
2212x621 David Timothy Peterson (7/10/1940-   )(b. Sao Paulo),
          m. Decatur, GA, 4/17/1970 Mary Louise York.
2212x6211 Tracie Michelle Peterson (2/7/1971-   )(b. Long
           Beach).
2212x622 Lois Jean Peterson (11/14/1941-   ), m. 1/4/1969
          Martin John Reilly.
2212x6221 Christina Marie Reilly (1/16/1971-   )(b. Fort
           Wayne).
2212x6222 Brian John Reilly (12/7/1972-   )(b. Fort Wayne).
2212x6223 Audrey Elizabeth Reilly (6/11/1974-   )(b. Fort
           Wayne).
2212x623 Rosalind Elaine Peterson (4/25/1944-   ), m. 12/1/
          1963 William ("Bill") Ryan.
2212x6231 David William Ryan (10/20/1964-   ).
2212x6232 Timothy Scott Ryan (10/2/1967-   ).
2212x6233 Matthew Jon Ryan (11/29/1968-   ).
2212x6234 Sean Michael Ryan (7/3/1973-   ).
2212x63 Ernest Linwood Maury, Jr. (2/1/1913-   )(b. Pennington,
         AL), m. Lillian Odessa Green (11/9/1915-   )(b. Ash-
         land, AL).
2212x631 Ernest Allen Maury (3/2/1937-   )(b. Birmingham), m.
          6/20/1958 Carolyn Faye Smith (10/13/1939-   )(b.
          Cullman, AL), dau. of Curgis Smith and his wife, the
          former Verde Lou Colier.
2212x6311 Dena Renee Maury (3/26/1960-   )(b. Birmingham).
2212x6312 Carmen Leilani Maury (7/3/1963-   )(b. New Orleans).
2212x6313 David Christopher Maury (9/24/1964-   )(b. New
           Orleans).
2212x64 Mary Maury (7/7/1918-   )(b. Jackson, AL), m. 8/29/1935
         John Horton Jones (3/28/1914-8/19/1966)(b. and bur.
         Birmingham).
2212x641 John Kenneth Jones (8/7/1936-   )(b. Birmingham),

m. 8/4/1956 Rachel Nell Owens (8/20/1938-   )(b.
Centerville, AL), dau. of David Herman Owens.
2212x6411 Maury Scott Jones (5/20/1961-   )(b. Birmingham).
2212x6412 Terri Lyn Jones (12/18/1962-   )(b. Birmingham).
2212x65 Harry Maury (4/23/1923-   )(b. Jackson, AL).
2212x7 Ruby Rolfe Maury (9/9/1883-   )(b. Pushmatah), m. 8/30/
1903 Johnston Frank Roberts (11/29/1883-   )(b. China
Spring, TX), son of Motley Maddux Roberts and his wife,
the former Hannah Margaret Evans.
2212x71 Scott Evans Roberts (8/30/1905-   )(b. China Spring).
M. (1st) Lucile Inex Clark. M. (2nd) 6/26/1946 Sybil
Morgan (12/22/   -   )(b. Louisiana).
   Child by first wife:
2212x711 Beverly Ann Roberts (10/8/1925-   )(b. Dallas), m. Earl
Henderson Rast.
2212x7111 Stephanie Ann Rast (7/30/1946-   )(b. Waco).
2212x7112 Susan Earle Rast (9/13/1947-   )(b. Waco).
2212x7113 Beverly Jan Rast (10/27/1959-   )(b. San Diego).
2212x72 Mary Randolph Roberts (3/4/1911-   )(b. China Spring),
m. 10/25/1936 James Hughey Coffman.
2212x721 James Hughey Coffman, Jr. (6/25/1940-   )(b. San
Francisco), m. Margo _____.
2212x7211 Jeffrey Howard Coffman (11/1/1964-   ).
2212x8 Mary Maury (8/6/1876-9/4/1879)(b. Alabama, bur. Kemper
County, MS).
2212x9 Henry Edwin Maury (2/28/1861-11/13/1863)(b. and d. Van
Buren County, AR).
2212xx Jefferson Davis Maury (7/2/1862-6/21/1863)(b. Van Buren
County)(twin).
2212xa Thomas Francis Maury (7/2/1862-12/1/1863)(twin).
2212xb Guy Francis Maury (10/12/1866-12/8/1867)(b. Alabama).

2215 Catherine Cochrane Randolph (d. 12/12/1862)(d. Richmond).
M. Richmond 8/7/1832.
22151 Walter Randolph Abbott (d. 6/30/1862)(b. Richmond), m.
Elizabeth Duval (2/11/1840-6/30/1909)(b. and d. Richmond)

221511 Walter Raleigh Abbott, Jr.(1861-5/   /1865)

22152 Virginia Trent Abbott (3/30/1835-10/26/1916)(b. Henrico
County, d. Richmond, bur. Hollywood). M. Richmond 3/6/
1856 Claiborne Watkins (1/18/1830-1/24/1842)(b. Powhatan
County, d. Richmond, bur. Hollywood), son of Henry W.
Watkins and his wife, the former Judith F. Hundley.
221521 Walter Abbott Watkins (4/3/1857-2/22/1935)(b. Richmond,
d. Staunton, bur. Hollywood), m. Isle of Wight County
6/5/1883 Mary Willie Spears (11/6/1859-3/9/1930)(b.
Chesterfield County, d. Richmond, bur. Hollywood), dau.
of Edward W. Spears and his wife, the former Rebecca
P. Hundley.
2215211 Claiborne Randolph Watkins (12/10/1885-10/30/1953)(b.
Chesterfield County, d. Richmond), m. Richmond 6/2/
1915 Virgina Whiteley (1890-1957).

2215212 Virginia Abbott Watkins (4/25/1000 7/4/1959)(d. Richmond), m. Richmond 4/28/1917 Paul Christian (1889-
1967).

2215213 Adelaide Ward Watkins (3/24/1899-11/22/1964)(b. Orange
County, d. Richmond), m. Richmond 11/17/1923 Charles
Terry (1896-1982).

2215214 Elizabeth Watkins (1/13/1901-   )(b. Richmond), m.
Haverford, PA, 12/9/1925 William Clarke (1897-1944).

221522 Charles Hunter Watkins (9/29/1858-2/20/1929)(b. and d.
Richmond, bur. Hollywood), m. (1st) Richmond 3/24/1898
Maude Hairston Ingles (2/15/1879-5/28/1911)(b. Martins-
ville, d. Richmond, bur. Hollywood), dau. of Cyrus H.
Ingles and his wife, the former Elizabeth Hairston.
M. (2nd) Elizabeth Ingles (1876-1952). No issue by
second wife.
   Children by first wife:

2215221 Charles Hunter Watkins, Jr. (7/14/1899-11/15/1980)(b.
and d. Richmond), m. New York, NY 10/2/1934 May Allen
(1908-   ).

2215222 Elizabeth Ingles Watkins (5/20/1901-2/5/1981)(b. and d.
Richmond), m. Richmond 6/10/1933 R. Carter Scott (1900-
1973).

2215223 Maude Randolph Watkins (8/23/1903-   /   /1969)(b. Richmond, d. New York, NY), m. James Galleher (1893-1982).

2215224 Catharine Montague Watkins (11/11/1905-   )(b. Richmond), m. Harrison Wiltshire (1902-   ).

2215225 Walter Abbott Watkins (11/26/1909-6/8/1910)(b. and d.
Richmond).

221523 Randolph Watkins (8/30/1860-4/27/1952)(b. and d. Richmond), m. Aiken County, SC, 2/26/1908 Lucie Lorenz
(1875-1961). No issue.

221524 Claiborne Watkins, Jr. (8/3/1863-2/27/1956)(b. and d.
Richmond). No issue.

221525 Kate Watkins (6/16/1866-4/4/1951)(b. Richmond, d. Laurel,
MD, bur. Arlington, VA), m. Richmond 11/19/1890 Charles
Gerhardt (3/19/1863-6/5/1957)(b. Baltimore, d. Mendham,
NJ, bur. Arlington, VA), son of Henry Gerhardt and his
wife, the former Emily Jane Carter. Charles Gerhardt
was a General in the U.S. Army.

2215251 Virginia Gerhardt (12/16/1891-3/19/1981)(b. Fort Assina-
boine, MT, d. San Francisco, bur. Arlington, VA), m.
New York, NY 8/12/1915 John Hale Stutesman (12/8/1883-
7/14/1966)(b. Peru, IND, d. Fairfax County, bur. Arlington, VA), son of Frank Mc. Stutesman and his wife,
the former Ada Dodds.

22152511 John Hale Stutesman, Jr. (12/16/1920-)(b. Washington,
DC), m. San Francisco 7/23/1949 Mary Ludekens (1922-
). Mr. Stutesman---officer in U.S. Foreign
Service.

221525111   John Rolfe Stutesman (1/10/1951-   )(b. Beirut,
                Lebanon).
221525112   Drake Hilbert Stutesman (1/8/1954-   )(b. Washing-
                ton, DC), m. London, England 3/19/1983 Arthur Ellis.
2215252   Charles Hunter Gerhardt (6/6/1895-10/9/1976)(b. Lebanon,
                TN, d. Winter Park, FL), m. Little Rock, AR, 6/14/1922
                Nina McCleskey (1900-   ). Charles Hunter Gerhardt
                was a Major General in the U.S. Army.
221526   Henry Watkins (4/22/1869-7/16/1869)(b. and d. Richmond).
221527   Virginia Watkins (6/6/1970-8/4/1872)(b. and d. Richmond).
221528   Elizabeth Watkins (12/28/1872-4/1/1951)(b. and d. Rich-
                mond).
221529   Adelaide Watkins (4/22/1875-4/29/1965)(b. and d. Rich-
                mond, bur. Hollywood), m. Richmond 1/7/1903 Alexander
                Barclay Guigon, Jr. (8/13/1858-5/15/1923)(b. and d.
                Richmond, bur. Hollywood), son of Judge Alexander
                Barlcay Guigon and his wife,the former Sarah Bates Allen
                of New Bedford, MA.
2215291   Lisa Guigon (baptised Elizabeth, and name legally
                changed to Lisa)(9/28/1907-   )(b. Richmond), m.
                11/29/1938 John Baird Shinberger.
2218   Georgianna Washington Randolph (1804-9/8/1841)(d. Richmond)
221x   Susan Frances Randolph (8/25/1800-7/4/1850), m. 1820
                Alexander Lithgow Botts.

222   Brett N. Randolph, Jr. (b. 2/21/1760)(b. Durlsey,
                Gloucestershire, County). M. Anne Meade Randolph.
                Matriculated 3/18/1777 at Oxford (St. Mary's Hall). 2 W
                (1) 23. Date of death (1/22/1828) is incorrect, as is the
                statement that he died in Mississippi. MEMORIAL, written
                by him in November of 1833, states that he was a resident
                of Amelia County, and this seems to be affirmed by the
                1830 Census of the household of Brett's eldest son,
                Richard Kidder Randolph (2221), which shows a member, male,

                70-80 years of age.
2221   Richard Kidder Randolph (b. 4/24/1794, d. 9/16/1846), m.
                1/28/1819 Elizabeth Jane ("Betsey") Montague (b. 8/4/1799)
                (d. Tuscaloosa), dau. of Dr. Mickelborough and Saraiah
                Moore Montague (or Ann Carter Vaughan Montague). In
                Reuben Vaughan Kidd's SOLDIER OF THE CONFEDERACY, p. 102,
                the spelling is Mickelboro, and Ann (no "e") Carter
                Vaughan. The surety on the marriage application of
                Richard Kidder Randolph and Elizabeth Jane ("Betsey")
                Montague was Brett N. Randolph (probably 2224).

22211   Brett Noel Randolph (b. 1819)
22212   George Washington Randolph (d. 11/1/1851), m. Cornelia C.
                Fleming

22213   Montague Mickelborough Randolph, d. 8/4/1826 (tombstone).

222131   Ann Elizabeth Randolph (1857-4/4/1930), m. 5/17/1874
                William Wallace Sumerall
222132   Nancy W. ("Nannie") Randolph, m. Robert Montieth
222133   John Mickelborough (d. 1936), m. Sally (Sarah) Darby.
                No issue.

222134 Alice Randolph (1863-1947), m _____ Morris. No issue.
222135 Virginia Randolph (1865-1934), m. James P. Botts
2221351 Son
2221352 Son
2221353 Dau.
222136 Richard Montague Randolph (b. 1866), m Elizabeth _____
2221361 Son
2221362 Dau.
2221363 Dau.
222137 Addie Randolph (d. 1936), m. Seab S. Jones. No issue.
222138 George Washington Randolph (b. 9/5 (or 7)/1874), m. 1899
        or 1900 Isabella ("Belle") Aldridge (d. 8/8/1941)
2221381 Chastain Morris Randolph (d. 8/21/1973), m. Clair Belle
         Eubanks, dau. of James William and Annie Pearl Berry
         Eubanks

22213821 George Gibson Randolph

2221382121 Megan Leigh (b. 8/18/1986)

22213822 Malcolm Montague Randolph

2221383 Armeade Randolph (1904-1904)
2221384 Joe Aldridge Randolph, m. Violet Speed Webb (b. 11/11/
         1909). Ancestor chart in Pocahontas Trails Quarterly,
         Vol. VI, No. 2, April 1988.

22218 Lucie Ann Randolph (6/10/1838-8/29/1872)(b. Greene County,
       AL; d. Eureka, Panola County, MS), m. Eureka 12/24/1864
       Rev. John Brewton Barry (10/2/1837-8/17/1907)(b. Ander-
       sonville District, SC; d. Vian, I.T.), son of William
       Harrison Barry and his wife, the former Harriet Lavinia
       Gambrell. Reverend Barry m. (2nd) 1873 Red Banks, MS,
       Rosa Clayton (1839-1917).

222181 Harriet Elizabeth ("Hattie") Barry (8/30/2865-2/21/1903)
        (b. Eureka Springs, MS; d. Stilwell, Cherokee Nation,
        I. T.). M. (1st) Hillsboro, TX, 5/20/1890, J. L.
        Bowers. M. (2nd) Hanson, I.T., 4/7/1896, Bruton Brewer
    Child by second husband:
2221811 Bruton Brewer, Jr. (b. 1901 or 1902)

222182 Kidder Stewart Barry (12/2/1867 or 1869-10/15/1854)(b.
        Oxford, MS; d. Tulsa). M. (1st) Adair, Sequoyah
        District, Cherokee Nation, 6/25/1891, Elizabeth
        ("Lizzie") Lane Weaver (d. 1896). M. (2nd) 7/10/1897,
        Elizabeth ("Liza") Arminda Hughes (8/14/1878-2/2/1931)
        (b. Atlanta, d. Adair, OK), dau. of Samuel Lindsey
        Hughes and his wife, the former Gracie A. Youngdeer
        Tidwell. M. (3rd).
    Children by first wife:

2221821 William Brewton Barry (5/31/1892-8/19/1950)(d. Nowata,
     OK, truck accident). M. Grace Lewis (1894-1976)
22218211 Robert Francis Barry (b. 5/5/1913)
22218212 Clarence Benjmain Barry (12/4/1914-4/23/1982), m. 9/11/
     1938 Lorene Rowlett (b. 5/29/1920), dau. of Lemuel Y.
     and Minnie D. Jackson Rowlett
222182121 Clarence Benjamin Barry, Jr. (10/26/1939-   ), m.
     12/23/1966 Marcia Lynn Kerr
2221821211 Katherine Lynn Barry (b. 5/18/1868)
2221821212 Kristine June Barry (b. 9/16/1970)
2221821213 Karla Jean Barry (b. 7/22/1972)
222182122 Elizabeth Ann Barry (b. 1/3/1941), m. 11/6/1964 Joseph
     Lemuel Johnson
2221821221 Thomas Johnson (b. 9/25/1965)
2221821222 Ann Letitia Johnson (b. 2/6/1967)
2221821223 Andrew Lemuel Johnson (b. 9/17/1970)
2221822 Stella M. Barry (6/7/1895-   ), m. Henry Behrens
22218221 Emma Lee Behrens (b. 2/12/1912), m. 8/28/1964 James
     Stevens
22218222 Raymond Behrens (8/4/1916-5/11/1970), m. Mary Winters,
     dau. of August and Minnie Teggmer Winters
222182221 Kenneth Behrens
222182222 Donald Behrens
222182223 Mary Ann Behrens
222182224 Linda Behrens
22218223 Vivian Behrens (b. 3/19/1917), m. William H. Winters
     (b. 4/7/1902), son of George and Pauline Meckling
     Winters
222182231 Robert Winters (b. 6/12/1935)
222182232 Evelyn Winters (b. 9/21/1938)
222182233 Harold Winters (b. 8/21/1947)
222182234 Carolyn Winters (b. 5/27/1949)
222182235 Darlene Winters (b. 6/18/1951)
22218224 Opal Behrens (b. 10/2/1918), m. Joe Ross
222182241 Maryland Ross
222182242 Gene Arthur Ross
222182243 Bertha Mae Ross

Children by second wife:

2221823 Clyde Eugene Barry (8/23/1898-5/31/1963)(b. Stilwell,
     OK; d. Claremore, OK), m. Ruby Othal Graves (3/7/1900-
     3/9/1979), dau. of Thomas Jefferson and Florence Yates
     Graves
22218231 Othell Eugene Barry (b. 7/16/1919), m. 7/ /1940
     William Hicks Doler (b. 1919), son of Calhoun and Mary
     Ethel Hicks Doler
222182311 David Fox Doler (b. 7/19/1941), m. (1st) Linda Glass,
     dau. of _____ and Dorothy Kendig Glass. M. (2nd)
     Kathleen Kircher
2221823111 David Fox Doler, Jr. (b. ca. 1957)
2221823112 Laura Ann Doler (b. 6/27/1963), m. 11/27/1982 Kenneth
     Jackson Pike

222182312 Othell Jean Doler (b. 3/16/1943), m. 6/3/1962 Robert
           Snowden (b. ca. 1939). Div. 1979
2221823121 Sherry Jeanette Snowden (b. 10/29/1964)
2221823122 Leslie Diane Snowden (b. 6/17/1967)

22218232 Elizabeth June Barry (b. 9/2/1923), m. (1st) _____.
          M. (2nd) Odis Parret (b. 1/16/1922)
222182321 Glenn Parret (b. 11/23/1951), m. to Gwen _____
2221824 Rena Clorena Barry (7/10/1900-11/14/1949)(b. Stilwell,
         OK; d. Claremore, OK), m. 5/21/1919, William L. Harris
         (12/2/1893-10/31/1951) adopted 8/31/1941 Jack Faye
2221825 Ralph Louis Barry (9/1/1902-10/7/1973)(b. Stilwell, OK;
         d. Ukiah, CA), m. 1/27/1928 Minnie Mae Gilbert
22218251 Ralph Louis Barry, Jr. (1/24/1929-9/20/1933)
22218252 Rena Elva (Renae Aaron) Barry (b. 2/10/1930), m. (1st)
          2/1/1946 William Edward Moat (b. 7/3/1927), son of
          Albert and Della Hill Moat. M. (2nd) 12/25/1979
          Julian A. Burgas-Dector. Rena Elva change name to
          Renae Aaron Barry Dector
222182521 William Randall Moat (b. 12/27/1948), m. 1/ /1966
           Cherrie Louise Marcotte. Div. 197___. Remarried
           198___
2221825211 William Ray Moat (b. 6/6/1969)
2221825212 Tammy Marie Moat (b. 12/27/1971)
222182522 Thomas Edward Moat (1/21/1951-8/7/1952)
222182523 Ralph Timothy Moat (4/16/1956), m. 5/22/1966 Linda
           Leisy
2221825231 Marni Lynn Moat (b. 10/7/1975)
222182524 Robert Thomas Moat (5/8/1957), m. Victoria Travis
           (b. 3/5/1959)
2221825241 Jaime Ray Moat (b. 12/1/1979)
222182525 Richard Barry Moat (b. 11/11/1961)

2221826 Emma Gertrude Barry (5/29/1904-5/31/1981)(b. Adair, OK;
         d. Tulsa; bur. Claremore, OK).

2221827 Albert Lee Barry (6/22/1906-   )(b. Chelsea, OK), m.
         (1st) Ethel Jackson (d. 4/4/1965). M. (2nd) Floy
         Gilbert
22218271 Mable Gene Barry (b. 8/28/1928), m. 9/8/1949 Leroy
          Gabbert (b. 10/2/1924), son of Charles H. and Ida
          Phillips Gabbert
222182711 Charles Leroy Gabbert (b. 7/3/1952), m. 10/8/1976
           Brenda Lou _____
2221827111 Melinda Dawn Gabbert (b. 6/5/1979)
222182712 Donald Wayne Gabbert (b. 12/10/1953), m. 12/18/1978
           Carla Gail _____
222182713 Barry Gene Gabbert (b. 8/13/1961)
22218272 John Samuel Barry (b. 10/11/1930)
22218273 Ramona Lee Barry (10/21/1933-3/4/1934)
22218274 William Donald Barry (b. 10/10/1935)

22218275 Jerry Wayne Barry (b. 9/28/1937), m. 10/4/1957 Margaret
          DaNell Stafford (b. 1/28/1940), dau. of Joseph B. and
          Leona Settliff Stafford
222182751 Jerry Wayne Barry, Jr. (9/16/1959), m. 9/21/1979
          Kimberly Melody Nitchell
2221827511 Amber Ann Barry (b. 7/22/1980)
222182752 Dana Sue Barry (b. 8/17/1965)
222182753 Rorin Renee Barry (b. 11/11/1968)
22218276 Phyllis Ann Barry (b. 9/28/1937)
22218277 Helen Susan Barry (b. 2/20/1941), m. 4/8/1967 Albert
          Frederick Tillock

222182771 Randall Lee Tillock (b. 9/5/1963)
222182772 Darrell Frederick Tillock (b. 10/2/1969)
222182773 Jerry Don Tillock (b. 10/2/1969)
222182774 Kevin Joe Tillock (b. 10/17/1973)
22218278 Terry Lee (b. 3/10/1951), m. (1st) _____ Vickers.
          M. (2nd) 1/1/1972 Ronald F. Fifer (b. 1/12/1952), son
          of Cleo and Elmore Waters Fifer
222182781 Melissa Kim Vickers (b. 6/4/1969)
222182782 Jacqulyne Michele Vickers (b. 1/18/1970)
222182783 Michael Shawn Fifer (b. 11/29/1972)
2221828   Haskell Clarence Barry (12/27/1907-   )(b. Bartles-
          ville, OK). M. (1st) 8/2/1931, Zella Leona Maxey (6/
          30/1907-6/15/1967)(b. Laclede County, MO; d. Vinita,
          OK), dau. of Thomas Daniel Maxey and his wife, the
          former Mopsie Elzora E. Cook. M. (2nd) Elsie Mae Shaw
          Hamady
22218281 Mary Lou Barry (3/8/1934-   )(b. Claremore, OK), m.
          Fayetteville, AR 6/10/1952, Sloan Flemmons Million
          (b. 2/10/1930 Lake City, AR), son of Amos Flemmons and
          Lila Gladys Rush Million
2221829   Raymond Homer Barry (9/3/1909-8/9/1973)(b. Adair, OK;
          d. Ponca City), m. Foyil, OK, 7/7/1929, Lucy Myrtle
          Mohon (6/10/1910-1/24/1952), dau. of Albert Lee and
          Nannie Lamb Mohon
22218291 Raymond Eugene Barry (b. 4/13/1930), m. (1st) 8/26/1951
          Georgia Ann Feguson (1/22/1932-10/18/1977), dau. of
          George R. and Lydia C. Blaser Ferguson. M. (2nd)(as
          second husband) 7/1/1978 Ruth C. Roper
222182911 Charlayne Rae Barry (b. 10/27/1963)
22218292 Robert Dean Barry (b. 7/21/1931), m. 1/28/1955 Carolyn
          Jean McClelland (b. 6/16/1936), dau. of William
          Raymond and Minnie Pearl Emmons McClelland
222182921 Mitzi Gail Barry (b. 5/27/1956), m. 4/6/1977 Jeffrey
          Allen Vanthournout (b. 1/10/1956), son of Arthur and
          Dorothy Nelson Vanthournout
2221829211 Matthew Barry Vanthournout (b. 6/17/1982)
222182922 Kirby Dean Barry (b. 9/25/1958)
22218293 Haskell Randall Barry (b. 7/14/1933), m. 6/30/1950
          Margaret Susan Lewis (b. 5/1/1932), dau. of Everett E.
          and Opal Johnson Lewis

222182931   Nancy Susan Barry (b. 1/12/1951)
222182932   Kent Wayne Barry (b. 1/23/1953)
222182x   Elva Maude Barry (2/22/1912-   )(b. Pryor, OK). M.
          (1st) Guy Heaton. M. (2nd) Tulsa 6/16/1951, Orville
          Edward Dykes (11/14/1904-12/11/1972), son of James
          Samuel and Ethel Edna Humb Dykes

222182a   Helen Louise Barry (1/22/1915-1/22/1915)(b. and d.
          Adair, OK.)

222183   Lucy Ada Barry (9/21/1870-2/7/1955)(b. Eureka Springs,
          MS; d. Muskogee; bur. Vian, OK), m. Muldrow, I.T., 2/1/
          1893 William ("Willie") Thomas Moss (3/10/1874-1/8/1927)
          (b. Cherokee or Choctaw Nation, I.T.; d. and bur. Vian,
          OK), son of James Layton Moss and his wife, the former
          Martha Ann Sanders Force Hunter. Lucy Ada was
          originally named Reithe Ada Dupree but after the death
          of her mother, her father renamed her.

2221831   Rosa Ann Moss (2/25/1895-4/21/1968)(b. at Vian, Cherokee
          Nation; d. Talihina, OK), m. Vian "At Ma Hunter's"
          3/12/1916 Joseph Alexander Morris (12/18/1885-   )
          (b. Elm Grove, Flint District, Cherokee Nation), son of
          John Gideon and Annie Morris.
          Note: Joseph Alexander Morris is listed on the Dawes
                 Roll (No. 17822) as 3/4 Cherokee. His father,
                 John Gideon Morris (b. Cherokee Nation, East,
                 NC) was the son of Willson Morris (b. Cherokee
                 Nation, East, NC) and his wife, the former Ellen
                 Elizabeth Powell. Willson's father was Gideon
                 Franklin Morris, son of Drewry and Rachel Morris
                 of Greenville District, SC, and his mother was
                 Che-ga-yu-ee, a full blooded Cherokee (her
                 mother was Co-lee-cha and her grandmother was
                 Oo-be-ja or cha). John Gideon Morris' wife
                 Annie was the dau. of Sar-tah-kah and Kah-hu-kah
                 of Flint District, I.T. Hence, Joseph Alexander
                 Morris may be 5/8 instead of 3/4 Cherokee.
22218311   James Ramsey Morris (3/3/1917-6/27/1918)(b. Badger Lee,
          OK; d. near Sallisaw; bur. Sequoyah County).

22218312   Lula Lee Morris (8/1/1918-   )(b. Badger Lee, OK).
          M. (1st) Roy O. Salee. M. (2nd) 2/1/1946 Earl Earnest
          Boggs (1/24/1923-   )(b. Cyril, OK), son of William
          Franklin and Pearl Beatrice Sullins Rogers Boggs
      Child by first husband:
222183121 Linda Rose Sallee Boggs (2/16/1940-   )(b. Vian,
          OK), m. William Wayne Perry (4/4/1939-   )(b.
          Butler, OK), son of Henry Thomas and Ruby Warren
          Perry
          Note: Linda was adopted by Earl Earnest Boggs in
                 1946.

2221831211 Vicki Lyn Perry (8/9/1957-   )(b. Muskogee, OK).
            M. (1st) Kenneth Barton (10/12/1950-   ). M. (2nd)
            Michael Lee Smith (7/11/1957-   ), son of Phillip
            Jackson Smith and his wife, the former Betty Ann
            Bell

22218312111 Melissa Ann Smith (6/15/1979-   )(b. Muskogee).
22218312112 Michaelyn Dawn Smith (7/27/1980-   )(b. Muskogee).
2221831212   Theresa Gail Perry (10/3/1958-   )(b. Muskogee),
             m. Charles W. Phillips (3/15/1955-   ), son of
             Bill and Lucille Phillips.
22218312121 Derek Wayne Phillips (11/19/1980-   )(b. Tahlequah,
             OK).
22218312122 Angela Renae Phillips (7/19/1982-   )(b. Tahlequah,
             OK).
2221831213   Billy Wayne Perry, Jr. (2/26/1962-   )(b. Muskogee).
2221831214   Keli Dian Perry (3/9/1969-   )(b. Muskogee).
22218313 Wilson Taylor Morris (7/21/1920-   )(b. Badger Lee,
          OK), m. Tahlequah, OK, 11/20/1942 Dorothy Frances
          Hogan (4/16/1923-   )(b. Kansas City, KS), dau.of
          Chester Leroy Hogan and his wife, the former Frances
          Louise Perkins.
             Note: Faith Frances Jones Morris (7/3/1939-   )(b.
                    Portland, OR). Adopted by Wilson Taylor Morris.
                    M. (1st)   . Div. M. (2nd) Earl William
                    Johnson (9/22/1930-   ). M. (3rd) Dan Danatt
                    (1960-   ). Child: Echo Faye Johnson (8/14/
                    1956-   )(b. Pleasanton, CA), m. Steve Bobair.
                    Div.
222183131   Doranna Lee Morris (6/13/1945-   )(b. Portland, OR),
            m. Portland, OR, 4/10/1965 David Stephen Peterson
            (4/2/1944-   )(b. Westland, OR), son of Arthur and
            Mable Peterson.
2221831311 Deanna Lynn Peterson (4/4/1969-   )(b. Portland, OR).
2221831312 Debbie Sue Peterson (4/21/1970-   )(b. Portland, OR).
222183132   Tana Louise Morris (6/12/1946-   )(b. Portland, OR),
            m. Portland, OR, 5/28/1965 David Schroeder (1/13/
            1947-   )(b. Tillamack, OR), son of Vern and Harriet
            Dietz Schroeder.
2221831321 Torace Gregory Schroeder (1/6/1966-   )(b. Portland,
            OR).
2221831322 Jeffrey Alan Schroeder (3/19/1970-   )(b. Portland,
            OR).
222183133   Melinda Kay Morris (7/18/1956-   )(b. Portland,
            OR). M. (1st) Larry D. Dunham (5/18/1955-   )(b.
            Michigan). M. (2nd) Portland, OR, 2/14/1980, Robert
            Arthur Struble (10/17/1942-   )(b. Burlington,
            IA), son of Arthur and Amy Watkins Struble.
        Child by second husband:
2221831331 Trebor Taylor Struble (9/29/1981-   )(b. Oregon).

22218314 Harriet ("Hattie") Ruth Morris (10/17/1924-   )(b.
          Badger Lee, OK), m. 10/20/1942 Goodlow Gay Young, Sr.
          (2/5/1922-   )(b. Marble City, OK), son of John
          Young

222183141 Goodlow Gay Young, Jr. (1/6/1943-   )(b. Tahlequah,
           OK), m. Edith Claus Chee (3/26/1943-   )(b.
           Arizona).
2221831411 Rhonda Jean Young (10/9/1965-   ).
2221831412 Renee Michelle Young (6/8/1968-   ).
222183142 Ronald Gene Young (7/13/1945-   )(b. Tahlequah, OK),
           m. Arizona, Estalla Moreno. Adopted: Brian Gene
           Young (3/7/1973-   ).
222183143 Brenda Lee Young (1/28/1948-   )(b. Tahlequah, OK),
           m. Arizona, Norris Alton Nordvold (3/30/1942-   ).
           Brenda retains her maiden name.
2221831431 Alexis Nordvold-Young (1984-   )(b. Nairobe, Kenya).
222183144 Phillip Glen Young (12/16/1949-   )(b. Tahlequah, OK),
           m. Arizona, Gloria Mose (7/28/1949-   ).
2221831441 Rollin Joel Young (10/18/1968-   ).
2221831442 Nikki Shannon Young (5/18/1973-   ).

22218315 Joseph Houston Morris (9/27/1926-   )(b. Vian, OK),
          m. Oregon, Dorothy Jean Grenbremer (6/27/1926-   )
          (b. Ashland, OR), dau. of William Grenbremer and his
          wife, the former Lillian Grace Rosencrans

222183151 Nancy Jo Morris (1/28/1948-   )(b. Portland, OR), m.
           Gardiner, OR 1/28/1968 Danny Alton Doyle (12/30/1946-
)(b. Coos Bay, OR), son of William Hubert
           Doyle and his wife, the former Annette Andrus.
2221831511 Keri Jo Doyle (1/28 or 30/1972-   )(b. Reedsport,
            OR).
2221831512 Jeffrey Alton Doyle (2/28/1977-   )(b. Reedsport, OR).
222183152 Janie Lynn Morris (9/1/1951-   )(b. Westlake, OR).
           M. (1st) 11/25/1972 Clifford Orlene Herrmann III (9/
           13/1948-   ). M. (2nd) 6/24/1978 Walter Weraska
           (7/4/1951-   ), son of Alexander Weraska (b. Russia
           12/12/1910) and his wife, the former Sophia Meir
           Weraska (b. Germany 9/2/1921).
      Child by first husband:
2221831521 Carly Ann Herrmann (6/16/1975-   )(b. Redding, CA).
      Child by second husband:
2221831522 Kristen Marie Weraska (1/27/1980-   )(b. Salem, OR).
22218316 David Gambrell Morris (10/7/1928-   )(b. Vian, OK), m.
          Muskogee 5/10/1949, Mary Shasta Coodey (8/2/1932-   )
          (b. Porum, OK), dau. of Daniel Coodey and his wife,
          the former Vetrx V. Brooks.
222183161 Charla Jean Morris (9/26/1950   )(b. Muskogee), m.
           Apison, TN, 12/26/1973 Ernest Alan Gentry (10/23/1945
           -    )(b. Streater, IL), son of Ernest W. Gentry
           and his wife, the former Joan Kolassa Gentry.
2221831611 Charla Janelle Gentry (9/5/1978-   )(b. Chattanooga).
2221831612 Ernest David Gentry (3/1/1984-   ).
222183162 David Lloyd Morris (9/3/1953-   )(b. Pryor, OK).

222183163   Katherine Denise Morris (1/19/1955-   ), m. Keene,
            TX, 7/6/1975, Michael Harvard Wiegand (7/11/1951-   )
            (b. Wilson, PA), son of Howard Clarence Wiegand and
            his wife, the former Arvilla Stitzer
2221831631 Matthew Michael Wiegand (6/23/1978-   )(b.
            Talihina, OK)
2221831632 Bryan Phillip Wiegand (8/14/ or 31/1982-   )(b.
            Louisiana)
2221831633 Benjamin Jonathan Wiegand (8/1/1984-   )

222183164   Patricia Annette Morris (11/13/1957-   )(b. Grand
            Island, NE), m. Keene, TX, 5/14/1978 Christopher
            Marion Schwach (12/20/1954-   )(b. Cape Girardeau,
            MO), son of Glen Schwach and his wife, the former
            Dorothy Holland.
2221831641 Karl Steven Schwach (6/30/1982-   )(b. Wheaton, MD).
2221831642 Angela Michelle Schwach (3/26/1984-   ).
222183165   Deborah Joyce Morris (11/15/1958-   )(b. Grand
            Island, NE), m. Keene, TX, 1/14/1979 Robert Preston
            Childress (4/15/1954-   )(b. Snyder, TX), son of

            Leonard Wesley Childress and his wife, the former
            Doris Allene Flournoy.
2221831651 Rachel Marie Childress (8/6/1979-   )(b. Lawton, OK).
2221831652 Daniel Lee Childress (2/21/1982-   )(b. Tahlequah,
            OK).
2221831653 Tashina Leia Childress (10/11/1984-   ).

22219317   Monta Lynn Morris (2/8/1936-   )(b. Vian, OK), m.
            Vian 6/16/1956 Frederick Leonidas Drew (5/19/1934-   )
            (b. Eufaula, OK), son of David Drew, and his wife,
            the former Ola McCombs

222183171   Frederick Leonidas Drew, Jr. (3/9/1957-   )(b.
            Tahlequah, OK).
222183172   Yvonne Ahniwake Drew (9/17/1958-   )(b. Sallisaw, OK).
222183173   Ramona Janette Drew (5/22/1960-   ).
222183174   Joseph Daniel Drew (6/9/1961-   ).
222183175   Monta Suzette Drew (8/24/1963-1/16/1964)(b. Tahlequah,
            OK; d. Oklahoma City; bur. Vian, OK).
22218318   Ada June Morris (7/19/1938-   )(b. Muskogee), m. Vian,
            OK, 12/25/1959 Cleo Wayne Leaf (6/13/1934-   )(b.
            Vian, OK), son of John Leaf and his wife, the former
            Maudine Shanks.
222183181   Phaedra Jai Leaf (5/3/1976-5/3/1976)(b. and d. Salli-
            saw, OK; bur. Vian, OK).
2221832   Helen Louise Moss (9/4 or 16/1897-7/8/1951)(b., d. and
            bur. Vian, OK), m. 10/22/1916 Austin Zachariah Young
            (5/29/1891-4/25/1939)(b. I.T., d. and bur. Vian, OK),
            son of Tom Ed Young and his wife, the former Matura
            ("Matierry") Cook.

22218321   Helen Austina Young (11/ /1917-10/ /1920)(b. Vian,
           OK).
22218322   Robert Randolph Young (9/6/1920-2/6/1982)(b. Vian,
           OK; d. Fort Smith AR; bur. Vian), m. 8/3/1944 Alice
           Virginia Trammell (6/24/1927-   )(b. Alabama),
           dau. of Robert Andrew Trammell and his wife, the
           former Nettie Virginia Culver. Div.
222183221 Donna Sue Young (11/26/1946-   )(b. Vian, OK), m.
           Vian, OK, 12/27/1965 James Enoch Anderson (12/12/
           1943-   ), son of James and Hazel Anderson.
2221832211 Monica Dawn Anderson (10/5/1972-   )(b. Fort Smith,
           AR).
2221832212 James Eric Anderson (1/12/1975-   )(b. Fort Smith,
           AR).
222183222 Dorinda Kay Young (8/21/1948-   )(b. Sallisaw, OK),
           m. Vian, OK, 8/2/1968 Johnny Wayne Riggs (1/1/1948-
)(b. Muskogee), son of John L. Riggs and
           his wife, the former Joan Davis.
2221832221 Michelle Desiree Riggs (8/27/1971-   )(b. Muskogee).
2221832222 Marcia Danielle Riggs (2/24/1972-   )(b. Fort Smith,
           AR).
2221832223 Dustin Wayne Riggs (7/23/1975-   )(b. Muskogee).
222183223 Michael Randolph Young (11/27/1949-   )(b. Sallisaw,
           OK). M. (1st) Vian, OK, 4/2 /1969 Paula Judelle
           Taylor (2/7/1950-   ), dau. of John Bill Taylor

           and his wife, the former Ruth Denny. Div. 1978. M.
           (2nd) 8/13/1981.
2221832231 Tara Leann Young (7/1/1973-   )(b. Fort Smith, AR).
2221832232 Jarrod Randolph Young (6/26/1974-   )(b. Fort Smith,
           AR).
222183224 Daryle DeWayne Young (7/12/1951-   )(b. Sallisaw,
           OK), m. Vian, OK, 1971 Loveda Joy O'Neal (3/19/1952-
)(b. Vian, OK), dau. of Charles O'Neal and his
           wife, the former Phyllis Risley. Div. 1980.
2221832241 Jason DeWayne Young (5/20/1978-   )(b. Muskogee).
2221832242 Kimberly Renee Young (10/26/1979-   )(b. Muskogee).
222183225 Christy Deanne Young (2/17/1955-)(b. Leadville, CO).
222183226 Shelly Renee Young (8/18/1961-   )(b. Sallisaw, OK),
           m. 6/9/1984 William Jacob Risenhoover (7/8/1960-   ),
           son of Theodore Risenhoover and his wife, the former
           Theodora Zevalakis.
22218323   Harry Keleen Young (8/29/1923-   )(b. Vian, OK). M.
           (1st) 12/1/1946 Patricia Louise Pillsbury Chapman
           (6/24/1928-   ), dau. of Malcolm Pillsbury and his
           wife, the former Laverne Eloise Brown. (Patricia
           Louise Pillsbury was adopted by the Chapmans. Div.
           M. (2nd) Dorothy Terzich (2/28/1930-   ).
    Children by first wife:
222183231 Keith Alden Young (10/12/1947-   )(b. Stockton, CA).
           M. (1st) Darcy Thompson, dau. of Jack and Shirley
           Thompson. Div. M. (2nd) 6/ /1973 Waynette Holland
           (6/15/1953-   )(b. Bakersfield, CA), dau. of Wayne
           Olaf Holland and his wife, the former Joan Horn.

Children by second wife:
2221832311 Keith Anthony Young (11/12/1979-   )(b. Las Vegas).
2221832312 Michael Wayne Young (7/23/1983-   )(b. Las Vegas).
222183232 Keleen Adel Young (7/24/1951-   )(b. Stockton, CA),
    m. Santa Cruz, CA 1/20/1977 Stanley Harris (2/15/
    1952-   )(b. Las Vegas), son of Jack Charles Harris
    and his wife, the former Flavia Lynn Pillow.
2221832321 Amber Louise Harris (1/12/1978-   )(b. Las Vegas).
2221832322 Stacy Keleen Harris (8/25/1979-   )(b. Las Vegas).
2221832323 Crystol Lynn Harris (2/23/1982-   )(b. Las Vegas).
2221832324 Alyssa Lauren Harris (12/23/1984-   )(b. Las Vegas).
22218324 William Thomas ("Bill Tom") Young (5/22/1925-   )(b.
    Vian, OK), m. Lawton, OK, 4/31/1950 Peggy Louise
    Hutton (1/21/1933-   )(b. Frederick, OK), dau. of
    James Augustus Hutton and his wife, the former Minnie
    Irene Parrott.
222183241 James Austin Young (12/6/1951-   )(b. Wewoka, OK), m.
    Broken Arrow, OK, 7/22/1972 Barbara Arline Smith (11/
    24/1942-   )(b. Eau Claire, WI), dau. of Jesse E.
    Smith and his wife, the former Berniece Reitmeier.
2221832411 Elizabeth Katherine Young (11/24/1974-   )(b. Wichita
    Falls, TX).
2221832412 Jamie Rebekah Young (10/5/1977-   )(b. Frederick,
    OK).
222183242 Roy Allen Young (5/3/1952-   )(b. Bristow, OK), m.
    Chelsea, OK, 8/8/1975 Lela Mae Pattison (10/16/1954
    or 1964-   )(b. Claremore, OK), dau. of Leroy
    Pattison and his wife, the former Maxine Copeland.
2221832421 Matthu Alden Young (5/15/1978-   )(b. Vinita, OK).
2221832422 Mark Anthony Young (4/30/1981-   )(b. Tulsa, OK).
222183243 Leslie Ray Young (7/28/1958-   )(b. Sallisaw, OK),
    m. Donna Lea Garris (11/22/1960-   )(b. Sallisaw,
    OK), dau. of Jimmy LeRoy Garris and his wife, the
    former Vera Coleen Cullum.
2221832431 Amy Michelle Young (8/28/1981-   )(b. Claremore,
    OK).
2221832432 Amanda Marlene Young (6/24/1983-   )(b. Claremore,
    OK).
222183244 Tina Lynn Young (7/19/1963-   )(b. Fort Smith, AR).
22218325 Winnie Lee Young (2/9/1927-   )(b. Vian, OK), m. 12/
    1/1943 Wade Stovall (7/5/1923-   ), son of William
    Henry Stovall and his wife, the former Minnie Lee
    Burnett.
222183251 Jackie Ray Stovall (11/7/1944-   )(b. Stockton, CA),
    m. Vian, OK, 9/25/1965 Sharon Ruth Tyler (1/5/1945-
)(b. Vian, OK), dau. of Ernest Tyler and
    his wife, the former Ruth Lancaster.
2221832511 Angela Denise Stovall (4/16/1967-   )(b. Fort
    Smith, AR).
2221832512 Delaina Ruth Stovall (9/15/1972-   )(b. Fort Smith,
    AR).

222183252   Theresa Gail Stovall (7/29/1948-10/30/1963)(b. Wood-
            land, CA, bur. Muskogee).
22218326   Helen Louise Young (4/26/1929-   )(b. Vian, OK), m.
            Byron Eugene Henning (8/22/1913-   )(b. Sperry, OK),
            son of Grover Cleveland Henning and his wife, the
            former Winifred Height.
222183261   Roger Eugene Henning (11/27/1949-   )(b. Sallisaw,
            OK).

222183262   Byrana Louise Henning (9/29/1951-   )(b. Sallisaw,
            OK). M. (1st) Ronald Eugene Turley (4/1/1949-   ).
            Div. M. (2nd) Charles Glenn Wesley (2/7/1949-   ),
            son of Charles Robert Wesley

    Children by first husband:
2221832621 Katrina Kae Turley (3/20/1972-)(b. Salida, CO).
2221832622 Cody Rae Turley (2/9/1973-   )(b. Salida, CO).

    Child by second husband:
2221832623 Anthony Glenn Wesley (11/11/1977-   )(b. Leadville,
            CO)

222183263   Barbara Mae Henning (11/23/1953-   )(b. Sallisaw, OK),
            m. Colorado Springs, CO, 9/8/1973 Stephen Robert
            McGinn (4/28/1953-   )(b. Prividence, RI), son of
            Robert Ed McGinn and his wife, the former Barbara
            Helen Vanner.
2221832631 Amy Henning McGinn (2/1/1983-   )(b. New Orleans).
222183264   Stanley Dwight Henning (9/1/1955-   )(b. Leadville,
            CO), m. Leadville 2/28/1981 Karen Christoph (12/2/
            1959-   ), dau. of Albert Christoph and his wife,
            the former Clara Ann Burress.
22218327   Austin Zachariah Young, Jr. (1/23/1931-   )(b. Vian,
            OK), m. Washington, D.C., 11/5/1953 Myrle Elizabeth
            Howell (11/27/1931-   )(b. Hopewell, VA), dau. of
            Claude Howell and his wife, the former Elizabeth
            McCoy.
            Note: Dau. Jessie Marie Young (12/16/1951-   )(b.
                Washington, D.C.)(adopted by Austin Zachariah
                Young, Jr.), m. David Wayne Young (9/25/1941-
)(b. Vian, OK).
222183271   Claudia Elizabeth Young (4/19/1957-   )(b. Cherry
            Point, NC). M. (1st) Daryl Lott. Div. M. (2nd).

2221832711 Tamara Lynn Lott (b. 10/9/1976)
222183272   Austin Zachariah Young III (7/21/1958-   )(b.
            Quantico, VA), m. Famara _____
2221832721 Austin Zachariah Young IV
2221832722 Katrina Young

222183273   Richard Young.

22218328   Sharlie Ann Young (2/15/1933-   )(b. Vian, OK), m.
             Reno 1/13/1952 Douglas Milton Ferguson (3/1/1927-   )
             (b. Glendale, CA), son of Barney Torrence Ferguson and
             his wife, the former Frances Edgerta Anderson
222183281   Sharlie Suzanne Ferguson (9/21/1953-   )(b. Stockton,
             CA), m. Sacramento, CA, 6/6/1976 Dennis Robert
             Petersen (10/16/1948-   )(b. Berkeley, CA), son of
             Robert P. Petersen and his wife, the former Pauline
             Maddox
2221832811   Laure Deborah Petersen (7/2/1982-   )(b. Walnut
             Creek, CA)
2221832812   Robert Douglas Petersen

222183282   Douglas Charles Ferguson (5/10/1955-   )(b. Stockton,
             CA). M. (1st) Valerie Jean Malka (10/13/1957-   ),
             (b. Sacramento, CA). Div. M. (2nd) 9/24/1981 Sheree
             Lynn Cogdill (4/1/1956-   )(b. Wichita, KS), dau.
             of Mr. Cogdill and his wife, the former Miss Brown.
2221832821   Jeffrey Douglas Ferguson (4/13/1982-   )(b.
             Sacramento, CA).
222183283   Jeffrey Torrence Ferguson (2/24/1958-   )(b. Stockton,
             CA), m. Reno 1/17/1981 Tracy Lynne Smith (4/30/1962-
)(b. Oceanside, CA), dau. of William and
             Judy Smith.
22218329   Child stillborn.
2221832x   Child stillborn (9/27/1919).

2221833   Harriet ("Hattie") Randolph Moss (7/15/1900-1/22/1977)
             (b. Vian, Cherokee Nation, I.T.; d. Muskogee; bur.
             Vian, OK), m. Kansas 9/21/1921 Harrison Whitfield
             Branscum (8/27/1890-4/9/1973)(b. Alco, AR; d. and bur.
             Vian, OK), son of George Whitfield Branscum and his
             wife, the former Mary Ann Goodman

22218331   Mary Lou Branscum (8/22/1932-   )(b. Vian, OK). M.
             (1st) Patrick P. Gordon (7/6/1931-   ). M. (2nd)
             Lawrence Millis (8/26/19 -   )(b. Brooklyn).
22218332   Peggy Ann Branscum (2/10/1934-   )(b. Vian, OK),
             m. Bernard Rosenberg (3/2/1933-   )(b. Boston).

222183321   Bernard Allen Rosenberg (b. 3/13/1955), m. 6/ /1975
             Anna Kathryn Ward
2221833211   Bryan Christopher Rosenberg (b. 3/4/1976)
2221833212   Kevin Michael Rosenberg (6/21/1978)
2221833213   Brent Allen Rosenberg (b. 7/17/1979)
222183322   Jack Randolph Rosenberg (b. 6/1/1956), m. 1975 Jackie
             Sue Catron (b. 9/19/1955), dau. of Vesper and Billie
             Marie Moss Catron
2221833221   Jeff(erson) Randolph Rosenberg (b. 8/14/1977)
2221833222   Jared Whitfield Rosenberg (b. 6/8/1980)
222183323   Richard Eugene Rosenberg (b. 7/5/1959)
222183324   Terri Lou Rosenberg (7/11/1960)

22218333 Harold Whitfield Branscum (5/11/1936-   )(b. Vian,
          OK). M. (1st) Susan Galbreath (8/29/1940-   ).
          Div. 4/22/1964.   M. (2nd) Myra Walbridge (12/8/1932-
).

2221834 Barry Thomas Moss (1/22/1903-6/14/1960)(b. Vian,
          Cherokee Nation, I.T.; d. and bur. Vian, OK). M. (1st)
          Box, OK, 1/17/1924 Katie Anne Young (10/20/1906-8/ /
          1982)(b. Vian, Blackgum, Cherokee Nation, I.T.; d.
          Tulsa), dau. of Tom Ed Young and his wife, the former
          Matura ("Matierry") Cook. Div. M. (2nd) Thelma Eva
          Duffield (7/26/1912-9/30/1947)(b. Shawnee, OK, d. Vian,
          OK)

     Children by first wife:
22218341 Ruby Bernice Moss (11/22/1924-   )(b. near Vian, OK),
          m. Tulsa, 8/4/1946 Edwin Lester Stone (10/13/1919-
)(b. Baxter, MO), son of Delmer Orval Stone
          and his wife, the former Infanta Delores ("Inta")
          Thompson.
222183411 Donna Joyce Stone (9/9/1948-   )(b. Bristow, OK), m.
          Tulsa 1/21/1978 Edward Patrick ("Pat") Kane (11/12/
          1943-   )(b. Bartlesville, OK), son of Edward
          Peter Kane and his wife, the former Alberta Mildred
          Armstrong.
2221834111 Meghan Arianne Kane (5/31/1979-   )(b. Tulsa).
222183412 Edwin Keith Stone (7/26/1950-   )(b. Bristow, OK),
          m. Okmulgee, OK, 12/26/1970 Sharon Rae Roulston (5/
          28/1950-   )(b. Okmulgee, OK), dau. of Enos Leonard
          Roulston and his wife, the former Betty Rae Southern.
          Adopted child: Emily Lauren Stone (2/7/1979-   )(b.
          Tulsa).
2221834121 Alison Lindsay Stone (10/29/1980-   )(b. Tulsa).
222183413 Susan Elaine Stone (2/21/1952-   )(b. Bristow, OK),
          m. Guthrie, OK, 7/4/1974 Dennis Ray Rone (3/28/1944-
                    ), son of Therman Austin Rone and his wife,
          the former Alma Jo Lee. Adopted child: Nathan David
          Rone (12/20/1977-   )(b. Oklahoma City).
22218342 Joseph Clifton Moss (1/25/1926-   )(b. Box, OK). M.
          (1st) Tulsa 6/15/1951 Mary Rosetta Hersh (8/9/1929-
                    ), dau. of Thomas Eugene Hersh and his wife,
          the former Rosetta Thelma Oliphant. Div. M. (2nd)
          Tulsa 2/26/1971 Jo Ann Green (3/25/   -   ).
     Children by first wife:
222183421 Gwendolyn Joetta Moss (4/13/1953-   )(b. Tulsa),
          m. Wichita 5/25/1974 Kevin Ray Holloway (5/26/1954-
)(b. Wichita). Div.
2221834211 Rebecca Lavonne Holloway (8/1/1975-   )(b. Wichita).
222183422 Joseph Clifton Moss, Jr. (11/7/1954-   )(b. Tulsa),
          m. Wichita 8/31/1976 Tammie Marie Harper (12/9/1957-
)(b. Wichita).
2221834221 Ryan Douglas Moss (7/3/1981-   )(b. Wichita).

Children by second wife:
222183423 Stacie Francene Moss (12/18/1971-   )(b. Tulsa)
       (twin).
222183424 Tracie Renee Moss (12/18/1971-   )(b. Tulsa)(twin).
22218343 Billy Royce Moss (1/18/1928-   ). M. (1st) Mary Lou
       Parks (9/16/1932-   ). Div. M. (2nd) Annette   .

   Child by first wife:
222183431 Billy Royce Moss, Jr. (9/14/1954-   ).
   Child by second wife:
222183432 Teresa Moss.
   Children by second wife:
22218344 James Allen Moss (2/2/1935-2/2/1935)(b. and d. Vian,
       OK).
22218345 Eva Lou Moss (12/10/1940-12/10/1940)(b. and d. Vian,
       OK).

22218346 Virginia Mae Moss (2/15/1936-   )(b. Vian, OK), m.
       5/11/1956 Robert Lee Lam (2/28/1932-   )(b. Marshall,
       OK), son of William Ebb and Frances Young Lam
222183461 Ginny Lee Lam (3/11/1957-   ), m. Charles Robin
       Andrews (b. 10/11/1955), son of Charles and Gladys
       Andrews
222183462 Teri Lynn Lam (12/30/1958-   ), m. James Mark Kemp
       b. 11/21/1957), son of James and Elizabeth Kemp
22218347 Ruth Lavonne Moss (2/20/1937-   )(b. Vian, OK), m. 1/
       14/1957 Jerry Gene Cawhorn (4/5/1937-   )(b. Pueblo,
       CO).
222183471 Sherry Sue Cawhorn (12/26/1957-   ).
222183472 Cindy Kay Cawhorn (1/7/1961-   ).

22218348 Thelma Marie Moss (4/4/1938-   )(b. Vian, OK), m.
       (1st) Robert Frederick Stahl (b. 12/17/1910). Div.
       8/10/1962. M. (2nd) Aubrey Keilberg
222183481 Sharon Lorraine Stahl (b. 5/5/1961)
222183482 Keith Keilberg
22218349 James Leon Moss (5/10/1939-   )(b. Vian, OK). M.
       (1st) Daphne Ann Moon (b. 7/15/1940). Div. M. (2nd)
       Linda Robinson Lee Gallion
2221834x Martha Ann Moss (9/24/1942-   )(b. Vian, OK), m.
       Ronald Rea Morris (b. 3/16/1937).
2221834x1 Ronald Barry Morris (b. 6/21/1974)
2221834a Eva Lou Moss (d. 12/10/1940)

2221835 Winnie Davis Moss (10/1/1905-6/18/1978)(b. Vian, OK, d.
       Reno), m. Tex Coleman-Callahan (10/18/1900-6/ /1982)
       (b. Porum, Cherokee Nation, I.T., d. Pawnee, OK).
22218351 Frank Edwin Coleman-Callahan (5/4/1932-), m. Kathleen
       Stone (11/3/1933-   ).
222183511 Gail Lynette Coleman-Callahan (8/6/1956-).
222183512 Cathy Coleman-Callahan.
2221836 Malcolm Pugh Moss (2/9/1909-   )(b. Vian, OK), m.
       Tahlequah, OK, 3/31/1934 Blanche Mae West (5/10/1914-
           ), dau. of George West and his wife, the former
       Ethel Gerard.

22218361 George Wayne Moss (8/4/1935-   )(b. Muskogee). M.
          (1st) Sharon Ann Gunderson (5/17/1939-   )(b. Oregon),
          dau. of "Gete" and "Babe" Gunderson. M. (2nd)
          Christine Perkins (4/12/1936-6/14/1977). M. (3rd)
          Norma Gullett (Arkin)(4/12/1936-   )
222183611 Lance Wayne Moss (11/13/1958)
222183612 Bardt Shannon Moss (8/30/1960)
22218362 Sandra Ann Moss (6/10/1938-   ), m. Ralph Donald
          Laws (4/2/1936-   ), son of Ralph James and Ella
          Margaret Nicholson Laws
222183621 Ralph Gordon Laws (b. 8/19/1960)
222183622 Curtis Fallon Laws (b. 6/17/1962)
222183623 Jason Bryan Laws (b. 11/13/1964)
22218363 Larry Malcolm Moss (12/19/1940-   ). M. (1st) June
          Elease Haylor (4/18/1945-   ), dau. of _____ and
          Susan Lestack Haylor. M. (2nd) Kathy _____
222183631 Lawrence Eugene Moss (b. 5/17/1961)
222183632 Stacy Lin Moss (b. 4/1/1968)
2221837   Lucy Lee Moss (8/1/1911-   )(b. Vian, OK). M (1st)
          Francis Bruce Richards (d. 4/28/1954). M. (2nd) Henry
          Harris (2/5/1912-   )(b. Vian, OK)

222184 Child (b. 1872). Possibly stillborn. Pocahontas Trails
        Quarterly. Vol. 3, No. 3.

22219   Maria ("Aunt Mariah") Louisa Randolph (6/20/1841-   )
        (b. Greene County, AL), m. 10/28/1858 W. Green Middleton
        (both were from Panola County, MS). Middleton, a Captain
        C.S.A., was killed in battle near Pontotoc, MS. (7/17/
        1864). Maria m. (2nd) in MS 8/18/1866 William Sidney
        Mills (d. 11/6/1899 at Hillsboro, TX, where the family
        moved in 1878).
222191 Willie Green Middleton (d. at 5 yrs. old)
222192 Frank M. Middleton (1864-   )(b. Mississippi), m.
        Tennie _____ (1867-   )(b. Tennessee). Lived in
        San Angelo, TX
2221921 Louise Middleton (1891-   )(b. Texas)
2221922 Nillis Middleton (1894-   )(b. Texas)
2221923 Chester Middleton (1898-   )(b. Texas)
2221924 Herman Middleton (1903-   )(b. Texas)
222193 Sidney M. Mills (1884-   ), m. Bessie _____. Lived
        in Hillsboro, TX
222194 Clara Mills

2223 Patrick H. Randolph, m. _____ Meade

2224 Brett N. Randolph III (d. 9/24/1819, age 29)(d. at
      residence of his father in Powhatan County). M. Mary
      Willing Byrd of "Westover". 34V72. The "N" probably
      stands for Noel (see 22211). This material from Kate
      Duvall Randolph Family Tree (Virginia Archives) may be
      erroneous.

22241 Evelyn Byrd Randolph, m. Benjamin ("Barry") Oxley.

222411 Jennie Willing Oxley, m. John Law Will of Idaho.

22251   Richard Randolph Michaux (1/22/1823-11/20/1899), m. (1st)
        4/25/1872, Anna Davis (3/ /1849-11/26(?)/1876, dau. of
        James Wortham and Mary D. Davis. 45V220-1. M. (2nd)
        Sarah Davis

    Child of first wife:
222511   Anna Meade Michaux, m. J. S. Williams of Asheville, NC.
         45 V 220-1.

2225213   Leonidas Macon Michaux, Jr.
22252131   Leonidas Macon Michaux III
222521311   Leonidas Macon Michaux IV

2225231   Mildred Randolph Michaux (b. 5/10/1907)

222524   Lucy Evelyn Michaux, m. (2nd) Thomas Maxwell McConnell,
         Presbyterian minister and author. 45 V 220-1.

2227   _____.
2228   _____.
2229   _____.
222x   _____.
            MEMORIAL states that 222 had ten children.

223   Susannah Randolph, m. 8/23/1783, Dr. Charles Douglass (10/
      11/1752-   ) of Essex, England. Heir presumptive
      of the Earl of Morton. Susannah was born in Dursey,
      Gloucester County, England, and was married in North
      Nobley, Gloucester County. Dr. Douglass was born in Saw-
      bridge Court, Herefordshire, and at the time of the
      marriage was living at Standes, Mt. Fitchet, Essex. They
      came to Virginia after the Revolution and lived in
      Alexandria on Prince Street, two lots up from Union Street.
2231   Susannah Mary Ann Douglass (5/ /1785-   ), m (1st)
       _____ Wallace. M. (2nd) 6/2/1808, Capt. John Tucker
       of Paget, Bermuda. He was a ship commander who moved to
       Alexandria (Washington, D. C.) in 1801 and became a
       vestryman at Christ Church in Alexandria.
22311   Susan Jane Tucker (6/20/1810-   ), m. (1st) Andrew
        McDonald Jackson (d. 1840), Purser, U.S.N. M. (2nd)
        Henry Chandler Holt, Surgeon, U.S.N. Washington, D.C.
223111   Thomas Alphonse Jackson, Chief Engineer, U.S.N.
         Resigned and joined the Confederates. M. Maria
         Douglas Marbury of Alexandria.
2231111   Mary St. George ("Saintie") Tucker Jackson, m. Prof.
          Benjamin William Arnold, Jr.
22311111   Benjamin William Arnold III
22311112   Douglas Anderson Arnold (daughter)
22311113   St. George Tucker Arnold, m. Elizabeth Poole. He is
           deceased.
22311114   Randolph McDonald Arnold (b. in Lynchburg), m. Otto
           E. Aufranc, M.D.
223111141   Otto William Randolph Aufranc. Died.
223111142   St. George Tucker Aufranc, M.D.
2231111421   Lisa Wescott Aufranc
2231111422   St. George Tucker Aufranc II

2231111423 Kaarina Elizabeth Aufranc
223112 Andrew St. George Jackson
22312 John Randolph Tucker (1/31/1812-6/12/1883), m. 6/7/1838,
        Virginia Webb (18 years old, d. 1/10/1858), dau. of
        Commandant (Commander) Thomas Tarleton and Harriet
        Doris Webb. He was born in Alexandria and died in
        Petersburg. Commander U.S.N. Commodore C.S.N. Admiral
        (Peru).
223121 John ("Jack") Tarleton Tucker (b. 5/ /1839-1/26/1880).
        Third Assistant Engineer, U.S.N. Resigned and joined
        the Confederates.
223122 Alfred Taylor Tucker (7/ /1841-1842)
223123 Charles Douglas Tucker (9/ /1842-3/ /1864). Acting
        Master, C.S.N. Lost in wreck of Juno, a blockade
        runner.
223124 Virginia Fleming Tucker (d. before her first birthday).
223125 Harriet Reilly Tucker (9/ /1847-11/ /1863)
223126 Randolph Tucker (b. 7/ /1849)
223127 Tarleton Webb Tucker (b. 2/ /1851)
223128 Harry Gringo Tucker (10/18/1856-1/1/1862). Henry
        Augustus Wise was "Harry Gringo".
223129 Virginius Tucker (1/1/1858-4/17/1925). Born and died in
        Norfolk. M. 8/5/1885, Kathreen Booker Rogers
2231291 Louise Rogers Tucker (b. 6/27/1886)
2231292 George Ansell Tucker (b. 2/2/1888)
2231293 Virginia Randolph Tucker (b. 8/23/1889)
2231294 Anna Douglas Tucker (b. 3/27/1892)
2231295 John Reilly Tucker (b. 5/30/1894)
2231296 Kathreen McConnell Tucker (b. 5/16/1898)
2231297 Ralph Douglas Tucker (6/28/1900-2/26/1927). Born
        Norfolk, died New Rockelle, NY). M. 12/15/1927, Edna
        Penn Warren
22312971 Lucy Penn Tucker (b. 9/6/1932)
22312972 Ralph Douglas Tucker, Jr. (b. 7/22/1934 in Atlanta).
          M. 5/16/1970, Nellie Faye Freeman
223129721 Randolph Douglas Tucker (b. 2/27/1971)

        NOTE: The following person is a descendant of Admiral
               Tucker (22312):
                   John Randolph ("Josh") Tucker of Pensacola - great
                   grandson
22313   Honoria ("Nora") Mary Tucker (b. 1816), m. 11/26/1842,
        Joseph Williamson Randolph (22113). Children under
        father.
22314   Douglas Adam Tucker (1818-   ) b. in Alexandria, m. 5/14/
        1846 in Cooper County. MO. Maria Elizabeth Bronough
        (1819-1875), b. in Mason County (now WV) died Pilot
        Grove, Cooper County. Tucker was a farmer.
223141 John Tucker (1847-   )
223142 Douglas Tucker (1849-   )
223143 Nola Virginia Tucker (4/23/1856-8/9/1938) b. Wayne
        County, d. Tulsa. m. Alexander H. Meredith (1848-1904)
        a butcher of Pilot Grove. D. Warrensburg, MO
2231431 Martha Meredith (1876-1957)
2231432 Lon Meredith (1878-1933)
2231433 Arthur F. Meredith (7/27/1882-3/24/1944) b. Pilot Grove,
         d. Lincoln, KS, m. 6/28/1911 at Lincoln, Sarah C.
         Jennings (1/17/1885-1979)

22314331 Janice Meredith (1914-1952)
22314332 William Hugh Meredith (9/6/1916-   ), m. 7/1/1947,
          Beulah Mae Weber (8/10/1920-   )
223143321 William Hugh Meredith, Jr. (1/28/1949-   ), m. 6/22/
          1974, Mardelle F. Parkinson (4/4/1943-   )
2231433211 Stacy Meredith (11/11/1977-   )
22314333 Robert Arthur Meredith (1920-1988)
223143331 Robert Meredith (b. 3/6/1949). Deceased.
223143332 Debra Meredith (b. 8/5/1953). Deceased.
223143333 James Meredith (b. 8/6/1950)
22314334 Anna Jean Meredith (1922-   ), m.   Burtley
223143341 Jeanne C. Burtley (b. 6/8/1949), m.   Hurlburt
223143342 Janet V. Burtley (b. 5/28/1952), m.   Adair
223143343 Theresa Ann Burtley (b. 10/8/1954). Deceased.
22314335 Virginia Meredith (1924-   ), m.   Ruf
223143351 Randy Ruf (b. 6/9/1948)
223143352 Richard Ruf (b. 6/19/1951)
223143353 Roger Ruf (b. 2/4/1957)
223143354 Lorraine Ruf (b. 12/16/1961), m.   Capri
2231434 Lon Meredith (1878-1933)
223144
223145
223146
2234 Abbadore Albert (or Albert Aberdeen) Douglas (12/31/1789-
      (twin)
2235 Eliza Randolph Douglas (1791-   )

24 Archibald Cary (d. 2/27/1787). **Magazine of Virginia
    Genealogy**, Vol. 23, No. 4, p. 39-41.

2411 Mary ("Molly") Randolph (8/9/1762-1828), m. 12/9/1780 David
      Meade Randolph.

2412 Henry Cary Randolph (1/8/1764-3/13/1765)
2413 Elizabeth Randolph (b. 6/19/1765)
24131 Robert Randolph Pleasants

24134633 Virginia Adair Minor (d. 1907)

241346352 Adair Anderson Ely (d. 4/27/1987)
241346353 Anna Morris Ely, m. _____ Starnes

241346412 Virginia Cary Barba (b. 1925)
24134642 John Adair Purcell, m. 1928, Rebecca Trapnell
24134643 Lydia Mosby Purcell, m. Frederick Pasonby Wilmer

2413465 Rosalie Harrison Pleasants, m. 5/28/1893

24134652 Sheppard Archer (d. 1899)
24134653 William Wharton Archer, Jr., m. 11/19/1927
24134654 Edmund Minor Archer (b. 9/22/1904)

241374 Matthew Franklin Pleasants, Jr.

2414   Thomas Mann Randolph (b. 10/1/1778)

24141   Ann Cary Randolph (d. 2/7/1826), m. Charles Lewis Bankhead, son of Dr. John and Mary Warner Lewis (Light-
        foot) Bankhead

241411111   Charles Archibald Cary Bankhead

241411132   William Everett Bell, Jr.

2414111332   Helen Catherine Marr

241411135   Kathleen Wheeler Blair and Kathleen Wheeler Blair Bell
2414111351   Robert Griffith Bell, Jr.

24141113611   Jane Cary Anne Bell

241411241   Cary Randolph Bankhead Gillum

241411242   Rachel Errett Gillum, m. 1917

241411251   Charles Lewis Bankhead, Jr.

2414112612   Anne Cary Moyer, m. (1st) William Waers, m. (2nd)
            Robert Davis

2414112943   Joseph Russell Bankhead, Jr.

24141132   Mary Norris and Mary Norris Wells and Mary Norris
           Sublette

241413   Ellen Wayles (or Monroe) Bankhead and Ellen Wayles (or
         Monroe) Carter

241413131   Preston Henry Bailey. His wife: Elizabeth Marie Left-
            wich, dau. of George Whitfield Leftwich and his wife,
            the former Ava C. Flournoy.
2414131311   Margaret Preston Bailey (5/12/1918-   ).

2414144   (dau.) Bankhead (b. 1860, d. inf.)

2414145523   John Daniel Wykes III and Elizabeth Bankhead Hotch-
            kiss Wykes

24141456111   John Fennel Mitchell

2414228   Moncure Robinson Taylor, m. Lucie Madison Willis (1871-
            ), dau. of John Willis and his second wife (m.
         1870), Mary Lupton of Clarke County. THE WILLISES OF
         VIRGINIA by Maud Potter.

2414242   Jefferson Randolph Ruffin, d.s.p.

24142431112   Anthony Page Case

2414?432   Francis Gildart Ruffin, d.s.p.
24142433   Caryanne Nicholas Randolph Ruffin and Caryanne Nicholas
          Randolph Ruffin McMurdo

24142435123   Peter Randolph Balyeat

24142443   Wilson Cary Nicholas Ruffin, Jr.
24142444   Francis Gildart Ruffin

2414246411   Joan Charlene Ruffin, m. Michael Woodrow Sharp

241425   Mary Buchanan Randolph. Principal of Edge Hill School
          for Girls. Unm.

24142621   Child by first wife instead of child by first husband.

2414263   Jefferson Randolph Harrison, d.s.p. Unm.
241427   Maria Jefferson Carr Randolph, m. 4/26/1848 Charles Mason

24142721   Charles Mason Smith, M.D.

241427212   Addison Gordon Billingsley, Jr. (b. 1/26/1912), son of
          Addison Gordon and Ellie Annis Leavell Billingsley

24142x   Jane Nicholas Randolph (b. 10/10/1831)(b. Albemarle
          County, d. Lynchburg), m. Albemarle County, Robert
          Garlick Hill Kean (10/7/1828-6/13/1898)(b. Caroline
          County, d. Lynchburg). He m. (2nd) 3/2/1874 Adelaide
          Navarro Demaret Prescott (11/5/1844-10/1/1922)(b. Wash-
          ington, LA; d. Providence, RI).
24142x1   Lancelot Minor Kean (b. Albemarle County, d. Louisiana),
          m. (1st) Elizabeth Tucker Prescott (6/5/1854-1/17/1902)
          (b. and d. Washington, LA)(she was younger sister of
          Lancelot's father's second wife).   M. (2nd) Martha
          Foster Murphy (b. 6/10/1879)(b. Jeanerette, LA).
24142x11   Jane Randolph Kean (b. Lynchburg), m. Alexandria, LA,
          John Samuel Butler (1861-10/6/1916)(b. Opelousas,
          LA; d. Baton Rouge).
24142x111   John Samuel Butler, Jr. (b. Chenneyville, LA), m.
          Abbeville, LA, Miriam Elizabeth Leguenee (b. 5/12/
          1907)(b. Abbeville, LA).
24142x1111   Miriam Elizabeth Butler (b. Abbeville, LA), m. New
          Orleans, Richard Joseph Moore (10/6/1936-   )(b.
          Denver).
24142x11111   Richard Joseph Moore, Jr. (b. New Orleans).
24142x11112   Sean Samuel Butler Moore (b. New Orleans).
24142x11113   Patrick Edward Moore (b. Charleston, SC)(twin).
24142x11114   Jefferson Randolph Kean Moore (b. Charleston, SC)
          (twin).

24142x113 Jane Randolph Butler, m. Wesley Cary Lancaster
24142x1131 Wesley Cary Lancaster, Jr.

24142x12 Lancelot Minor Kean, Jr. (1)
24142x13 Lancelot Minor Kean, Jr. (2)

24142x15 Maria Evalina Sanfrosa Prescott Kean (b. Sioux City,
          IA), m. Washington, DC, Constant Southworth (8/12/
          1894-1984)(b. Duluth, MN; d. Alexandria, VA).

24142x16 Elizabeth Caroline Hill Kean (b. Sioux City, IA; d. New
          Orleans), m. Raymond Henry Campbell (d. 10/21/1969)
          (d. New Orleans)

24142x163 Raymond Henry Campbell, Jr., m. Elizabeth Contelli

24142x17 James Louis Randolph Kean (b. New Orleans), m. Mary
          Louise McCarter (b. 12/8/1914).
24142x171 James Louis Randolph Kean, Jr. (b. New Orleans).
24142x2 Martha ("Pattie" or "Patsy") Cary Kean (b. Lynchburg, d.
          Annapolis), m. Lynchburg, John Speed Morris (4/1/1855-
          10/24/1928)(b. Lynchburg, d. Ancon, Panama Canel Zone).
24142x21 Robert Kean Morris (b. Lynchburg, d. Mexico City). M.
          (1st) Panama Canel Zone, Meta Elaine Thomas (7/20/
          1888-1/5/1963)(b. Brainerd, MN; d. Santa Barbara, CA).
          Div. 1922. M. (2nd) Panama Canel Zone, Louise Newcom
          Richards Baughman, formerly wife of William E.
          Baughman (Sr.).
24142x211 Dorothy Elaine Morris (b. Panama Canal Zone, d. Sunny-
          vale, CA).
24142x2111 Dorothy Elaine Lamar, m. Fred Rogers Saunders (b. 7/
          20/1923).

24142x212 Robert Kean ("Bert") Morris, Jr. (b. 12/24/1915)(b.
          Balboa, Panama Canal Zone), m. Pueblo, CO, Muriel
          Ellen Walker (b. 10/9/1917)(b. Pueblo, CO)

24142x2121 Robert Kean Morris III (b. San Diego).
24142x2122 Cynthia Anne Morris (b. San Diego).
24142x22 Mary Randolph Morris (b. 2/19/1885)(b. Lynchburg), m.
          Washington, DC, Allen Melancthon Sumner (10/1/1883-
          7/19/1918)(b. Boston, d. France).
24142x23 Page Waller Morris (d. 9/10/1956)(b. Albemarle County),
          m. Frederick Campbell Stuart Hunter II (d. 1930).
24142x232 John Morris Hunter, m. Juliet King Lehman (b. 1911).
24142x24 William Sylvanus Morris (b. 5/5/1887)(b. Campbell
          County, d. Duluth), m. Pearl Lenore Oberg (d. ca.
          1935)(d. Duluth).
24142x25 Pattie Nicholas Morris (b. Indian Territory), m.
          Washington, DC, Horace King Hutchens (d. 1972)(b.
          Pulaski, NY; d. Euclid, OH).

24142x251   Katherine King Hutchens (b. New York City). M. (1st)
            New Rochelle, NY, George William Wiley (7/13/1913-4/
            1/1970)(b. Oak Park, IL; d. Cleveland). M. (2nd)
            Cleveland, William Joseph Ermisch.
24142x26 Adelaide Prescott Morris (b. Indian Territory), m.
            Washington, DC, Thomas Ross Cooley (6/26/1893-11/28/
            1959)(b. Grass Valley, CA; d. Quantico, VA).

24142X261   Adelaide Morris Cooley, m. Hal (Henry?) Waugh Smith,
            M.D.

24142X3   Jefferson Randolph Kean (b. Lynchburg, d. Washington,
            DC). M. (1st) Louise Hurlburt Young (9/1/1877-12/10/
            1915)(b. St. Augustine; d. Fort Leavenworth). M. (2nd)
            Cornelia Butler Knox (3/1/1875-4/   /1954)(b. Tours,
            France; d. Washington, DC).
24142x31 Martha Jefferson Kean (b. Key West, d. Alexandria, VA),
            m. Washington, DC, William Chason. Div. 1932.

24142x311   William Randolph Chason (d. 1980)

24142x312   Louise Young Chason (b. Hopewell, VA).
24142x313   Robert Leonard Chason (b. Hopewell, VA).
24142x31311   Sara Elizabeth Bladon (last name changed by adoption
            to Chason).
24142x314   Helen Borodell Chason (b. Miami), m. Alexandria, VA,
            John Wesley Crump (b. 8/21/1923)(b. Philadelphia).
24142x3141   Sheila Kean Crump (b. Alexandria, VA), m. Cherry
            Hill, NJ).
24142x32 Robert Hill ("Bob") Kean (d. 1/16/1985)(b. Morristown,
            NJ; d. Alexandria, VA), m. New Orleans, Sarah Rice
            ("Sadie") Elliott (b. 6/19/1905)(b. Albemarle County).
24142x321   Jefferson Randolph ("Randy") Kean II (b. New Orleans).
            M. (1st) Evanston, IL, Barbara Miller (b. 5/4/1932)
            (b. Chicago). Div. 8/22/1968. M. (2nd) Alexandria,
            VA, Leah Jones Stevens (b. 6/30/1943)(b. West Point,
            NY).
24142x3211   Evalina Southworth Kean (b. Washington, DC).
24142x322   Margaret Young ("Peggy") Kean (b. Charlottesville), m.
            Charlottesville, Edward Alexander ("Sandy") Rubel (b.
            12/12/1934)(b. Brookline, MA).
24142x3221   Daniel Martin Rubel (b. Providence, RI).
24142x3222   Stephen Elliott Rubel (b. Providence).
24142x3223   Sarah Rice Rubel (b. Providence).
24142x4   Data is erroneous, and should be:
24142x4   Robert Garlick Hill Kean, Jr. (12/26/1861-   )(b. Albe-
            marle County). Disappeared in 1883. When last heard
            from he was in Colorado.

24142x41   Evalina Moore Kean, m. Edward Rolfe Ford Wells

24142x5   Louis Randolph Kean (b. and d. Albemarle County).
24142x6   George Wythe Randolph Kean (b. and d. Albemarle County).

24142a111 Virginius Randolph Shackelford, Jr. (1)
24142a113 Virginius Randolph Shackelford, Jr. (2)

24142b Meriwether Lewis Randolph, Captain, C.S.A.

24142c Sarah Nicholas Randolph. Principal of Patapsco, Ellicott
        City. Also, Miss Randolph's School for Girls, Eutaw
        Place, Baltimore. Also, an author.

241443111 Julia Gardner Coolidge

2414431251 Laura Elizabeth Richards, m. (1st) Harvey Milton
           Miller

2414431521 Albert Lamb Lincoln III, m. Joan Miller

2414431541 John Hamilton Coolidge

24144351 Harold Jefferson Coolidge, Jr. (d. 2/18/1985). His
          first marriage, to Helen Carpenter Isaacs, ended in
          divorce. He was an internationally known zoologist
          and conservationist.

24144353 Emily Fairfax Coolidge, m. (1st) Harry Adsit Woodruff
          (d. 1952)

241443611 Jane Coolidge Whitehill (and Jane Coolidge Whitehill
           Rotch). Death date is incorrect.

241443641 Helena Stacy French, m. Bertrand Israel Halperin

241444 Dr. Algernon Coolidge (twin to Philip Sydney Coolidge)
        (241445)

241444373 Francis Lowell Coolidge, Jr.

24144453 Mary Lowell Barton, m. Dr. Edmond Delos Churchill

241445 Philip Sydney Coolidge (d. 9/19/1864)(twin to Dr.
        Algernon Coolidge)(241444)
241446 Thomas Jefferson Coolidge. Minister to France.

24144611 Hetty (Mehitable?) Appleton Sargent

24144632 Thomas Jefferson Newbold, m. Katherine Hubbard (d. 7/4/
          1939)

2414611 Nicholas Philip Trist Burke, m. Jane Revere Reynolds
         (b. 6/3/1871)

241461121   Nicholas Randolph Burke, m. Claire Juliette (Greszty)
            Gardiner

2414614   Henry Randolph Burke, m. Rosella Gordon Trist (b. 5/26/
          1869)

24146143   Rosella Trist Burke, m. Robert Edwin Graham (b. 7/24/
           1899)

2414614411   Jane Randolph Burke (b. 5/15/1963)

2414631111   John William Fulton, Jr., m. Lotus Pua Kenaona

241463112   Virginia Jefferson Kenny (b. 3/13/1916), m. 6/8/1935
            Seward Davis, Jr.

2414631122   Katherine Ray Davis

2414634   Mary Helen Trist (b. 9/12/1865)

241491   Isaetta Carter Randolph, m. James Lenaeus Hubard (13423),
         Lt. Col. 44th Reg, Va. Col., CSA, son of Robert T. and
         Susan Bolling Hubard

241491111   Wiley Nelson Hubard, m. (2nd) Annie Irene Kemp

241491122   Robert King Hubard, m. (2nd) Frances Ruth Richenberger
241491123   Ramona Jean Hubard, m. (1st) Robet Alonzo Stokes

241491221   Harry Benjamin Munday, Jr., m. 10/25/1952 Pauline
            Vaughan

2414916   Mary Randolph Hubard, m. Edward Miles Mathewes (10/8/
          1868-12/ /1952)

241491642   Thomas Richard Waring, Jr.

241492   Lewis Carter Randolph (6/13/1838-5/29/1887), m. 1/29/
         1867, Louisa Hubard, only dau. of Robert Thruston
         Hubard (13426)

2414921   Robert Hubard (or Carter) Randolph

24149273   Elizabeth Carrier Randolph, m. (1st) 10/28/1928, Joseph
           D. Rivers. M. (2nd) Monroe Stanley Bopst
241492731   William Lord Rivers, m. (2nd)(as second husband)
            Sylvia Willis Griffin

241493   Robert Mann Randolph (b. 4/15/1851), m. 1885, Margaret
         Calhoun Harris

2414x Meriwether Lewis Randolph (b. 1/10/1810), m. Elizabeth
       Martin (niece of President Andrew Jackson. One source
       gives name as Elizabeth Wharton).

2414a Septima Anne Randolph (/16/1804-11/20/1849), m. Dr.
       David Scott Meiklehan (no dates)

2414b George Wythe Randolph (Secretary of War, C.S.A.), m.
       (as second husband) Mary Elizabeth (or Crittenden) Adams
       Pope. (221221)
2415   William Randolph (b. 6/16/1770) of "Chellew", Cumberland
       County

241511 William Mayer Randolph (b. 5/24/1815). Moved to St.
        Louis

24151336 DeBenville Keim (d. 1883)

2415162l1 Virginia Elizabeth Pochon, m. Harry Ustance Oxenham.
           She d. 3/1/1987. Burial at Millar Family Cemetery
           in Front Royal
241516211l Peter Rolfe Oxenham lives in Geneva. Born in
            Stuttgart, Germany
241516212 Erica Millar Pochon, m. (2nd) W. A. Samouce of
           Virginia Beach

241516213 Rolfe Millar Pochon. Lives in Lausanne.

241516215 Beverley Randolph Pochon. Lives in Lausanne.

241516217 Catherine DuBois Pochon, m. _____ Dike of Geneva

241518 Christopher Mayer Randolph (9/1/1830-9/22/1868). Captain
        C.S.A. M. (2nd) 4/11/1865 Frances ("Fannie") Bernard
        Lambeth (5/11/1840-1/24/1927), dau. of William Meredith
        Lambeth and his wife, the former Georgeanna Norris
        Slacum.
2415182 Son (b. 8/4/1859, d. infant).
    Children, etc., by second wife:
2415183 Lambeth Slacum Randolph (12/8/1865-4/26/1866).
2415184 Peyton Lambeth Randolph (5/14/1867-9/15/1895)(b. at
         "Lucky Hit" Plantation, Avoyelles Parish, LA; d. Los
         Angeles). M. ca. 1950 Rose Dorsey.
24151841 Beverley Lambeth Randolph (5/19/1894-8/19/1914)(b. Los
          Angeles, d. London).
2415185 Christopher Mayer Randolph, Jr. (10/25/1868-11/23/1937)
         (b. at "Lucky Hit" Planation, d. at "The Farm", Fairfax
         County, VA), m. Mary Frances Munro Bolling (1114212).

24152242 Alexander Tidball Jones, m. Emily Carr Whittle, dau. of
           Fortesque (Bishop) and Frances McNeece Whittle

24152431 Rebecca Hume Lewis

241524312 Rebecca Jean Tyndell (instead of Wyndell).

2415243112 Cary Randolph Marshall (1/6/1932-10/26/1985)(b. and
            d. in Winchester), m. John J. Cottingham.
24152431121 John J. Cottingham, Jr. (   ). Home: Washing-
             ton, DC.
24152431122 Randolph Marshall Cottingham (   ). Home:
             Centreville, VA.

241524522 Mary Chatard Doll

2415311 Ellen Randolph Tabb, m. Dr. Thomas Barkwell Lane, son of
          Walker Gardiner and Mary Anna Henry Barkwell Lane

241532 William Eston Randolph, m. Sarah Lavinia Epes. Lived in
         Millwood. 15W 252.

2415328 Benjamin Burn Randolph (d. 1870-inf.)

2415329 Lucy Wellford Randolph (b. 3/13/1873-d. 4 mos. old)

241533314 Rosalie O'Fallon Randolph (d. 7/19/1981)

241533531   Mary Carter Randolph (b. Kirkwood, MO). M. (1st)
            Beverley Tucker Nelson, son of William Meade Nelson
            and his wife, the former Jane ("Jennie") Stewart
            Robinson. M. (2nd) Kenneth D. Stabler (9/21/1892-
)(b. Salem).
2415335311 Mary Carter Randolph Nelson (b. St. Louis)(twin), m.
            Stuart S. Howards, M.D.
2415335312 Thomas Randolph Nelson (b. St. Louis)(twin), M.D.
2415335313 Page Nelson (b. Winchester), m. Rudolph Karl
            Loeser.
2415335321 Edward Fairfax Randolph, Jr. (12/11/1938-   )(b.
            Washington, D.C.), m. Patricia Louise Dolvin.
24153353211 Son.

241533533 Jane Cary Randolph, m. 3/15/1948 Benjamin Harrison III
            (24216431)
2415335331 Jane Cary Harrison (2/21/1949-   ). Also, Jane
            Cary Harrison Embury

24153353311 Taylor Harrison Embury (4/4/86-   ).

24153353312 Philip A. Embury, Jr. (8/28/1988-   )
2415335332 Nancy Randolph Harrison (5/12/1951-   ). Also,
            Nancy Randolph Harrison Thorpe

2415335333 Benjamin Harrison IV (12/18/1953-   )

24153353332 Benjamin Harrison V (2/17/86-   ).

24153353333 Stuart Randolph Harrison (10/11/1989-   )

241533541 Katherine Gratz Randolph, m. (2nd) Guy Snyder.

241533542 Rosalie Fitzhugh Randolph, m. Edgar Dickson.

2415338 Jane Cary Randolph (d. 3/15/1863)
2415339 Lucius Wilton Randolph (b. & d. 4/28/1866)
241534 Lucius Burwell Randolph, m. Isadora Preston (6/8/1836-
        5/8/1917)
2415341 Emma K. Randolph (10/20/1860-8/15/1928), m. (1st) 9/24/
         1881, Henry Winegard (6/12/1860-8/26/1894), son of
         Isaac W. and Mary Clarke Winegard. M. (2nd) W. W.
         Watson
24153411 Nellie Winegard (5/25/1882-9/11/1918), m. 1898, Joe
          Brewer (1/25/1876-9/27/1953)
241534111 Alonzo Brewer (b. 5/25/1899-d. as a young child.)
241534112 Henry Brewer (2/19/1901-8/14/1921). Unm.
241523113 Carol Brewer (3/30/1903-11/21/1973), m. (1st) Harry
           Hendrix. M. (2nd) George Hanson
2415341131 Nell Hendrix
2415341132 Myra Hendrix
2415341133 Carolyn Hanson
24153411 4 Murray Brewer (6/5/1905-1985), m. Camille Boatwright
2415341141 Murray Brewer, Jr.
2415341142 Gladys Brewer, m. _____ Landers
24153411421 (son), m.
2415341143 James Brewer, m.
24153411431 dau.
24153411432 dau.
2415341144 Kenneth Brewer, m.
24153411441 Shannon Brewer
24153411442 dau.
241534115 Elizabeth Brewer (3/28/1909-9/10/1938), m. (1st)
           Cardinal Henry

241534116 Charlotte Brewer (10/   /1911-11/14/1977), m. (1st)
           _____ Hornsby; m. (2nd) _____ Spooner;
           m. (3rd) _____ DeMay; m. (4th) Luther Lamb
2415341161 Doyle Hornsby
241534117 Howard Brewer (2/25/1913-7/12/1988), m. (1st) Evelyn
           Bennett; m. (2nd) Walton Cannon
  Child by second wife:
2415341171 Deborah Brewer

24153412 Arthur Cleveland Winegard (4/21/   -4/4/1945), m. 9/18/
          1910, Lillie Mae Davis (8/26/1886-8/14/1982), dau.
          of William Sampson and Susan Louise Collins Davis
241534121 Henrietta Jane Winegard (b. 9/23/1911), m. (1st)
           4/5/1930 Edward Otis Floyd (3/   /1899-2/23/1960),
           son of Eugene and Emma Roberts Floyd. M. (2nd)
           12/23/1960 James Guy Crew
2415341211 Velma Mary Lois Floyd (b. 5/6/1931), m. 7/29/1949,
            Cola Ellen Martin
24153412111 Gary Allen Martin
24153412112 Pamela Ann Martin (b. 10/   /1960), m. Mike Blackburn
241534121121 Mary Jane Blackburn
2415341212 Claude Edward Floyd (b. 6/16/1934), m. ca. 1955 Hazel
            Nell Dover
24153412121 Belinda Floyd (b. 3/18/1956)
24153412122 James Edward Floyd
241534122 William Sampson Winegard (b. 9/27/1913-2/2/1986), m.
           10/1/1932 Viola Baucom (b. 4/29/1912), dau. of James
           Holly and Mary Isabel McClelland Baucom
241534121 Helen Elizabeth Winegard (b. 11/3/1933), m. 8/29/1953
           Rufus Dause Albritton, Jr. (b. 9/24/1927), son of
           Rufus Dause and Florence Lastinger Albritton
24153412211 Rufus Dause Albritton III (b. 12/29/1955), m.
             12/27/1980 Caroline Elaine Fitzpatrick, dau. of
             James and June A. Harland Fitzpatrick. Div. 1984
24153412212 Samuel Gay Albritton (b. 12/17/1957), m. 1/30/1982
             Karen Denise Simpson, dau. of Marion Lavon and Ruby
             Nell Franks Simpson
24153412213 Michael Shawn Albritton (9/18/1970)
241534122 Mildred Charlotte Winegard (b. 1/5/1938), m. 6/19/
           1938 Raymond Andrew Mann (b. 2/14/1940), son of
           John Andrew and Jessie Mae Mann Mann
24153412221 Cynthia Rene Mann (b. 4/25/1962)
             John Andrew Mann (b. 2/10/1969). Adopted.
241534123 Roy Alton Winegard (b. 8/7/1939), m. 7/15/1960 Doris
           Addie Keene (b. 5/31/1939), dau. of Elmer and Addie
           Mae Rutledge Keene
24153412231 Sharon Denise Winegard (b. 10/7/1962)
24153412232 Richard Allen Winegard (b. 10/27/1967)
241534124 Ethel Irene Winegard (b. 1/10/1947), m. 7/11/1965
           Harold Eugene Childress (b. 11/28/1944), son of
           Harold Alexander and Flossie Viola Smith Childress
24153412241 Rachelle Lyn Childress (b. 3/13/1970)
24153412242 Shana Lenay Childress (b. 7/24/1979)

241534123 Arthur Randolph Winegard (b. 5/2/1921), m. (1st) Inez
           Gaylord; m. (2nd) Ina Pauline Patterson (b. 4/29/
           1931), dau. of Ira Patterson
2415341231 Arthur Randolph Winegard, Jr. (b. 8/18/1950), m.
           (1st) 4/1/1973 Cyndee Anderson; m. (2nd) 10/1/19____
           Pamela Kiravac
    Child by second wife:
24153412311 Kimberly Kay Winegard (b. 11/28/1982)
2415341232 Stephen Edward Winegard (b. 11/18/1954), m. 9/ /1974
           Kathy C. Justice

24153412321 Stephen Edward Winegard II (b. 2/4/1975)
24153412322 Christina Lee Winegard (b. 1982)
2415341233 Asa Cleveland Winegard (b. 5/6/1958)
24153413 Isadora Winegard (2/23/1886-5/11/1909). Unm.
24153414 Henrietta Winegard (9/14/1888-6/19/1907), m. _____
           Resurgam
24153415 Randolph Klein Winegard (5/ /1891-1952), m. (1st) Ora
           Whitfield
241534151 Helen Winegard (twin)
241534152 Vivian Winegard (twin)
24153416 Carlie Winegard (b. 1/ /1894), m. _____ Green
241534161 Mildred Green

2415343 Virginius Randolph (b. 11/11/1867)

2416 Archibald Cary Randolph 8/24/1771-10/3/1771)
2417 Judith Randolph (b. 8/24/1771-twin to Archibald Cary
       Randolph 2416), m. 12/31/1789 or 1793 Richard Randolph
2418 Anne Cary Randolph (9/16/1774-5/28/1837), m. 5/28/1795
       Gouverneur Morris, minister to France. Lived at
       Morrisania, NY

2419 Jane Cary Randolph (12/17/1776-3/2/1842), m. 5/11/1795,
       Thomas Eston Randolph (4/11/1767-4/11/1842). Inherited
       "Dungeness". Finally settled in Florida.
24191 William Eston Randolph (2/7/1796-6/17/1817), d.s.p.
24192 Thomas Mann Randolph (3/19/1798-8/20/1835), m. 4/11/1821,
        Susan Eaton Browne (d. 1835 or 1837)
241921 Thomas Eston Randolph (6/29/1823-9/26/1833)
241922 William Brown Randolph (b. 6/10/1825), m. to Annie
         Campbell or Jennie Turner
2419221 Jane Randolph
2419222 William Randolph
241923 Marian Symmes Randolph (3/28/1827-1859 or 1860), m. 1845,
         Joseph Yates Porter (1817-1847)
2419231 Joseph Yates Porter, Jr., M.D. (1847 or 1849-1927 or
          1929), m. Louise Curry (1849-1929)
24192311 Mary Louise Porter (1873-1945), m. William H. Harris
241923111 Mann Randolph Harris (b. 1898)
241923112 Minnie Porter Harris (b. 1900)
241923113 William H. Harris, Jr. (b. 1904, d. inf.)
241923114 William Curry Harris (b. 1909), m. Yolanda Mendoza

2419231141   _____ Harris
2419231142   _____ Harris
2419231143   _____ Harris
2419231144   _____ Harris
24192312 William Randolph Porter, M.D. (1871-1953), m. 1898
          Grace Dorgan (1875-1939)
241923121 Jessie Porter (b. 1898), m. (1st)1925 Wallace Kirke.
          M. (2nd) E. L. Newton
  Child by first husband:
2419231211 Jeane Porter Kirke (b. 1926), m. Arthur Poirer
24192312111 Porter Poirer
24192312112 Susan Poirer

  Child by second husband:
2419231212 Caroline Randolph Newton, m. (1st) Theodore Land. M.
          (2nd) William Horneck. M. (3rd) _____
24192313 Joseph Yates Porter III (1881-1955), m. (1st) 1907
          Alice Maloney. M. (2nd) 1924 Mary Baker. M. (3rd)
          Beulah Brantley
  Child by first wife:
241923131 Joseph Yates Porter IV (1909-1967), m. (1st) Anita
          Gato. M. (2nd) Harriet Stevens Wilson (d. 197__)
  Child by second wife:
241923132 Mary Louise Porter (b. 1925), m. (1st) Louis Smith.
          M. (2nd) Bascom Groom, Jr.
24192314 Roberta Porter (1874 or 1875-1922), m. 1897 Wilbert
          Montjoy
241924 Jane Cary Randolph (7/ /1829-1833?)
24193 Mary Elizabeth Cleland Randolph, m. (1st) Francis Wayles
          Eppes VII (b. 9/20/1801). He m. (2nd) 3/15/1837

241932 Dr. John Wayles Eppes (b. 7/4/1825), m. 11/10/1854
          Josephine H. Bellamy

24193221 Margaret Kennedy, m. 1915, Albert Hernandez Blanc
24193222 Josephine Bellamy Kennedy (5/6/1889-5/7/1961)

241932222 Marion Howard Bradley, Jr. (b. 12/11/1915), m. 12/30/
          1941 Joye Patricia Clark
2419322221 Ann Randolph Bradley (b. 1/28/1944), m. 12/1/1962
          Robert Bradford Bernette
2419322222 Josephine Eppes Bradley (b. 9/10/1947)
2419322223 Marion Howard Bradley III, m. 9/18/1951
24193223 Alexander Kennedy, Jr. (1885-1903)
24193224 Agnes Kennedy (b. 1882), m. James Washington Herbert
241932241 Elizabeth Eppes Herbert (b. 3/23/1921), m. 4/24/1943
          Joseph Byron Davis
2419322411 Joseph Byron Davis, Jr. (b. 3/10/1944)
2419322412 Ann Lynwood Davis (b. 8/7/1945)
2419322413 James Kennedy Davis (b. 9/18/1947)
2419322414 William Lewis Davis
241932242 Julia Frances Herbert (b. 6/15/1922), m. 9/ /1943
          Robert Edward Lee Hall Forbes
2419322421 Julia Lee Forbes

24193224222 Florence Patricia Kennedy Forbes (b. 10/8/1946)
24193224223 Robert Edward Lee Hall Forbes, Jr. (b. 9/29/1948)
241932424 George Joseph Forbes (b. 5/7/1951)
24193224225 Clarence Aloysius Hall Forbes (b. 7/18/1952)
24193224243 Agnes Kennedy Herbert (d. inf.)
24193225 Florence Patti Kennedy (b. 1891)
24193226 John Wayles Kennedy (6/15/1889-7/4/1932), m. 11/19/1921
        Laura Cecelia Hebb
241932261 John Wayles Kennedy, Jr. (b. 2/24/1923), m. 6/1/1949
            Dina Morelli
24193224611 Lisa Morelli Kennedy (b. 2/21/1952)
241932262 Margaret Combs Kennedy (b. 9/29/1924), m. 8/14/1954
            Eugene Hall Johnstone
24193224621 Eugene Hall Johnstone, Jr. (b. 7/19/1955)
24193224622 Laura Hebb Johnstone (b. 12/19/1956)
24193224623 Virginia Coad Johnstone (b. 12/ /1958)
241932263 Alexander Kennedy (b. 4/15/1926), m. 3/25/1957 Mary
            Collette Barrett
24193224631 Mary Grace Kennedy (b. 12/23/1957)
24193224632 John Wayles Kennedy (b. 8/24/1959)
241932264 Patricia Hebb Kennedy (b. 6/28/1928), m. 10/22/1955
            Samuel Robert Garrabrant
24193224641 Laura Wayles Garrabrant (b. 8/13/1956)
24193224642 Robert Bayard Garrabrant (b. 2/24/1957)
241932265 Anne Katherine Kennedy (b. 11/4/1929), m. 1/20/1953
            Owen William Hendon
24193224651 Nicole Hendon (b. 11/8/1955)
24193224652 McKim Kennedy Hendon (b. 3/19/1957)
24193224653 Robert Derek Hendon (b. 8/23/1959)
241933 Thomas Jefferson Eppes (6/29/1827-1860 or 1870), m. 4/28
        1859
2419331 Thomas Jefferson Eppes, Jr. (2/22/1861-11/2/1910), m.
        (2nd) Mamie Jeanette Shoemaker Gones
  Children by first wife:
24193311 Thomas Jefferson Eppes III (9/6/1884-2/1/1944)
24193312 Edna Bellamy Eppes (b. 12/12/1892), m. 9/1/1915
241933121 Edna Eppes Lattimore, m. 7/12/1941, Jack Stacy Clancy
2419331211 Helen Lattimore Clancy (b. 3/6/1943)
2419331212 Jack Stacy Clancy, Jr. (6/14/1947)
2419331213 Carol Clancy (b. 7/2/1949)
241933122 William Lattimore (b. 6/28/1818), m. 12/20/1943 Helen
            M. Clancy
2419331221 Anne Eppes Lattimore (b. 2/19/1947)
2419331222 Elizabeth Bellamy Lattimore (b. 11/24/1949)
2419331223 William Lattimore, Jr. (b. 5/25/1954)

24193331 Theodosia Bellamy Morrison, m. Dudley Shepard Shine
            (d. 6/ /1933), son of David Shepard and Caroline
            Matilda Eppes Shine. M. (2nd) Cyril Norman Boland
  Children by first husband:
241933311 Dudley Shepard Shine, Jr., m. 3/4/1936 Margaret
            Pinkham

2419333111 Dudley Shepard Shine III (b. 2/22/1938)
2419333112 Randolph Shine (b. 4/3/1942)
241933312 Theodosia Morrison Shine, m. Dean Rader
2419333121 Randolph Rader (b. 10/22/1945)

24193341 Francis Eppes, Jr.

241933412 Francis Eppes III

2419335 Paul Eppes (d. 1868)
2419336 Randolph Eppes (10/21/1868-12/5/1941), m. 12/15/1898,
          Sarah Josephine Mays
24193361 Edith Bellamy Eppes (b. 12/26/1899)
241933611 Edith Eppes Bass (b. 12/19/1921), m. 11/18/1944
           William Ellison Thompson, Jr.

2419336111 William Ellison Thompson III (8/29/1945)
2419336112 David Craig Thompson (b. 3/22/1947)
2419336113 Mark Randolph Thompson (b. 3/29/1952)
2419336114 Sarah Ann Thompson (b. 11/6/1953)
241933612 Eleanor Mays Bass (b. 1/23/1924), m. 10/19/1946 Dr.
           Joseph Brannen Ganey
2419336121 Joseph Brannen Ganey, Jr. (b. 7/25/1949)
2419336122 James Nowell Ganey (b. 7/15/1950)
2419336123 Thomas Harris Ganey (b. 11/15/1954)
241933613 Dr. Haskell Harris Bass, Jr. (b. 6/6/1936)
24193362 Martha Simpkins Eppes (b. 6/30/1903), m. (1st) 1923
          Edward Baldwin Young. M. (2nd) 4/26/1934 Francis
          Putney Wetherbee
   Child by first husband:
241933621 Meta/Margaret Baldwin Young (b. 11/6/1924), m. 4/12/
           1947 William Dyer Shackelford
2419336211 Martha Eppes Shackelford (b. 6/9/1950)
2419336212 Theresa Dyer Shackelford (b. 5/8/1956)
2419336213 Meta/Margaret Baldwin Shackelford (b. 2/22/1961)
2419336214 Maria Eppes Shackelford (b. 3/29/1962)
    Children by second husband:
241933622 Francis Putney Wetherbee, Jr. (b. 4/3/1935), m. 3/17/
           1959 Nancy Elizabeth Butts
241933623 James Roland Wetherbee (b. 1/4/1940)
241933624 Sarah Eppes Wetherbee (b. 1/23/1943)
241934 Rev. William Eston Eppes (b. 7/5/1830), m. (1st) 8/ /
        1854, Emily Bancroft. M. (2nd) 1877, Augusta Jones
        Kollock

24193432 William Eston Eppes (b. 6/10/1885)
24193433 James Bancroft Eppes, m. (1st) Elizabeth Walliford.
          M. (2nd) 1945 Carolyn Frances Walliford
   Children by first wife:

241934332 Caroline Frances Eppes (b. 1911), m. (1st) 1929
           Stanford Ivan Hoff. M. (2nd) 1934, William Bernard
           Loving

Child by first husband:
2419343321 Stanford Ivan Hoff, Jr. (1930-1950)
    Children by second husband:
2419343322 William Bernard Loving, Jr. (b. 1936), m. 1/7/1959
        Myna Joyce Bruner
2419343323 Clare Bancroft Loving (b. 1938), m. 3/2/1959 Dr.
        Merrill Eugene Speelman. Div.
241934333 James Bancroft Eppes, Jr. (b. 1913), m. 5/18/1946
        Elizabeth Claude Fuller
2419343331 John Williford Eppes (b. 6/21/1941)
2419343332 James Bancroft Eppes III (b. 11/1/1942)
2419343333 Thomas Jefferson Eppes (b. 5/21/1946)
2419343334 Lucy Elizabeth Eppes (b. 6/16/1956)
241934334 Emily Eppes (1910-1921)
241934335 Mary Eppes, m. 1943 Remus Strother Turner
2419343351 Remus Strother Turner, Jr. (b. 2/4/1945)
2419343352 Janet Elizabeth Turner (b. 4/6/1947)

2419343353 Joseph Eppes Turner (b. 6/11/1950)
2419343354 Paul Alan Turner (b. 4/27/1954)
241934336 Dr. Williford Eppes, m. 10/9/1948 Emily Mulligan
2419343361 Emily Elizabeth Eppes (b. 7/27/1949)
2419343362 Douglas Williford Eppes (b. 6/25/1950)
2419343363 Thomas Wayne Eppes (b. 9/24/1952)
2419343364 Barbara Carolyn Eppes (b. 7/30/1955)
2419343365 David Charles Eppes (b. 6/6/1957)

24193435 John Wayles Eppes (d. 11/6/1961)
241934351 John Francis Eppes (b. 4/4/1921), m. 8/27/1944
        Margaret Temple
2419343511 Constance Bancroft Eppes (b. 11/27/1953)

2419345 Lucy Randolph Eppes (d. 1896)

24193454 Emily Cleland Bancroft (d. 6/22/1956)
24193455 Matilda Eppes Bancroft (b. 10/10/1892), m. 9/27/1929
        Thomas Wetzell Richards
241934551 Thomas Edward Richards (2/26/1932), m. 9/6/1953
        Charlene Jeanette Ruark
2419345511 Keith Randolph Richards (b. 1/26/1955)
2419345512 Thomas Jeffrey Richards (b. 10/18/1958)

2419347 William Eston Eppes, Jr.
24193471 Adele Evelyn Eppes (b. 6/8/1890), m. 4/13/1913 James
        William Lockett
241934711 Martha Ann Lockett (b. 4/26/1914), m. (1st) 1935
        William Ewell Lewis. M. (2nd) 8/30/1957 Emory
        McNeille

241934713 Frances Hunter Lockett (b. 12/25/1917), m. 1938
        Alton A. Rogers
2419347131 Jane Elizabeth Rogers (b. 1939), m. 8/23/1958
        William Carl Quante

24193471311 William Carl Quante, Jr. (b. 5/17/1959)
24193471312 Albert John Quante (b. 2/16/1963)
241934713? Joyce Hunter Rogers (b. 1940)
241934714 James William Lockett, Jr. (b. 11/20/1920), m. 1941,
    Madie Sapp
2419347141 Evelyn Mae Lockett (b. 1943)
2419347142 Patricia Fay Lockett (b. 1945)
?419347143 Martha Ann Lockett (b. 1950)
2419347144 James William Lockett III (b. 6/24/1956)
241934715 Randolph Eppes Lockett (b. 5/11/1922), m. (1st) 1942
    Catherine C. Roberts. M. (2nd) 9/4/1951 Elizabeth
    Ruth Reynolds
  Child by second wife:
2419347151 Randolph Eppes Lockett, Jr. (b. 1/3/1956)
241934716 Frederick Buckner Lockett, m. Josephine Rodewalt
2419347161 Cynthia Diane Lockett (b. 6/ /1952)
24193472 William Randolph Eppes (8/20/1892-1/13/1919), m. 1/2/
    1919 Marion Grey McCorkle
241934721 Randolph Marion Eppes (b. & d. 6/ /1919)

24193473 Arthur Beverley Eppes (10/22/1893-8/8/1959), m. (2nd)
    6/9/1927, Klara Elizabeth Schmitt
  Child by second wife:
241934731 Clara Elizabeth Eppes (b.5/20/1928), m. 8/21/1948
    James Patrick Evans
2419347311 Lynn Carol Evans (b. 12/12/1952)
2419347312 James Randolph Evans (b. 2/13/9155)
2419347313 David Arthur Evans (b. 7/12/1957)
2419347314 Nancy Elizabeth Evans (b. 7/12/1959)
24193474 Irene Ada Eppes (b. 10/23/1895), m. 7/10/1939, Thomas
    Maloney Hallam
24193475 Catherine Eppes, m. (1st) 5/20/1925, Joseph Forrester
    Buckner. M. (2nd) 1952 William E. Ratcliffe
  Children by first husband:
241934751 Emily Bancroft Buckner (b. 4/16/1926), m. 5/ /1948
    Arthur Cody, Jr.
2419347511 Craig Stephen Cody (b. 7/29/1949)
2419347512 Donald Alan Cody (b. 8/23/1951)
2419347513 Arthur Gary Cody (b. 12/6/1954)
241934752 Joseph Forrester Buckner, Jr. (4/16/1928-5/30/1941)
24193476 Thomas Jefferson Eppes (2/7/1899-9/29/1961), m. 10/11/
    1919 Camille Hamilton. M. (2nd) Eunice Treadwell
    Burrell
  Child by first wife:
241934761 Gloria Camille Eppes, m. (1st) 7/29/1947 Francis
    Mulherrin. M. (2nd) 9/16/1949 Joseph T. McDavid
  Child by first husband:
2419347611 Linda Anne Mulherrin (b. 4/21/1948)
  Child by second husband:
2419347612 Gloria Elizabeth McDavid (b. 8/15/1953)
24193477 William Eston Eppes III (10/3/1901-1/11/1919)
24193478 Marion Theresa Eppes (b. 10/29/1904), m. 5/16/1928

241934781 William Lee Moss (b. 2/14/1929), m. 12/24/1950
           Elizabeth Ann Reibes
2419347811 Michael Moss (b. 10/6/1951)
2419347812 Theresa Anne Moss (b. 4/25/1954)
2419347813 William Scott Moss (b. 11/5/1959)
2419347814 Judith Marie Moss (b. 1/25/1963)
241934782 Mary Catharene Moss (b. 6/3/1931), m. 2/26/1949 Thomas
           James Woods
2419347821 James Anthony Woods (b. 12/14/1949)
2419347822 David William Woods (b. 11/19/1954)
2419347823 Richard Lee Woods (b. 12/4/1955)
241934783 John Hill Moss (b. 7/17/1937), m. 6/13/1959 Joy Louise
           Pickler
2419347831 Daniel Lee Moss (b. 9/1/1960?)
2419347832 John Eric Moss (b. 1/21/1961?)
24193479 Benjamin Scott Eppes (b. 8/15/1906), m. 6/28/1932
241934791 Frances Crane Eppes (b. 12/21/1933), m. 6/ /1954
           Albert Whitman Brame
241934792 Amalia (sic) Scott Eppes (b. 1/29/1937), m. 8/17/1960
           Howard Griffin Rodges
241934793 Benjamin Scott Eppes, Jr. (b. 4/17/1943)

241934x1 Dr. John Kendall Eppes, m. 7/16/1943 Nell Richardson
          Reiley
241934x11 John Kendall Eppes, Jr. (b. 12/9/1944)

241935 Mary Elizabeth Cleland Eppes (b. 7/3/1833). Unm.
241936 Francis Eppes (3/29/1835-9/10/1835)
24194 Harriet Tucker Randolph (b. 1/10/1803), m. 12/24/1831
24195 Lucy Beverley Randolph (11/14/1805-8/3/1884), m. 2/20/1838
241951 Harriet Parkhill (4/5/1841-d.s.p. 7/8/1926). Deaconess
        in Episcopal Church.
24196 Dr. James Henry Randolph (7/3/1809-5/31/1892), m. (1st)
       9/3/1840, Margaret Esther Hayward (d. 5/12/1851). M.
       (2nd) 1852 Elizabeth Kelly Beard (1823-1917)
241961 Dr. Arthur Lee Randolph (b. 1847), m. 1878
2419611 Vallee Joseph Randolph, m. (2nd) Anna Rice
2419612 Mary Page Randolph (b. 1879)
2419613 Arthur Lee Randolph, Jr.
24196131 Eleanor Page Randolph, m. William Cunningham Smith
241961311 Mary Page Randolph Smith, m. Robert G. Dulin
2419613111 Genevieve Dulin, m. _____ Lundburg
2419613112 Amy Marie Dulin

241962 Thomas Hayward Randolph (b. 6/6/1845), m. 6/6/1872 Julia
        Church Croom (10/5/1850-11/26/1915), dau. of George
        Alexander and Julia Moore Church Croom
2419621 Margaret Hayward Randolph (7/6/1873-9/16/1966), m. 6/12/
         1901, Judge James Bryan Whitfield (11/8/1860-8/20/
         1948), son of Richard Allen Whitfield
24196211 Mary Croom Whitfield (4/10/1902-1/3/1985)
24196212 James Bryan Whitfield, Jr. (5/20/1904-6/28/1982)
24196213 Julia Croom Whitfield (b. 7/11/1905), m. 10/12/1934
          Clarence Arendal Neeley (b. 2/20/1906)

241962131 Margaret Lawton Neeley (b. 7/19/1935), m. 12/23/1954
            Donald Richard Palmer (d. 1971)
2419621311 Kerry Kathleen Palmer (b. 4/18/1956), m. 7/29/1978
            Timothy S. Evavold
2419621312 Zachary Palmer (b. 7/24/1957), m. 11/26/1977 Shirley
            J. Kayne
241962132 Anne Arendal Neeley (b. 7/30/2944), m. 9/10/1946 Joel
            Philip Clark
2419621321 Jon Collins Clark (b. 10/19/1970)
2419621322 Jesse Lawton Clark (b. 9/6/1972)
24196214 Margaret Whitfield, d. inf.
24196215 Randolph Whitfield (b. 2/9/1909), m. 6/25/1931, Shirley
            Brown McPhail (b. 10/1/1910), dau. of Dr. William
            Ashley and Clara Grantham McPhail
241962151 Clare Grantham Whitfield (b. 4/16/1936), m. 4/7/1955
            Russell Brown Schweikart (10/25/1935-12/29/1983).
            Astronaut Appolo 9.
2419621511 Vicki Louise Schweikart (b. 9/12/1959)
2419621512 Randolph Barton Schweikart (b. 9/8/1960)(changed
            Barton to Whitfield). M. Michelle Heng
24196215121 Ashley Marie Schweikart (b. 4/13/1985)
2419621513 Russell Brown Schweikart, Jr. (b. 9/8/1960), m. 7/5/

            1986 Susan Joan Vaude Woude
2419621514 Elin Ashley Schweikart (b. 10/19/1961)
2419621515 Diana Croom Schweikart (b. 7/26/1964)
241962152 Dr. Randolph Whitfield, Jr. (b. 6/3/1938), m. 8/16/
            1963 Suzanne Sellers (b. 4/14/1943)
2419621521 Thomas Eston Randolph Whitfield (b. 2/27/1976)
2419621522 Louise Sellers Whitfield (b. 6/5/1978)
241962153 Mary Croom Whitfield (b. 7/6/1943), m. (1st) 9/12/1966
            Thomas F. McDow IV (b. 2/10/1942), m. (2nd) (Cmrd.)
            Ashury Coward IV
   Children by first husband:
2419621531 Thomas F. McDow (b. 11/17/1970)
2419621532 Randolph Whitfield McDow (b. 3/13/1972)
2419621533 Mary Croom McDow (b. 3/19/1975)

2419623 Annie Porter Randolph (1878-1931 or 1953)
2419624 Dr. James Henry Randolph (1876-1946), m. (1st) Evelyn
            Winthrop (1877-1962)
24196241 James Henry Randolph, Jr. (b. 11/27/1905), m. (1st)
            Mary Chatfield Anthony (7/9/1906-3/27/1959). M. (2nd)
            (as third husband) Kathleen Scott Borland Lowe. M.
            (3rd)(as second husband) Neva Matthews Bennett
   Children by first wife of 24196241:
241962411 Hilda Anthony Randolph (b. 1/8/1933), m. James Anthony
            Robida (2/1/1930-7/6/1977)
2419624111 James Randolph Robida (b. 12/15/1957)
241962412 James Henry Randolph III (b. 7/20/1937), m. Charlene
            Fay Clark (b. 2/18/1903)
2419624121 Robbie Rennie Randolph (b. 8/21/1964)

2419624122 Hilda Dawn Randolph (b. 12/25/1965)
2419624123 James Henry Randolph IV (b. 9/6/1967)
2419624124 Henry Armstrong Randolph (b. 3/4/1969)
24196242 John Winthrop Randolph (1907-1970), m. (1st) Maryine
          McCloren. M. (2nd) Virginia Davis
  Child by first wife:
241962421 Evelyn Malinda (or Melissa) Randolph (b. 9/19/1941),
       m. Charles W. Shueddig
  Children by second wife of 24196241:
24196243 Barbara Hope Randolph (b. 1/30/1927), m. Joseph Bartlet
       Raney
241962431 Diane Elizabeth Raney (b. 1/20/1949), m. 1970 Scott
       Dudley
241962432 Joseph Bartlett Raney, Jr. (b. 3/2/1951), m. Denver
       McLaren
241962433 Mary Annette Raney
241962434 James Randolph Raney (b. 8/25/1963)
24196244 Patricia Louise Randolph (b. 4/1/1928), m. 1952 Ralph
       S. Kaplan
241962441 David S. Kaplan (b. 5/28/1952), m. Dianne Powell
241962442 Ruth Barbara Kaplan (b. 12/17/1954 or 1955)
2419625 Hayward Randolph (1879-1939), m. 7/4/1904 Luella Clark
24196251 Elizabeth Clark Randolph (b. 5/6/1906), m. 1929 Dr.
       George Calloway
241962511 Nancy Randolph Calloway (b. 3/30/1931), m. 1954
       William Wayman
2419625111 Jeff Calloway Wayman (b. 1/ /1955)
2419625112 Wendy Calloway Wayman (b. 3/ /1958)
241962512 Judy Randolph Calloway (b. 7/6/1933), m. 8/11/1956
       Daniel McCook
2419625121 Peter Calloway McCook (b. 9/23/1957)
2419625122 Charles Calloway McCook (b. 12/19/1959)
24196252 John Hayward Randolph (6/21/1908-3/17/1972), m. 1939
       Ruth Moore
241962521 David Hayward Randolph (b. 1/8/1947), m. 7/1/1966
       Leona J. Fair
2419625211 Jeffrey Wade Randolph (b. 3/30/1970)
     Adopted child of 24196252:
     Deborah Ruth Randolph (b. 1/11/1949), m. 11/7/1969
     Kirby Jackson Brumby

  Children by second wife (of 24196):
24196 Maria Beard Randolph (1855-1949) m. 1892 Rev. John
       Chipman (1858-1931), son of William Colfax and Harriet
       Grosvenor Sumner Chipman
2419661 Randolph Chipman (1893-1895)
2419662 John Chipman, Jr. (4/25/1897-5/14/1983), m. 1923 Ruth
       Harriet Hayes
24196621 David Randolph Chipman (b. 1/23/1928), m. 6/7/1951
       Marsha Doolittle (b. 10/9/1928)
241966211 David Hillary Chipman (b. 7/9/1953), m. 5/27/1977 Jill
       Turner

241966212 Eric Hayes Chipman (b. 8/13/1958)
2419662?2 Ruth Elizabeth Chipman (b. 9/25/1931), m. 7/24/1953
        Charles David Busch (b. 12/28/1929)
241966221 Katherine Ann Busch (b. 3/21/1955)
241966222 John Victor Busch (b. 11/10/1956)
241966223 Brian David Busch (b. 6/16/1968)
241967 Elizabeth James Randolph (1857-1940), m. John Miller Cook
2419671 John Miller Cook, Jr. (1890-ca. 1935), m. Louise
        Williford
241968 Lucy Beverley Randolph, m. Theodore DuBose Bratton (1862-
        1944), son of Col. William Bratton
2419681 Rev. William DuBose Bratton (d. 1938), m. Ivy Wardlow
        Gass (1885-1969), dau. of Rev. John M. and Ivy Perrin
        Gass
24196811 Theodore DuBose Bratton (7/ /1916-7/25/1973), m. Mary
        Simpson Williams
241968111 Mary Anderson Bratton (b. 1962)
24196812 Lucy Randolph Bratton, m. John Waldrup Brown
241968121 Frances Waldrup Brown (b. 1941), m. Frank Adam
        Cianciola
2419681211 Lucy Randolph Cianciola (b. 1969)
241968122 Lucy Bratton Brown (b. 1943), m. George William Burton
2419681221 Alan Waldrup Burton (b. 1970)
241968123 John Waldrup Brown, Jr. (b. 1947), m. Dorothy Harris
        Gassaway
241968124 Kathryn Gass Brown (b. 1952)
241968125 Lincoln Palmer Brown (b. 1954)

24196813 Col. William DuBose Bratton, m. Eileen Skidmore
24196814 John Gass Bratton (b. 1/4/1929)

2419683 John Randolph Bratton (b. 9/3 or 25/1892), m. 12/3/1919
        Annie Lewis Drake (b. 5/29/1894)
24196831 Anne Lewis Bratton (b. 10/24/1920), m. 6/27/1942 Col.
        Hubert Eldridge Allen (b. 6/12/1917)
241968311 Anne Bratton Allen (b. 2/8/1945), m. 10/23/1971
        Vincent Robert Russo, M.D.
2419683111 Elizabeth Angela Russo (b. 12/4/1974)
241968312 Elizabeth Eldridge Allen (b. 6/18/1948), m. (1st)
        8/16/1969 Henry Warlick. Div. M. (2nd) 6/22/1974
        William Earl Brinkley, Jr. (b. 8/12/1942)
2419683121 John Henry Warlick II (b. 2/23/1971)
24196832 John Randolph Bratton, Jr. (b. 8/6/1922), m. 10/14/
        1944 Michelle Telfair (b. 9/16/1925)
241968321 Michelle Telfair Bratton (b. 7/25/1945), m. 2/5/1967
        Alton Person Parker, Jr. (b. 6/18/1943)
2419683211 Alton Person Parker III (b. 8/19/1967)
2419683212 John Bratton Parker (b. 2/11/1969)
241968322 John Randolph Bratton III (b. 1/6/1947)
241968323 Mary Constance Bratton (b. 7/5/1950), m. 4/22/1972
        Joseph Clayton Wine, Jr. (b. 3/2/1951)
2419683231 Joseph Clayton Wine III (b. 4/12/1975)

241968324 Lucy Beverley Bratton (b. 3/15/1954)
241968325 Theodore DuBose Bratton (b. 6/27/1955), m. 11/1/1980
           Margaret Foerster
241968326 Jane Telfair Bratton (b. 12/14/1957)
241968327 Samuel Telfair Bratton (b. 4/22/1964)
24196833   Lewis Palmer Bratton, D.D.S. (b. 12/2/1926), m. 9/9/
           1952 Audrey Marie Campbell (b. 3/21/1934)
241968331 Charles Campbell Bratton (b. 12/1/1957)
241968332 Audrey Pamela Bratton (b. 6/15/1959)
241968333 Lewis Drake Bratton (b. 2/29/1964)
2419684   Randolph B. Bratton (d. 1937), m. Eula Boulware (1900-
           1974), dau. of Thomas McDuffie and Isabel Stevenson
           Boulware
24196841   Randolph Bratton (1921-1946), m. Dorothy Williams
24196842   Lucy Beverley Bratton (12/15/1925-4/30/1975), m. Robert
           Crawford Alley
241968421 Fredericka Bratton Alley (b. 9/24/1951), m. 2/ /1981
           William Alexander Martin
241968422 Beverley Boulware Alley (b. 10/1/1952)
24196843   Isabel Bratton (b. 1923), m. 5/17/1945 Earl Wilson
           Kirkwood
241968431 Beverley Randolph Kirkwood (b. 11/12/1947), m. 4/20/
           1968 Julius French Haley II
2419684311 Julius French Haley III (b. 5/12/1970)
241968432 Katherine Harrison Kirkwood (b. 2/22/1949), m. 8/21/
           1970 Jack Richard Roper
241968433 Elizabeth Earle Kirkwood, m. 1979 Paul Bernard Sliger
241968434 Earle Wilson Kirkwood, Jr. (b. 12/17/1955)

2419687   Marion Randolph Bratton (d. 1961), m. Harris Brister
           (d. 1933)
24196871   Harris Brister, Jr. (d. 1965), m. Mary Stone
24196872   Ivy Bratton Brister (d. 1966), m. Gerald Wilford
           Hedgecock
241968721 Gerald Wilford Hedgecock, Jr. (b. 10/21/1949)
241968722 Marion Randolph Hedgecock (b. 6/10/1951), m. 8/ /1973
           Thomas M. Fennell
241968723 Ivy Bratton Hedgecock (b. 9/8/1952), m. George A.
           Frierson
24196873   Theodore Bratton Brister (5/ /1930 or 1931), m. 6/29/
           1958 Delores Wells
241968731 Dabney Anne Brister (b. 6/29/1959)
241968732 Kelley Diane Brister (b. 4/22/1961)
2419688   Mary Means Bratton, m. 12/17/1921 Robert Eldridge
           Connor, son of Dr. Augustus Camillus and Caroline Gayle
           Rivers Connor
24196881   Robert Eldridge Connor, Jr. (b. 8/6/1923)
24196882   Elizabeth Randolph Connor (b. 5/13/1927), m. Currin
           Rather Gass (b. 7/2/1921), son of Henry Markley and
           Marguerite Rather Gass
241968821 Henry Markley Gass (b. 12/3/1952)

241968822   Currin Rather Gass, Jr. (b. 1/10/1954)

241968823   Theodore DuBose Bratton Gass (b. 3/11/1957)

24106883   Theodore Bratton Connor (b. 6/30/1931), m. Jeanene
            Robbins

241968831   Reginald Robbins Connor (b. 7/20/1951), m. Vickie
            Monore

241968832   Caroline Rivers Connor (b. 5/24/1953), m. Michael
            Brady

241968833   Elizabeth DuBose Connor (2/24/1856-11/24/1911)

241968834   Jamie Randolph Connor (b. 9/25/1952)

24196884   Sydney Symington Connor (b. 5/12/1936), m. Phyllis
            Smith

241968841   Deborah Kaye Connor

2419689   Isabella Bratton 9d. 1954), m. Parham Bridges (d. 1969)

24196891   Parham Bridges, Jr. (9/18/1927), m. Loris Cayce

241968911   Theodore Bratton Bridges (b. 1965)

24198   Dr. Arthur Moray Randolph (1815-1867), m. 1/15/1840,
        Laura Harrison DuVal (1819-1907), dau. of Gov. (of
        Florida) William Pope and Nancy Haynes DuVal

241982   Elizabeth Eppes Randolph (b. 9/5/1845 or 1846), m.
         4/5/1866 Benjamin Franklin Whitner (Capt. C.S.A.)(4/5/
         1842-1913)

2419821   Benjamin Franklin Whitner, Jr. (d. 8/16/1868), m. (1st)
          11/22/1890 Carolyn Alexander (d. 2/ /1897). M. (2nd)
          10/7/1903 Annie Willard
  Child by first wife:
24198211   Benjamin Franklin Whitner III (b. 1897), m. 1923
           Dorothy Lynn Rumph (b. 1923)

241982111   Dorothy Ann Whitner (b. 1930), m. Frank H. Backes

2419821111   James W. Backes (b. 9/29/1953)

2419821112   Thomas W. Backes (b. 12/17/1956)

2419821113   Stephen C. Backes (b. 8/3/1958)

2419821114   Benjamin E. Backes (b. 5/9/1961)

241982112   Jane Randolph Whitner (b. 9/16/1931), m. 1953 Rogers
            Tibbets Grange, Jr.

2419821121   Dorothy Katherine Grange (b. 9/26/1954)

2419821122   Rogers Tibbetts Grange III (b. 11/10/1956)

2419821123   Thomas R. Grange (b. 10/2/1959)
  Child by second wife:
24198212   Elizabeth Whitner (b. 1909), m. 1941 Daniel C. Gallant,
           Sr.

241982121   Daniel C. Gallant, Jr. (b. 9/20/1943)

241982122   Franklin W. Gallant (b. 2/9/1945), m. 1970 Shirley
            Webb

2419821221   Nathan Daniel Gallant (b. 6/9/1976)

2419822   Laura Duval Whitner (10/22/1872-1940), m. Sydney
          Octavius Chase, Sr. (1860-1941)

2419822l   Randall Chase II (1898-1971), m. 1943 Julia Gehan

241982211 Laura Duval Chase (b. 4/1/1945)
241982212 Randall Chase III (b. 12/12/1946), m. 1976 Susan Jane
           Kreinke
241982?121 Peter Bradford Chase (b. 9/19/1977)
241982213 Joshua Coffin Chase (b. 11/17/1948), m. 1973 Christine
           Davis
24198222 Sydney Octavius Chase, Jr. (b. 1900), m. 1925 Margaret
           Lane
241982221 Sydney Octavius Chase III (b. 1935), m. 1970 Christel
           Bohne
2419822211 Roland S. Chase (b. 1972)
241982221? Torsten F. Chase (b. 1974)
(24198??2??)(adopted) Sara R. Chase, m. 1977 Dean Byers
2419822221 Ann Lane Byers (b. 1978)
24198223 Franklin W. Chase, Sr. (b. 1908), m. Helen Verney
241982231 Franklin W. Chase, Jr. (b. 1936), m. 1960 Joan Watzek
2419822311 Franklin W. Chase III (b. 1962)
241982231? Pamela H. Chase (b. 1964)
2419822313 Elizabeth R. Chase (b. 1966)
24198224 Lucia R. Chase (b. 1941), m. 1963 Converse Bright, Jr.
241982241 Thomas Chase Bright (b. 1965)
241982242 Elizabeth Chase Bright (b. 1970)
2419823 Eston Randolph Whitner (b. 1/27/1867), m. 1895 Ruth
           Brown
2419824 Sarah Jane Whitner (b. 9/24/1870), m. Joshua Coffin
           Chase, Sr.
24198241 Franklin Whitner Chase (b. 189____)
24198242 Joshua Coffin Chase, Jr. (1894-1877)
2419825 Elizabeth Randolph Whitner (b. 11/6/1875)
2419826 Arthur Randolph Whitner (b. 10/8/1881)
2419827 William Church Whitner (b. 11/17/1886)
241983 Thomas Eston Randolph (11/25/1841-12/8/1862)
241984 William Duval Randolph (b. 6/3/1844), m. Marion Elizabeth
           McKay
2419841 Sarah McKay Randolph (b. 4/10/1870), m. 2/4/1891 W. A.
           Carter
24198411 John Arthur Carter (11/4/1891-1/11/1898)

24198412 Shirley Randolph Carter (9/26/1896-11/29/1897)
24198413 William Alonzo McKay Carter (b. 11/26/1902), m. 11/30/
           1926 Virginia Harrison Hall
241984131 Virginia Randolph Carter (b. 4/22/1930)
241985 Laura Hines Randolph (7/12/1849-10/ /1881), m. (1st)
           1869 William Church. M. (2nd) 1875 Baxter Connell
2419851 Alonzo Church (b. 6/27/1870), m. 6/16/1901 Louise
           Mallory Rareshide
24198511 Whitner Church (5/20/1902-7/19/1923)
24198512 Louise Church (b. 10/16/1903)
24198513 Randolph Church (b. 4/14/1905), m. 2/5/1931 Eunice
           Louise Butler (b. 4/14/1905)
241985131 Randolph Butler Church (b. 11/ /1933)
24198514 Alonzo Lee Church (b. 10/14/1907)
2419852 Arthur Connell (b. 9/5/1875)
2419853 Jane Connell (b. 9/5/1875), m. William Ingersoll

241986   Arthur Moray Randolph, Jr. (b. 9/1/1851), m. (as second
         husband) _____
2419861 Laura Randolph
241987   Cary Randolph (7/1/1853-1935), m. 1886 Perry Clements
         (1867)(?)-1959)
2419871 George Clements
2419872 Frank Clements
2419873 Evelyn Clements
2419874 Lucy Beverley Clements. Twin to Mary Page.
2419875 Mary Page Clements. Twin to Lucy Beverley.
2419876 Elizabeth Clements
2419877 Robert Clements
241988   John Parkhill Randolph (b. 10/15/1855), m.
2419881 Joseph Randolph
2419882 Laura Randolph
241x Dr. John Randolph of "Middle Quarter " (9/11/1779-8/19/
      1834), m. 1804 Judith Lewis, dau. of Col. William lewis
      (b. in Ireland 1724, d. 1811). A colonel of colonial
      forces in Revolution.
241x1 William Mann Randolph and Margaret Smith Randolph lived
       at "Edgehill"

241x11 Jane Margaret Randolph (b. 5/7/1840), m. Edward Clifton
        Anderson

241x112322 Irenee DuPont May, Jr.

241x1142 Margaret Randolph Rotch, m. James Jackson Storrow

241x12 William Lewis Randolph, m. (1st) Agnes Dillon. M. (2nd)
        11/9/1887 Margaret Randolph Taylor from "Lego",
        Albemarle County

241x122 Thomas Jefferson Randolph IV, m. (2nd) Annie Clifton
         Marclay

241x12352 William Mann Randolph III (b. 4/20/1933)

241x123524 Susan Caroline Randolph

241x1237 Hollins Nicholas Randolph II, m. Mary Virginia Blue
          Hoge(9/12/1908-4/14/86). Bur. Monticello.

241x123711 Bonnie Sue Randolph (b. 1/8/1958)

241x5 Virginia Cary Randolph, m. Thomas Allen Omohundro
241x6 Beverley Randolph (d. young)
241x7 Powell Randolph
241x8 John Randolph
241x9 Lavinia Randolph
241a George Washington Randolph (12/19/1781-7/7/1785)
241b Harriet Randolph (11/24/1783-12/1/1839), m. 12/19/1805
      Richard S. Hackley

241b1   Harriet Randolph Hackley (6/26/1810-7/18/1880), m. 4/ /
         1832 Capt. Andrew Talcott (4/22/1797-4/25/1883), son of
         George Talcott and his second wife, Abigail Goodrich.
         Harriet was Andrew's second wife, his first wife,
         Catharine Thompson, d. 10/ /1828 without issue.
241b11   Ann Cary Talcott (5/27/1845-   ), m. 10/3/1865 Gustave
         Von Boleslowski of Vienna, Austria.
241b111 Maximiliana Carlotta Von Boleslowski (7/6/1866-1/18/
         1875).
241b112 Henri Richard Von Boleslowski (6/19/186 -   ).
241b113 Richard Franz Carl Von Boleslowski (1/20/1873-   ).
241b12   Mary Gray Talcott (2/8/1837-   ).
241b13   Frances Lewis Talcott (11/19/1843-   ).
241b14   Richard Hackley Talcott (7/14/1839-   ).
241b15   Thomas Mann Randolph Talcott (d. 5/7/1920), m. Nannie
         Carrington McPhail (d. 8/12/1922).
241b151 Mary Gray Talcott (6/11/1869-6/4/1956).
241b152 Harriet Randolph Talcott (12/28/1870-9/16/1956).
241b153 Eva Carrington Talcott (5/21/1876-2/1/1958).
241b154 Augusta McVickar Talcott (8/28/1877-5/13/1940), m. 4/22/
         1903, Dr. Truman Alfred Parker (d. 9/4/1949).
241b1541 Augusta McVickar Parker (4/20/1905-   ). M. (1st)
         1/7/1924 Ronald Parker King (d. 5/2/1933). M. (2nd)
         12/ /1957 Fried Hiat.
241b15411 Layton Judd King (11/7/1926-   ).
241b15412 Ronald Parker King (10/ /1931-   ).
241b15413 Augusta Talcott King (4/16/1934-   ).
241b1542 Truman Alfred Parker, Jr. (1/13/1907-   ), m. 9/6/
         1933 Maurine Brockett.
241b15421 Maurine Diannes Parker (7/28/1936-   ).
241b15422 Truman Alfred Parker III (7/10/1939-   ).
241b15423 Mary Gray Parker (12/31/1942-   ).
241b15424 Son (12/31/1942-1/1/1943).
241b1543 Thomas Mann Randolph Parker (8/27/1909-8/15/1953). M.
         (1st) 5/3/1942 Priscilla Somma. Div. M. (2nd) 3/23/
         1952 Marjorie Clum Barter.
   Child by first wife:
241b15431 Kristin Somma Parker (12/23/1944-   ).
   Child by second wife:
241b15432 Anne Randolph Parker (4/4/1953-   ).
241b1544 Nancy Carrington Parker (12/29/1911-   ), m. 12/25/
         1941 John Vaughan Hilton (d. 12/24/1957).
241b15441 Gwendolen Ruth Hilton (8/20/1944-   ).
241b15442 Ronald Vaughan Hilton (5/6/1950-   ).
241b155 Jennie McPhail Talcott (10/14/1879-1/20/1959).
241b156 Nannie C. Talcott (12/6/1867-12/24/1873).
241b157 Lilias Blair Talcott (2/18/1874-9/8/1874).
241b158 Thomas Mann Randolph Talcott (4/1/1875-6/ /1875).
241b16   George Russell Talcott (1/21/1841-2/18/1899), m. 11/8/
         1881 Frances Mason Berry, dau. of Nathaniel Edmondston
         and Juliet (?) Berry.

241b161   George Russell Talcott, Jr. (12/19/1882-12/25/1917), m.
       6/19/1915 Liesa Bolling Archer (4/22/1886-1/25/1971)
       (125112).
241b1611   Mary Archer ("Molly") Talcott (8/11/1916-   ), m. 10/
       26/1940 Edward Griffith Dodson, Jr. (2/11/1914-   ),
       son of Col. Edward Griffith Dodson and his wife, the
       former Harriotte Jones Winchester.
241b16111   Elizabeth Archer Dodson (4/7/1942-   ), m. 6/2/1973
       James D. Heinzen.
241b161111   Stearns Nicholas Heinzen (3/6/1974-   ).
241b161112   Molly Talcott Heinzen (5/11/1976-   ).
241b161113   Harriotte Winchester Heinzen (10/2/1982-   ).
241b16112   Harriotte Winchester Dodson (7/19/1943-   ), m. 1/
       25/1969 Eugene Russell McDannald, M.D.
241b161121   Mary Archer McDannald (3/1/1973-   ).
241b161122   George Hunt McDannald (7/31/1975-   ).
241b16113   Edward Griffith Dodson III (3/3/1950-   ).
241b162   Nathan Edmonston Berry Talcott (9/22/1884-12/23/1918),
       m. 2/19/1916 Maria Curtis Cocke (2/24/1882-4/4/1962),
       dau. of Thomas Lewis Preston Cocke and his second wife,
       the former Mary Booth Curtis.
241b1621   Nathan Edmonston Berry Talcott, Jr. (12/6/1916-   ), m.
       8/25/1956 Ann Sims Hamill, dau. of Francis Lincoln
       Hamill.
241b16211   Andrew Richard Talcott (10/17/1958-   ).
241b16212   Hugh Preston Talcott (11/27/1959-   ).
241b1622   George Russell Talcott (2/15/1918-   ), m. 2/16/1946
       Eleanor Watkins Moon (3/8/1920-   ), dau. of John
       Martin Moon and his wife, the former Mary Elizabeth
       Heath.
241b16221   Mary Martin Talcott (2/19/1950-   ), m. 6/3/1972 David
       Paul Hendrix (11/16/1949-   ), son of Paul Corneliason
       Hendrix and his wife, the former Mamie Catherine
       Kimble.
241b162211   Sarah Elizabeth Hendrix (10/15/1976-   ).
241b162212   Paul Randolph Hendrix (5/3/1979-   ).
241b16222   George Russell Talcott, Jr. (9/24/1953-   ), m. 5/20/
       1978 Barbara Jean Goodwin (9/14/1956-   ), dau. of
       William P. Goodwin.
241b162221   George Russell Talcott III (9/3/1980-   ).
241b162222   William James Talcott (10/3/1984-   ).
241b163   Juliet Dushane Talcott (11/15/1885-10/19/1918).
241b164   Frances Cary Talcott (11/1/1887-   ), m. 12/29/1917
       Elbert Ghenard Wood, M.D.

241b1641   Frances Cary Wood (10/16/1918-7/13/1939).
241b1642   Elbert Ghenard Wood, Jr. (12/25/1921-5/23/1944?).
241b1643   Edith Randolph Wood (12/29/1922-   ), m. Frances Henry
       Bongardt, Jr., M.D.
241b16431   Deborah Bongardt (10/26/1956-   ).
241b16432   Francis Henry Bongardt III (1/5/1958-   ).
241b1644   Ann Cary Wood (4/3/1926-5/24/1926).
241b165   Sarah Randolph Talcott (3/14/1891-   ),m. 11/17/1917
       Marion Nimmo Fisher.

241b1651   Juliet Talcott Fisher (4/9/1919-   ), m. 6/7/1941
           Winfield Firman.
241b16511 Frances Ann Firman (1/12/1943-   ).
241b16512 Thomas Randolph Firman (6/29/1945-   ).
241b16513 Dorothy Firman (10/8/1949-   ).
241b1652   Andrew Fisher (12/17/1920-   ), m. 10/10/1942 Cornelia
           Johnson.
241b16521 Peter Randolph Fisher (5/19/1944-   ).
241b16522 Carolyn Fisher (9/23/1947-   ).
241b16523 Andrew Randolph Fisher (7/14/1949-   ).
241b1653   Frances Randolph Fisher (12/28/1924-   ), m. 8/17/1947
           Clarke T. Merwin.
241b16531 Andrew Scott Merwin (10/2/1948-   ).
241b16532 Douglas Clarke Merwin (11/17/1949-   ).
241b16533 Michael Gains Merwin (11/11/1951-   ).
241b16534 Russell Talcott Merwin (7/22/1956-   ).
241b16535 Sinda Randolph Merwin (9/22/1958-   ).
241b17   Lucia Beverly Talcott (2/8/1833-11/27/1856).
241b18   Charles Gratiot Talcott (2/28/1834-9/15/1867), m. 10/18/
           1858 Theodosia L. Barnard.
241b181   Charles Gratiot Talcott, Jr. (9/14/1859-   ).
241b182   Harry Randolph Talcott (11/9/1861-   ).
241b183   Robert Barnard Talcott (12/3/1863-   ).
241b184   Lucia Beverly Talcott (12/3/1865-   ), m. Herman
           Hollerith.
241b1841   Lucia B. Hollerith.
241b1842   Nan Hollerith.
241b1843   Virginia Hollerith.
241b1844   Charles Hollerith.
241b1845   Richard Hollerith.
241b1846   Herman Hollerith, Jr.
241b185   Edmund Myers Talcott (11/17/1866-   ), m.
241b19   Harriet Randolph Talcott (11/9/1835-11/1/1858), m. Rev.
           William S. Southgate.
241b191   Randolph Southgate (8/8/1860-   ).
241b192   William Scott Southgate (1/2/1862-   ).
241b193   Mary King Southgate (1/2/1862-5/ 1863).
241b194   Grace Helen Southgate (6/19/1863-   ).
241b195   Frances Southgate (2/14/1865-   ).
241b196   Harry Randolph Southgate (6/9/1868-2/2/1869).
241b197   Eleanor Southgate (6/18/1869-   ).
241b198   Anita Mary Southgate (6/18/1871-   ).
241b199   George Talcott Southgate (7/25/1873-   ).
241b1x   Edward Talcott (9/4/1849-1849).
241b1a   Henry Cary Talcott (10/24/1851-1851).

241b3   Lucia Beverley Hackley, m. Dr. Lewis Byrd Willis (9/ /
        1801-10/3/1835). Maud Potter in THE WILLISES OF VIRGINIA
        states that he was a physician who settled in Florida
        after graduating from medical school. His father, Col.
        Byrd Charles Willis, was, in 1832, appointed Navy Agent
        for the Port of Pennsacola.
        Dr. Lewis Byrd Willis m. (3rd) Hester Savage of the
        Eastern Shore of Maryland. He was drowned (in Florida)
        while attempting to cross a big lagoon on horseback.
        See, also, 24194.

241b31 Lewis Byrd Willis, Jr., m. (2nd) Lucy Barkley

241b44 Harriet Randolph Cutts (1856-1856)

241c Virginia Randolph (d. 5/2/1852), m. 8/28/1805 William (or
      Wilson) Jefferson Cary. Lived at "Carysbrook".
241c1 Wilson Miles Cary, m. Jane Margaret Carr (1809-1903), dau.
      of Peter and hester Smith Stevenson Carr

241c1133 Juliana Howard McHenry
241c11331 Robert Lee Randolph III

241c11424 Gaylord Lee Clark, Jr.

241c11511 George Martin Gillet, Jr.

241c1152 Charles Morton Stewart, Jr.
241c11521 Charles Morton Stewart III

241c13 Mehitabel (?) Cary

241c15 Wilson Miles Cary, Jr.

241c161 Mehitabel (?) Cary, m. Fairfax Harrison (241c521)

241c3422 Donald S. MacRae, Jr.
241c34221 Donald S. MacRae III

241c383 Randolph Moncure (b. and d. 1886)

241c521 Fairfax Harrison, m. Mehitabel (?) Cary

242 Jane Cary (d. 1774), m. 1768 Thomas Isham Randolph.

24215461 Mary Cary Harrison (d. 11/2/1987)(born at Fire Creek,
          WV) and Mary Cary Harrison Mitchell. Also 24216432.

24216433 Virginia Gwynne Harrison, m. Sherman Brownell Joost,
          Jr.
242164331 Peter Harrison Joost (7/26/1942-   )
242164332 Derek Brownell Joost (7/10/1946-   ), m. Marie
          Walz
2421643321 Lauren Walz Joost (4/7/1979-   )
2421643322 Katharine Gwynne Joost (10/19/1982-   )
242164333 Gordon Murray Joost (2/3/1949-   ), m. Debbie Slavitt
2421643331 Henry Harrison Joost (/ /1982-   )

242171 Elizabeth Burwell Randolph, m. Warren Collier Smith

2421712 Warren Collier Smith, Jr.

2421715 Elizabeth Randolph Smith

2421721 Dr. Archiabld Cary Randolph III, m. (2nd)(as second
         husband) Rebecca Anne Dulany McElhone

24217212 Lt. Richard Hunter Dulany Randolph, m. Sara Sears.
          Had issue.

2421722 Robert Renshaw Randolph (12/5/1882-8/2/1883)

242174 Col. William Wellford Randolph was killed at the Battle
        of the Wilderness

24217712 Robert Carter ("Bobs") Randolph IV (d. 3/16/1959)(b. at
          "Powhatan", d. at "The Woodlands", Brunswick County).
          His widow, originally from Charlottesville, m. (2nd)
          A. Russell Meredith, Jr., of Broadnax, VA.
242177121 Robert Carter Randolph V. Jackson-Hope Medalist at
           V.M.I., a Rhodes Scholar, and a lawyer in Seattle.
242177122 Douglas Randolph.
242177123 Susan Gordon Dabney Randolph.
242177124 Bolling Harrison Randolph.
242177125 Thomas Nelson Carter Randolph.

24217822? Angus MacDonald Crawford Randolph, m.

2421782221 Robert Carter Randolph (4/17/1981-   ).

24217x Mary Cary Randolph

242331 Edward West.
242332 Thomas Ira West, Jr.
242333 Elizabeth West.
242334 Fannie West.
242335 Julia Page West (1830-   ), m. 2/7/1860 William Henry
        Pleasants (1818-1888). Children listed in 1880 Census
        of Henrico County, Lorton's Chart.
2423351 William Heth Pleasants (ca. 1862-1919).
2423352 Ella Leigh Pleasants ((1865-   ).
2423353 Mary Page Pleasants (1867-   ).
2423354 Howard Peterkin Pleasants (1868 or 1870-1901), m. 6/22/
         1892, Eleanor Hirshfield (-   ) of Ft. Worth, TX.
24233541 Julia (Mary?) Page Pleasants (8/9/1893-1985), m. 6/12/
          1917, Charles Grattan Price (1883-1981) of Harrison-
          burg.
242335411 Charles Grattan Price, Jr. (5/31/1919-   ), m.
           Kathleen V. Nutter.

2423354111 Julia Kathleen Price (1943-   ).
2423354112 Melinda Marshall Price (1944-   ), m.   /   /1963,
            Stuart Preston Childress.
24233541121 Melanie Marshall Childress (1964-   ).
2423354113 Charles Grattan Price III (1949-   ).

242335412 Page Pleasants Price (2/15/1924-   ). Home: Harrison-
            burg.
2423354121 Edmund Pleasants Price (1948-   ).
2423354122 William Marshall Price.
2423354123 Eleanor Page Price.
2423355 Charles Madison Pleasants (7/ 1871-7/21/1929), m. Mary
            Mayo (7/ /1875-   ), dau. of George and Lizzie Mayo.

242351 Mann Page (d. 1904), m. ca. 1860 Catherine Crane (1840-
).

2423831 Beverley Heth Page Randolph, Jr.

24238323 Henry Armistead Boyd, Jr.

242413513 Archibald Harrison

242417361 James Grover McCann, Jr. (d. 1980)

242417391 Leigh Randolph Harrison, m. Ede Capella
2424173911 Aleta Capella (b. 1966)
242417392 Benjamin Willis Harrison, m. Beverley Belton
2424173921 Michael Harrison (b. 1956)
242417392 Anne Carter Harrison
2424173923 Benjamin Leigh Harrison

242453 Julien Harrison (d. 7/17/1877)(b. Richmond). His second
            wife, Elizabeth ("Lilly") Johnston (d. 7/ 1917)(d. at
            Short Hills, NJ). Harrison served as a Major at the
            First Battle of Manassas, and later became Colonel of
            the 6th Virginia Cavalry. Severely wounded in 1863.
            Lived at "Elk Hill", Goochland County, and in Norfolk.

2424532 William Maury Hill (d. Richmond).
24245321 Mary Maury ("Mamie") Hill (b. Richmond), m. William S.
            P. Mayo, Jr., son of William S. P. Mayo and his wife,
            the former Katherine Cole Friend.
24245322 Julien Harrison Hill (9/15/1877-   )(b. Richmond), m.
            4/22/1903 Lucy Kearny, dau. of Gen. John Watts Kearny.
242453221 Lucy Kearny Hill (4/4/1904-   )(b. Richmond).
242453222 Frances Cadwallader Hill (12/6/1905-   )(b. Richmond).
242453223 Mary Kearny Hill (5/30/1907-   )(b. Waynesboro).
242453224 Mildred Irving Hill (11/29/1908-   ).
242453225 Anne Maury Hill (12/18/1914-   ).
242453226 Julien Harrison Hill, Jr. (6/5/1916-   ).

242453227 Diana Kearny Hill (1/19/1918-   )(b. Richmond).
24245323 Lily H. Hill, m. Wilson Lawrence Smith.
24245324 William Maury Hill, Jr. (1881-   ) d.s.p.
24245325 Mildred Hill, m. Shelton Strickler Fife. Had issue.

2424538 Hebe Harrison (d. 5/ /1838)(b. at "Elk Hill", d. Coral
         Gables, FL). M. (1st) Charlottesville, Upton Wilson
         Muir (d. 7/ /1904)(b. Bardstown, KY, d. Cape May, NJ),
         son of Peter Brown Muir and his wife, the former Soph-
         ronia Rizer. He was a Judge in Louisville.
         M. (2nd) Atlantic City 7/ /1907 Louis Emory McComas
         (10/28/1846-11/10/1907)(b. near Williamsport, MD, d.
         Washington, DC). He had two daughters by his first
         wife, the former Leah Humrichouse. M. (3rd) Cary
         Talcott Hutchinson (3/4/1866-1/18/1939)(b. St. Louis,
         d. Coral Gables).
24245381 Elizabeth Harrison Muir (2/14/1893-   )(Louisville).
         M. (1st) Harrisonburg, VA 11/23/1915 William Potter
         Waters (12/ /1893-   )(b. St. Louis, d. Richmond),
         son of William Darrah Waters and his wife, the former

         Ella Potter. M. (2nd) Coral Gables 12/13/1933 Charles
         Benjamin Lee, Jr. (8/7/1900-   )(b. Charleston, WV),
         son of Charles Benjamin Lee and his wife, the former
         Dora Workman.
242453811 Hebe Harrison Waters (b. at "Tallwood", Albemarle
         County). M. (1st) Washington, DC, 12/28/1940 Vance
         Jackson Alexander, Jr. (8/12/1916-   )(b. Nashville),
         son of Vance Jackson Alexander and his wife, the
         former Hazel Brock. Div. M. (2nd) 7/2/1948 James
         McClellan Peters (7/30/1913-   ). M. (3rd) Milton S.
         Ritzenberg of Washington, DC, and "North Hill",
         Clarke County. Div.
242453812 Elizabeth Darrah Waters (b. Charlottesville). M. (1st)
         Frederick, MD, 7/4/1936 Caskie Norvel (1919-   ), son
         of Caskie Norvel and his wife, the former Anne
         Provic. M. (2nd) 8/23/1940 David Madison Alger, son
         of James Alger and his wife, the former Margery Hill.
24245382 Peter Upton Muir (b. Louisville), m. Wilmington, DE,
         6/21/1941 Frances Corson Bates (5/8/1909-   )(b. Wil-
         mington, DE), dau. of Daniel Moore Bates and his wife,
         the former Bertha Corson Day.
2424539 Elizabeth Montgomery Harrison (b. at "Elk Hill", d.
         Charlottesville), m. Charlottesville 3/14/1898 her
         cousin, John Watts Kearny (7/25/1845-7/27/1933)(b.
         Paducah, KY, d. Cape May), son of Philip Kearny and his
         wife, the former Diana Moore Bullitt. In 1910, he
         built, in Charlottesville, his home called "Lewis
         Mountain". He had six children by his first wife, the
         former Lucy McNary.

24245391 Elizabeth Anderson Kearny (12/16/1899-   )(b. Washing-
          ton, DC), m. Charlottesville 5/5/1928 Ford Hibbard,
          son of Omri Ford Hibbard and his wife, the former
          Helen Dole Edwards.
242453911 John Watts Kearny Hibbard (3/12/1937-   )(b. New York
          City).
242453x   Peyton Randolph Harrison (b. "Elk Hill", d. Louisville).
          M. Louisville 6/ /1903 Louise Thomas Wheat (2/2/1880-
          4/15/1933), dau. of Milton Wheat and his wife, the for-
          mer Annie Thomas.
242453x1 Julien Harrison (1/30/1905-   )(b. Greenville, MS)
          (twin), m. Margaret Hanger, dau. of Harry Hanger and
          his wife, the former Martha Shelby.
242453x11 Martha Shelby Harrison.
242453x12 Peyton Randolph Harrison.
242453x2 Ann Thomas Harrison (1/30/1905-   )(b. Greenville, MS)
          (twin), m. Louisville 4/26/1930 Edward Moody Scay (1/
          16/1900-2/25/1953)(b. Canmer, KY), d. New York City),
          son of Robert Watson Scay and his wife, the former
          Elizabeth Jennings Cowherd.
242453b   Bernard Johnston Harrison (d. 12/29/1941)(b. at "Elk
          Hill", d. Tucson). M. 6/19/1901 Jane Dashiell Randolph
          (b. Fort D.A. Russell, Cheyenne).
242453b1 John Randolph Harrison (b. New York City), m. Villa
          Nova, PA, Emily Barclay McFadden (7/8/1909-   )(b.
          Newport, RI), dau. of George McFadden and his wife,
          the former Josephine McIlvaine. Ca. 1953, Harrison
          was ranching in Chihuahua, Mexico.
242453b11 Josephine Clement Harrison (b. New York City), m.
          New York City 6/9/1950 Maxwell Evarts, son of
          Jeremiah Evarts.
242453b14 Robert Carter Harrison (4/30/1938-   )(b. Houston).
242453b2 Bernard Johnston Harrison, Jr. (2/16/1907-   )(b. New
          York City), m. Roslyn, Long Island, Martha Barclay
          Kountze (11/28/1907-   )(b. New York City), dau. of
          DeLancey Kountze and his wife, the former Martha
          Johnston.
242453b21 Carter Henry Harrison (3/4/1935-   )(b. Washington,
          DC).

2424722   Lucia Cary Harrison (1856-1898), dau. of Benjamin and
          Molly Randolph (Page) Harrison of "The Fork", m. 1878
          Edmund Randolph Cocke(1841-1922). Edmund's first wife
          was Phoebe Alexander Preston.
24247221 Mary Randolph Page Cocke (1879-1879).
24247222 Lucia Cocke (1880-1880).
24247223 Elizabeth Randolph Cocke (1882-   ). Unm.
24247224 Edmund Randolph Cocke (1883-1966), m. 1919 Margaret
          Richie Harrison, dau. of Dr. George Byrd Harrison
          and his wife, the former Jane Marshall Stone.
24247225 Benjamin Harrison Cocke (1886-1887).
24247226 William Armistead Cocke (1888-1928). Unm.

24247227 Edmonia Preston Cocke (1890-   ). Unm.

24247220 Catherine Harrison McKim Cocke (9/16/1892-12/11/1985),
     m. 1918 William Cazenove Gardner (5/20/1875-0/1/1904),
     of Maryland. They lived at "Clover Lick".

242472281 William Cazenove Gardner, Jr. (5/6/1920-8/5/1986), m.
     1944 Pauline Swanson Buzzard (9/3/1926-   ).

2424722811 Carol Ann Gardner (3/31/1945-   ), m. Howard Newton
     Mullenax (11/27/1942-   )

24247228111 Jon Claude Mullenax (12/31/1963-   ), m. Regina
     Ann Kerr (7/26/1971-   )

242472281111 Shawnna Ann Mullenax (12/2/1989-   )

24247228112 Amber Lee Mullenax (4/22/1965-   ), m. Danny
     Oliver Rexrode (10/8/1952-   )

242472281121 Trista Lee Rexrode (9/23/1984-   )

242472281122 Dustin Jack Rexrode (10/5/1989-   )

2424722812 Rodney William Gardner (4/4/1948-   ), m. Linda
     Sue Singleton Nichols (8/28/1944-   )

24247228121 Justin Page Gardner (5/6/1983-   )

2424722813 Randolph Lee Gardner (12/3/1949-   ), m. Margaret
     Alice Geiger (10/4/1949-   )

24247228131 David Vaughn Gardner (6/10/1983-   )

2424722814 Frederick Page Gardner (1/21/1952-   ), m. Cathy
     Lynn Polk (10/30/1954-   )

24247228141 Leata Marie Gardner (7/11/1978-   )

24247228142 Phillip Daniel Gardner (8/23/1979-   )

242472282 Catherine Cocke Gardner (6/10/1921-6/10/1921)

242472283 Twin sister to Catherine Cocke Gardner (6/10/1921-6/
     10/1921)

242472284 Edmund Cocke Gardner (7/31/1922-   ), m. 1955 Jo Ann
     Beverage (3/1/1936-   )

2424722841 Catherine Elaine Gardner (5/15/1956-   ), m. Donald
     Nathan Ollis (1/7/1956-   )

24247228411 Matthew Garrett Ollis (9/14/1985-   )

24247228412 Sarah Brianne Ollis (7/4/1989-   )

242472285 Harrison McKim Gardner (7/1/1925-   ), m. 1950
     Gertrude Virginia Moss (5/23/1926-   )

2424722851 Elizabeth Ann Gardner (7/28/1957-   ), m. Benny E.
     Nini (2/26/1952-   )

24247228511 Jessica Elizabeth Nini (8/12/1981-   )

24247228512 Michael Benjamin Nini (5/26/1983-   )

24247228513 Nicholas Gardner Nini (5/9/1990-   )

2424722852 Mary Catherine Gardner (11/19/1960-   ), m. Marvin
     Ferguson (9/17/1959-   )

242472286 Harriet Rowland Gardner (8/20/1930-   ), m. 1948
     Aubrey Clayton Meadows, Jr. (6/5/1928-   )

2424722861 Mary McKim Meadows (6/21/1949-   ), m. Gary Niki
     Corley (11/5/1949-   )

24247228611 Robert Myles Corley (7/12/1976-   )

24247228612 Rebecca Michelle Corley (4/4/1979-   )

2424722862 Ann Gardner Meadows (11/30/1950-   ), m. Richard
     L. Church (5/30/1951-   )

24247228621 Christine McKim Church (11/22/1974-   )

24247228622 Richard David Church (8/1/1978-   )
2424722863 Aubrey Clayton Meadows III (4/15/1952-   )
2424722864 David Scott Meadows (9/16/1964-   )
242472287 Lucia Cary Gardner (4/19/1934-   ), m. 1956 Robert
          Carroll Phillips (5/28/1934-   )
2424722871 Catherine Mary Phillips (5/10/1961-   ), m. Robert
          Alden Rubin (7/18/1958-   )
2424722872 Elisabeth Sue Phillips (6/2/1964-   ), m. Jonathan
          Scott Taylor (3/10/1963-   )
24247228721 Carol Elisabeth Taylor (9/16/1990-   )
24247229 Nelson Page Cocke (1894-10/25/1990), m. 1942 Blanche
          Gertrude Jackson (1898-1978). Lived in Richmond.

2424722x Belle Harrison Cocke (1898-1898).

243 Elizabeth Cary (b. 1760), m. 7/12/1787 Robert Kincaid "Late
     of Buckingham County".

2431 Mary Kincaid, m. Charles Irving (dead by 1852) of Bucking-
      ham County.

24311 Charles Irving, Jr.

24312 Henry Page Irving, m. 10/5/1836 Williana Mortimer Harrison
       (5/8/1813-2/7/1847)(b. at "Clifton", d. Richmond), dau.
       of Randolph Harrison (1768-1839) of "Clifton" and his
       wife, the former Mary Randolph (1773-1835) of
       "Dungeness".

243121 James H. Irving
243122 Henry Page Irving, Jr.
243123 Joseph Kincaid Irving (d. 1864)
24313 Joseph Kincaid Irving

Grady Lee Randolph

Included in this volume is material taken from Grady Lee
Randolph's book "THE RANDOLPHS OF VIRGINIA" (AFTER THE AMERICAN
REVOLUTION)(1990).

Some of the material includes names or parts of names. Some
make corrections. And some seems to be in error.

For example, Mr. Randolph seems to be in error in his
listing of Amelia Randolph (number 811) and of her husband
William Bolling (4/5/1731-1776). See POCAHONTAS' DESCENDANTS
page 332.

Secondly, Mr. Randolph seems to be in error in his listing
of Jediah Randolph (number 5134) as the son of Thomas Mann
Randolph. Jediah's name does not appear in the several Randolph
family trees and genealogies and because of this, he and his
descendants are not included in POCAHONTAS' DESCENDANTS or in
this volume.

24314   Robert Kincaid Irving (d. 1894), m. Delia Eldridge (5614).
        For their child, etc., see under her number. In 20 W(1)
        207, the spelling is Kinkead.
243141 Joseph Kincaid Irving. See 56361.

24315   Carter Irving.
24316   Mary Irving, m. Anthony Thornton of New York.

243161 H. C. Thornton

24317   Mildred F. Irving, m. Samuel J. Booker "late of Buckingham
        County".
24318   Isabella Irving. Unm. in 1852.

244134 Virginia Page Hobson, m. 1863 Richard Archer of Powhatan
        County.
2441341
2441342
2441343

24425112 James Keith (4/25/1923-   )
24425113 Thomas Randolph Keith (12/22/1930-   )
24425114 Glamis Keith

244661x1   Jean Lewis, m. Thomas Russell Price
244661x11 Page Price, m. Parnell Lewis
244661x12 Ruth Price, m. _____ Casey
244661x13 Russell Price, m. Casey Whitehead
244661x2   Meriwether Lewis, m. (1st) Matthew Carter Stovall, m.
           (2nd)(as second wife) John Thomas Fargason, Jr.
           (b. 2/4/1925), son of John Thomas and Nell Cooke
           Fargason
244661x21 Meriwether Lewis Stovall (9/26/1950-   ), m. 8/4/
           1983 Charles McGettigan
244661x22 Matthew Carter Stovall II (1951-1957)
244661x23 Randolph Lee Fargason (11/13/1960-   )

245   Henry Cary (d. young).
246   Sarah Cary (2/23/1753-4/7/1773), m. 9/13/1770 Archibald
      Bolling.
247   Dau. (d. young).
248   Dau. (d. young).

251621 Charles Hansford Sheild II (b. 11/4/1867). Omit: (1796-
        1868). Lawyer of Louisville.
251622 George Norton Sheild (b. 7/22/1870)

251632363 Janet April Sheely, m. Vastuia Tavui (Vastuia Melepai)

27 Ryland Randolph (1738-12/ /1784).

331   Lucy Champe Fleming (1776-1840) of Goochland County, m. John
      Markham (1/20/1770-1821). The Markhams moved to
      Versailles, KY
3311 Bernard Markham (b. 1795)
3312 William Fleming Markham (1800-1860), m. at Versailles (7/9/
      1825 Sussana Railey (1801-1872)(d. Waco, Texas), dau. of
      Thomas and Martha Woodson Railey of Versailles. The
      Markhams lived at Vicksburg.
33121 Rev. Thomas Railey Markham (1828-1894), m. at Vicksburg
      11/30/1858 Mary Searles (d. 1863). Resided: New Orleans
331211 Charles Searles Markham (1859-1861)
331212 William Railey Markham (1861-1863)
331213 Henry Smith Markham (1863-1863)
331214 Robert Price Markham (1863-1863)
33122   William Fleming Markham, Jr. (died during Civil War).
        Omit of Huntersville, Texas. The Willima F. Martin of
        Huntersville was from a different branch of the Markham
        family.

33123 Martha Woodson Markham (1832-1910), m. at Vicksburg
       12/23/1858 Fabius M. Sleeper (1830-1881). son of Gideon
       and Margaret McDowell Sleeper. Sleepers resided at
       Waco.
331231 William Markham Sleeper (1859-1944), m. 4/26/1892 at
       Waco, TX, Laura Ben Risher (1867-1956). Resided:
       Liberty, MS; Waco, TX
3312311 Benjamin Risher Sleeper (1894-1972), m. 8/1/1923 at
        New York City, Frances Boyd (1898-1983). Resided:
        Waco, TX
33123111 Elisabeth Day Sleeper (1924-1939). Waco, TX
33123112 Martha Margaret "Patty" Sleeper (b. 1926), m. Robert
          Charles Jeep. Waco, TX
331231121 Elisabeth Day Jeep (b. 1948). Tekameh, NE
331231122 Victoria Jeep (1951-1951). Tekameh, NE
331231123 Robert Charles Jeep (1954-1973). D. Waco, TX

331231124 Robin Jeep (b. 1954). Tekameh, NE
3312312 Martha Margaret Sleeper (b. 1896) at Waco, TX, m. 4/17/
         1920 at Waco, TX, Harry Elias Sames (1897-1956). D. at
         Laredo, TX
33123121 Laura Sleeper Sames (1921-1971), m. (1st) Cecil Wade.
          M. (2nd) William Calohan. Resided: Laredo, TX
331231211 William Sames Wade (1946-1952)
331231212 Martha Margaret Wade (b. 1950). Laredo, TX
33123122 Mary Wright Sames (1923-1938). Laredo, TX
33123123 Harry Elias Sames (b. 1926), m. 12/25/1947 Lydia
          Jackson. Resided: Laredo, TX
331231231 Mary Loving Sames (b. 1951)
331231232 Harry E. Sames (b. 1952)
331231233 Richards Edwin Sames (b. 1954)
331231234 John Markham Sames (b. 1959)

33123124   Martha Margaret "Peggy" Sames (b. 1928) at Laredo, TX,
           m. (1st) 11/23/1948 Frank Burton Tirey (1924-1969).
           M. (2nd) 1971 Richard H. Harrison. Resided: Laredo,
           TX
331231241 Martha Margaret Tirey (b. 1949) at Austin, TX
331231242 Laura Alice Tirey (b. 1951) at Waco, TX
331231243 Frank B. Tirey (b. 1952) at Waco, TX
3312313   Alethea Halbert Sleeper (1898-1980), m. 1/29/1923 Walter
           Brown Dossett (1899-1973), b. Meridian, MS. Resided:
           Waco, TX
33123131   Jane Brown Dossett (b. 1924), m. 2/ /1944 J. Leigh
           Brooks (b. 1921). Resided: Waco, TX
331231311 Alethea Dossett Brooks (b. 1945) at Blytheville, AK
331231312 Sarah Elizabeth Brooks (b. 1947) at Waco, TX
33123132   Laura Risher Dossett (b. 1926), m. 2/6/1948 Curtis
           Cullen Smith (b. 1925). Resided: Waco, TX
331231321 Sallie Chesnutt Smith (b. 1950) at Waco, TX
331231322 Alethea Risher Smith (b. 1953) at Waco, TX
331231323 Elizabeth Brient Smith (b. 1958) at Waco, TX
33123133   Walter Brown Dossett (b. 1927), m. 8/4/1951 Mary Martha
           Dickie (b. 1931). Resided: Waco, TX
331231331 Walter Dickie Dossett (b. 1952) at Albequerque, NM
331231332 Markham Brown Dossett (b. 1953) at Waco, TX
331231333 Susan Sleeper Dossett (b. 1955) at Waco, TX
331231334 Martha Beckham Dossett (b. 1961) at Waco, TX
331231335 Pauline Reeder Dossett (b. 1964) at Waco, TX
33123134   Frances Sleeper Dossett (b. 1929), m. 7/30/1949 Thomas
           Rowland Swann (b. 1927) at Tyler, TX. Resided:
           Waco, TX; Tyler, TX
331231341 Thomas Dossett Swann (b. 1952) at Tyler, TX
331231342 Andrew Rowland Swann (b. 1954) at Tyler, TX
331231343 Alethea Evans Swann (b. 1958) at Tyler, TX
3312314   William Markham Sleeper (1900-1935) at Waco, TX
3312315   Frances Dinwiddie Sleeper (1902-1972), m. 6/8/1925
           Thomas ford Stone (1898-1955), d. Houston, TX.
           Resided: Waco, TX; Houston, TX
33123151   Ada Risher Stone (b. 1929) at Houston, TX, m. 10/12/
           1955 at Waco, TX, James Russell Patton (b. 1929) at
           Waco, TX
331231511 Laura Risher Patton (b. 1957) at Waco, TX
331231512 James Russell Patton (b. 1959) at St. Louis, MO
331232   Susan Margaret Sleeper (1861-1941). Never married.
331233   Lucy Fleming Sleeper (1863-1951), m. 2/21/1884 Robert
           Fonda Gribble (1857-1935). Gribbles resided at Waco.
3312331   Theodore Miles Gribble (1894-1971), m. 11/19/1919 Louise
           Ouida Irwin. Resided: Waco.
33123311   Louise Fonda Gribble (b. 1924), m. 7/21/1951 George
           Streeter ("Jack") Maxfield (1913-1893). Resided:
           Waco.
331233111 Martha Woodson Maxfield (b. 1952), m. 4/7/1979 Lon
           Worth Cottingham. Resided: Dallas.
3312331111 Lara Elizabeth Cottingham (b. 1983)
3312331112 Sara Worth Cottingham (b. 1988)

331233112 Elizabeth Fonda Maxfield (b. 1954), m. at Alexandria,
           VA 11/4/1989 William Ross Pumfrey
3312332   Elizabeth Fonda Gribble (1885-1948), m. 9/21/1913 Arthur
           Ewald Ruhmann. Resided: Waco.
33123321   Albert Edward Ruhmann (1914-1974), m. 7/25/1938 Ruth
           Hall. Resided: Waco and Normangee, TX
33123322   Lucy Bertha Ruhmann (b. 1915), m. 7/4/1944 Charles G.
           Danzau
33123323   Elizabeth Eleanor Ruhmann (b. 1917), m. 6/12/1945
           R. K. Robinson, Jr.
33123324   Henrietta Gribble Ruhmann (b. 1922). Never married.
33123325   Susanna Fonda Ruhmann (b. 1924), m. 3/24/1949 Grant
           Jensen
33123326   Helen Louise Ruhmann (b. 1928), m. ca. 1950 Rudolph
           Svadlemak
3312333   Robert Francis Gribble (1890-1928), m. 3/25/1916 Joyce
           Hudson
33123331   Nancy Joy Gribble (b. 1919 Dallas, TX), m. 7/8/1941
           Carl Ellis Nelson
33123332   Elizabeth Fonda Gribble (b. 1922 Mercedes, TX), m.
           11/29/1944 Stephen Cook
33123333   Robert Fonda Gribble (b. 1932 at Austin, TX), m.
           (1st) 1/23/1955 Nelda Behrens, m. (2nd) 7/11/1976
           Rita Montgomery
331234   Thomas Markham Sleeper (1866-1943), m. at Clarksville,
           TN 10/23/1890 Caroline Lacy Lockert (1868-1950).
           Resided: Waco.
3312341   James Lockert Sleeper (1893-1981), m. Hannee Hardy of
           Abilene, TX. Resided: Waco.
33123411   James Lockert Sleeper, Jr. (b. 1916), m. 10/29/1949
           Elizabeth Smith of Ft. Worth, TX. Resided: Midland,
           TX.
331234111 David Lockert Sleeper (b. 1951), m. 8/10/1974
           Barbara Snow
331234112 Frances Elizabeth Sleeper (b. 1954), m. 6/16/1977
           Carter Hayes Moore
3312342   Thomas Markham Sleeper (1895-1973), m. 9/8/1929 Jennie
           Bess Holmes. Resided: Waco.
33123421   Clarence Holmes Sleeper (b. 1932)
33123422   Dorothy Ruth Sleeper (b. 1936)

3312343   Mary Woodson Sleeper (1898-1986), m. 10/23/1922 Donald
           Montfort Bernard (1897-1989). Resided: Waco and
           Alexandria, VA
33123431   Donald Montfort Bernard, Jr. (b. 1923 at Austin), m.
           at Bronxville, NY 8/31/1946 Betsy Blakeney Hodges (b.
           1925)
331234311 Martha Blakeney Bernard (b. 1948 in New Orleans), m.
           at Vienna, Austria 6/8/1973 Eugen Karl Scherer
3312343111 Eugen Karl Michael Donald Scherer (b. 1977 Vienna,
           Austria)
3312343112 Stephen Arpid Scherer (b. 1981 Vienna, Austria)
331234312 Carol Woodson Bernard (b. 1950 New Orleans), m. at
           Elon College, NC, 11/24/1978 Todd Edward Snyder
           (b. 1950). Resided: Pittsburg.

3312343121 Donald Bernard Snyder (b. 1983)
3312343122 William Bernard Snyder (b. 1988)
3312343123 Thomas Bernard Snyder (b. 1988)
3312343124 Kenneth Bernard Snyder (b. 1988)
331234313 Donald Montfort Bernard III (b. 1955 Anacortes,
          Wash.), m. 1/6/1979 Ellen Corbin. Div. No issue.
3312343? William Markham Bernard (b. 1927 Wichita Falls, TX),
          m. at Washington, D.C. 6/14/1949 Ruth Bruninger
          Stickle (b. 1928)
331234321 Mary Louise Bernard (b. 1950), m. (1st) 5/1/1975
          Charles Palmer. Div. No issue. M. (2nd) 4/28/1990
          Thomas Richard Adams
331234322 William Markham Bernard, Jr. (b. 1953), m. 2/17/1989
          Maria Esposito. Resided: Baltimore.
3312343221 Laura Amanda Bernard (b. 1989)
33123433 Mary Caroline Bernard (b. 1933 at Nashville), m. at
          Chevy Chase 8/26/1955 David Henry Pace (b. 1934)
331234331 Julia Elizabeth Pace (b. 1959 Enid, OK), m. 3/16/
          1985 Robert Carrol May, Jr. (b. 1959). Resided:
          Dallas.
3312343311 Robert Carroll May (b. 1986)
3312343312 Stephen Barnard May (b. 1989)
331234332 David Henry Pace, Jr. (b. 1962 Enid, OK), m. 12/5/
          1987 Caroline Elizabeth Daly (b. 1961). Resided:
          Dallas.
3312343321 David Henry Pace (b. 1988)
3312343322 Alexander Daly Pace (b. 1988)
3312344 William Lacy Sleeper (1900-1986), m. (1st) Gladys
          Primm, m. (2nd) Norma Dew. No issue.
331235 Van Francis Sleeper (1868-1876)
33124 Lucy Fleming Markham (1836-1884), m. at Vicksburg 1/30/
          1862 Edward A. Jones (d. 1900), son of Alexander and
          Elizabeth Cary Jones of Princess Anne, MD. Resided:
          Waco.
331241 Elizabeth Cary Jones (b. 1862)
331242 Susan Markham Jones (b. 1866)
331243 George Woodson Jones (b. 1869)
331244 Martha Estelle Jones (b. 1871)
33125 George Washington Markham (1823-1853)
3313 George W. Markham (1807-after 1880), m. 11/8/1845 Alcey
          Jane Billingsley (1828-1893), dau. of Joseph and Sarah
          Simely Billingsley. Resided: Vicksburg.
33131 Walter B. Markham (b. 1849)
33132 Aubin Markham (b. 1851)
33133 Henry Markham (b. 1853)
33134 Mary Virginia Markham (b. 1855), m. F. M. Featherstone
33135 Sarah "Sallie" Markham (b. 1857 at Vicksburg), m. (1st)
          6/10/1877 John Birdsong. M. (2nd) Walter Folkes
331351 Markham Birdson (b. 1878)
33136 Lucy G. Markham (b. 1865)
3314 Linnaeus Markham (b. 1798), m. Elizabeth
          Resided: Yazoo County, Miss.
33141 Janetta Markham, m. 9/21/1840 Alexander Laws Thornton.
          Resided: Versailles, KY

331411   Sallie Thornton, m. Randolph Railey of Versailles, KY
331412   Charles Thornton. Never married.
331413   Catherine Thornton, m. Joseph Lewis
331414   Nannie Thornton, m. Richard Lyle
3315   Hugh Mercer Markham (1813-1864), m. at Vicksburg 5/19/1859
         Catherine Pearce Weller (1826-1899), dau of Rev. George
         Weller. First husband of Catherine Weller was Joseph Todd.
33151   Hugh Mercer Markham, Jr. (1861-1897). Never married.
         Resided: Vicksburg.
33152   Frank Devereux Markham (1862-1913), m. 6/16/1897 Anna
         Chapman DuBose (1870-1960). Resided: Vicksburg, MS
331521   Catherine Weller Markham (1898-1978), m. 9/2/1921
         William Bruce Montgomery (1897-1941)
3315211   Ann Wing Montgomery (b. 1922), m. 7/25/1965 James
         Robert Wilson (b. 1932)
3315212   William Bruce Montgomery (b. 1925), m. 6/30/1949
         Dorothy Jean Robinson (b. 1925)
33152121   Julie Ann Montgomery (b. 1954), m. 7/8/1978 James
         Whitted Witherspoon Guthrie (b. 1954)
331521211   William Montgomery Guthrie (b. 1982)
331521212   Catherine Bonifay Guthrie (b. 1985)
33152122   Melissa Lisle Montgomery (b. 1958), m. 6/21/1981
         Gregory Wayne Caudill (1958)
331521221   Ann Claire Caudill (b. 1987)
3315213   Alexander Brooks Montgomery (b. 1926), m. 8/30/1952
         Placida Mary Brazinski (b. 1930)
33152131   Alexander Brooks Montgomery (1954-1981)
33152132   Lisa Catherine Montgomery (b. 1955), m. 8/17/1980
         Gary Derr Schaffer (b. 1953)
331521321   Sarah Wing Schaffer (b. 1982)
331521322   Hannah Catherine Schaffer (b. 1983)
331521323   Brooks Montgomery Schaffer (b. 1985)
331521324   Peter James Schaffer (b. 1987)
33152133   Robert Clay Montgomery (b. 1959), m. 2/4/1984 Audrey
         Anne Rogers (b. 1958)
331521331   Alexander Clay Montgomery (b. 1986)
331521332   William Markham Montgomery (b. 1988)
331522   Frank Devereux Markham (1904-ca. 1980). No issue.
331523   Lucia Denny Markham (1907-1976), m. 11/13/1927 Spickard
         Perry Burton (1903-1966). Resided: Oklahoma City, OK
3315231   Perry Cooper Burton (b. 1928), m. 10/2/1951 Mary
         Latimore Wright (b. 1932)
33152311   Cady Burton (b. 1953), m. 12/28/1974 Michael Canapp
         (b. 1950)
33152312   John Markham Burton (b. 1955), m. 3/9/1985 Reba Robert
         (b. 1953)
331523121   Emily Ann Roberts Burton (b. 1990)
33152313   Jane Dubone Burton (b. 1958), m. 1984 Richard Miller
         (b. 1952)
331523131   Elizabeth Jane Miller (b. 1985)
331523132   Samantha Powell Miller (b. 1988)
331523133   Ian Michael Miller (b. 1989)

33152314   David Cooper Burton (b. 1962), m. 10/19/1984 Angela
             Kirtley Burton (b. 1963)
3315232   Frank Chapman Burton (b. 1933),m. (1st) 5/10/1958
             Madelyn Edwards. Div. M. (2nd) 5/ /1975 Esther
             Banitah. Div.
33152321   Robert Chapman Burton (child of Burton/Edwards)(b.
             1959), m. 3/7/1987 Charlotte Jean Cunningham (b. 1960)
33152111   Austin Chapman Burton (b. 1988)
33152322   Jacob William Burton (b. 1990)
33152322   Kathryn Burton (child of Burton/Edwards)(b. 1967)
33152323   Elizabeth Ellen (Esther) Burton (b.1972)(child of
             Burton/Edwards)
3315233   Carolyn Ann Burton (b. 1935), m. 6/27/1959 James S.
             Evans (b. 1936). Resided: Oklahoma City, OK
33152331   Cynthia Jane Evans (b. 1961), m. 2/7/1987 Larry Conant
             (b. 1955)
33152311   Jonathan Tyler Conant (b. 1988)
33152312   Lindy Carol Conant (b. 1989)
33152332   Stephen Burton Evans (b. 1967), m. 10/14/1989 Renee
             Dempsey
33152333   James Markham Evans (b. 1972)
3316   John N. Markham (b. 1821), m. Lucy Davidson. Resided:
             Versailles.
33161   James Markham (b. 1853)
33162   Lucy Aubin Markham (1854-1856)
33163   John W. Markham (1854-1861)
             Probably other children
3317   Mary Markham (b. 1803), m. 8/22/1837 Reuben B. Berry
             (b. 1798). Resided: Versailles.
33171   Benjamin Berry (b. 1838)
3318   Judith Markham is not a child of John and Lucy Champe
             Fleming Markham.
3319   Judith Virginia Markham (not Virginia Markham) b. ca. 1805-
             d. before 1835), m. 2/4/1829 Putnam T. Williams (1805-
             1835) of Jefferson County, MISS. No record of a marriage
             to Jesse Claiborne. Resided: Jefferson County, MS.
33191   Mary B. Williams (b. 1832), m. Field Dunbar. Resided:
             Natchez.
33192   John Williams (b. before 1835)
331x   Aubin Markham (1817-1868), m. ca. 1840 John Odlin Hutchins
             (1816-1890), son of John and Eliza Brooks (Towson)
             Hutchins. Resided: Natchez.
331x1   John Hutchins (b. 1841), m. 1878 Melissa Harrell.
             Resided: Arkansas.
331x2   Lucy Hutchins (b. 1843), m. 12/19/1868 Robert Wells
             (d. 1880), son of Richard and Jane Carson Wells.
             Resided: Mississippi and Princeton, NJ.
331x21   Robert William Wells (1869-1944), m. 12/24/1905 Madie
             Baggett (d. 1942). Resided: Gulfport, Vicksburg,
             Laurel, MS
331x211   Mary Lucy Wells (b. 1908). Unm.
331x22   McKim Holliday Wells (1877-1966), m. 10/28/1907 at
             Biloxi, MS, Sarah Antionette Lemon (1887-1959) of
             Gulfport, MS, dau. of Daniel and Mary Keel Lemon.
             Resided: Natchez, MS; Laurel, MS

331x221 McKim Holliday Wells (b. 1914), m. (1st) Mary Lynn
          Cuffe. Div. M. (2nd) 2/18/1950 Annis Massey at
          Laurel, MS
331x2211 Christy Lynn Wells (parents Wells/Cuffe)(b. 1943),
          m. 11/28/1966 Charles Wright Irby. Resided:
          Pascagoula, MS; Bedford, TX
331x22111 Kimberly Ann Irby
331x22112 Charles Wright Irby
331x222 Robert Wells (b. 1916) at Laurel, MS, m. 2/17/1939
          Ethel Wright (b. 1913) at Meridian, MS
331x2221 Robert William Wells (b. 1942), m. (1st) 1963 Margaret
          Cowart of Starkville, MS. M. (2nd) 1978 Patricia
          Marie Kelly at Salt Lake City, UT. Resided: Metairie,
          LA; Park City, UT
331x22211 Any Suzanna Wells (dau. of Wells/Cowart)
331x22212 Robert William Wells (son of Wells/Cowart)
331x22213 Kelly Marie Wells (dau. of Wells/Kelly)
331x2222 Sarah Ella Wells (b. 1947) at Laurel, MS, m. 8/30/1969
          Erwin Simerly. Div.
331x22221 Melissa Elise Simerly
331x22222 David Franklin Simerly
331x223 Aubin Markham Wells (b. 1911) at Hattiesburg, MS, m. 5/
          16/1936 Howard Clayton Clements (b. 1910) at Towns, GA,
          son of Clayton and Minnie Hutchinson Clements.
          Resided: Vancleave, MS
331x2231 Howard Clayton Clements (b. 1944) at Laurel, MS, m.
          6/9/1968 Kathy Pearl Ingram (b. 1949), dau. of Samuel
          and Ila Jay Ingram. Resided: Baker, LA; Clinto, LA
331x22311 Karon Michelle Clements (b. 1970)
331x22312 Leigh Aubin Clements (b. 1972)
331x22313 Lowell Clayton Clements (b. 1977)
331x22314 Ila Amanda Clements (b. 1980)
331x224 Jean Antoinette Wells (1908-1986), m. 8/10/1942 William
          Virgil Redmon (b. 1916). Resided: Louisville, KY
331x2241 Barbara A. Redmon (1944-1955)
331x23 Aubin Markham Wells (1873-1917), m. 5/11/1899 at
          Princeton, NJ, Robert Lansing Zabriskie (b. 1872).
          Resided: Princeton, NJ; Aurora, NY
331x231 Louise Zabriskie (b. 1901), m. 7/14/1928 William F.
          Redfield (1894-1989). Resided: New Jersey
331x2311 Aubin Wells Redfield (b. 1929), m. (1st) James Bryan.

          Div. M. (2nd) Robert Sanders (d. 1990)
331x23111 James H. Bryan, m. Nancy Luick
331x231111 Marjorie Bryan (b. ca. 1985)
331x231112 Robert Bryan (b. ca. 1989)
331x23112 William Redfield Bryan, m. Helen Sanderi
331x231121 Weston Bryan (b. ca. 1980)
331x231122 Lindsey Bryan (b. ca. 1982)
331x231123 Kathrine Louise Bryan (b. ca. 1985)
331x2312 William F. Redfield (b. 1930), m. (1st) Nancy Fawcett.
          Div. M. (2nd) Doris _____
331x23121 Julie Louise Redfield (dau. of Redfield/Fawcett), m.
          K. C. Spaan

331x231211 Melanie Spaan (b. ca. 1989)
331x23122 Frances Carey Redfield (dau. of Redfield/Fawcett), m.
          Bradley Reich
331x231221 Jason Reich (b. ca. 1988)
331x23123 Aubin Wells Redfield, m. 11/ /1989 Daniel Washburn
331x2313 Jane Wells Redfield (b. 1934), m. Robert Forsberg
331x23131 Katherine Louise Forsberg
331x23132 Robert Forsberg
331x23133 Kristen Forsbert, m. 1988 Mark Diepus
331x232 Robert Wells Zabriskie (b. 1911), m. Allie Prigg
331x233 Aubin Zabriskie (1905-1940), m. Samuel Fowler of
          Knoxville, TN
331x2331 Samuel Fowler (b. 1929), m. Joann _____
331x23311 Elizabeth Fowler, m. Michael Cassidy
331x23312 Aubin Fowler
331x23313 Frank Fowler
331x23314 Gordon Fowler
331x2332 Robert Zabriskie Fowler (b. ca. 1931), m. Marlene
          ___ _____. Resided: Ithaca, NY
331x23321 Jennifer Fowler
331x23322 Ruth Fowler
331x2333 James Lansing Fowler (b. ca. 1934), m. Nell _____.
          Resided: Brentwood, TN
331x23331 Catherine Chandler Fowler (b. 1963)
331x23332 James Fowler
331x23333 Thomas Wells Fowler (b. 1966)
331x24 Jane Wells, m. (1st) Harry Bunn. M. (2nd) Charles
          Parsons. No issue. Resided: Princeton, NJ
331x3 Eliza Brooks Hutchins (1844-1926), m. 1/15/1873 Reuben
          Macon Fry (1847-1905), son of Philip Slaughter and Mary
          Pamela Anderson Fry of Orange, VA. Resided: Lake
          Village, AR; Fort Smith, AR and Oklahoma City, OK
331x31 Edmund Mortimer Fry (1873-1945), m. 10/12/1908 Brunetta
          Esther Williams (1881-1945). Resided: Oklahoma
331x311 Philip Hutchins Fry (b. 1912), m. 9/28/1935 Helen
          Gaines (b. 1909). Resided: Oklahoma
331x3111 Philip Hutchins Fry (b. 1939), m. Janice Ehred
331x31111 Philip Hutchins Fry (b. 1962)
331x31112 Wendy Lynn Fry
331x3112 Anita Fry (b. 1942)
331x312 Edmund Mortimer Fry (b. 1916), m. Helen Lancaster.
          Resided: Oklahoma
331x3121 Edmund M. Fry
331x3122 Hunter Williams Fry
331x3123 Linda Fry
331x32 Reuben Macon Fry (1875-1956), m. (1st) 10/18/1905
          Louise Kerr (1878-1932). M. (2nd) 7/1/1933 Sarah
          Miller. Resided: Uniontown, PA
331x321 Reuben Macon Fry (b. 1906)
331x322 Joseph Kerr Fry (b. 1908)
331x33 Infant Fry
331x34 Aubin M. Fry (1877-1957), m. 4/19/1899 Samuel Edwin
          Clarkson (1875-1951), son of Richard Albert and
          Elizabeth Jane Robinson Clarkson. Resided: Fort
          Smith, AR and Oklahoma City, OK

331x341   Albert Luther Clarkson (1901-1981), m. 5/2/1927 Blanch
        Bernice Rowland (1905-1953), dau. of Robert and Laura
        Nichols Rowland. Resided: Oklahoma City, OK
331x3411   Rowland Clarkson (b. 1928), m. 11/22/1950 Germaine
        Millspaugh (b. 1929), dau. of Robert and Laura
        Millspaugh. Resided: Oklahoma City, OK and
        Greeneville, TN
331x34111 Lynn Aubin Clarkson (1952-1968)
331x34112 Leslie Germaine Clarkson (b. 1953), m. 4/4/1981
        Steve Richards (b. 1950), son of Vernon and Georgia
        Wood Richards
331x341121 Aubin Richards (b. 1988)
331x34113 Lance Clarkson (b. 1956), m. 5/20/1989 Judith Gay
        Hodges (b. 1947), dau. of Ned and Helen Archer
        Hodges. Resided: Greeneville, TN
331x34114 Laura Lee Clarkson (b. 1964)
331x3412   Blanche Aubin Clarkson (b. 1932), m. 9/16/1950 Robert
        Hutchison (b. 1928), son of Robert and Edith Walden
        Tanner Hutchison. Resided: Oklahoma City, OK and
        Gunnison, CO
331x34121 Robert Lawrence Hutchison (b. 1951), m. 5/ /1981
        Jane Himmelberg (b. 1952). Resided: Colorado
        Springs, CO
331x341211 Lark Marie Hutchison (b. 1983)
331x34122 Pamela Sue Hutchison (b. 1953),m. 6/18/1977 David
        Michael Garrett (b. 1953), son of Richard William
        and Aline Jewell Svejkovsky Garrett. Resided:
        Oklahoma City, OK
331x341221 Christin Aline Garrett (b. 1979)
331x341222 Elizabeth Michelle Garrett (b. 1981)
331x341223 Micah Hutchison Garrett (b. 1988)
331x34123 Stephanie Aubin Hutchision (b. 1956), m. 6/17/1978
        Stephen Craig Wallace (b. 1954). Resided:
        Oklahoma City, OK and Colorado Springs, CO
331x341231 Stephen Zachary Wallace (b. 1979)
331x341232 Justin Robert Wallace (b. 1980)
331x341233 Rainey Michelle Wallace (b. 1983)
331x341234 Bryan Thomas Wallace (b. 1987)
331x34124 Thomas Rowland Hutchison (b. 1959), m. 1986 Ann
        Brown (b. 1962). Div. 1987. Resided: Fort Collins,
        CO

331x341241 Terry Robert Hutchison (b. 1987)
331x34125 Susan Elizabeth Hutchison (b. 1961), m. 8/ /1984
        Charles Schmitt (b. 1959). Resided: Colorado and
        Scotts Bluff, NE
331x341251 David Schmitt (b. 1988)
331x4   Aubin Markham Hutchins (1847-1914), m. 10/27/1869 at
        Natchez, Frank F. Weller (1839-before 1910). Resided:
        Ascension County, LA
331x41 Frank F. Weller (b. ca. 1871)
331x42 George Todd Weller (1872-1894)
331x43 Aubin Markham Weller (1873-1915), m. J. E. Gonzales
331x44 Lilly Weller (b. ca. 1876)
331x45 Martha M. Weller (1877-1916), m. W. G. Delaune

331x46 Cassie Weller (ca. 1882)
331x47 Katie Weller (ca. 1884)
331x48 Mamie Weller (ca. 1886)
331x5 Hugh Hutchins (b. 1850), m. Gabriella Ligon
331x6 Mary Jane "Mamie" Hutchins (b. 1855), m. Charles E.
        Sessions (b. 1853). Resided: Memphis, TN
331x61 Richard R. Sessions (ca. 1881)
331x62 Auben Avant Sessions (ca. 1883)
331x63 Charles E. Sessions (ca. 1885)
331x64 Sidney D. Sessions (ca. 1888)
331a Osborne Markham. D. inf.
331b Martha Bolling Markham (1816-1906). Never married.
        Resided: Versailles.
331c Norbourne Markham. D. inf.
331d Champe Fleming Markham (b. 1797), m. (1st) at Goochland
        County 12/23/1818 Sally H. Cocke, m. (2nd) at Vicksburg,
        MS, 5/14/1840 Elizabeth Thompson

33242 Caroline Wooldridge (b. 8/3/1835).
332425 Mary Bolling Archer (b. 12/7/1859).

3324251 Virginia ("Jennie") Manuel

332426 John Walthall Archer (b. 12/7/1859)

33242642 Abbott Floyd Archer, Jr.

366 Thomas Bernard resided in Goochland County and served in the
        Revolution for four years in the regular service of the
        Army of the United States in the Virginia line (and
        possibly served under Capt. Charles Fleming). He was given
        land in Highland County, Ohio in recognition of his
        services. Moved to Ohio 6/ /1807.
3661 Elizabeth Bernard, m. Francis Smithson. She wwas about 58
        in 1850.
3662 John (Adams?) Bernard (b. 1800 Goochland County). Lived in
        Illinois.
36621 Harriet ("Hattie") Bernard (b. Galena, Ill.)
36622 Sarah Marie Bernard (b. 12/ /1835 in Galena, Ill), m.
        Galena, Ill Chester Anthony Coborn. Her mother was
        supposedly born in Ohio. Moved to Sauk Rapids, MN, where
        he was Depot Agent for Northern Pacific R.R.
366221 Eva Ellen Coborn (5/6/1856-5/9/1906)(born Galena, Ill.,
        d. Superior, Wisc., bur. Sauk Rapids, MN), m. Sauk

        Rapids, MN 10/25/1872 Samuel Perrin Carpenter (6/1/1835-
        7/10/1909)(b. Michigan, d. Superior, Wisc.), son of
        Justus and Wealthy Parsons Carpenter
3662211 Ora Lulu Carpenter (10/13/1873-4/16/1886)(d. injuries in
        Sauk Rapids cyclone)
3662212 Olive Mae Carpenter (9/23/1879-4/14/1886)(d. injuries in
        cyclone)
3662213 Horace Carpenter (1/ /1877-5/21/1945)(d. Hollywood, CA),
        m. (1st) Ella Hilger, m. (2nd) Beatrice _____.

3662214   Angeline Carpenter (10/ /1884-3/12/1890)(d. injuries in cyclone)

3662215   Samuel Justus Carpenter (2/15/1885-1/25/1950)(b. Sauk Rapids, Iowa, d. Little Falls, MN), m. Duluth, MN 9/25/1912 Mabel Emily Howson (6/5/2883-12/31/1968)(b. Wadena, MN). Both buried Crystal Lake Cemetery, Minneapolis.

36622151   Chester Charles Carpenter (10/14/1913-)(b. Minneapolis), m. Minneapolis 6/20/1941 Marian Eunice Shorts (5/16/1916-)(b. Coleraine, MN), dau. of Thomas Benjamin and Lily Merle McCormick Shorts. U.S. Army in World War II.

366221511   Susan Jane Carpenter (3/20/1948-)(b. Minneapolis), m. 6/6/1970 Terry John Hughes (b. Richfiled, MN). Home: Delta, CO. Have two adopted children.

36622152   Richard William Carpenter (8/9/1916-1/14/1985)(b. Minneapolis, d. Chisago City, MN)(bur. at Fort Swelling), m. Mora, MN 7/17/1954 Thea Mildred Horne (2/16/1915-)(b. Mora, MN), dau. of Mathias M. and Margaret Sophie Pederson Horne. U.S. Army in World War II.

366221521   Diane Evon Carpenter (8/15/1955-). Minneapolis.

36622153   Dorothy Jane Carpenter (9/11/1918-)(b. Minneapolis), m. Minneapolis 9/8/1939 Carroll Loerch Borne (5/3/1916-)(b. Minneapolis), son of Roy and Erna M. Loerch Borne.

366221531   Richard Phillip Borne (3/5/1942-)(b. Minneapolis), m. Minneapolis 9/11/1964 Susan B. Emerson (8/2/1944-)(b. Minneapolis), dau. of Clarence Waldo and Margaret Joyce Carter Emerson. Minneapolis.

3662215311   Peter Christian Borne (3/1/1967-)(b. Minneapolis), m. Minneapolist 12/30/1989 Michelle Marie Trudeau (b. Minneapolis)(9/10/1965-)(Mount Olivet Lutheran Church). Dau. of Charles J. and Elaine A. Knutson Trudeau. Minneapolis.

3662215312   Timothy Richard Borne (12/11/1968-). Minneapolis.

3662215313   Andrew Todd Borne (11/26/1973-). Minneapolis.

366221532   Marcia Emily Borne (11/24/1943-)(b. Minneapolis), m. Minneapolis 6/18/1966 Stephen J. Nelson (11/9/1943-)(b. Minneapolis), son of Eldred and Ida Mae Marwin Nelson. Div. Minneapolis.

3662215321   Michael Laird Nelson (1/29/1972-)(b. San Jose, CA)

3662215322   Scott Justus Nelson (6/11/1974-)(b. Kalamazoo, MI)

366221533   Robert Justus Borne (8/25/1951 or 7/28/1951-)(b. Minneapolis), m. Minneapolis 8/18/1972 Susan Rae Morgan (4/2/1950-)(b. Minneapolis), dau. of Donald W. and Beverly K. Pearson Morgan (Donald d. 8/9/1978 and Beverly married Marshall A. Griswold).

3662215331   Robert Ryan Borne (8/23/1978-)(b. Apple Valley, MN)

3662215332   Jamie Lynn Borne (4/4/1982-)(b. Apple Valley, MN)

36622154 Robert Justus Carpenter (7/11/1920-11/8/1948)(b.
          Minneapolis, d. Little Falls, MN)(bur. Crystal Lake
          Cemetery, Minneapolis). U.S. Army in World War II
          (d. injuries received in power saw accident).
3662216   Chester Eben Carpenter (7/23/1888-9/11/1974 or 11/26/
          1974)(b. Sauk Rapids, Iowa, d. Columbia, CA)(bur.
          Superior, WS), m. Camp Douglas, WS 6/28/1916 Lula
          Cecil Yates (9/12/1891-   )(b. Brainerd, MN), dau.
          of William and Rebecca Mitchell Yates
36622161 Doris Lou Carpenter (5/28/1918-   )(b. Superior,
          WS), m. Little Falls, MN 5/29/1949 Elvir Adolph Kazek
          (2/21/1918-12/14/1975)(b. and buried at Randall, MN)
          (d. Little Falls, MN)
366221611 Ruth Lois Kazek (11/30/1942-   )(b. Little Falls,
          MN), m. Little Falls, MN 7/13/1963 Wayne Robert
          Traaseth (7/12/1942-   )(b. Duluth, MN), son of
          Peter and Alma Olsen Traaseth
3662216111 Michelle Lynne Traaseth (5/2/1964-   )(b. Grand
          Forks, ND), m. 7/21/1990 Douglas Lusk
3662216112 Wendy Anne Traaseth (7/13/1967-   )(b. Burlington,
          WS)
3662216113 Kara Jeanne Traaseth (8/6/1971-   )(b. Minneapolis)
366221612 Dale Alfred Kazek (2/3/1946-   )(b. Little Falls, MN),
          m. Osage, Iowa 10/30/1971 Rebecca Marie Keinast (5/9/
          1950-   )(b. Osage, Iowa), dau. of Arnold and
          Jeanne Simon Keinast
3662216121 Kelly Jeanne Kazek (2/20/1972-   ). Minneapolis.
          Unm.
          She has a daughter:
36622161211 Kerry Justine Kazek (8/30/1989-   )(b. St. Cloud,
          MN)
3662216122 Nicole Renae Kazek (5/14/1975-   ). Monticello, MN
366221613 Lloyd Chester Kazek (11/14/1947-   )(b. Little Falls,
          MN), m. (1st) Little Falls, MN 2/17/1968 Karen Ellen
          Rahn (10/9/1950-   )(b. Little Falls, MN), dau. of
          Leonard and Lila Opsal Rahn. M. (2nd) Milbank, SD
          8/15/1975 Doris June Kemp (5/9/1951-   )(b. St.
          Paul), dau. of William and Lorraine Owens Kemp
3662216131 Lloyd Chester Kazek, Jr. (7/1/1968-7/2/1968)
3662216132 Leo Sherman Kazek (3/15/1969-3/16/1969)
3662216133 Lonnie Michael Kazek (3/1/1970-   )

          Doris June Kemp was married first to Armsberger and
          had a child by him, Joseph William Armsberger
          (11/21/1972-   )(b. St. Paul, MN)

3662216134 Jennifer Ann Kazek (8/29/1976-   )(b. Minneapolis)
366221614 Jean Lucille Kazek (4/14/1952-   )(b. Little Falls,
          MN), m. Memphis 8/6/1977 Tyrus Raymond Legge, Jr.
          (11/16/1952-   )(b. Memphis), son of Tyrus Raymond
          and Ida Adams Legge.
36622162 Verna Marie Carpenter (1/10/1920-   )(b. Superior, WS),
          m. Santa Ana, CA 7/25/1948 Paul Frederick Colbeck (7/
          4/1911-   )(b. Grand Rapdis), son of Rev. Edwin and
          Daisy White Colbeck

366221621 Connie Marie Colbeck (10/1/1949-   )(b. Escalon, CA)
366221622 Barbara Gail Colbeck (11/4/1951-   )(b. Colusa, CA),
           m. Columbia, CA 6/12/1971 Bruce Lewis Muzzey (8/29/
           1951-   )(b. San Jose, CA), son of Ralph Butler
           and Marjorie Spalding Muzzey
3662216221 Rebekah Sarah Muzzey (8/2/1974-   ). San Jose.
3662216222 Elspeth Daisy Muzzey (9/12/1977-   ). San Jose.
3662216223 Breanne Marie Muzzey (7/17/1980-   ). Redmond,
           Wash.
3662216224 Benjamin Butler Muzzey (10/15/1983-   ). Renton,
           Wash.
3662163 Donald Yates Carpenter (12/30/1929-   )(b. Little
           Falls, MN), m. Little Falls, MN 9/3/1952 Donna Mae
           Bloxham (3/21/1925-   )(b. Anoka, MN), dau. of Duran
           Dallas and Maude Stella Hunter Bloxham
366221631 Mark Jefferey Carpenter (9/14/1953-   )(b. St. Cloud,
           MN), m. Cincinnati 2/11/1982 Terrance Diane Frederick
           (4/22/1953-   )(b. Johnson Air Force Base, Honshue,
           Japan), dau. of Ronald Terrance and Marion Evelyn
           Doyle Frederick. Mark and Terrance are divorced.
3662216311 Vanessa Carpenter (11/9/1983-   )
366221632 Lori Marie Carpenter (9/22/1955-   )(b. Duluth, MN),
           m. Columbus, Ohio 8/26/1978 Robert Charles Becker (4/
           10/1956-   ), son of William Arthur and Julia Mae
           Fulton Becker
3662216321 Megan Marie Becker (12/6/1985-   )
3662216322 Kathryn Marie Becker (1/4/1988-   )
366221633 Bruce Timothy Carpenter (1/8/1958-   )(b. Des Moines),
           m. Worthington, Ohio (6/9/1979 Deborah Lynn Combs
           (7/23/1960-   )(b. Hazard, KY), dau. of Marshall E.
           and Alma Bryant Combs. Bruce and Deborah are
           divorced.
3662217 Mary Virginia Carpenter (3/7/1893-   )(d. Columbia, CA),
           m. 7/24/1925 Emil Williams Dahl. Minneapolis.
366222 Ora Otaitsa Coburn (1855-'9'6)(b. Galena, ILL), m. 3/21/
           1872 Fred Dane Carlton
366223 Chester Anthony Coburn, Jr. (b. St. Paul, MN 10/5/1867-
           ), m. 4/5/1896 Julia Stullich
366224 Robert Lee Coburn (b. St. Paul, MN 8/24/1869), m. 9/8/
           1898 Frances Gerard (b. 1878)
366225 Dead by 1900
366226 Dead by 1900
366227 Dead by 1900
366228 Dead by 1900
3663 Sarah Bernard, m. William Morris. About 54 in 1850.
3664 George Washington Bernard (9/ /1799-1895)(born in
           Virginia). About 51 in 1850. M. Harriet McConnel
3665 Thomas Jefferson Bernard (1801-1868)(born in Virginia).
           About 49 in 1850, m. (1st) Amanda Young, m. (2nd) Mary
           McConnel (1806-1838)
3666 Mary ("Polly") Bernard, m. John Underwood. About 45 in
           1850.
3667 Susan Bernard, m. William Rees (d. prior to 1850)

36671 Mary Ellen Rees
36672 Thomas Rees
36673 Harriett Rees
36674 John Rees
36675 Samuel Rees
3668 Nancy Bernard, m. Thomas Riley. She was about 38 in 1850.

Many of the children of Thomas and Mary Hicks Bernard were born in Virginia, and all resided (in 1850) in the Ohio counties of Clinton and Highland except 3662 John (Adams?) Bernard who resided in Illinois.

Much of the above information is from a Pension affidavit made in 1850 in Clinton County, Ohio, and signed ("his work") by George W. Bernard.

3711 Mary Deane Yates (d. by 5/10/1796), m. William Hamlin

41 Frances Trent (10/18/1753-3/ /1780), dau. of Alexander Trent III of "Barter Hill", Cumberland County, and his wife, the former Elizabeth Woodson. Pocahontas Trails Quarterly Vol. 3, No. 3.

Capt. William Gay (living December 1809). In place of "Cumberland" insert "Goochland".

41111 Letitia Christian Gay (d. age 18).
41112 Ann Manning Gay, m. Robert H. Gilliam of Richmond
41113 Lucy Harrison Gay, m. Henry Wilson of "Bon Brook", Cumberland County.
41114 Bettie Collier Gay. Teacher in Williamsburg. Unm. as of 1886.
4112 Benjamin Carter Gay (1818-1867), m. Elizabeth Cary Baptist.
41121 Lucy Harrison Gay, m. Frank Edward Whitfield of Memphis, later (1886) of Corinth, Miss.
411211 Frank Edward Whitfield, Jr.
411212 Carter Cary Whitfield.
411213 Lucy Gay Whitfield.
411214 Lizzie Carrie Whitfield.
41122 Edward Baptist Gay.
41123 George Minge Gay (twin).
41124 Richard A. Gay (twin).
41125 Benjamin Carter Gay, Jr.
41126 William Powhatan Gay.
41127 Lizzie Carrie Gay.
4115 Omit this number and both lines under it.

The following data is from Hearst's Sunday American, Atlanta, April 12, 1931:
412 Peter Efford Bentley (1759-1837) of Goochland County, son of Samuel Bentley. M. (1st) Martha Markham, dau. of Col. Bernard Markham and his wife, the former Elizabeth Harris.

```
4122    Wm. Field Bentley.
4127    Alexander Willis Bentley.  M. (1st) Margaret Newman.  M.
           (2nd) Julia Peter.
4128    Louisa Woodson Bentley, m. William N. Roper.
412x    Henry Hogue Bentley, slain at the Alamo.
41251   William Bentley, m. Nannie Abbott.
41252   Alexander Bentley, m. Josephine Harris.
41253   David Bentley.  Unm.
41254   John Eldridge Bentley, m. Blanche Spurlock.
41255   George Bentley, m. Miss Ware.
41256   Sarah Bentley, m. Polk Ware.
41257   Mary Bentley.  Unm.
41258   Robert Thompson Bentley.  Unm.


419    Sally Gay of "Fairfield", Goochland County


41d    John H. Gay (d. 8/7/1797).



43     Mary Gay (d. 11/  /1800), m. Neale ("Ugly Neale") Buchanan
          (d. 2/23/1793).  Neale is sometimes spelled Neil.
       ----------------------------------------------------------------

5   Martha Bolling, m. Thomas Eldridge.  "Rochedale Hundred" (now
       known as Jones' Neck) was on the south side of the James
       River, opposite Curle's Neck.  Elizabeth Jones, mother of
       Thomas Eldridge, is shown as the dau. of Sarah Howell Jones.
       Reference: John Bennett Boddie's HISTORICAL SOUTHERN
       FAMILIES.  Vol. Xx, page 32.
51  Thomas Eldridge III (ca. 1737 in Sussex County - 1822 in
       Madison County, AL).  A Revolutionary War soldier.  M.
       Winifred Jones Miller (b. 5/22/1843).
511 Thomas Eldridge IV (ca. 1777-ca. 1824 in Sussex County), m.
       3/24/1804 Elizabeth Hall (b. ca. 1780 in Virginia).

5118   Rolfe Eldridge (11/6/1807 in Sussex County-4/30/1859 in
          Woodruff County, AR), m. 11/28/1828, in Sussex County,
          Caroline Mary Hall (1/28/1807 in Sussex County-1890
          Woodruff County), dau. of Dr. John and Martha Hall.
          Rolfe and Caroline migrated on Germantown, Shelby County,
          TN between 1836 and early 1837.
             Sometime after 1850 Rolfe and Caroline Eldridge moved
          to the Gregory Community in Woodruff County, AR.  Ages
          for 51181-51184 are from 1850 Census.
51181   John Eldridge - 19
51182   Harriet Eldridge - 14 (7/4/1835-1888), m. 1/8/1857 Jesse
          T. Gray, son of Walter and Mary Carr Gray
51183   Laura Eldridge, b. in TN - 13
51184   Sarah Eldridge - 10
```

51185   Rolfe Eldridge (1/31/1840 in Germantown-2/15/1891 in
        Woodruff County), m. 3/25/1869 Ella Love Watson (12/29/
        1851 in Desoto, MS-2/18/1880 Woodruff County), dau. of
        Samuel and Mary Dupree Watson. Rolfe was educated at
        Hickory Plains, Prairie County, TN and at Trenton, Gibson
        County, TN.   In 1862 a CSA cavalryman under Captain
        Hooker.
  Children born in Arkansas (ages for 511851-511854 are from 1880
  Census):
511851 Jane Eldridge - 10
511852 Rolfe Eldridge - 8
511853 Robert Eldridge - 7
511854 John Dupree Eldridge - 5 (2/12/1876-5/3/1953 in Augusta,
        AR), m. (1st) 2/26/1896, in Woodruff County, Vertie
        Alexander Bell (2/4/1877-   ), dau. of W. J. Bell. M.
        (2nd) 9/16/1902 Kate Marie Nowlin (5/20/1891 in Carroll
        County, TN - 3/22/1949 in Memphis), dau. of George and
        Mollie Nowlin.
5118541   Rolfe   Eldridge   (12/12/1896-11/11/1968),   m. Ruth
        Elizabeth Conner
5118542 Willie Bell Eldridge (3/5/1899-3/7/1919)
5118543 Cora Virginia Eldridge (12/9/1903-   ),m. 6/16/1926
        Charles Rench Galloway
5118544 John Dupree Eldridge, Jr. (3/3/1909-   ), m. 10/18/
        1934 Carra Wood Mixon. He owns and maintains the
        original Eldridge and Watson farms at Gregory, AR
5118545 George Paul Eldridge (12/20/1915-9/2/1969), m. (1st)
        6/29/1937 Percy Katherine Steels, m. (2nd) 8/22/1959
        Shirley Elms
51186   Lucy Eldridge
51187   Robert Eldridge, b. in Tennessee
51188   Ella L. Eldridge, b. in Mississippi. Age 17 by 1870
        Census
51189   Samuel Eldridge. Age 3 mos. by 1870 Census. Born in AR

512   Judith Eldridge (b. Nottoway County - d. 8/30/1856 in
        Franklin County, AL), m. in Nottoway County, Henry Cox III
        (b. in Nottoway County 1/22/1774-11/26/1821 in Franklin
        County, AL)

5122   Ann Harris Cox (5/5/1800 in Nottoway County - 1/22/1864 in
        Franklin County), m. 12/5/1816, in Madison County, AL,
        William Stratton Jones (12/30/1798 in Amelia County-1/30/
        1870 in Franklin County, AL)

51225   Thomas Speck Jones, M.D. (9/4/1827 in Franklin County, AL-
        1/1/1913 in Baton Rouge), m.7/5/1849, in Franklin County,
        Eliza Perkins Perry (12/18/1828 in Brownsville, TN -
        3/10/1901 in Baton Rouge)
512251 Thomas Sembola Jones (10/5/1859 in Jackson, LA - 5/15/
        1933 in Baton Rouge), m. 11/7/1885, in Baton Rouge,
        Deborah Seldon Spencer (9/21/1858 at Vandalia, LA -
        1/2/1889 at Baton Rouge)
5122511 Eliza Perry Jones (1887 in Baton Rouge - 9/10/1916 in

New Orleans), m. 6/30/1908, at Baton Rouge, James
Edward Halligan (2/11/1879 in Boston - 1/30/1965 in
New Orleans)
51225111   Elizabeth Perry Jones Halligan (10/26/1914 in Baton
Rouge -   ), m. 4/15/1939, in Boston, John Burden
Toy (6/25/1914-   )

The following data is from Hearst's Sunday American,
Atlanta, April 12, 1931:
513   Rev. David Thompson, b, Glasgow (educated at University of
Edinburgh). In 1809, the Thompsons moved to Madison County,
AL.

52   Jenny Eldridge is Jane Eldridge known as Aunt Jenny.

541   Maj. James Boswell Ferguson (b. 1781-96 V 212).   The
Fergusons lived at "La Valee", Goochland County.

55211   Sarah H. May, m. 11/ /1829 Robert Burwell Page (1806-
1837)(b. at "The Fork"), son of Maj. Carter Page and his
wife, the former Lucy Nolan.
552111   Carter Page (d. young).
552113   Mary May Page (b. ca. 1835), m. 1860 Francis D. Irving
(she was his second wife). They moved to Farmville.
5521131   Dr. Paulus Irving of Danville.
5521132   Sarah May Irving.
5521133   Francis D. Irving, Jr.
5521134   Robert Paige Irving.

55217   Lucy Nolan Page (b. ca. 1837), m. Rev. James Grammar of
Ashland, VA.

5527   David Mann Branch (six lines)(Fouchee Street).

55274412   Alan Henry Branch, m. 7/3/1962 Judy Leach Lovinger.
552744121   Scott Alan Branch (6/3/1963-   ).

55274421   Charles Edward Johnston III, m. Polly _____.
552744211   Charles Edward Johnston IV (5/ /1963-   ).

552744221   Elizabeth Hertzog Jones (4/20/1963-   ).

561   Rolfe Eldridge, Jr. See 20 W (1) 207.

56191   Rolfe Eldridge Glover, m. 1885 Sarah Eyre Blair (1861-
        1929), eldest dau. of James Heron and Jane Blair. The
        Blairs lived in Richmond on the northwest corner of
        Third and Cary Streets.

5632   Ann Elizabeth Eldridge (d. 1848), m. Thomas Henry Garrett
        (3/12/1819-9/26/1906)
56321   Thomas William Garrett (6/5/1842-   ), m. Ann Elizabeth
        Wright
56322   Mary Ann Garrett (8/7/1846-   ), m. Capt. William
        Independence Raisin (7/4/1840-   )
5633   John Rolfe Eldridge, m. 9/20/1848 Eliza Maria Hanes (12/10/
        1827-8/8/1899)
56331   Annie Elizabeth Eldridge (6/27/1849-   ), m. 10/17/1872
        Julian Eugene Connor
563311 Rena Maud Connor, m. 6/5/1901 John Chambers Ayres, M.D.
        (4/2/1877-8/18/1952)(b. Weakley County, TN; d. Memphis)
5633111 Martha Eldridge Ayres (6/15/1904-   ), m. 12/27/1927
        Albert Madison Brinkley II (11/22/1905)
56331111 Albert Madison Brinkley III (8/10/1933-10/22/1952)
5633112 Kathryn Conner Ayres (2/26/1907-   ), m. 6/12/1928
        Floyd Benjamin James of Ruston, LA (1/4/1907-   ).
        Home: Knoxville.
56331121 Renna Kathryn James (12/17/1931-   ), m. 10/4/1958
        Lowell Orum Burkhalter
56331122 Floyd Benjamin James, Jr. (3/1/1936-   ), m. 1/26/1957
        Margaret Ann Riser of Ruston, LA
563311221 Floyd Benjamin James III
56331123 John Tom James (8/17/1941-   )
5633113 John Chambers Ayres, Jr. (1910-   )(b. Memphis), m.
        4/9/1937 Martha Ruth Turner (div.). M. (2nd) Edith
        Howard Dillon
   Children by first wife:
56331131 Martha Paige Ayres (8/14/1939-   )
56331132 John Chambers Ayres III (3/4/1943-   )
   Child by second wife:
56331133 Janie Dillon Ayres (2/20/1949-   )

5634   David Walker Eldridge, m. Amanda Hooker

56344   Thomas Walker Eldridge (7/16/1868-7/17/1935), m. 11/22/
        1906 Maude Fore
56345   George Rolfe Eldridge (9/21/1870-   ), m. Pearl Gill
56346   Robert Randolph Eldridge (10/8/1874-   ), m. Caroline
        Vaughan

5635   Susan Bolling Eldridge (5/10/1830-7/5/1896), m. 3/7/1855
        Peter Sipe
56351   Nora Ann Sipe (8/21/1856-9/24/1919), m. 2/27/1874 Harrison
        Brown Jones
56352   Mary Wythe Sipe (7/27/1859-2/18/1925). Unm.
56353   Henry Walker Sipe (3/24/1863-5/13/1919). Unm.
56354   Florence Eldridge Sipe (1/20/1866-   ), m. 11/8/1894 Rev.
        Albert Sidney Johnson Rice

54355   Charles Kidder Sipe (5/1/1865-   ), m. a Missouri widow,
      Mrs. Gill

54356   Katherine Moorman Sipe (6/3/1871-8/10/1932), m. 12/31/1907
      Edward W. Patterson (9/7/1872-3/1/1948). She is bur. at
      Hanes Chapel, Buckingham County

5636   Courtney Wythe Eldridge

56364   Thomas Fleming Turner (8/26/1868-   )
56365   Harry Fowles Turner (12/29/1869-   ). In 1936, he was
      living at the old homeplace in Buckingham County

56367   Rolfe Eldridge Turner (7/17/1874-   )
5637   Mary Virginia Eldridge (3/19/1836-   )
56371   Jeminie Hales (9/4/1864-   )
56372   Annie Kidder Hales (10/16/1866-   ), m. _____ Cheatham
56373   Peter Clements Hales (11/1/1869-   ). Unm.
56374   Mary Courtney Hales (3/30/1872-   ). In 1936, living
      in Sheppards, VA. Unm.
56375   Susan Rolfe Hales (11/27/1874-   ). Unm.

58   It is believed that Martha Eldridge who married John Harris
    of Goochland was a daughter of Thomas and Judith Kennon
    Eldridge, and was not a descendant of Pocahontas. Martha's
    daughter Pamela Harris married Rev. Christopher MacRae and
    Martha's son (Pamela's brother) was Eldridge Harris (1764-
    1803). Wyndham Robertson apparently is in error on pages
    39 and 34 of his work POCAHONTAS AND HER DESCENDANTS (1887).
    See 46 V 172 and 267.

6112 Robert Emmet Robinson (d. 4/1/1835), m. Adeline Dewees.
     Indiana Henley (b. 3/24/1818).
61121 Robert Emmet Robinson, Jr. (ca. 1846-1/14/1878).
6113 Powhatan Robinson (1819-10/ /1882).
6114 Rebecca Murray Robinson (d. 5/5/1882).

6123 George N. Skipwith (10/22/1819-8/31/1874).

6124 Cornelia Lotte Skipwith (1816-12/27/1851), m. James Murray
     Whittle (9/18/1806-4/8/1891). Cornelia was related to and
     named for Cornelia Greene Skipwith (daughter of Gen.
     Nathaniel Greene and wife of Peyton Skipwith)

61241 Matoaka Whittle

612411 Matoaka Sims (5/ /1874-8/ /1874)

612412 James W. Sims (naval officer), m.   . Lived in
      Hampton, VA

6124121   Annie ("Nan") Tremaine Sims. Unm.

6124122   , m. Col. Eugene Outen.

612413   John H. Sims (d. 8/6/1935), m. Lydia   . Lived in
          Washington, D.C.

6125   Thomas Bolling Skipwith (b. 8/4/18___).

62   John Murray was an officer in the Revolution.
621   Edmund Randolph Yates married first Mary Deane (371)

621312   John Murray Yates III

623   Susanna Murray (also Susanna Murray Ruffin) died in church
         just as services were concluded. Theodoric Bland Ruffin
         was raised by Frances Bland.
6231   Jean Bland Ruffin (died while 62311 was "quite a child") m.
         Richard cocke
62311   Eliza Edmunds Cocke (7/24/1808-12/7/1885), m. 5/17/1826
         John Royall Robertson (10/1/1796-10/12/1884), son of John
         Archer Robertson who m. 1795 Elizabeth (Ann?) Royall.
         Div. granted 1/22/1814. They removed from Petersburg to
         Selma, Alabama in 1829 or 1830.
623111   Jean Ruffin Robertson (4/10/1826-8/27/1912), m. 10/1/1850
         George William Adams (1815-1853)

The Pocahontas Jug

A 6 1/2 inch tall, mushroom colored. salt-glazed stoneware
jug was acquired in 1987 by the Jamestown-Yorktown Foundation
from one of the Elwins. See POCAHONTAS' DESCENDANTS, pages 310-
311, and this volume page vi.

The jug, attributed to Hans Hilgers, Siegburg, ca. 1590, has
an "almost contemporary" but not original silver collar mount
incised "TMR".

The "TMR" is said by some to be for Thomas (Rolfe), for
Matoaka and for Rebecca.

One idea is that the jug was a gift to Pocahontas from Queen
Anne, wife of King James I, and another is that it may have been
the King's 1617 New Year gift to Pocahontas.

6231111 Catherine ("Kittie") Innes Adams (8/17/1851-6/28/1929),
         m. 11/17/1874 Wilson Bills Dobbins
62311111 Innes Wilson Dobbins (5/4/1876-11/13/1945), m. 12/20/
         1906 Mignonne Kathleen Murphey
623111111 Innes Wilson Dobbins, Jr. (b. 2/16/1908), m. 10/26/
         1935 Anne Cooper Parker
6231111111 Anne Cooper Dobbins (b. 7/13/1936)
6231111112 Innes Wilson Dobbins III (b. 10/1/1939)
6231111113 Stephen Adams Dobbins (b. 9/12/1943)
623111112 Jane Adams Dobbins (b. 10/8/1911), m. 12/7/1935
         Joseph Radford Gathright
6231111121 Joseph Radford Gathright, Jr. (b. 9/4/1941)
623111113 John Dunlap Dobbins (b. 8/29/1915), m. 9/20/1941 Sarah
         Helm
6231111131 John Dunlap Dobbins, Jr. (b. 10/8/1942)
6231111132 Robert Helm Dobbins (b. 6/6/1951)
62311112 Louise Emily Dobbins (b. 10/15/1878), m. Joseph
         Thompson Meadors, D.D.S. (d. 11/17/1948)
623111121 John Allen Meadors (b. 10/16/1903), m. 4/27/1938 Alma
         Campbell
623111122 Lily Minge Meadors (b. 4/16/1907), m. 12/27/1937 Mark
         Alfred Grant (d. 7/26/1952)
6231111221 Marion Louise Grant (b. 10/4/1938)
6231111222 Mark Alfred Grant, Jr. (3/18/1940-3/30/1940)
62311113 Jean Ruffin Dobbins (11/3/1880-7/10/1950), m. 4/27/1914
         James Preston Hoskins (d. 8/2/1948)
62311114 Lily Evelyn Dobbins (1/20/1883-4/11/1908), m. 3/7/1904
         Jackson Chadwick Minge
62311115 Olivia Hill Dobbins (b. 11/26/1888), m. 4/18/1911
         Charles P. Hatcher (d. 1/1/1939)
6231112 Willie Georgine Adams (11/3/1853-1/9/1951), m. 8/14/1893
         Lemuel Durant Hatch
623112 Richard Montgomery Robertson, M.D. (10/29/1829-10/13/
         1879)(b. Petersburg, d. Selma, AL), m. 1/17/1870 Helen
         Eloise Ferguson (6/5/1847-6/20/1930)(b. and d. in Selma,
         AL)
6231121 Anthony Ferguson Robertson (11/5/1870-10/11/1919), m.
         6/6/1894 Gertrude Jenkins (b. 3/21/1873)
62311211 Danelson Caffrey Jenkins Robertson (3/8/1896-2/12/1955)
         m. 8/11/1917 Maude Ethelnayer Bates
623112111 Marjorie Jean Robertson (b. 4/16/1920), m. Jack
         McCormack Howell
6231121111 Pamela Howell (b. 6/24/1941)
623112112 Donelson Anthony Robertson (b. 9/26/1926)
62311212 Parker Anthony Robertson (b. 1/7/1901), m. 4/23/1928
         Constance Margaret Schaetzle
623112121 Anthony Keith Robertson (b. 2/11/1930)
6231122 Ella Robertson (11/26/1871-3/5/1946)(b. Demodolis, AL,
         d. Selam), m. 9/6/1893 in Selma, Calvin Young, Jr.
         (6/6/1870-1/5/1935)(b. Polk, AL, d. Selma)
62311221 Richard Robertson Young (7/17/1894-5/10/1946), m. (1st)
         10/20/1919 Marion Hollister (10/4/1894-2/6/1928); m.
         (2nd) 3/29/1937 Mrs. Violet Ferrell
    Child by first wife:

623112211 Richard Robertson Young, Jr. (b. 4/24/1922-d. mid
           1980's), m. June Sealey in Chapel Hill, NC. Adopted
           two children.
623112?2   Caroline Rutherford Young (b. 2/6/1898)(b. and d. in
           Selma), m. 3/8/1923 in Selma, Vickers Rives Allen (4/
           19/1887-3/9/1967)(b. and d. in Selma)
623112??1 Elizabeth ("Betty") Rives Allen (b. 1/17/1928)(b. in
           Selma), m. 9/3/1947 in Selma, John Furniss Callaway
           (b. 9/21/1926 in Selma). Div. 8/1/1977
623112??11 John Furniss Callaway, Jr. (b. 9/28/1948), m. 7/9/
           1977 Teressa Marten
62311222111 Rachel Callaway (b. 12/1/1982)
623112??112 Michael John Callaway (b. 4/5/1984)
62311222113 Clare Alison Callaway (b. 12/20/1985)
623112??12 Vickers Allen Callaway (b. 10/19/1949), m. 1/9/1981
           Marilyn Jeffcoat
623112??121 Caroline Allen Callaway (b. 11/14/1983)
62311222122 Vickers Allen Callaway, Jr. (b. 1/23/1986)
62311222123 William Benjamin Callaway (b. 12/7/1988)
623112??13 James Callaway (12/4/1950-12/6/1950)
623112??14 James Alison Callaway (b. 10/9/1952-11/22/1972)
623112??2 Nell Vickers Allen (b. 5/13/1936), m. 6/15/1955
           William James Samford II of Opelika, AL
623112??21 Mary Catherine Samford (b. 9/11/1958)
623112?222 William Allen Samford (b. 8/9/1960)
623112?2?3 Thomas Matthew Samford (b. 9/18/1962)
623112?3   Pauline Edmunds Young (b. 12/9/1902-3/28/1985), m. 3/
           31/1924 William Richard Thixton (8/9/1892-12/13/1977)
623112?31 William Richard Thixton, Jr. (b. 1/3/1930). M. Div.
           No issue.
623112?32 Thomas Calvin Thixton (b. 2/10/1932), m. 3/ /1956
           Audrey French. Div. 1978
623112?321 Thomas Calvin Thixton, Jr. (b. 8/18/1959)
623112?322 Daniel French Thixton (b. 5/2/1961)
623112?3?3 Pauline LaVere Thixton (b. 11/26/1962)
623112?33 Jane Thixton (b. 3/5/1937), m. (1st) Milton Lee
           Williams. Div. M. (2nd) Jerry McKenna
   Children by first husband:
623112?331 Mark Lawrence Williams (b. 12/24/1959)
623112?332 Melinda Lee Williams (b. 4/18/1963), m. Brad Deeman
623112?4   Calvin Young III (3/2/1905-10/18/1967), m. (1st) 8/31/
           1937 Sophia Murawiec. Div. M. (2nd) 10/10/1941 Florine
           Snider
623112?5   Emily Ferguson Young (b. 7/2/1909), m. 9/23/1931 Thomas
           Murray Greer (10/2/1901-1/26/1986)
623112?51 Emily Ann Greer (b. 4/10/1933), m. 7/14/1962 James G.
           Lockard
623112?511 Laura Ann Lockard (9/8/1963), m. 12/17/1988 Randall
           Huffman
623112?512 Elizabeth Irene Lockard (b. 1/13/1968)
623112?52 Eloise Greer (b. 7/29/1935), m. 10/6/1952 Ray Alen
           Moore
623112?521 Ray Alan Moore, Jr. (b. 7/22/1953), m. 4/25/1987
           Alison Byers McBryde

62311225P2 Thomas Greer Moore (b. 1/7/1955), m. 6/11/1977 Laurie
            Lyn Dean
62311225221 Amanda Michelle Moore (b. 4/17/1980)
62311225222 Shelby Lynn Moore (b. 10/9/1985)
62311225P3 Ann Young Greer (b. 4/11/1958), m. 3/17/1979 Wendell
            Fred Stephens
62311225231 Sara Louise Stephens (b. 3/25/1985)
62311225232 Murray Lee Stephens (b. 5/12/1987)
6231122253 Murray Thomas Greer, Jr. (b. 10/13/1940), m. 11/23/
            1962 Rosalie White
62311225231 Vivian Lee Greer (b. 10/13/1965)
62311225232 Susan Renee Greer (b. 3/1/1967)
62311225233 Murray Thomas Greer III (b. 10/13/1971)
623113 Julian Robertson (b. 9/10/1830-d. inf.)
623114 Elizabeth Royall Robertson (10/23/1832-11/30/1900), m.
        4/3/1856 Dr. Joseph Asbury Groves (6/5/1830-11/24/1923)
6231141 John Courtenay Groves (8/17/1857-1/3/1909), m. 1882
         Evelyn Vaughan
62311411 Joseph Courtenay Groves (legally changed to John
          Courtenay Groves, Jr.)(2/22/1883-4/29/1933), m. 6/1/
          1909 Lillian Newell
623114111 Lillian Evelyn Groves (b. 5/10/1911), m. (1st) 5/31/
           1933 Archie Van Aken. Div. M. (2nd) 12/ /1944 Nelson
           Newman
    Child by first husband:
623114111 Vivienne Elayne Van Aken (b. 2/10/1936)
    Children by second husband:
6231141112 Berry Newman (b. 2/23/1946)
6231141113 Barbara Newman (b. 1/18/1950)
623114112 Vivienne Elise Groves (b. 8/29/1912), m. (1st) 6/6/
           1934 Dr. Fred Keeler Shaw. Div. M. (2nd) 8/31/1944
           Dr. Ronald Lorne Hamilton
    Children by first husband:
6231141121 Mary Louise Shaw (b. 12/19/1936), m. 3/19/1955 Roger
            Glenn Teumer
6231141122 Robert Frederick Shaw (b. 7/7/1940)
623114113 John Courtenay Groves III (b. 10/11/1914), m. 1946
           Margaret Whitaker
6231141131 Vivienne Elise Groves (b. 8/27/1953)
623114114 George Cunningham Groves (10/25/1916-2/ /1948). Unm.
623114115 Elizabeth Groves (b. 5/11/1924), m. 5/ /1945 Louis
           Altamari
6231141151 Jeffrey George Altamari (b. 10/29/1949)
6231141152 Michael John Altamari (b. 12/29/1952)
6231141153 Christopher Louis Altamari (b. 5/10/1954)
623114P Joseph Asbury Groves, Jr. (7/21/1859-11/24/1894), m.
         1890 Drusilla Maryman (d. 10/27/1891)
6231143 Royall Robertson Groves (9/17/1860-10/29/1881). Unm.
6231144 William Harvie Groves (7/23/1865-1/26/1885). Unm.
6231145 Elizabeth Royall Groves (6/21/1868-2/17/1946). Unm.
6231146 Mary Louisa Harvie Groves (b. 1/31/1871), m. 5/3/1894
         Charles Henry Hopson (12/23/1865-1/2/1941)
62311461 Elizabeth ("Bessie") Louise Hopson (b. 6/13/1895). Unm.
62311462 Mary Evelyn Hopson (b. 5/22/1897). Unm.

6231147 James Alston Groves (10/28/1873-11/13/1945). Unm.
623115 Royall Robertson (b. 12/22/1834-d. inf.)
623116 Ann Eliza Robertson (b. 6/25/1836), m. 11/8/1855 Thomas
        Moseby Cunningham (7/24/1829-1878)
6231161 Mary Lee Cunningham (b. 8/17/1856), m. Peter Conrey
        James
6231162 Eliza Cunningham (b. 11/18/1858), m. 9/16/1879 Eyre
        Damer
62311621 Eyre Damer, Jr. (2/17/1883-6/1/1927), m. 8/22/1916
        Grace Lightbourn
623116211 Eyre Damer III (8/20/1919-1/4/1948). Unm.
623116212 Darrel Damer (b. 3/11/1922), m. 2/4/1942 Margaret
        Howard
6231162121 Darrel Willis Damer (b. 9/1/1944)
6231162122 Margaret Elaine Damer (b. 4/2/1948)
6231163 Anne Bondurant Cunningham (b. 2/7/1861). Unm.
6231164 George Adams Cunningham (3/23/1863-12/28/1928), m. 5/10/
        1893 Mary Gaillard Pickens
6231165 Leila Cunningham (1865-1878)
6231166 Carrie Shields Cunningham (10/10/1867-5/20/1894), m.
        Benjamin Diggs
62311661 Carrie C. Diggs (b. 5/20/1894), m. 6/30/1932 Walter
        Henderson-Cleland
623116611 John George Walter Henderson-Cleland (b. 7/10/1933)
6231167 Thomas Cunningham (1869-10/25/1885)
6231168 Loula Parke Cunningham (b. 11/18/1871-3/15/1950), m.
        12/11/1903 Frederick Bracey
62311681 Smith Herbert Bracey (b. 4/8/1905), m. 12/23/1938 Helen
        Paris
623116811 Helen Gaillard Bracey (b. 7/17/1943)
623116812 Linde Bracey (b. 12/31/1951)
62311682 William Gordon Bracey (b. 8/31/1910), m. 12/11/1934
        Myrtle Gragg
623116821 Margaret Ann Bracey (b. 1/9/1936)
623116822 William Gordon Bracey, Jr. (b. 2/7/1937)
62311683 Ann Elizabeth Bracey (b. 2/7/1907), m. 9/30/1931 Pryor
        Walker Fitts
623116831 Frederick Bracey Fitts (b. 9/27/1935). Adopted.
623116832 Mary Parke Fitts (b. 9/24/1949). Adopted.
6231169 Katherine Cunningham (b. 1874-d. inf.)
623116x William Gordon Cunningham (b. 9/15/1876). Unm.
623117 John Royall Robertson, Jr. (b. 11/23/1838). Unm.

63 Anne Murray, m. Neil Buchanan

631 Anne Buchanan, m. Richard Cross

6312 Richard Cross, m. Anna Macklin (Maclin)

63121 John Bolling Cross, m. Elizabeth Armstrong

631211 Richard Cross, m. Elizabeth McMillan

6312111 Kimball Allyn Cross, m. Fredonia Rosalie Perry

63121111 Thomas Jones Cross, m. May Barr

631211111 Bolling Allyn Cross, m. Nell Lemon

6312111111 Katherine Sterling Cross, m. Paul E. Haygood

63121111111 Paul Meriwether Haygood, m. Charlotte Smither

631211111111 Charlotte Hardie Haygood

631211111112 Katherine Sterling Haygood

63121111112 Dr. Bolling Cross Haygood

63121111113 Katherine Sterling Haygood, m. Dr. Walker Pettit
          McVea

6312111112 May Bolling Cross, m. Frederick Ancrum Lord Holloway

63121111121 Nell Cross Holloway, m. William Iselin

631211111211 Sarah Bolling Iselin

631211111212 Eleanor Jay Iselin

63121111122 Frederic Lord Holloway

63121111123 Mary Bolling Holloway, m. John Barto McEntire III

631211111231 Katherine Stirling McEntire

631211111232 Harriet Bolling McEntire

631211111233 John Barto McEntire IV

63121111124 Anne Howard Holloway, m. William Heywood Stone III

631211111241 William Heywood Stone IV

6312111113 Thomas Jones Cross II, m. Vivian Landry

63121111131 Thomas Jones Cross III

63121111132 Kimball Allyn Cross

63121111133 Perry Landry Cross

64 Thomas Gordon and his second wife, Elizabeth Baird, are
    buried in Blandford Cemetery, Petersburg.

6411121 through 641138 and 64114 through 6411452 probably should
    be Baskerville and not Baskervill.

64131 Ann Gordon Coleman, m. Mark Alexander.

652 Mary Ann Davies (1789-1869), m. 1804 Fortescue Whittle.

Peter Gay

        In   the   Paris   (Indiana)   Cemetery adjacent to Boyleston in
Clinton County, there is a simple,   rather old   stone marker that
reads:

> Peter Gay
> War 1812
> 1785-1865
> Descendant
> of
> Pocahontas

        Query: Is this Peter Gay a son of Capt. William Gay (41)
and of his third wife, Judith Scott?

        Peter Gay entered the service on 7/26/1812 at Sharpsburg,
Maryland, being drafted to serve a three month's term in Capt.
William Curtis' Company, Captain   Coles' Regiment, Maryland
Militia (Infantry), a unit that was under the command of General
Stansbury.

        Captain Coles' regiment, raised in Sharpsburg, consisted
of about 80 men.

        The Company marched to Baltimore (Fair Camp) and engaged in
the Battle of Bladensburg.   Distance travelled 200 miles.

        Peter Gay was discharged in Baltimore on 10/1/1813.

652185   Ruth Drewry Whittle (d. 2/26/1920), m. Robert Thruston
          Hubard III (d. 1963)(134231).
6521851   Walter Lee Penn, Jr. (d. 10/18/1975).
65218511 Walter Lee Penn III, m. (1st) 1/23/1971 (Div. 8/3/1976)
          Barbara Pierce, dau. of Frederick G. Pierce, M.D., and
          his wife, the former Dorothy Allen. Walter Lee Penn
          III and his wife Barbara adopted 12/3/1971 John
          Christian Penn (9/20/1970-   ).
          Walter Lee Penn III, m. (2nd) 4/23/1983 Melinda Hiscox
          Carter (4/18/1941-   ), dau. of Harold William Hiscox
          and his wife, the former Freda Elizabeth Meyer.
          Melinda's children by previous marriages:
          (a) William Letcher Pannill, Jr. (8/29/1968-   ).
          (b) Coates Randolph Carter (7/18/1971-   ).
65218512 Robert Hubard Penn (5/28/1945-   ), m. 7/28/1978,
          Carla Bearns Addicks (11/4/1946-   )(Div. 10/20/1980),
          dau. of Charles Berns and his wife, the former Ivah
          Lee.
6521852   Robert Thruston Hubard IV (11/25/1914-5/19/1982).
6521853   Ruth Whittle Hubard (9/21/1917-   ).
6521854   Mary Stafford Hubard (9/21/1917-   ), m. 6/16/1975
          Ralph Lucian Payne (1/16/1916-   )(Div. 12/11/1972),
          son of Grover Cleveland Payne and his wife, the former
          Ruth Virginia Deeton.
65218541 Mary Stafford Payne (12/19/1950-   ), m. 6/26/197__
          David Robert Wilson (7/11/1951-   ), son of Sam
          Wilson and his wife, the former Marjorie Alice
          Connolly.
652185411 Diana Broughton Wilson (9/16/1981-   ).
65218542 Sarah Hubard Payne (1/31/1953-   ), m. 8/12/1972
          Joseph Robert Beauchamp, Jr. (3/16/1951-   ), son of
          Joseph Robert Beauchamp and his wife, the former
          Elizabeth Lev Robinson.
652185421 Rebecca Lev Beauchamp (4/29/1976-   ).
652185422 Ann Sinclair Beauchamp (3/12/1979-   ).
652185423 Emily Whittle Beauchamp (5/5/1981-   ).
6521855   Stafford Whittle Hubard (3/1/1912-5/11/1912).

652187   Kennon Caithness Whittle (d. 11/10/1967).
6521871   Mary Holt Whittle, m. 10/19/1946 Horatio Nelson Woodson
          (3/26/1909-7/22/1970), son of Walter Henderson Woodson
          and his wife, the former Pauline Bernhardt.
65218711 Walter Nelson Woodson (2/2/1950-   ), m. 5/30/1981
          Alexandra Waschenko (1/2/1958-   ), dau. of Gleb
          Waschenko and his wife, the former Mary Gelement.
65218712 Mary Holt Woodson (5/27/1952-   ), m. 6/19/1982 James
          Gunn Murphy, Jr. (8/31/1952-   ), son of James Gunn
          Murphy and his wife, the former Stella Lasitter.
652187121 James Gunn Murphy III (11/16/1983-   ).
6521872   Stafford Gorman Whittle III (9/29/1924-   ), m. (1st)
          6/26/1947 Elizabeth Martin (1/2/1927-   ), dau. of
          Duval Martin and his wife, the former Maude _____.

Div. M. (2nd) 5/24/1981 Ethel Rakes Sharp (9/27/1923-
).
Children by first wife:
65218721 Mary Clark Whittle (5/13/1948-   ), m. 9/19/1981
Leslie Meriwether German (6/19/1947-   ), son of
Leslie German and his wife, the former Mary Elizabeth
Scales.
65218722 Stafford Gorman Whittle IV (11/17/1950-12/3/1983).
6521873 Kennon Caithness Whittle, Jr. (3/15/1932-   ), m. (1st)
6/30/1962 Jane Gregory (4/ /1941-   ), dau. of John
Gregory and his wife, the former Lou Dillard Nissen.
Div. M. (2nd) 11/ /1981 Sigrid Lynn Harrison.
Children by first wife:
65218731 Kennon Caithness Whittle III (12/8/1964-   ).
65218732 John Gregory Whittle (4/4/1968-   ).

652189 William Murray Whittle (d. 7/21/1960). His wife, the
former Alice Hairston Glenn, d. 3/7/1983. Her mother
(Mrs. James Dodge Glenn) was the former Sarah Staples
Hairston.

65218911 William Clarence Kluttz, Jr. (11/19/1946-   ), m.
7/5/1969 Susan Elizabeth Wear, dau. of John Edmund
Wear and his wife, the former Susie Nelson Hester.
652189111 William Clarence Kluttz III (10/5/1971-   ).
652189112 Susan Whittle Kluttz (5/21/1976-   ).
65218912 Robert Hairston Kluttz (8/3/1948-   ), m. 5/1/1971
Bess Acra Adams (2/5/1948-   ), dau. of George
Hackney Adams and his wife, the former Hennie Green
Wallace.
652189121 Robert Hairston Kluttz, Jr. (8/18/1974-   ).
652189122 Sarah Whittle Kluttz (10/27/1975-   ).
652189123 Branch Adams Kluttz (6/19/1982-   ).
65218913 Joseph Branch Craige Kluttz (3/2/1951-   ), m. 8/23
1975 Mary Carey Nealon (7/6/1951-   ), dau. of
William Kennedy Nealon and his wife, the former Rita
Marie Carey.
652189131 Carey Hairston Kluttz (9/14/1981-   ).
652189132 Joseph Branch Craige Kluttz, Jr. (8/2/1983-   ).
65218914 James Whittle Kluttz (9/7/1954-   ), m. 8/28/1982
Courtney Alston Horner, dau. of Guy Thomas Horner
and his wife, the former Katherine Brice Macon.
652189141 James Whittle Kluttz, Jr. (6/9/1984-   ).

661 Edmund Harrison (1764-1826) of "The Oaks", Amelia County.
M. (2nd) 1806 Martha Wayles Skipwith, dau. of Col. Henry
S. Skipwith, and had issue.

6616 Julia Harrison (b. 12/ /1796).

Memorial

of

Brett Randolph, Jr. (222)

The memorial of Brett Randolph a resident of the county of
Amelia state of Va. - Your Memorialist begs leave to represent
your Honb. body, that he was born in the county of Gloustershire,
of England, on the 17th of Feby. 1760 - that his father & grandfather were both natives of Va. - that his father was sent to
England for his education, & sometime in the year 1752 inter-
married with Mary Scott a native of Wales, being then about 20
years of age. On the 4th Septr. 1759 he departed this life
leaving to his posthumous son a moiety of his estate in Va.-
that his mother departed this life in the month of Novr. 1779---
Shortly afterwards your memorialist took passage on a Merchant-
man, one of the West India fleet bound to St. Christopher's
under convoy of Commodore Walsingham - From St. Eustatius he took
passage in a Brig bound to Baltimore & reached Richmond about the
20th of Augt. 1780 - The next day, having letters for Mr. Edmund
Randolph, from his father, then in London, waited on him &
delivered said letters & by his advice took the oath of
allegiance to the U.S. - After taking possession of his estate he
was enrolled in the militia, & served a short tour under Capt.
Robert Bolling, in Jany. 1781, now living in Petersburg, who was
dispatched to watch the movement of Arnold, then descending James
River. Shortly afterwards he joined a troop of Cavalry under
Capt. Carter Page, was with LaFayette when he cannonaded
Perersburg from Archer's hill opposite thereto, & continued in
the troop till Genl. LaFayette formed a junction with Genl. Wayne
wch. took place at Raccoon ford in the county of Orange - On one
occasion Genl. LaFayette addressed Capt. Page in the following
terms - "Capt. Page, the correct information respecting the
british army, which you have communicate to me, demands my
warmest acknowledgements to you & your troop of Cavalry, as
perhaps it has been the salvation of the american army; should we
come to an action, you shall be placed on the right wing"---
Some where in the upper end of Hanover Genl. Thos. Nelson stated
to Capt. Page that there were letters of great inportance to be
delivered to Thos. Jefferson then Governor of the State as soon
as possible - Your Memorialist undertook to deliver them, reached
Orange Court-house that night & got to Monticello next morning to
breakfast---After reading the letters, the contents of wch were
that it was probable that Col. Tarlton would make an attempt to
capture the Assembly then sitting at Charlottesville - Mr.
Jefferson began to pack up his books, & after finishing his
dispatches for Baron Steuben then stationed at the point of fork,
your memorialist left Monticello & delivered them the same day-
the next day he returned to headquarters which were at Orange
Court-house - The result of Tarlton's expedition is well known-
on his return from Charlottesville, he formed a junction with
Col. Simcoe at the point of Fork, but Baron Steuben had crossed
James River & retreated to the South ---when the assembly was

sitting in Staunton, your Memorialist was dispatched with letters
for Genl. Stevens - on ascending the blue ridge, he was arrested
by a party of riflemen, who insisted that he was one of Tarlton's
light-horse, that he was an an englishman, & that his cloaths
were made in England - the first assertion he denied, the fact he
agreed to having on a waistcoat wch was made in England -After
shewing them an appointment of a Lieutenancy (in one of the
Legions to be raised for the defense of the State) which he had
in his pocket, & stating to them that the detention of the letter
for Genl. Stevens might be of serious consequence, he was
suffered to proceed - staid that night at a tavern on the top of
the blue ridge & reached Staunton next morning before Genl.
Stephens had risen from his bed. On his return his horse gave
out & he was compelled to purchase another, having no authority
to impress one --- In conclusion your Memorialist takes leave to
observe that his services, tho humble, have been render'd at his
own expense - that he furnished a Negro man to work on the fort
then called Hood's on James river without receiving any
compensation---that he has been the father of ten children, two
of wch (died)--that soon after the death of his wife wch happen'd
in the month of Jany. 1820, he divided his property amongst his
surviving children they stipulating to pay him $30 cash annually
- some of them have failed to comply with the stipulation, wch is
the cause of this present application --- that he has suffered
much from Lawsuits & surety-ship, has been frequently warranted
for small sums, is now in the 73d year of his age, & as it is
natural for mankind at his time of life (such is his
temper) to seek repose & tranquility, your Memorialist solicits
some pecuniary aid from his adopted country, & as in duty bound
he will forever pray - Amelia County, Va.
Novr. 13th, 1833.
P.S. Altho the troop of cavalry under Captn. Page consisted of
nearly 100 - it is believed that your Memorialist is the only
survivor.

                    Memorial of Brett
                    Randolph
                to be delivered to Lawyer
                    Nash - Powhatan Cty.
                I have found the copy you gave
                me last year, & now return
                you the original by Mr.
                Stratton.
                        JMN

                        Notes

St. Christopher's or St. Kitts.
Commodore Walsingham - Commodore the Honorable Robert Boyle
Walsingham.
Col. Tarlton - Banastre Tarleton. (Note e in Tarleton).
Col. Simcoe - John Graves Simcoe (1752-1806).
Genl. Stevens/Stephens - Edward Stephens.
Lawyer Nash - James M. Nash.

Index

NOTE: The name of the spouse of a Pocahontas descendant is indexed even though that spouse is not a descendant of Pocahontas, but the name ·of a parent of such a spouse is not indexed unless, of course, that parent is a descendant of Pocahontas.

Allen, and Michael John 6231141152
Anderson, Cyndee 2415341231
Anderson, Donna Sue Young 222183221
Anderson, Edward Clifton 241x11
Anderson, James Enoch 222183221
Anderson, James Eric 2221832212
Anderson, Jane Margaret Randolph 241x11
Anderson, Monica Dawn 2221832211
Andrews, Alice Morse 1322988
Andrews, Alvaree 1322989
Andrews, Charles Phelps 132298712
Andrews, Charles Robin 222183461
Andrews, Colleen Frances Chambless 132298712
Andrews, Daniel 1322983
Andrews, Daniel Eddins III 132298322
Andrews, Daniel Eddins Jr. 13229832
Andrews, Deborah Lynn 1322987112
Andrews, Elizabeth Bland Armistead 1414x242
Andrews, Elizabeth Eddins 132298
Andrews, Eula Lee Seay 1322987
Andrews, Florence Crandall 13229871
Andrews, Ginny Lee Lam 222183461
Andrews, Glenda Faye Hudson 132298711
Andrews, Jack 13229823

Andrews, Josephus Green 1322987
Andrews, Josephus Green Jr. 13229871
Andrews, Lawrence Duane 1322987113
Andrews, Lawrence Ross 132298711
Andrews, Mae Decima 1322981
Andrews, Mark Phelps 1322987122
Andrews, Mary Elizabeth 132298321
Andrews, Mary Lou Ellen Wade 13229832
Andrews, Mary Lou Kennedy 1322982
Andrews, Michelia Jo 1322987111
Andrews, Dr. Reddin 132298
Andrews, Reddin 1322984
Andrews, Richard Warren 1322989
Andrews, Robert 1322985
Andrews, Ruth Dana 13229831
Andrews, Ruth Ford 1322983
Andrews, Travis 13229821
Andrews, Virginia Meredith 1322986
Andrews, William 1322982
Andrews, William Jr. 13229822
Andrews, William Ronald 1414x242
Anne, Queen p. 129
Antes, Leland 13229812
Antes, Leland Jr. 132298121
Antes, May Bess Wood 13229812
Anthony, Mary Chatfield 24196241
Archer, 125141
Archer, Alexander Hamilton 12116
Archer, Alexander Hamilton III 1211641
Archer, Alexander Hamilton IV 12116411
Archer, Alexander Hamilton, Jr. 121164
Archer, Alexander Hamilton V 121164111
Archer, Bessie Manning 121161
Archer, Catharine Jefferson 12517
Archer, Cornelia Whelan Randolph 125114
Archer, Cornelia Whelan Randolph 2211321
Archer, Dave Tibbs 12116414
Archer, Davis Manning 1211642
Archer, Dorothy Bryant 1251142
Archer, Dorothy Delores Bryant 22113212
Archer, Edmund Minor 24134654
Archer, Edward 1217
Archer, Edward Cunningham 12512
Archer, Col. Edward P. 125
Archer, Edwin 12111
Archer, Elizabeth 121
Archer, Elizabeth Carpenter 1211643
Archer, Elizabeth Featherstone Price 1211
Archer, Elva Sanford Bell 125113
Archer, Field 121
Archer, Field 1211
Archer, Field 1216
Archer, Frances Anne 12116413

Archer, Frances Tibbs 1211641
Archer, India Reeder 121162
Archer, Jacob 12112
Archer, Jacob Michaux 12514
Archer, James McIlwaine 125113

Archer, John Walthall 12513
Archer, John Walthall 332426
Archer, Liesa Bolling 12511?
Archer, Liesa Bolling 241b161
Archer, Littleton 12114
Archer, Margaret India 1211644
Archer, Margaret Jones Walthall 1211
Archer, Martha Bolling 121
Archer, Martha Elizabeth 125115
Archer, Martha Woodson 12518
Archer, Martha Woodson Michaux 1251
Archer, Mary Alabama Horn 121164
Archer, Mary Bell 1251131
Archer, Mary Bolling 332425
Archer, Mary Finley 125111
Archer, Mary Finley McIlwaine 12511
Archer, Mary Ilwaine 1251141
Archer, Mary Jefferson Bolling 125
Archer, Mary Rhodes 1211643
Archer, Mary Susan 12516
Archer, Norman Randolph 1251142
Archer, Norman Randolph 22113212
Archer, Peter Jefferson 1251
Archer, Peter Jefferson 125114
Archer, Peter Jefferson 2211321
Archer, Pocahontas Bolling 12519
Archer, Powhatan Bolling 1211
Archer, Richard 24134
Archer, Robert P. 12515
Archer, Sarah Walthall ("Sally") 12515
Archer, Sheppard 24134652
Archer, Taylor Clements 1211643
Archer, Taylor Manning 12116412
Archer, Terry Alan 12116431
Archer, Thomas Jefferson 12115
Archer, Virginia Page Hobson 24134
Archer, William 12113
Archer, William Segar 12511
Archer, William Wharton, Jr. 24134653
Archer, Willie Eilleen 121163
Archer, Winifred Trent 12116411
Arduino, Joanna 111326531
Arkin, Norma Gullett 222183361
Armistead, Ann Harrison 1414x6
Armistead, Anne 1414x23
Armistead, Eliza P. Trueheart 1651
Armistead, Elizabeth Bland 1414x242
Armistead, Estelle Ruffin Marks 1414x5
Armistead, George Ajax 1414x
Armistead, George Clayton 1414x2
Armistead, George Clayton III 1414x211
Armistead, George Clayton Jr. 1414x21
Armistead, Jeanne Banister 1414xx
Armistead, John Clayton 1414x5
Armistead, John Graff 1414x24
Armistead, John Grant III 12511411
Armistead, John Grant Jr. 1251141
Armistead, Margaret Bottomly 1414x212
Armistead, Margaret Skinner 1414x21
Armistead, Maria Page 1652
Armistead, Maria von Mebes 1414x241
Armistead, Maria von Mebes Perts 1414x24
Armistead, Mary Bland 1414x22
Armistead, Mary Jeffrey 1414x4
Armistead, Mary Ilwaine Archer 1251141
Armistead, Mary Susannah Bland 1414x
Armistead, Mary White Graff 1414x2
Armistead, Peter Jefferson 12511412
Armistead, Robert Fontaine 12511413
Armistead, Sallie Bland 1414xa
Armistead, Theodorick Bland 1414x3
Armistead, Theresa Simmons 1414x25
Armistead, Virginia Harrison 1414x1
Armistead, William Skinner 1414x213
Armstrong, Elizabeth 63121
Armstrong, Phillippa Alexander Bruce Shepperson 1653171
Armstrong, Tiffney Haley 1653171
Arnold, Prof. Benjamin William, Jr. 2231111
Arnold, Benjamin William III 22311111
Arnold, Carrie 1322844
Arnold, Douglas Anderson (daughter) 22311112
Arnold, Elizabeth Poole 22311113
Arnold, Mary St. George ("Saintie") Tucker Jackson 2231111

-G-

-I-

-J-

-K-

-L-

Randolph, Rebecca Anne Dulany McElhone 2421721
Randolph, Richard 21332
Randolph, Richard 2417
Randolph, Richard IV 211c
Randolph, Richard, Jr. 21
Randolph, Lt. Richard Hunter Dulany 24217212
Randolph, Richard Kidder 2221
Randolph, Richard Montague 222136
Randolph, Richard Rutherford III 21332421
Randolph, Richard Rutherford IV 213324211
Randolph, Rittenhouse S. 213322
Randolph, Robbie Rennie 241964121
Randolph, Dr. Robert Carter 2133
Randolph, Robert Carter ("Bobs") IV 24217712
Randolph, Robert Carter 2421782221
Randolph, Robert Carter V 242177121
Randolph, Robert Hubard (or Carter) 2414921
Randolph, Robert Lee III 241c11331
Randolph, Robert Mann 241493
Randolph, Robert Renshaw 2421722
Randolph, Robert Ryland 2141
Randolph, Rosalie Fitzhugh 241533542

Randolph, Rosalie O'Fallon 241533314
Randolph, Rose Dorsey 2415184
Randolph, Ruth Moore 24196252
Randolph, Ryland 2141
Randolph, Ryland 27
Randolph, Ryland McKenzie 213324212
Randolph, Sara Sears 24217212
Randolph, Sarah Lavinia Epes 241532
Randolph, Sarah McKay 2419841
Randolph, Sarah Nicholas 24142c
Randolph, Septima Anne 2414a
Randolph, Smith 213323
Randolph, Susan Caroline 241x123524
Randolph, Susan Eaton Browne 24192
Randolph, Susan Frances 221x
Randolph, Susan Gordon Dabney 242177123
Randolph, Susannah 223
Randolph, Theodorick Beverley 213x
Randolph, Theodorick Bland 213x
Randolph, Theodorick Tudor p. iv
Randolph, Thomas Eston 2419
Randolph, Thomas Eston 241921
Randolph, Thomas Eston 241983
Randolph, Thomas Hayward 241962
Randolph, Thomas Isham 242
Randolph, Thomas Jefferson IV 241x122
Randolph, Thomas Mann p. 108, 2414
Randolph, Thomas Mann 24192
Randolph, Thomas Nelson Carter 242177125
Randolph, Vallee Joseph 2419611
Randolph, Violet Speed Webb 2221384
Randolph, Virginia 222135
Randolph, Virginia 241c
Randolph, Virginia Cary 241x5
Randolph, Virginia Davis 24196242
Randolph, Virginius 2415343
Randolph, William 2415
Randolph, William 2419222
Randolph, William Brown 241922
Randolph, William Duval 241984
Randolph, William Eston 241532
Randolph, William Eston 24191
Randolph, William Lewis 241x12
Randolph, William Mann 241x1
Randolph, William Mann III 241x12352
Randolph, William Mayer 241511
Randolph, Col. William Wellford 242174
Raney, Barbara Hope Randolph 24196243
Raney, Denver McLaren 241962432
Raney, Diane Elizabeth 241962431
Raney, James Randolph 241962434
Raney, Joseph Bartlet 24196243
Raney, Joseph Bartlet, Jr. 241962432
Raney, Mary Annette 241962433
Rareshide, Louise Mallory 2419851
Rast, Beverly Ann Roberts 2212x711
Rast, Beverly Jan 2212x7113
Rast, Earl Henderson 2212x711
Rast, Stephanie Ann 2212x7111
Rast, Susan Earle 2212x7112

Ratcliffe, Catherine Eppes Buckner 24193475
Ratcliffe, William E. 24193475
Rawlings, Anne Tucker 142322113
Rawlings, Elizabeth Claxton 14232213
Rawlings, Elizabeth Tucker 1423221111
Rawlings, Emily Hume 14232214
Rawlings, Emily Hume Alfriend 1423221
Rawlings, Evelina Tucker Trapnell 14232211
Rawlings, Frances Bland 14232212
Rawlings, Hunter Ripley 1423221
Rawlings, Hunter Ripley III 142322111
Rawlings, Hunter Ripley IV 1423221112
Rawlings, Hunter Ripley Jr. 14232211
Rawlings, Irene M. Kukawa 142322111
Rawlings, Mary Blair 14232215
Rawlings, Rebecca Trapnell 142322112
Ray, Evelyn 22125313
Reade, Frank 111x411
Reade, Jean Cunningham 111x411
Redfield, Aubin Wells 331x2311
Redfield, Aubin Wells 331x23123
Redfield, Doris 331x2312
Redfield, Frances Carey 331x23122
Redfield, Jane Wells 331x2313
Redfield, Julie Louise 331x23121
Redfield, Louise Zabriskie 331x231
Redfield, Nancy Fawcett 331x2312
Redfield, William F. 331x231
Redfield, William F. 331x2312
Redmon, Barbara A. 331x2241
Redmon, Jean Antoinette Wells 331x224
Redmon, William Virgil 331x224
Reed, Brett Randolph 2135214
Reed, Gladys Dudley Hatfield 22125426
Reed, Loyd Lee 22125426
Reed, Marsha Carol 221254261
Reeder, Lloyd Richard 132298311
Reeder, Lloyd Richard Jr. 1322983112
Reeder, Michael Ray 1322983113
Reeder, Ruth Ann Williams 132298311
Reeder, Ruth Ellen 1322983111
Reeder, Susan Elizabeth 1322983114
Rees, Harriett 36673
Rees, John 36674
Rees, Mary Ellen 36671
Rees, Samuel 36675
Rees, Susan Bernard 3667
Rees, Thomas 36672
Rees, William 3667
Register, Estella Denise Brock 2212x41112
Register, Richard Carlton 2212x41112
Register, Travis 2212x411122
Register, Wendy Denise 2212x411121
Reihes, Elizabeth Ann 241934781
Reich, Bradley 331x23122
Reich, Frances Carey Redfield 331x23122
Reich, Jason 331x231221
Reid, Anne Randolph 21352162
Reid, Augusta Randolph 2135213
Reid, Barbara Jean Hillyer 21352151
Reid, Brett Bradley 21352164
Reid, Brett Elizabeth 213521522
Reid, Camilla 213521523
Reid, Carolyn Walker 21352161
Reid, Ellen Clarke 213521512
Reid, Evelin Svec 21352152
Reid, Capt. George Harrison 21352152
Reid, Ione Harrison 2135215
Reid, John Bryan 2135215
Reid, John Bryan III 213521514
Reid, John Bryan IV 213521521
Reid, John Bryan, Jr. 21352151
Reid, John Randolph 21352165
Reid, Laura 213521513
Reid, Linda 213521511
Reid, Madelon Calais 2135215
Reid, Marion Ethel 21352163
Reid, Oliver Fowlkes 2135216
Reid, Rubin Leroy 21352161
Reid, Victor Randolph 213521515
Reiley, Richardson 241934x1
Reilly, Audrey Elizabeth 2212x6223
Reilly, Brian John 2212x6222

-S-

-Y-

-Z-

Second

CORRECTIONS

and

ADDITIONS

to

POCAHONTAS' DESCENDANTS

by

Stuart E. Brown, Jr., Lorraine F. Myers
and Eileen M. Chappel

THE POCAHONTAS FOUNDATION

1994

The Powhatan group as well as other
Indians were "neither savages nor sons of
the devil, but human beings possessing some
of the virtues and voices common to mankind".
Robert Beverley, Jr.
(ca. 1667 or 1668-4/21/1722)

Acknowledgements

Much of the data included in this volume was obtained
from or through the assistance of the following persons and
organizations: Lorene Barry; Robert M. Bartell; Lula Lee Morris
Boggs; Jocelyn G. Bolling; Aubrey W. Booth, Randolph Wall Cabell;
Adelaide Leigh Cleere; Kevin Collier (Pocahontas Foods U.S.A.);
Mary Kate ("Kay") Copeland; Richard J. Cross, M.D.; Leila
Elizabeth Eldridge D'Aiutolo; Mr. and Mrs. William L. Evans;
Louise Harris; Anne D. Joyner; Sallye Koskie; Clare D'Artois
Leeper; David Barhydt Marshall; David Bowen McCandlish; William
("Bill") Hugh Meredith; Henry S. Middendorf, Jr.; Irene Randolph
Morrill; Lucia Gary Gardner Phillips; Katherine B. Rutledge; Sue
West Teague; Virginia Historical Society; Lois Choate Owen White;
and Claire Frederick Pence Woodward.

Additional Bibliography

NOTE: Books, etc., relied upon in whole or in part are noted
either in the text or in the following list.

Cabell, Randolph Wall. 20TH CENTURY CABELLS AND THEIR KIN.
1993.

Fauntleroy, Juliet. TOMBSTONE INSCRIPTIONS FROM CAMPBELL AND
OTHER VIRGINIA COUNTIES.

Stone, Letta Brock. THE WEST FAMILY REGISTER. 1928.

Introduction

A list of the names of the descendants of Pocahontas as presently prepared by The Pocahontas Foundation (hereinafter referred to as Foundation) is in the three volumes: POCAHONTAS' DESCENDANTS (1985) (hereinafter referred to as PD), CORRECTIONS AND ADDITIONS TO POCAHONTAS' DESCENDANTS (1992) (hereinafter referred to as C & A) and SECOND CORRECTIONS AND ADDITIONS TO POCAHONTAS' DESCENDANTS (1994).

But the list does not pretend to be complete and any and all proposed additions and corrections will be cordially invited.

Please write, sending a stamped and addressed envelope, to The Pocahontas Foundation, P. O. Box 431, Berryville, Virginia 22611.

Contents

Indian Queens

Maureen Barbara Snow doing some historical work on the Cornwall village of Indian Queens reports that the ship "Treasurer", because of bad weather, was diverted to Falmouth, and that Pocahontas, en route by road to London, stayed at an inn in the village known as Indian Queens.

The school badge of the Indian Queens County Private School is a representation of the head of Pocahontas.

The Rolfes

An article on the Rolfes appears in the third edition (1987) ADVENTURERS OF PURSE AND PERSON VIRGINIA 1607-1624/5, Revised and Edited by Virginia M. Meyer (1974-1981) and John Frederick Dorman (1981-1987) and on page 512 there is a note on the "non-existent" record evidence showing that Jane Rolfe who married Col. Robert Bolling was a daughter of Thomas Rolfe.

Indian Slave

Some material on Col. Robert Bolling (13) and Philip A. Bolling (1343) is in Eugene A. Maloney's A HISTORY OF BUCKINGHAM COUNTY and this includes, on page 37, an advertisement that appeared in the VIRGINIA GAZETTE for April 14, 1768, of Col. Robert Bolling offering a reward of 40 shillings for the return of his runaway Indian slave.

Richard Cross, m. (1st) 7/23/1770

In William Curry Harllee's KINFOLKS, Volume 3, page 2703, etc., there appears much material on Richard Cross, m. (1st) 7/23/1770 (wife Anna Maclin) and on their descendants. Some persons name him as a son of Anne Buchanan Cross (b. ca. 1764) (631) and as a grandson of Anne Murray Buchanan (8/30/1746 or 1779) (63). However, the dates make it difficult if not impossible to identify Richard Cross (m. 1st 7/23/1770) as a descendant of Pocahontas, but the naming of his second son John Bolling Cross and the naming of some of his descendants Bolling, Powhatan and Pocahontas gives reason to conclude that he was related to William Cross, husband of Anne Buchanan (b. ca. 1764) (631)

Duchess of Windsor and Lady Astor

Reports are that the Baltimorean, Wallis Warfield, late Duchess of Windsor, is a direct descendant of Pocahontas and the same is true as regards Nancy Langhorne Shaw, the Danville native who in 1906 married the second Viscount Astor and became the first female member of Britain's House of Commons. But a genealogical examination has failed to show that either of these two ladies is a descendant of Pocahontas.

Improved Order of Red Men
Degree of Pocahontas

In 1854 a resolution proposed a branch (Daughters of Pocahontas) for female relatives (wives, widows, daughters and sisters) of Red Men, but the resolution lay on the table.

In 1863, an effort proposed founding The Daughters of Powhatan but the effort fell by the wayside.

Then, in 1885, the Red Men established their women's auxillary, calling it Degree of Pocahontas.

In 1894, there was presented and adopted a Degree of Pocahontas badge and later, for a past local president ("Pocahontas"), there was presented a jewel badge bearing the letters "D.O.P." and the Red Men's motto: Freedom, Friendship and Charity.

In 1930, a resolution proposed changing the name Degree of Pocahontas to Daughters of Pocahontas but the resolution fell by the wayside.

In 1978-1984, Degree of Pocahontas raised money to pay for the erection of Pocahontas memorial gates and a walkway at the church of St. Agnes in Gravesend, England, and in an over-subscription $2000.00 was sent to the church and the balance of $1196.86 was donated to the Association for the Preservation of Virginia Antiquities to help make repairs and to do landscaping at the Pocahontas site in Jamestown.

In each year, on the last Saturday in June, the Virginia chapter of Degree of Pocahontas lays a wreath on the Pocahontas site in Jamestown.

Reference: HISTORY OF THE IMPROVED ORDER OF RED MEN AND DEGREE OF POCAHONTAS. 1765-1988 (1989) by Robert E. Davis.

vi
VIRGINIA 350th ANNIVERSARY COMMISSIO

SPONSORING ON BEHALF OF THE COMMONWEALTH THE JAMESTOWN FESTIVAL OF 1
THE TRAVIS HOUSE • WILLIAMSBURG, VIRGIN

GOVERNOR THOMAS B. STANLEY, HONORARY CHAIRMAN

HONORABLE LEWIS A. McMURRAN, JR., *Chairman*
HONORABLE LLOYD C. BIRD, *Vice-Chairman*

MISS ELLEN BAGBY
EDWARD L. BREEDEN, JR.
HARRY F. BYRD, JR.
RUSSELL M. CARNEAL
ADMIRAL ALVIN D. CHANDLER, USN Ret.

M. HALE COLLINS
JOHN WARREN COOKE
EDMUND T. DEJARNETTE
FELIX E. EDMUNDS
CARLISLE H. HUMELSINE

VERNON E. KEMP
ALLEN R. MATTHEW
W. MARVIN MINTER
W. TAYLOE MURPHY
FRED G. POLLARD

PARKE ROUSE, JR., EXECUTIVE DIRECTOR

27 March 1957

Dear Descendant of Pocahontas and John Rolfe:

The 343d anniversary of the marriage of Pocahontas and John Rolfe will be an epochal event in the history of the Commonwealth and one of the great days of the Virginia Festival.

More than a thousand descendants of the little Indian girl and the "most Worthy Maister Rolfe" have expressed interest in the occasion. You and all your relatives and friends are cordially invited. There will be registration of descendants and attractive name tags for all to wear.

At 11 o'clock on Friday morning, 5 April 1957, the wedding ceremony will be re-enacted. The officiating clergyman will be Dr. Churchill Gibson, wearing early 17th-century vestments. Powhatan's two representatives will be on hand, as will other appropriately costumed members of the bridal party. One of the attendants will be little Pocahontas Lamb, descendant of the Indian princess.

After the ceremony Paul Green, author of The Founders, The Common Glory, The Lost Colony, and other historical pageant-plays, will speak from the steps of the church. His subject will be "Pocahontas, America's First Heroine."

A picnic will follow, at which far-flung members of the Pocahontas-Rolfe family will be reunited. Box lunches, priced at one dollar, will be served, as well as cold drinks of many sorts.

During the afternoon guests will be free to visit Festival Park, to which the entrance fee of one dollar required of all visitors admits them. Perhaps they will want to roam around Williamsburg. Certainly many descendants will cross the river by ferry to visit the house erected in 1652 on land belonging to Pocahontas by "guifte of the Indyan King" and sold by Thomas Rolfe, son of Pocahontas and John Rolfe, to Thomas Warren.

I shall appreciate a card letting me know how many relatives and friends you plan to bring with you.

Sincerely yours,

Eudora Ramsay Richardson

Mrs. F. Briggs Richardson
Pocahontas Day Chairman

Minnecuttack
Skipwith Road
Richmond 26, Virginia

Corrections and Additions to PD and/or C & A

If a number is omitted, every name under that number that appears in a text or in an Index is to be omitted.

The theory of Florence Miriam Elizabeth Dorothea Wright Carson is disputed, conclusively we believe, by William Thorndale (see C & A, page vi), negating Mrs. Carson's allegations, in PD on pages 5 and 310-314, that Anne Rolfe, wife of Peter Elwyn V (1623-1695), was the daughter of Pocahontas' son Thomas Rolfe.

This negating also involves omitting all of the E numbers (in PD on pages 314-324).

Page v in C & A - under Page iii, first line, the word "in" should be "is"

Page 7 First line in the second paragraph of Blair Bolling List should have the word "differs" changed to read "suggests a minor name change and several minor date changes".

111326523 Hibernia McIlwaine ("Mac") Cuthbert, m. Dr. William J. Langley

111344311 Charlotte Nelson Munster, m. Stephen Landvoight

111344353 Robertson, John William Peyton, Jr. Index change in PD

1113812 Wyndham A. Robertson

1114243 Frances Evans Barksdale, m. Arthur Edward Ooghe

111x2145 Anne Byrd Symington, m. Thomas C. Platt

111x2611 Franklin Carter Blackford, m. K. Ray Iseman

111x611 Wyndham Robertson White, Jr., m. Judith Harriman Fernald
111x6111 Wyndham Robertson White III, m. Lois Choate Owen
111x61111 Allison Stuart White (b. 12/27/1961), m. Stephen Douglas Twente
111x61112 Wyndham Robertson White IV (b. 8/11/1964), m. Christine Brothers Birdsong
111x61113 John Owen White (b. 11/4/1968)

111x831 Margie W. Robertson

12 John Blair Bolling III. In a letter dated 7/26 or 27/1775 George Gilmer wrote to Jefferson "Poor Bob Bolling has run his race, adieu to Burgundy, died suddenly at "Richmond". THE PAPERS OF THOMAS JEFFERSON 238.

12412   William Holcombe Bolling lived in Wytheville where he was
        a Circuit Court Judge. The family moved to Washington,
        D.C., after the Civil War.

1241211 Elizabeth Bolling, m. Dr. Boyd
12412111 Lola Elizabeth Boyd (d. 2/10/1992), a resident of New
        York
12412112, 12412113, 12412114 Mildred Stuart Boyd, Edith Bolling
        (Nelson?) Boyd and Eleana Rolfe Boyd lived in California.

124122 Alexander Hunter Galt (d. 5/28/1935)
1241221 Alexander Bolling Galt (d. without issue)
124123 Matthew Hawes Maury (b. 6/19/1860)

1241232 Lucy Logwood Maury (d. 7/7/1980)
12412321 Anne Moeling
12412322 Lucy Moeling
124124 William Archibald Bolling (d. 10/23/1934)
124125 Bertha Bolling (d. 9/21/1937). Unm.
124127 Edith Bolling (d. 12/28/1961)
124128 John Randolph Bolling (d. 11/ /1950). Unm. Served as
        President Wilson's secretary.
124129 Richard Wilmer Bolling (d. 10/18/1951), m. Eleanor
        ("Nell") Hunter Lutz (d. 7/20/1960)
1241291 Clara Lutz Bolling (b. 6/10/1910), lives in Washington,
        D.C., m. 11/7/1931 Harry F. Fowler (8/22/1906-10/11/
        196?)
12412911 Lawrence A. Fowler (b. 8/19/1936). Lives in Alexandria.
1241292 Richard Wilmer Bolling, Jr. (6/11/1912-9/20/1952). Unm.
1241293 Sterling Ruffin Bolling (b. 3/7/1915), m. 5/20/1944 Jane
        Audrey Smith Sharon (b. 12/22/1916), dau. of Judge
        James Simeon and Audrey Smith Sharon of Sanford,
        Florida. Reside in Charleston, South Carolina.
12412931 Sterling Ruffin Bolling, Jr. (b. 8/25/1945 in Albany,
        Georgia), m. 8/9/1985 Jocelyn Angela Gernat (b. 3/17/
        1954 in Southington, Connecticut), dau. of William
        Lawrence and Margaret Alberta Yurcak Gernat. Reside
        in Maryland.
124129311 Ian Wilson Bolling (b. 10/29/1989)
1241294 Barbara Bolling (b. 6/6/1919), m. 2/6/1942 Cary Clarke
        Moody Fuller (b. 12/1/1912). Div. Barbara resides
        in Washington, D.C.
12412941 Cary Clarke Moody Fuller, Jr. (b. 9/8/1942). Resides
        in New York.
12412942 Richard Bolling Fuller (b. 12/15/1945). Resides in
        Washington, D.C.

132 Pocahontas Rebecca Bolling, m. Col. Joseph Cabell, Jr.
        (1762-8/31/1831)

1322 Sarah Bolling Cabell (5/29/1786-1851)

13228721 Robert Clement Trube III (b. 1938)
13228722 Jane Meredith Trube (b. 1941)

132295 Elizabeth Eddins (1855-1900), m. Reddin Andrews, Jr.
(1848-1923), of Texas. M.D.

1322951 Virginia Meredith Andrews (1884-1964), m. Joseph Theodor
Christian, Sr. (1885-1959)

13229511 Joseph Theodor Christian, Jr. (b. 1910), m. Bernardine
Henderson (b. 1912)

132295111 Virginia Christian (b. 1942), m. Irving Virgil Hayes,
Jr. (b. ca. 1942)

1322951111 Richard Christian Hayes (b. ca. 1964)

1322951112 Patrick David Hayes (b. ca. 1966)

132295112 Sybil Christian, M.D. (b. 1947), m. Donald Henry
Heise, M.D. (b. 1947)

1322951121 Ryan Henry Heise (b. ca. 1974)

1324 Joseph Megginson Cabell

1327 Benjamin William Sheridan Cabell

132721 Ann Elizabeth Cabell (3/27/1848-1892), m. John A. Coleman
(1845-1899)

1327212 John Roy Cabell Coleman (7/7/1877-1/10/1943) (twin).
Born at "BelGrade", Pittsylvania County. Spanish-
American War. Lawyer in Richmond and Danville.
Genealogist. M. 4/4/1904 Helen Louise Hobart (1879-
1962)

13272122 Lila Anne Coleman (b. 2/27/1909), m. 11/30/1930 Harry
Howe Heard (1893-1940)

132721221 Helen Lee Heard (b. 6/15/1932), m. 12/27/1952 Herbert
Carroll Etheridge (b. 1931)

1327212211 Ann Carol Etheridge (b. 12/17/1959), m. 11/23/1991
John Hayden Busch (b. ca. 1958)

1327212212 Janet Susan Etheridge (b. 3/2/1962), m. 6/15/1987
Thomas Burke (b. ca. 1961)

13272122121 Coleman Patrick Burke (b. 1989)

13272122122 William Avery Burke (b. 1992)

1327212213 Thomas Randall Etheridge (b. 9/23/1957)

1327212214 Patricia Gale Etheridge (b. 3/26/1956), m. 7/3/1982
Monte G. Plott (b. ca. 1955)

13272122141 Micah Etheridge Plott (b. 1992)

13272123 Martha Wilson Coleman (b. ca. 1913)

1327213 Daniel Coleman (b. 7/7/1877) (twin). A prominent
attorney in Norfolk-Tidewater area.

132723 Mary Winifred Cabell (b. 8/15/1853), m. Orthodox Creed
Smith (b. ca. 1853)

1327233 Roy Cabell Smith (b. ca. 1886), m. 4/10/1912 George
Wilson Cabell (7/28/1886-1966), son of Dr. Sears and
Althaea Spalding Cabell. No issue.

132724 Nathaniel Wilson Cabell (9/3/1855-1891), m. Ann Eskridge
Frederick (1859-1949)

1327241   John Roy Cabell II (1880-1955), m. Mary Ellison Robinson
          (1883-1970)
13272411 Carroll Hurtel Cabell (1905-1938), m. Louise McKagen
          (1905-1969)
132724111 Carroll Hurtel Cabell, Jr. (1938-1958)
13272412 Catherine Claiborne Cabell (b. 2/10/1907), m. 12/18/
          1928 Roy Markley King (1906-1978)
132724121 Joyce Catherine Cabell King (b. 8/12/1929), m. (1st)
          William Jackson Pearson III (b. 1925). Div., m.
          (2nd) 9/8/1957 Carl Samuel Pulkinen (b. 1924)
1327241211 William Jackson Pearson IV (b. 1951), m. 8/17/1973
          Julia Frances Otken (b. 1952)
13272412111 Cheryl Julia Pearson (b. 1975)
13272412112 William Jackson Pearson V (b. 1978)
13272412113 Paul Darlington Pearson (b. 1982)
13272412114 Claiborne Boyce Pearson (b. 1983)
1327241212 Elizabeth Flagg Pulkinen (5/23/1960), m. 7/4/1992
          Jeffrey Lee Ashworth (b. ca. 1958)
1327241213 Carl King Pulkinen (b. 8/28/1961)
1327241214 Edward Crew Pulkinen (b. 1/18/1963)
132724122 Margaret Elizabeth King (11/18/1930), m. 12/19/1950
          Robert Lee Greer (b. 1928). Div.
1327241221 Robert Lee Greer, Jr. (b. 12/16/1952), m. (1st)
          Judith Ann Smith (b. 1952). Div., m. (2nd) Mary
          Ellen Guy (b. 1952)
   Child by first wife:
13272412211 Amy Elizabeth Greer (b. 1980)
   Child by second wife:
13272412212 Robert Lee Greer III (b. 1985)
1327241222 Catherine Bowman Greer (b. 1954), m. 11/26/1988 Hugh
          Vernon Remmert (b. 1956)
13272412221 Kelly Elizabeth Remmert (b. 1991)
1327241223 Charles Cawood Greer (b. 2/18/1957), m. 11/18/1984
          Debra Louise Cole (b. 1952). Debra had three
          children by an earlier marriage.
13272412231 Margaret Cole Greer (b. 1985)
1327241224 Mary Cabell Greer (11/29/1959), m. John William
          McGinty III (b. ca. 1959). Div.
13272412241 John William McGinty IV (b. ca. 1983)
132724123 Anne Cabell King (b. 10/15/1933), m. 3/13/1954 John
          Howell Moye (1932-1979)
1327241231 John Howell Moye, Jr. (b. 11/30/1954), m. 6/15/1979
          Tandy Mitchell (b. 1958)
13272412311 Tiffany Marie Moye (b. 1980)
13272412312 John Howell Moye III (b. 1982)
13272412313 Catherine Elizabeth Moye (b. 1986)
1327241232 Thomas Markley Moye (1956-1991)
1327241233 Anne Claiborne Moye (b. 1958), m. (1st) 9/2/1978
          Richard Condon Robinson; m. (2nd) 2/21/1990 Kenneth
          Wayne Kinlaw (b. 1951)
13272412331 Richard Condon Robinson, Jr. (b. 1979)
13272412332 Michael Christopher Kinlaw (b. 1990)
13272413 John Roy Cabell III (1909-1982), m. Helen Lynch (b.
          1920)

132724131 Patricia Cabell (b. 1942)
132724132 Carole Cabell (b. 1943)
13272414   Agnes Rives Cabell (b. 1911), m. (1st) William Harold
           Lynch (b. ca. 1911); m. (2nd) James O. Burks (b. ca.
           1911)
132724141 William Harold Lynch, Jr. (b. 1943), m. Sharon
           (b. ca. 1943)
1327241411 Randy Lynch (b. ca. 1965)
132724142 Frances Cabell Lynch (b. 1945), m. Wayne Jackson (b.
           ca. 1945)
1327241421 Peggy Jackson (b. ca. 1970)
1327241422 Christopher Jackson (b. ca. 1972), m.
13272415   Nathaniel Wilson Cabell (b. 1914), m. Jean Warley
           Whitsell (b. 1924)
132724151 Helen Claiborne Cabell (b. 1949), m. (1st) Joseph
           Frederick Tucker (b. ca. 1949); m. (2nd) Frank
           Cheatham Parker (b. ca. 1949)
1327241511 Braxton Stuart Tucker (b. 1975)
1327241512 Caroline Claiborne Parker (b. 1982)
1327241513 Alice Cheatham Parker (b. 1988)
132724152 Mary Randolph Cabell (b. 8/1/1950), m. 8/24/1985 David
           James Prum (b. 2/12/1958), son of Bruce Edward and
           Joan Gahan Prum
1327241521 David Gahan Cabell ("Max") Plum (b. 1986)
1327241522 Hannah Randolph Cabell Plum (b. 1989)
1327241523 Mary ("Molly") Randolph Cabell Plum (1992-1992)
132724153 Nathaniel Wilson Cabell, Jr. (b. 1951), m. Lesley
           Schoepf (b. 1956)
1327241531 Nathaniel Wilson Cabell III (b. 1985)
132724154 John Witsell Cabell (b. 1953)
132724155 Thomas Leigh Cabell (b. 1956)
13272416   Mary Ellison Cabell (b. 1924), m. John Thomson Witsell
           (b. 1929)

1327244   George Craghead Cabell (6/24/1888-11/30/1962), m. 2/20/
          1919 Lewis Maney Childress (1/7/1884-10/10/1966), dau.
          of Horace and Shelley Maney Childress.
13272441 Shelley Childress Cabell (b. 5/11/1920), m. 1/30/1943
          William Homer Blitch, Jr. (6/10/1920-3/9/1984), son of
          William Homer and Lottie Parrish Blitch. He was a
          pilot in World War II.
132724411 Lewis Cabell Blitch (b. 1/22/1948), m. (1st) John
          Andrew Evans (b. ca. 1946);, m. (2nd) David Shoffner
          (b. ca. 1947)
   Child by first husband:
1327244111 John Claiborne Evans (b. 1979)

13273 Virginia Josephine Cabell (1815-1832)
13274 William Lewis Cabell (1/1/1827-2/22/1911). West Point.
       M. Harriette Amanda Rector (1837-4/16/1887). General
       Cabell was Mayor of Dallas for four terms. Book: OLD
       TIGE. GENERAL WILLIAM L. CABELL, C.S.A. by Paul Harvey,
       Jr.

132741   Benjamin Elias Cabell (11/18/1858-1931), m. Sarah Earle
         Pearre (1869-1921)
1327411 Benjamin Elias Cabell, Jr. (1899-1964), m. Olivia Halsey
         Glover (1896-1991)
13274111 Sarah Lee Cabell (1/12/1924), m. (1st) 11/21/1952
          Thomas Woodrow Massey (1914-1971); m. (2nd) George
          Madison Pavey, Jr. (b. ca. 1924)
132741111 Thomas Woodrow Massey, Jr. (b. 1953), m. Rebecca Ann
           Farrow (b. ca. 1955)
1327411111 Edwin Cabell Massey (b. 1984)
1327411112 Thomas Boone Massey (b. 1987)
1327412 Charles Pearre Cabell (10/9/1903-5/25/1971), General
         USAF, m. 9/18/1934 Octavia Jacklyn DeHymel (b. 10/9/
         1902), dau. of Franklin and Catherine DeWitt DeHymel.
13274121 Charles Pearre Cabell, Jr. (b. 7/12/1936). West Point.
          Brig. General USAF, m. 6/24/1966 Helena Spencer
          Callaway (b. 5/12/1941), dau. of Maj. Lambert Spencer
          and Sara Elizabeth Lupe Callaway.
132741211 Carrie Cartwright Cabell (b.1972)
132741212 Pearre Holman Spencer Cabell (b. 1974)
13274122 Catharine DeWitt Cabell (10/27/1938), m. 9/15/1962
          Charles Paul Bennett (b. 2/25/1938)
132741221 Charles Cabell Bennett (b. 1964)
132741222 Ben Paul Bennett (b. 1965)
13274123 Benjamin D. Cabell IV (b. ca. 1940)
1327413 Earle Cabell (10/27/1906-9/14/1975), m. Elizabeth Holder
         (1906-1991). Mayor of Dallas in 1961 when Kennedy was
         assassinated. Member of Congress. They adopted two
         children: Earle Cabell, Jr. (b. ca. 1932), and
         Elizabeth Lee Cabell (b. ca. 1934). With brother
         Pearre founded a very successful ice cream and dairy
         company later sold to 7-11 Stores.
132742 Catherine ("Katie") Doswell Cabell (1/6/1861-7/ /1927),
        m. (1st) 4/24/1889 John Rufus Currie (b. ca. 1865); m.
        (2nd) J. C. Muse (b. ca. 1860). No issue.
132743 John Joseph Cabell (11/28/1870-1903), m.   (b.
        ca. 1868)
1327431 Shingo Rector Cabell (b. 1898), m. Richard Paul Lemin
         (b. ca. 1895)
132744 Lawrence DuVal Cabell (8/22/1874-11/24/1946),Col. U.S.A.
        West Point. Spanish American War and World War I. M.
        9/3/1911 Frances Miller (1877-1949)
1327441 Frances Miller Cabell (b. 1918), m. Howard Stanley
         Aronson, M.D. (1901-1973)
13274411 Frances Miller Aronson (b. 1950)
13274412 Harriet Emilie Aronson (b. 1955)
132745 Lewis Rector Cabell (1/3/1879-1952), m. Marion Pierce (b.
        ca. 1898)
132746 William Lewis Cabell, Jr. (1867-1867)
132747 Pocahontas Rebecca Cabell (1871-1871)

132771 DeRosey Carroll Cabell, m. (1st) Marie Otis (b. ca.
        1865); m. (2nd) Martha Otis (b. ca. 1885)

Children by first wife:
1327711 Marie Otis Cabell (b. ca. 1886), m. Lee Armstrong (b.
         ca. 1886)
1327712 DeRosey Carroll Cabell, Jr. (b. ca. 1889), m.
         (b. ca. 1892)
13277121 DeRosey Carroll Cabell III (b. 1919)
1327713 Agnes Cabell (b. ca. 1890), m. Edward Isaacs (b. ca.
         1889)
132772 Sallie Doswell Cabell (b. ca. 1863), m. Will Greenwood
        (b. ca. 1864)
1327721 Will C. Greenwood (b. ca. 1891), m.   (b.
         ca. 1893)
13277211 Gladys Greenwood (b. ca. 1819)
13277212 Nell Greenwood (b. ca. 1920)
13277213 William Greenwood (b. ca. 1922)
1327722 Cabell Greenwood (b. ca. 1893)
1327723 Gladys Greenwood (b. ca. 1895), m. John McFodin (b. ca.
         1892)
13277231 Sawania McFodin (b. ca. 1923)
132773 Benjamin Cabell (b. ca. 1865-1886)
132774 Powhatan Joseph Cabell (b. ca. 1867), m. Gear Botefuhr
        (b. ca. 1873)
1327741 Alice Breckinridge Cabell (b. ca. 1896), m.   Reed
         (b. ca. 1895)
13277411 James Reed (b. ca. 1920-1944)
13277412 Robert Reed (b. ca. 1922)
1327742 Virginia Cabell (b. ca. 1898)
1327743 Joseph Cabell (b. ca. 1900)
1327744 Frederick Cabell (b. ca. 1903)
1327745 Gerald Cabell (b. ca. 1906)
132775 Mary Pocahontas Cabell (b. ca. 1870), m. Melvin Cornish
        (b. ca. 1868)
1327751 Cabell Carroll Cornish (b. ca. 1894)
1327752 Helen Carroll Cornish (b. ca. 1896), m. Robert B. Hutch-
         inson (b. ca. 1894)
13277521 Robert Hutchinson (b. ca. 1920)
13277522   Hutchinson (b. ca. 1923)
1327753 William Cornish (b. ca. 1899), m. Rita Pool (b. ca.
         1895)
13277531 Richard C. Cornish (b. ca. 1927)
132776 Virginia Josephine Cabell (b. ca. 1873), m. George A.
        Mansfield (b. ca. 1973)
1327761 Margaret Mansfield (b. ca. 1900), m. A. Hugo (b. ca.
         1898)
1327762 George Mansfield (b. ca. 1902)
1327763 William Mansfield (b. ca. 1906)
1327764 Charles Mansfield (b. ca. 1909)
132777 Inf. (b. & d. 1875)
132778 Inf. (b. & d. 1877)
132779 Breckinridge Cabell (b. ca. 1880), m. Ben Mills (b. ca.
        1876)
1327791 Dorothy Cabell Mills (b.ca. 1905), m. Thomas Christopher
         Allen (b. ca. 1903)
13277911 Thomas Allen (b. ca. 1927)

13277912 Robert Allen (b. ca. 1929)
1327792 Mary Carroll Mills (b.ca. 1907), m. John Allan Hattstrom
          (b. ca. 1905)
13277921 Dau. (b. ca. 1930)
13277922 Dau. (b. ca. 1933)
13277x Henry Sayre Cabell (1885-4/6/1933), m. Hazel Clyde Ransom
        (1888-8/2/1934-killed in automobile accident)
13277x1 Henry Bertrand Cabell (b. 12/25/1922), m. 1/10/1948
         Margaret E. Condray. Wounded at Okinawha.
13277x11 Anne Cabell (b. 1949), m. Robert O'Neil Warrington, Jr.
          (b. 1945)
13277x111 Robert O'Neil Warrington III (b. ca. 1970)
13277x112 Daniel Scott Warrington (b. ca. 1972)
13277x113 Kristy Cabell Warrington (b. 1979)
13277x12 Robert Bertrand Cabell (b. 1950)
13277x13 Terence Martin Cabell (b. 1955), m. Patricia Ann
          Rostkowski (b. 1953)
13277x2 Ben Mills Cabell (b. 3/8/1928), Colonel U.S.A., 2/11/
         1949 Virgie Mae Olle (b. 10/25/1929), dau. of Herman A.
         and Carmen Weisser Olle
13277x21 Cathleen Cabell (b. 5/27/1950), m. 7/5/1973 Peter Byron
          Cramblet (b. 1948). West Point. Three time All
          American Lacrosse "Attack". Colonel U.S.A.
13277x211 Courtney Brooke Cramblet (b. 1978)
13277x212 Tierney Ellen Cramblet (b. 1979)
13277x213 Gavin Peter Cramblet (b. 1981)
13277x214 Wyatt Tyler Cramblet (b. 1989)
13277x22 Ben Ransom Cabell (b. 1951) West Point. Lt. Col.
          U.S.A., m. 8/16/1980 Susan Dianne Beebe (b. 1956)
13277x221 Carolyn Ann Cabell (b. 1983)
13277x23 Michael Olle Cabell (b. 9/25/1955), m. 2/20/1982 Lynda
          Marie Cain (b. 2/10/1952), dau. of Zack Lindberg and
          Evelyn Marie Ball Cain
13277x231 Michael Cain Cabell (b. 1984)
13277x232 Kristen Marie Cabell (b. 1990)
13278 George Craghead Cabell (1/25/1836-1906), m. (1st) Mary
       Harrison Baird (1838-9/30/1890), m. (2nd) Ellen Virginia
       Ashton (1851-1904)
132781 Sarah ("Sallie") Doswell Cabell (1860-1933), m. (1st)
        Leonidus Howell Lewis (1853-1935); m. (2nd)
        Brady (b. ca. 1858); m. (3rd) W. T. Miles, Brig. Gen.
        (b. ca. 1870)
1327811 George C. Lewis (b. ca. 1881)
1327812 Benjamin Harrison Lewis (2/28/1882-3/18/1953), m. (1st)
         12/19/1904 Martha Valentine Ellis (2/14/1887-12/23/
         1975), dau. of John Howard and Martha Kidd Daubin
         Ellis. He met her when his father married her mother.
         Div. M. (2nd) Julia   . No issue by second
         wife.
13278121 Harrison Adolphus Lewis (1905-1989), m. Hilda Bruhm
          (b. ca. 1917)
132781211 Robert Cabell Lewis (b. 1949), m. Andrika Marion
           Donovan (b. ca. 1949)
1327812111 Johanna Drika Lewis (b. 1976)

132781212 Harrison Torick Lewis (b. ca. 1951)
13278122 Martha June Lewis (b. 6/30/1913), m. 11/27/1937 Richard
          Edgar Strauss (5/27/1913-12/9/1967), son of Edgar Leon
          and Esther Mariam Goodman Strauss
132781221 Richard Edgar Lewis Strauss (b. 5/14/1941), m. 7/16/
          1966 Linda Lee Kostelecky (b. 1944)
1327812211 Barbara Lee Strauss (b. 1970)
132781222 Martha Mariam Strauss (b. 10/25/1943), m. 12/18/1968
          Stephen Homer Kirby (b. 1943). Div. 1985.
1327812221 Adam Jefferson Kirby (b. 1977)
1327812222 Benjamin James Kirby (b. 1980)
132781223 Monica Mari Strauss (b. 10/5/1952), m. 2/14/1986
          Thomas Richard Spilker (b. 1952). Div. 1989.
1327812231 Amelia Valentine Spilker (b. 1986)
1327813 Willis Archibald Lewis (b. ca. 1885)
1327814 Dau. (b. and d. ca. 1880)
132782 Annie Atkinson Cabell (1862-1942), m. Garland Stone
       Wooding (1864-1933).

1327822 Mary Cabell Wooding (1891-1977), m. (1st) Samuel Addison
        Schoolfield (1889-1931); m. (2nd) Red James (b. ca.
        1881)
13278221 Samuel Addison Schoolfield, Jr. (b. 1918), m. Maurietta
         Jo Maurer (b. 1925)
132782211 Linda Wilson Schoolfield (b. 1949), m. Michael Charles
          Kessler (b. 1949)
1327822111 Margaret Leigh Kessler (b. 1973)
1327822112 Emily Beth Kessler (b. 1976)
1327822113 Bonnie Marie Kessler (b. 1979)
132782212 Peter Wooding Schoolfield (b. 1951), m. Diane Marie
          Barton (b. 1955)
1327822121 Jeremy Wooding Schoolfield (b. 1979)
1327822122 Kevin Andrew Schoolfield (b. 1983)
1327822123 Jeffrey Brian Schoolfield (b. 1985)
1327822124 Lucas Aaron Schoolfield (b. 1988)
132782213 David Perry Schoolfield (b. 1957), m. Gail Marie
          Atchison (b. 1959)
1327822131 Bradley James Schoolfield (b. 1987)
1327822132 Katelyn Ann Schoolfield (b. 1990)
1327823 William Henry Wooding (1899-1950), m. Louyse Ursula
        Wildman (1900-1984)
13278231 Nancy Cabell Wooding (b. 1927), m. Robert Lee Bonifant
         (1927-1983)
132782311 Nancy Lee Bonifant (b. 1946), m. William Eldridge
          McBride (b. 1941)
1327823111 Katherine Lisa McBride (b. 1969)
1327823112 William Eldridge McBride III (b. 1972)
1327823113 Margaret Bryant McBride (b. 1975)
132782312 Robert Lee Bonifant, Jr. (b. 1948), m. Robin Berlin
          (b. 1953)
1327823121 Kelly Bonifant (b. 1979)
1327823122 Sarah Bonifant (b. 1981)
1327823123 Ross Lee Bonifant (b. 1984)

132782313 William Wooding Bonifant (b. 1950), m. Victoria
    Lucille Haydon (b. 1950)
1327823131 William Wooding Bonifant, Jr. (b. 1976)
1327823132 Challice Lee Bonifant (b. 1978)
1327823133 Nancy Katherine Bonifant (b. 1981)
1327823134 Garland Parrish Bonifant (b. 1983)
132782314 George Christopher Bonifant (b. 1952), m. Cheryl Ann
    Arnold (b. 1952)
1327823141 George Cabell Bonifant (b. 1982)
1327823142 Robert Gregory Bonifant (b. 1984)
1327823143 James Michael Bonifant (b. 1991)
132782315 James Bonifant (b. 1956), m. Debra Anne Croft (b.
    1956)
1327823151 Matthew James Bonifant (b. 1984)
1327823152 Nancy Elizabeth Bonifant (b. 1986)
1327823153 John Croft Bonifant (b. 1990)
132782316 Garland Louyse Bonifant (b. 1960), m. Edward Joseph
    DeMarco (b. 1960)
1327823161 Robert Vincent DeMarco (b. 1986)
1327823162 Patricia Nan DeMarco (b. 1988)
1327823163 Claire Louise DeMarco (b. 1991)
132782317 Benjamin Cabell Bonifant (b. 1962)
13278232 Lois Elizabeth Wooding (b. 1928), m. (1st) Christie
    Radcliffe Middleton (b. 1929); m. (2nd) Charles Payne
    Morley (b. ca. 1926)
132782321 Kathryn Wooding Middleton (b. 1949), m. (1st) James
    Guest (b. ca. 1947); m. (2nd) James E. Lindblad (b.
    ca. 1947)
  Child by first husband:
1327823211 Dustin Guest (Adopted by second husband) Lindblad
  Children by second husband:
1327823212 Purdom Kathryn Lindblad (b. 1978)
1327823213 Laura Elizabeth Lindblad (b. 1979)
132782322 Christie Radcliffe Middleton III (b. 1951), m. Iris D.
    Rodriguez (b. 1950)
1327823221 Stephanie Kimberly Middleton (b. 1989)
132782323 William Wooding Middleton (b. 1954), m. Kathryn Louise
    Griffin (b. 1956)
1327823231 William Wooding Middleton, Jr. (b. 1979)
1327823232 Brandice Louise Middleton (b. 1982)
1327823233 Richard Kenneth Middleton (b. 1984)
132783 Benjamin William Sheridan Cabell, M.D. (2/24/1864-1/13/
    1920), m. 1/1/1895 Nancy Bradley (b. ca. 1868-1935),
    Born "Bridgewater", Pittsylvania County, the home of
    his grandfather Maj. B. W. S. Cabell. He graduated
    from Hampden-Sydney but the ceremony was delayed
    because of a cow in the tower - - - he had apparently
    placed the cow there.
1327831 George C. Cabell (b. ca. 1895)
1327832 Frances Isabel Cabell (11/26/1896-1984), m. 1927 Percy
    Paul Pratt (10/30/1896-1956), son of Burla and Lydia
    Ann Brand Pratt.

13278321 Benjamin Cabell Pratt, Col. USMC (b. 5/29/1730), m.
          8/31/1957 Jacquelyn Blanche Lusby (b. 2/4/1929), dau.
          of Jackson Cole and Blanche Mayo Lusby. They had one
          adopted child.
132783211 Timothy Cabell Pratt (b. 6/9/1958), m. 4/4/1987 Carol
           Metzger (b. 1959)
132783212 Kerry Mayo Pratt (b. 11/6/1959), m. 6/19/1982 Gregory
           Horne (b. 1953)
1327832121 Stephanie Alexis Horne (b. 1984)
1327832122 Rachel Allison Horne (b. 1991)
1327832123 Shaun Benjamin Horne (b. 1992)
13278322 Frances Sheridan Pratt (b. 1934), m. William Linwood
          Douglas Townsend (b. 1928)
132783221 William Linwood Douglas Townsend, Jr. (b. 1959), m.
           Margaret Elizabeth Mewborne (b. 1963)
1327832211 William Linwood Douglas Townsend III (b. 1992)
132783222 Sheridan Pratt Townsend (b. 1960), m. Albert Ray
           Newsome, Jr. (b. 1960)
132783223 Cabell Dupre Townsend (b. 1969)
1327833 Powhatan Algernon Cabell (1902-1958), m. Mary Coral
         Bland (b. 1903)
13278331 Nancy Bland Cabell (b. 1928), m. (1st) Walter Raleigh
          Sawyer (b. 1916); m. (2nd) Henry Stanley Zagray (b.
          ca. 1930)
132783311 Frances Sheridan Sawyer (b. 1947), m. (1st) Tom Harry
           Harmon (b. 1946); m. (2nd) Elbert Lee Palmer (b.
           1952)
1327833111 Gary Walter Harmon (b. 1967)
1327833112 Paul Shane Harmon (1971-1976)
1327833113 Catherine Dawn Harmon (b. 1979)
132783312 Walter James Sawyer (b. 1951), m. Donna DeLane Daniels
           (b. 1955)
1327833121 Ashley Elizabeth Sawyer (b. 1984)
1327833122 Walter James Sawyer, Jr. (b. 1990)
132783313 Robert Carroll Sawyer (b. 1954), m. Patricia Lynn
           Parker (b. 1954)
1327833131 Parker Elliott Sawyer (b. 1992)
132783314 William Cabell Sawyer (b. 1956), m. Deborah Elaine
           Gentry (b. 1959)
13278332 Mary Sheridan Cabell (b. 1930), m. Charles William
          Batts (b. 1925)
132783321 Charles William Batts, Jr. (b. 1952), m. Cathryn
           Chambers (b. 1959)
1327833211 Ryan Jeffrey Batts (b. 1987)
1327833212 Kevin Michael Batts (b. 1989)
132783322 Susan Elaine Batts (b. 1954), m. Michael Stephen
           Staley (b. 1951)
1327833221 Stephen Robert Staley (b. 1976)
1327833222 Bonnie Leigh Staley (b. 1980)
13278333 Benjamin William Sheridan Cabell IV (b. 1932), m.
          Shirley Anne Miller (b. 1936)
132783331 Constance Anne Cabell (b. 1962)
132783332 Robert Sheridan Cabell (b. 1964)
132783333 Deborah Lynn Cabell (b. 1969)

132784   George Craghead Cabell, Jr. (8/8/1868-8/ /1949). Born
         at "Bridgewater". Lived 1892-6 in Marlin, TX. Later,
         attorney in Danville and Norfolk. M. 8/31/1892 Kate
         ("Katie") Walters Graveley (b. 1873)
1327841 Mary B. Cabell (1893-1896)
1327842 George Craghead Cabell II (1892-1893)
132785   Powhatan Algernon ("Algie") Cabell (6/8/1876-1966).
         Described himself as a "degenerate son of a noble sire".
         M. (1st) 6/16/1909 Mary Jane Daisy Pope (1881-1918); m.
         (2nd) 3/9/1922 Elizabeth Gertrude Meyerhoffer (7/28/
         1893-9/18/1981), dau. of Robert Michael and Elizabeth
         Susie Perkey Meyerhoffer.
   Children by first wife:
1327851 Algernon Thomasson Cabell (1905-1906)
1327852 Virginia Elizbeth Baird Cabell (1908-1973), m. (1st)
         Wilson Reynolds (b. ca. 1906); m. (2nd) Raymond
         Williams (b. ca. 1908); m. (3rd) Bonny Thomas (b. ca.
         1910); m. (4th) Ellsworth Shumway (b. ca. 1910); m.
         (5th) Cecil Vance Tarter (1914-1965)
1327853 George Craghead Cabell III (1910-1981), m. Mary Bettie
         Felts (1902-1979)
13278531 George Craghead Cabell IV (b. 1929)
1327854 Benjamin William Sheridan Cabell (1912-1974), m. Ellen
         Hopkins (1918-1990)
13278541 Billy Cabell (1936-1942)
13278542 Betty Thomas Cabell (1939-1941)
13278543 Stanley Powhatan Cabell (b. 1941), m. Cynthia Louise
         Cook (b. 1947)
132785431 Jeffrey Douglas Cabell (b. 1972)
132785432 Todd William Cabell (b. 1974)
132785433 Amy Louise Cabell (b. 1977)
1327855 Newit Edward Cabell (7/2/1917-7/12/1979), m. (1st)
         Evelyn Susan Williams (b. 1915); m. (2nd) Virginia
         Elizabeth Jester (b. 1915)
   Child by first wife:
13278551 Newit Edward Cabell, Jr. (b. 1938), m. (1st) Nelda Page
         Holt (b. 1937); m. (2nd) Sybil Jean Harris (b. 1949)
   Children by first wife:
132785511 Debra Paige Cabell (b. 1961), m. Mayland Kemp Bradshaw
         (b. ca. 1959)
1327855111 Justin Kemp Bradshaw (b. 1987)
1327855112 Brent Cabell Bradshaw (b. 1989)
132785512 Stephen Brooks Cabell (b. 1964), m. Mary Beth Edmond-
         son (b. ca. 1966)
   Children by second wife:
13278552 Richard Howard Cabell (b. 1943), m. (1st) Lynn Kibler
         (b. 1941). Adopted a son. M. (2nd) Josephine Mallimo
         (b. 1955)
132785521 Karen Elizabeth Cabell (b. 1962)
132785522 John Edward Cabell (b. 1967)
13278553 Virginia Elizabeth Cabell (b. 1944), m. Michael James
         Greener (1944)
132785531 Clayton Thomas Greener (1970-1971)
132785532 Donald Michael Cabell Greener (b. 1971)

132785533 Darren Kendall Greener (b. 1975)
13278554 Mary Jane Cabell (1945-1993), m. Dennis Leslie Proctor
          (b. 1945)
132785541 Dennis Robert Proctor (b. 1962), m. Julie Hersman (b.
          1962)
1327855411 Beau Edward Proctor (b. 1985)
1327855412 Ben Hersman Proctor (b. 1988)
132785542 Danny Joe Proctor (b. 1966), m. Kelly Williams (b.
          1966)
1327855421 Megan Danielle Proctor (b. 1990)
   Children by second wife:
1327856 Robert Baird Cabell (b. 1/4/1923), m. (1st) 9/ /1946
          Jeanne Beatrice Quebodeaux (1923-1952); m. (2nd) 10/11/
          1953 Norma Anne Holloway (b. 1931)
   Children by second wife:
13278561 Robert Baird Cabell, Jr., Maj. USAF (b. 7/20/1954), m.
          5/12/1984 Catherine Florence Niles (b. 1958)
132785611 Angela Faith Cabell (b. 1986)
132785612 Christina Joy Cabell (b. 1990)
132785613 Sarah Hope Cabell (b. 1993)
13278562 Frank Holloway Cabell (b. 1/4/1957), m. 6/21/1986 Tammy
          Elizabeth Jenkins (b. 1958)
132785621 Joyce Elizabeth Cabell (b. 1988)
132785622 Frank Tyler Cabell (b. 1990)
13278563 Anne Elizabeth Cabell (b. 10/3/1958), m. 5/30/1987
          Charles Aden Wiley III (b. 1962)
13278564 William Sheridan Cabell (b. 8/26/1961)
1327857 Mary Gertrude Cabell (b. 1925), m Hubert Bridges (1913-
          1953)
13278571 Mary Hu Bridges (b. 1946)
13278572 Warren Cabell Bridges (b. 1948), m. Nancy Virginia
          Bradshaw (b. 1949)
132786 Henry Ruffin Cabell (1866-1867)
132787 John Lewis Cabell (1871-1872)
132788 Mary Baird Cabell (1873-1876)

1331 Martha West, m. 12/24/1811 James Saunders Jones

13311x9 Rosa Maria Gilliam. Residence: "Landover"

133121 (page 53) through 1331212Bx11 (page 57). Omit.

13312 Thomas West Jones (b. 1816), m. Martha West
133121 William Jones (1846-1867). Only child. Unm.

1342 Susan Pocahontas Bolling, m. Robert Thruston Hubard (9/26/
          1808-10/19/1871). Member of Virginia Legislature.
13421 William Bolling Hubard (b. 12/24/1836)
13422 Edmund Wilcox Hubard (b. 2.17.1841), m. Julia Taylor of
          Louisa County. He was named for his uncle, a Member of
          Congress.
13423 James Lenaeus Hubard (b. 2/27/1835), m. 11/13/1860 Isaetta
          Carter Randolph
13424 Eugene Hubard (died at 8 years)

13425   Robert Thruston Hubard, Jr., m. Sarah Edmunds. Member of
        Virginia Legislature and on Governor Cameron's staff
        (Colonel).

13427   Philip A. Hubard, m. Mary Wilson. Residence: Cumberland
        County
13428   Bolling Hubard, m. Julia Chapman

14   Mary Bolling (d. 8/9/1812)
141   Richard Bland IV of "Jordan's" of Nottoway Parish, Amelia
        County.
1411   Richard Bland V (d. 6/29/1864), m. (1st) Adeline Manton
        (d. 1828); m. (2nd) 8/13/1829 Martha Elizabeth Ledbetter
        (d. 6/25/1886)
   Children by first wife:
14111   Anne Bland, m. Edward Turner
14112   Unnamed child. Adeline died during birth of this child.
   In C & A improperly numbered Peter Bland (see 14115 below).
   Children by second wife:
14113   John Bolling Bland "of Richmond and Baltimore" (1844-   ),
        m. Miss Boyd
141131   Boyd Bland
141132   Fanny Bland
141133   Unnamed child
141134   Unnamed child
14114   Susan Bland (1834-   )
14115   Peter Bland (1835-   )
1412   John Bolling Bland (b. 7/17/1798)

   Child by second wife:
14122   Robert Epes Bland (d. 1892), m. Miss Hettie Rivers

   Child by first wife:
14123   John Theodorick Bland, m. (1st) Bettie Marks; m. (2nd)
        Miss Ruffin; m. (3rd) Priscilla Read Watkins

   Children by third wife:
14124   William Epes Bland, m. at Petersburg 6/10/1863 Sarah
        Russell Bland, a cousin, dau. of Theodorick Bland (1414)

141246   Magdalen Pickett Bland, m. William Temple

14126   Mary Harrison Bland, m. (1st)   Bryant; m. (2nd)
        Johnson

1414   Theodorick Bland, m. 12/18/1834 Mary Brooke Harrison. Both
        d. at "Jordan's Point".
14141   Theodorick Bland, Jr. Family historian. Served 44th
        Battalion, Co. C, and during 1864-5, in Co. E, 5th
        Regiment. Captured at Farmville after Battle of Peters-
        burg. Imprisoned at Point Lookout.

14143   Sarah ("Sally") Russell Bland, m. her cousin, William Epes
        Bland (14124)

14144 Anne Bland, m. Charles Gee

14147 Susannah Poythress Bland, m. Edgar (Edward?) Temple

1415 Mary Bolling Bland (d. 12/25/1824)

1419 Peter Poythress Bland (d. 1820)

14232252 Alfriend, Robert Whitehead, M.D. Add to C & A Index.

1423242 Elizabeth Vickery ("Bill" or "Billie") Alfriend

143 Elizabeth Blair Bland, m. 2/10/1787 William Poythress

144 Dau. b. 8/ /1771, died same day.

1534 Mary Louisa Tazewell (1823-7/15/1851), m. 6/20/1847 Dr.
       J. B. Southall (1810-12/12/1862). He m. (2nd) 10/5/1854
       Mary's sister, Martha Jefferson Tazewell (1536)
15341 Mary Whitfield Southall (1849-1915), m. 1/8/1879 George
       Watson James, Ltt. D. (12/20/1846, Richmond-12/1/1918)
153411 George Watson James, Jr., m. Annie Rhinehart
1534111 Dr. George Watson James III
153412 John Quarles James (1883-1974), m. Elsie Bogert
153413 Mary Schoolcraft James (11/28/1881, Richmond-3/20/1977),
       m. 12/1/1904 Victor Balmer Shelburne (8/19/1880-1/19/
       1954)
1534131 Louise Balmer Shelburne (10/30/1905-   ), m. 10/11/
       1933 Edward Hilton Satterthwaite (1903-1955)
1534132 Emily Watson Shelburne (8/14/1907-5/26/1953), m. 6/20/
       1936, Francis Leonidas Joyner (8/6/1909-   )
15341321 Emily Shelburne Joyner (10/21/1938-   ), m. 9/1/1962
       Jack Riley Poteet (4/27/1939-   )
153413211 Emily Ellen Poteet (1/19/1964-   ), m. 9/22/1990
       John Douglas Roberts (9/18/1964-   )
153413212 Mary Frances Poteet (4/16/1966-   )
15341322 Francis Leonidas Joyner, Jr. (10/9/1942-   ), m.
       2/10/1968 Anne Dulin Joyner (5/2/1946-   )
1534133 Mary Southall Shelburne (5/20/1915-   ), m. (1st)
       4/15/1939 William Redditt Crawford (9/9/1914-2/6/1945),
       m. (2nd) 6/11/1949 James Leroy McLaurin (12/8/1901-   )
1534134 Victor Balmer Shelburne, Jr. (2/21/1922-   ), m. 5/8/
       1948 Jane Elizabeth Becker (10/19/1921-   )
15341341 Brian James Shelburne (9/7/1949-   ), m. 8/6/1988
       Yvonne Weakland (4/24/1963-   )
15341342 Victor Balmer Shelburne III (5/10/1952-   )
15341343 Jane Louise Shelburne (12/3/1955-   ), m. 1/7/1978
       Henry Jay Fisher (6/13/1956-   )
153413431 Jayson Henry Fisher (5/10/1980-   )
153413432 Mary Jean Fisher (4/9/1987-   )
153414 Louise Tazewell James, m. George W. Balmer
1534141 Mary Southall Balmer

16   Archibald Bolling. M. (2nd) 2/17/1774 or 10/1/1774 Jane
     Randolph
161   Sarah Bolling (1772-1837), m. Joseph Cabell Megginson

1611a   Frances Cabell Megginson (12/6/1844-   ), m. 11/14/1865,
        Dr. William N. Horsley (b. 1829) of Nelson
1611a1   William N. Horsley, Jr. (b. 8/7/1866)

1611a3   Anne Horsley (10/10/1871-6/4/1874)

1613141   Mattie Blain Megginson (b. 1889)
1613142   Clara Virginia Megginson (b. 1893)

1613x   Joseph Cabell Megginson
1613a   Archibald Bolling Megginson

16141   Sarah Jane Megginson, m. Hamilton Leftwich Blaine, M.D.

161412   Mary Frances Louise Blaine (6/11/1853-1903), m. Metellus
         Woods Tompkins, M.D.
1614121   Mary Elizabeth Tompkins (1876-1972), m. James Broadus
          Stringfellow (1872-1935)
16141211   Ann Stringfellow (b. 1903), m. Richard Anderson Forbes
161412111   Ann Stringfellow Forbes (b. ca. 1925)
161412112   Richard Anderson Forbes, Jr.
161412113   Charles Harrison Forbes
16141212   Mary Blaine Stringfellow (b. 1906), m. Metellus
           Tompkins Craig (b. 1912)
16141213   Robert Bruce Stringfellow (b. ca. 1910), Col. U.S.A.
1614122   Caroline Virginia Tompkins (1878-1961), m. Robert
          Alexander Craig (1881-1943)
16141221   Metellus Tompkins Craig (b. 1912), m. Mary Blaine
           Stringfellow (16141212)

1615   Samuel Bolling Megginson, m. Mary Ann Johnston (3/19/1809-
       1875)
16151   Joseph Cabell Megginson (8/14/1829-1917), m. (1st) Eliza
        Susan Alvis (10/12/1823-1862)

161512   James Bolling Megginson (1857-1889), m. Elizabeth Bagby
         Lewis (1858-1952)
1615121   William James Bolling Megginson (1884-1954), m. Annie
          McLaughlin (1883-1956)
16151211   Emma Guy Megginson (b. 1914), m. 12/12/1937 Howard
           Arthur Felder (1913-1976). Residence: Charleston,
           SC. M. (2nd) 1984 William Swinton Anderson (b. 1907)
   Children by first marriage:
161512111   Howard Arthur Felder, Jr. (b. 1938), m. Lela Rebecca
            Cozzens (b. 1941)
       NOTE: Howard Arthur Felden, Jr., adopted children
       of his wife (they were Howard Richard, James Richard
       and Deanna Richard and they took the name Felder).
161512112   William Hall Felder (b. 1940), m. Patricia Myers
            (b. 1937)

1615121121   Jennifer Felder (b. 1972)
1615121122   William Hall Felder, Jr. (b. 1974)
161512113   James Norwood Felder (b. 1943), m. C. Ann Gilland
            (b. 1945)
1615121131   Katherine A. Felder (b. 1972)
1615121132   James Norwood Felder, Jr. (b. 1975)
161512114   Alton Hayne Felder II (b. 1947), m. Ruth Barksdale
            (b. ca. 1947)
1615121141   Zachary Hayne Felder (b. 1982)
161512115   Ellen Felder (1956-1978), m. John Arcand (b. ca.
            1956)
161513   Ida Branch Megginson (1857-1881), m. Thomas Edwin Coleman
         (1856-1929)
1615131   Mabel Bertha Coleman (1879-1970), m. John Richard Booker
          (1870-1952)
16151311   Sue Booker (b. 1899), m. William Diuquid Christian II
           (1900-1945)
161513111   Peggy Sue Christian (b. 1928)
161513112   Katherine Sue Christian (b. 1935)
16151312   Edna Olivia Booker (b. 1906), m. George Malcom Thomas
           Ewing (1895-1961)
161513121   Lucy Ewing (b. 1940), m. Bernard Elmore Martin (b. ca.
            1940)
16151313   John Richard Booker, Jr. (1917-1972), m. Lillian
           Roeblad (1921-1972)
161513131   Janet Booker (b. 1947), m. (1st) Walter Henry Dondero
            (b. 1939); m. (2nd)
1615131311   Leanne M. Dondero (b. 1967)
1615131312   Richard John Dondero (b. 1969)
1615131313   Stephen Henry Dondero II (b. 1977)

1624   John Breckinridge Cabell, m. (2nd) Martha Anne Posey (b.
       1815)

16245   Sears Cabell, M.D. (5/10/1848-1897), m. Althaea Spalding
        Cabell (1847-1933) (16267)
162451   William Nicholas Cabell (1/11/1875-1949), m. 5/24/1919
         Alla Spyker (b. ca. 1875). No issue.

162453   Sears Ted Cabell (7/29/1878-2/9/1953), m. 2/21/1902
         Martha Ella Lewis (1881-1961)
1624531   Martha Cabell (b. 1902)
1624532   Ted Sears Cabell, Jr. (b. 1909), m. (1st) Elsie Myrtle
          Lemmons (1913-1961); m. (2nd) Louise Rosebloom (b. ca.
          1915); m. (3rd) Bernise Kerch (b. 1918)
   Children by first wife:
16245321   Ted Sears Cabell III (b. 1930), m. (1st) Dorothy
           Frances Herzwurm (b. ca. 1930); m. (2nd) Carol
           Jeannine Daly (b. 1930)
   Children by first wife:
162453211   Gregory Brian Cabell (b. b. 1957)
162453212   Deborah Ann Cabell (b. 1958)
   Children by second wife:
162453213   Laura Leigh Cabell (b. 1961)

162453214   Anne Marie Cabell (b. 1963)
16245322 Patricia Elsie Cabell (b. 1934), m. William George
          Ringling (b. 1923)
162453221   David Alan Ringling (b. 1959)
162453222   Jeffrey Lane Ringling (b. 1961)
162453223   Andrew Dallas Ringling (b. 1964)
162453224   Joseph Tyler Ringling (b. 1966)
162453225   John Douglas Ringling (b. 1968)
162453226   Gayna Marie Ringling (b. 1969)
162453227   Ted Christopher Ringling (b. 1972)
   Child by second wife:
16245323 Jacqueline Cabell (b. 1939), m. Paul R. Dixon (b. ca.
          1939)
162453231   Desiree Nicole Dixon (b. 1962)
162453232   Paula Michelle Dixon (b. 1964)
   Child by third wife:
16245324 James ("Jimmy") Cabell (b. 1947)

1624533 Sara Otis Cabell (b. 1911), m. Julius Thompson Warren
         (1910-1968)
16245331 Sarah Jean Warren (b. 1933), m. (1st) Seymour Adam
          Spiegelman (b. ca. 1933); m. (2nd) Thomas Waddell
          Nichols, M.D. (b. 1929)
162453311   Penny Warren Spiegelman (b. 1956)
162453312   Suellyn Tyler Spiegelman (b. 1958)
162453313   Bret Spiegelman (b. 1960)
162453314   Heather Welch Nichols (b. 1970)
16245332 Phyllis Mareve Warren (b. 1939), m. Douglas Cordoza
          (b. ca. 1939)
162453321   Lisa Cordoza (b. 1959)
162453322   Douglas Cordoza, Jr. (b. ca. 1961)
162453323   Gianna Cordoza (b. ca. 1963)
162453324   Daren Cordoza (b. ca. 1965)
162453325   Tiffany Cordoza (b. 1969)

162455 Frank Murray Cabell (2/1/1882-3/10/1960), m. Emma Pickens
        Thompson (b. ca. 1882-1938)
1624551 Muriel Eleanor Cabell (b. 1908), m. (1st) Robert James
         McMillan (1899-1971); m. (2nd) La Cari Long (b. ca.
         1908-1989)
16245511 Murray Cabell McMillan (1929-1983), m. Patricia
          Isabelle Brady (b. 1929). Adopted one son.
162455111 Scott Shorey McMillan (b. 1963), m. Holly Joanne
           Garrison (b. 1965)
1624551111   Megan Anne McMillan (b. 1991)
162455112   Robert Murray McMillan (b. 1966), m. Patricia Dawn
            Falk (b. ca. 1968)
16245512 Robert James McMillan, Jr. (b. 1936), m. Elaine Ruth
          Mueller (1941-1989)
162455121   Jeffrey Robert McMillan (b. 1974)
1624552 Sarah Pickens Cabell (1909-1975)
1624553 Murray William Cabell (b. 1911), m. Helen Antoinette
         Nicholson (b. 1920)
16245531 Christine Cabell (b. 1944)

16245532 Thomas Nicholson Cabell (b. 1948), m. Vickie Joy Rice
          (b. 1948)
162455321 Emily Christine Cabell (b. 1975)
16245533 Therese Cabell (b. 1949)
162456 Allie Spalding Cabell (6/13/1884-11/10/1958), m. 9/2/1913
          Edmund Taylor Woolfolk (1884-1972)
1624561 Anne Woolfolk (b. 1915), m. Robert Sidney White, Jr. (b.
          1915)
16245611 Molly Bain White (b. 1956)
1624562 Edmund Taylor Woolfolk, Jr. (b. 1917), m. Frances Louise
          Courtney (b. 1918)
16245621 Edmund Taylor Woolfolk III (b. 1945), m. Carolyn Diane
          Williams (b. 1951)
162456211 Courtney Leigh Woolfolk (b. 1976)
16245622 Douglas Courtney Woolfolk (b. 1945), m. Mary Lylia
          Toups (b. 1953)
1624563 Allie Woolfolk, M.D. (b. 1919)
162457 George Wilson Cabell (7/28/1886-1966), 4/10/1912 Roy
          Cabell Smith (b. ca. 1886). No issue.
162458 Eleanor ("Ellen") Cabell (9/13/1888-1973), m. 9/18/1926
          William Abram Lobdell (1882-1947)
1624581 Eleanor Lobdell (b. 2/2/1928), m. 10/18/1946 Coleman
          Lilley McVea (b. 1920)
16245811 Ellen Louise McVea (b. 2/16/1948), m. 4/3/1969 Alan
          Roger Hall (b. 1946)
162458111 Kirsten Margrethe Hall (b. 1971), m. Jay Garrett
          Poelman (b. 1973)
162458112 Ann-Marie Kristine Hall (b. 1975)
162458113 David Alan Hall (b. 1977)
16245812 Anne Lilley McVea (b. 6/9/1949), m. 12/10/1977 Rodney
          Glen Kendall (b. 1955)
162458121 Karl Robert Kendall (b. 1981)
162458122 James Lawrence Kendall (b. 1983)
162458123 Paul Thomas McVea Kendall (b. 1985)
162458124 Grant Michael Kendall (b. 1988)
16245813 Coleman Lilley McVea, Jr. (b. 10/1/1951), m. 8/25/1979
          Valli Vaun Nichols (b. 1956)
162458131 Seth Michael McVea (b. 1980)
162458132 Sarah Love McVea (1981)
162458133 Melissa Grace McVea (b. 1983)
162458134 Lael Lilley McVea (b. 1985)
162458135 Joshua Coleman McVea (b. 1988)
162458136 Emily Kate McVea (b. 1992)
16245814 Sarah Grace McVea (b. 11/20/1954), m. 6/9/1976 John
          Wendell Hall (b. 1951)
162458141 John Richard Hall (b. 1977)
162458142 Ammon Wendell Hall (b. 1979)
162458143 Jared Coleman Hall (b. 1980)
162458144 Rachel Sarah Hall (b. 1982)
162458145 Joseph Cabell Hall (b. 1985)
162458146 Aaron Russell Hall (b. 1989)
16245815 Russell Lobdell McVea (b. 7/24/1957), m. 8/28/1982
          Peggy Washburn (b. 1962)
162458151 Nicholas Russell McVea (b. 1983)

162458152   Alayna Kristy McVea (b. 1985)
162458153   Lucas L. McVea (b. 1987)
162458154   Hannah Elizabeth McVea (b. 1990)
16245816   Virginia Love McVea (b. 11/4/1962), m. 6/30/1984
            Jack Burnett Smith (b. 1950)
162458161   Paul Charles Smith (b. 1989)
162458162   Brian Burnett Smith (b. 1992)
162459   Susan Cabell (4/10/1892-5/14/1942), m. 6/18/1912 Isidore
            Larguier IV (1891-1939)
1624591   Billy Cabell Larguier (b. 1913), m. Wilford Paul Hamil-
            ton (b. 1911)
16245911   John Burgoyne Hamilton (b. 1933), m. Cynthia Segrest
            (b. 1933)
162459111   Cynthia Lee Hamilton (b. 1956)
162459112   John Burgoyne Hamilton, Jr. (b. 1958)
162459113   William Cabell Hamilton (1961-1971)
162459114   Elizabeth Caroline Hamilton (b. 1970)
16245912   Wilford Paul Hamilton, Jr. (b. 1935), m. Frances
            Virginia Jordan (b. 1936)
162459121   Holly Jordan Hamilton (b. 1963)
16245913   Mary Sue Hamilton (b. 1942), m. Byron Richard Bolen
            (b. 1939)
162459131   Amy Hamilton Bolen (b. 1963)
162459132   Trudy Saison Bolen (b. 1965)
162459133   Leigh Durham Bolen (b. 1969)
162459134   Byron Richard Bolen, Jr. (b. 1972)
16245914   Sara Ellen Hamilton (b. 1944), m. William Allen Nabors
            III (b. 1941)
162459141   William Allen Nabors IV (b. 1966)
162459142   Hamilton Hughes Nabors (b. 1970)
162459143   Mary Ellen Nabors (b. 1974)
162459144   Samuel Stuart Nabors (b. 1977)
16245915   Martha Larguier Hamilton (b. 1950), m. John Bradford
            Gray (b. 1948)
162459151   John Bradford Gray, Jr. (b. 1973)
162459152   Kathrine Rivers Gray (b. 1975)
1624592   Isidore Larguier V (b. 1915), m. Emily Lou Fleniken
            (b. 1919)
16245921   Isidore Larguier VI (b. 1939), m. Masil Richard (b.
            1938)
162459211   Christina Marie Larguier (b. 1963)
162459212   Monique Noel Larguier (b. 1964)
16245922   Rebecca Anne Larguier (b. 1946), m. John Dale Facundus
            (b. 1946)
162459221   John Dale Facundus II (b. 1966)
1624593   Sue Cabell Larguier (b. 1918), m. Homer Dale Spaht (b.
            1915)
16245931   Homer Dale Spaht, Jr. (b. 1942), m. Anita Louise Fife
            ((b. 1942)
162459311   Ashley Elizabeth Spaht (b. 1974)
16245932   Susan Louise Spaht (b. 1944)
16245933   Kay Elizabeth Spaht (b. 1948), m. John Coyt Hutchison,
            Jr. (b. 1938)
162459331   Susan Elizabeth Hutchison (b. 1974)

162459332 Virginia Lott Hutchison (b. 1975)
16245934 Charles William Spaht (b. 1950), m. Frances Abigail
          Morgana (b. 1951)
1624594 Calvin Woodbridge Larguier (1921-1970), m. Iris Melba
          Vine (b. 1924)
16245941 Johnnie Sue Larguier (b. 1948), m. William Ewell
          Cooper, Jr. (b. 1926)
16245942 Iris Mellisa Larguier (b. 1951)
1624595 Margery Louise Larguier (b. 2/16/1930), m. 7/9/1948
          Clifton Frank Fabre (b. 1923)
16245951 Clifton ("Kip") Frank Fabre, Jr. (b. 1949), m. Emily
          Dupuy (b. 1944)
162459511 Ryan Clifton Fabre (b. 1972)
162459512 Brad Kenneth Fabre (b. 1975)
16245952 John Bradford Fabre (b. 1955)
16245953 David Larguier Fabre (b. 1957)
16245954 Farin Louise Fabre (b. 1959)
16245955 Calvin Isidore Fabre (b. 1967)

1626 Robert Bolling Cabell II, m. (2nd) Eleanor Hart (1816-1904)

16262 Mary Frances Cabell

162651 Mary ("Mamie") Cabell Taylor (10/31/1873-1940), m. Silas
          Lucas Lee (1859-1954)
1626511 Joseph Cabell Lee (b. 1917), m. Alice Jaseta Kopetzky
          (b. 1926)
16265111 Harold Michael Lee (b. 1949)
16266 Susan Cowan Cabell (11/6/1845-1911), m. John Posey
          Beverley (b. ca. 1839)

162663 Eleanor Hodge Beverley (1874-1923), m. Frank Lyle Hays
          (b. ca. 1874)
1626631 Georgia Hopkins Hays (b. 1904), m. William Ralph
          McConnell (b. 1900)
16266311 William Ralph McConnell, Jr. (b. 1929), m. Jackie Lee
          Almes (b. 1932)
162663111 John Robert McConnell (b. 1955)
162663112 Leeann McConnell (b. 1957)
162663113 Thomas Dean McConnell (b. 1962)
16266312 Frank Emory McConnell (b. 1931), m. Barbara Walton
          Drake (b. 1932)
162663121 Susan Georgia McConnell (b. 1955)
162663122 Ann Stoddard McConnell (b. 1956)
162663123 James Edward McConnell (b. 1959)
1626632 Frank Lyle Hays, Jr. (ca. 1906-1973), m. Hazel
          (b. ca. 1906)

162664 Susan ("Sudie") Rudy Beverley (1883-1976), m. Dr. Ben-
          jamin Yeager Jaudon (1874-1949)
1626641 Benjamin Anderson Jaudon (b. 1903)
1626642 Joseph Cabell Jaudon, M.D. (b. 1904), m. Ruth Elizabeth
          Bulla (b. 1906)

16266421 Anne Elizabeth Jaudon (b. 1935), m. James Campbell VII
          (b. 1935)
162664211 Elizabeth Anne Campbell (b. 1959)
162664212 James Douglas Campbell (b. 1962)
162664213 Joseph Kevin Campbell (b. 1963)
162664214 Dorothy Carolyn Campbell (b. ca. 1965)
16266422 Joseph Cabell Jaudon, Jr. (b. 1937), m. Helen Shirley
          Forsee (b. 1937)
162664221 Jennifer Elizabeth Jaudon (b. 1963)
162664222 Joseph Cabell Jaudon III (b. 1965)
16266423 Robert Crandall Jaudon (b. 1941), m. Ferrin Louise
          Leresche (b. 1940)
162664231 Robert Crandall Jaudon, Jr. (b. 1972)
1626643 Frances Elizabeth Jaudon (1908-1977), m. August Rophe
          Boden (b. ca. 1908)
16266431 August Rophe Boden, Jr. (b. 1930), m. Lila Dale Barrett
          (b. ca. 1930)
162664311 Dale Jaudon Boden (b. 1956)
162664312 Charles Henry Boden (b. 1957)
1626644 Beverley Yeager Jaudon (1908-1941)

16268 Laura Bradford Cabell (2/24/1851-1947)

1626a Inah Gabriella Cabell (6/27/1858-1947)
1626b Joseph Benjamin Cabell (5/3/1862-1935)
1627 George Washington Cabell , m. Mary Redd Williams (b. ca.
      1820)

16273 Joseph Joel Cabell (2/12/1842-1868), m. Rhoda Williams (b.
      ca. 1843-6/24/1868)
162731 George Benjamin Cabell, m. Annie Abbott (b. 1873)
1627311 Fenley Abbott Cabell (b. 1895), m. Ruth Thomas (b. ca.
          1896)
1627312 Lillian Cabell (b. 1895), m. William H. Jones (b. ca.
          1893)
16273121 Virginia Jones (b. 1916)
16273122 Dorothy Jones (b. 1918)
16273123 Barbara Jones (b. 1919)
162732 Louisa Cabell, m. Stanley Choatham (b. ca. 1865)
1627321 Ollie Choatham (b. ca. 1889)
1627322 Joe Choatham (b. ca. 1891)
1627323 Clint Choatham (b. ca. 1893)
1627324 Virginia Choatham (b. ca. 1895)
1627325 John Choatham (b. ca. 1897)

162771 Sears Wilson Cabell (1874-1943), m. Brenda Haines (b. ca.
      1875)
1627711 Virginia Cabell (b. ca. 1888)
1627712 Helen Cabell (b.ca. 1900)
1627713 Laura Cabell (b. ca. 1902)

1627a Virginia Margaret Cabell (10/5/1857-1940), m. George W.
      McKendrick (1855-1931)
1627a1 Mary Cabell McKendrick, m. Charles H. Tyler (1878-1905)

1627a11 Margaret Rebecca Tyler (1908-1919)
1627a12 John Calvin Tyler (b. 1911), m. Margaret Angela Proctor
     (b. 1916)
1627a121 Stephen Proctor Tyler (b. 1943)
1627a122 Louisa Angela Tyler (b. 1945)
1627a2 Calvin Carlisle McKendrick (12/26/1884-1904)
1627b William Henry Cabell (1/31/1861-4/5/1926) (killed in an
     automobile accident), m. Georgia C. Cooper (1868-1947)
1627b1 Mary Elizabeth Cabell (6/1/1906-5/28/1985), m. 1925 Earl
     Clarkston Akin (1894-1959)
1627b11 Samuel Cabell Akin (b. 1928), m. (1st) Mary Ruth Dillen
     (b. 1927); m. (2nd) Charlotte Womack (b. 1935)
  Child by first wife:
1627b111 Bruce Earl Akin (b. 1955)
  Child by second wife:
1627b112 Elizabeth Leigh Akin (b. 1964), m. Damon Wade Yost (b.
     ca. 1963)
1627b2 George Breckenridge Cabell (7/2/1907-2/7/1984), m. 9/6/
     1936 Tybera Wilson (b. 1913)
1627b21 Stephen Carrington Cabell (b. 1945), m. Mary O'Flynn
     Barr (b. 1949)
1627b211 Meredith Glenn Cabell (b. 1978)
1627b212 Stephen Carrington Cabell, Jr. (b. 1984)

162x Richard Randolph Cabell

162b George C. Cabell (4/16/1825-d. inf.)

173 Nathaniel West Dandridge (1/14/1771-7/26/1847), m. 7/13/
     1797, Martha H. Fontaine (7/4/1781-9/12/1845) (grand-
     daughter of Patrick Henry). Home: Pontotoc, Mississippi.
1731 Charles Fontaine Dandridge, M.D., m. Tabitha Anne McGhee.
     Home: Sardis, Mississippi
17311 McGhee Dandridge. Killed in the Battle of Shiloh.
1732 William Fontaine Dandridge, m. 11/20/1825 Susan Stith in
     Brunswick County.
17321
1733 Eliza Ann Dandridge, m. William Hereford, M.D.
1734 Martha Lightfoot Dandridge (6/3/1850-   ), m. Col.
     Richard R. Bolton
1735 Nathaniel West Dandridge III, m. Harriet A. Wylie
1736 Rosalie Spotswood Dandridge, m. William Daugherty Bradford
1737 Henry Bolling Dandridge, M.D., m. Adeline Kenon Wilbourn
17371 Lightfoot ("Lightie") Dandridge, m. Henry Woodson Baker
173711 Katie Jenkins Baker, m. Marvin N. Fogleman
1737111 Mary Kate Fogleman, m. Thomas Dove Copeland
17371111 Sharon Diane Copeland, m. Stephen M. Barrager
173711111 Katherine Copeland Barrager (b. 6/11/1978)
173711112 Meghan Douglas Barrager (b. 8/23/1979)
17371112 Connie Sue Copeland, m. Gerald Dan Crockett
173711121 Bradford Thomas Crockett (b. 12/11/1966)
173711122 Dana Sue Crockett (b. 1/10/1969)

174a312211 Laura Michelle Giese

2122 William Beverley Randolph (6/11/1799-5/15/1868), m. 5/21/
       1816, Sarah Lingan
21221 James Lingan Randolph (6/11/1817-9/17/1888), m. 11/23/1848
       Emily Strother
212211 John Strother Randolph (11/1/1849-11/7/1850)
212212 Beverley Strother Randolph (7/17/1851-   ), m. 9/20/
       1882 Mary Jewett
212213 Edmund Strother Randolph (4/30/1855-8/25/1866)
212214 Lingan Strother Randolph (5/13/1859-3/7/1922), m. 10/15/
       1890 Fanny Robbins (2/18/1867-   )
2122141 James Robbins Randolph (8/4/1891-   )
2122142 Orlando Robbins Randolph (7/11/1894-   ), m. 10/24/
       1923 Jean Graham McAllister (12/6/1897-   )
21221421 Beverley Randolph (dau.) (12/5/1924-   )
21221422 Jean Graham Randolph (10/7/1929-   )
2122143 Emily Randolph (1/13/1897-   ), m. 10/12/1918 Stapleton
       Conway Deitrick

21221432 Frances Randolph Deitrick (7/13/1922-   )
21221433 Lingan Randolph Deitrick (4/26/1925-   ) (twin)
21221434 Elsie Payne Deitrick (4/26/1925-   ) (twin)
21221435 Emily Lynn Deitrick (11/18/1926-   )
2122144 Lingan Strother Randolph, Jr. (2/12/1903-   ), m. 5/9/
       1931 Anne Elizabeth Wallace (4/13/1910-   )
21221441 Joan Overton Randolph (4/25/1933-   )
21221442 Lingan Strother Wallace Randolph (1/8/1936-   )
21222 Martha Jane Randolph (11/16/1818-   ), m. 6/23/1840
       Charles Ferdinand Codwise
212221 Mary Byvanck Codwise (7/18/1842-3/1/1890)
212222 Beverley Randolph Codwise (6/5/1844-   )

21223 William Moray Randolph (1/24/1821-11/14/1890), m. 6/5/1851
       Sarah Seymour
212231 William Seymour Randolph (9/28/1857-   ), m. 10/19/
       1881 Lucy Cunningham
212232 Felix Seymour Randolph (3/29/1859-   ), m. 9/22/1891
       Lelia Little
212233 Richard Beverley Randolph (5/28/1861-   ). Unm.
212234 Emma Stark Randolph (3/1/1863-   ), m. 6/5/1890
       Benjamin Daily
212235 Mary Meade Randolph (6/28/1870-   ), m. 4/20/1892
       Albert Livingston Johnson
21224 Emma Beverley Randolph (5/5/1823-10/9/1864), m. 6/1/1855
       Henry Stark
21225 Cornelia Patterson Randolph (2/10/1825-   ). Unm.
21226 Richard Randolph (1/29/1827-2/9/1893). Unm.
21227 Mary Meade Randolph (9/23/1828-   ), m. 9/13/1855
       W. W. Turner
21228 Harriet Isabel Randolph (7/19/1830-7/5/1879), m. 6/14/
       1860 John A. Pickett
212281 George Randolph Pickett (3/31/1861-10/31/1885). Unm.
21229 Elizabeth Gibbon Randolph (4/1/1833-   ), m. 10/28/
       1863 Washington Custis Calvert
2122x David Meade Randolph (7/30/1836-8/3/1837)

2124 Burwell Starke Randolph (1800-10/22/1854), d.s.p.

216 Jane Randolph, m. 2/17/1774 or 10/1/1774 Archibald Bolling

2184 Rebecca Meade (180 -   ), m. James Lea
21842 Howard Fairfax Lea (18 -   )
218421 Leisa Fairfax Lea (1900-   ), m.   MacBride
2184211 Pamela Fairfax MacBride (19 -   ), m. Austen Bayard
        Colgate (192 -   )
21842111 Sarah Colgate
21842112 Bruce Colgate

219221 George Fleming Jones. Omit: General C.S.A.
21932 Julia Calvert ("Pink") Bolling, m. Rev. Philip Barraud
        Cabell of "Edgewood" Nelson County, son of Nathaniel
        Francis and Anne Blaws Cocke Cabell of "Liberty Hall")
        Warminster, VA.
219321 Elizabeth Nicholas Cabell (1861-1862)
219322 Joseph Hartwell Cabell (12/24/1863-12/11/1955), m. (1st)
        Margaret Polk Logan (1875-1904); m. (2nd) Louise Telford
        Groesbeck (1881-1965)
   Children by first wife:
2193221 Philip Francis Cabell (11/22/1896-2/15/1927), m. 9/6/
        1918 Constance Hollingsworth in Dallas.
21932211 Barbara Dallas Cabell
2193222 Margaret Logan Cabell (2/12/1902-   ), m. 6/11/1921
        Sydney B. Self (1896-1980). Authoress: RED CLAY
        COUNTRY, etc.
21932221 Sydney B. Self, Jr.
21932222 Shirley Self
21932223 Hartwell Cabell Self
21932224 Virginia Self
   Child by second wife:
2193223 Mary Groesbeck Cabell, m. (1st) Parker Crenshaw; m.
        (2nd) George Selden Somerville (-1973)

2193241 Julia Calvert Cabell (1896-1984), m. (1st) James Van
        Wyck Osbourne (d. 1939 in automobile accident); m.
        (2nd) 1935 Igor Moravsky, a Captain in the Czarist
        Russian Army. Osbournes built house "Rock Castle"
        on James River near "Bolling Hall".

221112 Virginia Randolph, m. James Baugh Mallory

2211123 James Baugh Mallory, Jr.

22115 Elizabeth Anna Randolph, m. Richard Channing Hall, son of
        Jacob and Catherine Elizabeth Moore Hall
221151 Catherine Elizabeth Hall

2211512 Katherine Randolph Brown

221156 Frances McMurdo Hall

2212   Mary Goode Randolph had a child by her first husband George
          Washington Thornton. See 2212a

22121   Henry Randolph Thornton, m. (1st) 6/18/1828 Mary Agnes
          Bradford

221211   George Thornton, m. Frances ("Fannie") Rew

2212113   Katherine ("Kate") Thornton

2212116   Frances ("Fannie") Thornton

221221   Mary Elizabeth Adams (d. 1971)

221224   Maria Critenton Adams

22123   Mary Goode Thornton. First husband was the son of Philip
          P. Maury

221251   Seth Thornton Maury, m. Kathryn Elizabeth Stevenson

2212512   Zaidee Elizabeth Maury (b. 12/14/1886)
22125121   Maurine Zada DeBusk (b. 11/17/1907)
221252   Richard Randolph ("Dick") Maury (b. 1/2/1850)
2212521   Annie Lena Maury (b. 8/16/1881) (d. young)
2212522   Lottie Stewart Maury (b. 5/29/1883)

2212531   Cora G. Maury, m. 1906 William Henry Guinn

2212532   Margaret Fontaine Maury

22125322   Alton Ray Ferguson (1907-1907) (b. Waco, TX)

221254   Edmund Kimbro Maury, m. (1st) Annie Foster
2212541   Caroline Elizabeth Maury (b. 11/7/1882)

221254222   Earl Grey Hatfield
22125423   Annie Lee Hatfield

22125426   Gladys Dudly Hatfield (9/2/1915-   )

2212544   Flora Lee Maury, m. Joseph Samuel McFall
22125441   Joseph Samuel McFall, Jr.

22125444   Son (d. young)

221257   Mary Lucy Maury, m. James Benjamin Stevenson whose
          mother was the former Susan Barns

221257431   David Maury Griffith (b. 11/7/1951)

22125751   Hermione Stevenson. Her husband Gene Arthur Franklin
          (b. 1/8/1920)

221257512   John Patrick Franklin. First wife was Nancy Granville

2212575122   Johanna Susanne Franklin

2212575131   Diana Thompson

22125752   Jeanne Dee Stevenson. Husband's name is Attebery
221257521   Robert Craven Carter Attebery
221257522   Penelope Susan Attebery
221257523   Michael Gordon Attebery
221257524   Allen Addison Attebery
22125753   James Gordon Stevenson. Mother of his wife was the
           former Lulu Vaugn Morgridge

22125754   Marjorie Ann Stevenson, m. 6/2/1951 Robert Franklin
           Hummer

2212581   Gilbert Lafayette Maury II

2212583   John Cason Maury (11/18/1900-   )

221259   Elizabeth Greene Maury
22126   James Woodville Maury (d. 10/19/1822)

221271   Richard Harris Maury. Unm.

2212723   Irene ("Renie") Kittrell Maury (b. Wahalak)

2212725   James Randolph Maury. Unm.

2212731   James Berkeley ("Berk") Maury, m. Renna Agnes Burks
          (d. 3/17/1968), dau. of George Samuel Burks
22127311   Mary Agnes Maury, m. John W. Cox. No issue.

22127342   Edward Wright Maury, m. (2nd) Rose Mary Sasek

221273432   Michael Maury (2/13/1947-   ). Adopted by his
            mother's second husband, a Mr. Sellman.
221273433   Letitia Lynn Maury (8/27/1955-   ). Goes by name
            of Peister.

221273521   Richard Daniel Humpries (b. 7/14/1946)

2212741   Richard Gathright Maury (killed ca. 1914 when a bull
          crossed in front of an automobile that he was driving).
2212742   Kate Harris Maury

22128   Catherine Mildred Washington Maury (d. 8/18/1826)
22129   Agnes Gray Maury (d. 8/16/1831)

2212x41   Ruby Randolph Maury (d. 2/19/1987) (bur. Birmingham).
          The mother of her first husband Horace Lee Crabtree
          was the former Halia West.
2212x411   Nell Virginia Crabtree. Her second husband was
           Clarence Carl Bookout.

2212x411111   Christopher Wayne Chenry (11/22/1975-   )
2212x41112 Estella Denise Brock. Her husband Richard Carlton
           Register was the son of Giford Franklin Register.

2212x4112   Roslyn Lanel Brock. The mother of her husband Henry
           Julius Stern was the former Hedwig Israelsohn.

2212x412   Horace Jackson Crabtree's wife Mildred Byrd was the
          daughter of James Ira Robert Byrd.
2212x4121 Jacquelyn Crabtree (b. New Brockton)

2212x4122   Judy Dianne Crabtree (b. 8/22/1947)

2212x414   Ruby Frances Crabtree (d. 5/9/1923) (bur. New Brockton)
2212x415   Helen Sue Crabtree (b. New Brockton). Her third
          husband Herbert William Teague, Jr. (b. 6/26/1919)

2212x416   Jean Frederica Crabtree (b. New Brockton)

2212x417   Betty Joan Crabtree (d. 5/25/1991) (b. New Brockton)

2212x41711   Erik Stephen West (b. 3/8/1971)
2212x4172 Michael Leslie West, m. Jeannie Austen
2212x41721   Aubrey West
2212x41722   Michael Austen West

2212x41732 Sarah Ashleigh (b. 10/21/1983)

2212x42 Lucie Gaines Maury (d. 12/30/1989) (bur. Birmingham)
2212x421 Byron Barnes Brice (6/16/1925-1/31/1983) (bur. Birm-
         ingham)
2212x4211 Beverley Brock Brice. Her husband James Carl Cooper
          (d. 6/1/1972) (bur. Birmingham)

2212x43 Gilbert Wallace Maury. His wife the former Clarice
        Adella Parks (d. 12/6/1987) (bur. Talladega, AL)
2212x431 Katherine Virginia Maury. Her husband James Gibson
         Stringer (d. 6/24/1991) (bur. Talladega, AL) was
         the son of the former Willie Caludine Sanders

2212x43111   Katherine Leigh Stringer

2212x43113 Laura McLane Stringer (b. Birmingham)
2212x4312 Robert Sanders Stringer, m. Carol Layne Trice
2212x4313 Virginia Clarice Stringer (b. 3/2/1951)
2212x4314 David Lee Stringer, m. Sharon Kay Gray (b. 1/1/1952)
          (b. Birmingham)

2212x4414 Nona Christine Maury (b. 11/11/1961)

2212x611 Maury Odell Dorriety (b. 7/13/1936)

2212x6312 Carmen Leilani Maury (b. 7/23/1963)
2212x6313 David Christopher Maury (b. 9/22/1964)

2212x6411 Maury Scott Jones (b. 5/30/1961)

2212x7 Ruby Rolfe Maury (d. 1/4/1982) (bur. Waco). Her husband
     Johnston Frank Roberts (d. 11/28/1972) (bur. Waco)
2212x71 Scott Evans Roberts (d. 8/25/1983) (bur. Waco). His
     first wife was the former Lucile Inez Clark

2212xa Thomas Francis Maury (d. 12/ /1863)

2212a Jan Thornton, m. 9/21/1805 Dr. Scott
2212a1 Frances Scott, d. 12/29/1848

2221821211 Kathy Lynn Barry (b. 5/18/1968)
2221821212 Kristy June Barry (b. 9/16/1970)
222182122 Elizabeth Ann Barry (b. 1/31/1941), m. 11/6/1964,
     Joseph Leo Johnson
2221821223 Andrew Lem Johnson (b. 9/17/1970)

222183 Lucy Ada Barry (b. Eureka, MS)
2221831 In the 16th line Oo-be-ja should read Oo-lu-ja (or cha).
     Note: The name may be Wilson instead of Willson and
     he might not have been a son of Gideon Franklin Morris
     . . . in 1838, when Wilson/Willson was trying to find
     his mother, he was captured and one of the guards,
     given $100.00 to release him, chose from among five
     young men, all of whom claimed to be Gideon's son.
     However, the choice made seemed to please Gideon who,
     in his will, recognized Wilson/Willson as his son.

22314332 William Hugh ("Bill") Meredith

241 Anne Cary, m. Thomas Mann Randolph. After her death he m.
     9/15/1790 Gabrielle Harvie (age 18), dau. of Col. John
     Harvie of "Belvedere"
2411 Mary ("Molly") Randolph, m. David Meade Randolph. She
     wrote THE VIRGINIA HOUSE-WIFE, published in 1824 and
     often reprinted, and in her later years she was called
     "Old Queen".

241346352 Adair Anderson Ely (1921-4/27/1987)
241346353 Anna ("Nancy") Morris Ely, m.   Starnes

2414111211 Marie Elizabeth Bankhead, m. Lloyd R. Miller

24141113431 Robert M. Solberg
241411134311 Jennifer Leigh Solberg
241411134312 Michael Paul Solberg
241411134313 Nathaniel James Solberg
24141113432 Janet Solberg

24142 Col. Thomas Jefferson Randolph, m. Jane Hollins Nicholas

241424 In the Index of PD (page 422) Francis Gildart Ruffin is
     improperly labelled 24142444

24142x   Jane Nicholas Randolph, m. Robert Garlick Hill Kean. He m. (2nd) Adelaide Navarro Demarest Prescott. In PD, under 24142x4, omit:

        Children by second wife:
        24142x41 Evalina Moore Kean
        24142x42 Caroline Hill Kean
        24142x43 Marshall Prescott Kean
        24142x44 Otho Vaughan Kean

      And in C & A, under 24142x4, omit:
      24142x41 Evalina Moore Kean, m. Edward Rolfe Ford Wells

24142x261   Adelaide Morris Cooley, m. (1st) Hal Waugh Smith (omit Henry from CORRECTIONS AND ADDITIONS), m. (2nd) Burnette Lawrence Gadeberg

24142x2613   Adelaide Leigh (Smith) Gadeberg, m. William James Cleere
24142x26131 William Burnett Cleere (b. 11/15/1974)
24142x26132 Lawrence Ryan Cleere (b. 8/8/1978)

2414431541   John Hamilton Coolidge, m. Anne Hallowell Richards

2414435111   Nicole Rousmaniere Coolidge

241446   Thomas Jefferson Coolidge. In the Paris Salon of 1882, Coolidge purchased off the wall for 10,000 francs, John Singer Sargeant's eight foot by eleven foot masterpiece "El Jaleo" (hubbub, ruckus, noise), now the property of the Boston art museum, and just cleared of years of dust and grime by Alain Goldrach. It is being exhibited ("John Singer Sargeant's El Jaleo") in 1992 at the National Gallery of Art and at the Isabella Stewart Gardner Museum in Boston.
2414461   Marian Appleton Coolidge, m. Lucius Manlius Sargent

241446111   Francis Lee Higginson III. Under him change "Child by second wife" to read "Children by second wife". Omit "Children by third wife".

241446112   John Higginson, m. Lida Wendover Riesmeyer

24144611231 Wingate Joan Mackay-Smith, m. John Campbell Dalton
24144611232 Juliet Higginson Mackay-Smith, m. George Scott Winslow McCagg
24144611233 Emily Austin Mackay-Smith, m. James Michael Day

241446331   Emily Redmond Cross, m. Sir John Kenyon Vaughan-Morgan (b. 1905). Cr. Baron Reigate (1970)
2414463311 Julia Redmond Vaughan-Morgan, m. (1st) Henry Walter Wiggin (b. 1939). Div. 1977. M. (2nd) 11/1/1986 Joseph King (b. 1936)

24144633111 Lucy Redmond Wiggin, m. 10/20/1990 Joel Patrick Ford

24144633112 Deborah Mary Vaughan-Morgan, m. Michael Whitfield
     (b. 1939)

241446332 Richard James Cross, m. Margaret Whittemore Lee
     (b. 1916)
2414463321 Richard James Cross, Jr., m. Anne Marie Dyman
     (b. 1942)

2414463322 Margaret Lee Cross, m. William Martin Brodsky
     (b. 1941)

24144633222 Rachel Lee Brodsky
2414463323 Alan Whittemore Cross, m. Marion Morgan Johnson
     (b. 1944)

24144633233 Caroline Whittemore Cross
24144633234 Susannah Hunt Cross

2414463325 Jane Randolph Cross, m. 1985 Paul David Spector
24144633251 Jessie Cross Spector (b. 9/22/1986)
24144633252 Abby Cross Spector (b. 9/1/1989)

2414463331 William Redmond Cross III, m. 12/23/1989 Ellen
     Patricia Healy
2414463332 Pauline Curtis Cross, m. 1985 Brock Reeve
24144633321 Nathaniel Cross Reeve (b. 10/24/1988)
24144633322 Adam Cross Reeve (b. 11/25/1990)
2414463333 Frederick Newbold Cross, m. 1991 Jane Frances
     Griffern

241446335 Mary Newbold Cross, m. Donald Pond Spence (b. 1926)
2414463351 Alan Keith Spence, m. (1st) Pamela Whitten Hughes
     (b. 1953). Div. 1983. M. (2nd) 7/4/1992 Bonnie
     Joseph Carey
2414463352 Sarah Coolidge Spence, m. 1985 James Harvey McGregor
24144633521 Edward ("Neddy") Isham Spence McGregor (b. 11/18/
     1992)

2414616311 Nicholas Porter Thorndike

241492721 Catharine Randolph Russell, m. James Leake Little
2414927211 Catharine Randolph Little

2414b George Wythe Randolph, m. (as second husband) Mary Eliza-
    beth Adams Pope

2415162 Samuel Rolfe Millar (5/21/1857-9/20/1927), m. Bertha
    Marie Riedel of Heidelberg

2415333111 Ann Tate Randolph, m. Wayne Lilley
24153331111 William Randolph Lilley (11/16/1976-   )
24153331112 Phyllis Ann Lilley (12/11/1978-   )

2415333112   Carol Gillis Randolph (12/10/1952-   ), m. John
            Collier Hart Sumner
24153331121   Wendy Randolph Sumner (12/8/1970-   ), m. 6/8/1991
            John Haas
24153331122   John Collier Hart Sumner, Jr. (10/1/1972-   )
24153331123   Jessica Elaine Sumner (9/29/1977-   )
241533312   Ruth Caroline Randolph (d. 3/26/1992), m. John Lamb
            Gillis (d. 3/17/1976)
2415333121   John Lamb Gillis, Jr., m. Nichole Mitchell
24153331211   John Mitchell Gillis (11/21/1966-   ), m. 8/17/
            1991 Jennifer Storey
24153331212   Suzanne Lamb Gillis (12/2/1969-   )
2415333122   Carol Randolph Gillis, m. William D. Manning, Jr.
24153331221   Carol Randolph Manning (4/2/1963-   ), m. Luke
            Dauchot
241533312211   Nicholas Dauchot
241533312212   Christopher Dauchot
24153331222   Rebecca Barrett Manning (9/18/1964-   ), m.
            Anthony Scaletto
24153331223   Anne Gillis Manning (10/5/1969-   )
2415333123   Anne Carter Gillis
2415333124   Mary Barrett Gillis (11/16/1949-   ), m. John
            Francis Menousek
24153331241   Mary Barrett Menousek (2/6/1978-   )
24153331242   Caroline Carter Menousek (12/31/1980-   )
24153331243   James Randolph Menousek (9/6/1984-   )
24153331244   Elizabeth Lamb Menousek (9/30/1988-   )
241533313   Irene Randolph, m. 5/23/1951 Henry Leighton Morrill
            (5/12/1911-   ), son of Charles Henry and Lenita
            Collins Morrill
2415333131   Lenita Collins Morrill (2/11/1952-   ), m. 9/11/
            1982 Mads Emanuelsen
2415333132   Ann Randolph Morrill (11/25/1954-   ), m. 6/2/1979
            Leo B. Schmid
24153331321   Andrew Leighton Schmid (5/1/1983-   )
24153331322   Carter Randolph Schmid (12/9/1989-   )

2415335413   Camilla Cary Thompson, m.   Braver

241632162   on page 234 of PD should be 241632612

2419335113   Mark Randolph Thompson. In C & A page 88 this
            number should be 2419336113

2419335114   Sarah Ann Thompson. In C & A page 88 this number
            should be 2419336114

241c52   Constance Fairfax Cary (1843-1920), m. Burton Norvell
            Harrison. Mrs. Harrison was a well-known novelist.

24218   Lucy Burwll Randolph, m. Rev. Eleazer Carter Hutchison
            who was "shocked" that his family owned slaves and
            insisted that they sell them, which they did. 4 CCHA 34.

2421883   Donald Roy Anderson (d. 1889, age 4)

2421885   Infant (d. 1886)

2442511   Omit 24425111, 244251111, 244251112 and 244251113
     Insert:
24425111 Ellie Wood Page Keith (9/10/1921-   )

25   Jane Bolling Randolph (1728-1756), m. Col. Anthony Walke, Jr.
     (or II) (d. 1782). He is bur. at "Greenwich", Princess Anne
     County. He m. (2nd) 5/8/1757 Mary Mosely (d. 11/22/1785).
     He was a merchant and Member of H. of B.

251   Rev. Anthony Walke III (d. 1814) of "Fairfield" (Princess
     Anne County), m. (1st) 1/15/1776 Anne McColley McClanahan
     (d. 1809). His second wife was the widow of Charles
     Fisher.
2511 Edwin Walke (second child of 251)

2513 John Newton Walke (a child by second marriage) m. Mary Land

2514 Anthony Walke IV (oldest child of 251), m. (2nd) 6/27/1811
     Ann Livingston. Anthony inherited the "Fairfield" estate.
2515 Jane E. Walke (fourth child of 251)
2516 Susan Meade Walke (third child of 251) (1795 or 1798-1833),
     m. at "Fairfield", Charles Hansford Sheild (10/23/1796-
     1868), son of Robert Sheild VI and his wife Martha
     Hansford. A lawyer of Louisville.

25163   Anne Walke Sheild (d. 10/21/1904) (born in York County),
     m. 5/21/1846 Robert John McCandlish of Norfolk (1/27/
     1820-2/22/1890). Parkersburg, WV
251631 Charles Sheild McCandlish, m. about 1880 Elizabeth Putnam
2516311 Randolph Walke McCandlish, m. Frances ("Pepper") Archer

25163112 Charles Sheild McCandlish II (1922-5/27/1985), m.
         Winifred Thompson (b. 1921), dau. of Ernest Hamblin
         and Genevieve Wickham Thompson.
251631121 Charles Sheild McCandlish III (11/6/1949-   ), m.
         6/17/1967 Anne Leake (b. 5/13/1945), dau. of Evans
         Mundy and Gladys Maupin Leake.
2516311211 Charles Sheild McCandlish IV (b. 1969)
251631122
2516311221 Leslie Ann Murdock
2516311222 Alexander Murdock
251631123 Thomas Wickham McCandlish (10/11/1950-   ), m. Nancy
         Lynne Friedberg (12/24/79-   ), dau. of Isadore
         Hirsh and Evelyn Shenfeld Friedberg.
2516311231 Laura Elizabeth McCandlish (11/25/1979-   )
2516311232 Eline Thompson McCandlish (7/27/1981-   )
2516311233 Carolyn Anne McCandlish (3/8/1985-   )
251631124 Ellen Archer McCandlish, m. 2/1/1957 John Martin
         Melville (7/8/1937-   )
2516311241 John D'Wolf Melville (12/6/1895-   )

2516311242 Alysse Wickham Melville (7/2/1987-   )

251632 Upton Beall McCandlish (b. Norfolk, d. Hancock, Western-
        port, MD). Cashier of a bank. M. Margaret ("Maggie")
        Lindsay Landstreet of Fauquier County (d. 1919), dau. of
        Rev. John Landstreet and his wife Mary Frances Swink.

2516321 Lindsay McCandlish (d. about 1926), m. Elizabeth Lee
        Rick
25163211 Jane Randolph McCandlish, m. Harold N. Boyer

2516322 Robert John McCandlish (10/18/1879-8/12/1955), m. 4/22/
        1908 Jane Charlton Graves (1887-1970), dau. of Ralph
        Charlton and Laura Stephens Carter Graves. Piedmont,
        WV.
25163221 Sarah ("Sally") Graves McCandlish (10/28/ -   ), m.
        Richard Huse Crane
251632211 Jane McCandlish Crane (10/3/1946-   ), m. 10/19/1968
        Lt. Col. Thomas Clyde McSwain, Jr. (12/29/1945-   ),
        son of Thomas Clyde and Isabel Sterrett McSwain.
2516322111 Kristin Bunker McSwain (5/1/1969-   )
2516322112 Kimberly Sterrett McSwain (2/21/1973-   )
251632212 Richard Huse Crane, Jr. (3/21/1943-   )
25163222 Robert John McCandlish, Jr. (b. 3/8/1909, at Hancock,
        MD), m. 5/24/1941, at Richmond, Josephine Meredith
        Sutton, dau. of Frank Taylor Sutton, Jr. and his wife
        Rebekah Shore Watson
251632221 Rebekah ("Beck") Sutton McCandlish (7/10/1945-   ),
        m. Lawrence Loring Burckmyer (5/3/1930-   )
2516322211 Sarah Lindsay Burckmyer (5/17/1974-   )
2516322212 Charles Loring Burckmyer (12/31/1976-   )
251632222 Charles Sheild McCandlish (11/15/1948-   ), m. 8/7/
        1976 Mary William Smith (1/31/1951-   ), dau. of
        David Ames and Caroline Hatten Nash Smith.
2516322221 Robert John McCandlish II (9/6/1980-   )
2516322222 Caroline Nash McCandlish (5/16/1982-   )

2516323 Edward Gerstell McCandlish. Illustrator, cartoonist,
        author.
25163231 Margaret Belle McCandlish (4/30/1920-   )
251632311 Douglas Ray Edwards, m. 11/22/1977 Gail Lynne Pardo,
        dau. of Dorsey and Ethel Maur Pardo.
2516323111 Susan ("Suzy") Belle Edwards (5/21/1984-   )
2516323112 Connie Lynne Edwards (9/4/1985-   )
2516323113 Carla Jean Edwards (8/19/1987-   )

2516323122 Eric Owen Lindsay (3/22/1985-   )
2516323123 Mitchell Ross Lindsay (3/23/1987-   )

251632313 Keith Anson Edwards, m. (1st) 8/22/1976 Catherine
        S. Heid, dau. of Daniel and Katie Heid, m. (2nd)
        11/7/1987 Deborah Kay Sykes-Bruce (3/22/19 -   ).
        She had two children from an earlier marriage.

2516323132   Brittany Marie Edwards (12/6/1988-   )

25163233   Phoebe Grey McCandlish
251632331   Mary Jane Cochran, m. (1st) Jim Wallain. Div., m.
            (2nd) Michael Christopher Neal. Div. 1988.
2516323311   Jeffrey Todd Neal was adopted by Michael Christopher
            Neal

251632332   Nancy Hope Wetzler (8/15/1954-   )
2516323321   Brett Hunter Mormann (10/8/1985-   )
2516323322   Laura Katherine Mormann (6/2/1988-   )
251632333   Raymond Edwin Wetzler, m. Dondi Lee Medlin. Div.

251632341   Stephen Claude McCandlish (6/22/1962-   ), m. (never
            married) Rochelle Lorie Lodar (4/14/1967-   ), dau.
            of Raymond Charles Lodar and his wife Beverly Lillian
            Lodar. The family name was Lodarski but was changed
            before Rochelle was born. Stephen m. 6/25/1988 in
            Rochester, Angela April ("Lee") King (1/14/1966-   )
            (b. at Kansas City), dau. of James Monroe King and
            his wife Wilma Cordelia Guy.
2516323411   Allen Dennis Lodar (11/24/1988 in Rochester-   )
   Children by second wife:
2516323412   Stephanie Cordelia Marie McCandlish (12/19/1989-   )
2516323413   Erin-Casey Lee McCandlish (9/23/1991-   )
251632342   Peter David McCandlish, m. 7/20/1992 Patricia ("Pat")
            Waters (b. 11/27/1959). Her first husband was Morgan
            A. Smith.
251632343   Karen Louise McCandlish

25163235   Doris King McCandlish, m. Charles A. Kurzius (3/10/
            1926-2/9/1983)
251632351   Mathew Charles Kurzius (5/25/1954-   ), m. Teresa
            ("Terry") Kotz (12/8/1946-   )

2516323512   Janice Lynn Kurzius (8/4/1984-   )
251632352   Hope Marie Kurzius, m. (2nd) 2/5/1985 at Hoboken,
            NJ, Daniel Wayne Zelinski (11/2/1956-   )

25163236   Anne Walke McCandlish, m. 2/15/1928 Ronald Carroll
            Marshall
251632361   Ronald Edward Marshall, m. 12/30/1971 Joyce Jones
            (adopted name) (11/14/1953-   ), dau. of Rev. Jack
            R. and Ida Mae Gardner Jones.

2516323613   Anne Sheely (b. 8/7/1986)

251632363   Janet April Sheely, m. Vastuia Tavui (vas means
            "ship" or "outrigger"; tuia makes it read a "big
            ship or outrigger).

2516323632   Kavika (English translation is David) Andreas Tavui
            (b. 7/5/1986)

25163238 Evelyn Hope McCandlish, m. Frank Milton Rider (b. 10/
          3/1931)
251632381 John Frederick Rider III, m. 10/19/1986 Karen C.
          Zobel, R.N., dau. of Tom Zobel.
251632382 Karl Thomas Rider (b. 9/19/1958), m. 6/16/1990 Sally
          Joanna Bedwell. Sally's first husband was David M.
          Bowling.
   Son of Jane Alice Bender (not wife)
2516323821 Matthew Gary Rider (b. 11/8/1988)
25163239 Jean Landstreet McCandlish, m. William Robert ("Bob")
          Hoffman, son of Paul Preston and Emma Lucille Pendle-
          ton Hoffman.
2516324   Katherine Davis McCandlish (b. 1888), m. 6/4/1913
          Frederick Dawson Richardson
25163241 Evelyn Randolph ("Randy") Richardson (8/12/1914-3/8/
          1988), m. Dr. George Edward Frederick Macatee, Jr.
          (3/1/1913-8/15/1987), son of George and Anne Forney
          LeGrand Macatee.
251632411 George Edward Frederick Macatee III (7/12/1944-   ),
          m. Mary Locke Davis (12/20/1953-   ), dau. of Walter
          Hamlet and Mary Locke Craig Davis.
2516324111 Mary Locke Macatee (1/24/1983-   )
2516324112 Rebecca Taylor Macatee (1/17/1986-   )
251632412 John Randolph Macatee (4/15/1950-   )
251632413 Phyllis Lee Macatee

25163242 Phyllis Walke Richardson (6/16/1921-   ), m. (1st)
          George J. Barnes (d. 1984), m. (2nd) Henry Lyle Millan
          (12/12/1921-   )
251632421 John Alden Millan (11/19/1962-   )

2516325   Evelyn Orme McCandlish (3/3/1888-   ), m. Ralph Kerper
          Tallant. Piedmont, WV
2516326   Ruth McCandlish (12/17/1892-2/22/1987), m. (1st) 12/25/
          1917 Robert Doddridge Graham (d. 1972), m. (2nd) Ralph
          Kerper Tallant (d. 1981). No children.
25163261 Roberta McCandlish Graham (10/ /1934-   ), m. 12/ /
          1957 Frank Mayer Carter II (9/12/1924-   )
251632611 Anne Lindsay Carter (11/5/1958-   ), m. 8/1/1981
          James Lillard
2516326111 Lindsay Carter Lillard (1/ /1987-   ), b. in Rich-
          mond.
251632612 Frank Graham Carter III (3/28/1962-   )

2516327   Beverly Diggs McCandlish (7/23/1896-8/16/1896).
          Westernport, MD.
2516328   Upton L. McCandlish, Jr. (6/ /1876-   ). Mineral
          County.
2516329   Mary McCandlish (4/7/1878-1881). Mineral County.
251632x   Henry Alvord McCandlish (12/ /1882-5/1/1883).
          Westernport, MD.

251633 Ann ("Nannie") Walke McCandlish (12/31/1850-11/23/1903)

251634 Sarah ("Sally") Sheild McCandlish, m. about 1980 Thomas
Hardaway Hawks of Vicksburg, son of Joseph and Rebecca
Randolph Hawks.

251634221 Thomas Holmes Hawks, m. 5/17/1980 Katherine ("Kate")
Janie Thomson (b. 4/24/1955), dau. of John Donald
Gunn Thomson and his wife Barbara Anne Robb.
2516342211 Gordon Thomson Hawks (b. 7/26/1986)
2516342212 Heather Barbara Hawks (b. 3/18/1988)
2516342213 Ian James Hawks (b. 10/19/1991)

251635 Robert Coleman McCandlish (1862 or 1866 in WV-5/30/1925
in Akron), m. (1st) Maude L. Yeager (of Marlinton, WV),
m. (2nd) 6/9/1908 Ann Verlinda Landstreet (1856 or 1858-
1945), dau. of John and Mary Francis Swink. She was
sister to Margaret who m. Upton Beall McCandlish. No
issue.
2516351 Henry Yeager McCandlish (second child). D. Florida
age 65.
2516352 Anne Walke McCandlish (first child) (6/28/1901-11/13/
1984), m. 2/25/1925 in Akron, Ohio, William Edwin
Bartell (1891-6/8/1971)
25163521 Robert ("Bob") McCandlish Bartell (b. 4/12/1926), m.
9/20/1952 Lanier Higginbotham (widow Bennett). No
children. She has two children by her first marriage.
2516353 Virginia McCandlish (d. child birth - mother also died).

25165 William Francis Sheild, m. Mrs. Lizzie Armistead Booker
(or Miss Lizzie Stribling)

3 Mary Bolling. The date of her wedding is 1731, of her death
is 1770, and the date of the death of her husband, Col. John
Fleming, is 1766.

32312152 David Parish Barhydt Marshall

323121522 David Barhydt Marshall (omit "Jr.)

35 Charles Fleming (8/9/1745-1778). Lt. Col. of 8th Va. Reg.
M. 6/1/1768 or 2/14/1768 at "Warner Hall" Lucy Lewis (6/12/
1747-7/6/1797 or 1798), dau. of Warner Lewis. They had
only one child. Fleming was commissioned Captain of Company
A, 7th Virginia Regiment on 2/29/1776. Wounded at the
Battle of Brandywine 9/11/1777. On 6/28/1778 he was commissioned Lieut. Col. on the eve of the Battle of Monmouth,
New Jersey, where he was wounded and died. It has been
stated that he resigned in December of 1778 but this is
error. See No. 67,817 and War Department, Washington, D.C.,
No. 105778.
351 Lucy Lewis Fleming (1/27/1770-7/6/1815), m. 6/1/1793 William
Evans of Scotland (1758-1800)
3511 Fleming Bolling Evans (6/6/1795-8/9/1861), m. 12/30/1819
Mary Ann Atkinson (4/15/1802-4/25/1877)

35111   William Leroy Evans (6/6/1822 Rogersville, TN-7/9/1857),
        m. 12/27/1843 Martha Ellen Veale (11/22/1822 Knoxville,
        TN-10/31/1918 Sherman, TX)
351111 John Fleming Evans (5/19/1849 Rogersville, TN-1933 or
        1/11/1935 Altus, OK), m. 2/16/1876 at Denton, TX,
        Elizabeth ("Lizzie") Peyton Davis (12/14/1854 Columbia,
        LA-1/3/1924 Fort Worth)
3511111 Alma Leroy Evans
3511112 Guy Hart Evans (b. and d. Sherman, TX)
3511113 Warren Evans
3511114 May Davis Evans
3511115 Elizabeth Peyton Evans
3511116 Virginia Evans
3511117 John Fleming Evans, Jr.
3511118 William Leroy Evans (9/23/1888 Sherman, TX-12/25/1947
        Fort Worth), m. 4/1/1920 Annie Loraine Zinn (6/11/1894
        Fort Worth-7/10/1981)
35111181 Ann Elizabeth Evans
35111182 William Leroy Evans, Jr. (8/31/1920 Colorado Springs-
                ), m. 3/1/1946 at Sledge, MS (Baptist Church,
        Quitman County) Dorothy Eloise Taylor (6/28/1922
        Memphis-   ) (b. Baptist Memorial Hospital,
        Shelby county)
351111821 William Taylor Evans (3/29/1947-   ), m. Winna Lee
        Wilson
3511118211 Lee-Taylor Evans (dau.) (2/28/1981 Houston-   )
3511118212 Pamela Adele Evans (12/19/1984 Houston-   )
351111822 John Scott Evans (8/31/1949-   )
351111823 James Randall Evans (4/14/1952-   )
351111824 Cynthia Ann Evans (8/28/1953-   )

412 Elizabeth Gay (1772-   ), m. 1795 Peter Efford Bentley
     (1757 or 1761-1857)

4124 Efford Bolling Bentley (9/21/1801-8/8/1882), m. Lucy
      Williamson Chamberlayne, dau. of William Byrd and Ann
      Williamson Mosby Chamberlayne

41245 William Chamberlayne Bentley (2/25/1852-   ), m. Lulu
       Logan (11/19/1865-   ), dau. of General Logan of
       Louisiana
412451 William Chamberlayne Bentley, Jr. (7/28/1903-   ),
        m. Barbara Townsend Greene (3/14/1911-   )
4124511 Stewart Woodruff Bentley (6/9/1938-   ), m. Claire
         Frederick Pence (9/7/1942-   )
41245111 Stewart Woodruff Bentley, Jr. (10/5/1962-   ), m.
         Gabriele Greim (6/22/1951-   )
41245112 Elizabeth (Catherine) Bentley (3/3/1964-   ), m.
         Jon Allen Brouelette (11/13/1945-   )
412451121 Adam Bentley Brouelette (10/24/1989-   )
41245113 William Chamberlayne Bentley III (6/24/1969-   ),
         m. Tammy Helms (2/21/1966-   )
412451131 Lauren Elizabeth Bentley (2/11/1992-   )

5   Martha Bolling, m. Thomas Eldridge. Elizabeth Jones, second
    wife of Thomas Eldridge, is shown as the dau. of Sarah
    Edmunds Jones

56 Rolfe Eldridge (12/29/1744 or 5-1806), of "Subpoena", Buck-
    ingham County, m. (MB 11/26/1773 Brunswick County), Susannah
    Everard Walker (1754-3/27/1821), dau. of Col. George Walker,
    originally of Elizabeth City County, and his wife, the
    former Mary Meade.

5617   Benjamin Eldridge, m. Eliza Perkins, a near kinswoman to
       Monroe Perkins of Richmond who married Elizabeth
       ("Lizzie") Langhorne, eldest of the famed Langhorne
       sisters.
56171 Benjamin Rolfe Eldridge, m. Letitia Terry of Bedford
       County. He served for many years as treasurer of the
       Richmond Cedar Works
561711 Edward F. Eldridge. Attorney in Richmond.

56181 Paul Eldridge (10/18/1858-   ), m. 10/6/1886 Bessie
       Duncan (2/11/1868-   )
561811 Paul Eldridge, Jr. (ca. 1888-11/ /1960), m. ca. 1948
       Frances   . No issue.
56182 Grandison Moseley Eldridge (12/10/1861-8/ /1899)
56183 William Moseley Eldridge (10/18/1863-   ), m. 1/22/
       1891 Emma Morton
561831 Elizabeth Eldridge, m.   Bet, a lawyer in SC
561832 Jeanette Eldridge. Lived in Kentucky
5618321 Son
5618322 Son
56184 Elizabeth Fearn Eldridge (12/11/1867-   ), m. 9/2/1899
       Albert Dabney Barnes
561841 Elizabeth Barnes, m.
5618411 Patricia
561842 Dabney Barnes
561843 Eldridge Barnes
46185 Rolfe Eldridge, m.
561851 Sally Rolfe Eldridge

56186 John Eldridge, Jr. (11/24/1864-9/6/1951) (b. Buckingham
       County, d. Atlanta), m. Lillian Emma Moorman (6/1/1877-
       12/30/1946) (b. and d. Buckingham County). She was the
       widow of Benjamin F. Spencer.
561861 John Eldridge III (10/10/1903-5/ /1942). Died in Battle
       of Coral Sea. M. Dorothy Greenwood (d. 1/ /1991) (b.
       British Columbia, d. "Alcoma", Buckingham County)
5618611 Barbara Eldridge (b. ca. 1931), m. Kenneth Whitney
        Weihe
56186111 Elizabeth Greenwood Weihe (b. 8/30/1959), m. 1/18/1986
         (U.S. Naval Academy) Marc Louis Dapas
561861111 Matthew Dapas (b. 7/24/1988)
56186112 John Gibson Weihe (9/ /1961-   ), m. (before 5/28/
         1988) Lucia Ann Detrick, dau. of John Samuel and Lydia
         Chawner Hadley

56186113 Ellen Whitney Weihe (b. 11/8/1965-   )
56186114 Richard Weihe
5618612 Joan Eldridge (b. ca. 1933), m. Donald Janak
56186121 Ann Blair Janak (1/25/1971-   )
5618613 Constance Eldridge (b. ca. 1935)
561862 Thomas Moorman Eldridge (9/23/1906-   ) (b. Buckingham
        County), m. Atlanta 10/8/1931 Leila Venable Mason (1/19/
        1909-4/8/1959), dau. of Frank Tucker and Elizabeth
        Richard Venable Mason
5618621 Leila Elizabeth Eldridge (10/23/1933-   ), m. Douglas-
        ville, GA, Domenic Robert D'Aiutolo (7/29/1927-   ),
        son of Vito P. and Louise Tedesco D'Aiutolo
56186211 Thomas Vito D'Aiutolo (8/20/1954-   ), m. 5/5/1977
        Maureen Lorraine Mede (8/15/1957-   ), dau. of John
        Lawrence and Mary Driscoll Mede
561862111 Eric Thomas D'Aiutolo (9/24/1985-   )
56186212 Louise Leila D'Aiutolo (6/25/1956-   ), m. 8/19/1978
        John William Poole (2/18/1956-   ), son of George
        Bayliss and Valerie Laura Gough Poole
561862121 Leila Whitney Poole (4/19/1985-   )
561862122 John William Poole, Jr. (7/4/1987-   )
561862123 Laura Elizabeth Poole (12/19/1991-   )
56186213 Leila Elizabeth D'Aiutolo (10/25/1957-   ), m. 7/30/
        1983 Kevin Ralph Parke (12/14/1959-   ) son of Ralph
        Leon and Janet Ruth Eshelman Parke
561862131 Christopher James Parke (9/18/1987-   )
5618622 Frank Mason Eldridge (3/26/1939-   ), m. 7/8/1967
        Gladney L'Angel Cureton (1/21/1943-   ), dau. of
        Fred Cureton
56186221 Elizabeth Cureton Eldridge (4/10/1971-   )
56186222 Frank Mason Eldridge, Jr. (3/24/1976-   )
5618623 Thomas Moorman Eldridge, Jr. (11/29/1942-   ), m.
        (1st) Gloria Campbell, m. (2nd) 2/27/1971 Frances Buff
        Fleming, dau. of Lake Little Fleming
   Children by first wife:
56186231 Thomas Moorman Eldridge III (ca. 1959-   )
56186232 Christa Eldridge (ca. 1962-   )
   Children by second wife:
56186233 Thomas Moorman Eldridge III (10/24/1972-   )

561863 William Rolfe Eldridge (11/6/1911-3/29/1931). No issue.

5636211 Eldridge Hoyle ("Coots") Turner

56411 Benjamin Rolfe Williams, m. Willie Sue Thatcher
564111 Lela Williams, m. John Paul Penland
5641111 William Rolfe Penland, m. Martha Fink
56411111 David Penland

5642 Susannah Walker Williams (10/ /1821-12/13/1906) (died in
        Mobile), m. 10/26/1848 in Mobile, AL, Michael Threefoot
        (1822-4/30/1902) (born in Germany, died in Mobile)

56421   Courtney Eldridge Threefoot (11/12/1844-12/12/1900) (born
        and died in Mobile), m. 11/20/1873 John Francis Mahon
        (1847-1899) (born in London, Ontario, Canada-died in
        Sidney, Australia)
564211 John Aldolphus Mahon (6/28/1875-8/16/1954) (born in
        London, Ontario-died Baltimore), m. 8/3/1896 in Mobile,
        AL, Ethel Jacob (5/27/1879-8/18/1948) (born Selma, AL-
        died Baltimore)
5642111 Marie Clayton Mahon (4/17/1897 at Meridian, AL-d. New
        Orleans), m. 6/15/1915 in Mobile, George Clarke
        Marlette (2/5/1888 in Trilla, IL-4/14/1950 in Mobile)
56421111   Sarah Janice Marlette (12/12/1922 in Mobile-12/18/1978
        in New Orleans), m. 7/31/1946 in New Orleans, Cyril
        Busing Burck (b. 7/18/1914 in New Orleans)
564211111 Martha Elizabeth Burck (b. 2/5/1948 in New Orleans),
        m. William Giles Shackelford, Jr. (b. 3/2/1949)
   Children (born in New Orleans):
5642111111 William Giles Shackelford III (b. 1/28/1982)
5642111112 Scott Marlette Shackelford (b. 7/14/1984)
5642111113 Elizabeth Burck Shackelford (b. 11/22/1986)
564211112 Cyril Busing Burck, Jr. (b. 12/9/1950 in New Orleans),
        m. 7/19/1974 Pamela Dale Richmond (b. 12/28/1950 in
        New Orleans)
   Children (born in New Orleans):
5642111121 Christian Richmond Burck (b. 8/29/1979)
5642111122 Robin Marlette Burck (b. 7/2/1982)
5642111123 Elizabeth Clark Burck (b. 9/9/1986)
564211113 Katherine Augusta Burck (b. 3/16/1949), m. 4/24/1982
        in Baton Rouge, Clayton Fenton Rutledge (b. 4/13/1939
        in Francisville)
56421112   Ethel Pauline Marlette, m. Charles Anepohl
56421113   Geraldine Maurice Marlette (b. 12/29/1916 in Haney-
        ville, AL), m. 12/24/1937 William I. Little (9/3/1913-
        7/5/1969)
   Children (born in New Orleans):
564211131 Geraldine Marlette Little (b. 12/4/1939), m. 11/21/
        1969 Joseph Gilbert
564211132 Mildred Marie Little (b. 1/24/1943), m. 1/1/1990)
        David Henry
564211133 Carole Lynn Little (b. 11/16/1946), m. 11/8/1985
        Randy Caruthers
564211134 Deborah Ann Little (b. 4/3/1949), m. 8/20/1980 Charles
        Suhor

631 through 63121111133 in C & A to be omitted.

631 Anne Buchanan, m. William Cross. Married in Scotland.
6311 Anna Cross, m. Robert Yuille
6312 Marion Cross, m. James W. Alston
6313 John Cross, m. Jean Waldrop He may have called himself
        Cross-Buchanan
6314 Neil Cross

6315　William Cross (1809-1862), m. Anna Chalmers Wood (1812-
　　　　1878), dau. of John Wood (1779-1821) and his wife Eliza-
　　　　beth Denniston (1787-1837)
63151　Elizabeth Cross (1836-1869), m. Henry Hall
631511　Alexander Hall (b. 1869), m. Favel Mortimer Jones
6315111　John Alexander Hall (b. 1900)
6315112　Hugh Hall (b. 1901)
6315113　Favel Elizabeth Gertrude Hall (b. 1908), m. 1939 John
　　　　L. C. Shedden
63152　William Cross (1838-1916)
63153　John Walter Cross (1840-　　　), m. Marian Evans (Lewis)
63154　Anna Buchanan Cross (1841-　　　), m. Albert Druce
631541　William Druce (1869-1908), m. Ruby Vetch
6315411　Dorothy Cross Druce (b. 1897), m. Charles Onslow-Graham
6315412　Joan Cross Druce (b. 1899), m. Stanislaus Osiakovski
63154121　Felicia Osiakovski
631542　Nina Druce (1870-1907), m. Alick A. H. Maclean
6315421　Ian Maclean (b. 1902), m. Diana Marsden-Smedley (Wise)
63154211　Lowry Druce Maclean (b. 1939) (twin)
63154212　John Faitways Maclean (b. 1939) (twin)
6315422　Mary Maclean (b. 1903), m. Ian Maclean
63154221　Adrian Maclean (b. 1937)
63154222　Belinda Maclean (b. 1940)
63155　Mary Finlay Cross (1843-1902)
63156　Richard James Cross (1845-1917), m. (1st) 1872 Matilda
　　　　Redmond (1847-1883), dau. of William Redmond (1804-1874)
　　　　and his wife Sabina Elizabeth Hoyt (1812-1870), m. (2nd)
　　　　1886 Annie Redmond (1852-1929)
631561　Eleanor Cross (1873-1950), m. 1890 Allan Marquand
6315611　Eleanor Marquand (b. 1897), m. George Forsyth
63156111　Eleanor Forsyth (b. 1928)
63156112　Mary Blaikie Forsyth (b. 1929)
63156113　Allan Forsyth (b. 1931)
6315612　Mary Elizabeth Marquand (b. 1900)
6315613　Sarnia Marquand (b. 1902)
6315614　Allan Marquand, Jr. (1912-1938), m. 1937 Gertrude Palmer
63156141　Marilyn Marquand (b. 1938)
631562　William Redmond Cross (1874-1940), m. 1913 Julie Appleton
　　　　Newbold (1891-1972), dau. of Thomas Newbold (1849-1929)
　　　　and his wife Sarah Lawrence Coolidge (1858-1922). For
　　　　the descendants, see 24144633, etc.
631563　Mary Redmond Cross (1875-1942)
631564　Richard James Cross (1876-1877)
631565　John Walter Cross (b. 1878-1951), m. (1st) 1808 Lily Lee
　　　　Page (d. 1920), m. (2nd) 1932 Katherine B. Hoyt (Mather)
6315651　John Walter Cross, Jr. (b. 1990), m. (1st) 1930 Marian
　　　　Moore (Div. 1937), m. (2nd) 1939 Jane Foster (Douglas)
63156511　John Walter Cross III (b. 1931)
63156512　Michael McGinley Cross (b. 1934)
6315452　Howard Page Cross (b. 1910)
631566　Emily Redmond Cross (1879-1955)
631567　Eliot Buchanan Cross (1883-1949), m. 1920 Martha McCook
6315671　James Eliot Cross (b. 1921)
6315672　Martha A. Cross (b. 1923)

63157   Eleanor Cross (1847-1895)
63158   Emily Cross (1849-1907), m. Frank Otter
631581   Gwendolyn Otter (b. 1876)
631582   Frank Otter, Jr. (b. 1877)
631583   Harry Otter
63159   Alexander Cross (1851-1865)
6315x   Florence Cross (1857-1915), m. Henry Eve
6316   Richard Cross

641   Ann ("Nancy") Gordon, m. Henry Embry Coleman

6411121   In the changes in C & A on page vi and on page 135 the
          figure 6411452 should read 64114552

6413   John Coleman, m. (1st) Elizabeth Sims Clarke, m. (2nd)
       Mary Love
   By first wife:
64131   Ann Gordon Coleman (1826-1850), m. Mark Alexander (1825-
        1906)
641311   Elizabeth ("Betty") Clark Alexander (1849-1895), m. Gen.
         James Rawlings Herbert (1833-1884) of Baltimore.
6413111   Anne Gordon Herbert (1869-1940), m. William Kennedy
          Boone (1868-1947)
64131111   Elizabeth Alexander Boone (1895-1897). D. infant.
64131112   William Kennedy Boone, Jr. (1897-   ), m. (1st) Sarah
           Blackwell Field (189 -   ), m. (2nd) Thelma Bowra
           (Griffin)
64131113   James Rawlings Herbert Boone (1899-   ), m. Muriel
           Harmar Wurts-Dundas (1903-   )
64131114   John Marshall Boone (1900-   ), m. Ula Claire March
64131115   Sarah Kennedy Boone (1902-   ), m. Henry Stump
           Middendorf (1893-   )
641311151   Henry Stump Middendorf, Jr. (1923-   )
641311152   John William Middendorf II (1924-   ), m. Isabelle
            Jackson Paine (1930-   ). Secretary of the Navy
            under Presidents Nixon and Ford.
6413111521   Frances Paine Middendorf (1954-   )
6413111522   Martha Middendorf (1957-   )
641311153   William Kennedy Boone Middendorf (1926-   ), m. Mary
            Gardner Reynolds (1929-   )
6413111531   Jean Reynolds Middendorf (1950-   )
6413111532   Christopher Stump Middendorf (1952-   )
641311154   Sarah Kennedy Boone Middendorf (1930-   ), m. Iver
            Edward Lofving (1931-   )
64131116   Carlyle Fairfax Boone (1905-1931), m. Charles Rowland
           Posey (1905-   )
641311161   Carlyle Fairfax Posey (1931-   )
64131117   Camilla Hammond Boone (1908-   ), m. (1st) Howard
           Percival Snyder (1907-   ), m. (2nd) Shephard
           Vogelgesang (1901-   ), m. (3rd) Leopold Richard
           Gellert (1896-   )
   Child by second marriage:
641311171   Carlyle Boone Vogelgesang (1943-   )

64131118 Alexander Gordon Boone (1910-   ), m. Edith Dean Flint
          (1913-   )
641311181 Alexander Gordon Boone, Jr. (1933-   ), m. Sylvia J.
          Hayes (1936?-   )
6413111811 Alexander Gordon Boone III (1957-   )
641311182 William Kennedy Boone II (1942-   )
6413112 Camilla Hammond Herbert (1871-1943), m. William Pinkney
          White, Jr. (187 -1931). No children.
6413113 Mark Alexander Herbert (187 -1899). Unm.
6413114 Mary Coleman Herbert (1877-1961), m. Humphrey Warren
          Buckler (18   -1949)
64131141 Alice Lawrason Buckler (1803-   ), m. (1st) Dr.
          William Neill, Jr. (188 -1936), m. (2nd) Robert
          Shafer
     Child by Dr. Neill:
641311411 William Neill III (1925?-   ), m. Henriette S. Hopper
6413114111   Neill (1956-   )
64131142 Humphrey Warren Buckler, Jr. (1906-   ), m. Helen
          Rutherford McCormick
641311421 Humphrey Warren Buckler III (1935-   )
641311422 Joan Rutherford Buckler 91937-   ), m. Robert L.
          Claybrook (193 -   )
641311423 Lewis Morris Buckler (1940-   )
64131143 Mary Herbert Buckler (1913-   ), m. (1st) William
          Pinkney Craig (1906-   ), m. (2nd) Judge James
          MacGill (1912-   )
     Child by first marriage:
641311431 Sally K. Craig
     Child by second marriage:
641311432 Dau.   MacGill
641311433   MacGill
6413115 Sarah Carlyle Fairfax Herbert (18   -1947), m. (1st)
          Courtland Hawkins Smith, m. (2nd) Charles Rapley Hooff
     Child by first marriage
64131151 Courtland Hawkins Smith, Jr. (1900-   ), m. (1st)
          Nancy D. Jackson, m. (2nd)
     Child by first marriage:
641311511 Nancy J. Smith
     Children by second marriage:
641311512 Camilla (?) Smith, m. (?)
641311513 Jacqueline (?) Smith
64131152 Col. Mark Alexander Herbert Smith (1901-   ), m. Anne
          C. MacGill
641311521 Mark Alexander Herbert Smith, Jr.
64131153 Charles Rapley Hooff, Jr. (1910-   ), m. Elizabeth T.
          Dunn
641311531 Charles Rapley Hooff III
641311532   Hooff (?)
64131154 John Carlyle Herbert Hooff (1918-   ), m.
641311541
6413116 Elizabeth Snowden Herbert (18   -1925). Unm.

     By first or second wife:
64132 Patricia Coleman, m.   . No children.

Index

NOTE: The name of the spouse of a Pocahontas descendant is indexed even though that spouse is not a descendant of Pocahontas, but the name of a parent of such a spouse is not indexed unless, of course, that parent is a descendant of Pocahontas.

Bentley, Tammy Helms 41245113
Bentley, William Chamberlayne 41245
Bentley, William Chamberlayne III
   41245113
Bentley, William Chamberlayne, Jr.
   412451
Berlin, Robin 132782312
Bet, Elizabeth Eldridge 561831
Bet, Mr. 561831
Beverley, Eleanor Hodge 162663
Beverley, John Posey 16266
Beverley, Robert, Jr. ii
Beverley, Susan ("Sudie") Rudy 162664
Beverley, Susan Cowan Cabell 16266
Birdsong, Christine Brothers 111x61112
Blackford, Franklin Carter 111x2611
Blaine, Hamilton Leftwich, M.D. 16141
Blaine, Mary Frances Louise 161412
Blaine, Sarah Jane Megginson 16141
Bland, Adeline Manton 1411
Bland, Anne 14111
Bland, Anne 14144
Bland, Bettie Marks 14123
Bland,   Boyd 14113
Bland, Boyd 141131
Bland, Elizabeth Blair 143
Bland, Fanny 141132
Bland, Hettie Rivers 14122
Bland, John Bolling 14113
Bland, John Bolling 1412
Bland, John Theodorick 14123
Bland, Magdalen Pickett 141246
Bland, Martha Elizabeth Ledbetter 1411
Bland, Mary Bolling 1415
Bland, Mary Brooke Harrison 1414
Bland, Mary Coral 1327833
Bland, Mary Harrison 14126
Bland, Peter 14115
Bland, Peter Poythress 1419
Bland, Priscilla Read Watkins 14123
Bland, Richard IV 141
Bland, Richard V 1411
Bland, Robert Epes 14122
Bland,   Ruffin 14123
Bland, Sarah ("Sally") Russell 14124,
   14143
Bland, Sarah ("Sally") Russell Bland
   14124, 14143
Bland, Susan 14114
Bland, Susannah Poythress 14147
Bland, Theodorick 1414
Bland, Theodorick, Jr. 14141
Bland, William Epes 14124, 14143
Blitch, Lewis Cabell 132724411
Blitch, Shelley Childress Cabell
   13272441
Blitch, William Homer, Jr. 13272441
Boden, August Rophe 1626643
Boden, August Rophe, Jr. 16266431
Boden, Charles Henry 16266312
Boden, Dale Jaudon 162664311
Boden, Frances Elizabeth Jaudon 1626643
Boden, Lila Dale Barrett 16266431
Bogert, Elsie 153412
Bolen, Amy Hamilton 162459131
Bolen, Byron Richard 16245913
Bolen, Byron Richard, Jr. 162459134
Bolen, Leigh Durham 162459133
Bolen, Mary Sue Hamilton 16245913
Bolen, Trudy Saison 162459132
Bolling, Archibald 16, 216
Bolling, Barbara 1241294
Bolling, Bertha 124125
Bolling, Clara Lutz 1241291

Bolling, Edith 124127
Bolling, Eleanor ("Nell") Hunter Lutz
   124129
Bolling, Elizabeth 1241211
Bolling, Ian Wilson 124129311
Bolling, Jane Audrey Smith Sharon
   1241293
Bolling, Jane Randolph 16, 216
Bolling, Jane Rolfe iv
Bolling, Jocelyn Angela Gernat 12412931
Bolling, John Blair III 12
Bolling, John Randolph 124128
Bolling, Julia Calvert ("Pink") 21932
Bolling, Martha 5
Bolling, Mary 14
Bolling, Mary 3
Bolling, Phillip A. (1343) iv
Bolling, Pocahontas Rebecca 132
Bolling, Richard Wilmer 124129
Bolling, Richard Wilmer, Jr. 1241292
Bolling, Col. Robert (13) iv
Bolling, Sarah 161
Bolling, Sterling Ruffin 1241293
Bolling, Sterling Ruffin, Jr. 12412931
Bolling, Susan Pocahontas 1342
Bolling, William Archibald 124124
Bolling, William Holcombe 12412
Bolton, Col. Richard R. 1734
Bolton, Martha Lightfoot Dandridge 1734
Bonifant, Benjamin Cabell 132782317
Bonifant, Challice Lee 1327823132
Bonifant, Cheryl Ann Arnold 132782314
Bonifant, Debra Anne Croft 132782315
Bonifant, Garland Louyse 132782316
Bonifant, Garland Parrish 1327823134
Bonifant, George Cabell 1327823141
Bonifant, George Christopher 132782314
Bonifant, James 132782315
Bonifant, James Michael 1327823143
Bonifant, John Croft 1327823153
Bonifant, Kelly 1327823121
Bonifant, Matthew James 1327823151
Bonifant, Nancy Cabell Wooding 13278231
Bonifant, Nancy Elizabeth 1327823152
Bonifant, Nancy Katherine 1327823133
Bonifant, Nancy Lee 132782311
Bonifant, Robert Gregory 1327823142
Bonifant, Robert Lee 13278231
Bonifant, Robert Lee, Jr. 132782312
Bonifant, Robin Berlin 132782312
Bonifant, Ross Lee 1327823123
Bonifant, Sarah 1327823122
Bonifant, Victoria Lucille Haydon
   132782313
Bonifant, William Wooding 132782313
Bonifant, William Wooding, Jr.
   1327823131
Booker, Edna Olivia 16151312
Booker, Janet 161513131
Booker, John Richard 1615131
Booker, John Richard, Jr. 16151313
Booker, Lillian Roeblad 16151313
Booker, Lizzie Armistead 25165
Booker, Mabel Bertha Coleman 1615131
Booker, Sue 16151311
Bookout, Clarence Carl 2212x411
Bookout, Nell Virginia Crabtree _____
   2212x411
Boone, Alexander Gordon 6413118
Boone, Alexander Gordon III 6413111811
Boone, Alexander Gordon, Jr. 641311181
Boone, Anne Gordon Herbert 6413111
Boone, Camilla Hammond 64131117
Boone, Carlyle Fairfax 64131116

Cross, Richard James, Jr. 2414463321
Cross, Susannah Hunt 24144633234
Cross, William iv
Cross, William 631
Cross, William 6315
Cross, William 63152
Cross, William Redmond 631562
Cross, William Redmond III 2414463331
Cross-Buchanan, Jean Waldrop 6313
Cross-Buchanan, John 6313
Cunningham, Lucy 212231
Cureton, Gladney L'Angel 5618622
Currie, Catherine ("Katie") Doswell
    Cabell 132742
Currie, John Rufus 132742
Cuthbert, Hibernia McIlwaine ("Mac")
    111326523

-D-

D'Aiutolo, Domenic Robert 5618621
D'Aiutolo, Eric Thomas 561862111
D'Aiutolo, Leila Elizabeth 56186213
D'Aiutolo, Leila Elizabeth Eldridge
    5618621
D'Aiutolo, Louise Leila 56186212
D'Aiutolo, Maureen Lorraine Mede
    56186211
D'Aiutolo, Thomas Vito 56186211
Daily, Benjamin 212234
Daily, Emma Stark Randolph 212234
Dalton, John Campbell 24144611231
Dalton, Wingate Joan Mackay-Smith
    24144611231
Daly, Carol Jeannine 16245321
Dandridge, Adeline Kenon Wilbourn 1737
Dandridge, Charles Fontaine, M.D. 1731
Dandridge, Eliza Ann 1733
Dandridge, Harriet A. Wylie 1735
Dandridge, Henry Bolling, M.D. 1737
Dandridge, Lightfoot ("Lightie") 17371
Dandridge, Martha H. Fontaine 173
Dandridge, Martha Lightfoot 1734
Dandridge, McGhee 17311
Dandridge, Nathaniel West 173
Dandridge, Nathaniel West III 1735
Dandridge, Rosalie Spotswood 1736
Dandridge, Susan Stith 1732
Dandridge, William Fontaine 1732
Daniels, Donna DeLane 132783312
Dapas, Elizabeth Greenwood Weihe
    56186111
Dapas, Marc Louis 56186111
Dapas, Matthew 561861111
Dauchot, Carol Randolph Manning
    24153331221
Dauchot, Christopher 241533312212
Dauchot, Luke 24153331221
Dauchot, Nicholas 241533312211
Davis, Elizabeth ("Lizzie") Peyton
    351111
Davis, Mary Locke 251632411
Day, Emily Austin Mackay-Smith
    24144611233
Day, James Michael 24144611233
DeBusk, Maurine Zada 22125121
DeHymel, Octavia Jacklyn 1327412
Deitrick, Elsie Payne 21221434
Deitrick, Emily Lynn 21221435
Deitrick, Emily Randolph 2122143
Deitrick, Frances Randolph 21221432

Deitrick, Lingan Randolph 21221433
Deitrick, Stapleton Conway 2122143
DeMarco, Claire Louise 1327823163
DeMarco, Edward Joseph 132782316
DeMarco, Garland Louyse Bonifant
    132782316
DeMarco, Patricia Nan 1327823162
DeMarco, Robert Vincent 1327823161
Detrick, Lucia Ann 56186112
Dillen, Mary Ruth 1627b11
Dixon, Desiree Nicole 162453231
Dixon, Jacqueline Cabell 16245323
Dixon, Paul R. 16245323
Dixon, Paula Michelle 162453232
Dondero, Janet Booker 161513131
Dondero, Leanne M. 1615131311
Dondero, Richard John 1615131312
Dondero, Stephen Henry II 1615131313
Dondero, Walter Henry 161513131
Donovan, Andrika Marion 132781211
Dorriety, Maury Odell 2212x611
Douglas, Jane Foster 6315651
Drake, Barbara Walton 16266312
Druce, Albert 63154
Druce, Anna Buchanan Cross 63154
Druce, Dorothy Cross 6315411
Druce, Joan Cross 6315412
Druce, Nina 631542
Druce, Ruby Vetch 631541
Druce, William 631541
Duncan, Bessie 56181
Dunn, Elizabeth T. 64131153
Dupuy, Emily 16245951
Dyman, Anne Marie 2414463321

-E-

Eddins, Elizabeth 132295
Edmondson, Mary Beth 132785512
Edmunds, Sarah 13425
Edwards, Brittany Marie 2516323132
Edwards, Carla Jean 2516323113
Edwards, Catherine S. Heid 251632313
Edwards, Connie Lynne 2516323112
Edwards, Douglas Ray 251632311
Edwards, Gail Lynne Pardo 251632311
Edwards, Keith Anson 251632313
Edwards, Susan ("Suzy") Belle 2516323111
Eldridge, Barbara 5618611
Eldridge, Benjamin 5617
Eldridge, Benjamin Rolfe 56171
Eldridge, Bessie Duncan 56181
Eldridge, Christa 56186232
Eldridge, Constance 5618613
Eldridge, Dorothy Greenwood 561861
Eldridge, Edward F. 561711
Eldridge, Eliza Perkins 5617
Eldridge, Elizabeth 56181
Eldridge, Elizabeth Cureton 56186221
Eldridge, Elizabeth Fearn 56184
Eldridge, Emma Morton 56183
Eldridge, Frances 561811
Eldridge, Frances Buff Fleming 5618623
Eldridge, Frank Mason 5618622
Eldridge, Frank Mason, Jr. 56186222
Eldridge, Gladney L'Angel Cureton 5618622
Eldridge, Gloria Campbell 5618623
Eldridge, Grandison Moseley 56182
Eldridge, Jeanette 561832
Eldridge, Joan 5618612
Eldridge, John III 561861

-K-

-L-

McConnell, Georgia Hopkins Hays 1626631
McConnell, Jackie Lee Almes 16266311
McConnell, James Edward 162663123
McConnell, John Robert 162663111
McConnell, Leeann 162663112
McConnell, Susan Georgia 162663121
McConnell, Thomas Dean 162663113
McConnell, William Ralph 1626631
McConnell, William Ralph, Jr. 16266311
McCook, Martha 631567
McCormick, Helen Rutherford 64131142
McFall, _____ (son) 22125444
McFall, Flora Lee Maury 2212544
McFall, Joseph Samuel 2212544
McFall, Joseph Samuel, Jr. 2212544
McFodin, Gladys Greenwood 1327723
McFodin, John 1327723
McFodin, Sawania 13277231
McGhee, Tabitha Anne 1731
McGinty, John William III 1327241224
McGinty, John William IV 13272412241
McGinty, Margaret Cole Greer 1327241224
McGregor, Edward ("Neddy") Isham Spence
    24144633521
McGregor, James Harvey 2414463352
McGregor, Sarah Coolidge 2414463352
McKagen, Louise 13272411
McKendrick, Calvin Carlisle 1627a2
McKendrick, George W. 1627a
McKendrick, Mary Cabell 1627a1
McKendrick, Virginia Margaret Cabell
    1627a
McLaughlin, Annie 1615121
McLaurin, James Leroy 1534133
McLaurin, Mary Southall Shelburne
    Crawford 1534133
McMillan, Elaine Ruth Mueller 16245512
McMillan, Holly Joanne Garrison 162455111
McMillan, Jeffrey Robert 162455121
McMillan, Megan Anne 1624551111
McMillan, Muriel Eleanor Cabell 1624551
McMillan, Murray Cabell 16245511
McMillan, Patricia Dawn Falk 162455112
McMillan, Patricia Isabelle Brady
    16245511
McMillan, Robert James 1624551
McMillan, Robert James, Jr. 16245512
McMillan, Robert Murray 162455112
McMillan, Scott Shorey 162455111
McSwain, Jane McCandlish Crane 251632211
McSwain, Kimberly Sterrett 2516322112
McSwain, Kristin Bunker 2516322111
McSwain, Lt. Col. Thomas Clyde, Jr.
    251632211
McVea, Alayna Kristy 162458152
McVea, Anne Lilley 16245812
McVea, Coleman Lilley 1624581
McVea, Coleman Lilley, Jr. 16245813
McVea, Eleanor Lobdell 1624581
McVea, Ellen Louise 16245811
McVea, Emily Kate 162458136
McVea, Hannah Elizabeth 162458154
McVea, Joshua Coleman 162458135
McVea, Lael Lilley 162458134
McVea, Lucas L. 162458153
McVea, Melissa Grace 162458133
McVea, Nicholas Russell 162458151
McVea, Peggy Washburn 16245815
McVea, Russell Lobdell 16245815
McVea, Sarah Grace 16245814
McVea, Sarah Love 162458132
McVea, Seth Michael 162458131
McVea, Valli Vaun Nichols 16245813

McVea, Virginia Love 16245816
Meade, Rebecca 2184
Mede, Maureen Lorraine 56186211
Medlin, Dondi Lee 251632333
Megginson, Annie McLaughlin 1615121
Megginson, Archibald Bolling 1613a
Megginson, Clara Virginia 1613142
Megginson, Eliza Susan Alvis 16151
Megginson, Elizabeth Bagby Lewis 161512
Megginson, Emma Guy 16151211
Megginson, Frances Cabell 1611a
Megginson, Ida Branch 161513
Megginson, James Bolling 161512
Megginson, Joseph Cabell 161
Megginson, Joseph Cabell 1613x
Megginson, Joseph Cabell 16151
Megginson, Mary Ann Johnston 1615
Megginson, Mattie Blain 1613141
Megginson, Samuel Bolling 1615
Megginson, Sarah Bolling 161
Megginson, Sarah Jane 16141
Megginson, William James Bolling
    1615121
Melville, Alysse Wickham 2516311242
Melville, Ellen Archer McCandlish
    251631124
Melville, John D'Wolf 2516311241
Melville, John Martin 251631124
Menousek, Caroline Carter 24153331242
Menousek, Elizabeth Lamb 24153331244
Menousek, James Randolph 24153331243
Menousek, John Francis 2415333124
Menousek, Mary Barrett 24153331241
Menousek, Mary Barrett Gillis 2415333124
Meredith, William Hugh ("Bill") 22314332
Metzger, Carol 132783211
Mewborne, Margaret Elizabeth 132783221
Meyerhoffer, Elizabeth Gertrude 132785
Middendorf, Christopher Stump 6413111532
Middendorf, Frances Paine 6413111521
Middendorf, Henry Stump 64131115
Middendorf, Henry Stump, Jr. 641311151
Middendorf, Isabelle Jackson Paine
    641311152
Middendorf, Jean Reynolds 6413111531
Middendorf, John William II 641311152
Middendorf, Martha 641311522
Middendorf, Sarah Kennedy Boone 64131115
Middendorf, Sarah Kennedy Boone 64131115
Middendorff, Mary Gardner Reynolds
    641311153
Middendorff, William Kennedy Boone
    641311153
Middleton, Brandice Louise 1327823232
Middleton, Christie Radcliffe 132782232
Middleton, Christie Radcliffe III
    132782322
Middleton, Iris D. Rodriguez 132782322
Middleton, Kathryn Louise Griffin
    132782323
Middleton, Kathryn Wooding 132782321
Middleton, Lois Elizabeth Wooding
    13278232
Middleton, Richard Kenneth 1327823233
Middleton, Stephanie Kimberly 1327823221
Middleton, William Wooding 132782323
Middleton, William Wooding, Jr.
    1327823231
Miles, Sarah ("Sallie") Doswell Cabell
    Lewis Brady 132781
Miles, W. T. 132781
Millan, Henry Lyle 25163242
Millan, John Alden 251632421

Sheild, Lizzie Armistead Booker 25165
Sheild, Lizzie Stribling 25165
Sheild, Susan Meade Walke 2516
Sheild, William Francis 25165
Shelburne, Brian James 15341341
Shelburne, Emily Watson 1534132
Shelburne, Jane Elizabeth Becker 1534134
Shelburne, Jane Louise 15341343
Shelburne, Louise Balmer 1534131
Shelburne, Mary Schoolcraft James 153413
Shelburne, Mary Southall 1534133
Shelburne, Victor Balmer 153413
Shelburne, Victor Balmer, Jr. 1534134
Shelburne, Victor Balmer III 15341342
Shelburne, Yvonne Weakland 15341341
Shoffner, David 132724411
Shoffner, Lewis Cabell Blitch Evans
    132724411
Shumway, Ellsworth 1327852
Shumway, Virginia Elizabeth Baird Cabell
    Reynolds Williams Thomas 1327852
Smith, Adelaide Leigh 24142x2613
Smith, Adelaide Morris Cooley 24142x261
Smith, Anne C. MacGill 64131152
Smith, Brian Burnett 162458162
Smith, Camilla 641311512
Smith, Courtland Hawkins 6413115
Smith, Courtland Hawkins, Jr. 64131151
Smith, Hal Waugh 24142x261
Smith, Jack Burnett 16245816
Smith, Jacqueline 641311513
Smith, Judith Ann 132724 1221
Smith, Col. Mark Alexander Herbert
    64131152
Smith, Mark Alexander Herbert, Jr.
    641311521
Smith, Mary William 251632222
Smith, Mary Winifred Cabell 132723
Smith, Nancy D. Jackson 64131151
Smith, Nancy J. 641311511
Smith, Orthodox Creed 132723
Smith, Paul Charles 162458161
Smith, Roy Cabell 1327233
Smith, Roy Cabell 162457
Smith, Sarah Carlyle Fairfax Herbert
    6413115
Smith, Virginia Love McVea 16245816
Snow, Maureen Barbara iv
Snyder, Camilla Hammond Boone 64131117
Snyder, Howard Percival 64131117
Solberg, Janet 24141113432
Solberg, Jennifer Leigh 241411134311
Solberg, Michael Paul 24141113 4312
Solberg, Nathaniel James 24141113 4313
Solberg, Robert M. 24141113431
Somerville, George Selden 2193223
Somerville, Mary Groesbeck Cabell
    Crenshaw 2193223
Southall, Dr. J. B. 1534
Southall, Mary Louisa 1534
Southall, Mary Whitfield 15341
Spaht, Anita Louise Fife 16245931
Spaht, Ashley Elizabeth 162459311
Spaht, Charles William 16245934
Spaht, Frances Abigail Morgana 16245934
Spaht, Homer Dale 1624593
Spaht, Homer Dale, Jr. 16245931
Spaht, Kay Elizabeth 16245933
Spaht, Sue Cabell Larguier 1624593
Spaht, Susan Louise 16245932
Spector, Abby Cross 24144633252
Spector, Jane Randolph Cross 2414463325

Spector, Jessie Cross 24144633251
Spector, Paul David 2414463325
Spence, Alan Keith 2414463351
Spence, Bonnie Joseph Carey 2414463351
Spence, Donald Pond 241446335
Spence, Mary Newbold Cross 241446335
Spence, Pamela Whitten Hughes 2414463351
Spence, Sarah Coolidge 2414463352
Spiegelman, Bret 162453313
Spiegelman, Penny Warren 162453311
Spiegelman, Sarah Jean Warren 16245331
Spiegelman, Seymour Adam 16245331
Spiegelman, Suellyn Tyler 162453312
Spilker, Amelia Valentine 132781 2231
Spilker, Monica Mari Strauss 132781223
Spilker, Thomas Richard 132781223
Spyker, Alla 162451
St. Agnes Church v
Staley, Bonnie Leigh 1327833222
Staley, Michael Stephen 132783322
Staley, Stephen Robert 1327833221
Staley, Susan Elaine Batts 132783322
Stark, Emma Beverley Randolph 21224
Stark, Henry 21224
Starnes, Anna ("Nancy") Morris Ely
    241346353
Starnes, Mr. 241346353
Stern, Henry Julius 2212x4112
Stern, Roslyn Lanel Brock 2212x4112
Stevenson, Hermione 22125751
Stevenson, James Benjamin 221257
Stevenson, James Gordon 22125753
Stevenson, Jeanne Dee 22125752
Stevenson, Kathryn Elizabeth 221251
Stevenson, Marjorie Ann 22125754
Stevenson, Mary Lucy Maury 221257
Stith, Susan 1732
Storey, Jennifer 24153331211
Strauss, Barbara Lee 1327812211
Strauss, Linda Lee Kostelecky 132781221
Strauss, Martha June Lewis 13278122
Strauss, Martha Mariam 132781222
Strauss, Monica Mari 132781223
Strauss, Richard Edgar 13278122
Strauss, Richard Edgar Lewis 132781221
Stribling, Lizzie 25165
Stringer, Carol Layne Trice 2212x4312
Stringer, David Lee 2212x4314
Stringer, James Gibson 2212x431
Stringer, Katherine Leigh 2212x43111
Stringer, Katherine Virginia Maury
    2212x431
Stringer, Laura McLane 2212x43113
Stringer, Robert Sanders 2212x4312
Stringer, Sharon Kay Gray 2212x4314
Stringer, Virginia Clarice 2212x4313
Stringfellow, Ann 16141211
Stringfellow, James Broadus 1614121
Stringfellow, Mary Blaine 16141212,
    16141221
Stringfellow, Mary Elizabeth Tompkins
    1614121
Stringfellow, Robert Bruce 16141213
Strother, Emily 21221
Suhor, Charles 564211134
Suhor, Deborah Ann Little 564211134
Sumner, Carol Gillis Randolph 2415333112
Sumner, Jessica Elaine 24153331123
Sumner, John Collier Hart 2415333112
Sumner, John Collier Hart, Jr.
    24153331122
Sumner, Wendy Randolph 24153331121
Sutton, Josephine Meredith 25163222
Symington, Anne Byrd 111x2145

-T-

Tallant, Evelyn Orme McCandlish 2516325
Tallant, Ralph Kerper 2516325
Tallant, Ralph Kerper 2516326
Tallant, Ruth McCandlish Graham 2516326
Tarter, Cecil Vance 1327852
Tarter, Virginia Elizabeth Baird Cabell
  Reynolds Williams Thomas Shumway
  1327852
Tavui, Janet April Sheely 251632363
Tavui, Kavika (David) Andreas 2516323632
Tavui, Vastuia 251632363
Taylor, Dorothy Eloise 35111182
Taylor, Julia 13422
Taylor, Mary ("Mamie") Cabell 162651
Tazewell, Mary Louisa 1534
Teague, Helen Sue Crabtree _____ _____
  2212x415
Teague, Herbert William, Jr. 2212x415
Temple, Edgar (Edward") 14147
Temple, Magdalen Pickett Bland 141246
Temple, Susannah Poythress Bland 14147
Temple, William 141246
Terry, Letitia 56171
Thatcher, Willie Sue 56411
Thomas, Bonny 1327852
Thomas, Ruth 1627311
Thomas, Virginia Elizabeth Baird Cabell
  Reynolds Williams 1327852
Thompson, Camilla Cary 2415335413
Thompson, Diana 2212575131
Thompson, Emma Pickens 162455
Thompson, Mark Randolph 2419335113
Thompson, Sarah Ann 2419335114
Thompson, Winifred 25163112
Thomson, Katherine ("Kate") Janie
  251634221
Thorndike, Nicholas Porter 2414616311
Thornton, Frances ("Fannie") 2212116
Thornton, Frances ("Fannie") Rew 221211
Thornton, George 221211
Thornton, George Washington 2212
Thornton, Henry Randolph 22121
Thornton, Jan 2212a
Thornton, Katherine ("Kate") 2212113
Thornton, Mary Agnes Bradford 22121
Thornton, Mary Goode 22123
Thornton, Mary Goode Randolph 2212
Threefoot, Courtney Eldridge 56421
Threefoot, Michael 5642
Threefoot, Susannah Walker Williams
  5642
Tompkins, Caroline Virginia 1614122
Tompkins, Mary Elizabeth 1614121
Tompkins, Mary Frances Louise Blaine
  161412
Tompkins, Metellus Woods, M.D. 161412
Toups, Mary Lylia 16245622
Townsend, Cabell Dupre 132783223
Townsend, Frances Sheridan Pratt
  13278322
Townsend, Margaret Elizabeth Mewborne
  132783223
Townsend, Sheridan Pratt 132783222
Townsend, William Linwood Douglas
  13278322
Townsend, William Linwood Douglas III
  1327832211
Townsend, William Linwood Douglas, Jr.
  132783221

"Treasurer" iv
Trice, Carol Layne 2212x4312
Trube, Jane Meredith 13228722
Trube, Robert Clement III 13228721
Tucker, Braxton Stuart 1327241511
Tucker, Helen Claiborne Cabell
  132724151
Tucker, Joseph Frederick 132724151
Turner, Anne Bland 14111
Turner, Edward 14111
Turner, Eldridge Hoyle ("Coots")
  5636211
Turner, Mary Meade Randolph 21227
Turner, W. W. 21227
Twente, Allison Stuart White 111x61111
Twente, Stephen Douglas 111x61111
Tyler, Charles H. 1627a1
Tyler, John Calvin 1627a12
Tyler, Louisa Angela 1627a122
Tyler, Margaret Angela Proctor 1627a12
Tyler, Margaret Rebecca 1627a11
Tyler, Mary Cabell McKendrick 1627a1
Tyler, Stephen Proctor 1627a121

-V-

Vaughan-Morgan, Deborah Mary 24144633112
Vaughan-Morgan, Elily Redmond Cross
  241446331
Vaughan-Morgan, Julia Redmond 2414463311
Vaughan-Morgan, Sir John Kenyon 241446331
Veale, Martha Ellen 35111
Vetch, Ruby 631541
Vine, Iris Melba 1624594
Vogelgesang, Camilla Hammond Boone Snyder
  64131117
Vogelgesang, Carlyle Boone 641311171
Vogelgesang, Shephard 64131117

-W-

Waldrop, Jean 6313
Walke, Ann Livingston 2514
Walke, Anne McColley McClanahan 251
Walke, Col. Anthony, Jr. 25
Walke, Rev. Anthony III 251
Walke, Anthony IV 2514
Walke, Edwin 2511
Walke, Jane Bolling Randolph 25
Walke, Jane E. 2515
Walke, John Newton 2513
Walke, Mary Land 2513
Walke, Susan Meade 2516
Walker, Susannah Everard 56
Wallace, Anne Elizabeth 2122144
Wallain, Jim 2516332331
Wallain, Mary Jane Cochran 2516332331
Warfield, Wallis v
Warren, Julius Thompson 1624533
Warren, Phyllis Mareve 16245332
Warren, Sara Otis Cabell 1624533
Warren, Sarah Jean 16245331
Warrington, Anne Cabell 13277x11
Warrington, Daniel Scott 13277x112
Warrington, Kristy Cabell 13277x113
Warrington, Robert O'Neil III 13277x111
Warrington, Robert O'Neil, Jr. 13277x11
Washburn, Peggy 16245815
Waters, Patricia ("Pat") 251632342
Watkins, Priscilla Read 14123

9 780806 314075